Paris Metro

*The stations Liège and Rennes are closed after 8pm and on Sundays and holidays.

Beyond the city limits, *Métro Urbain* tickets are not valid on the RER

13 Line Terminus
● Station
○ Transfer Station

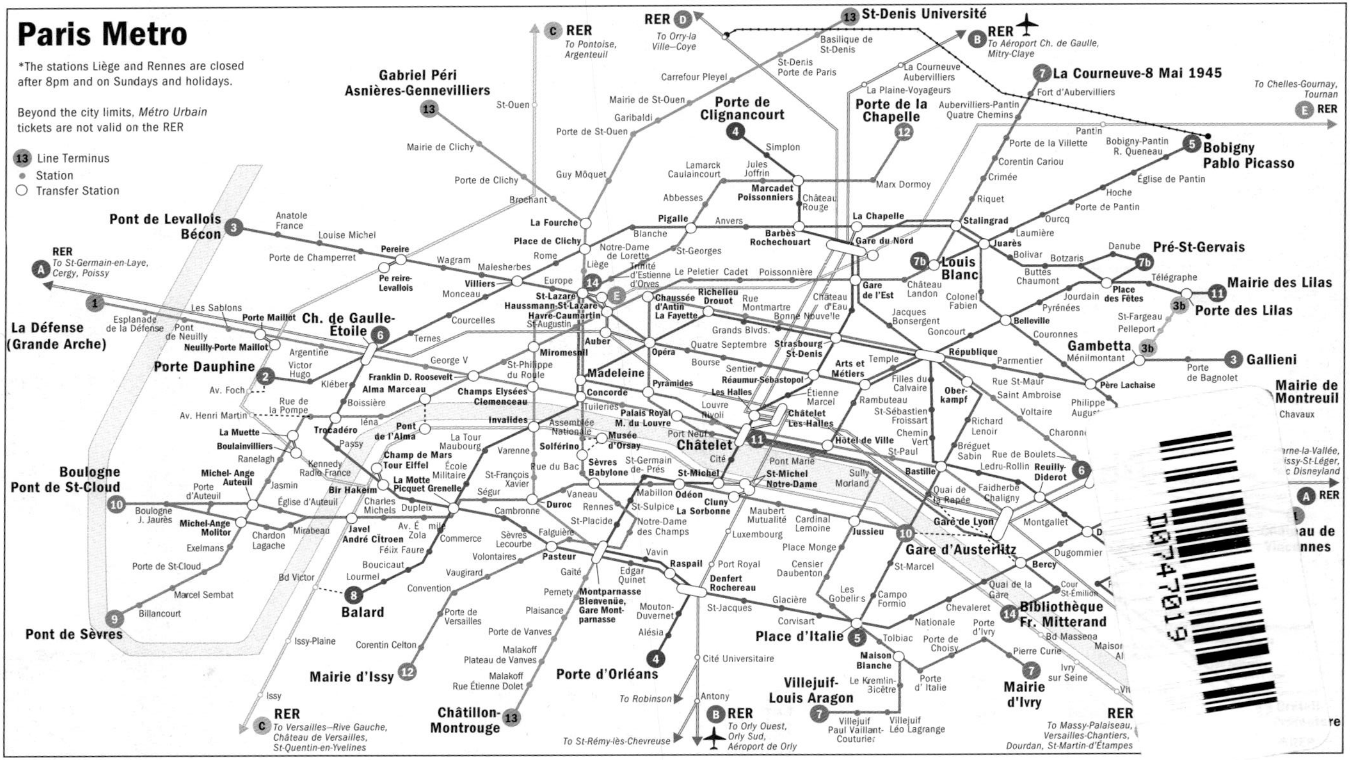

Paris: Overview and Arrondissements

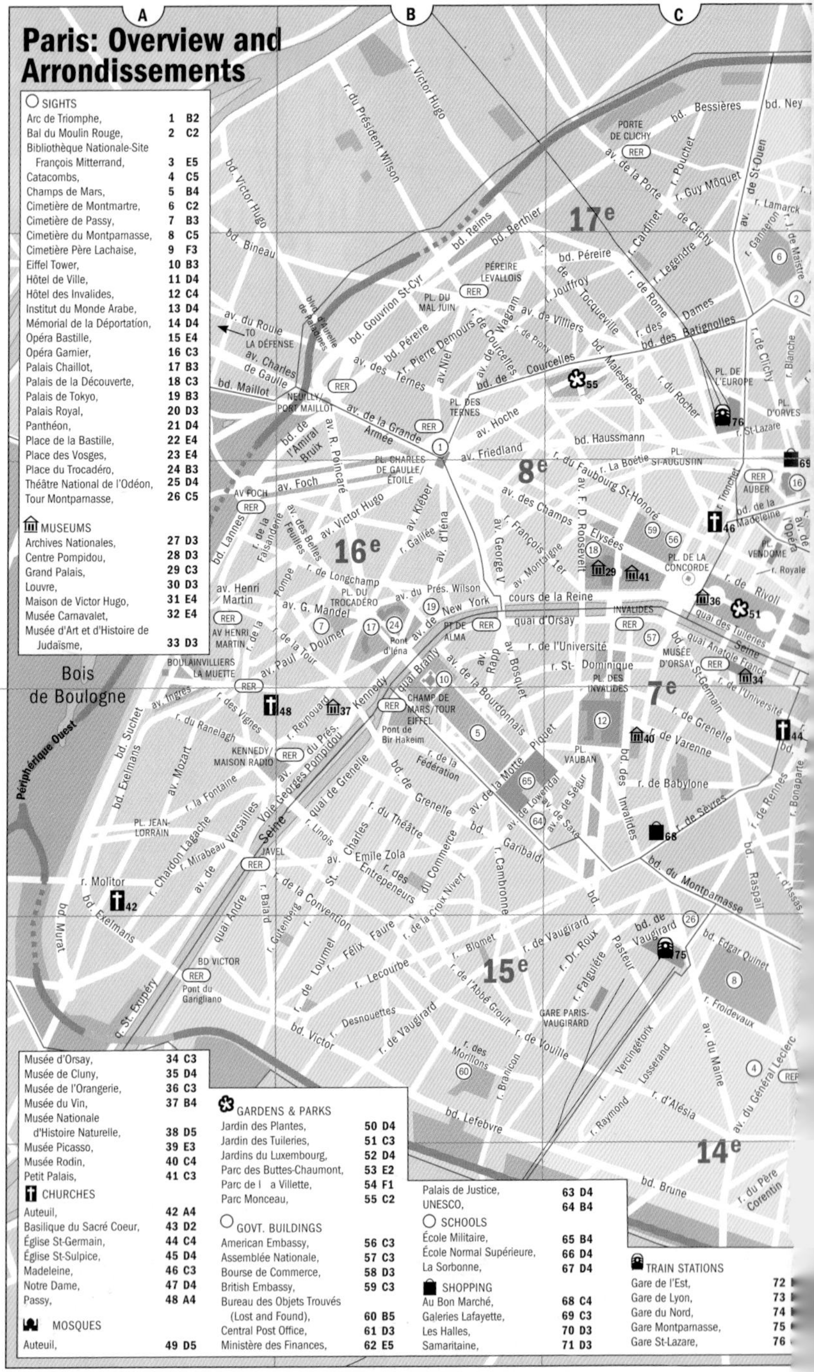

○ SIGHTS

Arc de Triomphe,	1	B2
Bal du Moulin Rouge,	2	C2
Bibliothèque Nationale-Site François Mitterrand,	3	E5
Catacombs,	4	C5
Champs de Mars,	5	B4
Cimetière de Montmartre,	6	C2
Cimetière de Passy,	7	B3
Cimetière du Montparnasse,	8	C5
Cimetière Père Lachaise,	9	F3
Eiffel Tower,	10	B3
Hôtel de Ville,	11	D4
Hôtel des Invalides,	12	C4
Institut du Monde Arabe,	13	D4
Mémorial de la Déportation,	14	D4
Opéra Bastille,	15	E4
Opéra Garnier,	16	C3
Palais Chaillot,	17	B3
Palais de la Découverte,	18	C3
Palais de Tokyo,	19	B3
Palais Royal,	20	D3
Panthéon,	21	D4
Place de la Bastille,	22	E4
Place des Vosges,	23	E4
Place du Trocadéro,	24	B3
Théâtre National de l'Odéon,	25	D4
Tour Montparnasse,	26	C5

MUSEUMS

Archives Nationales,	27	D3
Centre Pompidou,	28	D3
Grand Palais,	29	C3
Louvre,	30	D3
Maison de Victor Hugo,	31	E4
Musée Carnavalet,	32	E4
Musée d'Art et d'Histoire de Judaïsme,	33	D3
Musée d'Orsay,	34	C3
Musée de Cluny,	35	D4
Musée de l'Orangerie,	36	C3
Musée du Vin,	37	B4
Musée Nationale d'Histoire Naturelle,	38	D5
Musée Picasso,	39	E3
Musée Rodin,	40	C4
Petit Palais,	41	C3

CHURCHES

Auteuil,	42	A4
Basilique du Sacré Coeur,	43	D2
Église St-Germain,	44	C4
Église St-Sulpice,	45	D4
Madeleine,	46	C3
Notre Dame,	47	D4
Passy,	48	A4

MOSQUES

Auteuil,	49	D5

GARDENS & PARKS

Jardin des Plantes,	50	D4
Jardin des Tuileries,	51	C3
Jardins du Luxembourg,	52	D4
Parc des Buttes-Chaumont,	53	E2
Parc de l a Villette,	54	F1
Parc Monceau,	55	C2

○ GOVT. BUILDINGS

American Embassy,	56	C3
Assemblée Nationale,	57	C3
Bourse de Commerce,	58	D3
British Embassy,	59	C3
Bureau des Objets Trouvés (Lost and Found),	60	B5
Central Post Office,	61	D3
Ministère des Finances,	62	E5
Palais de Justice,	63	D4
UNESCO,	64	B4

○ SCHOOLS

École Militaire,	65	B4
École Normal Supérieure,	66	D4
La Sorbonne,	67	D4

SHOPPING

Au Bon Marché,	68	C4
Galeries Lafayette,	69	C3
Les Halles,	70	D3
Samaritaine,	71	D3

TRAIN STATIONS

Gare de l'Est,	72
Gare de Lyon,	73
Gare du Nord,	74
Gare Montparnasse,	75
Gare St-Lazare,	76

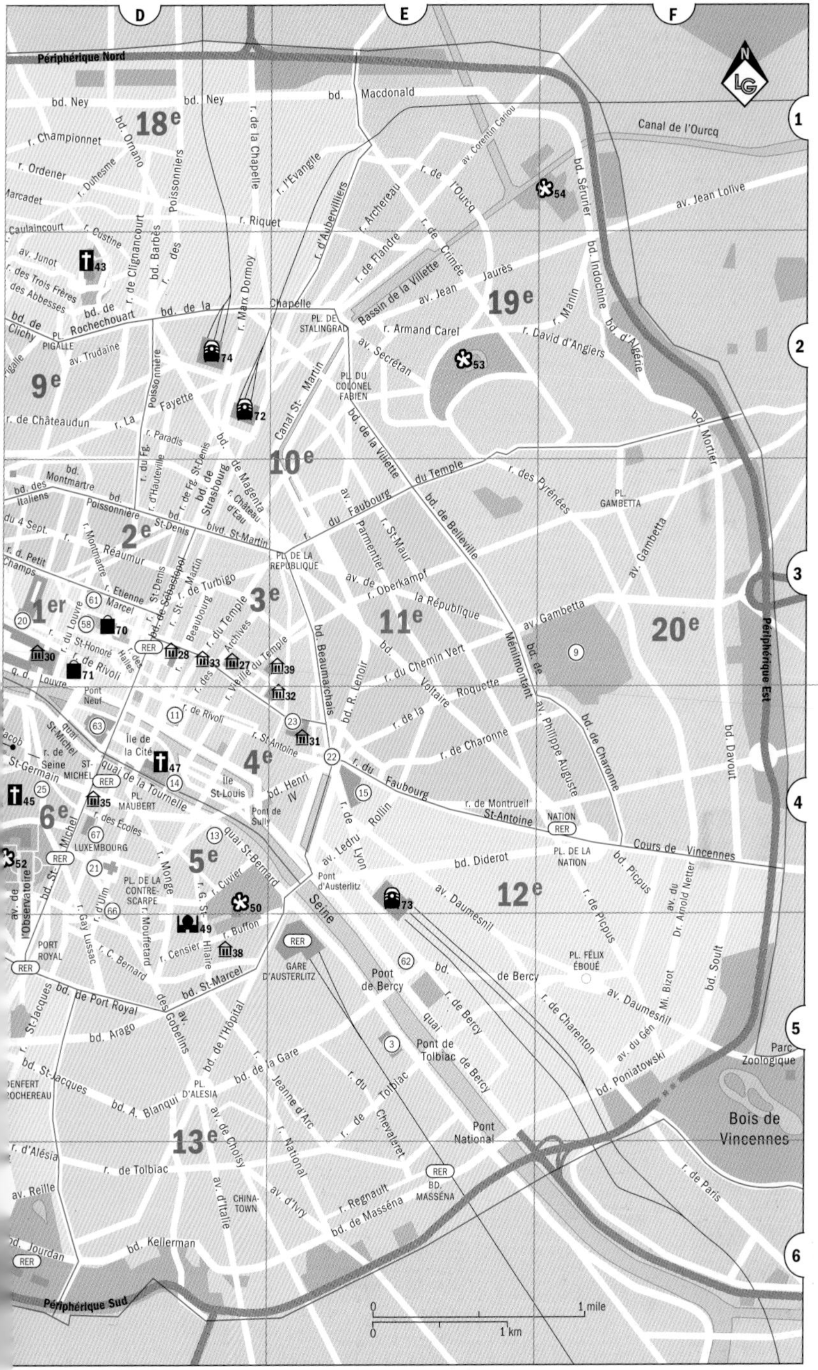

D
E
F
1
2
3
4
5
6
N
LG
Périphérique Nord
bd. Ney
bd. Ney
bd. Macdonald
18e
r. Championnet
bd. Ornano
r. Poissonniers
r. de la Chapelle
r. Ordener
r. Duhesme
Marcadet
r. l'Evangile
r. de l'Ourcq
av. Corentin Cariou
Canal de l'Ourcq
bd. Sérurier
av. Jean Lolive
r. Archereau
r. d'Aubervilliers
r. Riquet
r. Caulaincourt
r. Custine
av. Junot
43
r. des Trois Frères
r. des Abbesses
r. de Clignancourt
bd. Barbès
r. des
r. Marx Dormoy
r. de Flandre
r. de Crimée
bd. Indochine
av. Jean Jaurès
Bassin de la Villette
19e
r. Manin
54
bd. de Clichy
PL. PIGALLE
bd. de Rochechouart
bd. de la Chapelle
PL. DE STALINGRAD
r. Armand Carel
r. David d'Angiers
bd. d'Algérie
av. Trudaine
74
av. Secrétan
53
9e
Canal St-Martin
PL. DU COLONEL FABIEN
r. Poissonnière
r. La Fayette
72
r. de Châteaudun
r. Paradis
bd. de la Villette
bd. Mortier
r. du Fg. Poissonnière
r. d'Hauteville
r. du Fg. St-Denis
bd. de Strasbourg
bd. de Magenta
r. Château d'Eau
10e
bd. Montmartre
bd. des Italiens
bd. Poissonnière
bd. St-Denis
r. du Faubourg du Temple
r. des Pyrénées
PL. GAMBETTA
av. Parmentier
r. St-Maur
bd. de Belleville
r. du 4 Sept.
r. Montmartre
2e
r. Réaumur
bd. de Sébastopol
blvd. St-Martin
av. Gambetta
r. d. Petit Champs
r. St-Denis
r. St-Martin
r. de Turbigo
PL. DE LA RÉPUBLIQUE
av. de la République
r. Oberkampf
3
1er
r. Etienne Marcel
3e
61
20
58
70
r. du Louvre
r. St-Honoré
r. Beaubourg
r. du Temple
r. des Archives
11e
av. Gambetta
20e
Périphérique Est
RER
28
33
27
r. Vieille du Temple
39
bd. Beaumarchais
bd. Voltaire
r. du Chemin Vert
Ménilmontant
bd. de Ménilmontant
9
30
r. de Rivoli
r. des Halles
71
q. d. Louvre
32
Pont Neuf
r. des
bd. R. Lenoir
r. de la Roquette
av. Philippe Auguste
quai St-Michel
11
r. de Rivoli
63
23
r. St-Antoine
31
r. de Charonne
bd. de Charonne
bd. Davout
Jacob
r. de Seine
Île de la Cité
47
4e
22
r. du Faubourg St-Antoine
bd. St-Germain
ST-MICHEL
quai de la Tournelle
Île St-Louis
bd. Henri IV
15
r. de Montreuil
45
25
RER
14
35
PL. MAUBERT
Pont de Sully
r. Rollin
r. de Lyon
NATION
RER
6e
r. des Écoles
13
quai St-Bernard
av. Ledru Rollin
Cours de Vincennes
52
bd. St-Michel
67
LUXEMBOURG
RER
5e
bd. Diderot
PL. DE LA NATION
bd. Picpus
21
r. Monge
r. Cuvier
Pont d'Austerlitz
av. de l'Observatoire
PL. DE LA CONTRESCARPE
r. G. St-Hilaire
Seine
73
av. Daumesnil
12e
r. de Picpus
av. du Dr. Arnold Netter
r. d'Ulm
66
r. Mouffetard
50
49
r. Buffon
r. Gay Lussac
PORT ROYAL
r. C. Bernard
r. Censier
38
RER
GARE D'AUSTERLITZ
PL. FÉLIX ÉBOUÉ
RER
Pont de Bercy
62
bd. de Bercy
bd. St-Marcel
bd. de Port Royal
av. des Gobelins
r. de Bercy
quai de Bercy
r. de Charenton
av. Daumesnil
bd. Mi. Bizot
bd. Soult
r. St-Jacques
bd. Arago
bd. de l'Hôpital
3
Pont de Tolbiac
av. du Gén
Parc Zoologique
bd. St-Jacques
r. de la Gare
bd. Poniatowski
DENFERT ROCHEREAU
PL. D'ALESIA
bd. A. Blanqui
r. Jeanne d'Arc
r. du Chevaleret
r. de Tolbiac
Bois de Vincennes
Pont National
13e
av. de Choisy
r. National
r. d'Alésia
r. de Tolbiac
RER
r. de Paris
av. Reille
av. d'Italie
CHINA-TOWN
av. d'Ivry
r. Regnault
BD. MASSÉNA
bd. de Masséna
bd. Jourdan
RER
bd. Kellerman
Périphérique Sud
0
1 mile
0
1 km

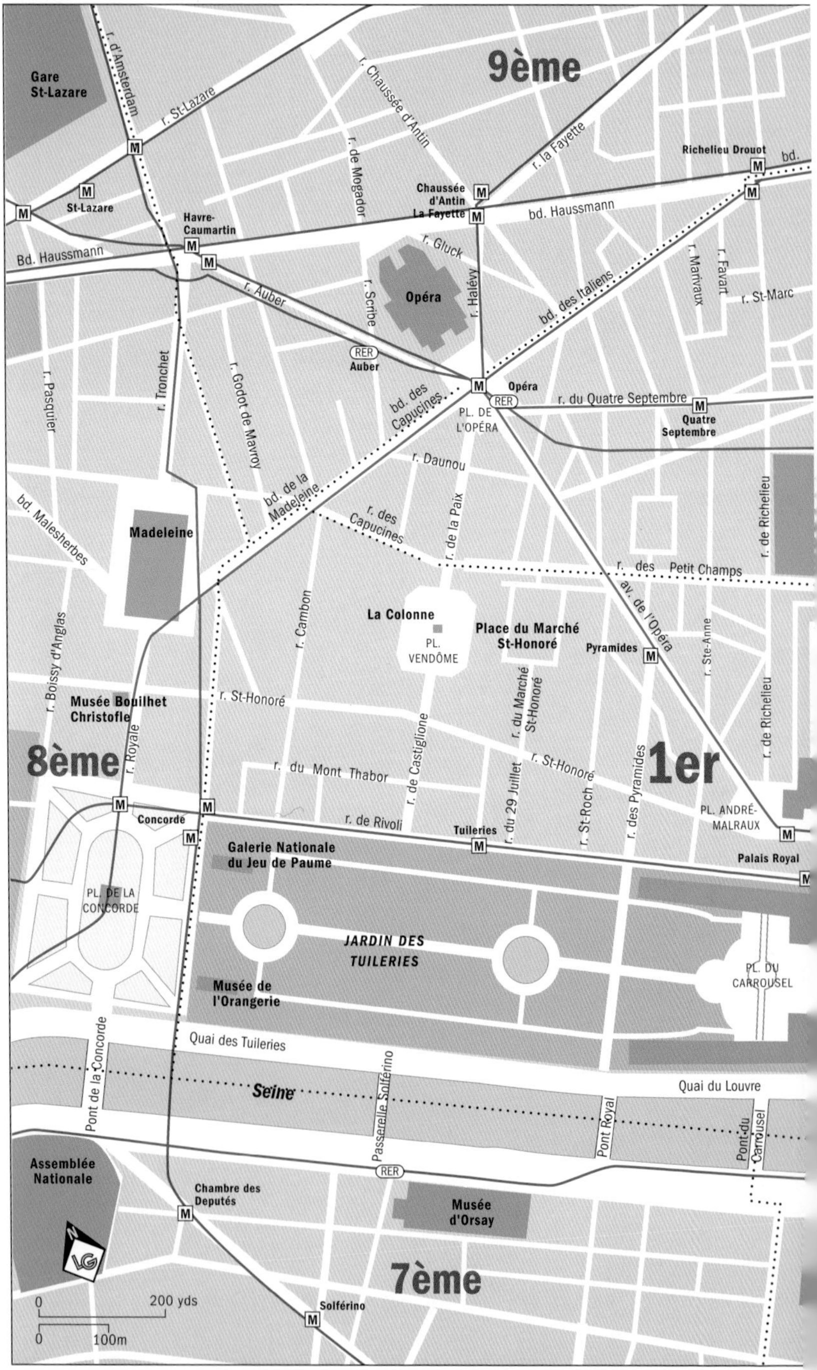

9ème
8ème
1er
7ème
Gare St-Lazare
r. d'Amsterdam
r. St-Lazare
r. Chaussée d'Antin
r. de Mogador
r. la Fayette
Richelieu Drouot
bd.
St-Lazare
Chaussée d'Antin La Fayette
bd. Haussmann
Havre-Caumartin
Bd. Haussmann
r. Gluck
r. Auber
r. Scribe
Opéra
r. Halévy
bd. des Italiens
r. Marivaux
r. Favart
r. St-Marc
RER
Auber
r. Pasquier
r. Tronchet
r. Godot de Mavroy
bd. des Capucines
PL. DE L'OPÉRA
r. du Quatre Septembre
Quatre Septembre
r. Daunou
bd. Malesherbes
Madeleine
bd. de la Madeleine
r. des Capucines
r. de la Paix
r. de Richelieu
r. des Petit Champs
av. de l'Opéra
r. Cambon
La Colonne
Place du Marché St-Honoré
PL. VENDÔME
Pyramides
r. Ste-Anne
r. Boissy d'Anglas
Musée Bouilhet Christofle
r. St-Honoré
r. du Marché St-Honoré
r. Royale
r. du Mont Thabor
r. de Castiglione
r. du 29 Juillet
r. St-Roch
r. des Pyramides
PL. ANDRÉ-MALRAUX
Concorde
r. de Rivoli
Tuileries
Palais Royal
Galerie Nationale du Jeu de Paume
PL. DE LA CONCORDE
JARDIN DES TUILERIES
PL. DU CARROUSEL
Musée de l'Orangerie
Quai des Tuileries
Pont de la Concorde
Passerelle Solférino
Seine
Quai du Louvre
Pont Royal
Pont du Carrousel
Assemblée Nationale
Chambre des Deputés
Musée d'Orsay
Solférino
0
200 yds
100m

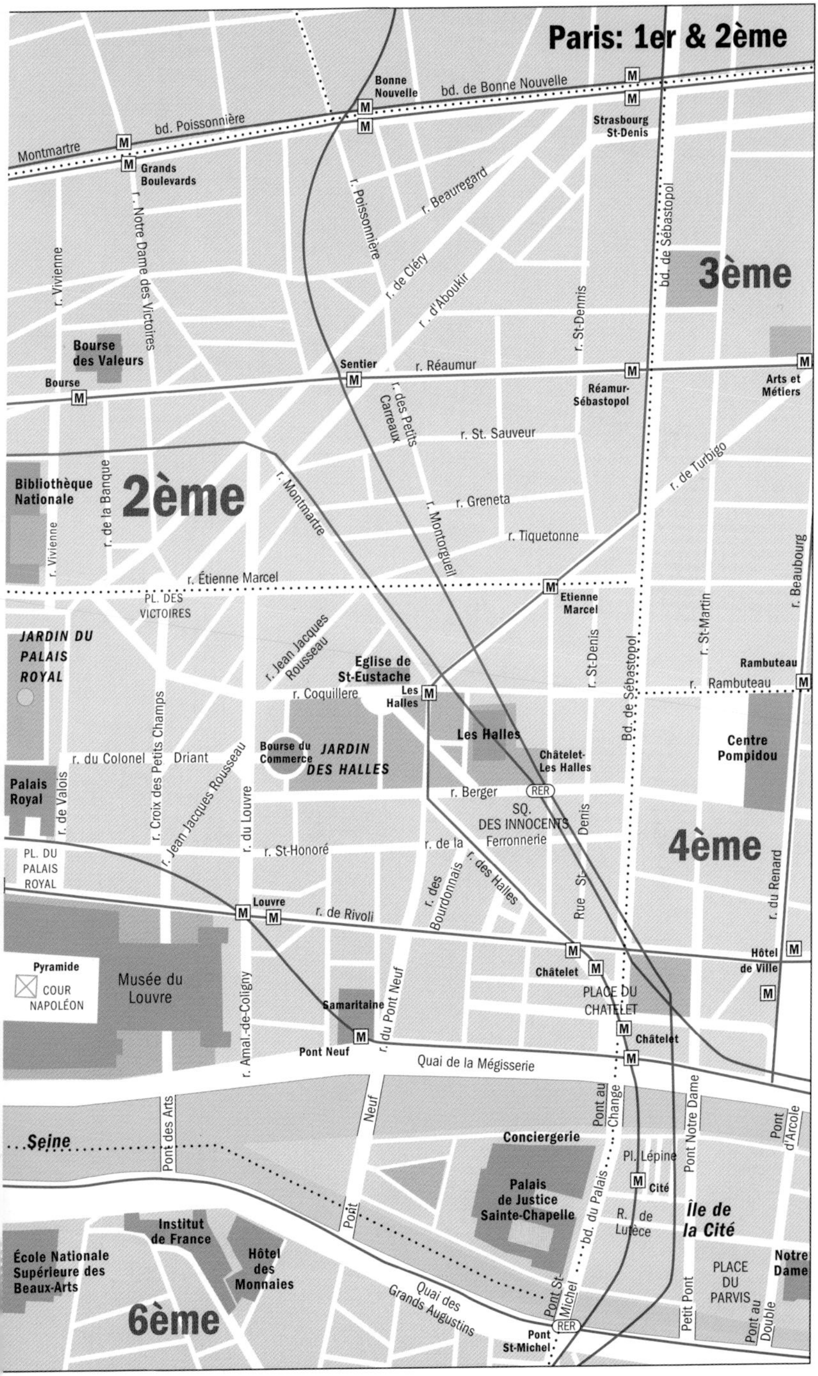
Paris: 1er & 2ème
2ème
3ème
4ème
6ème
bd. de Bonne Nouvelle
bd. Poissonnière
Montmartre
Bonne Nouvelle
Strasbourg St-Denis
Grands Boulevards
r. Notre Dame des Victoires
r. Vivienne
r. Poissonnière
r. Beauregard
r. de Cléry
r. d'Aboukir
bd. de Sébastopol
r. St-Dennis
Bourse des Valeurs
Bourse
Sentier
r. Réaumur
Réaumur-Sébastopol
Arts et Métiers
r. des Petits Carreaux
r. St. Sauveur
Bibliothèque Nationale
r. de la Banque
r. Montmartre
r. Greneta
r. de Turbigo
r. Montorgueil
r. Tiquetonne
r. Vivienne
r. Étienne Marcel
PL. DES VICTOIRES
Etienne Marcel
r. Beaubourg
JARDIN DU PALAIS ROYAL
r. Jean Jacques Rousseau
Eglise de St-Eustache
r. St-Denis
Bd. de Sébastopol
r. St-Martin
Rambuteau
r. Rambuteau
r. Coquillere
Les Halles
r. Croix des Petits Champs
Bourse du Commerce
JARDIN DES HALLES
Les Halles
Châtelet-Les Halles
Centre Pompidou
r. du Colonel Driant
Palais Royal
r. de Valois
r. du Louvre
r. Berger
RER
SQ. DES INNOCENTS
Rue St-Denis
r. St-Honoré
r. de la Ferronnerie
PL. DU PALAIS ROYAL
r. des Bourdonnais
r. des Halles
r. du Renard
Louvre
r. de Rivoli
Châtelet
Hôtel de Ville
Pyramide
COUR NAPOLÉON
Musée du Louvre
r. Amal.-de-Coligny
r. du Pont Neuf
Samaritaine
PLACE DU CHATELET
Châtelet
Pont Neuf
Quai de la Mégisserie
Pont au Change
Pont Notre Dame
Pont d'Arcole
Seine
Pont des Arts
Pont Neuf
Conciergerie
Pl. Lépine
Palais de Justice Sainte-Chapelle
Cité
bd. du Palais
R. de Lutèce
Île de la Cité
Institut de France
Hôtel des Monnaies
École Nationale Supérieure des Beaux-Arts
Quai des Grands Augustins
Pont St Michel
RER
Pont St-Michel
Petit Pont
PLACE DU PARVIS
Pont au Double
Notre Dame

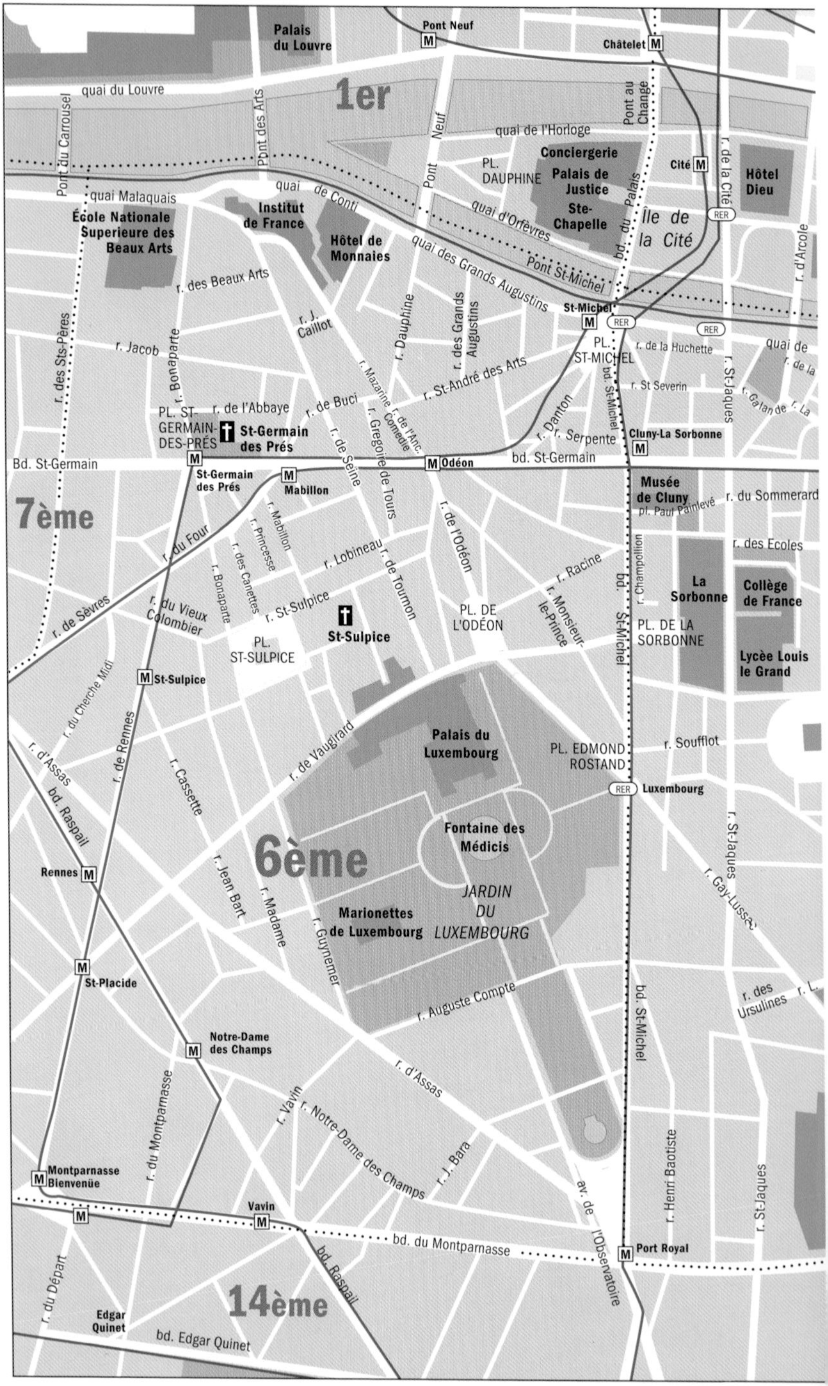

1er
6ème
7ème
14ème
Palais du Louvre
Pont Neuf
Châtelet
quai du Louvre
Pont du Carrousel
Pont des Arts
Pont Neuf
quai de l'Horloge
Pont au Change
Conciergerie
Palais de Justice
Ste-Chapelle
PL. DAUPHINE
Cité
Hôtel Dieu
r. de la Cité
quai Malaquais
quai de Conti
Institut de France
Hôtel de Monnaies
École Nationale Superieure des Beaux Arts
quai d'Orfèvres
Île de la Cité
bd. du Palais
quai des Grands Augustins
Pont St-Michel
r. d'Arcole
St-Michel
RER
r. des Beaux Arts
r. J. Caillot
r. Dauphine
r. des Grands Augustins
r. des Sts-Pères
r. Jacob
r. Bonaparte
PL. ST-MICHEL
r. de la Huchette
quai de
r. St-Jaques
r. Mazarine
r. de l'Anc. Comédie
r. St-André des Arts
r. St Severin
r. Galande
r. de l'Abbaye
r. de Buci
PL. ST-GERMAIN-DES-PRÉS
St-Germain des Prés
r. Danton
r. Serpente
bd. St-Michel
Cluny-La Sorbonne
r. de Seine
r. Gregoire de Tours
Bd. St-Germain
Odéon
bd. St-Germain
St-Germain des Prés
Mabillon
Musée de Cluny
pl. Paul Painlevé
r. du Sommerard
r. Mabillon
r. Princesse
r. des Canettes
r. de l'Odéon
r. du Four
r. Lobineau
r. de Tournon
r. des Ecoles
r. Champollion
r. Racine
La Sorbonne
Collège de France
r. Bonaparte
r. St-Sulpice
r. Monsieur-le-Prince
bd. St-Michel
r. de Sèvres
r. du Vieux Colombier
St-Sulpice
PL. DE L'ODÉON
PL. DE LA SORBONNE
PL. ST-SULPICE
Lycée Louis le Grand
St-Sulpice
r. du Cherche Midi
r. de Rennes
r. de Vaugirard
Palais du Luxembourg
PL. EDMOND ROSTAND
r. Soufflot
r. d'Assas
bd. Raspail
r. Cassette
Luxembourg
Fontaine des Médicis
Rennes
r. Jean Bart
r. Madame
JARDIN DU LUXEMBOURG
r. St-Jaques
r. Gay-Lussac
Marionettes de Luxembourg
r. Guynemer
St-Placide
r. Auguste Compte
r. des Ursulines
Notre-Dame des Champs
r. d'Assas
bd. St-Michel
r. du Montparnasse
r. Vavin
r. Notre-Dame des Champs
r. J. Bara
Montparnasse Bienvenüe
av. de l'Observatoire
r. Henri Baotiste
r. St-Jaques
Vavin
bd. du Montparnasse
Port Royal
bd. Raspail
r. du Départ
Edgar Quinet
bd. Edgar Quinet

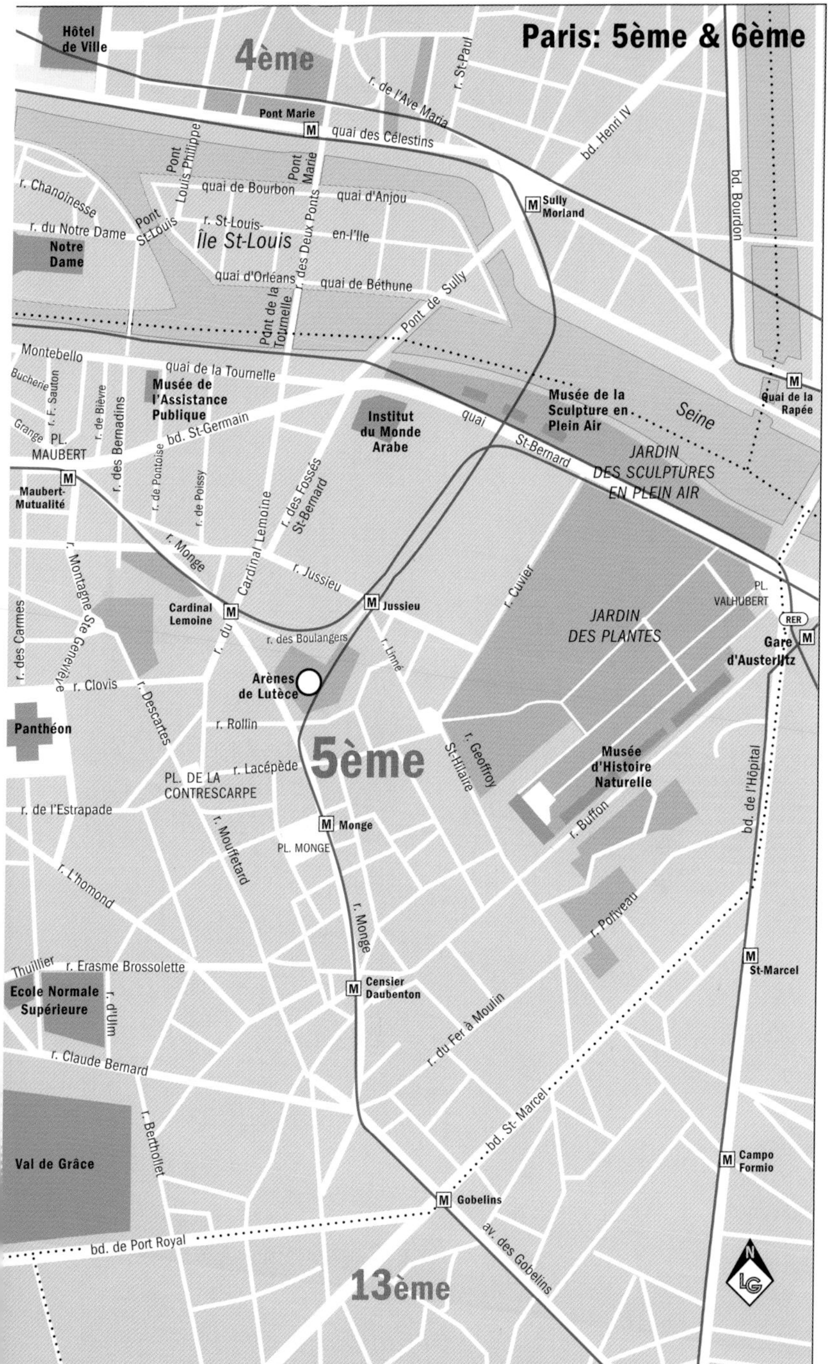

Paris: 5ème & 6ème
4ème
5ème
13ème
Hôtel de Ville
Pont Marie
r. de l'Ave Maria
r. St-Paul
quai des Célestins
bd. Henri IV
bd. Bourdon
Pont Louis Philippe
Pont Marie
quai de Bourbon
quai d'Anjou
r. Chanoinesse
Pont St-Louis
r. St-Louis-en-l'Ile
Île St-Louis
r. du Notre Dame
Notre Dame
r. des Deux Ponts
Sully Morland
quai d'Orléans
quai de Béthune
Pont de la Tournelle
Pont de Sully
Montebello
quai de la Tournelle
Bucherie
r. F. Sauton
r. de Bièvre
r. des Bernadins
Musée de l'Assistance Publique
bd. St-Germain
Grange
PL. MAUBERT
Maubert-Mutualité
r. de Pontoise
r. de Poissy
Institut du Monde Arabe
quai St-Bernard
Musée de la Sculpture en Plein Air
Seine
JARDIN DES SCULPTURES EN PLEIN AIR
Quai de la Rapée
r. Cardinal Lemoine
r. des Fossés St-Bernard
r. Monge
r. Montagne Ste Geneviève
r. Jussieu
Jussieu
r. Cuvier
PL. VALHUBERT
RER
Gare d'Austerlitz
Cardinal Lemoine
r. du
r. des Carmes
r. des Boulangers
r. Linné
JARDIN DES PLANTES
r. Clovis
Arènes de Lutèce
Panthéon
r. Descartes
r. Rollin
r. Geoffroy St-Hilaire
Musée d'Histoire Naturelle
r. Lacépède
PL. DE LA CONTRESCARPE
r. de l'Estrapade
r. Mouffetard
Monge
PL. MONGE
r. Buffon
bd. de l'Hôpital
r. L'homond
r. Monge
r. Poliveau
St-Marcel
Thuillier
r. Erasme Brossolette
Ecole Normale Supérieure
r. d'Ulm
Censier Daubenton
r. du Fer à Moulin
r. Claude Bernard
bd. St. Marcel
Campo Formio
Val de Grâce
r. Berthollet
Gobelins
bd. de Port Royal
av. des Gobelins
N
LG

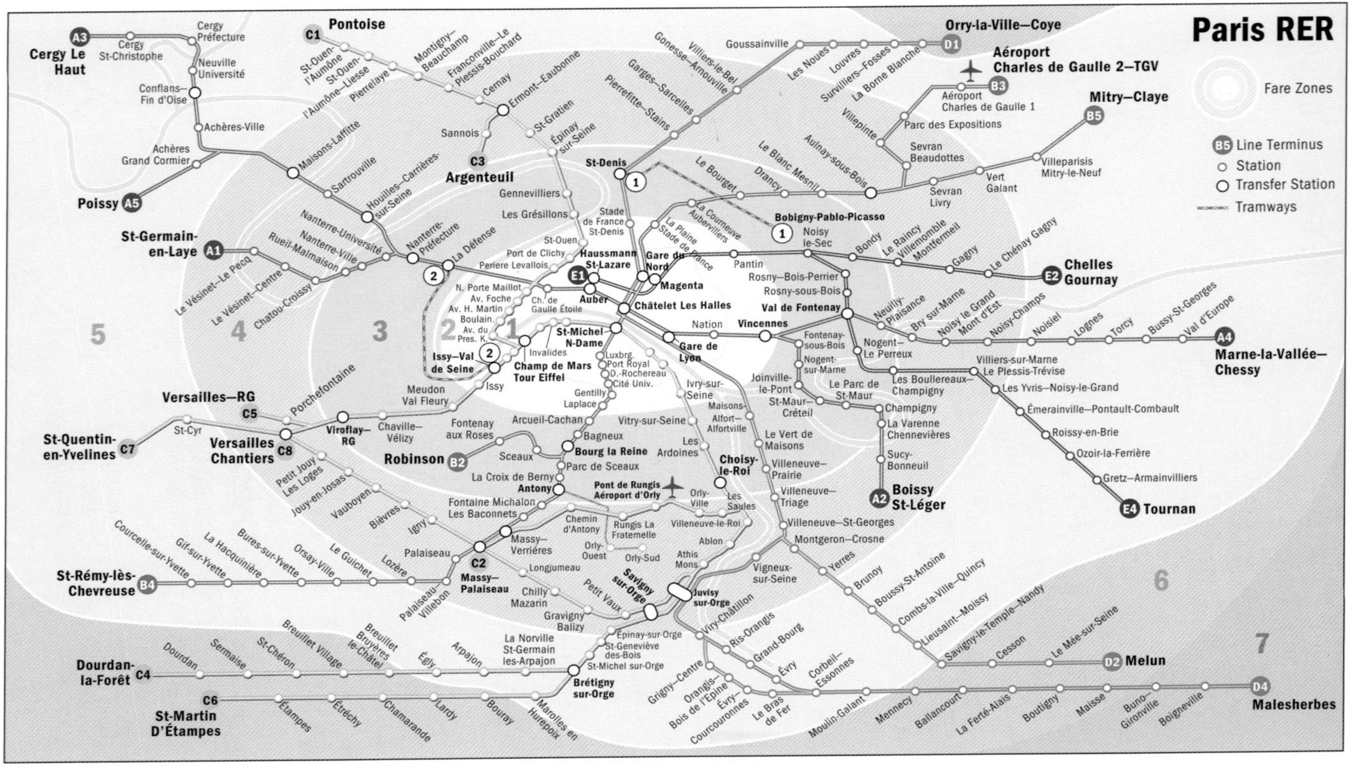
Paris RER
Fare Zones
B5 Line Terminus
Station
Transfer Station
Tramways
1
2
3
4
5
6
7
A1 St-Germain-en-Laye
Le Vésinet–Le Pecq
Le Vésinet–Centre
Chatou-Croissy
Rueil-Malmaison
Nanterre-Ville
Nanterre-Université
A3 Cergy Le Haut
Cergy St-Christophe
Cergy Préfecture
Neuville Université
Conflans–Fin d'Oise
Achères-Ville
Achères Grand Cormier
A5 Poissy
Maisons-Laffitte
Sartrouville
Houilles–Carrières-sur-Seine
Nanterre-Préfecture
La Défense
Charles de Gaulle Étoile
Auber
Châtelet Les Halles
Gare de Lyon
Nation
Vincennes
Val de Fontenay
Neuilly-Plaisance
Bry sur-Marne
Noisy le Grand Mont d'Est
Noisy-Champs
Noisiel
Lognes
Torcy
Bussy-St-Georges
Val d'Europe
A4 Marne-la-Vallée–Chessy
Fontenay-sous-Bois
Nogent-sur-Marne
Joinville-le-Pont
St-Maur–Créteil
Le Parc de St-Maur
Champigny
La Varenne Chennevières
Sucy-Bonneuil
A2 Boissy St-Léger
D1 Orry-la-Ville–Coye
La Borne Blanche
Survilliers–Fosses
Louvres
Les Noues
Goussainville
Villiers-le-Bel
Gonesse–Arnouville
Garges–Sarcelles
Pierrefitte–Stains
St-Denis
Stade de France St-Denis
Gare du Nord
St-Michel N-Dame
Gare de Lyon
Maisons-Alfort–Alfortville
Le Vert de Maisons
Villeneuve-Prairie
Villeneuve-Triage
Villeneuve–St-Georges
Montgeron–Crosne
Yerres
Brunoy
Boussy-St-Antoine
Combs-la-Ville–Quincy
Lieusaint–Moissy
Savigny-le-Temple–Nandy
Cesson
Le Mée-sur-Seine
D2 Melun
Vigneux-sur-Seine
Juvisy sur-Orge
Viry-Châtillon
Ris-Orangis
Grand-Bourg
Évry
Corbeil-Essonnes
Grigny–Centre
Orangis–Bois de l'Épine
Évry–Courcouronnes
Le Bras de Fer
Moulin-Galant
Mennecy
Ballancourt
La Ferté-Alais
Boutigny
Maisse
Buno–Gironville
Boigneville
D4 Malesherbes
B3 Aéroport Charles de Gaulle 2–TGV
Aéroport Charles de Gaulle 1
Parc des Expositions
Villepinte
Sevran Beaudottes
B5 Mitry–Claye
Villeparisis Mitry-le-Neuf
Vert Galant
Sevran Livry
Aulnay-sous-Bois
Le Blanc Mesnil
Drancy
Le Bourget
La Courneuve Aubervilliers
La Plaine Stade de France
Luxbrg.
Port Royal
D.-Rochereau
Cité Univ.
Gentilly
Laplace
Arcueil-Cachan
Bagneux
Bourg la Reine
Parc de Sceaux
La Croix de Berny
Antony
Fontaine Michalon
Les Baconnets
Massy–Verrières
Massy–Palaiseau
Palaiseau
Palaiseau-Villebon
Lozère
Le Guichet
Orsay-Ville
Bures-sur-Yvette
La Hacquinière
Gif-sur-Yvette
Courcelle-sur-Yvette
B4 St-Rémy-lès-Chevreuse
Sceaux
Fontenay aux Roses
B2 Robinson
Pont de Rungis Aéroport d'Orly
Orly-Ville
Les Saules
Villeneuve-le-Roi
Ablon
Athis Mons
Choisy-le-Roi
Les Ardoines
Vitry-sur-Seine
Ivry-sur-Seine
Chemin d'Antony
Rungis La Fraternelle
Orly-Ouest
Orly-Sud
Longjumeau
Chilly Mazarin
Gravigny Balizy
Petit Vaux
Savigny sur-Orge
Epinay-sur-Orge
St-Geneviève des-Bois
St-Michel sur-Orge
Brétigny sur-Orge
La Norville St-Germain les-Arpajon
Arpajon
Égly
Breuillet Bruyères le-Châtel
Breuillet Village
St-Chéron
Sermaise
Dourdan
C4 Dourdan-la-Forêt
Marolles en Hurepoix
Bouray
Lardy
Chamarande
Étrechy
Étampes
C6 St-Martin D'Étampes
C1 Pontoise
St-Ouen-l'Aumône
St-Ouen-l'Aumône–Liesse
Pierrelaye
Montigny–Beauchamp
Franconville–Le Plessis-Bouchard
Cernay
Ermont–Eaubonne
Sannois
C3 Argenteuil
St-Gratien
Épinay sur-Seine
Gennevilliers
Les Grésillons
St-Ouen
Port de Clichy
Periere Levallois
N. Porte Maillot
Av. Foche
Av. H. Martin
Boulain.
Av. du Pres. K.
Invalides
Champ de Mars Tour Eiffel
Issy–Val de Seine
Issy
Meudon Val Fleury
Chaville–Vélizy
Viroflay–RG
Porchefontaine
C5 Versailles–RG
C8 Versailles Chantiers
St-Cyr
C7 St-Quentin-en-Yvelines
Petit Jouy Les Loges
Jouy-en-Josas
Vauboyen
Bièvres
Igny
Haussmann St-Lazare
E1
Magenta
Pantin
Rosny–Bois-Perrier
Rosny-sous-Bois
Noisy le-Sec
Bobigny-Pablo-Picasso
Bondy
Le Raincy Villemomble Montfermeil
Gagny
Le Chénay Gagny
E2 Chelles Gournay
Nogent–Le Perreux
Les Boullereaux–Champigny
Villiers-sur-Marne Le Plessis-Trévise
Les Yvris–Noisy-le-Grand
Émerainville–Pontault-Combault
Roissy-en-Brie
Ozoir-la-Ferrière
Gretz–Armainvilliers
E4 Tournan

LET'S GO

■ PAGES PACKED WITH ESSENTIAL INFORMATION

"Value-packed, unbeatable, accurate, and comprehensive."

—The Los Angeles Times

"The guides are aimed not only at young budget travelers but at the independent traveler; a sort of streetwise cookbook for traveling alone."

—The New York Times

"Unbeatable; good sight-seeing advice; up-to-date info on restaurants, hotels, and inns; a commitment to money-saving travel; and a wry style that brightens nearly every page."

—The Washington Post

■ THE BEST TRAVEL BARGAINS IN YOUR BUDGET

"All the dirt, dirt cheap."

—People

"Let's Go follows the creed that you don't have to toss your life's savings to the wind to travel—unless you want to."

—The Salt Lake Tribune

■ REAL ADVICE FOR REAL EXPERIENCES

"The writers seem to have experienced every rooster-packed bus and lunar-surfaced mattress about which they write."

—The New York Times

"[Let's Go's] devoted updaters really walk the walk (and thumb the ride, and trek the trail). Learn how to fish, haggle, find work—anywhere."

—Food & Wine

"A world-wise traveling companion—always ready with friendly advice and helpful hints, all sprinkled with a bit of wit."

—The Philadelphia Inquirer

■ A GUIDE WITH A SPIRIT AND A SOCIAL CONSCIENCE

"Lighthearted and sophisticated, informative and fun to read. [Let's Go] helps the novice traveler navigate like a knowledgeable old hand."

—Atlanta Journal-Constitution

"The serious mission at the book's core reveals itself in exhortations to respect the culture and the environment—and, if possible, to visit as a volunteer, a student, or a teacher rather than a tourist."

—San Francisco Chronicle

LET'S GO PUBLICATIONS

TRAVEL GUIDES

Australia 9th edition
Austria & Switzerland 12th edition
Brazil 1st edition
Britain 2008
California 10th edition
Central America 9th edition
Chile 2nd edition
China 5th edition
Costa Rica 3rd edition
Eastern Europe 13th edition
Ecuador 1st edition
Egypt 2nd edition
Europe 2008
France 2008
Germany 13th edition
Greece 9th edition
Hawaii 4th edition
India & Nepal 8th edition
Ireland 13th edition
Israel 4th edition
Italy 2008
Japan 1st edition
Mexico 22nd edition
New Zealand 8th edition
Peru 1st edition
Puerto Rico 3rd edition
Southeast Asia 9th edition
Spain & Portugal 2008
Thailand 3rd edition
USA 24th edition
Vietnam 2nd edition
Western Europe 2008

ROADTRIP GUIDE

Roadtripping USA 2nd edition

ADVENTURE GUIDES

Alaska 1st edition
Pacific Northwest 1st edition
Southwest USA 3rd edition

CITY GUIDES

Amsterdam 5th edition
Barcelona 3rd edition
Boston 4th edition
London 16th edition
New York City 16th edition
Paris 14th edition
Rome 12th edition
San Francisco 4th edition
Washington, D.C. 13th edition

POCKET CITY GUIDES

Amsterdam
Berlin
Boston
Chicago
London
New York City
Paris
San Francisco
Venice
Washington, D.C.

LET'S GO

FRANCE

2008

Andrea Halpern Editor
Sara O'Rourke Associate Editor
Caitlin Marquis Associate Editor

Researcher-Writers

Aliza Aufrichtig
Richard Beck
Mathieu Desruisseaux
David Haussman
Anna Polonyi
Harker Rhodes
John Stroh

Joy Ding Map Editor
Calina Ciobanu Managing Editor

St. Martin's Press New York

HELPING LET'S GO. If you want to share your discoveries, suggestions, or corrections, please drop us a line. We read every piece of correspondence, whether a postcard, a 10-page email, or a coconut. **Address mail to:**

Let's Go: France
67 Mount Auburn St.
Cambridge, MA 02138
USA

Visit Let's Go at **http://www.letsgo.com,** or send email to:

feedback@letsgo.com
Subject: "Let's Go: France"

In addition to the invaluable travel advice our readers share with us, many are kind enough to offer their services as researchers or editors. Unfortunately, our charter enables us to employ only currently enrolled Harvard students.

Distributed outside the USA and Canada by Macmillan.

ISBN-13: 978-312-37453-2
ISBN-10: 0-312-37453-4
First edition
10 9 8 7 6 5 4 3 2 1

Let's Go: France is written by Let's Go Publications, 67 Mount Auburn St., Cambridge, MA 02138, USA.

HOW TO USE THIS BOOK

COVERAGE LAYOUT. *Let's Go: France* launches out of **Paris** and continues with a whirlwind tour of the diverse *départements* of this often-stereotyped country. Beginning with the **Loire Valley,** a land of castles and real-life fairy tales, we head to the craggy coasts of fiercely-Celtic **Brittany** and war-torn **Normandy.** We then travel to **The North,** where vestiges of its war-ridden past coexist with romantic retreats. Then it's on to **Champagne**—for just that. In **Alsace, Lorraine,** and **Franche-Comté,** the German influence pervades more than the meat-and-cheese-drenched cuisine, and the food and wine tradition continues in **Burgundy.** Venture into the adventure meccas of the **Rhône-Alpes** and the volcanic **Massif Central,** whose beauty is on a higher plane, then dive into the caves of **Dordogne** and **Limousin.** Discover the quirky coast of **Poitou-Charentes** and a Spanish spirit in luxurious **Aquitaine and Pays Basque** and fiercely independent **Languedoc-Roussillon.** Visit the southeast, where world-famous festivals (with the young, restless, and ultra-glamorous) sweep through picturesque **Provence** and the notoriously naughty **Côte d'Azur.** Finish on the Mediterranean island of **Corsica,** which is as diverse as its mainland counterpart.

TRANSPORTATION INFO. For making connections between destinations, information is generally listed under both the arrival and departure cities. Parentheticals usually provide the trip duration followed by the frequency, then the price. For more general information on travel, consult the **Essentials** (p. 9) section.

COVERING THE BASICS. The first chapter, **Discover France** (p. 1), contains highlights of the country, complete with **Suggested Itineraries.** The **Essentials** (p. 9) section contains practical information on planning a budget, making reservations, and other useful tips for traveling in France. Take some time to peruse the **Life and Times** (p. 58) section, which introduces France, briefly summing up its history, culture, and customs. The **Appendix** (p. 797) has climate information, a list of bank holidays, measurement conversions, a phrasebook, and a glossary. For study abroad, volunteer, and work options in France, **Beyond Tourism** (p. 82) is all you need.

SCHOLARLY ARTICLES. Three contributors with unique regional insight wrote articles for *Let's Go: France.* Harvard graduates and Let's Go veterans (and also sisters) **Charlotte** and **Sara Houghteling** provide insight into Haussman's revamping of Paris (p. 137), and Harvard graduate **Cat Walleck** chronicles her experience restoring ancient buildings in the Côte d'Azur (p. 93).

PRICE DIVERSITY. Our researchers list establishments in order of value from best to worst, with absolute favorites denoted by the *Let's Go* thumbs-up (👍). Since the cheapest price does not always mean the best value, we have incorporated a system of price ranges for food and accommodations; see p. XVIII.

PHONE CODES AND TELEPHONE NUMBERS. Area codes for each region appear opposite the name of the region and are denoted by the ☎ icon. Phone numbers in text are also preceded by the ☎ icon.

A NOTE TO OUR READERS. The information for this book was gathered by *Let's Go* researchers from May through August of 2007. Each listing is based on one researcher's opinion, formed during his or her visit at a particular time. Those traveling at other times may have different experiences since prices, dates, hours, and conditions are always subject to change. You are urged to check the facts presented in this book beforehand to avoid inconvenience and surprises.

Hotel du Lion d'Or
Room (Double)
Hôtel du Lion D'Or
5 rue de la Sourdière
75001 PARIS
Tel: 33 (0) 1 42 60 79 04
Fax: 33 (0) 1 42 60 09 14
info@hotelduliondor.com
CyberCafe
Studio Apartment
Budget hotel
in the heart of Paris
Minutes from the most beautiful landmarks in Paris, and with its own
CyberCafe, Hôtel du Lion d'Or is the perfect choice for Let's Go Travelers.
Only a two minute walk away from the Louvre!
www.hotelduliondor.com

CONTENTS

RESEARCHER-WRITERS

Aliza Aufrichtig *Alsace, Lorraine, and Franche-Comté; Burgundy; Champagne; The North*

Whether it meant making her own mustard (it turned out "a bit runny") or pretending to have a child to complete her Bastille Day experience (anything to get a glow stick), Aliza was determined to drink in (often literally) all that her route had to offer. With unquestionable wit, this Hemingway expert found cool, quirky, or fun sights (Metz's train station?) that the towns themselves didn't know they had—and on her days off, jet-setted to Paris, her true love.

Richard Beck *Paris*

Rich may be the only person who has refused to be wooed by Paris's many distractions (including an overly aggressive prostitute). More than your average blond, Rich stripped the City of Love of its lustre: he stormed the Bastille (finding little of interest), rooted through the Louvre (unfazed by even the Mona Lisa), and uncovered unofficial Paris politics (i.e., cutting culinary rivalries). From an apartment in the outlying *arrondissements*, this Literature major got the inside scoop—all while fiercely defending his beloved pastries from persistent Parisian pigeons.

Mathieu Desruisseaux *Corsica, Côte d'Azur*

A savvy Québec native, Mathieu saw his itinerary—packed with the most glamorous, posh, pricey, and snooty places in France, where many have lost their fame, fortune, and minds—and partied through it with a sniff (in Grasse, the perfume capital) and maybe the occasional "O.M.D." (French for "Oh My God"). Mopeding around Corsica and scuba diving at every chance, Mathieu only fell once—in love, that is, with the town of Cannes.

David Hausman *Aquitaine and Pays Basque, Languedoc-Roussillon, Provence*

Armed with biting honesty and a tiny French car, David ventured through landscapes made famous by countless Impressionists—and revealed which actually deserved to be painted. This Social Studies major explored his love of cooking in food write-ups that could make anyone drool, and infused more spark (if it were possible) into lively student centers Toulouse and Montpellier—all while meeting months of downpour with infectious optimism.

RESEARCHER-WRITERS

Anna Polonyi *Loire Valley, Poitou-Charentes*

Despite being a French native, Anna definitely took the country by surprise. Within the first few days, she had talked herself out of a €300 fine, drudged up scandal in one of the Loire Valley's most sophisticated châteaux, and partied at every happening spot on the west coast. Anna took on abbeys and found their dirty little secrets, took on ugly cities and found their hidden beauty, and took on some of the most worn regions and left them renewed.

Harker Rhodes *Brittany, Normandy*

With the word "budget" deeply imprinted on his mind, Harker took every *crêperie*, supermarket, and hostel in northwestern France by storm. Calling Harker's copy impeccable would be an understatement, as would be calling his notes extensive. A Linguistics major and history lover, this New Hampshire native thrived in fiercely-cultural Brittany and war-torn Normandy—overcoming weeks of rain, runaway luggage, and bitter post office workers.

John Stroh *Dordogne and Limousin, Massif Central, Rhône-Alpes*

A Varsity rower and French history buff, John was the perfect person to take on the rugged terrain of the Massif and Alps. Biking sometimes over 60km (one time fixing his own tire in a torrential downpour), hiking anywhere and everywhere (again, usually during a deluge), and using French bread as his main fuel, this Iowa native found adventure at every turn—without ever losing his cool.

CONTRIBUTING WRITERS

Charlotte Houghteling has worked on *Let's Go: Middle East*, *Egypt*, and *Israel* titles. She wrote her senior thesis on the development of department stores during the Second Empire and, in 2004, completed her M.Phil at Cambridge University on the consumer society of Revolutionary Paris. She recently graduated from Columbia Law School.

Sara Houghteling was a researcher-writer for *Let's Go France: 1999*. She spent a year teaching at the American School in Paris in 2000 and holds a Masters in Fine Arts from the University of Michigan. Funded by a Fulbright Grant, Sara spent 2006 in Paris researching her upcoming novel on the recovery of Jewish artwork in Paris after WWII.

Cat Walleck graduated from Harvard University in 2006 with a degree in Romance Language Studies (French, English, and Italian). She is currently attending the American Conservatory Theater to pursue a career in acting.

ACKNOWLEDGMENTS

TEAM FRANCE THANKS: Our RWs, for being brave/hilarious/brutally honest. Italy, for Disney/country/laughs. Joy, for fashion. Vicki, for 'getting' Frame. Bri and Inès, for repping FRA in EUR. Calina, for endless support. Opening hours in France, for keeping things complicated.

ANDREA THANKS: David, Mathieu, and Rich for making me laugh and making my job easy. Caitlin, for meticulous work and putting Vinnie in his place. Sara, for BLWAH, dancing in our chairs, and lunchtime talks. Vinnie, for teaching me Army values. Stefan, for ratatouille. Victoria, for pod dates. FRITA, for making the office a home. Tom, for a shoulder. Georgia, for email love from far away. Tish, for my daily phone call. Mom and Dad, for Brookline, Basie, and more than I could ever fit in this paragraph.

SARA THANKS: Aliza, Anna, and John for letting me live vicariously through their copy. Caitlin, for presents and sanity. Dre, for sharing my obsessions with Jane Austen, food, awkward pronunciations, and everything French. Vinnie, for metaphors, Ghostwriter, similarly-random music taste, and conceding defeat. Stefan, for cheery mornings. Victoria, for patience/support. FRITA for amazing dates/chats. France, esp. Paris. Dad, for keeping things humorous. Mike, for listening to my stories. Mom, for everything.

CAITLIN THANKS: Harker, for flawless copy. The ladies of Team France: Sara, for 'generalizations'; Dre, for responding with a reassuring 'amazing.' The men of Team Italy: Vinnie, for reminding us the '07 book was already perfect; Stefan, for keeping us grounded. Victoria, for stories. Susan and Ez, for understanding. Hope, for summer. Sheena, for so much more than a place to stay. M&D, for more than I deserve.

JOY THANKS: Team FRA; rocking maps. BShiz; ADD, coffee, pad thai, a second home. Gihi & Dlou; my dose of science. Mom & Dad; because.

Editor
Andrea Halpern
Associate Editors
Sara O'Rourke, Caitlin Marquis
Managing Editor
Calina Ciobanu
Map Editor
Joy Ding
Typesetter
Victoria Esquivel-Korsiak

LET'S GO

Publishing Director
Jennifer Q. Wong
Editor-in-Chief
Silvia Gonzalez Killingsworth
Production Manager
Victoria Esquivel-Korsiak
Cartography Manager
Thomas MacDonald Barron
Editorial Managers
Anne Bensson, Calina Ciobanu, Rachel Nolan
Financial Manager
Sara Culver
Business and Marketing Manager
Julie Vodhanel
Personnel Manager
Victoria Norelid
Production Associate
Jansen A. S. Thurmer
Director of E-Commerce & IT
Patrick Carroll
Website Manager
Kathryne A. Bevilacqua
Office Coordinators
Juan L. Peña, Bradley J. Jones

Director of Advertising Sales
Hunter McDonald
Senior Advertising Associate
Daniel Lee

President
William Hauser
General Managers
Bob Rombauer, Jim McKellar

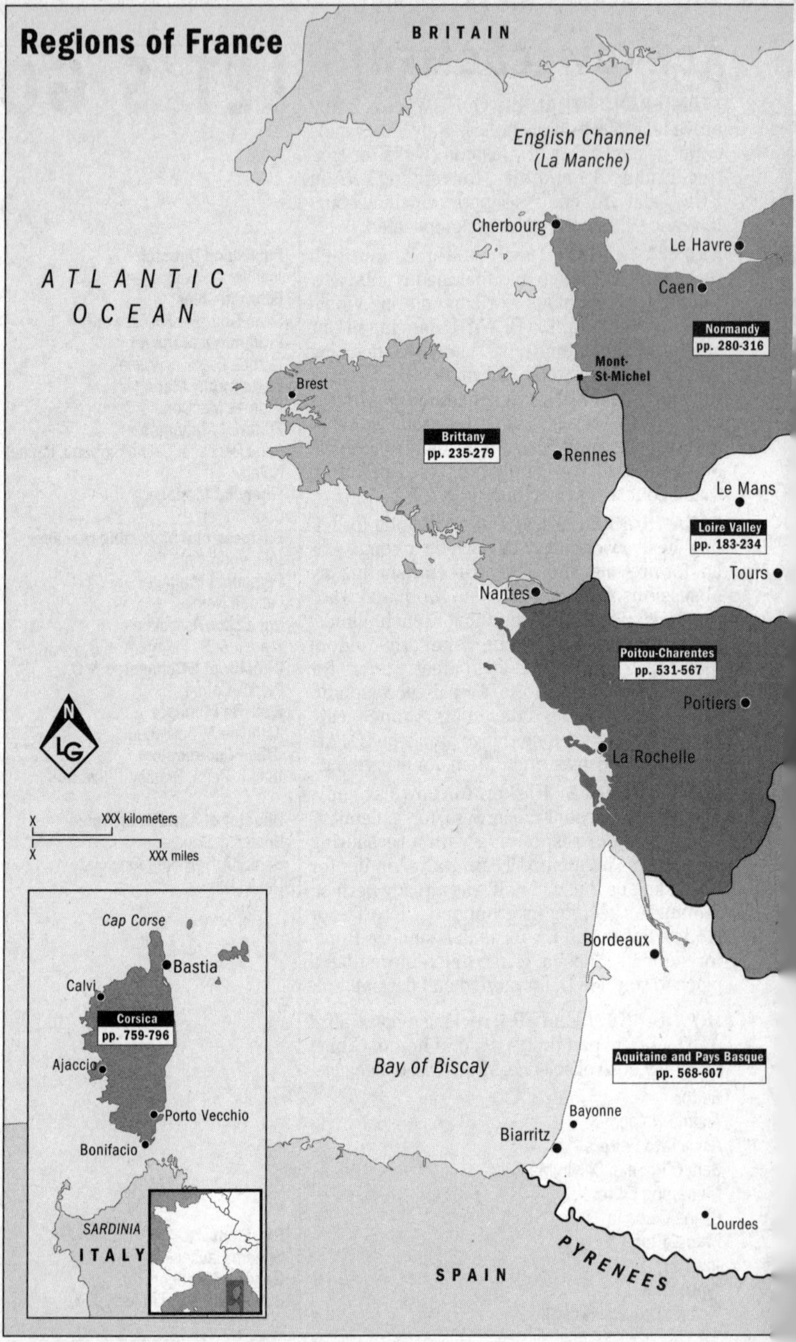
Regions of France
BRITAIN
English Channel
(La Manche)
ATLANTIC
OCEAN
Cherbourg
Le Havre
Caen
Normandy
pp. 280-316
Mont-
St-Michel
Brest
Brittany
pp. 235-279
Rennes
Le Mans
Loire Valley
pp. 183-234
Tours
Nantes
Poitou-Charentes
pp. 531-567
Poitiers
La Rochelle
N
LG
X
XXX kilometers
X
XXX miles
Cap Corse
Bastia
Calvi
Corsica
pp. 759-796
Ajaccio
Porto Vecchio
Bonifacio
SARDINIA
ITALY
Bordeaux
Bay of Biscay
Aquitaine and Pays Basque
pp. 568-607
Bayonne
Biarritz
Lourdes
PYRENEES
SPAIN

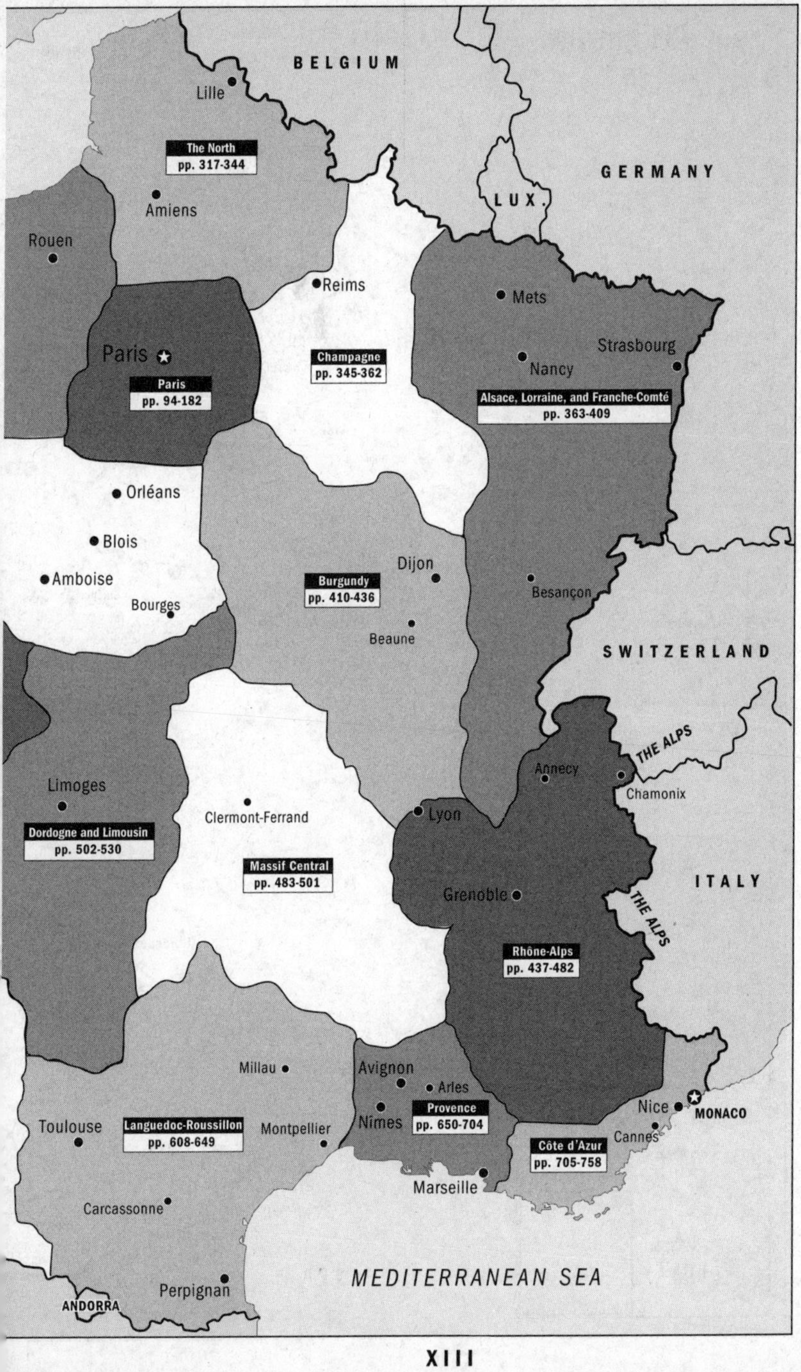
BELGIUM
GERMANY
LUX.
SWITZERLAND
ITALY
MONACO
ANDORRA
MEDITERRANEAN SEA
THE ALPS
THE ALPS
Lille
The North
pp. 317-344
Amiens
Rouen
Reims
Paris
Paris
pp. 94-182
Champagne
pp. 345-362
Mets
Nancy
Strasbourg
Alsace, Lorraine, and Franche-Comté
pp. 363-409
Orléans
Blois
Amboise
Bourges
Dijon
Burgundy
pp. 410-436
Beaune
Besançon
Annecy
Chamonix
Lyon
Limoges
Dordogne and Limousin
pp. 502-530
Clermont-Ferrand
Massif Central
pp. 483-501
Grenoble
Rhône-Alps
pp. 437-482
Millau
Avignon
Arles
Nîmes
Provence
pp. 650-704
Nice
Cannes
Côte d'Azur
pp. 705-758
Toulouse
Languedoc-Roussillon
pp. 608-649
Montpellier
Marseille
Carcassonne
Perpignan

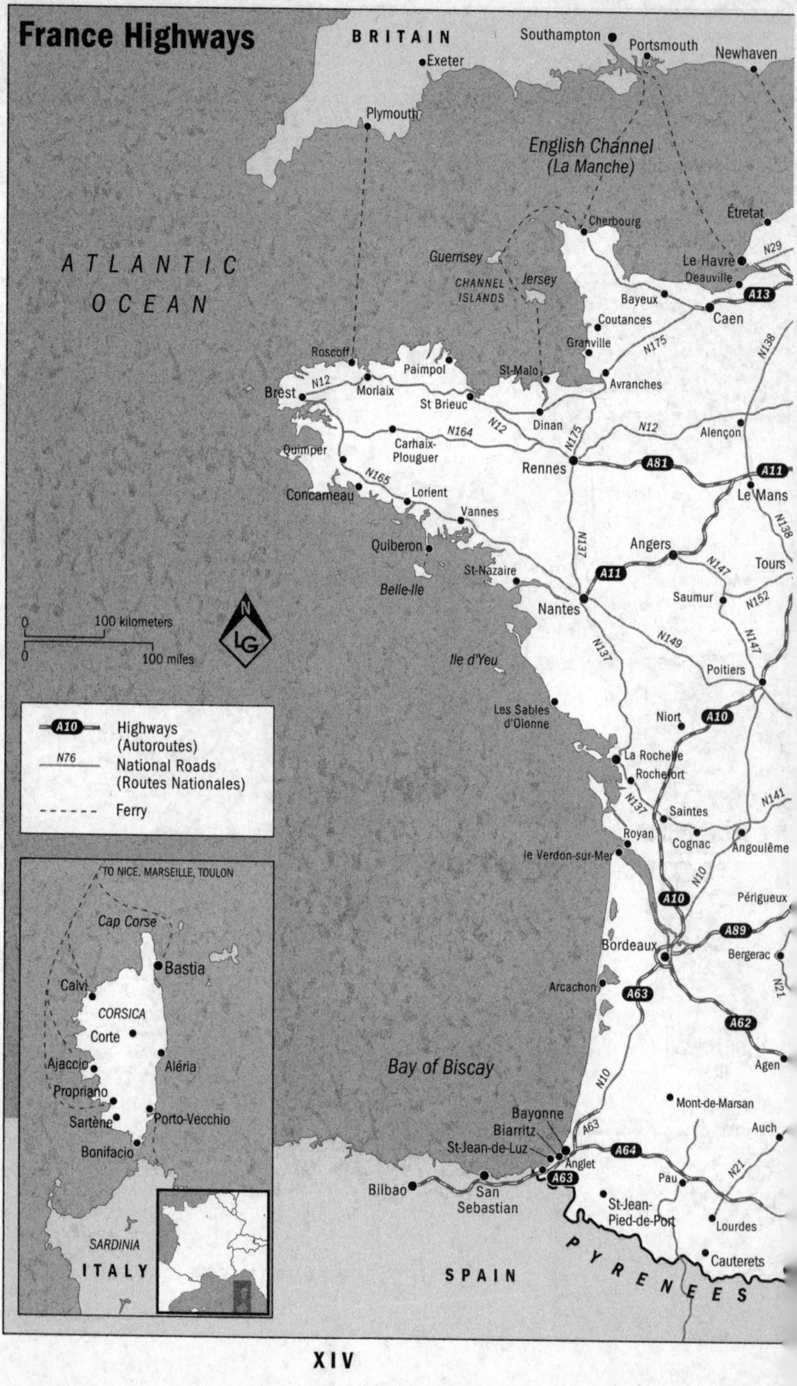
France Highways
BRITAIN
Southampton
Portsmouth
Newhaven
Exeter
Plymouth
English Channel
(La Manche)
ATLANTIC
OCEAN
Cherbourg
Étretat
Guernsey
CHANNEL
ISLANDS
Jersey
Le Havre
Deauville
Bayeux
Caen
Coutances
Granville
Roscoff
Paimpol
St-Malo
Avranches
Brest
Morlaix
St Brieuc
Dinan
Alençon
Quimper
Carhaix-
Plouguer
Rennes
Le Mans
Concarneau
Lorient
Vannes
Quiberon
Angers
Tours
St-Nazaire
Belle-Ile
Saumur
Nantes
0
100 kilometers
0
100 miles
Ile d'Yeu
Poitiers
Les Sables
d'Olonne
Niort
Highways
(Autoroutes)
National Roads
(Routes Nationales)
Ferry
La Rochelle
Rochefort
Saintes
Royan
Cognac
Angoulême
le Verdon-sur-Mer
TO NICE, MARSEILLE, TOULON
Périgueux
Cap Corse
Bordeaux
Bergerac
Bastia
Calvi
Arcachon
CORSICA
Corte
Ajaccio
Aléria
Bay of Biscay
Agen
Propriano
Sartène
Porto-Vecchio
Mont-de-Marsan
Bayonne
Biarritz
Auch
Bonifacio
St-Jean-de-Luz
Anglet
Pau
Bilbao
San
Sebastian
St-Jean-
Pied-de-Port
Lourdes
SARDINIA
ITALY
SPAIN
Cauterets
PYRENEES
A10
A11
A13
A62
A63
A64
A81
A89
N10
N12
N21
N29
N76
N137
N138
N141
N147
N149
N152
N164
N165
N175

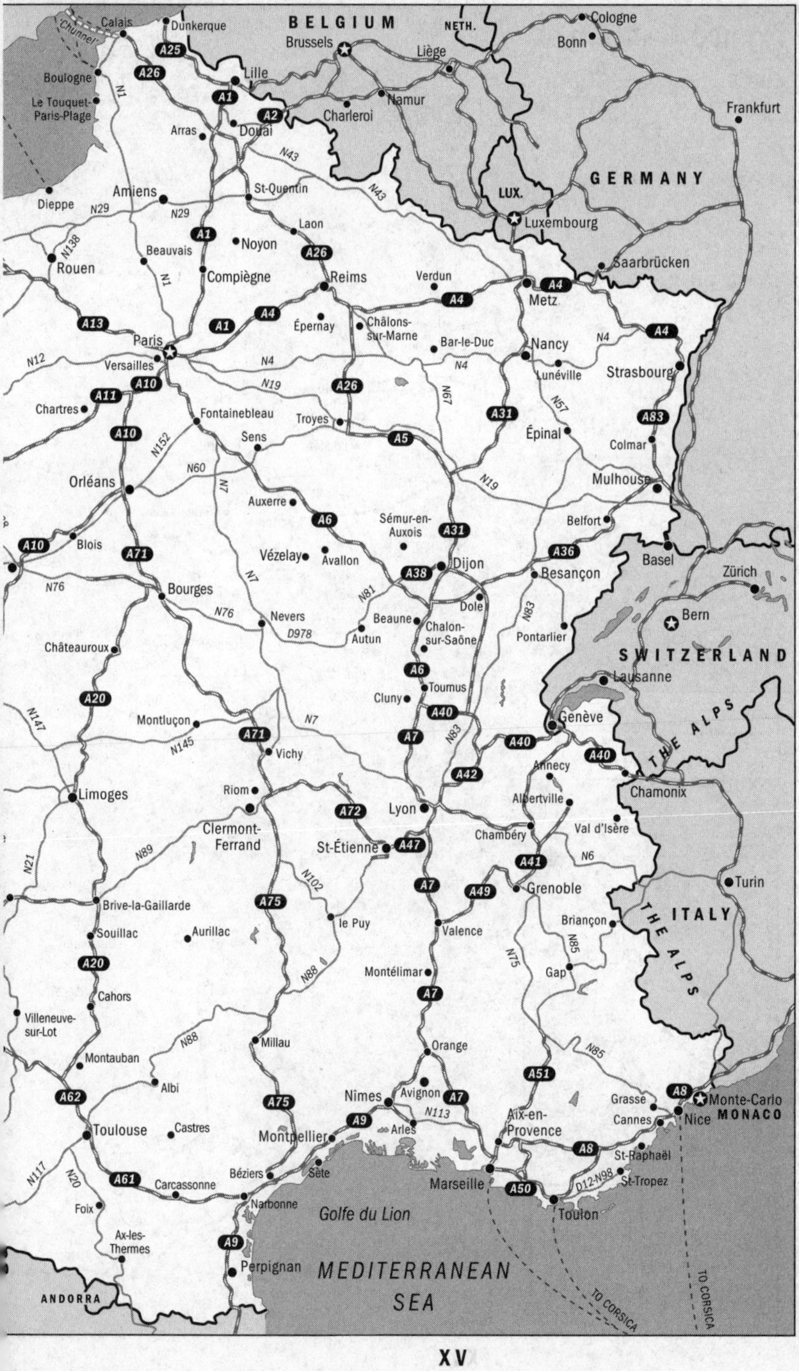
BELGIUM
NETH.
GERMANY
LUX.
SWITZERLAND
ITALY
THE ALPS
THE ALPS
MONACO
ANDORRA
MEDITERRANEAN
SEA
Golfe du Lion
'Chunnel'
TO CORSICA
TO CORSICA
Calais
Dunkerque
Brussels
Liège
Cologne
Bonn
Frankfurt
Boulogne
Le Touquet-Paris-Plage
Lille
Namur
Charleroi
Arras
Douai
Amiens
Dieppe
St-Quentin
Laon
Noyon
Beauvais
Rouen
Compiègne
Reims
Verdun
Luxembourg
Saarbrücken
Metz
Paris
Versailles
Épernay
Châlons-sur-Marne
Bar-le-Duc
Nancy
Lunéville
Strasbourg
Chartres
Fontainebleau
Troyes
Épinal
Colmar
Sens
Orléans
Mulhouse
Auxerre
Sémur-en-Auxois
Belfort
Blois
Vézelay
Avallon
Dijon
Basel
Zürich
Bourges
Besançon
Dole
Bern
Nevers
Beaune
Chalon-sur-Saône
Autun
Pontarlier
Châteauroux
Tournus
Cluny
Lausanne
Montluçon
Genève
Vichy
Annecy
Riom
Lyon
Albertville
Chamonix
Limoges
Clermont-Ferrand
St-Étienne
Chambéry
Val d'Isère
Grenoble
Turin
Brive-la-Gaillarde
le Puy
Valence
Briançon
Souillac
Aurillac
Montélimar
Gap
Cahors
Villeneuve-sur-Lot
Millau
Orange
Montauban
Albi
Nîmes
Avignon
Grasse
Monte-Carlo
Nice
Cannes
Toulouse
Castres
Montpellier
Arles
Aix-en-Provence
St-Raphaël
Sète
Béziers
Marseille
St-Tropez
Carcassonne
Narbonne
Toulon
Foix
Ax-les-Thermes
Perpignan
A1
A2
A4
A5
A6
A7
A8
A9
A10
A11
A13
A20
A25
A26
A31
A36
A38
A40
A41
A42
A47
A49
A50
A51
A61
A62
A71
A72
A75
A83
N1
N4
N6
N7
N12
N19
N20
N21
N29
N43
N57
N60
N67
N75
N76
N81
N83
N85
N88
N89
N102
N113
N117
N138
N145
N147
N152
D978
D12-N98

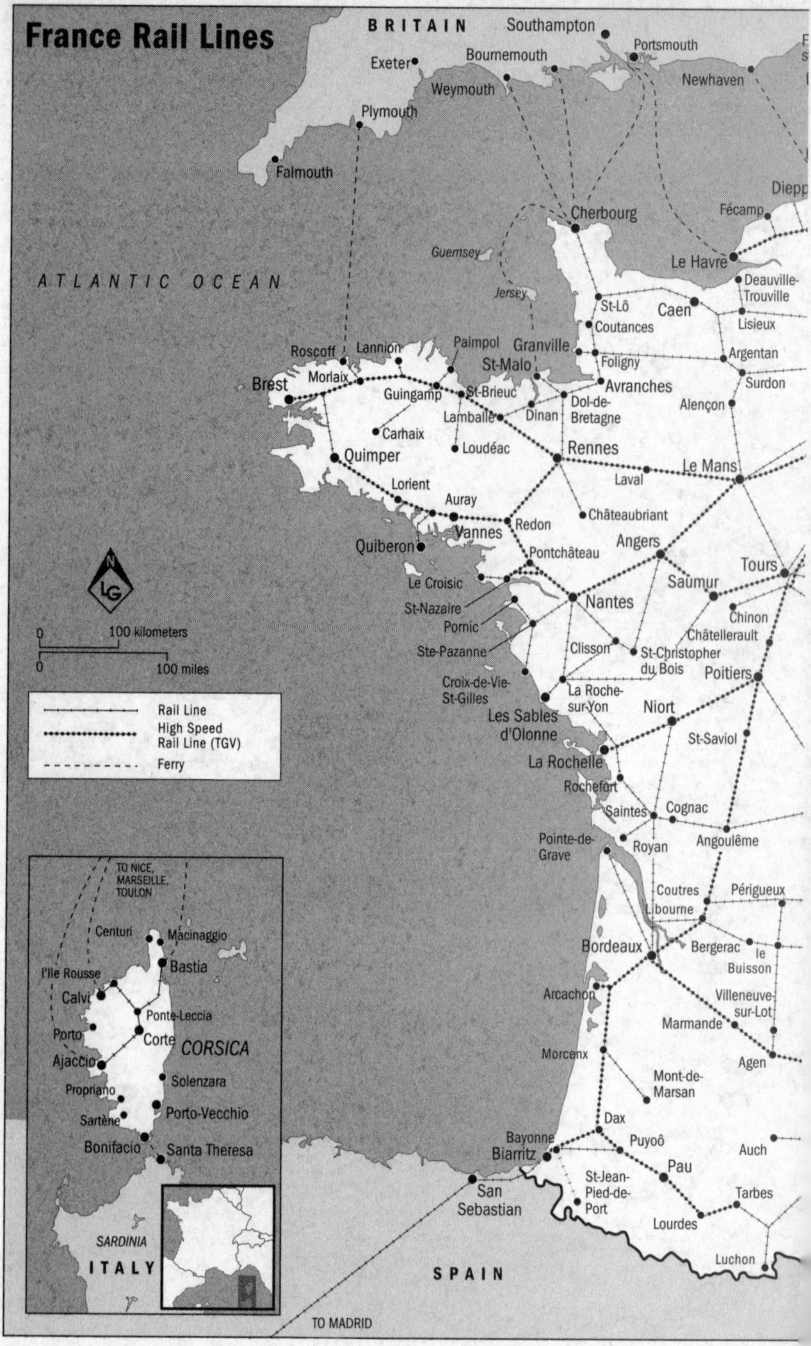
France Rail Lines
BRITAIN
Southampton
Portsmouth
Exeter
Bournemouth
Weymouth
Newhaven
Plymouth
Falmouth
Cherbourg
Fécamp
Le Havre
Guernsey
Jersey
ATLANTIC OCEAN
Deauville-Trouville
St-Lô
Caen
Lisieux
Coutances
Roscoff
Lannion
Paimpol
Granville
Argentan
St-Malo
Foligny
Brest
Morlaix
Avranches
Surdon
Guingamp
St-Brieuc
Dol-de-Bretagne
Alençon
Lamballe
Dinan
Carhaix
Loudéac
Rennes
Quimper
Le Mans
Laval
Lorient
Auray
Châteaubriant
Redon
Vannes
Quiberon
Angers
Pontchâteau
Tours
Le Croisic
Saumur
St-Nazaire
Nantes
Chinon
Pornic
Châtellerault
100 kilometers
Ste-Pazanne
Clisson
St-Christopher du Bois
100 miles
Poitiers
Croix-de-Vie-St-Gilles
La Roche-sur-Yon
Rail Line
Niort
High Speed Rail Line (TGV)
Les Sables d'Olonne
St-Saviol
Ferry
La Rochelle
Rochefort
Saintes
Cognac
Pointe-de-Grave
Royan
Angoulême
TO NICE, MARSEILLE, TOULON
Coutres
Périgueux
Libourne
Centuri
Macinaggio
Bordeaux
Bergerac
le Buisson
Bastia
l'Ile Rousse
Calvi
Arcachon
Villeneuve-sur-Lot
Ponte-Leccia
Porto
Corte
CORSICA
Marmande
Ajaccio
Morcenx
Agen
Solenzara
Propriano
Mont-de-Marsan
Porto-Vecchio
Sartène
Dax
Bonifacio
Santa Theresa
Bayonne
Puyoô
Auch
Biarritz
Pau
St-Jean-Pied-de-Port
Tarbes
San Sebastian
Lourdes
SARDINIA
ITALY
Luchon
SPAIN
TO MADRID

TO ANTWERP
BELGIUM
Cologne
Dover
Folke-
stone
Calais
Dunkerque
Boulogne
Brussels
Etaples
Béthune
Lille
Valenciennes
Douai
Montreuil
Maubeuge-
le-Bois
Arras
Le Tréport-
Mers
Abbeville
GERMANY
Amiens
St-Quentin
Hirson
LUX.
Luxembourg
Abancourt
Charleville-
Mézières
Laon
Beauvais
Longuyon
Thionville
Rouen
Compiègne
Saarbrücken
Reims
Verdun
Soissons
Metz
Epernay
Saverne
Sarrebourg
Château-
Thierry
Châlons-
sur-Marne
Bar-le-Duc
Versailles
Paris
Nancy
Strasbourg
Dreux
Lunéville
Toul
Molsheim
Neufchâteau
Chartres
Sélestat
Troyes
Epinal
St-Dié
Colmar
Châteaudun
Sens
Chaumont
Montargis
Mulhouse
Orléans
Culmont-
Chalindrey
Vendôme
Auxerre
Belfort
Vesoul
Basel
Blois
Avallon
Montbéliard
Vézelay
TO MILAN
TO ZURICH
Vierzon
Dijon
Besançon
Corbigny
Beaune
TO ZURICH
Loches
Bourges
Dole
Mouchard
Nevers
Bern
Autun
SWITZERLAND
Chagny
Pontarlier
Châteauroux
Paray-
le-Monial
Lons-le-
Saunier
Lausanne
Moulins
Montluçon
Geneva
Bourg-
en-Bresse
Annecy
Vichy
Guéret
Roanne
Aix-les-
Bains
Chamonix-
Mont-Blanc
Albertville
Limoges
Lyon
Riom
Satolas
Eygurande-
Merlindes
Bourg-St-Maurice
St-
Etienne
Chambéry
Clermont-
Ferrand
Vienne
ITALY
Meymac
Arvant
Grenoble
Moirans
Brive
Turin
Modane
Neussargues
Le Puy-
en-Velay
Briançon
Sarlat
Souillac
Aurillac
Valence
Gap
Figeac
La Bastide
Montélimar
Veynes-
Dévoluy
Rodez
Cahors
Mende
Orange
Montauban
Millau
St-Auban
MONACO
TO FLORENCE
Alès
Ventimiglia
Albi
Avignon
Nîmes
St-Sulpice
Tarascon
Monte-Carlo
Grasse
Toulouse
Castres
Montpellier
Arles
Miramas
Aix-en-
Provence
Cannes
Nice
St-Raphaël
Mazamet
Béziers
Antibes-
Juan-les-Pins
Sète
Marseille
Carcassonne
Narbonne
Hyères
Toulon
Foix
Quillan
MEDITERRANEAN
SEA
Ax-les-
Thermes
Prades
Perpignan
ANDORRA
Villefranche
TO CORSICA
TO BARCELONA

1 2 PRICE RANGES 3 4
FRANCE 5

Our researchers list establishments in order of value from best to worst; our favorites are denoted by the Let's Go thumbs-up (). However, because the best value is not always the cheapest price, we have also incorporated a system of price ranges, based on a rough expectation of what you'll spend. For **accommodations,** we base our range on the cheapest price for which a single traveler can stay for one night. For **restaurants** and other dining establishments, we estimate the average amount a traveler will spend. The table tells you what you'll *typically* find in France at the corresponding price range; keep in mind that no system can allow for every individual establishment's quirks. You'll typically get more for your money in larger cities, although Paris, the Riviera, and Corsica are always pricey. In other words: expect anything.

ACCOMMODATIONS	RANGE	WHAT YOU'RE *LIKELY* TO FIND
1	under €20	Campgrounds, dorm rooms, or dorm-style rooms. Expect bunk beds and a communal bath; you may have to provide or rent towels and sheets.
2	€20-32	Upper-end hostels or lower-end pensions, *chambres d'hôtes,* and *gîtes.* May have a private bathroom, or there may be a sink in your room and a communal shower in the hall.
3	€33-42	A small room with a private bath, probably in a budget hotel or pension. Should have decent amenities, such as phone and TV. Breakfast may be included in the price of the room.
4	€43-60	Similar to ❸, but may have more amenities or be in a more highly touristed or centrally located area. Will usually have TV, A/C, phone, and full bath.
5	over €60	Larger or more upscale hotels. If it's a ❺ and it doesn't have the perks you want, you've paid too much.

FOOD	RANGE	WHAT YOU'RE *LIKELY* TO FIND
1	under €10	Sometimes a sit-down lunch *menu* at a budget restaurant. More likely a full meal at a kebab stand, sandwich shop, street-corner *crêperie,* or bakery.
2	€10-16	Appetizers at a café or low-priced *plats* at a budget restaurant. You can find a fuller meal at an ethnic establishment. May be a two-course *formule.*
3	€17-25	*Plats* at a sit-down restaurant or a limited three-course *menu.* Chances are, you're paying for décor and ambience.
4	€26-35	Expect an appetizer, main dish, and wine (sometimes dessert). Often bistro or *brasserie* setting. Location may be especially convenient or highly touristed.
5	over €35	Your meal might cost more than your room, but there's a reason--it's something fabulous or famous, or both, and you'll probably need to wear something other than sandals and a T-shirt.

DISCOVER FRANCE

France is often distilled down to a pretty picture: the Eiffel Tower illuminated against the night sky, a field of lavender in Provence, or an extravagant château reflected in the still water of the Loire River. While these postcard images may be beautiful, to truly appreciate France you have to go beyond tourist icons and explore the diverse mix of people, cultures, and foods that make up this ever-changing nation. France's long and storied past fills the pages of textbooks with tales of revolutions, conquests, intrigues, and, well, more revolutions, but it is the nation's present that brings people back again and again. Cities bustling with diverse immigrant populations, businessmen, and students are surrounded by tiny towns that don't bustle at all. Visitors will not find themselves alone here; the tourist hordes can be overwhelming, and even the most magical of places can seem less so when shared with a bus tour of camera-toting travelers. However, it is not difficult to step off the beaten path: an abandoned beach on Corsica's wild peninsula or the humbling WWI monuments in the northern province of Pas de Calais are only a train ride and a world apart from Paris's crowded attractions.

France lives up to its stereotypes, providing the best in fine wine, strong cheese, and that certain romantic *je ne sais quoi*, but it also goes beyond its clichés. Maybe you'll first experience the French spirit as you watch a fierce game of *pétanque* in a *provençal* village. Maybe you'll taste it in a warm croissant eaten at dawn after a night of clubbing in Lille, or in a Moroccan pastry purchased at a street market in Marseille. France does not fit within the confines of this page; it offers something different for everyone. Whether it's a nine-course meal in one of Lyon's famous restaurants, a hike to a hidden waterfall in the Pyrénées, or a stroll through one of Paris's less frequented parks, something in France will leave you breathless, and it probably won't be what you expected. Look beyond the postcard images, and France will never fail to surprise you.

FACTS AND FIGURES

OFFICIAL NAME: République française.

POPULATION: 63,714,000.

CAPITAL: Paris.

GDP PER CAPITA: US$30,100.

PRESIDENT: Nicolas Sarkozy.

MAJOR RELIGIONS: 88% Catholic, 9% Muslim, 2% Protestant, 1% Jewish.

AVERAGE LIFE EXPECTANCY: 80 years.

LITERACY RATE: 99% of those over 15.

WINE PRODUCED PER YEAR: Approximately 9 billion bottles.

FROGS CONSUMED PER YEAR: 60-80 million amphibians, or 120-160 million legs.

ESTIMATED NUMBER OF ROMANTIC ENCOUNTERS PER DAY: 4,959,476 in Paris alone. *Ah, l'amour!*

WHEN TO GO

In July, Paris's population starts to thin out; by August, it has positively vanished, leaving only tourists and pickpockets. During this month of national

TOP 10 FRENCH FESTIVALS

1. Festival d'Avignon. Early July transforms Avignon's streets into a craze of theater and dance (p. 677).

2. Festival International du Film. This famous film festival brings equally famous celebrities to Cannes in May (p. 745).

3. Bastille Day. On July 14th, Paris lights up with parades and fireworks to celebrate its independence (p. 175).

[redacted]estival de Cornouaille. Quimper's Breton extravaganza features traditional costumes and bagpipes at the end of July (p. 266).

5. Jazz d'Orléans. At the end of June, Orléans hosts a gathering of top international jazz musicians who perform for large and enthusiastic crowds (p. 191).

6. La Fête du St-Emilion. Drink all the wine you can handle for €2 in this *vin*-crazy town outside Bordeaux (p. 575).

7. Mondial Pétanque. The *pétanque* elite descend upon Millau in mid-August for the national tournament of Provence's favorite sport (p. 639).

8. Les Tombées de la Nuit. This party brings theater, music, and a 14hr. dance fest to Rennes in July (p. 241).

9. Fêtes de la Vigne. Song, dance, and wine fill Dijon for a week every summer (p. 416).

1[redacted]êtes Traditionnelles. In early August, Bayonne gets wild with fireworks, concerts, and a frenzied cow race (p. 587).

vacation, the French hop over to the Norman coast, storm the beaches of the western Atlantic from La Rochelle down to Biarritz, and hike the shores of rocky Corsica. From June to September, the Côte d'Azur becomes one long tangle of halter-topped, khaki-shorted Anglophones—a constant, exhausting party. Late spring and autumn are the best times to visit Paris and the south; winter in Paris can be grim, presided over by a terrible *grisaille*—chilly "grayness"—and the south gets hot and sticky in the summer. The rest of the country is relatively untouristed and easy to visit year-round. In terms of weather, the north and west of France are best in summer, while the center and east of the country, generally the least touristed areas of France, are ideal in spring and autumn. During the winter, the Alps provide some of the world's best skiing, while the Pyrénées offer a calmer, if less climatically dependable, alternative.

As a rule, the farther south you travel in the summer, the more crucial hotel reservations become. Reserve a month ahead for the Côte d'Azur, Corsica, Languedoc, Provence, and the Pays Basque. Paris requires reservations year-round.

WHAT TO DO

WHERE ALL THE LIGHTS ARE BRIGHT

While **Paris** (p. 94) is one of the world's best-known cities (for good reason), you'll also find plenty to do in France's regional centers. **Lyon** (p. 437) has had a reputation for boring *bourgeoisie*, but today it provides nonstop action and the nation's best cuisine. Throughout its 2600-year history, multicultural **Marseille** (p. 650) has consistently been an action-filled melting pot. **Nice** (p. 705), only a short distance from the rest of the Côte d'Azur, is a party town packed with equally exciting museums. With a hybrid Franco-German culture and world-class museums, **Strasbourg** (p. 378) was the obvious choice to house the European Parliament. Students are the heart of northern **Lille** (p. 317) and Breton **Rennes** (p. 235), which mixes a medieval *vieille ville* (old town) and major museums with a frenzied club scene. In the southwest, **Bordeaux** (p. 568) has both great wine and great architecture, sophisticated **Montpellier** (p. 640) is the gay capital of France, and rosy **Toulouse** (p. 608) livens up the Languedoc with student-filled nightlife and modern art.

ONCE UPON A TIME...

French châteaux range from imposing feudal ruins to the well-preserved country homes of 19th-century industrialists. The greatest concentration is found in the **Loire Valley** (p. 183), where the defensive hilltop fortresses of **Chinon** (p. 211) and **Saumur** (p. 212) contrast with the Renaissance grace of **Chambord** (p. 197), **Chenonceau** (p. 208), and **Cheverny** (p. 198). But the Loire has no monopoly on châteaux. At **Versailles** (p. 176), you can find a tribute to the great "Sun King" Louis XIV and bear witness to his enormous ego—in case his nickname wasn't proof enough. In Provence, you'll be hard-pressed to decide whether the Palais des Papes in **Avignon** (p. 670) is a castle or a palace, while the craggy ruins of nearby **Les Baux** (p. 681) will take you back to the age of chivalry. Perhaps the most impressive château is the fortress of **Carcassonne** (p. 620), a medieval citadel which still stands guard over the Languedoc. If you prefer more intimate, less-touristed castles, head to the **Route Jacques Cœur** near **Bourges** (p. 226). Religion has also played its part, giving rise to a wealth of architectural gems. Paris's **Notre Dame** (p. 127) is the most famous cathedral in France, but a more exquisite Gothic jewel is the nearby **Sainte-Chapelle** (p. 129). The Gothic style of architecture first reached maturity in the majestic cathedral at **Chartres** (p. 180), though several other medieval masterpieces await in **Strasbourg** (p. 386) and **Reims** (p. 345). A more modern sensibility animates Le Corbusier's post-war masterpiece chapel at **Ronchamp** (p. 401).

AU NATUREL

The Alps deserve their fame, offering thrilling skiing at **Val d'Isère** (p. 477) and **Chamonix** (p. 469), but they are just one of France's four mountain ranges. To the north, you'll find the rolling **Jura** mountains (p. 398) in **Franche-Comté,** while **Le Mont-Dore** (p. 490), in the **Massif Central,** provides spectacular hiking near extinct volcanoes. To the southwest, you can climb through the **Pyrénées** (p. 602) into Spain. If snow-capped peaks aren't your thing, discover lowland pleasures in the flamingo-filled plains of the **Camargue** (p. 694). Advanced hikers can trek the length of **Corsica's** interior (p. 759), but the less dedicated can find great day and overnight hikes everywhere on the island, especially on the **Cap Corse** (p. 788).

LET THEM EAT CAKE

Paris (p. 94) has its share of Michelin three-star restaurants, but **Lyon** (p. 437) is the true capital of French cuisine, brimming with inventive—and pricey—culinary gems. Though the French hate to admit it, much of their cuisine bears the influence of other nations—tapas sneak onto menus in **Biarritz** (p. 579), Swiss *tartiflette* dominates in the Alps resort of **Chamonix** (p. 469), and beer and sausages prove **Strasbourg's** (p. 378) German influence. France's cuisine is also infused with hints of the ocean, due to over 3000km of seaside real estate. Whether it's Atlantic mussels in the port towns of **Normandy** (p. 280), *bouillabaisse* in **Marseille** (p. 650), or oysters in **Bordeaux** (p. 568), the bounty of the sea never fails to disappoint. Finally, don't forget France's most famous exports—mustard from **Dijon** (p. 410) or olive oil from **Provence** (p. 650) are excellent ways to bring a piece of France home with you.

LA VIE EN ROSÉ

France produces—and consumes—some of the world's finest inebriants. Start with a champagne aperitif from one of **Reims's** spectacular *caves* (wine cellars; p.

345). To sample a bit of everything, try the red wines in **Bordeaux** (p. 568) and **Burgundy** (p. 410) and the whites of Alsace's **Route du Vin** (p. 386) and the **Loire Valley** (p. 183). Top it all off with an after-dinner drink—either **Cognac,** crafted in its namesake town (p. 544) or Calvados, an apple brandy made in **Normandy** (p. 280).

HERE COMES THE SUN

The Côte d'Azur attracts two types of people—the stars who create its glamor, and the masses who come looking for it. Party among Europe's tanned youth in **Nice** (p. 705) and **Juan-les-Pins** (p. 737). Surfers should head straight for the Atlantic waves in **Anglet** (p. 587). If sun and sand are your only desires, try **Ile Rousse** (p. 778) in Corsica or the dune beaches near **Arcachon** (p. 577). Some of France's most beautiful beaches await in rugged Brittany, at **Belle-Ile** (p. 270) and **St-Malo** (p. 243). Find solitude on the pristine *plages* of **Ile d' Yeu** (p. 565) and **Ile d'Aix** (p. 559).

FINE FRENCH WARES

Those with refined taste decorate their homes with Brittany's *faïence*—brightly painted porcelain sold in quaint towns like **Quimper** (p. 263)—and the bubble glass unique to **Biot** (p. 736). **Strasbourg** (p. 386), the birthplace of the Christmas tree, is a one-stop shopping center for charming Christmas decorations of all kinds. For a sampling of the biggest names in France's *haute couture*, visit the high-end boutiques in **Nice** (p. 705). A stop in nearby **Grasse** (p. 745), the capital of the world's perfume industry, can make even the grimiest backpacker smell sweet.

LET'S GO PICKS: FRANCE

BEST PLACE TO KISS: On the steps leading to **Montmartre** (p. 107), the longest and most panoramic climb in Paris, especially at dusk.

BEST PRE-HISTORIC DECOR: The awesome cave paintings at **Lascaux** (p. 520) and **Les-Eyzies-de-Tayac** (p. 518), the world's oldest art displays.

BEST EXCUSE FOR DRINKING WINE: The free *dégustations* don't stop as you stumble merrily along the **avenue de Champagne** in **Epernay** (p. 354)—and neither should you.

BEST PLACES TO LOSE YOUR TAN LINES: The delightfully debaucherous city of **St-Tropez** (p. 751) or clothing-optional beaches in **Corsica** (p. 759).

LONGEST SHOTS: The still-loaded **German artillery** in Longues-sur-Mer (p. 307); your chances at the famous **Monte-Carlo Casino** (p. 726).

MOST UNUSUAL FOODS: Blood sausage in **Alsace** (p. 378); bone marrow in **Paris** (p. 94).

BEST LIVING CANVASES: The gorgeous orchards and harbor of **Collioure** (p. 634), which inspired Matisse, Dalí, and Picasso; **Arles** (p. 688), where Van Gogh painted cafés and starry nights—and left his ear; the fruit in **Aix-en-Provence** that Cézanne made famous (p. 664).

BEST WAYS TO LOSE YOUR BREATH: Hiking **Mont Blanc** (p. 469); crossing the border into Spain through the **Pyrénées** (p. 602); biking to the **Loire Valley's** (p. 183) famous châteaux.

MOST COMPELLING REASONS FOR WORLD PEACE: Normandy's WWII **D-Day Beaches** (p. 303); tiny **Oradour-sur-Glane** (p. 508), untouched since Nazis massacred its entire population; the bones of 130,000 unknown soldiers at the Ossuaire outside **Verdun** (p. 377).

BIGGEST EGOS: Louis XIV, responsible for **Versailles** (p. 176); Napoleon, who still haunts his hometown of **Ajaccio** (p. 762); Francois I, creator of France's biggest party house, **Chambord** (p. 197).

SUGGESTED ITINERARIES

The following itineraries are designed to lead you to the highlights of France's distinct regions, from cosmopolitan hubs to sleepy villages. While these itineraries are intended for those who haven't traveled around France very much, even seasoned Francophiles can use them as a template for additional daytrips and excursions. However, there are many ways to explore the country, not all of which we can cover. For more ideas, especially on less-touristed spots that you might otherwise skip over, see **Don't Miss,** below, or the regional chapter introductions.

LA CRÈME DE LA CRÈME (1 MONTH)

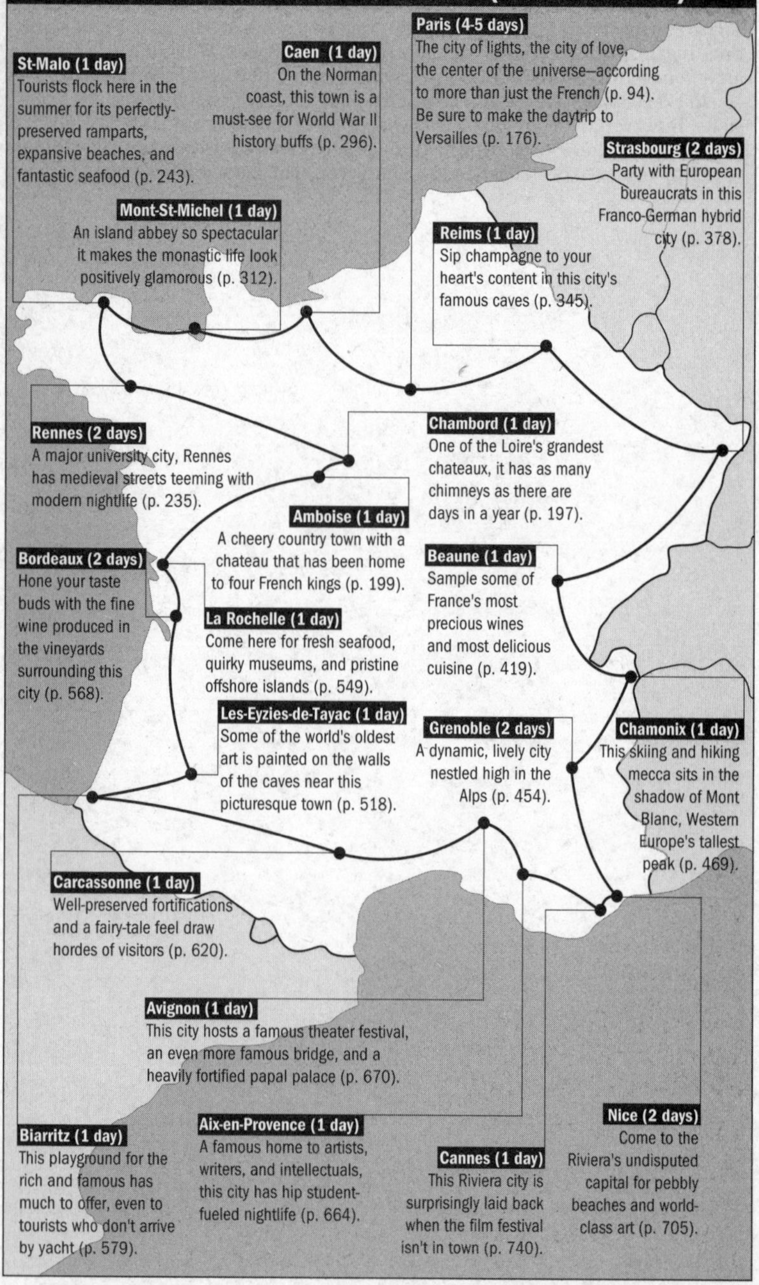

St-Malo (1 day)
Tourists flock here in the summer for its perfectly-preserved ramparts, expansive beaches, and fantastic seafood (p. 243).
Caen (1 day)
On the Norman coast, this town is a must-see for World War II history buffs (p. 296).
Paris (4-5 days)
The city of lights, the city of love, the center of the universe—according to more than just the French (p. 94). Be sure to make the daytrip to Versailles (p. 176).
Strasbourg (2 days)
Party with European bureaucrats in this Franco-German hybrid city (p. 378).
Mont-St-Michel (1 day)
An island abbey so spectacular it makes the monastic life look positively glamorous (p. 312).
Reims (1 day)
Sip champagne to your heart's content in this city's famous caves (p. 345).
Rennes (2 days)
A major university city, Rennes has medieval streets teeming with modern nightlife (p. 235).
Chambord (1 day)
One of the Loire's grandest chateaux, it has as many chimneys as there are days in a year (p. 197).
Amboise (1 day)
A cheery country town with a chateau that has been home to four French kings (p. 199).
Bordeaux (2 days)
Hone your taste buds with the fine wine produced in the vineyards surrounding this city (p. 568).
Beaune (1 day)
Sample some of France's most precious wines and most delicious cuisine (p. 419).
La Rochelle (1 day)
Come here for fresh seafood, quirky museums, and pristine offshore islands (p. 549).
Les-Eyzies-de-Tayac (1 day)
Some of the world's oldest art is painted on the walls of the caves near this picturesque town (p. 518).
Grenoble (2 days)
A dynamic, lively city nestled high in the Alps (p. 454).
Chamonix (1 day)
This skiing and hiking mecca sits in the shadow of Mont Blanc, Western Europe's tallest peak (p. 469).
Carcassonne (1 day)
Well-preserved fortifications and a fairy-tale feel draw hordes of visitors (p. 620).
Avignon (1 day)
This city hosts a famous theater festival, an even more famous bridge, and a heavily fortified papal palace (p. 670).
Biarritz (1 day)
This playground for the rich and famous has much to offer, even to tourists who don't arrive by yacht (p. 579).
Aix-en-Provence (1 day)
A famous home to artists, writers, and intellectuals, this city has hip student-fueled nightlife (p. 664).
Cannes (1 day)
This Riviera city is surprisingly laid back when the film festival isn't in town (p. 740).
Nice (2 days)
Come to the Riviera's undisputed capital for pebbly beaches and world-class art (p. 705).

DE-BEACHERY (2 WEEKS)

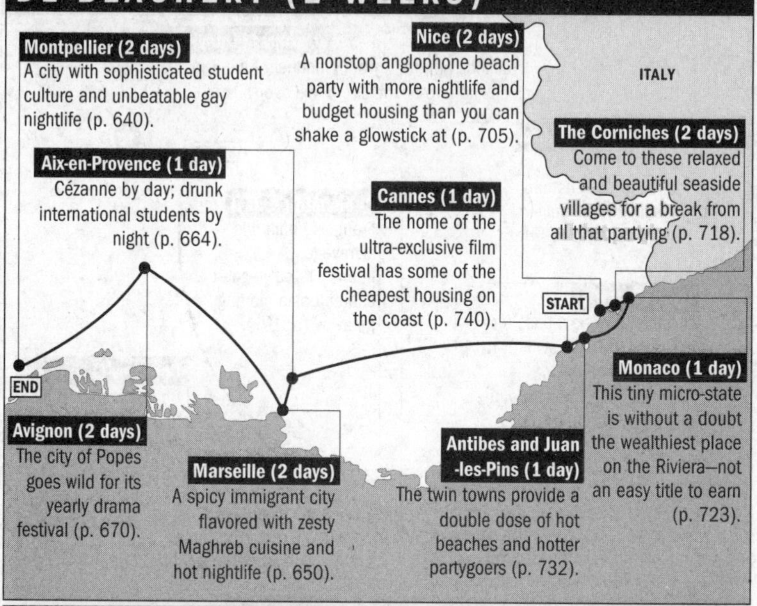

Montpellier (2 days) A city with sophisticated student culture and unbeatable gay nightlife (p. 640).

Nice (2 days) A nonstop anglophone beach party with more nightlife and budget housing than you can shake a glowstick at (p. 705).

The Corniches (2 days) Come to these relaxed and beautiful seaside villages for a break from all that partying (p. 718).

Aix-en-Provence (1 day) Cézanne by day; drunk international students by night (p. 664).

Cannes (1 day) The home of the ultra-exclusive film festival has some of the cheapest housing on the coast (p. 740).

Monaco (1 day) This tiny micro-state is without a doubt the wealthiest place on the Riviera—not an easy title to earn (p. 723).

Avignon (2 days) The city of Popes goes wild for its yearly drama festival (p. 670).

Marseille (2 days) A spicy immigrant city flavored with zesty Maghreb cuisine and hot nightlife (p. 650).

Antibes and Juan-les-Pins (1 day) The twin towns provide a double dose of hot beaches and hotter partygoers (p. 732).

ROUTE GOURMANDE (3 WEEKS)

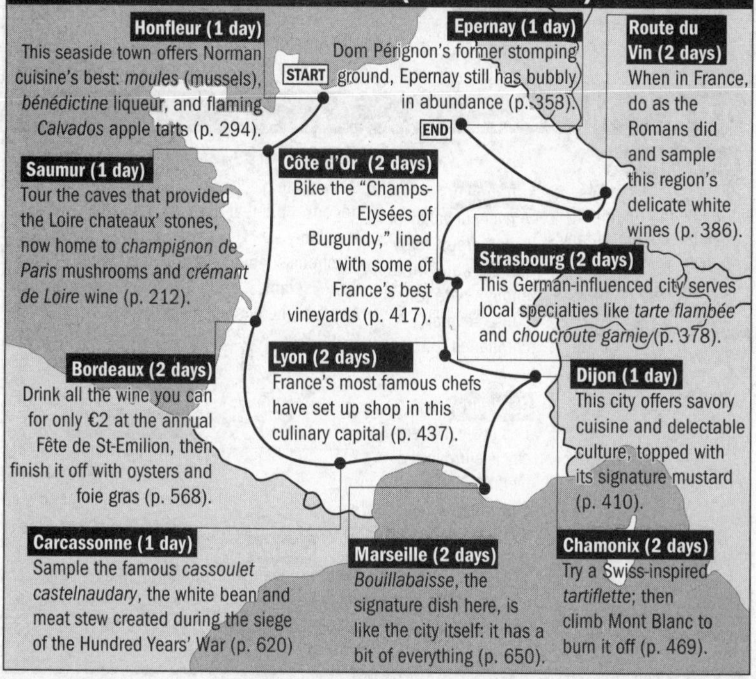

Honfleur (1 day) This seaside town offers Norman cuisine's best: *moules* (mussels), *bénédictine* liqueur, and flaming *Calvados* apple tarts (p. 294).

Epernay (1 day) Dom Pérignon's former stomping ground, Epernay still has bubbly in abundance (p. 358).

Route du Vin (2 days) When in France, do as the Romans did and sample this region's delicate white wines (p. 386).

Saumur (1 day) Tour the caves that provided the Loire chateaux' stones, now home to *champignon de Paris* mushrooms and *crémant de Loire* wine (p. 212).

Côte d'Or (2 days) Bike the "Champs-Elysées of Burgundy," lined with some of France's best vineyards (p. 417).

Strasbourg (2 days) This German-influenced city serves local specialties like *tarte flambée* and *choucroute garnie* (p. 378).

Bordeaux (2 days) Drink all the wine you can for only €2 at the annual Fête de St-Emilion, then finish it off with oysters and foie gras (p. 568).

Lyon (2 days) France's most famous chefs have set up shop in this culinary capital (p. 437).

Dijon (1 day) This city offers savory cuisine and delectable culture, topped with its signature mustard (p. 410).

Carcassonne (1 day) Sample the famous *cassoulet castelnaudary*, the white bean and meat stew created during the siege of the Hundred Years' War (p. 620)

Marseille (2 days) *Bouillabaisse*, the signature dish here, is like the city itself: it has a bit of everything (p. 650).

Chamonix (2 days) Try a Swiss-inspired *tartiflette*; then climb Mont Blanc to burn it off (p. 469).

KNIGHTS AND CASTLES (1 WEEK)

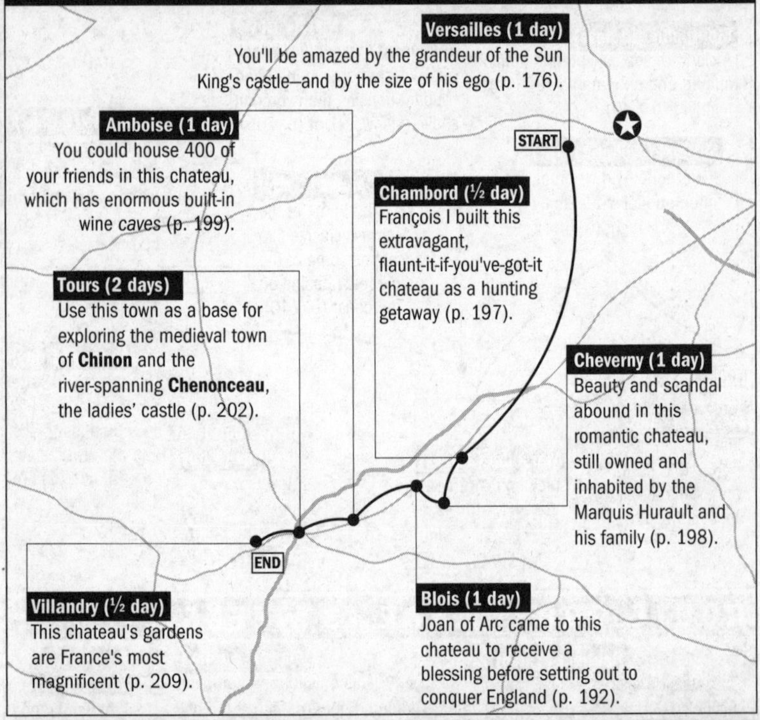
Versailles (1 day)
You'll be amazed by the grandeur of the Sun King's castle—and by the size of his ego (p. 176).
START
Amboise (1 day)
You could house 400 of your friends in this chateau, which has enormous built-in wine *caves* (p. 199).
Chambord (½ day)
François I built this extravagant, flaunt-it-if-you've-got-it chateau as a hunting getaway (p. 197).
Tours (2 days)
Use this town as a base for exploring the medieval town of **Chinon** and the river-spanning **Chenonceau**, the ladies' castle (p. 202).
Cheverny (1 day)
Beauty and scandal abound in this romantic chateau, still owned and inhabited by the Marquis Hurault and his family (p. 198).
END
Villandry (½ day)
This chateau's gardens are France's most magnificent (p. 209).
Blois (1 day)
Joan of Arc came to this chateau to receive a blessing before setting out to conquer England (p. 192).

DON'T MISS...

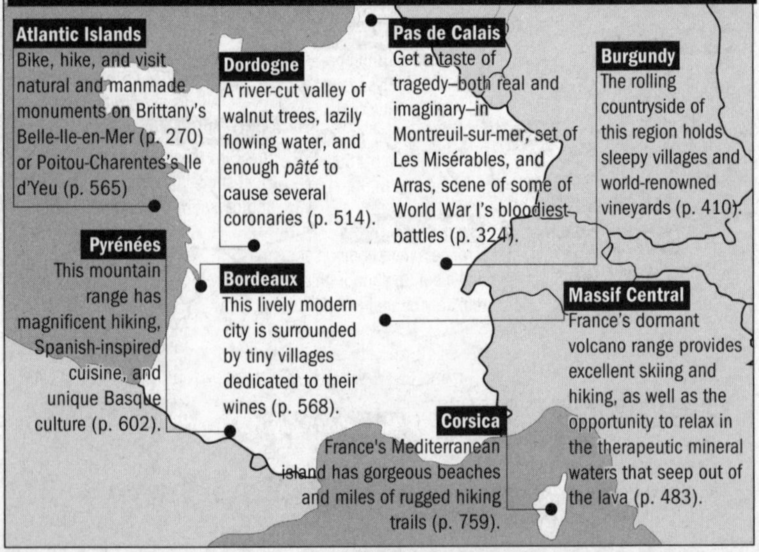
Atlantic Islands
Bike, hike, and visit natural and manmade monuments on Brittany's Belle-Ile-en-Mer (p. 270) or Poitou-Charentes's Ile d'Yeu (p. 565)
Dordogne
A river-cut valley of walnut trees, lazily flowing water, and enough *pâté* to cause several coronaries (p. 514).
Pas de Calais
Get a taste of tragedy—both real and imaginary—in Montreuil-sur-mer, set of Les Misérables, and Arras, scene of some of World War I's bloodiest battles (p. 324).
Burgundy
The rolling countryside of this region holds sleepy villages and world-renowned vineyards (p. 410).
Pyrénées
This mountain range has magnificent hiking, Spanish-inspired cuisine, and unique Basque culture (p. 602).
Bordeaux
This lively modern city is surrounded by tiny villages dedicated to their wines (p. 568).
Massif Central
France's dormant volcano range provides excellent skiing and hiking, as well as the opportunity to relax in the therapeutic mineral waters that seep out of the lava (p. 483).
Corsica
France's Mediterranean island has gorgeous beaches and miles of rugged hiking trails (p. 759).

ESSENTIALS

PLANNING YOUR TRIP

ENTRANCE REQUIREMENTS.

Passport (p. 10). Required for non-EU citizens, as well as citizens of the UK and Ireland.

Visa (p. 12). France does not require visas for EU citizens and residents of Australia, Canada, New Zealand, Switzerland, Japan, the US, and many more countries, except for visits of more than 90 days. To find out if you will need a visa, check out this link from the French Ministry for Foreign Affairs (available only in French): http://www.diplomatie.gouv.fr/en/france_159/entering-france_2045/index.html.

Work Permit (p. 12). Required for all non-EU citizens planning to work in France.

EMBASSIES AND CONSULATES

FRENCH CONSULAR SERVICES ABROAD

All consulates will provide information on obtaining visas and travel to France in general. The hours listed below are for visa concerns unless otherwise stated. Most consulates will receive inquiries by appointment.

Australia: Consulate General, Level 26, St-Martins Tower, 31 Market St., Sydney NSW 2000 (☎02 9268 2400; www.ambafrance-au.org). Open M-F 9am-noon.

Canada: Montréal: Consulat Général de France à Montréal, 1 pl. Ville-Marie, Bureau 2601, 26th fl., Montréal, QC H3B 4S3 (☎514-878-4385; www.consulfrance-montreal.org). Open M-F 8:30am-noon. **Québec:** Consulat Général de France à Québec, Maison Kent, 25 rue Saint-Louis, Québec, QC G1R 3Y8 (☎418-694-2294; www.consulfrance-quebec.org). Open M-F 8:30am-noon without appointment and 2-5pm with appointment. **Toronto:** Consulat Général de France à Toronto, 2 Bloor St. East, Ste. 2200, Toronto, ON M4W 1A8 (☎416-847-1900; www.consulfrance-toronto.org). Open M-F 9am-12:30pm. By appointment only.

Ireland: French Embassy, Consulate Section, 36 Ailesbury Rd., Ballsbridge, Dublin 4 (☎01 277 5000; www.ambafrance.ie). Open M-F 9:30am-12:30pm.

New Zealand: New Zealand Embassy and Consulate, 34-42 Manners St., P.O. Box 11-343, Wellington (☎64 43 84 25 55; www.ambafrance.net.nz). Open M-F 9:15am-1:15pm.

United Kingdom: Consulate General, 21 Cromwell Rd., London SW7 2EN (☎020 7073 1200; www.consulfrance-londres.org). Open M-Th 8:45am-noon, F 8:45-11:30am. Visa service: P.O. Box 57, 6a Cromwell Pl., London SW7 2EW (☎020 7073 1250).

United States: Consulate General, 4101 Reservoir Rd. NW, Washington, D.C. 20007 (☎202-944-6195; www.consulfrance-washington.org). Open M-F 8:45am-12:45pm. Visa service ☎202-944-6200. Open M-F 8:45am-12:30pm. Operator 8:45am-12:45pm and 2-5pm. Consulates also in Atlanta, Boston, Chicago, Houston, Los Angeles, Miami, New Orleans, New York, and San Francisco. See www.info-france-usa.org/intheus/consulates.asp for more info.

CONSULAR SERVICES IN FRANCE

Travelers visit these embassies only when they encounter trouble and need assistance. The most common concern is the loss of a passport or a question about potentially dangerous local conditions. If you encounter serious trouble, your home country's embassy or consulate can usually provide legal advice, and may even be able to advance you money in emergency situations. But don't expect them to get you out of every scrape; you must always follow French law in France. In the case of arrest, your consulate can do little more than suggest a lawyer. Dual citizens of France cannot call on the consular services of their second nationality for assistance. Hours vary; call before visiting. Visa services tend to be available only in the morning.

Australia: Australian Embassy and Consulate, 4 rue Jean Rey, 75724 Paris Cédex 15 (☎33 1 4059 3300; www.france.embassy.gov.au). Open M-F 9am-5pm.

Canada: Canadian Embassy and Consulate, 35 av. Montaigne, 75008 Paris (☎01 44 43 29 00; www.international.gc.ca/canada-europa/france). Open daily 9am-noon and 2-5pm.

Ireland: Embassy of Ireland, 12 ave. Foch, 75116 Paris (☎01 44 17 67 00; embassyofirelandparis.netfirms.com). Open M-F 9:30am-noon. Also in **Antibes, Cherbourg,** and **Lyon.**

New Zealand: New Zealand Embassy and Consulate, 7ter rue Léonard de Vinci, 75116 Paris (☎01 45 01 43 43; www.nzembassy.com/france). Open July-Aug. M-Th 9am-1pm and 2-4:30pm, F 9am-2pm; Sept.-June M-Th 9am-1pm and 2-5:30pm, F 9am-1pm and 2pm-4pm.

United Kingdom: British Embassy, Consulate Section, 18bis rue d'Anjou, 75008 Paris (☎01 44 51 31 02; www.amb-grandebretagne.fr). Open M-F 9:30am-12:30pm and 2:30pm-4:30pm. Also in **Bordeaux, Lille, Lyon,** and **Marseille.**

United States: Consulate General, 2 ave. Gabriel, 75008 Paris Cédex 08 (☎01 43 12 22 22, 24hr. emergency assistance; www.amb-usa.fr). Send mail to 2 rue St-Florentin, 75382 Paris Cédex 08. Open M-F 9am-noon. Tell guard you want American citizen services. Also in **Bordeaux, Lille, Lyon, Marseille, Nice, Rennes, Strasbourg,** and **Toulouse;** visa services Paris only.

TOURIST OFFICES

The **French Government Tourist Office (FGTO),** also known as "Maison de la France," runs tourist offices in French cities and offers tourist services to travelers visiting France. The FGTO runs the useful website **www.franceguide.com.** *Let's Go* lists the tourist office in every town where one exists.

Australia: Maison de la France, 25 Bligh St., level 13. Sydney 2000, NSW (☎61 2 9231 5244; au.franceguide.com).

Canada: Maison de la France, 1800 av. McGill College, Ste. 1010, Montréal, QC H3A 3J6 (☎514 288 2026; ca-en.franceguide.com).

United Kingdom: Maison de la France, 178 Piccadilly, London W1J9AL (☎090 6824 4123; uk.franceguide.com).

United States: New York: Maison de la France, 444 Madison Ave., 16th fl., New York, NY 10022 (☎514-288-1904; us.franceguide.com). **California:** Maison de la France, 9454 Wilshire Bd., Ste. 210, Beverly Hills, CA 90212 (☎514-288-1904; fax 310-276-2835). **Chicago:** Consulate General of France, 205 N. Michigan Ave., Ste. 3770, Chicago, IL 60601 (☎514-288-1904).

DOCUMENTS AND FORMALITIES

PASSPORTS

REQUIREMENTS

Citizens of Australia, Canada, Ireland, New Zealand, the UK, and the US need valid passports to enter France and to re-enter their home countries. France does not allow entrance if the holder's passport expires in under three months; returning home with an expired passport is illegal and may result in a fine.

NEW PASSPORTS

Citizens of Australia, Canada, Ireland, New Zealand, the UK, and the US can apply for a passport at any passport office or at selected post offices and courts of law. Citizens of these countries may also download passport applications from the official website of their country's government or passport office. Any new passport or renewal applications must be filed well in advance of the departure date, though most passport offices offer rush services for a very steep fee. Note, however, that "rushed" passports may still take up to two weeks to arrive.

ONE EUROPE. European unity has come a long way since 1958, when the European Economic Community (EEC) was created to promote European solidarity and cooperation. Since then, the EEC has become the European Union (EU), a mighty political, legal, and economic institution. On May 1, 2004, 10 South, Central, and Eastern European countries—Cyprus, the Czech Republic, Estonia, Hungary, Latvia, Lithuania, Malta, Poland, Slovakia, and Slovenia—were admitted to the EU, joining 15 other member states: Austria, Belgium, Denmark, Finland, France, Germany, Greece, Ireland, Italy, Luxembourg, the Netherlands, Portugal, Spain, Sweden, and the UK. In 2007, Bulgaria and Romania became the EU's most recent additions.

What does this have to do with the average non-EU tourist? The EU's policy of **freedom of movement** means that border controls between the first 15 member states (minus Ireland and the UK, and plus Norway and Iceland) have been abolished, and visa policies harmonized. Under this treaty, formally known as the **Schengen Agreement,** you're still required to carry a passport (or government-issued ID card for EU citizens) when crossing an internal border, but once you've been admitted into one country, you're free to travel to other participating states. On June 5, 2005, Switzerland ratified the treaty but has yet to implement it. The 10 newest member states of the EU are anticipated to begin implementing the policy in October of 2007. Britain and Ireland have also formed a **common travel area,** abolishing passport controls between the UK and the Republic of Ireland.

For more important consequences of the EU for travelers, see **The Euro** (p. 14) and **European Customs** and **EU customs regulations** (p. 14).

PASSPORT MAINTENANCE

Photocopy the page of your passport with your photo, as well as your visas, traveler's check serial numbers, and any other important documents. Carry one set of copies in a safe place, apart from the originals, and leave another set at home. Consulates also recommend that you carry an expired passport or an official copy of your birth certificate in a part of your baggage separate from other documents.

If you lose your passport, immediately notify the local police and the nearest embassy or consulate of your home government. To expedite its replacement, you must show ID and proof of citizenship; it also helps to know all information previously recorded in the passport. A replacement usually takes two weeks to process, although it may be longer, and it may be valid only for a limited time. Any visas stamped in your old passport will be irretrievably lost. In an emergency, ask for immediate temporary traveling papers that will permit you to re-enter your home country.

VISAS, INVITATIONS, AND WORK PERMITS

VISAS

EU citizens do not need a visa. Citizens of Australia, Canada, New Zealand, and the US do not need a visa for stays of up to 90 days, though this three-month period begins upon entry into any of the countries that belong to the EU's **freedom of movement** zone. For more information, see **One Europe** (p. 11). Those staying longer than 90 days may purchase a **long-stay visa** *(long séjour)* at their local French consulate; all forms and fees must be presented in person. A visa costs US$132 and allows the holder to spend one year in France. All foreigners (including EU citizens) who plan to stay over 90 days must apply for a **temporary residence permit** *(carte de séjour temporaire)* at the prefecture in their town of residence within eight days of their arrival in France.

Double-check entrance requirements at the nearest French embassy or consulate (see **Embassies and Consulates Abroad,** p. 9) for up-to-date info before departure. US citizens can also consult http://travel.state.gov.

Entering France to study for more than 90 days requires a *carte de séjour*. For more information, see **Beyond Tourism** (p. 82).

WORK PERMITS

Admission as a visitor does not include the right to work, which is authorized only by a work permit. For more information, see the **Beyond Tourism** chapter (p. 82).

IDENTIFICATION

When you travel, always carry at least two forms of identification on your person, including a photo ID; a passport and a driver's license or birth certificate is usually an adequate combination. Never carry all of your IDs together; split them up in case of theft or loss, and keep photocopies of all of them in your luggage and at home.

STUDENT, TEACHER, AND YOUTH IDENTIFICATION

The **International Student Identity Card (ISIC),** the most widely accepted form of student ID, provides discounts on some sights, accommodations, food, and transportation; access to a 24hr. emergency helpline; and insurance benefits for US cardholders. In France, cardholders may receive discounts on prepaid phone cards, movie tickets, and drinks at certain bars. Applicants must be full-time secondary or post-secondary school students at least 12 years of age. Because of the proliferation of fake ISICs, some services (particularly airlines) require additional proof of student identity.

The **International Teacher Identity Card (ITIC)** offers teachers the same insurance coverage as the ISIC and similar but more limited discounts. To qualify for the card, teachers must be currently employed and have worked a minimum of 18hr. per week for at least one school year. For travelers who are under 26 years old but are not students, the **International Youth Travel Card (IYTC)** also offers many of the same benefits as the ISIC.

Each of these identity cards costs US$22. ISICs, ITICS, and IYTCs are valid for one year from the date of issue. To learn more about ISICs, ITICs, and IYTCs, try www.myisic.com. Many student travel agencies (p. 26) issue the cards; for a list of issuing agencies and more information, see the **International Student Travel Confederation (ISTC)** website (www.istc.org).

The **International Student Exchange Card (ISE Card)** is a similar identification card available to students, faculty, and youths aged 12 to 26. The card provides discounts, medical benefits, access to a 24hr. emergency helpline, and the ability to purchase student airfares. An ISE Card costs US$25; call ☎800-255-8000 (in North America) or ☎480-951-1177 (from all other continents) for more info, or visit www.isecard.com.

CUSTOMS

Upon entering France, you must declare certain items from abroad and pay a duty on the value of those articles if they exceed the allowance established by France's customs service. Note that goods and gifts purchased at **duty-free** shops abroad are not exempt from duty or sales tax; "duty-free" merely means that you need not pay a tax in the country of purchase. Duty-free allowances were abolished for travel between EU member states on June 30, 1999, but still exist for those arriving from outside the EU. Upon returning home, you must likewise declare all articles acquired abroad and pay a duty on the value of articles in excess of your home country's allowance. In order to expedite your return, make a list of any valuables brought from home and register them with customs before traveling abroad, and be sure to keep receipts for all goods acquired abroad.

France requires a **value added tax (VAT)** of up to 19.6% (see **Taxes,** p. 18). Non-EU tourists bringing purchased goods home with them can usually be refunded this tax for purchases of over €175 per store. Ask for VAT forms at the time of purchase and present them at the *détaxe* booth at the airport. You must carry these goods with you at all times—at the airport and on the airplane. You must claim your refund within six months; it generally takes one month to process.

MONEY

CURRENCY AND EXCHANGE

The currency chart below is based on August 2007 exchange rates between the European Union euro (EUR€) and Australian dollars (AUS$), Canadian dollars (CDN$),

CUSTOMS IN THE EU. As well as freedom of movement of people within the EU (see p. 11), travelers in the 15 original EU member countries (Austria, Belgium, Denmark, Finland, France, Germany, Greece, Ireland, Italy, Luxembourg, the Netherlands, Portugal, Spain, Sweden, and the UK) can also take advantage of the freedom of movement of goods. This means that there are no customs controls at internal EU borders (i.e., you can take the blue customs channel at the airport), and travelers are free to transport whatever legal substances they like as long as it is for their own personal (non-commercial) use—up to 800 cigarettes, 10L of spirits, 90L of wine (including up to 60L of sparkling wine), and 110L of beer. Duty-free allowances were abolished on June 30, 1999 for travel between the original 15 EU member states; this now also applies to Cyprus and Malta. However, travelers between the EU and the rest of the world still get a duty-free allowance when passing through customs.

New Zealand dollars (NZ$), British pounds (UK£), and US dollars (US$). Check the currency converter on websites like www.xe.com or www.bloomberg.com, or a large newspaper for the latest exchange rates.

EURO (€)

AUS$ = €0.63	€1 = AUS$1.59
CDN$ = €0.70	€1 = CDN$1.44
NZ$ = €0.56	€1 = NZ$1.78
UK£ = €1.48	€1 = UK£0.68
US$ = €0.75	€1 = US$1.34

As a general rule, it's cheaper to convert money in France than at home. While currency exchange will probably be available in your arrival airport, it's wise to bring enough foreign currency to last for the first 24 to 72 hours of your trip (€100).

When changing money abroad, try to go only to banks or *bureaux de change* that have at most a 5% margin between their buy and sell prices. Post offices in France exchange currency for a universal €5 commission. Since you lose money with every transaction, **convert large sums** (unless the currency is depreciating rapidly), but **no more than you'll need.**

If you use traveler's checks or cash, carry some in small denominations (the equivalent of US$50 or less) for times when you are forced to exchange money at disadvantageous rates, but bring a range of denominations since charges may be levied per check cashed. Store your money in a variety of forms; ideally, at any given time you will be carrying some cash, some traveler's checks, and an ATM and/or credit card. All travelers should also consider carrying some US dollars (about US$50 worth), which are often preferred by local tellers.

THE EURO. The official currency of 13 members of the European Union—Austria, Belgium, Finland, France, Germany, Greece, Ireland, Italy, Luxembourg, the Netherlands, Portugal, Slovenia, and Spain—is now the euro.

The currency has some important—and positive—consequences for travelers hitting more than one euro-zone country. For one thing, money-changers across the euro-zone are obliged to exchange money at the official, fixed rate (see above), and at no commission (though they may still charge a small service fee). Second, euro-denominated traveler's checks allow you to pay for goods and services across the euro-zone, again at the official rate and commission-free.

TRAVELER'S CHECKS

Traveler's checks are one of the safest and least troublesome means of carrying funds, but they are difficult to cash in France. Post offices are the best bet for cashing checks, although even they will often refuse them. Fees for exchangings checks are generally much higher than for exchanging cash. American Express and Visa are the most recognized brands. Ask about toll-free refund hotlines and the location of refund centers when purchasing checks, and always carry emergency cash.

American Express: Checks available with commission at select banks, at all AmEx offices, and online (www.americanexpress.com; US residents only). American Express cardholders can also purchase checks by phone (☎800-528-4800). Checks available in Australian, British, Canadian, European, Japanese, and US currencies, among others. American Express also offers the Travelers Cheque Card, a prepaid reloadable card. Cheques for Two can be signed by either of two people traveling together. For purchase locations or more information, contact AmEx's service centers: in Australia ☎61 29 271 8666, in New Zealand 649 367 4567, in the UK 441 273 696 933, in the US and Canada 800-221-7282; elsewhere, call the US collect at 1 336 393 1111. In France, call ☎00 331 4777 7000.

Travelex: Visa TravelMoney prepaid cash card and Visa traveler's checks available. For information about Thomas Cook MasterCard in Canada and the US call ☎800-223-7373, in the UK 0800 622 101; elsewhere call the UK collect at +44 1733 318 950. For information about Interpayment Visa in the US and Canada call ☎800-732-1322, in the UK 0800 515 884; elsewhere call the UK collect at +44 1733 318 949. For more information, visit www.travelex.com.

Visa: Checks available (generally with commission) at banks worldwide. For the location of the nearest office, call the Visa Travelers Cheque Global Refund and Assistance Center: in the UK ☎0800 895 078, in the US 800-227-6811; elsewhere, call the UK collect at +44 2079 378 091. Checks available in British, Canadian, European, Japanese, and US currencies, among others. Visa also offers TravelMoney, a prepaid debit card that can be reloaded online or by phone. For more information on Visa travel services, see http://usa.visa.com/personal/using_visa/travel_with_visa.html.

CREDIT, DEBIT, AND ATM CARDS

Where they are accepted, credit cards often offer superior exchange rates—up to 5% better than the retail rate used by banks and other currency

TOP 10 WAYS TO SAVE IN FRANCE

If you plan to spend money —and you will—we can't think of a better place for you to do it than in France. Just make sure you spend every euro wisely.

1. Buy food at markets (especially open-air markets) and grocery stores instead of restaurants. Lunch of a baguette and piece of cheese will be under €3.

2. Buy the Delta "Buraliste" card for the best long-distance rates.

3. Purchase excellent wines at vineyards to avoid retail markups. Cheap wines in supermarkets often cost less than €5 and still taste good.

4. Rent a bike, not a moped or motorcycle.

5. Bring a sleepsack to save money on sheets in hostels

6. Be on the lookout for days when you can get into sights and museums for free.

7. Take advantage of flyers and coupons (in weekly papers or from promoters) that will allow you to bypass cover charges at clubs.

8. Drink your coffee at the bar of a café rather than at a table.

9. Build more outdoors activities into your itinerary.

10. If you're dead set on buying Chanel, wait until the massive sales in January and June.

> **TIP** **TAKE THE CREDIT.** Don't be surprised if a French shopkeeper in a small town doesn't know what to do with your credit card. In France, most people use the *carte bancaire,* which has a small chip rather than a magnetic strip. Ask the shopkeeper if he has a swipe reader before making your purchase.

exchange establishments. Credit cards may also offer services such as insurance or emergency help, and are sometimes required to reserve hotel rooms or rental cars. **MasterCard** (a.k.a. EuroCard in Europe) and **Visa** (a.k.a. Carte Bleue in France) are the most frequently accepted; **American Express** cards work at some ATMs and at AmEx offices and major airports. The use of ATM cards is widespread in France in both cities and rural areas. Depending on the system your home bank uses, you can most likely access your personal bank account from abroad. ATMs get the same wholesale exchange rate as credit cards, but there is often a limit on the amount of money you can withdraw per day (usually around US$500). There is typically also a surcharge of US$1-5 per withdrawal. **Debit cards** are as convenient as credit cards but withdraw money directly from the holder's checking account. A debit card can be used wherever its associated credit card company (usually MasterCard or Visa) is accepted. Debit cards often also function as ATM cards and can be used to withdraw cash from associated banks and ATMs throughout France. The two major international money networks are **MasterCard/Maestro/Cirrus** (for ATM locations: ☎800-424-7787 or www.mastercard.com) and **Visa/PLUS** (for ATM locations: ☎800-847-2911 or www.visa.com). **American Express** and **Diners Club** cards are not as prevalent in France as elsewhere, but may be accepted in more upscale restaurants and accommodations, or in heavily touristed areas. Most ATMs charge a transaction fee that is paid to the bank that owns the ATM, although **Bank of America** cardholders can use **BNP/Paribas** ATMs without a charge.

> **PINS AND ATMS.** To use a cash or credit card to withdraw money from a cash machine (ATM) in Europe, you must have a four-digit **Personal Identification Number (PIN).** If your PIN is longer than four digits, ask your bank whether you can just use the first four, or whether you'll need a new one. **Credit cards** don't usually come with PINs, so if you intend to hit up ATMs in Europe with a credit card to get cash advances, call your credit card company before leaving to request one.
>
> Travelers with alphabetical, rather than numerical, PINs may also be thrown off by the lack of letters on European cash machines. The following are the corresponding numbers to use: 1=QZ; 2=ABC; 3=DEF; 4=GHI; 5=JKL; 6=MNO; 7=PRS; 8=TUV; and 9=WXY. Note that if you mistakenly punch the wrong code into the machine three times, it will swallow your card for good.

GETTING MONEY FROM HOME

If you run out of money while traveling, the easiest and cheapest solution is to have someone back home make a deposit to your bank account. Failing that, consider one of the following options.

WIRING MONEY

It is possible to arrange a **bank money transfer,** which means asking a bank back home to wire money to a bank in France. This is the cheapest way to transfer cash, but it's also the slowest, usually taking several days. Note that some banks may only release your funds in local currency, potentially sticking you with a poor exchange rate; inquire about this in advance. If your home bank has a relationship with a bank in France, make sure to use that bank, as the rate will be better. Money transfer services like **Western Union** are faster and more convenient than bank transfers—but also pricier. Western Union has many locations worldwide. To find one, visit www.westernunion.com, or call in Australia ☎1800 173 833, in Canada and the US 800-325-6000, in the UK 0800 833 833, in France 08 25 82 58 42. To wire money using a credit card (Discover, MasterCard, Visa), call in Canada and the US 800-CALL-CASH, in the UK ☎0800 833 833. Money transfer services are also available to **American Express** cardholders and at selected **Thomas Cook** offices.

US STATE DEPARTMENT (US CITIZENS ONLY)

In serious emergencies only, the US State Department will forward money within hours to the nearest consular office, which will then disburse it according to instructions for a US$30 fee. If you wish to use this service, you must contact the Overseas Citizens Service division of the US State Department (☎202-647-5225, toll-free 888-407-4747).

COSTS

The cost of your trip will vary considerably, depending on where you go, how you travel, and where you stay. The most significant expenses will probably be your round-trip (return) **airfare** to France (see **Getting to France: By Plane,** p. 26) and a **railpass** or **bus pass** (see **Getting Around France: By Train,** p. 32). Before you go, spend some time calculating a reasonable daily **budget.**

STAYING ON A BUDGET

To give you a general idea, a bare-bones day in France (camping or sleeping in hostels/guesthouses, buying food at supermarkets) would cost about US$32 (€24); a slightly more comfortable day (sleeping in hostels/guesthouses and the occasional budget hotel, eating one meal per day at a restaurant, going out at night) would cost US$58 (€43); and for a luxurious day, the sky's the limit. Don't forget to factor in emergency reserve funds (at least US$200) when planning how much money you'll need.

TIPS FOR SAVING MONEY

Some simpler ways to save include searching out opportunities for free entertainment, splitting accommodation and food costs with trustworthy fellow travelers, and buying food in supermarkets rather than eating out. Bring a sleepsack (p. 18) to save on sheet charges in European hostels, and do your **laundry** in the sink (unless you're explicitly prohibited from doing so). Museums often have certain days once a month or once a week when admission is free; plan accordingly. If you are eligible, consider getting an ISIC or an IYTC (p. 13); many sights and museums offer reduced admission to students and youths. For getting around quickly, bikes are the most economical option. Renting a bike is cheaper than renting a moped or scooter. Don't forget about walking, though; you can learn a lot about a city by seeing it on foot. Drinking at bars and clubs quickly becomes expensive. It's cheaper to buy alcohol at a supermarket and imbibe (responsibly, of course) before going out. That said, don't go overboard. Though staying within your budget is important, don't do so at the expense of your health or a great trip

TIPPING AND BARGAINING

By French law, service must be included at all **restaurants, bars,** and **cafés.** Look for *service compris* on the menu. If service isn't included, tip 15-20%. Even when it's included, it is polite to leave a *pourboire* (€0.50 to 5% of the bill) at a café, restaurant, or bar. Tip your hairdresser 20%; tip taxis 15%. Concierges and other hotel staff may expect to be tipped for extra services (never less than €1.50).

You should inquire about discounts and less pricey options, but don't try to bargain at established places like hotels, hostels, restaurants, cafés, museums, and nightclubs. Bargaining is acceptable at markets.

TAXES

The **value added tax (VAT)** is a general tax on doing business in France; it applies to a wide range of services and goods (e.g., entertainment, food, and accommodations). The tax can be up to 19.6% of the price of the good, although there is a reduced 5.5% tax on food. Some of the VAT can be recovered (see **Customs,** p. 13).

PACKING

Pack lightly: Lay out only what you absolutely need, then take half the clothes and twice the money. The Travelite FAQ (www.travelite.org) is a good resource for tips on traveling light. The online **Universal Packing List** (http://upl.codeq.info) will generate a customized list of suggested items based on your trip length, the expected climate, your planned activities, and other factors. If you plan to do a lot of hiking, also consult **The Great Outdoors,** p. 49. Some frequent travelers keep a bag packed with all the essentials: passport, money belt, hat, socks, etc. Then, when they decide to leave, they know they haven't forgotten anything.

Luggage: If you plan to cover most of your itinerary by foot, a sturdy **frame backpack** is unbeatable. (For the basics on buying a pack, see p. 51.) Toting a **suitcase** or **trunk** is fine if you plan to stay in one or two cities and explore from there, but not a great idea if you plan to move around frequently. In addition to your main piece of luggage, a **daypack** (a small backpack or courier bag) is useful.

Clothing: No matter when you're traveling, it's a good idea to bring a warm jacket or wool sweater, a rain jacket (Gore-Tex® is both waterproof and breathable), sturdy shoes or hiking boots, and thick socks. Flip-flops or waterproof sandals are must-haves for grubby hostel showers, and extra socks are always a good idea. You may also want one outfit for going out, and maybe a nicer pair of shoes. If you plan to visit religious or cultural sites, remember that you will need modest and respectful clothing. See **Customs and Etiquette** (p. 67) for more info on fitting in. To get an idea of the climate, see the **Appendix** (p. 797); in general, France tends to be fairly temperate, but the August 2003 heat wave, killed an estimated 14,802 people as it reached temperatures of up to 104°F, reminding all to come prepared for any weather.

Sleepsack: Some hostels require that you either provide your own linen or rent sheets from them. Save cash by making your own sleepsack: fold a full-size sheet in half the long way, then sew it closed along the long side and one of the short sides. However, note that some hostels are catching on and have begun to prohibit sleepsacks.

Converters and Adapters: In France, electricity is 230 volts AC, enough to fry any 120V North American appliance. 220/240V electrical appliances won't work with a 120V current, either. Americans and Canadians should buy an adapter (which changes the shape of the plug; US$5) and a converter (which changes the voltage; US$10-30), or a device that does both. Make sure your converter works for your appliance; small electronics require different converters than heating devices. Don't make the mistake of using only an adapter (unless appliance instructions explicitly state otherwise; laptops, for example, are often made for universal usage). Europeans, along with Australians and New Zealanders (who use 230V at home), won't need a converter but will need a set of adapters to use anything electrical. For more on all things adaptable, check out http://kropla.com/electric.htm.

Toiletries: Condoms, deodorant, razors, tampons, and toothbrushes are available everywhere, but it may be difficult to find your preferred brand; bring extras. Contact lenses are likely to be expensive and difficult to find, so bring enough extra pairs and solution for your entire trip. Bring your glasses and a copy of your prescription in case you need emergency replacements. If you use heat-disinfection, either switch temporarily to a chemical disinfection system (check first to make sure it's safe with your brand of lenses), or buy a converter to 230V.

First-Aid Kit: For a basic first-aid kit, pack bandages, a pain reliever, antibiotic cream, a thermometer, a multifunction pocketknife, tweezers, moleskin, decongestant, motion-sickness remedy, diarrhea or upset-stomach medication (Pepto Bismol® or Imodium®), an antihistamine, sunscreen, insect repellent, and burn ointment.

Film: If you don't want to bother with film, consider using a digital camera. Although it requires a steep initial investment, a digital camera means you never have to buy film again. Just be sure to bring along a large enough memory card and extra (or rechargeable) batteries. For more info on digital cameras, visit www.shortcourses.com/choosing/contents.htm. Less serious photographers may want to bring a disposable camera or two. Despite disclaimers, airport security X-rays can fog film, so buy a lead-lined pouch at a camera store or ask security to hand-inspect it. Always pack film in your carry-on luggage, since higher-intensity X-rays are used on checked luggage.

Other Useful Items: For safety purposes, you should bring a **money belt** (not to be confused with a conspicuously non-French fanny pack) and a small **padlock.** Basic **outdoors equipment** (plastic water bottle, compass, waterproof matches, pocketknife, sunglasses, sunscreen, hat) may also prove useful, although some of these items can be left at home if you're not planning on camping or hiking. **Quick repairs** of torn garments can be done on the road with a needle and thread; also consider bringing electrical tape for patching tears. If you want to do laundry by hand, bring detergent, a small rubber ball to stop up the sink, and string for a makeshift clothes line. Other things you're liable to forget include: an umbrella, sealable **plastic bags** (for damp clothes, soap, food, shampoo, and other spillables), an **alarm clock,** safety pins, rubber bands, a flashlight, earplugs, garbage bags, and a small calculator. A **cell phone** can be a lifesaver on the road; see p. 42 for information on acquiring one that will work in France.

Important Documents: Don't forget your passport, traveler's checks, ATM and/or credit cards, adequate ID, and photocopies of all of the aforementioned in case these documents are lost or stolen (p. 10). Also check that you have any of the following that might apply to you: a hosteling membership card (p. 46); driver's license (p. 12); travel insurance forms, ISIC (p. 13), and/or rail or bus pass (p. 32).

SAFETY AND HEALTH

GENERAL ADVICE

In any type of crisis situation, the most important thing to do is **stay calm.** Your country's embassy abroad (p. 9) is usually your best resource when things go wrong; registering with that embassy upon arrival in the country is often a good idea. The government offices listed in the **Travel Advisories** box (p. 21) can provide information on the services they offer their citizens in case of emergencies abroad.

LOCAL LAWS AND POLICE

The police in France *(la police)* are generally very responsive to requests for help. The emergency call number is ☎ 17. Possession of illegal drugs is punished severely. The legal blood alcohol level for driving is **0.05%,** 0.03% lower than in New Zealand, Ireland, the United Kingdom, and the United States—so exercise caution.

DRUGS AND ALCOHOL

Possession of **illegal drugs** (including marijuana) in France can result in a substantial jail sentence or fine. Police may arbitrarily stop and search anyone on the street. **Prescription drugs,** particularly insulin, syringes, or narcotics, should be left in their original, labeled containers and accompanied by their prescriptions and a doctor's statement. In case of arrest, your home country's consulate can suggest attorneys and inform your family and friends but can't get you out of jail. For more info, US citizens can contact the Office of Overseas Citizens Services (☎202-501-4444; http://travel.state.gov).

The French love alcohol, but they drink carefully. Though there is no law prohibiting open containers, drinking on the street is considered uncouth. Restaurants may serve alcohol to anyone 16 years or older. People light up almost anywhere: some eateries have non-smoking sections, but they're often not respected. Times are changing, however, as some parts of France are in the process of outlawing smoking in public places.

SPECIFIC CONCERNS

DEMONSTRATIONS AND POLITICAL GATHERINGS

In France, past demonstrations by students, labor groups, and other routine protesters have grown into more violent confrontations with the police. In 2006, opponents to a controversial labor deregulation bill sparked protests throughout France in February, March, and April. Millions of young protesters converged on France's urban centers to show their dissatisfaction in demonstrations that frequently turned violent and required police intervention. Although tensions have calmed somewhat, protests are a continual threat in France. The most common form of violence when demonstrations get out of hand is property damage, and tourists typically are not targets, but travelers are still advised to avoid demonstrations. In general, use common sense in conversation and, as in dealing with any sensitive cultural issue, be respectful of political and religious perspectives.

TERRORISM

Terrorism has not been as serious a problem in France as in other European countries, but after September 11, 2001, the French government heightened security in public places. For example, most train stations no longer permit luggage storage. Al Qaeda cells, as well as other terrorist groups, can be found in France. Since its colonial period, France has had a tense relationship with Algeria, a situation that has been a source of sporadic violent outbursts. Domestic anti-Semites have firebombed several Jewish synagogues in the past few years. The box on **Travel Advisories** lists helpful offices and webpages where you can find the most up-to-date list of your home country's government's advisories about travel.

PERSONAL SAFETY

EXPLORING AND TRAVELING

To avoid unwanted attention, try to blend in as much as possible. Respecting local customs (in many cases, dressing more conservatively than you would at home) may placate would-be hecklers. Familiarize yourself with your surroundings before setting out, and carry yourself with confidence. Check maps in shops and restaurants rather than on the street. If you are traveling alone, be sure someone at home knows your itinerary, and never tell anyone you meet that you're by yourself. When walking at night, stick to busy, well-lit streets and avoid dark alleyways.

TRAVEL ADVISORIES. The following government offices provide travel information and advisories by telephone, by fax, or via the web:

Australian Department of Foreign Affairs and Trade: ☎612 6261 1111, 24 hour consular emergency center: ☎612 6261 3305; www.dfat.gov.au.

Canadian Department of Foreign Affairs and International Trade (DFAIT): Call ☎800-267-8376; www.dfait-maeci.gc.ca. Download or call for their free booklet, *Bon Voyage...But.*

New Zealand Ministry of Foreign Affairs: ☎044 398 000; www.mfat.govt.nz.

United Kingdom Foreign and Commonwealth Office: ☎020 7008 1500; www.fco.gov.uk.

US Department of State: ☎888-407-4747; http://travel.state.gov. Visit the website for the booklet *A Safe Trip Abroad.*

As a rule, areas around train stations are almost always unsafe. If you ever feel uncomfortable, leave the area as quickly as you can.

There is no sure-fire way to avoid all the threatening situations you might encounter while traveling, but a good **self-defense course** will give you concrete ways to react to unwanted advances. **Impact, Prepare,** and **Model Mugging** can refer you to local self-defense courses in Australia, Canada and the US. Visit the website at www.modelmugging.org for a list of nearby chapters.

If you are using a **car,** find out about local driving etiquette and wear a seatbelt. Children under 40 lbs. should ride only in specially designed car seats, available for a small fee from most car rental agencies. Study route maps before you hit the road, and if you plan on spending a lot of time driving, consider bringing spare parts. For long drives in desolate areas, invest in a cellular phone and a roadside assistance program (see p. 38). Park your vehicle in a garage or well-traveled area, and use a steering wheel locking device in larger cities. **Sleeping in your car** is the most dangerous way to get your rest. For info on the perils of **hitchhiking,** see p. 40.

POSSESSIONS AND VALUABLES

Never leave your belongings unattended; crime occurs in even the safest-looking hostels and hotels. Bring your own padlock for hostel lockers, and don't ever store valuables in a locker. Be particularly careful on **buses** and **trains;** horror stories abound about determined thieves who wait for travelers to fall asleep. Carry your bag or purse in front of you where you can see it. When traveling with others, sleep in alternate shifts. When alone, use good judgment in selecting a train compartment: never stay in an empty one, and use a lock to secure your pack to the luggage rack. Use extra caution if traveling at night or on overnight trains. Try to sleep on top bunks with your luggage stored above you (if not in bed with you), and keep important documents and other valuables on you at all times.

There are a few steps you can take to minimize the financial risk associated with traveling. First, **bring as little with you as possible.** Second, buy a few combination **padlocks** to secure your belongings either in your pack or in a hostel or train station locker. Third, **carry as little cash as possible.** Keep your traveler's checks and ATM/credit cards in a **money belt**—not a "fanny pack"—along with your passport and ID cards. Fourth, **keep a small cash reserve separate from your primary stash.** This should be about US$100 (US$ or euro are best) sewn into or stored in the depths of your pack, along with your traveler's check numbers and photocopies of your passport, your birth certificate, and other important documents.

In large cities **con artists** often work in groups and may involve children. Beware of certain classics: sob stories that require money, rolls of bills "found" on the street, mustard spilled (or saliva spit) onto your shoulder to distract you while they snatch your bag. **Never let your passport and your bags out of your sight.** Beware of **pickpockets** in city crowds, especially on public transportation. Also, be alert in public telephone booths: If you must say your calling card number, do so very quietly; if you punch it in, make sure no one can look over your shoulder.

If you will be traveling with electronic devices, such as a laptop computer or a PDA, check whether your homeowner's insurance covers loss, theft, or damage when you travel. If not, you might consider purchasing a low-cost separate insurance policy. **Safeware** (☎800-800-1492; www.safeware.com) specializes in covering computers and charges $90 for 90-day comprehensive international travel coverage up to $4000.

PRE-DEPARTURE HEALTH

In your **passport,** write the names of any people you wish to be contacted in case of a medical emergency, and list any allergies or medical conditions. Matching a prescription to a foreign equivalent is not always easy, safe, or possible, so if you take prescription drugs, consider carrying up-to-date prescriptions or a statement from your doctor stating the medication's trade name, manufacturer, chemical name, and dosage. While traveling, be sure to keep all medication with you in your carry-on luggage. For tips on packing a **first-aid kit** and other health essentials, see p. 19. The French names for common drugs are: *aspirine* (aspirin), *pénicilline* (penicillin), *antihistaminique* (antihistamines), and *ibuprofène* (ibuprofen).

IMMUNIZATIONS AND PRECAUTIONS

Travelers over two years old should make sure that the following vaccines are up to date: MMR (for measles, mumps, and rubella); DTaP or Td (for diphtheria, teta-

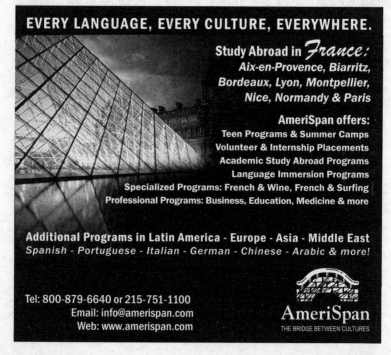

nus, and pertussis); IPV (for polio); Hib (for *Haemophilus influenzae* B); and HepB (for Hepatitis B). For recommendations on immunizations and prophylaxis, consult the Centers for Disease Control and Prevention (CDC; see below) in the US or the equivalent in your home country, and check with a doctor for guidance.

USEFUL ORGANIZATIONS AND PUBLICATIONS

The American **Centers for Disease Control and Prevention** (**CDC;** ☎877-FYI-TRIP; www.cdc.gov/travel) maintains an international travelers' hotline and an informative website. Consult the appropriate government agency of your home country for consular information sheets on health, entry requirements, and other issues for various countries (see the listings in the box on **Travel Advisories**, p. 21). For quick information on health and other travel warnings, call the **Overseas Citizens Services** (M-F 8am-8pm from US ☎888-407-4747, from overseas 202-501-4444), or contact a passport agency, embassy, or consulate abroad. For information on medical evacuation services and travel insurance firms, see the US government's website (http://travel.state.gov/travel/abroad_health.html) or the **British Foreign and Commonwealth Office** (www.fco.gov.uk). For general health information, contact the **American Red Cross** (☎202-303-4498; www.redcross.org).

STAYING HEALTHY

Common sense is the simplest prescription for good health while you travel. Drink lots of fluids to prevent dehydration and constipation, and wear sturdy, broken-in shoes and clean socks to keep your feet blister-free.

ONCE IN FRANCE

ENVIRONMENTAL HAZARDS

Travelers should exercise extra caution in mountainous regions like the Alps, Pyrénées, and Massif Central, which often remain cold throughout the summer and are risky areas for altitude sickness. During the summer, be especially careful in southern regions like Provence and the Cote d'Azur, as they can get extremely hot and sunny.

Heat exhaustion and dehydration: In 2003, heat exhaustion killed over 14,800 people in France, so exercise extreme caution to prevent it. Heat exhaustion leads to nausea, excessive thirst, headaches, and dizziness. Avoid it by drinking plenty of fluids, eating salty foods (e.g., crackers), abstaining from dehydrating beverages (e.g., alcohol and caffeinated beverages), and wearing sunscreen. Continuous heat stress may eventually lead to heatstroke, characterized by a rising temperature, severe headache, delirium and cessation of sweating. Victims should be cooled off with wet towels and taken to a doctor immediately.

Sunburn: Always wear sunscreen (SPF 30 or higher) when spending a lot of time in the sun. If you get sunburned, drink more fluids than usual and apply an aloe-based lotion. Severe sunburns can lead to sun poisoning, a condition that can cause fever, chills, nausea, and vomiting. Sun poisoning should always be treated by a doctor.

Hypothermia and frostbite: A rapid drop in body temperature is the clearest sign of overexposure to cold. Victims may also shiver, feel exhausted, have poor coordination or slurred speech, hallucinate, or suffer amnesia. *Do not let hypothermia victims fall asleep.* To avoid hypothermia, keep dry, wear layers, and stay out of the wind. When the temperature is below freezing, watch out for frostbite. If skin turns white or blue, waxy, and cold, do not rub the area. Drink warm beverages, stay dry, and slowly warm the area with dry fabric or steady body contact until a doctor can be found.

High Altitude: Allow your body a couple of days to adjust to less oxygen before exerting yourself. Note that alcohol is more potent and UV rays are stronger at high elevations. At especially high altitudes, acute mountain sickness (AMS; a.k.a. altitude sickness) is a risk, and is characterized by lack of appetite, nausea, fatigue or dizziness, insomnia and swelling of extremities, though most extreme symptoms include fluid in the lungs or swelling of the brain. To cure minor symptoms, victims can try taking a series of deep breaths every couple minutes; all symptoms can be cured by moving to a lower altitude.

INSECT-BORNE DISEASES

Many diseases are transmitted by insects—mainly mosquitoes, fleas, ticks, and lice. Be aware of insects in wet or forested areas, especially while hiking and camping; wear long pants and long sleeves, tuck your pants into your socks, and use a mosquito net. Use insect repellents such as DEET and soak or spray your gear with permethrin (licensed in the US only for use on clothing). **Ticks**—which can carry Lyme and other diseases—can be particularly dangerous in rural and forested regions. If you find a tick attached to your skin, grasp the head with tweezers as close to your skin as possible and apply slow, steady traction. Removing a tick within 24 hours greatly reduces the risk of infection. Do not try to remove ticks with petroleum jelly, nail polish remover, or a hot match. Ticks usually inhabit moist, shaded environments and heavily wooded areas. If you are going to be hiking in these areas, wear long clothes and DEET.

Tick-borne encephalitis: A viral infection of the central nervous system transmitted during the summer by tick bites (primarily in wooded areas) or by consumption of unpasteurized dairy products. The risk of contracting the disease is relatively low in France, especially if precautions are taken against tick bites.

Lyme disease: A bacterial infection carried by ticks and marked by a circular bull's-eye rash of 2 in. or more. Later symptoms include fever, headache, fatigue, and aches and pains. Antibiotics are effective if administered early. Left untreated, Lyme can cause problems in joints, the heart, and the nervous system.

FOOD- AND WATER-BORNE DISEASES

Prevention is the best cure: be sure that your food is properly cooked and the water you drink is clean. In France, most tap water is clean, but outdoor water sources, such as rivers and wells, may not be. Watch out for food from markets or street vendors that may have been cooked in unhygienic conditions. Other culprits are raw shellfish, unpasteurized milk, and sauces containing raw eggs. If you must use outdoor water sources, purify water with **iodine tablets;** note, however, that some parasites such as *giardia* have exteriors that resist iodine treatment, so if you can, boil water. Always wash your hands before eating or bring a quick-drying purifying liquid hand cleaner.

Traveler's diarrhea: Results from drinking contaminated water or eating uncooked and contaminated foods. Symptoms include nausea, bloating, and urgency. Try quick-energy, non-sugary foods with protein and carbohydrates to keep your strength up. Over-the-counter anti-diarrheals (e.g., imodium) may counteract the problem. The most dangerous side effect is dehydration; drink 8 oz. of water with ½ tsp. of sugar or honey and a pinch of salt, try decaffeinated soft drinks, or eat salted crackers. If you develop a fever or your symptoms don't go away after 4-5 days, consult a doctor. Consult a doctor immediately for treatment of diarrhea in children. Risk of contracting diarrhea in France is very low, but travelers should always be cautious.

OTHER INFECTIOUS DISEASES

The following diseases exist in every part of the world. Travelers should know how to recognize them and what to do if they suspect they have been infected.

Rabies: Transmitted through the saliva of infected animals; fatal if untreated. By the time symptoms (thirst and muscle spasms) appear, the disease is in its terminal stage. If you are bitten, wash the wound, seek immediate medical care, and try to have the animal located.

Hepatitis B: A viral infection of the liver transmitted via blood or other bodily fluids. Symptoms, which may not surface until years after infection, include jaundice, appetite loss, fever, and joint pain. It is transmitted through unprotected sex and unclean needles. A 3-shot vaccination sequence is recommended for sexually-active travelers and anyone planning to seek medical treatment abroad; it must begin 6 months before traveling. Risk of contracting Hep B is relatively low in France, but travelers should always be cautious.

Hepatitis C: Like Hepatitis B, but the mode of transmission differs. IV drug users, those with occupational exposure to blood, hemodialysis patients, and recipients of blood transfusions are at the highest risk, but the disease can also be spread through sexual contact or sharing items like razors and toothbrushes that may have traces of blood on them. No symptoms are usually exhibited. If untreated, Hepatitis C can lead to liver failure.

AIDS and HIV: For detailed information on Acquired Immune Deficiency Syndrome (AIDS) in France, call the 24hr. National AIDS Hotline at ☎800-342-2437.

Sexually transmitted infections (STIs): Gonorrhea, chlamydia, genital warts, syphilis, herpes, HPV, and other STIs are easier to catch than HIV and can be just as serious. Though condoms may protect you from some STIs, oral or even tactile contact can lead to transmission. If you think you may have contracted an STI, see a doctor immediately.

OTHER HEALTH CONCERNS

MEDICAL CARE ON THE ROAD

Medical care in France is as good (and as expensive) as anywhere in the world. All but the smallest towns have a hospital, generally with English-speaking staff, which is listed under the Practical Information in each city listing. Every town has a **24hr. pharmacy** *(pharmacie de garde)*. Pharmacies assume this duty on rotation; check with the police or on pharmacy doors for location.

If you are concerned about obtaining medical assistance while traveling, you may wish to employ special support services. The *MedPass* from **GlobalCare, Inc.**, 6875 Shiloh Rd. East, Alpharetta, GA 30005, USA (☎800-860-1111; www.globalcare.net), provides 24hr. international medical assistance, support, and medical evacuation resources. The **International Association for Medical Assistance to Travelers** (**IAMAT;** US ☎716-754-4883, Canada 519-836-0102; www.iamat.org) has free membership, lists English-speaking doctors worldwide, and offers detailed info on immunization requirements and sanitation. If your regular **insurance** policy does not cover travel abroad, you may wish to purchase additional coverage.

Those with medical conditions (such as diabetes, allergies to antibiotics, epilepsy, or heart conditions) may want to obtain a **MedicAlert** membership (US$40 per year), which includes among other things a stainless steel ID tag and a 24hr. collect-call number. Contact the MedicAlert Foundation International, 2323 Colorado Ave., Turlock, CA 95382, USA (☎888-633-4298, outside US ☎209-668-3333; www.medicalert.org).

WOMEN'S HEALTH

Women traveling in unsanitary conditions are vulnerable to **urinary tract (including bladder and kidney) infections.** Over-the-counter medicines can sometimes alleviate symptoms, but if they persist, see a doctor. **Vaginal yeast infections** may flare up in hot and humid climates. Wearing loosely fitting trousers or a skirt and cotton underwear will help, as will over-the-counter remedies like Monistat or Gynelotrimin. Bring supplies from home if you are prone to infection, as they may be difficult to find on the road. **Tampons, pads,** and **contraceptive devices** are widely available, though your favorite brand may not be stocked—bring extras of anything you can't live without. **Abortion** is legal in France. Recent changes have relaxed restrictions on surgical and pharmaceutical abortions, permitting them up to 12 weeks into pregnancy. The **morning-after pill** (*la pillule du lendemain*) is legal and available at pharmacies. Contact the French branch of the International Planned Parenthood Federation, the **Mouvement Français pour le Planning Familial** (**MFPF;** ☎01 48 07 29 10; www.planning-familial.org), which can supply the names of French hospitals and OB/GYN clinics performing abortions. More info about family planning centers can also be obtained through the **International Planned Parenthood Federation,** European Regional Office, Rue Royale 146, Brussels 1000, Belgium (☎32 22 50 09 50; http://www.ippfen.org/site.html.)

GETTING TO FRANCE

BY PLANE

When it comes to airfare, a little effort can save you a bundle. Courier fares are the cheapest for those whose plans are flexible enough to deal with the restrictions. Tickets sold by consolidators and standby seating are also good deals, but last-minute specials, airfare wars, and charter flights often beat these fares. The key is to hunt around, be flexible, and ask about discounts. Students, seniors, and those under 26 should never pay full price for a ticket.

AIRFARES

Airfares to France peak between June and September; holidays are also expensive. The cheapest times to travel is between November and April (excluding the Christmas season). Midweek (M-Th morning) round-trip flights run US$40-50 cheaper than weekend flights, but they are generally more crowded and less likely to permit frequent-flier upgrades. Failing to fix a return date ("open return") or arriving in and departing from different cities ("open-jaw") can be pricier than round-trip flights. Patching one-way flights together is the most expensive way to travel. Flights between France's regional hubs—Bordeaux, Lyon, Marseille, Nice, Paris, Strasbourg, and Toulouse—tend to be cheaper.

If France is only one stop on a more extensive globe-hop, consider a round-the-world (RTW) ticket. Tickets usually include at least five stops and are valid for about a year; prices range US$1200-5000. Try **Northwest Airlines/KLM** (☎800-225-2525; www.nwa.com) or **Star Alliance,** a consortium of 16 airlines including United Airlines (www.staralliance.com).

Fares for roundtrip flights to Paris from the US or Canada cost US$600-1500 pretax, US$400-750 in the low season (Nov.-Mar.); from the UK, £50-200/£25-100; from Australia AUS$2000/AUS$3000; from New Zealand NZ$2000-3500/NZ$1000-3500.

BUDGET AND STUDENT TRAVEL AGENCIES

While knowledgeable agents specializing in flights to France can make your life easy and help you save, they may not spend the time to find you the lowest possible fare—they get paid on commission. Travelers holding **ISICs** and **IYTCs** (see p. 13) qualify for big discounts from student travel agencies. Most flights from budget agencies are on major airlines, but in peak season some may sell seats on less reliable chartered aircraft.

STA Travel, 5900 Wilshire Blvd., Ste. 900, Los Angeles, CA 90036, USA (24hr. reservations and info ☎800-781-4040; www.statravel.com). A travel organization for students and youths with over 150 offices worldwide (check their website for a listing of all their offices), including US offices in Boston, Chicago, Los Angeles, New York, Seattle, San

Francisco, and Washington, D.C. Ticket booking, travel insurance, railpasses, and more. Walk-in offices are located throughout Australia (☎03 9207 5900), New Zealand (☎09 309 9723), and the UK (☎08701 630 026).

Travel CUTS (Canadian Universities Travel Services Limited), 187 College St., Toronto, ON M5T 1P7, Canada (☎888-592-2887; www.travelcuts.com). Offices throughout Canada and the US including Los Angeles, New York, Seattle, and San Francisco.

USIT, 19-21 Aston Quay, Dublin 2, Ireland (☎01 602 1904; www.usit.ie), Ireland's leading student/budget travel agency has 20 offices throughout Northern Ireland and the Republic of Ireland. Offers programs to work, study, and volunteer worldwide.

Wasteels, Skoubogade 6, 1158 Copenhagen K., Denmark (☎3314 4633; www.wasteels.com). A huge chain with 180 locations across Europe. Sells Wasteels BIJ tickets discounted 30-45% off regular fare and 2nd-class international point-to-point train tickets with unlimited stopovers for those under 26 (sold only in Europe).

ESSENTIALS

FLIGHT PLANNING ON THE INTERNET. The Internet may be the budget traveler's dream when it comes to finding and booking bargain fares, but the array of options can be overwhelming. Many airline sites offer special last-minute deals on the Web. Try **Air France** (www.airfrance.com) for tickets to France from all over the world.

STA (www.statravel.com) and **StudentUniverse** (www.studentuniverse.com) provide quotes on student tickets, while **Orbitz** (www.orbitz.com), **Expedia** (www.expedia.com), **Travelocity** (www.travelocity.com), and **Opodo** (www.opodo.com) offer full travel services. **Priceline** (www.priceline.com) lets you specify a price, and obligates you to buy any ticket that meets or beats it; **Hotwire** (www.hotwire.com) offers bargain fares, but won't reveal the airline or flight times until you buy; **Kayak** (www.kayak.com) gives you the option of searching without specifying dates or precise location, so you can plan your vacation around the cheapest flight. Other sites that compile deals include www.bestfares.com, www.flights.com, www.lowestfare.com, www.onetravel.com, and www.travelzoo.com.

SideStep (www.sidestep.com) and **Booking Buddy** (www.bookingbuddy.com) are online tools that can help sift through multiple offers; these two let you enter your trip information once and search multiple sites.

Air Traveler's Handbook (www.faqs.org/faqs/travel/air/handbook) is an indispensable resource on the Internet, with a comprehensive listing of links to everything you need to know before you board a plane.

COMMERCIAL AIRLINES

The commercial airlines' lowest regular offer is the **APEX** (Advance Purchase Excursion) fare, which provides confirmed reservations and allows "open-jaw" tickets. Generally, reservations must be made seven to 21 days ahead of departure, with seven- to 14-day minimum-stay and up to 90-day maximum-stay restrictions. These fares carry hefty change and cancellation penalties, which rise in summer. Book peak-season APEX fares early. Use **Expedia** (www.expedia.com) or **Travelocity** (www.travelocity.com) to get an idea of the lowest published fares, then use the resources outlined here to try to beat those fares. Low-season fares should be appreciably cheaper than the **high season** (June-Aug.) ones listed here.

TRAVELING FROM NORTH AMERICA

Basic round-trip fares to Paris cost roughly US$400-800. Standard commercial carriers like **American** (☎800-433-7300; www.aa.com), **United** (☎800-538-2929;

www.ual.com), **US Airways** (☎800-428-4322; www.usairways.com), **Delta** (☎800-221-1212 from US; www.delta.com) and **Northwest** (☎800-447-4747; www.nwa.com) will probably offer the most convenient flights, but they may not be the cheapest. Check **Lufthansa** (☎800-399-5838; www.lufthansa.com), **British Airways** (☎800-247-9297; www.britishairways.com), **Air France** (☎800-237-2747; www.airfrance.us), and **Alitalia** (☎800-223-5730; www.alitaliausa.com) for cheap tickets from destinations throughout the US to all over Europe. You might find an even better deal on one of the following airlines, if any of their limited departure points is convenient for you.

Icelandair: ☎800-223-5500; www.icelandair.com. Stopovers in Iceland for no extra cost on most transatlantic flights. Service from 5 US hubs to Paris and other European destinations. For last-minute offers, subscribe to their email, "Lucky Fares."

Finnair: ☎800-950-5000; www.finnair.com. Cheap round-trips from San Francisco, New York, and Toronto to Paris; connections throughout Europe.

TRAVELING FROM THE UK AND IRELAND

Because of the many carriers flying from the British Isles to the continent, we only include discount airlines or those with cheap specials here. The **Air Travel Advisory Bureau** in London (☎870 737 0021; www.atab.co.uk) provides referrals to travel agencies and consolidators that offer discounted airfares out of the UK. **Cheapflights** (www.cheapflights.co.uk) publishes airfare bargains.

Aer Lingus: Ireland ☎0818 365 000; www.aerlingus.ie. Return tickets from Dublin, Cork, Galway, Kerry, and Shannon to Paris, Rennes, and Nice (approximately EUR€40-50). Also offers flights from the US via Ireland (approximately US$300-600).

bmibaby: UK ☎08702 642 229; www.bmibaby.com. Departures from multiple cities in the UK to Paris (approximately UK£20-50).

easyJet: UK ☎08712 442 366; www.easyjet.com. Services various destinations in Europe; offers flights from London to Paris and Lyon (approximately UK£20-50).

KLM: UK ☎08705 074 074; www.klmuk.com. Cheap return tickets to numerous destinations in France.

Ryanair: Ireland ☎0818 303 030, UK 08712 460 000; www.ryanair.com. From Dublin, Glasgow, Liverpool, London, and Shannon to destinations throughout Western Europe, including Paris (UK£20-50).

TRAVELING FROM AUSTRALIA AND NEW ZEALAND

Qantas Air: Australia ☎13 13 13, New Zealand ☎0800 808 767; www.qantas.com.au. Flights from Australia and New Zealand to Paris for around AUS$2500.

Singapore Air: Australia ☎13 10 11, New Zealand ☎0800 808 909; www.singaporeair.com. Flies from Auckland, Christchurch, Melbourne, Perth, and Sydney to international destinations including Paris (approximately AUS$2500).

Thai Airways: Australia ☎1300 65 19 60, New Zealand ☎09 377 38 86; www.thaiair.com. Flights to international destinations including Paris.

AIR COURIER FLIGHTS

Those who travel light should consider courier flights. Couriers help transport cargo on international flights by using their checked luggage space for freight. Generally, couriers are limited to carry-ons and must deal with complex flight restrictions. Most flights are round-trip only, with short fixed-length stays (usually one week) and a limit of one ticket per issue. Most of these flights also operate only out of major gateway cities, mostly in North America. Generally, you must be over 18 (in some cases 21). In summer, the most popular destinations require an advance reservation of about two weeks (you can usually book up to two months in advance). Super-discounted fares are common for "last-minute" flights (3 to 14 days ahead).

FROM NORTH AMERICA

Round-trip courier fares from the US to Western Europe run about US$200-500. Most flights leave from New York, Los Angeles, San Francisco, or Miami in the US; and from Montreal, Toronto, or Vancouver in Canada. The organizations below provide members with lists of opportunities and courier brokers for an annual fee. Prices quoted below are round-trip.

Air Courier Association, 1767 A Denver West Blvd., Golden, CO 80401 (☎800-211-5119; www.aircourier.org). Ten departure cities throughout the US and Canada to Paris and other Western European cities (high season US$130-640). One-year membership US$49.

International Association of Air Travel Couriers (**IAATC;** www.courier.org). From 7 North American cities to Western European cities, including **Paris.** One-year membership US$45.

Courier Travel (www.couriertravel.org). Searchable online database. Multiple departure points in the US to various European destinations, including Paris.

FROM THE UK, AUSTRALIA, AND NEW ZEALAND

The minimum age for couriers from the **UK** is usually 18. The **International Association of Air Travel Couriers** (see above) often offers courier flights from London and **Courier Travel** (see above) offers flights from London and Sydney.

STANDBY FLIGHTS

Traveling standby requires considerable flexibility in arrival and departure dates. Companies dealing in standby flights sell vouchers rather than tickets, along with the promise to get you to your destination (or near your destination) within a certain window of time (typically 1-5 days). You call in before your specific window of time to hear your flight options and the probability that you will be able to board each flight. You can then decide which flights you want to try to catch, show up at the appropriate airport at the appropriate time, present your voucher, and board if space is available. Vouchers can usually be bought for both one-way and round-trip travel. You may receive a monetary refund only if every available flight within your date range is full; if you opt not to take an available (but perhaps less convenient) flight, you can only get credit toward future travel. Read agreements with any company offering standby flights with care, as tricky fine print can leave you in the lurch. To check on a company's service record in the US, contact the Better Business Bureau (☎703-276-0100; www.bbb.org). It is difficult to receive refunds, and clients' vouchers will not be honored if an airline fails to receive payment in time.

TICKET CONSOLIDATORS

Ticket consolidators, or **"bucket shops,"** buy unsold tickets in bulk from commercial airlines and sell them at discounted rates. The best place to look is in the Sunday travel section of any major newspaper (such as *The New York Times*), where many bucket shops place tiny ads. Call quickly, as availability is extremely limited. Not all bucket shops are reliable, so insist on a receipt that gives full details of restrictions, refunds, and tickets, and pay by credit card (in spite of the 2-5% fee) so you can stop payment if you never receive your tickets. For more info, see www.travel-library.com/air-travel/consolidators.html.

TRAVELING FROM CANADA AND THE US

Some consolidators worth trying are **Rebel** (☎800-732-3588; www.rebeltours.com), **Cheap Tickets** (www.cheaptickets.com), **Flights.com** (www.flights.com), and **TravelHUB** (www.travelhub.com). *Let's Go* does not endorse any of these agencies. As always, be cautious, and research companies before you hand over your credit card number.

CHARTER FLIGHTS

Tour operators contract charter flights with airlines in order to fly extra loads of passengers during peak season. These flights are far from hassle free. They occur less frequently than flights through major airlines, make refunds particularly difficult, and are almost always fully booked. Their scheduled times may change and they may be cancelled at the last moment (as late as 48 hours before the trip, and without a full refund). And check-in, boarding, and baggage claim for them are often much slower. However, they can be much cheaper.

Discount clubs and fare brokers offer members savings on last-minute charter and tour deals. Study contracts closely; you don't want to end up with an unwanted overnight layover. **Travelers Advantage** (☎800-835-8747; www.travelersadvantage.com; US$90 annual fee includes discounts and cheap flight directories) specializes in **European** travel and tour packages.

BY CHUNNEL FROM THE UK

Traversing 27 mi. under the sea, the Chunnel is undoubtedly the fastest, most convenient, and least scenic route from England to France.

BY TRAIN. Eurostar, Eurostar House, Waterloo Station, London SE1 8SE (UK ☎08705 186 186; www.eurostar.com) runs frequent trains between London and the continent. Ten to 28 trains per day run to 100 destinations including Paris (4hr., US$75-400, 2nd class), Disneyland Paris, Brussels, Lille, and Calais. Book online, at major rail stations in the UK, or at the office above.

BY BUS. Both **Eurolines** (www.eurolines.com) and **Busabout** (www.busabout.com) provide bus-ferry combinations (see p. 34).

BY CAR. Eurotunnel, Customer relations, P.O. Box 2000, Folkestone, Kent CT18 8XY (UK ☎08705 353 535; www.eurotunnel.co.uk) shuttles cars and passengers between Kent and Nord-Pas-de-Calais. One-way tickets for a car and up to 8 passengers start at UK£49. If you plan to return before midnight on your second day, it will cost you UK£22 each way; a two- to five-day return for a car costs UK£39 one-way. Book online or via phone. Travelers with cars can also look into sea crossings by ferry (see below).

BY BOAT FROM THE UK AND IRELAND

The fares below are for **one-way** tickets for **adult foot passengers** unless otherwise noted. Though standard return fares are usually just twice the one-way fare, **fixed-period returns** (usually within five days) are almost invariably cheaper. Ferries run **year-round** unless otherwise noted. **Bikes** are usually free, although you may have to pay up to UK£10 in high season. For a **camper/trailer** supplement, you will have to add UK£20-140 to the "with car" fare. If more than one price is quoted, the price in UK£ is valid for departures from the UK and the price in euro is valid for departures from France. A directory of ferries in this region can be found at www.seaview.co.uk/ferries.html.

Brittany Ferries: UK ☎08703 665 333, France ☎0033 298 800; www.brittany-ferries.com. **Plymouth** to **Roscoff, France** (6hr.; in summer 1-3 per day, off-season 1 per week; UK£20-58 or €21-46). **Portsmouth** to **St-Malo, France** (10¾hr., 1 per day, €23-49) and **Caen, France**

(5¾hr., 2-4 per day, €21-44). **Poole** to **Cherbourg, France** (4¼hr., 2-3 per day, €21-44). **Cork** to **Roscoff, France** (14hr., mid-Mar. to early Nov. 1 per week, €52-99).

Irish Ferries: France ☎1 56 93 43 40; Ireland ☎353 818 300 400; UK ☎8705 17 17 17; www.irishferries.ie. **Rosslare** to **Cherbourg** and **Roscoff** in France (18hr., €49-99).

P&O Ferries: UK ☎08705 980 333; www.posl.com. **Dover** to **Calais, France** (1¼hr., every 40min.-1hr., 50 per day; from UK£10).

SeaFrance: France ☎08 25 08 25 05; www.seafrance.com. **Dover** to **Calais, France** (1½hr., 15 per day, UK£7-11).

GETTING AROUND FRANCE

France is blessed with a well-maintained and exceptionally complete network of roads, and traveling by car, though more expensive, can offer greater freedom to explore the countryside than trains. Many of the country's most popular monuments are inconvenient or expensive to reach except by car. Nevertheless, traveling by train is probably the most comfortable way to get where you're going. France's system of high-speed and local trains connects all but the most minor towns. There are many discounts available for travel within certain regions, as well as for students or seniors. For those places unreachable by train, there is usually a bus system, though sometimes they can be unreliable. Fares are either **one-way** *(aller simple)* or **round-trip** *(aller-retour)*. "Period returns" require you to return within a specific number of days; "day return" means you must return on the same day. Unless stated otherwise, *Let's Go* always lists single fares. Round-trip fares on trains and buses in France are double the one-way fare.

BY PLANE

The recent emergence of no-frills airlines has made hopscotching around Europe by air increasingly affordable and convenient. While these flights often feature inconvenient hours or serve less popular regional airports, with one-way flights averaging US$80, it's never been faster or easier to jet set across the Continent.

easyJet: UK ☎0871 244 2366; www.easyjet.com. Serves 72 destinations in Belgium, the Czech Republic, Denmark, Estonia, France, Germany, Greece, Hungary, Italy, Latvia, the Netherlands, Poland, Portugal, the Slovak Republic, Slovenia, Spain, Switzerland, and the UK.

Ryanair: Ireland ☎0818 303 030, UK 0871 246 00 00; www.ryanair.com. Serves 120 destinations in Austria, Belgium, the Czech Republic, France, Germany, Ireland, Italy, Latvia, the Netherlands, Poland, Portugal, Scandanavia, Spain, and the UK.

The **Star Alliance European Airpass** offers economy class fares as low as US$65 for travel within Europe to more than 200 destinations in 42 countries. The pass is available to non-European passengers on Star Alliance carriers, including Air Canada, Austrian Airlines, BMI British Midland, Lufthansa, Scandinavian Airlines System, Thai International, United Airlines, and Varig, as well as on certain partner airlines. See www.staralliance.com for more information. In addition, a number of European airlines offer discount coupon packets. Most are only available as tack-ons for transatlantic passengers, but some are stand-alone offers. Most must be purchased before departure, so research in advance.

Europe by Air: ☎888-321-4737; www.europebyair.com. *FlightPass* allows you to country-hop to over 150 European cities. US$99 per flight.

Iberia: ☎800-772-4642; www.iberia.com. *Europass* allows Iberia passengers flying from the US to Spain to add a min. of 2 additional destinations in Europe. US$133 each.

BY TRAIN

TRANSPORTATION LISTINGS: CENTER-OUT. *Let's Go* employs the "center-out" principle for transportation listings: for each town, we describe only how to reach towns of similar or greater importance. If you're in a big city, information on reaching neighboring small towns will be in the small town listings themselves rather than in the big city.

Trains in France are generally comfortable, convenient, and reasonably swift. Second-class compartments, which seat two to six, are great places to meet fellow travelers. Trains, however, are not always safe; for **safety tips,** see p. 20. For long trips, make sure you are on the correct car, as trains sometimes split at crossroads. Towns listed in parentheses on European train schedules require a train switch at the town listed immediately before the parenthesis. Locate the *guichets* (ticket counters), the *quais* (platforms), and the *voies* (tracks), and you will be ready to roll. Terminals can be divided into *banlieue* (suburb) and *grandes lignes* (bigger, inter-city trains). Yellow *billetteries* (ticket machines) sell tickets for credit cards with PINs.

You can either buy a **railpass,** which allows unlimited travel in Europe within a particular region for a given period of time, or purchase individual **point-to-point** tickets as you go. French trains offer discounts of 25% to 50% on tickets for travelers under 26 with the **Carte 12-25** (€49, good for 1 year). Once in France, call SNCF at ☎08 92 30 83 08 or visit www.sncf.com for **train info** or **tickets.**

TIP **EVERYONE NEEDS VALIDATION.** Be sure to validate *(composter)* your ticket! Orange and yellow validation boxes can be found in every station, usually in front of the doors leading to the tracks, and you must have your ticket stamped with date and time by the machine before boarding the train.

RESERVATIONS. While seat reservations are required only for selected trains (usually on major lines), you are not guaranteed a seat without one (usually US$5-30). You should strongly consider reserving in advance during peak holiday and tourist seasons (at least a few hours ahead). You will also have to purchase a **supplement** (US$10-50) or special fare for high-speed or high quality trains such as TGVs. InterRail holders must also purchase supplements (US$3-20) for TGVs; supplements are often unnecessary for Eurailpass and Europass holders.

OVERNIGHT TRAINS. On night trains, you won't waste valuable daylight hours traveling and you can avoid the hassle and expense of staying at a hotel. However, the main drawbacks include uncomfortable, sleepless nights, and a lack of scenery—not to mention compromised safety (See **Personal Safety: Exploring and Traveling,** p. 20). You can either sleep upright in your seat (supplement about US$2-10) or pay for a separate space. **Couchettes** (berths) typically have four to six seats per compartment (supplement about US$10-50 per person); **sleepers** (beds) in private sleeping cars offer more privacy and comfort, but are much more expensive (supplement US$40-150). When using a railpass valid only for a restricted number of days, inspect train schedules to maximize the use of your pass: an overnight train or boat journey often uses up only one of your travel days if it departs after 7pm.

SHOULD YOU BUY A RAILPASS? Railpasses were conceived to allow you to jump on any train in Europe, go wherever you want, and change your plans at will. In practice, it's not so simple. You still must stand in line to validate your pass, pay for supplements, and fork over cash for seat and *couchette* reservations. More importantly, railpasses don't always pay off. For ballpark estimates, consult the **RailEurope** railpass brochure for prices of point-to-point tickets. Alternatively, try the **Railsaver** tool at www.railpass.com/new, which calculates whether or not you would save money using a railpass and recommends the most appropriate railpass for your trip. If you are planning to spend extensive time on trains between big cities, a railpass will probably be worth it. But in many cases, especially if you are under 26, point-to-point tickets may prove less expensive.

MULTINATIONAL RAILPASSES

EURAIL PASSES. Eurail is valid in most of Western Europe: Austria, Belgium, Denmark, Finland, France, Germany, Greece, Hungary, Italy, Luxembourg, the Netherlands, Norway, Portugal, the Republic of Ireland, Spain, Sweden, and Switzerland. It is **not valid** in the UK. **Eurail Global Passes,** valid for a consecutive given number of days, are best for those planning on spending extensive time on trains every few days. Other types of global passes are valid for any 10 or 15 (not necessarily consecutive) days within a two-month period, is more cost-effective for those traveling longer distances less frequently. **Eurail Pass Saver** provides first-class travel for travelers in groups of two to five (prices are per person). **Eurail Pass Youth** provides parallel second-class perks for those under 26.

EURAIL GLOBAL PASSES	15 DAYS	21 DAYS	1 MONTH	2 MONTHS	3 MONTHS
Eurail Pass Adult	US$675	US$879	US1089	US$1539	US$1899
Eurail Pass Saver	US$569	US$745	US$925	US$1309	US$1615
Eurail Pass Youth	US$439	US$569	US$709	US$999	US$1235

OTHER GLOBAL PASSES	10 DAYS IN 2 MONTHS	15 DAYS IN 2 MONTHS
Eurail Pass Adult	US$799	US$1049
Eurail Pass Saver	US$679	US$895
Eurail Pass Youth	US$519	US$679

Passholders receive a timetable for major routes and a map with details on bike rental, car rental, hotel, and museum discounts. Passholders often also receive reduced fares or free passage on many boat, bus, and private railroad lines.

The **Eurail Select Pass** is a slimmed-down version of the Eurailpass: it allows five to 15 days of unlimited travel in any two-month period within three, four, or five bordering countries of 23 European countries. **Eurail Select Passes** (for individuals) and **Eurail Select Pass Saver** (for people traveling in groups of two to five) range from US$429/365 per person (5 days) to US$949/805 (15 days). The **Eurail Select Pass Youth** (second-class), for those ages 12-25, costs US$279-619. You are entitled to the same **freebies** afforded by the Eurailpass, but only when they are within or between countries that you have purchased.

SHOPPING AROUND FOR A EURAIL. Eurailpasses are designed by the EU itself, and can be bought only by non-Europeans almost exclusively from non-European distributors. These passes must be sold at uniform prices determined by the EU. However, some travel agents tack on a US$10 handling fee, and others offer certain bonuses with purchase, so shop around. Also, keep in mind that pass prices rise annually, so if you're planning to travel early in the year, you can save cash by purchasing before January 1 (you have three months from the purchase date to validate your pass in Europe).

It is best to buy your Eurail before leaving; only a few places in major European cities sell them, and at a marked-up price. You can get a replacement for a lost pass only if you have purchased insurance on it under the Pass Security Plan (US$14). Eurail Passes are available through travel agents, student travel agencies like STA (p. 26), and **Rail Europe** (Canada ☎800-361-7245, US 877-257-2887; www.raileurope.com) or **Flight Centre** (☎866-967-5351; www.flightcentre.com). It is also possible to buy directly from **Eurail's** website, www.eurail.com. Shipping is free to North America, Australia, New Zealand, and Canada.

OTHER MULTINATIONAL PASSES. If you have lived for at least six months in one of the European countries where **InterRail Passes** are valid, they prove an economical option. The Inter Rail Pass allows travel within 30 European countries (excluding the passholder's country of residence). The **Global Pass** is valid for a given number of days (not necessarily consecutive) within a 10 day-1 month period. (5 days within 10 days, adult 1st class €329, adult 2nd class €249, youth €159; 10 days within 22 days €489/359/239; 1 month continuous €809/599/399. The **One Country Pass** limits travel within one European country (€33 for 3 days). Passholders receive free admission to many museums, as well as **discounts** on accommodations, food, and many ferries to Ireland, Scandinavia, and the rest of Europe. Passes are available at www.interrailnet.com, as well as from travel agents, at major train stations throughout Europe, and through online vendors (www.railpassdirect.co.uk).

DOMESTIC RAILPASSES

If you are planning to spend a significant amount of time within one country or region, a national pass—valid on all rail lines of a country's rail company—may be more cost-effective than a multinational pass. But many national passes are limited and don't provide the free or discounted travel on private railways and ferries that Eurail does. Some of these passes can be bought only in Europe, some only outside of Europe; check with a railpass agent or with national tourist offices.

NATIONAL RAILPASSES. The domestic analogs of the Eurailpass, national railpasses are valid either for a given number of consecutive days or for a specific number of days within a given time period. Usually, they must be purchased before you leave. A four-day Eurail Spain Pass is US$295-225, and a four-day Eurail Portugal Pass is US$165. For more information on national railpasses, check out www.raileurope.com/us/rail/passes/single_country_index.htm.

RAIL-AND-DRIVE PASSES. In addition to simple railpasses, many countries (as well as Eurail) offer rail-and-drive passes, which combine car rental with rail travel—a good option for travelers who wish both to visit cities accessible by rail and to make side trips into the surrounding areas. Prices range from US$605-2056, depending on the type of pass, type of car, and number of people included. Children under the age of 11 cost $183, and adding more days costs $72-105 per day (see **By Car,** p. 36).

BY BUS

Though European trains and railpasses are extremely popular, in some cases buses prove a better option. Often cheaper than railpasses, **international bus passes** allow unlimited travel on a hop-on, hop-off basis between major European cities. The prices below are based on high-season travel.

Eurolines, 28 ave Du Genéral de Gaulle, Bagnolet, Paris (☎0870 514 3219, France 08 92 89 90 91; www.eurolines.com). The largest operator of Europe-wide coach services. Unlimited 15-day (high season €329, under 26 and over 60 €279; low season €199/169) or 30-day (high season €439/359; low season €229/299) travel passes that offer unlimited transit between 35 major European cities.

FURTHER READING & RESOURCES ON TRAIN TRAVEL.

Info on rail travel and railpasses: www.raileurope.com.

Point-to-point fares and schedules: www.raileurope.com/us/rail/fares_schedules/index.htm. Allows you to calculate whether buying a railpass would save you money.

Railsaver: www.railpass.com/new. Uses your itinerary to calculate the best railpass for your trip.

European Railway Server: www.railfaneurope.net. Links to rail servers throughout Europe.

Thomas Cook European Timetable, updated monthly, covers all major and most minor train routes in Europe. Buy directly from Thomas Cook (www.thomascooktimetables.com).

Busabout, 258 Vauxhall Bridge Rd., London SW1V 1BS, UK (☎0207 950 1661; www.busabout.com). Offers 5 interconnecting bus circuits covering 60 cities and towns in Europe. Unlimited (consecutive-day) Passes, Flexipasses, and Add On Passes are available. Unlimited standard/student passes are valid for 2 weeks (US$469/419), 4 weeks (US$739/659), 6 weeks (US$919/819), 8 weeks (US$1049/939), 12 weeks (US$1319/1179), or for the season (US$1649/1469).

BY CAR

Cars offer speed, freedom, access to the countryside, and an escape from the town-to-town mentality induced by train travel. Although a single traveler won't save by renting a car, four usually will. If you can't decide between train and car travel, you may benefit from a combination of the two; RailEurope and other railpass vendors offer rail-and-drive packages. Fly-and-drive packages are also often available from travel agents or airline/rental agency partnerships.

Many places in France—especially many of the most popular tourist attractions, like the Loire châteaux or the D-Day beaches—are best reached by car. Other attractions can be reached in no other way. However, those renting cars should be aware that parking is often difficult to find and rarely free, and that in small towns streets are excessively narrow. Speed limits are high in France but come with strict policing. French drivers have been known to make last-minute maneuvers and fail to yield the right of way, so beware.

DRIVING PERMITS AND CAR INSURANCE

INTERNATIONAL DRIVING PERMIT (IDP)

If you plan to drive a car in **France**, you must **be over 18 and** have a valid driver's license (a valid American license is usually sufficient). It may be a good idea to obtain an **International Driving Permit (IDP)** in case you are stranded or in an accident and the police don't speak English; **information on the IDP is printed in 11 languages, including French**.

Your IDP, valid for one year, must be issued in your own country before you depart. An application for an IDP usually requires one or two photos, a current local license, an additional form of identification, and a fee. To apply, contact your home country's automobile association. Be vigilant when purchasing an IDP online or anywhere other than your home automobile association. Many vendors sell permits of questionable legitimacy for higher prices.

CAR INSURANCE

Most credit cards cover standard insurance. If you rent, lease, or borrow a car, you will need a **Green Card,** or **International Insurance Certificate,** to certify that you have liability insurance and that it applies abroad. Green cards can be obtained at car rental agencies, car dealers (for those leasing cars), some travel agents, and some border crossings.

RENTING

You can rent a car from a US-based firm (Alamo, Avis, Budget, or Hertz) with European offices, from a European-based company with local representatives (Europcar), or from a tour operator (Auto Europe, Europe By Car, and Kemwel Holiday Autos) that will arrange a rental for you from a European company at its own rates. Multinationals offer greater flexibility, but tour operators often strike better deals. It is often cheaper to pick up a car in Belgium, Germany, or the Netherlands than in Paris. It is always significantly less expensive to reserve a car from the US than from Europe. Ask airlines about special fly-and-drive packages; you may get up to a week of free or discounted rental. Expect to pay US$80-400 per week, plus tax (5-25%), for a tiny car. Reserve ahead and pay in advance if at all possible. Always check if prices quoted include tax and collision insurance; some credit card companies provide insurance, allowing their customers to decline the collision damage waiver. Ask about discounts and check the terms of insurance, particularly the size of the deductible. To rent a car from most agencies in France, you need to be at least 21 years old. Some require renters to be 25, and most charge those aged 21-24 an additional insurance fee (around €20-25 per day). Small local operations occasionally rent to people under 21, but be sure to ask about the insurance coverage and deductible, and always check the fine print.

Many rental packages offer unlimited kilometers, while others offer a limited number of kilometers per day with a surcharge per kilometer after that. Return the car with a full tank of gasoline (petrol) to avoid high fuel charges at the end. Be sure to ask whether the price includes **insurance** against theft and collision. Remember that if you are driving a conventional rental vehicle on an **unpaved road** in a rental car, you are almost never covered by insurance; ask about this before leaving the rental agency. Be aware that cars rented on an **American Express** or **Visa/MasterCard Gold** or **Platinum** credit card in France might not carry the automatic insurance that they would in some other countries; check with your credit card company. Many rental companies in France require you to buy a **Collision Damage Waiver (CDW),** which costs about US$10-80 per day. **Loss Damage Waivers (LDWs)** do the same in the case of theft or vandalism.

National chains often allow one-way rentals (picking up in one city and dropping off in another). There is usually a minimum hire period and sometimes an extra drop-off charge of several hundred dollars. Rental companies in France include:

Auto Europe (☎888-223-5555 or 207-842-2000; www.autoeurope.com).

Avis (Australia ☎136 333; Canada 800-331-1212; France 00 34 93 344 3715; UK 870 010 0287; US 800-331-1212; www.avis.com).

Budget (Canada ☎800-268-8900; New Zealand 0800-283-438; UK 870 156 5656; US 800-527-0700; www.budgetrentacar.com).

Europe by Car (US ☎800-223-1516 or 212-581-3040; www.europebycar.com).

Europcar International, 3 av. du Centre, 78 881 Saint Quentin en Yvelines Cedex, France (France ☎02 25 35 83 58; UK 870 607 5000; US 877-940-6900; www.europcar.com).

Hertz (☎800-654-3001 for international reservations or 800-654-3131 for local reservations; www.hertz.com).

Kemwel (US ☎877-820-0668; www.kemwel.com).

ESSENTIALS

ESSENTIALS

ON THE ROAD

It is mandatory for all passengers to wear seatbelts both in the front and back seats. French police can fine anyone who does not comply with these laws. To receive directions, estimates of driving time, and toll and gas costs, check out **Itinéraire** (www.iti.fr). **Gas stations** in most towns won't accept cash after 7pm, but they will take the French *Carte Bleue* (analogous to Visa). Gasoline generally costs around €1.60 per liter. Diesel *(gazole)* fuel tends to be cheaper than unleaded *(essence sans plomb)*. Ask at a French Government Tourist Office for *la carte de l'esssence moins chère*, a map of supermarkets close to highway exits, where gas is cheaper. Tolls in France are high. *Autoroutes* (marked on signs with an A) are tolled express highways. *Routes nationales* (marked with an N) and the smaller, more scenic *routes départementales* (marked with a D) do not have tolls.

DRIVING PRECAUTIONS. When traveling in the summer, bring substantial amounts of water (a suggested 5 liters of **water** per person per day) for drinking and for the radiator. Check with the local automobile club for details. When traveling for long distances, make sure tires are in good repair and have enough air, and get good maps. A **compass** and a **car manual** can also be very useful. You should always carry a **spare tire** and **jack, jumper cables, extra oil, flares,** a **flashlight,** and **heavy blankets** (in case your car breaks down at night or in the winter). If you don't know how to **change a tire,** learn before heading out, especially if you are planning on traveling in deserted areas. Blowouts on dirt roads are very common. If your car breaks down, **stay in your vehicle;** if you wander off, there's less likelihood trackers will find you.

For an informal primer on French road signs and conventions, check out www.travlang.com/signs and www.franceguide.com. The **Association for Safe International Road Travel (ASIRT),** 11769 Gainsborough Rd., Potomac, MD 20854, USA (☎301-983-5252; www.asirt.org), provides specific information about road conditions in France.

DANGERS

In France, the most dangerous aspects of driving include narrow streets, careless drivers, and high speed limits. Make sure you are comfortable driving under these conditions. Generally, the speed limits are as follows: 130kph (81mph) on autoroutes, 90-110kph (56-68mph) on highways and open roads, and 50 kph (30mph) in towns. Note that police can collect up to €380 in fines on the spot if you are caught breaking the law. Exercise caution on mountainous regions, where roads can be narrow and unpaved—as well as icy in the winter. Almost all roads in Corsica are mountainous and narrow, so be extra vigilant about following the rules of the road. Most accidents occur during the tourist season, when streets are crowded with unfamiliar drivers. For more info on the driving conditions in France specific to your time of visit, see the website of **Bison Futé** (www.bison-fute.equipement.gouv.fr.), an organization geared toward reducing road congestion.

CAR ASSISTANCE

If your car breaks down on the road, go to one of the nearby orange SOS phones, which are stationed every 2km on motorways and every 4km on two-way highways. You will be expected to give your identity, location, and vehicle description. Dial ☎15 for an ambulance and ☎17 for the police. In addition, most car rental agencies offer 24/7 roadside assistance; check before you rent your car.

BY BOAT

Most European ferries are quite comfortable; the cheapest ticket typically includes a reclining chair or *couchette.* Fares jump sharply in July and August. Ask for discounts; ISIC holders can often get student fares, and Eurail Pass holders get many reductions and free trips (for examples of popular freebies, see p. 19). You'll occasionally have to pay a port tax (under US$10).

ENGLISH CHANNEL AND IRISH SEA FERRIES

Ferries are frequent and dependable. The main route across the **English Channel,** from England to France, is Dover-Calais, though ferries also travel frequently to and from Brittany. The main ferry port on the southern coast of England is Portsmouth, with connections to France and Spain. Ferries also cross the **Irish Sea,** connecting Northern Ireland with Scotland and England, and the Republic of Ireland with Wales. (See **Getting to France,** p. 26 for more information.)

MEDITERRANEAN AND AEGEAN FERRIES

Mediterranean ferries may be the most glamorous, but they can also be the most rocky. Bring toilet paper. Ferries run from France to Morocco and Tunisia. Reservations are recommended, especially in July and August. Schedules are erratic and prices vary. Shop around, and beware of dinky, unreliable companies that don't take reservations.

BY BICYCLE

With a mountain bike, you can do some serious natural sightseeing. Many airlines will count your bike as your second free piece of luggage; a few charge extra (around US$80). Bikes must be packed in a cardboard box with the pedals and front wheel detached; many airlines sell bike boxes at the airport (US$15). Most ferries let you take your bike for free or for a nominal fee, and you can always ship your bike on trains. Renting a bike beats bringing your own if you plan to stay in one or two regions. In addition to **panniers** (US$10-40) to hold your luggage, you'll need a good **helmet** (US$15-50) and a **sturdy lock** (from US$25). For more books on biking through France, try **Mountaineers Books,** 1001 S.W. Klickitat Way, Suite 201, Seattle, WA 98134, USA (☎206-223-6303; www.mountaineersbooks.org).

If you are nervous about striking out on your own, **Blue Marble Travel** (Canada ☎519-624-2494, France 01 42 36 02 34, US 215-923-3788; www.bluemarble.org) offers bike tours for small groups of ages 20 to 49 throughout Europe. **CBT Tours,** P.O. Box 27640, San Francisco, CA 94127, USA (☎800-736-2453; www.cbttours.com), offers full-package culinary, biking, hiking, and sightseeing tours (US$2000-2500) to France, as well as custom-designed trips.

> **HEADS UP!** While avid cyclists, the French aren't always as keen on cycling safety. When renting a bike, you may have to insist on being given *un casque* (a helmet) and *un anti-vol* (a lock). Don't be afraid to stand your ground; even if helmets aren't legally required, most bike shops have a few in their back room waiting for "crazy" customers like you.

BY MOPED AND MOTORCYCLE

Motorized bikes and **mopeds** don't use much gas, can be put on trains and ferries, and are a good compromise between costly car travel and the limited range of bicycles. However, they're uncomfortable for long distances, dangerous in the rain, and unpredictable on rough roads. Always wear a helmet, and never ride with a backpack. If you've never ridden a moped before, a twisting Alpine road is not the place to start. Expect to pay about US$20-35 per day; try auto repair shops, and remember to bargain. **Motorcycles** are more expensive and normally require a license, but are better for long distances. Before renting, ask if the price includes tax and insurance or you may be hit with an unexpected fee. Avoid handing over your passport as a deposit; if you have an accident or mechanical failure you may not get it back until you cover all repairs. Pay ahead of time instead.

BY THUMB

> **!** *Let's Go* never recommends hitchhiking as a safe means of transportation, and none of the information presented here is intended to do so.

Let's Go strongly urges you to consider the risks before you choose to hitchhike. Hitching means entrusting your life to a stranger and risking assault, sexual harassment, theft, and unsafe driving. The choice, however, remains yours. France is the hardest country in Europe in which to get a lift, though in Corsica—particularly along hiking routes—it is more common than elsewhere. If you do decide to hitchhike *(faire du stop)*, remember that thumbing is tolerated only at rest stops, tollbooths, and highway entrance ramps; hitching, or even standing, along *autoroutes* is illegal. Hitchhiking at night can be particularly dangerous; experienced hitchers stand in well-lit places. For women traveling alone (or even in pairs), hitching is just too dangerous. A man and a woman are a less dangerous combination; two men will have a harder time getting a lift, while three men will go nowhere. Experienced hitchers pick a spot outside of built-up areas, where drivers can stop, return to the road without causing an accident, and have time to look over potential passengers as they approach. Finally, success will depend on appearance. Drivers prefer hitchers who are neat and wholesome-looking.

Most Western European countries offer a ride service, which pairs drivers with riders for a fee. **Eurostop** (www.taxistop.be/index_ils.htm), Taxistop's ride service, is one of the largest in Europe. Also try **Allostop** (www.allostop.net) in France. Not all organizations screen drivers and riders; ask in advance.

KEEPING IN TOUCH

BY EMAIL AND INTERNET

Internet access is readily available throughout France. Only the smallest villages lack Internet cafés, and in larger towns Internet cafés are well equipped and widespread, though often pricey. Although in some places it's possible to forge a remote link with your home server, in most cases this is a much slower (and thus more expensive) option than taking advantage of free web-based email accounts (e.g., www.gmail.com and www.hotmail.com). Internet cafés and the occasional free Internet terminal at a public library or university are listed in the Practical Information sections of major cities. For lists of additional cybercafés in France, check out www.cybercaptive.com. One of the challenges of checking email at internet cafés is that the French keyboard is different from the American, Australian, and British keyboard; in order to avoid confusing emails home where Zs and As are swapped, go to the control panel or system preferences, select keyboard, and change the settings.

Increasingly, travelers find that taking their **laptop computers** on the road with them can be a convenient option for staying connected. Laptop users can call an Internet service provider via a modem using long-distance phone cards specifically intended for such calls. They may also find Internet cafés that allow them to connect their laptops to the Internet. And most excitingly, travelers with wireless-enabled computers may be able to take advantage of an increasing number of Internet "hot spots," where they can get online for free or for a small fee (many McDonald's offer free Wi-Fi). Newer computers can detect these hot spots automatically; otherwise, websites like www.jiwire.com, www.wififreespot.com, and www.wi-fihotspotlist.com can help you find them. You might consider insuring your laptop while traveling.

WARY WI-FI. Wireless hot spots make Internet access possible in public and remote places. Unfortunately, they also pose **security risks.** Hot spots are public, open networks that use unencrypted, unsecured connections. They are susceptible to hacks and "packet sniffing"—ways of stealing passwords and other private information. To prevent problems, disable ad hoc mode, turn off file sharing, turn off network discovery, encrypt your e-mail, turn on your firewall, beware of phony networks, and watch for over-the-shoulder creeps. Ask the establishment whose wireless you're using for the name of the network so you know you're on the right one. If you are in the vicinity and do not plan to access the Internet, turn off your wireless adapter completely.

BY TELEPHONE

CALLING HOME FROM FRANCE

TIP **BE A CHATTERBOX.** If you buy an international phone card and are staying in a room with a telephone, make sure to call from your room rather than from a payphone—*télécabines* charge large fees, reducing your talk time by half.

You can usually make direct international calls from pay phones, but if you aren't using a phone card, you may need to feed the machine regularly. **Prepaid phone cards are a common and relatively inexpensive means of calling abroad.** Each one comes with a Personal Identification Number (PIN) and a toll-free access number. You call the access number and then follow the directions for dialing your PIN. To purchase prepaid phone cards, check online for the best rates; www.callingcards.com is a good place to start. Online providers generally send your access number and PIN via email, with no actual "card" involved. You can also purchase cards in France (see **Calling Within France,** p. 42).

COMPANY	TO OBTAIN A CARD:	TO CALL ABROAD:
AT&T (US)	800-364-9292 or www.att.com	0800 99 00 11
Canada Direct	800-561-8868 or www.infocanadadirect.com	0800 99 00 16 or 0800 99 02 16
MCI (US)	800-777-5000 or www.minutepass.com	0800 99 00 19
Telecom New Zealand Direct	www.telecom.co.nz	0800 90 42 80
Telstra Australia	1800 676 638 or www.telstra.com	0800 99 00 61

Another option is to purchase a **calling card,** linked to a major national telecommunications service in your home country. Calls are billed collect or to your account. To obtain a calling card, contact the appropriate company listed below. Where available, there are often advantages to purchasing calling cards online, including better rates and immediate access to your account. To call home with a calling card, contact the operator for your service provider in France by dialing the appropriate toll-free access number (listed below in the third column).

PLACING INTERNATIONAL CALLS. To call France from home or to call home from France, dial:

1. The **international dialing prefix.** To call from **Australia,** dial 0011; **Canada** or the **US,** 011; **Ireland, New Zealand,** or the **UK,** 00; **France,** 00.
2. The **country code** of the country you want to call. To call **Australia,** dial 61; **Canada** or the **US,** 1; **Ireland,** 353; **New Zealand,** 64; the **UK,** 44; **France,** 33.
3. The **city/area code.** *Let's Go* lists the city/area codes for cities and towns in France opposite the city or town name, next to a ☎. If the first digit is a zero (e.g., 01 for Paris), omit the zero when calling from abroad (e.g., dial 011 33 1 from the US to reach Paris).
4. The **local number.**

Placing a collect call through an international operator can be expensive, but may be necessary in case of an emergency. You can frequently call collect without even possessing a company's calling card just by calling its access number and following the instructions.

CALLING WITHIN FRANCE

The simplest way to call within the country is to use a card-operated pay phone. **Prepaid phone cards** (*Télécartes*, available at newspaper kiosks and *tabacs*), which carry a certain amount of phone time depending on the card's denomination, are usually the only way to pay, as coin-operated phones have largely been phased out. The computerized phone will tell you how much time, in units, you have left on your card. Another kind of prepaid telephone card comes with a PIN and a toll-free access number. Instead of inserting the card into the phone, you call the access number and follow the directions on the card. These cards can be used to make international as well as domestic calls. *Télécartes* are available in 50-unit (€7.50) and 120-unit (€15) denominations; one minute of a local call uses about one unit. Emergency numbers, directory information (☎12), and toll-free numbers (*numéros verts*) beginning with 0800 can be dialed without a card.

If the phone you use does not provide English commands, proceed with caution; French payphones are notoriously unforgiving. *Décrochez* means pick up, *patientez* means wait. Do not dial until you hear *numérotez* or *composez*. *Raccrochez* means "hang up." To make another call, press the green button instead of hanging up. Phone rates typically tend to be highest in the morning, lower in the evening, and lowest on Sunday and late at night.

CELLULAR PHONES

If you plan to stay in France for several months, buying a French cell phone is worth the cost. Incoming calls to cell phones are often free (even from abroad), and local calls are charged the local rate. The cheapest phones are relatively inexpensive (from €40), and French phones do not require a long-term plan. **Orange** and **SFR** generally provide the best deals and reception. Cell phone calls can be paid for without signing a contract if you purchase a **Mobicarte,** a prepaid card available in denominations of €15, €25, or €35.

TIP **CABINE CALL-BACK.** Making international calls from France is easy—but getting the best deal on the dizzying array of phone cards offered at *tabacs* and post offices is anything but. While the spiffy public phone booths *(cabines)* that sit on most major streets have slots in which to insert a *télécarte* with a microchip, this is the most expensive way to call internationally. Savvy travelers ask for a *carte téléphonique internationale* at a *tabac*. These cards have a hidden trick which gets you more minutes: *cabine call-back.* When using a non-*télécarte* phone card, don't dial the large, obvious four-digit number marked "free" on the instructions. Instead, when using a *cabine,* dial the smaller, less-obvious 0800 number labelled *cabine call-back* or just *call-back.* Dial the number, and an automated voice will tell you, in French, to hang up. Do so, and in a minute or so the phone will ring. Pick up, and dial your PIN and the number you're calling. It's a bit tedious, but this method will save you precious phone-card minutes otherwise wasted entering your pin and dialing.

The international standard for cell phones is the **Global System for Mobile Communication (GSM).** To make and receive calls in France you will need a **GSM-compatible phone** and a **SIM (Subscriber Identity Module) card,** a country-specific, thumbnail-sized chip that gives you a local phone number and plugs you into the local network. Many SIM cards are **prepaid,** meaning that they come with calling time included and you don't need to sign up for a monthly service plan. Incoming calls are frequently free. When you use up the prepaid time, you can buy additional cards or vouchers (usually available at convenience stores) to "top up" your phone. Another option is to get a SIM card from **Call-in-Europe** (www.call-in-europe.com), which bills your credit card for the minutes you use and offers good rates and excellent plans for frequent travelers to France. For more information on GSM phones, check out www.telestial.com, www.orange.co.uk, www.roadpost.com, or www.planetomni.com. Companies like **Cellular Abroad** (www.cellularabroad.com) and **Mobile Planet** (www.mobileplanet.com) rent cell phones that work in a variety of destinations around the world, providing a simpler option than picking up a phone in-country.

TIP **GSM PHONES.** Just having a GSM phone doesn't mean you're necessarily good to go when you travel abroad. The majority of GSM phones sold in the United States operate on a different **frequency** (1900) than international phones (900/1800) and will not work abroad. Tri-band phones work on all three frequencies (900/1800/1900) and will operate throughout most of the world. Additionally, some GSM phones are **SIM-locked** and will only accept SIM cards from a single carrier. You'll need a **SIM-unlocked** phone to use a SIM card from a local carrier when you travel.

Check with your service provider to see if your phone's band can be switched to 900/1800, which will register your phone with one of the three French servers: **Bouyges** (www.bouygtel.com), **Itineris** (www.ifrance.com/binto/itineris.htm), or **France Télécom** (www.agence.francetelecom.com).

TIME DIFFERENCES

France is 1 hour ahead of Greenwich Mean Time (GMT) and observes Daylight Saving Time (beginning in March and ending in October).

4AM	5AM	6AM	7AM	8AM	NOON	1PM	10PM
Vancouver Seattle San Francisco Los Angeles	Denver	Chicago	New York Toronto	New Brunswick	London	**PARIS**	Sydney Canberra Melbourne

BY MAIL

SENDING MAIL HOME FROM FRANCE

Airmail is the best way to send mail home from France. **Aerogrammes,** printed sheets that fold into envelopes and travel via airmail, are available at post offices. Write "airmail" and "par avion" on the front. Most post offices will charge exorbitant fees, or simply refuse to send aerogrammes with enclosures. To send a package, use one of the boxes provided by the post office—using your own will cost significantly more. **Surface mail** is by far the cheapest and slowest way to send mail. It takes one to two months to cross the Atlantic and one to three to cross the Pacific—good for heavy items you won't need for a while, such as souvenirs that you've acquired along the way. These are standard rates for mail from France to:

Australia: Allow 8 days for regular airmail home. Postcards/aerogrammes €0.85. Letters up to 20g €0.85; packages up to 0.5kg €7.20, up to 2kg €16.50.

Canada: Allow 6 days for regular airmail home. Postcards/aerogrammes €0.85. Letters up to 20g €0.85; packages up to 0.5kg €7.20, up to 2kg €16.50.

Ireland: Allow 3 days for regular airmail home. Postcards/aerogrammes €0.60. Letters up to 20g €0.60; packages up to 0.5kg €6, up to 2kg €12.30.

New Zealand: Allow 8 days for regular airmail home. Postcards/aerogrammes €0.85. Letters up to 20g €0.85; packages up to 0.5kg €7.20, up to 2kg €16.50.

UK: Allow 3 days for regular airmail home. Postcards/aerogrammes €0.60. Letters up to 20g €0.60; packages up to 0.5kg €6, up to 2kg €12.30.

US: Allow 6 days for regular airmail home. Postcards/aerogrammes €0.85. Letters up to 20g €0.85; packages up to 0.5kg €7.20, up to 2kg €16.50.

SENDING MAIL TO FRANCE

To ensure timely delivery, mark envelopes "airmail" and "par avion." In addition to the standard postage system whose rates are listed above, **Federal Express** (Australia ☎13 26 10, Canada and the US 800-463-3339, Ireland 1800 535 800, New Zealand 0800 733 339, the UK 08456 070 809; www.fedex.com) handles express mail services from most countries to France. Sending a postcard within France costs €0.20, while sending letters (up to 20g) domestically requires €0.54.

There are several ways to arrange pick up of letters sent to you while you are abroad. Mail can be sent via **Poste Restante** (General Delivery) to almost any city or town in France with a post office, but it is not very reliable. Address *Poste Restante* letters (max. 20g) like so:

Napoleon BONAPARTE
Poste Restante
Postal Code, City
FRANCE

The mail will go to a special desk in the central post office, unless you specify a post office by street address or postal code. It's best to use the largest post office, since mail may be sent there regardless. Bring your passport (or other photo ID) for pick up; there may be a small fee. If the clerks insist that there is nothing for you, ask them to check under your first name as well. *Let's Go* lists post offices in the **Practical Information** section for each city and most towns.

TRAVELING EUROPE THIS SUMMER?
Get connected before you go!
• Don't miss your calls from home!
• Get your US phone calls forwarded to a local phone!
• Get a phone and local number of your destination country before you leave home!
PLATFORM.
3000
www.platform3000.com

ESSENTIALS

ACCOMMODATIONS

HOSTELS

TIP **PUTTING THE YOUTH IN YOUTH HOSTEL.** Outside of July and August, school groups often take over hostels, transforming them into playgrounds. That means noise, dirty bathrooms, and long lines at breakfast. Ask at the hostel when you reserve to ensure that you won't be the only one over 12.

Many hostels are laid out dorm-style, often with large single-sex rooms and bunk beds, although private rooms that sleep two to four are becoming more common. They sometimes have kitchens and utensils for use, bike or moped rentals, storage areas, transportation to airports, breakfast and other meals, laundry facilities, and Internet access. There can be drawbacks: some hostels close during certain daytime "lockout" hours, have a curfew, don't accept reservations, impose a maximum stay, or, less frequently, require that you do chores. In France, a dorm bed in a hostel will average around €10-15 and a private room around €15-25; *Let's Go* lists all hostel dorm and room prices per person.

A HOSTELER'S BILL OF RIGHTS. There are certain standard features that we do not include in our hostel listings. Unless we state otherwise, you can expect that every hostel has no lockout, no curfew, free sheets, free hot showers, some system of secure luggage storage, and no key deposit.

HOSTELLING INTERNATIONAL

Joining the youth hostel association in your own country (listed below) automatically grants you membership privileges in **Hostelling International (HI),** a federation of national hosteling associations. **Over 150** HI hostels are scattered throughout France and **are typically less expensive and nicer than private hostels.** HI's umbrella organization's website (www.hihostels.com), which lists the web addresses and phone numbers of all national associations, can be a great place to begin researching hosteling. Other comprehensive hosteling websites include www.hostels.com, www.hostelplanet.com, and www.eurotrip.com.

LIVING THE HI-LIFE. All HI hostels in France are open to non-HI members. However, HI members are entitled to a €2.90 discount. The prices that *Let's Go* lists are for non-members.

Most HI hostels also honor **guest memberships**—you'll get a blank card with space for six validation stamps. Each night you'll pay a non-member rate and earn one guest stamp; get six stamps and you're a member. A new membership benefit is the FreeNites program, which allows hostelers to gain points toward free rooms. Most student travel agencies (see p. 26) sell HI cards, as do the national hosteling organizations listed below; most hostels in France will also sell them. All prices listed below are valid for **one-year memberships** unless otherwise noted.

Australian Youth Hostels Association (AYHA), 422 Kent St., Sydney, NSW 200 (☎02 9261 1111; www.yha.com.au). AUS$52, under 18 AUS$19.

Hostelling International-Canada (HI-C), 205 Catherine St. Ste. 400, Ottawa, ON K2P 1C3 (☎613-237-7884; www.hihostels.ca). CDN$35, under 18 free.

An Óige (Irish Youth Hostel Association), 61 Mountjoy St., Dublin 7 (☎830 4555; www.irelandyha.org). €20, under 18 €10.

Hostelling International Northern Ireland (HINI), 22-32 Donegall Rd., Belfast BT12 5JN (☎02890 32 47 33; www.hini.org.uk). £15, under 25 £10.

Youth Hostels Association of New Zealand Inc. (YHANZ), Level 1, 166 Moorhouse Ave., P.O. Box 436, Christchurch (☎0800 278 299 in NZ or 03 379 9970; www.yha.org.nz). NZ$40, under 18 free.

Scottish Youth Hostels Association (SYHA), 7 Glebe Cres., Stirling FK8 2JA (☎01786 89 14 00; www.syha.org.uk). £8, under 18 £4.

Youth Hostels Association (England and Wales), Trevelyan House, Dimple Rd., Matlock, Derbyshire DE4 3YH (☎08707 708 868; www.yha.org.uk). £16, under 26 £10.

Hostelling International USA, 8401 Colesville Rd., Ste. 600, Silver Spring, MD 20910 (☎301-495-1240; www.hiayh.org). US$28, under 18 free.

Fédération Unie des Auberges de Jeunesse, 27 rue Pajol, 75018 Paris (☎0033-1 44 89 87 27; www.fuaj.org).

ESSENTIALS

BOOKING HOSTELS ONLINE. One of the easiest ways to ensure you've got a bed for the night is by reserving online. Connect to the **Hostelworld** booking engine through **www.letsgo.com,** and you'll have access to bargain accommodations from Paris to Pontorson with no added commission.

HOTELS, GUESTHOUSES, AND PENSIONS

Hotel singles in France cost about €25 (approximately US$35) per night, doubles €35 (US$47). If you want a double with two twin beds instead of one double, ask for *une chambre avec deux lits.* All accredited hotels are ranked on a zero- to four-star system by the French government according to factors such as room size, facilities, and plumbing. You'll typically share a hall bathroom; a private bathroom may cost extra, as may hot showers. Some hotels offer *pension complet* (all meals) and *demi pension* (no lunch). Smaller **guesthouses** and **pensions** are often cheaper than hotels. If you make **reservations** in writing, indicate your night of arrival and the number of nights you plan to stay. The hotel will send you a confirmation and may request payment for the first night. Often it is easiest to make reservations over the phone or online with a credit card.

Hotels listed in the **Accommodations** section for each town or city in *Let's Go* are generally small, family-run establishments close to sights of interest. *Let's Go* doesn't list budget chains like Hôtels Formule 1, Etaps Hôtel, and Hôtels Première Classe, which can usually be found on the outskirts of town. They typically charge €29-33 for one- to three-person rooms with sink, TV, hall showers, toilets, and telephones and are sometimes the cheapest, though least charming, option.

TIP **CHEAPER SLEEPER.** Many smaller, private hotels do not list their cheapest accommodations on the sign downstairs that lists prices of rooms. Especially if you are looking for a single room with one bed, ask if the hotel has anything *"moins cher."* They may tell you, "*Oui,* but it has a poor view," or "*Oui,* but the room is very small," but *oui,* it will always have a bed. Always ask if there is something cheaper than the first quoted price for a room.

CAMPING

The French are avid campers but approach the outdoors in a civilized and organized way. After 3000 years of settled history, there is little wilderness in France.

Even if you find any, forget those romantic dreams of roughing it unless your definition of 'roughing it' involves a stint in jail; it is illegal to camp in public spaces or light your own fires. Organized campings (campsites) are ranked on a four-star system and often include amenities such as bars, supermarkets, playgrounds, and swimming pools. Campgrounds generally charge separately for the use of their sites (€1.50-7 per site or tent) and for the number of people staying in them (€3-6 per person, less for children). Most campsites have toilets, showers, and electrical outlets, though often at extra expense (€2-5). Where relevant, campsites are listed at the end of the Accommodations section of towns in Let's Go. A comprehensive search by region or criteria of over 10,000 campsites in France can be found at www.campingfrance.com. Some campsites rent tents or RVs. For more information on outdoor activities in France, consult the following resources or see The Great Outdoors, below.

Sites & Paysages de France, Avenue des Côteaux, 66140 Canet en Roussillon (☎820 20 46 46). Publishes a brochure featuring regional campsites and outdoor activities.

Camping and Caravaning Guide France (Michelin Travel Publications, US$14).

OTHER TYPES OF ACCOMMODATIONS

BED & BREAKFASTS (B&BS)

For a cozy alternative to impersonal hotel rooms, B&Bs (private homes with rooms available to travelers; *chambres d'hôtes)* range from acceptable to sublime. Rooms in B&Bs generally cost **€30** for a single and **€35-45** for a double in France. Though they are not extremely common in France, B&Bs can be found online through **Bed & Breakfast Inns Online** (www.bbonline.com), **InnFinder** (www.inncrawler.com), **InnSite** (www.innsite.com), **BedandBreakfast.com** (www.bedandbreakfast.com), **Pamela Lanier's Bed & Breakfast Guide Online** (www.lanierbb.com), or **BNBFinder.com** (www.bnbfinder.com).

CHAMBRES D'HÔTE. France's *chambres d'hôte,* or bed and breakfasts, give you the chance to stay with local families. Organized through the **Gîtes de France,** *chambres d'hôte,* or *ferme auberges* if they are located on a working farm, provide an unparalleled glimpse into French culture. Many also offer *tables d'hôte,* where guests are served a full French-style dinner with the hosts. Check tourist offices for extensive listings of *chambres d'hôte* in the region.

UNIVERSITY DORMS

Many **colleges** and **universities** open their residence halls to travelers when school is not in session; some do so even during term-time. Getting a room may take a couple of phone calls and require advanced planning, but rates tend to be low, and many offer free local calls and Internet access. For information on universities in France, consult the following source:

Centre National des Œuvres Universitaires et Scolaires (CNOUS), 69 quai d'Orsay, 75007 Paris (☎01 44 18 53 00; www.cnous.fr). A regional guide of universities and lodgings throughout France available on the website, under 'La Vie Etudiante,' subheading: Logement. Click on 'Carte des Cités U' at the bottom. Or, when in France, inquire at a relevant Student Welcome Center *(service d'accueil des étudiants)*.

YMCAS AND YWCAS

Young Men's Christian Association (YMCA) and **Young Women's Christian Association (YWCA)** lodgings are usually cheaper than a hotel but more expensive than a hostel. Not all 30 French locations offer lodging; those that do are often located in urban downtowns. Although most YWCAs won't take men, many YMCAs accept women and families; some will not lodge those under 18 without parental permission.

World Alliance of YMCAs, 12 Clos Belmont, 1208 Geneva, Switzerland (☎+41 22 849 5100; www.ymca.int). Listings of Ys worldwide.

HOME EXCHANGES AND HOSPITALITY CLUBS

Home exchange offers the traveler various types of homes (houses, apartments, condominiums, villas, even castles), plus the opportunity to live like a native and cut down on accommodation fees. For more information, contact HomeExchange.com Inc., P.O. Box 787, Hermosa Beach, CA 90254, USA (☎310 798 3864 or toll free 800-877-8723; www.homeexchange.com), **or** Intervac International Home Exchange (**01 43 70 21 22;** www.intervac.com).

Hospitality clubs link their members with individuals or families abroad who are willing to host travelers for free or for a small fee to promote cultural exchange and general good karma. In exchange, members usually must be willing to host travelers in their own homes; a small membership fee may also be required. **The Hospitality Club** (www.hospitalityclub.org) is a good place to start. **Servas** (www.servas.org) is an established, more formal, peace-based organization, and requires a fee and an interview to join. An Internet search will find many similar organizations, some of which cater to special interests (e.g., women, GLBT travelers, or members of certain professions). As always, use common sense when planning to stay with or host someone you do not know.

LONG-TERM ACCOMMODATIONS

Travelers planning to stay in France for an extended period of time may find it most cost-effective to rent an **apartment.** A basic one-bedroom (or studio) apartment in Paris will range €650-3000 per month. If you want to be super-hip (but possibly broke), stay in the Latin Quarter (5ème or 6ème). To save money, consider renting near a Metro station in an outlying neighborhood, where you'll still have fast and easy access to the Paris without the city prices. Besides the rent itself, prospective tenants usually are also required to front a security deposit (frequently one month's rent) and sometimes the last month's rent.

A good place to check for apartments is **craigslist** (www.craigslist.org), a forum for renters and rentees where you can see others' listings. You may have more success if you post your own housing needs and allow renters to contact you. For apartments and houses to buy or rent throughout France, try **Go-To-France** (www.go-to-france.co.uk); the site also offers practical advice for prospective renters.

THE GREAT OUTDOORS

The **Great Outdoor Recreation Page** (www.gorp.com) provides general information for travelers planning on camping or spending time in the outdoors.

USEFUL RESOURCES

A variety of publishing companies offer hiking guidebooks to meet the educational needs of novice or expert. For information about camping, hiking, and biking,

LEAVE NO TRACE. Let's Go encourages travelers to embrace the "Leave No Trace" ethic, minimizing their impact on natural environments and protecting them for future generations. Trekkers and wilderness enthusiasts should set up camp on durable surfaces, use cookstoves instead of campfires, bury human waste away from water supplies, bag trash and carry it out with them, and respect wildlife and natural objects. For more detailed information, contact the **Leave No Trace Center for Outdoor Ethics,** P.O. Box 997, Boulder, CO 80306 (☎800-332-4100 or 303-442-8222; www.lnt.org).

write or call the publishers listed below to receive a free catalog. Campers heading to Europe should consider buying an International Camping Carnet. Similar to a hostel membership card, it's required at a few campgrounds and sometimes provides discounts. It is available in North America from the Family Campers and RVers Association and in the UK from The Caravan Club (see below).

Automobile Association, Member Administration Contact Centre, Lambert House, Stockport Road, Cheadle SK8 2DY, UK (☎08706 000 371; www.theAA.com). Publishes *Caravan and Camping Europe* as well as road atlases for Britain, Europe, France, Germany, Ireland, Italy, Spain, and the US.

The Caravan Club, East Grinstead House, East Grinstead, West Sussex, RH19 1UA, UK (☎01342 326 944; www.caravanclub.co.uk). For UK£34, members receive access to sites, insurance services, equipment discounts, maps, and a monthly magazine.

The Mountaineers Books, 1001 SW Klickitat Way, Ste. 201, Seattle, WA 98134, USA (☎206-223-6303; www.mountaineersbooks.org). Over 600 titles on hiking, biking, mountaineering, natural history, and conservation.

Sierra Club Books, 85 Second St., 2nd fl., San Francisco, CA 94105, USA (☎415-977-5500; www.sierraclub.org). Publishes general resource books on hiking and camping.

NATIONAL PARKS

France has a system of six national parks; all are in mountainous regions, except the Parc National de Port Cros, which is on a Mediterranean island near Toulon. National parks make up 0.7% of France's overall area. Check out the extensive www.parcsnationaux-fr.com for helpful information. All national parks have visitor centers with knowledgeable helpful staff; be sure to stop there before setting out on strenuous hikes. Most parks have camping areas and many have *gîtes*, if you prefer not to rough it. France also has numerous locally-run regional parks *(parc naturels régionaux)* and natural reserves *(réserves naturales)*.

WILDERNESS SAFETY

Staying **warm, dry,** and **well hydrated** is key to a happy and safe wilderness experience. For any hike, prepare yourself for an emergency by packing a first-aid kit, a reflector, a whistle, high-energy food, extra water, rain gear, a hat, mittens, and extra socks. For warmth, wear wool or insulating synthetic materials designed for the outdoors. Cotton is a bad choice as it dries painfully slowly.

Check **weather forecasts** often and pay attention to the skies when hiking, as weather patterns can change suddenly. Always let someone—a friend, your hostel, a park ranger, or a local hiking organization—know when and where you are going. Know your physical limits, and do not attempt a hike beyond your ability. See **Safety and Health,** p. 19, for information on outdoor medical concerns.

CAMPING AND HIKING EQUIPMENT

WHAT TO BUY

Good camping equipment is both sturdy and light. North American suppliers tend to offer the most competitive prices.

Sleeping Bags: Most sleeping bags are rated by season; "summer" means 30-40°F (around 0°C) at night; "four-season" or "winter" often means below 0°F (-17°C). Bags are made of **down** (warm and light, but expensive, and miserable when wet) or of **synthetic** material (heavy, durable, and warm when wet). Prices range US$50-250 for a summer synthetic to US$200-300 for a good down winter bag. **Sleeping bag pads** include foam pads (US$10-30), air mattresses (US$15-50), and self-inflating mats (US$30-120). Bring a **stuff sack** to store your bag and keep it dry.

Tents: The best tents are free-standing (with their own frames and suspension systems), can be set up quickly, and only require staking in high winds. Low-profile dome tents are the best all-around. Worthy 2-person tents start at US$100, 4-person tents start at US$160. Make sure your tent has a rain fly and seal its seams with waterproofer. Other useful accessories include a **battery-operated lantern,** a plastic **groundcloth,** and a nylon **tarp.**

Backpacks: Internal-frame packs mold well to your back, keep a lower center of gravity, and flex adequately to allow you to hike difficult trails, while **external-frame packs** are more comfortable for long hikes over even terrain, as they carry weight higher and distribute it more evenly. Make sure your pack has a strong, padded hip-belt to transfer weight to your legs. There are models designed specifically for women. Any serious backpacking requires a pack of at least 4000 cu. in. (16,000cc), plus 500 cu. in. for sleeping bags in internal-frame packs. Sturdy backpacks cost anywhere from US$125 to $420–your pack is an area where it doesn't pay to economize. On your hunt for the perfect pack, fill up prospective models with something heavy, strap it on correctly, and walk around the store to get a sense of how the model distributes weight. Either buy a **rain cover** (US$10-20) or store all of your belongings in plastic bags inside your pack.

Boots: Be sure to wear hiking boots with good **ankle support.** They should fit snugly and comfortably over 1-2 pairs of **wool socks** and a pair of thin **liner socks.** Break in boots over several weeks before you go to spare yourself blisters.

Other Necessities: Synthetic layers, like those made of polypropylene or polyester, and a pile jacket will keep you warm even when wet. A **space blanket** (US$5-15) will help you to retain body heat and doubles as a groundcloth. Plastic **water bottles** are vital; look for shatter- and leak-resistant models. Carry **water-purification tablets** for when you can't boil water. Although most campgrounds provide campfire sites, you may want to bring a small **metal grate** or **grill.** For those places (including virtually every organized campground in France) that forbid fires or the gathering of firewood, you'll need a **camp stove** (the classic Coleman starts at US$50) and a propane-filled **fuel bottle** to operate it. Also bring a **first-aid kit, pocketknife, insect repellent,** and **waterproof matches** or a **lighter.**

WHERE TO BUY IT

The online and mail-order companies listed below offer lower prices than many retail stores. A visit to a local camping or outdoors store will give you a good sense of the look and weight of certain items before you buy.

Campmor, 400 Corporate Dr., PO Box 680, Mahwah, NJ 07430, USA (☎800-525-4784; www.campmor.com).

Cotswold Outdoor, Unit 11 Kemble Business Park, Crudwell, Malmesbury Wiltshire, SN16 9SH, UK (☎08704 427 755; www.cotswoldoutdoor.com).

Discount Camping, 833 Main North Rd., Pooraka, South Australia 5095, Australia (☎618 8262 3399; www.discountcamping.com.au).

Eastern Mountain Sports (EMS), 1 Vose Farm Rd., Peterborough, 03458 NH, USA (☎888-463-6367; www.ems.com).

Gear-Zone, 8 Burnet Rd., Sweetbriar Rd. Industrial Estate, Norwich, NR3 2BS, UK (☎1603 410 108; www.gear-zone.co.uk).

L.L. Bean, Freeport, ME 04033, USA (Canada and the US ☎800-441-5713; UK 0800 891 297; www.llbean.com).

Mountain Designs, 443a Nudgee Rd., Hendra, Queensland 4011, Australia (☎7 3114 4300; www.mountaindesigns.com).

Recreational Equipment, Inc. (REI), Sumner, WA 98352, USA (Canada and the US ☎800-426-4840, elsewhere 253-891-2500; www.rei.com).

CAMPERS AND RVS

Renting an RV costs more than tenting or hosteling but less than staying in hotels while renting a car (see **Rental Cars,** p. 36). The convenience of bringing along your own bedroom, bathroom, and kitchen makes RVing an attractive option, especially for older travelers and families with children.

Rates vary widely by region, season (July and August are the most expensive months), and type of RV. Rental prices for a standard RV are around US$1050 (€783) per week.

Auto Europe, 39 Commercial St., P.O. Box 7006, Portland, ME 04112, USA (☎888-223-5555; www.autoeurope.com). Rents RVs in Paris and Nice.

ORGANIZED ADVENTURE TRIPS

Organized adventure tours offer another way of exploring the wild. Activities include hiking, biking, skiing, canoeing, kayaking, rafting, climbing, and archaeological digs. Tourism bureaus often can suggest parks, trails, and outfitters. Organizations that specialize in camping and outdoor equipment like REI and EMS (see above) also are good sources for information.

Specialty Travel Index, P.O. Box 458, San Anselmo, CA 94979, USA (US ☎888-624-4030, elsewhere 415-455-1643; www.specialtytravel.com).

SPECIFIC CONCERNS

SUSTAINABLE TRAVEL

As the number of travelers on the road continues to rise, the detrimental effect they can have on natural environments becomes an increasing concern. With this in mind, *Let's Go* promotes the philosophy of **sustainable travel.** Through a sensitivity to issues of ecology and sustainability, today's travelers can be a powerful force in preserving as well as restoring the places they visit.

Ecotourism, a rising trend in sustainable travel, focuses on the conservation of natural habitats and how to use them to build up the economy without exploitation or overdevelopment. Travelers can make a difference by doing research in advance and by supporting organizations and establishments that pay attention to their impact on their natural surroundings and that strive to be environmentally friendly.

France has a number of resources for travelers interested in ecotourism, some of which are listed below. National parks and the island of Corsica provide myriad opportunities for ecotourism (see **Beyond Tourism: Volunteering,** p. 82).

L'Association Française d'Ecotourisme (AFE), 31 rue des Filatiers, Toulouse 31000, France (☎06 76 26 93 55; www.ecotourisme.info/). Gives advice on ecotourism in France and lists other relevant websites.

UNAT Tourisme Solidaire, 8 rue César Franck, Paris 75015, France (☎01 47 83 21 73; www.unat.asso.fr/f/ts/). Helps travelers plan environmentally responsible and socially conscious trips to France.

RESPONSIBLE TRAVEL

The impact of tourist euros on the destinations you visit should not be underestimated. The choices you make during your trip can have powerful effects on local communities—for better or for worse. Travelers who care about the destinations and environments they explore should make themselves aware of the social and cultural implications of the choices they make when they travel. Simple decisions such as buying local products instead of globally-available ones, paying fair prices for products or services, and attempting to say a few words in the local language can have a strong, positive effect on the community.

Community-based tourism aims to channel tourist euro into the local economy by emphasizing tours and cultural programs that are run by members of the host community and that often benefit disadvantaged groups. This type of tourism also benefits the tourists themselves, as it often takes them beyond the traditional tours of the region. **Fugues en France,** 8 place de l'Hôtel de Ville, Mersault 21190, France (☎03 80 21 71 18; www.bonappetit-france.com) provides extensive information on multilingual tours of vineyards and culinary centers in Bordeaux, Burgundy, and Provence. For more on French environmental concerns, see the **French Institute for the Environment** website: www.ifen.fr. The *Ethical Travel Guide* (UK£13), a project of **Tourism Concern** (☎020 7133 3330; www.tourismconcern.org.uk), is an excellent resource for information on community-based travel with a directory of 300 establishments in 60 countries.

TRAVELING ALONE

There are many benefits to traveling alone, including independence and a greater opportunity to connect with locals. On the other hand, solo travelers are more vulnerable targets of harassment and street theft. If you are traveling alone, look confident, try not to stand out as a tourist, and be especially careful in deserted or very crowded areas. Stay away from areas that are not well lit. If questioned, never admit that you are traveling alone. Maintain regular contact with someone at home who knows your itinerary, and always research your destination before traveling. For more tips, pick up *Traveling Solo* by Eleanor Berman (Globe Pequot Press, US$18), visit www.travelaloneandloveit.com, or subscribe to **Connecting: Solo Travel Network,** 689 Park Rd., Unit 6, Gibsons, BC V0N 1V7, Canada (☎604-886-9099; www.cstn.org; membership US$30-48).

WOMEN TRAVELERS

Women exploring on their own inevitably face some additional safety concerns, but it's easy to be adventurous without taking undue risks. If you are concerned, consider staying in hostels which offer single rooms that lock from the inside or in religious organizations with single-sex rooms. Stick to centrally located accommodations, and avoid solitary late-night treks or Metro rides.

Always carry extra cash for a phone call, bus, or taxi. **Hitchhiking** is never safe for lone women, or even for two women traveling together. Look as if you know where you're going, and approach older women or couples for directions if you're lost or uncomfortable.

Generally, the less you look like a tourist, the better off you'll be. Dress conservatively, avoiding short shorts or skirts, especially in rural areas. Wearing a conspicuous **wedding band** sometimes helps to prevent unwanted advances.

Young women in France will frequently face verbal harassment; while most of it is harmless, it can be very uncomfortable. Your best answer to verbal harassment is no answer at all; feigning deafness, sitting motionless, and staring straight ahead at nothing will usually do the trick. The extremely persistent can sometimes be dissuaded by a firm, loud, and very public "Va-t-en!" ("VAH-TON;" "Go away!" in French). Don't hesitate to seek out a police officer or a passerby—particularly an older woman—if you are being harassed. Memorize the emergency numbers in places you visit (police ☎ 17), and consider carrying a whistle on your keychain. A self-defense course will both prepare you for a potential attack and raise your level of awareness of your surroundings (see **Personal Safety,** p. 20). Also be sure you are aware of the health concerns that women face when traveling (see p. 25).

GLBT TRAVELERS

France is fairly liberal toward gay, lesbian, bisexual, and transgendered travelers, and there are prominent gay and lesbian communities in Paris, Marseille, and other southern towns. In most larger cities, GLBT travelers are welcome and in good company. However, overt displays of sexual identity can evoke an unfriendly response in more remote regions of the country. To avoid hassles at airports and border crossings, transgendered travelers should make sure that all of their travel documents consistently report the same gender. Listed below are contact organizations, mail-order catalogs, and publishers that offer materials addressing some specific concerns. **Out and About** (www.planetout.com) offers a comprehensive website and a weekly newsletter addressing gay travel concerns. The online newspaper **365gay.com** also has a travel section (www.365gay.com/travel/travelchannel.htm).

Gay's the Word, 66 Marchmont St., London WC1N 1AB, UK (☎ 020 7278 7654; http://freespace.virgin.net/gays.theword/). The largest gay and lesbian bookshop in the UK, with both fiction and non-fiction titles. Mail-order service available.

Giovanni's Room, 345 South 12th St., Philadelphia, PA 19107, USA (☎ 215-923-2960; www.queerbooks.com). An international lesbian and gay bookstore with mail-order service (carries many of the publications listed below).

International Lesbian and Gay Association (ILGA), Avenue des Villas 34, 1060 Brussels, Belgium (☎ 32 2 502 2471; www.ilga.org). Provides political information, such as homosexuality laws of individual countries.

ADDITIONAL RESOURCES: GLBT.

Spartacus 2005-2006: International Gay Guide. Bruno Gmunder Verlag (US$33).

The Gay Vacation Guide: The Best Trips and How to Plan Them, Mark Chesnut. Kensington Books (US$15).

TRAVELERS WITH DISABILITIES

The French Ministry of Tourism includes a branch called *Tourisme et Handicap,* which is devoted to providing information about access for disabled travelers at tourist sights and amenities in Paris and its suburbs. Check out http://english.pidf.com/page/p-894/art_id-955 for a list of accommodations, attractions, and associations approved by *Tourisme et Handicap*. Disabled travelers can stay in France on a budget but may need to pay more than the average backpacker.

Those with disabilities should inform airlines and hotels of their disabilities when making reservations; some time may be needed to prepare special accommodations. Airports in France have published a guide for passengers with restricted mobility *(mobilité réduite)* that can be found at http://www.aeroportsdeparis.fr/Adp/fr-FR/Passagers/Departs/PersonnesAMobiliteReduite/BienPreparerVotreVoyage/bien_preparer_votre_voyage.htm. Call ahead to restaurants, museums, and other facilities to find out if they are wheelchair accessible. **Guide dog owners** should inquire as to the quarantine policies of each destination country.

Rail is probably the most convenient form of travel for disabled travelers in Europe: many stations have ramps, and some trains have wheelchair lifts, special seating areas, and specially-equipped toilets. The French national railroad offers wheelchair compartments on all TGV (high speed), Conrail, and CityNightLine trains. All Eurostar, some InterCity (IC) and some EuroCity (EC) trains are also wheelchair-accessible. For those who wish to rent cars, some major **car rental** agencies (e.g., Hertz) offer hand-controlled vehicles.

USEFUL ORGANIZATIONS

Accessible Journeys, 35 West Sellers Ave., Ridley Park, PA 19078, USA (☎800-846-4537; www.disabilitytravel.com). Designs tours for wheelchair users and slow walkers. The site has tips and forums for all travelers.

Flying Wheels Travel, 143 W. Bridge St., Owatonna, MN 55060, USA (☎507-451-5005; www.flyingwheelstravel.com). Specializes in escorted trips to Europe for people with physical disabilities; plans custom trips worldwide.

Society for Accessible Travel and Hospitality (SATH), 347 Fifth Ave., Ste. 610, New York, NY 10016, USA (☎212-447-7284; www.sath.org). An advocacy group that publishes free online travel information. Annual membership US$49, students and seniors US$29.

MINORITY TRAVELERS

Like much of Europe, France has experienced a wave of immigration from former colonies in the past few decades. The *Mahgreb*, an ethnic group composed of North Africans and Arabs, makes up the greatest percentage of the immigrants, at over a million, followed by West Africans and Vietnamese. Many immigrants are uneducated and face discrimination, which leads to poverty and crime in the predominately immigrant *banlieues* (suburbs). In the fall of 2005, riots swept France in retaliation for the deaths of two Parisian immigrant teenagers following an altercation with the police. In turn, there has been a surge of support for the far-right National Front party and its cry, "*La France pour les français.*" Anyone who might be taken for a **North African** or a **Muslim** may encounter verbal abuse and is more likely than other travelers to be stopped and questioned by the police. Racism is especially prevalent in the Southeast. The following organizations can give you advice and help in the event of an encounter with racism.

S.O.S. Racisme, 51 av. de Flandre, 75019 Paris (☎01 40 35 36 55; www.sos-racisme.org). Provides legal services and helps negotiate with police.

Mouvement contre le racisme et pour l'amitié entre les peuples (MRAP), 43 bd. Magenta, 75010 Paris (☎01 53 38 99 99; www.mrap.asso.fr). Handles immigration issues; monitors publications and propaganda for racism.

DIETARY CONCERNS

While France is renowned for its food, this culinary empire is rather exclusive when it comes to those with special dietary requirements. Vegetarians will find few options when dining out, and vegans will find even fewer, while kosher diners will struggle outside large cities. Supermarkets are a savior, and the resources listed here can help lead you to restaurants that will be more accommodating to dietary restrictions.

The travel section of the The Vegetarian Resource Group's website, at www.vrg.org/travel, has a comprehensive list of organizations and websites that are geared toward helping vegetarians and vegans traveling abroad. They also publish Vegetarian France, a guide which can be purchased at www.vegetarian-guides.co.uk. For more information, visit your local bookstore or health food store, and consult *The Vegetarian Traveler: Where to Stay if You're Vegetarian, Vegan, Environmentally Sensitive* (Larson Publications; US$16). Vegetarians will also find numerous resources on the web; try http://vegelist.online.fr/resto.htm, which lists vegetarian restaurants and *chambres d'hôtes* in France, www.vegdining.com, www.happycow.net, and www.vegetariansabroad.com, for starters. In restaurants, say *"je ne mange pas de viande, je suis végétarien(ne)"* (I don't eat meat, I'm a vegetarian) to your waiter.

Travelers who keep kosher should contact synagogues in larger cities for information on kosher restaurants. Your own synagogue or college Hillel should have access to lists of Jewish institutions across the nation. A useful worldwide kosher restaurant database with numerous listings in France is http://shamash.org/kosher/. If you are strict in your observance, you may have to prepare your own food on the road. A good resource is the Jewish Travel Guide, edited by Michael Zaidner (Vallentine Mitchell; US$18). Travelers looking for halal restaurants may find www.zabihah.com a useful resource, although most large cities have a significant Muslim population and thus provide numerous halal dining opportunities.

OTHER RESOURCES

Let's Go tries to cover all aspects of budget travel, but we can't put *everything* in our guides. Listed below are books and websites that can serve as jumping-off points for your own research.

USEFUL PUBLICATIONS

Au Contraire! Figuring Out the French, Gilles Asselin. Intercultural Press, 2001 (US$25). Provides a look into subtle cultural patterns.

Culture Shock! France, Sally Adamson Taylor. Graphic Arts Center Publishing Company, 2003 (US$14). Tips and warnings.

Fragile Glory: A Portrait of France and the French, Richard Bernstein. Plume, 1991 (US$15). A witty look at France by the former *New York Times* Paris bureau chief.

French or Foe? Getting the Most Out of Visiting, Living and Working in France, Polly Platt. Distribooks Intl., 1998 (US$17). A popular guide to getting by in France.

WORLD WIDE WEB

Almost every aspect of budget travel is accessible via the web. In 10min. at the keyboard, you can make a hostel reservation, get advice on travel hot spots from other travelers, or find out how much a train from Marseille to Paris costs.

Listed here are some regional and travel-related sites to start off your surfing; other relevant websites are listed throughout the book. Because website turnover is high, use search engines (e.g., www.google.com) to strike out on your own.

WWW.LETSGO.COM. Our website features extensive content from our guides; a community forum where travelers can connect with each other, ask questions or advice, and share stories and tips; and expanded resources to help you plan your trip. Visit us to browse by destination and to find information about ordering our titles!

THE ART OF TRAVEL

Backpacker's Ultimate Guide: www.bugeurope.com. Tips on packing, transportation, and where to go. Also tons of country-specific travel information.

How to See the World: www.artoftravel.com. A compendium of great travel tips, from cheap flights to self defense to interacting with local culture.

Travel Intelligence: www.travelintelligence.net. A large collection of travel writing by distinguished travel writers.

INFORMATION ON FRANCE

CIA World Factbook: www.odci.gov/cia/publications/factbook/index.html. Tons of vital statistics on France's geography, government, economy, and people.

Geographia: www.geographia.com. Highlights, culture, and people of France.

PlanetRider: www.planetrider.com. A subjective list of links to the "best" websites covering the culture and tourist attractions of France.

TravelPage: www.travelpage.com. Links to official tourist office sites in France.

World Travel Guide: www.travel-guides.com. Helpful practical info.

LIFE AND TIMES

LAND

Some things are ubiquitous in France—wine, cheese, châteaux, and charm; yet France is also a land packed with varied geography and diverse culture. A roughly hexagonal territory about 80% the size of Texas, France occupies 545,630 sq. km of mountains and islands, volcanoes and river valleys. Laden with waterfalls, the **Pyrenees** mountains form the border with Spain to the southwest, while the snow-capped peaks of the **Alps** and **Jura** separate France from Italy and Switzerland to the east. North of the Jura, the rambling **Rhine River** divides France and Germany. France shares its only artificial boundary with Belgium, in the northeast corner of the country. The English Channel (known in France as "La Manche," meaning "the sleeve") separates Normandy's chalky cliffs from England's stony shoreline by a mere 34km at its narrowest point. The Atlantic Ocean laps onto fine sand beaches in the west, while the Mediterranean sparkles alongside pebbly seashores in the south. Low-lying plains and river valleys comprise most of France's interior, with the exception of the rugged **Massif Central**—an expansive plateau of extinct volcanoes, gorges, and caves—in the country's center. **Corsica,** France's Mediterranean island, sits 170km off the French coast. Its mountainous 8680 sq. km, adored by hikers from the mainland, consist of craggy rocks and cliffs to the west and a lagoon-dotted coast to the east. For information about French national parks, check out www.parcsnationaux-fr.com, and for more on French environmental concerns, see the French Institute for the Environment's website, www.ifen.fr.

DEMOGRAPHICS

ETHNIC MINORITIES

The influx of immigrants from France's former colonies in North Africa and the Caribbean has diversified its cuisine, music, and art. Ethnic minorities face hostility at times, as immigration is a contentious issue and foreigners are often blamed for France's social ills. The ultra-conservative, anti-immigrant *Front National* party strengthened throughout the late 1990s, particularly along the Riviera and in the countryside, although its popularity has recently waned. The party's controversial leader, **Jean-Marie Le Pen,** made it to the second round of the 2002 election before losing to Jacques Chirac, but came in fourth in the first round of the 2007 election, with only 10% of the vote. Ethnic minorities are concentrated in the low-income suburbs *(banlieues)* surrounding major cities. In the fall of 2005, the unemployment and racial discrimination facing the children of Arabic and African immigrants ignited the Paris region in a series of riots that led to almost 3000 arrests. While the problems behind the riots persist, tensions seem to have cooled, at least for the moment.

RELIGIOUS MINORITIES

A secular nation, France still bears the stamp of centuries of dominant Catholicism; for example, the feast of the Assumption remains a national holiday.

Meanwhile, religious intolerance of Muslim (9%) and Jewish (1%) communities has recently increased. The 2004 controversy following the ban of religious symbols, including the Muslim headscarf, in public schools brought to the forefront tensions lurking beneath the official platform of state neutrality toward religion. French sympathies with Palestinian concerns have sparked anti-Semitic rhetoric and violence among extremists, and Muslims have fallen victim to similar discrimination and attacks.

GLBT

Major French cities are generally tolerant and many have vibrant homosexual communities, with Paris and Montpellier taking the lead. The mayor of Paris, **Bertrand Delanoë** of the Green Party, is openly gay and quite popular. In small towns, however, homophobia and hate crimes are recurring problems. In 1999, France became the first traditionally Catholic country to recognize homosexual civil unions with the **Pacte Civil de Solidarité,** known by its acronym **PACS,** but these unions do not receive the same state benefits as marriage. Discrimination based on sexual orientation is illegal in the workplace, though gay activists continue to struggle to attain the same rights to adoption and reproductive technologies that married couples enjoy.

WOMEN

Progressive national legislation criminalizes sexual harassment, ensures paid maternity leave, and finances government-run day care. Still, women are seen primarily as wives and mothers and remain severely underrepresented in high-paying careers and top government positions. There is also a double standard within marriage, as infidelity is generally accepted for men but not for women. Male infidelity is so acceptable that at former President François Mitterand's funeral, both his wife and mistress were included in the official procession. A permanent government committee monitors and promotes gender equality.

HISTORY

FROM GAULS TO GOTHS

Human life first appeared in France over two million years ago, but recognizable humans didn't hit the scene until 25,000 BC when Cro-Magnons (cavemen and cavewomen) began roaming the **Dordogne Valley.** While one man left his skull for railroad workers to dig up in 1868, the rest of the Cro-Magnon race also made sure to bequeath something to its descendants—namely, the vast and elaborate graffiti-filled caves of Périgord. Unwilling to be overlooked, Neolithic peoples carved their own mark in the stone monoliths *(menhirs)* at **Carnac** (p. 271) in Brittany by 4500 BC. Peace continued through 500 BC, when the Celtic **Gauls** came from the east to join the Greek colonists who settled at Massalia—modern day **Marseille** (p. 650)—during the seventh century BC. But the tranquility was not everlasting. Inevitably, the force of Rome soon hit town, making **Provence** a province in 121 BC

25000 BC
The first "Frenchmen" (Cro-Magnons) appear on the scene, creating cave paintings that would foreshadow France's rich cultural legacy.

4500 BC
Neolithic peoples "make their mark" at Carna with strategically-placed stone *menhirs*.

500 BC
Gauls settle in with Greeks; the two communities happily trade together.

121 BC
Romans colonize the south and spoil its inhabitants' peaceful coexistence.

52 BC
Caesar conquers Vercingetorix's band of northern rebels and names present-day Paris "Lutetia Parisiorum."

AD 486
Clovis I founds the Frankish Empire.

AD 511
First Council of Orleans seals the bond between the Merovingian Crown and the Church.

AD 768
Charlemagne becomes king of the Franks and founds the Carolingian Dynasty.

AD 800-888
The Carolingian Empire is plagued by Vikings.

AD 987
Hugh Capet is crowned king in Picardie.

1137
Capetian king Louis VII and Eleanor of Aquitaine wed.

1146
Louis VII and wife Eleanor set out together to join the Crusades.

1309
Pope Clement moves the Vatican to Avignon

and quickly conquering the rest of the south. Fierce resistance from France's northern Gauls under the leadership of **Vercingétorix** (to this day, arguably France's greatest hero) kept the Romans out of their territory until Vercingétorix surrendered himself to **Julius Caesar** at Alesia in 52 BC. By the time Rome fell in AD 476, Gaul had suffered Germanic invasions for centuries, and in AD 481 the **Franks** came to dominate. Frankish **Clovis I** began the Merovingian dynasty, converting himself and his kingdom to Christianity in AD 496. Clovis established **Paris** as his capital and became the first in a long line of French kings, who—dropping the "C" and changing the "v" to a "u"—took the name "Louis." **Charlemagne,** named Holy Roman Emperor in AD 800, inaugurated the more expansive Carolingian dynasty.

NEXT TIME, SIGN A PRENUP

The Carolingian dynasty soon gave way to the Capetian, when **Hugh Capet** consolidated power in AD 987. The line started strong, with the first four kings ruling for over a century, but then Louis the Fat came to power. Oddly enough, his gluttony was not the deadliest of the dynasty's sins. Instead, it was the carelessness of his successor, **Louis VII,** who inadvertently set off 500 years of fighting between France and England by failing to gain legal rights to the estate of his first wife, **Eleanor of Aquitaine.** When this ex-queen ran off with England's Henry II in 1152, a broad swath of French land stretching from the Channel to the Pyrénées went with her. The plot only grew thicker when England's **Edward III** tried to claim the throne of France in 1337. He landed his troops in Normandy, triggering the 116-year-long **Hundred Years' War.** The English crowned their own **Henri VI** king of France 90 years later, but salvation for France arrived in the form of a 17-year-old peasant girl. **Joan of Arc,** allegedly inspired by the voice of God, won several victories, turning the English tides before being burned at the stake for heresy in 1430.

POPES AND PROTESTANTS

During the Middle Ages, **Pope Innocent II** called for the **First Crusade** at the **Council of Clermont** in his quest to wrest Jerusalem from the Saracens. The ensuing wave of religious furor left a legacy of cathedrals, convents, and monasteries, including the haunting isle of **Mont-St-Michel** (p. 312), in its wake. Dismayed by the Church's growing power, King **Philip IV** arrested—and all but killed—**Pope Boniface VIII** in 1303. Unsurprisingly, Boniface died soon after, and his French successor, **Pope Clement V,** moved the pope's court from Rome to Church-owned **Avignon** (p. 670), where it remained until 1378. The **"Western Schism"** of the next 40 years split the Catholic church in two, as rival popes competed for influence from their respective thrones in Avignon and Rome. By the end of the conflict, the Church—in an attempt to solve the problem—had only complicated the situation by declaring a third pope. By 1414, divine rule had once again been consolidated under one man, Pope Martin V.

In the 16th century, religious conflict between **Huguenots** (French Protestants) and **Catholics** sparked the **Wars of Religion.** The fervently Catholic queen **Catherine de Medici** orchestrated a marriage between her daughter and the Protestant **Henri de Navarre** in 1572. The Medicis then trapped celebratory Huguenots in Paris, arranging a string of assassinations that triggered the 24 hours of country-wide carnage known as the **St-Bartholomew's Day Massacre.** Henri, who quickly converted to Catholicism, ascended to the throne as the first **Bourbon** monarch. In 1598 he eased tensions with the **Edict of Nantes,** which granted tolerance to French Protestants.

BOURBON ON THE ROCKS

In the 17th century, a series of dynamic cardinal-king teams brought the Bourbon monarchy to the height of its power and extravagance. **Louis XIII** and his capable and ruthless minister, **Cardinal Richelieu,** centralized power in the hands of the monarchy and in 1642 passed the scepter to **Cardinal Mazarin** and the five-year-old **Louis XIV.** By 1661, the young monarch decided he was ready to rule alone and went on to become the most self-indulgent king France had ever known. Humbly, Louis declared himself the **Sun King** and adopted the motto *"l'état, c'est moi"* ("I am the state"). He began renovations on the magnificent palace of **Versailles** (p. 176) in 1668, moving political power out of Paris and into his personal *appartements.* The king's astounding extravagance, however, nearly bankrupted his treasury and aggravated the growing resentment among the lower classes.

SO YOU WANT A REVOLUTION

By the time **Louis XVI** inherited the throne in 1774, peasants had come to blame the monarchy for their terrible poverty. To quell the unrest, in 1789 Louis called a last-resort meeting of delegates from the three classes of society (clergy, nobility, and everybody else). The proceedings were dominated by the First Estate, and the bourgeois-dominated Third Estate, whose thoughts and opinions were constantly silenced, soon broke away and proclaimed itself the **National Assembly.** On June 17th, the Assembly arrived at the proceedings only to find that the other Estates—in a demonstration of power and maturity—had locked them out of their chamber. The Assembly responded by congregating on the tennis courts of Versailles instead, where they signed the aptly-named **Tennis Court Oath,** which promised to draft a new constitution. News of these radical political moves spurred on the bourgeois and working-class activists of Paris, who stormed the **Bastille** prison on July 14, 1789 and overtook this powerful symbol of the monarchy. The crowd liberated the political prisoners within and seized the arms for themselves—thus sparking a national revolt aimed at overturning the **Old Regime.** However, despite the Assembly's utopian principles—*liberté, égalité,* and *fraternité* (liberty, equality, fraternity)—and its **Declaration of the Rights of Man,** the Revolution soon turned ugly. In 1793, after the people had overthrown the monarchy and officially replaced

1337
The Hundred Years' War against England begins and lasts 116 years.

1378
After the papacy has been moved back to Rome, an anti-pope is established at Avignon, beginning the "Western Schism."

1424
Joan of Arc claims the voice of God has inspired her to defeat the English at Orléans.

1431
Joan of Arc is burned at the stake by the English, who are not amused by her claims.

1562-98
Feuding between Catholics and Protestants escalates into extensive massacre during the Wars of Religion.

1618-48
During the Thirty Years' War, the Catholic French begrudgingly side with the Protestant Dutch and Swedes to challenge the German Habsburg dynasty.

1682
Louis XIV officially establishes his court in the completed Château de Versailles.

1744
The famous quote *"Qu'ils mangent de la brioche"* ("Let them eat cake") is misattributed to Marie Antoinette, making her perhaps the most hated woman in French history.

1788
France comes to the rescue of rebellious colonists in the American Revolution.

June 1789
The French Revolution begins with the Tennis Court Oath and the storming of the Bastille.

August 1789
The National Assembly signs the Declaration of the Rights of Man.

1791
Olympe de Gouges publishes the Declaration of the Rights of Woman and the Female Citizen.

1792
The guillotine is invented; France is declared a republic by the National Convention.

1793
Louis XVI and Marie Antoinette are executed by guillotine.

1794
Maximilien Robespierre heads to the guillotine, officially ending the Reign of Terror.

it with the **First Republic,** the radical **Jacobins** came to power. This faction, led by **Maximilien Robespierre,** took over the Convention and guillotined the Louis XV, his young queen **Marie Antoinette,** and anyone else suspected of royalism. This period of arbitrary mass slaughter, known as the **Reign of Terror,** finally expired when Robespierre himself met the guillotine in 1794; afterward, power was entrusted to a five-man **Directory.**

THE LITTLE DICTATOR

The crafty Directory ruled France for half a decade, but one young general had different plans for the country. After overthrowing the Directory in 1799, **Napoleon Bonaparte** and a handful of supporters established the **Consulate.** Time revealed this new government to be a dictatorship, as Napoleon obtained the title First Consul for Life in 1802, only to crown himself **Emperor** two years later. His **Napoleonic Code** created a centralized government and streamlined France (and later much of Europe) into a more efficient state, but it also reestablished slavery, limited the rights of women, and promoted censorship throughout France. Yet France was not enough; Napoleon constantly sought to expand his newfound empire. After his army crushed the Austrians, Prussians, and Russians, only Britain remained undefeated, successfully defended by her Royal Navy at the 1805 **Battle of Trafalgar.** But Napoleon could not conquer nature herself: in 1812, his army of 700,000 captured Moscow only to find the city deserted with winter approaching—a winter that froze to death all but 200,000 of his troops. A war-weary France then turned against Napoleon, and in return for his abdication in 1814, he was "given"—or rather exiled to—the Mediterranean island of **Elba.** The Bourbon **Louis XVIII** restored the monarchy, but Napoleon abandoned Elba and landed with a small party at Cannes in 1815. He marched north, once again rallying France behind him as the king fled to England. The ensuing **Hundred Days** rule ended on the field of **Waterloo** in Flanders, where England's **Duke of Wellington** triumphed. Napoleon was banished to **St-Helena** in the Atlantic and died there in 1821.

TAKE TWO (OR THREE)

Though quick to step into the power vacuum left by Napoleon, the Bourbon dynasty never fully regained its former glory. **Charles X** attempted to follow the Bourbon legacy by restricting the press and the electorate but instead merely incited the **July Revolution of 1830.** Charles, with a clear memory of the sharp fate that befell the previous monarch, quickly abdicated, and **Louis-Philippe** established a **constitutional monarchy.**

France's industrialization created a class of urban poor; receptive to new socialist ideas, they provided the muscle behind the **Revolution of 1848,** which culminated in the declaration of the **Second Republic** and the adoption of universal male suffrage. The people gave a clean slate to Louis Napoleon, nephew of Napoleon Bonaparte, and elected him as their president; predictably enough, the apple did not fall far from the tree, and in an 1851 coup he seized power and declared himself **Emperor Napoleon III.** During his **Second Empire** reign, Napoleon III revived the French economy and hired **Baron Haussmann** to bring Paris to its modern grandeur by replacing webs of narrow alleys with broad boulevards.

Across the Rhine, **Otto von Bismarck,** a crafty nation-builder, goaded France into declaring war on Germany, beginning the 1870-71 **Franco-Prussian War.** Forced to cede Alsace-Lorraine to the Germans after defeat, the Second Empire collapsed, giving rise to the **Third Republic.** Dissatisfied with the conservatism of the new government, the Parisian masses revolted by establishing the radical **Commune** of 1871. Ultimately the government's weapons prevailed over the Commune's utopian ideals, and over 10,000 *communards* perished. Although the Republican government stabilized, the **Dreyfus Affair** soon undermined its credibility. A Jewish captain in the French army, Alfred Dreyfus was wrongly convicted in 1894 of leaking military documents to the Germans. The unfounded treason charges sparked a decade of heated controversy. Despite the repression associated with the Third Republic, its Universal Expositions crowned an era of technological and cultural modernization.

THE TWO GREAT WARS

Germany's 1871 unification changed the balance of power in Europe. In 1907, France formed the **Triple Entente** with Britain and czarist Russia, while Germany, Italy, and the Austro-Hungarian Empire formed the **Triple Alliance.** When **World War I** erupted in 1914, German armies advanced on France, but a stalemate developed as both armies dug trenches, with so-called victories based on advances of mere meters. France and her allies triumphed in 1918 after US troops arrived. Devastated by four years of combat and the loss of 1.3 million men—both of which left a bitter aftertaste—France demanded crippling reparations from Germany.

During the depression of the 1930s, tensions between Fascists and Socialists left France ill-equipped to confront the massive mobilization of **Adolf Hitler's** Germany. In May 1940, a short time after the beginning of **World War II,** the Germans swept through Belgium and into France, causing the government to capitulate in June—a defeat made more humiliating by the sight of Nazi troops marching beneath the Arc de Triomphe. The Germans occupied the north and directed a French collaborationist puppet state in the south, ruled from **Vichy** (p. 498). While a small percentage of France's population formed the heroic **Résistance** to Nazi rule, most Frenchmen simply stood by, some even helping round up Jews to send to death camps. **General Charles de Gaulle** led the government-in-exile from London, insisting that French troops spearhead the **liberation of Paris** on August 25th, 1944.

FOURTH REPUBLIC AND POST-COLONIAL FRANCE

De Gaulle proclaimed the **Fourth Republic** in 1944, nationalizing industry and extending suffrage to women. The general

1806
Jacques-Louis David reinvents history, depicting Napoleon crossing the Alps on a white stallion instead of his actual vehicle of choice, a mule.

1812
Napoleon's troops occupy Moscow, freeze in the Russian winter, and the few that survive ignobly withdraw.

1830
Louis-Philippe forms a constitutional monarchy.

1853-70
Baron Haussmann reconstructs Paris—thus paving the way for its *haute couture* status.

1862
Victor Hugo publishes *Les Misérables* while in exile in Britain.

1898
The Dreyfus Affair exposes French anti-Semitism.

1914-18
World War I breaks out across Europe.

1919
The Treaty of Versailles officially ends World War I, but France makes demands of Germany that sow the seeds for World War II.

1940-1944
The Nazi Occupation of Paris leads to the establishment of a puppet regime in Vichy.

1940
Charles de Gaulle encourages the French *Résistance* in his June 18 radio address.

1944
De Gaulle declares the Fourth Republic after the liberation of Paris.

1944
French women attain the right to vote.

1954
The Algerian National Liberation Front (FLN) launches the colony's war of independence.

1968
Student protesters cripple France with massive strikes.

1977
The controversial Centre Pompidou, one of the many *Grands Projets* of the 70s and 80s, opens in Paris.

1981
Socialist François Mitterand ascends to the presidency.

1995
Center-rightist Jacques Chirac elected to succeed Mitterand.

stepped down in 1946, leaving behind a weak parliamentary government unable to control rising turmoil in the quickly disintegrating 19th-century **colonial empire.**

After a violent struggle for independence, the town of **Dien Bien Phu** in Vietnam achieved liberation in 1954, helping to mobilize the native inhabitants of France's other protectorates and colonies. **Morocco** and **Tunisia** gained independence in 1956, followed by **Mali, Senegal,** and the **Côte d'Ivoire** in 1960. When France refused to grant Algerian nationalists independence in 1954, the result was one of the ugliest and bloodiest decolonization processes in history. At a peaceful 1961 demonstration against curfew restrictions for Algerians in Paris, police opened fire on the largely North African crowd, killing hundreds and dumping their bodies into the Seine. The French people turned to their favorite general to deal with the impending crisis, and in 1958 de Gaulle was re-elected president. With a new constitution allowing for a stronger presidency, France once again changed the name of its government in hopes of effecting actual governmental change, this time declaring itself the **Fifth Republic.** In 1962, a referendum from the new government reluctantly granted independence to Algeria, the last existing French colony, finally ending eight years of brutal conflict.

Meanwhile, the country was becoming disillusioned with the de Gaulle administration. In **May 1968,** a series of strikes, protests, and insurrections shook Paris and all of France. The uprising involved a broad cross-section of French society. Students battled police in university hallways and in the narrow streets of the Latin Quarter, nearly two-thirds of the French workforce went on strike, and intellectuals championed the ever-popular revolutionary concept of free love, as well as political and artistic freedom. The government responded by deploying tank and commando units in Paris, and the National Assembly was dissolved. Ultimately, de Gaulle once again succeeded in restoring order, but the ideals of May '68 remain salient in the French national consciousness to this day.

THE 80S, 90S, AND TODAY

In 1981, Socialist **François Mitterrand** won the presidency and the Socialists gained a majority in the National Assembly. They raised the minimum wage and began widespread nationalization, but the socialist economy did not fare well in the global environment of the late 20th century. At the same time, the far-right began to flourish under the leadership of **Jean-Marie Le Pen.** He formed the **Front National (FN)** party on an anti-immigration platform with racist overtones, attacking the new working class from North Africa. In 1995, Mitterrand did not seek reelection, and center-rightist **Jacques Chirac** was elected president, a post he occupied until 2007.

The question of European integration has been one of the biggest challenges facing France in recent decades (see **One Europe,** p. 11). Led by Charles De Gaulle, who famously—and with just a touch of hubris—declared, "It is Europe, from the Atlantic to the Urals...that will decide the destiny of the world,"

France was an early advocate of a unified Europe. Nevertheless, in June 2005 it was the French electorate that dashed Europe's hopes for a constitution. France's Euro-skeptics expressed fears that the country's jobs were being lost to Eastern Europe, but the electorate also seems to have used the Europe vote to express discontent about domestic issues such as a stagnant economy and an unresponsive government. After the political failure caused by the constitution's defeat, Jacques Chirac was forced to dismiss his prime minister **Jean-Pierre Raffarin** in favor of the poet-philosopher **Dominique de Villepin.** The job was almost up for grabs again in 2006, when de Villepin falsely accused **Nicolas Sarkozy,** then Interior Minister, of corruption, but the controversy calmed in the face of the upcoming 2007 presidential election. Sarkozy escaped the cloud of the charges and went on to win that election, beating out Socialist female candidate **Ségolène Royal.** His election cemented the power of the center-right and demonstrated that the economy is still the most important issue in France.

While Sarko, as he is known to the French, bested Royal by a comfortable margin, he begins his presidency facing a number of challenges. Racist treatment of Arabic and African immigrants and increasingly high levels of unemployment continue to plague the country. In October of 2005, riots erupted across France after two teenage immigrants were killed in an altercation with the police in a Parisian suburb; while few were injured, thousands of cars were torched in nearly 300 towns before the violence stopped. An economy beset by debt and French fears of globalization also promise to test Sarko during his first years in office.

1998
France wins the World Cup.

1999
The Euro is introduced as the official currency, but the franc will not be forgotten.

2002
Conservative Jean-Marie Le Pen receives unprecedented support in the presidential election; France rallies to reelect Chirac in the final round.

2004
France outlaws religious symbols in public schools.

May 2005
France rejects the European constitution.

Fall 2005
A storm of racial tension erupts as riots sweep France.

Summer 2006
Soccer star Zinedine Zidane headbutts an Italian opponent during the World Cup Final, which France goes on to lose in penalty kicks.

May 2007
Conservative Nicolas Sarkozy is elected President of France, beating out his female opponent, Socialist Ségolène Royal.

CULTURE

America is like your mother—you go there for comfort. France is like your mistress—you go there for pleasure!
—*Anonymous*

FOOD AND DRINK

De Gaulle complained that no nation with 400 types of cheese could ever be united; certainly France's wide variety of provincial specialties reflects its unique cultural variety and commitment to great food. Street-side markets provide fresh ingredients every day, and many people continue to forgo supermarkets for their local *boulangeries* and *charcuteries.* Restaurants expect customers to spend multiple hours savoring their meal, and even the cheapest bistros serve three courses or more. When traveling through France, make sure to try region-specific dishes and drinks—from seafood and hot chocolate in the Pays Basque to apple tarts and calvados in Normandy, these carefully-prepared meals are often the best (and most flavorful) way to experience the French *joie-de-vivre.*

MEALS. The French ease into their day with a light breakfast *(le petit déjeuner)*, consisting largely of bread *(le pain)* or sometimes croissants and espresso with hot milk *(café au* *lait)* or a hot chocolate *(le chocolat chaud)*. The largest meal is lunch *(le déjeuner)* served between noon and 2pm, though in larger cities, the traditional leisurely lunch is disappearing, chased away by the demands of a global economy. Dinner *(le dîner)* begins late, around 8pm, and involves less cooking and less food than lunch, sometimes consisting of no more than cheese, *pâté*, and bread. A complete French meal includes an *apéritif* (before-dinner drink), an *entrée* (appetizer), a *plat* (main course), salad, cheese, dessert, coffee, and a *digestif* (after-dinner drink). While a home-cooked meal may cut out most of these courses, restaurants tend to offer the full experience (for a price, *bien sûr*).

deal **THE REAL DEAL: FAST FOOD.** Can't finish those last bites of your *plat principal*? The waitstaff will cast looks of confusion or downright scorn if you ask for a doggie bag—or dare to say you're in a hurry. The French take food quite seriously and resent those who wish to alter the complete dining experience. If you're in a rush or trying to save money, look for cafés advertising meals *à emporter* (to go), grab a ready-made sandwich at a *boulangerie* (bakery), or buy bread and produce from a nearby market and make your own *déjeuner sur l'herbe* (picnic).

MENUS. Most restaurants offer a *menu à prix fixe* (fixed-price meal) that costs less than ordering a la carte. The *menu* may include an appetizer, *plat* (main course), *fromage* (cheese), and dessert. The *formule* is a cheaper, two-course version. Sparkling water *(eau gazeuse)* or flat mineral water *(eau plate)* are always offered first; for a free pitcher of tap water, ask for *une carafe d'eau* (if the stubborn waitstaff still brings you water you have to pay for, adding a "*du robinet*," or "from the tap", should do the trick). The meal isn't complete without coffee *(un café)*. When *boisson comprise* is written on the menu, you are entitled to a free drink (usually wine) with the meal. Vegetarians will have the best luck at *crêperies*, ethnic restaurants, and establishments catering to a younger crowd, although aversion to meat will sometimes be taken as culinary sacrilege.

GROCERIES. For a €15 spree you can eat a marvelous restaurant meal, but it's easy to assemble inexpensive meals yourself with a ration of cheese, *pâté*, bread, and wine. Start with bread from the *boulangerie* (bakery), and then proceed to the *charcuterie* (delicatessen) for *pâté*, *saucisson* (hard salami), or *jambon* (ham), or buy a freshly roasted chicken from the *boucherie* (butcher shop). *Charcuteries* also tend to offer a surprising selection of side dishes, both vegetarian and not; *tabouli*, a North African inspired couscous dish, is a popular option. If you want someone else to do the work, *boulangeries* often sell fresh sandwiches. *Pâtisseries* (cake shops) will sate nearly any sweet tooth with treats ranging from the decadent, layered *mille-feuille* to the crunchy-on-the-outside-and-moist-on-the-inside *macaron au chocolat*.

TIP **THE BEST BAKERS.** France is packed with *boulangeries* and *pâtisseries*—so many, in fact, that it's hard to tell the good from the bad. Look for a bakery with a blue sticker featuring a chef's hat, which declares the house a *pâtisserie artisanale,* where master bakers prepare breads on the premises.

CAFÉS. Cafés on a major boulevard can be more expensive than smaller establishments a few steps down a side street. Prices in cafés are two-tiered: cheaper at the counter *(au comptoir)* than in the seating area *(en salle)*. Outdoor seating *(à la terrasse)* may charge even more. Beer and (in the south) the anise-flavored *pastis* are the staple café drinks, while coffee, *citron pressé* (lemonade), and *diabolo menthe* (peppermint soda) are popular non-alcoholic choices. If you order *café*, you'll get espresso; for coffee with milk or cream, ask for a *café crème*. *Bière à la pression*, or draft beer, is 660ml of either pale *(blonde)* or dark *(brune)* lager; for something smaller, ask for *un demi* (330ml). Beware fresh-squeezed juices, such as *citron pressé*, which contain nothing but fruit juice and water; add your own sugar or practice your best pucker-face.

WINE: IT DOES A BODY GOOD

Wine *(le vin)* is an integral component of French cultural heritage. Though consumption is slowing as the French keep pace with the sobriety of modern life, this cultural treasure continues to play a major role in social occasions. France produces an astoundingly diverse array of reds, whites, and rosés; each varies according to the grape, region, and method of production. French wine makers place great importance on the concept of *terroir*, the combination of soil composition, sunlight, and rain unique to each hectare of carefully cultivated land. The **Bordeaux** region, along the Dordogne and Garonne rivers of the southwest, is famous for its bold, full-bodied reds and sweet white Sauternes. Connoisseurs prize the reds and whites of **Burgundy,** the region centered around Dijon and Beaune, for their subtle refinement. Farther south, the region of **Côtes du Rhône** turns out richly flavored reds, while the even warmer **Côtes de Provence** region is known for its rosés. The whites of the **Loire** Valley tend to be delicate and aromatic, while those of **Alsace,** along the border with Germany, are fruitier. The sparkling whites of **Champagne** are synonymous with celebration worldwide. By law, only wines produced in this region may bear its name.

Though French wines are expensive in the US, quality wine is surprisingly affordable in France. Budget travelers can pick up decent bottles in supermarkets for as little as €3-4. Those looking to splurge should head to the shops of *cavistes* (wine merchants), where knowledgeable staff can point out quality bottles in the €10-15 range. Visiting the vineyards where wine is produced makes for an educational experience and a great bargain; tours typically end with free tastings, after which travelers can buy homegrown wines without the middleman markup.

While wine is king in France, it is not the nation's only claim to alcoholic fame. Regional specialties such as Provence's potent licorice-flavored *liqueur*, *pastis*, Normandy's *bénédictine liqueur* and *calvados* (hard cider), and Cognac's self-titled drink are all worth a stop on the traveler's tour of France's Bacchanalian delights.

CUSTOMS AND ETIQUETTE

> In Paris they simply stared when I spoke to them in French; I never did succeed in making those idiots understand their language.
>
> —*Mark Twain*

LOOKING GOOD. Style and fashion are important in France, and dressing well is not taken lightly. The more of an effort you make to blend in, the better your experience in France will be. For dress, what may look perfectly innocuous in Miami will mark you out instantly in Marseille. The French are known for their conservative stylishness: go for dressy sandals or closed-toe shoes, jeans or khakis, and stylish shirts, rather than Teva sandals and baggy pants. The French rarely wear shorts; if you choose to wear shorts, make sure they are not too short. Skirts or dresses (knee-length or longer) are generally most appropriate for women. Sneakers, athletic t-shirts, baseball caps, or any kind of sloppy clothing will mark you as a tourist immediately. Conservative and respectful clothing (covered shoulders for women) is mandatory when visiting places of worship.

LES CHIENS. The French *adore* their dogs. Don't be surprised to find a pampered pet in your hotel, on your train, or even sitting under the table next to you in a restaurant. Perhaps because they are so well traveled, most French pooches are also well-behaved. However, this civility has not yet translated to toilet use, so watch out on sidewalks—even the threat of a $600 fine doesn't seem to inspire the French to pick up after their dogs.

SMOKING. Despite recent government efforts to curb the habit, one third of the French population smokes. A proposed ban on smoking in public was defeated in 2006, so expect smoke-filled cafés, bars, and sidewalks. Some restaurants have started designating non-smoking sections, but don't count on them, especially in smaller cities.

ETAGES. The French call the ground floor the *rez-de-chaussée* and start numbering with the first floor above it *(le premier étage)*. The button labeled "R" (not "1") is typically the ground floor. The *sous-sol* is the basement.

HOURS. Most restaurants open at noon for lunch and close in the afternoon before re-opening for dinner. For those craving a light meal at 3pm, some bistros and cafés remain open throughout the day. Small businesses, banks, and post offices close daily noon-2pm. Many establishments shut down on Sundays and take half-days on Wednesdays, while most museums are closed on Mondays.

SHOPPING. Shopping in France is a joy and an art form. Fashion is serious business among the French, both men and women. Stores nationwide have *soldes* (sales) in January and July, which is when you can get the best bargains. France uses the continental European sizing system, which differs from both American and British sizes.

Type of Clothing	French Sizes	American Sizes	British Sizes
Women's Clothing	36	6	8
	38	8	10
	40	10	12
	42	12	14
	44	14	16
	46	16	18
Women's Shoes	36	5	4
	37	6	5
	38	7	6
	39	8	7
	40	9	8
	41	10	9
Men's Suits	44	34	34
	46	36	36
	48	38	38
	50	40	40
	52	42	42
	54	44	44
	56	46	46
	58	48	48
Men's Shoes	39.5	7	6
	41	8	7
	42	9	8
	43	10	9
	44.5	11	10
	46	12	11
	47	13	12

LANGUAGE. The French are extremely proud of their native tongue. When English words began sneaking in (*le jogging* is an example), the government took action, creating a Law for the Protection of the French Language, in 1994. As English has become the international language of business, the French have made some accommodations, but not many, and English speakers are often met with scorn. If your French is anything but fluent, waiters and salespeople who detect the slightest accent will often immediately respond in English. If you continue to speak in French, more often than not, the waiter or salesperson will respond in French. Those without knowledge of the most beautiful language in the world (according to the French) will fare well with English in most parts of the country; in rural areas and less-touristed areas, such as the Massif Central or Flanders, some working knowledge of French is a major asset. Believe it or not, French is not France's only language; while regional dialects such as Basque, Corsican, and Breton are in steep decline, they continue to hang on, infusing their regions with a proud linguistic tradition and culture.

TIP **VERLAN: A USER'S GUIDE.** French youngsters have developed a very particular form of slang, called *verlan,* which is genuinely decipherable, once the basic concept is grasped. Verlan is based on the idea of reversing the order of syllables: the word Verlan itself is a reversed form of *l'envers,* which means backwards. One syllable words such as *femme* (woman) or *mère* (mother) are simply reversed to form what is pronounced as 'mef' or 'rem'. Two syllable words such as *crayon* are broken up according to syllable, and the order is changed, to make words like 'yoncré.' So when you hear an unfamiliar word, don't assume it's brand-new to your vocabulary; try deciphering it first–it might be *verlan.* Try this: *cainri*–it comes from *ricain,* an abbreviated form of *American.*

POLITESSE. The French put a premium on polite pleasantries. Always say *"Bounder Madame/Monsieur"* when entering a business, restaurant, or hotel, and *"Au Revoir"* or *"Bonne journée"* (Good day) when leaving. If you bump into someone, drop him or her a quick *"Pardon."* When meeting someone for the first time, a handshake is appropriate. However, friends and acquaintances—except two men, who often stick to a handshake—greet each other with *bisous,* an airy kiss on each cheek. There's even more love in the South of France, where three kisses are the norm.

TIP **PILLOW TALK.** The French often mock English-speakers for unwittingly making sexual references in French. Here are a couple of commonly used expressions you should know about:

Je suis excité(e) might be an attempt to express excitement at a new museum or a film but actually means "I am sexually aroused."

Je suis plein(e) may seem to translate to "I am full (of food)" but for a girl, this means "I have been sexually satisfied," or, even worse, "I'm pregnant."

Oh my God! This English expression may seem harmless, but in French, *godde* means vibrator, so what you're really saying is "Oh my vibrator!"

PUBLIC RESTROOMS. French public toilets are worth the €0.30 they require, as the newer models of these machines magically self-clean after each use. Older public restrooms are often dirty or broken. Toilets in train stations and public gardens are tended by *gardiens* and generally cost €0.40-0.60, often in exact change. Public restrooms can sometimes prove elusive, but private establishments do not look kindly on being used solely for their facilities; in an urgent situation, you may have to buy a drink or snack first. In rural areas, public restrooms often consist of a very basic shack without toilet paper; always carry tissues and hand sanitizer.

SERVICE. There is no assumption in France that "the customer is always right," and complaining to managers about poor service is rarely worth your while. When engaged in any official process (e.g., opening a bank account, purchasing insurance), don't fret if you get shuffled from one desk to another. Hold your ground, patiently explain your situation, and (maybe) you will eventually prevail.

TIPPING. In restaurants and cafés, the tip is almost always included in the tab, as indicated by the words *"service compris"* on the check. To acknowledge particularly good service, the French usually leave a euro or two in change on the table. Cab drivers should be tipped 15% of their fare. It's also a good idea to tip museum tour guides €1 after a free tour and tour guides for official tour companies 20%.

TABLE MANNERS. Bread is served with every meal; it is perfectly polite to use a piece to wipe your plate. Etiquette dictates keeping one's hands above the table, not in one's lap, and forearms, not elbows, should rest on the table. In restaurants, waiters will not bring the check until you ask. When you are ready to pay, say, *"L'addition, s'il vous plaît."* And, no matter what movies suggest, it is extremely impolite to address your waiter as *"garçon"* (boy). Call him *"Monsieur"* instead.

KNOW YOUR REPUBLICS. Everyone knows the French have gone through a number of governments; it's often difficult to keep them straight. Here's a short tutorial so you can keep up with at least the most basic political discussions:

Valois Dynasty (1328-1589): Rulers included the Fortunate, the Wise, the Well-Beloved (later the Mad), the Victorious or Well-Served, the Universal Spider, and the Affable, as well as such bigwigs as Francois I and Catherine de Medici.

Bourbon Dynasty (1589-1792): Protestant Henry IV defeated the Medicis to launch this dynasty, converting to Catholicism in the process. It took a Revolution to finish them off—at least for the time being.

First Republic (1792-1804): This government had its own chaotic jumble of sub-governments. They included the National Convention (when France adopted universal male suffrage), the Directory (when five men shared power—a.k.a. four too many), and the Consulate (Napoleon's debut).

First Empire (1804-1814): Napoleon became—er, named himself—Emperor. The Napoleonic Code he established still rules French Law.

House of Bourbon (1814-1830): France just couldn't shake those Bourbons.

House of Orléans (1830-1848): Also known as the July Monarchy—a constitutional monarchy in which the bourgeois ruled. A little too tumultuous.

Second Republic (1848-1852): Began with a (comparatively) mini-Revolution and ended with a (comparatively) mini-coup d'Etat.

Second Empire (1852-1870): Another Napoleonic coup began this empire—this time, it was Napoleon III (the I's nephew).

Third Republic (1870-1940): Adolph Thiers said in 1870 that a republic was "the form of government that divides France least." At this point, however, it wasn't enough.

Vichy France (1940-1944): Named for the southern French town where the Nazis ran a puppet government. Led by Pétain; opposed by de Gaulle.

Provisional Government of the French Republic: While the Allies got their act together post-victory.

Fourth Republic (1946-1958): Revival of the Third, meaning the same problems still existed. After the Algiers Crisis, de Gaulle took over—under the precondition that there would be a Fifth Republic.

Fifth Republic (1958-any day now): de Gaulle made the presidency stronger. A half-decade later, it's still alive. At least for now.

THE ARTS

ARCHITECTURE

ANCIENT BEGINNINGS. The ancient peoples of France proved their artistic and engineering finesse independent of the 'civilizing' effect of the Romans when creating prehistoric murals in **Lascaux** (p. 520) and *menhirs* (enormous upright stones) in **Carnac** (p. 271). This does not mean, however, that the Roman Empire has been erased from the visual memory of France; its remnants are especially visible in Provence, with the theater at **Orange** (p. 702) and the ruins of the amphitheater at **Nîmes** (p. 697). Nearby, the Roman arches of the **Pont du Gard** aqueduct (p. 701) brought some 10 million gallons of water daily to Nîmes's thirsty citizens.

MEDIEVAL CATHEDRALS. Although ruins of the empire may be scarce, lasting evidence of Roman influence can be seen in the arches, thick walls, and barrel vaults of **Romanesque** churches built in the 11th- to 12th-century. Their quiet simple beauty, relatively speaking, is epitomized by churches like the **Basilique St-Sernin** in Toulouse (p. 608) and the **Basilique Ste-Madeleine** at Vézelay (p. 434). Later, **Gothic** architecture enabled vaults to soar skyward with arches that distributed weight outward to walls supported by dramatic flying buttresses. These exterior supports permitted thinner walls to showcase intricate stained glass. The cathedrals at **Amiens** (p. 337), **Chartres** (p. 180), and **Reims** (p. 345) exemplify the intricate sculptural details that define Gothic style.

RENAISSANCE, BAROQUE, AND NEOCLASSICISM. During the Renaissance, the infusion of Italian influence produced buildings such as King Francois I's elaborate **Chambord** (p. 197). châteaux sprung up in the Loire Valley as aristocrats scrambled to keep up with this royal example. Meanwhile, in response to his finance minister's 17th-century Baroque **Château de Vaux-le-Vicomte** outside Paris, Louis XIV converted his father's small hunting lodge at **Versailles** (p. 176) into the world's largest and most impressive royal residence. The mid-18th century welcomed the columns and clean lines of Neoclassicism, exemplified by **Soufflot's** grandiose **Eglise Ste-Geneviève** in Paris, known since the Revolution by its secular name, the **Panthéon** (p. 132).

19TH-CENTURY HAUSSMANIA. Although 'Capital of the World' may not be one of Paris's many nicknames, the city does owe its current organization to Napoleon III's vision that it would one day become just that. From 1852 to 1870, Baron Georges-Eugène Haussmann (see **Haussmania,** p. 137) plowed long, straight boulevards through the tangled clutter and narrow alleys of medieval Paris. The wide avenues not only supported the city's now-famous street-café culture but also impeded insurrection by diminishing the effectiveness of barricades. In the late 19th century, engineering entered the architectural scene when Gustave Eiffel created the star exhibit of 1889's International Exhibition. First decried by Parisians as hideous and unstable, the Eiffel Tower (p. 135) is now France's most iconic landmark. At the same time, Art Nouveau style was emerging, evident today in the swirling lines of Paris Metro stations where Hector Guimard's vinelike signs sprout from the ground.

20TH-CENTURY MODERNISM AND SUBURBAN MISERY. In contrast to the decorative flair of Art Nouveau, the prolific Swiss architect, painter, and writer known as **Le Corbusier** brought modernism to France with his creative use of concrete in individual homes, housing projects, urban planning, and even a mushroom-like chapel commemorating World War II at **Ronchamp** (p. 401). In the post-war years, housing projects, or **HLMs** *(habitations à loyer modéré)*, were originally intended as affordable housing, but are now associated with unemployment, racism, and the plight of poor immigrants. In the 1980s, Mitterand's 15 billion franc endeavor, known as the *Grands Projets*, heralded the construction of such icons as the **Parc de la Villette** (p. 144), the **Opéra** at the Bastille (p. 140), and **I. M. Pei's** glass pyramid at the **Louvre** (p. 148). Skyscrapers built in the 1980s and 1990s are confined to the business suburb of **La Défense.**

FINE ARTS

MEDIEVAL MASTERPIECES. Religion ruled the arts, with cathedrals, reliquaries, and religious texts as the dominant creative outlets. Brilliant stained glass and expertly chiseled stone at **Chartres** (p. 180), **Reims** (p. 345), and Paris's **Ste-Chapelle** (p. 129) translated between God (or King) and a largely illiterate parish by telling a royally-selected program of Bible stories. Monks created beautiful **illuminated manuscripts** by painstakingly adding gold and silver illustrations to sacred texts. The middle ages also saw the creation of Normandy's 11th-century **Bayeux tapestry,** a 70m long narrative of the Battle of Hastings (p. 302).

THE RENAISSANCE IN FRANCE. The art of 16th-century France drew its inspiration from the painting, sculpture, and architecture of the **Italian Renaissance.** At the invitation of François I, **Leonardo da Vinci** trekked up from Florence, bearing the smiling **Mona Lisa** in tow, but producing little in France. Visitors can breathe the air that was Leonardo's last in **Amboise** (p. 199).

BAROQUE AND ROCOCO. Also influenced by Italy, the French Baroque style brought masterpieces such as Louis XIV's Versailles and the realist paintings of the brothers **Le Nain** and **Georges de La Tour.** Entrance into the 1648 **Académie Royale,** which involved meeting specific standards, came to define artistic success. At the same time, artists such as **Le Brun** dominated its **salons,** the country's "official" art exhibitions. The early 18th century brought on the opulent **Rococo** style. Catering to the tastes of the nobility, **Antoine Watteau** painted the fantastic *fêtes* and secret *rendez-vous* of the aristocracy, while **François Boucher** depicted landscapes and rosy-cheeked shepherdesses.

NEOCLASSICAL AND ROMANTIC SCHOOLS. The French Revolution inspired painters such as **Jacques-Louis David** to stray from the history-painting genre and instead depict contemporary figures, as in his *Death of Marat.* David was a key figure in **Neoclassicism,** which emerged as Napoleon I emulated the Roman empire, and brought dramatic, large-scale paintings which often depicted the emperor as a hero or God. Napoleon's rule also saw the Louvre, which opened as a museum in 1792, grow in importance. Later, the paintings of **Eugène Delacroix** shocked the salons of the 1820s and 1830s with their **Romantic** and colorful melodrama. Both he and **Jean-Auguste-Dominique Ingres** pursued Asian-inspired subjects, as in the latter's seductive masterpiece, *La Grande Odalisque* (The Tall Concubine), now on display in the Louvre.

REALISM AND IMPRESSIONISM. After the Revolution of 1848, **Realists** like **Gustave Courbet** shifted their artistic focus to the humble aspects of peasant life. His *Burial at Ornans* caused a scandal when first exhibited because its huge canvas depicted a simple village scene instead of a historical one. **Edouard Manet's** *Luncheon on the Grass* was rejected by the Salon for its inclusion of nudes in an otherwise commonplace scene but held center stage among other rejected works at the **Salon des Refusés** in 1863. By the late 1860s, Manet's new aesthetic had set the stage for **Impressionists** such as **Claude Monet, Camille Pissarro,** and **Pierre-Auguste Renoir,** whose careful use of light and color earned them post-mortem fame outside the art historical community. Monet's garden at **Giverny** (p. 182), the source of his monumental *Water Lilies* series, is almost synonymous with Impressionism. This famous movement in turn inspired **Edgar Degas's** ballerinas, **Gustave Caillebotte's** rainy Paris streets, and **Berthe Morisot's** tranquil studies of women, as well as sculptor **Auguste Rodin's** *The Kiss* and **Camille Claudel's** *The Waltz*.

POST-IMPRESSIONISM. This color burst began with **Paul Cézanne's** work in **Aix-en-Provence** on colorful still lifes, portraits, and geometric landscapes (including his many versions of *Mont Ste-Victoire*) that unsettled traditional spacial relationships. **Georges Seurat** developed **Pointillism,** painting thousands of tiny dots to form a unified picture. **Paul Gauguin** painted large, flat blocks of color with bold outlines to depict "primitive" scenes of Arles, Brittany, Martinique, and Tahiti. Also in **Arles** (p. 688), his Dutch friend **Vincent Van Gogh** became famous for his mesmerizing brush strokes and intense colors--and for cutting off his ear. **Henri Matisse** became the forerunner of colorful **Fauvism** (from *fauves*, wild animals), evident in works like *The Dance*.

CUBISM AND BEYOND. In the 1910s, former Fauvist artist **Georges Braque** and Spanish-born **Pablo Picasso** (living in Paris) developed **Cubism,** which uses shaded planes to reassemble familiar images and objects in abstract form. Picasso's constant stylistic innovation set the course of modern art for decades. The **Musées Picasso** in Paris (p. 152) and Antibes (p. 734) pay tribute to his extensive career.

DADAISM, SURREALISM, AND THE SCENE TODAY. Prompted by their sense of loss after WWI, a group of artists sought to expose the constructed nature of modern consumer culture. The deliberate chaos of the **Dada** movement found its best expression in the works of **Marcel Duchamp,** who defied artistic conventions by signing his name on a factory-made urinal *(The Fountain)* and placing it in an art show. **Surrealism,** on the other hand, strove to unify fantasy and the everyday world, creating "an absolute reality, a surreality," according to **André Breton,** the movement's leader. The movement's exemplary works—**René Magritte's** apples and pipes, **Joan Mirò's** dreamscapes, **Max Ernst's** birds, and **Salvador Dalí's** melting timepieces—arose out of the 1920s Parisian art scene. Modern 20th-century experiments in photography, installation art, and sculpture are on view at the **Centre Pompidou** (p. 149) and the **Fondation Cartier pour l'Art Contemporain** (p. 160).

LITERATURE AND PHILOSOPHY

MEDIEVAL AND RENAISSANCE LITERATURE. Medieval aristocrats enjoyed tales of knightly honor and courtly love penned by **Marie de France** and **Chrétien de Troyes,** or the famous **Roman de la Rose,** an elaborate allegory about *l'amour*. The medieval masses, meanwhile, indulged in *chansons de gestes*, which told of eighth-century crusades and conquests. **John Calvin** ignited the ill-fated Protestant Reformation by criticizing the Catholic Church in his 1536 *"Institutes of the Christian Religion."* Around the same time, **François Rabelais** criticized French society in his satiric *Gargantua and Pantagruel*, told from the perspective of two comical giants. Later, **Michel de Montaigne** ensured himself eternal enemies, as students everywhere continue to struggle with writing essays, a literary form he pioneered in his 1588 *Essais*.

THE ENLIGHTENMENT. Although the French Enlightenment did not technically begin until the 1700s, its seeds were sewn a century earlier when **Cardinal Richelieu** founded the **Académie Française** in 1635 to codify and regulate French literature and language. Shortly thereafter, **René Descartes** used the Enlightenment ideal of **rationalism** to prove his own existence in the famously catchy--and logical--deduction, "I think, therefore I am." In the 18th-century, **Denis Diderot** ambitiously set out to accumulate and record no less than everything in his *Encylopédie*. Meanwhile, **Voltaire** critiqued social norms in his sharply witty *Candide*, and **Molière** did the same with comedic plays such as *Tartuffe*. **Jean-Jacques Rousseau,** who laid the foundation for modern democracy in *The Social Contract*, promoted the Enlightenment ideals of tolerance and equality in his argument for sovereign rule by common popular contract.

ROMANTICISM AND REALISM. During the 19th century, French literature adopted the expressive ideals of **Romanticism,** which had first come to prominence in Britain and Germany. Great writers such as **Henri Stendhal** helped to establish the novel as the preeminent literary medium, but the novels of **Victor Hugo,** most famously *Les Misérables* and *The Hunchback of Notre Dame*, dominated the Romantic movement. During the same period, the young Aurore Dupin left her husband, took the *nom de plume* **George Sand,** and published passionate novels condemning sexist conventions. Novelists **Honoré de Balzac, Emile Zola,** and **Gustave Flaubert** contributed to the movement of **Realism** in literature, creating detailed characters and settings that endeavored to be true to life. Flaubert's characters may have become a little too real, however; when the middle-class heroine of *Madame Bovary* spurned provincial life in favor of adulterous daydreams, Flaubert only narrowly escaped charges of immorality. Poet **Charles Baudelaire** was not so lucky—the same tribunal fined him 50 francs for obscenity in his verses. Despite his reputation for crudeness during his lifetime, today Baudelaire's poetry collection *Les Fleurs du Mal* (1857) is considered among the most influential from 19th-century France.

BELLE EPOQUE TO WWII. Toward the end of the 19th century, the dream reality of **Symbolism** replaced the daily reality of Realism. Poets such as **Stéphane Mallarmé,**

THE BEST EXPATRIATE LITERATURE

Julian Barnes. *Flaubert's Parrot.* An elderly English doctor journeys to France to research Flaubert's life and find inspiration for his short story *Un Coeur Simple.*

F. Scott Fitzgerald. *Tender is the Night.* No one captures the 1920s flapper set quite like Fitzgerald—his story of scandal and intrigue on the Riviera is a classic.

Adam Gopnik. *Paris to the Moon.* A *New Yorker* journalist settles down in Paris with his family. Observations on Parisian life are lyrically woven into larger cultural themes.

Ernest Hemingway. *A Moveable Feast.* The quintessential tale of a young expat in Paris. F. Scott Fitzgerald and Gertrude Stein make colorful cameo appearances.

W. Somerset Maugham. *The Moon and Sixpence.* A dull London businessman leaves his family to paint in Paris and Tahiti. Loosely based on the life of Paul Gauguin.

George Orwell. *Down and Out in London and Paris.* A writer takes grimy jobs in the dark underbelly of Paris. Beautifully descriptive and funny.

David Sedaris. *Me Talk Pretty One Day.* The wickedly irreverent expat delights in exposing the idiosyncrasies of life in France.

Paul Verlaine, and the precocious **Arthur Rimbaud** rejected mere description. **Modernism,** which began to take hold in the early 20th century, is perhaps best realized in the writings of **Marcel Proust,** who investigated the nature of time and love in the seven volumes of his *Remembrance of Things Past.* After World War II, **Existentialism** expressed **Jean-Paul Sartre's** theory that life gains meaning only through individual choice and action. Nobel laureate **Albert Camus,** an Algerian-born novelist, shared Sartre's theoretical beliefs; the two were good friends until political conflicts divided them.

FEMINISM AND LA PRÉSENCE AFRICAINE. Feminist **Simone de Beauvoir,** also tied to Jean-Paul Satre through existentialist ideas and a personal relationship (in her case as a lover), attacked the mistreatment of women and the stereotypes of femininity in *The Second Sex*, inspiring a generation of second-wave **feminists** starting in the 1950s. In turn, writers like **Marguerite Duras** *(The Lover)*, **Hélène Cixous** *(The Laugh of the Medusa)*, and **Luce Irigaray** *(This Sex Which Is Not One)* sparked feminist movements both in France and abroad.

Throughout the 20th century, writers from the French colonies of **Haiti, Québec,** the **Antilles,** the **Maghreb** (Algeria, Tunisia, Morocco), and **West Africa** condemned France's rampant racism and colonial exploitation. These ideas were channeled into the **Négritude** movement in the 1930s by intellectuals **Aimé Césaire** (Martinique) and **Léopold Sédar Senghor** (Senegal). Similarly, **Mehdi Charef** (Maghreb) wrote provocative novels about *beur* (slang for Arab-French) culture and the difficulties of cultural assimilation.

POSTMODERNISMS. France boasts many prominent figures of **Postmodernism,** which still influences literary, political, and intellectual thought. Despite its universality, the movement resists definition and is best described as a rejection of stable meaning and identity. Its roots can be traced to the **Structuralist** theories of 20th-century anthropologist **Claude Lévi-Strauss,** who argued that society determines behavior. **Post-Structuralist** theorists, influenced by the revolutionary moment of May 1968, argued that language itself is inherently controlled. **Jacques Derrida's** theory of **deconstruction,** a way of reading texts by seeking to uncover the internal tensions they suppress, transformed philosophy, literary theory, and cultural criticism in France and across the globe. Influential historian and philosopher **Michel Foucault,** author of *Madness and Civilization* and *The History of Sexuality*, argued that society, including institutions like hospitals and schools, can only be understood in terms of the power dynamics it enforces.

FILM

A MEDIUM WITHOUT A FUTURE? After inventing the *cinématographe*—a device that was able to record, develop, and project motion pictures—the aptly-named **Lumière** brothers, **Louis** and **Auguste,** screened the world's first film in a Parisian café in 1895. Soon thereafter Auguste remarked, "The cinema is a medium without a future." Luckily, he was better at inventing than at predicting trends, and Paris became the Hollywood of early cinema, dominating production and distribution worldwide. Although WWI stunted growth, the inter-war period yielded a large number of diverse and influential films. Envisioned by **Fernand Léger** and **Dudley Murphy,** the 1924 experimental film *Ballet Mécanique* mesmerized viewers with its disorienting and fast-paced montages. In 1937 **Jean Renoir,** son of the Impressionist painter, directed the powerful *La Grande Illusion* (Grand Illusion), a startling anti-war film that was banned in Germany.

POST-WAR INNOVATION. The 1950s was a pivotal decade for French film. In 1956, a star was born when **Jean Vadim** sent **Brigitte Bardot** shimmying naked across the screen in *Et Dieu Créa la Femme* (And God Created Woman). The **French New Wave** movement, an iconoclastic rejection of traditional cinematic form that blurred linear time and the distinction between fiction and reality, was captured in films like **François Truffaut's** coming-of-age story *Les 400 Coups* (The 400 Blows), **Jean-Luc Godard's** gangster flick *A Bout de Souffle* (Breathless), and **Alain Resnais's** *Hiroshima, Mon Amour* (Hiroshima, My Love). Famed critic **André Bazin,** mentor to Godard and Truffaut, played a crucial part in bringing the movement to fruition.

CONTEMPORARY CLASSICS AND CINEMA BEUR. French talent enjoyed international recognition in the 1960s, producing stars such as the stunning **Catherine Deneuve** and omnipresent **Gérard Depardieu.** Released in 1966, **Gillo Pontevorco's** powerful *The Battle of Algiers* portrayed the violent French occupation of the African city. Later, *La Cage aux Folles* (The Birdcage), a 1978 film about a gay couple by **Edouard Molinaro,** itself a remake of Jean Poiret's 1973 play, inspired a popular American remake in 1996. Meanwhile **Claude Berri's** *Jean de Florette* and Polish **Krzysztof Kieslowski's** *Three Colors* trilogy became instant classics of late 20th-century French cinema. Several recent French films have explored the issue of gay identity and sexual orientation, including Belgian **Alain Berliner's** transgender tragicomedy *Ma Vie en Rose* (My Life in Pink). Meanwhile, charming **Audrey Tautou** earned international fame for her role in **Jean-Pierre Jeunet's** *Le Fabuleux Destin d'Amélie Poulain* (Amélie). **Cinéma Beur,** a movement exploring second-generation North Africans coming to terms with life in Parisian housing projects, has produced explosive films like **Mehdi Charef's** *Le thé au harem d'Archi Ahmed* (Tea in the Harem) and **Mathieu Kassovitz's** *La Haine* (Hate).

MUSIC

The early sounds of French music could be heard in monasteries, where Gregorian chants gained popularity around the 12th century. Medieval troubadours entertained with narrative ballads, and during the Renaissance **Josquin des Prez** composed revered masses. Baroque composer **Jean-Baptiste Lully** entertained the court of **Louis XIV** with his lavish operas, and later **Robespierre's** reign of terror witnessed a people rallying to strains of revolutionary music. **Rouget de Lisle's** epic *War Song of the Army of the Rhine* inspired volunteers from Marseille to dub the song **La Marseillaise** and designate it as the national anthem in 1795.

In the 19th-century, Paris became the center of European music, serving as a center for influential foreign composers, including **Frédéric Chopin, Franz Liszt,** and **Félix Mendelssohn. Grand opera** merged with the simpler **Opéra comique** to produce the **Romantic lyric opera,** an exotic amalgam of soaring arias and tragic death best exemplified by **Georges Bizet's** *Carmen.* Music at the turn of the 20th century began a new period of intense, often abstract invention, heralding the impressionistic **Claude Débussy** and unsentimental **Eric Satie. Maurice Ravel's** Basque origins surfaced in the Spanish rhythms of his most famous work, *Boléro*, and the violently dissonant sounds of **Igor Stravinsky's** *Rite of Spring* caused a riot at its 1913 premiere at the Théâtre des Champs-Elysées.

JAZZ AND CABARET. Though a thoroughly American musical form, **Jazz** found a welcoming second home in France during its formative years. Jazz crooner **Josephine Baker** left the US for Paris in 1925, finding France more accepting than her segregated home. In the years following WWII, a stream of American jazz musicians, including a young **Miles Davis,** flowed onto the Paris music scene. The hundreds of jazz clubs in France today are testament to the enduring popularity of this American tradition. **Cabaret,** which came to prominence around the same time as jazz, brought song, dance, comedy, and theater to smoky nightclubs across the country. **Edith Piaf's** iconic voice popularized Cabaret music with such sultry ballads as "*La Vie en Rose.*"

CLASSICS OF THE 60S AND BEYOND. In the second half of the 20th century, French music was dominated by two opposing ambitions: to emulate the sound of American pop, and to maintain a distinctly French musical tradition. The French love of rock 'n' roll inspired **yé-yé,** a genre whose sound was unmistakably borrowed from the American version. Parisian Jean-Phillips Smet Americanized his name to **Johnny Hallyday** before bursting into the pop scene as a teen idol in the

1960s, gyrating his hips to Elvis-inspired tunes. The same decade produced the more unique guitar-strumming **Georges Brassens,** who sang lyrically complex and often subversive ballads but became famous for his handlebar moustache and ever-present pipe. Belgian songwriter **Jacques Brel** performed impassioned songs of love, loneliness, and despair. The undisputed bad boy of the era, **Serge Gainsbourg,** shocked and delighted audiences with his crass lyrics and pleasure-seeking nihilism. Even the pope took notice of Gainsbourg, condemning the immorality of the artist's biggest hit, "*Je t'aime...Moi non plus*" ("I Love You...Me Neither").

The French contemporary music scene offers a diverse mix of sounds. Full of catchy beats and sugary choruses, French pop has a lot of style, but many complain that it lacks substance. American pop is also wildly popular on the French sound waves, though a national law mandates that at least forty percent of programming be in French. Hip-hop and rap have entered the scene, led by the poetic **MC Solaar** and the often-violent sounds of **NTM.** France also welcomes musicians from across the globe, such as North African **Cheb Khaled** and **Faudel,** Middle Eastern **Natacha Atlas,** and Latin American **Manu Chao.** French pop icons like **Jean-Jacques Goldman, Gérald de Palmas,** and the band **Noir Désir** bring the sounds of 80s and 90s rock to the French language. Meanwhile, the creative contributions of young singer-songwriters like **Bénabar, Thomas Fersen, Keren Ann,** and supermodel **Carla Bruni** are infusing the French music scene with talent and sophistication.

SPORTS AND RECREATION

SOCCER

The French take their *football* very seriously. Their national team, *Les Bleus*, emerged from a half-century of mediocrity to capture the 1998 **World Cup,** igniting an explosion of celebration from Paris to the Pyrenees. The charismatic star of the team, **Zinedine Zidane,** or "Zizou," has become a national hero, dominating billboards nationwide. After a devastating first-round elimination in the 2002 World Cup, Zizou led the French squad to the 2006 World Cup Finals, where it was defeated in penalty kicks by the Italians. Now that Zidane has retired—going out with a head-butting bang in the final match—France is looking to its next star, cool-headed **Thierry Henri,** to lead the team to international glory.

CYCLING

Cycling is more than a national obsession—it's an addiction. France gets its annual dose when it hosts the grueling three-week, 3500km **Tour de France,** which celebrated its 100th anniversary in 2003. Unfortunately, France's love for the sport hasn't necessarily translated to victory: American **Lance Armstrong** survived testicular cancer to capture a record-setting seven consecutive championships before retiring in 2005. The 2006 race brought controversy to the Tour when the first-place finisher, American Floyd Landis, tested positive for testosterone use. The Tour currently does not recognize him as champion, and official proceedings have begun to determine whether or not to strip him of the title. In the meantime, the second-place finisher, Spain's Oscar Pereiro, considers himself the winner. 2007's race saw more controversy, as one-time leader, Patrik Sinkewitz, was fired by his T-Mobile® team for suspicious behavior, leaving Spaniard Alberto Contador, who has denied dope-usage, to take the victory.

RECREATIONAL SPORTS

As much a French staple as wine or cheese, **pétanque,** once dominated by old *provençal* men, has been gaining popularity among all ages. The basic premise of

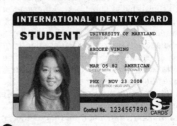

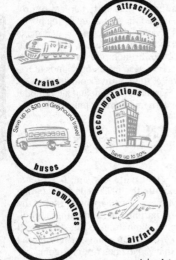

the game, like Italian bocce or British lawn bowls, is to throw a large metal ball as close as possible—or more importantly, closer than the opponent—to a smaller metal ball. Thanks to the country's several mountainous regions, **Alpine** and **cross-country skiing** are also popular. Despite objections by French traditionalists, other non-indigenous sports, particularly **rugby** and **golf,** continue to gain a foothold.

HOLIDAYS AND FESTIVALS

The French love to celebrate. Thus, it is unsurprising that French festivals pervade the country year-round, commemorating almost any imaginable occasion. They are a wonderful way to experience a region's best-loved traditions. The most important national holiday is **Bastille Day,** July 14, the anniversary of the storming of the Bastille in 1789. In Paris, this celebration begins with a solemn military march up the Champs-Elysées, followed by dancing, drinking, and fireworks—the latter three also occurring throughout the country. When Bastille Day falls on a Tuesday or Thursday, the French often also take off Monday or Friday, a crafty practice known as *faire le pont* (making the bridge). In addition to the following National holidays, French law allows citizens five weeks of vacation per year; most locals travel during July and August, causing businesses to close and transportation outlets to become clogged. The holiday dates listed below are for 2008. For more information on specific or regional events, check out "Festival" listings for individual cities in the guide, or visit www.franceguide.com.

DATE	NATIONAL HOLIDAY
January 1	Le Jour de l'An (also called la St-Sylvestre); New Year's Day
March 24	Le lundi de Pâques; Easter Monday
May 1	La Fête du Travail; Labor Day
May 1	L'Ascension; Ascension Day
May 8	Fête de la Victoire 1945; Celebrates the end of World War II in Europe
May 12	Le Lundi de Pentecôte; Whit Monday
July 14	La Fête Nationale; Bastille Day
August 15	L'Assomption; Feast of the Assumption
November 1	La Toussaint; All Saints' Day
November 11	L'Armistice 1918; Armistice Day
December 25	Noël; Christmas

LIFE AND TIMES

BEYOND TOURISM

A PHILOSOPHY FOR TRAVELERS

HIGHLIGHTS OF BEYOND TOURISM IN FRANCE
DIG UP skulls and other treats at archaeological sites or restore Roman ruins (p. 85).
FIGHT for immigrant healthcare benefits with **Doctors Without Borders** (p. 83).
STUDY in the hallowed halls of the **Sorbonne,** France's oldest university (p. 88).
COOK up gourmet eats at one of France's most prestigious culinary institutes (p. 88).

As a tourist, you are always a foreigner. While hostel-hopping and sightseeing can be great fun, you may want to consider going *beyond* tourism. Experiencing a foreign place through studying, volunteering, or working can help reduce that touristy stranger-in-a-strange-land feeling. Furthermore, travelers can make a positive impact on the natural and cultural environments they visit. With this Beyond Tourism chapter, *Let's Go* hopes to promote a better understanding of France and to provide suggestions for those who want to get more than a photo album out of their travels. The "Giving Back" sidebar feature (p. 678) also highlights regional Beyond Tourism opportunities.

There are several options for those who seek to participate in Beyond Tourism activities. Opportunities for **volunteerism** abound, with both local and international organizations. **Studying** in a new environment can be enlightening, whether through direct enrollment in a local university or in an independent research project. **Working** is a way to immerse yourself in the local culture while financing your travels.

As a **volunteer** in France you can participate in projects that vary from repairing crumbling mountains to reconstructing ancient châteaux. Later in this chapter, we recommend organizations that can help you find the opportunities that best suit your interests, whether you're looking to get involved for a day or for a year.

Studying at a college or language program is another option. France is home to some of the world's oldest universities, including the Sorbonne, founded in 1257, and has been renowned for centuries for its programs in philosophy and literature. If existentialism isn't your thing, France's fantastic array of culinary and fine arts schools, from the world-famous Cordon Bleu in Paris to painting classes in the Provence of Van Gogh and Matisse, are the perfect way to escape the tourist masses and experience real French culture.

Many travelers structure their trips around the **work** available to them along the way, ranging from odd jobs on the go to full-time, long-term stints in cities. While long-term work is tough to find for non-EU citizens without a professional specialty, English and especially English-French bilingual skills are desirable and can help in the job search. Short-term work is more readily available and can range from picking grapes off the vine to picking up the mess at a hostel. Both long-term and short-term jobs require a work permit, which is discussed further in the upcoming sections.

VOLUNTEERING

Volunteering can be a powerful and fulfilling experience, especially when combined with the thrill of traveling in a new place. Though France is considered wealthy by Western standards, there is no shortage of aid organizations to address the social issues that the country faces. Short-term volunteering positions can be found in virtually every city.

WHY PAY MONEY TO VOLUNTEER? Many volunteers are surprised to learn that some organizations require large fees or "donations." While this may seem ridiculous at first glance, such fees often keep the organization afloat, in addition to covering airfare, room, board, and administrative expenses for the volunteers. (Other organizations must rely on private donations and government subsidies.) If you're concerned about how a program spends its fees, request an annual report or finance account. A reputable organization won't refuse to inform you of how volunteer money is spent.

Pay-to-volunteer programs might be a good idea for young travelers who are looking for more support and structure (such as pre-arranged transportation and housing), or anyone who would rather not deal with the uncertainty implicit in creating a volunteer experience from scratch.

Most people who volunteer in France do so on a short-term basis, at organizations that make use of drop-in or once-a-week volunteers. The best way to find opportunities that match your interests and schedule may be to check with the local or national volunteer centers listed below.

Those looking for longer, more intensive volunteer opportunities usually choose to go through a parent organization that takes care of logistical details and often provides a group environment and support system—for a fee. There are two main types of organizations—religious and non-sectarian—although there are rarely restrictions on participation for either.

GENERAL VOLUNTEER ORGANIZATIONS

Care France, CAP 19, 13 rue de Georges Auric, 75019 Paris (☎01 53 19 89 89; www.carefrance.org). An international organization providing volunteer opportunities that range from combating AIDS to promoting human rights to improving urban development. Over 130,000 supporting offices throughout France.

France Bénévolat, 127 rue Falguière Hall B1, 75015 Paris (☎01 40 61 97 98; www.francebenevolat.org). 70 offices in France place volunteers with organizations that match their interests.

International Volunteer Program, 678 13th St., Ste. 100, Oakland, CA 94612, USA (☎1-866-614-3438; www.ivpsf.org). 1- to 3-month programs in arts and culture, humanitarian relief, environmental conservation, and community development. Fee of US$1850 for a 6-week program includes in-country transportation and room and board. Application fee $100. Intermediate knowledge of French required. Ages 18+.

International Volunteer Programs Association, 31 73rd St., Ste. 2, North Bergen, NJ 07047, USA (☎201-221-4105; www.volunteerinternational.org). International search site for volunteer and internship opportunities that includes general information about volunteering abroad.

Volunteers for Peace, 1034 Tiffany Rd., Belmont, VT 05730, USA (☎802-259-2759; www.vfp.org). 2- to 3-week work camps provide international volunteers the opportunity to live and work together in host communities, while contributing to one of several projects, ranging from archaeological restoration to AIDS education. US$250 fee covers food, lodging, and supplies. Membership fee $30.

YOUTH AND THE COMMUNITY

Community-based projects involve close work with disadvantaged populations in France. A high unemployment rate has left many communities reliant on social programs, which range from elderly care to prison reform. These programs are usually among the most rewarding of all volunteer experiences, but due to their one-on-one nature, knowledge of French is often necessary.

Action Contre la Faim, 4 rue Niepce, 75662 Paris (☎01 43 35 88 88; www.actioncontrelafaim.org). International organization that combats hunger and helps countries attain autonomy. Volunteers organize the Race Against Hunger to raise money for the cause.

Centre de Sculpture, Fonderie de la Dure, Montolieu 11170, Toulouse (☎04 68 24 81 81; louise.sculpture@gwanadoo.fr). Non-profit rural art center in Toulouse. Volunteers assist with community development programs.

Fédération Familles de France, 28 pl. St-Georges, 75009 Paris (☎01 44 53 45 90; www.familles-de-france.org). Volunteers help the organization support families and children in need by providing assistance with education and resumés.

Fondation Claude Pompidou, 42 rue du Louvre, 75001 Paris (☎01 40 13 75 00; www.fondationclaudepompidou.asso.fr). Aids the sick, elderly, and disabled through home care and companionship. Volunteers are generally expected to commit to 1 year.

GENEPI, 12 rue Charles Fourier, 75013 Paris (☎01 45 88 37 00; www.genepi.fr). Students work with inmates to promote the social rehabilitation of those in French prisons. Offices throughout France.

International Partnership for Service-Learning and Leadership, 815 Second Ave., New York, NY 10017, USA (☎212-986-0989; www.ipsl.org). Matches volunteers with host families, provides intensive French classes, and requires 10-12hr. per week of service for a year, semester, or summer. Beginner level of French recommended. Ages 18-30. Based in Montpellier. Program fees US$7200-$27,500.

L'Arche les Sapins, Domaine des Abels, Lignières-Sonneville, 16130 Charente (☎05 45 80 50 66; www.archesapins.org). Christian organization that places volunteers in a community home for the mentally challenged or those with learning disabilities. Ages 18-28. Central location in Poitou-Charentes.

Marseille Volontariat, 14 rue Paul Casimir, 13010 Marseille (☎04 91 79 70 72; www.marseille-volontariat.com). Helps volunteers find opportunities by field of civic interest–including elderly care, insurance disputes, and prison education–in Marseille. Contact the Marseille Centre Regional Information Jeunesse (☎04 91 24 33 50; www.crijpa.com) for housing assistance.

Médecins Sans Frontières (Doctors without Borders), 8 rue St-Sabin, 75011 Paris (☎01 40 21 29 29; www.msf.fr). Coordinates volunteers with at least 2 years of professional experience to provide healthcare to recent immigrants. Interview required. Must be ready to leave within 3 months and volunteer for a minimum of 6 months.

Secours Catholique: Delegation de Paris, 13 rue St-Ambroise, 75011 Paris (☎01 48 07 58 21; www.quiaccueillequi.org). Catholic organization that works to support unemployed adults, children with social problems, immigrants, and other marginalized groups in Paris.

Secours Populaire Français, 9/11 rue Froissart, 75140 Paris (☎01 44 78 21 00; www.secourspopulaire.asso.fr). Provides food and clothing to poor children and families, and arranges sporting and cultural activities. Aims to improve the quality of life of disadvantaged communities.

ENVIRONMENTAL CONSERVATION

After oil spills in 1999 and 2002, France enacted strict pollution controls to protect the coastal areas of the Mediterranean. However, French natural resources still face challenges, and individual volunteers continue to aid the environment where the government cannot.

Canadian Alliance for Development Initiatives and Projects (CADIP), 129-1271 Howe St., Vancouver, BC V6Z 1R3, Canada (☎604-628-7400; www.cadip.org). Offers programs in environmental activism and historical renovation throughout France. Most projects last 2 to 4 weeks. Program fee US$235. Includes room and board.

Centres Permanents d'Initiatives pour l'Environnement (CPIE), 26 rue Beaubourg, 75003 Paris (☎01 44 61 75 35; www.cpie.fr). Organizes environmentally-centered volunteer programs and courses throughout mainland France and Corsica.

Jeunesse et Reconstruction, 10 rue de Trevise, 75009 Paris (☎01 47 70 15 88; www.volontariat.org). Database of volunteer opportunities in environmental preservation and historical reconstruction for young people ages 15+.

Organisation Mondiale de Protection de la Nature, 1 Carrefour de Longchamp, 75116 Paris (☎01 55 25 84 84; www.wwf.fr). Offers various opportunities for environmental activism regarding issues like climate change, endangered species, and sustainable living. Part of the World Wildlife Fund. Sites around France and the EU. Membership fee $30.

World-Wide Opportunities on Organic Farms (WWOOF), WWOOF France, 2 pl. Diderot, 94300 Viennes (www.wwoof.fr). Provide volunteers the opportunity to learn first-hand organic farming techniques, such as bio-dynamic, permaculture, and micro-agriculture. Must purchase book with a list of 300+ farms (€20, €15 for electronic version).

HISTORICAL RESTORATION

The preservation and reconstruction of French landmarks is an ongoing concern. Volunteers looking for a more labor-intensive experience, as well as a great opportunity to learn about France's architectural history, can find groups assisting this process. Also see Jeunesse et Reconstruction and Council on International Educational Exchange above.

APARE, 25 bd. Paul Pons, 84800 L'Isle sur la Sorgue (☎04 90 85 51 15; www.apare-gec.org). Arranges short-term historical restoration projects in Avignon for young people from France and abroad. 3- to 5-week projects for ages 16-18 and 6- to 12-month projects for ages 18-25.

Association CHAM, 5/7 rue Guilleminot, 75014 Paris (☎01 43 35 15 51; www.cham.asso.fr). Organizes groups to restore medieval French landmarks in Francophone countries. Open M-F 9am-12:30pm and 1:30-5:30pm.

Club du Vieux Manoir, Ancienne Abbaye du Moncel, 60700 Pontpoint (☎03 44 72 33 98; http://cvmclubduvieuxmanoir.free.fr). Year-long and summer work restoring castles and churches. Membership and insurance fee €14 per year. Program fee €14 per day, not including food and tent.

GEC, 25 bd. Paul Pons, 84800 L'Isle sur la Sorgue (☎04 90 27 21 20; www.apare-gec.org). Opportunities including long-term projects in historical and environmental preservation for volunteers ages 18-25 and short-term projects for younger students.

REMPART, 1 rue des Guillemites, 75004 Paris (☎01 42 71 96 55; www.rempart.com). Union of 170 non-profit French organizations that offers summer and year-long programs for monument restoration. Most projects last 2 to 3 weeks and charge €5-8 per day and a small membership fee. Ages 18+.

La Sabranenque, rue de la Tour de l'Oume, 30290 St-Victor la Coste (☎04 66 50 05 05; www.sabranenque.com). Restoration of Mediterranean architecture in Provence. Programs from June-Sept. and Mar.-Oct. Ages 18+.

STUDYING

Study-abroad programs range from basic language and culture courses to college-level classes, often for credit. In order to choose a program that best fits your needs, research as much as you can before making your decision—determine costs and duration, as well as what kind of students participate in the program and what sort of accommodations are provided. France has a wide range of study options that provide different experiences, from direct enrollment in French universities to American programs with American professors using French resources.

VISA INFORMATION. Non-EU citizens hoping to study abroad in France must apply for a special student visa from the French consulate. There is a **short-stay** visa for stays up to 90 days, as well as two **long-stay** visas: one for three to six months, and one for six months to a year. Prospective students must fill out two applications for the appropriate visa and provide a passport valid for up to three months after the student's last day in France and two extra passport photos. Additionally, students must give proof of enrollment or admission in a French learning institute, a letter from the home university or institution certifying current registration as a student, a financial guarantee with a monthly allowance of US$600 per month during the intended stay, and proof of medical insurance. Finally, there is a visa fee that can be paid during the time of application (€99). When in France, students with long-stay visas for more than six months must obtain a **carte de séjour** (a student residency card) from the local Préfecture de Police; students should obtain the card within the first week of their stay in France and will be required to undergo a medical check-up. EU citizens do not need a visa but must obtain a carte de séjour with proof of enrollment, proof of health insurance, and proof of sufficient financial resources. See www.diplomatie.gouv.fr/en for more information.

In programs that have large groups of students who speak the same language, there is a trade-off. You may feel more comfortable in the community, but you will not have the same opportunity to practice a foreign language or to befriend other international students. For accommodations, dorm life provides a better opportunity to mingle with fellow students, but there is less of a chance to experience the local scene. If you live with a family, there is a potential to build lifelong friendships with natives and to experience day-to-day life in more depth, but conditions can vary greatly from family to family.

UNIVERSITIES

Most university-level study-abroad programs are conducted in French, although many programs offer classes in English and beginner and lower-level language courses. Those who are relatively fluent in French may find it cheaper to enroll directly in a university abroad, although getting college credit may be more difficult. As a student at a French university, you will receive a student card (*carte d'étudiant*) upon presentation of a residency permit and a receipt for your university fees. The **Centre Régional des Oeuvres Universitaires et Scolaires (CROUS)** (www.crous.fr) offers benefits and discounts to students, including cheap meals and housing assistance. You can search www.studyabroad.com for various semester-abroad programs that meet your criteria, including your desired location and focus of study. The following is a list of organizations that can help place students in university programs abroad, or have their own branch in France.

AMERICAN PROGRAMS

American Institute for Foreign Study, College Division, River Plaza, 9 West Broad St., Stamford, CT 06902, USA (☎800-727-2437; www.aifsabroad.com). Organizes programs for high school and college study in universities in Cannes, Grenoble, and Paris. Program fees are around US$6000 for the summer, US$15,000 per semester, and US$29,000 per academic year.

Council on International Educational Exchange (CIEE), 7 Custom House St., 3rd fl., Portland, ME 01401, USA (☎800-407-8839; www.ciee.org/study). Sponsors work, volunteer, academic, and internship programs in Paris and Rennes. At least 2 years of college French required. Program fees are US$11,600-13,250 per semester and US$21,500-23,800 per year.

Cultural Experiences Abroad, France, 2005 W. 14th St., Ste. 113, Tempe, AZ 85281, USA (☎800-266-4441; www.gowithcea.com). Programs in Aix-en-Provence, Grenoble, the Riviera, and Paris. Students can take classes in both English and French. US$4000 for the summer, US$8000-12,000 per semester, and US$18,000-US$27,000 per academic year.

European Institute for International Education, The Eur-Am Center, 32500 Telegraph Rd., Ste. 209, Bingham Farms, MI 48025, USA (☎248-988-9341; www.euram-center.com). Provides both educational and private-sector opportunities for people of all ages. Run by the University of Southern Mississippi. Tuition from US$3800-4000 for the summer to US$9900 for a semester.

Institute for American Universities, 1830 Sherman Ave., Ste. 402, Evanston, IL 60201, USA (☎800-221-2051; www.iaufrance.org). University-affiliated summer and school-year programs in Aix-en-Provence and Avignon. Tuition from US$4860 for the summer to US$13,080 for a semester.

International Association for the Exchange of Students for Technical Experience (IAESTE), 10400 Little Patuxent Pkwy. Ste. 250, Columbia, MD 21044, USA (☎410-997-3068; www.iaeste.org). Offers 8- to 12-week internships in France for college students who have completed 2 years of technical study.

School for International Training, College Semester Abroad, Kipling Rd., P.O. Box 676, Brattleboro, VT 05302, USA (☎888-272-7881 or 802-257-7751; www.sit.edu/studyabroad). Semester-long programs in France cost US$21,000. Also runs **The Experiment in International Living** (☎800-345-2929; www.usexperiment.org). 3- to 5-week summer programs that offer high-school students cross-cultural homestays, community service, ecological adventure, cultural activities, and language training in France for US$4700-6200.

BEYOND TOURISM

FRENCH PROGRAMS

French universities are far cheaper than their American equivalents; however, it can be hard to receive academic credit at home for a non-approved program. Expect to pay at least €800 per month (€1100 in Paris) in living expenses. EU citizens studying in France can take advantage of the three- to 12-month **SOCRATES** program (www.europe-education-formation.fr; available in French only), which offers grants to support inter-European educational exchanges. For info on programs of study, requirements, and grants, visit www.egide.asso.fr.

French universities are segmented into three degree levels: the first level involves a basic university degree, the second is the equivalent of a Master's degree, and the third is a *Doctorat*, or PhD. Programs at the first level (except the Grandes Ecoles, described below, p. 89) are two or three years long and generally focus on science, medicine, and the liberal arts. They must admit anyone holding a *baccalauréat* (French graduation certificate) or recognized equivalent to their first year of courses (British A levels or two years of college in the US). The more selective and demanding **Grandes Ecoles** cover specializations from physics to photography to veterinary medicine. These have notoriously difficult entrance examinations that require a year of preparatory schooling.

Foreign students can study throughout France at the many regional universities, although Paris is the hub of France's best-known universities and Grandes Ecoles.

Many French universities offer French language and cultural programs as well as general university classes, particularly during the summer.

Agence EduFrance (www.edufrance.fr). A 1-stop resource for North Americans thinking about studying for a degree in France. Info on courses, costs, and grant opportunities. Housing options available in universities or with French families.

American University of Paris, 6 rue du Colonel Combes, 75007 Paris (☎01 40 62 07 20; www.aup.fr). US admissions office: 950 S. Cherry St., Ste. 210, Denver, CO 80246 (☎303-757-6333). Offers US-accredited degrees and summer programs in English on its Paris campus. Intensive French language courses offered. Tuition €12,172 per semester and €23,864 per year, not including living expenses.

Université Paris-Sorbonne, 1 rue Victor Cousin, 75230 Paris (☎01 40 46 22 11; www.paris4.sorbonne.fr). The grandfather of French universities; founded in 1257 and still going strong. Also offers 3- to 9-month programs for American students. Tuition €520-2500 for summer and semester French culture courses.

LANGUAGE SCHOOLS

Language schools can be independently run international or local organizations or divisions of foreign universities. They rarely offer college credit but are a good alternative to university study if you desire a deeper focus on the language or a slightly less rigorous course load. These programs are also good for high school students who might not feel comfortable with older students in a university program. Some worthwhile programs include:

Alliance Française, Ecole Internationale de Langue et de Civilisation Française, 101 bd. Raspail, 75270 Paris Cédex 06 (☎01 42 84 90 00; www.alliancefr.org). Instruction at all levels, with courses in legal, medical, and business French. Courses last 1 to 12 weeks and cost approximately €50 per week for daily 2-hour sessions. Enrollment fee €55.

Eurocentres, Seestr. 247, CH-8038 Zurich, Switzerland (☎+41 1 485 50 40; www.eurocentres.com). Another location at 55 Eccleston Sq., London SW1V 1PH (☎207 963 84 50). Language programs for beginning to advanced students with homestays in France. In Paris, Amboise, and La Rochelle.

Institut de Langue Française, 3 av. Bertie-Albrecht, 75008 Paris (☎01 45 63 24 00). Language, civilization, and literature courses.

Language Immersion Institute, SCB 106, State University of New York at New Paltz, 1 Hawk Dr., New Paltz, NY 12561, USA (☎845-257-3500; www.newpaltz.edu/lii). Summer language courses and some overseas courses in French. Program fees are around US$1000 for a 2-week course, not including accommodations.

World Link Education: Study French and Experience France, 24 Storgatan, 302 43 Halmstad, Sweden (☎+46 35 106680; www.wle-france.com). US Office: 1904 3rd Ave., Ste. 633, Seattle, WA 98101 (☎800-621-3085 or 206-264-0941). French language and culture classes in different cities around the country for all ages. Tuition fees vary. In Paris, Annecy, Bordeaux, and Chambery.

CULINARY AND ART SCHOOLS

One final—and pricier—study abroad option for experts and novices alike is enrollment in a French culinary institute or art school. There is no place better than the artistic and culinary capital of the world to learn to paint or cook. These schools allow budding chefs and Van Goghs to participate in semester- or year-long programs. For smaller, more intimate courses based in farms and homes, often with well-known chefs or food critics, amateur cooks should check out **www.cookingschools.com,** which lists private schools in France.

Cordon Bleu Paris Culinary Arts Institute, 8 rue Léon Delhomme, 75015 Paris (☎01 53 68 22 50; www.cordonbleu.edu). The *crème de la crème* of French cooking schools. Programs range from the decadent *Grand Diplôme* (€32,500) to 1-day workshops on specific culinary themes (€30-200).

Eurolingua Institute, 5 rue Henri Guinier, 34000 Montpellier (☎33 467 15 04 73; www.eurolingua.com/French_in_Montpellier.htm). Language school that offers internships in hotel work and culinary arts in Montpellier and Nice (intermediate French level required). Prices range from €750 (3 months) to €1350 (1 year); full-time work pays €200 per month.

Gastronomicom—French Language and Gastronomy School, Résidence St-Loup, 1 Avenue des Soldats, 34300 Cap d'Agde (☎04 67 32 15 07; www.gastronomicom.fr). Located in seaside resort on the Mediterranean coast, this school offers 3 programs of study for students ages 18-60. 4-, 12-, 28-week courses in cooking, wine appreciation, and intensive French (€1980/4800/5400). All plans of study include lectures and free tastings. 28-week course includes 4-month internship. €150 enrollment fee.

Grande Ecole des Arts Culinaires et de l'Hôtellerie de Lyon (Lyon Culinary Arts and Hotel Management School), Château du Vivier, BP 25, 69131 Ecully Cédex, Lyon (☎04 72 18 02 20; www.each-lyon.com). Premier school affiliated with world-famous chef Paul Bocuse, located in France's capital city of *haute cuisine*. 6- and 12-week summer courses in English and French for amateurs (€3500-6500).

The International Kitchen, 330 N. Wabash, Ste. 2613, Chicago IL 60611 (☎800-945-8606 or 312-467-0560; www.theinternationalkitchen.com). Offers 2- to 7-night "cooking vacations" with famous chefs in Burgundy, Champagne, the Loire Valley, Paris, Provence, the Côte d'Azur, and the Southwest (US$785-3000). Also offers 1-day course in the Rhône-Alpes, Paris, Provence, and the Côte d'Azur ($170-290), as well as wine- and chocolate-tastings ($65-170).

Lacoste School of Art, 201 E. Broughton St., Savannah, GA 31401, USA (☎912-525-4786; www.scad.edu/lacoste). French location at Rue du Four, 84480 Lacoste. In the *provençal* town of Lacoste, this school is administered by the Savannah College of Art and Design. Summer and fall courses in architecture and painting preservation. Tuition €2550 per course with minimum of 2 courses for undergraduates. €4300 program fee includes room, board, weekend excursions, and museum admissions.

The Marchutz School, 1830 Sherman Ave., Ste. 402, Evanston, IL 60201, USA (☎800-221-2051; www.iaufrance.org/Marchutz). Run by the Institute for American Universities. Interdisciplinary programs in multiple media on the outskirts of Aix-en-Provence. Classes, seminars, private instruction, painting supplies, and excursions included. In English. Semester courses US$14,640; summer courses US$5265.

Painting School of Montmiral, rue de la Porte Neuve, 81140 Castelnau de Montmiral (☎05 63 33 13 11; www.painting-school.com). 2-week classes at student or professional levels in English or French. With accommodations and half-board €1304. €500 deposit required.

Pont Aven School of Art, 269 S. Main St., Providence, RI 02903, USA (☎401-272-5445; www.pontavensa.org). French location at Pension Gloanec, 5 pl. Paul Gaugin, 29930 Pont-Aven (☎02 98 09 10 45). English-speaking school in Brittany offers courses in art history and studio art. 4- and 5-week summer sessions €4700-7400.

WORKING

As with volunteering, work opportunities tend to fall into two categories. Some travelers want long-term jobs that allow them to integrate into a community, while others seek out short-term jobs to finance the next leg of their travels. With unemployment stubbornly staying at 9%, finding long-term jobs in France is almost impossible for non-EU citizens. Employers must prove that an employee can perform a task that cannot be performed by a French employee, making it slightly easier for people to get managerial jobs or work as highly skilled technicians. If you're undeterred by the less-than-welcoming attitude toward foreign workers, you may want to try a job that requires English-language skills, as bilingual candidates have a better chance of finding work. Note that working abroad often requires a special work visa; see the box below for information about obtaining one.

VISA INFORMATION. **EU citizens** have the right to work and study in France without a visa, and can easily obtain a **residency permit** *(carte de séjour)* by presenting a passport or other ID and proof of employment. By law, all EU citizens must be given equal opportunity when applying to jobs not directly related to national security. In addition, **non-EU citizens** wishing to **work** in France for more than 90 days must have an offer of employment authorized by the French Ministry of Labor (www.travail.gouv.fr/) before applying for a **long-stay visa** (US$135) through their local French consulate. Within 8 days of arrival, holders of long-stay visas must apply for a *carte de séjour*. International students looking for part-time work (up to 19½hr. per week during the academic year) can apply for a temporary work permit upon completing their first academic year in a French university. For **au pairs, scientific researchers,** and **teaching assistants,** special rules apply; check with your local consulate. For more info, see www.consulfrance-washington.org.

LONG-TERM WORK

If you're planning on spending a substantial amount of time (more than three months) working in France, search for a job well in advance. International placement agencies are often the easiest way to find employment abroad, especially for those interested in teaching English. Although they are often only available to college students, **internships** are a good way to segue into working abroad; although they are often un- or underpaid, many say the experience is well worth it. Be wary of advertisements for companies claiming to be able get you a job abroad for a fee—often the same listings are available online or in newspapers. Some reputable organizations include:

Association for International Practical Training (AIPT), 10400 Little Patuxent Pkwy., Ste. 250, Columbia, MD 21044, USA (☎410-997-2200; www.aipt.org). Offers assistance to students and professionals in variety of fields.

American Chamber of Commerce in France, 156 Boulevard Haussmann, 75004 Paris, France (☎33 01 56 43 45 67; www.amchamfrance.org). Supports American and Franco-American businesses in France and Europe.

Centre d'Information et de Documentation Jeunesse, 101 quai Branly, 757015 Paris, France (☎01 44 49 12 00; www.cidj.com). Provides information on work opportunities in France. Open M-W and F 10am-6pm, Th 1-6pm and Sa 9:30am-1pm. Job search engine in French at www.jobs-ete.com.

French-American Chamber of Commerce (FACC), 122 E. 42nd St., New York, NY 10168, USA (☎212-867-0123; www.faccnyc.org). Information on international career development programs including work, internship, and teaching opportunities.

TEACHING ENGLISH

Teaching jobs abroad are rarely well-paid, although some elite private American schools offer competitive salaries. Volunteering as a teacher in lieu of getting paid is a popular option; even then, teachers often receive some sort of a daily stipend to help with living expenses. In almost all cases, you must have at least a bachelor's degree to be a full-fledged teacher, though college undergraduates can often get summer positions teaching or tutoring. Because many bosses require that employees take English classes, demand for teachers is fairly high despite France's resilient pride in its language.

Many schools require teachers to have a **Teaching English as a Foreign Language (TEFL)** certificate. You may still be able to find a teaching job without certification, but certified teachers often find higher-paying jobs. Native English speakers working in private schools are most often hired for English-immersion classrooms where no French is spoken. Those volunteering or teaching in public schools are more likely to be working in both English and French. Placement agencies or university fellowship programs are the best resources for finding teaching jobs. The alternative is to contact schools directly or to try your luck once you arrive in France. If you are going to try the latter, the best time to look is several weeks before the start of the school year. The following organizations are helpful in placing teachers in France.

French Ministry of Education Teaching Assistantship in France, French Embassy, 4101 Resevoir Rd., Washington, D.C., 20007, USA (☎202-944-6294; http://frenchculture.org/the_education.cfm). Program for US citizens sends up to 1700 recent grads to teach English in France on a €900 monthly stipend.

International Schools Services (ISS), 15 Roszel Rd., P.O. Box 5910, Princeton, NJ 08543, USA (☎609-452-0990; www.iss.edu). Hires teachers for more than 200 overseas schools including 9 in France. Candidates should have experience in teaching or international affairs; 2-year commitment expected.

AU PAIR WORK

Au pairs are typically women (although sometimes men), aged 18-27, who work as live-in nannies, caring for children and doing light housework in foreign countries in exchange for room, board, and a small spending allowance or stipend. One perk of the job is that it allows you to get to know France without the high expenses of traveling. Drawbacks, however, can include mediocre pay and long hours. In France, this means between €50 and €75 per week. Much of the au pair experience depends on the family with whom you are placed. The agencies below provide a good starting point for looking for employment.

Childcare International, Ltd., Trafalgar House, Grenville Pl., London NW7 3SA (☎+44 020 8906 3116; www.childint.co.uk).

InterExchange, 161 Sixth Ave., New York, NY 10013, USA (☎800-287-2477; www.interexchange.org). Matches prospective au pairs with families. Childcare experience recommended.

L'Accueil Familial des Jeunes Etrangers, 23 rue du Cherche-Midi, 75006 Paris (☎01 42 22 50 34; www.afje-paris.org). Arranges summer and 18-month au pair work for college graduates which require 30 hours of work per week in exchange for €267 per month and employment benefits, and room and board.

SHORT-TERM WORK

Traveling for long periods of time can be hard on the finances; therefore, many travelers try their hand at odd jobs for a few weeks at a time to help pay for another month or two of touring around. Opportunities can be found at **Regional Youth Information Centers (CRIJ)** in France or in the "Positions Vacants" section of papers such as the "Guide du Job Trotter." Seasonal work can be found in the hotel and restaurant businesses, in markets, and in agriculture. EU citizens can earn about €50 a day picking grapes in France through **Appellation Contrôlée,** Neutronstraat 10, 9743 AM Groningen, Holland. The program charges a €99 placement cost and provides room and board (☎050-549-2434; www.apcon.nl). Another popular option is to work several hours a day at a hostel in exchange for free or discounted room and/or board. Most often, these short-term jobs are found by word of mouth, or by expressing interest to the owner of a hostel or restaurant. Due to high turnover in the tourism industry, many places are eager for help, even if it is only temporary. *Let's Go* lists temporary jobs of this nature whenever possible; look in the practical information sections of larger cities or check out the list below for some of the available short-term jobs in popular destinations.

FURTHER READING ON BEYOND TOURISM.

Alternatives to the Peace Corps: A Guide of Global Volunteer Opportunities, by Paul Backhurst. Food First Books, 2005 (US$12).

The Back Door Guide to Short-Term Job Adventures: Internships, Summer Jobs, Seasonal Work, Volunteer Vacations, and Transitions Abroad, by Michael Landes. Ten Speed Press, 2005 (US$22).

Green Volunteers: The World Guide to Voluntary Work in Nature Conservation, ed. Fabio Ausenda. Universe, 2007 (US$15).

How to Get a Job in Europe, by Cheryl Matherly and Robert Sanborn. Planning Communications, 2003 (US$23).

How to Live Your Dream of Volunteering Overseas, by Joseph Collins, Stefano DeZerega, and Zahara Heckscher. Penguin Books, 2002 (US$20).

International Job Finder: Where the Jobs Are Worldwide, by Daniel Lauber and Kraig Rice. Planning Communications, 2002 (US$20).

Live and Work Abroad: A Guide for Modern Nomads, by Huw Francis and Michelyne Callan. Vacation-Work Publications, 2001 (US$16).

Overseas Summer Jobs 2002. Peterson's Guides and Vacation Work, 2002 (US$18).

Volunteer Vacations: Short-Term Adventures That Will Benefit You and Others, by Doug Cutchins, Anne Geissinger, and Bill McMillon. Chicago Review Press, 2006 (US$18).

Work Abroad: The Complete Guide to Finding a Job Overseas, by Clayton Hubbs. Transitions Abroad Publishing, 2002 (US$16).

Work Your Way Around the World, by Susan Griffith. Vacation-Work Publications, 2007 (US$22).

ancient fixer-uppers

The summer before my junior year of high school, I went to France for one month to work with *L'Association pour la Participation et l'Action Régionale* (Association for Participation and Regional Action). Established in 1979, this group is an educational youth organization based in Avignon that organizes young volunteers from around the world to come to southern France (Provence Alpes-Côte d'Azur region and the Mediterranean) and work on the restoration and management of 25-30 sites. Projects last from three weeks to six months and are highly subsidized: a three-week trip averages €200-300 and includes food, housing, training, materials, weekend trips, and transportation around France. APARE focuses on areas of architectural heritage and on maintaining the natural environments in which they are found.

"As the sun lifted over the rocky hillside, we trudged uphill with our pick-axes."

My *chantier*, or work site, was in St-Tropez, situated on the Mediterranean among 500-year-old stone ruins, snobby cafés, and beautiful people. We lived in the Citadel, camping underneath tents and on army cots. I was the only American volunteer among a group of 12 other European teenagers, the majority of whom were French. We woke up each day at 7am and headed off to the site—a 17th-century coastal arms battery called Point-Sur-Capon. As the scorching sun lifted over the rocky hillside, we trudged uphill with our pick-axes, hoes, rakes, and cement shovels.

There were two areas to the site: below, an old stone building where arms had been stored, and farther up the craggy hillside, a stone arc that once housed cannons. We spent the first week clearing away the undergrowth in the area. When we had finished, we could not only see the amazing stone work on the site but also, suddenly, the Mediterranean's deep blue water. The second week focused on the lower site, where we made our own cement with lime and sand from the beach below and filled in the dilapidated walls. After that, we moved up to the top for the third week and rebuilt the wall with stones found in the area. Afternoons were spent drinking beer in the cafés, playing on the stone beaches of St-Tropez, or sleeping under the pine canopies of the Citadel.

This was no vacation; I got to experience a taste of southern French life and cultural history for very little money. Every weekend we took trips to visit other *chantiers*, where we stayed up all night in centuries-old castles draining liters of wine from the next-door vineyard. We day-tripped into little villages dotting Provence, visiting leather fairs and wine festivals where the only other people there were locals.

"I got to experience French life and cultural history for very little money."

This is the perfect trip for the enthusiastic Francophile because you not only experience the ancient castles, the fragrant hillsides, the incredible food, and the warm people, but also help to maintain and rebuild some of France's most majestic locales.

For more info on L'Association pour la Participation et l'Action Régionale, see listing for APARE on p. 85.

***Cat Walleck** graduated from Harvard University in 2006 with a degree in Romance Language Studies (French, English, and Italian). She plans to attend the American Conservatory Theater to pursue a career in acting.*

PARIS

Paris (PAH-ree; pop. 2,153,600) has been a center of culture and commerce for over 2000 years. In the midst of it all, it has become a symbol of romance, revolution, heroism, and hedonism. Paris draws millions of visitors per year, but despite its iconic status as a tourist destination, its ever-changing and accessible image keeps it fresh. From students who come to study at the Sorbonne to tourists who wonder why the French ignore so many consonants, anyone can enjoy the city where buildings don't exceed six stories *pour que tout le monde ait du soleil* (so that all can have sunshine). The City of Light, Paris twinkles with magnetic charm. Only in Paris are baguettes as satisfying as *haute cuisine* and excellent musicians as common in the Metro as in concert halls. The City of Love, Paris is a source of inspiration unrivaled in beauty. Art seeps from the many world-class museums and history from every Roman ruin, Renaissance hotel, and 19th-century boulevard. A vibrant political and commercial center, Paris blends the spirit of revolution with a reverence for tradition, devoting as much energy to preserving conventions as it does to shattering them.

HIGHLIGHTS OF PARIS

SHARE the view with: Quasimodo atop **Notre Dame** (p. 127); gargoyles on the stairs of Montmartre's **Sacré-Coeur** (p. 138); tourists at the **Arc de Triomphe** (p. 136); trendsetters on the 56th floor of **Tour Montparnasse** (p. 141); and lovebirds at the top of the **Eiffel Tower** (p. 135).

WANDER through halls filled with intimidatingly impressive art at the **Louvre** (p. 145), **Musée d'Orsay** (p. 156), **Centre Pompidou** (p. 149), **Musée Rodin** (p. 157), and **Musée Picasso** (p. 152).

STORM the **Bastille** district (p. 173)–once home to the legendary prison, now a center of Parisian partying. Or, enjoy a beer next to a real guillotine in the **Quartier Latin** (p. 171), where much of 20th-century radicalism found its start.

INTERCITY TRANSPORTATION

BY AIRPLANE

ROISSY-CHARLES DE GAULLE

Flights: Transatlantic flights use **Charles de Gaulle** (☎3950; www.adp.fr). The airport has a 24hr. English-speaking info center.

Trains: RER. To **Paris** from Roissy-CDG, the RER B (one of the Parisian commuter rail lines) runs to central Paris from Terminals 1 and 2. To transfer to the Metro, get off at "Gare du Nord," "Châtelet-Les-Halles," "St-Michel," or "Denfert Rochereau." To **Roissy-CDG** from Paris, take the RER B to "Roissy," the end of the line. (30-35min.; RER every 15min. 5am-midnight; €7.75, under 18 €5.50).

Buses: Roissybus runs between the intersection of rue Scribe and rue Auber, near M: Opéra, and terminals 1, 2, and 3. Tickets can be purchased on the bus (45min.; to airport every 15min. 5:45am-7pm, every 20min. 7-11pm; from airport every 15min. 6am-7pm, every 20min. 7-11pm; €8.50, under 5 free). **Air France Buses** (recorded info in English ☎08 92 35 08 20) run to 2 sections of the city. Stops at or between terminals 2A and 2F and at Terminal 1 on the "Departures" level. Buy tickets on board. Line #2 runs to the **Arc de Triomphe** (M: Charles de Gaulle-Etoile) at 1 av. Carnot and **place de**

la Porte de Maillot/Palais des Congrès (M: Porte de Maillot) on bd. Gouvion St-Cyr (both 35min.; every 15min. 5:45am-11pm; €13, under 18 €6.50; 15% group discount). Line #4 runs to **rue du Commandant Mouchette** opposite the Hôtel Méridien (M: Montparnasse-Bienvenüe) and **Gare de Lyon** (M: Gare de Lyon) at 20bis bd. Diderot (both every 30min. 7am-9:30pm; €14, under 18 €7; 15% group discounts).

ORLY

Flights: Charters and many continental flights use **Orly,** 18km south of the city. Info in English (☎3950). Open daily 6am-11:45pm.

Trains: RER. From "Orly Sud: Gate G" or "Gate I: Platform 1," or "Orly Ouest Level G: Gate F," take the **Orly-Rail** shuttle (every 15min. 6am-11pm; free) to the "Pont de Rungis/Aéroport d'Orly" stop, where you can board the RER C2 to a number of Paris destinations. (35min.; every 20min. 5am-11:30pm; €5.75, under 18 €4.) The **Jetbus** (every 15min. 6:20am-10:50pm, €5.70) provides a quick connection between "Orly Sud: gate H: platform 2" or "Orly Ouest Level 0: Gate C" and **M: Villejuif-Louis Aragon** on Metro Line 7.

Bus: RATP Orlybus runs to Metro and RER stop **Denfert-Rochereau,** 14ème, from "Orly Sud" (30min.; every 15-20min. 6am-11:30pm from "Orly" to "Denfert-Rochereau," 5:35am-11pm from "Denfert-Rochereau" to "Orly;" €6). You can also board the Orlybus at "Dareau-St-Jacques," "Glacière-Tolbiac," and "Porte de Gentilly." **Air France** buses run between Orly and **Gare Montparnasse,** near 6ème (M: Montparnasse-Bienvenüe), and the

Invalides Air France agency, pl. des Invalides (30min.; every 15min. 6am-11:30pm; €9, under 18 €4.50). **Air France shuttles** stop at Orly Ouest and Orly Sud's departures levels.

Orlyval: RATP also runs **Orlyval,** a combination of Metro, RER, and VAL rail shuttles, and probably your fastest option. The VAL shuttle goes from "Antony" (a stop on RER Line B) to "Orly Ouest" and "Orly Sud." Tickets for the VAL (€7.20) or a combination VAL-RER ticket (from €9.10) are available. Buy tickets at any RATP booth or from the Orlyval agencies at Orly Ouest, Orly Sud, and Antony. **To Orly:** Be careful when taking the RER B from Paris to Orly, because it splits into 2 lines before the Antony stop. Get on the train that says "St-Rémy-Les-Chevreuse" or just look for the track that has a lit-up sign saying "Antony-Orly" ("Antony" to "Orly Sud" 8min., every 4-7min. 6am-11pm). **From Orly:** Trains arrive at "Orly Ouest" 2min. after reaching "Orly Sud" ("Orly Sud" to "Antony" 8min., every 4-7min. 6am-11pm).

BEAUVAIS

Flights: Ryanair, easyJet, and other intercontinental airlines fly to **Aéroport Beauvais.**

Buses: run between the airport and bd. Pershing in the 17ème, near Hôtel Concorde Lafayette (M: Porte Maillot). Tickets (€13) can be purchased in the arrivals lounge of the airport or on the bus. Call ☎03 44 11 46 86 for bus schedules and other info.

BY TRAIN

If you're traveling between Paris and another European city, trains are a scenic and convenient option. The prices below are the full fares for one-way, second-class tickets unless otherwise noted. Timetables and prices vary greatly according to the time of day, day of the week, and season; for the most current listings, consult the difficult-to-navigate and impossibly-slow-to-load SNCF website at www.sncf-voyages.fr.

Gare d'Austerlitz: To the Loire Valley, southwestern France (Bordeaux, Pyrénées), Portugal, and Spain. To **Barcelona** (12hr., €125) and **Madrid** (12-13hr., €125).

Gare de l'Est: To eastern France (Alsace, Champagne, Lorraine, Strasbourg), Austria, southern Germany (Frankfurt, Munich), Hungary, Luxembourg, Prague, and parts of Switzerland (Basel, Lucerne, Zürich). To: **Luxembourg** (4-5hr., €67); **Munich** (9hr., €154); **Prague** (14hr., €152); **Vienna** (15hr., €154); **Zürich** (7hr., €105).

Gare du Nord: To northern France, Britain, Belgium, Eastern Europe, northern Germany (Cologne, Hamburg), the Netherlands, and Scandinavia. To **Amsterdam** (4-5hr., €100), **Brussels** (1½hr., €78), and **London** (by the Eurostar Chunnel; 3hr., €230).

Gare de Lyon: To southern and southeastern France (Lyon, Provence, Riviera), Greece, Italy, and parts of Switzerland (Berne, Geneva, Lausanne). To **Florence** (13hr., €130), **Geneva** (4hr., €72), and **Rome** (15hr., €130).

Gare Montparnasse: To Brittany and southwestern France on the TGV.

Gare St-Lazare: To Normandy.

BY BUS

International buses arrive in Paris at the **Gare Routière Internationale du Paris-Gallieni** (M: Gallieni) outside Paris at 28 av. du Général de Gaulle. **Eurolines** (☎49 72 57 80, €0.34 per min.; www.eurolines.fr) sells tickets to most destinations in France and bordering countries.

ORIENTATION

The **Seine River** (SEHN) flows from east to west through the heart of Paris. Two islands in the Seine, **Ile de la Cité** and **Ile St-Louis,** are situated in the city's geographical center. The Seine splits Paris into two sections: the **Rive Gauche** (REEV go-sh; Left Bank) to the south and the **Rive Droite** (REEV dwaht; Right Bank) to the north. Modern Paris is divided into **20 arrondissements** (districts) that spiral clockwise outward from the center of the city. Each *arrondissement* is referred to by its number (e.g. the Third, the Sixteenth). In French, "Third" is said *troisième* (TWAZ-yem) and abbreviated "3ème"; "Sixteenth" is said *seizième* (SEZ-yem) and abbreviated "16ème." The same goes for every *arrondissement* except the First, which is said *premier* (PRUHM-yay) and abbreviated 1er. Sometimes it is helpful to orient yourself around central Paris's major monuments: on Rive Gauche, the sprawling Jardin du Luxembourg lies in the southeast; the Eiffel Tower, visible from many points in the city, stands in the southwest; moving clockwise and crossing the Seine to Rive Droite, the Champs Elysées and Arc de Triomphe occupy the northwest and the Sacré-Coeur stands high in the northeast. *Let's Go* splits Paris into neighborhoods according to divisions used by most Parisians: the Seine Islands, Châtelet-les-Halles and Opéra, the Marais, the Latin Quarter and St-Germain, Invalides, Champs-Elysées, Montmartre, the Bastille, the Thirteenth Arrondissement, Montparnasse and the Fifteenth Arrondissement, and the Outlying Arrondissements. These divisions are not the same as the official *arrondissement* boundaries, so each neighborhood introduction indicates the *arrondissements* that correspond to the area.

LOCAL TRANSPORTATION

The **RATP (Régie Autonome des Transports Parisiens)** coordinates a network of subways, buses, and commuter trains in and around Paris. For info, contact **La Maison de la RATP,** 190 rue de Bercy, across the street from M: Gare de Lyon or the **Bureau de Tourisme RATP,** pl. de la Madeleine, 8ème (M: Madeleine; ☎40 06 71 45; open daily 8:30am-6pm). The RATP also has a helpful English website (www.ratp.fr/ParisVisite) with info on fares, routes, passes, and services for disabled visitors.

FARES AND PASSES

Paris's ticket system changed in July, 2007, abandoning the purple tickets for white ones and raising prices. Individual tickets for the Metro now cost €1.50 each and €11.10 for a *carnet* of 10. Each Metro ride requires only one ticket. The bus requires at least one, sometimes more, depending on connections and the time of day. The new Metro tickets allow for free transfers between the train and the bus and between buses. If you're staying in Paris for several days or weeks, a **Carte Orange** can be very economical. Bring an ID photo (taken by machines in most major stations; €3.81) to the ticket counter and ask for a weekly *carte orange hebdomadaire* (€16) or the monthly *carte orange mensuelle* (€53). Beware: the weekly pass does not allow for a week of unlimited travel from the day you buy the ticket but rather a week of travel starting on a Monday and ending on Sunday. The monthly pass works in the same fashion, starting on the first of the month. If you're taking your photo at a Metro booth, select the smallest size; if you already have a passport photo you will have to cut it so it fits on the card. The tickets with prices quoted here are for passes in Zones 1 and 2 (the Metro and RER in Paris) and work on all Metro, bus, and RER modes of transport. If you're in town for only a day or two, a cheap option is the **Carte Mobilis** (☎08 91 36 20 20; available in Metro stations; 1-day pass in Zones 1 and 2 €5.50), which provides unlimited Metro, bus, and RER transportation within Paris. More expensive **Paris Visite** tickets are valid for unlimited travel on the bus, Metro, and RER. They also give discounts on sightseeing trips, museum admission, and stores like Galeries Lafayette, though the discounts are not necessarily worth the cost. (Available at the airport, Metro, and RER stations. 1-day pass €8.50, 2-day

€14, 3-day €19, 5-day €28; under 12 approximately ½-price.) Visitors can also purchase **Carte Musée** (2-day pass €35, 4-day €55, and 6-day €75).

METRO

TIP **LATE-NIGHT LOCOMOTIVE.** The Paris Metro shuts down for the night at 12:30am, but don't despair if the magic hour has passed you by and you're far from home or hostel. All that happens when the clock strikes 12:30am is that the last trains of the night leave from the ends of each line. If you're near the center of the city, you'll be able to catch a ride until 1am or so.

Entrances to most Metro stations are marked with an "M" or with fancy *"Métropolitain"* lettering designed by Art Nouveau legend Hector Guimard; for each listing in the guide, *Let's Go* indicates the corresponding Metro station with an "M:" designation. Paris boasts one the world's most impressive subway systems, with approximately 375 stations. The Metro runs from 5:30am-12:30am, and the specific times of the first and last trains for each line and station are displayed on the platform. Connections to other lines are indicated by orange *correspondance* signs; exits by blue *sortie* signs. Transfers are free if made within a station; it is not always possible to reverse direction on the same line without exiting the station. **To avoid fines, hold on to your ticket** until you pass the point marked **Limite de Validité des Billets** on the way to the exit. Do not count on buying a Metro ticket late at night; some ticket windows close by 10pm.

STATION SAVVY. The following stations can be dangerous at night: Barbès-Rochechouart, Pigalle, Anvers, Châtelet-Les-Halles, Gare du Nord, Gare de l'Est, château d'Eau. If concerned, take a taxi (p. 99) or Noctambus.

RER

The RER *(Réseau Express Régional)* is the RATP's commuter rail. It passes through central Paris. Within the city, the RER travels much faster than the Metro. There are five RER lines, marked A-E, with different branches designated by a number, like the C5 line to Versailles-Rive Gauche. The newest line, the E, is called the EOLE (Est-Ouest Liaison Express), and links Gare Magenta to Gare St-Lazare. Within Paris, the RER works the same as the Metro, running from about 5:30am to about 1:20am. Tickets for the Metro cannot be used for RER trains, even though both run through some of the same stations.

BUS

Though slower and often more costly than the Metro, buses can serve as cheap sightseeing tours and helpful introductions to the city's layout. The *Grand Plan de Paris* (free at Metro stations) includes a map of the bus lines. The free bus map *Autobus Paris-Plan du Réseau* is available at the tourist office and Metro information booths. Bus tickets are the same as those used on the Metro and can be purchased either in Metro stations or on the bus from the driver; however, if you buy a ticket at a Metro station, you can make both bus-bus and bus-train free transfers, whereas if you buy a ticket on the bus, you cannot transfer for free. *Cartes oranges* and other transport passes *(Paris Visite, Carte Mobilis)* are valid on buses and subways (see **Metro,** p. 98). When you wish to leave the bus, press the red button to illuminate the *arrêt demandé* (stop requested) sign.

NIGHT BUSES. Most buses run daily 7am-8:30pm; those marked **Autobus de nuit** continue until 1:30am. The **Noctilien** (tickets €1.40) operates within Paris as well as the suburbs from 12:30-5:30am. The frequency of buses varies widely, from every 10min. at some stops on weekends to every hour at other stops; check www.noctilien.fr. Noctilien bus stops are marked with a blue "N" inside a white circle, with a red star on the upper-right hand side. The system comprises 40 lines. Free maps are available at Metro stations. All RATP passes are valid.

TOUR BUSES. Balabus (☎44 68 43 35) stops at virtually every major sight in Paris (Bastille, St-Michel, Louvre, Musée d'Orsay, Concorde, Champs-Elysées, Charles de Gaulle-Etoile; whole loop 1hr.). It only runs on Sundays and public-holiday afternoons between April and September. The circuit requires three standard bus tickets and starts at the Grande Arche de La Défense or Gare de Lyon.

> TIP **HIT THE ROAD.** In the summer, take the bus instead of the Metro—you'll see more of Paris and avoid the jostling, sweaty Metro crowd. Those handy little purple tickets can be used on the Metro and the bus.

TAXIS

Taxis take three passengers; a fourth person is an additional €2-3. Companies include: **Aero Taxi** (☎47 39 01 47; for airport destinations), **01 Taxi** (☎49 17 01 01), **Alpha Taxis** (☎45 85 85 85), **Taxis Bleus** (☎08 25 16 24 24), and **Taxis G7** (☎47 39 47 39). **Tarif A,** the basic rate, is in effect in Paris 7am-7pm (€0.62 per km). **Tarif B** is in effect Monday through Saturday 7pm-7am, all day Sunday, and 7am-7pm from airports and close suburbs (€1.06 per km). **Tarif C** is in effect from the airports 7pm-7am (€1.24 per km). There's also a *prix en charge* (base fee) of €2, and a minimum charge of €5. It's customary to tip 15% and polite to add an extra €1.

CARS

Traveling by car in Paris is only convenient if your plans include significant travel outside the city. Parisian drivers are merciless. **Priorité à droite** gives the right of way to the car approaching from the right, regardless of the size of the streets, and Parisian drivers exercise this right even in the face of grave danger. Technically, drivers are not allowed to honk their horns within city limits unless they are about to hit a pedestrian, but this rule is often broken. The legal way to show discontent is to flash your headlights. A map of Paris marked with one-way streets is indispensable for drivers. **Parking** is expensive and hard to find. For information on car rental agencies, licenses, and insurance, see **Essentials,** p. 36.

TOP TEN METRO STATIONS

1. Concorde, 1er, has mosaic-covered walls—each tile displays a different letter. Take a stab at solving the world's largest word search (actually a series of long quotes).

2. Cluny La Sorbonne, 5ème, has signatures of the Sorbonne's luminaries all over the ceiling.

3. Arts et Metiers [redacted] ème, is covered entirely in copper, reminiscent of Captain Nemo's submarine—or plumbing, depending on how you look at things.

4. Louvre, 1er, features replicas of the museum's artwork.

5. Montparnasse-Bienvenüe, 15ème, is a mega-station where you can choose your speed of moving sidewalk—either 3km per hour or a daunting 9km per hour on the *trattoir rouland rapide* (fast-rolling sidewalk).

6. Bastille, 11ème, beneath the site of the former prison, has murals depicting the events of the Revolution.

7. Varenne, 7ème, displays replicas of Rodin sculptures.

8. Châtelet, 1er, is a large, grimy, and disorienting station, but the excellent array of musicians that play near the transfer to Line 4 are sure to brighten your commute.

9. Palais Royal, 1e [redacted] boasts a lavishly bejeweled entrance.

10. Porte Dauphine, 16ème, has a florid Art Nouveau entrance, designed by Hector Guimard.

BICYCLES

During Parisian Metro strike after Metro strike, bike shops have come to the rescue of stranded citizens, and an emergent cycling community has approached its dream of an auto-free Paris. If you have never ridden a bike in heavy traffic, however, don't use central Paris as a testing ground. Safer, shaded bike paths wind through the Bois de Boulogne and the Bois de Vincennes, on the city's periphery. Bicycles can be transported on all RER lines anytime except during rush hour (M-F 6:30-9am and 4:30-7pm) and on Metro line 1 Sunday before 4:30pm. Ask for a helmet (not legally required, but always a good idea) and inquire about insurance.

Paris à vélo, c'est sympa!, 22 rue Alphonse Baudin, 11ème (☎48 87 60 01; www.parisvelosympa.com). M: St-Richard Lenoir. 9am-2pm or 2-7pm €10, 9am-7pm €13, 24hr. €17; €250 deposit. Open M and W-F 9am-1pm and 2-5:30pm, Sa-Su 9:30am-1pm and 2-6pm.

Paris-Vélo, 2 rue de Fer-à-Moulin, 5ème (☎43 37 59 22). M: Censier-Daubenton. €14 per day. Open Apr.-Sept. M-Sa 10am-7pm, Su 10am-2pm and 5-7pm; Oct.-Mar. M-Sa 10am-6pm, Su 10am-2pm and 5-7pm.

Roulez Champions, 5 rue Humblot, 15ème (☎40 58 12 22; www.roulezchampions.com). €15 per day. Also rents in-line skates. Open Mar.-Oct. Tu-Sa 10:30am-1pm and 3:30-7:30pm, Su 10am-7pm; Nov.-Feb. 10:30am-1pm and 3:30-7pm.

SEjEM, 144 bd. Voltaire, 11ème (☎44 93 04 03). Rents bikes and scooters. Open daily 9am-7pm.

PRACTICAL INFORMATION

TOURIST AND FINANCIAL SERVICES

Tourist Offices:

Bureau Pyramides, 25 rue des Pyramides, 1er (☎08 92 68 30 00). M: Pyramides. Open June-Oct. daily 9am-7pm; Nov.-May M-Sa 10am-7pm, Su 11am-7pm.

Bureau Gare de Lyon, 20 bd. Diderot, 12ème (☎08 92 68 30 00). M: Gare de Lyon. Open M-Sa 8am-6pm.

Montmartre Tourist Office, 21 pl. du Tertre, 18ème (☎42 62 21 21). M: Anvers. Open daily 10am-7pm.

Tours:

Bateaux-Mouches (☎42 25 96 10, info ☎40 76 99 99; www.bateaux-mouches.fr.) M: Alma-Marceau. 70min. tours in English. Departures every 45min. 10:15am-8pm from the Right Bank pier near Pont d'Alma.

Fat Tire Bike Tours, 24 rue Edgar Faure, 15ème (☎56 58 10 54; www.fattirebiketoursparis.com). Tours mid-May to mid-Sept. 11am and 3pm; mid-Sept. to Nov. and mid-Feb. to mid-May 11am. Ask about the tour of Monet's Garden. €24, students €22.

Consulates and Embassies: See **Essentials,** p. 9.

American Express: 11 rue Scribe, 9ème (☎47 77 79 28). M: Opéra or Auber. Open M-Sa 9am-6:30pm.

LOCAL SERVICES

GLBT Resources:

ACT-UP Paris, 45 rue de Sedene, 11ème (☎48 06 13 89). M: Bréguet-Sabin.

Boobs Bourg, 26 rue de Montmorency, 3ème (☎42 72 80 86). Sign up at this bar to join a Paris-wide lesbian email list with information on lectures and social events.

Centre Gai et Lesbien, 3 rue Keller, 11ème (☎43 57 21 47). M: Ledru-Rollin or Bastille. Open M-F 4-8pm.

Ecoute Gaie, ☎44 93 01 02. Crisis hotline. Open M and W-Th 8-10pm, Tu and F 6-10pm.

GLBT Crisis Line: SOS Homophobie, ☎48 06 42 41. Takes calls M and F 6-10pm, Tu-Th and Su 8-10pm, Sa 2-4pm.

Laundromats: Ask at your hostel or hotel for the closest laundry facilities. Some options include: **Marass,** 21 rue Debelleyme, 3ème; **La Pince à Linge,** 3 pl. Monge, 5ème; **Redon Blanc Service,** 2 rue Comète, 7ème; **Selsa Service,** 70 bd. Picpus, 12ème; **Multiservices,** 75 rue Ouest, 14ème; **Lav'story,** 140 av. Jean Jaurès, 19ème.

EMERGENCY AND COMMUNICATIONS

PHONE CODE. The phone code for Paris is ☎**01.**

Crisis Lines:

Alcoholics Anonymous (AA), ☎46 34 59 65; www.aaparis.org. Holds both English and French meetings.

Free Anglo-American Counseling Treatment and Support (FACTS): ☎44 93 16 69. HIV/AIDS information line. Open M and W 6-10pm.

Doctor: SOS Médecins, ☎47 07 77 77. Makes house calls.

Dentist: SOS Dentaire, 87 bd. Port-Royal (☎40 21 82 88). RER: Port-Royal. Open daily 9am-6pm and 8:30-11:45pm. No walk-ins.

Eyes: SOS Oeil, ☎40 92 93 94. Open daily 9am-5pm.

Poison: ☎40 05 48 48. In French, but some English assistance is available.

Rape: SOS Viol, ☎08 00 05 95 95. Open M-F 10am-7pm.

English-Language Crisis Line: SOS Help!, ☎46 21 46 46. Open daily 3-11pm.

Pharmacies: Look for the neon green crosses that indicate pharmacies all over the city. Call the police for the **pharmacies de garde,** the rotating pharmacies in different *arrondissements* that handle emergencies.

Medical Services:

American Hospital of Paris, 63 bd. Hugo, Neuilly (☎46 41 25 25). M: Port Maillot, then bus #82 to the end of the line.

Hertford British Hospital (Hôpital Franco-Britannique de Paris), 3 rue Barbès (☎46 39 22 22), in the Parisian suburb of Levallois-Perret. M: Anatole France. Specializes in gynecology. Has some English-speaking doctors.

Hôpital Bichat, 46 rue Henri Buchard, 18ème (☎40 25 80 80). M: Port St-Ouen. Emergency services.

Internet Access: Internet is not hard to find in Paris; cheap Internet, however, is scarce. Some establishments bill by the minute (usually €0.15 per min.), or by the hour (€2-6). Hotels and hostels tend to charge more. If you are traveling with a computer with wireless capabilities, take a trip to McDonald's, where customers can access the Wi-Fi network for as long as they desire (in most locations). Many cafés also have Wi-Fi access.

FRENCH CONNECTION

If you choose to stay in Paris for longer than a few days, it can become inconvenient (and expensive) to have to trek to the nearest Internet café to get your fill of Google and email. While investing in Wi-Fi for your apartment is only advisable for those who, well, have an apartment, there are ways to avoid spending exorbitant amounts just to stay in touch.

At many cafés, including the trendy La Sancerre in the 18ème (p. 110), customers can tap into a "free" Wi-Fi connection as long as they buy something to eat or drink. In theory, you could try to sit unnoticed and connect on the down-low, but some places foil would-be Wi-Fi pirates by mandating the purchase of an access card. Check out www.hotcafe.fr, a site that lists over thirty Wi-Fi cafés, for more information.

Your best bet, however, is to find a McDonald's. Many branches of the fast-food giant offer absolutely free Wi-Fi inside. Look for the Wi-Fi sticker on the window (or just go in and try, and if it doesn't work, pretend you came for the atmosphere). No purchase is necessary.

Hostels that offer free Internet on common computers are also available for those without a laptop. It is important to check before you book, however, as some cheaper hostels charge rather high rates for a connection.

Post Office: There are several post offices in each *arrondissement.* Most are open M-F 8am-7pm, Sa 8am-noon.

Federal Express, 63 bd. Haussmann, 8ème (☎40 06 90 16). Call M-F before 5pm for pickup. Open M-Sa 9am-7pm, dropoff by 4:45pm.

Poste du Louvre, 52 rue du Louvre, 1er (☎40 28 20 40). M: Louvre. Open daily 24hr.

PARIS BY NEIGHBORHOOD

SEINE ISLANDS (4ÈME)

It's appropriate that all distance points in France are measured from *kilomètre zéro,* a circular sundial in front of Notre Dame on Ile de la Cité. After all, if any place can be called the heart of Paris, it is this slip in the Seine. Ile de la Cité is situated in the very center of the city and at the center of the Ile de France, the region surrounding Paris. Construction of the **Cathedral of Notre Dame** began here in 1163 and—along with other historically significant buildings, including **Ste-Chapelle** and **La Conciergerie**—ensured that the island would remain a center of Parisian religious, political, and cultural life—and, now, thrive as a major center of tourism.

Ile St-Louis had less illustrious beginnings. Originally composed of two small islands—Ile aux Vaches (Cow Island) and Ile de Notre Dame—Ile St-Louis was considered suitable for duels, cows, and little else throughout the Middle Ages. In 1267, the area was renamed for Louis IX after he departed for the Crusades. Ile St-Louis still retains a certain remoteness from the rest of Paris. Older residents say *"Je vais à Paris"* (I'm going to Paris) when leaving by one of the four bridges linking Ile St-Louis and the mainland. All in all, the island looks remarkably similar to its 17th-century self, retaining a rich depth of history as well as a genteel tranquility. While tourists might clog the streets on weekends, the island is nonetheless an easily walkable haven of boutiques, specialty food shops, and art galleries.

CHÂTELET-LES-HALLES AND OPÉRA (1ER, 2ÈME)

Châtelet-les-Halles (CHAT-a-lay-lays-all) is home to much of Paris's royal history, and the ritzy area lives up to its past. Its most famous sight, the **Louvre,** was home to French kings for four centuries, and the surrounding **Jardin des Tuileries** was redesigned in 1660 by Louis XIV's favored architect, André Le Nôtre. Today, the bedchambers and dining rooms of the *ancien régime* house the world's finest art, and the Sun King's prized gardens are a playground for sunbathers, children, and tourists alike. However, royalty still dominates Châtelet-les-Halles: Chanel, Cartier, and the Ritz hold court here in the imposing **place Vendôme.** Less glamorous souvenir shops crowd **rue du Rivoli** and **Les Halles,** while elegant boutiques line **rue St-Honoré,** also home to the Comédie Française, where actors preserve the tradition of Molière. Farther west, jazz clubs rule the night on **rue des Lombards.**

> **LET'S NOT GO.** Although the 1er is one of the safest regions of Paris above ground, the area's Metro stops (Châtelet and Les Halles) are dangerous and best avoided at night.

The Opéra area has a long history of trade and commerce, from the lovely 19th-century **passages** (prototypical shopping malls) to the **Bourse,** where stocks have been traded for hundreds of years. The oldest and most enduring trade of all—prostitution—has thrived on **rue St-Denis** since the Middle Ages. **Rue Montorgeuil** is lined with old-fashioned *boulangeries* and other food shops and cafés. The area known as **Etienne-Marcel** bursts with fabulously cheap clothing and great sales in more expensive stores—come here to get outfitted for wild nights of clubbing. For those tired of searching for the perfect top and up for a laugh, the Opéra Comique, now the **Théâtre Musicale,** is between bd. des Italiens and rue de Richelieu.

THE MARAIS (3ÈME, 4ÈME)

The Marais is Paris's comeback kid. Nothing more than a bog—*marais* literally means "swamp"—until monks drained the area in the 13th century, the Marais became the city's center of fashionable living when Henri IV built the glorious **Place des Vosges** in the early 1800s. Under Louis XV, however, the fashionable crowds fled to St-Honoré and St-Germain, and slums and tenements began to replace the elegant *hôtels* during the Revolution. In the last 30 years, gentrification and construction have restored the Marais's royal lustre.

Today, once-palatial mansions have become exquisite museums; tiny, twisting streets have been taken over by hip bars, avant-garde galleries, and some of the city's most intriguing boutiques. Home to the center of Paris's Jewish population, **Rue des Rosiers,** in the heart of the 4ème, has superb kosher delicatessens; Middle Eastern and Eastern European restaurants also abound. The Marais is unquestionably the center of GLBT Paris, with its hub at the intersection of **rue Ste-Croix de la Bretonnerie** and **rue Vieille-du-Temple;** its clubs stay lively even on Sundays. Recent heavy tourism has encroached upon the Marais's eclectic personality, threatening to reduce it to commercial blandness. Yet the district retains its signature charm: an accessible, fun, and friendly mix of old and new, queer and straight, cheap and chic, classic and alternative, hip and historic. No Paris pilgrim should miss it.

LET'S NOT GO. Be alert in the northern Marais at night. Though galleries, boutiques, and restaurants have started to move into the area, it's not as consistently occupied by crowds as the Marais's southern half and can feel eerily isolated. Don't walk to bars and clubs alone.

LATIN QUARTER AND ST-GERMAIN (5ÈME, 6ÈME)

This area is known as the *Quartier Latin,* named for the language used in the 5ème's prestigious *lycées* and universities prior to 1798. The 5ème has been in the intellectual thick of things since the founding of the **Sorbonne** in 1263, and its hot-blooded student population has played a role in uprisings from the French Revolution to the May 1968 insurrection. In the 6ème, cafés on the legendary **boulevard St-Germain** were the stomping grounds of Hemingway, Sartre, Picasso, Camus, and just about everyone else in Paris during the first half of the 20th century.

While the reasons aren't easy to pin down—some cite the replacement of the old cobblestones, used by students as projectiles in the old days—it's a fact that the Latin Quarter has lost its rebellious vigor. Yet while areas like **boulevard St-Michel** (the boundary between the 5ème and 6ème), with their chain stores and hordes of camera-toting tourists, are notable victims of commodification, the smaller student quarter byways hold fast to their progressive, multiethnic tone. The bars in this area are some of the best in Paris, and it's difficult to walk a block without running into a bookshop. The Latin Quarter is also the defiantly beating heart of that quintessentially Parisian passion: art house cinema. The area's final claim to fame is as a great place to walk; **place de la Contrescarpe** and **rue Mouffetard,** both in the 5ème, are good for people-watching, and the Mouff has one of the liveliest street markets in Paris. As for food, you'll probably have to drop some cash if you want more than a *crêpe;* the area's accommodations aren't any more economically forgiving. However, if money is no object, there is terrific boutique shopping to be had to the west and south of Eglise St-Germain-des-prés.

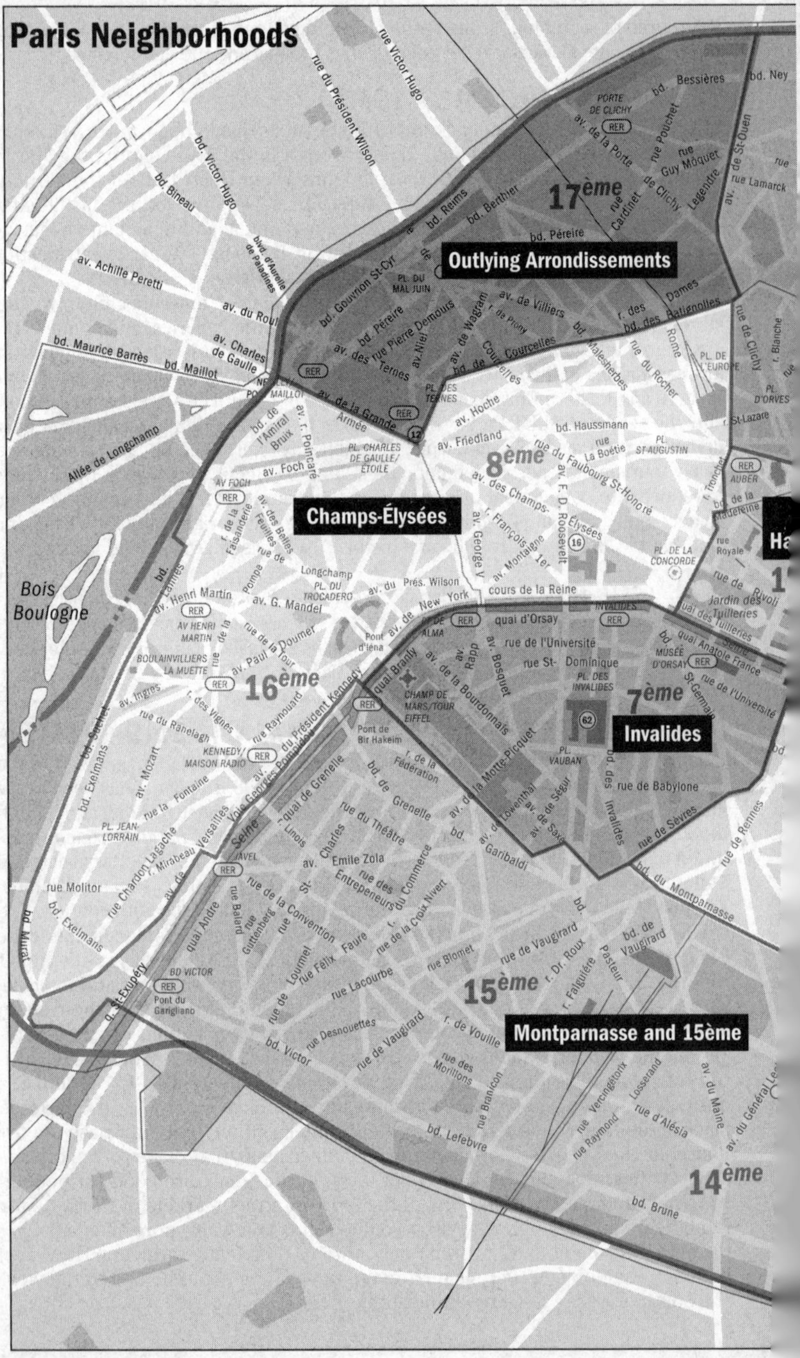
Paris Neighborhoods
Outlying Arrondissements
Champs-Élysées
Invalides
Montparnasse and 15ème
17ème
8ème
16ème
7ème
15ème
14ème
Bois Boulogne
Seine
PL. CHARLES DE GAULLE/ ÉTOILE
PL. DE LA CONCORDE
PL. DU TROCADERO
CHAMP DE MARS/TOUR EIFFEL
PL. DES INVALIDES
PL. VAUBAN
PORTE DE CLICHY
PL. DU MAL JUIN
PL. DES TERNES
PL. DE L'EUROPE
PL. ST-AUGUSTIN
MUSÉE D'ORSAY
KENNEDY/ MAISON RADIO
PL. JEAN-LORRAIN
BD VICTOR
Pont du Garigliano
Pont de Bir Hakeim
Pont d'Iéna
av. des Champs-Élysées
av. Foch
av. de la Grande Armée
av. Victor Hugo
bd. Haussmann
quai d'Orsay
rue de Vaugirard
bd. du Montparnasse
bd. Lefebvre
bd. Brune
bd. Victor
rue de Rivoli
Jardin des Tuileries
bd. Exelmans
bd. Murat
bd. Suchet
Allée de Longchamp
av. de New York
av. du Président Kennedy
rue de la Convention
rue de Sèvres
rue de Babylone
av. Bosquet
rue de Grenelle
cours de la Reine
rue du Faubourg St-Honoré
bd. Malesherbes
bd. Berthier
bd. Bessières
bd. Péreire
av. de Wagram
av. de Villiers
av. Hoche
av. Friedland
av. Kléber
av. Henri Martin
av. G. Mandel
av. Paul Doumer
rue de Passy
rue du Ranelagh
av. Mozart
rue La Fontaine
av. de Versailles
rue Molitor
quai André Citroën
rue Lecourbe
rue de Rennes
av. du Maine
av. du Général Leclerc
rue d'Alésia
rue Raymond Losserand
av. Émile Zola
bd. de Grenelle
bd. Garibaldi
av. de Suffren
av. de Ségur
av. de Saxe
av. de la Motte-Picquet
av. de la Bourdonnais
av. Rapp
quai Branly
rue de l'Université
rue St-Dominique
bd. St-Germain
quai Anatole France
rue Royale
bd. de la Madeleine
rue de Clichy
rue Blanche
av. de St-Ouen
rue Lamarck
rue Legendre
av. de Clichy
rue Cardinet
rue de Rome
rue du Rocher
r. Tronchet
bd. des Batignolles
rue St-Lazare
av. Montaigne
av. George V
av. F. D. Roosevelt
cours Albert 1er
rue la Boétie
av. de la Porte de Clichy
rue Pouchet
rue Guy Môquet
bd. de Courcelles
rue de Prony
av. Niel
rue Pierre Demours
av. des Ternes
bd. Gouvion St-Cyr
av. Charles de Gaulle
av. du Roule
av. Achille Peretti
bd. Maurice Barrès
bd. Maillot
bd. Bineau
bd. Victor Hugo
rue du Président Wilson
rue Victor Hugo
bd. de l'Amiral Bruix
av. Raymond Poincaré
bd. Lannes
rue de la Pompe
rue de Longchamp
av. du Prés. Wilson
rue des Vignes
rue Raynouard
rue Chardon Lagache
r. Mirabeau
rue Balard
rue de Lourmel
rue Félix Faure
rue St-Charles
rue des Entrepreneurs
rue du Commerce
rue de la Croix Nivert
rue Blomet
rue Desnouettes
r. de Vouillé
rue des Morillons
rue Brancion
r. Falguière
bd. Pasteur
rue Vercingétorix
bd. de Vaugirard
r. Dr. Roux
av. de Lowenthal
bd. des Invalides
rue Linois
rue du Théâtre
r. de la Fédération
quai de Grenelle
Voie Georges Pompidou
RER

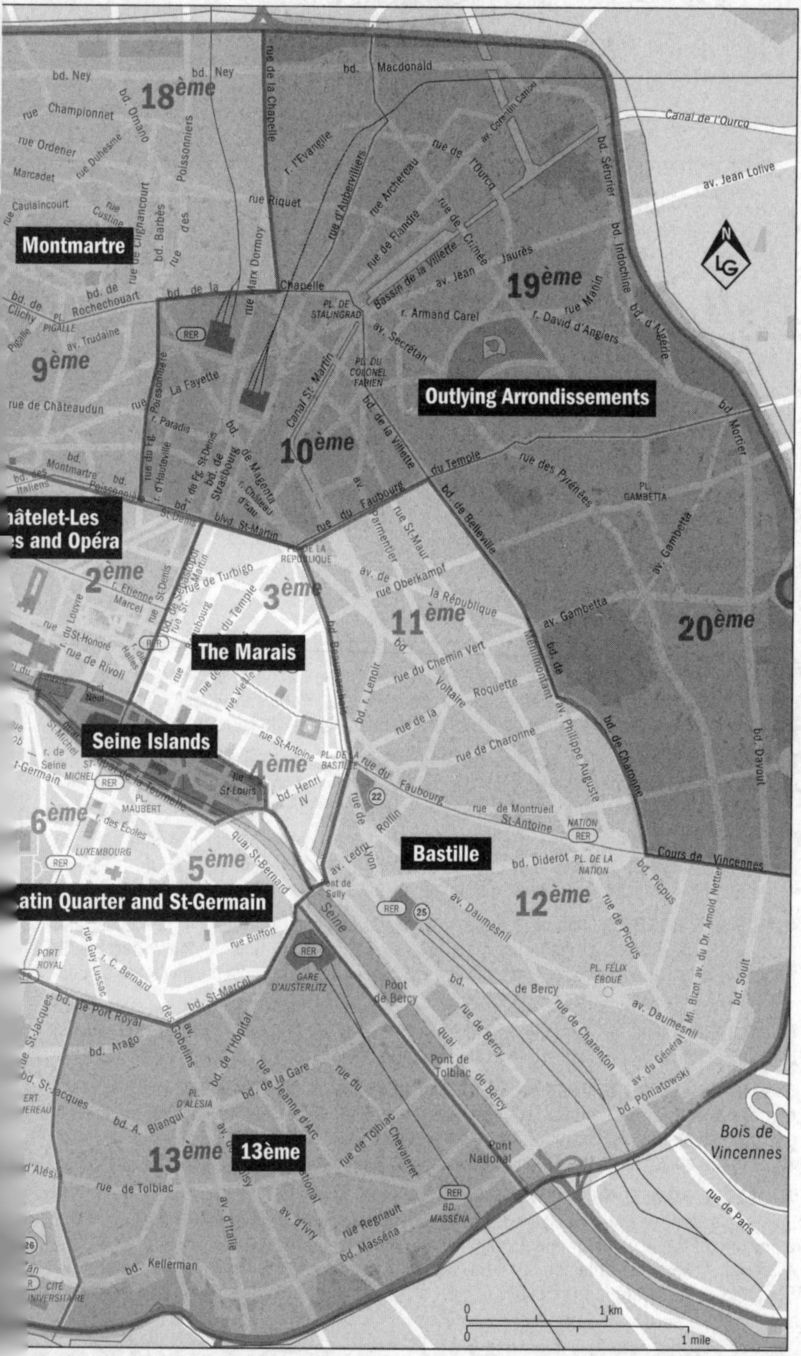
Montmartre
Châtelet-Les Halles and Opéra
The Marais
Seine Islands
Latin Quarter and St-Germain
Outlying Arrondissements
Bastille
13ème
18ème
19ème
9ème
10ème
2ème
3ème
11ème
20ème
4ème
6ème
5ème
12ème
13ème
bd. Ney
bd. Macdonald
Canal de l'Ourcq
av. Jean Lolive
rue de la Chapelle
bd. de la Chapelle
bd. de Rochechouart
PL. PIGALLE
av. Trudaine
rue de Châteaudun
PL. DE STALINGRAD
Bassin de la Villette
av. Jean Jaurès
r. Armand Carel
r. David d'Angiers
av. Secrétan
PL. DU COLONEL FABIEN
Canal St-Martin
bd. de la Villette
bd. de Magenta
bd. de Strasbourg
bd. Montmartre
bd. des Italiens
bd. Poissonnière
bd. St-Denis
blvd. St-Martin
PL. DE LA REPUBLIQUE
rue du Faubourg du Temple
bd. de Belleville
rue des Pyrénées
PL. GAMBETTA
av. Gambetta
bd. Mortier
rue Oberkampf
rue du Chemin Vert
rue de la Roquette
rue de Charonne
bd. de Ménilmontant
av. Philippe Auguste
bd. de Charonne
bd. Davout
rue de Turbigo
rue St-Honoré
rue de Rivoli
rue St-Antoine
PL. DE LA BASTILLE
rue du Faubourg St-Antoine
rue de Montreuil
NATION
PL. DE LA NATION
bd. Diderot
Cours de Vincennes
bd. Picpus
rue de Picpus
av. Daumesnil
PL. FÉLIX ÉBOUÉ
bd. de Bercy
rue de Charenton
bd. Poniatowski
Bois de Vincennes
rue de Paris
bd. St-Germain
bd. St-Michel
PL. MAUBERT
r. des Écoles
LUXEMBOURG
quai St-Bernard
Seine
rue Buffon
PORT ROYAL
bd. de Port Royal
bd. St-Marcel
GARE D'AUSTERLITZ
Pont de Bercy
Pont de Tolbiac
Pont National
quai de Bercy
bd. Arago
bd. St-Jacques
PL. D'ALESIA
bd. A. Blanqui
av. des Gobelins
bd. de l'Hôpital
bd. de la Gare
rue de Tolbiac
rue du Chevaleret
av. d'Italie
av. d'Ivry
rue Regnault
bd. Masséna
BD. MASSÉNA
bd. Kellerman
CITÉ UNIVERSITAIRE
RER
0
1 km
0
1 mile

START: St-Paul Metro station

FINISH: Rambuteau Metro station

DISTANCE: 2.1km/1¼ mi.

DURATION: 4hr.

WHEN TO GO: In the morning.

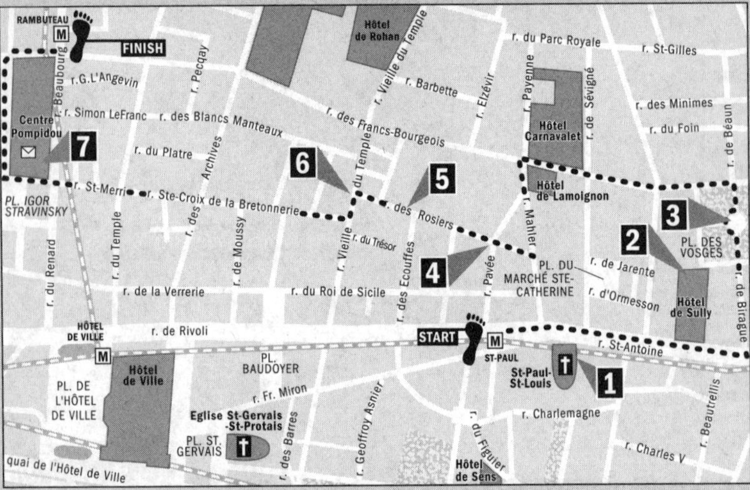

1. EGLISE ST-PAUL-ST-LOUIS. Exit the Metro station and walk east toward the large dark church. Inside are paintings of kings Clovis, Charlemagne, Robert the Pious, and St-Louis. The site once held the embalmed hearts of Louis XIII and Louis XIV (p. 131).

2. HÔTEL DE SULLY. Walk down rue St-Antoine toward pl. de la Bastille. You will see the *place*'s Colonne de Juillet marking the spot of the famous prison. A great example of how aristocratic wealth transformed this swampy area, Hôtel de Sully boasts a private *orangerie.*

3. PLACE DES VOSGES. Continue in the direction of pl. de la Bastille and turn left onto rue de Birague, which leads directly onto pl. des Vosges. Built by Henri IV in 1605, the *place* attracted aristocrats who built chic apartments nearby. Victor Hugo lived at #6.

4. RUE DES ROSIERS. Return to rue des Frances Bourgeois. Turn left on rue Mahler and right on rue des Rosiers to get to the main Jewish neighborhood. Since before World War II, when the Nazis sent over 75% of Parisian Jews to concentration camps, the city's Jewish population has been on the decline (p. 131).

5. FALAFEL. Facing off from either end of rue des Rosiers are Paris's best falafel stands: L'As du Falafel and Chez Hannah (p. 119). Both do takeout, so you can keep walking.

6. RUE VIEILLE DU TEMPLE AND RUE ST-CROIX DE LA BRETTONERIE. At the other end of rue des Rosiers, pause on rue Vieille du Temple. Enjoy Orthodox Jewish bookshops and swanky boutiques. On rue St-Croix de la Bretonnerie, trendy meets chic. The street is the epicenter of the Marais's thriving gay community (p. 131).

7. CENTRE POMPIDOU. Follow rue St-Croix la Brettonerie. This modern museum's controversial design contrasts with the streets around it. Enjoy one of the world's foremost collections of contemporary art and a fabulous view from the top. Exit the complex at the north to the Rambuteau Metro station (p. 149).

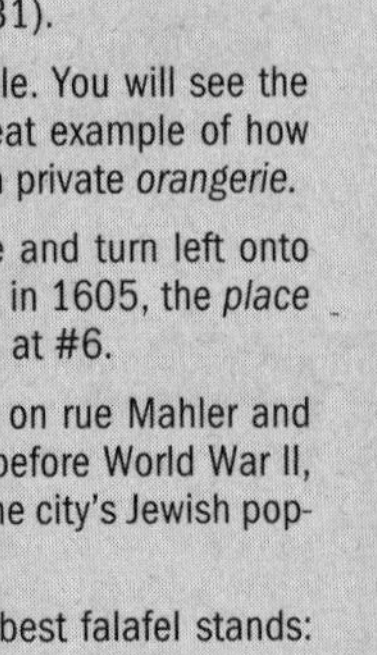

INVALIDES (7ÈME)

Between the grass of the **Champ de Mars** and the fashionable side streets surrounding **rue de Sèvres,** the Invalides area offers both the most touristy and the most intimate sights in Paris. The area known as Invalides became Paris's most elegant residential district in the 18th century, although many of the neighborhood's stunning residences have been converted to foreign embassies. Though the 1889 completion of the **Eiffel Tower** at the river's edge sparked outrage, it has since secured Invalides's reputation as a Parisian landmark. The **National Assembly** and the **Hotel National des Invalides** add historical substance and traditional French character to this section of the Left Bank. While the area's accommodations are uniformly expensive, vigilant budget-hungry travelers will be rewarded with cheap eats, particularly on **rue Cler** between rue de Grenelle and av. de la Motte-Picquet.

CHAMPS-ELYSÉES (8ÈME, 16ÈME)

The Champs-Elysées area is past its prime. Its boulevards are still lined with the vast mansions, expensive shops, and grandiose monuments that keep tourists coming, but there's little sense of movement or style. The **Champs-Elysées** itself, once synonymous with fashion, now houses charmless establishments ranging from cheap to exorbitant. Much of the neighborhood is occupied by office buildings and car dealerships; these areas are comatose after dark. Only the Champs itself throbs late into the night, thanks to flashy nightclubs, cinemas, and the droves of tourists that spill onto its sidewalks. A stroll along **avenue Montaigne,** on **rue du Faubourg St-Honoré,** or around the **Madeleine** will give a taste of what life in Paris is like for those with money to burn. While it's usually the case that low prices mean low quality here—particularly for accommodations—there are a few good restaurant deals to be found. The northern part of the neighborhood, near the **Parc Monceau,** is a lovely, quiet area for walking, as are the manicured, tree-lined streets of **Passy, Auteuil,** and **Chaillot,** southwest of the Champs. This area also offers some of the best views of the Eiffel Tower, framed by immaculate Art Nouveau and Art Deco architecture. An impressive number of **museums** showcase everything from cutting-edge contemporary art to second-century Asian statuary.

MONTMARTRE (9ÈME, 18ÈME)

The southern Montmartre area is a diagram of Paris's cultural extremes. The area bordering Châtelet-les-Halles boasts the high art of the magnificent **Opéra Garnier** and the *haute couture* of swanky department stores **Galeries Lafayette** and **Au Printemps.** The middle of the district, however, offers a striking contrast: porn shops, X-rated cinemas, and often aggressive prostitution characterize the neon-lighted area known as **Pigalle.** Separating these two sectors is a sleepy, residential neighborhood. There are plenty of hotels, but many to the north are used for the local flesh trade. Nicer but not-so-cheap hotels are available near the respectable and central bd. des Italiens and bd. Montmartre.

Upper Montmartre is a mix of nostalgic history (rue Lepic), pseudo-artistic schmaltz (pl. du Tertre), upscale bohemia (above rue des Abbesses), and sleaze (along bd. de Clichy). The rather strenuous climb (or relaxing ride on the funicular) up to the **Basilique du Sacré-Coeur** is worth it for the sprawling panoramas of the city. The northwestern corner retains some village charm, with breezy, cobbled streets speckled with interesting shops and cafés. At dusk, gas lamps illuminate the stairways that lead up the hillside to the basilica. Hotel rates rise as you climb the hill to Sacré-Coeur. Downhill and south at seedy pl. Pigalle, accommodations tend to rent by the hour.

LET'S NOT GO. **Place Pigalle** and **M: Barbès-Rochechouart** are notorious for prostitution and drugs, both of which become apparent at an early hour. The area is heavily policed, but travelers (particularly young women and those traveling alone) should still exercise caution. At night **M: Abesse** is safer than **M: Anvers, M: Pigalle,** and **M: Barbès-Rochechouart.** Always be careful in the central Montmartre district.

BASTILLE (11ÈME, 12ÈME)

As its name attests, the Bastille (bah-STEEL) area is most famous for hosting the Revolution's kick-off at the **Bastille** prison on July 14, 1789. The French still storm this neighborhood nightly in search of the latest cocktail, culinary innovation, or up-and-coming artist. Five Metro lines converge at M: République and three at M: Bastille, making the Bastille district a transport hub and mammoth center of action—the hangout of the young and fun (and frequently drunk). The 1989 opening of the glassy **Opéra Bastille** on the bicentennial of the Revolution was supposed to breathe new cultural life into the area, but the party atmosphere has yet to give way to galleries and string quartets. Today, with numerous bars along **rue de Lappe,** international dining options on **rue de la Roquette,** and young designer boutiques throughout, the Bastille is a great area for unwinding after a day at the museums—even if the neighborhood's museums themselves are less than impressive. Indeed, the area is still a little rough, and the wide commercial boulevards that run through Bastille lack the refined charm of many Paris *arrondissements.*

North of the Bastille on **rue Oberkampf** and **rue Ménilmontant,** eclectic neighborhood bars provide the perfect end to a pub crawl. Budget accommodations also proliferate in the area. **Place de la Nation,** farther south, was the setting for Louis XIV's wedding in 1660 and the site of revolutionary fervor in 1830 and 1848. Today, this part of the Bastille district borrows youthful momentum from the neighboring 4ème and 11ème *arrondissements.* Its northwestern fringes are funky—the **Viaduc des Arts, rue de la Roquette,** and **rue du Faubourg St-Antoine** are lined with galleries and stores—and its core is working class, with a large immigrant population.

THIRTEENTH ARRONDISSEMENT

LET'S NOT GO. While the area is generally safe during the day, **place de la République** and **boulevard Voltaire** are best avoided after sunset. Also be careful around **Gare de Lyon** all the time, especially at night, and near the sleazy nightlife at **avenue du Maine's** northern end.

Until the 20th century, the 13ème was one of Paris's poorest *arrondissements,* with conditions so terrible that Victor Hugo set *Les Misérables* in parts of the neighborhood. Traversed by the **Bièvre,** a stagnant stream clogged with industrial refuse, the 13ème was also the city's worst-smelling district.

The 20th and 21st centuries have brought many changes to the 13ème, olfactory and otherwise. In 1910, the Bièvre was filled in. Environmentalists eventually won a campaign to close the neighborhood's tanneries and paper factories. The construction that began with Mitterrand's ultra-modern **Bibliothèque de France** in 1996 has continued with the MK2 entertainment complex and other developments associated with **ZAC (Zone d'Aménagement Concerté),** a project that will make the banks of the 13ème into the largest cultural center in Paris. The area is also home to several immigrant communities residing in the thriving **Chinatown.**

MONTPARNASSE AND THE FIFTEENTH ARRONDISSEMENT (14ÈME, 15ÈME)

The Montparnasse area is no longer haunted by such legendary visitors as Hemingway, Modigliani, and Henry Miller, but the area's continued affordability and well entrenched café culture still attract young artists and students. Restaurants (of both the cheap and Lost Generation-chic varieties), cafés, and artists' havens make Montparnasse well worth a visit.

Unlike its neighbor to the east, the 15ème has never been a legendary area. Today, the city's most populous *arrondissement* has been predominantly middle-class for decades. The modern **Parc André Citroën** attracts families from all over Paris on weekends, but aside from the park, the 15ème has no tourist sights to speak of, and its atmosphere is often crowded, busy, and—around **Gare Montparnasse**—very industrial (a.k.a. ugly). As a result, the 15ème is one of Paris's least touristed areas, and streetwise travelers can benefit from low room rates and affordable restaurants. Locals have their pick among the many shops on **rue du Commerce,** the cafés at the corner of **rue de la Convention** and **rue de Vaugirard,** and the specialty shops along **av. Emile Zola.**

OUTLYING ARRONDISSEMENTS (10ÈME, 17ÈME, 19ÈME, 20ÈME)

LET'S NOT GO. Especially at night, be careful at the border of the 17ème and the 18ème near pl. de Clichy, in the emptier northwestern corner of the 19ème, along rue David d'Angiers, bd. Indochine, av. Corentin Cariou, and by the *Portes* in the 19ème.

The 10ème, 17ème, 19ème, and 20ème *arrondissements* comprise Paris's outskirts. All are good areas to find budget accommodations and tasty cheap meals, but because they are far from the city's center and can be seedy at night, they rarely make it onto tourists' itineraries.

The 17ème is a diverse district where bourgeois turns working class and back again within a block. In general, the southern and eastern parts of the *arrondissement* share the aristocratic bearing of the neighboring 8ème and 16ème, while the western half resembles the more tawdry 18ème and Pigalle. Thanks in large part to its multicultural population, the 17ème offers a fabulous variety of restaurants across the spectrum of prices. The **Village Batignolles** is a nice change of pace from central Paris and a great place for a stroll—during daylight hours. Upscale neighborhood bars like **L'Endroit** cater to stylish young crowds.

The 19ème and 20ème, both primarily working class, have recently flourished as new centers of Parisian bohemia. Between the romantic **Parc des Buttes Chaumont** and the famed **Cimetière du Père Lachaise,** clusters of performance spaces, artsy cafés, and galleries have joined the neighborhood's ethnic eateries, shops, and markets. Home to a population of Asian, Greek, North African, Russian, and Jewish communities, these *arrondissements* include Paris's most dynamic neighborhoods.

ACCOMMODATIONS

Accommodations in Paris are expensive—you don't need *Let's Go* to tell you that. At the absolute minimum, expect to pay €20 for a dorm bed in a hostel and €28 for a single in a hotel. It is more economical for groups of two or more to stay in a **hotel** rather than a hostel, since hotels charge by the room and not per person.

> **TIP** **BEFORE YOU GET HOSTEL.** If you arrive in Paris without a hostel reservation—or if you arrive in Paris with a hostel reservation that falls through—head for the information desk at a major train station. The employees there will often agree to call hostels and book a room for you.

Paris's **hostels** generally don't charge for sheets and tend to have flexible maximum stays. The city has six HI hostels, which offer discounts to members (see **Hostels,** p. 46). The rest of Paris's dorm-style beds are either private hostels or quieter *foyers* (student dorms). In cheaper hotels, few rooms have private baths. Rooms fill quickly after morning check-out, so arrive early or reserve ahead—from one week to one month or more in summer. Most hostels and *foyers* include the **taxe de séjour** (€0.10-2 per person per day) in listed prices, but some do not.

Hidden gems are extremely hard to come by in Paris; chances are you will get what you pay for. The cheapest accommodations are found in the outer *arrondissements*, particularly in the **13ème, 14ème,** and **15ème.** There are also many cheap hotels in the **Marais,** some with old-fashioned character.

BY PRICE

CHO Châtelet-Les Halles and Opéra. **Seine** Seine Islands. **LQ** Latin Quarter and Saint-Germain. **Montparnasse** Montparnasse and 15ème. **Out** Outlying Arrondissements.

€18-30 (❷)	
Aloha Hostel (115)	Montparnasse
Aub. de Jeun. "Le D'Artagnan" (115)	Out
Aub. de Jeun. "Jules Ferry" (114)	Bastille
CISP "Kellerman" (114)	13ème
CISP "Ravel" (114)	Bastille
Ctr. Int'l (BVJ) Paris Louvre (112)	CHO
Ctr. Int'l (BVJ) Paris Quartier Latin (112)	LQ
Hôtel Caulaincourt (114)	Montmartre
Hôtel des Jeunes (MIJE) (111)	Marais
Hôtel des Médicis (112)	LQ
Hôtel Palace (116)	Out
Hôtel Tiquetonne (111)	CHO
Ouest Hôtel (115)	Montparnasse
Three Ducks Hostel (115)	Montparnasse
Le Village Hostel (114)	Montmartre
Woodstock Hostel (113)	Montmartre
Young and Happy Hostel (111)	LQ
€33-42 (❸)	
Hôtel Esmeralda (112)	LQ
Hôtel de Milan (116)	Out
Hôtel Montebello (112)	Invalides
Hôtel Picard (111)	Marais
Hôtel Printemps (115)	Montparnasse
Hôtel du Séjour (111)	Marais
Hôtel Stella (112)	LQ
€43-60 (❹)	
Hôtel de l'Aveyron (114)	Bastille
Hôtel de Blois (115)	Montparnasse
Hôtel Marignan (112)	LQ
Perfect Hôtel (113)	Montmartre
Rhin et Danube (116)	Out
OVER €60(❺)	
Grand Hôtel Jeanne d'Arc (111)	Marais
Hôtel Beaumarchais (114)	Bastille
Hôtel Boileau (113)	Champs-Elysées
Hôtel Eiffel Rive Gauche (113)	Invalides
Hôtel Europe-Liège (113)	Champs-Elysées
Hôtel St-Jacques (112)	LQ

CHÂTELET-LES-HALLES AND OPÉRA

Centre International de Paris (BVJ): Paris Louvre, 20 rue Jean-Jacques Rousseau (☎53 00 90 90; www.bvjhotel.com). M: Louvre or Palais-Royal. From M: Louvre, take rue du Louvre away from the river, turn left on rue St-Honoré and right on rue Jean-Jacques Rousseau. This large hostel draws an international crowd and offers a central common area with a skylight, brass lanterns, and *brasserie*-style tables. Bright, dorm-style rooms with 2-8 beds per room. English spoken. Breakfast and showers included. Lockers €2. Internet access €1 per 10min. Reception 24hr. Guests must be ages 18-35. Reservations recommended 2 weeks in advance. Rooms held for 5-10min. after your expected check-in time; call if you'll be late. Dorms €27; doubles €29. ❷

Hôtel Tiquetonne, 6 rue Tiquetonne (☎42 36 94 58; fax 42 36 02 94). M: Etienne-Marcel. Walk against traffic on rue de Turbigo; turn left on rue Tiquetonne. Located near Marché Montorgueil and rue St-Denis's sex shops. The rooms are generously sized, considering the ritzy area and low price. Elevator. Breakfast €6. Hall showers €6. Closed Aug. and 1 week at Christmas. Reservations recommended 1 month in advance. Singles €30, with shower €40; doubles €50. AmEx/MC/V. ❷

THE MARAIS

Hôtel des Jeunes (MIJE) (☎42 74 23 45; www.mije.com). Books beds in Le Fourcy, Le Fauconnier, and Maubuisson (below), 3 small hostels on cobblestone streets in beautiful old Marais residences recognized as historical 17th-century monuments. Few 5-star hotels occupy such gorgeous buildings. No smoking. English spoken. The restaurant at Le Fourcy offers a main course with drink (€8.50, lunch only) and 3-course "hosteler special" (€11). Breakfast, in-room shower, and sheets included (no towels). Public phones and free lockers (with a €1 deposit). Internet €0.10 per min. with €0.50 initial connection fee. Max. stay 7 days. Reception 7am-1am. Lockout noon-3pm. Curfew 1am; notify in advance if coming back later. Quiet hours after 10pm. Arrive before noon the 1st day of reservation (call in advance if you'll be late). Groups of 10 or more may reserve a year in advance. Individuals can reserve months ahead online and 2-3 weeks ahead by phone. MIJE membership required (€2.50). 4- to 9-bed dorms €28; singles €43; doubles €66; triples €87; quads €108. Cash only. ❷

Maubuisson, 12 rue des Barres. M: Hôtel de Ville or Pont Marie. From M: Pont Marie, walk against traffic on rue de l'Hôtel-de-Ville and turn right on rue des Barres. A half-timbered former girls' convent on a quiet street by the St-Gervais monastery. Accommodates more individual travelers than groups, as there are only singles, doubles, triples, and quads.

Le Fourcy, 6 rue de Fourcy. M: St-Paul or Pont Marie. From M: St-Paul, walk against traffic down rue St-Antoine and turn left on rue de Fourcy. Hostel surrounds a large, social courtyard—think miniature Tuileries—ideal for picnicking.

Le Fauconnier, 11 rue du Fauconnier. M: St-Paul or Pont Marie. From M: St-Paul, take rue du Prevôt, turn left on rue Charlemagne, then right on rue du Fauconnier. Ivy-covered, sunny building steps away from the Seine and Ile St-Louis.

Grand Hôtel Jeanne d'Arc, 3 rue de Jarente (☎48 87 62 11; www.hoteljeannedarc.com). From M: St-Paul, walk against traffic on rue de Rivoli and turn left on rue de Sévigné, then right on rue de Jarente. Gorgeous, well-appointed rooms with shower, toilet, TV, and windows overlooking a peaceful street. Beautiful mosaic mirror in the reception area. 1 wheelchair-accessible double on ground fl. English spoken. Breakfast €6. Reserve 3 months in advance by email or phone with credit card. Singles €60-84; doubles €84-97; triples €116; quads €146. MC/V. ❺

Hôtel du Séjour, 36 rue du Grenier St-Lazare (☎48 87 40 36). From M: Etienne-Marcel, follow traffic on rue Etienne-Marcel, which becomes rue du Grenier St-Lazare. 1 block from Les Halles and the Centre Pompidou, this family-run hotel offers 20 bright, clean rooms and a very warm welcome. Showers €4. Reception 7:30am-10:30pm. Reservations recommended 1 month in advance. Singles €35; doubles €47, with shower and toilet €58. Extra person €22. Cash only. ❸

Hôtel Picard, 26 rue de Picardie (☎48 87 53 82; fax 48 57 62 56). M: République. Follow bd. du Temple and turn right on rue Charlot. Take the 1st right onto rue de Franche Comté, which becomes rue de Picardie. Superb location barely makes up for decaying stairs and hallways. TVs in rooms with showers. Breakfast €4.50. Hall showers €3 (1 shower per day included with stay). Reserve 2-3 weeks ahead. Singles €37, with shower €56, with shower and toilet €64; doubles €47/72/94; triples €114. 5% discount with *Let's Go.* MC/V. ❸

LATIN QUARTER AND ST-GERMAIN

Young and Happy (Y&H) Hostel, 80 rue Mouffetard (☎47 07 47 07; www.youngandhappy.fr). M: Monge. Cross rue Gracieuse and take rue Ortolan to rue Mouffetard. A funky, lively, and friendly hostel. Laid-back staff and clean–if basic–rooms, some with showers and toilets. Kitchen. English spoken. Breakfast included. Sheets €2.50 with €5 deposit, towels €1. Internet access €2 per 30min. Lockout 11am-4pm. 4- to 10-bed dorms €23; doubles €26. Jan.-Mar. €2 discount. ❷

Hôtel Stella, 41 rue Monsieur-le-Prince (☎40 51 00 25; http://site.voila.fr/hotel-stella). M: Odéon. Walk against traffic on bd. St-Germain and make a left onto rue Monsieur-le-Prince. Takes the exposed-beam look to a whole new level with centuries-old woodwork. Rooms are huge, with high ceilings and an atmosphere that makes you glad to call this place home; some even have pianos. Reserve ahead. Singles €35-45; doubles €55-65; triples €75-85; quads €85-95. ❸

Hôtel Marignan, 13 rue du Sommerard (☎43 54 63 81; www.hotel-marignan.com). From M: Maubert-Mutualité, turn left on rue des Carmes, then right on rue du Sommerard. Clean, freshly decorated rooms can sleep up to 5–almost an impossibility in the rest of Paris–but are only a great deal if more than 3 people share. English-speaking owner welcomes backpackers and families to a place with the privacy of a hotel and the friendliness of a hostel. TV upon request. Kitchen available. Breakfast included. Hall showers open until 10:45pm. Free laundry. Internet. Reserve ahead. Singles €45-60; doubles €55-85; triples €75-110; quads €85-135; quints €90-150. Cash only. ❹

Hôtel Esmeralda, 4 rue St-Julien-le-Pauvre (☎43 54 19 20). M: St-Michel. Walk along the Seine on quai St-Michel toward Notre Dame, then turn right at Parc Viviani. Antique wallpaper, ceiling beams, and red velvet create an atmosphere that totters between rustic and Victorian. Adjacent to a small park, less than a block from the Seine, and within earshot of Notre Dame's bells–the location is truly outstanding. Breakfast €6. Singles €35, with shower and toilet €65; doubles €85-120; triples €110. ❸

Hôtel des Médicis, 214 rue St-Jacques (☎43 54 14 66). RER: Luxembourg. Turn right on rue Guy-Lussac and left on rue St-Jacques. Jim Morrison slummed in room #4 for 3 weeks in 1971. You get what you pay for, and in what may be the least expensive place in the *arrondissement,* that means peeling paint, broken-down furniture, and a dose of ragged charm. Some rooms with balcony. 1 shower and toilet per fl. Reception 24hr. Singles €30; doubles €31; triples €45. ❷

Centre International de Paris (BVJ): Paris Quartier Latin, 44 rue des Bernardins (☎43 29 34 80). M: Maubert-Mutualité. Walk with traffic on bd. St-Germain and turn right on rue des Bernardins. A boisterous hostel that tries to class itself up with posters of jazz and film greats in the lobby. Large cafeteria downstairs. Microwave and TV. 100 beds. English spoken. Breakfast included. Showers in rooms. Lockers €2. Internet access €1 per 10min. Reception 24hr. Reserve at least 1 week in advance or arrive at 9am to check availability. 10-bed dorms €28; singles €40; doubles €60; quads €120. ❷

Hôtel St-Jacques, 35 rue des Ecoles (☎44 07 45 45; www.paris-hotel-stjacques.com). M: Maubert-Mutualité. Turn left on rue des Carmes, then left on rue des Ecoles and cross the road. Cary Grant filmed *Charade* here. Spacious, elegant rooms with balcony, bath, and TV come at surprisingly reasonable rates. Chandeliers and walls decorated with *trompe-l'oeil* designs give it a regal feel. English spoken. Breakfast €9-11. Free Wi-Fi. Singles €58-88; doubles €100-130; triples €160. AmEx/MC/V. ❺

INVALIDES

Hôtel Montebello, 18 rue Pierre Leroux (☎47 34 41 18; hmontebello@aol.com). M: Vaneau. Sparsely furnished but exceptionally clean rooms and a welcoming English-speaking staff. Exposed wood beams and curving stairways contribute to the hotel's distinctive atmosphere. A bit far from the 7ème's sights, but unbeatable rates for this upscale neighborhood. Breakfast served 7:30-9:30am, €4. Reservations recommended 2 weeks in advance. Singles €25-42; doubles €40-49. Extra bed €10. ❸

Hôtel Eiffel Rive Gauche, 6 rue du Gros Caillou (☎45 51 24 56; www.hotel-eiffel.com). M: Ecole Militaire. Walk up av. de la Bourdonnais, turn right onto rue de Grenelle, then left onto rue du Gros Caillou. On a quiet street. Comfortably traditional and refreshingly bright family-run hotel. Rooms have cable TV, phone, Internet jack, and bath; some have Eiffel Tower views. Breakfast buffet €9.50. Safe deposit box €3. Singles €75-115; doubles €75-125; triples €95-145; quads €105-175. Extra bed €10. MC/V. ❺

CHAMPS-ELYSÉES

Hôtel Europe-Liège, 8 rue de Moscou (☎42 94 01 51; fax 43 87 42 18). M: Liège. Turn left onto rue de Moscou; the hotel is on the right. As a rule, budget travelers will want to stay outside of the 8ème, but within the area this is the best bet. Cheerful, sparkling clean rooms and a lovely interior courtyard. Many restaurants nearby. All rooms have TV, hair dryer, phone, and shower or bath. Breakfast €7. Reservations recommended 3-4 weeks in advance, especially July-Aug. Singles €71; doubles €86. AmEx/MC/V. ❺

Hôtel Boileau, 81 rue Boileau (☎42 88 83 74; www.hotel-boileau.com). M: Exelmans. Walk down bd. Exelmans away from its curving corner and turn right on rue Boileau. A stay here will put you far away from most of Paris's sights, and while the spotless rooms come with cable TV and a telephone, they also come with peeling wallpaper. Breakfast €8.50-10. Internet available. Reservations recommended 1 month in advance June-Sept. Singles €70-77; doubles €80-95; triples €125-130. AmEx/MC/V. ❺

MONTMARTRE

Woodstock Hostel, 48 rue Rodier (☎48 78 87 76; www.woodstock.fr). M: Anvers. From the Metro, walk against traffic on pl. Anvers, turn right on av. Trudaine, and left on rue Rodier. A hippie vibe and serious case of Beatles worship contribute to the Woodstock's fun, friendly atmosphere. Rooms are basic, but the lovely terrace is worth your euro. English spoken. Breakfast included. Sheets €2.50; towels €1. Communal kitchen, safe deposit box, and Internet access (€2 per 30min.). Max. stay 2 weeks. Lockout 11am-3pm. Curfew 2am. Reserve ahead. 4- or 6-person dorms €22; doubles €50. ❷

Perfect Hôtel, 39 rue Rodier (☎42 81 18 86 or 42 81 26 19; www.paris-hostel.biz). M: Anvers. Across from the Woodstock. This hotel lives up to its name. Some rooms have balconies, and the upper floors have a beautiful view. Fun atmosphere. English-speaking staff. Phones, communal refrigerator, kitchen access, free

HELPING THROUGH HUMOR

At the age of 26, Michel Colucci adopted the name Coluche and—like so many before him with only one appellation—embarked on an entertainment career. Sure enough, the man with the razor-sharp political wit quickly became one of France's most beloved comedians. He ran for president in 1981—"I'll quit politics when politicians quit comedy"—but dropped out of the race when polls showed that he actually had a chance of winning. Before a motorcycle accident ended his life in 1986, Coluche founded the charity **Restos du Cœur** (Restaurants of the Heart), leaving a permanent mark on France.

Restos du Cœur is a network of soup kitchens and other volunteer activities. Their emphasis on fostering personal relationships between those who volunteer and those who receive aid, along with their good humor—would a comedian have it any other way?—has set them apart as a uniquely positive force of goodwill. Volunteers can work the kitchens, provide face-to-face companionship, or help combat illiteracy, but they have to be able to do it for a few months. Coluche knew the importance of consistency and trust; it almost made him president.

Paris office: 4 cité d'Hauteville (☎53 24 98 00; www.restosducoeur.org). Meals distributed daily in different regions of the city.

coffee, and a beer vending machine (€1.50). Breakfast included. Reservations recommended 1 week ahead. Singles €44, with toilet €60; doubles €50/60. MC/V. ❹

Hôtel Caulaincourt, 2 pl. Caulaincourt (☎46 06 46 06; www.caulaincourt.com). M: Lamarck-Caulaincourt. Walk up the stairs to rue Caulaincourt and proceed to the right, between no. 67 and 69. One of the best values around. Formerly used as artists' studios, the simple rooms have wonderful views of Montmartre and the Paris skyline. TVs and phones in every room. Breakfast €5.50. Free Internet access. Reservations recommended 1 month ahead. Singles €25, with shower €50, with shower and toilet €60; doubles €63-76; triples with shower €89. MC/V. ❷

Le Village Hostel, 20 rue d'Orsel (☎42 64 22 02; www.villiagehostel.fr). M: Anvers. Walk uphill on rue Steinkerque and turn right on rue d'Orsel. In the midst of the Sacré-Coeur tourist traffic but clean, cheap, and comfortable. Some rooms with a view of Sacré-Coeur, some off a patio, and some on the street. Toilet and shower in every room. Kitchen, TV, stereo, telephones, and Internet access in the lounge. Breakfast included. Sheets €2.50; towel €1. Max. stay 1 week. Lockout 11am-4pm. Reserve online. For same-day phone reservations, call at 8am. 4-, 6-, or 8-bed dorms €24; singles €27; doubles €60; triples €81. Cash only. ❷

BASTILLE

Auberge de Jeunesse "Jules Ferry" (HI), 8 bd. Jules Ferry (☎43 57 55 60; auberge@micronet.fr). M: République. Walk east on rue du Faubourg du Temple and turn right on bd. Jules Ferry. Wonderful location in front of a park and next to pl. de la République. 100 beds. Modern, clean, and bright rooms with sinks, mirrors, and tiled floors. Doubles with big beds. Party atmosphere. Breakfast and showers included. Laundry €3, dry €2. Lockers €2. Internet access in lobby €1 per 10min. Max. stay 1 week. Reception and dining room 24hr. Lockout 10:30am-2pm. No reservations; arrive between 8am and 11am to secure a bed. If there are no vacancies, the staff will try to book you in a nearby hostel. 4- to 6-bed dorms and doubles €21. MC/V. ❷

Centre International du Séjour de Paris: CISP "Ravel," 6 av. Maurice Ravel (☎44 75 60 00; www.cisp.asso.fr). M: Porte de Vincennes. Walk east on cours de Vincennes and take the 1st right on bd. Soult. Turn left on rue Jules Lemaître and right on av. Maurice Ravel. It's a hike to Paris's main attractions from this less-appealing part of town, but it's worth it. Large, clean rooms, art displays, and an outdoor pool (€3-4). Cafeteria open daily 7:30-9:30am, noon-1:30pm, and 7-10:30pm (meal €11). Breakfast included. Free Internet access. Reception 24hr. Curfew 1:30am; make arrangements with the night guard to be let in later. Reservations recommended 1-2 months ahead. 8-bed dorm with shower and toilet in hall €19; 2- to 4-bed dorm €25; singles with shower and toilet €37; doubles with shower and toilet €27 per person. AmEx/MC/V. ❷

Hôtel Beaumarchais, 3 rue Oberkampf (☎53 36 86 86; www.hotelbeaumarchais.com). M: Oberkampf. Exit on rue de Malte and turn right on rue Oberkampf. This spacious hotel is worth the extra money. Painted in eye-popping colors, the atmosphere is as fun and hip as the nearby nightlife. Suites include TV room with desk and breakfast table. A/C. Buffet breakfast €10. Reserve 2 weeks in advance. Singles €75-90; doubles €110-130; suites €150-170; triples €170-190. AmEx/MC/V. ❺

Hôtel de l'Aveyron, 5 rue d'Austerlitz (☎43 07 86 86; fax 43 07 85 20). M: Gare de Lyon. Walk away from the station on rue de Bercy and turn right on rue d'Austerlitz. On a quiet street. Small, thoughtfully decorated rooms. Lounge and bar. English-speaking staff is eager to help. Breakfast €5. 1 wheelchair-accessible room. Reservations recommended 2-3 months ahead for Mar.-Oct., 1 week ahead otherwise. Singles with shower €55; doubles with shower €59, with bath €65; triples €70; quads €100. MC/V. ❹

THIRTEENTH ARRONDISSEMENT

Centre International du Séjour de Paris: CISP "Kellerman," 17 bd. Kellerman (☎44 16 37 38; www.cisp.asso.fr). M: Porte d'Italie. Cross the street and turn right onto bd.

Kellerman. This 396-bed hostel resembles a retro spaceship on stilts. Clean rooms are adequate. Breakfast included (7-9am). TV room, laundry, Internet access, and cafeteria (open daily noon-1:30pm and 6:30-9:30pm). Reception 6:30am-1:30am. Reservations recommended 1 month ahead. 8-bed dorms €19; 2- to 4-bed dorms €26; singles with shower and toilet €39; doubles with shower and toilet €28. MC/V. ❷

MONTPARNASSE AND THE FIFTEENTH ARRONDISSEMENT

Aloha Hostel, 1 rue Borromée (☎42 73 03 03; www.aloha.fr). M: Volontaires. Walk against traffic on bd. de Vaugirard, then turn right on rue Borromée. Frequented by a lively international crowd, with brightly colored varnished doors and cheery checkered sheets. No outside alcohol allowed on the premises; drinks available in the café. Breakfast included. Sheets €3, €7 deposit; towels €2/3. Internet access €2 per 30min.; free Wi-Fi. Reception 7am-2am. Lockout 11am-5pm. Curfew 2am. Reserve at least 1 week ahead; doubles can't be guaranteed. No groups in Aug. Apr. to mid-Sept. dorms €23; doubles €25. Mid-Sept. to Mar. €19/23. ❷

Hôtel de Blois, 5 rue des Plantes (☎45 40 99 48; www.hoteldeblois.com). M: Mouton-Duvernet. Turn left on rue Mouton Duvernet, then left on rue des Plantes. One of the best deals in Paris. Each room has floral wallpaper, moldings, and lush carpets, as well as TV, phone, hair dryer, and a clean bathroom. The welcoming owner keeps thank-you notes from former guests in a proudly displayed scrapbook. 26 rooms on 5 floors, but no elevator. Breakfast €6.30. Reservations recommended for rooms on lower floors. Singles and doubles with shower and toilet €60-65, with bath €65-82. MC/V. ❹

Three Ducks Hostel, 6 pl. Etienne Pernet (☎48 42 04 05; www.3ducks.fr). M: Félix Faure. Head toward the church from the Metro and walk against traffic; the hostel is on the left. With palm trees in the courtyard, beach-style shower sheds, airy rooms, and a fully equipped bar (open until 1am), this hostel is aimed at fun-seeking Anglos. Small 4- to 12-bed dorm rooms with sink. Equally small kitchen. 2 doubles available; must be reserved far in advance. Breakfast included. Sheets €3.50; towels €1. Free Internet access in lobby. Max. stay 2 weeks. Reception 8am-2am. Lockout daily noon-4pm. Reserve online with credit card 1 week ahead. Dorms €23-25; doubles €27. MC/V. ❷

Ouest Hôtel, 27 rue de Gergovie (☎45 42 64 99; fax 45 42 46 65). M: Pernety. Walk against traffic on rue Raymond Losserand and turn right on rue de Gergovie. A modest hotel with rooms stuck in the 70s and dark but clean bathrooms. A small lending library behind the lobby has books left by previous guests. Breakfast €5. Hall shower €5. 1-bed doubles €22-28, with sink €28-34, with shower €37-39. MC/V. ❷

Hôtel Printemps, 31 rue du Commerce (☎45 79 83 36; www.hotelprintemps15.com). M: La Motte-Picquet-Grenelle. In a busy neighborhood, surrounded by shops and small restaurants, this 52-room hotel is relatively cheap and reasonably clean. English-speaking staff is cooperative. Guests are counted upon entering the lobby, so don't try to smuggle in extra people! Breakfast €5. Curfew 2:30am. Reservations recommended. Singles and doubles €37, with shower €43, with bath €46. MC/V. ❸

OUTLYING ARRONDISSEMENTS

Auberge de Jeunesse "Le D'Artagnan" (HI), 80 rue Vitruve (☎40 32 34 56; www.hihostels.com). M: Porte de Bagnolet. From the Metro, walk south on bd. Davout and make a right on rue Vitruve. Neon lights and funky decorations welcome legions of boisterous young people as well as older single travelers and families. Despite the large number of guests, the hostel's dorm rooms are generously sized and very well lit. Breakfast served 7-11am. Lockers €2 per day. Towel €2.50. Laundry €3; dry €1. Internet access €2 per 30min. Restaurant (open noon-2pm and 6:30-9:30pm; *plat* €4.50), bar (Happy hour 9-10pm; open 9pm-2am), and a small cinema (free films nightly at 6:30pm). Max. stay 8 nights. Reception

PARIS

A BITE IN THE DARK

It's no secret that Paris's cuisine is some of the world's best; what sets the restaurant **Dans le noir** apart is that you can't see your gourmet meal.

Founded in 2004 by Edouard de Broglie and Etienne Boisrond, the restaurant has charged itself with awakening senses other than sight—patrons at this restaurant dine in total darkness. After passing through a series of heavy curtains, diners are led to their table by the restaurant's staff. While you're free to order a la carte—the menu consists of inventive takes on traditional French cuisine—the more adventurous will opt for *le menu surprise.* You won't know what's on your plate until you taste it.

You may wonder how your servers are able to move through the dining room so easily. They're used to it—Dans le noir employs only blind waiters. In addition to its lofty ambitions of sensory awakening, the restaurant has partnered with the Association Paul Guinot to help the blind find employment. Combining a uniquely disorienting, exciting experience with social change, Dans le noir is money well spent.

51 rue Quincampoix. M: Hôtel de ville. ☎42 77 98 04; www.danslenoir.com. Reservations recommended 3-5 days ahead. Dinner €30-39. Sa-Su lunch €31-37. Su brunch €26.

8am-1am. Lockout noon-3pm. Reservation by fax or email required. 2-bed dorms €26; 3-, 4-, and 5-bed dorms €22; 9-bed dorms €20. Under 10 half-price, under 5 free. ❷

Rhin et Danube, 3 pl. de Rhin et Danube (☎42 45 10 13; fax 42 06 88 82). M: Danube; or bus #75 from M: Châtelet (30min.). Just steps from the Metro, the R&D is a real deal. The suites are not fancy, but they are spacious and many look onto a pretty *place.* Each room has kitchen, fridge, dishes, shower, toilet, phone, and color satellite TV. Reservations recommended 1 month in advance. Singles €46; doubles €61; triples €73; quads €83; quints €92. MC/V. ❹

Hôtel Palace, 9 rue Bouchardon (☎40 40 09 45). M: Strasbourg-St-Denis. Walk against traffic on bd. St-Denis until you reach the small arch; follow rue René Boulanger on the left, then turn left on rue Bouchardon. As centrally located as you'll find in the 10ème, this hotel charges hostel rates. You get what you pay for, including sagging stairways and scuffed walls. Breakfast €3.50. Shower €3.50. Reserve 2 weeks ahead. Singles €24, with shower €33; doubles €25/38; triples €51; quads €61. AmEx/MC/V. ❷

Hôtel de Milan, 17 rue de St-Quentin (☎40 37 88 50; www.hoteldemilan.com). M: Gare du Nord. Follow rue de St-Quentin from the Metro for 3 blocks. The hotel's hospitality and location near the *gares* more than compensate for the fact that the rooms themselves may not make visitors swoon. Breakfast €5. Hall showers €4. Singles €31, with toilet and shower €54; doubles €38, with toilet €43, with toilet and shower €54, with bathtub €58, with 2 beds €61; triples with toilet and shower €72. MC/V. ❸

FOOD

When in doubt, spend your money on food in Paris. Skip the museum, sleep in the dingy hotel, but **eat well.** Paris's culinary scene has been justly famous for centuries, and eating in the City of Light remains as exciting today as it was when Sun King Louis XIV made feasts an everyday occurrence. The city's strong suit, sensibly enough, is French food; sausage and sauerkraut from Alsace and seafood *bouillabaisse* from the Riviera all hold their own. An expensive meal in a really terrific bistro—easily a three-hour endeavor if you don't rush things—is something that you'll remember long after your passport has expired. Paris's other great gift to travelers is the pastry, which is cheap and everywhere. A croissant will never cost more than €1, and when the butter starts to seep through the paper bag, you'll know you've found the real thing.

Beyond traditional French cuisine, Paris offers delicious international dishes. Don't miss the kosher delis and falafel stands in the Marais on **rue des Rosiers,** or the North African flavors at *djerbas* near the **Pigalle** Metro station in Montmartre. In the Latin Quarter, head to the area around the **Panthéon** for sidewalk bistros; the streets around **place St-Michel** for tiny, bustling restaurants; and **rue St-André-des-Arts** for *crêperies* and *panini* vendors. Check out **Chinatown** in the 13ème and the cluster of Asian diners in the western portion of the 1er. Avoid a pricey sit-down meal and stop by an *épicerie* to create a picnic to eat in Luxembourg Gardens, Parc Buttes Chaumont, or on the steps at Sacré-Coeur. *Bon appétit!*

BY TYPE

CHO Châtelet-Les Halles and Opéra. **Seine** Seine Islands. **LQ** Latin Quarter and Saint-Germain. **Montparnasse** Montparnasse and 15ème. **Out** Outlying Arrondissements.

AFRICAN
- Babylone Bis (118) — CHO ❶

AMERICAN/ANGLO
- Chez Haynes (123) — Montmartre ❷
- James Joyce Pub (125) — Out ❷
- No Stress Café (122) — Montmartre ❸

ASIAN
- L'Etoile du Kashmir (125) — Out ❶
- Foyer Vietnam (121) — LQ ❶
- Lao Siam (125) — Out ❶
- Thai Phetburi (124) — Montparnasse ❷
- Tricotin (124) — 13ème ❶

BISTRO
- Café des Musées (124) — Bastille ❸
- Chez Janou (120) — Marais ❷
- Chez Paul (124) — Bastille ❸
- Le Comptoir du Relais (120) — LQ ❹
- Le Dix Vins (124) — Montparnasse ❹
- Les Noces de Jeannette (118) — CHO ❹

CAFÉ/TEA ROOM
- Café de l'Industrie (123) — Bastille ❸
- Café Vavin (121) — LQ ❷
- La Flèche d'Or (125) — Out ❷
- Ladurée (122) — Champs-Elysées ❸
- Mariage Frères (119) — Marais ❹
- Le Sancerre (123) — Montmartre ❶

CRÊPERIE/ICE CREAM
- Amorino (118) — Seine ❶
- Berthillon (118) — Seine ❶
- Breizh Café (119) — Marais ❷
- Crêperie Saint Germain (121) — LQ ❶
- Ty Yann (122) — Champs-Elysées ❷

MIDDLE EASTERN
- L'As du Falafel (119) — Marais ❶
- Babylone (123) — Bastille ❶
- Café de la Mosquée (121) — LQ ❷
- Chez Hannah (119) — Marais ❶
- Chez Omar (120) — Marais ❸
- Savannah Café (121) — LQ ❷
- Tourace (122) — Invalides ❶

SPECIALTY STORES
- Davoli (121) — Invalides ❶
- Gusto Italia (121) — Invalides ❷
- La Fournée d'Augustine (125) — Out ❶

TRADITIONAL AND MODERN FRENCH
- Au Petit Fer à Cheval (120) — Marais ❸
- Le Bar à Soupes (123) — Bastille ❶
- Brasserie de l'Ile St-Louis (118) — Seine ❸
- Les Broches à l'Ancienne (123) — Bastille ❸
- Le Caveau du Palais (118) — Seine ❹
- L'Ebauchoir (123) — Bastille ❸
- Pain, Vin, Fromage (120) — Marais ❷
- Refuge des Fondues (123) — Montmartre ❸
- Le Scheffer (122) — Champs-Elysées ❸
- Severo (124) — Montparnasse ❸
- Le Soleil Gourmand (122) — Montmartre ❷
- Le Temps des Cerises (124) — 13ème ❸
- Taxi Jaune (119) — Marais ❸

TRENDY/INTELLIGENTSIA
- Aux Artistes (124) — Montparnasse ❷
- Curieux Spaghetti Bar (120) — Marais ❷
- L'Endroit (125) — Out ❸
- Le Fumoir (119) — CHO ❹
- Mood (122) — Champs-Elysées ❸

VEGETARIAN AND VEGAN
- Bioboa (118) — CHO ❶
- Bob's Juice Bar (125) — Out ❶
- Piccolo Teatro (120) — Marais ❷
- La Victoire Suprême (118) — CHO ❷

SEINE ISLANDS

Amorino, 47 rue St-Louis-en-l'Ile (☎44 07 48 08). M: Pont Marie. Cross the Pont Marie and turn right on rue St-Louis-en-l'Ile. With a selection of 20 *gelati* and *sorbetti* flavors (more in summer), Amorino serves amazing concoctions and more generous servings than its more famous neighbor, Berthillon. You can ask for as many flavors as you want at no extra charge. Your cone (€3-5.50) or cup (€3-8.50) will look like a work of art. The champion should watch out for this fiery underdog. ❶

Le Caveau du Palais, 19 pl. Dauphine (☎43 26 04 28). M: Cité. Le Caveau serves up hearty French fare under timbered ceilings. Well-heeled locals crowd the terrace in the summer. The meat-heavy menu is pricey but worth the splurge. Appetizers €8.50-20. Main dishes €17-50. Desserts €8-9. Open daily 12:15-2:30pm and 7:15-10:30pm. Reservations necessary for dinner and recommended for lunch. AmEx/MC/V. ❹

Berthillon, 31 rue St-Louis-en-l'Ile (☎43 54 31 61). M: Cité or Pont Marie. Berthillon plays up its own celebrity so well—it's reputed to have Paris's best ice cream—that you may even trick yourself into believing that your tiny scoop was worth €2. The line is usually filled with English-speakers. Look for stores nearby that sell Berthillon indulgences; the wait is shorter, they usually offer a wider selection of flavors, and they're open in late July and Aug., when the main outfit is closed. Single scoop €2; double €3; triple €4. Open Sept. to mid-July W-Su 10am-8pm. Closed 2 weeks in both Feb. and Apr. ❶

Brasserie de l'Ile St-Louis, 55 quai de Bourbon (☎43 54 02 59). M: Pont Marie. Cross Pont Marie and turn right on rue St-Louis-en-l'Ile; continue to the end of the island. An old-fashioned *brasserie*. Serves up large portions of über-rich Alsatian cuisine. Don't make any other significant culinary plans for the day. *Plats* include *choucroute garnie* (sausages and pork on a bed of sauerkraut; €17). Also an array of omelettes and other typical café fare (€7-15). Outdoor seating with a view of the Panthéon through the Left Bank rooftops. Open M-Tu and Th-Su noon-midnight. No reservations. AmEx/MC/V. ❸

CHÂTELET-LES-HALLES AND OPÉRA

Bioboa, 3 rue Danielle Casanova (☎42 61 17 67). M: Pyramides. Cheap, delicious, organic lunches in a bright, trendy atmosphere. It's hard to know what else you could want from this exceptional eatery. Prepared foods are available from the refrigerated shelves if you're in a hurry. It's worth sticking around for a hot panini with *chèvre* and grilled vegetables (€7). A constantly rotating selection of smoothies (€5-7) is also available. Open daily 11am-6pm. MC/V. ❶

La Victoire Suprême du Cœur, 41 rue des Bourdonnais (☎40 41 93 95). M: Châtelet. Walk down rue de Rivoli and turn right onto rue des Bourdonnais. With a relaxed crowd and breezy décor, this is one of the best lunch options in the area. Tasty vegetarian dishes highlight a health-conscious menu. Meals marked with a "V" can be made vegan. Fresh smoothies made daily (€5.50). 2-course *menu* €12.50. Open M-F 11:45am-10pm, Sa noon-10pm. AmEx/MC/V. ❷

Babylone Bis, 34 rue Tiquetonne (☎42 33 48 35). M: Etienne-Marcel. Walk against traffic on rue de Turbigo and turn left onto rue Tiquetonne. With zebra skin on the walls, banana leaves on the ceiling, and loud *zouk* music blasting from the speakers, this eatery fits right into its quirky neighborhood. Serves Antillean and African cuisine, including delicious *aloko* (fried bananas; €5.50) and stuffed crab (€9). It is also a late-night destination for celebrity musicians: pictures of Snoop Dogg, Stevie Wonder, and Marvin Gaye decorate the walls. Open daily 8pm-8am. MC/V. ❶

Les Noces de Jeannette, 14 rue Favart and 9 rue d'Amboise (☎42 96 36 89). M: Richelieu-Drouot. Exit onto bd. des Italiens, then turn left onto rue Favart. This elegant and diverse restaurant is a reminder of what a great bistro can be. *Menu du Jeanette* (€27) includes salads, grilled meat, roasted fish *plats,* and fabulous desserts. *Kir* included with meal. Open daily noon-1:30pm and 7-9:30pm. Reservations recommended. ❹

Le Fumoir, 6 rue de l'Amiral Coligny (☎42 92 00 24; www.lefumoir.com). M: Louvre. As you cross rue de Rivoli on rue du Louvre, it becomes rue de l'Amiral Coligny. Though you may hear as much English as French while you sip a beverage on the deep leather sofas—proximity to the Louvre is the likely culprit—Le Fumoir still draws a contingent of elegantly-dressed locals with its old-world ambience. Part bar, part tea house, it serves one of Paris's best brunches (€21). Coffee €2.60. Brunch Su noon-3pm. Open daily 11am-2am. Reservations strongly recommended for brunch. AmEx/MC/V. ❹

THE MARAIS

Breizh Café, 109 rue Vieille du Temple (☎42 72 13 77; www.breizhcafe.com). M: St-Sebastien. With a wonderful neighborhood atmosphere, this place is too good to be true. While *crêpes* aren't exactly hard to find in Paris, inexpensive and inventive *crêpes* made with the highest-possible quality ingredients around (raw milk cheese and organic veggies) are rare. The best thing about the already delicious *crêpe* with potatoes, herring, crème fraîche, and caviar is the €11 price tag. Also carries a wide selection of regional ciders and Breton beers (€3.50). Open M and W-Su noon-11:30pm. MC/V. ❷

Chez Hannah, 54 rue des Rosiers (☎42 74 74 99). M: St-Paul. L'As du Falafel's resentful younger sibling serves up a near-identical menu just down the street. Many believe that the falafel (€8.50, takeout €4) here is better than at its more celebrated counterpart. The lines are almost always more manageable. Open Tu-Su noon-midnight. ❶

L'As du Falafel, 34 rue des Rosiers (☎48 87 63 60). M: St-Paul. Allegedly credited by Lenny Kravitz as having "the best falafel in the world," this kosher falafel stand and restaurant will probably make you agree with the rock star. The falafel special (€6.50, takeout €4) is indeed special, and it goes well with a glass of the house lemonade (€4). Open M-Th and Su 11am-midnight, F 11am-6pm. MC/V. ❶

Au Petit Fer à Cheval, 30 rue Vieille du Temple (☎42 72 47 47). M: Hôtel de Ville or St-Paul. From M: St-Paul, walk with traffic on rue de Rivoli and turn right; the restaurant is on the right. An oasis of *kir* and *Gauloises* graced by a low-key (but never boring) crowd of locals. One of the best spots in Paris to enjoy a morning coffee. Hidden behind the bar are a few tables where you can order *filet mignon de veau* (€16). Delicious *tarte tatin* €7.50. Open daily 9am-2am. Kitchen open noon-1:15am. MC/V. ❸

AN EPICUREAN EMPIRE. The same fellow who owns Au Petit Fer à Cheval also runs 2 equally fantastic restaurants nearby—**Les Philosophes** and **La Chaise au Plafond,** which are great alternatives if Au Petit Fer is crowded.

Mariage Frères, 30 rue du Bourg-Tibourg, 4ème (☎42 72 28 11). M: Hôtel-de-Ville. Started by 2 brothers who found British tea shoddy, this salon offers 500 varieties of tea (€7-15). While the sophisticated clientele contribute to the salon's refined atmosphere, the waiters in cream-colored linen suits push things over the top. Tea *menu* includes sandwiches, pastries, and tea (€30). Classic brunch *menu* is excellent (brioche, eggs, tea, cakes; €30-36), as is the decadent Snob Salad (€24) which comes piled high with *foie gras* and smoked salmon. Open daily 10:30am-7:30pm; lunch M-Sa noon-3pm, afternoon tea 3-6:30pm, Su brunch 12:30-6:30pm. Reservations recommended for brunch. AmEx/MC/V. Also at 13 rue des Grands Augustins, 6ème (☎40 51 82 50), and at 260 rue du Faubourg St-Honoré, 8ème (☎46 22 18 54). ❹

Taxi Jaune, 13 rue Chapon (☎42 76 00 40). M: Arts et Métiers. Walk along rue Beaubourg and turn left onto rue Chapon. An intimate and convivial atmosphere reminiscent of a 1930s French diner brings a crowd of devoted regulars who delight in the creative, neatly presented dishes. Appetizers €8. *Plats* €17. Lunch *menu* €14. Open M-F 9am-

1am. Closed 3 weeks in Aug. and winter holidays. Kitchen open noon-3pm and 8-10:30pm. Reservations strongly recommended. V. ❸

Piccolo Teatro, 6 rue des Ecouffes (☎42 72 17 79). M: St-Paul. Walk with traffic down rue de Rivoli and take a right on rue des Ecouffes. A romantic vegetarian hideout draped in red velvet. Dishes like veggie lasagna (€12) and carrot cake (€5) reflect a fondness for home-style cooking. Appetizers €4-6.50. *Plats* €11-12. Desserts €5-6. Open daily noon-3pm and 7-11pm. AmEx/MC/V. ❷

Pain, Vin, Fromage, 3 rue Geoffrey L'Angevin (☎42 74 07 52). M: Rambuteau or Hôtel de Ville. On a small side street right near the Centre Pompidou, this cozy Parisian classic (complete with rustic basement wine cellar) takes an original spin on France's 3 basic food groups—fondue (€14-15), salad (€4-9), and wine. Open M-Sa 7-11:30pm. Reservations recommended. AmEx/MC/V. ❷

Chez Janou, 2 rue Roger Verlomme (☎42 72 28 41). M: Chemin-Vert. From the Metro, take rue St-Gilles and turn left on rue des Tournelles; it's on the corner of rue Roger Verlomme. Hidden in a quiet section of the 3ème, this bustling Parisian bistro is lauded for its inexpensive gourmet food. The salad with avocado, grapefruit, and crayfish is only the beginning of an unusually creative menu. Shady terrace is superb for summer dining *al fresco. Plats* €15. Open daily noon-3pm and 7pm-midnight. Reservations recommended, as this local favorite is packed every night of the week. Cash only. ❷

Curieux Spaghetti Bar, 14 rue St-Marri (☎42 72 75 97; www.curieuxspag.com). M: Rambuteau or Hôtel de Ville. Light mist welcomes you into this trendy restaurant. Fashionable serving staff busily caters to a youngish clientele who chain-smoke while dining on generous helpings of pasta (€9-18). Doubles as a bar. Try the shots of perfumed vodka in fanciful flavors such as bubble gum and mojito. Daily special €10. *Menu* €12. Happy hour 4-8pm. Open M-W and Su noon-2am, Th-Sa noon-4am. MC/V. ❷

Chez Omar, 47 rue de Bretagne (☎42 72 36 26). M: Arts et Métiers. Walk along rue Réamur away from rue St-Martin. Rue Réamur turns into rue de Bretagne. One of the better Middle Eastern eateries in town, featuring bright décor. Come at 7:30pm for peace and quiet; the local intelligentsia crowds in later. In a city overflowing with *steak-frites,* vegetarians will swoon over the couscous (€10-22), *brochettes* (€13), and *ratatouille* (€16). Open M-Sa noon-2:30pm and 7-11pm, Su 7-11pm. Cash only. ❸

LATIN QUARTER AND ST-GERMAIN

Le Comptoir du Relais, 9 carrefour de l'Odeon (☎44 27 07 97). M: Odéon. Though the focus is on pork and other meats at this truly outstanding bistro, there's

TOP TEN WEIRD ANIMAL PARTS TO EAT IN FRANCE

While contemporary French cuisine is renowned for its sophistication, the roots of French cooking can be found in some not-so-sophisticated parts of nature's most delicious creatures.

1. Pied de Porc (pig's feet). They're usually chopped, seasoned, and delicately fried.

2. Tête de Veau (calf's head). Rolled up, sliced, and served to the applause of French diners everywhere. A national favorite.

3. L'Os à moelle (bone marrow). Served on its own with salt, parsley, and a little spoon.

4. Boudin (blood sausage). Mentioned as far back as Homer's *Odyssey*. Now you too, sitting "beside a great fire," can fill "a sausage with fat and blood and turn it this way and that."

5. Foie Gras (goose liver). American cities have banned the food, but the French seem to be holding fast to their tradition.

6. Whole Fish. The best meat on any fish is just behind the eye. So when the whole thing arrives on a plate, carpe diem!

7. Escargots. These you've heard about before. They come with garlic and parsley butter.

8. Tail. Can be eaten on its own, in a stew, you name it.

9. Groin. In French, pigs say "groin" instead of "oink." So when you order this, you're also imitating it. Ironic?

10. Filet (cow muscle). Talk about weird!

really not a weak link in Le Comptoir's menu. *Foie gras* on toast (€11) is a good starter for those who don't feel guilty, and a beef stew with noodles, onions, and refreshing hints of lemon (€16) will keep you going on a rainy (or snowy) day. The locals-heavy, hyper-crowded atmosphere makes the whole experience a lot of fun. Show up for a late lunch (after 3pm) or early dinner (before 8pm Sa-Su) to avoid a wait. Open M-F noon-6pm and for 8:30 dinner seating; Sa-Su noon-10pm. Reservations strongly recommended for weekday dinner, not accepted on weekends. MC/V. ❹

Foyer Vietnam, 80 rue Monge (☎45 35 32 54). M: Place Monge. It's a little out of the way, but this eatery—a local favorite if ever there was one—serves large portions and charges small prices. The 2-course lunch *menu* is only €7 with a student ID; try starting with the tasty *Pho* and then moving on to the *Porc au caramel* or duck with bananas (€8.50). You'll have trouble finding another restaurant that offers lychees in syrup (€2.50) for dessert. Open M-Sa noon-2pm and 7-10pm. ❶

Café de la Mosquée, 39 rue Geoffrey St-Hilaire (☎43 31 38 20). M: Censier-Daubenton. In the Mosquée de Paris. Adorned with fountains and white marble floors, this café deserves a visit. Even Parisian pigeons know how good it is—watch your food on the patio. Persian mint tea (€2.50) and *maghrebain* pastries (€2.50), make for a great late-afternoon snack. Inside, the restaurant serves couscous (€9-25) on gorgeous copper tabletops. For dessert, the *Coupe Orientale* (2 scoops of mint tea ice cream and 1 scoop of honey nougat; €6.50) is tasty. Open daily 9am-11pm. MC/V. ❷

Savannah Café, 27 rue Descartes (☎43 29 45 77). M: Cardinal Lemoine. Follow rue du Cardinal Lemoine uphill, turn right on rue Clovis, and walk 1 block to rue Descartes. Decorated with eclectic knick-knacks, this cheerful restaurant serves Lebanese food. Dishes include eggplant caviar, tabouli, and a selection of pasta dishes (€13). Try the perfectly composed starter sampler for 2 (€16), with warm goat cheese, tabouli, and baba ganoush, among others. *Plats* €13-15. Open M-Sa 7-11pm. MC/V. ❷

Crêperie Saint Germain, 33 rue St-André-des-Arts (☎43 54 24 41). M: St-Michel. Cross pl. St-Michel and walk down rue St-André-des-Arts. Gets the job done. Serves filling wheat-flour *galettes,* like the Chihuahua (chicken cooked with peppers, tomatoes, and onions; €9). Sweet dessert *crêpes* like the Zanzibar (pear ice cream, raspberries, chocolate sauce, and whipped cream; €7.50). €9 *menu* (M-F noon-3pm) includes 2 *crêpes* and a *cidre* or soda. Open daily noon-midnight. AmEx/MC/V. ❶

Café Vavin, 18 rue Vavin (☎43 26 67 47). M: Vavin. While the food here doesn't leap out from the rest of the café pack, the students and professors-gone-bonkers that pack its tiny tables make for a terrific atmosphere. Vavin inhabits the part of Montparnasse that spills over into the 6ème and is surrounded by small boutiques. *Entrecôte* and fries €13. Salads €9.50-12. Open M-Sa 8am-1am, Su 8am-8:30pm. MC/V. ❷

INVALIDES

Davoli, 32 rue Cler (☎45 51 23 41). M: Ecole Militaire. Budget travelers in a not-so-budget neighborhood can have it both ways at this gourmet paradise. A closet-sized food market with a celebrity pedigree (Catherine Deneuve and Jeanne Moreau have both been spotted picking up groceries here). For those in search of a lunch or snack, Davoli's selection of meats, cheeses, baked goods, and prepared foods is a guaranteed hit. Try their *quiche lorraine* (€2.20) or go out on a limb with *escargots de bourgogne* (€8.20 per dozen). Open Tu and Th-Sa 8am-1pm and 3:30-7:30pm, Su 8am-noon. ❶

Gusto Italia, 199 rue de Grenelle (☎45 55 00 43). M: Ecole Militaire. Walk toward the Eiffel Tower on av. de la Bourdonnais, then turn right on rue de Grenelle. This unassuming spot spends the bulk of its time catering and selling a small selection of cheeses, meats, and wines, but for a few hours each day it is one of the better deals in the neighborhood. €11 can buy a well-dressed salad, an authentically Italian lasagna, or pizza big enough to share (try the "4 cheeses" pizza). Lunch served daily noon-3pm. ❷

Tourace, 47 rue Babylone (☎06 86 73 11 46). M: St-François Xavier. Cheap lunch counter fare with a Lebanese flair. While the sandwiches (around €4.50) and lunch plates (around €9.50) won't blow you away, the prices for combos are another matter: €6.20 for any sandwich, drink, and dessert–the baklava is very tasty. You will have a hard time finding a better deal in Invalides. Open daily 10am-11pm. ❶

CHAMPS-ELYSÉES

Ty Yann, 10 rue de Constantinople (☎40 08 00 17). M: Europe. Turn right on rue de Rome and left on rue de Constantinople. The welcoming Breton chef and owner, M. Yann, cheerfully prepares outstanding yet inexpensive *galettes* (€7-10) and *crêpes* in this tiny restaurant, decorated with his mother's pastoral paintings. *La vaniteuse* (€8), with sausage sautéed in cognac, Emmental cheese, and onions, is highly recommended. Create your own *crêpe* (€5.50-6.50) for lunch. Takeout available for 15% less. Open M-F noon-2:30pm and 7-10:30pm, Sa 7-10:30pm. MC/V. ❷

Le Scheffer, 22 rue Scheffer (☎47 27 81 11). M: Trocadero. Walk down av. Paul Doumer, then make a right on rue Scheffer. From the sounds of clattering pans to the red checkered tablecloths, Le Scheffer is an unpretentious stronghold of traditional French cuisine. Slow service around lunchtime and suspicion of tourists add to the authenticity of this local favorite. Appetizers (€6-7.50) include a tasty salad topped with warm goat cheese. Of the *plats,* the steak tartare (raw ground beef with mustard and capers, €14) is extremely popular. Open M-Sa 10:30am-11pm. ❸

Mood, 114 av. des Champs-Elysées and 1 rue Washington (☎42 89 98 89). M: George V. A sensuously elegant melange of Western contemporary décor and delicate Japanese accents reflects the fusion cuisine. Dine on the *prix-fixe* lunch (a great value at €20) in the upper dining room, or indulge your hedonistic side on the lower level's plush beds at night. A drink list with poetic mixed drinks (€9-11) such as *septembre en attendant* (waiting for September). Appetizers €9-18. *Plats* €12-15. Live music and DJ in the evenings. Reservations recommended for the restaurant and required for the lounge. Restaurant open daily 10am-4am, lounge open 10pm-4am. AmEx/MC/V. ❸

Ladurée, 16 rue Royale (☎42 60 21 79) and 75 av. des Champs-Elysées, 8ème (☎40 75 08 75). M: Concorde or FDR. Ever wondered what it would be like to dine inside a Fabergé egg? The Rococo décor of this tea salon attracts a jarring mix of well-groomed shoppers and tourists. Famous for the mini macaroons in the window (€1.30, in 16 different varieties), this spot offers little that hasn't been soaked in vanilla or caramel. Boxes of *"Chocolats Incomparable"* from €17. Box of candied orange peel €19. Specialty tea *Ladurée mélange* €6.50. Su brunch €29. Open daily 8:30am-7pm, lunch served until 3pm. AmEx/MC/V. ❸

PARIS

MONTMARTRE

No Stress Café, 2 pl. Gustave Toudouze (☎48 78 00 27). M: St-Georges. Walk uphill on rue Notre Dame de Lorette and turn right onto rue H. Monnier. A French crowd comes for American-sized salads: enormous, flamboyant piles of vegetables and enthusiastically seasoned meats (€13-16). Also serves fried onion rings with a tasty, spicy sauce (€5). Massages are available after 9pm (W-Sa). Vegetarian options abound. Open Tu-Su 11am-2am. Su brunch noon-3:30pm. MC/V. ❸

Le Soleil Gourmand, 10 rue Ravignan (☎42 51 00 50). M: Abbesses. Facing the church on pl. des Abbesses, head right down rue des Abbesses and turn right (uphill) on rue Ravignan. Local favorite serves light *provençal* fare in a cheerful, half-underground dining room decorated to match the restaurant's name. Try the *bricks* (grilled stuffed filo dough; €11), the 5-cheese *tartes* (€11), and the delicious homemade cakes (€5). The menu is rounded out with vegetarian options like the *assiette sud* (€13), a generous collection of grilled and marinated vegetables. Open daily 12:30-2:30pm and 7:30-11pm. Evening reservations recommended. Cash only. ❷

Chez Haynes, 3 rue Clauzel (☎48 78 40 63). M: St-Georges. Head uphill on rue Notre Dame de Lorette and turn right on rue H. Monnier, then right again on rue Clauzel to the end of the block. Opened in 1949, this was Paris's first African-American-owned restaurant, though it is now run by a Portuguese/Brazilian couple. A former hangout of Louis Armstrong, James Baldwin, and Richard Wright, Haynes is famous for its New Orleans soul food and complimentary cornbread. Generous portions are mostly under €16. Ma Sutton's fried honey chicken €14. Sister Lena's BBQ spare ribs €14. Banana split €8. Chez Haynes's soul food *menu* Tu-Sa, Brazilian food Su. Live music F-Sa nights; €5 cover. Open Tu-Su 7pm-midnight. AmEx/MC/V. ❷

Refuge des Fondues, 17 rue des Trois Frères (☎42 55 22 65). M: Abbesses. Walk down rue Yvonne le Tac and take a left on rue des Trois Frères. Only 2 main dishes: *fondue bourguignonne* (meat fondue) and *fondue savoyarde* (cheese fondue). The wine (2 choices: red or white) is served in baby bottles with rubber nipples. Yum? *Menu* €16. Open July-Aug. Tu-Sa 5pm-2am; Sept.-June daily 5pm-2am; food from 7pm. No new diners after 12:30am. Reservations recommended. ❸

Le Sancerre, 35 rue des Abbesses (☎42 58 08 20). M: Abbesses. Facing the church on pl. des Abbesses, head right on rue des Abbesses. A modernized café with a topless mermaid on the ceiling and simple but delicious dishes like tomato and mozzarella salad (€7). Hip 20-somethings while away the evening with mixed drinks on the terrace. Beer €3.50-5.50. *Apéritifs* €3.50-8. Wines €3-5. Open daily 7am-2am. MC/V. ❶

BASTILLE

Le Bar à Soupes, 33 rue Charonne (☎43 57 53 79; www.lebarasoupes.com). M: Bastille. Walk down rue Faubourg St-Antoine and turn left on rue Charonne. Features big bowls of tasty soup (€5.50). The €9.50 lunch *menu,* which comes with soup, a crusty roll, wine or coffee, and salad or a cheese plate, is an astonishing deal. The staff is friendly enough to put you in a good mood for the rest of your day. Try the gooey *gâteau chocolat* (€3) for dessert. Open M-Sa noon-3pm and 6:30-11pm. MC/V. ❶

Café de l'Industrie, 15-17 rue St-Sabin (☎47 00 13 53). M: Breguet-Sabin. A happening café frequented by funky 20-somethings. L'Industrie may be the only restaurant in Paris to straddle a street. Both sides serve the same diverse menu: tagliatelle with pesto (€9.50) rubs elbows with marlin (€14). Coffee €2.50. *Vin chaud* €4.50. Salads €8.50-9. Popular fruit-filled brunch Sa-Su €18. Open daily 10am-2am. MC/V. ❸

Babylone, 21 rue Daval (☎47 00 55 02). M: Bastille. In an area packed with cheap sandwich shops and *crêpe* stands, this shawarma and falafel spot stands out. With a flickering neon sign and a checkered tile floor, the tiny space feels a little bit like a 50s diner. But don't even think about asking for a burger. You order a falafel (€4), shawarma (€5), or falafel and shawarma (€5) sandwich, or you don't order at all. Beer €2.50. Open M 10am-7pm, Tu-Sa 10am-12:30am. Cash only. ❶

Les Broches à l'Ancienne, 21 rue St-Nicolas (☎43 43 26 16). M: Ledru-Rollin. Walk along rue du Faubourg St-Antoine away from the Bastille column and turn right onto rue St-Nicolas. Follow your nose: the meats here are slow-cooked over flames in a stone oven. Dark wood sets the tone for serious food at surprisingly low prices. Appetizers €5-8.50. Shoulder of lamb with *frites* €18. Jazz some F nights starting at 8pm; dinner and performance about €25. Open M-Sa noon-2:30pm and 7-10:30pm. Closed 2nd and 3rd weeks of Aug. Reservations recommended. AmEx/MC/V. ❸

L'Ebauchoir, 45 rue de Citeaux (☎43 42 49 31). M: Faidherbe-Chaligny. Walk down rue du Faubourg St-Antoine and turn left on rue de Citeaux. Funky decorations create a nice, informal atmosphere. €14 lunch *menu* is a bargain. *Plats* from €15. *Menu* €23. Open M 8-11pm, Tu-Sa noon-11pm. Food served noon-2:30pm and 8-11pm. MC/V. ❸

PARIS

Café des Musées, 49 rue Turenne (42 72 96 17). M: Chemin-Vert. Part bar, part café, part bistro—this intimate restaurant may be undergoing something of an identity crisis, but it draws in a diverse crowd: businessmen finishing the workday, students with tattered paperbacks, and families out for a meal. The restaurant's bistro fare is delicious, and at €19, the rotating 3-course *prix-fixe menu* is a steal. Appetizers €5-15. *Plats* €12-24. Desserts €5-12. Open daily 11:30am-2pm and 7:30-11pm. MC/V. ❸

Chez Paul, 13 rue de Charonne (☎47 00 34 57). M: Bastille. Go east on rue du Faubourg St-Antoine and turn left on rue de Charonne. Downstairs has a classic bistro feel; upstairs has a romantic atmosphere; both have a fun, witty staff. The food? Not as fun and witty. Those looking to avoid the bland takes on bistro fare can attempt St-Antoine's Temptation (€18), a dish of pig ear, foot, tail, and groin. Open daily noon-2:30pm and 7pm-2am. Kitchen closes 12:30am. Reservations required for dinner. AmEx/MC/V. ❸

THIRTEENTH ARRONDISSEMENT

Tricotin, 15 av. de Choisy (☎45 84 74 44). M: Porte de Choisy. 6 chefs prepare delicious food from Cambodia, Thailand, and Vietnam, which is served in 2 large, enthusiastically decorated rooms. Try the Cambodian fried rice with beef (€7.50) or any of the *vapeur* (dim sum) foods, such as the steamed shrimp ravioli (€3.50). Always busy, but Tricotin has diligent service. Open daily 9:30am-11:30pm. MC/V. ❶

Le Temps des Cerises, 18 rue de la Butte-aux-Cailles (☎45 89 69 48). M: Place d'Italie. Take rue Bobillot and turn right on rue de la Butte-aux-Cailles. A local restaurant cooperative. All of Le Temps's workers, from cook to bartender, have shared ownership since 1976. Specializes in classic dishes like *andouillette* (€14); try the *assiette Grècque,* piled high with cold cuts (€14), or the excellent *magret de canard* (€18). Lunch *menu* €9.50. Other *menus* €15-23. Open M-F 11:45am-2:15pm and 7:30-11:45pm, Sa 11:45am-2:15pm. Reservations recommended for dinner. AmEx/MC/V. ❸

MONTPARNASSE AND THE FIFTEENTH ARRONDISSEMENT

Le Dix Vins, 57 rue Falguière (☎43 20 91 77; www.le-dix-vins.com). M: Pasteur. Follow bd. Pasteur up the hill and make a right onto rue Falguière. This intimate bistro has an appropriate pun for a name—both the meals and the wines (fortunately numbering more than 10) are indeed *divin* (divine). The *menus,* while not exactly cheap (€20-24), offer diners a classic French meal with a tame *nouvelle cuisine* (new, light cuisine) twist. *Plats* €15. Open M-F noon-2:30pm and 8-11pm. MC/V. ❹

Thai Phetburi, 31 bd. de Grenelle (☎40 58 14 88; www.phetburi-paris.com). M: Bir-Hakeim. Head away from the river on bd. de Grenelle; the restaurant is on the left. Minutes from the Eiffel Tower. Award-winning food, friendly service, and reasonable prices. The *tom yam koung* (shrimp soup flavored with lemongrass; €7.30) and *lab kai* (chicken in thai grass; €9.10) are both favorites, though they come in modest portions. Many vegetarian options. Lunch *menu* €11. 10% off for takeout. Open M-Sa noon-2:45pm and 7-11pm. AmEx/MC/V. ❷

Severo, 8 rue des Plantes (☎45 40 40 91). M: Mouton Duvernet. Exit the Metro and walk down rue Brézin; cross av. du Maine and make a quick left onto rue des Plantes. The out-of-the-way location may be a blessing in disguise: a prominent shout-out in *The New York Times* hasn't altered its fiercely local following. The owner is a former butcher, and it shows; this is some of the best meat in the city, and while a splurge on some of the more expensive cuts is worth your while, an inexpensive meal is both possible and delicious. Anything with *frites* (€14-29) is highly recommended. *Mousse au chocolat* €6. Open M-F noon-2:30pm and 7:30-10:30pm. MC/V. ❸

Aux Artistes, 63 rue Falguière (☎43 22 05 39). M: Pasteur. Walk up the hill and turn right onto rue Falguière. One of the 15ème's cooler spots, this lively restaurant draws a mix of professionals, students, and artists—including Modigliani in his time. Don't be put off by the surfboards and American license plates covering every inch of the place; the *artistes* serve typical modest French food. *Plats* €10. Lunch *menu* €10. Dinner *menu* €13. Open M-F noon-2:30pm and 7:30pm-midnight, Sa 7:30pm-midnight. ❷

OUTLYING ARRONDISSEMENTS

Lao Siam, 49 rue de Belleville (☎40 40 09 68). M: Belleville. Even before your food arrives, you'll be impressed—or at least amused—by the wall of articles singing this Chinese and Thai eatery's praises. Thai-dried calamari salad (€6.30) makes for a light preamble to the *poulet royal au curry* (royal chicken curry; €8.40) or *filet du poisson* with "hip-hop" sauce (€8.60). Wash it down with a *citron pressé* (lemonade; €2.30) and finish it off with kumquats (€2.80). Open daily noon-3pm and 7-11pm. MC/V. ❶

La Fournée d'Augustine, 31 rue des Batignolles (☎48 89 91 54). M: Rome. With Gare St-Lazare to your right, walk down bd. des Batignolles, then turn left on rue des Batignolles. This closet-sized *pâtisserie* bakes an absolutely fantastic baguette (€1), and with lines out the door at lunchtime, it's hard to miss. Their sandwiches (€3-4), always made with fresh bread, range from light fare like goat cheese and cucumber to the more substantial grilled chicken and veggies. Grab a *pain au chocolat* (€1) or a *congolais* (individually-sized coconut cake; €2) for later. Rotating schedule of bread; check the chalkboards on the back wall. Open M-Sa 7am-8pm. MC/V. ❶

Bob's Juice Bar, 15 rue Lucien-Sampaix (☎06 82 63 72 74; www.bobsjuicebar.com). M: Jacques Bonsergent. Tucked away in the 10ème, this cheap vegetarian eatery serves up delicious sandwiches, soups, salads, freshly made juices, and pancakes—yes, that's right, pancakes. A large communal table creates a social atmosphere, and the cool indie tunes add style points. A dozen *formules* (€5-9) ensure a budget-friendly option no matter what you're in the mood for. Juice €3-4.50. Pancakes €2. Open Tu-F 7:30am-6pm, Sa-Su 7:30am-4pm. Cash only. ❶

The James Joyce Pub, 71 bd. Gouvion St-Cyr (☎44 09 70 32; www.kittyosheas.com). M: Porte Maillot (exit at Palais de Congrès). Take bd. Gouvion St-Cyr past Palais de Congrès. Stained-glass windows dedicated to Joyce's novels brighten the upstairs restaurant and the downstairs bar. While a traditional Irish meal like stew with bacon and cabbage or ham with spuds and cheese (from €9.50) is good anytime, the Joyce truly becomes a destination whenever an important rugby match is on TV. An informal tourist office for middle-aged and younger Anglophone expats. Free "Funky Maps," which list all the English-speaking bars and pubs in Paris. F nights live Irish rock from 9:30pm, except in summer. Open daily 11am-2am. Food served noon-9pm. AmEx/MC/V. ❷

La Flèche d'Or, 102bis rue de Bagnolet (☎44 64 01 02; www.flechedor.fr). M: Alexandre Dumas. Follow rue de Bagnolet until it crosses rue des Pyrénées; the café is on the right. In a defunct train station, this bar/café/performance space serves internationally-inspired dishes (the "New York" is a bacon cheddar cheeseburger; €15). Nightly entertainment includes live bands. *Menus* €12-15. Open daily from whenever the show starts, usually 7-8pm, to 2am. Dinner served 8pm-midnight. MC/V. ❷

L'Endroit, 67 pl. du Dr. Félix Lobligeois (☎42 29 50 00). M: Rome. Follow rue Boursault to rue Legendre and turn right. Look for the blue exterior, the waitstaff's cutting-edge haircuts, and the revolving tower of liquor. As cool during the day as it is at night, L'Endroit is the place to be seen in the 17ème. 4-course weekend brunch (noon-3:30pm; €20, children's brunch €6) headlines a long menu packed with an array of big salads (€11-16) and toasted sandwiches (€12). Open daily 10am-2am. MC/V. ❸

L'Etoile du Kashmir, 3 rue des Batignolles (☎45 22 44 70). M: Rome. With Gare St-Lazare to your right, walk down bd. des Batignolles and turn left on rue des Batignolles. Serves Indian classics at low prices in a colorfully-lit interior. A 2-course lunch *formule* (vegetarian menu available; €7.50) and spicy curry with potatoes (€9) appeal to the budget-conscious, but the adventurous spring for the "chef's surprise for two people" (€28). Takeout for 15% less. Open daily noon-3pm and 7-11:30pm. ❶

SUPERMARKETS AND OUTDOOR MARKETS

It may be the food capital of Europe, but eating out in Paris can put a serious dent in your wallet—in only a few days. Fortunately, the city is packed with alternatives. Like any city, Paris has many **supermarkets.** One of the largest chains is **Monoprix,** which sells a comprehensive selection of high quality food at relatively high prices. Two less expensive options are **Casino** and **Franprix;** large and small branches of both can be easily found all over the city. **Lidl** and **Leader Price** are cheapest. The best way to find a supermarket is to check branch locations online or to ask on the street. Chances are, a supermarket is only a few blocks away.

Those looking for a more quintessentially Parisian way to pinch pennies will relish the city's **outdoor markets;** the Mayor's office website lists more than 80 (www.v1.paris.fr/EN/Living/markets/markets.asp). These markets, which frequently shut down entire streets, are a paradise for budget travelers. Vendors from stores all over Paris sell produce, cheese, wine, and prepared foods, among other things. If you're planning to do some serious shopping and have a small suitcase with wheels, bring it along. It will substitute for the small wheeled carts that many Parisian shoppers use for easy outdoor shopping.

Saxe-Breteuil Outdoor Market, av. de Saxe. M: Ségur. Exit the Metro and walk against traffic on rue Perignon, which leads directly to the market. With the Eiffel tower poised gracefully in the distance, the Saxe-Breteuil is a Parisian institution. It backs up its impeccable style with an incredible selection of produce, seafood, and cheese. A wine vendor frequently hands out samples of the day's stock; ask nicely. There's even a falafel stand. It's best to arrive before noon. Open Sa 7am-3pm.

Belleville Outdoor Market. M: Belleville. Not for the faint of heart, this middle-eastern influenced market can provide a thrilling experience. Produce, spices, sneakers, belts, and everything else you can think of are squeezed onto bd. de Belleville. It's best to know what you're coming for; vendors behind the tables bellow at anyone who walks by, leaving browsers bewildered. This is the place for dates and figs. Look out for pickpockets. Open Tu and F 7:30am-2:30pm.

St-Germain Covered Market. M: Mabillon. Exit the Metro and walk down rue de Montfaucon. The market is inside the large building at the end of the street, at the back. While this market cannot keep up with its outdoor cousins in terms of size or ambience, it will appeal to travelers looking to get their food and go. Its selection–particularly of fresh seafood–is great. Open Tu-Sa 8:30am-1pm and 4-7:30pm, Su 8:30am-1pm.

Batignolles Organic Produce Market. M: Rome. Exit the Metro and, with Gare St-Lazare on your right, walk down bd. des Batignolles. The market is on the traffic divider in the middle of the street. For those looking to live green while traveling, this market brings in the best organic produce around. Open Sa-Su 10am-2pm.

SIGHTS

To see most of what makes Paris Paris—medieval passageways, sidewalk cafés, the gleaming white **Sacré-Coeur Cathedral,** 19th-century boulevards, the majestic **Arc de Triomphe,** regal gardens—doesn't require much more than open eyes and a penchant for wandering. From **Notre-Dame** on Ile de la Cité to the **Père Lachaise Cemetery** in the 20ème, the City of Light brims with history, intrigue, and architectural splendor. Paris is embarrassingly pretty, particularly at night; it's well worth setting aside time after dinner for a stroll. Unlike its museums, most sights in Paris are either free or reasonably priced, so anyone can get a gorgeous eyeful while still saving enough to splurge on a fancy Parisian dinner (always keep your priorities in mind). Expect many of the more popular sights to be particularly crowded in the summer, and know that the **Eiffel Tower** will be mobbed almost all the time. Most sights are open daily, but many have alternate weekend hours during French school holidays.

SEINE ISLANDS

TIP **THE EARLY BIRD BEATS THE CROWDS.** Ile de la Cité can seem like the apocalyptic center of European tourism sometimes, but you can avoid the crowds if you're willing to get an extra-early start. While Notre Dame is open at 7:45am, the tourists don't arrive until 9am, and a line doesn't form at Ste-Chapelle until the late morning.

NOTRE DAME

M: Cité. ☎42 34 56 10; crypt ☎55 42 50 10. Cathedral open daily 7:45am-7pm. Towers open Jan.-Mar. and Oct.-Dec. daily 10am-5:30pm; Apr.-Sept. daily 10am-6:30pm; June-Aug. Sa-Su 10am-11pm. €7.50, ages 18-25 €5, under 18 free. Audio tours €5. Tours begin at the entrance booth. In French M-F 2, 3pm; call ahead for English tours. Free. Mass M-F 8, 9am (except July-Aug.), noon, 6:15pm; Sa 9am, 6:30pm; Su 8:30, 9:30, 11:30am, 12:45, 6:30pm. Gregorian chant 10pm. Free recital by a cathedral organist 4:30pm. Vespers M-Sa 5:45pm. Treasury open M-F 9:30am-6pm, Sa 9:30am-5pm, Su 1-1:30pm and 6-6:30pm, last entry 15min. before closing. €3, under 26 €2, under 18 €1. Crypt open Tu-Su 10am-6pm, last entry 5:30pm. €3.50, over 60 €2.50, under 27 €1.50, under 13 free. MC/V over €15.

Nothing in Paris lives a double-life quite like Notre Dame. Since its beginnings in 1163, the world-famous cathedral has been turned into a "Temple of Reason" by secular revolutionaries, used for the papal coronation of Napoleon, served as housing for livestock, been home to Victor Hugo's famous hunchback, and provided shelter for Parisians facing the imminent invasion of the Nazis. It has held royal weddings—including that of Henri of Navarre and Marguerite—and major trials—such as Joan of Arc's heresy hearings in 1455. The cathedral seems to be front and center for every major French event—Charles de Gaulle was almost shot by Nazi snipers on the way to give thanks here for France's liberation during WWII. Despite the close ties between Parisians and their cathedral, visiting Notre Dame itself can be a depressing experience. At 9am, hundreds of tourists descend upon the building, tramp around, gawk, and snap as many photos as they can. As a site of architectural interest, Notre Dame remains the arch-example of the Gothic style, but the spiritual awe it was built to provoke is probably a thing of the past.

Newly cleaned, Notre Dame's **exterior** looks better than it has in decades. The oldest work is above the **Porte de Ste-Anne** (right), dating from 1165 to 1175. After sending Louis XIV to the guillotine, Revolutionaries attacked the Kings of Judah above the doors. The heads are now exhibited in the Musée de Cluny (p. 153). Watch for the lazy gargoyle looking bored on the tower. The cathedral's **interior** seems to be constructed of weightless walls, thanks to the flying buttresses that support the vaulted ceiling from outside. The transept's **rose windows,** nearly 85% 13th-century glass, are the most spectacular feature. A chart on the right side of the cathedral outlines the progression of the Gothic style in French cathedrals, lending some useful context to Notre Dame itself. The **treasury,** south of the choir, contains an assortment of artifacts. The famous **Crown of Thorns,** allegedly worn by Jesus, was moved to Notre Dame at the end of the 18th century and is presented only on Fridays during Lent (5-6pm). The **Crypte Archéologique,** pl. du Parvis du Notre Dame, houses artifacts unearthed in the construction of a parking garage.

Two years of sandblasting have brightened the **towers,** revealing the rose windows and rows of saints. The claustrophobia-inducing staircase leads out onto a

DISTANCE: 3.5km/2¼ mi.

DURATION: 4½ hr.

WHEN TO GO: In the afternoon.

THE HEART OF THE CITY OF LOVE

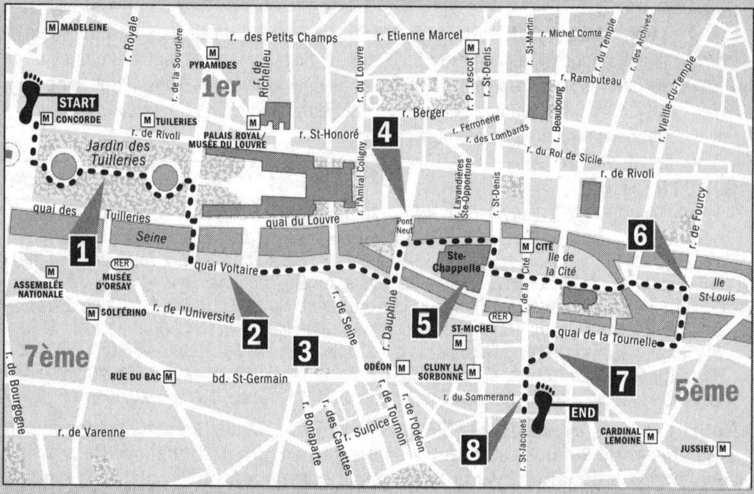

1. JARDIN DES TUILERIES. Like the nearby sidewalks of the Champs-Elysées, this garden features broad pathways perfect for people-watching. Unlike the Champs-Elysées, it has not been taken over by traffic, fast-food joints, and car dealerships (p. 130).

2. QUAI VOLTAIRE. Head for the Seine and cross Pont Royal, then turn left onto quai Voltaire. Name an artist. That artist probably lived on this block. Baudelaire, Wagner, Delacroix, and Sibelius are a few examples. Check the plaques on the buildings for others (p. 135).

3. SEINE BOOKSELLERS. Working out of stands along the Seine, these vendors may be the best resource in Paris for cheap used books, old magazines, and 19th-century comics.

4. PONT NEUF. Paris's oldest bridge links Ile de la Cité to the right and left banks. If you've brought a significant other along, it's the best place in the city to make out (p. 129).

5. SAINT-CHAPELLE. Walk down the island and turn inward at bd. du Palais. Built in the 13th century to house relics of Christ, the chapel now serves as the foremost example of Gothic architecture, with hundreds of magnificent panels of stained glass (p. 129).

6. BERTHILLON AND AMORINO. Walk to the far end of the island on rue Lutece. Cross the bridge onto Ile St-Louis. Behold the great ice-cream rivalry! Berthillon is the heavyweight, but Amarino, which offers more generous helpings, makes for a scrappy challenger (p. 118).

7. SHAKESPEARE & CO. Cross Pont de Tournelle and make a right onto quai de la Tournelle. This English-language bookshop had the foresight to publish "Ulysses" in 1922—its role as a Parisian literary hub has not changed (p. 164).

8. NATIONAL MUSEUM OF THE MIDDLE AGES. One of Paris's best museums is housed in a medieval mansion. With the famed "Lady and the Unicorn" tapestries, it can be easy to miss the wood-carved Romanesque altarpieces or the dazzling manuscripts that fill out the collection (p. 153). The Cluny-La Sorbonne Metro stop is two blocks away.

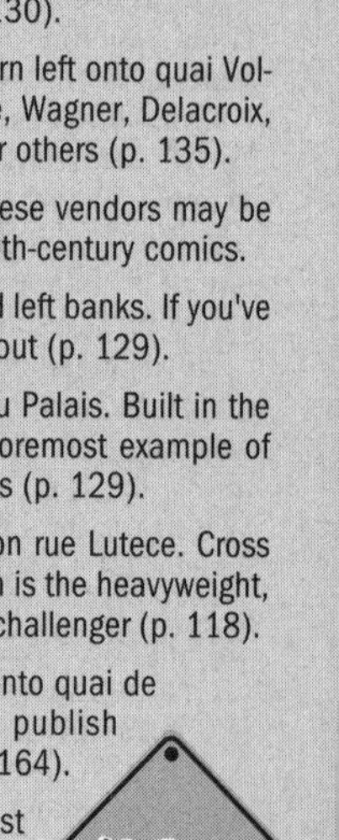

spectacular perch, where troops of gargoyles survey the city. In the south tower, a tiny door opens onto the 13-ton bell that even Quasimodo couldn't ring; it requires the force of eight people to move.

STE-CHAPELLE. Ste-Chapelle remains the foremost example of flamboyant Gothic architecture and a tribute to the craft of medieval stained glass. The Lower Chapel has a blue vaulted ceiling dotted with golden *fleurs-de-lis*, but the real star is the Upper Chapel. When light pours through its stained-glass windows on sunny days, illuminating frescoes of saints and martyrs, it's one of the most breathtaking sights in Paris. The windows, dating from 1136, narrate the Bible from Genesis to the Apocalypse; read them from bottom to top, left to right. *(6 bd. du Palais. M: Cité. Within Palais de la Cité. ☎53 40 60 93; www.monum.fr. Open daily Nov.-Feb. 9am-5pm; Mar.-Oct. 9:30am-6pm; last entry 30min. before closing. €7.50, seniors and ages 18-25 €4.80, under 18 free. Ticket with Conciergerie €9.50, seniors and ages 18-25 €7, under 18 free. Cash only. Occasional candlelit classical music concerts held in the Upper Chapel Mar.-Nov. €16-25. Check the FNAC website, www.fnac.fr, or the booth to the left of the ticket-taker for details.)*

PONT NEUF. The Pont Neuf (New Bridge) is, logically enough, the oldest bridge in Paris. Once Paris's most popular thoroughfare, it's now Paris's most popular make-out spot. *(M: Pont Neuf.)*

MÉMORIAL DE LA DÉPORTATION. This memorial commemorates the 200,000 French victims of Nazi concentration camps. Inside, the focal point is a tunnel lined with 200,000 quartz pebbles, reflecting the Jewish custom of placing stones on graves of the deceased. A barred window that looks out over the Seine is particularly moving. *(M: Cité. At the very tip of the island on pl. de l'Ile de France, a 5min. walk from the back of the cathedral, and down a narrow flight of steps. Open daily Apr.-Sept. 10am-noon and 2-7pm; Oct.-Mar. 10am-noon and 2-5pm. Last admission 10min. before closing. Free.)*

RUE ST-LOUIS-EN-L'ILE. The main thoroughfare of Ile St-Louis, this narrow, cobblestone street is home to an enticing collection of clothing boutiques, gourmet food stores, ice cream shops, and galleries. A charming, quiet oasis, the *rue* is a relief in such a hyper-touristed area of town. *(This street bisects the island lengthwise.)*

QUAI DE BOURBON. Sculptor Camille Claudel lived and worked at **no. 19** from 1899 until her brother, poet Paul Claudel, committed her to an asylum in 1913. Camille was driven mad by the rejection of her mentor and lover, sculptor Auguste Rodin. Her most striking work is displayed in the Musée Rodin (p. 157). At the intersection of the quai and rue des Deux Ponts sits the café **Au Franc-Pinot,** whose wrought-iron facade is almost as old as the island itself. Closed in 1716 when authorities discovered anti-government tracts, the café-cabaret reemerged as a center for treason during the Revolution: the daughter of the proprietor made an unsuccessful attempt on Robespierre's life in 1794 and was guillotined. *(Visible to the left after crossing Pont St-Louis; the quai wraps around the northwest edge of the island.)*

PALAIS DE JUSTICE. Built after the great fire of 1776, the Palais is home to the district courts of France. All trials are open to the public; choose a door and make your way through the green gates that stand beyond *Egalité*. Climb the stairs to the second floor and immediately go left (look for "Cour d'Appel" signs); guards will let you into a courtroom viewing gallery. *(Within Palais de la Cité, 4 bd. du Palais; use the entrance for Ste-Chapelle at 6 bd. du Palais. M: Cité. ☎44 32 51 51. Courtrooms open M-F 9am-noon and 1:30-end of last trial. Free.)*

CHÂTELET-LES-HALLES AND OPÉRA

EGLISE DE ST-EUSTACHE. There is a reason why Richelieu and Molière were baptized in the Eglise de St-Eustache, why Louis XIV received communion in its

PARIS

sanctuary, and why Mozart had his mother's funeral here: it is magnificent—at least on the outside. Construction of the church began in 1532 and wasn't completed until the mid-1700s. The chapels contain paintings by Rubens, a joyous bronze panel by former phenom Keith Haring, and the British artist Raymond Mason's bizarre relief *Departure of the Fruits and Vegetables from the Heart of Paris*, commemorating the closing of the market at Les Halles. The art makes for a fascinating contrast with the deteriorating interior. A large, ongoing restoration process is underway, but even under scaffolding, the church is a treat. *(M: Les Halles. Above rue Rambuteau. ☎42 36 31 05; www.saint-eustache.org. Open M-F 9:30am-7pm, Sa 10am-7pm, Su 9am-7:15pm. Mass M-F 12:30, 6pm; Sa 6pm; Su 9:30, 11am, 6pm.)*

GALERIES AND PASSAGES. Paris's *passages* (and their posh siblings, *galeries*) are considered the world's first shopping malls. In the early 19th century, speculators built shopping arcades in alleys all over central Paris. They designed panes of glass, held in place by lightweight iron rods, to attract window shoppers. Most have disappeared because of urban development, but the 20 or so that remain have been restored and are perfect for a rainy-day stroll. The *galeries* that surround the Jardins du Palais Royal are the most famous in Paris, but others in the 1er and 2ème are also worthwhile; keep your eyes out for arched doorways. Today, they house upscale clothing boutiques, cafés, and gift shops (several sell antique postcards). They are also great places to find antique bookstores.

PLACE VENDÔME. Stately pl. Vendôme, by the Tuileries, was constructed in 1702 as a monument to the military prowess of Louis XIV. Designed by Jules Hardouin-Mansart, the square was built to house embassies, but bankers liked the place and bought it, constructing lavish private homes behind the elegant facades. Today, the smell of money is still in the air: shop windows filled with perfumes, jewelry, designer clothes, and other unaffordable luxuries line the square. *(M: Tuileries.)*

JARDIN DES TUILERIES. Sweeping down from the Louvre to pl. de la Concorde, the Jardin des Tuileries celebrates the victory of geometry over nature. Missing the public promenades of her native Italy, Catherine de Médici had the gardens built in 1564. In 1664, André Le Nôtre (the mastermind behind the Versailles gardens) imposed straight lines and topiaries on the grounds. Sculptures of figures from classical mythology line the pathways, and cafés and courts are scattered throughout the park. In the summer, rue de Rivoli's terrace becomes an amusement park with rides, food stands, and a huge ferris wheel. *(M: Tuileries. ☎40 20 90 43. Open daily Apr.-Sept. 7am-11pm; Oct.-Mar. 7:30am-7:30pm. English tours from the Arc de Triomphe du Carrousel. Amusement park open July to mid-Aug.)*

BIBLIOTHÈQUE NATIONALE: SITE RICHELIEU. Site Richelieu was the main branch of the **Bibliothèque Nationale de France** (National Library) until 1998, when most of the collection was moved to the new Site Mitterrand in the 13ème (p. 140). Housed in this fortress are collections of stamps, money, photography, medals, maps, and manuscripts. Scholars must pass through a strict screening process to gain access to the main reading room, but temporary exhibits are open to the public. *(58 rue de Richelieu. M: Bourse. Just north of the Galeries Vivienne and Colbert, across rue Vivienne. Info line ☎53 79 87 93, tours ☎53 79 86 87; www.bnf.fr. Library open M-F 9am-6pm, Sa 9am-5pm. Books available only to researchers who prove they need access to the collection. Tours of the former reading room, La Salle Labrouste, 1st Tu of the month 2:30pm in French; €7. Reservations recommended. Galleries open only when there are exhibits Tu-Sa 10am-7pm, Su noon-7pm. Admission depends on the exhibit but is usually €5-7, students €4-5.)*

LES HALLES. A sprawling market since 1135, Les Halles received its first face-lift in the 1850s with the addition of large iron-and-glass pavilions. In 1970, the market was torn down and replaced with a cinema called Forum des Halles, as well as the

PARIS

depressing underground shopping mall that still stands today—it looks like a cross between an airport and a Soviet *gulag*, with the addition of a Starbucks. The urban renewal above ground brought gardens and futuristic structures that break up the bleakness underground, shedding some light on subterranean shoppers. Beware of pickpockets. *(M: Les Halles.)*

THE MARAIS

PLACE DES VOSGES. The magnificent pl. des Vosges, at the end of rue des Francs-Bourgeois, is Paris's oldest public square and one of its most charming spots. Kings built several mansions on this site, including the Palais de Tournelles, which Catherine de Médici ordered destroyed after her husband Henri II died there in a jousting tournament in 1563. Henri IV subsequently had it rebuilt. Each of the 36 buildings lining the square has an arcade on street level, two stories of pink brick, and a slate-covered roof. Molière, Racine, and Voltaire filled the grand parlors with their *bons mots*, and Mozart played a concert here at age seven. During the Revolution, the statue of Louis XIII in the center of the park was destroyed (the current one is a copy), and the park was renamed pl. des Vosges, after the first department in France to pay its taxes. Victor Hugo lived at no. 6, now a museum (see p. 152) devoted to his life and work. *(M: Chemin Vert or St-Paul.)*

RUE DES ROSIERS. In the heart of the Marais Jewish community, rue des Rosiers is refreshingly bistro-free. Instead, the locals and tourists who stroll down this street head for the kosher deli and the best falafel in Paris. When Philippe-Auguste expelled Jews from the city in the 13th century, many families moved to this area, which lay just outside the city walls. Since then, the quarter has seen an influx of Russian Jews in the 19th century, and of North African Sephardim, who fled Algeria in the 1960s. *(4 blocks east of Beaubourg, parallel to rue des Francs-Bourgeois. M: St-Paul.)*

RUE VIEILLE-DU-TEMPLE AND RUE STE-CROIX DE LA BRETONNERIE. Winter, spring, summer, or fall—the intersection of these two streets is always hot. The epicenter of Paris's GLBT community, this area has recently seen tourists joining beautiful boys in skin-tight jeans and girls walking hand-in-hand. Although many establishments fly the rainbow flag, queer and straight go together: people of all stripes wander through trendy boutiques while intellectuals sip merlot. *(M: St-Paul or Hôtel de Ville. 1 block north of rue de Rivoli, where rue du Roi de Sicile becomes rue de la Verrerie; rue Vieille-du-Temple meets it and, 1 block north, crosses rue Ste-Croix de la Bretonnerie.)*

ARCHIVES NATIONALES. At the **Musée de l'Histoire de France,** curators draw on documents held in France's National Archives to put together rotating temporary exhibits. While their focus tends to be narrow, the museum's sheer wealth of material compensates somewhat. The exhibits are housed in the plush 18th-century Hôtel de Soubise. Call ahead for upcoming exhibitions. *(60 rue des Francs-Bourgeois. M: Rambuteau. ☎40 27 60 00. Open M-F 10am-12:30pm and 2-5:30pm, Su 2-5:30pm.)*

EGLISE ST-PAUL-ST-LOUIS. The dome of the 17th-century Eglise St-Paul-St-Louis is visible from a distance. Up close, the church's exterior, desperately in need of a good scrub-down, is less appealing. Paintings inside depict four French kings: Clovis, Charlemagne, Robert the Pious, and St-Louis. There's even a painting by Delacroix, *Le Christ au Jardin des Oliviers*, on the left side of the transept. Before being destroyed during the Revolution, Louis XIII and Louis XIV's embalmed hearts were kept in vermeil boxes guarded by silver angel statues. The holy-water vessels were gifts from Victor Hugo. Around dusk, many homeless individuals call the church steps home. *(99 rue St-Antoine. M: St-Paul. ☎42 72 30 32. Open M-W and F-Su 8am-8pm, Th 8am-10pm. Free tours in French at 3pm every 1st and 2nd Su of the month, or call to arrange special visits. Mass M 7pm; Tu-F 9am, 7pm; Sa 9am, 6pm; Su 9:30, 11am, 7pm.)*

HÔTEL DE VILLE. Paris's grandiose city hall dominates a large square filled with fountains and Belle Epoque lampposts. The present edifice is a 19th-century replica of the original medieval structure, which was a meeting hall for the cartel that controlled traffic on the Seine. Municipal executions took place on pl. Hôtel-de-Ville; in 1610, Henri IV's assassin, Ravaillac, was drawn and quartered here. In 1871, *communards* doused the building with gasoline and set it on fire, creating a blaze that lasted eight days and left only the frame. Today, the square occasionally hosts concerts. *(Information office, 29 rue de Rivoli. M: Hôtel de Ville. ☎ 42 76 43 43. Open M-F 9am-7pm when there is an exhibit, until 6pm otherwise. Group tours available with advance reservations, call for available dates. Special exhibit entry on rue de Lobau.)*

HÔTEL DE SENS. The Hôtel de Sens houses the **Bibliothèque Forney** and provides one of the city's few surviving examples of medieval residential architecture. Built in 1474 for Tristan de Salazar, the Archbishop of Sens, its military adornments reflect the violence of its time. The *hôtel* is well fortified against invaders, with turrets to guard the surrounding streets, a dungeon in the square tower, and chutes for pouring boiling water down on unwanted visitors in its Gothic arch entrance. A former residence of Queen Margot, Henri IV's first wife, the Hôtel also saw its share of royal scandal. In 1606, the 55-year-old queen drove up to her courtyard to find her two lovers-of-the-month arguing. When one opened the lady's carriage door, the other shot him dead. Unfazed, the queen ordered the perpetrator's execution. The Hôtel recently underwent a significant renovation; as a result, hours and admission prices may have changed. Call ahead for details. *(1 rue du Figuier. M: Pont Marie. ☎ 42 78 14 60. Open Tu-Sa 1:30-7pm. Special exhibits €4, seniors and under 26 €3.)*

LATIN QUARTER AND ST-GERMAIN

JARDIN DU LUXEMBOURG AND PALAIS DU LUXEMBOURG. Parisians flock to these spectacular formal gardens, violent winds be damned (seriously, there are violent winds here). With chairs conveniently placed along the paths and big, open views of the sky, it's difficult to walk through without pausing to take a seat. A residential area in Roman Paris, the site of a medieval monastery, and later the home of 17th-century French royalty, the gardens were liberated during the Revolution and are now free to all. *(6ème. M: Odéon or RER: Luxembourg. The main entrance is on bd. St-Michel. Open daily dawn-dusk. Guided tours in French Apr.-Oct. 1st W of every month at 9:30am; depart from pl. André Honorat behind the observatory.)* The Palais du Luxembourg, located within the park and home to the French Senate (and thus closed to the public), was built in 1615 for Marie de Médicis. Homesick for Florence, the queen tried to recreate her native architecture and gardens in her new home in Paris. In 1630, during a titanic power play between Marie and her erstwhile ally Cardinal Richelieu, Marie threw such a legendary tantrum that her son, Louis XIII, kicked her off the royal council and exiled her to Cologne. During WWII, the palace was used by the Nazis as headquarters for the *Luftwaffe*. *(6ème. www.monum.fr.)*

PANTHÉON. Ascribing his recovery from grave illness to the powers of Ste-Geneviève, Louis XV vowed to build a memorial in her name. The first stone was laid in 1764. In 1791, Revolutionaries converted the church into a mausoleum of heroes. Some of France's most distinguished citizens are buried here, including Marie and Pierre Curie, Jean Jaurès, Voltaire, Jean-Jacques Rousseau, Emile Zola, and Victor Hugo. The crypt also contains the heart of Léon Gambetta in a big red urn, which is pretty gross. The Panthéon's other main attraction is **Foucault's Pendulum.** The pendulum's plane of oscillation stays fixed as the Earth rotates around it, confirming the Earth's rotation for nonbelievers like Louis Napoleon III. *(pl. du Panthéon. M: Cardinal Lemoine or RER Luxembourg. From rue Cardinal Lemoine, turn right on rue Clovis; walk around to* *the front of the building to enter. ☎44 32 18 04. Open daily Apr.-Sept. 10am-6:30pm; Oct.-Mar. 10am-6pm; last admission 45min. before closing. Free 1st Su of the month Oct.-Mar. Guided tours in English, French, German, and Spanish leave from inside the main door; call ahead for times. The Panthéon is* tenue correcte; *visitors must dress conservatively and silence their cell phones. €7.50, ages 18-25 €5, under 18 free.)*

EGLISE ST-GERMAIN-DES-PRÉS. The Eglise de St-Germain-des-Prés, the oldest standing church in Paris, is the last remnant of what was once one of the richest abbeys in the world. Completed in AD 558, the church was the centerpiece of the Abbey of St-Germain-des-Prés, a center of Catholic intellectual life until it was disbanded during the Revolution. Worn away over the years by fire and even a saltpeter explosion, what remains of the abbey's exterior looks appropriately world-weary. The magnificent interior, completely redone in the 19th century, is painted in maroon, deep green, and gold; especially striking are the royal blue and gold-starred ceiling, frescoes depicting the life of Jesus, and decorative mosaics along the archways. The information window at the church entrance has a schedule of the church's frequent concerts. *(3 pl. St-Germain-des-Prés. M: St-Germain-des-Prés. Walk into pl. St-Germain-des-Prés to enter the church from the front. ☎55 42 81 18. Open daily 8am-7:45pm. Info office open M 2:30-6:45pm, Tu-F 10:30am-noon and 2:30-6:45pm, Sa 3-6:45pm.)*

EGLISE ST-SULPICE. The Neoclassical facade of the Eglise St-Sulpice dominates the enormous square by the same name. Designed by Servadoni in 1733, the church is both unfinished and in need of a restoration. Scaffolding surrounding the North Tower is scheduled to come down in mid-2008. Look for the set of Delacroix frescoes in the first chapel on the right, Jean-Baptiste Pigalle's *Virgin and Child* in a rear chapel, and a large organ used in frequent concerts. The stark, dirty, legitimately unattractive interior provides a contrast to these three gems. *(M: St-Sulpice or Mabillon. From M: Mabillon, walk down rue du Four and make a left onto rue Mabillon. Rue Mabillon intersects rue St-Sulpice at the entrance to the church. ☎42 34 59 60; www.paroisse-saint-sulpice-paris.org. Open daily 7:30am-7:30pm. Guided tour in French Su 3pm.)*

MOSQUÉE DE PARIS. Built in 1920 to honor the role of North African countries in WWI, the **Institut Musulman** houses the elaborate minaret and shady porticoes of the Mosquée de Paris. The dense cedar doors lead to ascetic prayer rooms (visible from the courtyard but closed to the public). Additional amenities include a soothing café (p. 121), relaxing steam bath, and *hammam. (39 rue St-Hilaire, behind the Jardin des Plantes at pl. du Puits de l'Ermite. M: Censier Daubenton. Walk down rue Daubenton and turn left at the end of the street onto rue Georges Desplas; the mosque is on the right. ☎43 31 38 20; www.la-mosquee.com. Open daily 10am-noon and 2-5:30pm.* Hammam *open for men Tu 2-9pm, Su 10am-9pm; women M, W-Th, Sa 10am-9pm, F 2-9pm. €15. Massage €10 per 10min., €30 per 30min. Guided tour €3, under 18 €2. MC/V.)*

RUE MOUFFETARD. The 5ème's rue Mouffetard, south of pl. de la Contrescarpe, hosts one of Paris's oldest and liveliest street markets. Hemingway lived on the Mouff at 74 rue du Cardinal Lemoine. The stretch up rue Mouffetard, past pl. de la Contrescarpe, and onto rue Descartes and rue de la Montagne Ste-Geneviève is the quintessential Latin Quarter stroll, which attracts a mix of Parisians and visitors. *(M: Cardinal Lemoine, Place Monge, or Censier Daubenton.)*

ODÉON. The **Cour du Commerce St-André** is one of the most picturesque walking areas in the 6ème, with cobblestone streets, centuries-old cafés (including **Le Procope**), and outdoor seating. Beyond the arch stands the **Relais Odéon,** a Belle Epoque bistro whose stylishly painted exterior is a fine example of the Art Nouveau style. The **Carrefour d'Odéon,** just to the south of bd. St-Germain-des-Prés, is a favorite Parisian hangout filled with sidewalk bistros and cafés. *(M: St-Germain-des-Prés.)*

BOULEVARD ST-GERMAIN. While this street is famous as the former stomping grounds of existentialist artists and intellectuals, the literary café culture here has gone the way of the dodo—now it's devoted to *haute couture*. Bd. St-Germain displays an unabashed indulgence in all things fashionable and cutting edge. While upscale chains dominate the street itself, excellent designer boutiques have made inroads into the area in recent years. *(M: St-Germain-des-Prés.)*

CAFÉ DE FLORE AND LES DEUX MAGOTS. These two literary landmarks, once the hangouts of Brigitte Bardot and Jean-Paul Sartre, are now sadly filled with crowds of tourists and businessmen willing to pay for the history with exorbitantly priced coffee (€4-7). While they are not worth a culinary stop, both cafés offer plenty of opportunities for intellectual idolatry. Sartre composed his famous *Being and Nothingness* in Café de Flore, and you can see the booth he used to share with lover Simone de Beauvoir in the upstairs Art Deco seating, on the left. Not to be outdone, Les Deux Magots boasts a cloistered area behind high hedges that was home to literati from Mallarmé to Hemingway. *(M: St-Germain-des-Prés. Café de Flore, 172 bd. St-Germain. ☎45 48 55 26. Open daily 7:30am-1:30am. AmEx/MC/V. Les Deux Magots, 6 pl. St-Germain-des-Prés. ☎45 48 55 25. Open daily 7:30am-1am. AmEx/MC/V.)*

LA SORBONNE. Founded in 1253 by Robert de Sorbon as a dormitory for 16 poor theology students, the Sorbonne has since diversified its curriculum and earned a place among the world's most esteemed universities. In accordance with its elite status, the Sorbonnne is not open to the public—but only until 2009, when the undergoing renovations on the **Chapelle de la Sorbonne** finish up. **Place de la Sorbonne** is sprinkled with an assortment of cafés, bookstores, and—during termtime—students. *(45-47 rue des Ecoles. M: Cluny-La Sorbonne or RER: Luxembourg. Walk away from the Seine on bd. St-Michel and turn left on rue des Ecoles to see the main building.)*

JARDIN DES PLANTES. The Jardin des Plantes has 45,000 square meters of carefully tended flowers and lush greenery. Opened in 1640 by Louis XIII's doctor, the gardens originally grew medicinal plants to promote His Majesty's health. Today, it seems like the soil is as good for nine-year-old French children as it is for flowers, and the constant hum of construction detracts from the peaceful atmosphere. The **Ecole de Botanique** is a landscaped garden tended by students, horticulturists, and amateur botanists. The **Roserie** has roses from all over the world, which are in full bloom in mid-June. The gardens also include the **Musée d'Histoire Naturelle** and the **Ménagerie Zoo,** with 1100 animals. During the 1871 siege of Paris, starving Parisians ate a few of the elephants, which you can bet the pachyderms' relatives never forgot. *(M: Gare d'Austerlitz, Jussieu, or Censier-Daubenton. ☎40 79 37 94. Jardin des Plantes, Ecole de Botanique and Roserie open daily in summer 7:30am-8pm; in winter 8am-5:30pm. Free. Grandes Serres, 57 rue Cuvier. Due to reopen in late 2007. Ménagerie Zoo, 3 quai St-Bernard and 57 rue Cuvier. Open daily Apr.-Sept. 10am-6pm; Oct.-Mar. 10am-5:30pm. Last entrance 30min. before closing. €6, students €4.)*

COLLÈGE DE FRANCE. Created by François I in 1530 as an alternative to the Sorbonne, the prestigious Collège de France stands just behind its more prestigious counterpart. The humanist motto *Doce Omnia* ("Teach Everything") is in mosaics in the interior courtyard. Courses at the college—given in the past by such luminaries as Henri Bergson, Pierre Boulez, Michel Foucault, Milan Kundera, and Paul Valéry—are free for all. The Collège is otherwise closed to the public. *(11 pl. Marcelin-Berthelot. M: Maubert-Mutualité. Walk against traffic on bd. St-Germain, turn left on rue Thenard; the entrance to the Collège is at the end of the road, across rue des Ecoles and up the steps. ☎44 27 12 11 or 44 27 11 47; www.college-de-france.fr. Courses Oct.-May. Closed Aug.)*

PLACE ST-MICHEL. The Latin Quarter meets the Seine at this monumental locale where the 1871 Paris Commune and the 1968 student uprising began. Tourists—no locals here, thank you—pose for photos in front of the *place*'s centerpiece, a majestic 1860 fountain featuring St-Michel slaying a demon. **Eglise St-Séverin** has spiraling columns and modern stained glass. Follow rue de la Harpe away from the square and turn left on rue St-Séverin. The 1170 **Eglise St-Julien-le-Pauvre,** across bd. St-Jacques from St-Séverin, is one of Paris's oldest churches. Visitors can check out the traditional bistros on nearby **rue Soufflot** and **rue des Fossés St-Jacques.** *(M: St-Michel.)*

INVALIDES

EIFFEL TOWER. Gustave Eiffel wrote about his tower: "France is the only country in the world with a 300m flagpole." Designed in 1889 as the tallest structure in the world, the Eiffel Tower was conceived as a monument to engineering in the modern age and intended to surpass the Egyptian pyramids in size and notoriety. Critics dubbed it a "metal asparagus" and a "Parisian Tower of Babel." Writer Guy de Maupassant ate lunch every day at its ground-floor restaurant—the only place in Paris, he claimed, from which he couldn't see the offensive thing. Nonetheless, when it was inaugurated in March 1889 as the centerpiece of the *Exposition Universelle* (World's Fair), the Tower earned Parisians' love; nearly two million people ascended during the fair alone. Some still criticize its glut of tourists, trinkets, and con artists (beware the "refugees" who ask for money) but don't believe the anti-hype—the tower is a wonder of design and engineering, and is truly stunning up close. *(M: Bir-Hakeim or Trocadéro. ☎44 11 23 23; www.tour-eiffel.fr. Open daily mid-June to Aug. 9am-midnight; Sept. to mid-June 9:30am-11pm; stairs 9:30am-6pm. Last access to top 30min. before closing. Elevator to 1st fl. €4.50, under 12 €2.30; 2nd fl. €7.80/4.30; top €11.50/6. Stairs to 1st and 2nd fl. €3.50, under 3 free.)*

TIP **DON'T GET A-WRIST-ED.** If you are approached near a popular tourist spot by someone with colorful string, watch your wrists. Once he starts tying the "bracelet" that he completed in less than a minute, the only way to get out of paying for it is karate.

HÔTEL NATIONAL DES INVALIDES. The Hôtel des Invalides's gorgeous gold-leaf dome can be seen throughout the neighborhood. Built by Napoleon as a hospital for soldiers wounded in the service of the Empire, it is both ironic and appropriate that Invalides would come to house a complex of museums glorifying French military history. The **Musée de l'Armée,** which has Napoleon's hat and not much else of interest, and the **Musée de l'Ordre de la Liberation** are worth a look; but the real star is the **Musée des Plans-Reliefs,** which houses dozens of enormous, detailed models of French fortresses and towns, all made around 1700. Don't miss the model of **Mont St-Michel** or the hilarious **Fort Paté,** which looks like its namesake meat spread. The **Eglise St-Louis** also has **Napoleon's tomb,** which compensates for its startling simplicity through sheer enormity. *(127 rue de Grenelle. M: Invalides. Enter from pl. des Invalides or pl. Vauban and av. de Tourville. Open daily Apr.-Sept. 10am-6pm; Oct.-Mar. 10am-5pm.)*

CHAMPS DE MARS. The Champs de Mars, a tree-lined expanse stretching from the Ecole Militaire to the Eiffel Tower, is named, appropriately enough, after the god of war. Close to the 7ème's monuments and museums, the field was a drill ground for the Ecole Militaire under Napoleon. Today, kids may be frolicking and birds twittering, but the Champs isn't maintained very well and certainly can't hold a candle to Paris's many spectacular public parks and gardens. *(M: La Motte Picquet-Grenelle or Ecole Militaire. From the av. de la Motte-Picquet, walk towards Ecole Militaire.)*

QUAI VOLTAIRE. The quai Voltaire boasts an artistic heritage more distinguished than any other Parisian block, although there's not much to see aside from a few small plaques. No. 27 is where Voltaire spent his last days. No. 19 was home to Baudelaire while he wrote *Les Fleurs du Mal* from 1856 to 1858, to Richard Wagner as he composed *Die Meistersinger* between 1861 and 1862, and to the exiled Oscar Wilde. Eugène Delacroix, and later Jean-Baptiste-Camille Corot, lived at no. 13. Jean-Auguste-Dominique Ingres died at no. 11 in 1867. The Russian ballet dancer Rudolf Nureyev lived at no. 23 from 1981 until his death in 1993. *(Along the Seine between Pont Royal and Pont du Carrousel. M: rue du Bac. Walk up rue du Bac to the river.)*

CHAMPS-ELYSÉES

PARC MONCEAU. This lush urban retreat, encircled by gold-tipped iron gates, borders the elegant bd. de Courcelles. A number of architectural oddities—covered bridges, Dutch windmills, Roman ruins, and roller rinks—make this a kids' romping ground as well as a formal garden. As it is slightly out of the way, this local afternoon hangout has few tourists. *(M: Monceau or Courcelles. Open daily Apr.-Oct. 7am-10pm; Nov.-Mar. 7am-8pm; last entry 15min. before closing.)*

PALAIS DE TOKYO. Built for the 1937 World Expo, this austere, neoclassical, and ugly Palais is home to the world-class **Musée d'Art Moderne de la Ville de Paris,** which offers free admission to its brilliantly curated permanent collection. For those emerging from the fray at the Louvre or Musée d'Orsay, the unhurried atmosphere and spacious architecture will be a welcome relief. Be sure to set aside time for two monumental paintings of dancers by Matisse, as well as a room devoted to the outrageous neo-expressionism of Georg Baselitz, Gerhard Richter, and others. *(11 av. du Président Wilson. M: Iéna. ☎53 67 40 00; www.mam.paris.fr. Open Tu and Th-Su 10am-6pm, W 10am-10pm. Permanent collections free; call ahead for prices for temporary exhibitions.)* The Palais's west wing houses the excellent **site de création contemporaine,** which exhibits today's hottest art. *(11 av. du Président Wilson. M: Iéna. ☎47 23 38 86; www.palaisdetokyo.com. Open Tu-Su noon-midnight. €6; seniors, under 25, groups of 10 or more €4.50; artists and art students €1.)*

ARC DE TRIOMPHE. The arch is situated at the top of a hill and offers a stunning view down the Champs-Elysées to the Tuileries and Louvre. In 1758, architect Charles François Ribart envisaged the spot as a monument to France's military prowess—in the form of a giant, bejeweled elephant. Fortunately for France, construction of the monument was not undertaken until 1806, when Napoleon imagined a less kitschy tribute with which to welcome his troops home. On July 14, 1919, the Arc provided the backdrop for the Allied victory parade. During WWII, Frenchmen were reduced to tears as the Nazis goose-stepped through their beloved monument. Today, this 165 ft. arch is dedicated to all French army soldiers and veterans. Don't miss the **tomb of the unknown soldier,** where an eternal flame has been burning since WWI. Inside the Arc, visitors can climb up to the **terrasse** observation deck to catch a brilliant view of the "Historic Axis," from the Arc de Triomphe du Carrousel and the Louvre Pyramid at one end to the Grande Arche de la Défense at the other. *(M: Charles de Gaulle-Etoile. Wheelchair-accessible. Expect lines even on weekdays, although you can escape the crowds if you go before noon. You will kill yourself (and face a hefty fine) trying to dodge the 10-lane merry-go-round of cars around the arch, so use the pedestrian underpass on the right side of the Champs-Elysées facing the arch. Buy your ticket in the pedestrian underpass before going up to the ground level. Open daily Apr.-Sept. 10am-11pm; Oct.-Mar. 10am-10:30pm. Last entry 30min. before closing. €8, ages 18-25 €5, under 17 free. MC/V.)*

GRAND AND PETIT PALAIS. At the foot of the Champs-Elysées, the Grand and Petit Palais face one another on av. Winston Churchill. Built for the 1900 World's Fair, they exemplify Art Nouveau architecture; the Petit Palais's golden gate is especially dazzling. Today, the Petit Palais houses an eclectic mix of artwork, while the Grand Palais holds temporary exhibits on art, architecture, and French

haussmania

How Paris Cleaned Up Its Act

Like a clock, 12 straight boulevards radiate outward from pl. Charles de Gaulle. Café-lined streets and wide boulevards seem as organic to Paris as the snaking Seine. Yet none of this is an accident. The city's charm is calculated—it wasn't always so beautiful.

> **"Paris, as we find it in the period following the Revolution...was uninhabitable."**

Social commentator Maxime du Camp observed in the mid-19th century: "Paris, as we find it in the period following the Revolution of 1848, was uninhabitable. Its population...was suffocating in the narrow, tangled, putrid alleyways in which it was forcibly confined." Sewers were not used until 1848, and waste and trash rotted in the Seine. Streets followed a maddening 12th-century design; in some *quartiers*, winding thoroughfares were no wider than 3.5m. In the hands of Seine prefect Baron Georges-Eugène Haussmann, social architect under Emperor Louis Napoleon, the city's layout was demolished and reconstructed to embody a new urban vision.

> **"Like a clock, 12 straight boulevards radiate outwards from pl. de Gaulle."**

Haussmann replaced the medieval streets with his sewers and *grand boulevards;* he proclaimed the necessity of unifying Paris and promoting trade among *arrondissements*, viewing the old streets as impediments to commercial and political progress. His wide boulevards swept through whole neighborhoods of cramped row houses and passageways, displacing 350,000 of Paris's poorest residents.

The widespread rage at Haussmann's plans cemented the emperor's desire to use the city's layout to reinforce his authority. Haussmann believed that creating *grands boulevards* and carefully mapping the city could prevent future uprisings. However, during the 1871 revolt of the Paris Commune, which saw the rise of the Third Republic, the *grands boulevards* proved ideal for constructing protest barricades.

Despite the questionable underlying political agenda of Haussmannization, most of the prefect's changes were for the better. Haussmann transformed Montfauçon into the Parc des Buttes-Chaumont, replacing the open-air dump with pleasant waterfalls and grottoes. Paris became eminently navigable, and while it is hard to imagine the city as a sewer-less, alley-ridden metropolis, perhaps such a picture makes it seem all the more beautiful today.

Charlotte Houghteling *has worked on the* Let's Go's Middle East, Egypt, *and* Israel *titles. She completed her M.Phil. at Cambridge on the consumer society of Revolutionary Paris.*

Sara Houghteling *was a Researcher-Writer for* Let's Go: France 1999 *and holds a Masters in Fine Arts from the University of Michigan. Funded by a Fulbright Grant, Sara spent a year in Paris researching her upcoming novel.*

history. The Grand Palais also houses the **Palais de la Découverte,** a children's science museum. The complex is most beautiful at night, when its statues are backlit and the glass dome glows from within. *(M: Champs-Elysées-Clemenceau.)*

PLACE DU TROCADÉRO. In the 1820s, the Duc d'Angoulême built a memorial to his victory in Spain at Trocadéro. For the 1937 World's Fair, Jacques Carlu added two mirror-image white stone buildings called the **Palais de Chaillot,** which look more Soviet than French, as well as an austere veranda between them. The terrace attracts tourists, vendors, and roller bladers and offers the best Eiffel Tower view, day or night. Beware pickpockets and traffic as you gaze upward. *(M: Trocadéro.)*

AVENUE DES CHAMPS-ELYSÉES. Extending outward from the Louvre along its central axis, this wide thoroughfare is the most famous street in Paris. While it was the center of Parisian opulence in the early 20th century—with flashy mansions towering above exclusive cafés—the Champs has since undergone a bizarre kind of democratization. Shops along the avenue now range from designer fashion to low-budget tchotchkes; while it may be an inelegant spectacle, the Champs offers some of the best people-watching in Paris—tourists, wealthy bar-hoppers, and even Parisians crowd its broad sidewalks throughout the week. *(M: Charles de Gaulle-Etoile. The Champs runs from pl. Charles de Gaulle-Etoile southeast to pl. de la Concorde.)*

PLACE DE LA CONCORDE. Paris's most infamous public square, built between 1757 and 1777, is the eastern terminus of the Champs-Elysées. During the Revolution and Reign of Terror, the *place* became an epicenter of public grievance, where heads rolled—literally. Louis XVI, Marie Antoinette, and Robespierre all met their ends here. It was optimistically renamed pl. de la Concorde in 1830, and a 3200-year-old obelisk pilfered from temples at Luxor has replaced the guillotine. Beware: navigating the numerous wide crosswalks that lead to the obelisk can be exasperating. *(M: Concorde.)*

PASSY AND AUTEUIL. Located southwest of Trocadéro, these two buildings, famous for their flamboyant neo-Baroque architecture, once attracted such visitors as Molière, Proust, and Racine. Now, the area features pricey boutiques and lavish apartments. *The Last Tango in Paris* was filmed here. The vibrant streets around La Muette Metro stop make for a nice informal walking tour. *(M: Passy.)*

MADELEINE. Mirrored by the Assemblée Nationale across the Seine, the Madeleine was begun in 1763 by Louis XV and modeled after a Greco-Roman temple. Construction of the church was halted during the Revolution but completed in 1842. The structure has four domes that light the interior, 52 exterior Corinthian columns, and a curious altarpiece depicting the Mary Magdalene with angels. Besides the captivating facade, there is little to see, except the flower market outside. *(Pl. de la Madeleine. M: Madeleine. ☎ 44 51 69 00; www.eglise-lamadeleine.com. Open daily for visiting 9:30am-7pm. Regular organ and chamber concerts; contact the church for a schedule or call Virgin or FNAC for tickets. Mass M-F 7:45am, 12:30, 6:30pm; Sa 11am, 6pm; Su 9:30, 11am, 12:30, 6pm.)*

CATHÉDRALE ALEXANDRE-NEVSKY. Known as the Eglise Russe, this onion-domed cathedral is Paris's primary Russian Orthodox church and Russian cultural center. The spectacular, recently restored interior, lavishly decorated with icons, was painted by artists from St-Petersburg in gold, reds, blues, and greens, in the classic Byzantine style. *(12 rue Daru. M: Ternes. ☎ 42 27 37 34. Open Tu, F, Su 3-5pm. Services in French and Russian Sa 6-8pm, Su 10am-12:30pm; additional times on church calendar.)*

MONTMARTRE

BASILIQUE DU SACRÉ-COEUR. This ethereal basilica, with its signature shining white onion domes, was commissioned to atone for France's war crimes in the

Franco-Prussian War. Begun in 1876, it was fully funded by the working class and ultimately completed in 1919. During WWII, 13 bombs were dropped on Paris, all near the structure, but miraculously no one was killed. This inspired fervent devotion and made Sacré-Coeur an even holier site. The covered passage that curves behind the high altar—called the ambulatory—was originally designed as a way to accommodate the hordes of pilgrims who would otherwise interrupt the prayers of the parishioners. Today's pilgrims are a touristy secular bunch, but the ambulatory still does a fine job. If you have energy left after climbing to the base of the basilica, ascend the structure for the perfect panoramic view of the city. *(35 rue du Chevalier-de-la-Barre. M: Anvers, Abbesses, or Château-Rouge. ☎53 41 89 00. Basilica open daily 6am-11pm. Dome open daily 9am-6pm. Wheelchair-accessible around the back. Basilica free. Dome €5. Call ahead for crypt hours.)*

RUES DES ABBESSES, LEPIC, AND D'ORSEL. These days, tasty restaurants, trendy cafés, and traditional *boulangeries* crowd the corner of Montmartre around rue des Abbesses and rue Lepic. The international hit film *Amélie* (2002) was filmed in the area, and fans have since been making pilgrimages to the title character's home. Predictably, longtime residents are complaining about the "*Amélie Poulainization*" of their neighborhood, but truth be told, the damage isn't too conspicuous. Tall iron gates hide the beautiful gardens of several 18th-century townhouses. Walking down rue Lepic will take you past the **Moulin Radet,** one of the last remaining windmills in Montmartre. Farther down is the site of the now-demolished **Moulin de la Galette,** which Auguste Renoir depicted in a sun-dappled painting during one of the frequent dances held there (*Bal au Moulin de la Galette*, 1876; now in the Musée d'Orsay, p. 156). Even farther down, at 54 rue Lepic, lies one of Vincent van Gogh's former homes. Attractive boutiques cluster along rue d'Orsel near M: Abbesses. *(M: Abbesses.)*

OPÉRA GARNIER. The exterior of the Opéra Garnier—with its newly restored multi-colored marble facade, sculpted golden goddesses, and ornate columns and friezes—is one of Paris's most impressive sights. On bright days, its recently renovated exterior shimmers like gold. It's no wonder that Oscar Wilde once swore he saw an angel floating on the sidewalk while he was sitting next door at the Café de la Paix. *(M: Opéra. ☎08 92 89 90 90; www.operadeparis.fr. Concert hall and museum open mid-July to Aug. 10am-5:30pm; Sept. to mid-July daily 10am-4:30pm. Concert hall closed during rehearsals; call ahead. €8, students and under 25 €4. English tours daily 11:30am, 2:30pm; €12, seniors €10, students €9, under 10 €6.)*

PIGALLE. On the border of the 18ème, the generally naughty Pigalle area is a **salacious, simmering stew of sleaze.** Stretching along bd. de Clichy from pl. Pigalle to pl. Blanche, this neighborhood is home to famous cabarets (Folies Bergère, Moulin Rouge, Folies Pigalle) and overtly raunchy newcomers like Le Coq Hardy and Dirty Dick. Visitors traveling alone should exercise caution. *(M: Pigalle.)*

BAL DU MOULIN ROUGE. Along bd. de Clichy and bd. de Rochechouart are many Belle Epoque cabarets and nightclubs, but none have achieved the stardom—or notoriety—of the infamous Bal du Moulin Rouge. At the turn of the century, Paris's bourgeoisie came to the Moulin Rouge to play at being bohemian. Today, despite the famous, reconstructed windmill, there's not much to see from the street. If you're looking to splurge on one of the world-famous cabaret's splashy shows, see **Entertainment,** p. 167. *(82 bd. de Clichy. M: Blanche. Across from the Metro.)*

BASTILLE

PLACE DE LA BASTILLE. On July 14, 1789, Parisians stormed the Bastille Prison, sparking the French Revolution. Two days later, the National Assembly ordered the prison demolished, but the ground plan of the prison's turrets remains embedded near rue Saint-Antoine. Today, this busy intersection mainly ignores its past—except on Bastille Day, of course. At the center of the square is a monument of winged Mercury holding a torch of freedom, symbolizing France's movement towards democracy. *(M: Bastille.)*

OPÉRA BASTILLE. One of Mitterrand's *Grands Projets* (p. 72), the Opéra opened in 1989 with the hopes of attracting a more "cultured" public. It has been described as a huge toilet because of its resemblance to the coin-operated *pissoirs* on the streets of Paris. An ongoing debate centers on the cultural worth of this gargantuan center for the arts, since it attracts more tourists than locals. The complex is in fact the largest theater in the world—the immense auditorium seats 2703 people—but 95% of the building is taken up by exact replicas of the stage, which are used for rehearsals and workshops. *(130 rue de Lyon. M: Bastille. Look for the words "Billeterie." ☎40 01 19 70; www.operadeparis.fr. 1hr. tour almost every day, usually at 1 or 5pm; call ahead for schedule. Tours are in French, but groups of 15 or more can arrange for English. €11, over 60 and students €9, under 10 €6.)*

THIRTEENTH ARRONDISSEMENT

BIBLIOTHÈQUE NATIONALE DE FRANCE: SITE FRANÇOIS MITTERRAND. This library is the last and most expensive of Mitterrand's *Grands Projets* (p. 72). It was built to accommodate the ever-increasing number of books housed in the old Bibliothèque Nationale in the 2ème—since 1642, every book published in France has entered the national archives, housed in the library. The four L-shaped towers of Dominique Perrault's stunning, controversial design look like open books, and the pines emerging from the enormous sunken garden at the center of the courtyard help to soften the library's glassy planes and straight lines. Inside the imposing buildings you'll find large, underground reading rooms. *(Quai F. Mauriac. M: Quai de la Gare or Bibliothèque François Mitterrand. ☎53 79 59 79; www.bnf.fr. Open M 2-7pm, Tu-Sa 9am-7pm, Su 1-7pm; closed 1st, 2nd, 3rd Su of Sept. Ages 16+. €3.50. Annual membership €35, students €18. MC/V.)*

QUARTIER DE LA BUTTE-AUX-CAILLES. Historically a working-class neighborhood, the Butte-aux-Cailles (Quail Knoll) district is like a mini-village in the heart of the big city, with old-fashioned lampposts and cobblestone streets. **Rue de la Butte-aux-Cailles** and **rue des Cinq Diamants** share duties as the *quartier*'s main drags. Funky new restaurants and drinking holes have cropped up amongst the old standards, the Butte's cooperative bar, **La Folie en Tête,** and the intellectual hang-out **Le Temps des Cerises.** The nascent gentrification of the entire *arrondissement* has attracted trendsetters, artists, and intellectuals to this area, but, luckily for long-time residents, this process is still slow-moving. *(M: Corvisart. Exit onto bd. Blanqui and turn onto rue Barrault, which will intersect rue de la Butte-aux-Cailles.)*

CHINATOWN (QUARTIER CHINOIS). The heart of Paris's Chinatown is south of rue Tolbiac on av. de Choisy, av. d'Ivry, and the surrounding blocks. Home to a large population of Chinese, Vietnamese, Thai, and Cambodian immigrants, this vibrant community—you guessed it—offers the best Asian food in Paris. The area's eateries focus on *à la vapeur* (steamed) dishes, and an afternoon of window shopping can turn up some unexpected finds among the legions of ceramic Buddhas. *(M: Porte d'Ivry, Porte de Choisy, Tolbiac, and Maison Blanche are near Chinatown.)*

JOSÉPHINE BAKER SWIMMING POOL. Paris's 37 thriving municipal swimming pools are a wonderful way to escape the heat—and the tourists. This particular pool does swimming as only Paris can, offering a relaxing dip in the middle of the Seine. Yes, the pool itself is floating on the river. An attached spa is available for your post-swim indulgence. *(Quai François Mauriac. M: Quai de la Gare. Exit the Metro, walk to the Seine, and turn right. ☎56 61 96 50. Hours vary widely depending on the day of the week and the academic year, so call ahead. Entry €2.60, students and under 18 €1.50. Spa €5.50.)*

MONTPARNASSE AND THE FIFTEENTH ARRONDISSEMENT

PARC ANDRÉ CITROËN. The futuristic Parc André Citroën was created by landscapers Alain Provost and Gilles Clément in the 1990s, after Citroën's factory had closed down. This jaded Parisian's jungle is located alongside the Seine and contains fountains, tall greenhouses, and a "wild" garden whose plants change each year. In the summer, the grass is crowded with sunbathers and picnickers. Hot-air balloon rides launch from the central garden and offer spectacular aerial views of the park and the city. *(M: Javel or Balard. ☎44 26 20 00; www.aeroparis.com. Park open 24hr. Balloon rides M-F 7am-9:30pm, Sa-Su 9am-9:30pm. Weekends and holidays 10min. balloon rides €12, ages 12-17 €10, ages 3-11 €6, under 3 free; weekdays €10/9/5/free.)*

TOUR MONTPARNASSE. Affectionately known as Paris's "other" tower, Tour Montparnasse has been considered an eyesore among locals since it was built in 1973. A monument to commercialism with offices filling its 56 stories, it stands at 209m and boasts an incredible 360° view of Paris from the 56th floor (newly renovated with a full bar), where you can see for 40km on a clear day. The best way to avoid seeing this looming edifice is from the Trocadéro, where it disappears perfectly behind the Eiffel Tower—or, you can actually ascend to see the view. *(33 av. du Maine. M: Montparnasse-Bienvenüe. Entrance on rue de l'Arrivée. ☎45 38 52 56. Open May-Sept. daily 9:30am-11:30pm; Oct.-Apr. M-F 9:30am-10:30pm. Bar open until 1am. Admission €9.50, students €6.80, ages 7-15 €4.)*

CATACOMBS. The Catacombs were originally excavated to provide stone for building the city. By the 1770s, much of the Left Bank was in danger of caving in, so digging promptly stopped. The former quarry was converted into a mass grave in 1785 when the stench of the city's public cemeteries became unbearable. Built twice as far underground as the Metro, Paris's "municipal ossuary" now comprises dozens of winding tunnels and hundreds of thousands of bones. They line the walls in gruesomely artful patterns, with skulls arranged into lines and crosses. After a long, dizzying descent down a spiral staircase, it's a half-kilometer walk to the Catacombs themselves. While barred gates and signs rule out any possibility of getting lost, the dim lighting and frequent turns can make for a surprisingly isolated experience. It takes 45min. to walk through, and the self-guided tour finishes with a long climb—another narrow spiral staircase—that spits you out two Metro stops away from where you started. Because only 200 people are allowed in at a time, the line can be long and slow-moving. Show up as early as possible, preferably just before opening time, to minimize your wait. *(1 av. du Colonel Henri Roi-Tanguy. M: Denfert-Rochereau. Take exit pl. Denfert-Rochereau, and cross av. du Colonel Henri Roi-Tanguy with the lion on your left. You exit the Catacombs at 36 rue Rémy-Dumoncel. M: Mouton Duvernet is 2 blocks to the right at av. du Général Leclerc. ☎43 22 47 63. Open Tu-Su 10am-4pm. €7, over 60 €5.50, ages 14 to 26 €3.50, under 14 free. MC/V over €15.)*

BOULEVARD DU MONTPARNASSE. In the early 20th century, avant-garde artists like Modigliani, Duchamp, Chagall, and Léger moved to Montparnasse, many of them fleeing Montmartre's rising rents. Soviet exiles Lenin and Trotsky talked strategy over cognac in cafés like Le Dôme, Le Sélect, and La Coupole. Between the World Wars, Montparnasse attracted the "Lost Generation"—brooding disillusioned American expatriates like Calder, Hemingway, and Henry Miller. Now heavily commercialized, Montparnasse is crowded with chain restaurants and

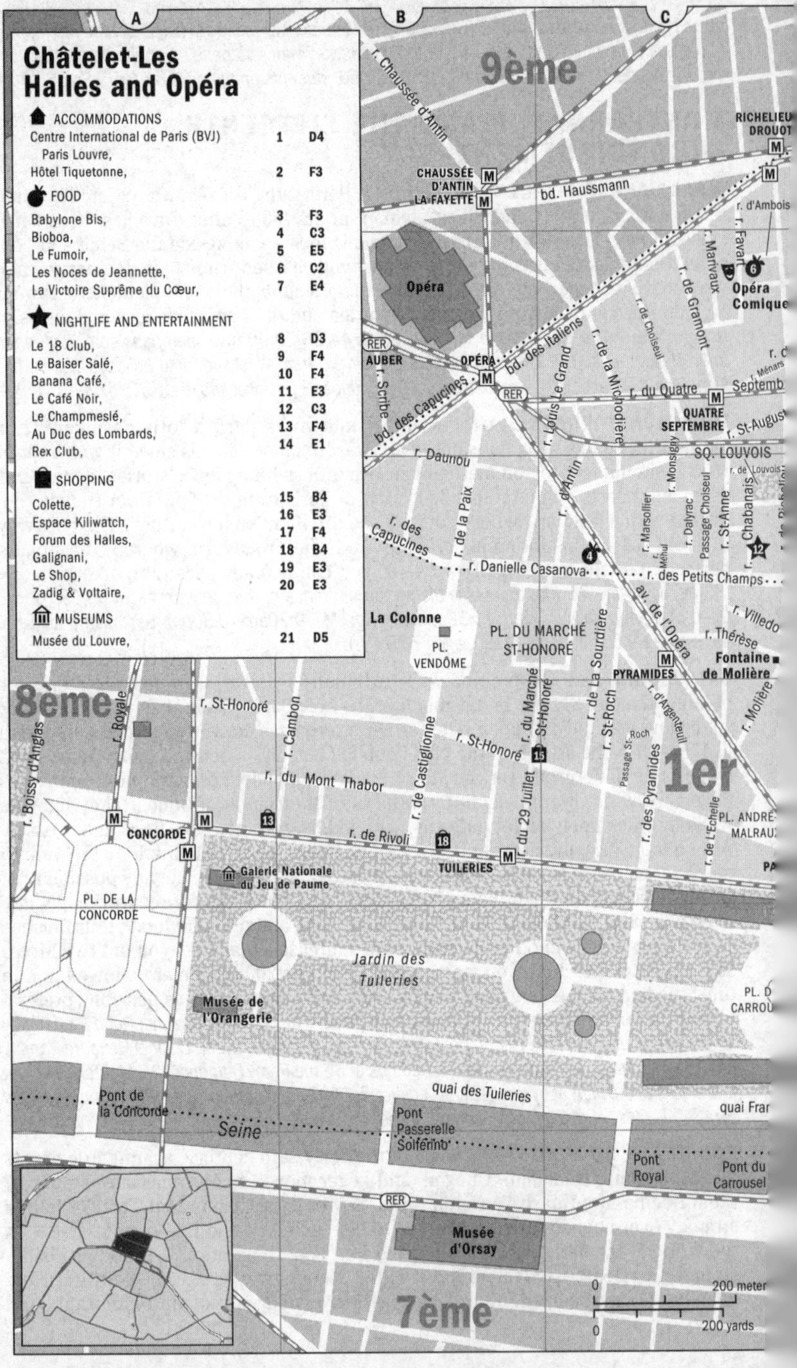
A
B
C
Châtelet-Les Halles and Opéra
ACCOMMODATIONS
Centre International de Paris (BVJ) 1 D4
Paris Louvre,
Hôtel Tiquetonne, 2 F3
FOOD
Babylone Bis, 3 F3
Bioboa, 4 C3
Le Fumoir, 5 E5
Les Noces de Jeannette, 6 C2
La Victoire Suprême du Cœur, 7 E4
NIGHTLIFE AND ENTERTAINMENT
Le 18 Club, 8 D3
Le Baiser Salé, 9 F4
Banana Café, 10 F4
Le Café Noir, 11 E3
Le Champmeslé, 12 C3
Au Duc des Lombards, 13 F4
Rex Club, 14 E1
SHOPPING
Colette, 15 B4
Espace Kiliwatch, 16 E3
Forum des Halles, 17 F4
Galignani, 18 B4
Le Shop, 19 E3
Zadig & Voltaire, 20 E3
MUSEUMS
Musée du Louvre, 21 D5
9ème
8ème
1er
7ème
r. Chaussée d'Antin
CHAUSSÉE D'ANTIN LA FAYETTE
bd. Haussmann
RICHELIEU DROUOT
r. d'Ambois
r. Favart
r. Marivaux
Opéra Comique
Opéra
r. de Gramont
r. de Choiseul
r. de la Michodière
r. Louis Le Grand
bd. des Italiens
RER
AUBER
OPÉRA
r. Scribe
bd. des Capucines
r. du Quatre Septembre
QUATRE SEPTEMBRE
r. St-Augustin
SQ. LOUVOIS
r. de Louvois
r. Daunou
r. d'Antin
r. Monsigny
r. Dalyrac
Passage Choiseul
r. Marsollier
r. Méhul
r. St-Anne
r. Chabanais
r. des Capucines
r. de la Paix
r. Danielle Casanova
r. des Petits Champs
av. de l'Opéra
r. Villedo
r. Thérèse
La Colonne
PL. VENDÔME
PL. DU MARCHÉ ST-HONORÉ
r. de La Sourdière
PYRAMIDES
Fontaine de Molière
r. d'Argenteuil
r. Molière
r. St-Honoré
r. Royale
r. Boissy d'Anglas
r. Cambon
r. de Castiglionne
r. du Marché St-Honoré
r. St-Roch
Passage St-Roch
r. des Pyramides
r. du Mont Thabor
r. du 29 Juillet
r. de l'Echelle
PL. ANDRÉ MALRAUX
CONCORDE
r. de Rivoli
TUILERIES
Galerie Nationale du Jeu de Paume
PL. DE LA CONCORDE
Jardin des Tuileries
Musée de l'Orangerie
quai des Tuileries
Pont de la Concorde
Seine
Pont Passerelle Solférino
Pont Royal
Pont du Carrousel
RER
Musée d'Orsay
0 200 meter
0 200 yards

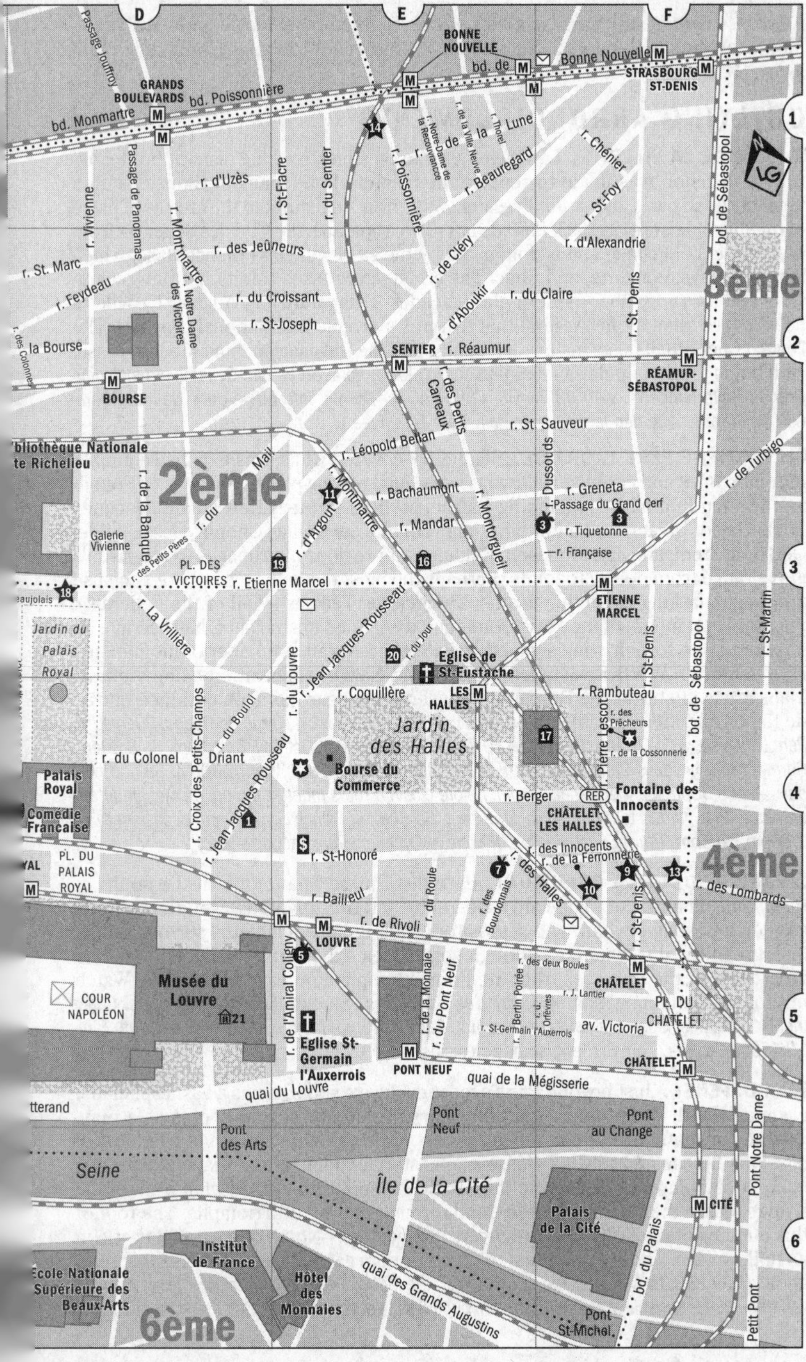
GRANDS BOULEVARDS
BONNE NOUVELLE
bd. Poissonnière
bd. Monmartre
bd. de Bonne Nouvelle
STRASBOURG ST-DENIS
Passage Jouffroy
Passage de Panoramas
r. d'Uzès
r. St-Fiacre
r. du Sentier
r. Poissonnière
r. Beauregard
r. de la Lune
r. Chénier
r. St-Foy
bd. de Sébastopol
r. Vivienne
r. Montmartre
r. des Jeûneurs
r. St. Marc
r. Feydeau
r. Notre Dame des Victoires
r. du Croissant
r. St-Joseph
r. de Cléry
r. d'Aboukir
r. d'Alexandrie
r. du Claire
3ème
r. St. Denis
la Bourse
BOURSE
SENTIER
r. Réaumur
RÉAMUR-SÉBASTOPOL
r. des Petits Carreaux
r. St. Sauveur
r. Léopold Bellan
Bibliothèque Nationale site Richelieu
2ème
r. du Mail
r. Bachaumont
r. Montorgueil
r. Dussoubs
r. Greneta
Passage du Grand Cerf
r. de Turbigo
r. de la Banque
Galerie Vivienne
r. Mandar
r. Tiquetonne
r. Française
r. d'Argout
PL. DES VICTOIRES
r. des Petits Pères
r. Etienne Marcel
ETIENNE MARCEL
Jardin du Palais Royal
r. La Vrillière
r. Jean Jacques Rousseau
r. du Jour
Eglise de St-Eustache
r. St-Martin
r. Coquillère
LES HALLES
r. Rambuteau
r. du Louvre
Jardin des Halles
r. Croix des Petits-Champs
r. du Bouloi
r. des Prêcheurs
r. de la Cossonnerie
r. Pierre Lescot
r. du Colonel Driant
Bourse du Commerce
Palais Royal
Comédie Française
r. Berger
RER
Fontaine des Innocents
CHÂTELET LES HALLES
PL. DU PALAIS ROYAL
r. St-Honoré
r. des Innocents
r. de la Ferronnerie
4ème
r. des Halles
r. des Lombards
r. Bailleul
r. du Roule
r. des Bourdonnais
r. de Rivoli
LOUVRE
r. de l'Amiral Coligny
r. des deux Boules
CHÂTELET
Musée du Louvre
COUR NAPOLÉON
r. de la Monnaie
r. du Pont Neuf
r. Bertin Poirée
r. J. Lantier
r. d. Orfèvres
r. St-Germain l'Auxerrois
av. Victoria
PL. DU CHÂTELET
Eglise St-Germain l'Auxerrois
PONT NEUF
quai du Louvre
quai de la Mégisserie
Pont Neuf
Pont au Change
Pont des Arts
Pont Notre Dame
Seine
Île de la Cité
CITÉ
Palais de la Cité
bd. du Palais
Institut de France
Ecole Nationale Supérieure des Beaux-Arts
Hôtel des Monnaies
quai des Grands Augustins
Pont St-Michel
Petit Pont
6ème
PARIS

tourists. Classics still hold their own, however (the pricey La Coupole, for example), providing a wonderful place to sip coffee, read Apollinaire, and daydream away. (*M: Montparnasse-Bienvenüe or Vavin*).

OUTLYING ARRONDISSEMENTS

PARC DE LA VILLETTE. La Villette used to be a meatpacking district, but thankfully a decision was made to replace the neighborhood slaughterhouses with a neighborhood park, and *voilà:* President Mitterrand inaugurated the area as a "place of intelligent leisure" in 1985. Parc de la Villette separates the Cité des Sciences from the Cité de la Musique and is dominated by the steel-and-glass **Grande Halle,** which features plays, concerts, and films. The architecture fuses traditional Haussmann style and swirling, über-modern glass facades. Every July and August, La Villette hosts a free open-air **film festival** that features a diverse international program. The **Zénith** concert hall hosts major rock bands, and the **Trabendo** jazz and modern music club holds a very popular annual jazz festival. *(M: Porte de Pantin. General info including Grande Halle concerts ☎40 03 75 03. Call FNAC for tickets. Info office open daily 9:30am-6:30pm. Promenade des Jardins open daily 6am-1am. Free.)*

CIMETIÈRE PÈRE LACHAISE. Behind ivy-covered walls, this expansive jumble of tombstones and cobbled walkways is the final resting place of dozens of French and foreign luminaries, including Balzac, Molière, Proust, Haussmann, Jacques Louis David, Delacroix, La Fontaine, and Collette, as well as Chopin, Oscar Wilde, Gertrude Stein, and Jim Morrison. Evidence of previous pilgrimages to Morrison's grave range from poetry to joints. Perhaps the most moving sites in Père Lachaise are those marking collective deaths. The **Mur des Fédérés** (Wall of the Federals), where 147 members of the Paris Commune were lined up and shot, has become an important site for left-wing sympathizers. Near the wall, a number of monuments commemorate WWII Resistance fighters and Nazi concentration camp victims. Maps are available at the Bureau de Conservation near the main entrance on rue de Repos and are advisable if you don't want to get lost. *(16 rue du Repos, 20ème. M: Père Lachaise. ☎55 25 82 10; tours ☎40 71 75 60. Open Mar.-Oct. M-F 8am-6pm, Sa 8:30am-6pm, Su and holidays 9am-6pm; Nov.-Feb. M-F 8am-5:30pm, Sa 8:30am-5:30pm, Su and holidays 9am-5:30pm. Last entrance 15min. before closing. Tours meet at the bd. de Ménilmontant entrance. 2hr. guided tour in English June-Sept. Sa 3pm; in French Sa 2:30pm, occasionally Tu 2:30pm, Su 3pm. Tours €6, students €3. Entry to Cimetière Père Lachaise free.)*

PARC DES BUTTES-CHAUMONT. Parc des Buttes-Chaumont, in the south of the 19ème, is a mix of manmade topography and transplanted vegetation, all created on a nostalgic whim. Today's visitors walk the winding paths surrounded by lush greenery and dynamic—though sometimes exhausting—hills, and enjoy a great view of the *quartier* from the Roman temple atop cave-filled cliffs. Watch out for the ominously named *Pont des Suicides* (Suicide Bridge). *(M: Buttes-Chaumont or Botzaris. Open daily June to mid-Aug. 7am-10:15pm; May and mid-Aug. to Sept. 7am-10:15pm; Oct.-Apr. 7am-8:15pm; some gates close early.)*

LA DÉFENSE. Just beyond Paris's most exclusive suburbs lies a vast esplanade, crammed with eye-popping contemporary architecture, that serves as a playground for many of the city's biggest corporations. The centerpiece is hard to miss: the **Grande Arche de la Défense** is a 35-story building in the shape of a hollow cube. It completes the axis from the Arc de Triomphe du Carrousel in front of the Louvre, down the Champs-Elysées, and through the Arc de Triomphe. The roof of this unconventional office space covers one hectare—Notre Dame could nestle in its hollow core. There's not much to do other than gawk, but the gawking is pretty great. *(M or RER: La Défense. The RER is faster; the Metro is cheaper. Note: RER ticket may get you through the turnstile at the Paris station, but it won't get you out at La Défense without a fine.)*

VILLAGE BATIGNOLLES. The Village Batignolles, in the eastern half of the 17ème, is a dynamic neighborhood that houses both working-class and bourgeois residents. It centers around **rue des Batignolles,** stretching from **boulevard des Batignolles** at the southern end to **place du Dr. Félix Lobligeois,** where a cluster of hip cafés overlooks the tree-lined square. Just north of this *place* are the craggy waterfalls and duck ponds of the English-style park, **square des Batignolles.** To the west, **rue des Dames** is lined with restaurants and cafés, and **rue de Lévis** with shops. At the intersection of rue des Batignolles and bd. des Batignolles, there is an **organic produce market** on the traffic divider every Saturday. **La Cité des Fleurs,** 59-61 rue de la Jonquière (at the intersection with rue des Epinettes), is a row of exquisite private homes and gardens. Designed in 1847, this prototypical condominium complex required each owner to plant at least three trees in his garden. *(M: Villiers.)*

BOIS DE BOULOGNE. A former royal hunting ground, the Bois de Boulogne contains over 2000 acres of green canopy. Parisians walk, jog, bike, boat, and picnic among manmade lakes and waterfalls. The Bois has served many functions, from aristocratic playground to firewood supplier during the Revolution. More recently, the Bois has become a bazaar of sex and drugs, with prostitutes and violent crime at night. It is best avoided after dark. *(M: Porte Maillot, Sablons, Pont de Neuilly, Porte Dauphine, or Porte d'Auteuil. Open 24hr.)*

PUCES DE ST-OUEN. The granddaddy of all flea markets, the Puces de St-Ouen is an overwhelming smorgasbord of random stuff. Over 270 stalls sell everything from lighting systems to porcelain pottery. In general, merchandise is either dirt-cheap and shoddy or expensive and antique, but if you're willing to slog through the sneaker stands and smoking paraphernalia, you may find a great deal. If you are a savvy rock 'n' roll connoisseur—and patient—this is the place to find rare records. Record peddlers generally know what they have, but if you look long enough, you might just find a priceless LP for next to nothing. *(Just north of the 18ème. M: Porte-de-Clignancourt. www.parispuces.com. Open M and Sa-Su 7am-7:30pm, although most stalls open 9-10am. Most vendors open only 9am-6pm; many of the official stalls close early, but renegade vendors may open at 5am and stay open until 9pm.)*

MUSEUMS

Paris's museums are universally considered to be among the world's best, and even if some may be a splurge, no visitor to the city should miss them. If you're going to be doing the museum circuit while in Paris, you may want to invest in a **Carte Musées et Monuments,** which offers admission to 65 museums in greater Paris. The card is cost-effective if you plan to visit more than three museums or sights every day and will enable you to sail past admission lines. It is available at major museums, tourist office kiosks, and many Metro stations. Ask for a brochure listing participating museums and monuments. A pass for one day is €15, for three days €30, for five days €45. For more information, call the **Association InterMusées,** 4 rue Brantôme, 3ème (☎44 61 96 60; www.intermusees.com). Most museums, including the **Musée d'Orsay,** are closed on Mondays, while the **Louvre, Centre Pompidou,** and **Musée Rodin** are closed on Tuesdays.

CHÂTELET-LES-HALLES AND OPÉRA

LOUVRE

M: Palais-Royal-Musée du Louvre. ☎40 20 53 17; www.louvre.fr. Open M, Th, and Sa 9am-6pm; W and F 9am-10pm. Last entry 45min. before closing; visitors are asked to leave 15-30min. before closing. Sign up for the English, French, or Spanish tours (1-1½hr.) at the info desk; daily at 11am, 2, 3:45pm. There are also tours in French sign lan-

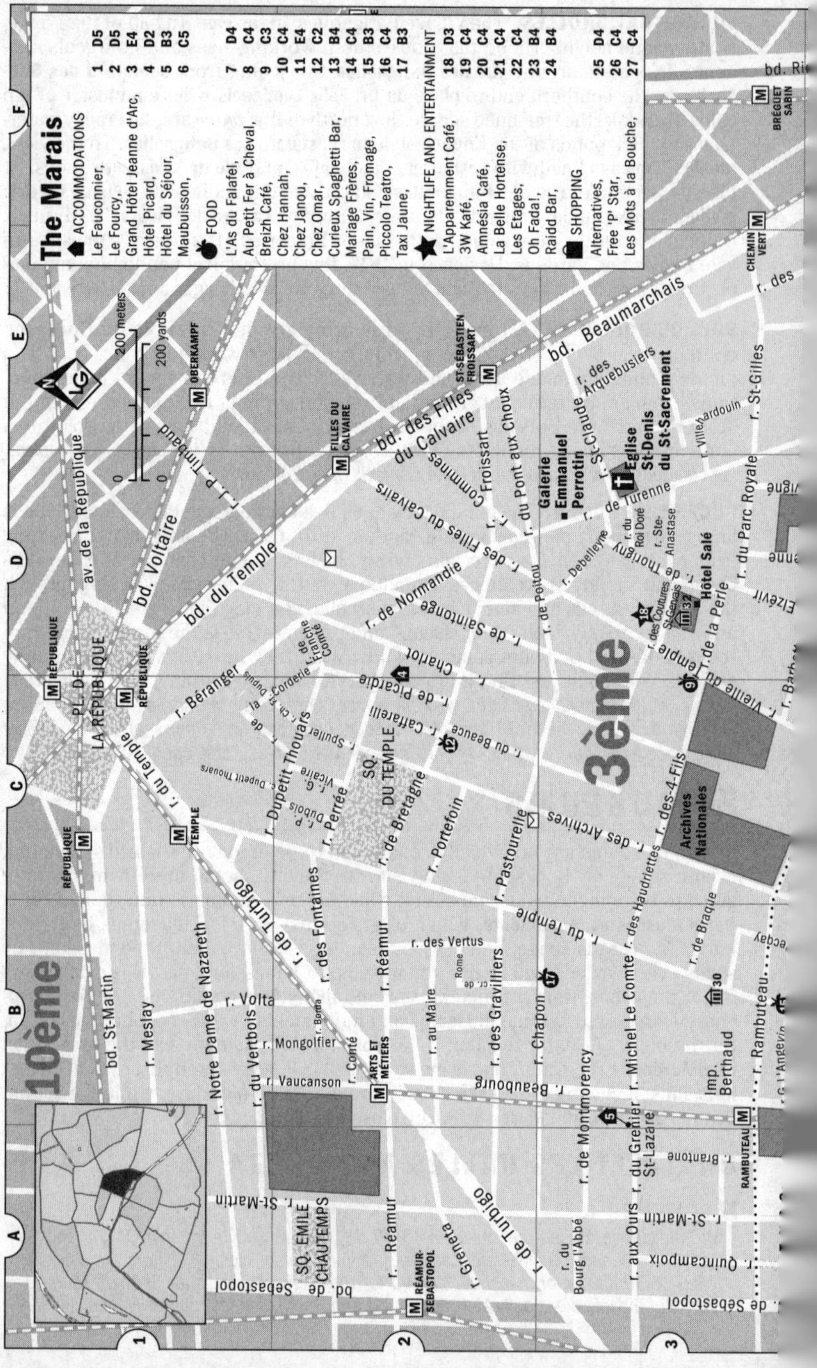
The Marais
ACCOMMODATIONS
Le Fauconnier, 1 D5
Le Fourcy, 2 D5
Grand Hôtel Jeanne d'Arc, 3 E4
Hôtel Picard, 4 D2
Hôtel du Séjour, 5 B3
Maubuisson, 6 C5
FOOD
L'As du Falafel, 7 D4
Au Petit Fer à Cheval, 8 C4
Breizh Café, 9 C3
Chez Hannah, 10 C4
Chez Janou, 11 E4
Chez Omar, 12 C2
Curieux Spaghetti Bar, 13 B4
Mariage Frères, 14 C4
Pain, Vin, Fromage, 15 B3
Piccolo Teatro, 16 C4
Taxi Jaune, 17 B3
NIGHTLIFE AND ENTERTAINMENT
L'Apparemment Café, 18 D3
3W Kafé, 19 C4
Amnésia Café, 20 C4
La Belle Hortense, 21 C4
Les Etages, 22 C4
Oh Fada!, 23 B4
Raidd Bar, 24 B4
SHOPPING
Alternatives, 25 D4
Free 'P' Star, 26 C4
Les Mots à la Bouche, 27 C4
10ème
3ème
PL. DE LA RÉPUBLIQUE
SQ. DU TEMPLE
SQ. EMILE CHAUTEMPS
Archives Nationales
Hôtel Salé
Eglise St-Denis du St-Sacrement
Galerie Emmanuel Perrotin
bd. Beaumarchais
bd. des Filles du Calvaire
bd. du Temple
bd. Voltaire
av. de la République
r. de Turbigo
r. du Temple
r. Réaumur
bd. de Sébastopol
200 meters
200 yards

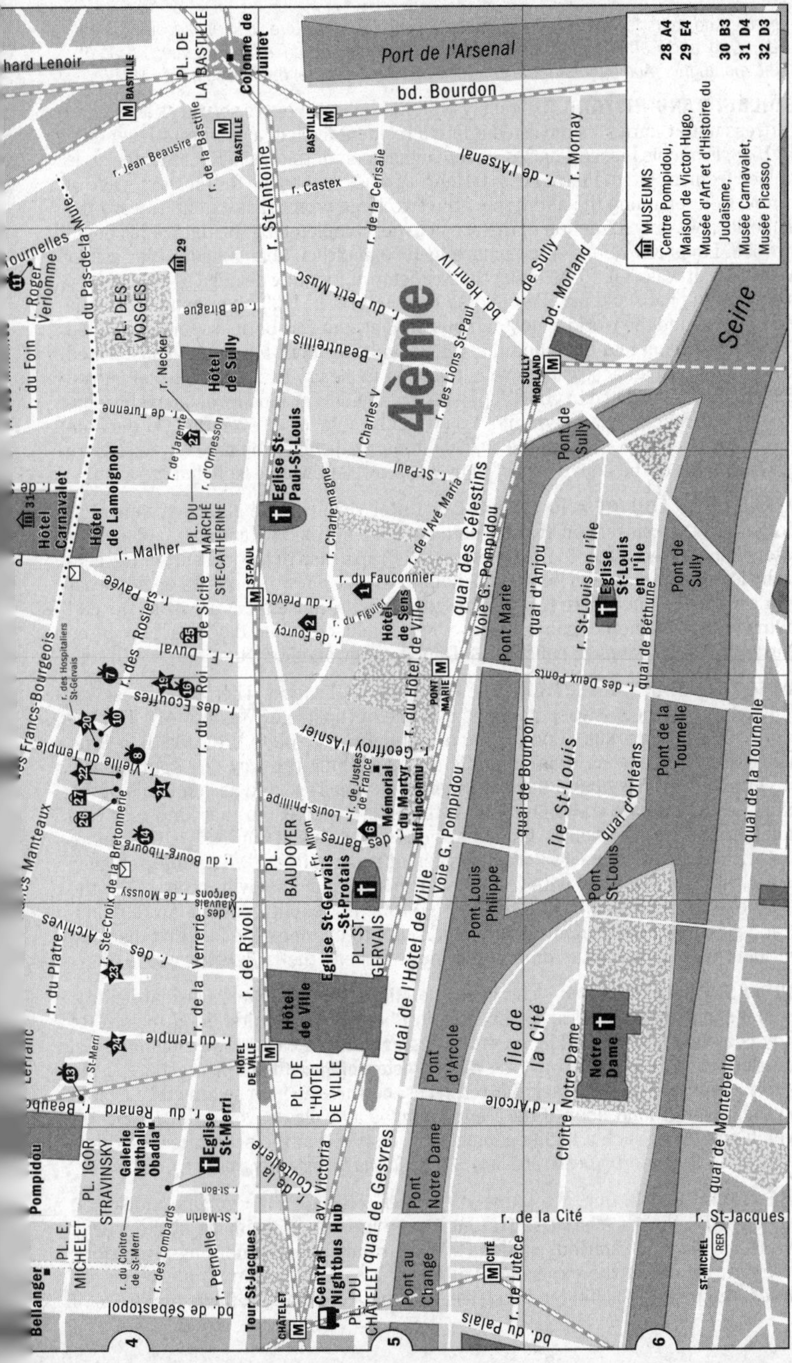
MUSEUMS
Centre Pompidou, 28 A4
Maison de Victor Hugo, 29 E4
Musée d'Art et d'Histoire du Judaïsme, 30 B3
Musée Carnavalet, 31 D4
Musée Picasso, 32 D3
Port de l'Arsenal
bd. Bourdon
PL. DE LA BASTILLE
Colonne de Juillet
BASTILLE
r. St-Antoine
PL. DES VOSGES
Hôtel de Sully
Hôtel Carnavalet
Hôtel de Lamoignon
Eglise St-Paul-St-Louis
4ème
Seine
bd. Henri IV
bd. Morland
SULLY MORLAND
quai des Célestins
Pont de Sully
Eglise St-Louis en l'Île
Île St-Louis
quai d'Orléans
quai de Béthune
quai d'Anjou
quai de Bourbon
Pont Marie
Pont Louis Philippe
Pont de la Tournelle
quai de la Tournelle
Pont St-Louis
Île de la Cité
Notre Dame
Cloître Notre Dame
quai de Montebello
Pont d'Arcole
Pont Notre Dame
Pont au Change
quai de Gesvres
quai de l'Hôtel de Ville
Voie G. Pompidou
Hôtel de Ville
PL. DE L'HOTEL DE VILLE
Eglise St-Gervais-St-Protais
PL. ST. GERVAIS
PL. BAUDOYER
Mémorial du Martyr Juif Inconnu
Hôtel de Sens
PONT MARIE
ST-PAUL
HÔTEL DE VILLE
CHÂTELET
CITÉ
ST-MICHEL
RER
Central Nightbus Hub
PL. DU CHÂTELET
av. Victoria
Tour St-Jacques
r. de Rivoli
bd. de Sébastopol
Eglise St-Merri
PL. IGOR STRAVINSKY
Galerie Nathalie Obadia
PL. E. MICHELET
Pompidou
r. de la Cité
r. St-Jacques
bd. du Palais
r. de Lutèce
r. d'Arcole
r. Vieille du Temple
r. des Rosiers
r. des Francs-Bourgeois
r. du Roi de Sicile
r. des Écouffes
r. du Temple
r. de la Verrerie
r. Ste-Croix de la Bretonnerie
r. des Archives
r. du Platre
r. Pavée
r. Malher
PL. DU MARCHÉ STE-CATHERINE
r. de Turenne
r. du Foin
r. Roger Verlomme
r. du Pas-de-la-Mule
r. de Birague
r. Beautreillis
r. du Petit Musc
r. Charles V
r. des Lions St-Paul
r. St-Paul
r. Charlemagne
r. de l'Avé Maria
r. du Fauconnier
r. du Figuier
r. de Fourcy
r. du Prévôt
r. Geoffroy l'Asnier
r. François Miron
r. des Barres
r. Louis-Philippe
r. de Sully
r. Mornay
r. de l'Arsenal
r. de la Cerisaie
r. Castex
r. Jean Beausire
r. de la Bastille
r. Necker
r. de Jarente
r. d'Ormesson
r. des Deux Ponts
r. St-Louis en l'Île
r. du Renard
r. des Lombards
r. Pernelle
r. St-Martin
r. du Cloître de St-Merri
r. de la Coutellerie
r. du Bourg-Tibourg
r. de Moussy
r. des Mauvais Garçons
r. des Hospitaliers St-Gervais
r. F. Duval
r. de Justes de France

PARIS

guage and tours for the visually impaired; check the website or call ahead. Admission €8.50, W and F after 6pm €6; under 26 and the unemployed F after 6pm free; 1st Su of the month free. Audio tours at the entrance to each branch of the museum, €5. MC/V.

BUILDING AND HISTORY. Originally built in 1190, the Louvre served as a Parisian fortress until Charles V converted it into a residential château in the 14th century. In 1528, François I razed Charles's château and commissioned a Renaissance-style palace from architect Pierre Lescot. Henri IV was responsible for the next stage of renovation, planning the addition of the two large wings that extend toward the Tuileries, but only a fraction of the project was completed by the time of his death in 1610. Louis XIV adopted the palace in 1650 and then abandoned it for flashier Versailles. It wasn't until 1725 that the Academy of Painting decided to hold annual salons in the halls and put the building back to use. In 1793, their exhibit became permanent, and the world's most famous art museum was born. Napoleon fulfilled Henri IV's dream and extended the wings, and President Mitterand transformed the Louvre into an accessible, well-organized museum. Architect I.M. Pei moved the museum's entrance to cour Napoléon, on an underground level below his controversially modern glass pyramid. You won't be able to see everything at the Louvre. A comprehensive tour of the 30,000+ items on display would take weeks. Here are highlights of the Louvre selected by *Let's Go*. Allow at least half a day.

PYRAMID DU LOUVRE AND ENTRANCE. Enter through the glass pyramid that dominates the central courtyard. Purchase tickets from any automatic dispenser after riding the escalator to the basement. Pick up a map of the museum at the centrally located information booth. It is helpful to take a few minutes to decide what you want to see and where you want to go within the museum. A trip from one end of the Louvre to another can take more than 20min. on a busy day. There are three entrances to the wings of collections: Denon, Sully, and Richelieu.

MESOPOTAMIAN COLLECTION. The cradle of civilization. The fertile crescent. The land of epithets. Mesopotamia is also the birthplace of Western Art. The **Victory Stela of Naram Sim** (Room 2) is a highlight. It depicts the Akkadian King ascending the heavens, trampling his enemies along the way and sporting the crown of a god. **The Winged Bulls of Sargon II** (Room 4) served as guardians of the king's Assyrian palace. While modern times have delegated that kind of job to highly trained armed guards, the bulls' massive size is still impressive. On a more historical note, **Hammurabi's Code** holds center stage in Room 3. The object itself is a modest stela inscribed with 282 laws for his Babylonian civilization. It's in the Louvre because it is a physical memento of the first public codified law, a democratic gesture of such importance that it's easy to overlook the fact that dismemberment was the sentence for minor crimes like petty theft. *(Richelieu; ground fl.)*

GREEKS, ROMANS, & CO. The **Venus de Milo** is the ultimate classical beauty, even if she is missing her arms. Located in Room 74 on the first floor, the size-14 lady is always surrounded by an enthusiastic horde of camera-waving admirers. Overlooking a nearby stairway, the **Winged Victory of Samothrace** proves that a head is not a prerequisite for Greek masterpieces; beware the intense crowds. Located on the lower ground floor of the Denon wing is a display devoted to **Cycladic Art,** which employed such a highly geometricized style that the sculptures and idols actually look modern. *(Denon and Sully; 1st fl., ground fl., and lower ground fl.)*

THE ITALIANS. Ok, fine. We know you didn't come for the Cycladic Idols. You came for Da Vinci's **Mona Lisa** (Room 6), the most famous image in the world. While the lady's mysterious smile is still charming, there is nothing mysterious or charming about the experience of looking at it in person. The crowds are fierce, the painting is hidden in a glass box that constantly reflects hundreds of camera flashes, and you won't be allowed within 15 ft. We here at *Let's Go* don't want to be heretical, but if you're pressed for time you might consider skipping the lady. In the adjacent hall, an astonishing group of Renaissance masterpieces awaits—everything from Da Vinci's **Virgin on the Rocks** to Raphael's **Grand Saint Michel** to Fra Angelico's **Calvary.** It's an impressive bunch that outlines the rise of Humanism in the West. This wing is best visited as soon as the museum opens, as it turns into a circus within 30min. *(Denon; 1st fl.)*

HOLLAND, FLANDERS, THE NETHERLANDS. A more civilized museum experience awaits on the less crowded second floor. Vermeer's astonishing **Astronomer** and **Lacemaker** occupy Room 38. While the lifelong resident of Delft left behind no drawings or other clues to his preparatory methods, some scholars believe that he used a *camera obscura* in composing his works. One can make out subtle effects of light that could not have appeared to Vermeer's naked eye without a little assistance. This section is also filled with works by Rembrandt, Van Eyck, and Van der Weyden, as well as a monumental **24-painting cycle** by Rubens. *(Richelieu; 2nd fl.)*

FRANCE. It is only fitting that a French palace would be filled with so many French paintings. The 17th-, 18th-, and 19th-century works that occupy the second floor of the Sully wing can be as fluffy and sugary as a chocolate soufflé, but don't lose interest quite yet. Keep an eye out for Watteau's **Pilgrimage to Cytheria** (Room 36), a melancholy ode to the impermanence of love. La Tour's fascination with hidden sources of light produced the haunting works that occupy Room 28. Once you've had your fill of peace and quiet, head back to the first floor of Denon, where the French heavyweights keep a close eye on the Mona Lisa. In Rooms 75, 76, and 77, large-format works dominate the walls. Géricault's **Raft of the Medusa,** ripped straight from the headlines in 1819, depicts the Medusa's abandoned passengers struggling to survive as they try to catch the attention of a passing ship. A large "X" formed by the bodies on the raft lends the painting its compositional stability, and the horrifying depiction of hunger and despair packs an emotional wallop. The second most famous painting in these galleries is Delacroix's **Liberty Leading the People,** in which Liberty, like almost everything in Western Art, is symbolized by a partially nude woman. David's enormous paintings **The Coronation of Napoleon, The Oath of the Horatii,** and **Sabine Women** all showcase the painter's Neoclassical style. Finally, check out Ingres's body-twisting **Grande Odalisque** (go ahead, try and put your legs like that) and Delacroix's **Death of Sardanopolous.** They are both examples of Orientalism, a product of France's imperial adventures in North Africa. Within France itself, the "Orient" was imagined as a paradise of indulgence, sexually generous women, and crazy drugs. *(Sully, 2nd fl.; Denon, 1st fl.)*

THE MARAIS

CENTRE POMPIDOU. The **Musée National d'Art Moderne** is the Centre Pompidou's main attraction. While its collection spans the 20th century, the art from the last 50 years is particularly brilliant. It features everything from Philip Guston's uncomfortably adorable hooded figures to Eva Hesse's uncomfortably anthropomorphic sculptures. Those looking to escape the discomfort will want to see Cai Guo-Qang's *Bon Voyage,* an airplane made of wicker and vine hanging from the ceiling and studded with objects confiscated from passengers' carry-on luggage at the Tokyo airport. On the museum's second level, early 20th-century heavyweights like Duchamp and Picasso hold court. The **Salle Garance** hosts an adventurous film series, and the **Bibliothèque Publique d'Information** (entrance on rue de Renard) is a free, non-circulating library. *(Pl. Georges-Pompidou, rue Beaubourg. M: Rambuteau or Hôtel de Ville. RER: Châtelet-Les Halles. ☎44 78 12 33; www.centrepompidou.fr. Centre open M and W-Su 11am-9:50pm. Museum open M and W-Su 11am-8:50pm, last ticket sales 8pm. Library open*

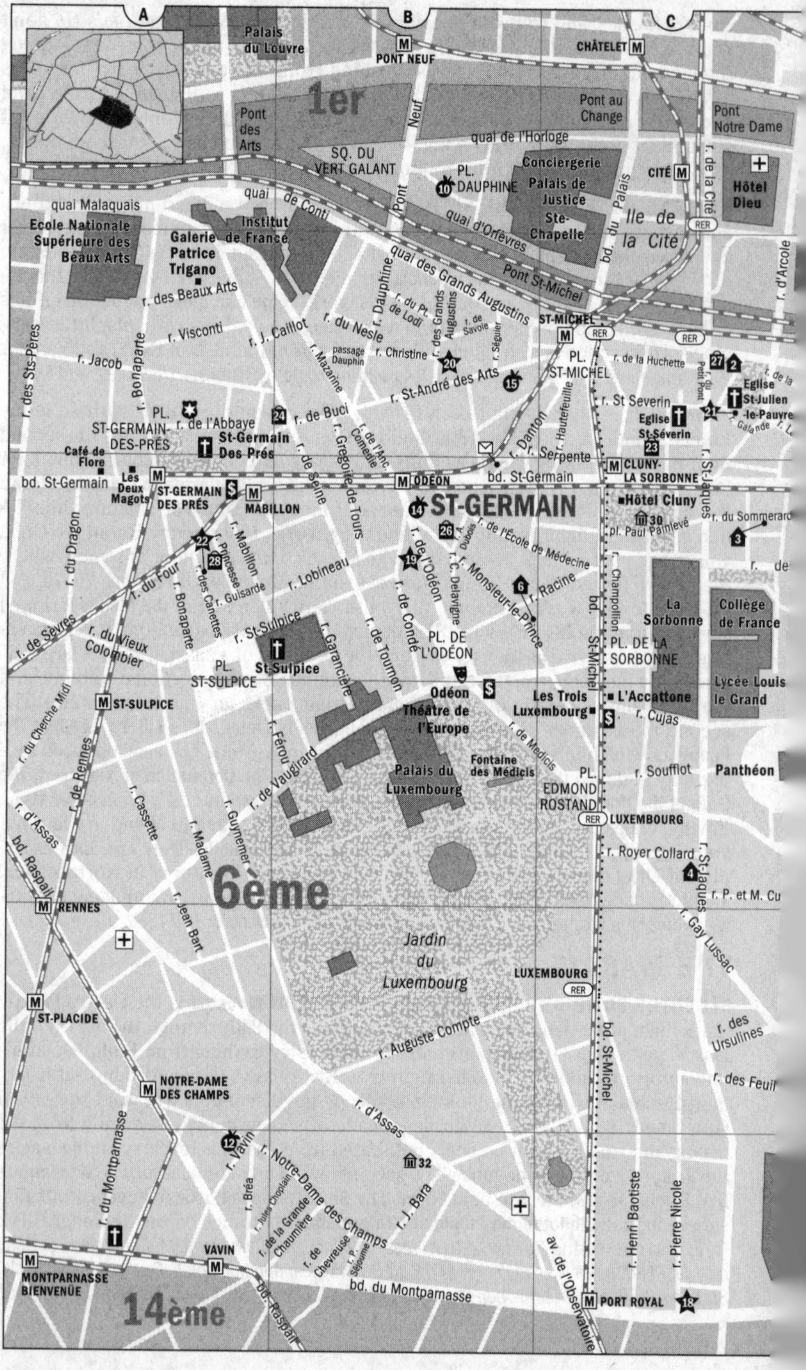
A
B
C
Palais du Louvre
PONT NEUF
CHÂTELET
1er
Pont des Arts
Pont Neuf
Pont au Change
Pont Notre Dame
quai de l'Horloge
SQ. DU VERT GALANT
PL. DAUPHINE
Conciergerie
Palais de Justice
Ste-Chapelle
CITÉ
Hôtel Dieu
r. de la Cité
bd. du Palais
Ile de la Cité
quai Malaquais
quai de Conti
quai d'Orfèvres
Ecole Nationale Supérieure des Beaux Arts
Institut de France
Galerie Patrice Trigano
quai des Grands Augustins
Pont St-Michel
r. d'Arcole
r. des Beaux Arts
r. Visconti
r. J. Caillot
r. du Nesle
r. Dauphine
r. du Pt. de Lodi
r. des Grands Augustins
r. de Savoie
r. Séguier
ST-MICHEL
RER
r. Jacob
r. Bonaparte
r. des Sts-Pères
passage Dauphin
r. Christine
r. Mazarine
r. St-André des Arts
PL. ST-MICHEL
r. de la Huchette
Eglise St-Julien -le-Pauvre
r. Galande
r. du Petit Pont
PL. ST-GERMAIN-DES-PRÉS
r. de l'Abbaye
St-Germain Des Prés
r. de Buci
r. de l'Anc. Comédie
r. Hautefeuille
r. St Severin
Eglise St-Séverin
Café de Flore
Les Deux Magots
bd. St-Germain
ST-GERMAIN DES PRÉS
MABILLON
r. de Seine
r. Grégoire de Tours
ODÉON
r. Danton
r. Serpente
CLUNY-LA SORBONNE
r. St-Jacques
ST-GERMAIN
Hôtel Cluny
pl. Paul Painlevé
r. du Sommerard
r. du Dragon
r. Mabillon
r. Princesse
r. des Canettes
r. Guisarde
r. du Four
r. Lobineau
r. de l'Odéon
r. A. Dubois
r. de l'Ecole de Médecine
r. C. Delavigne
r. Monsieur-le-Prince
r. Racine
r. Champollion
bd. St-Michel
La Sorbonne
Collège de France
r. de Sèvres
r. du Vieux Colombier
r. Bonaparte
r. St-Sulpice
St-Sulpice
PL. ST-SULPICE
r. Garancière
r. de Tournon
r. de Condé
PL. DE L'ODÉON
PL. DE LA SORBONNE
Lycée Louis le Grand
ST-SULPICE
r. du Cherche Midi
Odéon Théâtre de l'Europe
Les Trois Luxembourg
L'Accattone
r. Cujas
r. Férou
r. de Médicis
r. de Rennes
r. de Vaugirard
Palais du Luxembourg
Fontaine des Médicis
PL. EDMOND ROSTAND
r. Soufflot
Panthéon
r. d'Assas
r. Cassette
r. Madame
r. Guynemer
LUXEMBOURG
bd. Raspail
r. Royer Collard
6ème
r. P. et M. Cu
RENNES
r. Jean Bart
r. Gay Lussac
Jardin du Luxembourg
ST-PLACIDE
r. Auguste Comte
r. des Ursulines
NOTRE-DAME DES CHAMPS
r. des Feuil
r. Vavin
r. Notre-Dame des Champs
r. du Montparnasse
r. Bréa
r. Jules Chaplain
r. de la Grande Chaumière
r. J. Bara
r. de Chevreuse
r. P. Séjourné
av. de l'Observatoire
r. Henri Baotiste
r. Pierre Nicole
VAVIN
MONTPARNASSE BIENVENÜE
bd. du Montparnasse
bd. Raspail
PORT ROYAL
14ème
2
3
4
6
10
12
14
15
18
19
20
21
22
23
24
26
27
28
30
32

PARIS

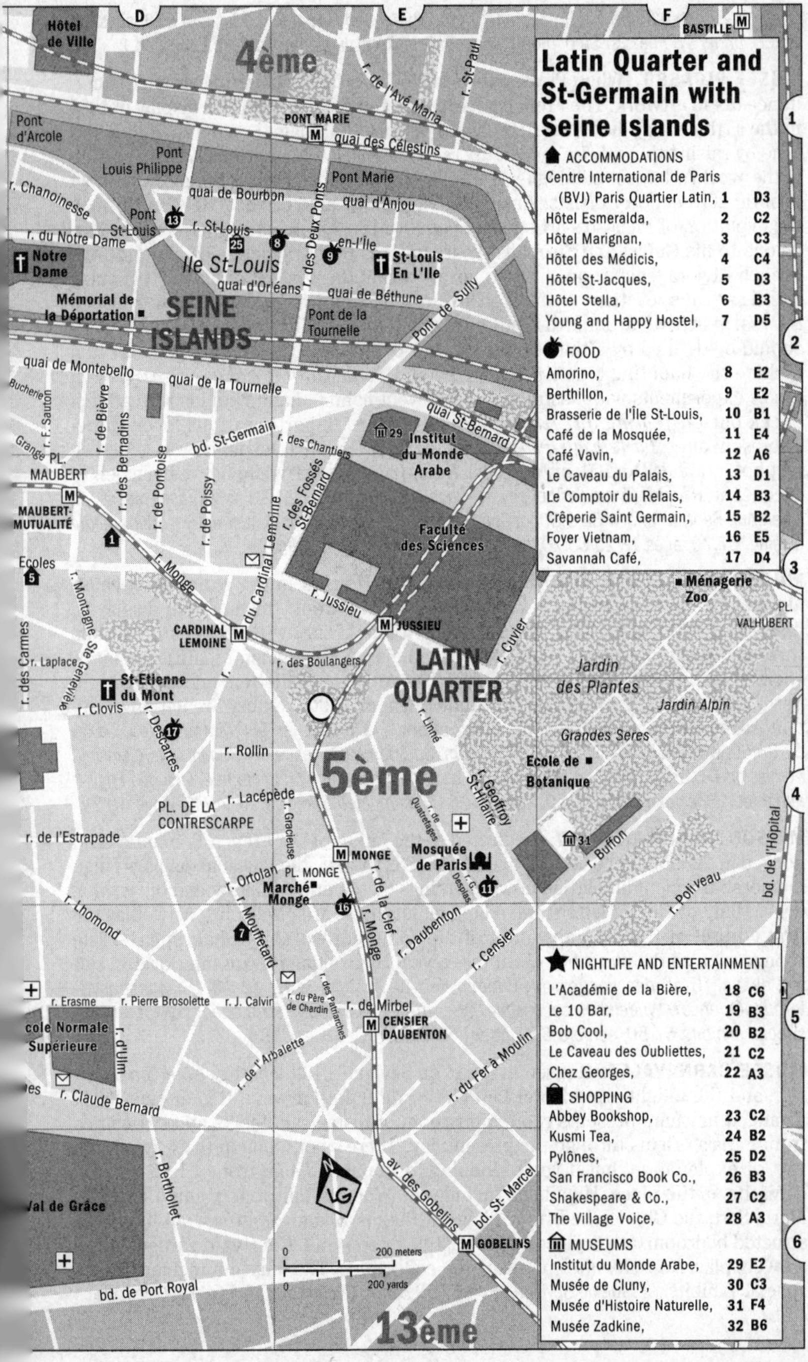
Latin Quarter and St-Germain with Seine Islands
ACCOMMODATIONS
Centre International de Paris (BVJ) Paris Quartier Latin, 1 D3
Hôtel Esmeralda, 2 C2
Hôtel Marignan, 3 C3
Hôtel des Médicis, 4 C4
Hôtel St-Jacques, 5 D3
Hôtel Stella, 6 B3
Young and Happy Hostel, 7 D5
FOOD
Amorino, 8 E2
Berthillon, 9 E2
Brasserie de l'Île St-Louis, 10 B1
Café de la Mosquée, 11 E4
Café Vavin, 12 A6
Le Caveau du Palais, 13 D1
Le Comptoir du Relais, 14 B3
Crêperie Saint Germain, 15 B2
Foyer Vietnam, 16 E5
Savannah Café, 17 D4
NIGHTLIFE AND ENTERTAINMENT
L'Académie de la Bière, 18 C6
Le 10 Bar, 19 B3
Bob Cool, 20 B2
Le Caveau des Oubliettes, 21 C2
Chez Georges, 22 A3
SHOPPING
Abbey Bookshop, 23 C2
Kusmi Tea, 24 B2
Pylônes, 25 D2
San Francisco Book Co., 26 B3
Shakespeare & Co., 27 C2
The Village Voice, 28 A3
MUSEUMS
Institut du Monde Arabe, 29 E2
Musée de Cluny, 30 C3
Musée d'Histoire Naturelle, 31 F4
Musée Zadkine, 32 B6
D
E
F
1
2
3
4
5
6
BASTILLE
Hôtel de Ville
4ème
r. de l'Avé Maria
r. St-Paul
Pont d'Arcole
PONT MARIE
quai des Célestins
Pont Louis Philippe
Pont Marie
quai de Bourbon
quai d'Anjou
r. Chanoinesse
Pont St-Louis
r. St-Louis-en-l'Île
r. du Notre Dame
Notre Dame
Ile St-Louis
St-Louis En L'Ile
quai d'Orléans
r. des Deux Ponts
quai de Béthune
Mémorial de la Déportation
SEINE ISLANDS
Pont de la Tournelle
Pont de Sully
quai de Montebello
quai de la Tournelle
quai St-Bernard
r. de Bièvre
r. des Bernadins
r. F. Sauton
bd. St-Germain
r. des Chantiers
Institut du Monde Arabe
PL. MAUBERT
MAUBERT-MUTUALITÉ
r. de Pontoise
r. de Poissy
r. du Cardinal Lemoine
r. des Fossés St-Bernard
Faculté des Sciences
Ecoles
r. Monge
r. Jussieu
Ménagerie Zoo
PL. VALHUBERT
r. Montagne Ste Geneviève
CARDINAL LEMOINE
JUSSIEU
r. des Carmes
r. Laplace
r. des Boulangers
LATIN QUARTER
r. Cuvier
Jardin des Plantes
Jardin Alpin
St-Etienne du Mont
r. Clovis
r. Descartes
r. Linné
Grandes Seres
r. Rollin
5ème
Ecole de Botanique
r. Lacépède
r. Geoffroy St-Hilaire
PL. DE LA CONTRESCARPE
r. Gracieuse
r. de Quatrefages
r. de l'Estrapade
MONGE
Mosquée de Paris
r. Buffon
bd. de l'Hôpital
r. Ortolan
PL. MONGE
Marché Monge
r. G. Desplas
r. de la Clef
r. Poliveau
r. Lhomond
r. Mouffetard
r. Monge
r. Daubenton
r. Censier
r. Erasme
r. Pierre Brosolette
r. J. Calvin
r. du Père de Chardin
r. des Patriarches
r. de Mirbel
CENSIER DAUBENTON
Ecole Normale Supérieure
r. d'Ulm
r. de l'Arbalète
r. du Fer à Moulin
r. Claude Bernard
r. Berthollet
av. des Gobelins
bd. St- Marcel
Val de Grâce
GOBELINS
0
200 meters
200 yards
bd. de Port Royal
13ème

M and W-F noon-9:50pm, Sa-Su 11am-9:50pm. Library and Forum free. Museum €10, ages 18-26 €8, under 18 free; 1st Su of month free for all. Visitors' guides available in bookshop.)

MUSÉE PICASSO. When Picasso died in 1973, his family paid their French inheritance tax in artwork. The French government put the collection on display in 1985 in the 17th-century **Hôtel Salé,** so named because its original owner made his fortune by raising the *gabelle*, or salt tax (*salé* means salted in French). The museum is the world's largest catalogue of the life and 70-year career of one of the most prolific 20th-century artists. Arranged chronologically, it leads viewers through the evolution of Picasso's artistic and personal life. From his earliest work in Barcelona to his Cubist and Surrealist years in Paris to his Neoclassical work on the French Riviera, each room situates his art within the context of his life: his many mistresses, his reactions to the World Wars, and so forth. You can follow the *Sens de Visite* arrows around the building—or, if you don't believe an artist's work should be defined by a time frame, go your own way. Highlights of the collection include the haunting blue *Autoportrait* and *Still-life with chair-caning*. Picasso's experiments with abstraction often went hand in hand with his love affairs: check out *La femme qui lit (Woman Reading)*, a portrait of his lover Marie-Thérèse Walter; *La femme qui pleure (Woman Crying)*, inspired by the Surrealist photographer Dora Maar; and *The Kiss*, painted later while he was married to Jacqueline Roque. *(5 rue de Thorigny. M: Chemin Vert. ☎42 71 25 21; www.musee-picasso.fr. Open Apr.-Sept. M and W-Su 9:30am-6pm; Oct.-Mar. 9:30am-5:30pm; last entry 45min. before closing. €7.70, ages 18-25 €5.70, under 18 free; 1st Su of month free.)*

MUSÉE D'ART ET D'HISTOIRE DU JUDAÏSME. Housed in the grand **Hôtel de St-Aignan,** once a tenement for Jews fleeing Eastern Europe, this museum displays a history of Jews in Europe, France, and North Africa, with a focus on rituals throughout the diaspora. Modern testimonials on the Jewish identity are interspersed among exquisite ancient relics. The collection of letters and newspapers pertaining to the Dreyfus Affair—the indictment of a 19th-century French Jew, Captain Alfred Dreyfus, for treason—is excellent. *(71 rue de Temple. M: Rambuteau. ☎53 01 86 60; www.mahj.org. Open M-F 11am-6pm, Su 10am-7pm; last entry 30min. before closing. Admission €7, ages 18-26 €4.50, under 18 and art or art history students free; includes English audio tour. Special exhibits €5.50, ages 18-26 €4, combined ticket €9.50/7. MC/V over €12.)*

PARIS

MAISON DE VICTOR HUGO. Dedicated to the father of the French Romantics and housed in the building where he lived from 1832 to 1848, the museum displays Hugo memorabilia, including little-known paintings by the artist's family and his writing desk. Many of Hugo's letters and edited manuscripts are on display, as well as the first edition of Hugo's translation of the complete works of Shakespeare. The rooms, such as the *chambre chinoise*, reveal Hugo's flamboyant interior decorating skills. *(6 pl. des Vosges. M: Chemin Vert or Bastille. ☎42 72 10 16; maisonsvictorhugo@paris.fr. Wheelchair-accessible. Open Tu-Su 10am-6pm. Permanent collection free; special exhibits €7.50, seniors €5, under 26 €3.50. MC/V over €15.)*

MUSÉE CARNAVALET. Housed in Mme. de Sévigné's 16th-century *hôtel particulier* and the neighboring Hôtel Le Peletier de Saint-Fargeau, this meticulously arranged museum presents room after room of historical objects and curiosities from Paris's origins through the present day. There's not much in the way of context or explanation, but if you're looking for a painted sign from a 19th-century café, this is the place. Highlights include the Wendel Ballroom, painted by Jose-Maria Sert, the Charles Le Brun ceilings in Rooms 19 and 20, Proust's fully reconstructed bedroom, and a piece of the Bastille prison wall. Courtyard gardens make a lovely place to relax after perusing the collections. The museum regularly hosts special exhibits. *(23 rue de Sévigné. ☎44 59 58 58. M: Chemin Vert. Take rue St-Gilles, which* *turns into rue de Parc Royal, and turn left on rue de Sévigné. Open Tu-Su 10am-6pm; last entry 5pm. Free. Special exhibits €7, seniors €5.50, under 26 €3.50, under 14 free. MC/V over €15.)*

LATIN QUARTER AND ST-GERMAIN

MUSÉE DE CLUNY. The **Hôtel de Cluny** houses the **Musée National du Moyen Âge,** one of the world's finest collections of medieval art, including jewelry, sculpture, and tapestries. The *hôtel* itself is a flamboyant 14th-century manor built on top of first-century Roman ruins. In the 15th century, the *hôtel* became home to the monastic Order of Cluny, and in 1843, the state converted the *hôtel* into the medieval museum. The museum's collection, which is brilliantly curated so as to be impressive without being overwhelming, includes art from Paris's most important medieval structures: Ste-Chapelle, Notre Dame, and St-Denis. Panels of brilliant stained glass in ruby reds and royal blues from Ste-Chapelle line the ground floor. The brightly lit *Galerie des Rois* contains sculptures from Notre Dame—including a series of marble heads of the kings of Judah, severed during the Revolution. A collection of medieval jewelry includes royal crowns, brooches, and daggers. Perhaps the most impressive work of goldsmithing is the exquisite 14th-century **Gold Rose** on the first floor. And tucked away among gilded reliquaries and ornate illuminated manuscripts, there is a gruesome sculpture of the head of St-John the Baptist on a platter. But the star of the museum is the series of allegorical tapestries, **La Dame à la Licorne** *(The Lady at the Unicorn)*, which visually depict the five senses. The centerpiece of the museum's collection of 15th- and 16th-century Belgian weaving, this complete cycle was made famous by George Sand, who discovered the tapestries hanging in the Château Broussac in Chantelle, south of Paris. *(6 pl. Paul-Painlevé. M: Cluny-La Sorbonne. ☎53 73 78 00, concert info 53 73 78 16. Open M and W-Sa 9:15am-5:45pm. Last entry 5:15pm. Garden open 9am-9:30pm summer, until 5:30pm winter. €7.50, ages 18-25 and 1st Su of each month €5.50, under 18 free. Garden free.)*

MUSÉE D'HISTOIRE NATURELLE. This museum packs it in, housing three science museums in one, all beautifully situated within the Jardin des Plantes. The four-floor **Grande Galerie de l'Evolution** would have you think it's Darwin's sort of place, but the Noah's Arc parade of naturalistic stuffed animals betrays more conservative ideological tendencies. A section of the permanent exhibit is dedicated to human interaction with the environment, with displays on farming and sustainable development, as well as a slightly alarmist world population counter that estimates our numbers in the future. Next door, the **Musée de Minéralogie,** surrounded by luscious rose trellises, contains lovely diamonds, rubies, and sapphires in addition to other surprisingly beautiful minerals. The mood lighting makes this feel like a romantic spot—until the hordes of children that these three museums attract remind you where you are. Look toward the back of the main hall to find gems glowing eerily under the black light. The **Galeries d'Anatomie Comparée et de Paléontologie** are at the far end of the garden, with an exterior that looks like a Victorian house of horrors. Inside, the museum is a ghastly cavalcade of femurs, ribcages, and vertebrae formed into pre-historic animals. Horrifying? Yes. Inescapably compelling? Surprisingly so. Despite snazzy new placards, the place doesn't seem to have changed much since its 1898 opening; it's more notable as a museum of 19th-century *grotesquerie* than as an anatomy catalogue. Check out the fossils, lined up in a grand procession of death, on the first floor. *(57 rue Cuvier, in the Jardin des Plantes. M: Gare d'Austerlitz or Jussieu. ☎40 79 32 16; www.mnhn.fr. Grande Galerie de l'Evolution open M and W-Su 10am-6pm. €8, ages 4-14 and students under 26 €6. Musée de Minéralogie open M and W-Su 10am-5pm, Apr.-Sept. Sa-Su until 6pm. €6, students €4. Galeries d'Anatomie Comparée et de Paléontologie open M and W-Su 10am-5pm; Apr.-Oct. Sa-Su until 6pm. €6, students €4. Weekend passes for the 3 museums and the ménagerie €20, students €15; valid for both weekend days, but no re-entry to any museum.)*

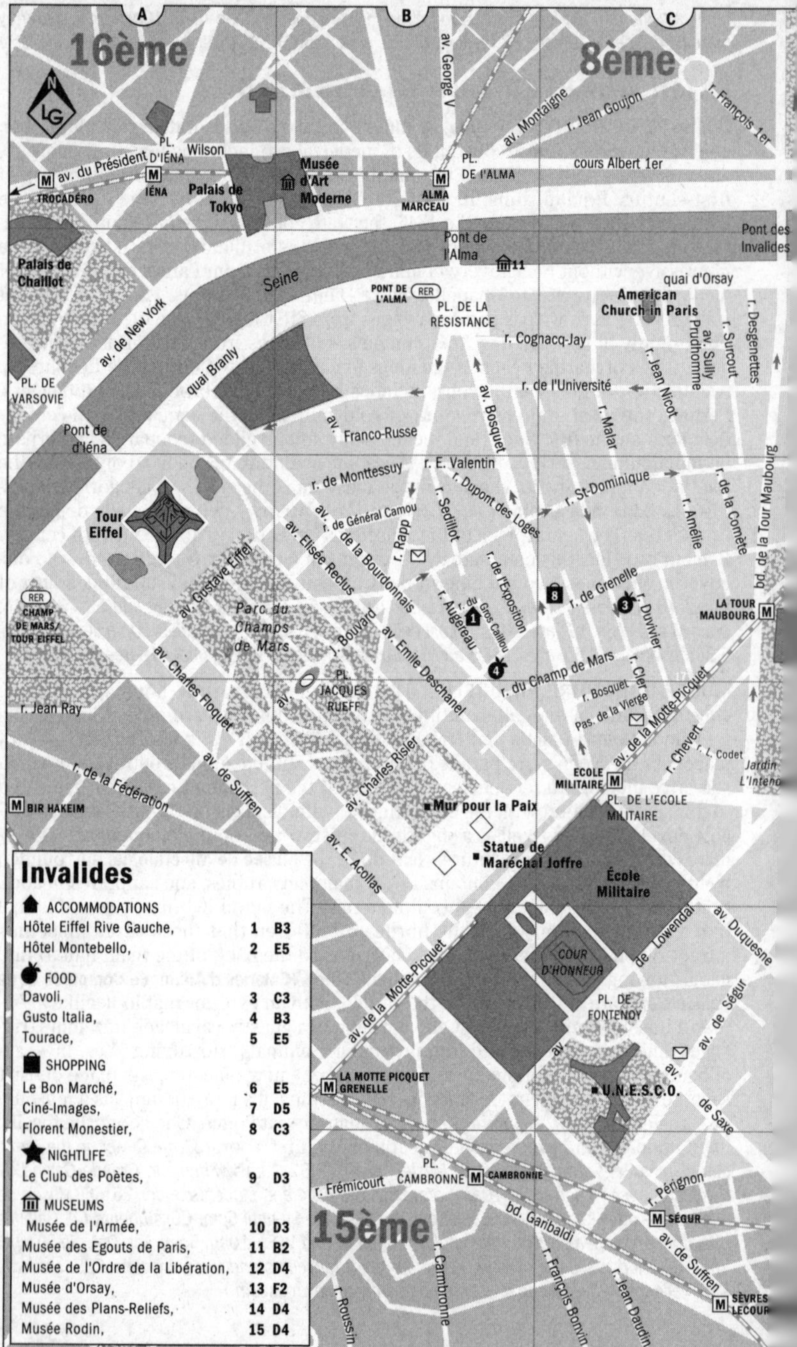
A
B
C
16ème
8ème
15ème
av. George V
av. Montaigne
r. Jean Goujon
r. François 1er
PL. D'IÉNA
av. du Président Wilson
TROCADÉRO
IÉNA
Palais de Tokyo
Musée d'Art Moderne
PL. DE l'ALMA
ALMA MARCEAU
cours Albert 1er
Pont de l'Alma
11
Pont des Invalides
Palais de Chaillot
Seine
PONT DE L'ALMA
RER
quai d'Orsay
American Church in Paris
PL. DE LA RÉSISTANCE
r. Cognacq-Jay
av. de New York
quai Branly
PL. DE VARSOVIE
Pont de d'Iéna
av. Franco-Russe
r. de l'Université
av. Bosquet
r. Malar
r. Jean Nicot
av. Sully Prudhomme
r. Surcout
r. Desgenettes
r. E. Valentin
r. de Monttessuy
r. Dupont des Loges
r. St-Dominique
r. Amélie
r. de la Comète
bd. de la Tour Maubourg
Tour Eiffel
av. r. de Général Camou
r. Rapp
r. Sedillot
av. Elisée Reclus
av. de la Bourdonnais
r. de l'Exposition
8
r. de Grenelle
3
LA TOUR MAUBOURG
RER
CHAMP DE MARS/ TOUR EIFFEL
av. Gustave Eiffel
Parc du Champs de Mars
av. J. Bouvard
r. Augereau
1
r. du Gros Caillou
av. Emile Deschanel
r. Duvivier
4
r. du Champ de Mars
av. Charles Floquet
PL. JACQUES RUEFF
r. Cler
r. Bosquet
Pas. de la Vierge
av. de la Motte-Picquet
r. Jean Ray
av. Charles Risler
r. Chevert
r. L. Codet
Jardin L'Inten
r. de la Fédération
av. de Suffren
ECOLE MILITAIRE
PL. DE L'ECOLE MILITAIRE
BIR HAKEIM
Mur pour la Paix
Statue de Maréchal Joffre
École Militaire
av. E. Acollas
av. Duquesne
av. de Lowendal
COUR D'HONNEUR
PL. DE FONTENOY
av. de Ségur
av. de la Motte-Picquet
U.N.E.S.C.O.
av. de Saxe
LA MOTTE PICQUET GRENELLE
PL. CAMBRONNE
CAMBRONNE
r. Frémicourt
r. Pérignon
SÉGUR
bd. Garibaldi
av. de Suffren
r. Cambronne
r. François Bonvin
r. Jean Daudin
r. Roussin
SÈVRES LECOUR
Invalides
ACCOMMODATIONS
Hôtel Eiffel Rive Gauche, 1 B3
Hôtel Montebello, 2 E5
FOOD
Davoli, 3 C3
Gusto Italia, 4 B3
Tourace, 5 E5
SHOPPING
Le Bon Marché, 6 E5
Ciné-Images, 7 D5
Florent Monestier, 8 C3
NIGHTLIFE
Le Club des Poètes, 9 D3
MUSEUMS
Musée de l'Armée, 10 D3
Musée des Egouts de Paris, 11 B2
Musée de l'Ordre de la Libération, 12 D4
Musée d'Orsay, 13 F2
Musée des Plans-Reliefs, 14 D4
Musée Rodin, 15 D4

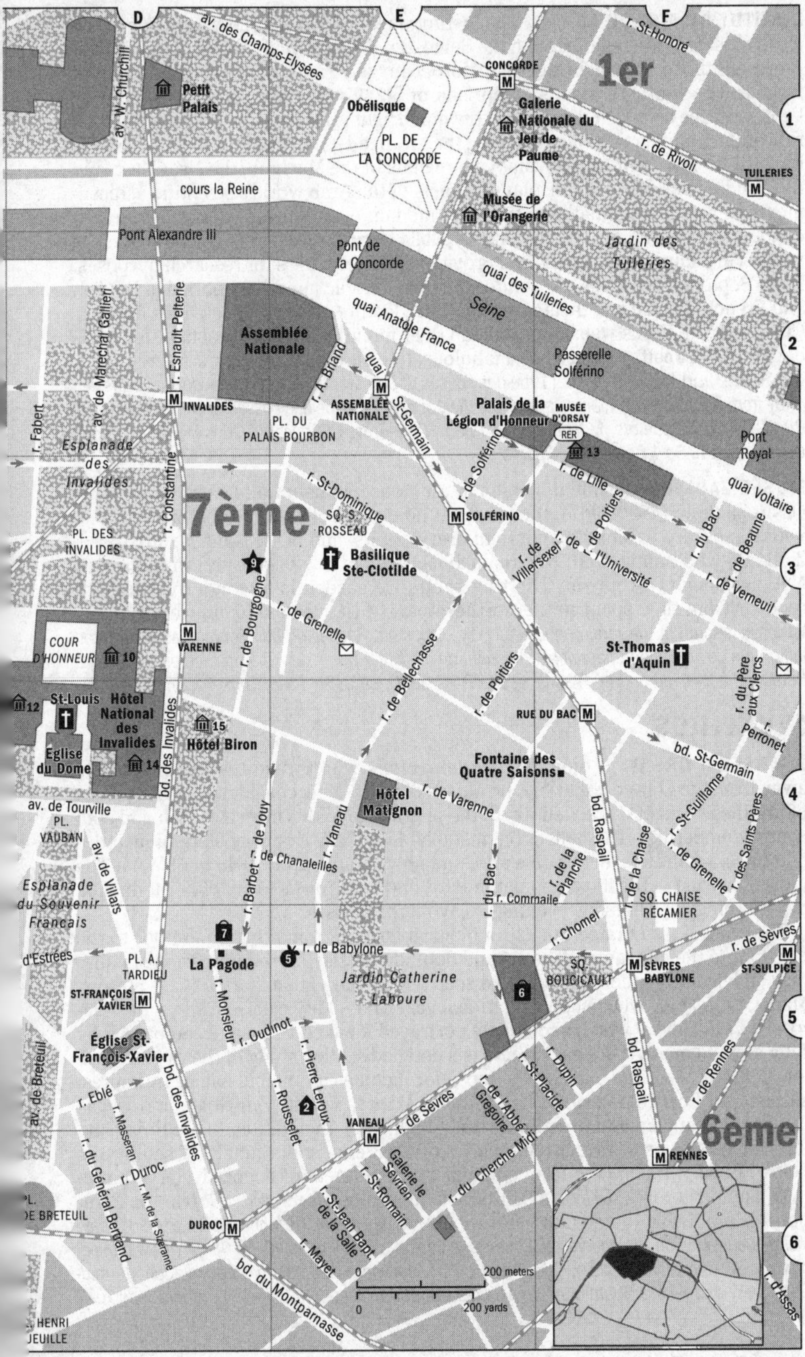

1er
7ème
6ème
av. des Champs-Elysées
Petit Palais
av. W. Churchill
CONCORDE
Obélisque
PL. DE LA CONCORDE
Galerie Nationale du Jeu de Paume
r. St-Honoré
r. de Rivoli
TUILERIES
cours la Reine
Musée de l'Orangerie
Pont Alexandre III
Pont de la Concorde
Jardin des Tuileries
quai des Tuileries
Seine
quai Anatole France
Assemblée Nationale
r. Esnault Pelterie
av. de Marechal Gallieni
r. A. Briand
quai St-Germain
Passerelle Solférino
ASSEMBLÉE NATIONALE
INVALIDES
PL. DU PALAIS BOURBON
Palais de la Légion d'Honneur
MUSÉE D'ORSAY
RER
13
Pont Royal
quai Voltaire
r. Fabert
Esplanade des Invalides
r. Constantine
r. St-Dominique
SQ. S. ROSSEAU
SOLFÉRINO
r. de Solférino
r. de Lille
r. de Poitiers
r. du Bac
r. de Beaune
PL. DES INVALIDES
9
Basilique Ste-Clotilde
r. de Villersexel
r. de l'Université
r. de Verneuil
COUR D'HONNEUR
10
VARENNE
r. de Bourgogne
r. de Grenelle
r. de Bellechasse
St-Thomas d'Aquin
r. du Père aux Clercs
12
St-Louis
Hôtel National des Invalides
Église du Dome
14
bd. des Invalides
15
Hôtel Biron
r. de Poitiers
RUE DU BAC
r. Perronet
Fontaine des Quatre Saisons
bd. St-Germain
av. de Tourville
PL. VAUBAN
Hôtel Matignon
r. de Varenne
r. St-Guillame
r. Barbet de Jouy
r. de Chanaleilles
r. Vaneau
bd. Raspail
r. de la Chaise
r. de Grenelle
r. des Saints Pères
Esplanade du Souvenir Francais
av. de Villars
r. du Bac
r. Comnaile
r. de la Planche
SQ. CHAISE RÉCAMIER
r. Chomel
r. de Sèvres
7
5
r. de Babylone
d'Estrées
PL. A. TARDIEU
La Pagode
Jardin Catherine Laboure
SQ. BOUCICAULT
SÈVRES BABYLONE
ST-SULPICE
6
ST-FRANÇOIS XAVIER
r. Monsieur
r. Oudinot
Église St-François-Xavier
r. Pierre Leroux
r. Dupin
r. St-Placide
bd. Raspail
r. de Rennes
av. de Breteuil
r. Eblé
r. Masseran
r. Rousselet
2
VANEAU
r. de Sèvres
r. de l'Abbé Gregoire
r. du Cherche Midi
RENNES
r. du Général Bertrand
r. Duroc
r. M. de la Sizeranne
Galerie le Sevrien
r. St-Romain
PL. DE BRETEUIL
DUROC
r. St-Jean Bapt. de la Salle
r. Mayet
bd. du Montparnasse
0
200 meters
200 yards
PL. HENRI QUEUILLE
r. d'Assas
D
E
F
1
2
3
4
5
6

PARIS

INSTITUT DU MONDE ARABE. The Institut du Monde Arabe (IMA) is in one of the city's most striking buildings. On the Seine, the IMA was built to look like a ship to represent those on which Algerian, Moroccan, and Tunisian immigrants sailed to France. The southern face is comprised of ■**240 Arabesque portals,** powered by light-sensitive cells that determine how much light is needed to illuminate the interior of the building without damaging the art. Inside, the spacious museum exhibits third- to 18th-century art from Arab regions of the Maghreb, the Near East, and the Middle East. Level Six displays artifacts of the Arab world's scientific achievements in astronomy, mathematics, and medicine, and Level Four is devoted to contemporary Arab art. The extensive **public library** houses over 50,000 works, as well as an audio-visual center, and provides Internet access for research purposes. From September to June, the auditorium hosts Arabic movies (subtitled in English and French), music and theater productions, lecture series, and activities for kids. Check out the IMA's website or pick up their monthly IMAInfo brochure for more details. The ■**rooftop terrace** has a fabulous, free view of Montmartre, Sacré Coeur, the Seine, and Ile de la Cité. *(1 rue des Fossés St-Bernard. M: Jussieu. Walk down rue Jussieu away from the Jardin des Plantes and make the 1st right onto rue des Fossés St-Bernard. ☎ 40 51 38 38; www.imarabe.org. Museum open Tu-Su 10am-6pm. €5, ages 12-26 €4, under 12 free. Library open Tu-Sa 1-6pm. Free. Cinema €4.)*

MUSÉE ZADKINE. Installed in 1982 in the house and studio of Russian sculptor Ossip Zadkine (1890-1967), the museum houses a collection of his work, along with temporary exhibits by contemporary artists, and is pleasantly tourist-free. Zadkine, who immigrated to Paris in 1909, worked in styles from Primitivism to Neoclassicism to Cubism. The tiny sculpture garden is a wonderful place to recover from time spent in the northern part of the 6ème. *(100bis rue d'Assas. M: Vavin. Just south of the Jardin du Luxembourg. Cross bd. Raspail on bd. Montparnasse and turn left on rue de la Grande Chaumière; then right on rue Notre Dame des Champs, left on rue Joseph Bara, and a final left on rue d'Assas. ☎ 55 42 77 20. Open Tu-Su 10am-6pm. €4, under 26 €2.)*

INVALIDES

■**MUSÉE D'ORSAY.** If only the *Académiciens* who turned the Impressionists away from the Louvre could see the Musée d'Orsay. Now considered masterpieces of art, these "rejects" are well worth the pilgrimage to this mecca of 19th and 20th century modernity. The collection, installed in a former railway station, includes paintings, sculptures, decorative arts, and photography from 1848 until WWI. The museum is one of the most popular in Paris and has crowds to match. Visit on Sunday mornings or Thursday evenings to avoid the masses.

The museum is curated in a chronological fashion from the ground floor to the top floor to the mezzanine. The ground floor, dedicated to Pre-Impressionist paintings and sculpture, contains the two scandalous works that started it all, both by Manet: *Olympia*, whose confrontational gaze and nudity caused a stir, and *Déjeuner sur L'Herbe*, which shockingly portrayed a naked woman accompanied by fully-clothed men. At the back, there is a detailed section study of the Opera Garnier, definitely worth a glance. The top floor includes all the big names in Impressionist and Post-Impressionist art: Monet, Manet, Seurat, Van Gogh, and Degas (his famed dancers and prostitutes are a highlight). In addition, the exterior and interior balconies offer supreme views of the Seine and a jungle of sculptures below. Finally, the middle level contains an assortment of decorative arts, paintings, and sculptures. Don't miss Rodin's imperious *Honoré de Balzac* or Pompon's adorably big-footed *Ours Blanc*. *(62 rue de Lille. M: Solférino, RER Musée d'Orsay. Visitor's entrance on the square off 1 rue de la Légion d'Honneur. ☎ 40 49 48 14; www.musee-orsay.fr. Wheelchair-accessible; call ☎ 40 49 47 14 for more information. Open mid-June to mid-Sept. Tu-W and F-Sa 9:30am-6pm, Th 10am-9:45pm, Su 9am-6pm; mid-Sept. to mid-June Tu-W and F-Sa 9:30am-6pm, Th 10am-9:45pm. Last ticket sales 30min. before closing. €7.50, M-W and F-Sa after 4:15pm, Th after 8pm, Su €5.50; ages 18-25 €5, under 18 free. 1hr. English-language tours Tu-Sa 11:30am and 2:30pm; call ahead to confirm. €6.50/5/free. Bookstore open Tu-W and F-Su 9:30am-6:30pm, Th 9:30am-9:30pm. AmEx/MC/V.)*

MUSÉE RODIN. Located in the elegant 18th-century Hôtel Biron, where Auguste Rodin lived and worked at the end of his life, the museum displays the vast majority of his better-known sculptures, including his best-known, *The Thinker*. His mournful masterpiece *Bourgeois de Calais*, which depicts the tragedy of men facing their death; and his horrifying *La Porte d'Enfer (Gates of Hell)*, in bronze, are incongruous additions to the lush garden. The museum also boasts several sculptures by Camille Claudel, Rodin's muse, collaborator, and lover. A Sunday afternoon would be well spent reading amid the graceful flowers and sculptures. *(79 rue de Varenne. M: Varenne. ☎44 18 61 10; www.musee-rodin.fr. Touch tours for the blind and educational tours available; ☎44 18 61 24. Ground floor and gardens wheelchair-accessible. Open Apr.-Sept. Tu-Su 9:30am-5:45pm; Oct.-Mar. Tu-Su 9:30am-4:45pm. Last entry 30min. before closing. €6, seniors and ages 18-25 €4; special exhibits €7/5. First Su of the month free. Garden exhibits may be closed in bad weather. Audio tour €4 each for permanent and temporary exhibits, combined ticket €6. Temporary exhibits housed in the chapel, to the right of the entrance. Café open Tu-Sa Apr.-Sept. 9:30am-6:30pm, Oct.-Mar. 9:30am-4:30pm. MC/V.)*

MUSÉE DES EGOUTS DE PARIS (MUSEUM OF THE SEWERS OF PARIS). Part public service announcement from the Mayor's office, part sewer, this may be the strangest museum in Paris. Guided tours take visitors through still-working sewer tunnels—yes, they smell like a sewer—and give an animated account of Paris's struggles for potable water and waste-free streets. The signs, mannequins dressed as sewer workers, and displays may not be worth your time, but in a city that goes all out to beautify itself, this is a unique opportunity to see the underbelly of Paris. *(Pont de l'Alma. Across from 93 quai d'Orsay. M: Alma-Marceau. ☎53 68 27 81. Open M-W and Sa-Su May-Sept. 11am-5pm, Oct.-Apr. 11am-4pm. Closed 2 weeks in Jan. €4.10; students, over 60, and under 10 €3.30. English and French tours depending on number of visitors.)*

CHAMPS-ELYSÉES

MUSÉE JACQUEMART-ANDRÉ. Nélie Jacquemart's passion for art and her husband Edouard André's wealth combined to create this extensive collection. During the couple's lifetime, Parisian high society admired their double-corniced marble and iron staircase; however, only very special guests got a glimpse of their precious collection of English, Flemish, and Italian Renaissance artwork, which included a *Madonna and Child* by Botticelli, *St-George and the Dragon* by Ucello, and *Pilgrims at Emmaus* by Rembrandt. Now you can wander through the gorgeous late 19th-century home, furnished with a collection worthy of the most prestigious museums. The couple imported the magnificent Italian fresco on the upper level, set above a walled indoor garden. Visitors can enjoy a light lunch in the tea room (open 11:45am-5:30pm; *plat chaud du jour* €14), or admire the museum's facade while resting in the courtyard. *(158 bd. Haussmann. ☎45 62 11 59. M: Miromesnil. Open daily 10am-6pm. Last entry 5:30pm. €9.50, students and ages 7-17 €7, under 7 free. 1 free child ticket per 3 purchased tickets. English headsets free with admission. AmEx/MC/V.)*

MAISON DE BALZAC. Honoré de Balzac hid from bill collectors (under the pseudonym of M. de Breugnol) in this three-story hillside *maison*, his home from 1840-47. In this tranquil retreat, he completed a substantial part of *La Comédie Humaine*. Visitors can see the desk and beautifully embroidered chair where Balzac wrote and edited for a reported 17 hours a day. In the fantastic Manuscript Room, you can observe his excruciating editing process. View over 400 printing block portraits of his characters, organized into genealogical sequences, in one of

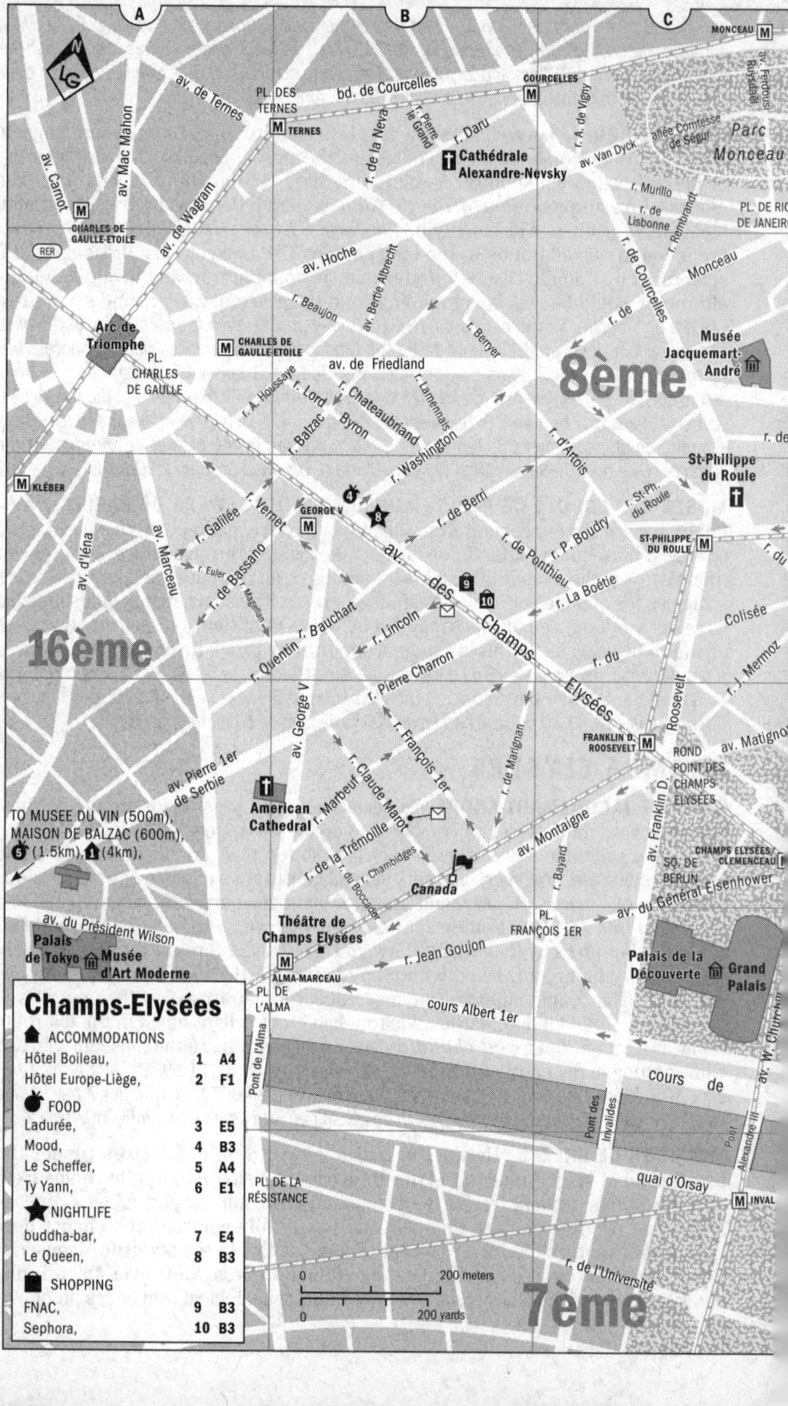
A
B
C
av. de Ternes
PL. DES TERNES
TERNES
bd. de Courcelles
COURCELLES
MONCEAU
av. Mac Mahon
av. Carnot
av. de Wagram
r. de la Neva
r. Pierre le Grand
r. Daru
Cathédrale Alexandre-Nevsky
r. A. de Vigny
av. Van Dyck
allée Comtesse de Ségur
Parc Monceau
av. Ferdousi
Ruysdaël
r. Murillo
r. de Lisbonne
r. Rembrandt
PL. DE RIO DE JANEIRO
CHARLES DE GAULLE-ETOILE
RER
av. Hoche
r. Bertie Albrecht
r. de Courcelles
r. de Monceau
r. Beaujon
r. Berryer
Arc de Triomphe
PL. CHARLES DE GAULLE
av. de Friedland
Musée Jacquemart-André
8ème
r. A. Houssaye
r. Lord Byron
r. Chateaubriand
r. Lamennais
r. Balzac
r. Washington
r. d'Artois
St-Philippe du Roule
KLÉBER
GEORGE V
r. Galilée
r. Vernet
r. de Berri
r. St-Ph. du Roule
r. P. Boudry
ST-PHILIPPE DU ROULE
av. d'Iéna
av. Marceau
r. Euler
r. de Bassano
r. Magellan
r. de Ponthieu
r. La Boétie
av. des Champs-Elysées
r. Bauchart
r. Lincoln
r. Quentin
r. du Colisée
r. J. Mermoz
16ème
r. Pierre Charron
av. George V
r. François 1er
r. de Marignan
FRANKLIN D. ROOSEVELT
av. Franklin D. Roosevelt
av. Matignon
ROND POINT DES CHAMPS ELYSÉES
av. Pierre 1er de Serbie
American Cathedral
r. Marbeuf
r. Claude Marot
r. de la Trémoille
r. Chambiges
r. du Boccador
av. Montaigne
r. Bayard
Canada
CHAMPS ELYSÉES/CLEMENCEAU
SQ. DE BERLIN
av. du Général Eisenhower
TO MUSEE DU VIN (500m),
MAISON DE BALZAC (600m),
5 (1.5km), 1 (4km),
av. du Président Wilson
Palais de Tokyo
Musée d'Art Moderne
Théâtre de Champs Elysées
ALMA-MARCEAU
PL. DE L'ALMA
PL. FRANÇOIS 1ER
r. Jean Goujon
cours Albert 1er
Palais de la Découverte
Grand Palais
Pont de l'Alma
Pont des Invalides
cours de
av. W. Churchill
Pont Alexandre III
quai d'Orsay
PL. DE LA RÉSISTANCE
INVAL
r. de l'Université
200 meters
200 yards
7ème
Champs-Elysées
ACCOMMODATIONS
Hôtel Boileau, 1 A4
Hôtel Europe-Liège, 2 F1
FOOD
Ladurée, 3 E5
Mood, 4 B3
Le Scheffer, 5 A4
Ty Yann, 6 E1
NIGHTLIFE
buddha-bar, 7 E4
Le Queen, 8 B3
SHOPPING
FNAC, 9 B3
Sephora, 10 B3

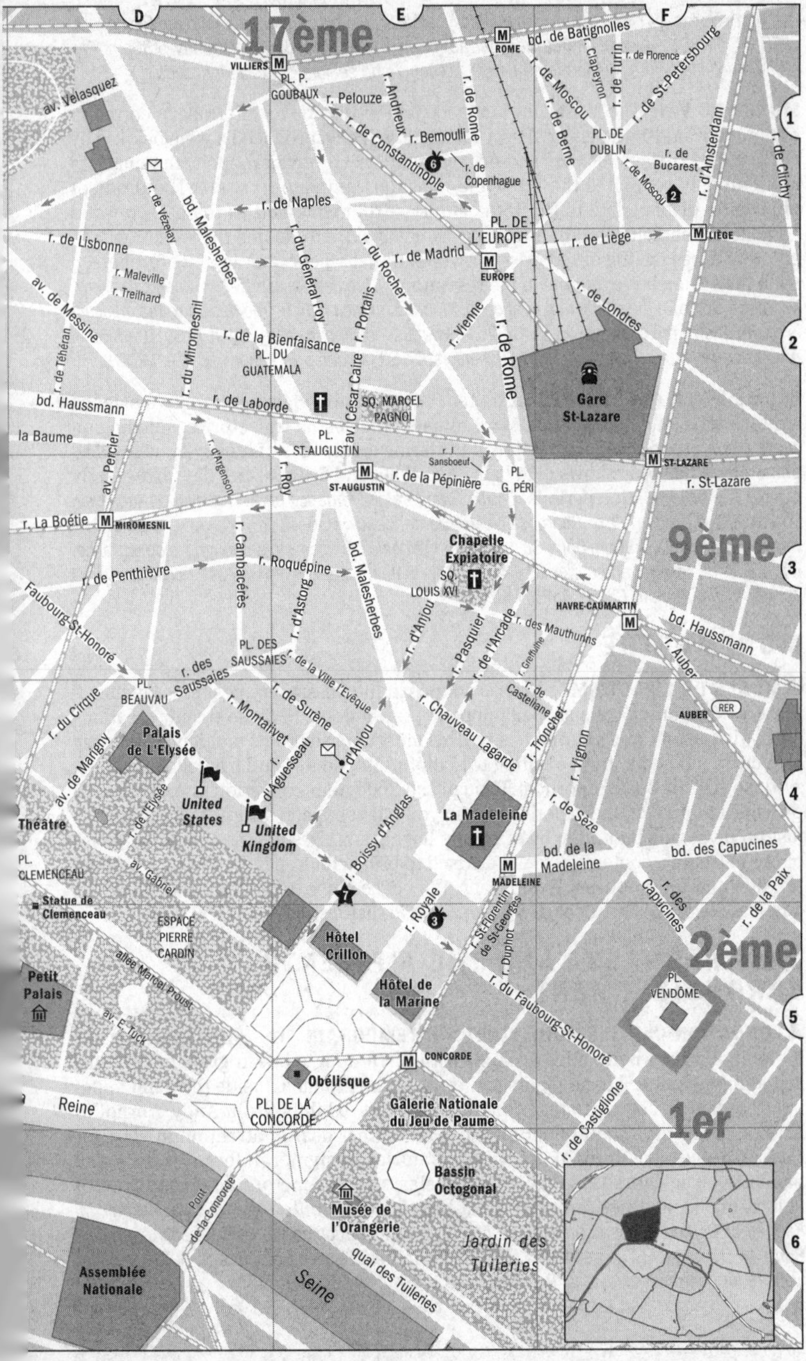
17ème
9ème
2ème
1er
Gare St-Lazare
Chapelle Expiatoire
La Madeleine
Palais de L'Elysée
United States
United Kingdom
Hôtel Crillon
Hôtel de la Marine
Obélisque
PL. DE LA CONCORDE
Galerie Nationale du Jeu de Paume
Bassin Octogonal
Musée de l'Orangerie
Jardin des Tuileries
Petit Palais
Assemblée Nationale
Seine
quai des Tuileries
Statue de Clemenceau
ESPACE PIERRE CARDIN
PL. VENDÔME
bd. Haussmann
bd. Malesherbes
r. de Rome
r. de Rivoli
r. du Faubourg-St-Honoré
r. Royale
bd. de la Madeleine
bd. des Capucines
r. St-Lazare
r. de Londres
r. de Madrid
r. de Lisbonne
r. de Naples
r. de Constantinople
bd. de Batignolles
r. d'Amsterdam
r. de Clichy
ROME
VILLIERS
EUROPE
LIÈGE
ST-LAZARE
ST-AUGUSTIN
MIROMESNIL
HAVRE-CAUMARTIN
AUBER
MADELEINE
CONCORDE
PARIS

the last rooms. *(47 rue Raynouard. M: Passy. Walk up the hill and turn left onto rue Raynouard. ☎55 74 41 80; www.paris.fr/musees/balzac. Open Tu-Su 10am-6pm. Last entry 5:30pm. Permanent collection free. Guided tours €4.50, students and seniors €4; call for schedule.)*

MUSÉE DU VIN. The Musée du Vin is located in the cool, subterranean corridors of the renovated 15th-century Passy Monastery, which produced a wine beloved by Louis XIII. With whimsical (and occasionally creepy) wax models, the museum meticulously recreates the life cycle of wine from vine to *verre*. Hundreds of objects on display date to the 18th century—from wine bottles to corkscrews to agricultural implements. After the tour, you may have to remind the receptionist to give you a free tasting of red, *rosé*, or white. If that whets your appetite for more, a wine-heavy lunch is available in the restaurant. *(Rue des Eaux, or 5-7 pl. Charles Dickens. M: Passy. Go down the stairs, turn right on pl. Alboni, and then right on rue des Eaux; the museum is at the end of the street. ☎45 25 63 26; www.museeduvinparis.com. Open Tu-Su 10am-6pm. Admission (includes 1 glass of wine) €9, seniors €7.50, students €7, under 18 free. MC/V.)*

PALAIS DE LA DÉCOUVERTE. Kids tear around the Palais's interactive science exhibits, pressing buttons that start comets on celestial trajectories, spinning on seats to investigate angular motion, and staring at all kinds of creepy-crawlies. The **planetarium** has four shows (11:30am, 3:15, 4:30, and 5:45pm) per day; arrive early during school vacation periods. *(In the Grand Palais, entrance on av. Franklin D. Roosevelt. M: Franklin D. Roosevelt or Champs-Elysées-Clemenceau. ☎56 43 20 20; www.palais-decouverte.fr. Open Tu-Sa 9:30am-6pm, Su 10am-7pm. Wheelchair-accessible through a side entrance. €7; students, seniors, and under 18 €4.50; under 5 free. Families with at least 2 children €4.50 per adult. Planetarium €3.50. AmEx/MC/V.)*

MONTMARTRE

MUSÉE DE L'EROTISME. Bronze statues in the missionary position, Japanimation sex cartoons, vagina-shaped puppets—seven floors of these steamy creations await visitors at Paris's shrine to sex. This museum celebrates multicultural erotic art across all media, from painting to sculpture to video—and even includes King Alfonso XIII of Spain's pornos! Though the 2000-item collection is organized to provide a more edifying experience than you might expect, it turns out that there's just no un-sexing photographs of people having sex. Despite the scholarly nature of the museum's contents, it is not advised to bring children here. The upper floors are devoted to temporary exhibitions. *(72 bd. de Clichy. M: Blanche. ☎42 58 28 73; www.musee-erotisme.com. Open daily 10am-2am. €8, students and groups €6.)*

MONTPARNASSE AND THE FIFTEENTH ARRONDISSEMENT

FONDATION CARTIER POUR L'ART CONTEMPORAIN. The Fondation Cartier looks like a futuristic indoor forest, with a stunning modern glass facade surrounding the natural local plants and trees of the grounds. Inside the main building, the gallery hosts rotating contemporary art exhibits, from Andy Warhol to African sculpture. The Fondation received a great deal of attention in 2004 for *Pain Couture*, a show of Jean-Paul Gaultier designs rendered in rolls and baguettes. On Thursdays, gallery enthusiasts can scope out an eclectic set of dance, music, and performance art at the *Soirées Nomades*. *(261 bd. Raspail. M: Raspail or Denfert-Rochereau. ☎42 18 56 50; www.fondation.cartier.com. Open Tu-Su noon-8pm. €7.50, students and seniors €5.50, under 10 free.* Soirées Nomades *Th 8:30pm; check website for performance details. Reserve ahead at ☎42 18 56 72.)*

OUTLYING ARRONDISSEMENTS

EXPLORA SCIENCE MUSEUM. Dedicated to bringing science to young people, the Explora Science Museum is the star attraction of La Villette, located in the complex's Cité des Sciences et de l'Industrie. The monumental, futuristic architecture rocks on its own, but the displays inside are even better. Kids will love them, and adult visitors may find themselves equally enthralled. The museum boasts close to 300 exhibits on topics ranging from astronomy and mathematics to computer science and sound. Explora also features a **planetarium** (level 2), the **Cinéma Louis Lumière** (level 0) with 3D movies, a modest **aquarium** (level 2), and **Médiathèque,** a multimedia science and technology library that has over 3500 films. The museum's **Cité des Enfants** offers one set of programs for kids ages 3-5 and another for ages 5-12. Both require that children be accompanied by an adult but admit no more than two adults per family. Most programs are in French, but the interactive exhibits are just as fun for English-speaking explorers, as many are in English. The *vestiaire* on the ground floor rents strollers and wheelchairs. *(M: Porte de la Villette. 30 av. Corentin-Cariou. ☎ 40 05 80 00; www.cite-sciences.fr. Museum open Tu-Sa 10am-6pm, Su 10am-7pm. Last entry M-Sa 5:30pm, Su 6pm. €8, under 25 or families of 5 or more €6, under 7 free. Planetarium supplement €3, under 7 free. Médiathèque open Tu noon-7:45pm, W-Su noon-6:45pm; free. 1½hr. Cité des Enfants programs Tu-Su about every 2hr.; €5.)*

GALLERIES

After seeing the art hanging in Paris's museums, take home a piece for yourself; many galleries display the work of both established and up-and-coming artists. The **Marais** has recently become the center of Paris's contemporary art scene, and the city's best galleries cluster in the area's northern half. The 6ème's **St-Germain-des-Prés** is home to a handful of more conservative galleries. Those around the **Champs-Elysées** contain more traditional Impressionist and post-Impressionist works. The *portes Ouvertes* festival (May-June; check *Pariscope* for information) allows visitors to watch artists work in their studios. Most galleries close at lunchtime, on Mondays, and in August.

GALERIE EMMANUEL PERROTIN. Set in a courtyard, this large gallery displays everything from installation art to painting to sculpture. The permanent display of a miniature metal cathedral with X-rays for stained-glass windows is a must-see. *(76 rue du Turenne. M: St-Sebastien Froissart. 3ème. ☎ 42 16 79 79. Open Tu-Sa 11am-7pm.)*

ATELIER CARDENAS BELLANGER. This gallery doesn't let its tiny size stand in its way. Recent exhibitions include Henry Taylor's wickedly funny paintings on race and a salon on contemporary drawing. Bearded freak-folk hero Devendra Banhart has exhibited and curated here. *(43 rue Quincampoix. M: Rambuteau. 4ème. ☎ 48 87 47 65. Open Sept. to mid-July Tu-Sa 11am-7pm.)*

FAIT & CAUSE. This gallery with a heart aims to spread humanist and humanitarian consciousness, mostly through documentary photography. Exhibits understandably draw large crowds; past artists have included Jacob Riis, Jane Evelyn Atwood, and Robert Doisneau. *(58 rue Quincampoix. M: Rambuteau or Etienne-Marcel. 3ème. ☎ 42 74 26 36. Open Tu-Sa 1:30-6:30pm.)*

GALERIE NATHALIE OBADIA. This gallery features new works by young painters who just might make it into the nearby Centre Pompidou someday. The witty, angry paintings frequently on display are desperate attempts to get the medium of painting back on the road to glory. *(3 rue du Cloître St-Merri. M: Hôtel de Ville. 4ème. ☎ 42 74 67 68. Open M-Sa 11am-7pm.)*

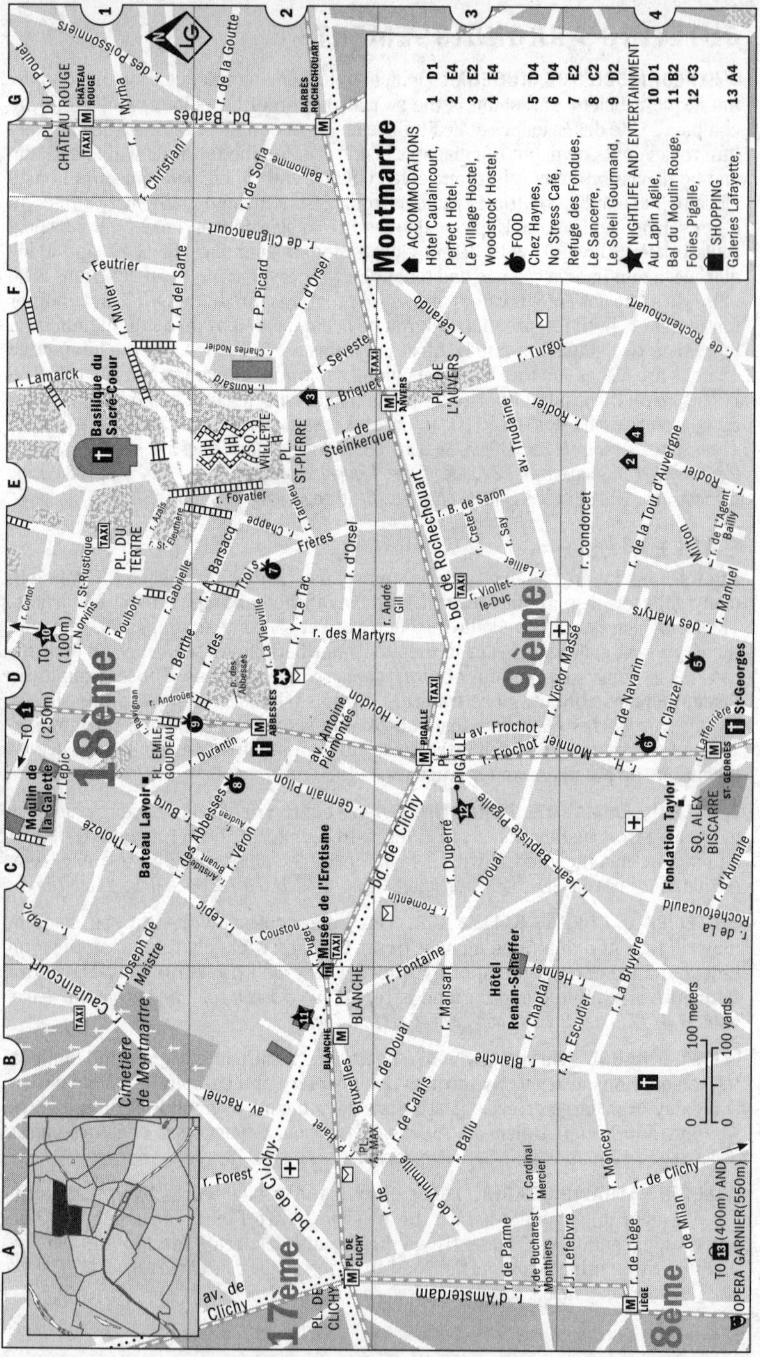
Montmartre
ACCOMMODATIONS
Hôtel Caulaincourt, 1 D1
Perfect Hôtel, 2 E4
Le Village Hostel, 3 E2
Woodstock Hostel, 4 E4
FOOD
Chez Haynes, 5 D4
No Stress Café, 6 D4
Refuge des Fondues, 7 E2
Le Sancerre, 8 C2
Le Soleil Gourmand, 9 D2
NIGHTLIFE AND ENTERTAINMENT
Au Lapin Agile, 10 D1
Bal du Moulin Rouge, 11 B2
Folies Pigalle, 12 C3
SHOPPING
Galeries Lafayette, 13 A4
18ème
9ème
17ème
8ème
Basilique du Sacré-Coeur
Moulin de la Galette
Bateau Lavoir
Musée de l'Erotisme
Cimetière de Montmartre
Hôtel Renan-Scheffer
Fondation Taylor
TO 1 (250m)
TO 10 (100m)
TO 13 (400m) AND OPERA GARNIER (550m)
0 100 meters
0 100 yards

FONDATION TAYLOR. Run as a non-profit art space and serving the Parisian and international artistic community with annual prizes in painting, sculpture, and engraving, the Fondation displays year-round exhibits ranging from figurative to non-objective work. *(1 rue la Bruyère, 9ème. Take rue Notre Dame de Lorette away from pl. St-Georges and turn left onto rue la Bruyère. M: St-Georges. ☎48 74 85 24. Open Tu-Sa 1-7pm when there is an exhibition. Call for details.)*

GALERIE PATRICE TRIGANO. Down the street from the Ecole des Beaux-Arts, Trigano yearns for a return to the 20th century. While the works on display may have been created in the last few years, the abstract expressionist and photorealist styles they embody have been around for decades. Don't forget to check out the basement and the small sculpture garden in the back. *(4bis rue des Beaux-Arts, 6ème. ☎46 34 15 01; www.od-arts.com/patricetrigano. Open Tu-Sa 10am-1pm and 2:30-6:30pm.)*

SHOPPING

In a city where Hermès scarves function as slings for broken arms and department store history stretches back to the mid-19th century, shopping is nothing less than an art form. Be prepared to expend every ounce of your energy while out in the boutique battlefield, but take comfort in the knowledge that your efforts will pay off. Almost everything in this city, from the world's most expensive dresses to the quirkiest kitchen appliances, is astoundingly stylish. The brave and experimental, willing to splurge on independent designs by off-the-beaten path boutiques in the **18ème** or the **Marais,** will be especially rewarded with one-of-a-kind pieces—wearable evidence of your exploits in the fashion capital of the world.

Shopping in Paris is as diverse as the city itself, from the wild club wear near **rue Etienne-Marcel** to the Marais's unique and funky emporiums to the upscale designer shops of **St-Germain-des-Prés.** The great *soldes* (sales) of the year begin after New Year's and at the very end of June, with the best prices at the beginning of February and the end of July. If at any time of year you see the word *braderie* (clearance sale) in a store window, enter without hesitation.

PARIS COUTURE FOR POCKET CHANGE. A *stock* is the French version of an outlet store, selling big name clothing for less—often because it has small imperfections or dates from last season. Many are on rue d'Alésia in the 14ème (M: Alésia), including **Cacharel Stock,** no. 114 (☎45 42 53 04; open M-Sa 10am-7pm; AmEx/MC/V); **S.R. Store** (Sonia Rykiel) at no. 112 and no. 64 (☎43 95 06 13; open Tu 11am-7pm, W-Sa 10am-7pm; MC/V); and **Stock Patrick Gerard,** no. 113 (☎40 44 07 40). A large **Stock Kookaï** bustles at 82 rue Réamur, 2ème (☎45 08 17 91; open M 11:30am-7:30pm, Tu-Sa 10:30am-7pm); **Apara Stock** sits at 16 rue Etienne Marcel (☎40 26 70 04); and **Haut-de-Gomme Stock,** with names like Armani, Christian Dior, and Dolce & Gabbana, has 2 locations: 9 rue Scribe, 9ème (M: Opéra; ☎40 07 10 20; open M-Sa 10am-7pm) and 190 rue de Rivoli, 1er (M: Louvre-Rivoli; ☎42 96 97 47; open daily 11am-7pm).

CLOTHING

Colette, 213 rue St-Honoré, 1er (☎55 35 33 90; www.colette.fr). M: Pyramides. This über-cool, multi-level boutique has an uncanny knack for knowing what you want before you do. T-shirts, dresses, handbags, jeans, sneakers, art books, DVDs, perfumes, and stylish gadgets from Japan, the US, and Europe are collected here in a constantly rotating selection. There's even a water bar on the lower level. A range of prices makes this a destination for too-cool-for-school kids with some extra cash as well as tried-and-true fashionistas. T-shirts from €50. Pants from €180. Open M-Sa 11am-7pm. AmEx/MC/V.

Espace Kiliwatch, 64 rue Tiquetonne, 2ème (☎42 21 17 37). M: Etienne-Marcel. Walk east down rue Etienne-Marcel and turn right onto rue Tiquetonne. One of Paris's coolest, most popular shops. Second-hand shirts from €20, pants from €30. Open M 2-7pm, Tu-Th 11am-7pm, F-Sa 11am-8:30pm. MC/V.

Zadig & Voltaire, 15 rue du Jour, 1er (☎42 21 88 70). M: Etienne-Marcel. 6 other locations in the city. Stylish, sexy women's clothes and accessories. You won't have any trouble fitting your newly empty wallet into your newly purchased handbag. Tops around €130, pants around €150. Opening hours vary by branch. Main branch open M 1-7:30pm, Tu-Sa 10:30am-7:30pm, Su 1:30-7:30pm. AmEx/MC/V.

Le Shop, 3 rue d'Argout, 2ème (☎40 28 95 94). M: Etienne-Marcel. If you're looking for something a little "euro" to put on for a night at the club, this is the place. If you're looking for a shirt that doesn't feature "edgy" detailing, go somewhere else. 2 levels, 1200 sq. meters, and 24 "corners" of club wear, plus a live DJ. Shirts and pants start at around €50. Open M 1-7pm, Tu-Sa 11am-7pm. AmEx/MC/V.

Free 'P' Star, 8 rue Ste-Croix-de-la-Bretonnerie, 4ème (☎42 76 03 72). M: Hôtel de Ville. Enter as Plain Jane and leave as a star. Selection of vintage dresses (€20), velvet blazers (€40), and a €10 jean pile all crammed into an extremely narrow space. The store also features the largest selection of track jackets and zip-up hoodies you've ever seen. Worn military-style blazers €20. Open M-Sa noon-11pm, Su 2-10pm. MC/V over €20.

Alternatives, 18 rue du Roi de Sicile, 4ème (☎42 78 31 50). M: St-Paul. This upscale second-hand shop sells an eclectic collection, including reasonably-priced designer digs. Bottoms under €100. Christian Louboutin heels as low as €50. Only a few customers allowed at a time to ensure quality service. Open Tu-Sa 1-6:30pm. MC/V.

BOOKS AND MUSIC

Abbey Bookshop, 29 rue de la Parcheminerie, 5ème (☎46 33 16 24; www.abbeybookshop.net). M: St-Michel or Cluny. Located on a road steeped in literary history, this laid-back shop overflows with new and used English-language titles, as well as Canadian pride furnished by its friendly expat owner Brian. A good selection of travel books (everything from Paris to the Columbia Icefield in Canada). Impressive basement collection of anthropology, sociology, history, and literary criticism titles. Also carries English-language fiction and French-Canadian work. Brian occasionally gives out cups of the best coffee in Paris for free, complete with a dollop of maple syrup for Canadian flair. Ask about the Canadian club's author events and Su hikes, or add your name to their email list. Open M-Sa 10am-7pm, sometimes later.

Shakespeare & Co., 37 rue de la Bucherie, 5ème (☎43 25 40 93; www.shakespeareco.org). M: St-Michel. A terrific English-language bookshop and miniature socialist utopia, where the books on the 2nd fl. are just for reading (not for buying) and you can sleep for free if the owner likes you. An adjacent storefront holds an impressive collection of first editions, with emphasis on the Beat Generation. Scenes from the film *Before Sunset* were shot here. Open daily noon-midnight. MC/V.

Galignani, 224 rue de Rivoli, 1er (☎42 60 76 07). M: Tuileries. Opened in 1810, this was the 1st English-language bookshop in Europe. Today, it divides its shelves between French and English-language books and magazines, with a great selection of modern fiction and French classics. Open M-Sa 10am-7pm. AmEx/MC/V.

Les Mots à la Bouche, 6 rue Ste-Croix-de-la-Bretonnerie, 4ème (☎42 78 88 30; www.motsbouche.com). M: Hôtel de Ville. Walk with traffic along rue du Temple, then turn right onto rue Ste-Croix-de-la-Bretonnerie. A 2-story bookstore offering queer literature, photography, magazines, and art. Don't miss the international DVD collection (with titles somewhere between art and porn) in the corner of the lower level (€10-28). Open M-Sa 11am-11pm, Su 1-9pm. AmEx/MC/V.

The Village Voice, 6 rue Princesse, 6ème (☎46 33 36 47; www.villagevoicebookshop.com). M: Mabillon. Takes its name less from the Manhattan paper than from the Parisian neighborhood. An excellent Anglophone bookstore and the center of the city's English literary life, featuring 3-4 readings, lectures, and discussions every month (Sept. to early July). A good selection of English-language travel books. Open M 2-7:30pm, Tu-Sa 10am-7:30pm, Su 1-6pm. AmEx/MC/V.

San Francisco Book Co., 17 rue Monsieur le Prince, 6ème (☎43 29 15 70). M: Odéon. This old bookshop's towering shelves hold scads of secondhand English-language books, both literary and pulp—including some rare and out-of-print titles. A great place to trade in used paperbacks. Open M-Sa 11am-9pm, Su 2-7:30pm. MC/V.

Ciné-Images, 68 rue de Babylone, 7ème (☎47 05 60 25; www.cine-images.com). M: St-François-Xavier. A cinephile's paradise, this boutique has endless stock: original movie posters, from Bergman's austere classic *The Silence* (€200) to Delavena's less serious *Le Vampire Sexuel* (€30). Prices can run as high as €20,000 (for the original German poster for Fritz Lang's *M*), but it's worth browsing through the shelves even if you can't afford a thing. Open Tu-F 10am-1pm and 2-7pm, Sa 2-7pm. MC/V.

FNAC (Fédération Nationale des Achats et Cadres), is the big Kahuna of Parisian music chains and has 9 locations throughout the city. The Champs-Elysées (74 av. des Champs-Elysées; ☎53 53 64 64), Bastille (4 pl. de la Bastille; ☎43 42 04 04) and Etoile (26-30 av. des Ternes; ☎44 09 18 00) branches are the largest, with comprehensive selections of music, stereo equipment, and, in some cases, books. Use scanners to listen to any CD in the store. Tickets to nearly any concert and many theater shows can be purchased at the FNAC ticket desk located on the ground level of the store. For detailed and helpful information (in French), visit the website at www.fnac.com. All branches open at 10am and most close at 7:30 or 8pm. The Champs-Elysées branch closes at midnight. MC/V.

GIFTS AND MISCELLANY

Kusmi Tea, 56 rue de Seine, 6ème (☎46 34 29 06; www.kusmitea.com). M: Mabillon. Walk away from l'Eglise St-Germain-des-prés on bd. St-Germain; turn left on rue de Seine. Founded in 1867, Kusmi first made teas for Russia's Tsars. The 1917 October Revolution put a dent in their consumer base, so they fled to Paris. The sleek white décor and trim tins may be a bit

BEST OF THE BASTILLE

Tucked behind the Bastille are the newest names in Paris fashion. Up-and-coming labels may have the same moneyed interiors as their Marais counterparts, but the prices are more reasonable. The area draws a mix of punks, who frequent the shops that line rue Keller, and trendy young folks.

1. **Roucou Paris,** 30bis rue de Charonne. Sleek bags for 60s-style mods. A small wallet is €90, so come ready to spend.

2. **Des Petits Hauts,** 5 rue Keller. The bright pink exterior is as girly as the clothes inside. Delicate knits in sorbet colors, from €40.

3. **Anne Willi,** 13 rue Keller. The minimalist, pastoral collections on display here are perfect for your inner zen-librarian.

4. **Gaële Barré,** 17 rue Keller. Unexpected juxtapositions of prints and polka dots adorn tops, dresses, and skirts—all cut in graceful, wispy shapes. Vintage-style sundress €150.

too pretty, but don't worry—the tea is outstanding. Try Prince Vladimir (black tea, citrus, and vanilla). 125g tins from €9.50. Open daily 11am-8pm. Cash only.

Pylônes, 57 rue St-Louis-en-l'Ile, 4ème (☎46 34 05 02). M: Pont Marie. Sells all the items you'll never really need (but certainly want). Exuberantly whimsical, feminine, and adorable. If the CD case that looks like a huge die (€33) and the snake-shaped bike lock (€20) don't charm you, a brightly colored toaster (€47) is always useful. Open daily 10:30am-7:30pm. Also at 13 rue Ste-Croix-de-la-Bretonnerie, 4ème. AmEx/MC/V.

Sephora, 70-72 av. des Champs-Elysées, 8ème (☎53 93 22 50). M: Charles de Gaulle-Etoile. The fairest cosmetics store of them all offers an enormous array of beauty products to color your world pretty. The welcoming carpeted corridor is lined with almost every *eau-de-toilette* on the market for both men and women, making it the perfect place to go wild before a night out. Frequent makeover promotions by prestigious cosmetics companies on the premises. Prices run the gamut from reasonable to absurd: a 900ml bottle of Chanel No. 5® can be yours for €2000. Open daily 10am-midnight. AmEx/MC/V.

Florent Monestier, 47bis av. Bosquet, 7ème (☎45 55 03 01). M: Ecole Militaire. Nostalgic bric-a-brac to perfect that cluttered, shabby-chic look. Those searching for a Mother's Day gift—€28 for bubble-bath in a hand-labeled bottle—need look no farther; there are unexpected finds as well, like an egg cup (€4) or an enormous ceramic rooster (€40). Open M-Sa 10:30am-7pm. MC/V.

DEPARTMENT STORES

Galeries Lafayette, 40 bd. Haussmann, 9ème (☎42 82 34 56). M: Chaussée d'Antin. Chaotic (the equivalent of Paris's entire population visits here each month), but carries it all, including Kookaï, agnès b., and Cacharel. It can be difficult to find a middle ground between high-end labels that make you pay in doubloons and ultra-distressed, ultra-edgy "streetwear." The astounding food annex on the 1st fl., Lafayette Gourmet, has everything from a sushi counter to a mini-*boulangerie.* Open M-W and F-Sa 9:30am-7:30pm, Th 9:30am-9pm. AmEx/V.

Le Bon Marché, 24 rue de Sèvres, 7ème (☎44 39 80 00). M: Sèvres-Babylone. Paris's oldest department store, Le Bon Marché has it all, from scarves to smoking accessories, designer clothes to home furnishings. Don't be fooled by the name (*bon marché* means cheap)—this is Paris's most exclusive and expensive department store. Across the street is **La Grande Epicerie de Paris** (38 rue de Sèvres), Bon Marché's celebrated gourmet food annex, featuring all things dried, canned, smoked, and freshly baked. Store open M-W and F 9:30am-7pm, Th 10am-9pm, Sa 9:30am-8pm. La Grande Epicerie open M-Sa 8:30am-9pm. AmEx/MC/V.

PARIS

FLEA MARKETS

PUCES DE ST-OUEN

TIP **COMMENT DIT-ON "RIP-OFF"?** First-time flea market visitors should note some important tips. There are no €1 diamond rings here. If you find the Hope Diamond in a pile of schlock jewelry, think again: you haven't. Be prepared to bargain; sellers at flea markets don't expect to get their starting prices. Pickpockets love crowded areas, and "three Card Monte" con artists proliferate. Don't be pulled into the game by seeing someone win lots of money; he's part of the con, planted to attract suckers.

Official Market (www.parispuces.com). M: Porte-de-Clignancourt. On rue des Rosiers and rue Jules Vallès, the regular market is officially divided into 15 sub-markets, each theoretically specializing in a certain type of item. Don't try to follow a set path or worry about hitting every *marché,* as they all generally have the same eclectic collection of every antique you could ever imagine. Your best bet is to get lost and then keep browsing. Most of the official markets have posted maps of their layout and stalls; these are very helpful once inside. Open M and Sa-Su 7am-7:30pm, although most stalls open around 9am and close at 6pm; on M most vendors are open fewer hours.

ENTERTAINMENT

Paris satisfies all entertainment tastes. The best resources are the weekly bulletins **Pariscope** (€0.40) and **Figaroscope** (€1), both on sale at newsstands. Even if you don't understand French, you should be able to decipher the listings of times and locations. Similarly, you don't need to speak fluent French to enjoy Parisian theater. Entertainment establishments present music, physical comedy, and experimental abstraction for any audience. The comedy-oriented **café-théâtres** and music-oriented **cabarets** recall 1930s Paris. Be warned: the cabarets's crowd is distinctly 21st-century and distinctly touristy. Ballet and modern dance companies often host prominent visiting companies, and the city's new **Stade de France** offers spectator and participatory sports galore.

Among Paris's many treasures, music and film top the list. West African music, Caribbean calypso and reggae, Latin American salsa, North African *raï*, European house, techno, and rap are fused by the hippest of DJs in the coolest of Paris's **clubs.** While Paris's classical music scene can't hold a candle to Berlin, London, or Vienna, classical concerts are staged in both concert halls and churches. For concert listings, check the free magazine *Paris Selection,* available at tourist offices throughout the city. Parisians are also inveterate film-goers, and the city's art-house cinemas are fantastic, even if they do take themselves a bit too seriously. Frequent English-language film series and festivals make the cinema accessible, inventive, challenging, and entertaining.

FREE CONCERTS

Free concerts are often held in churches and parks, especially during summer festivals, and are very popular, so plan to arrive at the host venue early. The **American Church in Paris,** 65 quai d'Orsay, 7ème, sponsors free concerts. (M: Invalides or Alma Marceau. ☎40 62 05 00. Sept.-May Su 6pm.) **Eglise St-Germain-des-Prés** also has free concerts; check the information booth just inside the door for times. **Eglise St-Merri,** 78 rue St-Martin, 4ème; contact **Accueil Musical St-Merri,** 76 rue de la Verrerie, 4ème (M: Châtelet; ☎42 71 40 75 or 42 71 93 93). Concerts take place Wednesday to Sunday in the **Jardin du Luxembourg's** band shell, 6ème (☎42 34 20 23); show up early if you don't want to stand. Occasional free concerts are held in the **Musée d'Orsay,** 1 rue Bellechasse, 7ème. (M: Solférino. ☎40 49 49 66.)

OPERA AND BALLET

Opéra Garnier, pl. de l'Opéra, 9ème (☎08 92 89 90 90; www.operadeparis.fr). M: Opéra. Hosts symphonies, chamber music, and ballet. Tickets are usually available 2 weeks before the show. Box office open M-Sa 10am-6:30pm. Last-minute discount tickets go on sale 1hr. before show-time. For wheelchair access call 2 weeks in advance (☎40 01 18 08). Ticket prices vary. AmEx/MC/V.

Opéra Comique, 5 rue Favart, 2ème (☎42 44 45 46; www.opera-comique.com). M: Richelieu-Drouot. Operas on a lighter scale. Founded in 1714 to give theatergoers an alternative to the dominant Italian opera, the company has produced operas composed by Berlioz and Bizet, as well as the premiere of Debussy's only opera. Upcoming shows include *Porgy and Bess* in June 2008. Box office open M-Sa 9am-9pm. Tickets €6-95. Cheapest tickets (limited visibility) usually available until the show starts. MC/V.

Opéra de la Bastille, pl. de la Bastille, 12ème (☎08 92 89 90 90; www.operadeparis.fr). M: Bastille. Opera and ballet with a modern spin. Subtitles in French. Check website for the season's events. Tickets can be purchased by Internet, mail, phone (M-Th 9am-6pm, Sa 9am-1pm), or in person (M-Sa 10:30am-6:30pm). Rush tickets 15min. before show for students under 25 and seniors. For wheelchair access, call 2 weeks ahead (☎40 01 18 50). Tickets €5-160. AmEx/MC/V.

CABARET

Au Lapin Agile, 22 rue des Saules, 18ème (☎46 06 85 87). M: Lamarck-Coulaincourt. Turn right on rue Lamarck, then right up rue des Saules. Picasso, Verlaine, Renoir, and Apollinaire hung out here in Montmartre's heyday; now, a touristy audience crowds in for comical poems and songs. The *chansonnier* inspired Steve Martin's 1996 hit play *Picasso at the Lapin Agile.* Shows Tu-Su 9pm-2am. Admission and 1st drink €24, M-F and Su (except holidays) students €17. Drinks €6-7. MC/V.

Bal du Moulin Rouge, 82 bd. de Clichy, 9ème (☎53 09 82 82; www.moulinrouge.com). M: Blanche. Directly across from the Metro. This world-famous cabaret has hosted such international stars at Ella Fitzgerald and Elton John. The crowd consists of tourists out for an evening of sequins, tassels, and skin. The revues are still risqué, but the price of admission is prohibitively expensive. A ticket with a half-bottle of champagne is €99 for the 9pm show. Catch the late show at 11pm for €89, but be prepared to stand if it's a busy night. Shows nightly 7, 9, 11pm. MC/V.

THEATER

La Comédie Française, pl. Collette, 1er (☎44 58 15 15; www.comedie-francaise.fr). M: Palais-Royal. Founded by Molière, this is now the granddaddy of all French theaters. Expect wildly gesticulated slapstick farce; you don't need to speak French to understand the jokes. Performances take place in the 862-seat *Salle Richelieu.* Box office open daily 11am-6pm and 1hr. before shows. Tickets €11-35. Rush tickets available 1hr. before show. Disabled patrons are asked to make reservations in advance. If you plan to stay in Paris for a long time, invest in the *Passeport Comédie-Française,* which allows you to make reservations at reduced prices. Check the website (in French) for details. The *comédiens français* perform the same sort of plays in the 300-seat **Théâtre du Vieux Colombier,** 21 rue des Vieux Colombiers, 6ème (☎44 39 87 00 or 44 39 87 01). M: St-Sulpice or Sèvres-Babylone. AmEx/MC/V.

Odéon Théâtre de l'Europe, 1 pl. Odéon, 6ème (☎44 85 40 40 or 44 85 40 00; www.theatre-odeon.fr). M: Odéon. Programs in this elegant Neoclassical building range from classics to avant-garde, but the Odéon specializes in foreign plays in their original language. 1042 seats. Call ahead for wheelchair access. Box office open daily 11am-6pm and 2hr. before the show. Tickets €7.50-30 for most shows; fewer than 30 rush tickets (€7.50 or €13) available 1½hr. before performance. Affiliate **Petit Odéon** has 82 seats. Tickets €10. MC/V.

Bouffes du Nord, 37bis bd. de la Chapelle, 10ème (☎46 07 34 50; www.bouffesdunord.com). M: La Chapelle. Bouffes du Nord is an experimental theater (headed by Micheline Rozan and famous British director Peter Brook) that produces cutting-edge performances and concerts and offers occasional productions in English. Call ahead for wheelchair access. Open Sept.-July. Box office open M-Sa 11am-6pm. Concerts €22, under 26 and over 60 €11; plays €8-23. MC/V.

JAZZ

Le Baiser Salé, 58 rue des Lombards, 1er (☎42 33 37 71; www.lebaisersale.com). M: Châtelet. From rue de Rivoli exit, walk down rue des Lavandières St-Opportune. Cross the street and follow rue St-Opportune, then turn right onto rue des Lombards. Cuban, African, and Antillean music featured together with modern jazz and funk in a welcoming, mellow space. Month-long African music festival in July. Beer €6.50-12. Mixed drinks €9. Jazz concerts start at 10pm, *chanson* earlier on some nights; music until 2:30am (2-3 sets). Mainly new talent. Free jam sessions M at 10pm; 1-drink min. Cover €12-18. Happy hour 5-8:30pm. Open daily 5pm-6am. AmEx/MC/V.

Au Duc des Lombards, 42 rue des Lombards, 1er (☎42 33 22 88; www.ducdeslombards.fr). M: Châtelet. Down from Le Baiser Salé; see directions above. One of France's premier jazz spots. Renovated for 2008. Cover €19-23; in advance students €12, couples €30. Beer €7-10. Mixed drinks €10. Music 10pm-1:30am. Open M-Sa 5pm-2am. MC/V.

New Morning, 7-9 rue des Petites Ecuries, 10ème (☎45 23 51 41; www.newmorning.com). M: Château d'Eau. This 400-seat former printing plant now plays host to some of the biggest global headliners in the city. Dark, smoky, and crowded, New Morning is everything a jazz club should be. The venue's best acoustics are in the lower front section or near the wings of the stage. All the greatest names in jazz have played here—from Chet Baker to Stan Getz and Miles Davis. These days it continues to attract big names like Wynton Marsalis, Betty Carter, and Eddie Palmieri. Drinks €6-10. Tickets can be purchased from the box office, any FNAC branch, or the Virgin Megastore and average €16-20. Open Sept.-July from 8pm; exact times vary. Concerts begin 8-9:30pm. MC/V.

CINEMA

Accattone, 20 rue Cujas, 5ème (☎46 33 86 86). M: Luxembourg. Setting the gold-standard for art-house atmosphere, the lineup at the Accattone is carefully selected to ensure an exciting cinematic experience. Antonioni, Salvador Dalí, and Eisenstein are deities here. All with subtitles. €6.50, students €5.50.

Musée du Louvre, 1er (info ☎40 20 53 17; schedules www.louvre.fr). M: Louvre. Art films, films on art, and silent movies. Some films in English. Open Sept.-June. Free.

Les Trois Luxembourg, 67 rue Monsieur-le-Prince, 6ème (☎46 33 97 77). M: Cluny. Turn left onto bd. St-Michel, right onto rue Racine, and left onto rue M-le-Prince. Independent, classic, and foreign films, all with subtitles. €7, students and seniors €5.50.

La Pagode, 57bis rue de Babylone, 7ème (☎45 55 48 48). M: St-François-Xavier. A French-designed Japanese pagoda built in 1895 and re-opened as a cinema in 2000, La Pagode screens independent and classic French films, as well as the occasional American new release (in English, *bien sûr*). Stop in at the café between shows. Tickets €8; over 60, under 21, students, and M and W €6.50.

NIGHTLIFE

BARS AND PUBS. Paris's bars are either chic nighttime cafés or more laid-back neighborhood spots that often double as Anglo havens. In the **5ème** and **6ème,** bars draw French and foreign students, while the **Marais** teems with Paris's young and hip, queer and straight. Great neighborhood spots are springing up in the outlying areas of the Left Bank, particularly in the **13ème** and **14ème. Les Halles** and surroundings draw a slightly older set, while the outer *arrondissements* cater to a full range of locals. The **Bastille** is another central party area, but it's more suited to pounding flavored vodka shots than slowly sipping Bordeaux.

CLUBS. Clubbing in Paris is less about hip DJs' beats than about dressing up and getting in. Drinks are expensive, and Parisians drink little beyond the first round. Many clubs accept reservations, so there's no available seating on busy nights. Dress well and be confident but not aggressive. Come early and as a couple if you can. Bouncers like tourists because they generally spend more money, so speak

English. Clubs are usually busiest between 2 and 4am. Tune in to *Radio FG* (98.2 FM) or *Radio Nova* (101.5 FM) to find out about upcoming events.

GLBT NIGHTLIFE. The **Marais** is the center of Parisian GLBT life. Most queer bars and clubs are in rue du Temple, rue Ste-Croix de la Bretonnerie, rue des Archives, and rue Vieille du Temple in the **4ème** (p. 171). Lesbian bars abound in the **3ème** (p. 171). For the most comprehensive listing of GLBT organizations and services, consult *Illico* (free at queer bars and restaurants), *Gai Pied's* annually updated book *Guide Gai* (€15 at kiosks and bookstores), or Zurban's annual *Paris Gay and Lesbian Guide* (€5 at any kiosk). **Les Mots à la Bouche,** Paris's largest GLBT bookstore, serves as an unofficial information center for queer life.

CHÂTELET-LES-HALLES AND OPÉRA

BARS

Le Champmeslé, 4 rue Chabanais (☎42 96 85 20). M: Pyramides. Walk down ave. de l'Opéra, make a right on rue des Petits Champs, and then a left onto rue Chabanais. This welcoming lesbian bar is Paris's oldest and most famous. Both men and women come to enjoy the popular cabaret shows (Th 10pm), the Tu *soirée voyance,* and the monthly art exhibits. Beer €4 before 10pm, €5 after. Mixed drinks €8. Enjoy a free drink on your birthday. No cover. Open M-Sa 3pm-dawn.

Banana Café, 13 rue de la Ferronnerie (☎42 33 35 31; www.bananacafeparis.com). M: Châtelet. Take rue Pierre Lescot to rue de la Ferronnerie. This *très branché* (way cool) evening spot is the most popular GLBT bar in the 1er, and it draws a mixed group. Patrons can enjoy the loud dance music and tropical décor while watching scantily-clad male pole dancers. Head downstairs for a lively piano bar and another dance floor. Beer €4-5.50. Mixed drinks €8.50. Legendary theme nights. "Go-Go Boys" Th-Sa midnight-dawn. F-Sa €10 cover includes drink. 2-for-1 drinks during nightly Happy hour 6-9pm; mixed drinks excluded. Open daily 5:30pm-6am. AmEx/MC/V.

Le Café Noir, 65 rue Montmartre (☎40 39 07 36). M: Sentier. Turn down rue d'Aboukir and make a left onto rue Montmartre. With a plastic solar system dangling from the ceiling, a leopard-skin covered bike in a window, and bartenders who leap onto the bar to get a laugh, this is one of the least predictable spots in Paris. A true mix of locals and Anglophones; patrons gladly overcome language barriers to meet one another. Beer €2.50-3.50. Open M-F 8am-2am, Sa 4pm-2am. MC/V.

CLUBS

Le 18 Club, 18 rue Beaujolais (☎42 97 52 13; www.club18.fr). M: Pyramides. The oldest gay club in Paris is still going strong. Drawing a mostly male crowd to its intimate bar and dance floor, lighthearted Le 18 Club spins fun pop music. Mixed drinks €6-9. Cover €10, includes 1 drink. Open W 7pm-3am, F-Sa midnight-6am.

Rex Club, 5 bd. Poissonnière (☎42 36 10 96; www.rexclub.com). M: Bonne-Nouvelle. This non-selective club presents the most selective DJ line-up. Young clubbers, including some high-schoolers, crowd this casual venue to hear cutting-edge techno, jungle, and house fusion from international DJs on one of the best sound systems in Paris. Large dance floor and lots of seats. Beer €7.50-8. Mixed drinks €9-10. Cover around €15, some nights free. Open W-Th 11:30pm-6am, F-Sa midnight-6am.

THE MARAIS

BARS

Oh Fada!, 35 rue Ste-Croix de la Bretonnerie (☎40 29 44 40). M: Hôtel de Ville. With its outstanding musical taste and self-deprecating sense of fun ("This bar kills me" is written on the wall), Oh Fada! is the most likeable GLBT spot in the Marais. Mostly gay men, but women and straight men are welcome. Drinking gives way to dancing later at night. Beer €4-6. Open M-W and Su 5pm-2am, Th-Sa 5pm-4am. Cash only.

La Belle Hortense, 31 rue Vieille du Temple (☎48 04 71 60). M: St-Paul. Walk with traffic along rue de Rivoli and turn right onto rue Vieille du Temple. Though the philosophy books lining the walls and wannabe philosophers lining the bar may be intimidating, this is a great place to strike up a conversation over mellow music and Merlot. Frequent exhibits, readings, lectures, book signings, and discussions held in the small leather-couch-filled back room; advertised on the front window. Coffee €1.30-2. Great selection of wines from €4 per glass, €8 per bottle. Open daily 5pm-2am. MC/V.

L'Apparemment Café, 18 rue des Coutures St-Gervais (☎48 87 12 22). M: Chemin Vert. Beautiful red lounge with games and a chill, young crowd. Those looking for a momentary escape from the Marais's thumping beats will be happy to find that there is frequently no music here, just the murmur of conversation. Displays local artists' paintings, all for sale. Late-night meals €12-15, served until 11:30pm. Mixed drinks €9.

Amnésia Café, 42 rue Vieille du Temple (☎42 72 16 94). M: St-Paul or Hôtel de Ville. A largely queer crowd comes to lounge on plush sofas in Amnésia's sleek wood-paneled interior. 1st fl. café, 2nd fl. lounge and basement club with music beginning 9pm. This is one of the Marais's top see-and-be-seen spots, especially on Sa nights. Espresso €2. *Kir* €4. Mixed drinks €7.50-10. Open daily 11am-2am. MC/V.

3W Kafé, 8 rue des Ecouffes (☎48 87 39 26). M: St-Paul. Walk with traffic along rue de Rivoli and turn right onto rue des Ecouffes. The Marais's hippest lesbian bar got a face-lift and a new name—3W stands for "Women With Women." Sleek interior, smooth beats, and a laid-back atmosphere make it a great hangout. Men welcome when accompanied by women. Beer €3.30-5. Mixed drinks €8-9. Downstairs club with DJ F-Sa from 10pm. Open M-Th and Su 5:30pm-2am, F-Sa 5:30pm-4am. MC/V.

Les Etages, 35 rue Vieille du Temple (☎42 78 72 00). M: St-Paul or Hôtel de Ville. Set in an 18th-century hotel-turned-bar. 4 floors populated by dressed-down 20-somethings. Selection of €4 mixed drinks during Happy hour (5-9pm), brought with a side of nuts and olives. Beer €4-6. Mixed drinks €7.50-9. Open daily 5pm-2am. MC/V over €15.

CLUB

Raidd Bar, 23 rue du Temple. M: Hôtel de Ville. The most hip and happening GLBT club in the Marais and perhaps even Paris. Spinning disco globes cast undulating shadow and light in the intimate space, illuminating the muscular bartenders' topless torsos. Watch performers strip in a glass shower stall built into the wall (they take it *all* off in shows at 11pm, midnight, 1, 2am). Tu disco night, W 80s and house, Su 90s. Beer €4.

LATIN QUARTER AND ST-GERMAIN

Le 10 Bar, 10 rue de l'Odéon (☎43 26 66 83). M: Odéon. Walk against traffic on bd. St-Germain and make a left on rue de l'Odéon. Le 10 Bar is a classic student hangout where Parisian youth indulge in philosophical and political discussion. Either that or they're getting drunk and making inside jokes. After several glasses of their famous spiced sangria (€3.50), you might feel inspired to join in. Jukebox plays everything from Edith Piaf to Aretha Franklin. Open daily 6pm-2am.

Chez Georges, 11 rue des Cannettes (☎43 26 79 15). M: Mabillon. Walk down rue du Four and turn left on rue des Cannettes. Upstairs is a wine bar with a crowd spanning the ages: chain-smoking college students, 30-somethings, and quiet types playing chess against themselves are equally at home here—maybe it's the cheap wine. Downstairs is a smoky, candlelit cellar rampant with students drinking and dancing. Beer €3.50-4. Wine €1.50-4. Upstairs open Tu-Sa noon-2am; cellar 10pm-2am. Closed Aug.

L'Académie de la Bière, 88bis bd. Port Royal (☎43 54 66 65; www.academie-biere.com). RER: Port Royal. With 12 kinds of beer on tap and more than 300 more in bottles, this bar doesn't mess around. Fortunately, it doesn't matter what you pick—there's not a weak link on the menu. The outdoor tent seating is a plus. Beer €6.50-8.50. Happy hour nightly 3:30-7:30pm. Open M-Th 10am-2am, F-Sa 10am-3am.

Le Caveau des Oubliettes, 52 rue Galande (☎46 34 23 09). M: St-Michel. Head away from pl. St-Michel on quai de Montebello and turn right on rue Petit Pont, then left onto rue Galande. 2 scenes in 1, both with a mellow, funky vibe. The upstairs bar (La Guillotine) has sod carpeting, ferns, and a real guillotine. The downstairs cellar is an outstanding jazz club. The cellar's previous incarnation as an actual *caveau des oubliettes* (cave of the forgotten ones), where criminals were locked up and forgotten, makes the night more exciting. Free *soirée boeuf* (jam session) M-Th and Su 10pm-1:30am; F-Sa concerts free. Beer from €4. Mixed drinks from €4.50. Open daily 5pm-2am.

Bob Cool, 15 rue des Grands Augustins (☎46 33 33 77). M: Odéon. Walk up rue de l'Ancienne Comédie, turn right on rue St-André-des-Arts and left onto the small rue des Grands Augustins. One of the city's best expat hangouts, Bob Cool has a laid-back clientele, a friendly vibe, and colorful paintings and photographs covering the walls. The music is at the discretion of the bartender and ranges from salsa to The Corrs to Buddy Holly. Beer by the pint €4.50. Mixed drinks €5-6. Open daily 5pm-2am.

INVALIDES

Le Club des Poètes, 30 rue de Bourgogne (☎47 05 06 03; www.poesie.net). M: Varenne. Walk up bd. des Invalides with the Invalides behind and to the left; turn right on rue de Grenelle and left onto rue de Bourgogne. In 1961, Jean-Pierre Rosnay took it upon himself to make "poetry contagious and inevitable—*vive la poésie!*" Now his son Blaise has inherited the mission; a restaurant by day, Le Club des Poètes is transformed at 10pm on Tu, F, and Sa nights, when a troupe of readers and comedians, including Rosnay's family, bewitch the audience with poetry from Petrarch and Lorca. If you arrive after 10pm, wait until you hear a break to enter. Le Club is not cheap (dinner without wine €20) but great for a drink. Mixed drinks €7.50. Lunch *menu* €15. Open Tu-Sa noon-3pm and 8pm-1am. Kitchen closes 10pm. Closed Aug. MC/V.

CHAMPS-ELYSÉES

BAR

buddha-bar, 8 rue Boissy d'Anglas (☎53 05 90 00; www.buddha-bar.com). M: Madeleine or Concorde. Perhaps the most glamorous drinking hole in the world (Madonna drops by when she's in town). If you're sufficiently attractive, wealthy, or well-connected, you'll be quickly led to 1 of the bar's 2 dim, candlelit levels, where your internal organs will gently vibrate to the hypnotic "global" rhythms permeating the air. A giant Buddha watches over the chic ground-floor restaurant, while an elegant bar serves creative mixed drinks (€15) upstairs. You'll break the bank, but it just might be worth it. Beer €8-9. Wine €10-12. Open M-F noon-3pm and 6pm-2am, Sa-Su 6pm-2am.

CLUB

Le Queen, 102 av. des Champs-Elysées (☎53 89 08 90). M: George V. Where drag queens, superstars, tourists, and go-go boys get down to the mainstream rhythms of a 10,000-gigawatt sound system. Her Majesty is one of the cheapest and most accessible GLBT clubs in town, but it caters to a mix of tastes. Women have better luck with the bouncer if in the company of at least one male. M disco, W Ladies' Night, Th-Sa house, Su 80s. Cover M-Th and Su €15, F-Sa €20; includes 1 drink. Bring an ID and avoid coming in large groups. All drinks €10. Open daily midnight-dawn. AmEx/MC/V.

MONTMARTRE

Folies Pigalle, 11 pl. Pigalle (☎48 78 55 25; www.folies-pigalle.com). M: Pigalle. The largest, wildest club in the sleazy Pigalle *quartier*—not for the faint of heart. A former strip joint, the Folies is popular with both GLBT and straight clubbers and is probably the most trans-friendly club in the city. Mostly house and techno. *Soirées Transsexuelles* every Su and 1st M of each month, although all nights welcome all types. Usually crowded. Drinks €10. Cover €20; includes 1 drink. Open M-Th and Su midnight-dawn, F-Sa midnight-noon. AmEx/MC/V.

BASTILLE

! **LET'S NOT GO.** While much of Paris's best nightlife centers around the Bastille, stay away from bd. Richard Lenoir, which runs north-northwest from the Bastille, at night. It is sparsely populated and dangerous.

BARS

Le Pop In, 105 rue Amelot (☎48 05 56 11). M: St-Sébastien Froissart. Living a double life as a neighborhood bar and rock club, this broken-in, crowded spot is a favorite hangout for Paris's young, carefully bedraggled cool kids. Tiny concert venue; both the live music and the tunes on the stereo are pop and rock, which will be a welcome change from all the raves. Beer €2.50-5. Open Tu-Su 6:30pm-1:30am.

Le Bar Sans Nom, 49 rue de Lappe (☎48 05 59 36). M: Bastille. Take rue de la Roquette and make a right onto rue de Lappe. Packed amidst a terrific variety of bars and hangouts, this one sticks out even though it's "nameless." Cluttered décor gives the impression of a Victorian lair. The bar's famed mixed drinks, listed on oversized wooden menus, are consumed by a calm crowd. Don't leave Paris without trying their mojito (€8.50). Free tarot-card reading Tu 5:30pm (come early to grab a seat), when the bar is mobbed by young Parisian women seeking their destiny. Beer €5-6.20. Shots €6.20. Mixed drinks €9. Open Tu-Th 6pm-2am and F-Sa 6pm-4am. MC/V over €16.

Barrio Latino, 46-48 rue du Faubourg St-Antoine (☎55 78 84 75; www.buddha-bar.com). M: Bastille. Shares the same swanky owners as buddha-bar (see p. 172). No wallflowers on this hot Latin dance floor, and not an empty barstool on weekends. Crowds here come looking good; if you want to avoid bouncer troubles you should probably ditch the flip-flops and **Let's Go** T-shirt. Shake it on the packed ground floor, or take your potent strawberry margarita (€12) for a stroll up to the 4th fl. to relax on the leather couches. Su brunch is an institution among locals (noon-4pm; €28) and includes a free salsa lesson. DJ from 10pm. Open daily noon-2am. AmEx/MC/V.

CLUB

Wax, 15 rue Daval (☎48 05 88 33). M: Bastille. Head north on bd. Richard Lenoir and make a right on rue Daval. Always free and fun, as long as you dress smart. Set up in a concrete bunker with retro orange-and-white couches, this mod club gets crowded at night with a mix of locals and tourists. W and Su disco and funk, Th R&B, F-Sa house. Open daily 9pm-dawn. Beer €5.50-7. Mixed drinks €9.50. MC/V over €15.

THIRTEENTH ARRONDISSEMENT

BAR

La Folie en Tête, 33 rue de la Butte-aux-Cailles (☎45 80 65 99). M: Corvisart. The 13ème's artsy *axis mundi*. Exotic instruments line the walls of this beaten-up neighborhood hangout, which stands out on an otherwise quiet street. Crowded concerts Sept.-June Sa nights, usually Afro-Caribbean music (€8). Beer €3. *Ti* punch €5.50. Happy hour 6-8pm; *kir* €1.50. Open M-Sa 6pm-2am; service ends at 1:30am. MC/V.

CLUB

Batofar (☎53 60 17 42), facing 11 quai François-Mauriac. M: Quai de la Gare. Facing the river, walk right along the *quai;* Batofar has the red lights. This 45m long, 520-ton barge/club has made it big with the electronic music crowd but maintains a friendly vibe. Live artists and DJs. "Electronic brunch" Su afternoon. Cover €8-15; includes 1 drink. Open M-Th 11pm-6am, F-Su 11pm-dawn; hours change for special film and DJ events. Buy tickets through FNAC, ☎03 60 17 30. MC/V.

MONTPARNASSE AND THE FIFTEENTH ARRONDISSEMENT

L'Entrepôt, 7-9 rue Francis de Pressensé (☎45 40 07 50; www.lentrepot.fr). M: Pernety. From the Metro, turn right, walk down rue Raymond Losserand and turn right onto rue Francis de Pressensé. Proving that intellectualism and good times can indeed go together, this savvy establishment offers a quadruple combo: a 3-screen independent cinema; a restaurant with a garden patio; a modern art gallery; and a trendy bar that features live jazz, Latin, and world music. This contained explosion of art is somewhat overwhelming–you may need to come a few times to see it all. Jazz and poetry readings Th 9:30pm (€5-7). *Ciné-Philo*–a screening, lecture, and discussion café–is held every other Su 2:20pm (€8); check the monthly schedule in the main foyer. Improvisational theater takes up the alternate Su 6:30pm (free). World music concerts F-Sa; cover €5-7. A multitude of other events, including jams sessions and slams; check website. Beer €3.50. Su brunch noon-3pm (€22). Open M-Sa 11am-1am (usually later F-Sa), Su 11am-midnight. Kitchen open daily noon-3pm and 8-11pm.

Smoke Bar, 29 rue Delambre (☎43 20 61 73). M: Vavin. Walk down rue Delambre past pl. Delambre; the bar is on the left. Local bar filled with lively regulars and cheap drinks that undercut Paris prices. A place where you might be able to strike up a conversation with a stranger without feeling like an outsider–depending on how many drinks you've had. Starting next year, the name will no longer be fitting, due to Paris's new non-smoking rules. Occasional live performances; open mic Su. Beer €2.30-3. Mixed drinks €5-6.50. Open M-F noon-2am, Sa 6pm-2am. MC/V.

OUTLYING ARRONDISSEMENTS

Café Flèche d'Or, 102bis rue de Bagnolet (☎44 64 01 02; www.flechedor.fr). This rock club/art space may put on a tough act with its graffiti-covered bathroom walls, but it's actually quite welcoming. Bespectacled indie kids with neat haircuts come for art videos, dance classes, and crazy theater on the tracks below the terrace. Live music nightly, from rock and alternative to trip-hop and electro-pop. Beer M-Th and Su €4.50, F-Sa €5. Mixed drinks €8. DJ set Th-Sa midnight-6am. Cover €5-20, but often free. Open M-W 8pm-2am, Th-Sa 8pm-6am. MC/V.

L'Endroit, 67 pl. du Dr. Félix Lobligeois (☎42 29 50 00). M: Rome. Follow rue Boursault to rue Legendre and turn right. Hip, young 17ème-ers come for the snazzy bar and idyllic spot on a tree-lined *place*. Popular choices include the mojito and the apple martini. Wine €3-4. Beer €4. Mixed drinks €8-9. Open daily 10am-2am, often later F-Sa. MC/V.

Café Chéri(e), 44 bd. de la Villette (☎42 02 02 05). M: Belleville. With cheap drinks, nightly DJ sets, and outdoor seating, this is quickly becoming one of the hottest spots in the 19ème. Beer starts at €3 and comes with free chips. Indie atmosphere. Nightly DJ sets (pop and electronic) start around 10pm. No cover. Open daily 8am-2am.

FESTIVALS

Paris has a festival (or 20) for every season; check with the Paris tourist offices (p. 100), or consult listings in *Pariscope* and *Time Out*. These are only some of the best—all are guaranteed to keep you fat, happy, or drunk (or all three).

Bastille Day (Fête Nationale), July 14. France's Independence Day. Festivities begin the night before, with traditional street dances at the tip of Ile St-Louis. The free *Bals des Pompiers* (Firemen's Balls) take place inside every Parisian fire station the night of July 13 and/or 14th from 9pm-4am, with DJs, bands, and cheap alcohol (€5). These balls are the best of Paris's Bastille Day celebrations. The fire stations on rue Blanche, bd. du Port-Royal, rue des Vieux-Colombiers, and the Gay Ball near quai de la Tournelle in the 5ème are probably your best bets for a rollickin' good time. For information on the *Bals*, call the **Sapeurs Pompiers** (☎47 54 68 22) or visit them at 1 pl. Jules Renard in the 17ème. There is dancing at pl. de la Bastille with a concert, but be careful, as kids sometimes throw fireworks into the crowd. July 14 begins with an army parade down the Champs-Elysées at 10:30am (get in place by 8 or 9am) and ends with fireworks at 10:30-11pm. The fireworks can be seen from any bridge on the Seine or from the Champs de Mars (get there as early as 3-4hr. beforehand to snag a decent spot). During the parade and fireworks, the Metro stations along the Champs and at Trocadéro are closed. Groups also gather in the 19ème and 20ème (especially in the Parc de Belleville) where the hilly topography allows for a long-distance view of Trocadéro. Unfortunately, the entire city also becomes a combat zone, with firecrackers underfoot; avoid the Metro and deserted areas if possible. *Vive la France!*

Jazz à la Villette, early Sept. (☎40 03 75 75 or 44 84 44 84; www.villette.com). M: Porte de Pantin. At Parc de la Villette. A week-long celebration of jazz, from big bands to new international talents, as well as seminars, films, and sculptural exhibits. Past performers include Herbie Hancock, Ravi Coltrane, Wayne Shorter, and Sonic Youth. Marching bands parade every day, and an enormous picnic closes the festival. Concerts €12-30. For reduced price tickets, call ahead.

Gay Pride, last Sa in June (www.gaypride.fr). See **A Gay Old Time,** p. 175. For additional information on dates and events, call the **Centre Gai et Lesbien** (☎43 57 21 47), **Le Duplex bar** (☎42 72 80 86), or **Les Mots à la Bouche bookstore** (☎42 78 88 30; www.motsbouche.com). Or check Marais bars and cafés for posters.

Fête de la Musique, June 21 (☎40 03 94 70). Also called "Faîtes de la Musique" ("Make Music"), this

GAY OLD TIME

Boasting a substantial GLBT population and the first openly gay mayor of a major European city, Paris is a queer-friendly city bursting at the seams with entertainment and resources. Most notably, the City of Light participates in a campaign of marches across France to celebrate and raise awareness for queer communities. The highlight is the annual **Gay Pride Festival,** held on the last Saturday of June.

Nearly all of Paris's vibrant queer communities turn out for this infectiously exuberant parade. The festive din can be heard from several Metro stops away; attendance is only partially optional if you're within the city limits, but that's for the best. A fabulous Carnaval scene greets visitors as they reach the festival. Drag queens in feathered costumes pose daintily next to scantily clad dancers shimmying, bumping, and grinding on floats.

This might be the only time the Communist Party, the Socialist Party, and the UMP (Chirac's right-wing party) root for the same cause. A sense of organized chaos ensues as the crowds and floats wiggle and bob from Montparnasse to the Bastille, dancing, chanting, and waving banners. While there is a hint of political consciousness, it hardly distracts from the parade's glittery, muscled, and celebratory mood.

Gay Pride Paris (p. 167), last weekend in June (www.gaypride.fr).

summer solstice celebration gives everyone the chance to make a racket, as Paris's noise laws don't apply for the festival. The Metro runs all night to transport tired revelers home (unlimited pass for the night of the 21st €2.50).

Fête du Cinéma, late June (www.feteducinema.com). Started in 1984, this festival aims to bring cheaper movies to all Parisians. Purchase 1 ticket at regular movie price (€6-8) and receive a passport for unlimited showings (during the 3-day festival) of participating films for €2 each. Arrive early for favorites and expect long lines. Full listings of movies and events can be found online, at theaters, or in Metro advertisements. Don't miss this opportunity to join the millions of movie-goers who relish the blockbusters, indie flicks, imports, and ever-enduring classics that make the Parisian cinema scene one of the most diverse and enjoyable in the world.

DAYTRIPS FROM PARIS

VERSAILLES

One look inside Versailles (VEHR-sye) is enough to explain why the French Revolution happened. Once a simple hunting lodge, this enormously opulent palace is a testament to the incredible power—and ego—of the self-named Sun King, Louis XIV, who made the town his royal seat in 1682. The palace's gilded sculptures, painted ceilings, inlaid furniture, and expansive gardens exemplify the luxurious decadence that blinded the French royalty to the needs of their suffering people for over a century. After seeing her luxurious flowered bedroom and mock peasant village, you can almost understand how Marie Antoinette could (allegedly) say "Let them eat cake" when told that Parisians were starving for lack of bread.

After the French Revolution removed the French monarchy—and their belongings—the château lay in disrepair until Louis-Philippe decided to make it a national museum, adding the inscription *"A Toutes Les Gloires De La France"* ("To All the Glories of France") on the front of both wings of the palace. In 1871, the château took the limelight again when Wilhelm of Prussia was proclaimed Kaiser Wilhelm I of Germany in the Hall of Mirrors after winning the Franco-Prussian War. On June 28, 1919, at the end of WWI, France forced Germany to sign the ruinous Treaty of Versailles in the same room. Today, the château is an easy daytrip from Paris, but beware: every other tourist will be making the same trek.

TRANSPORTATION AND PRACTICAL INFORMATION

RER Line C5 runs from Paris (M: Invalides and others) to the "Versailles Rive Gauche station," the end of this line (30-40min., every 15min., €2.80). Make sure to buy an RER ticket to Versailles, not a regular Metro ticket, and hold onto it until you leave the Versailles station; both types will get you onto the RER, but you'll need the correct RER ticket to exit at Versailles. From the RER station, turn right down av. de Général de Gaulle, walk 200m, and turn left at the first big intersection on av. de Paris; the entrance to the château is straight ahead. On the way back, take any train; they're all headed toward Paris.

To get to the **Office de Tourisme de Versailles,** 2bis av. de Paris, from the RER Versailles station, start by following the directions to the château; the office will be on the left when you turn onto av. de Paris. The tourist office gives a patient explanation of your options in Versailles before you reach the mayhem ahead. The tourist office also provides a detailed map of the town and brochures on accommodations, restaurants, and events. (☎39 24 88 88. Open Apr.-Sept. M 10am-6pm, Tu-Su 9am-7pm; Oct.-Mar. M and Su 11am-5pm, Tu-Sa 9am-6pm.)

ROYALTY FOR A DAY. If you're planning on buying the **Château Passeport** (Apr.-Oct. M-F €20, Sa-Su €25; Nov.-Mar. €16), pick it up at the tourist office to avoid long lines at the château itself. Unfortunately, the office doesn't sell tickets to the individual sights, but if you're planning on seeing more than just the château, the pass will pay for itself. **Paris Museum Pass** (p. 145) holders get into the château for free, so they'll also avoid the ticket lines. You can even skip the security line by buying a combined château-guided tour pass.

While there are a number of tourist dining options along the walk from the train station to the palace, your best warm-weather bet is to bring a picnic (and a blanket) to enjoy in the gardens after you tour the palace; picnicking is allowed by the **Pièce d'Eau des Suisses,** in the park by the **Grand Canal,** and on other sites marked on the château map. Continue straight on av. du Général de Gaulle past av. de Paris to find a **Monoprix** supermarket, av. de l'Europe, on the left. (Open 8:30am-8:55pm.) There are also snack bars in various corners of the gardens.

TIP **ROYAL FLUSH.** Don't waste time waiting in the line for the public toilets at the château in Versailles. If you walk a few hundred meters, there are several more with a much shorter wait inside the gardens—and they're free.

SIGHTS

THE PALACE OF VERSAILLES.

☎30 83 78 00; www.chateauversailles.fr. Passeport *(day pass) including admission to all sights and audio tours Apr.-Oct. M-F €20, Sa-Su €25; Nov.-Mar. €16; under 18 free. Individual tickets to the château, Trianons, or gardens only also available (see below). Wheelchair-accessible entrance. Info desks by the ticket office or inside the château provide maps.*

TIP **LET THEM WAIT IN LINE.** Try to arrive before the château opens to beat the lines. See the château first, before the onslaught of tourists, then wander at leisure through the gardens and make it to the Grand and Petit Trianon around noon when they open. Crowds are largest on weekends and in summer. Planning to see it all? The château and its grounds are vast, so move fast!

CHÂTEAU. The main attraction at Versailles is the richly decorated rooms of its main château; enter the north wing through the **chapelle (chapel),** a two-story masterpiece built by Hardouin-Mansart from 1699 to 1710. Head farther into the wing to the **Musée de l'Histoire de France,** created in 1837 by Louis-Philippe to celebrate his nation's glory. Portraits of French royalty and nobility from the 17th and 18th centuries hang on colorful, textured walls. However, a shortage of security guards often causes the museum to close unexpectedly, so don't count on seeing it.

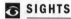

Coming back towards the center of the palace on the second floor, you'll get another view of the chapel from its upper entrance on your way to the palace's most ornate rooms: the **Grandes Appartements (State Apartments).** Each gilded and ostentatious salon is named after a Roman god, such as Hercules, Mars, or Apollo (the Sun King's favorite), lavishly depicted on the ceiling. The next rooms are the palace's best—the **War Salon, Peace Salon,** and the great **Galerie des Glaces (Hall of Mirrors).** Facing out towards the gardens from the center of the palace, the mirrors (masterpieces of 17th-century technology and unthinkably expensive at the time) double the feel of light and space in the room. It was in this room that Germany signed the Treaty of Versailles in 1919. The entire Hall of Mirrors has just undergone its first complete restoration, costing 12 million euro. A door in the side of the long hallway leads to the **Cabinet du Roi (King's Bedroom),** where Louis XIV woke up, had breakfast, and received his morning visitors, and to the **Cabinet du Conseil (Council Chamber),** from which he ran his kingdom.

The **Chambre de la Reine (Queen's Apartments)** run along the south side of the palace's center, mirroring the State Apartments on the north side. Here is Marie Antoinette's bedroom, with the secret door through which she (temporarily) escaped the angry Parisian mob on October 6, 1789. After the queen's rooms is the **Salle du Sacré (Coronation Room),** devoted to Napoleon and dominated by David's painting of the Emperor's coronation (another version hangs in the Louvre.) The last rooms in the main château are the **1792** and **1830** rooms, dedicated to heroes of the Revolution and Restoration, respectively. These rooms stem off of the long **Galerie des Batailles (Hall of Battles),** which chronicles 13 centuries of French victories, including the Battle of Yorktown, just of the hall center. These three rooms were established by Louis-Philippe as part of the Musée de l'Histoire and—like the Musée—may close unexpectedly. *(Château open Tu-Su Apr.-Oct. 9am-6:30pm; Nov.-Mar. 9am-5:30pm; last admission 30min. before closing. Château only €14, 2½hr. before closing €10; under 18 free. Audio tour €6, Apr.-Sept. Sa-Su €10. Included on Paris Museum Pass, see* p. 145.)

ROYAL PRIVILEGES. Several rooms in the château, including the apartments of Louis XV and Louis XVI and the Opéra, are only accessible via 1½hr. guided tours in English or French. The schedule of tours offered changes daily; if you're considering taking one, check what's available and reserve a space on the morning of your visit in the room to the right inside the main ticket office entrance. Tickets for the guided tour don't include entry to the rest of the château, unless you buy a combo ticket. (☎30 83 77 88. Reservations 9am-3:45pm. Tour alone €15, combo ticket €22; under 18 or handicapped €5.50.)

GARDENS. Planned by master gardener Le Nôtre and filled with over 400 sculptures by artists such as Le Brun, Coysevox, and Mansart, the gardens of Versailles remain a testament to Louis XIV's attempt to master nature. Make sure you've got a copy of the château map before you start wandering through them—the gardens are vast (90 hectares), and many of the best fountains and colonnades are hidden inside tall groves. That said, don't pressure yourself to see every sight; these gardens were built for relaxation—and for show—not for rushed visits.

The main entrance is through the courtyard on the left side of the château, which leads to the terrace and its breathtaking view of the gardens' expanse. To the left, the flowerbeds of the **Parterre Sud** lead to a stone balcony high above the neatly organized **Orangerie,** and to the vast lake of the **Pièce d'Eau des Suisses.** After admiring the view, come back down the center steps past the **Bassin de Latone,** decorated with a sculpture of Latona shielding her children as the evildoers climbing towards her are transformed into frogs.

The manicured lawn, or **Tapis Vert** (Green Carpet), stretches down the center of the garden to the **Bassin d'Apollon,** where the Sun King's beloved sun god rises out of the water on his gilded chariot, pulled by four noble horses. Past the fountain, the **Grand Canal** stretches into the distance. In the nearest grove on the north side of the garden is the incredible **Bosquet de l'Encelade,** with a fountain featuring an enormous gold-plated statue of Enceladus (a Titan) half-buried under the rocks he hurled against heaven. This grove is also the closest to the Trianons (see below)—head up along the Grand Canal and follow the signs to get to them. Still on the north side of the gardens, but back toward the château, are an impressive collection of fountains, starting with the three-leveled **Bosquet des Trois Fontaines.** The exit at the bottom of this grove leads to the enormous **Bassin de Neptune,** the largest fountain in the gardens, decorated with sculptures of Neptune, Tritons, and cupids riding fantastic sea monsters. The smaller **Bassin du Dragon,** with dolphins and cupids surrounding the dragon-shaped center fountain, stands in front. From here, the fountain-lined **Allée d'Eau** leads towards the château.

The best time to visit the gardens are the summer weekends of the **Grandes Eaux Musicales,** the only time when the gardens' many fountains are turned on. To enhance the atmosphere, classical music plays over surprisingly innocuous loudspeakers. The spectacle, which lasts a few hours, comes at a price, but it's well worth it to see the beauty of the sparkling water added to the long alleys of hedges and flowers. Tickets (available at the gardens' entrance) are required to enter the gardens at any point during the day. Even more impressive (and more expensive) are the nighttime **Grandes Eaux Nocturnes,** when the fountains are accompanied by a dazzling sound and light show. To be sure to get in, reserve tickets for the Grandes Eaux Nocturnes in advance at the tent to the left of the Versailles courtyard (open June-Sept. Tu-Su 10am-6pm), which also has info and tickets for special performances in the gardens. *(Gardens open daily Apr.-Oct. 7:30am-8:30pm; Nov.-Mar. 8am-8pm. Free except on weekends of Les Grandes Eaux. Les Grandes Eaux ☎30 83 78 89, www.chateauversailles-spectacles.fr; Apr.-Oct. Sa-Su 11am-noon (some fountains) and 3:30-5:30pm (all fountains). €7, students and under 18 €5.50. Les Grandes Eaux Nocturnes run most Sa July-Aug. 9:30-11:30pm; call ahead. €17, students and under 18 €15.)*

TRIANONS AND MARIE ANTOINETTE'S GARDENS. A racier side of Versailles—where kings trysted with lovers and Marie Antoinette lived like the peasant she wasn't—lies just a 25min. walk (or a shorter tram ride) away. Follow the diagonal path northwest from the right side of the Grand Canal's base to reach the **Grand Trianon,** with its stunning pink marble colonnade. Built by Hardouin-Mansart for Louis XIV, it was later one of Napoleon's choice dwellings; inside one of the palace's rooms is an impressive set of green malachite furniture belonging to the Emperor. From here, head northeast to the **Petit Trianon,** built between 1762 and 1768 for Louis XV and his mistress Madame de Pompadour. Marie Antoinette made the Petit Trianon her own in 1774, and the building with its gardens became known as the **Domaine de Marie Antoinette.** The queen's gardens, behind the Petit Trianon, are dotted with ludicrous follies such as the **Temple of Love,** a domed rotunda of carved stone, and **Le Rocher,** an artificial rock spring. The most absurd, however, is the **Hameau,** Marie Antoinette's own pseudo-peasant "hamlet" at the back of the gardens.

THE LOCAL STORY

LET THEM STEAL FURNITURE

October 5, 1789 was a good day for the French Revolution and a very bad one for Versailles. Taking a cue from the crowd that stormed the Bastille prison, another, even larger group made their way to Versailles, hijacked the king and queen, and brought them back to Paris.

After those shenanigans, the revolutionaries auctioned off several of the chests, chairs, and tables that filled the Versailles palace. All of the artwork was transported to the Louvre for safekeeping. Many of the rooms and buildings at Versailles were later restored to their pre-Revolutionary glory, with reproductions put in place of the original furnishings; however, of the roughly 17,000 items sold off at public auction, a majority have been lost forever.

Gerald van Kemp, a French curator who died in January 2002, made it his life's work to track down missing pieces and return them to their rightful place. Nicknamed "The Man Who Gave Us Back Versailles," he retrieved some Riesener commodes made for Marie Antoinette and a Savonnerie carpet, for which the Versailles estate paid millions of dollars. Versailles's most prized former possession is Leonardo da Vinci's *Mona Lisa,* but let's hope she doesn't leave the Louvre anytime soon—the lines at Versailles are long enough already.

In an attempt to live the simple life, she commissioned Richard Mique to construct 12 buildings in the style of a small French village—complete with a water mill and lighthouse. The original lavish furnishings of these cottages have all gone, but the facades give some idea of how far the queen's idea of country life was from reality. *(Shuttle trams to the Trianons leave from station by Parterre Nord, on the north side of the château terrace. Round-trip €6, ages 11-18 €4.50. Audio tours for the ride through the gardens €1.20; ID deposit. Grand Trianon open daily Apr.-Oct. noon-6:30pm; Nov.-Mar. noon-5:30pm; last entrance 30min. before closing. Petit Trianon open daily Apr.-Oct. noon-6pm; closed Nov.-Mar. Marie Antoinette's gardens open daily Apr.-Oct. noon-7:30pm. Ticket including both Trianons and Marie Antoinette's gardens Apr.-Oct. €9, after 4pm €5; under 18 free. Grand Trianon Nov.-Mar. €5, under 18 free; Nov.-Mar. free.)*

CHARTRES

Just as it did centuries ago, Chartres (SHAR-t) revolves around its cathedral. The town dates back to Roman times, but its real history begins in the ninth century with the construction of its first cathedral and the arrival of its most holy relic, the Sancta Camisia (once allegedly worn by the Virgin Mary). That cathedral burned down in the 12th century, but its replacement, built in the height of the early Gothic style, has survived against all odds. Crowds have flocked here for hundreds of years, but tourists have largely replaced the Medieval pilgrims. Today's visitors may be more awed by the cathedral's sculpted facades and radiant stained-glass windows rather than by its religious relics, but no one leaves unmoved.

TRANSPORTATION AND PRACTICAL INFORMATION

Chartres is accessible by frequent SNCF **trains** from Gare Montparnasse on the line towards Nogent-le-Rotrou and Le Mans. (1¼hr., every hr., round-trip €26.) The cathedral's mismatched towers are visible on the left from the station's exit.

The Chartres **tourist office** is in front of the cathedral entrance at pl. de la Cathédrale. The staff provides an excellent map and practical guide, including a walking tour of the city's sights and information on hotels and restaurants. They also help find accommodations (€2) and offer an audio tour to the medieval town in English and French (€5.50). **Guided tours** (1½hr.) of the city leave from the tourist office in July and August. (☎ 02 37 18 26 26; www.chartres-tourisme.com. Tours in French Tu, Th, Sa 2:30pm; English Sa 4:15pm. €5, under 14 €3.50.) You can pick up the Chartres Pass (€15) here to get free admission and discounts at many of the city's sights, but it will only be worthwhile if you're visiting nearly every sight in town. (Open Apr.-Sept. M-Sa 9am-7pm, Su 9:30am-5:30pm; Oct.-Mar. M-Sa 10am-6pm, Su and holidays 10am-1pm and 2:30-4:30pm.) There's a **Monoprix** supermarket in the center of modern Chartres, with entrances on rue Noel Ballay and rue du Bois Merrain. Head straight out of the train station and bear right onto bd. Maurice Violette, then turn left at pl. des Epars. (Open M-Sa 9am-7:30pm.)

SIGHTS

THE CATHEDRAL

☎ 02 37 21 75 02; www.diocese-chartres.com/cathedrale. Open daily 8:30am-7:30pm. No sightseers during masses not held in the crypt. Mass not in crypt M and W- Th 6:15pm; Tu and Th 9am, 6:15pm; Sa 6pm; Su 9:15am in Latin, 11am. Mass in crypt M-F 11:45am; Su 6pm. Free entry to cathedral. Guided tour info ☎ 02 37 28 15 58. French tours Apr. to early Nov. M-Sa 10:30am and 3pm, Su 3pm; Nov.-Apr. daily 2:30pm. €6.20, students and seniors €4.20. English tours Mar.-Oct. M-Sa noon and 2:45pm; meet outside cathedral gift shop.

€10, students €5. ID deposit required for headset. 15-person min. Audio tours: choir (25min., €3.20), cathedral (45min., €4.20), both (70min., €6.20). ID deposit.

Chartres's cathedral—having miraculously escaped major damage during the French Revolution and WWII—is Europe's best-preserved medieval church. Most of the cathedral, including its nave and transept, was built in only 25 years by a single generation of devoted worshippers, after a fire destroyed their former church in 1194. Inside the cathedral is the world's largest collection of medieval stained glass, famously responsible for the uniquely bright tint "Chartres Blue." Guided tours of the cathedral are available in several languages (1hr.). On Sundays in July and August, the Chartres cathedral holds free organ concerts in the cathedral at 4:30pm as part of its International Organ Festival.

JEHAN-DE-BEAUCE TOWER. A 300-step spiral staircase leads to the top of this Flamboyant Gothic tower on the left of the cathedral's facade, built in the early 16th century and named after its architect. Unparalleled views stretch in all directions, taking in the mismatched 12th-century Romanesque tower on the right, the flying buttresses, and a 360° panorama of the landscape. Acrophobes beware: the tower feels miles above the ground. *(Open May-Aug. M-Sa 9:30am-12:30pm and 2-6pm, Su 2-6pm; Sept.-Apr. M-Sa 9:30am-12:30pm and 2-5pm, Su 2-5pm. Last admission 30min. before closing. €6.50, ages 18-25 €4.50, under 18 free; Nov.-May 1st Su of month free.)*

STAINED GLASS. At a time when books were rare and the vast majority of people illiterate, the cathedral served as a multimedia teaching tool with stained-glass windows for books. Most of the 176 windows date from the early 13th century and were preserved through both World Wars by devoted town authorities, who dismantled over 2000 sq. meters of glass and stored the windows pane by pane in the Dordogne. The oldest windows are the three lancets over the church's entrance, which survived the 1194 fire and depict the *Passion and Resurrection of Christ* and the *Tree of Jesse*. A map with the locations of each window can be picked up from the right transept. Binoculars are useful for viewing high windows.

SANCTA CAMISIA. The year after he became emperor in AD 875, Charlemagne's grandson, Charles the Bald, gave Chartres this piece of cloth, believed to have been worn by the Virgin Mary either during the Annunciation or when she gave birth to Jesus. When the relic survived the 1194 fire, it was taken as a miraculous sign that the Virgin wanted a new cathedral built. The cloth was torn to pieces during the Revolution and much of it lost; the largest remaining piece was returned to Chartres and is preserved behind glass in the back of the church on the left.

CRYPT. The cathedral's basement isn't nearly as impressive as the sights upstairs and is only accessible as part of a guided tour. Most of the foundations date back to the ninth century, though some parts—including an impossibly deep well where Viking raiders disposed of massacred citizens—already existed early in the AD first century. *(Tours in French leave Apr.-Oct. from the crypt, and Nov.-Mar. from the cathedral gift shop. ☎02 37 21 75 02. 30min. tours Apr.-Oct. M-Sa 11am, 2:15, 3:15, 4:30pm; mid-June to mid-Sept. also 5:15pm; Nov.-Mar. 11am, 4:15pm. €2.70, students €2.10, under 7 free.)*

OTHER SIGHTS

When you've seen your fill of the cathedral, head to the **Musée des Beaux-Arts,** in the former Bishop's Palace next door. The museum has preserved the bishop's chapel, designed by artists from Veronese's studio. Exhibits include a small 17th-century harpsichord collection and plaster death-masks of bandits executed in the 18th century. *(29 rue du Cloître Notre-Dame, next to the cathedral. ☎02 37 36 41 39. Open May-Oct. M and W-Sa 10am-noon and 2-6pm, Su 2-6pm; Nov.-Apr. M and W-Sa 10am-noon and 2-5pm, Su 2-5pm. €4.20, students and seniors €2.80, under 12 free.)* A small center for stained glass, **Centre International du Vitrail,** 5 rue du Cardinal Pie (facing the cathedral) changes its temporary exhibit once a year. Permanent models of some cathedral windows give you an idea of the incredible detail of these masterpieces, while studios show visitors glassmakers at work. (☎ *02 37 21 65 72; www.centre-vitrail.org. Open M-F 9:30am-12:30pm and 1:30-6pm, Sa-Su 10am-12:30pm and 2:30-6pm. €4, students €3.)*

GIVERNY

In 1883, Claude Monet and his family settled in Giverny (JHEE-vayr-nee) to escape the ever-quickening pace of Paris. By 1894, John Singer Sargent, Auguste Rodin, Paul Cézanne, and Mary Cassatt had all visited and turned the village into a major artists' colony. This sleepy riverside hamlet has retained its original charm, though it is now a major tourist destination, filled with those paying homage to the great Impressionist. When planning your visit, keep in mind that the town's two museums are closed from November to March and on Mondays.

TRANSPORTATION. SNCF **trains** run regularly from Paris's Gare St-Lazare to Vernon, the station nearest Giverny (40min., 13 per day, round-trip €24). A **shuttle bus** runs in sync with the train schedule from the Vernon station to Giverny (☎ 08 25 07 60 27; Apr.-Oct. Tu-Su). Connection times can be as short as 4min., so don't dawdle (20min., 6-7 per day, round-trip €4; schedules available at train station). You can rent a **bike** and get a basic map showing the start of the 5km route to Giverny from the **Café du Chemin de Fer,** opposite the Vernon station. (☎ 02 32 21 16 01. Open daily 7am-2am. €12 per day; ID deposit.) **Taxis** (☎ 02 32 54 56 45) run from the Vernon train station to Giverny for €10.

SIGHTS. Monet's beautiful house and gardens have become the **Fondation Claude Monet,** 84 rue Claude Monet. Visitors enter and exit the grounds through the studio in which Monet painted his large canvases of water lilies—it's now the gift shop. Rooms in Monet's house are restored to their original décor. The artist's collection of 18th- and 19th-century Japanese prints covers the walls of several rooms. Outside is the **Clos Normand,** a Norman-style walled garden, filled from April to July with overflowing rows of wild roses, hollyhocks, poppies, and honeysuckle. An underground passage (indicated by signs to the Jardin des Nymphéas) leads you straight into one of Monet's canvases: the water lilies, wisteria-covered Japanese bridge, and weeping willows of the Orientalist Water Gardens. To avoid crowds, show up early in the morning and, if possible, early in the season. (☎ 02 32 51 28 21; www.fondation-monet.com. Open Apr.-Oct. Tu-Su 9:30am-6pm; last entry 5:30pm. €5.50, students and ages 12-18 €4, ages 7-11 €3. Gardens only €4. AmEx/MC/V.) Giverny's other museum is the **Musée d'Art Américain,** 99 rue Claude Monet, which has no permanent collection but displays several temporary exhibitions of American art from 1750 to the present. (☎ 02 32 51 94 65; www.maag.org. Open Apr.-Oct. Tu-Su 10am-6pm; closed 1 week in early July. €5.50, students and seniors €4, ages 12-18 €3; 1st Su of month free. Audio tours €1.50.) **Monet's tomb,** where he is buried with his family, lies farther west along rue Claude Monet, behind the church. The simple grave is covered with the flowers he loved to paint.

DISNEYLAND RESORT PARIS

Seriously? You sure there's not any Parisian treat or attraction that you missed? Okay: www.disneylandparis.com.

LOIRE VALLEY (VAL DE LOIRE)

Welcome to the land of castles, where fairytales were born and where floppy-eared hunting hounds still bound eagerly through the woods. Captured on postcards, posters, and 3D puzzles, the châteaux of the Loire Valley are deeply historic, breathtakingly beautiful, and shamelessly extravagant. During the Renaissance, many were converted into residential palaces, framed by spectacular gardens and heaped with artistic masterpieces. Today, the rolling hills of the "Garden of France" are perfect for an afternoon bike ride, while their fertile soil also nurtures some of the nation's best wines. Visitors drift through the gilded salons and sigh-inducing gardens of the region's many castles, including Chenonceau (p. 208), whose arches span the Cher River; Cheverny (p. 198), replete with romance; and the impressive masterpiece of pomp known as Chambord (p. 197). Meanwhile, the southern Loire Valley benefited from the lavish attentions of Charles VII's financier, Jacques Cœur. Before being imprisoned for embezzlement, the extravagant Cœur built a string of châteaux through the heart of Berry, most of which are uninhabited and open to visitors. Found along the Route Jacques Cœur, they are easily accessible from Bourges (p. 226) or the medieval St-Amand-Montrond (p. 231).

The cities of the Loire are convenient bases for exploring the châteaux, but they are also exciting destinations in their own right. In Saumur (p. 212), truffles are practically worth their weight in gold. Fun, affordable Tours (p. 202) offers student-centered nightlife. Amboise (p. 199) is home to Leonardo da Vinci's final residence and resting place, as well as to mysterious troglodyte dwellings. Most of these towns also boast their own castles, which rise above centuries-old cobblestone streets, which may charm you to the point of giving clichés a second chance.

HIGHLIGHTS OF THE LOIRE VALLEY

MARVEL at the mix of beauty and scandal at **Fontevraud-l'Abbaye** (p. 216).

PROPOSE in the gallery of **Chenonceau** (p. 197); it doesn't get more romantic.

FACE YOUR DOOM at the world-renowned Apocalyptic Tapestry in **Angers** (p. 220), in which St-Jean battles evil and a seven-headed Satan gobbles down babies.

ORLÉANS ☎02 38

Today, the lively city of Orléans ("OHR-lay-ahn;" pop. 113,000) recalls its former prominence in French history as the thriving capital of the Loire valley. Indeed, many streets are named after or in relation to the famous Joan of Arc, who in 1429 was dubbed "Maiden of Orléans" after she liberated the city from a seven-month English siege, leading the French to victory in the Hundred Years' War. Now, skirted by sprawling commercial and suburban quarters, Orléans nevertheless boasts a charming *vieille ville* with well-preserved marble Renaissance architecture. Admittedly a stepping-stone to the valley's romantic châteaux, Orléans, with its small-town character and big-city fun, is itself a crucial stop.

YOUR CARRIAGE (OF CHOICE) AWAITS. When deciding how to get around the Loire, it's important to first pinpoint your priorities. The most cost-efficient way to travel is by **bike.** Flat roads connect the châteaux, all of which lie relatively close together; however, biking will limit how many châteaux you can see in a day. **Trains** travel to most châteaux and require little exertion but often have inconvenient schedules. The city of Tours is the best rail hub, with connections to 12 châteaux, while the smaller city of Blois is also a convenient base. An ambitious itinerary in the Loire Valley can only be accomplished with a **car,** and three châteaux a day is a healthy limit. A group of four renting a car can generally undercut **tour bus** prices; this will still be more expensive than taking a train or biking. The Michelin map of the region and tourist biking guides steer cyclists away from busy truck-laden highways.

TRANSPORTATION

Trains: A trolley shuttles passengers between the 2 stations every 30min. (€1.20). Tramway 'A' also runs between the stations every 4min. (€1.30).

Gare d'Orléans: (☎79 91 00), on pl. Albert I in the center of town. Info office and ticket booths open daily 5:30am-8:30pm. Trains go to: **Blois** (40min.; at least 15 per day; €9.20, under 26 €7); **Nantes** (2½hr.; M-F 3 per day, Sa-Su 2 per day; €35); **Paris** (1¼hr., every hr., €17); **Tours** (1½hr., every 30min., €16).

Gare Les-Aubrais, rue Pierre Semard (☎79 91 00), a 40min., 2.5km walk north of the town center. Walk north on rue du Faubourg Bannier, make a right on rue de Joie, then a left onto rue Louis Labonne. Stay on the left when the road forks and continue onto rue Lamartine, which turns into rue Pierre Semard; the station will be on your left. Trains go to **Paris** (1hr., every 30min., €17).

Buses: Gare Routière, 2 rue Marcel Proust, connects to the Gare d'Orléans. Info desk upstairs open July 11-Aug. 15 M-F 11:30am-1pm and 4:30-6pm; Aug. 16-July 10 M-F 7:30-9am, 11am-1pm, 1:30-7pm, Sa 10:30am-1:30pm. **Les Rapides du Val de Loire** (☎53 94 75; www.ulys-loiret.com) at the Gare Routière runs buses to **Sully** (1hr., 1-3 per day, €2) via **Germigny** and **St-Benoît-sur-Loire** (1¼hr., 1-3 per day, €2). **Transbeauce** (☎02 37 18 59 00) runs to **Chartres** (1¼hr.; M-F 4-8 per day, Sa-Su 2-3 per day; €12). Tickets sold on bus.

Public Transportation: SEMTAO, 2 rue de la Hallebarde and pl. d'Arc (☎08 00 01 20 00; www.semtao.fr), outside the Gare d'Orléans and under pl. d'Arc shopping mall, runs city buses. Info desk open M-F 6:45am-7:15pm, Sa 8am-6:30pm. 1hr. ticket €1.30, *carnet* of 10 €11.60, day pass €3.40.

Taxis: Taxi Radio d'Orléans (☎53 11 11), outside the Gare d'Orléans, at the Carrefour Parking exit. €2.10 base; €1.36 per km during day, €1.90 at night; €5.50 min. 24hr.

Car Rental:

Ecoto, 19 av. Paris (☎77 92 92). From €29 per day; €800 deposit. 21+ and licensed for 3+ years. Open M 8am-noon and 2-6pm, Tu-F 9am-noon and 2-6pm, Sa 9am-10am and 4-6pm.

Rent A Car, 3 rue des Sansonnières (☎62 22 44), a 4min. walk up the street from Ecoto; keep right when the road splits. Some English spoken. From €30 per day. Open daily 8am-noon and 2-6:30pm.

Bike Rental: CAD, 95 Faubourg Bannier (☎81 23 00). €11 per day, €20 per 2 days. Open M-F 9am-noon and 2-7pm, Sa 9am-5pm.

ORIENTATION AND PRACTICAL INFORMATION

Most spots of interest in Orléans are located in the *vieille ville,* which sits on the north bank of the Loire, a 2min. walk south of the train station. To reach the city center from

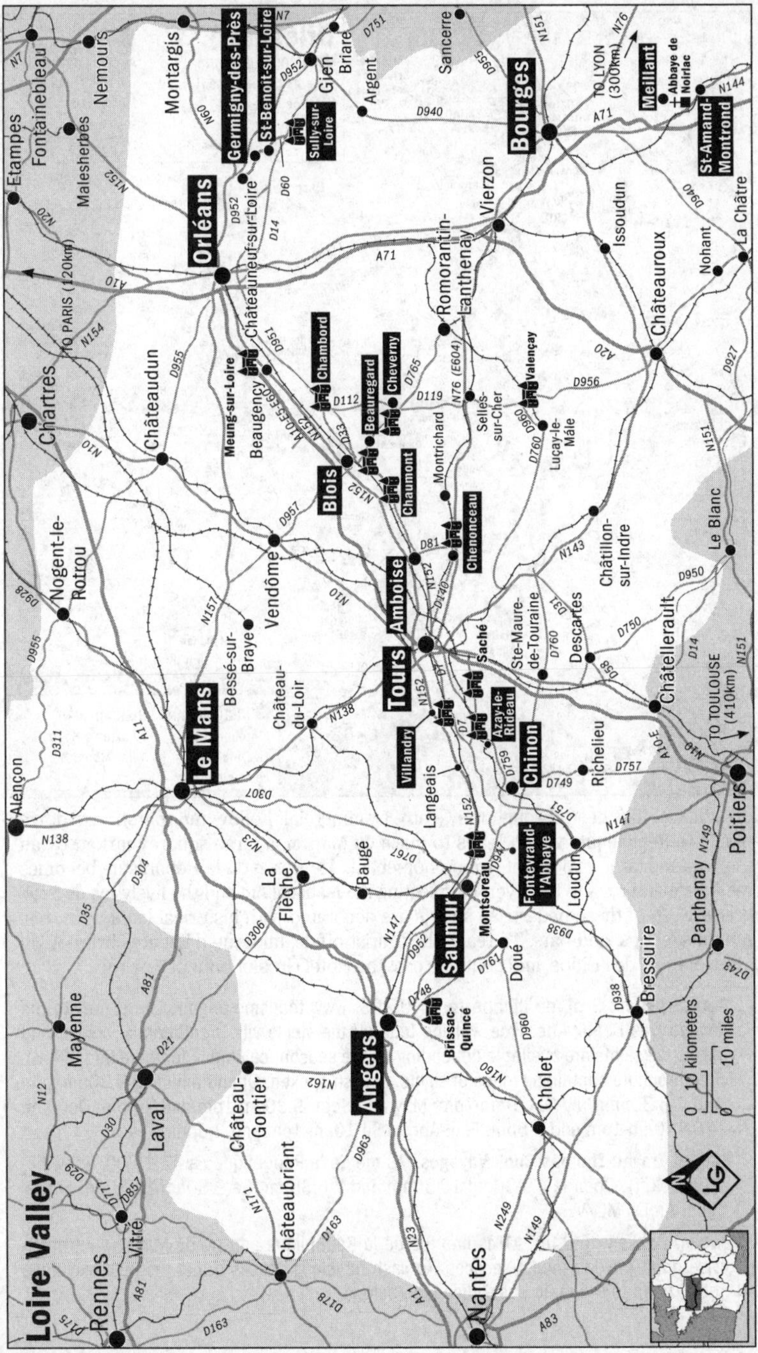

LOIRE VALLEY

the station, first head through the Centre Commercial. Follow the tram tracks down **rue de la République,** which leads to **place du Martroi,** a large square marked by an impressive statue of Joan of Arc on horseback. Here, rue de la République becomes **rue Royale** and runs to the river, intersecting **rue Jeanne d'Arc** and the lively **rue de Bourgogne.** Both of these pedestrian streets are decorated with historical landmarks, restaurants, shops, and bars. To reach the tourist office, take rue d'Escures from pl. du Martroi to pl. de l'Etape, and continue past the Hôtel Groslot onto pl. St-Croix.

Tourist Office: 2 pl. de l'Etape (☎24 05 05; www.tourisme-orleans.com), next to the Musée Des Beaux Arts. Free walking tours of the vieille ville's cathedrals, crypts, and nighttime sights are available depending on the season; call office for more info (€4-6). Free brochure containing maps of sights. English spoken. Open daily June 9:30am-1pm and 2-6:30pm; July-Aug. 9am-7pm; May and Sept. 9:30am-1pm and 2-6pm; Oct.-Jan. M-Sa 10am-1pm and 2-5pm; Feb.-Apr. M-Sa 10am-1pm and 2-6pm.

Budget Travel: Thomas Cook Voyages, 38 rue de la République (☎42 11 80; www.thomascook.fr). Open M-F 9:30am-12:30pm and 2-6:30pm, Sa 9:30am-12:30pm and 2-6pm. AmEx/MC/V.

Banks: Banks with 24hr. **ATMs** line rue de la République and pl. du Martroi, but otherwise don't provide tourist services. To cash traveler's checks or get the best exchange rates, head to the main post office (see below).

English Language Bookstore: Librairie Paes, 184 rue de Bourgogne (☎54 04 50). Also carries books in German, Italian, Portuguese, Russian, and Spanish. Call or stop by to order books not in stock. Open Tu-Sa 10am-12:30pm and 1:30-7pm. MC/V.

Internet Access and Youth Center: Centre Régional d'Information Jeunesse (CRIJ), 5 bd. de Verdun (☎78 91 78; www.informationjeunesse-centre.fr). Provides info on studying, jobs, housing, volunteer opportunities, and travel. Internet access 1hr. free (M-F 2-6pm). Open M-W and F 10am-1pm and 2-6pm, Th and Sa 2-6pm.

Laundromat: Laverie Bourgogne, 176 rue de Bourgogne. Wash €3.50 per 5kg, dry €1 per 9min. Open daily 7am-9pm.

Police: 63 rue du Faubourg St-Jean (☎24 30 00).

Crisis Line: Rape crisis line: ☎08 00 05 95 95.

Red Cross: ☎08 00 85 88 58.

Pharmacy: daily 7-9pm, call ☎15. After 9pm, call police with ID card and prescription.

Hospital: Centre Hospitalier Régional, 1 rue Porte Madeleine (☎51 44 44).

Post Office: pl. du Général de Gaulle (☎77 35 14). **Currency exchange.** Open M-F 8:30am-7pm, Sa 8:30am-12:15pm. **Postal Code:** 45000.

ACCOMMODATIONS

Cheap hotels are hard to find, and some accommodations close in August.

Hôtel de L'Abeille, 64 rue Alsace-Lorraine (☎53 54 87; www.hoteldelabeille.com), 1 block from the station. Owned by the same family since 1919; celebrated its 100th anniversary in 2003. The 31 fresh, comfortable rooms with antique furniture, (non-functional) fireplaces, and often fresh flowers, are worth the price. Continental breakfast €7.50, in bed €8. Wi-Fi in lobby. Singles with shower €42, with bath €47-52; doubles €45-58/89; triples €59/89; quads €75/110. AmEx/MC/V. ❹

Hôtel Charles Sanglier, 8 rue Charles Sanglier (☎53 38 50; hotelsanglier@wanadoo.fr). Boasts friendly service and a location in the heart of the city. Geranium-decorated 60s-style rooms are soon to be modernized. All have a screened-off bath area and cable TV. Breakfast in bed €4. Reservations recommended. Singles €40-45; doubles €50-55. Extra bed €10-12. Cash only. ❸

Hotel Bannier, 13 rue Faubourg Bannier (☎53 25 86), 2 blocks from the train station. Also serves as a *brasserie* and bar. 17 clean and well-equipped rooms with wood-paneled ceilings; some overlook a quiet yard. Breakfast €4.30. Reception M-Th 7:30am-9pm, F-Sa 7:30am-10pm. Singles and doubles €26-30; triples €31; quads €49. ❷

Auberge de Jeunesse (HI), 7 av. Beaumarchais (☎53 60 06). From the train station, take tram A to "Université-L'Indien" (35min.). From the stop, take a left down av. de Président John Kennedy then another left onto rue de Beaumarchais. The hostel is behind Tribune A of the Stade Omnisport. The cheapest option around but quite a trek from town. Rooms are dark and bare but clean. Bunk beds and shared bathrooms. Breakfast €3.50. Parking available. Reception M-F 8am-noon and 4-7pm. 4-bed single-sex dorms €8.80; singles €20, under 26 €11. Cash only. ❶

FOOD

In late summer and fall, locals feast on fresh *gibier* (game), once hunted in the nearby forests. Sausage, such as *andouillette de Jargeau* (tripe sausage), and *saumon de Loire* (salmon) are regional specialties. Local cheeses, like *frinault cendré* (a mild relative of Camembert), complement fresh river fare, and buttery *sablés* cookies make for a nice dessert. However, Orléans's most important culinary contributions are its tangy wine vinegars, which many local *brasseries* serve on salads and in marinades. *Gris Meunier* or *Auvergnat* wines, or nearby Olivet's pear and cherry brandies provide a nice finishing touch to any meal.

The extensive **Carrefour** supermarket, which occupies the back of a mall behind the train station at pl. d'Arc, is close to the *centre-ville.* (Open M-Sa 8:30am-9pm. AmEx/MC/V.) **Les Halles Châtelet,** pl. du Châtelet, is an enclosed ensemble of shops and food stands across the street from Galeries Lafayette, a large department store. Make a meal from the produce, cheese, bread and, meat sold at the various booths. (Open Tu-Sa 7:30am-7:30pm, Su 7:30am-1:30pm. Cash only.) *Brasseries* and bars around Les Halles Châtelet and **rue de Bourgogne** are the best bet for bargain food options and a lively atmosphere. Sandwiches with *frites* and Turkish *Shaorma* (kebab) are a good deal (€4-7). Chinese, Indian, and Middle Eastern restaurants lie between **rue de la Fauconnerie** and **rue de l'Université.**

Mijana, 175 rue de Bourgogne (☎62 02 02; www.mijanaresto.com). A charming Lebanese couple prepares—you guessed it—gourmet Lebanese cuisine, including vegetarian options such as falafel, *baba ghanoush* or hummus (€7 each). An intimate, authentic ambience perfect for a tête-à-tête, with Lebanese music and wine, and tables named after friends and family. Take-out sandwiches €4-6. Appetizers €6-9. *Plats* €12-25 Lunch *menu* €18. Open M-Sa noon-1:30pm and 7-10pm. AmEx/MC/V over €16. ❸

Au Don Camillo, 54 rue Ste-Catherine (☎53 38 97). A trendy, 2-story hangout offering thin crust pizzas (€6.80-9.40) and a surprising variety of salads (€12). With filling portions and fair prices, this place is a favorite of younger locals and tourists alike. *Plat du jour* €11. Lunch and dinner pizza or pasta *menus* with salad and drink €11/14. House *menu* €22. Open daily noon-3pm and 7pm-midnight. AmEx/MC/V. ❸

Bar des Tribunaux, 29 rue de la Bretonnerie (☎62 71 86). A local favorite, this café is often justifiably packed with lawyers from the nearby *Palais de la Justice*. Sports an appealing authentic atmosphere, a group of energetic waiters, and a playlist of French oldies to set the mood. It's a shame the kitchen's only open for lunch. Salads €7.90-8.30. Traditional fish and meat dishes €7.10-12. *Plat du jour* €7.60. Open M-F 8am-7pm. Food served until 2pm. AmEx/MC/V. ❷

Les Musardises, 38 rue de la République (☎53 30 98). A classic *salon de thé,* complete with waitresses in uniform and large embellished mirrors. Regional treats like *macarons d'Orléans* and *chocolat Cyrano*, as well as savory treats (€3 and up) are icing on the already-colorful cake. If left undaunted by the intensely yellow interior, stay and try the Chef's special *plat du jour* (€8.40), served only during lunch. Tea €3. Cakes €4-6. Chocolate €5.80 per 100g. Open M-Sa 8am-7:20pm, Su 8am-12:30pm MC/V. ❷

Le Vol-Terre, 253 rue Bourgogne (☎54 00 79). For those inclined to try out the philosophy of *bio* (organic) food, this small but lively restaurant offers an inventive dining experience. Salads (€12) use a variety of ingredients and explore a range of tastes. Menu in braille. Open M-Th noon-2pm and 7:30-11pm, F noon-2pm and 7:30-11:30pm, Sa noon-2pm and 7:30pm-midnight. ❷

SIGHTS

Most of Orléans's highlights—including the Eglise St-Paterne, remarkable for its stained-glass artwork ranging from the 11th century to modern times—are not far from pl. St-Croix. It is here that in 1429, Joan of Arc marched the triumphant French Army down the city's oldest—and now hippest—street, **rue de Bourgogne.**

CATHÉDRALE ST-CROIX. With towering Gothic buttresses and dramatic interior arches, this cathedral is Orléans's crown jewel. Its spire rises over 88m and can be seen from almost anywhere in town. Originally erected in the 13th century, the cathedral was under construction for more than two centuries before its completion. The two golden leopards cowering at Joan of Arc's feet in the north wing and the hand of God drawn directly above the altar are not to be missed. *(Pl. St-Croix. Open daily June-Aug. 9:15am-7pm; Sept. 9:15am-5:45pm; Oct.-May 9:15am-noon and 2:15-5:45pm. In summer Mass Su 10:30am. Contact tourist office for tours. Free.)*

HÔTEL GROSLOT D'ORLÉANS. Built in 1550 for bailiff Jacques Groslot, this beautiful Renaissance mansion was the king's local residence for two centuries and Orléans's city hall until the 1970s. One room is filled with Joan of Arc memorabilia, and another served as the final resting place of 16-year-old François II, who died from an ear infection in 1560. Unblemished by its history, the regally furnished rooms now host many of Orléans's receptions and weddings. A peaceful 19th-century garden provides respite from the busy city. *(Pl. de l'Etape, left of the Musée des Beaux Arts. Walk up the stairs to the entrance. ☎79 22 30; hotelgroslot@ville-orleans.fr. Open July-Sept. M-F and Su 9am-7pm, Sa 5-8pm; Oct.-June M-F and Su 10am-noon and 2-6pm. Garden open daily Apr.-Sept. 7:30am-8pm; Oct.-Mar. 8am-5:30pm. Contact tourist office for tours. For English guides call ahead. Brochure €1.)*

PARC FLORAL DE LA SOURCE. Originally created to host the International Flower Show of 1967, this 30-acre park contains the mysterious source of the Loiret river, a petting zoo and a butterfly reserve of 50 exotic species, which glide amid tropical flora. The picnic areas and playgrounds are ideal for a family outing—especially every Easter, when a giant egg hunt takes place. For €2 extra, travel around the park in the *petit train*. *(By car, take RN-20 dir.: Vierzon-Bourges and exit at "St-Cyr-En-Val." By tram, take dir.: Orléans-La Source and exit at "Université-Parc Floral" (30min). From Gare d'Orléans, take a right, cross the tracks, and walk down the path to the park entrance. ☎49 30 00; www.parc-floral-la-source.com. Open daily Apr. to mid-Oct. 10am-7pm; mid-Oct. to Mar. 2-5pm. Butterfly reserve open Apr.-Oct. Ticket booth closes 1hr. prior to closing. €4, students €3.50, ages 6-16 €2.50; under 6 free. Butterfly reserve €2.10-2.70 extra.)*

MUSÉE DES BEAUX ARTS. This fine collection—housed in a modern building next to the cathedral—boasts Italian, Flemish, and French paintings and sculptures from the last five centuries. Like most places in Orléans, Joan of Arc has a strong presence here; notice the large painting of the heroine on horseback in the main lobby. In addition to a particularly strong collection of 17th- and 18th-century French art, the museum hosts modern art and archaeological exhibits. The 19th- and 20th-century exhibits include paintings by Van Dyck, Boucher, Delacroix, and Gauguin. *(1 rue Fernand Rabier, to the right of the tourist office. ☎79 21 55; www.ville-orleans.fr.*

THE BONES AREN'T JOAN'S

Joan of Arc's legend is usually considered more fact than fiction, but new findings suggest her remains may be more fiction than fact. After extensively analyzing Joan's relics, French forensic scientist Philippe Charlier and his research team were "astonished" to find that two bones said to belong to the Maid of Orléans are actually a rib and a cat femur from Egyptian mummies.

The relics, kept in a museum in Chinon, were found in an apothecary's shop in Paris in 1867 and recognized as genuine by the Catholic Church shortly thereafter. Among the techniques used by Charlier is a French specialty: odor analysis. The scientist enlisted the help of two leading French perfume 'noses' to sniff the remains for any unusual scents that could provide a clue to their identity. Both 'noses' smelled vanilla, a scent found in mummified bodies, but not ones burnt at the stake. Corroborating that finding, carbon-14 dating placed the year of death between the 3rd and 6th centuries BC, which is at least 1700 years too early for Joan. Finally, chemical analysis showed traces of vegetative and mineral matter typical of Egyptian embalming, but no traces of charring or scorching. All evidence seems to indicate that these bones are from Cairo rather than Rouen; from now on, they'll be venerated for their age, and not for any aura of sanctity.

Open Tu–Sa 9:30am-12:15pm and 1:30-5:45pm, Su 2-6:30pm. €3, students under 25 and seniors over 65 €1.50, under 16 free; 1st Su of the month free.)

MAISON DE JEANNE D'ARC. This two-room museum is located in the house where the ill-fated saint stayed during her short sojourn in Orléans. An automated narration reconstructs the seven-month siege with miniature models of the ancient city, creating a unique interactive learning experience. The third floor is dedicated to Joan's helpers and patrons in Orléans. *(3 pl. Charles de Gaulle, across from the post office. ☎52 99 89. Headsets available with narration in English, French, German, Italian, and Spanish. Open May-Oct. Tu-Su 10am-noon and 2-6pm; Nov.-Apr. 2-6pm. €2; students, under 16, and groups over 10 €1.)*

OTHER SIGHTS. Popular with local schoolchildren and nature enthusiasts alike, the curious **Musée des Sciences Naturelles** makes natural history surprisingly fun. Make sure to visit the *cabinet des curiosities*, which features skeletons and stuffed bats accompanied by agreeable 1920s decor and cheery opera music. Live fish brighten the otherwise-gloomy aquarium on the first floor, and a greenhouse on the fourth floor provides a relaxing but humid end to the tour. *(6 rue Marcel Proust. ☎54 61 05. Open daily 2-6pm. €3, students €1, under 16 and school groups free.)* The **Musée Historique et Archéologique de l'Orléannais,** housed in the courtyard of the **Hôtel Cabu,** collects odd tidbits such as glass portraits of Sun King Louis XIV and an anonymous cross-eyed ecclesiastic, as well as a sculpture of Joan of Arc that gives new meaning to the word "bust." *(Sq. Abbé Desnoyers. ☎79 21 55. Open July-Aug. M-Sa 9:30am-12:15pm and 1:30-5:45pm, Su 2-6:30pm; May-June and Sept. Tu-Sa 1:30-5:45pm, Su 2-6:30pm; Oct.-Apr. W 1:30-5:45pm, Su 2-6:30pm. €3, students €1.50, under 16 free. Admission to Musée Historique included with admission to Musée des Beaux Arts. Call the tourist office for tour reservations; €3.80, €5 for tours in languages other than French.)* The **Centre Jeanne d'Arc,** at the **Médiathèque d'Orléans,** a modern building on pl. Gambetta, has a library with over 16,000 documents related to the city's heroine. *(www.jeannedarc.com.fr. Open Tu-W and F-Sa 10am-6pm, Th 1-8pm.)*

NIGHTLIFE

The campus of Orléans's university is on the outskirts of town, so the city's nightlife is usually lively only on weekends. Like most French towns, Orléans has a token pub-crawl street—**rue de Bourgogne**—strewn with bars to suit all tastes.

L'Atelier, 203 rue de Bourgogne (☎53 08 27). Small, rustic and a lively bar offers free concerts, debates, readings, and exhibitions. Cheap prices will remain so–they are etched into the wall and wooden staircase. Regulars–garrulous artists and musicians–are usually eager for conversation or a game of cards. Mixed drinks from €2.50. Open M-W and Sa 5:30pm-2am, Th-F 5:30pm-3am.

La Datcha, 205 rue Bourgogne (☎81 00 11). This Slavic-style bar offers 27 different vodka drinks named after famous Russians ("Julianov," €6) and related cultural spin-offs ("Big Lebowski," €6). Popular with a young, laid-back crowd. Dark wooden pillars, tables decorated with clients' graffiti, and ever-present funk music create a trendy vibe. Open M-Sa 5pm-2am.

Paxton's Head, 264-266 rue de Bourgogne (☎81 23 29). Suave leather couches, monogrammed carpets and occasional live jazz music give this bar its distinctly classy feel. Although the posh gilded fireplace and dark felt walls may suggest high prices, the pub caters to a mixed crowd. If asked, the owner will open private rooms in the back for large groups. Karaoke Th-Sa from 10pm. Beer €2.50-9.20. Mixed drinks €6.90-7.70. Open daily 3pm-3am.

Moog, 38 rue de l'Empereur (☎54 93 23). A classy crowd enjoys hard liquor (€5) while surrounded by stainless steel, sultry red lighting, and sassy pop music. The terrace, furnished with orange chairs, is oddly reminiscent of a playground. Beer from €2.80. Mixed drinks €6.80. Open July-Aug. M-Sa 6pm-2am; Sept.-June M-Sa 6pm-1am.

Le Decibel, 229 rue de Bourgogne (☎77 28 71). A regular destination for upbeat and rowdy *Orléanais*. A warm-up for a night out or a post-disco hangout. Functions as a café during the day. Wi-Fi available. Beer €2-4.50. Mixed drinks €3.50-5. Student nights Th-Sa; cover determined by students; 4th drink free. Open M-Sa 8am-1am.

FESTIVALS

Orléans comes alive with parades, music, and food for the **Fête de Jeanne d'Arc** (May 7-8 in 2008) in commemoration of the heroine's miraculous victory over the British. During the last two weeks of June, Orléans hosts **Jazz d'Orléans,** a festival with musicians from around the world. (www.orleans.fr/orleansjazz. Tickets €10-20, under 26 €10; some concerts free.) Every two years, in the last week of September, the **Fête de Loire** (next in 2009) explodes in fireworks, theatrical events, and nautical displays on the banks of the Loire (☎24 05 05). On weekends in November and December, the Orchestre National de France comes to town for the **Semaines Musicales Internationales d'Orléans (SMIO).** Finally, the **Marché de Noel,** or traditional Christmas market, sells candied apples and local goods on Pl. Martroi in the weeks leading up to the holiday.

DAYTRIPS FROM ORLÉANS

GERMIGNY. A day's drive eastward along the Loire reveals these three small villages, each dating from a different era of French history. About 30km southeast of Orléans lies the Carolingian church of Germigny-des-Prés. Originally constructed in AD 806 but thoroughly restored in the late 18th century, it is one of the three oldest churches in France. Enhancing the simple re-plastered interior are the original pillar-headings and a startling ninth-century "golden" mosaic in the demi-cupola of the oratory. Hidden for "protection" behind a white wash, the mosaic was rediscovered in 1830 by a group of children who were playing underneath it. *(Les Rapides du Val de Loire buses run from Orléans to Germigny (45min., 1-3 per day 6:45am-6:30pm, €2). Church ☎58 27 97. Church open daily Apr.-Oct. 9am-7pm; Nov.-Mar.10am-5pm. Museum open daily Apr.-Oct. 9am-12:30pm and 2-7pm; Nov.-Mar. 10am–noon and 2-5pm. Closed Jan. to mid-Feb. Guided tours for groups over 15 with reservation. Church free. Museum €2, ages 10-18 €1, under 10 free.)*

ST-BENOÎT-SUR-LOIRE. A Romanesque basilica 35km southeast of Orléans, St-Benoît is home to a community of Benedictine monks. An important cultural center in the ninth-12th centuries, it is still a site of pilgrimage, perhaps because Saint Benedict's relics, over 1000 years old, lie in an iron casket in the candlelit crypt. Above, Philip I lies on an original fourth-century Roman marble mosaic, transported to the Fleury Abbey at his own bidding. The monks offer six services a day, including Gregorian chants and a tour of the basilica every Sunday. *(Les Rapides du Val de Loire buses run from Orléans to Germigny (50min., 1-3 per day 6:45am-6:30pm, €2). Church ☎35 72 43. Open daily 6:30am-10pm. Abbey office open M-F 9-11:40am and 2-5:50pm. Services M-Sa 6:30am, noon, 2:30, 6:10, 9pm; Su 7:15, 11am, 3, 6:10, 9pm. French tour Su 3:15pm; €3. Write to Monastère de Fleury, 45730 St-Benoît-sur-Loire to book ahead.)*

SULLY-SUR-LOIRE. Described by Voltaire as "the most likeable of castles," this white-turreted and moat-surrounded château 40km southeast of Orléans has been visited by the likes of Charles VII, Joan of Arc, and Louis XIV. Particularly noteworthy is the suite dedicated to Psyche (a Greek mythical character), which was constructed during the Enlightenment and includes 17th-century tapestries bearing the Sully family's coat of arms. The château, which was meticulously maintained by the family until the 1960s, has recently undergone extensive renovations. Climb up to the chamber of the guards to steal a glimpse of the peaceful Loire stretching through the countryside. Throughout the year, themed tours are given in French; call ☎78 04 04 for reservations. The 17th-century forest surrounding the château offers a peaceful respite from the summer crowds. *(Les Rapides du Val de Loire buses run from Orléans to Germigny (1hr., 1-3 per day 6:45am-6:30pm, €2). Château open daily Apr.-Sept. 10am-6pm; Feb.-Mar. and Oct.-Dec. Tu-Su 2-5pm. Forest open daily 8am-sunset. ☎36 36 86; www.loiret.com. €7, families €6, free with prior visit to Chambrol and Gien.)* A historical festival is held outside the castle on the third weekend in May. In mid-June, the grounds stage the Festival de Sully et du Loiret, a world-famous classical music festival. *(www.festival-sully.com. For reservations call toll-free ☎08 00 45 28 18.)*

BLOIS ☎02 54

Topped with myriad brick chimneys and trimmed with narrow meandering cobblestone lanes, Blois ("BLWAH;" pop. 49, 171) is a sleepy town that bears witness to centuries of French architectural styles. A former medieval capital, Blois was home to François I and Louis XIII and served as the site from which Joan of Arc gathered the army that would liberate Orléans. Today, Blois makes a relaxing base for visits to Chambord and Cheverny, two of the Loire Valley's most famous châteaux; each is a short bike or bus trip away.

TRANSPORTATION

Trains: pl. de la Gare (☎08 92 35 35 35). Open M-Sa 5:30am-8:15pm, Su 7:15am-10pm. Trains go to: **Amboise** (20min., 15 per day, €5.80); **Angers** via **Tours** (1½hr., 9-11 per day, €22); **Orléans** (30-50min., 14 per day, €9); **Paris** via **Orléans** (1¾hr., 8 per day, €23); **Tours** (40min., 8-13 per day 8am-7pm, €8.70).

Buses: Point Bus, 2 pl. Victor Hugo (☎78 15 66; www.tub-blois.fr). Open M 1:30-6pm, Tu-F 8am-noon and 1:30-6pm, Sa 9am-noon and 1:30-4:30pm. **Transports Loir-et-Cher (TLC)** (☎02 54 58 55 44; www.TLCinfo.net) sends buses from the train station to **Chambord** and **Cheverny** (3 per day mid-May to early Sept.; €12; students, under 12, and over 65 €8.96; reduced entry to châteaux with bus ticket). Buy tickets on board. Open M-F 9am-noon and 2-6pm. For schedules contact TLC or the tourist office.

Taxis: Taxis Radio, pl. de la Gare (☎78 07 65). €5-6 from the station to the *vieille ville,* €26 to the castles. 24hr.

Bike Rental: Bike in Blois, 8 rue Henri Drussy (☎56 07 73; www.locationdevelos.com), near pl. de la Résistance. €14 standard bike or €38 tandem bike per day; price reduction for extra days. Open M-F 9:15am-1pm and 3-6:30pm, Su 10:30am-1pm and 3-6:15pm. Cash only. **Cycles LeBlond,** 44 Levée des Tuileries (☎74 30 13; cycle.leblond@caramail.com). A 20min. walk along the Loire, to the left of pl. de la Résistance. €12 per day, €25 per 3 days. Open daily 9am-9pm. Cash only.

ORIENTATION AND PRACTICAL INFORMATION

The château and city center are 5min. from the train station, left down **avenue Jean Laigret.** Between the château and **rue Denis Papin** is a bustling pedestrian quarter. When in doubt, descend: all roads lead to the river and town center.

Tourist Office: pl. du Château (☎90 41 41; www.bloispaysdechambord.com). Provides free maps of the city and biking routes in the Loire Valley, complete info on châteaux, tickets for bus circuits, and a reservation service (€2.30). Offers excellent themed tours of the area (€5-7; call office for reservations). Open Apr.-Sept. M-Sa 9am-7pm, Su and holidays 10am-7pm; Oct.-Mar. M-Sa 9:30am-12:30pm and 2-6pm, Su 10am-4pm.

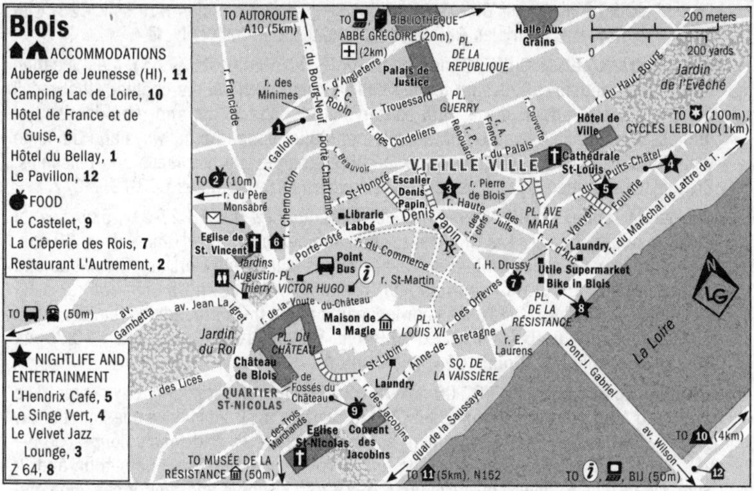

English-Language Bookstore: Librairie L'abbé, 9 rue Porte Chartraine. Open M 2-7:15pm, Tu-F 9:30am-7:15pm, Sa 9am-7:15pm. MC/V.

Youth Center: Bureau d'Information Jeunesse (BIJ), 7 av. Wilson (☎78 54 87). Free Internet access, no chatting. Reservations recommended. Brochures on accommodations, job info, cultural events, health, sports, and travel tips. Open M-Tu and Th-F 1-6pm, W 9am-noon and 1-6pm.

Laundromat: Laverie, 6 rue St-Lubin and 1 rue Jeanne d'Arc. Open daily 7am-9pm. Wash €4.30 per 6kg, dry €1 per 10min.

Pharmacy: Pharmacie des 3 Clefs, 30 rue Denis Papin (☎74 01 35). Open Tu-F 9am-7pm, Sa 8:30am-7pm.

Police: 42 quai St-Jean (☎90 09 00).

Red Cross: ☎55 65 45.

Hospital: Centre Hospitalier de Blois, Mail Pierre Charlot (☎55 66 33; www.ch-blois.fr).

Library and Internet Access: Bibliothèque Abbé Grégoire, pl. Jean Jaurès (☎56 27 40). No email or chatting. Limit 1hr. €0.20 per 5min., €2.40 per hr. Free for travel or job research. Library open M-Tu and F 1-6:30pm, W and Sa 10am-noon and 2-5pm. Free Internet at BIJ (see **Youth Center,** above).

Post Office: 2 rue Gallois (☎57 17 17). **Currency exchange.** Open M-F 8am-7pm, Sa 8am-12:30pm. **Postal Code:** 41000.

ACCOMMODATIONS AND CAMPING

Hôtel du Bellay, 12 rue des Minimes (☎78 23 62; http://hoteldubellay.free.fr), at the top of porte Chartraine, to the right of the Old Quarter. This rustic old house, hidden away in a quiet, centrally-located nook of the city, contains 12 clean but well-lived in rooms. Breakfast €5. Reception 24hr. Reservations recommended at least 3 weeks ahead. Singles and doubles with sink €25, with toilet €27, with shower €28, with bath €37; triples and quads €54-62. Tax €0.60. MC/V. ❷

Le Pavillon, 2 av. Wilson (☎74 23 27; fax 74 03 36), on the Loire, across the Pont Gabriel. Walk (10min.) or bus #3A from the train station. Bright, comfortable, simply furnished rooms, half of which overlook the Loire and château. Owner describes herself as "strict." Under renovation. Breakfast €6.50. Singles and doubles with sink €28, with shower and toilet €35; triples €50-55; family suite €65. Cash only. ❷

Hôtel de France et de Guise, 3 rue Gallois (☎78 00 53; fax 78 29 45). Ideal location next to the château. 50 elegant rooms–half of which overlook the château–that recall the decadent splendor of the 19th century. Glass chandeliers and reproductions of Impressionist works by Van Gogh, Renoir, and Monet adorn the hallways and the large dining area. All rooms with TV, phone, and bath; some with fireplaces and balconies. Breakfast €6; in bed €7. Singles €42-54; doubles €48-61; triples €63-79. MC/V. ❹

Auberge de Jeunesse (HI), 18 rue de l'Hôtel Pasquier (☎/fax 78 27 21), 5km west of Blois. Take bus #4 (dir.: Les Grouets) to "Auberge de Jeunesse" (10min., every 30 min. 7am-7:35pm). Pleasant 24-bed single-sex dorms with limited privacy. Spacious and well-equipped kitchen, hot showers and toilets in the yard, and a common room for lounging and reading. Manager is knowledgeable about the surrounding area. Breakfast €3.60. Reception 6:45-10am and 6-10:30pm. Lockout 10am-6pm. Curfew 10:30pm. Open Mar. to mid-Nov. Dorms €14. Cash only. ❶

Camping Lac de Loire (☎78 82 05; fax 78 62 03). From the station or city center, take bus S7 to "Lac de Loire" (20min., July-Aug. 3 per day, €1). 2min. bike ride from the city center. Site has 220 spots, swimming pool, mini-golf (€2), and tennis courts (€6 per hr.). Reception July-Aug. 8:30am-noon and 4-7pm; June and Sept. 8am-noon and 2-8pm. Open June to mid-Sept. July-Aug. €15-18 per 2 people and tent or car; June and Sept. €13. €3 per extra person. Electricity €3. Hot showers free. AmEx/MC/V. ❶

FOOD

Traditional *blésois* restaurants line **rue St-Lubin** and **place Poids du Roi,** and relatively inexpensive Chinese, Italian, and Greek restaurants surround the lively **place de la Résistance.** An **Intermarché** supermarket is at 16 av. Gambetta (open M-Sa 9am-7pm) and a **8 à huit** is at 11 rue du commerce (open M-Sa 8am-8pm and Su 8am-noon). Across the Point Gilbert, **place Louis XII** bustles with an open-air food and clothing **market** (open Sa 8am-1pm).

Le Castelet, 40 rue St-Lubin (☎74 66 09). A local fave by day and tourists' choice at night. Medieval regional specialties (cider-marinated chicken, €11) and local wines, such as the *touraine amboise* (by the glass, €38) can be enjoyed in the rustic interior or on the outdoor terrace on summer evenings. The good-humored owner gladly helps customers with their choices and explains the preparation of each dish. Vegetarian *menu* available. *Plats* €10-15. *Menus* €15-25. Open daily noon-1:45pm and 7-9:45pm. Dinner reservations highly recommended. MC/V. ❸

La Crêperie des Rois, 3 rue Denis Papin (☎90 01 90). *Crêperies* are a dime a dozen in most French towns, but this antique-decorated restaurant offers the widest selection in Blois. Try the "Texas" (steak, egg, tomatoes, and potatoes; €7.45) the more exotic "Martinique" (pineapple, ham, cheese, and egg; €6.15), or one of the several dessert *crêpes* (€1.75-6.45). Open Tu-Su noon-2pm and 7-10pm. MC/V. ❶

Restaurant L'Autrement, 5 rue du Pont du Gast (☎58 89 08), behind St-Vincent. Outgoing waiters serve a variety of affordable pizzas (€6.80-14), salads (€8-10), pastas (€6-12), and bargain *formules* (appetizer *du jour* and *plat du jour;* €10). Open Tu-Th noon-3pm and 7-10:30pm, F-Sa noon-3pm and 7-11:30pm. MC/V. ❷

SIGHTS

CHÂTEAU DE BLOIS. Brilliant gold trimming and carved pillars give this château more than just a touch of elegance. Home to Louis XII (1462-1515) and

François I (1494-1547), Blois's château was as prominent in the 15th and early 16th centuries as Versailles became in later years. The motto of François I, *Nutrisco et extingo* ("I feed on fire and I extinguish it"), explains the abundance of carved and painted fire-breathing salamanders, an icon peppered throughout the entire Loire Valley. As for the porcupines, they were the trademark of Louis XII, who embodied the french saying "*Qui s'y frotte, s'y pique*" ("Those who bother him will suffer the consequences"). The newest wing, part of the château's third major expansion, is a grandiose monument to French Classicism. It now houses two museums: the recently renovated **Musée des Beaux-Arts,** featuring a gallery of 16th- to 19th-century paintings, and the **Musée Lapidaire,** exhibiting sculpted rock pieces taken from nearby 16th- and 17th-century châteaux. Don't miss the four secret cabinets in the royal study, where Alexandre Dumas told Catherine de Medici to store her numerous poisons. Finally, you may want to take the 25min. carriage tour of the city, which departs from the château entrance. *(☎90 33 33; www.ville-blois.fr. Open daily Apr.-Sept. 9am-6:30pm; Oct.-Mar. 9am-noon and 2-5:30pm. Ticket booth closes 30min. before château. Admission including 2 museums €6.50, students under 25 €5, under 17 €3. Historical French tours depart from courtyard May-Sept. every hr.; call ahead to request 20min. English presentation in courtyard. Free with admission. Carriage tours daily July-Aug. 11am-7pm; Sept.-June 2:30-6:30pm. €6, under 18 €4.* **son-et-lumière** show *daily mid-Apr. to late May and Aug.-Sept. 10pm; June-July 10:30pm. €7, students €5, under 17 €3. English show W. Ticket to château and light show €11, students €8.50, under 18 €5.50. Ticket to château and Maison de la Magie €12/8.50/5.50. Ticket for all 3 attractions €16/11/9. MC/V.)*

VIEILLE VILLE. The most enjoyable attractions in Blois might be its hilly streets and ancient staircases. Bars and bakeries on **rue St-Lubin** and **rue des Trois Marchands** tempt those en route to the 12th-century Abbaye St-Laumer, now the **Eglise St-Nicolas.** *(Open daily 9am-6:30pm. Mass Su 9:30am.)* The winding streets east of **rue Denis Papin** are especially beautiful. Meanwhile, 500 years of expansions have endowed **Cathédrale St-Louis,** one of Blois's architectural jewels, with a beautiful mix of styles. *(Open daily 7:30am-6pm. Crypt open June-Aug.)* A spectacular view from the **Jardin de l'Evêché,** behind the cathedral, reaches over the roof tops of the old quarter, stretching along the brilliant Loire. On your way down, rest at the top of the Denis Papin stairs and watch the city unfold into the distance.

OTHER SIGHTS. The **Musée de la Résistance, de la Déportation, et de la Libération** is a powerful memorial to

TOP TEN LIST

KING OF HEARTS

The Loire Valley is renowned for extravagance and romance. Ideal places to propose include:

1. Atop the **Denis Papin staircase** (see left) in **Blois** at sunset: pretend the breathlessness is due to all those stairs you climbed.

2. Under the gaze of the eternally star-crossed lovers in the **King's Chambers** at **Cheverny** (p. 198): just hope your relationship isn't as doomed.

3. On **Chambord's** (p. 197) **rooftop terrace,** gazing up at the 365 chimneys—one for every day of the year you're in love.

4. The abandoned **cave-dwellings** of **Amboise** (p. 199): your love will be set in stone.

5. In **Beauregard's** (p. 198) ruined **chapel:** you might find someone to marry on the spot.

6. Among the lucky relics of St. Benedict in the dark crypt of **St. Benoît's basilica** (p. 191): at least no one will see you blush.

7. In **Fontevraud-L'Abbaye** (p. 216): forget syneisaktism—just give into temptation.

8. On the **balcony** of **Chaumont** (p. 199), overlooking the Loire: if you're lucky, the dizzying view will cause your lover to swoon—into your arms.

9. In **Chenonceau's gallery** (p. 208): try to forget that this palace was born out of adultery.

10. Under **Chinon's Tour Marie-Javelle** (p. 211): hope that your love is as strong as the tower, which survived the Hundred Years' War, Wars of Religion, and the Revolution *sans marque.*

local French Holocaust victims and the city of Blois during the war. Though the photographs and memorabilia may be a bit cheesy, the stories—including those about the GI who nearly crashed into the Château of Chambord and the circus elephants that were used to pull down crumbling houses in the town center—make it worth the visit. The museum is staffed by WWII veterans and Resistance members, who give excellent tours. *(1 pl. de la Grève. ☎56 07 02. Open M-F 9am-noon and 2-6pm, Sa 2-6pm. €3, students and under 18 €1. For guides in English, call ahead. Translations of tours available.)* The **Maison de la Magie,** next to the château, entertains with mildly amusing films, optical illusions, and displays dedicated to famous *blésois* magician Robert Houdin (Houdini's stage-name was a tribute to him). The **"hallucinoscope,"** a large optical illusion device, is the most popular attraction. The *spectacle* (magic show), performed three to four times a day, is a bit tacky but provides a half-hour of light-hearted entertainment—especially for children. *(1 pl. du Château. ☎90 33 33; www.maisondelamagie.fr. Open July-Aug. daily 10am-12:30pm and 2-6:30pm; Apr.-June and Sept. Tu-Su 10am-12:30pm and 2-6pm. Free guided tours with reservation. 1½hr. live shows 11:15am, 3:15, 5:15pm; July 20-Aug. 20 11:15am, 2:45, 4, 5:15pm. €7.50, students under 25 €6.50, under 17 €5.)*

NIGHTLIFE AND FESTIVALS

From October through April, the city hosts world-class jazz and classical musicians, dancers, and actors in the **Halle Aux Grains,** 1 pl. de la République. Schedules are available by phone. (☎90 44 00. Performances Tu-F 1:30-6:30pm, Sa 2-5pm. Tickets €19-23, students €16-21.) **Le Soleil à Rendez-Vous avec la Lune** has recently been replaced by **Tous sur le Pont.** Now in its third year, the music festival rocks the town for the first half of July; 2007 featured artists like Iggy & the Stooges. (☎08 92 68 36 22; www.toussurlepont.com. Festival daily 9am-7pm. Festival pass €35.)

Nightlife in Blois may be somewhat toned down, but that does not mean that there aren't a variety of places to finish the night off right. Not too far from the center of the action, **rue de Foulerie** has its own set of less-touristy restaurants and bars, whose crowds spill into the street in the summer.

Le Velvet Jazz Lounge, 15 rue Haute (☎78 36 32), just off rue Denis Papin. Holds weekly jazz concerts (€10 cover, some free) in a casually classy bar with high-vaulted ceilings that testify to its past as a 13th-century abbey. Blois's first non-smoking establishment. Reservations for concerts recommended. Beer €2.50-3.30. Mixed drinks €6.50-8. Concerts held 1st and/or last F of every month 8-11pm. Open Tu-Su 3pm-2am; *salon de thé* open 3-7pm. AmEx/MC/V.

Le Singe Vert, 8 rue de Foulerie (☎78 18 87). This jungle-themed bar serves pint-sized glasses of every cocktail imaginable to the young crowd of regulars. Two goldfish guard the counter. Mixed drinks €6-9.50. Guest DJs F. Open June-Sept. M and W-Su 7pm-2am; Oct.-Apr. Th-Su 7pm-2am. MC/V.

Z 64, 6 rue Maréchal de Lattre de Tassigny (☎74 27 76). Around midnight most–if not all–20-somethings in Blois flock to the neon lights of this downtown club, which is furnished with velvet zebra-patterned couches, Egyptian-like décor, and a large screen showing music videos. Mixed drinks €7.50-9. €4.50 min. Open Th-Sa 10:30pm-5am.

L'Hendrix Café, 1 rue du Puits Châtelet (☎58 82 73). Music and posters from rock icons abound in this popular and boisterous bar. Hang out among young local goths and rockers and sip a "Led Zeppelin" or "Pink Floyd." Beer €2.30-3.80. Mixed drinks €7. Terrace extra €0.20. Open daily June-Sept. 3pm-3am; closed W Oct.-Mar.

DAYTRIPS FROM BLOIS

TLC buses, outside the Blois train station, run a châteaux circuit to **Chambord** and **Cheverny** (3hr. with 1½hr. for each castle). For those who prefer to go at their own pace, the châteaux are within relatively easy **biking** distance through spectacular scenery. From Blois, it's 16km to **Chaumont,** 10km to Cheverny and 6km to **Beauregard.** The châteaux and towns are well marked along the roads. Cyclists should stay off the major highways. The **tourist office** branch across from the Château de Blois distributes maps of safe and efficient routes. The **Regional Tourism Committee** (☎78 62 52; www.loire-valley-travel.com) offers one-week cycling packages.

CHAMBORD

Take the TLC bus from the left of the Blois SNCF station (45min.; May-Sept. 9:10, 11:10am, 1:42pm; €11.20, students €8.90), or bike 1hr. To bike or drive, cross the Loire and ride 1km on av. Wilson. At the roundabout, go straight until St-Gervais-la-Forêt, then turn left onto D33. Château ☎50 40 00; www.chambord.org. Open daily mid-July to mid-Aug. 9am-7:30pm; Apr. to mid-July and mid-Aug. to Sept. 9am-6:15pm; Oct.-Mar. 9am-5:15pm; last entry 30min. before closing. €8.50, July-Aug. €9.50, ages 18-25 €6.50, under 17 free. MC/V.

Built by François I between 1519 and 1545 as a hunting lodge and party house, Chambord (shahm-BOHR) is perhaps the largest and most extravagant of the Loire châteaux. A testament to the monarch's desire to flaunt his flourishing power, the castle could accommodate the entire royal court—up to 10,000 people. With 426 rooms, 365 chimneys, 282 fireplaces and 77 staircases, the castle is a surprising synthesis of forms inherited from past centuries and innovations from Renaissance Italy, bearing the mark of François's interest in a variety of architectural styles. The Greek cross floor design used for the keep (the main tower) was formerly reserved only for sacred buildings, but 25-year-old François co-opted it in his quest for self-deification. In the center of the castle, he built a spectacular double-helix staircase, whose design is attributed to Leonardo da Vinci, and whose hollow, high interior mimics the architecture found in cathedrals. The chapel in the château's right wing has a symmetrical twin in the left wing, but that room was François's bedroom, indicating his desire to be worshipped—even in bed.

The ornamentation of Chambord represents the first influence of the Italian Renaissance on French architecture. François stamped Chambord with 200 of his trademark stone salamanders, commissioned 14m tapestries of his hunting conquests, splayed his initials across the large stone chimneys on the rooftop terrace, and scattered the royal *fleurs de lis* liberally throughout the chambers. After all this, François graced Chambord with his presence for only 72 days; he died before he ever saw his fantastic dream completed. In the 17th century, a new wing was built for Louis XIV. Busts of Molière and Lully—who performed in the castle in 1669—adorn the antechamber to his room. Rooms are labeled in English, but more detailed explanations of the château are available through an audio tour (€4) in many languages. Also available are half-hour historical presentations, guided tours (€4, students €3), and advanced French tours (€6, weekends and holidays) of the castle, as well as a variety of guided excursions into the surrounding forest.

An **ATM** stands next to the snack shops outside the tourist office. To explore the surrounding forests, rent a **boat** or **bike** through **Traineur de Loire** near the château. The boat tour around the castle (€6.50, students €5.50; with castle entrance €12.50/11.50) affords the chance to count the myriad chimneys. (☎33 37 54. 2-person boats €13.50 per hr., 3-person €14.50 per hr., 4-to 5-person €16 per hr. Bikes €5.50 per hr., €10 per ½-day, €13 per day. Tandem €11 per hr. €12 for 15min. boat ride and bottle of wine. Open daily July-Aug. 10am-7:30pm; Sept.-Oct. and Apr.-June 10am-6pm. MC/V.) Medieval shows occur on castle grounds in summer. (☎20 31 01. July-Aug. daily 11:45am and 4:30pm. €8.50, under 18 €6.50). Campers can trek to **Huisseau-sur-Cosson ❶**, 6 rue de Châtillon, 5km southwest of Chambord on D33. (☎20 35 26. Open May-Sept. 9am-noon and 3-8pm. €3.50 per adult, €2.60 per child under 7. €3.50 per tent. Electricity €3.)

CHEVERNY

To bike or drive to the château, head across the Loire on Pont Gabriel and continue straight on av. Wilson. For a long (16-20km) but scenic route, veer toward Chailles when the road splits to Chambord and Chailles. 4km down, turn toward Celletes. Follow signs to Château Troussay, and then Cheverny. Alternatively, take D765 south for 12km. ☎ 79 96 29; www.chateau-cheverny.fr. Open daily July-Aug. 9:15am-6:45pm; Apr.-June and Sept. 9:15am-6:15pm; Jan.-Mar. and Nov.-Dec. 9:45am-5pm; Oct. 9:30am-5:30pm. €6.80, students €5, ages 7-14 €3.40. Call for guided tours in English, German, and Spanish. The same bus that leaves from the SNCF station to Chambord continues to Cheverny.

Ever since its completion in 1634, Cheverny (shay-vayr-NEE) has been privately owned by the Hurault family, whose members have served as financiers and officers to the kings of France. The marquis, his wife, and their three children currently live in the castle, which in 1922 became one of the first privately owned castles to open its doors to visitors. Murals, armor, and elegant tapestries recounting romantic stories cover every inch of the walls in the luxurious Chambre du Roi. In the dining room, a series of paintings by Jean Monier recreate the story of Don Quixote. The portrait of Jeanne d'Aragon in the salon is attributable to the world-famous Renaissance painter Raphael. Fans of Hergé's Tintin books may recognize Cheverny's Renaissance facade as the inspiration for the design of Captain Haddock's mansion, Moulinsart. A gallery of Hergé's art and comics is adjacent to the château's souvenir shop. As well known as the château itself, Cheverny's kennels are home to 120 English-Poitevin hounds still used in hunting expeditions. The *repas de la meurte de chiens* offers a unique opportunity to see these hounds gulp down their chicken and duck dinner at their master's command in less than 60 seconds. (Open Apr. to mid-Sept. M-F 5pm.) Next to the kennels, in the trophy room, thousands of antlers surround a striking stained-glass window depicting a hunt.

Luxurious (but expensive) **Camping Les Saules** ❷ is located 2km south on the road to Contres. Swimming pool and bike rental are on-site. An 18-hole golf course is close by. (☎ 79 90 01; www.camping-cheverny.com. Open daily Apr.-Oct. 8:30am-8:30pm. €15.50-25.50 per site depending on the season; includes 2 people, 1 car, tent, or caravan. €4.50 per extra person, ages 4-10 €2.)

BEAUREGARD

A 30min., 6-8km bike ride from Blois. Left Off D765, en route to Cheverny. A taxi from Blois costs €26. Château: ☎ 70 40 05. Open July-Aug. daily 9:30am-6:30pm; Sept. and Apr.-June daily 9:30am-noon and 2-6pm; Oct.-Nov., mid-Dec. to early Jan., and early Feb.-Mar. M-Tu and Th-Su 9:30am-noon and 2-5pm. €6.50, students and ages 7-18 €4.50, under 8 free. Gardens alone €4.50. Hourly tours are available in French. For English, call ☎ 70 36 74. Information sheets available in multiple languages.

Before François I unleashed his fantasies on Chambord, he designed Beauregard (boh-ruh-GAHR), 6km south of Blois, as a hunting lodge for his uncle René, nicknamed the Bastard of Savoie. Though the château belonged to nobility, it is cozier than its flashy cousin. The portrait gallery, which was commissioned by Paul Ardier, treasurer to Louis XIII, is the world's largest. Today, this collection of 327 wall-to-wall paintings, called the *"Galerie des Illustres,"* is a *Who's Who* of European powers—including the likes of Philippe de Valois, Louis XIII, Elizabeth I, and Columbus. Though unfurnished, the Chamber of Bells *("Cabinets des Grelots")* in the south wing, is covered with remarkable decorative oak paneling, skillfully carved by Jean du Thier, who also worked for Diane de Poitiers. Added in 1996, *Le Jardin Des Portraits*, behind the château, is a classic French garden, with floral sections arranged by color. On your way back out, the ruins of a 15th-century chapel peek through the trees, inviting a walk into the woods.

CHAUMONT

Chaumont is accessible by a 1½hr. bike ride or 20min. car ride from Blois (16km on N152 dir. Tours). By bike, make a right after crossing pont Gabriel and follow D751 to Chaumont. The tourist office directions may suggest you take N152, but it is a large highway. The train that goes from Blois to Tours also runs through Onzain (10min.; M-F 10 per day, Sa-Su 9 per day; €3), From there, it's a 15min. walk to the castle, across the bridge and to the right. The Chaumont tourist office, 24 rue Maréchal Leclerc (☎20 91 73), across the bridge from N152, rents bikes (€8-10 per ½-day, €13 per day. Open W-F 9:30am-7pm, Su 9:30am-1pm and 1:30-6pm). Château ☎51 26 26. Open daily early May to mid-Sept. 9:30am-6:30pm; Apr. to early May and mid-Sept. 10:30am-5:30pm; Oct.-Mar. 10am-12:30pm and 1:30-5pm; last entrance 30min. before closing. €6.50, students €4.50, under 18 free.

Built on a precipice, Chaumont (SHOH-mohn) looks as though it were painted into the sky. The castle stands strikingly—and strategically—overlooking the Loire and was originally built in the 10th century by the Comte de Blois to protect his territories from his rival, the Comte d'Anjou. The marriage of Denise de Fougères to Sulpice d'Amboise delivered Chaumont into the Amboise family's hands. Following Henri II's death in 1559, his widow Catherine de Medici bought the castle in revenge against Diane de Poitiers, Henri's mistress, who resided in the nearby Château of Chenonceau, a royal architectural jewel that Catherine had coveted for years. She then forced Diane to move out of Chenonceau and into Chaumont. While Chaumont is not the most lavish of the Loire châteaux, it is one of the most creatively decorated, with intricate designs on the tile floor and paneled ceilings. Throughout the visit, the history of the castle unfolds, ending with a billiard and sitting room furnished in the style of the 1920s. The grounds and gardens of Chaumont are spectacular, as is the view of the Loire Valley. An international garden festival is also hosted here every year, as gardeners from all over the world compete with impressive botanical displays—which all must accord with the annual theme. The festival is a favorite with children. (☎20 99 22; www.chaumont-jardins.com. Festival daily May to mid-Oct. 9:30am-dusk. Gardens €9, students €6.50, ages 6-18 €3.50. Ticket booth closes at 7pm.)

AMBOISE ☎02 47

Compared to Orléans or Tours, Amboise (am-BWAHZ; pop. 12,000) seems tiny. Its peaceful and picturesque surroundings, however, ensure the town's popularity with visitors—indeed, tourism is its lifeline. One of the oldest cities in the Loire Valley, Amboise produced Charles VIII, Louis XI, Louis XII, Catherine de Medici, and François I. However, Amboise's most famous former resident was actually Italian: Leonardo da Vinci passed his last years here. The town's castle, mysterious cave-dwellings, and breathtaking views of the Loire more than make up for the shamelessly overpriced restaurants and accommodations that pepper Amboise's streets—and budget options can be found if you look hard enough.

TRANSPORTATION. **Trains** run to: Blois (20min., 10 per day, €5.80); Orléans (1hr., every 1½hr., €13); Paris (2¼hr., 1 per hr., €26); Tours (20min., 24 per day, €4.60) from the station at 1 rue de Jules-Ferry. (☎23 47 23. Open M-F 6:15am-9pm, Sa 7:15am-9pm, Su 9am-9:15pm.) **Fil Vert buses** (www.touraine-filvert.com) leave the tourist office for Chenonceau (30min., 2 per day, round-trip €3) and Tours (35min., 1-2 per day, €3). For **Taxis,** 12 quai du Général de Gaulle, call ☎45 19 55. To rent **bikes,** head to **Loca Cycles,** 2bis Jean-Jacques Rousseau, off quai du Général de Gaulle when walking toward the château. (☎57 00 28. €14 per day, €37 per 3 days; passport deposit. Open Mar.-Oct. daily 9am-12:30pm and 2-7pm. Cash only.)

ORIENTATION AND PRACTICAL INFORMATION. To reach the **tourist office,** take a left from the station and follow rue Jules-Ferry until it ends, then take a right. Cross the first bridge to your left and pass the residential Ile d'Or. After crossing the second bridge, turn right immediately; the office is 30m down in a circular building across from the shops on quai du Général de Gaulle. The office posts a list of hotels with vacancies and makes reservations for a €2.50 fee. To avoid the fee, call the hotline (☎23 27 42). A flyer with a self-guided walking tour, as well as maps and discount tickets for various châteaux on the Loire are available year-round. Call the tourist office to reserve. (☎57 09 28; www.amboise-valdeloire.com. Open M-Sa 9am-1pm and 2-6:30pm; schedules change frequently; call for the most up-to-date information. Tours for groups of at least 20 people available daily; €6, students €5. Some tours available in English. Call ahead for individual guided tours). The quai du Général de Gaulle is full of **banks** and **ATMs.** The most central **laundromat** is **LavCentre,** 5 allée du Sergent Turpin, across the road from the tourist office. (Open daily 7am-9pm. Last wash 8pm. Wash €3.70 per 7kg, dry €1 per 10min.) The **police** are at 1 bd. Anatole France (☎30 63 70), and the **hospital, Hôpital Robert Debre,** is on rue des Ursulines (☎23 33 33). Across the street from Ile d'Or Camping, **Pole Jeunesse,** 19 rue d'Ile d'Or, caters to youths' needs and has free **Internet** access. (☎30 55 98; pij.amboise@wanadoo.fr. Internet access M-F 2-5pm. Open M and W-F 9am-noon and 2-5pm, Tu 2-5pm.) **Cyber Café,** 119 rue Nationale, also provides Internet access. (☎57 18 04. €1 per 15min., €3 per hr. Sandwich, drink, and 1hr. Internet access noon-2pm €5. Open M and Su 3-10pm, Tu-Sa 10am-10pm.) Facing the tourist office, turn left and walk three blocks to the **post office** at 20 quai du Général de Gaulle. **Currency exchange** available. (Open M-F 8:30am-12:30pm and 2-6pm, Sa 8:30am-12:30pm.) **Postal Code:** 37400.

ACCOMMODATIONS AND CAMPING. The best budget accommodations are at the **Centre International de Séjour Charles Péguy (HI) ❶,** Ile d'Or. Follow rue Jules Ferry from the station, cross the first bridge on your left, and head downhill to the right immediately after the bridge. The clean and friendly hostel, which doubles as a youth center, is at the edge of the tiny residential island. For a view of the Loire, ask for a room on the third floor. TV room, game room and dining room are reserved for groups. (☎30 60 90; www.mjcamboise.fr. Breakfast €3. Sheets €3. Reception 10am-noon and 2-8pm. Reservations highly recommended. 1- to 4-bed dorms €12. Cash only.) **Hôtel Café des Arts ❷,** 32 rue Victor Hugo, is at the foot of the castle and offers wooden bunk beds in rooms with vibrantly colored décor. There is a sink in each room, and an older but well-maintained bathroom with tub and toilet in the hall. (☎/fax 57 25 04. Reception M and W-F 9am-11pm, Sa-Su 9am-midnight. Closed in Mar. July-Aug. Singles €25; doubles €36; triples €58; quads €73. Sept.-June €25/33/47/58. MC/V.) The three-star **Hôtel Belle-Vue ❹,** 12 quai Charles Guinot, offers tastefully furnished rooms with wooden beds. The terrace overlooking the Loire lends this hotel its name, though only half of the rooms have a view. (☎57 02 26; fax 30 51 23. Breakfast €9. Reception daily 7am-11pm. Singles €49; doubles €59-67; triples €78, quads €88. MC/V.) Located inside a beautiful park, **Ile d'Or camping ❶,** offers such clean, well-maintained facilities that it feels like an outdoor hotel. The riverside campsite has a multilingual staff, pool (€2.20), minigolf (free for guests), and restaurant—all with a view of the Loire. (☎02 46 57 23 37; Oct.-Mar. ☎23 47 38. Reception July-Aug. 7am-9:30pm, June 8am-12:15pm and 2:30-7:30pm, Apr.-May and Sept. 8:30am-12:15pm and 2:30-7:30pm. Apr. to early Sept. July-Aug. €2.45 per adult, €1.70 per child, €3.25 per site. Electricity €2. Shower free; €1.40 for non-campers. Prices drop Apr.-June and Sept. MC/V.)

FOOD. **Rue Victor Hugo** and **rue Nationale,** both at the base of the château, are lined with *brasseries* and bakeries. For a cheap picnic on the Loire, stop by

Marché Plus, 5 quai du Général de Gaulle. (Open M-Sa 7am-9pm, Su 9am-1pm. AmEx/MC/V.) Friday and Sunday mornings, a **market** unfolds along the banks of the river. One of the very first markets in the region, it offers a wide selection of fruits, vegetables, and other regional products (check tourist office for details). The good-humored staff at **Café des Arts ❶,** on the ground floor of the hotel bearing the same name, serves inexpensive sandwiches (€3.10-4.20), hot snacks (€4-6.50), and salads (€2-8.50). Occasional concerts, art exhibits and book readings attract a young, amiable crowd. (Open M and W-F 9am-9pm, Sa-Su 10am-10pm. MC/V.) Locals are willing to bear the tourist crowds to eat at **Chez Hippeau ❸,** 1 rue François 1er, which serves delicious regional treats on a classy terrace or in a sleek, cool interior. The proud owner will be happy to guide you through the many menu options. (☎57 26 30. Variety of large salads €6.80-15. *Menus* €15-24. Open daily July-Aug. noon-3:30pm and 7-10:30pm; Sept.-June noon-2:30pm and 7-9pm. MC/V.) Bountiful books and breakfast (€7.50) welcome you to **Art Thé ❶,** 6 pl. Michel Debre, where customers read, play board games, and drink tea. (Ice cream €2.50. Coffee €2.10. Open daily 9am-7pm. Cash only.)

SIGHTS AND ENTERTAINMENT. Perched atop a precipice overlooking the Loire, the **Château Royal d'Amboise,** between rue Victor Hugo and rue de la Concorde, was once considered one of the most beautiful in France. At one time, its battlements housed as many as 4000 people. In 1560, a failed Protestant conspiracy to kidnap the young king from the influential arch-Catholic family de Guise led to grisly murder: some of the rebel Huguenots were thrown into the Loire in sacks, while others were decapitated or hung on the château balcony, now described by smiling tour guides as the "Balcony of the Hanging People." The **Logis du Roi,** the main part of the château, still holds 2m carved chairs fashioned to prevent surprise attacks from behind. Most of the château was destroyed or sold off during Napoleon's reign; the current building has been heavily restored. The impressive **Tour des Minimes** remains to attest to the size of the original castle; descend its to less-frequented twin, the **Tour Hertault,** as you exit the château's gift shop to get an insider's view of the castle. For a more popular and outstanding view, ascend the **Tour Cavalière** and watch the Loire pass below. The jewel of the visit, however, is the **Chapelle St-Hubert,** an unassuming Gothic chapel next to the château, which holds Leonardo da Vinci's remains. Dim light, delicate stained-glass windows, fresh flowers, and a stone likeness of da Vinci's face all lend the chapel an air of grace. On a less graceful note, if you look toward the ceiling as you enter the chapel, you'll get a glimpse up the stone king's skirts. (☎57 00 98. www.chateau-amboise.com. Open daily July-Aug. 9am-7pm; Apr.-June 9am-6:30pm; Sept. 9am-6pm, Mar. and early to mid-Nov. 9am-5:30pm; mid-Nov. to Jan. 9am-12:30pm and 2-4:45pm; Feb. 9am-12:30pm and 1:30-5pm. €8.50, students €7, ages 7-14 €5. MC/V.)

Built under the walls of the château, the **Caveau des vignerons,** pl. Michel Débre, offers free tastings of locally made wine, goat cheese, *foie gras*, and preserved meats. All products are sold by a friendly staff at affordable prices. (☎57 23 69. Wine €5-40 per bottle. *Foie gras* €2.10-17. Goat cheese €2.10-6.35. Open daily Apr.-Nov. 10am-7pm. MC/V.) From the château, follow the cliffs along narrow and sinuous rue Victor Hugo beside the centuries-old **maisons troglodytiques,** houses built in hollowed-out cliffs. These hollows, originally created during the construction of the château, were used by modest factory workers, who grew gardens on the roofs and carved additional rooms into the rock. Today, many of the houses are abandoned; to peer into abandoned hollows, walk up the dead-end rue Leonard Perrault. **Clos Lucé,** Amboise's quirkiest attraction, rests 400m up rue Victor Hugo. This Renaissance manor and its sprawling gardens were given to Leonardo da Vinci in his last years by his most generous patron, François I, who often visited da Vinci using an underground tunnel that connects Clos Lucé to the château. Da Vinci's bedroom, library, and drawing room, have been renovated to resemble their 16th-century selves, while models of da Vinci's drawings—including one representing the first machine gun in history—rest in the cellar near the entrance to the king's underground tunnel. Twelve giant machines and 32 reproductions of da Vinci's paintings provide ample entertainment in the park. (☎57 00 73. Open daily July-Aug. 9am-8pm; Apr.-June and Sept.-Oct. 9am-7pm; Feb.-Mar. and Nov.-Dec. 9am-6pm; Jan. 10am-5pm. July-Aug. €12, students €9.50, under 18 €7; Sept.-Dec. and Feb.-June €9/7/6. Gardens closed in low season. MC/V.)

The enormous and imaginative drinks at **Le Shaker,** 1 rue de l'Entrepont, on Ile d'Or, come shaken—not stirred—and test even the highest tolerances. A young, rowdy crowd from nearby campsites and hostels gathers in the evenings to drink to the gorgeous Loire River backdrop. (☎23 24 26. Beer €3-6. Mixed drinks €8-10. Snacks €6-8. Open June-Sept. M-Th 6pm-3am and F-Sa 6pm-4am. MC/V.) In the last week of June through the first week of July, 2008, the seventh annual **Les Courants,** a music, film, and art festival, will bring popular French ska, jazz, and rock bands to the region. Amboise's parks usually burst with tents and campers as French youth from around the country come to see their favorite bands. (☎57 09 28; www.lescourants.com. Tickets €15-40.) A **brass band** festival also visits on the second weekend of June, bringing with it marching tunes and classical music. (Tickets €6-15. Call the tourist office for more info.)

TOURS ☎02 47

According to famous French author Balzac, Tours (TOOR; pop. 137,000) is "laughing, in love, fresh, flowery and perfumed better than all the other cities of the world." Although Balzac might have been confusing his birthplace with his idea of the perfect woman, Tours has charmed travelers and the French alike since the Roman era. Born out of the chaos of the Hundred Years' War (1337-1453), it reigned as the heart of the French kingdom in the 15th and 16th centuries. During WWII, the city sustained enormous losses, and few monuments remain to attest to its former status. Today, joggers fill the paths along the banks of the Loire, and after sunset the city's 30,000 local and foreign students take over the café-lined boulevards and the animated pl. Plumereau ("place Plum" to locals). Famous for its lack of a local accent, this capital of *"le bien-parlé"* ("the well-spoken") is the best place to perfect your French while visiting the valley's châteaux.

TRANSPORTATION

Trains: Pl. du Général Leclerc. Info office open M-Sa 5:50am-9:30pm, Su 5:50am-11:30pm. Trains go to **Paris** (3hr., every hr., €28.20), **Poitiers** (50min., 6 per day, €15), and **Saumur** (40min., 12 per day, €10) via St-Pierre-des-Corps. TGV runs to **Bordeaux** (4½hr., every hr., €44), **Paris** (1hr., every hr., €53), and **Poitiers** (1hr., 13 per day, €18) via St-Pierre-des-Corps.

Public Transportation: Fil Bleu, 5 rue de la Dolve (☎66 70 70). Office open M-F 7:30am-7pm, Sa 8:30am-1:30pm. Buses run daily 6am-8:30pm and occasionally at night; map available from the Fil Bleu office near the train station. Tickets €1.20, weekly passes €12 with ID photo.

Taxis: Taxis-Radio, 13 rue de Nantes (☎20 30 40). €1.40 per km during the day, €2.10 at night. 24hr.

Car Rental: Avis (☎20 53 27) in the train station. From €91 per day. Under-25 surcharge €25. Open M-F 8am-12:30pm and 1:30-6:30pm, Sa 9am-noon and 2-6pm. AmEx/MC/V. **Europcar,** 76 rue Bernard Palissy (☎64 47 76). From €91 per day.

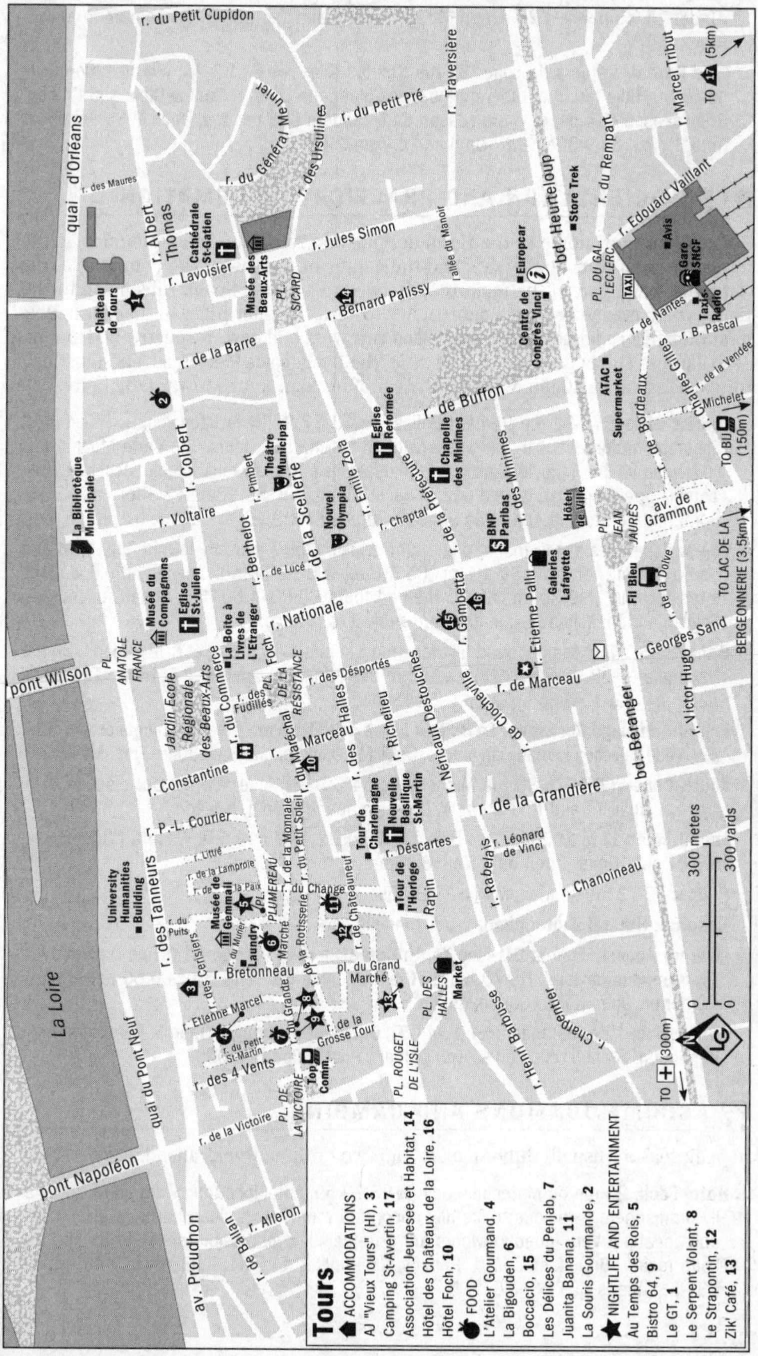

LOIRE VALLEY

Under-25 insurance €25. Open M-F 8am-noon and 2-6:30pm, Sa 9am-noon and 2-6pm. MC/V.

Bike Rental: Détours de Loire, 35 rue Charles Gîles. (☎61 22 23; www.locationdevelos.com). Bike return at different locations along the Loire, including Blois and Chinon. High season €14 per day, low season €11; tandem €38 per day. Open M-Sa 9am-1pm and 2-7pm, Su 9:30am-12:30pm and 6-7pm. MC/V.

ORIENTATION AND PRACTICAL INFORMATION

Place Jean Jaurès, home to the Hôtel de Ville and two bombastic fountains, is the intersection of four boulevards and the center of the town. The commercial **rue Nationale,** once part of the main road between Paris and Spain, runs north to the Loire, while **avenue de Grammont** reaches toward the Cher River to the south. **Boulevard Béranger** and **boulevard Heurteloup** run west and east, respectively, from pl. Jean Jaurès. The pedestrian *vieille ville*, the lively **place Plumereau,** and most historical sights are a 10min. walk northwest of pl. Jean Jaurès toward the Loire.

Tourist Office: 78-82 rue Bernard Palissy (☎70 37 37; www.ligeris.com). Free maps, accommodations booking, and reservations for châteaux tours. The Carte Multi-Visites (€7; valid for 1 yr.) provides access to 6 museums and a city tour. Internet access €1 per 15min. Open mid-Apr. to mid-Oct. M-Sa 8:30am-7pm, Su 10am-12:30pm and 2:30-5pm; mid-Oct. to mid-Apr. M-Sa 9am-12:30pm and 1:30-6pm, Su 10am-1pm.

Tours: Schedules at the tourist office. 2hr. walking tours mid-July to mid-Aug. M-Th and Sa-Su 10am; Apr.-Nov. Su 10am. €5.50, ages 6-12 €4.50. 2hr. nighttime walking tours July-Aug. F 9:30pm. €9/7. Themed tours €5.50/4.50. Call ahead for tours in English and for schedules, as they are subject to change.

Bank: 24hr. ATMs can be found all along rue Nationale, including at BNP Paribas, 86 rue Nationale (☎08 92 70 57 05), near rue des Minimes. Open M 2-5:45pm, Tu-F 9am-12:15pm and 1:30-6pm, Sa 9am-12:45pm.

English-Language Bookstore: La Boîte à Livres de l'Etranger, 2 rue du Commerce (☎05 67 29). Wide selection in many languages. Open M 10am-7pm, Tu-Sa 9:30am-7pm. MC/V.

Youth Center: BIJ, 78-80 rue Michelet (☎64 69 13). Free Internet access with daily sign-up. Open Tu and Th 1-6pm, W 10am-noon and 1-6pm, F 1-4pm.

Laundromat: Lavo 2000, 17 rue Bretonneau (☎02 47 73 14 69). Wash €3.80 per 8kg, dry €1 per 10min. Open daily 7am-8:30pm.

Police: 70-72 rue de Marceau (☎33 80 69).

Hospital: Hôpital Bretonneau, 2 bd. Tonnellé (☎47 47 47).

Internet Access: Free at **BIJ** (see **Youth Center**) and at the **Tourist Office** (see above). **Top Communications,** 68-70 rue du Grand Marché (☎76 19 53). €0.50 per 10min., €2 per hr. Open daily 10am-midnight.

Post Office: 1 bd. Béranger (☎60 34 05). **Currency exchange.** Open M-F 8am-7pm, Sa 8am-noon. Branch office on 92 rue Colbert. **Postal Code:** 37000.

ACCOMMODATIONS AND CAMPING

In peak season (usually July-August), call two or three weeks ahead.

Hôtel Foch, 20 rue du Maréchal Foch (☎05 70 59; hotel-foch.tours@wanadoo.fr). Family atmosphere, spacious, tastefully decorated rooms, and clean baths in an unbeatable location. Very friendly owners are extremely knowledgeable about Tours and the Loire region. Breakfast €5.50. Parking €5. Singles €20-34; doubles €23-46; triples €37-58; quads €51-58. MC/V. ❷

AJ "Vieux Tours," (HI), 5 rue Bretonneau (☎37 81 58; www.ajtours.org). Former student dorm with 146 rooms. Doubles, triples, and quads with single beds, sink, and balcony. Shared bathroom and kitchen. TV lounge on every fl. Breakfast included. Internet €1.50 per 15min. Reception daily 8am-noon and 5-11pm. Dorms €18. AmEx/MC/V. ❶

Association Jeunesse et Habitat, 16 rue Bernard Palissy (☎60 51 51; ajn.ufjt.tours@numericable.fr). Centrally located hostel with long-term housing for workers and students. Large, renovated rooms are pristine and have personal baths. Kitchen on 1st and 3rd floors. Small gym with climbing wall and ping-pong table. Breakfast €1.95, other meals €5.40-7.60. Laundry €3, €2 dry. Free Internet access. Reception M-Sa 8am-7pm. Singles with shower €18; doubles with bath €26. MC/V. ❶

Hôtel des Châteaux de la Loire, 12 rue Gambetta (☎05 10 05; www.hoteldeschateaux.fr). Rooms with garishly floral wallpaper and bedspreads. Amiable staff and elegant lobby make up for lack of taste elsewhere. All rooms with shower or bath, toilet, and cable TV. Breakfast €6.60. Parking €6. Open mid-Feb. to mid-Dec. Singles €43-52; doubles €43-61; triples €62-67. AmEx/MC/V. ❹

Camping St-Avertin, 61 rue de Rochepinard in St-Avertin (☎27 27 60). Take bus #5 from rue Nationale to Cottier stop, take a left over the bridge, and follow the signs (30 min., every 15min., €1.20). Tennis, volleyball and swimming nearby. Rather small sites with limited shade. Reception 8am-10pm. Curfew 10pm. In summer, reserve 1-2 mo. ahead. Open Apr. to mid-Oct. €3.60 per adult, €2.40 per child under 10, €3.60 per site, €6 per car, €6.50 per caravan. Electricity €3-4.80. AmEx/MC/V. ❶

FOOD

Rue Colbert and the streets around **place Plumereau** have dozens of pleasant outdoor options, including many *crêperies* with *menus* under €12. Bistros and pubs crowd **place Jean Jaurès.** Be sure to try the melt-in-your-mouth *macarons à l'ancienne* and anything *aux pruneaux* (with prunes). The light, fruity white wines of Vouvray, Monmousseau, and Montlouis are all worth a sip. In the summer, **place des Halles,** the indoor food market (M-Sa 7:30am-noon and 2-7pm, Su 7:30am-1pm), extends outdoors Wednesday and Saturday mornings (7am-noon). On the first Friday of the month (4-10pm), the *marché gourmand,* **place de la Résistance** sells gourmet products. A *marché traditionnel* sells fresh produce Tuesdays (8am-noon) in front of the tourist office. Find groceries at the **ATAC** supermarket, 5 pl. du Maréchal Leclerc (open M-Sa 7:30am-8pm; AmEx/MC/V) or at the supermarket in **Galeries Lafayette,** north of pl. Jean Jaurès. (Open M-Sa 9am-7:30pm. AmEx/MC/V.)

La Souris Gourmande, 100 rue Colbert (☎47 04 80). Cheese lovers congregate here for the delicious selection of *fromage* dishes, which are almost overshadowed by the astonishingly omnipresent bovine décor. Fondue €13-14 (min. 2 people). *Crêpes* €6.50. Omelettes €8-9. Open Tu-Sa noon-2pm and 7-10:30pm. MC/V. ❶

Juanita Banana, 13 rue du Change (☎64 91 12). Keeps its customers coming back with experimental dishes (foie gras bathed in Coca Cola €16) and an all-encompassing dining experience. Definitely on the new wave of French cuisine, this unique restaurant bases its menu and décor on a theme that changes every few months. Salads €10. *Plats* €10-20. Open Tu-Sa 10am-3pm and 6pm-2am. MC/V. For more information about Juanita Banana, see p. 206. ❸

L'Atelier Gourmand, 37 rue Etienne Marcel (☎38 59 87). Enjoy international variations on traditional dishes at this contemporary restaurant in the heart of *vieux* Tours. Art exhibits and a pleasant terrace add to the experience. An affordable lunch *menu* (€10) makes fine cuisine accessible to students. Appetizers €8-10. *Plats* €15-20. Desserts €6. Open M and Sa 7:30-10pm, Tu-F noon-2pm and 7:30-10pm. MC/V. ❸

FOOD FOR THOUGHT

The Loire Valley may be deeply set in its culinary ways, but one man in Tours is pushing the limits. His name is François Barbato, and his restaurant, **Juanita Banana** (p. 205), has set the pace for a new dining trend in one of France's most historic cities. Barbato's restaurant embraces a new style called "Fooding," a term coined by French journalist Alexandre Camas in January 1999. The word comes from the combination of "food" and "feeling" and offers a way for chefs to emancipate themselves from strict French culinary traditions by intellectualizing cooking—bringing psychology, philosophy, chemistry, and physics into food.

In his restaurant, Barbato carefully engineers the combination of food and atmosphere to create a complete dining experience. The menu—and its complementary décor—changes every few months based on a theme Barbato has thoroughly researched beforehand. Often inspired by the work of local artists, past themes have included "melting pot," "the particle," and "the Renaissance." If Barbato's dishes disturb his guests—if someone won't eat their rice because it's pink—he knows he is doing something right. Best of all, Barbato's innovative cuisine comes without designer prices, as delectable *plats* start at €10.

Juanita Banana, 13 rue du Change. ☎02 47 64 91 12.

La Bigouden, 3 rue du Grand Marché (☎64 21 91). Stands out among *crêperies* near pl. Plumereau. The camembert and jam *crêpe* (€4.80) is a local favorite. *Galettes* €2-7.60. Desserts €1.70-8.10. Open M-Tu and F-Sa noon-2pm and 7-11pm, Th and Su 7-11pm. Reservations recommended in high season. MC/V. ❷

Les Délices du Penjab, 53 rue du Grand Marché (☎28 64 06). Indian restaurant offering healthy vegetarian dishes for surprisingly low prices. Small, family-run feel. Take-out also available. Appetizers €2.90-3.90. Lassi €3.50. *Plats* €4.50-6.90. *Menus* €15-18. Open Tu-Su noon-2pm and 7-11pm. AmEx/MC/V. ❷

Boccacio, 9 rue Gambetta (☎05 45 22). Tucked-away pizzeria with slick brick décor. Locals come for crisp wood-oven pizzas (€9-11) and thick tiramisu (€5). Lunch *menus* €12-14. Open Th noon-2pm and 7-9:30pm, F-Sa noon-2pm and 7:30-10pm. MC/V. ❷

SIGHTS

You may be surprised to find that there is no château drenched in Renaissance pomp waiting for you in this Loire Valley city. Tours's château deteriorated due to neglect long ago, leaving only one tower to tell the tale. Henri III had his archrival's son, the second Duc de Guise, imprisoned here during the Wars of Religion, but the duke escaped by tricking his guards into hopping on one foot as he ran away. The tower now holds free temporary art exhibits. (☎70 88 46.) If you seek peace and quiet instead of museums and churches, head to **Lac de la Bergeonnerie** (also called Lac de Tours), a 10min. bus ride away on line #1. Don't forget that the **Carte Multi-Visites** (€7; valid for 1 year), available at the tourist office, offers access to Tours's five museums and includes one guided tour of the city.

CATHÉDRALE ST-GATIEN. Though not much is known about Saint Gatien, this flamboyant gothic edifice was erected in his name. As this cathedral was built and rebuilt a total of five times over 1100 years, the intricate facade combines centuries of architectural caprice. The two Renaissance spires are unusually asymmetrical, the south being significantly shorter. Allegedly, this one symbolizes royal power, while the north spire stands for spirituality—a message that the king's power does not outlast that of God. The **Psalette Cloister,** on the north end of the cathedral, holds a model of François I's staircase from the Château de Blois, and was the location of a scene in Balzac's *La Comédie Humaine.* *(Pl. de la Cathédrale. Cathedral ☎70 21 00, cloister ☎47 05 19. Cathedral open daily 9am-7pm. Free. Cloister open May-Sept. M-Sa*

9:30am-12:30pm and 2-6pm; Apr. daily 10am-noon and 2-5:30pm; Oct.-Mar. Th-Sa 9:30am-12:30pm and 2-5pm. €3, students and under 18 free.)

TOWERS OF BASILIQUE ST-MARTIN. The Tour de l'Horloge and Tour de Charlemagne reveal the incredible proportions of the fifth-century Basilique St-Martin. As the building was destroyed due to neglect and pillage after the Revolution, the two towers, fenced off due to their fragility, are all that remain. Saint Martin, the city's first bishop, now rests in the Nouvelle Basilique St-Martin, an ornate *fin-de-siècle* church designed by Victor Laloux, the architect of the Musée d'Orsay in Paris. *(Entrance on Rue Descartes. ☎05 63 87. Open daily 8am-8pm. Mass daily 11am.)*

MUSÉE DE COMPAGNONS. The ancestor of France's famous unions, the Compagnons, is a semi-secret society that produces the nation's most talented workers and craftsmen. Though legend claims *compagnons* have been in existence since King Solomon first gathered men to build the temple of Jerusalem, their origins can be officially traced back only to the Middle Ages, when the French first started building cathedrals. Discover their centuries of legacy and impressive handiwork—such as a sugar palace the size of a table. *(8 rue Nationale. ☎21 62 20. Open mid-June to mid-Sept. M and W-Su 9am-12:30pm and 2-6pm; mid-Sept. to mid-June 9am-noon and 2-6pm. €4.90, students and seniors €2.90, under 12 free.)*

MUSÉE DES BEAUX-ARTS. A succession of stunning salons, the Musée des Beaux-Arts is located in what was once the archbishop's palace. The architecture and outdoor gardens are as much—if not more—of an attraction as the art within. The upper floors house pieces from the 17th to 19th centuries, including works by Delacroix, Rembrandt, Monet, and Rodin. Outside, an impressive **Lebanese cedar,** planted during Napoleon's reign in 1804, stretches its tortuous branches over 800 square meters. *(18 pl. François Sicard, next to the cathedral. ☎05 68 73; museebeauxarts@ville-tours.fr. Museum open M and W-Su 9am-12:45pm and 2-6pm. Gardens open daily in high season 7am-8:30pm; in low season 7am-6pm. €4, students and seniors €2.)*

MUSÉE DU GEMMAIL. Located in an ivy-strewn courtyard, this unique museum is dedicated to an art form that originated in Tours in the 1950s. *Gemmail* is brightly colored glass melded together to form mosaics. Unlike stained-glass windows, the pieces do not include any form of metal. Works range from original pieces to interpretations of classics, including Leonardo da Vinci's *Mona Lisa* (p. 145) and Picasso's *Deux Femmes*. Don't miss the pieces in the 12th-century underground chapel, accessible through the door below the entrance. *(7 rue du Murier. Off rue Bretonneau, near pl. Plumereau. ☎61 01 19. Open Mar.-Oct. Tu-Su 2-6:30pm. €5.50, students €4, ages 13-18 €3, under 12 €2.)*

FESTIVALS AND NIGHTLIFE

Late June brings the **Fêtes Musicales en Touraine,** a 10-day celebration of classical music. (☎21 65 08; www.fetesmusicales.com. €12-23 per night.) Tours also hosts the 10-day **Jazz en Touraine** (☎50 72 70) festival every September, and the **Acteurs-Acteurs** (☎38 29 29; www.ciecanolopez.fr.) film and theater festival in the spring. The **Olympia,** 7 rue de Lucé (☎4 50 50), and **Le Grand Théâtre de Tours,** 34 rue de la Scellerie (☎60 20 00; www.tours.fr.), put on productions year-round. Call the tourist office for info on all festivities.

The most happening nightlife is on **place Plumereau,** whose lively cafés and bars overflow with chatty students in the summer. Three clubs on the square cluster together, while **rue du Commerce,** off pl. Plumereau, booms with busy bars.

Au Temps des Rois, 3 pl. Plumereau (☎05 04 51). A doll, a barrel, T-shirts, and old theater posters hang from the ceiling at this local favorite, known for its catchy music and cheap prices. Mingle with an international crowd while enjoying a beer (€2.50-5) in the city's liveliest district. Open daily 8:30am-2am. AmEx/MC/V.

Bistro 64, 64 rue du Grand Marché. Jazz lovers unite in this mellow bar, housed in one of Tours's restored medieval buildings. Enjoy concerts (Sept.-June Th 9:30pm) and a boisterous atmosphere while sipping on one of their famously plentiful mojitos (€6). Beer €4. Open M-Sa 11am-2am, Su 3pm-2am. Cash only.

Le Strapontin, 23-25 rue de Chateauneuf (☎47 02 74). A blood red décor designed by the artist-owner is punctuated by oversized cartoons and original pieces. A classy crowd sips fair-trade cocktails (€5.50) to revamped electro. Open M-Sa 5pm-2am. MC/V.

Le Serpent Volant, 54 rue du Grand Marché (☎38 59 10). This intimate, well-worn bar is a local favorite. An eclectic literary crowd enjoys occasional book readings, chess tournaments, slam poetry, and open mic nights. Beer €2.30-3.40. Mixed drinks €2.50-4.50. Open M 5pm-2am, Tu-Sa 11am-2am. Cash only.

Zik' Café, 5 rue des 3 Ecritoires (☎38 81 00). Caters to music lovers of all stripes. Locals can occasionally play DJ and spin their own mixes amid more typical rock, reggae, and electro. Homemade punch €2. Pint of beer €2.20. Mixed drinks €2.50. Happy hour daily 6-8:30pm. Open M-Sa 5pm-2am. MC/V.

Le GI, 13 rue Lavoisier (☎66 29 96). House, disco, and techno throb in blue and black lighting for a gay crowd of all ages. Mirrors and a zebra-motif set the scene on the 1st fl., as the sounds of themed soirées blast from the basement. Mixed drinks €8. 18+. Cover F €7, Sa €10; includes 1 drink. Open W-Su 11:30pm-5am. MC/V.

DAYTRIPS FROM TOURS: NEARBY CHÂTEAUX

Dozens of beautiful castles lie within 60km of Tours. Driving is an effective, though generally expensive, way to visit towns that cannot be reached by public transportation. Biking among châteaux is more economical and scenic (see p. 209). Minibus tours depart from Tours every day. **Alienor,** 35 rue Charles Gîles, is staffed by a very friendly English-speaking tour guides. (☎06 10 85 35 39. Tours €18-47.) For other tour companies, contact **St-Eloi Excursions** (☎06 70 82 78 75; www.saint-eloi.com; ½-day excursions €19-31, full-day €43-49), **Acco-Dispo Excursions** (☎06 82 00 64 51; www.accodispo-tours.com. ½-day excursions €19-31, full-day €43-49), or **Quart de Tours** (☎06 30 65 52 01; www.quartdetours.com. ½-day excursions €20-34, full-day €44-50). All tours have English-speaking guides. Most châteaux have free guided tours and performances during the summer.

The Loire Valley is known not just for its royal châteaux, but also its fantastic wines. Cellars often offer free *dégustations*. Ask for a free copy of the *Route des Vignobles* at the tourist office, which contains a comprehensive list of the 618 wine cellars with their contact information and hours of operation. **The Wine Tour,** also run by Alienor, 35 rue Charles Gîles, offers tours of some of the region's most famous vineyards. By bus, take #61 (20min., M-Sa 7 per day, €1.15) from pl. Jean Jaurès to les Patis. (☎06 10 85 35 39. Red tour €60, lunch included; white tour €35.) In Montlouis, across the river to the south, 10 *caves* pour wonderful dry whites. Trains run from Tours (10min., M-Sa 3 per day, €2.40).

CHENONCEAU

Trains run to Chenonceau from Tours (30min., 8 per day 9am-9pm, €5.70). The station is directly in front of the château entrance. Fil Vert buses leave for Chenonceau from Amboise (25min., M-Sa 2 per day, €1.50) and Tours (1hr., M-Sa 2 per day, €1.50). Château ☎23 90 07. Open daily July-Aug. 9am-8pm; June and Sept. 9am-7:30pm; Apr.-May 9am-7pm; Oct. 1-Oct. 27 9am-6:30pm; Oct. 28-Nov. 4 9am-6pm; Nov. 5-Feb. 9 9:30am-5pm; Feb.10-Mar. 15 9:30am-6pm; Mar. 16-Mar. 31 9:30am-7pm. Light show 9:30-

TIP **CHÂTEAUX HOPPING.** Few châteaux are accessible by public transportation, but travelers have other options. Renting a car provides the most freedom, but often at prohibitive prices. **Biking** is cheapest. With several dropoff locations along the Loire, **Détours de Loire** (☎61 22 23; www.locationdevelos.com) offers convenience and competitive prices for bicycles (€14 per day), but it's hard to cover more than 2 châteaux per day. For those in a hurry, plush minibuses depart from Tours every day at 9am or 1pm and visit 2 to 3 châteaux in a half-day (€19-31) or 4 to 5 in a full day (€43-49). Companies include: **Acco-Dispo Excursions** (☎06 82 00 64 51); **Alienor** (☎06 10 85 35 39); **Quart de Tours** (☎06 30 65 52 01); **St-Eloi Excursions** (☎06 70 82 78 75).

11pm. Castle €9.50, students €7.50. Entry to Château des Dames *wax museum €1.50 extra. Ipod audio tour in 12 languages €4.*

Perhaps the most elegant castle in France, Chenonceau (shuh-nohn-SOH) arches gracefully over the Cher River. Take the less-traveled pedestrian walk for a view of the donkeys' field, the 16th-century farm, and the flower garden.

This *château des dames* (castle of the ladies) owes its beauty to centuries of female designers. Royal tax collector Thomas Bohier originally commissioned the Venetian-inspired château. However, while he fought in the Italian Wars (1513-21), his wife Katherine oversaw the château's practical design, which features Italian staircases and four rooms branching from a central chamber. In 1547, King Henri II gave the château to his mistress, Diane de Poitiers, in line with official court rules, for her "great and commendable services." Endowed with beauty, intelligence, and a thirst for wealth and fame, Diane turned the castle into a profitable venture, considerably boosting its value by adding luxurious gardens and an arched bridge over the Cher so she could hunt in the nearby forest. Later, Henri's wife, Catherine de Medici, forced Diane to give up the castle in exchange for the less spectacular Chaumont (see p. 199). She designed her own gardens and the magnificent two-story gallery atop Diane's bridge as a way to assert her domination over her late husband's mistress. You may notice that Diane's chambers are stamped with 'H's and 'C's, the initials of the royal couple. When intertwined, these initials form the letter D (for Diane), an ambiguity that amused Henri but not his wife. The 60m long gallery is lit by 18 windows (nine on each side) overlooking the Cher and often hosts art exhibitions. During the world wars, the gallery served as a hospital and a means of smuggling Jews across the border—its north end being in occupied territory and its south end leading to the Petains's "free" (a.k.a safe) zone. Perhaps the most peculiar chamber is that of Louise de Lorraine, which is paneled all in black to accommodate the 12 years during which Lorraine mourned the mysterious death of her husband, Henri III. In the 18th and 19th centuries the Dupin family—who still owns the château today—lightened the mood, welcoming such visitors as Voltaire, Rousseau, and Flaubert. **La Cave des Domes,** next to the restaurant, offers wine tastings for €1. (Open daily 10:30am-1pm and 2-6:15pm.)

VILLANDRY

Trains leave from Tours to Savonnières (10min., 3 per day, €2.80). Fil Vert makes 2 trips W and Sa from the halte routière *to the tourist office in Villandry (2:10 and 6pm, return 1:15 and 5:15pm; €1.50). Many tour agencies run buses to the castle (see p. 209). From Tours, cyclists can travel 15km west along D16, a road that winds past Villandry; drivers should take D7. Château ☎50 02 09; www.chateauvillandry.com. Open daily July-Aug. 9am-6:30pm; late Mar. to June and Sept.-Oct. 9am-6pm; early Mar. 9am-5:30pm; Feb. 9am-5pm; Christmas holidays open 9:30am-4:30pm. Gardens open daily July-Aug. 9am-7:30pm; Sept. and late Mar. to June 9am-7pm; Oct. 9am-6:30pm; early Mar. 9am-6pm; Feb. and early Nov. 9am-*

LOIRE VALLEY

5:30pm. Château and gardens €8, students €5. Gardens only €5.50/3.50. Free tours in French. The tourist office, across D7 from the château, has maps and train schedules. ☎50 12 66. Open July-Aug. M-Sa 10am-7pm, Su 10am-noon and 1-7pm; Apr.-June daily 9:30am-12:30pm and 2-6pm; Jan.-Mar. and Sept.-Oct. M-Sa 9:30am-12:30pm and 2-6pm; Nov. to mid-Dec. M-Sa 9:30am-12:30pm and 2-5pm.

Villandry (VEEL-ahn-DREE) lives up to its claim of having the most beautiful gardens in France. With 125,000 flowers and 85,000 vegetables (all weeded by hand) it is certainly among the largest. Built on the banks of the Cher by Jean le Breton, minister to François I, the château was falling to pieces when the Spanish couple, the Carvallos, stumbled upon it in the 1920s. They fell in love with Villandry on the spot and decided to dedicate their lives to the renovation of the building and the reconstruction of the gardens. Save some euro and settle for a walk through Villandry's main attraction—which is vastly more interesting than the castle itself.

The château's elegant grounds are designed according to three historical styles. The *Potager*, filled with aromatic and medicinal herbs, follows medieval tradition. The middle level unfolds into symmetric patterns typical of the Renaissance—each of its four square "gardens of love" creates an allegory for a different type of love: tender, passionate, fickle, and tragic. The upper-level, lined with lime groves, contains a Classical swan pool, with waterfalls that provide irrigation for the rest of the grounds. An overgrown labyrinth completes the botanical experience.

AZAY-LE-RIDEAU

Trains run from Tours to the town of Azay-le-Rideau (25min.; M-F 9 per day 7:35am-7:29pm, Sa 5 per day 9am-6:30pm, Su 3 per day 2-9pm; €4.70). Turn right from the station and head left on D57 for 20min. Buses run from the Tours train station to the tourist office (50min.; 3 per day 6:40am-5:50pm; €5.20). Château ☎45 42 04. Open daily July-Aug. 9:30am-7pm; Apr.-June and Sept. 9:30am-6pm; Oct.-Mar. 9:30am-12:30pm and 2-5:30pm. Last entrance 45min. before closing. Light show daily early to mid-July 9:45-10:15pm; mid-July to mid-Aug. 10pm; mid-Aug. to mid-Sept. 9pm. Château €7.50, show €9, both €12; under 25 €4.80/5/7; under 18 free. Gardens €3. Guided tour €4, students €3; audio tour €4. The tourist office is at 4 rue du Château. (☎45 44 40; www.ot-paysazaylerideau.fr. Open July-Aug. M-Sa 9am-7pm, Su 10am-6pm; May-June and Sept. M-Sa 9am-1pm and 2-6pm, Su 10am-1pm and 2-5pm; Oct.-Apr. M-Sa 9am-1pm and 2-6pm.)

Surrounded by acres of trees and grass atop a dreamy island in the Indre river, the flamboyant château at Azay-le-Rideau (AH-zay luh ree-DOH) stands on the ruins of a fortress. The village acquired the nickname "Azay-le-Brûlé" (Azay the Burned) during the Hundred Years' War, when Charles VII, insulted by a castle guard rooting for the British, razed it to the ground in revenge. The corrupt financier Gilles Berthelot bought the land and built a new castle on the ruins of the old—with state money. Though smaller than François I's Chambord, the château was intended to rival its contemporary in beauty, and Berthelot succeeded so thoroughly that he had to flee the country before the king could have him executed, leaving his wife and beloved, unfinished castle. In symbolic punishment, François seized the château as royal property, which explains the crownless salamanders—marking a non-royal building built under François—on the external walls above the doors.

Azay's Renaissance style is apparent in the furniture and the ornate Italian second-floor staircase carved with the faces of 10 Valois kings and queens and lit by open windows. Portraits of the royal family and other members of the 16th- and 17th-century French aristocracy hang on the walls. The Gothic influence appears in the *grande salle* (grand drawing room), where 16th-century tapestries still hang. Before leaving Azay, take a romantic stroll through the misty grounds and listen to the croaking of the frogs living in the moat.

CHINON

Trains buses run from the Tours station to Chinon (45min.; M-F 8 per day, Sa 4 per day, Su 3 per day; €7.90. SNCF buses also leave the Tours station for Chinon (M-F 3 per day, Su 1 per day; €7.90). To drive from Tours, take highway D751 southwest (dir.: Azay le Rideau).

Resting between the banks of the Vienne River and the crumbling château where Richard the Lionheart drew his last breath, Chinon (SHEE-nohn) was one of the most important cities in France under the reign of Henri II, King of England and Anjou. Its glory days left behind a charming town whose narrow, café-filled streets rest at the foot of the hill crowned by Chinon's former fortress. In honor of native son and great Renaissance philosopher-writer François Rabelais, the town's streets and establishments bear his characters' names. Vineyards that produce the region's renowned red wines and the distinctive *confiture de vin de Chinon*, a delicious wine jam, surround Chinon.

For a charming stroll from town, take the less-traveled Impasse du Roberdeau past the ivy-covered ramparts to reach the ruins of Chinon's 10th-century **château,** scheduled to be under extensive restoration until early 2009. The grounds host three main fortresses, each constructed in a different era, which are connected by secret underground tunnels. The 14th-century **Tour de l'Horloge** has withstood the Hundred Years' War, the Wars of Religion, and the French Revolution without a blemish, protected by the popular legend that anyone who captured the bell tower would die a horrible death. Its bell, called *Marie Javelle*, has allegedly struck every half-hour since 1399. The **Musée de Jeanne d'Arc** that occupies the three-story tower is dedicated to the young warrior, who met with the dauphin in the *grande salle* of the château in 1429. As the story goes, the dauphin, to make sure she was not a fake, hid in the crowd while a mere guard sat in his throne. Joan was not fooled and noticed the dauphin, thus dispelling all doubts Charles VII might have had about her intuition. Slide shows detailing Joan's military campaigns are screened in French. (☎93 13 45; www.cg37.fr. Open daily Apr.-Sept. 9am-7pm; Oct.-Mar. 9:30am-5pm. Ticket office closes 30min. early. For free tours in English, French, or German call ahead. €3 during renovations. MC/V.)

After the climb down from the castle, enjoy a **wine tasting** at **Caves Plouzeau,** 94 rue Haute St-Maurice, in the heart of the *vieille ville*. Marc Plouzeau conducts **free tours** in a *cave* (wine cellar) beneath the château. (☎93 32 11; www.plouzeau.com. Open Apr.-Sept. Tu-Sa 11am-1pm and 3-7pm; Oct.-Mar. Sa only) The **Caves Painctes de Chinon,** rue Voltaire, form an extensive network of underground tunnels and cellars running beneath Chinon's castle. Adorned with chandeliers constructed from empty wine bottles and a natural fountain, this *cave* was where Rabelais stored his wine. (☎93 30 44; www.caves-painctes.abc-salles.com. Tours July-Aug. Tu-Su 11am, 3, 4:30, 6pm. €3; includes *dégustation*.)

On the third Saturday in August, all of Chinon turns out for **Marché à l'Ancienne,** which features regional foods like **fouaces** (a popular medieval pastry immortalized by Rabelais in one of his novels) and a parade of citizens costumed in late 19th-century garb. The **Avoine Zone Blues** brings jazz, blues, and rock groups from France and elsewhere in the first weekend of July. (Info ☎02 47 98 11 15. Tickets from €30, students from €15; some concerts free.) **Cinéma Le Rabelais,** 31bis pl. du Général de Gaulle, plays French and American films nightly. (☎08 92 68 47 07. Tickets €6.80, students €5.80.)

There is a **Shopi** supermarket at 22 pl. de l'Hôtel de Ville (open M-Sa 7:30am-7:30pm, Su 8:30am-12:30pm; AmEx/MC/V) and an **open-air market** every Thursday (open 7am-1pm) on pl. Jeanne d'Arc and every Sunday (open 7am-1pm) on pl. de l'Hôtel de Ville.

Stroll along rue Voltaire and around pl. de l'Hôtel de Ville to find the best cheap meals in town. For local cuisine, try **La Bonne France ❸,** 4 pl. de la Victoire. In a

LOIRE VALLEY

15th-century house, this quiet spot offers regionally themed *formules*, such as the "Provence" or "Touraine" (€15), as well as tasty €25 *menus*. (☎98 01 34. Open M-Tu and F-Su noon-1:30pm and 7-9pm, Th noon-1pm. MC/V.)

To reach the **tourist office,** pl. d'Hofheim, from the station, take a left and walk beside the river along rue Descartes—which becomes quai Jeanne d'Arc—for 20min., then turn right at Rabelais's statue onto pl. de l'Hôtel de Ville. Continue onto pl. du Général de Gaulle and turn onto rue Jean-Jacques Rousseau at the back right corner of the square. The office is on the left. (☎93 17 85. Hotel reservation service €2.50. Themed walking tours May-Sept. €4.70, students €2.50. Night tours €5/2.80. *Petit train* tour July-Aug. 6 times per day, €4. Office open May-Sept. daily 9am-7pm; Oct.-Apr. M-Sa 10am-12:30pm and 2-6pm.)

Bikes are available at **Detours de Loire,** 12 pl. Jeanne d'Arc, which offers several pickup and dropoff locations along the Loire, including Blois and Tours. (☎93 36 92; www.locationdevelos.com. Bikes €13 per day; tandems €38 per day. Open daily 9am-7pm. Cash only.) **L'Etape en Chinonais,** 27 rue Jean-Jacques Rousseau, in front of the tourist office, also rents bikes. (☎95 92 08; www.loirevelonature.com. €8 per ½-day, €15 per day. Open Tu-Su 9am-8pm.)

SAUMUR ☎02 41

A small town spliced by the sprawling Loire, Saumur (soh-MOOR; pop. 30,000) is one of the valley's most picturesque stops. Best known for its wine, mushrooms, and equestrian tradition, the city has also profited the past two centuries from an abundance of *tuffeau*, the stone used to build the Loire châteaux. Damp, chilly caves bear witness to years of stone excavation and endow the region with an environment prime for mushroom cultivation. In addition to *champignons de Paris* (button mushrooms), Saumur's fertile soil nurtures high-quality vineyards. However, this wide palette of discoveries is somewhat tempered by the fact that many sights are only accessible by car or infrequent buses.

LOIRE VALLEY

TRANSPORTATION

Trains: station on av. David d'Angers, 10min. from pl. Bilange. Take bus #11 from Pole Balzac (dir.: Gare SNCF/St-Lambert, €1.20). Ticket office open M-Sa 6:05am-8:45pm, Su 8:05am-9:45pm. SNCF trains and buses run to **Angers** (30min., 10 per day, €7.30); **Nantes** (1hr., 14 per day, €18-21); **Paris** (1½-3hr., 20 per day, €34-58); **Poitiers** (2½hr., 8 per day, €24); **Tours** (40min., 10 per day, €11-13).

Buses: Agglobus, 19 rue F. D. Roosevelt (☎51 11 87). Office open M 2-6pm, Tu-F 9am-noon and 2-6pm, Sa 9am-noon. Buses M-Sa 7am-7pm. Tickets €1.20.

Car rental: Europcar, 40 av. du Général de Gaulle (☎67 30 89). From €59 per day. 21+. Under-25 surcharge €30. Open M-F 8am-noon and 2-6pm, Sa 9am-noon and 2-6pm. AmEx/MC/V. **Hertz,** 78-80 av. du Général de Gaulle (☎67 20 06). From €41 per day. 21+. Under-25 surcharge €35. Open M-F 8:15am-noon and 2-6:15pm, Sa 8:30am-noon and 2-5:30pm. AmEx/MC/V.

Bike Rental: Détours de Loire, 1 rue David d'Angers (☎53 01 01; www.locationdevelos.com). Several pickup and dropoff locations along the Loire, including Blois and Tours. Bikes €14 per day; tandems €38 per day. Open M-Sa 9:30am-12:30pm and 4:30-7:30pm, Su 9:30am-12:30pm and 8-7pm. Cash only.

ORIENTATION AND PRACTICAL INFORMATION

Saumur's sights are best reached from the center of town by bus or bike.

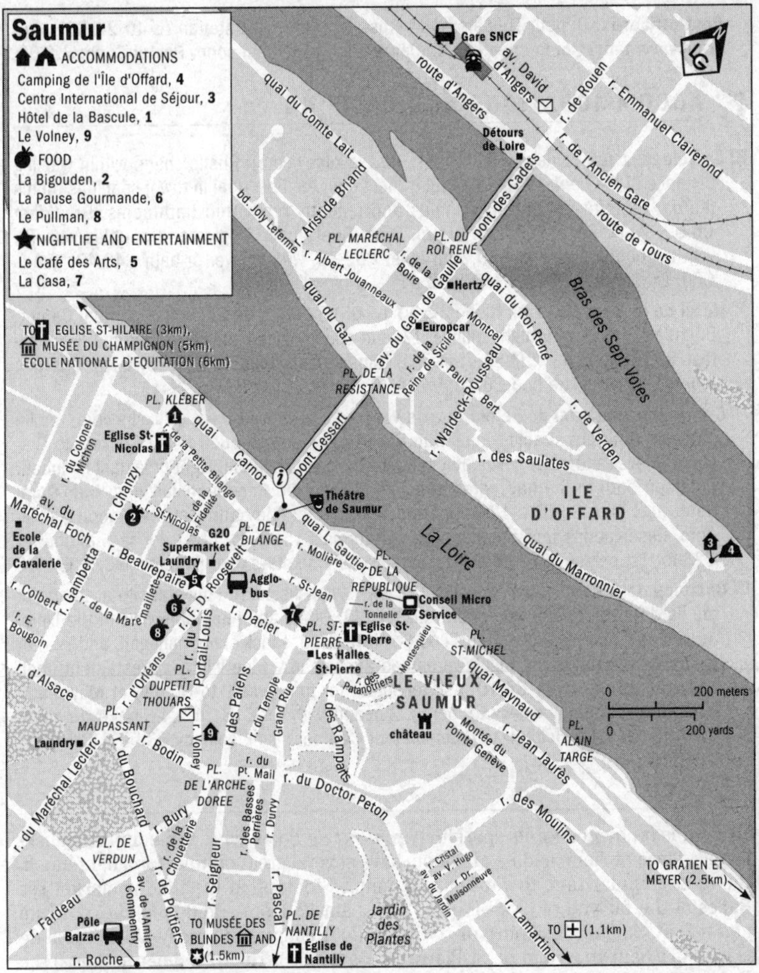

Tourist office: pl. de la Bilange (☎40 20 60; www.saumur-tourisme.com), across 2 bridges from the train station. Multilingual staff books accommodations, offers city tours by carriage (1½hr.; every hr. July-Aug.; €6, under 11 €4) and by boat on the Loire (☎06 61 92 08 74; €8, under 12 €4.50; sunset tour €9/5), as well as equestrian tours of the city in summer. Open mid-May to Sept. M-Sa 9:15am-7pm, Su 10:30am-5:30pm; Oct. to mid-May M-Sa 9:15am-12:30pm and 2-6pm, Su 10am-noon.)

Laundromats: 12 rue du Maréchal Leclerc. Wash €3.50 per 7kg. Open daily 7am-9:30pm. Also at 16 rue Beaurepaire. Wash €3.80 per 7kg. Open daily in high season 7:30am-10pm; in low season 7:30am-9:30pm.

Police: 415 rue du Chemin Vert (☎83 24 00).

Urgent Care: rte. de Fontevraud (☎53 30 30).

Internet Access: Conseil Micro Service, 69 quai Mayaud (☎67 15 30; www.conseil-micro-service.com). €1.50 per 30min. Open Tu-Sa 10am-6pm, Su 2-6pm.

Post office: Pl. Dupetit Thouars and across from the train station (☎40 22 08). **Currency exchange.** Both open M-F 8:30am-6pm, Sa 8:30am-noon. **Postal Code:** 49400.

ACCOMMODATIONS AND CAMPING

Le Volney, 1 rue Volney (☎51 25 41; www.levolney.com). Rustic charm within walking distance of the *centre-ville.* Cheerful owners offer the best deal in town; spacious rooms feature tasteful antique furnishings and recently renovated bathrooms. Breakfast €6.50. Wi-Fi. Reception 7am-10pm. Open Sept.-June. Singles and doubles with TV, with telephone and sink €30, with toilet €32-34, with shower or bath €40-49; quads €60. Extra bed €6. AmEx/MC/V. ❷

Hôtel de la Bascule, 1 pl. Kléber (☎50 13 65), near Eglise St-Nicolas on quai Carnot. Bright bedrooms with high ceilings, TV, and sparkly clean shower or bathroom. Breakfast €5.50. Reception M-Sa 7am-7pm. Singles and doubles €37-45; 2- to 4-person rooms €39-43. Extra bed €6.10. MC/V. ❸

Centre International de Séjour, rue de Verden (☎40 30 00; www.cvtloisirs.com), on Ile d'Offard. Bare but sizable rooms with bunk beds. Ask reception for free tickets to Gratien et Meyer and other *caves.* Kitchen and TV room available. Light breakfast included. Common bath in the hall. Internet access €8 per hr. Reception July-Aug. 8am-9pm; Sept. and June 8:30am-12:30pm and 2-7pm; Mar.-May and Oct. 9am-noon and 2-7pm. Reservations recommended. 8-bed dorms €15; 2- to 4-bed dorms with shower €23 for 1st person, €10 additional person. 10% off stays over 5 nights. MC/V. ❶

Camping de l'Ile d'Offard (☎40 30 00; www.cvtloisirs.com). Four-star site at the tip of the Ile d'Offard. Shares reception with the CIS. Offers an unbeatable view of the Loire, as well as a pool, laundry, tennis courts, playground, snack shop, mini-golf, and TV—not to mention brand-new bungalows named after nearby wine villages. Restaurant open daily 6-9:30pm. *Plats* €4-10. Ask reception for free tickets to Gratien et Meyer and other *caves.* Internet access €8 per hr. 2 people with car €16-24, €4-5 per extra adult, €2-2.50 per extra child. 4- to 6-person tent €40 per day. Electricity €3.50. MC/V. ❶

FOOD

Saumur is renowned for its sparkling *crémant de Loire* wine and bountiful mushrooms. **Place St-Pierre** and its offshoots have several great options for a light lunch, the most popular time to eat out in Saumur. Stock up at the indoor market **Les Halles** at the far end of pl. St-Pierre (Tu-F 8am-12:30pm and 3-7pm, Sa 7am-1pm and 3-7pm, Su 9am-12:30pm), or try its outdoor equivalents on av. du Général de Gaulle (Th 8am-1pm) and pl. St-Pierre (Sa 8am-1pm). The **G20** supermarket, 6 rue Roosevelt, sits inside a shopping center on the main street. (☎02 41 53 71 20. Open M-Sa 9am-7:30pm, Su 9am-12:30pm. AmEx/MC/V.)

Le Pullman, 52 rue d'Orléans (☎051 31 79). Intimate, family-run restaurant. Decorated like a 1920s Orient Express dining car, with baggage compartments and scenic window views. Back terrace is delightfully green in the summer. Pleasant owners and great lunch deals keep customers coming back. Lunch specials €7-9. *Plats* €9.50-15. *Menus* €13 and €26. Open M and Th-Su 10am-4pm and 7-10pm, Tu 10am-4pm. MC/V. ❸

La Pause Gourmande, 39 rue d'Orléans (☎38 32 52). Small but popular lunch spot run by a young Parisian couple. Fresh salads (€5-6.70), fast service and distinctly French feel. Traditional *plats* €8-10. *Menus* €11-17. Open M 7-9pm, Tu-W and F-Sa noon-2pm and 7-10pm, Th noon-2pm. Lunch reservations recommended. MC/V. ❷

La Bigouden, 67 rue St-Nicolas (☎67 12 59). Pink-clad table and fresh flowers only add to the already sentimental mood set by sweet *crêpes* with romantic names like the *Belle*

Angèle ("beautiful angel"; sautéed apples, corinthian grapes, and honey; €6.30) and *Nid de Coucou* ("cuckoo's nest"; whipped cream, maple syrup, and almonds; €6.30). Choose from over 35 savory *crêpes* (€6-10), 35 dessert *crêpes* (€5-8) and 12 salads (€5.50-9). Open July-Aug. daily noon-1:30pm and 7-9:30pm; Sept.-June M and Th-Su noon-1:30pm and 7-9:30pm. MC/V. ❷

SIGHTS

Three 12th- to 15th-century churches brighten downtown Saumur, and a soothing **Jardin des Plantes** is tucked between av. du Docteur Peton and rue Marceau, on the other side of the château. The picturesque **Pont Cessart** provides a panorama of the château towering above the city. Unfortunately, the city's most interesting sights can only be reached by car or the somewhat unreliable buses. Exercise caution if biking to these destinations, as most country roads lack sidewalks or bike paths.

ECOLE NATIONALE D'EQUITATION. In 1763, Louis XV chose Saumur as the location for his cavalry training camp, thereby establishing this town as France's top center for horsemanship. Since 1815,when the Ecole became a civilian national riding school, Saumur has continued the *Cadre Noir* tradition—having acquired this name due to the color of its uniforms, which set it apart from other, lesser-trained, blue-clad cavalry. Students and *écuyers* (professional riders) alike compete internationally and often go on to train equestrians around the country. The palatial premises, located 15min. from the center of town by car, contain over 50km of training grounds, 400 horses, and one of Europe's best veterinarian clinics. Tours pass through the facilities and training grounds; morning visits often include a 30min. viewing of daily warm-ups. *(☎53 50 60; www.cadrenoir.fr. Take bus 31, dir.: St-Hilaire, to "Alouette," then follow signs (25min. walk). No sidewalk; exercise caution. Grounds accessible by tour only. 1hr. tour every 30min. Apr.-Sept. M 2-4:30pm, Tu-F 9:30-11:30am and 2-4:30pm, Sa 9am-noon. €7.50, under 18 €4.50. Daily training routines and shows year-round €15, under 18 €8. Call for more info.)*

GRATIEN ET MEYER. Saumur's effervescent wines have been in high demand since the 12th century, when *Plantagenêt* kings took their favorite casks with them to England and then needed a constant supply. Countless wine cellars on the outskirts of Saumur offer tours and tastings. This well-known vineyard, perched atop a steep hill with a spectacular view of the valley, presents its cellars and small museum in a 40min. tour in English or French. The visit ends with a tasting of their award-winning vintages. Over five million bottles are kept in galleries dating from the Middle Ages. *(Rte. de Montsoreau. Take bus #1, dir.: Fontevraud, from "Pôle Balzac" to "Beaulieu," then walk up the hill. ☎83 13 32; www.gratienmeyer.com. Store open Apr.-Oct. daily 9:30am-6pm. Visits 10-11am and 2-5pm, tours depart every hr. €2.50, under 18 free. Nov.-Mar. open only to groups of 10 or more by reservation.)*

MUSÉE DES BLINDES. Commonly known as "the tank museum," Saumur's armed vehicle collection is the largest in the world—with over 200 pieces—and follows the evolution of 20th-century warfare. An ex-tobacco factory now curated by a Lieutenant Colonel and brimming with these intimidating killing machines, this museum is not for the faint-hearted. Keep an eye out for the Schneider, France's first tank; the camouflaged Tiger I, a monstrous German cruiser; and the Leclerc, currently the world's best-designed tank. Hidden among the massive machines are more subtle vehicles of war like the Nazi bicycle. A wing displaying memorabilia from the French Resistance is scheduled to be added in winter 2007. *(1043 rte. de Fontevraud. 40min. walk from the town center, or take bus #34, dir.: Chemin Vert, to "Fricotelle," and walk left 100m. ☎83 69 95; www.musee-des-blindes.asso.fr. Open daily May-Sept. 9:30am-6:30pm; Oct.-Apr. 10am-7pm. 30min. group visits. €7, students €4.50, under 18 €3.50.)*

MUSÉE DU CHAMPIGNON. Located in the dark caves that were once *tuffeau* mines, this museum explores the history of mushroom cultivation in the Saumur region. A variety of mushroom species grows in its dank interior—from classic white-button mushrooms to colorful velvet shank—and lend the caves their characteristic smell. In October, a month-long mushroom festival takes place in the museum. *Dégustation* of local produce (€2-4.50) and fresh varieties of mushrooms, such as *champignons de Paris* (€3 per kg, others €12 per kg), are available at reception. Museum patrons can also ask for regional mushroom recipes. Don't forget to bring an extra layer, as the caves are kept at a constant 14°C. *(Rte. de Gennes, Ste-Hilaire-St-Florent. Take bus #5, dir.: Villemole, to stop bearing the museum's name. ☎02 41 50 31 55; www.musee-du-champignon.com. Open daily Feb. to mid-Nov. 10am-7pm. €7, students €6, under 18 €4.60.)*

ENTERTAINMENT AND FESTIVALS

The **Théâtre de Saumur** (☎83 30 83), next to the tourist office, hosts everything from *galas de danse* to jazz concerts in its 19th-century hall. (Schedules are irregular, check with the tourist office.) Saumur residents line up to catch the latest flicks at **Cinéma Le Palace,** 13 quai Carnot. (☎51 00 00; www.cinefil.com. Tickets €7.50, afternoons and all day W €6.20; under 18 €6.20.) Late-night crowds gather in **place St-Pierre** next to the illuminated cathedral and in the numerous Irish pubs at **place de la République,** but for the most part Saumur has few nightlife options. Offering salsa lessons, ballroom dancing, and poker nights, **La Casa,** rue du Marché, caters to a classier crowd, who twirl and swirl among dark wooden furnishings. (☎40 36 02. Beer €2.80-3.20. Mixed drinks €5-7. Open Tu-Su 5pm-2am.) Shoot some darts at **Le Café des Arts,** 4 rue Beaurepaire, a large and popular bar in the *centre-ville*, strung with christmas lights and furnished with heavy black leather. The exotic "beer cocktails" (€3-5.20), including the "Singapour" (Malibu, cherry, pineapple, and, of course, beer), keep the crowds coming back. (☎51 21 72. Open M-Th 8:30am-9:30pm, F-Sa 9:30am-2am. MC/V.)

In the third week of September, the Cadre Noir shows off its horsemanship with shows at **La Grande Semaine de Saumur** (☎53 50 50; www.cadrenoir.fr). The **International Festival of Military Music** and the **Festival des Géants,** a march of oversized puppets, alternate years, taking over the town in late June. (☎51 25 69. *Des Géants* is scheduled for 2008.) In late July, the **Carrousel** organized by the Ecole de la Cavalerie and Ecole Nationale d'Equitation draws large crowds. After two hours of horse performances, the elite Cadre Noir enters the stage for a demonstration of equestrian dressage. Though still a favorite, the spectacle unfortunately no longer includes the motorcycle show or tank parade that originally made it popular. (☎40 20 66. Tickets €26-32.) Saumur also hosts many free equestrian events each year, including several horse-ball matches. (Call the *Cadre Noire* at ☎53 50 50 for more info.)

DAYTRIP FROM SAUMUR

FONTEVRAUD-L'ABBAYE

The best way to reach the abbey is by car, but the #1 bus makes the 17km trip from the Pole Balzac to Fontevraud Mairie (25min., M-Sa 2 per day, €1.20). Call ahead to for particular times at ☎08 00 50 77 82). Last return from Fontevraud M-F at 6:12pm, Sa 1:05pm. The tourist office, pl. St-Michel, dispenses free maps. (☎51 79 45. Themed tours of Fontevraud July-Aug. €4. Open Easter-Sept. M-Sa 9:30am-1:30pm and 2-7pm.) One stop before Fontevraud, in Montsoreau centre, there are curious troglodyte cliff dwellings and a well-kept château. Call the Montsoreau tourist office (☎51 70 22) for more info.

One of the largest—and oddest—monastic complexes in Europe, the **Abbaye de Fontevraud** (ah-BAY duh fohn-teh-VROH), has awed visitors for over nine centuries. Robert d'Arbrissel, who built the abbey in the forest of Fontevraud in 1101, failed to be canonized because he founded a community around the controversial practice of "*martyr blanc*," or "syneisaktisme," a particularly grueling act of faith wherein men and women sleep naked together, thus arousing each other only to practice ignoring their worldly desires. Church officials, unamused with the scandalous reputation attached to Arbrissel's now-defunct religious traveling group, gave Arbrissel land on the condition that he 'clean up his act'. To increase the humility of his monks, Arbrissel demanded that women rule the order, if not in the 'terrestrial' world, then at least in the 'spiritual' one. Needless to say, this power was somewhat abused in the creation of questionable rules such as those governing daily wine intake (½-L for women, ¼-L for men). Of Fontevraud's 36 abbesses, over half were of royal—including Bourbon—blood. Under the rule of these noble ladies, the abbey was coquettishly expanded in the style of the royal Loire châteaux: it is peppered with their initials and portraits, and its chapter house is painted with scenes of Christ's sufferings, upon which 16 abbesses intrude, having added themselves as they came to power, to the point of painting over each other. Following the Revolution, the abbey became a prison, and remained so from 1804 until 1963, housing minor criminals incarcerated for such petty crimes as sticking their tongues out at guards. The 12th-century church also serves as a *Plantagenêt* necropolis; Henri II was buried here in 1189 and his wife, Eleanor of Aquitaine, lies here as well, after having been imprisoned under his orders for 15 years. Their legendary son, Richard the Lionheart, completes the family burial site. Twenty-one chimneys herald the 12th-century Romanesque kitchens, inspired by sketches brought back from the Crusades. Unique in their fascinating architecture, the chimneys designed to clear the kitchen of smoke as effectively as possible, while accommodating seven simultaneously burning fires. An English booklet and signs help visitors along, but the 1hr. tour gives the best sense of the abbey's amazing history. (☎51 87 97; www.abbaye-fontevraud.com. Abbey open daily June-Sept. 9am-6:30pm; Jan.-Mar. 10am-5:30pm; Apr.-May and Oct. 10am-6pm. €7.90, students €5.90; mid-May to mid-Nov. €6.50/5.90. Tours free with admission; in English July-Aug.)

ANGERS ☎02 41

Bustling with shops, bars, and excellent restaurants, cosmopolitan Angers (ahn-JHAY; pop. 156,000) is a modern, sophisticated city still in touch with its illustrious royal roots. From behind the imposing walls of their fortress, the medieval dukes of Anjou once ruled over the surrounding territory as well as an insignificant island across the channel called Britain. Today, alongside Angers's 13th-century château and cathedral and its world-famous apocalyptic tapestry, the town offers first-class art museums housed in edifices as refined as the pieces residing within.

TRANSPORTATION

Trains: Pl. de la Gare. Info desk open M-Sa 6am-9:15pm, Su 8:45am-7pm. To: **Le Mans** (40min., 15 per day, €14); **Nantes** (1hr., every hr., €13); **Orléans** (3hr., 8 per day, €27-29) via **St-Pierre-des-Corps; Paris** (3-4hr., 15 per day, €39-46); **Poitiers** (2-3hr., 7 per day, €26-30) via **St-Pierre** or **Tours** (1hr., 10 per day, €16). **TGV** trains run to **Le Mans** (€17), **Nantes** (€16), and **Paris** (€46).

Buses: AnjouBus Buses (☎08 20 16 00 49), leave from outside the train station on Esplanade de la Gare for **Rennes** (3hr., 2 per day, €14) and **Saumur** (1½hr., 2 per day, €7.20). Check the ticket office, as schedules vary seasonally. Open M-Sa 6:30am-

7:30pm. **COTRA** buses (☎33 64 64; www.cotra.fr). Run from the train station and provide local service from pl. Lorraine. Open M-F 7:45am-6:30pm, Sa 8:45am-5:30pm. Tickets €1 from booth or machine, €1.20 on board.

Taxis: Allo Anjou Taxi ☎87 65 00. €1.32 per km. 24hr.

Car Rental: Avis (☎88 20 24). From €124 per day. 21+. Under-25 surcharge €25. Open M-F 7:30am-7pm, Sa 8am-noon and 2-6pm. **Europcar** (☎87 87 10). From €90 per day. 21+. Under-25 surcharge €33. Open M-F 7:30am-7pm, Sa 8am-noon and 2-6pm. Both in the train station.

Bike rental: At the tourist office. €10 per ½-day, €14 per day.

ORIENTATION AND PRACTICAL INFORMATION

Most restaurants and nightlife hot spots in Angers are on the pedestrian-only streets leading into **place du Ralliement.** To reach the château from the train station, follow rue de la Gare, then turn right at pl. de la Visitation onto rue Targot.

Tourist office: 7 pl. Kennedy (☎02 41 23 50 00; www.angersloiretourisme.com), just across from the castle. Follow directions to the château to rue Targot, then turn left at the traffic light onto bd. du Roi-René. Organizes tours of the city (€7.50, students and under 18 €5.50), reserves accommodations, offers **currency exchange** (€4.20 fee), and provides free maps. Open May-Sept. M-Sa 9am-7pm, Su 10am-7pm; Oct.-Apr. M 2-6pm, Tu-Sa 9am-6pm, Su 10am-1pm.

Centre d'Information Jeunesse, 5 allée du Haras (☎87 74 47). Offers info on employment, lodging, outdoor activities and cultural events. Free Internet access for research only; 30min. max. Open M-Tu and Th-F 1-6pm, W 10am-6pm, Sa 10am-noon.

Laundromat: 15 rue Valdermaine. Open daily 7am-10pm.

Police: 33 rue Nid de Pie (☎22 94 00).

Hospital: 4 rue Larrey (☎35 36 37).

Urgent Care: ☎35 37 12.

Internet access: Cyber Espace, 25 Rue de la Roë (☎24 92 71). €1 per 15min., €2 per 30min., €3 per hr. Open M-Th 9am-10pm, F-Sa 9am-midnight, Su 2-8pm.

Post office: 1 rue Roosevelt (☎20 81 82), just off rue Corneille near rue Voltaire. **Currency exchange.** Open M-F 9am-6:30pm, Sa 9am-12:30pm. **Postal Code:** 49100.

ACCOMMODATIONS AND CAMPING

Hôtel Continental, 12-14 rue Louis de Romain (☎86 94 94; www.hotellecontinental.com), near pl. du Ralliement in the center of town. Offers 25 newly renovated rooms that include double beds, cable, phone, Internet access (€4 per day), and stylish new furnishings. Buffet breakfast €8. Singles with shower or bathtub €55-63; doubles €65, with shower or bathtub €70; triples €76. AmEx/MC/V. ❹

Royal Hôtel, 8bis pl. de la Visitation (☎88 30 25; fax 81 05 75). Don't be discouraged by the fake-marble lobby, this place offers spacious rooms with double beds, big windows, and cable TV. Breakfast €5. Free Internet access in lobby. Reception M-Sa 6:45am-midnight, Su 7:15am-midnight. Singles €30-42; doubles €31-51, with private shower or bath €49; triples €56; quads €65. AmEx/MC/V. ❸

Hôtel de l'Univers, 2 pl. de la Gare (☎88 43 58; www.citotel.com/hotels/univ_fr). 5-10min. from downtown. Expect 45 well-kept rooms with comfortable double beds, telephones, and cable TV. Breakfast €6.20. Hall shower €4. Singles and doubles with sink €31, with shower €42-44, with bath €53-58; quads €66-73. AmEx/MC/V. ❷

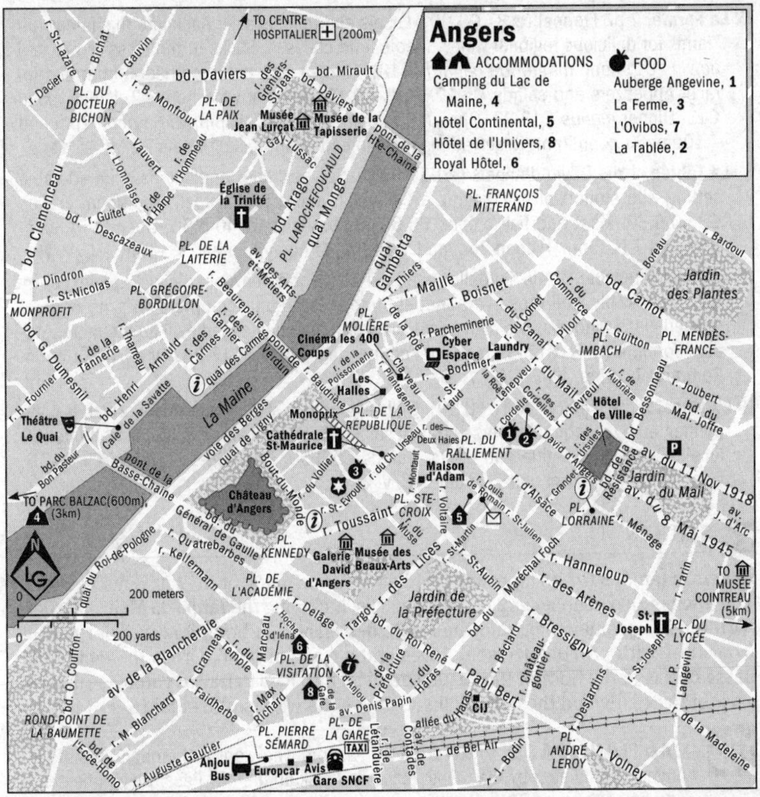

Centre d'Accueil du Lac de Maine, 49 av. du Lac de Maine (☎22 32 10; www.lacdemaine.fr). Take bus #6 or 16 to "Lac de Maine (Accueil)," (15min.; every 10min., last bus 12:45am from pl. du Ralliement; €1.20). Cross the street and turn right, then left at the roundabout; the hostel is a 5min. walk. Next to mirror-calm Lac du Maine. All rooms have bath and modern furniture. TV room, bar, billiards, pinball, video games. Breakfast included. Free Internet access. 10-day max stay. Reserve within 3 weeks of stay. Singles €37; doubles €41; 3- to 5-bed dorms €17. AmEx/MC/V. ❸

Camping du Lac de Maine, av. du Lac de Maine (☎02 41 73 05 03; www.lacdemaine.fr). Take bus #6 to "Camping du Lac de Maine" and follow signs. 4-star site. Offers a pool, foosball, ping pong, clean bathrooms, bike rental (€8.50 per day), free hot showers, and laundry. Open late Mar. to mid-Oct. Reception July-Aug. 8am-7pm; Sept.-June 8am-12:30pm and 2-7pm. 2 people with tent and car €12-17, €3 per extra adult, €2 per extra child. Electricity €3.30. Bungalow €153-572 per week. MC/V. ❶

FOOD

Angers caters to its student population with everything from *crêpes* to Chinese food, particularly along **rue St-Laud, rue St-Aubin,** and **boulevard Maréchal Foch.** A **Monoprix** grocery store resides on the ground floor of Les Halles, on pl. de la République (Open M-Sa 8:30am-9pm).

La Ferme, 2 pl. Freppel (☎87 09 90). Locals and tourists alike pack into this family-run "farm" for delicious regional wines, meats, and cheeses. Sticks to the classics like *coq au vin* (€11) and *magret de canard* (€13). Enjoy a view of the cathedral from the terrace. Appetizers and salads €5-10. *Plats* €9-12. Glass of wine from €2. Lunch *menu* €13. Dinner *menus* €18-33. Open M-Tu noon-2pm and 7-10pm, Th-Sa noon-2pm and 7-10pm, Su noon-2pm. Reservations recommended on weekends. AmEx/MC/V. ❸

La Tablée, 1 rue David d'Angers (☎05 12 50). Serves *crêpes* and salads in an adorable setting with stone walls, changing art exhibits, and a Breton feel. Traditional *crêpes* €3.50-6.60. Meat and fish *crêpes* €6.50-13. Desserts €2.40-5.80. Open M-Th noon-2pm and 7-9:30pm, F noon-2pm and 7-10pm, Sa noon-2pm and 7-11pm. MC/V. ❷

Auberge Angevine, 9 rue Cordelle (☎20 10 40). For a heavenly dining experience, try this remarkably well-preserved chapel-turned-restaurant—complete with its original stained-glass windows. The high prices are worth the unique medieval atmosphere. Student *formule* (M-F; €17) is highly recommended. *Menus* €17-38. Open Tu-Su noon-2pm and 7-10pm. AmEx/MC/V. ❸

L'Ovibos, 3 rue d'Anjou (☎87 48 90). Grills a variety of steaks and meats, which is complemented by an equally diverse array of salads. Salads and *menus* are named after US locales, so pick a region and dig in. Salads €5-8.50. *Plats* €8-18. *Menus* €9.80-18. Open M-Sa noon-2pm and 7-11pm. MC/V. ❷

SIGHTS

Angers is famous for its tapestries, which decorate many of the city's main sights. The town is also near several beautiful parks, including the **Jardin du Mail,** a garden with terrific promenades, and the **Jardin des Plantes,** a botanical wonder dating from 1901 with provocative sculptures and a tranquil pond. Cross the **Pont de la Basse Chaine** at the floor of the castle and head into **Parc Balzac** to catch a romantic view of the castle and the old city lights above the waters of La Maine.

TIP **CAUTION: PASS D'ANGERS.** Visitors who want a thorough visit of Angers should stop by the tourist office and pick up the City Pass, which offers admission to over 10 sites and some guided tours. (€14 for a 1-day pass, €21 for 2 days, €26 for 3 days.) Extra perks include free bus rides and parking, as well as discounts at the tourist office and cinema.

CHÂTEAU D'ANGERS. Bristling with 17 towers and protected by a 900m long, 15m high wall, the eerie medieval fortress was erected over Gallo-Roman ruins in the 13th century. Behind it, however, is a more pleasant residence: the palace of the Duke d'Anjou. Built in the Renaissance era, the flamboyant Gothic-style mansion stands inside a pleasant inner courtyard, also built in the 14th and 15th centuries. Next to the château stands a 15th-century chapel whose humble interior is overshadowed by fading red frescoes. These intricate buildings make it easy to forget that the château served as a prison for seven centuries—and as an asylum until the late 1940s. Tapestries with religious and regal scenes adorn the royal residence, but Angers's prized possession, the **Tapisserie de l'Apocalypse,** is secured in a gallery below. Commissioned by Louis I and completed in 1382, its 74 scenes depict Saint John's visions of the battle between good and evil. Created during the Hundred Years' War, it subtly weaves in references to the war between France, represented by John, and Britain, depicted as a menacing, lion-like monster. *(2 promenade du Bout du Monde, on pl. Kennedy. ☎86 48 77. Open daily May-Aug. 9:30am-6:30pm; Sept.-Apr. 10am-5:30pm. Last entrance 45min. before closing. €7.50, ages 18-25 €4.80, under 18 free. Free tours in French leave from the chapel 5 times daily.)*

LOIRE VALLEY

GALERIE DAVID D'ANGERS. This restored 11th-century Toussaint Abbey, now with a soaring glass roof, holds a collection of David d'Angers's 19th-century sculptures. D'Angers produced 23 vibrant life-size figures and over 50 busts. His subjects include major literary and historical characters, such as Goethe, Lafayette, and Washington, as well as personal friends Victor Hugo and Balzac. *(34bis rue Toussaint. ☎05 38 90. Open June-Sept. daily 10am-7pm; late Oct.-May Tu-Su 10am-noon and 2-6pm. €4; students €3; under 18 and history of art, architecture, and tourism students free.)*

MUSÉE JEAN LURÇAT. The Musée Lurçat, formerly one of France's most ancient hospitals, is now home to Angers's second woven masterpiece. The 80m long **Chant du Monde** (Song of the World) offers a symbolic journey through history, including a depiction of the atomic bombings of WWII. The neighboring **Musée de la Tapisserie Contemporaire** has a permanent textile and tapestry collection, which highlights pieces by Jean Lurçat and Grau-Garriga, though works by other artists are also on display. The monographic tapestries, including Thomas Gleb's *Zohar*, should not be missed. *(4 bd. Arago. ☎24 18 45. Open June-Sept. daily 10am-7pm; Oct.-May Tu-Su 10am-noon and 2-6pm. €4 for both museums, ages 18-25 €3, under 18 free.)*

MUSÉE COINTREAU. This factory, owned by the Cointreau family, has been making a *liqueur* native to Angers since 1849. The exhibit includes documents related to the production of the *liqueur*, advertisements, and a 10min. historical film. Free tastings follow. *(Bd. des Bretonnières, St-Barthélemy-d'Anjou. Take bus #7 to Cointreau. ☎31 50 50; www.cointreau.com. Visit by guided tours only; must reserve ahead.)*

CATHÉDRALE ST-MAURICE. The 12th-century building is a hodgepodge of styles—with a Norman porch, a 13th-century chancel intersecting a fourth-century Gallo-Roman wall, and some of the oldest stained glass in France. Atop the cathedral's main entrance, a trumpet-playing angel rises above an illuminated *vitrage* from 1944. The single nave of the church, with heavily decorated vault, is in the classic style of the Angevin Plantagenêt (Anjou) dynasty. Like everything in Angers, the church has a rotating exhibit of rare tapestries. *(Pl. Chappoulie. ☎87 58 45. Open daily 8:30am-7pm. Mass daily 9:30am, 7pm.)*

OTHER SIGHTS. The **Musée des Beaux-Arts** houses a small exposition on the history of the city, with relics uncovered in the region. The upper floors feature paintings from the 14th to 20th centuries. Arranged by century, the second floor houses earlier art, primarily from the Italian Renaissance era. Temporary exhibits feature contemporary painting, sculpture, and graphic art. *(14 rue du Musée. ☎05 38 00. Open June-Sept. M-Th and Sa-Su 10am-7pm, F 10am-9pm; Oct.-May Tu-Su 1-6pm; 1st F of the month 1-8pm. €4, students €3.)* Though dominated by modern architecture and flashy café umbrellas, the *vieille ville* retains some of its 16th-century stone houses. The most renowned, **La Maison d'Adam,** 1 pl. St-Croix, has its own plaque to inform passersby that this timber-framed house is Angers's oldest and grandest medieval residence. Originally called the "House of the Tree of Life" because of the sculpture on the corner, its name was changed when the scandal hit the home 200 years ago, and two wooden figures of Adam and Eve were stolen from the tree. On its bottom floor, the **Maison des Artisans** sells hand-crafted objects from the region; the upper floors remain inhabited. *(On the corner of pl. St-Croix and rue Montault. ☎88 06 27. Open M 2-7pm, Tu-Sa 9:30am-7pm.)*

ENTERTAINMENT AND FESTIVALS

The discos have been exiled to the suburbs, but cafés along **rue St-Laud** are always packed, and bars on student-dominated **rue Bressigny** get down before the sun does. Music echoes through the streets from behind dark red doors at **Le Bolero,** 38 rue St-Laud, a classy club in a beautiful Art Nouveau building. (☎88 61 19. Min. Tu-

Th €7, F-Sa €10. Open Tu-Th 11:30pm-3am, F-Sa 11:30pm-4am. AmEx/MC/V.) **Cinéma Les 400 Coups,** 12 rue Claveau, shows international films with French subtitles. (☎42 87 39. €7, students €5.80, Su 11am matinee €4.50.) The **Théâtre Le Quai,** opened in 2007 across the river from the château, presents cutting-edge avant-garde plays year-round. (☎22 20 20. Tickets €5-10. Open daily noon-6pm.)

From mid-June to early July, Angers attracts renowned French comedy and drama troupes to the château and other regional sights for the **Festival d'Anjou,** one of the largest theater festivals in France. (Info office at 1 rue des Arènes. ☎88 14 14; www.festivaldanjou.com. €20-30 per show, students €14.) In July and August, **Angers l'Eté** brings musicians from around the world, as well as prestigious jazz bands. Most concerts take place in the fabulous *cloître Toussaint.* (☎05 41 48. Tickets on sale at tourist office, 7 pl. Kennedy. €9, students €7.50.)

LE MANS ☎02 43

Though Le Mans (luh MAHN; pop. 146,100) may not be the most beautiful city in the Loire Valley, its central location, *brasseries* and bars, and old Roman city center make for a low-key stay. Currently undergoing massive reconstruction, the city has many unsightly areas, but pedestrian pathways preserve the *vieille ville*, one of the most enchanting in the entire region. Most travelers will want to make Le Mans a daytrip or return at the end of 2008 when the construction projects are scheduled to be completed, but for car racing fans, the city is worth a night's stay.

TRANSPORTATION

Trains: Bd. de la Gare. Ticket windows open M-F 6am-8pm, Sa 6am-7pm, Su 8:15am-9:30pm. To: **Nantes** (1½hr., 20 per day, €24-27); **Paris** (1-3hr., over 10 per day, €26-47); **Rennes** (1½hr., 10 per day, €22-25); **Tours** (1hr., 6 per day, €14).

Buses: SNCF (☎08 91 70 58 05) sends buses from the station to **Saumur** (2¾hr.; M-Sa 2 per day, Su 9:10pm; €15). **SETRAM,** 65 av. Général de Gaulle (☎24 76 76). Carts pedestrians around the city during the day. Info office open M-F 7am-7pm, Sa 8:30am-6:30pm. Buses run 5:30am-8pm. Ticket €1.20, *carnet* of 10 €8.80; sold on bus or in office. MC/V. The city's **Hi'bus** lines take over until 1:30am every night.

Taxis: Radio Taxi, 188 rte. de Beauge (☎24 92 92). Also across from the train station, including **Avis** (☎ 24 30 50). From €90. 21+. Under-25 surcharge €25. Open M-F 7:30am-7pm, Sa 9am-noon and 2-6pm. AmEx/DC/MC/V.

Car Rental: Rent A Car, 102 av. du Général Leclerc (☎24 50 50). Weekday deals from €39. Open M-F 8:30am-noon and 2-6:30pm, Sa 9am-noon. AmEx/MC/V.

PRACTICAL INFORMATION

Tourist office: rue de l'Etoile (☎28 17 22; www.lemanstourisme.com), in the 17th-century Hôtel des Ursulines. Walk down av. du Général Leclerc from the train station, and keep going on av. François Mitterand. The staff distributes free city maps, bike maps, and info booklets and runs French tours of the city (M-F 4:30pm) and cathedral (Su 3pm) in summer (€5.50, under 18 €3). English tours are available by reservation. Open July-Aug. M-Sa 9am-6pm, Su 2-6pm; Sept.-June M-F 9am-6pm, Sa 9am-noon and 2-6pm, Su 10am-noon.)

Beyond Tourism: France Bénévolat, 5 rue des Jacobins (☎87 50 40). Volunteer restoration with **Rempart** (☎01 42 71 96 55; www.rempart.com) during the summer (See **Beyond Tourism,** p. 85.)

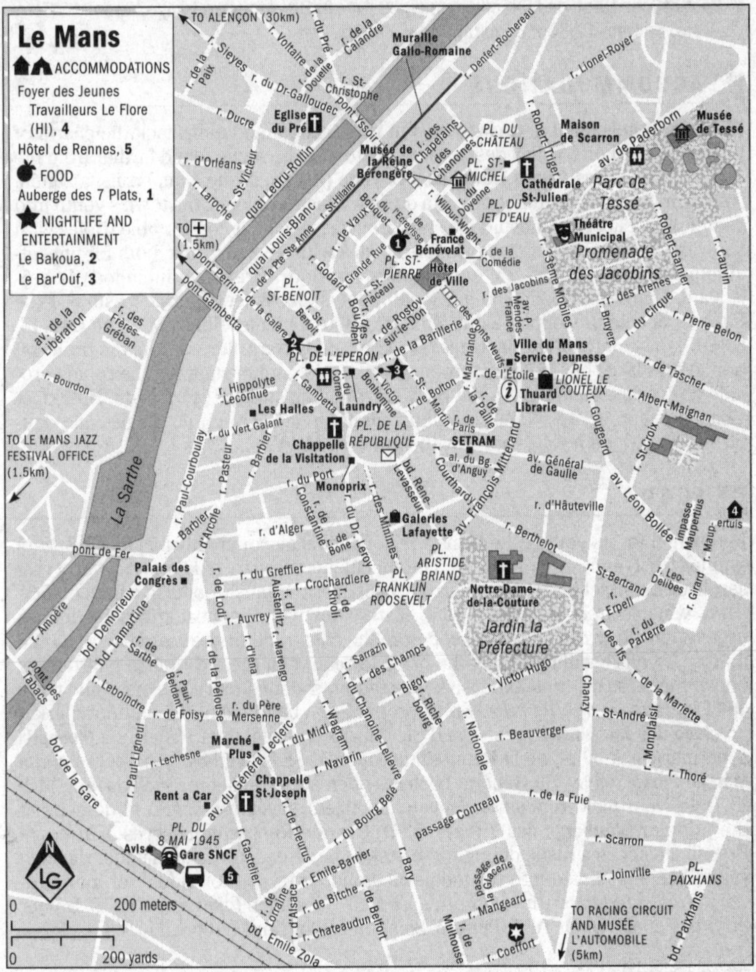

English-language bookstore: **Thuard Librairie,** 24 rue de l'Etoile (☎82 22 22). Open M-F 9am-7pm, Sa 9am-7:30pm. MC/V.

Youth center: Ville du Mans Service Jeunesse, 13 rue de l'Etoile (☎47 38 95). Offers student tips, sports trips, info on jobs and housing, and a booklet of all cultural events. Open M, W, F 10am-noon and 1:30-6pm, Tu and Th 1:30-6pm, Sa 2-6pm. Closed Sa during school holidays.

Laundromat: Lav'Ideal, 4 pl. l'Epéron. Wash €3.60, dry €1.10 per 10min. Open daily 7am-9pm.

Police: 6 rue Coeffort (☎78 55 00).

Hospital: 194 av. Rubillard (☎43 43 43).

Urgent Care: ☎51 15 15.

Post office: 13 pl. de la République (☎39 14 10). **Currency exchange.** Open M-F 8am-7pm, Sa 9am-12:30pm. **Postal Code:** 72000.

ACCOMMODATIONS

Plenty of hotels line bd. de la Gare, but most accommodations lack the charm of those in other Loire Valley destinations. Better deals can be found farther from the station. **Foyer des Jeunes Travailleurs Le Flore (HI) ❶,** 23 rue Maupertuis, a 25min. walk from the station, functions as a dorm for local students, the town's youth info center, and a hostel. A hospitable staff provides small but comfortable triples with shower, as well as spacious dorm-like singles with desk and sink, both for unbeatable prices. (☎81 27 55. TV lounge on every floor. Breakfast included M-Sa 5-8:30am. Cafeteria €5.25-6.50 per meal. Sheets €3. Wheelchair-accessible. Free Internet access. Reception 24hr. Max. stay 3- to 4-nights. Bunks M-F and Su €13, Sa €10. Cash only.) **Hôtel de Rennes ❸,** 43 bd. de la Gare, across from the train station, offers large but expensive rooms. Quiet and cool in summer, the rooms provide a pleasant escape from the busy surrounding streets. (☎24 86 40. Breakfast €6.20. Reception M-Sa 7am-11pm, Su 7am-noon and 5:30-11pm. Singles and doubles €38, with bath €45; triples with bath €54. MC/V.)

FOOD

Renowned for its poultry, Le Mans's regional cuisine commonly includes *pintade* (guinea fowl) and *canard* (duck). The succulent *marmite sarthoise*, a warm casserole of rabbit, chicken, ham, carrots, cabbage, and mushrooms in a bath of *Jasnière* wine, is an omnivore's dream. *Brasseries* with the most affordable menus used to line **place de la République,** before the construction site scared away all the diners. If you're willing to pay the price for eating in the old Roman quarter, try one of the pleasant—but expensive—restaurants along **Grande Rue** or behind **place de l'Eperon** in the *vieille ville.* Fresh produce can be found at the outdoor market on **place des Jacobins.** (Open W and Su 7am-1pm, F 8am-6pm.) There's a **Monoprix** supermarket at 30 pl. de la République (open M-Sa 8:30am-8:30pm; MC/V) and a **Marché Plus** at 68 av. du Général Leclerc (open M-Sa 7am-9pm, Su 9am-1pm; MC/V). Take your pick from among seven appetizers, seven *plats*, and 14 desserts at the popular **Auberge des 7 Plats ❸,** 79 Grande Rue, which serves *à la carte* French cuisine in a rustic dining room. Ask to be seated downstairs under the high vaulted ceiling carved into the medieval stone, or try the top floors for more privacy. Free *calvados* with your coffee. (☎24 57 77. Lunch *formules* €12-15. Dinner *menus* €20-28. Open Tu 7-10pm, W-Sa noon-1:30pm and 7-10pm. MC/V.)

SIGHTS

Unlike most cities in the valley, Le Mans's main attractions date to antiquity or the Middle Ages, including churches like the **Maison-Dieu,** founded by Henry Plantagenêt, and the Romanesque **Notre Dame-de-la-Couture,** near the station. The *billet inter-musée* (€6, students €3) can be found at any museum and includes visits to two of the following: Musée de Tessé, Musée Vert, or Musée de la Reine-Bérengère.

VIEILLE VILLE. Rising up behind thick Roman walls and the river Sarthe, Le Mans's *vieille ville* is one of the most picturesque in France. 15th- to 17th-century houses line the winding streets, and crumbling pillars that once served as street signs—the *Pilier Rouge* and the *Pilier aux Clefs*—mark the corners. Historical Tours depart from the Pilier Rouge. *(Tours M-F 4:30pm. 2hr. €5.50, students €3. In French only.)* In the summer, after sundown, fantastic figures illuminate the cathedral and the roman walls in *La Nuit des Chimères* (nightly July-Aug., 2hr., free). Housed in three 15th-century residences, the **Musée de la Reine Bérengère** displays artifacts from Le Mans's past, including 16th-century ceramic works from the houses's original weathervanes. A well-preserved 18th-century *métier à tisser* (loom) in the attic is perhaps the most impressive piece, while the 16th-century facade, depicting the Virgin Mary with Angel Gabriel, is as interesting as the museum's contents. *(7-11 rue de la Reine Bérengère. ☎47 38 80. Open Tu-Su July–Sept. 10:30am-12:30pm and 2-6:30pm; Oct.-June 2-6pm. €2.80, students €1.40, under 18 free; Su ½-price.)*

CATHÉDRALE ST-JULIEN. Built and rebuilt between the 11th and 15th centuries, Le Mans's cathedral stretches over 5000 square meters; its facade tells the story of Le Mans. Legend has it that Charles VI, on a visit to Le Mans in 1392, was seized by a fit of insanity and was patiently nursed back to health in the cathedral by Saint Julien, who later gave the building his name. Donations from the grateful King helped build the great chancel, which doubled the size of the cathedral, and resulted in the addition of impressive flying buttresses. A celtic *menhir* dating to 5000 BC still rests against the western side of the cathedral; nicknamed the 'belly button of Le Mans,' it was believed to have fertile powers due to its phallic form. Much of the stained glass dates back to the 11th century, while other *vitrages* pay a colorful tribute to Joan of Arc. Notice that there seems to be something missing from the cathedral: in 1832, lightning struck and destroyed its main spire; the cathedral is currently trying to raise the €2.5 million needed to regain its full 15th-century elegance. *(Pl. des Jacobins. Open daily July to mid-Sept. 8am-7pm; mid-Sept. to June 9am-noon and 2-5:30pm. Tours given by tourist office Su 3pm. Tours €5.50, under 18 €3.)*

MURAILLE GALLO-ROMAINE. The stocky fourth-century walls hugging the city's southwestern edge helped make the town of *Vindinium* (Le Mans's original name) a strong base for protection against the 'barbarous' tribes of ancient Roman times. Built by the Romans primarily to showcase their refinement, *lozanges*, intricate mosaics in 14 different patterns, adorn the outside. Punctuated by three arched gates and 10 massive towers, the 1.3km wall is the longest and perhaps best preserved Roman fortification to be found in France. Steep staircases leading into the *vieille ville* penetrate the robust stretch of molded stones.

MUSÉE AND PARC DE TESSÉ. Housed in the former 19th-century bishop's palace, the museum's collection celebrates over 600 years of art. The heavily restored modern interior displays 14th- to 20th-century paintings (including some works by Le Sueur) with a special emphasis on the Italian Renaissance. In 2008, exhibits will include Paraguayan Baroque sculptures (January) and *"Japon de legende"* (summer), which will explore aspects of Japanese culture. In the depths of the museum lie Egyptian artifacts from 1230 BC, including a reproduction of the **underground tomb of Nofetari,** one of the wives of Pharaoh Ramses II. The **tomb of Sennefer,** the mayor of Thebes around 1400 BC, contains a dizzying replica of the cave's original ceiling, accompanied by atmospheric lighting. Call ahead for guided tours in English and French. *(2 av. Paderborn, a 15min. walk from pl. de la République. Take bus #3, dir.: Bellevue, from rue Gastelier by the station or from av. du Général de Gaulle to Musée. ☎47 38 51. Open July-Aug. Tu-Su 10am-12:30pm and 2-6:30pm; Sept.-June Tu-Sa 9am-noon and 2-6pm, Su 10am-noon and 2-6pm. €4, students €2, under 18 free; Su ½-price.)* Behind the museum lies the spacious **Parc de Tessé,** where open-air concerts are hosted every weekend in the summer. Though bustling with families and students during the day, the park should be avoided after sunset, as it becomes dangerous.

RACING CIRCUIT AND MUSÉE AUTOMOBILE. Le Mans has a world-famous tradition of cars—Amédée Bollée and his sons allegedly invented the steam car and the gas car here in the 20th century. The 4km stretch of racetrack south of the city is a must-see for car enthusiasts. Since 1923 the circuit has hosted the annual **24**

Heures du Mans, a grueling test of endurance held in June. *(Tickets ☎40 24 75 or 72 72 24. Tickets to the tracks sold by the museum; €2.)* The massive **Musée Automobile de la Sarthe** traces the evolution of motor vehicles in racing with vintage and high-tech models, including the slick "Socema Gregoire" that Bollée drove 18hr. to introduce to Paris in 1952. Over 140 vehicles are displayed in this giant futuristic garage. *(At the corner of rue de l'Etoile and av. F. Mitterand. Take bus #6 to Raineries to the end of the line. 30min., every 10 min., €1.20. Take a right onto rue de Laigné, following signs to the museum. Schedules at SETRAM office. ☎72 72 24. Open June-Aug. daily 10am-7pm; Sept.-May 10am-6pm; Jan. Sa-Su 10am-6pm. €8, students and ages 12-18 €5, ages 7-11 €2.)*

NIGHTLIFE AND FESTIVALS

Le Mans packs most of its nocturnal revelry into the side streets off **place de la République.** A younger scene is down **rue du Dr. Leroy,** where bars resonate with techno or rock. **Rue des Ponts Neuf** has its own share of bars, decorated with everything from model cars to film projections. Caribbean-themed **Le Bakoua,** 5 rue de la Vieille Porte, off pl. de l'Eperon, draws crowds with calypso and DUB music (a mix of electro and reggae), tropical rum-based drinks, and cheap prices. A small rickety staircase leads to the teenage scene on the second floor. (☎23 30 70. Punch €2.50. Mixed drinks €4-8. Open M-Sa 6pm-2am. MC/V.) **Le Bar'Ouf,** 8 rue Victor Bonhommet, attracts a friendly mixed crowd with its obscure music, artsy vibe—enhanced by a mosaic stone floor and recycled ceiling ornaments—and weekly concerts. (☎24 19 01. Free Wi-Fi. DJ or concerts Th and Sa 10pm-1:30am. Beer €2-3.20. Shots €2.50-3. Mixed drinks €5.70. Open M-F noon-2am, Sa 2pm-2am. MC/V).

Cannes festival winners, independent films, and lesser-known international productions are featured nightly at **Les Cinéastes,** 42 pl. des Comtes du Maine. (☎51 28 18. €6.70, students €5.70, under 13 €3.70.) From mid-April to mid-May, the city hosts contemporary jazz artists for the **Europa Jazz Festival.** (☎23 78 99; www.europa.jazz.fr. Info and tickets at 9 rue des Frères Gréban.) **Les Soirs d'Eté** features around 50 free theater, comedy, and music performances, which take place throughout the city on Thursdays and Fridays in July and August. Pick up an *A l'Affiche* supplement from the tourist office for more info. Late in June, parades and circus performances take over pl. des Jacobins for **Le Mans fait son Cirque.** Last year's event featured Group F, a group dedicated to 'pyrotechnic' *spectacles.* (☎47 36 57. €2 for tent events; most events free.)

BOURGES ☎02 48

Staked in the heart of the lower Loire Valley, Bourges (BOORJH; pop. 75,000) attracts visitors with its flamboyant Gothic architecture, half-timbered houses, and shop-filled medieval streets. Bourges's wealth originated in 1433, when Jacques Cœur, financier of Charles VII, chose the humble city as the site for his palatial home. The city is also a convenient base for daytrips to the secluded châteaux tucked into the thick forests and rolling vineyards of the surrounding region.

TRANSPORTATION

Trains: pl. du Général Leclerc (☎08 92 35 35 35). Info office open M-F 9:30am-7:30pm, Sa 9:30am-6pm. Ticket office open M-Th 5:50am-8:25pm, F 5:50am-9:20pm, Sa 6:25am-7:35pm, Su 7:40am-9:05pm. To: **Lyon** (3½hr., 3 per day, €36); **Nevers** (45min., 8 per day, €7.80); **Paris** (2hr., 8 per day, €28); **Tours** (1½hr., 4 per day, €20). Many trains require a change at nearby Vierzon.

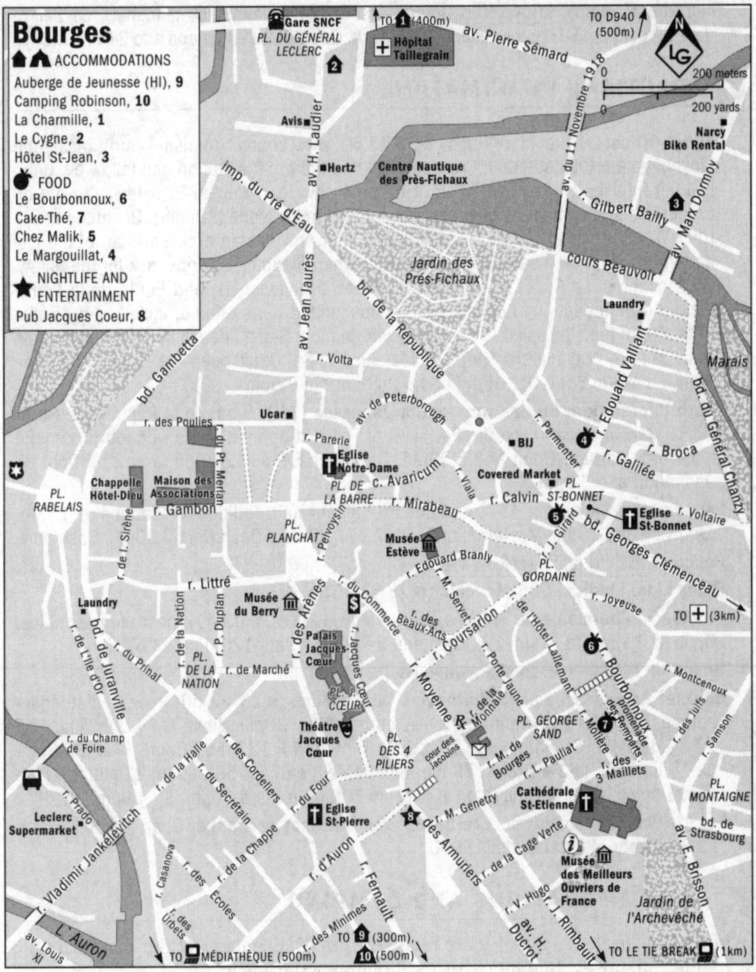

Buses: rue du Champ de Foire (☎24 36 42). Office open M-Tu and Th-F 8-9:30am and 4-6pm, W and Sa 8am-noon. Most buses stop at the train station.

Public Transportation: CTB (☎27 99 99) serves all areas of the city. All schedules are posted at the bus stops and available at the tourist office or 1 pl. de la Nation. Tickets €1.25, *carnet* of 10 €9.

Taxis: (☎24 50 00). €5 from the train station to tourist office. 24hr.

Car Rentals: Hertz, 4 av. Henri Laudier (☎70 22 92), near train station. From €46 per day; under 25 surcharge €35 per day. 21+. Open M-F 8am-noon and 2-6pm. AmEx/MC/V. **Avis,** 23 av. Henri Laudier (☎24 38 84). From €47 per day. Open M-F 8am-noon and 2-6pm and Sa 8am-1pm. AmEx/MC/V. **Ucar,** 21 av. Jean Jaurès (☎70 63 33), halfway between the station and the *centre-ville*. Under-25 insurance fee doubles. 21+. Open M-Sa 8am-noon and 2-6pm. MC/V.

Bike Rental: Narcy, 39 av. Marx Dormoy (☎70 15 84; narcyvelo@nerim.net). €7 per ½-day, €8 per day, €16 per weekend; ID deposit. Open Tu-Su 9am-noon and 2-6pm. MC/V.

PRACTICAL INFORMATION

Tourist Office: 21 rue Victor Hugo (☎23 02 60; www.bourges-tourisme.com), facing rue Moyenne near the cathedral. Cross the street in front of the station and follow av. Henri Laudier into the *vieille ville,* where it becomes av. Jean Jaurès. Bear left onto rue du Commerce and continue straight as it becomes rue Moyenne (18min.). Or catch bus #1 (dir.: Val d'Auron) to "Victor Hugo." Helpful staff provides an excellent map of the city and information on museums and festivals. When planning daytrips, ask for the following brochures: *La Route Jacques-Cœur, Route des Vignobles,* and *Route de la Porcelaine.* Accommodations booking €1. Various guided tours offered, including a 45min. tram tour of the city; ask office for more information. Self-guided illuminated night tours at sunset July-Aug. nightly; Sept. and May-June Tu-Sa. Office open Apr.-Sept. M-Sa 9am-7pm, Su 10am-6pm; Oct.-Mar. M-Sa 9am-6pm, Su 2-5pm.

Youth Information: Bureau Information Jeunesse (BIJ), 8 bd. de la République (☎24 77 19; bij@bourges.fr), on the 2nd level of Halle St-Bonnet. Helps with job placement and study abroad. Open M 2-5:30pm, Tu and Th-F 9am-12:30pm and 2-5:30pm, W 9am-noon and 2-6pm.

Laundromat: Lavmatic, 117 rue Edouard Valliant and additional locations at 15 bd. Juranville and 79 rue M. Haeselen (☎06 72 77 32 05). Open 8am-8:30pm. Cash only.

Police: 6 av. d'Orléans (☎23 77 17).

Crisis Line: Medical SOS Médecin (☎23 33 33).

Pharmacy: Pharmacie du Progrès, 27 rue Moyenne (☎24 00 41), near the post office. Open M 2-7pm, Tu-F 9am-12:30pm and 2-7pm, Sa 9am-12:30pm. MC/V.

Hospital: 145 rue François Mitterand (☎48 48 48).

Internet Access: Free at **Médiathèque,** bd. Lamarck (☎23 22 50; www.mediatheque-bourges.fr), a library 10min. from the tourist office. 30min. limit. Open July-Aug. Tu-F 12:30-6:30pm, Sa 9am-noon; Sept.-June Tu-W and F 12:30-6:30pm, Th 12:30-8pm, Sa 10am-5pm. **Le Tie Break,** 78 rue Jean Baffier (☎67 94 58), about 12min. from the tourist office. €4.80 per hr. Open M-F 11am-10:30pm, Sa 3-10pm, Su 4-8pm. MC/V.

Post Office: 29 rue Moyenne (☎68 82 82). **Currency exchange.** Open M-F 8am-7pm, Sa 8am-noon. **Postal Code:** 18000.

LOIRE VALLEY

ACCOMMODATIONS AND CAMPING

While hotels in the city center are relatively pricey, cheaper options can be found a 10min. walk away. Summer visitors should reserve ahead.

Hôtel St-Jean, 23 av. Marx Dormoy (☎24 13 48; hotelstjean.bourges@wanadoo.fr), in a quiet neighborhood 10min. from both the train station and the center of town. A gracious owner lets small, carpeted rooms with hard beds, TV and clean bath. Elevator. Breakfast €6. Reception 24hr. Singles €35; doubles €45; triples €55. MC/V. ❸

Le Cygne, 10 pl. du Général Leclerc (☎70 51 05; www.hotel-lecygne.com), across from the train station. Despite somewhat thin walls, rooms off colorful hallways are comfortable and equipped with shower, toilet, Wi-Fi, and TV. Elevator and attached restaurant. Breakfast €6. Singles and doubles €35-45; triples and quads €50-58. MC/V. ❸

Auberge de Jeunesse (HI), 22 rue Henri Sellier (☎24 58 09; bourges@fuaj.org), 10min. from town center. From the station, take av. Henri Laudier, which becomes av. Jean Jaurès, to pl. Planchat. Follow rue des Arènes, which becomes rue Fernault and then rue René Ménard. Turn left at rue Henri Sellier. Hostel is on the right, behind a brown and white building (25-30min.). Or, take bus #1 (dir.: Golf) or 2 (dir.: Hôpital) to "Auron."

Recently-renovated, clean, and colorful 2- to 5-bunk rooms, some with showers. Grassy garden overlooks small river. Access to kitchen and free parking. Breakfast €3.50. Reception 8-10am and 6-10pm. Dorms €16. Cash only. ❶

Centre International de Séjour: La Charmille, 17 rue Félix-Chédin (☎23 07 40; www.lacharmille.asso.fr). From the station, cross the tracks and walk 5min. up rue Félix-Chédin. Buses #1 and 2 run to the *centre-ville* (dir.: Golf or Hôpital, respectively). Next to a skate park. Clean, dorm-like rooms with shower. Loud and social atmosphere with a diverse array of guests–mostly young families, teenagers, and 20-somethings. Breakfast included. Lunch and dinner €9.50. Laundry. Dorms €14; singles €20. One-time membership fee €4.40, good for a year. MC/V. ❶

Camping Robinson, 26 bd. de l'Industrie (☎20 16 85; www.ville-bourges.fr). Follow directions to Auberge de Jeunesse (see above). Turn right at the end of rue Henri Sellier onto bd. de l'Industrie. Landscaped riverside campground near a residential area, 12min. from the city center. Free swimming pool nearby open in summer. Reception June-Aug. 7am-10pm; Sept. to mid-Nov. and mid-Mar. to May 8am-9pm. €3.70 per person, €2 per child, €3.70 per tent. Electricity €3-7.50. AmEx/MC/V over €15. ❶

FOOD

Locals fill the outdoor tables on **place Gordaine** and **rue des Beaux-Arts** during the spring and summer. For a touch of elegance, try the tasty regional cuisine in one of the many timber-framed restaurants on **rue Bourbonnoux** or **rue Girard.** Look for specialties like *poulet en barbouille* (chicken roasted in aromatic red wine), *crottin de chavignol* (the area's most famous goat cheese), and *oeufs en meurette* (eggs in red wine). The largest market is held on **place de la Nation** (Sa morning); another livens up **place des Marronniers** (Th until 1pm). There is a smaller, covered market permanently at **place St-Bonnet,** though it moves outdoors on Sunday mornings. (Tu-Th 8am-12:45pm and 3:30-7:30pm, F-Sa 8am-1pm and 3-7:30pm, Su 8am-1pm.) The **Leclerc** supermarket, rue Prado off bd. Juranville, next to the bus station, boasts an enormous selection. (Open M-Sa 8:30am-7:20pm. MC/V.)

Chez Malik, 7 rue Jean Girard (☎24 59 85). Serves almost-impossible-to-finish portions of the house specialty, couscous, in an exotic African-themed interior. Friendly staff and a vast menu of flavorful lamb, beef, and chicken combinations (€9.90-19). Open Tu-Sa noon-2pm and 7:30-10:30pm. MC/V. ❷

Cake-Thé, 74bis rue Bourbonnoux (☎24 94 60; www.cak-t.com). An intimate, storybook tearoom lodged into a lavender-lined passage between rue Bourbonnoux and rue Molière. Floral tablecloths, candles, and small bowls of dried fruit welcome you to this *salon de thé,* where delicious desserts (€4-5) and exotic teas (€3-4) provide a sweet, satisfying escape. Open M and Su 3-7pm, Tu-Sa 11am-7pm. MC/V. ❶

Le Margouillat, 53 rue Edouard Vaillant (☎24 08 13), offers flavorful cuisine inspired by France's ex-colonies in the Indian Ocean. A tropical atmosphere is complemented by an equally colorful menu. Creole fish (€12-15) is the house specialty, but the menu has other French favorites charmed with island accents. *Menus* €17-23. Open M and Sa 7-11pm, Tu-F noon-2pm and 7-11pm. MC/V. ❸

Le Bourbonnoux, 44 rue Bourbonnoux (☎24 14 76). On a quiet street of half-timbered houses. Serves regional fare in a bright, unpretentious atmosphere. *Canard* (duck) plays a central role in the dishes and décor; figurines line the walls. *Menus* €12-28. Open M-Th noon-2pm and 7:30-9:15pm, Sa 7-9pm, Su noon-2pm. AmEx/MC/V. ❸

SIGHTS

Bourges's past has endowed its *vieille ville* with outstanding museums, a pretty palace, and a stunning cathedral, all of which are clustered closely enough to be seen in one afternoon. The **Palais Jacques Cœur, Cathedral Tower,** and **Cathedral Crypt** are the only paid entry sites, and they sell either individual tickets or a combined *billet jumelé*, which will save you money if you plan to go to all three attractions. Bourges's many parks, including the rose-filled **Jardin de l'Archevêché** and the peaceful **Jardin des Prés-Fichaux,** provide plenty of places for a lovely stroll.

CATHÉDRALE ST-ETIENNE. This gargantuan thirteenth-century cathedral is a masterpiece of Gothic architecture, with gargoyles and flying buttresses reminiscent of Paris's Notre-Dame (p. 127). A soaring vaulted ceiling creates a cavernous interior illuminated by light from windows high above the nave, where impressive brass chandeliers also hang. The Great Tower, a copy of one of the Louvre's towers, is a symbol of royal power. Entrance to the church is free, but tickets are required to visit the cathedral's crypt or to climb the northern tower for a breathtaking view of the city. *(Cathedral open daily Apr.-Sept. 8:30am-7:15pm; Oct.-Mar. 9am-5:45pm. Tours led by parishioners available inside. June-Sept. 10:30am-12:30pm and 4-6pm. Mass Tu-Sa 6:30pm, Su 11am. Tours of crypt and tower daily except Su mornings July-Aug. 9:30am-12:30pm and 2-6pm; May-June 9:30-11:30am and 2-5:30pm; Apr. and Sept. 9:45-11:45am and 2-5:30pm; Oct.-Mar. 9:30-11:30am and 2-4:45pm. €6.50, ages 18-25 €4.50, under 18 free; tower €5/3.50/free). Ask at tourist office for schedule.)*

PALAIS JACQUES-CŒUR. Commissioned in 1443 by Jacques Cœur, finance minister to Charles VII, this palace was intended to flaunt Cœur's personal fortune to his high-society guests. Unfortunately, he was imprisoned for embezzlement in 1451, years before its completion. Today, the palace lies unfurnished but remains an exquisite example of the flamboyant architectural style of the late Middle Ages, with an exterior dotted with daunting gargoyles and an interior decorated with carved mantelpieces and vaulted ceilings. *(10bis rue Jacques-Cœur. ☎24 79 42. Mandatory guided tour in French. Short English text available. Open daily July-Aug. 9:30am-noon and 2-7pm; Sept.-Oct. and May-June 9:30am-noon and 2-6pm; Nov.-Mar. 9:30am-noon and 2-5pm. €6.50, ages 18-25 €4.50, under 18 free. Tours every 45min.)*

MUSEUMS. Bourges has several small, free museums with regionally-focused exhibits. The **Musée des Meilleurs Ouvriers de France,** housed in the 17th-century archiepiscopal residence, pays homage to superior local craftsmanship. Each year, the French government bestows a medal of honor, the *Meilleur Ouvrier*, on a number of artists and professionals who produce exceptional work in fields ranging from hairstyling to leatherwork to lighting; the museum chronicles the award's history and highlights recent winners within the year's featured craft. "*Les Accessoires*" (accessories) are the focus for 2008. *(Pl. Etienne Dolet. ☎57 82 45. Open Tu-Sa 10am-noon and 2-6pm, Su 2-6pm.)* Observe the diverse artistic style of the late Maurice Estève at the **Musée Estève,** which displays modern paintings, tapestries, and drawings by this local artist. The museum offers brochures in English and French. *(13 rue Edouard Branly. ☎24 75 38. Open M and W-Sa 10am-noon and 2-6pm, Su 2-6pm.)* The **Musée du Berry** showcases prehistoric, Gallo-Roman, and medieval artifacts excavated from the region, along with displays featuring local ceramic work and 19th-century farming implements. *(4 rue des Arènes. ☎70 41 92. Open M and W-Sa July-Aug. 10am-12:30pm and 1:30-6pm, Su 2-6pm; Apr.-June and Sept. to early Jan. 10am-noon and 2-6pm; early Jan.-Mar. 10am-noon and 2-5pm.)*

LOIRE VALLEY

ENTERTAINMENT AND FESTIVALS

Bars and cafés cluster in the *vieille ville*, but nightlife in Bourges is fairly subdued. On the weekends, the stone-walled **Pub Jacques Cœur,** 1 rue d'Auron, fills with a mixed-age crowd who comes for live music and DJs. Waitresses dressed in Jameson whiskey skirts and alcohol-inspired memorabilia add to the typical pub atmosphere. (☎70 72 88. Open M 10am-8pm, Tu-Sa 10am-2am.)

Les Nuits Lumière de Bourges, a self-guided nighttime tour of the city, presents Bourges in a whole new light. The tour begins with music and a slide show on local history, then follows a route through Bourges lit by glowing blue lampposts. Classical music plays while representations of medieval and Renaissance artwork are illuminated on major monuments, creating a fantastical effect. Tours start at nightfall in the Jardin de l'Archevêché and last about 2hr. (At sunset July-Aug. daily and May-June; Sept. Tu-Sa. Tourist office offers brochures. Free.) Free concerts and performances reign over the gardens, museums, and streets of Bourges every night from mid-June to mid-September during **Un Eté a Bourges.** (☎24 93 32; www.bourges.fr.) Over 100,000 ears perk up in April for the **Festival Printemps de Bourges.** (☎27 28 29; www.printemps-bourges.com. Most tickets €7-28; some informal folk, jazz, classical, and rock concerts free). Visual arts take center stage in early October at the **BulleBerry Festival Bande Dessinée** ("Bubbleberry Comic Book Festival"). Cartoonists and their fans converge on Bourges's historic sites for a weekend of displays and discussion. (☎23 02 60; www.bulleberry.com.)

DAYTRIPS FROM BOURGES: ROUTE JACQUES CŒUR

Jacques may have left his *cœur* in Bourges, but his ego spilled far into the surrounding countryside. The Route Jacques Cœur consists of a string of 13 châteaux, along with a 12th-century abbey, stretching from La Buissière in the north to Culan in the south. Less ostentatious than those of the Loire, these castles see far fewer tourists each year; visitors often receive more personal attention during tours. Many of the families who made them famous still live in the châteaux and enjoy sharing their homes. Most of the châteaux in this section can be seen only by guided tour. English brochures are often available; English tours are uncommon.

The châteaux make for relaxing daytrips, but most can be reached only by car or bike; routes are usually well marked. If you plan to stay overnight, arrange lodging ahead. The tourist offices in Bourges (p. 228) and St-Amand-Montrond (see below) have free English maps of the route and info on excursions. Although *Let's Go* highlights several châteaux below, the area is a treasure-trove of sights; this list should be considered merely a starting point for further exploration.

ST-AMAND-MONTROND

To get to St-Amand from Bourges, take the train (50min.; M-Sa 8 per day, Su 3 per day; €9), or drive south on N144 or A71. From there, a short bike or car ride takes you to nearby sights.

Forty-five kilometers south of Bourges lies St-Amand-Montrond (sehn ah-MAHN mohn-TROHN), an accessible starting point for explorations of the southern part of the route. Though the surrounding châteaux and stretches of forest are the real draw, St-Amand itself makes for an interesting half-day visit. The tourist office arranges a walking tour in French that takes visitors past the city's medieval churches, **Paroisse de St-Amand** and the **Eglise des Carmes.** Meanwhile, the ruins of the medieval **Forteresse de Montrond** can be seen from afar, or up close if you reserve ahead. (☎96 79 64. Mid-June to mid-Sept. 3 times a day, or call to schedule a visit.)

The **tourist office,** pl. de la République, provides free maps highlighting sights both within the city and in its surroundings. From the train station, follow av. de la Gare straight through the rotary; continue on as it becomes av. Jean Jaurès and, later, rue Henri Barbusse. After 20min., the road runs into pl. de la République; the tourist office is on the left. (☎96 16 86. Open daily 9am-noon and 2-6:45pm.) For a **taxi,** call ☎06 09 94 69 34. **Bike rental** is available at **Cycles HANTZ,** a branch of **Vélo & Oxygen,** 72 av. Général Charles de Gaulle. Head toward the tourist office from the station and when av. Jean Jaurès becomes rue Henri Barbusse, turn left onto rue 14 Juillet; at the T-intersection with N144, turn left (dir.: Bourges) and walk for

5min. The shop is on the right. (☎96 00 80. Open M 2-7pm, Tu-Sa 9am-noon and 2-7pm. Bikes €5 per hr., €10 per 4hr., €13 per 8hr.; €120 or ID deposit. MC/V.)

CHÂTEAU DE MEILLANT

If you plan on seeing the Abbey de Noirlac and the château by bike, go to the abbey first; otherwise you'll bike 7km uphill. To get to the town of Meillant from St-Amand, take rue Nationale, starting near the tourist office, and head north to the D10.

A beautiful but difficult 8km bike ride from St-Amand through the **Forêt de Meillant** leads to the impressive Renaissance Château de Meillant (shah-TOH duh may-YAHN). In the 15th century, it was purchased by the Amboise family, who imported Italian architects, sculptors, and decorators to infuse the castle with extravagant Renaissance accents. Its ornate stone carvings are especially visible on the **Tour du Lion,** a turret partially designed by Leonardo da Vinci. Excellent French guided tours of the château point out fascinating features of its architecture and interior decoration, describe the living habits of past inhabitants, and display the incredible range of art and weapons in the castle. The babbling brook and winding paths encircling the château provide a number of spots for visitors to admire its exterior. A small building near the castle contains intricate miniature models of castle life from the Middle Ages to the 18th century. (☎63 32 05. Open daily July-Aug. 9:30am-6pm; Sept. to mid-Nov. and Mar.-June 9:30am-noon and 2-6pm. Visit only by guided tour in French; English translation available. Château and gardens €7, students €5.50, ages 5-15 €5. MC/V.)

ABBAYE DE NOIRLAC

To get to the abbey from St-Amand, take rue Henri Barbusse to rue 14 Juillet. After crossing the river, turn left onto N144 (dir.: Bourges); the well-marked turn-off for the abbey is on the left. Be careful while crossing the wide road if you are on a bike.

Just 3km west of St-Amand-Montrond lies the Abbaye de Noirlac (ah-BAY duh nwahr-LAHK), a peaceful haven for city-weary travelers. The former Cistercian abbey now has vacant stone rooms with simple stained glass. The **cloister** at the center is framed by Gothic arcades and fringed by roses. Most of the monks' **chapter house** dates from its 12th-century construction; the rest was renovated in the 18th century. The abbey hosts annual exhibits on regional arts and culture. During June and July, the popular **L'Eté de Noirlac** energizes the abbey's spacious and otherwise serene rooms with an excellent selection of live music. (☎48 00 27; www.festivaldenoirlac.com. Tickets €12-22.) For larger groups, the abbey will host a special dinner of traditional monastery fare, dramatically reenacting the everyday life of a monk. (Call for reservations at least 15 days ahead. Groups of 20 or more only; €50 per person.) (☎62 01 01. Open daily July-Aug. 9:45am-6:30pm; Sept. and Apr.-June 9:45am-12:30pm and 2-6:30pm; Oct.-Mar. 9:45am-12:30pm and 2-5pm. Ticket office closes 1hr. before abbey. Call ahead for schedule of French tours; English explanations available. Call ahead to arrange English guided tours. €6, students €4.50. MC/V.)

MENETOU-SALON AND MAUPAS

To get to Menetou-Salon, take D940 (av. du Général de Gaulle in the city) north for 5km, continue straight through the roundabout, and bear right onto D11, following the signs. To get to Maupas from Menetou-Salon, follow the signs to Parassy and Morogues as the road passes through 7km of scenic, vineyard-covered countryside. The château is on the left, about 1km before Morogues. From Bourges, take rue de la Charité east as it becomes N151. Take a left on D955 and another left on D46. Enter through the white gates on the curbside.

A bit closer to Bourges and easier to reach by bike, Maupas and Menetou-Salon combine to make an ideal daytrip. Situated 20km north of Bourges, **Menetou-Salon** (mehn-TOO sah-LOHN) is the closer of the two. Leaving Bourges, the cityscape quickly recedes, replaced by endless rolling hills sprinkled with farms and vineyards, which are picturesque but often prove difficult for bikers. Many of these *vignobles* (vineyards) offer tours and sell their wine on-site. Jacques bought the Menetou-Salon castle in 1448, but his subsequent imprisonment, as well as the later Revolution, left the castle temporarily in ruins. In the 19th century, the Prince of Arenberg stepped in and decided to finish it. Though the current prince lives in the US, he often visits his château to hunt; the staff keeps his home prepared for his arrival by filling the rooms with fresh flowers daily. A video of the prince's fairytale-like wedding and several family photos add personal touches. Tour guides dressed in Romantic era costumes lead visitors through the castle's luxurious interior, pointing out antique wonders and showing off the Prince's magnificent vintage car collection, which includes a limited edition 1937 Rolls Royce. (☎64 80 54. Open daily July-Aug. 10am-7pm; May-June and Sept. 2-6pm. Visit by tour only; last tour 5pm. Tours in French with English brochure available; ends with free wine tasting; 1¼ hr. €8.50, students €6, under 7 free. AmEx/MC/V.)

The small but exquisitely preserved 13th-century castle of **Maupas** (moh-PAH) is decorated with beautiful antique furniture, tapestries, and *faïences* (decorative crockery) collected by Jerome Agard de Maupas, whose family has lived there since 1688. The 1hr. French tour showcases a staircase lined with an impressive collection of 887 painted plates from around the world, a beautiful Louis XIV-style canopy bed, 19th-century doll houses, and the famous flag of the Comte de Chambord, the last royalist Bourbon pretender to the throne, who insisted upon replacing the tricolor flag with the monarchy's white *fleur-de-lis*. (☎64 41 71. English brochures available. Call ahead for English tours. Open Palm Su-June M-Sa 2-7pm, Su 10am-noon and 2-7pm; July-Sept. daily 10am-noon and 2-7pm; early- to mid-Oct. daily 2-6pm; mid-Oct. to mid-Dec. Su 2-6pm. €7, students €5, ages 7-12 €4.50. Tours available by reservation mid-Dec. to May. Wine-tasting available for groups, €8. Cash only.)

BRITTANY (BRETAGNE)

Brittany has the *centre-villes*, *crêperies*, and châteaux that give France its superficial unity, but the region still holds fast to a separate cultural identity rooted in a long history of independence. Its Celtic roots date back to pre-Roman times, when Bretons began settling the region; since then, France has tried repeatedly to win over the province, finally succeeding in 1491 when the duke's daughter, Anne de Bretagne, married two successive French kings to protect her beloved Brittany from war with Paris. The châteaux of Nantes and Dinan are remnants of the region's fight for freedom, but Brittany's cultural independence is most noticeable in omnipresent black-and-white Breton flags, street signs written in the traditional Celtic language *Brezhoneg*, and traditional costumes worn during festivals. The sweetest part of Breton culture, though, is the cuisine—especially pastries like the sticky *kouing-amann* and the plum-filled *far breton*.

For its modern visitors, Brittany has something to satisfy every taste, from the millennia-old rows of Neolithic *menhirs* (standing stones) at Carnac (p. 271) to the centuries-old château of Nantes (p. 273), to the brand-new nightlife of Rennes. Meanwhile, the province's exceptional natural beauty is visible in the stunning seascapes of its offshore islands and in the woodland streams of Pont-Aven (p. 267), which inspired Paul Gauguin and other 19th-century artists to found a new school of painting. In the summer, locals and tourists enjoy the beaches and water sports in sun-drenched St-Malo and Quiberon (p. 268). Even in low season, when the churches, beaches, and cliffs become eerily romantic, these seaside destinations are far from dormant.

HIGHLIGHTS OF BRITTANY

ESCAPE the mainland and head to the rugged cliffs and rolling pastures of the western-most point in France: the **Ile d'Ouessant** (p. 261).

SUNBATHE in **St-Malo** (p. 243), which offers the same sandy beaches as the Côte d'Azur—without the high prices.

MIX UP a cocktail of old and new in **Rennes** (p. 235), a lively university town where you can party until dawn in centuries-old buildings and even a former prison.

RENNES ☎02 99

Rennes (REN; pop. 213,000), two hours from Paris, has the cosmopolitan atmosphere of the French capital and the independent spirit of the Breton countryside. The cityscape has everything from medieval half-timbered houses to ornate Neoclassical facades, and harbors colorful nightclubs at every turn. No question about it—this university town is the party mecca of northwest France. Unlike Brittany's coast, Rennes is most alive from September to June, when its 60,000 students are in town. Come summer, the city is more dormant—or just hungover.

TRANSPORTATION

Trains: Pl. de la Gare. Info and ticket office open M-Th 5:40am-9:05pm, F 5:40am-9:15pm, Sa 6:45am-8:05pm, Su 7:40am-10:05pm. To: **Brest** (2½hr., every hr., €30); **Caen** (3hr., 4 per day, €31); **Nantes** (1¼-2hr., 6-11 per day, €21); **Paris** (2hr., every hr., €53-65); **St-Malo** (1hr., 15 per day, €13); **Tours** (2½-3hr., every hr., €37).

Buses: 16 pl. de la Gare (☎30 87 80; www.gare-routière-rennes.fr), to the right of the train station's north entrance. **Illenoo** (☎30 87 80; www.illenoo.fr) serves **Dinan** (1¼hr.; M-Sa 5 per day, Su 4 per day; €3) and **St-Malo** (2hr.; M-Sa 5 per day, Su 3 per day; €3); ages 10-26 tickets 20% off. **Anjou Bus** (☎08 20 16 00 49; www.cg49.fr) goes to **Angers** (2½hr.; 2 per day; €14). **Regional buses** run to **Mont-St-Michel** (1½hr.; 4 per day; €11, under 25 or over 60 €9).

Public Transportation: Star, 12 rue du Pré Botté. (☎08 11 55 55 35; www.star.fr). Office open M-F 7am-7:30pm, Sa 9am-6:30pm. **Buses** run M-Sa 5:15am-12:30am, Su 7:25am-midnight. Buy tickets onboard, from the bus office, or at *tabacs.* A **Metro** line runs through the heart of Rennes and accepts the same ticket. Tickets €1.10, 1-day pass €3.20, *carnet* of 10 €11.

Taxis: (☎30 79 79). Stands at train station and on pl. de la République. 24hr.

Bike Rental: Guedard, 13 bd. Beaumont (☎30 43 78). €13 per day. Open M noon-7pm, Tu-F 9am-12:30pm and 2-7pm, Sa 9am-6pm. AmEx/MC/V.

ORIENTATION AND PRACTICAL INFORMATION

Avenue Jean Janvier, at the north exit of the station, runs over the Vilaine River, which separates the train station from the *vieille ville.* Turn left and walk along quai Chateaubriand to reach **place de la République,** the city's cultural center. To the north on rue d'Orléans lies **place de la Mairie,** in the heart of the *vieille ville.*

Tourist Office: 11 rue St-Yves (☎67 11 11; www.tourisme-rennes.com). From pl. de la République, turn right onto rue George Dottin, then right on rue St-Yves. The office is on the right. Free maps; directions; and lists of hotels, restaurants, and shops. 1-2hr. tours of sights in downtown Rennes in French July-Aug. daily, Sept.-June 1-3 per week; in English or Spanish Aug. 2 per week. €6.80, students €4, under 7 free. Ticket office for tours, festivals, and concerts. Open July-Aug. M-Sa 9am-7pm, Su 11am-1pm and 2-6pm; Sept.-June M 1-6pm, Tu-Sa 10am-6pm, Su 11am-1pm and 2-6pm.

Consulate: US, 30 quai Duguay Trouin (☎02 23 44 09 60; fax 35 00 92). By appointment only.

English-Language Bookstore: operated by the **Institut Franco-Américain,** 7 quai Chateaubriand (☎79 89 22; www.ifa-rennes.org). The largest English-language bookstore in Brittany. Open Tu 10am-noon and 1-6pm, W 10am-noon and 1-6:30pm, Th 1-6:30pm, F 1-5:30pm, Sa 10am-1pm.) **Comédie des Langues,** 25 rue de St-Malo (☎36 72 95; www.comediedeslangues.fr). Carries books in a variety of foreign languages (including German, Italian, Portuguese, and Spanish). Open M-F 9:30am-7pm, Sa 10am-6pm.

Youth Center: Centre Régional Information Jeunesse Bretagne (CRIJB), Maison du Champ de Mars, 6 cours des Alliés (☎31 47 48; www.crij-bretagne.com). Info on summer jobs, vacations, and safety. Free anonymous counseling Sept.-June. Internet for research free. Personal Internet annual membership €3; members €1 per hr., non-members €2 per hr. Open July-Aug. Tu 2-9pm, W-Sa 2-6pm; Sept.-June Tu 10am-9pm, W-F 10am-6pm, Sa 2-6pm.

Laundromats: 18 rue du Robien, near the hostel. Home to a café (☎38 86 62). Open Tu-W 11am-8pm, Th-F 11am-1am, Sa 1pm-1am, Su 3pm-1am. Also at 23 rue de

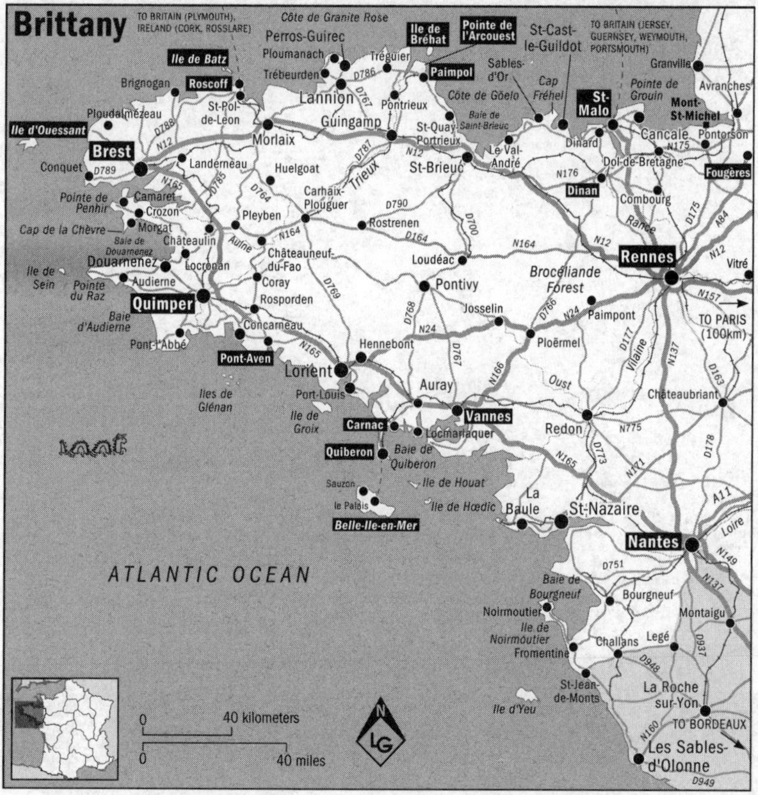

Penhoët (open daily 7am-8pm), 59 rue Duhamel (open daily 7am-10pm), and 3 pl. de Bretagne (open daily 7am-10pm).

Hiking and Biking Information: France Randonnée, 9 rue Portes Mordelaises (☎67 42 21; www.france-randonnee.fr). Info on *Grande Randonnée* (GR) trails (several day-to week-long hikes), as well as shorter walks. Open mid-Mar. to mid-Oct. M-F 10am-12:30pm and 2-6pm, Sa 10am-1pm; mid-Oct. to mid-Mar. closed Sa.

Police: 22 bd. de la Tour d'Auvergne (☎65 00 22).

Hospital: Centre Hospitalier Régional Hôtel Dieu, 2 rue de l'Hôtel Dieu (☎28 43 21).

Pharmacy: Across from the train station at **Pharmacie de la Gare,** 9 pl. de la Gare (☎30 83 27). Open M-F 8:30am-7:30pm, Sa 9am-12:30pm.

Internet Access: At **CRIJB** (see p. 236). **Rennes L@N,** 16 sq. de la Rance (☎08 77 82 54 63), near the hostel. €1 per 15min., €1.60 per 30min., €2.80 per hr. ½-price "Happy hours" July-Aug. 2-2:30pm and 6-7pm; Sept.-June 1-1:30pm and 6-7pm. Open July-Aug. M 2-10pm, Tu-Sa 2pm-1am, Su 2-11pm; Sept.-June M noon-10pm, Tu-Sa 11am-1am, Su 2-11pm. **Neurogame,** 2 rue de Dinan (☎65 53 85). €3 per hr. Open July-Aug. M-F noon-midnight, Sa 2pm-midnight, Su 2-10pm; Sept.-June M noon-midnight, Tu-F 10am-midnight, Sa 2pm-midnight, Su 2-10pm. **Cybernet Online,** 22 rue St-Georges (☎36 37 41). €0.80 per 5min., €2.50 per 30min., €4 per hr. Open M 2-8pm, Tu-F 10:30am-8pm. Closed Aug.

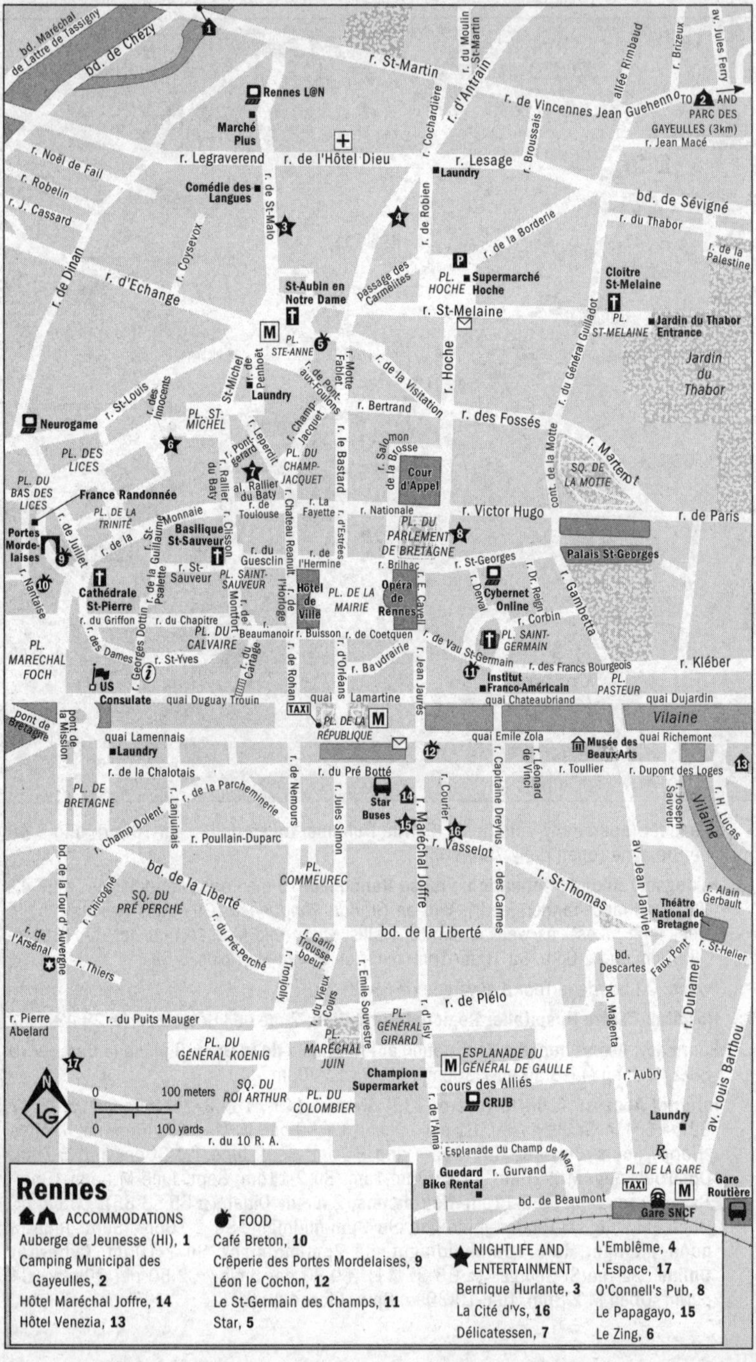
bd. Maréchal de Lattre de Tassigny
bd. de Chézy
r. St-Martin
r. du Moulin St-Martin
r. d'Antrain
r. de Vincennes
Jean Guehenno
TO 2 AND PARC DES GAYEULLES (3km)
allée Rimbaud
r. Brizeux
av. Jules Ferry
r. Jean Macé
Rennes L@N
Marché Plus
r. Noël de Fail
r. Robelin
r. J. Cassard
r. Legraverend
r. de l'Hôtel Dieu
r. Lesage
Laundry
r. Cochardière
r. Broussais
bd. de Sévigné
r. du Thabor
r. de la Palestine
Comédie des Langues
r. de St-Malo
r. de Robien
r. de la Borderie
r. Coysevox
r. de Dinan
r. d'Echange
passage des Carmélites
PL. HOCHE
Supermarché Hoche
Cloitre St-Melaine
St-Aubin en Notre Dame
r. St-Melaine
PL. ST-MELAINE
Jardin du Thabor Entrance
Jardin du Thabor
PL. STE-ANNE
r. de Penhoët
St-Michel
r. de Pont-aux-Foulons
r. Motte Fablet
r. de la Visitation
r. Hoche
r. du Général Guillaudot
Laundry
r. St-Louis
r. des Innocents
Neurogame
PL. ST-MICHEL
r. Bertrand
r. des Fossés
PL. DES LICES
r. Leperdit
r. Champ-Jacquet
r. le Bastard
r. Salomon de la Brosse
Cour d'Appel
r. Martenot
SQ. DE LA MOTTE
cont. de la Motte
PL. DU BAS DES LICES
r. Pont-gerard
r. Rallier du Baty
PL. DU CHAMP-JACQUET
al. Rallier du Baty
France Randonnée
r. de Toulouse
r. La Fayette
r. Nationale
r. Victor Hugo
r. de Paris
PL. DE LA TRINITÉ
r. de la Monnaie
Basilique St-Sauveur
r. Clisson
PL. DU PARLEMENT DE BRETAGNE
Portes Mordelaises
r. de Juillet
r. St-Guillaume
r. du Guesclin
r. de l'Hermine
r. d'Estrées
r. Brilhac
r. St-Georges
Palais St-Georges
r. Nantaise
r. St-Sauveur
PL. SAINT-SAUVEUR
r. de la Psalette
Hôtel de Ville
PL. DE LA MAIRIE
Opéra de Rennes
r. E. Cavell
r. Derval
Cybernet Online
r. Dr. Regnault
r. Gambetta
Cathédrale St-Pierre
r. du Griffon
r. du Chapitre
r. Montfort
r. de l'Horloge
r. Chateau Renault
r. Corbin
PL. DU CALVAIRE
r. Beaumanoir
r. Buisson
r. de Coetquen
r. de Vau St-Germain
PL. SAINT-GERMAIN
PL. MARECHAL FOCH
r. des Dames
r. St-Yves
r. Georges Dottin
r. du Cartage
r. de Rohan
r. d'Orléans
r. Baudrairie
r. Jean Jaurès
r. des Francs Bourgeois
r. Kléber
Institut Franco-Américain
PL. PASTEUR
US Consulate
quai Duguay Trouin
quai Lamartine
quai Chateaubriand
quai Dujardin
TAXI
PL. DE LA RÉPUBLIQUE
Vilaine
pont de Bretagne
pont de la Mission
quai Lamennais
Laundry
quai Emile Zola
Musée des Beaux-Arts
quai Richemont
r. de la Chalotais
r. du Pré Botté
r. Léonard de Vinci
r. Toullier
r. Dupont des Loges
PL. DE BRETAGNE
r. Lanjuinais
r. de la Parcheminerie
r. de Nemours
r. Jules Simon
Star Buses
r. Maréchal Joffre
r. Courier
r. Capitaine Dreyfus
r. Joseph Sauveur
r. H. Lucas
r. Champ Dolent
r. Poullain-Duparc
r. Vasselot
av. Jean Janvier
bd. de la Tour d'Auvergne
bd. de la Liberté
PL. COMMEUREC
r. St-Thomas
r. des Carmes
r. Alain Gerbault
Théâtre National de Bretagne
r. Chicogné
SQ. DU PRÉ PERCHÉ
r. du Pré-Perché
r. Garin Trousseboeuf
bd. de la Liberté
r. de l'Arsénal
r. Thiers
r. Tronjolly
r. du Vieux Cours
r. Emile Souvestre
bd. Descartes
Faux Pont
r. St-Helier
r. Duhamel
r. de Plélo
r. Pierre Abelard
r. du Puits Mauger
PL. DU GÉNÉRAL KOENIG
PL. MARÉCHAL JUIN
PL. GÉNÉRAL GIRARD
r. d'Isly
ESPLANADE DU GÉNÉRAL DE GAULLE
bd. Magenta
av. Louis Barthou
r. Aubry
Champion Supermarket
cours des Alliés
CRIJB
SQ. DU ROI ARTHUR
PL. DU COLOMBIER
r. de l'Alma
Laundry
0
100 meters
100 yards
r. du 10 R. A.
Esplanade du Champ de Mars
Guedard Bike Rental
r. Gurvand
PL. DE LA GARE
TAXI
Gare Routière
bd. de Beaumont
Gare SNCF
Rennes
ACCOMMODATIONS
Auberge de Jeunesse (HI), 1
Camping Municipal des Gayeulles, 2
Hôtel Maréchal Joffre, 14
Hôtel Venezia, 13
FOOD
Café Breton, 10
Crêperie des Portes Mordelaises, 9
Léon le Cochon, 12
Le St-Germain des Champs, 11
Star, 5
NIGHTLIFE AND ENTERTAINMENT
Bernique Hurlante, 3
La Cité d'Ys, 16
Délicatessen, 7
L'Emblême, 4
L'Espace, 17
O'Connell's Pub, 8
Le Papagayo, 15
Le Zing, 6

Post Office: Pl. de la République (☎78 43 32). Open M-F 8:30am-7pm, Sa 9am-12:30pm. **Currency exchange,** fax, photocopies, and Western Union. Branch at 24 pl. Hoche (☎02 23 20 02 05). Open M 10am-6pm, Tu-F 8:45am-12:15pm and 1:45-6pm, Sa 8:45am-12:15pm. **Postal Code:** 35000.

RENNES FOR POCKET CHANGE. Like many university towns, Rennes offers plenty of budget-friendly options. A relaxing walk past the rose bushes and trimmed trees of the **Jardin du Thabor** (p. 240) comes at no charge. For nighttime entertainment, check out the **Orchestra de Bretagne** (p. 241), which gives free summer concerts. On Wednesdays in July, head back to the garden for **Les Mercredis du Thabor** (p. 241), traditional Breton music and dance performances that are colorful, dynamic, and—you guessed it—free.

ACCOMMODATIONS AND CAMPING

Hotels cluster around the train station and along the south bank of the Vilaine; cheaper options tend to be slightly farther from the center. Consider reserving ahead, especially the first week of July during the Tombées de la Nuit festival.

SLEEPING AROUND. Breizhtrotters (Brittany's regional tourism department) now offers a 'stay 5 get one free' deal for regional hostels. Called the Pass Bretagne, this pass is accepted at 21 hostels in Brittany, including those in Rennes, Quimper, Quiberon, St-Malo, and Nantes. No more than two consecutive nights at the same hostel can be counted for the pass. For more info, inquire at your hostel or the Breizhtrotters website, www.breizhtrotters.com. For hostel info, contact the Fédération Unie des Auberges de Jeunesse (☎89 87 27; www.fuaj.com).

Auberge de Jeunesse (HI), 10-12 canal St-Martin (☎33 22 33; rennes@fuaj.org). From the station, take the Metro (dir.: Kennedy) to "Ste-Anne." Walk past the church onto rue de St-Malo, which turns into rue St-Martin. Continue over the bridge; the hostel is on the right. Simple 2- to 4-bed rooms with lockers and shower, some with views of the canal. Kitchen, common room with TV, cafeteria, and Internet access (€0.50 per 30min.). Breakfast included. Laundry (wash €3, dry €2). Reception 7am-11pm. Night guard after 1am. Lockout M-Sa 10am-3:30pm, Su 10am-1pm. €17. MC/V. ❶

Hôtel Maréchal Joffre, 6 rue Maréchal Joffre (☎79 37 74; fax 78 38 51). Small, simple, and quiet rooms over a tiny lunch counter in the center of town. Breakfast €5. Reception M-Sa 24hr., closed Su 1-8pm. Closed late July to early Aug. Singles €25, with shower and toilet €34; doubles €25-38; triples €40-44. AmEx/MC/V. ❷

Hôtel Venezia, 27 rue Dupont des Loges (☎30 36 56; hotel.venezia@wanadoo.fr), on an island in the Vilaine River. Behind the faded facade are small but cozy rooms. More expensive ones are decorated with rugs and marble mantels. An intellectual spot frequented by university administrators and professors. All rooms with TV. Breakfast €5. Reception 7am-11:30pm. Reservations recommended. Singles €28-36, with shower and toilet €38-46; doubles €38/48. Extra bed €10. AmEx/MC/V. ❸

Camping Municipal des Gayeulles, rue Maurice Audin in Parc des Gayeulles (☎36 91 22; www.camping-rennes.com). Take bus #3 (dir.: St-Laurent) from pl. du Colombier or pl. de la République to "Piscine/Gayeulles" (M-Sa every 10min., Su every 40min.; last bus midnight). Follow the path around the swimming pool on the right until the paved road; turn left and follow signs. Deep within the Parc des Gayeulles, these spots are separated by bushes, with additional spots in a field in July and Aug. Small snack bar. Internet access €1 per 30min. Reception mid-June to mid-Sept. daily 7:30am-1pm and

2-8pm; mid-Sept. to Oct. and Apr. to mid-June daily 9am-12:30pm and 4:30-8pm; Nov.-Mar. M-Sa 8-9am and 6-8pm. Gates closed mid-June to mid-Sept. 11pm-7am; mid.-Sept. to mid-June 10pm-7am. €3.30 per adult, under 10 €1.50, €2.50-5.50 per tent, €1.50 per car, €6.40-7.30 per caravan. Electricity €3. AmEx/MC/V. ❶

FOOD

Rennes's culinary center, northwest of the city, boasts an astounding quantity of ethnic restaurants; **rue de St-Malo** alone sports Haitian, Lebanese, Indian, and Chinese cuisine, with Greek and Italian restaurants nearby. There are plenty of kebab stands on and around **place Ste-Anne,** and more traditional restaurants around **place St-Michel** and in the city center. On the other side of the city, *brasseries* and *crêperies* line **rue St-George.** The city's largest market is on **place des Lices** (open Sa 7am-1pm); others are held Tu-Su throughout the city (ask at the tourist office for a list). Local **supermarkets** include a **Champion,** 20 rue d'Isly, in a mall near the train station (open M-Sa 9:30am-8pm), a **Supermarché Hoche,** 9 pl. Hoche (open M-Sa 8am-9pm, Su 9am-noon), and a **Marché Plus,** 43 pl. de la Rance, in an apartment complex off rue de St-Malo near the hostel (open M-Sa 7am-9pm, Su 9am-noon). There are several local grocery stores along **rue Jean Janvier** by the train station.

Le St-Germain des Champs (Restaurant Végétarien-Biologique), 12 rue du Vau St-Germain (☎79 25 52). Friendly chefs serve lunch at this popular organic and vegetarian spot accented with plants, jars of seeds, cloth lanterns, and nature photos. Lunch *plat* €10, with appetizer or dessert €14, with both €18. Open M-Sa noon-2:30pm. MC/V. ❸

Crêperie des Portes Mordelaises, 6 rue des Portes Mordelaises (☎30 57 40). Startlingly blue and pink, this small, simple, and authentic *crêperie* is one of the city's best, as crowds of students attest. Salads €2-7.50. Carefully crafted *galettes* and *crêpes* €3-10. Open M-Sa 11:30am-2pm and 6:30-11pm. Closed July. MC/V. ❷

Star, 3 pl. Ste-Anne (☎79 07 34). One of the best (and cheapest) *kebaberies* around pl. St-Anne; enjoy the delicious *sauce blanche* while people-watching from the tables outside. Kebab-*frites* €4. *Plats* €6.50-9.50. Cash only. ❷

Café Breton, 14 rue Nantaise (☎30 74 95). A stylish restaurant serving an ever-changing menu of market-fresh cuisine in a warm, dimly-lit dining room. Salads €5-9. *Plats* €12-16. Desserts €4-6. Open M noon-3pm, Tu-W noon-3pm and 7:30-10pm, Th-Sa noon-3pm and 7-11pm. Reservations recommended. Closed several weeks in Aug. ❸

Léon le Cochon, 1 rue Maréchal Joffre (☎79 37 54; www.leonlecochon.com). Enticing local dishes fuse modern and traditional at this elegant restaurant. The restaurant's pig theme, made visible by the giant "chef pig" statue and pig paintings, extends to the menu, although there are plenty of other options. Lunch *formule* €12. *Plats* €11-23. Open M-Th noon-2pm and 8-10:30pm, F-Sa 8-11pm. AmEx/MC/V. ❸

SIGHTS

The beautiful *vieille ville* is a quintessential medieval village. Half-timbered buildings—now filled with bars and modern storefronts—pepper the old city from **place Ste-Anne** and **place St-Michel** to **place du Calvaire** and on narrow **rue St-Georges.**

JARDIN DU THABOR. Some of the most beautiful gardens in France, these lush grounds feature fountains, giant trees, beautiful flower beds punctuated by statues, an aviary of parakeets, and "hell"— once a duelists' *rendez-vous*, now a pit with a performance stage. The target-shaped rose garden alone holds 980 varieties of the *fleur d'amour*. On Wednesdays in July, **Les Mercredis du Thabor** brings Breton song and dance to the gardens. *(☎30 06 87; http://skeudenn.ouestfrance.fr. Free shows at 8:30pm.)* A small gallery on the north side exhibits local artwork. *(☎28 56*

62. Entrances at pl. St-Melaine, rue de la Palestine, rue de Paris, and bd. de la Duchesse Anne. Open daily June-Aug. 7:30am-8:30pm; Sept.-June 7:30am-6:30pm.)

MUSÉE DES BEAUX-ARTS. Rennes's art museum is one of the city's lesser-known treasures, featuring a range of art, from ancient Egyptian to modern abstract works, but with few well-known pieces. The Baroque collection is impressive, especially Rubens's *The Tiger Hunt;* another hallway is devoted to Breton painters. *(20 quai Emile Zola. ☎02 23 62 17 45; www.mbar.org. Open Tu 10am-6pm, W-Su 10am-noon and 2-6pm. €4.30, students €2.20, under 18 free. €5.40/2.70 for special exhibits.)*

PARC DES GAYEULLES. Gayeulles's forests are interspersed with an indoor pool, several lakes (with paddle-boats in the summer), sports fields, tennis courts, mini-golf, and a campground. Many walking and bike paths cut through the park; posted maps appear at regular intervals. The park is also home to a working farm for children and an animal reserve. *(15min. bus ride; see Camping Municipal directions. ☎28 56 62. Open July-Aug. 8am-8:30pm; Sept.-June 8am-5:45pm. Free.)*

OTHER SIGHTS. Construction on the **Cathédrale St-Pierre** began in 1787 but was soon interrupted by the French Revolution; the building wasn't finished until 1844. Standing on a site previously occupied by a pagan temple, a Roman church, and a Gothic cathedral, the church is a 19th-century masterpiece, with a massive Neoclassical facade and huge columns inside holding up the painted and gilded ceiling. The one noticeable 20th-century addition to the cathedral is its altar, a large block of green bronze. The fifth chapel on the right houses the cathedral's treasure: a delicately carved 16th-century wooden altarpiece that traces the life of the Virgin Mary. *(Open daily 9:30am-noon and 3-6pm. Closed to visitors during high mass Su 10:30-11:30am.)* Across the street, tucked in an alleyway bearing the same name, the unassuming **Portes Mordelaises** are the last vestige of the medieval city walls.

NIGHTLIFE AND FESTIVALS

In summer, the **Orchestre de Bretagne** (☎27 52 75; www.orchestra-de-bretagne.com) offers a few free concerts along with its regular performances. During the best-known of Rennes's summer festivals, the week-long **Les Tombées de la Nuit** in early July, a riot of music, theater, mime, dance, and interactive performances overtakes the city. (☎32 56 56; www.tdn.rennes.fr.) The **Rencontres Transmusicales** (☎31 13 10; www.lestrans.com) in early December fills the city with high-quality international musicians and bands. April brings the **Festival Les Mythos** (☎79 26 07; www.festival-mythos.com), a celebration of *contes* (fairytales) and other oral traditions. Consult the tourist office for a guide of upcoming theater, dance, and classical music performances, and for festival tickets and info.

After the sun sets, the city's population seems to double, and the party doesn't calm down until dawn. Much of the action centers around **place Ste-Anne, place St-Michel,** and **place des Lices,** but don't stop there—hot nightspots pervade the city, with some great bars and discotheques south of the Vilaine. When heading outside the center, however, be careful and don't travel alone.

BRITTANY

BARS

La Cité d'Ys, 31 rue Vasselot (☎78 24 84). Named after a legendary Breton city, this bar is full of mythic atmosphere, enhanced by Celtic knots and crosses. 2 floors are linked by a twisting spiral staircase, and even the bar is a spiral. Fabulous variety of live traditional music twice a month. Coreff €2.40. Open daily noon-1am. AmEx/MC/V.

Le Zing, 5 pl. des Lices (☎79 64 60). 2 floors, 4 bars, and 8 rooms fill up around midnight with young and beautiful partyers, who appear even more alluring under flattering amber lights. Beer €2.50 before 10pm, €3 10pm-midnight, €4 thereafter. Mixed drinks €8/8.50/9. Open daily 3pm-3am. MC/V.

O'Connell's Irish Pub, 6-7 pl. du Parlement de Bretagne (☎79 38 76). Anglophones, Anglophiles, and locals alike come for pints of Beamish (€5.90), poured by Irish expats. Live Irish jigs Su 8:30pm. Beer €2.50-6. Whiskey €5.20-16. Happy hour M 7-10pm and Th 7pm-1am. Open M-Sa 11am-1am, Su 5pm-1am. MC/V.

Bernique Hurlante, 40 rue de St-Malo (☎38 70 09). Welcomes a diverse crowd in an intimate, funky space with modern art and a mosaic on the back wall. The house specialty is the "rum surprise" (€3.50)—as unique a concoction as the bar itself. Beer €2.40-2.70. Open Aug. Tu-Sa 6pm-1am; Sept.-July Tu-Sa 4pm-1am, Su 6pm-1am. AmEx/MC/V.

L'Emblême, 24 rue d'Antrain (☎38 71 88). A small gay bar with eclectic décor and a red-and-black striped floor. Theme nights Sa. Open M-Sa 5pm-1am. MC/V.

Le Papagayo, 10 rue Maréchal Joffre (☎79 65 13). An unassuming lunch counter by day, this tropical spot is a party after dark—especially on the twice-monthly theme nights. Beer €2.30-5. Sangria €3. Open M-Sa 7am-1am. MC/V.

CLUBS

Délicatessen, 7 impasse Rallier du Baty (☎78 23 41), near pl. St-Michel. Housed in a former prison, this club has swapped jailhouse rock for flashing lights and electronic beats. Drinks €6, after 1:30am €10. Cover Tu-Th €5, after 1:30am €10; F-Sa €8/15; includes 1 drink. Women free before 1am. Mandatory coat-check €2, bags €5. Open Tu-Sa midnight-5am.

L'Espace, 45 bd. de la Tour d'Auvergne (☎30 21 95). After 2am, a young and lively crowd fills the stage, cage, and two floors of L'Espace, grinding to thumping music under video screens, strobe lights, and disco balls. Shots €6. Beer €6-8. Mixed drinks €10. Cover Th-F €10, Sa €12; students free Th until 1am, €8 Th after 1am and F-Sa; includes 1 alcoholic or 2 non-alcoholic drinks. Mandatory coat-check €2, bags €5. Happy hour Th 11:30pm-1am. Open Th-Sa 11pm-5am. MC/V.

DAYTRIPS FROM RENNES

FOUGÈRES

Illenoo buses (☎30 87 80; www.illenoo.fr) depart from Rennes (1¼hr.; M-F 15 per day, Sa 9 per day, Su 2 per day; €3). The Fougères gare routière, *rue des Frères Deveria, is the end of the line. (☎99 08 77. Open July-Aug. M-F 9:30am-1pm and 2:30-5:30pm; Sept.-June M-F 6:30-11am and 4:20-6:20pm, Sa 9am-noon. Save yourself a short walk by getting off at "Fougères Jean Jaurès" for the historical city center, but return buses do not stop there; there's also a stop at the château. To reach the "Jean Jaurès" stop in the city center from the* gare routière, *turn left out of the station onto rue des Frères Deveria and then right at the roundabout onto rue de Sévigné. Continue past the roundabout and the large fountain onto bd. Jean Jaurès, and head uphill; the stop will be on your left.*

Fougères has a perfectly preserved historical center and a stunning **château,** 83 pl. Pierre Symon. The ancient castle sits on a promontory flanked by rock walls and a moat filled by the Nançon River. Its construction began around AD 1000 as part of a plan to reinforce the entire Breton duchy; though it has fallen into some disrepair in the centuries since, the ramparts and towers remain standing, and stairways with guardrails give visitors free access. **Tour Mélusine,** built by the Lusignan family of Poitou and named for their half-human, half-snake ancestress, is the castle's tallest tower, with walls 3m thick. Peek through the window in the floor to check out the tower's dungeon, then climb the spiral staircase for an incredible view of the surrounding countryside. (☎99 79 59. Open daily mid-June to mid-Sept. 9am-7pm; late Sept. and Apr. to mid-June 9:30am-noon and 2-6pm; Nov.-Dec. and

Feb.-Mar. 10am-noon and 2-5pm. 45min. tour included with castle admission in English and French July-Aug. every hr. 9am-noon and 2-6pm; Sept.-June in French every hr. 10am-noon and 2-5pm. €4.80, students €3.65, ages 10-16 €2.15.) Look for signs to the **Jardin Public,** cut into the hillside of the *haute-ville*, which has fountains, flowers, and panoramic views of the château and surrounding countryside. (Open mid-Apr. to mid-Oct. 8am-midnight; mid-Oct. to mid-Apr. 8am-10pm.)

To reach the **tourist office,** 2 rue Nationale, from the "Jean Jaurès" bus stop, walk uphill from the traffic circle on rue de Paris; pl. Aristide Briand will be on the right. At the end of the *place*, turn left at the **Marché Plus** (open M-Sa 7am-9pm, Su 9am-1pm); the tourist office is ahead, left of the Théâtre. (☎94 12 20; www.ot-fougeres.fr. Open July-Aug. M-Sa 9am-7pm, Su 10am-noon and 2-4pm; late June and early Sept. M-Sa 9:30am-12:30pm and 2-6pm, Su 1:30-5:30pm; mid-Apr. to mid-June and mid-Sept. to mid-Nov. M-Sa 9:30am-12:30pm and 2-6pm; mid-Nov. to mid-Apr. M 2-6pm, Tu-Sa 10am-12:30pm and 2-6pm.) Turn left out of the tourist office, then immediately left on **rue de la Pinterie,** the main artery of the medieval city, to reach the château.

ST-MALO ☎02 99

Scenic St-Malo (SEHN-mah-lo; pop. 53,000) deserves its reputation as a prime tourist destination. It combines the best of France's northern villages: rich history, delicious seafood, postcard-perfect vistas, and brilliant beaches. Though 80% of the town was destroyed in 1944, meticulous stone-by-stone reconstruction has made it difficult to distinguish the old from the new. The town's ramparts and towers fortify the scenic *vieille ville* and overlook miles of gorgeous coast.

TRANSPORTATION

Trains: SNCF station between av. Aristide Briand and rue d'Alsace. Ticket office open M-F 5:30am-8pm, Sa 5:30am-7:45pm, Su 7:30am-8:50pm. Trains run via **Dol** to: **Caen** (3½hr., 2-4 per day, €27); **Dinan** (1½hr., 5 per day, €8.20); **Paris** (4hr., 14 per day, €59-73); **Pontorson** (1½hr., 2-3 per day, €7.30); **Rennes** (1hr., 14 per day, €12).

Buses: Main office on espl. St-Vincent, beside tourist office (☎40 85 96). **Illenoo** (☎19 70 80; www.illenoo.fr) runs via **Pontorson** to **Mont-St-Michel** (2hr., 2 per day, €4.50). Office open July-Aug. M-F 8:30am-noon and 1:30-6pm, Sa 8:30am-noon; Sept.-June M-F 8:30am-12:30pm and 2-6pm. **Tibus** (☎08 10 22 22 22; www.cotesdarmor.fr) runs to **Dinan** (1hr., 3-5 per day, €2) and smaller towns to the west. **Courriers Bretons** (☎19 70 80; www.lescourriersbretons.fr) runs special summer lines several times per week to nearby sights including Mont-St-Michel, Dinan, and Ile de Bréhat. An office (☎40 19 27) in the train station has info on all buses. Open daily 8:45am-1:30pm and 2:30-6:30pm. Most buses stop at the main office, train station, and hostel.

Ferries: Gare Maritime du Naye and Gare Maritime de la Bourse. **Brittany Ferries** (☎08 25 82 88 28, www.brittanyferries.com; office open daily 7:30am-6pm) serves **Portsmouth** (9hr., 1 per day, €60-75). See **Getting There: By Boat,** p. 30. **Condor Ferries** (☎08 25 13 51 35; www.condorferries.com) runs to **Jersey** (1¼hr., 1-3 per day, €34-63) and **Guernsey** (2hr., 1-2 per day, €34-68).

Public Transportation: Keolis, Esplanade St-Vincent, by the tourist office, runs local buses (☎56 06 06) that also serve **Cancale** (30min., 7-14 per day). Buy tickets at the office or on board. Office open M-F 8:15am-12:15pm and 1:45-6pm, Sa 8:15am-noon; varies seasonally. Info also available at train station (see **Buses**). Buses run daily July-Aug. 7am-midnight; Sept.-June 6am-8pm. Tickets €1 (valid 1hr.), *carnet* of 10 €8.50, 24hr. pass €3.

Taxis: Taxi Malouins (☎81 30 30) or **Taxi Petit** (☎21 06 01). At St-Vincent and the train station.

BRITTANY

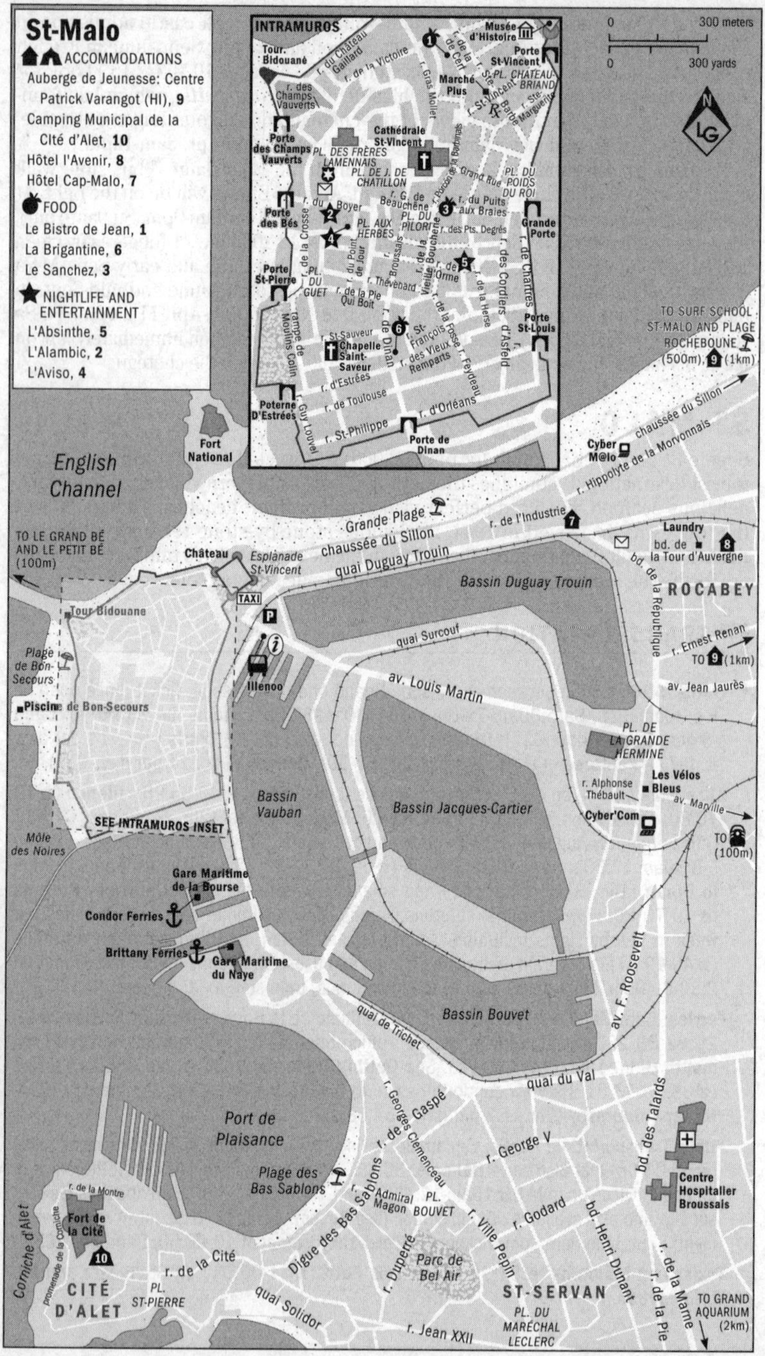
St-Malo
ACCOMMODATIONS
Auberge de Jeunesse: Centre Patrick Varangot (HI), 9
Camping Municipal de la Cité d'Alet, 10
Hôtel l'Avenir, 8
Hôtel Cap-Malo, 7
FOOD
Le Bistro de Jean, 1
La Brigantine, 6
Le Sanchez, 3
NIGHTLIFE AND ENTERTAINMENT
L'Absinthe, 5
L'Alambic, 2
L'Aviso, 4
INTRAMUROS
Tour. Bidouané
r. du Château Gaillard
r. de la Victoire
Musée d'Histoire
Porte St-Vincent
PL. CHATEAU-BRIAND
Marché Plus
r. des Champs Vauverts
Porte des Champs Vauverts
Cathédrale St-Vincent
PL. DES FRÈRES LAMENNAIS
PL. DE J. DE CHATILLON
Grand Rue
PL. DU POIDS DU ROI
Porte des Bés
r. du Boyer
PL. AUX HERBES
PL. DU PILORI
r. du Puits aux Braies
Grande Porte
Porte St-Pierre
PL. DU GUET
r. de la Crosse
r. Thévenard
r. de la Pie Qui Boit
r. de l'Orme
r. des Cordiers
r. de Chartres
r. d'Asfeld
Porte St-Louis
rampe de Moulins Colin
Chapelle Saint-Sauveur
r. de Dinan
r. des Vieux Remparts
r. Feydeau
r. d'Estrées
r. de Toulouse
r. d'Orléans
Poterne D'Estrées
r. Guy Louvel
r. St-Philippe
Porte de Dinan
0 300 meters
0 300 yards
TO SURF SCHOOL ST-MALO AND PLAGE ROCHEBOUNE (500m), 9 (1km)
Fort National
English Channel
Cyber M@lo
chaussée du Sillon
r. Hippolyte de la Morvonnais
Grande Plage
r. de l'Industrie
TO LE GRAND BÉ AND LE PETIT BÉ (100m)
Château
Esplanade St-Vincent
quai Duguay Trouin
Laundry
bd. de la Tour d'Auvergne
Bassin Duguay Trouin
bd. de la République
ROCABEY
Tour Bidouane
TAXI
quai Surcouf
r. Ernest Renan
TO 9 (1km)
Plage de Bon-Secours
Illenoo
av. Louis Martin
av. Jean Jaurès
Piscine de Bon-Secours
PL. DE LA GRANDE HERMINE
Les Vélos Bleus
r. Alphonse Thébault
av. Maville
Bassin Vauban
Bassin Jacques-Cartier
Cyber'Com
SEE INTRAMUROS INSET
TO (100m)
Môle des Noires
Gare Maritime de la Bourse
Condor Ferries
Brittany Ferries
Gare Maritime du Naye
av. F. Roosevelt
quai de Trichet
Bassin Bouvet
quai du Val
r. Georges Clemenceau
r. de Gaspé
bd. des Talards
Port de Plaisance
r. George V
Plage des Bas Sablons
r. Admiral Magon
PL. BOUVET
Centre Hospitalier Broussais
r. de la Montre
Fort de la Cité
Corniche d'Alet
Digue des Bas Sablons
r. Ville Pepin
r. Godard
bd. Henri Dunant
r. de la Marne
r. Duperré
Parc de Bel Air
r. de la Cité
promenade de la Corniche
CITÉ D'ALET
PL. ST-PIERRE
quai Solidor
ST-SERVAN
r. de la Pie
TO GRAND AQUARIUM (2km)
PL. DU MARÉCHAL LECLERC
r. Jean XXII

Bike Rental: Les Vélos Bleus, 19 rue Alphonse Thébault (☎40 31 63; www.velos-bleus.fr). €9 per ½-day, €12 per day; €150 deposit. Open daily 9am-noon and 2-6pm; reduced hours in low season and on weekends.

Windsurfer Rental: Surf School St-Malo, 2 av. de la Hoguette (☎40 07 47; www.surf-school.org). Along Grande Plage de Sillon, 1km from the *intra-muros,* near the hostel. Rental €25 for 1st hr., €17 per hr. thereafter; €42 per ½-day, €37 per additional ½-day. Lessons €35 per hr. Open daily 9am-6pm. AmEx/MC/V.

ORIENTATION AND PRACTICAL INFORMATION

The *intra-muros,* or old walled city, atop a rocky peninsula at the northernmost point of the modern town, is the heart of St-Malo's shopping and restaurant district. The harbor entrance is to the south, while the large, sandy beach runs east. Inland and eastward lies a less expensive but less colorful area where you'll find the train station, the youth hostel, and cheaper restaurants and hotels.

Tourist Office: Esplanade St-Vincent (☎08 25 13 52 00; www.saint-malo-tourisme.com), just outside the city walls. Turn right on the road outside the train station, then left onto av. Jean Jaurès at the roundabout. Make a left onto rue de l'Astrolabe; at the roundabout, make a right onto av. Louis Martin and follow it to Esplanade St-Vincent (15min.). Alternatively, take bus C1 or C2 (dir.: St-Vincent). From the *gare maritime,* turn left onto chausée Eric Tabarly, which becomes quai St-Louis and then Esplanade St-Vincent. **Free city guide** contains a map, walking tours, and tide tables; a more detailed map (€0.50), a list of accommodations, and *L'Omnibus* (a list of cheap current concerts) are also available. Open July-Aug. M-Sa 9am-7:30pm, Su 10am-6pm; Sept. and Apr.-June M-Sa 9am-12:30pm and 1:30-6:30pm, Su 10am-12:30pm and 2:30-6pm; Oct.-Mar. M-Sa 9am-12:30pm and 1:30-6pm.

Laundromat: 27 bd. de la Tour d'Auvergne. Open daily July-Aug. 7am-8:30pm; Sept.-June 7am-8pm.

Police: 3 pl. des Frères Lamennais (☎20 69 40), next to the post office.

Pharmacy: 8 rue Vincent (☎40 86 47), across the street from Marché Plus. Open M 2-7:30pm, Tu-Sa 9am-12:30pm and 2-7:30pm.

Hospital: Centre Hospitalier Broussais, 1 rue de la Marne (☎21 21 21).

Internet Access: Cyber M@lo, 68 chausseé du Sillon (☎56 07 78; cyberstmalo@yahoo.fr). €2.50 per 30min., €4 per hr. Open mid-June to mid-Sept. M-Sa 10am-11pm, Su 3-8pm; mid-Sept. to mid-June Tu-Th 11am-9pm, F-Sa 11am-11pm, Su 3-8pm. **Cyber'Com,** 26bis bd. des Talards (☎56 05 83) €2.05 per 30min. Open M-Tu and F 9am-noon and 1:30-6pm, W 1:30-6pm, Th 10am-noon and 1:30-7pm. Also at **L'Alambic** (see **Entertainment,** p. 247).

Post Office: 1 bd. de la République (☎20 51 78). **Currency exchange,** fax, and photocopies. Open M-F 8am-6:30pm, Sa 9am-12:30pm. Branch at pl. des Frères Lamennais (☎40 89 90), next to the police station. Open M-F 9am-noon and 2-5:30pm, Sa 9:30am-12:30pm. **Postal Code:** 35400.

ACCOMMODATIONS AND CAMPING

Rooms inside the walls of the city don't come cheap, but there are budget options within a few minutes' walk outside. Reserve at least a few days ahead, especially in summer, when the town becomes a magnet for French and foreign beach-goers.

Auberge de Jeunesse: Centre Patrick Varangot (HI), 37 av. du Révérend Père Umbricht (☎40 29 80; www.centrevarangot.com). From the train station, take bus #5 (dir.: Croix Désilles) or #10 (dir.: Cancale). On foot from the station, turn right on the road running by the station, then follow it for 10min. before turning right on av. Pasteur. This-becomes av. du Rév. Père Umbricht; keep right at the "Auberge de Jeunesse" sign (30min.) Large stone building 3 blocks from beach. Plain rooms with large windows. Popular with school groups. Tennis, volleyball, and basketball courts. Bar and common room with TV. Kitchen with individual refrigerators (€1.50). Accepts the Pass Bretagne (see p. 239). Breakfast included. Luggage storage €2. Laundry €4. Free Wi-Fi. Wheelchair-accessible. Bike rental €11 per ½-day, €15 per day. Reception 8am-11pm. July-Aug. dorms €16, with shower and toilet €19; singles €26. Sept.-June €15/18/28. MC/V. ❶

Hôtel l'Avenir, 31 bd. de la Tour d'Auvergne (☎56 13 33), 5min. from the station, 10min. from the *vieille ville*. Simple rooms with boats and seagulls decorating the blue walls and linens. Located above a quiet bar. Breakfast €5.50. Reception 7:30am-8:30pm. Singles €23, with shower €28; doubles €26/32; quads €60. Cash only. ❷

Hôtel Cap-Malo, 53 quai Duguay Trouin (☎40 39 58), at the end of the *bassin* parallel to the Grande Plage, near intersection of Quai Duguay Trouin and bd. de la République. A 5min. walk from the old city, this small hotel over a bar offers rooms overlooking the *bassin*. All with toilet. Breakfast €5.50. Reception Tu-Sa 8am-midnight, Su 8am-noon. Singles €35, with shower €40; doubles with shower €50. AmEx/MC/V. ❸

Camping Municipal de la Cité d'Alet (☎81 60 91; www.ville-saint-malo.fr/campings), southwest of the city. Take bus #6 (dir.: Quelmer/La Passagère) to "Alet." Head uphill and left at the ruins of Cathédrale St-Pierre onto allée Gaston Buy; the campground is 50m ahead. 285 gently-sloped, scenic spots near the beach. Reception May-Sept. M-F 9am-12:30pm and 3-6pm, Sa-Su 8:30am-7pm; hours extended July-Aug. Gates closed 11pm-7am; after 8pm see the night guard. 2 people and tent €13, 2 people and caravan with electricity €17. Extra adult €5.70, extra child 2-12 €2.65. MC/V. ❶

FOOD

Generic, overpriced restaurants huddle just within the *intra-muros*. **Outdoor markets** (8am-1pm) are held inside the walls and on **place Bouvet** in St-Servan (both Tu and F), and on **boulevard de la Tour d'Auvergne** (M, Th, Sa). There is a **Marché Plus** supermarket, 10bis rue Ste-Barbe, underground near the entrance to the city walls at Porte St-Vincent (open M-Sa 7am-9pm, Su 9am-1pm), and a **Champion** supermarket on av. Pasteur near the hostel. (Open June-Sept. M-Sa 8:30am-8pm, Su 9:30am-2:30pm; Oct.-Apr. M-Sa 8:30am-8pm, Su 9:30am-12:30pm.)

Le Sanchez, 9 rue de la Vieille Boucherie (☎56 67 17). Gluttonous servings of gelato both traditional and adventurous—anchovy, anyone?—are worth the long line. Order to go and you'll get more for less. 1 scoop €2, 2 scoops €3, 3 scoops plus toppings €4.80. Open mid-June to mid-Sept. daily 8:30am-midnight; mid-Sept. to Mar. M-Tu and Th-Su 8:30am-7:30pm; Apr. to mid-June daily 8:30am-7:30pm. MC/V over €15. ❶

La Brigantine, 13 rue de Dinan (☎56 82 82). Offers cheap but satisfying *galettes* (€1.60-10) and *crêpes* (€1.70-6.10), though service can be slow. Open July-Aug. daily noon-3pm and 7-11pm; Sept.-June M and Th-Su noon-3pm and 7-11pm. MC/V. ❶

Le Bistro de Jean, 6 rue de la Corne de Cerf (☎40 98 68). The freshest market fare is given traditional French bistro treatment at this stylishly simple restaurant scattered with old-fashioned sporting equipment and sepia photographs. Chalk menu changes daily. Appetizers €7.50-15. *Plats* €14-28. Lunch *menus* €14-19. Desserts €6.60. Open M-Tu and Th-F noon-1:45pm and 7-9:45pm; W and Sa 7-9:45pm. AmEx/MC/V. ❸

SIGHTS AND BEACHES

The town's **ramparts,** on the northern side of the city, look out over the beach toward a series of small, fortified islands that once guarded St-Malo's harbor. At low tide, pebbly causeways strewn with stranded mollusks emerge from the sea, giving access to the two closest islands, Fort National and Grand Bé; check the tide schedules at the tourist office before you visit. **Fort National** was designed in the 17th century by the French military's master architect, Vauban, to protect St-Malo from the English. He did his job well, as the fort has never been taken by sea. It's not really worth paying for a tour of the empty, stony fortresses, except for the fabulous view of the bay and the city from the top. (☎06 72 46 66 26. Open daily June-Sept. Hours depend on the tides; ask the tourist office. Tours in French at low tide. Pamphlets in English, German, Italian, and Spanish. €4, ages 6-15 €2.) The strange rocky seclusion of **Le Grand Bé,** west of the Fort and near the Piscine de Bon-Secours, offers a moment of solitude. The only permanent resident is St-Malo's native son and French Romantic author **Chateaubriand** (1768-1848), who asked to be buried where he could hear nothing but the wind and waves. Farther out to sea is **Le Petit Bé,** defended by another, smaller fort. Tours are available, but the causeway leading to Petit Bé from Grand Bé isn't exposed at every low tide. (☎06 08 27 51 20; www.petit-be.com. Hours depend on the tides; ask the tourist office. €5, under 8 free.) Those who prefer dry excursions should heed the posted warnings not to set out for any islands if the tide is within 10m of the causeway.

The **Grand Aquarium,** av. du Général Patton, is decidedly kid-friendly. Older visitors will enjoy the wide collection of fish, arranged thematically by habitat, and the 360-degree wrap-around shark tank. The aquarium's pride and joy is the **Nautibus,** an underwater ride. Take bus #C1 or C2 (dir.: St-Servan or Découverte) from the station or the tourist office. (☎21 19 00; www.aquarium-st-malo.com. Open daily mid-July to mid-Aug. 9:30am-10pm; early July and late Aug. 9:30am-8pm; Sept. and Apr.-June 10am-7pm; Oct.-Mar. 10am-6pm. Closed 3 weeks in Nov. and 3 weeks in Jan. Last entry 1hr. before closing. €15, ages 4-14 €10, under 4 free.) St-Malo native Jacques Cartier, famous for his Canadian explorations, is buried in the 12th-century **Cathédrale St-Vincent,** which has been carefully restored following heavy damage in WWII. Purists may disdain them, but the distinctively modern 20th-century iridescent stained-glass windows have an undeniable kaleidoscopic allure. (Mass Tu-Sa 6:30pm; Su 10 and 11:30am.) In July and August, the cathedral presents a series of concerts during the **Festival de Musique Sacrée.** (☎56 05 38, reservations 06 08 31 99 93. Tickets €20-25, students €17.)

It's hard to go wrong with the world-famous **beaches** in St-Malo. On the western side of the *intra-muros*, best accessed by stairwells that lead down from the walls, **plage de Bon-Secours** is sheltered on both sides by rocky outcroppings. It features the curious **Piscine de Bon-Secours,** three cement walls that hold in a pool's worth of salt water even at low tide, with a diving platform for the adventurous. To the east is the larger **Grande Plage,** a vast expanse of sand. Farther up the coast is the romantic **plage Rochebonne.** On the other side of the old city, to the south and protected from the sea by a marina, lies the more family-oriented **Plage des Bas Sablons,** popular with waders and school groups. The city's **château,** on the north-east corner of the ramparts, dates back to the 14th century. It now holds the town hall and the **Musée d'Histoire,** which fills two huge towers with artifacts illustrating St-Malo's maritime history. Climb to the top of the watchtower for the city's best views. (☎40 71 57; musee@ville-saint-malo.fr. Open Apr.-Sept. daily 10am-12:30pm and 2-6pm; Oct.-Mar. Tu-Su 10am-noon and 2-6pm. €5.10, students €2.55.)

NIGHTLIFE AND FESTIVALS

At the tourist office, pick up *L'Omnibus*, a small brochure that lists cheap contemporary concerts in town. **L'Alambic,** 8 rue du Boyer, with distillery equipment hanging from the ceiling, feels like a cross between a brewery and an enchanted forest and draws a young crowd every night. (☎40 86 41. Internet access €1 per

10min. Beer €2.50-3.60. Hard liquor €5.50. Open daily May-Oct. 10am-2am; Nov.-Apr. 11am-1am.) **L'Absinthe,** 1 rue de l'Orme, attracts a varied clientele to a spacious four-floored, wood-paneled interior with red lights, comfortable nooks, and an oversized clock. (☎40 85 40. Beer €2.50-4.50. Frozen margaritas €3.50. Whiskey €5.50. Open daily in high season 4pm-2am; low season noon-1am. MC/V.) **L'Aviso,** 12 rue du Point du Jour, sells 300 types of beer (from €3.40) and 20 kinds of whiskey to a predominantly middle-aged crowd. (☎40 99 08. Open daily 5pm-3am.)

St-Malo's many yearly festivals draw crowds almost as big as its beaches. Writers pour in and book fairs abound at the end of May or beginning of June for **Etonnants Voyageurs** (☎31 05 74; www.etonnants-voyageurs.net), the preeminent international literary and film festival in France. In the first week of July, **Festival des Folklores du Monde** attracts international folk musicians and dancers (☎40 42 50). The **Route du Rock** draws both famous and unknown rock, techno, and pop bands to the city during the second weekend in August (☎54 01 11; www.laroutedurock.com). Finally, the **Quai des Bulles,** held the last weekend in October, celebrates comic books (☎40 39 63; www.quaidesbulles.com).

DINAN ☎02 96

Dinan (dee-NAHN; pop. 11,000), on a hill above the river Rance, has all the charms of a well-preserved medieval Breton village—cobblestone streets, local artisans, and traditional *crêperies.* Outside the ramparts, the lush river valley and wooded countryside make for a natural beauty as appealing as the town's architecture.

TRANSPORTATION AND PRACTICAL INFORMATION. **Trains** leave from pl. du 11 Novembre 1918 (office open M 6am-7pm, Tu-F 7:25am-7pm, Sa 9am-7pm, Su 10:20am-12:50pm and 2:15-7:20pm) for Paris (3¾hr., 6 per day, €59) via Rennes (1hr., 8 per day, €13), and St-Malo (1hr., 6 per day, €8.10) via Dol. Tibus **buses** (☎39 21 05; www.cotesdarmor.fr; office open M-F 8am-noon and 2-6pm) leave from the train station and pl. Duclos Pinot, going to St-Malo (1hr., 3-6 per day) and Dinard (1hr.; M-F 3 per day, Sa 1 per day). There is a set price of €2 for all destinations. **Taxis** stand outside the train station; call ☎39 06 00.

The train station lies to the northwest of the walled city in the commercial district. To get to the **tourist office,** 9 rue du Château, from the station, bear left across pl. du 11 Novembre 1918 onto rue Carnot, then right onto rue Thiers, which brings you to pl. Duclos Pinot. Turn left to go inside the old city walls and bear right onto rue du Marchix, which becomes rue de la Ferronnerie. Pass parking lots on pl. du Champ and pl. Duguesclin to the left; the tourist office is ahead on the right. A multilingual staff provides a free walking-tour city map, an excellent historical guide with tours of the city and region (€2), and a reservations service for €2. (☎87 69 76; www.dinantourisme.com. Open July-Aug. M-Sa 9am-7pm, Su 10am-12:30pm and 2:30-6pm; Sept.-June M-Sa 9am-12:30pm and 2-6pm. Tours in French daily July-Aug. 3pm; Apr.-June and Sept. Sa 3pm. €5, under 18 €3.) Other services include: a **laundromat,** 19 pl. Duclos Pinot on rue des Rouairies, which becomes rue de Brest (open Tu-F 8:30am-noon and 1:45-7pm, Sa 8:30am-6pm); **public restrooms** underground by the *Mairie* on pl. Duclos Pinot; **police,** 16 pl. Duguesclin (☎87 74 00); a **hospital,** rue Chateaubriand (☎85 72 85); a **pharmacy,** 4 rue de l'Apport (☎39 21 31; open M 10am-12:30pm and 2-7pm, Tu-Sa 9am-12:30pm and 2-7pm); and **Internet** access at **Zonzon.com,** 9 rue Rouairies, near pl. Duclos Point (☎87 95 86; www.zonzon.com.fr; €3 per hr.; open M-W noon-8pm, F-Sa 10am-midnight, Su 3pm-10pm). The **post office,** pl. Duclos, has **currency exchange.** (☎85 83 50. Open M-F 8am-6:30pm, Sa 9am-12:30pm.) **Postal Code:** 22100.

ACCOMMODATIONS. The **Auberge de Jeunesse "Moulin du Méen" (HI)** ❶ is housed in a beautiful old mill outside of town in Vallée de la Fontaine-des-Eaux and offers clean two- to eight-bed rooms and a communal kitchen. Start the 20-30min. walk from the train station by exiting left, then turning left across tracks. Make a right onto rue du Clos du Hêtre, which becomes rue de l'Ecuyer and then rte. de Dinard; follow the tracks and signs downhill for 2km. Turn right on rue de la Fontaine des Eaux and continue through wooded lanes for another 2km. (☎39 10 83; dinan@fuaj.org. Accepts the Pass Bretagne, see p. 239. Breakfast €3.50. Free Internet access. Bike rental €6 per ½-day, €10 per day; deposit €50. Reception July-Aug. 8am-noon and 5-9pm; Sept.-June 9am-noon and 5-8pm. Dorms €15. MC/V.) The only disadvantage of the prime location of **Hôtel du Théâtre ❷,** 2 rue Ste-Claire, above a quiet bar in the heart of the *vieille ville*, is the noise of tourists outside. Large windows with flower boxes brighten several rooms. (☎39 06 91. Breakfast €5. Reception 9am-9pm. Singles and doubles €23, with shower and toilet €29; triples with shower and toilet €39. AmEx/MC/V.) At **Hôtel de la Gare ❷,** pl. de la Gare, next to the train station but 10min. from the *vieille ville*, friendly owners rent large and clean—if somewhat bare—rooms over a corner bar. (☎39 04 57; fax 39 02 29. Breakfast €5. Shower €2. Reception M-Sa 7am-8pm, Su 7am-2pm. Singles and doubles €25, with shower and toilet €32; triples and quads €50-55. AmEx/MC/V.)

FOOD. Simple bars and *brasseries* line the streets linking rue de la Ferronnerie with pl. des Merciers, especially narrow **rue de la Cordonnerie.** A **Monoprix** supermarket is at 7 pl. du Marchix. (Open M-Sa 9am-7pm.) There is also a **Marché Plus** at 28 pl. Duclos. (Open M-Sa 7am-9pm, Su 9am-1pm.) On Thursdays, head to the outdoor **market** (open 9am-1pm) on **pl. du Champ Clos,** near the tourist office, to grab some fruit and a box of the town's specialty cookies: *gavottes* (dried, crystallized *crêpes*). Small restaurants and cafés cluster outside the ramparts, especially along the port, which is down the steep Rue du Jerzual from the *vieille ville*. Within the walls of the old city, you'll find *crêperies* at every turn; one of the best is **Crêperie le Roy ❶,** 15 rue de la Lainerie, where an attentive staff serves up filling *galettes* (€2.30-7.70), sweet *crêpes* (€2.30-7), and dinner salads for €6.50-7.50. (☎39 29 72. Open July to mid-Sept. daily 11:30am-11pm; mid-Sept. to June Tu-Su 11:30am-2:30pm and 6-10pm.) For authentic Indian delights with an abundance of vegetarian options, head to **Taj Mahal ❸,** 9 rue Ste-Claire. Fixed *menus* (lunch €11, dinner €15-25) come with exotic desserts. (☎85 43 30; www.restaurant-indien-dinan.com. Appetizers €5.50-11. *Plats* €11-16. Open daily noon-2pm and 7-11pm. AmEx/MC/V.) Though it doesn't serve food, **ArThé ❶,** 19 rue de l'Apport, overflows with hundreds of intricate porcelain teapots and the atmosphere of an antique shop. With 60 varieties of exquisite teas (€4.20-6), you're sure to find a melange that suits you in this tiny treasure trove. (☎87 48 45. Open Tu-Su July-Aug. 7:30am-10:30pm; Sept.-June 10:30am-12:30pm and 2:15-7:30pm.)

SIGHTS. Spanning nearly 3km, the town's **ramparts** are the longest and oldest in Brittany and a sight in themselves. Their remains completely encircle the *vieille ville*, but if all you see is the 13th-century **Porte du Guichet**—which marks the original entrance to the **Château de Dinan**—you'll still get the picture. Formerly a military stronghold, ducal residence, and dungeon, the château today houses a small and unimpressive museum of local art and history in its fifth-floor *donjon* (keep). It's worth the visit just to wander around the keep itself. Helpful placards on each floor note what each room was originally used for, and a great view of the town greets those who make it up all 150 steps of the 34m tower. The museum also includes the 15th-century **Tour de Coëtquen,** across the Porte du Guichet from the keep. Along with the occasional temporary exhibit, its dank, drafty basement houses dimly-lit medieval tomb statues. (☎39 45 20. Open daily June-Sept. 10am-6:30pm; Oct.-Dec. and Feb.-May 1:30-5:30pm. Guided tours July-Aug. 11am. €4.25, students and ages 12-18 €1.70, under 12 free. Cash only.)

The **Basilique St-Sauveur** was built by a local noble grateful to have been spared in the Crusades. The Romanesque facade, which dates back to 1120, features a winged lion and bull above the doorway and four eroded statues on the side arches. Within are 12 wooden altars made by local craftsmen, as well as the heart of French military hero Bertrand du Guesclin. Begun in the 15th century, the **Eglise St-Malo,** on Grande Rue, contains a remarkable 19th-century English organ with blue and gold pipes and a massive Baroque altar. (Mass M-Th 8am, F 10am, Su 10:30am.) The summit of the 43m, 15th-century **Tour de l'Horloge,** on rue de l'Horloge, commands a brilliant view of Dinan's jumbled streets and the Rance Valley, though there's nothing to see on your way to the top. The bells ring every quarter-hour. (☎87 02 26. Open daily June-Sept. 10am-6:30pm; Apr.-May 2-6pm. Tour pamphlets available in English. €2.80, students and ages 12-18 €1.80, under 12 free.) Leaving the *vieille ville,* rue du Jerzual holds shops of local artisans selling sculptures, leatherwork, ceramics, and other *objets d'art.* Outside the walls, rue du Jerzual becomes rue du Petit Fort, which leads to the port; a left turn here takes you to **Maison d'Artiste de la Grande Vigne,** 103 rue du Quai, the former home of painter Yvonne Jean-Haffen (1895-1993), who moved here in 1937. Visitors are free to wander through the rooms, all designed by the artist, whose Breton-themed murals and paintings adorn the walls (yearly exhibitions show different themes in Jean-Haffen's work). Leave by the back door to descend through a flowery hillside garden. (☎87 90 80. Open daily mid-May to Sept. 2-6:30pm. Last entry at 5:45pm. €2.80, students and ages 12-18 €1.75, under 12 free.)

NIGHTLIFE AND FESTIVALS. The new **Le Patio,** 9 pl. du Champ Clos, has hands-down the best ambiance in town, with a backlit bar and leopard-skin chairs reflected in its wall-length mirror. It also offers food and a lovely secluded garden. (☎39 84 87. Beer €2.50-4. *Aperitifs* €2.20-6. Open mid-May to mid-Sept. M 2pm-2am, Tu-Sa 11am-2am, Su 3pm-2am; mid-Sept. to mid-May closes at 1am. MC/V.) **L'Absinthe,** 15 pl. St-Sauveur, near the basilica, feels a little like an old-fashioned speakeasy, with soft jazz and exposed-brick walls. On sunny days, the porch outside makes a lovely spot for a quiet coffee. (☎87 39 28. Beer €1.30-4. *Aperitifs* €2-6. Open 9am-11pm mid-Apr. to mid-Sept. daily; mid-Sept. to mid-Apr. Tu-Sa.) Every other year (next in 2008), Dinan hosts the two-day **Fête des Remparts** during the second half of July, when the whole town dons medieval garb for jousting tournaments and merrymaking. (☎87 94 94; http://perso.wanadoo.fr/fete-remparts.dinan. Presentations daily 10am-9pm. All-day access €10, under 10 and those in medieval garb free; tournaments €10, ages 5-9 €6.)

PAIMPOL ☎02 96

Featuring a port packed with impressive yachts and sailboats, Paimpol (PEM-pohl; pop. 8300) has made a visible transition from fishing village to seaside vacation spot. Though it offers few sights of its own, the town provides easy access to the beautiful islands, cliffs, beaches, and hiking trails on this stretch of French coast. Meanwhile, its seafood, *crêperies,* regional specialty shops, and surprisingly vibrant nightlife give it a festive atmosphere with strong Breton flavor.

TRANSPORTATION. Trains run to Rennes (2hr., 4 per day, €25) via Guingamp. The station is located at av. du Général de Gaulle. (Office open M-F 6:30-7am and 8am-7pm, Sa 8am-7pm, Su and holidays 8:30am-7pm.) Tibus **buses** (☎08 10 22 22 22) run from the train station to destinations throughout the Côtes d'Armor. **Bikes** can be rented at Intersport, zone de Kerpuns, at the mall on rue Raymond Pellier. (☎20 59 46. €7 per ½-day, €12 per day, €55 per week; under 18 €5/8/40. Open M-Sa 9:30am-12:15pm and 2-7pm. AmEx/MC/V.)

ORIENTATION AND PRACTICAL INFORMATION. To get to the **tourist office,** 19 rue Général Leclerc, from the train station, turn right on av. du Général de Gaulle, follow it to the roundabout, and turn down the second street on the right. The office is on the left; it plans to move to pl. de la République after 2009. The staff provides a useful practical guide in English and French and organizes summer tours of the city in French. (☎20 83 16; www.paimpol-goelo.com. Open July-Aug. M-Sa 9:30am-7:30pm, Su 10am-1:30pm; Sept.-June M-Sa 9:30am-12:30pm and 1:30-6:30pm. Tours €3-6, under 12 free; reserve ahead.) **Laundry** is available at **Au Lavoir Pampolais,** 23 rue du 18 Juin 1940, near the station (☎20 96 41; open daily 7am-10pm) or on rue de Labenne, near the port (open daily 7am-10pm). Other services include: **public restrooms** on the port between the *bassins;* **police,** 2 rue Jean Moulin (☎20 80 17), off rue Raymond Pellier; a **pharmacy,** 6 rue Georges Brassens, near Marché Plus (☎20 80 31; open M 2-7pm, Tu-Sa 9am-12:30pm and 2-7pm); a **hospital** on chemin de Malabry (☎55 60 00); and **Internet** access at **Cybercommune,** Centre Dunant, on the corner of rue Henry Dunant and rue Pierre Feutren (☎20 74 74; http://cybercommune.paimpol-goelo.com; €5 per hr.; open M 2-7pm, Tu-Sa 9:30am-12:30pm and 2:30-7pm). The **post office,** 10 av. du Général de Gaulle, has **currency exchange.** (☎20 82 40. Open M and W-F 8am-noon and 1:30-5:30pm, Tu 8am-12:30pm and 1:30-5:30pm, Sa 8am-12:30pm.) **Postal Code:** 22500.

ACCOMMODATIONS AND CAMPING. True budget options lie 2hr. away in Rennes, but if you're willing to pay a little more, you can find comfortable accommodations in Paimpol. Your best bet is **Hôtel Berthelot ❷,** 1 rue du Port, off quai Morand. A giant blue "H" sticking out of a pink facade marks the hotel's entrance on the right. An exceedingly cheerful staff oversees small but tidy and well-lit rooms. (☎20 88 66. Breakfast €5. Reception 7:30am-8:30pm. Singles and doubles €31, with shower €38, with bath €42, with bath and TV €44. MC/V.) The cheapest stay on the waterfront is **Le Terre-Neuvas ❸,** 16 quai Duguay-Trouin, over a restaurant by the same name (see **Food**). The rooms are on the small side but come with shower, toilet, TV, and phone; some have a harbor view. (☎55 14 14; fax 20 47 66. Breakfast €5. Reception 8am-11pm. Reservations recommended in summer. July-Aug. singles €34, with harbor view €40; doubles €42/48. Sept.-June singles €32/38; doubles €40/46. MC/V.) For a splurge, try the modern **Hôtel Le Goëlo ❹,** 4 quai Duguay-Trouin, with a welcoming staff and comfortable rooms. (☎20 82 74; www.legoelo.com. All rooms with TV, shower, and toilet; some with harbor views. Breakfast €6.50. Free Wi-Fi. Wheelchair-accessible. In summer, reserve 3-4 days ahead. July-Aug. singles and doubles €51-67; triples €80; quads €85. Sept.-June €45-57/75/80. AmEx/MC/V.) The seaside **Camping Municipal de Cruckin ❶,** rue de Cruckin, is a 30min. walk outside of town. From the station, turn right on av. du Général de Gaulle and right again at the roundabout, onto rue du Général Leclerc. Follow the street as it twists several kilometers uphill through four name changes; take a left on rue de Cruckin. The entrance is 100m down the hill on the right. Sparse hedges separate 130 flat plots. (☎20 78 47; fax 20 75 00. Laundry €4, dry €3.50. Wheelchair-accessible. Bike rental €3-4 per ½-day, €4-6 per day; €150 deposit. Reception July-Aug. daily 8:30am-8pm; Apr.-June and Sept. M-Sa 9am-12:30pm and 4:30-7:30pm, Su 9-10:30am and 6-7:30pm. Gates closed 10pm-8am. Open Apr.-Sept. July-Aug. €7 per site, €3.20 per adult, €2 per child under 7. Sept.-June €5.60/2.90/1.50. Electricity €3. AmEx/MC/V.)

FOOD. The **market** throughout the *vieille ville* provides picnic supplies (Tu morning), as does the **Marché Plus** supermarket, 11 rue St-Vincent, left at the roundabout from the train station. (Open M-Sa 7am-9pm, Su 9am-1pm.) Find seafood along quai Morand and *crêperies* lining rue des 8 Patriotes. The cheery staff at **Le**

TOP TEN LIST

GET YOUR BRET-ON

Brittany is one of few regions in which French doesn't hold a language monopoly, but instead competes with Brezhoneg (Breton), which descends from the language of the original Celtic inhabitants of Brittany. Here are the most helpful words to know:

1. **Breizh:** Brittany itself. Often in c[redacted]pounds, like Breizhtrotters.

2[redacted]**Ty,** also spelled Ti: translates approximately to "the house of[redacted]ike *chez.* You'll see it in resta[redacted]nt names.

3. **Penn:** not a Quaker, but a rocky point. These are everywhere along the Breton coast, so you'll see this word a lot on maps.

4. **Pesk:** fish. Given the importance of seafood in the Breton diet, this word is vital to survival.

5. **Kouing-aman:** another regional specialty, this time a sweet and sticky pastry.

6. **Kroaz:** cross. One of the few Breton words that sounds like its English equivalent, and a reminder of the historic power of Catholicism in the region.

7[redacted]**Krampouezh:** *crêpe.* The impo[redacted]ance is self-explanatory.

8. **Tour-tan:** lighthouse. This will help you locate some of the most beautiful sights along Brittany's jagged coastline.

[redacted]**Glav:** rain. Hope that you w[redacted]be hearing this word too oft[redacted]The one you want to hear is *heol,* meaning sun.

10. **Yec'hed mat:** Cheers! The most important phrase in any language.

Penn Ty ❷, 20 rue des 8 Patriotes, serves up great *galettes* at great prices (€1.60-7.90) while light Celtic music plays in the background. (☎55 11 41. Salads €4.90-8.90. *Menus* €7.90-20. Open July-Aug. M-Tu and F-Su 11:30am-3pm and 6:30-10:30pm; Nov.-Mar. M and F-Su 11:30am-3pm and 6:30-10:30pm, Tu 11:30am-3pm. MC/V.) Portside **Le Terre-Neuvas ❸,** quai Duguay-Trouin, serves an array of elegant seafood dishes, ranging from traditional *moules-frites* (mussels and fries) for €9 to gourmet *plats* for €23-39. (☎55 14 14. *Menus* €15-29. Open July-Aug. daily noon-2pm and 7-10pm; Sept.-June Tu-Su noon-2pm and 7-10pm. MC/V.)

SIGHTS. A half-hour's walk outside of Paimpol, hidden from the road by vegetation, lie the ruins of the **Abbaye de Beauport,** chemin de l'Abbaye. Built in 1202 and abandoned after the French Revolution, the abbey has found a new charm in its disrepair; soft green grass and colorful flowers sprout from its flying buttresses. The book-guided tour (in Dutch, English, French, German, Italian, or Spanish), included with admission, gives a complete account of the abbey's history and describes each of the abbey's sections in detail, from the intact cellars to the picturesque garden. In summer, the abbey puts on an award-winning light show, which illuminates the ruins (July-Aug. W and Su 10pm-1am; adults €8, ages 5-18 €4). To get there, follow directions to the campground but continue past rue de Cruckin to the next major left turn; the abbey is at the end of the lane. (☎55 18 54; www.abbaye-beauport.com. Open daily mid-June to mid-Sept. 10am-7pm; mid-Sept. to mid-June 10am-noon and 2-5pm. Last entry 30min. before closing. 4-6 tours in French per day. Apr.-Aug. €5, students €4, ages 11-18 €3, ages 5-10 €2; Sept.-Mar. €4.50/4/2/1.)

NIGHTLIFE AND FESTIVALS. Paimpol may be small, but it knows how to party. As the sun sets, crowds head to bars on side streets off the port, or to quai de Kernoa on the waterfront. Escape Brittany on a fun and relaxed safari at **Zanzi'Bar,** 10 quai de Kernoa. Reggae music, décor reminiscent of a thatched jungle hut, and playful toy giraffes complete the scene. (☎20 75 15. Beer €2.20. Hard cider €2.10. Open daily July-Aug. 3pm-2am; June-Sept. 5pm-1am. MC/V.) Named after a popular comic book character, **Le Corto Maltese,** 11 rue du Quai, earns its popularity among locals with its loud mix of classic rock, flashing lights, and Belgian and Irish beers on tap. (☎22 05 76. Beer €2.80-4. Irish coffee €6.50. Open mid-May to mid-Sept. daily 10am-2am; mid-Sept. to mid-May Tu-Su 10am-1am. AmEx/MC/V.) The heavy oak door of **Le Pub,** 3 rue Islandais, can't contain the revelry inside in the early morning hours. At 1am, a club opens upstairs, and Thursdays at 9:30pm Irish folk music adds flavor. (☎20 82 31. Beer €2.50-7. Mixed drinks €6-8. Prices rise when the disco opens. Open July-Aug. daily 9:30pm-5am; Sept.-June Th-Su 9:30pm-5am. AmEx/MC/V.)

Every other year in early August (next in 2009), the **Fête du Chant de Marin,** "Festival of Sailors' Songs," draws sailor-musicians from around the globe for three days of dancing, boating, and general merriment. (☎55 12 77; www.paimpol-festival.com.)

DAYTRIP FROM PAIMPOL

POINTE DE L'ARCOUEST AND ILE DE BRÉHAT

To get to Pointe de L'Arcouest, take a Tibus bus (☎20 94 58) from Paimpol (15min.; M-Sa 6 per day, Su 2 per day, more July-Aug.; €2). Drivers follow clearly marked GR34. Les Vedettes de Bréhat (☎55 79 50; www.vedettesdebrehat.com) runs boats to Ile de Bréhat (10min.; 5-16 per day; round-trip €8, ages 4-11 €6.50, with bike €15). For a few extra euro, take a 45min. circuit of the island from the sea (€13, ages 4-11 €9).

Six kilometers north of Paimpol, the peninsula ends in a tumble of pink granite called the **Pointe de l'Arcouest.** Although the Pointe itself is a worthy destination, it is usually used as a jumping-off point for the Ile de Bréhat. The surrounding blue-green waters provide some of France's best sea kayaking; the Centre Nautique de Loguivy-de-la-Mer, 5km outside the Pointe, rents **kayaks** and **catamarans.** (☎20 94 58; www.voile-kayak-mer.com. Kayak rental with guide €30 per ½-day, €49 per day. Catamarans €40 per 2hr. Open M-Sa 9am-noon and 2-5:30pm.)

Two kilometers out to sea lies the **Ile de Bréhat**—a mesh of rocky pink beaches, small tracts of farmland, flower-draped cottages, and fields of elbow-high grass and full trees. The Ile de Bréhat is actually the largest landmass in an archipelago of 96 islets, some of them so minute that they amount essentially to single rocks. Only 3.5km in length, Bréhat (BRAY-hah) is divided in the center by a small bridge. The southern half contains the *bourg* (town center) and the port, while the rugged northern half is mostly farmland, with a few scattered houses and the island's two lighthouses. To get the most out of your visit, take the earliest boat you can catch, then head north to avoid the crowds. Plan to take at least half a day to see the island; the trip from Paimpol to the island takes about 45min. if you time it right, and the island itself deserves at least 3hr. of exploration.

Follow signs from the *bourg* to the tiny, white-walled and orange-roofed **Chapelle St-Michel,** on a hilltop on the west side of the island, for a marvelous view of the island's green fields and houses and a rock-speckled bay. The natural beauty of this panorama is only matched by the eroded pink granite rock piles at the island's northern tip, on which the **Phare du Paon** lighthouse sits. According to legend, when unwed women throw a pebble between the rocks, the number of bounces indicates the years that they must wait until marriage. The lighthouse and its scenic surroundings are well worth the 40-50min. walk from the center of town.

From the port, follow the signs for a 15min. walk to the *bourg*. Here, you can find restaurants and a **8 à Huit** supermarket (open July-Aug. M-Sa 9am-7pm, Su 9am-1pm; Sept.-June M-Sa 9am-12:30pm and 3-7pm, Su 9:30am-12:30pm). The island's restaurants serve similar, overpriced dishes, and its cafés mainly sell *crêpes*, sandwiches, ice cream, and *frites*. Picnicking is both inexpensive and more enjoyable; come prepared or pick up supplies at the supermarket.

The best way to tackle the island is by foot or bicycle; paths to major sights are clearly marked. Of the many **bike** rental options, the closest to the port lies at the end of the walkway leading to the boats, marked by the sign "Vélos à Louer." (€6 per 2hr., €10 per 5hr., €15 per day; under 18 €5/8/13. Open Apr.-Sept. daily 9am-7pm, depending on ferry schedules. MC/V.) Although some paths take quick ups and downs and are packed with pedestrians during high season, biking is an easy and effective way to cover ground. To reach the **tourist office,** or "Syndicat d'Initiative," follow the main road toward the *bourg*, past the supermarket to the main square; the office is on the right. The staff sells a map (€1) of the island, although the *Vedettes de Bréhat* brochure offers an equivalent map for free. **Public restrooms** next door. (☎20 04 15; syndicatinitiative.Brehat@wanadoo.fr. Open July-Aug. M-Sa 10am-5pm; Sept. and Apr.-June M-Tu and Th-Sa 10am-12:30pm and 2-4:30pm; Oct.-Mar. M and Th 10am-12:30pm and 2-4:30pm, Sa 10am-1pm.)

ROSCOFF ☎02 98

With a bevy of seafood restaurants, a central port, and several beaches, Roscoff (ROSS-koff; pop. 3550) is a city of the sea. The town has been everything from a base for pirates and smugglers to the birthplace of *thalassothérapie* (sea-water therapy), a treatment popular in France today. There's not much to see besides sun and water, but Roscoff's strong nautical character and proximity to Ile de Batz make it worth a quick stop.

TRANSPORTATION AND PRACTICAL INFORMATION. SNCF **trains** and **buses** run via Morlaix (30-45min., 4-6 per day, €5.10) to Brest (2hr., 5 per day, €13-15), Rennes (4¼hr., 4 per day, €27-30), and Paris (5hr., 4 per day, €76-79). Penn-ar-Bed **buses** (☎76 24 58; http://infotransports.cg29.fr) leave from stops at the *centre-ville* and the ferry terminal and go to Morlaix (1hr., M-Sa 5 per day, €2) and Quimper (2½hr., 1 per day, €2). **Ferries** leave from the Port du Bloscon, outside of town. Brittany Ferries (☎08 25 82 88 28; www.brittanyferries.com) serves Plymouth, England (5-6hr., 1-2 per day, €124), and Cork, Ireland (10-11hr., 1 per week, €309). Irish Ferries (☎61 17 17; www.irishferries.com) serves Rosslare, Ireland, about twice per week. Irish Ferries offers Eurail discounts up to 30%. Clear signs mark the way to the *centre-ville* from the train station or ferry terminal.

The **tourist office,** 46 rue Gambetta, set back from the port, has transportation schedules, walking tours, maps, a visitor's guide, a separate guide to *chambres d'hôte*, and free **Internet** access on one computer. (☎61 12 13; www.roscoff-tourisme.com. Open July-Aug. M-Sa 9am-12:30pm and 1:30-7pm, Su 10am-12:30pm; Sept.-June M-Sa 9am-noon and 2-6pm.) There is a **laundromat** at 3 rue Jules Ferry. (Open daily 7:30am-9pm.) **Public restrooms** can be found near the tourist office, at the train station, and at the ferry terminal. **Police** are at 16 rue Jules Ferry (☎19 33 74). The **post office,** 19 rue Gambetta, offers **currency exchange** and photocopying. (☎69 71 28. Open July-Aug. M-F 9am-12:30pm and 1:30-5:30pm, Sa 9am-12:30pm; Sept.-June M-F 9am-noon and 2-5pm, Sa 9am-12:30pm.) **Postal Code:** 29680.

ACCOMMODATIONS AND FOOD. Roscoff has few budget hotels; cheaper options can be found on Ile de Batz. At **Hôtel d'Angleterre ❸,** 28 rue Albert de Mun, a delightful staff offers large rooms with Breton furniture in an old mansion. A sunroom with wicker chairs looks onto a backyard garden. Enjoy the restaurant, TV room with a pool table, and sunny sitting room with chessboards. (☎69 70 42; fax 69 75 16. Breakfast €6. Reception 8am-11pm. Open Easter to mid-Oct. July-Aug. singles and doubles €35, with toilet €45, with bath or shower €57; Apr.-May and Sept.-Oct. €28/37/50. *Demi-pension* €38/41/48 per person. Extra bed €16. MC/V.) Roscoff's only camping option is **Camping de Perharidy "Aux 4 Saisons" ❶,** near allée des Chênes Verts, 2km from the train station. From the station, turn left on rue Ropartz Morvan, right on rue des Capucins, left on rue Laënnec, and right on rue de la Baie. Turn left at the coast, following rte. du Laber past the Jardin Louis Kerdilés, and then right; the campsite will be on your left (30min.). About 200 spots by the beach include access to a volleyball court, mini golf, bowling, hot showers, and laundry. (☎69 70 86 or 06 07 41 28 53; www.camping-aux4saisons.com. Reception July-Aug. daily 9am-noon and 2-8pm; Apr.-June and Sept. to mid-Oct. 9-11:30am and 5:30-7:30pm. Reservations recommended. Open Apr. to mid-Oct. July-Aug. 2 adults with tent €9.60, with tent and car €11, with caravan or RV €12. Extra adult €3.10, child under 7 €1.80. Apr.-June and Sept. to mid-Oct. €7.60/8.40/13/2.80/1.70. Electricity €2.60-4.10. Cash only.)

Restaurants serving seafood *menus* (€13-25) line the port. There is a market (W 9am-1pm) on **quai Auxerre,** and a **Casino** supermarket a 15min. walk out of town on the right side of rue du Pontigou. (Open M-F 9am-12:30pm and 2-6pm, Sa 9am-6pm, Su 9am-noon; longer hours July-Aug.) One of Roscoff's most distinctive *crêperies,* **Ti Saozon ❶,** 30 rue Gambetta, just past the tourist office, feels like a traditional Breton home. (☎69 70 89. *Galettes* and *crêpes* €2.50-8.50. Open M-Sa from 6:30pm. Reservations recommended.) **Le Surcouf ❸,** 14 rue Amiral Réveillère, dishes up fresh seafood in a simple but elegant interior with crisp white tablecloths. (☎69 71 89; www.jalima.fr. *Plat du jour* €8. Seafood *plats* €14-19. Lunch *menu* €10, dinner *menus* €15-26. Open July-Sept. M-Th and Sa-Su noon-2:15pm and 7-9:30pm, F noon-2pm and 6:30-9:30pm. Oct.-June M-Tu, Th, Sa-Su noon-2:15pm and 7-9:30pm; F noon-2pm and 6:30-9:30pm. AmEx/MC/V.)

SIGHTS. The most popular sight in Roscoff is **Le Jardin Exotique,** a well-tended jungle featuring over 3000 species of tropical flora and a panoramic view of the bay of Morlaix. The garden is a 30min. walk outside of town past the ferry terminal; from the tourist office, walk to the dock and turn right. Follow quai d'Auxerre, bear left on rue Jeanne d'Arc, and continue through pl. de Keradraon onto rue Plymouth. Turn right on rue de Great Torrington and then left, following the signs. (☎61 29 19; www.jardinexotiqueroscoff.com. Open daily July-Aug. 10am-7pm; Apr.-June and Sept.-Oct. 10:30am-12:30pm and 2-6pm; Mar. and Nov. 2-5pm. €5, students and seniors €4, ages 12-18 €2.) The 16th-century **Eglise Notre Dame de Croaz-Batz** is reminiscent of an overgrown sand castle, with turreted spires and a Renaissance-style belfry. Twin stone cannons carved into the church's main tower point toward the sea, symbolically defending the city. (Open daily 9am-noon and 2-6pm.) On the far right side of the port is the **Pointe Ste-Barbe,** with spiraling stone steps leading up to a white chapel. Look out over a local shellfish farm for a view of Roscoff's port and the rocky islands of the Bay of Morlaix. If the weather's nice and you feel like a hike, take a walking tour (6-12km, 1½-3hr.) around Roscoff using the free *Circuits Pedestre* guide on the back of the town map.

ILE DE BATZ ☎02 98

Fifteen minutes off the coast of Roscoff sits Ile de Batz (EEL duh BAHTSS; pop. 500, in summer 3500), a wind-swept sanctuary of natural beauty only 3.5km long and 1.5km wide. Small farms and cottages stand in acres of green grass dotted with duck ponds, while winding paths lead through the countryside and along an unspoiled coastline. The island's many small beaches, said to have some of the finest sand in France, are perfect spots for a secluded dip.

TRANSPORTATION AND PRACTICAL INFORMATION. Three allied **ferry** companies—Armein (☎61 77 75), Armor Excursions (☎61 79 66), and CFTM (☎61 78 87)—connect Roscoff and Batz (10-15min.). Boats leave from Roscoff's port at high tide and from the walkway at the harbor at low tide. (Late June to Aug. every 30min., last boat from island 7:30pm; Sept. to late June 8-10 per day, last boat from island 6pm. Round-trip €7, ages 4-11 €4.) Circle the island or tour the Bay of Morlaix for a few more euro. (Tours July-Aug. 1hr. island circuit Su 3pm; €10, ages 4-11 €6. 2-5hr. Bay of Morlaix circuit daily 2:30pm; €13-14, under 18 €6-7.) There are a number of **bike rental** places in convenient locations on the island, including Vélos le Saoût; follow the signs uphill from the ferry dock. (☎61 77 65. €3 per hr., €9 per ½-day, €10 per day. Hours depend on ferry schedules, but generally 9am-8pm.)

The island's tiny **tourist office** is in the town hall from September to June, then moves to the port in July and August. To get to the town hall, turn left out of the port and follow signs. The staff hands out a small but sufficient guide, complete with 2hr. walking tours, as well as a detailed map. (☎61 75 70; www.iledebatz.com. Open July-Aug. M-F 10am-1pm and 2-5pm, Sa 9:30am-1pm; Sept.-June M-F 9am-noon and 1:30-4:30pm, Sa 10am-noon.) The Ile de Batz **post office,** with **currency exchange** and fax, is a pink building with a mural of children painted on the side, in the center of town; look for signs. (☎61 76 46. Open July-Aug. M-F 9am-noon and 1:30-4:30pm, Sa 9am-noon; Sept.-June M-F 9:30am-noon and 1:30-4pm, Sa 9:30am-noon.) **Postal Code:** 29253.

ACCOMMODATIONS AND FOOD. Make reservations in advance if you're staying on the island, especially in summer. The cheapest bed for miles around can be found at **Auberge de Jeunesse Marine (HI) ❶,** even if the facilities aren't the cleanest. To reach the hostel from the port, take the uphill road to the left of the hotel. Signs clearly mark the path to the hostel (5-10min.). Hidden among pines atop one of the island's hills, the five-building complex has the rustic air of a private lodge and access to a secluded beach. (☎61 77 69; www.aj-iledebatz.org. Breakfast included. Sheets €4. Reception daily July-Aug. 6:30-8:30pm; Apr.-June and Sept.-Oct. 6:30-7:30pm. Building open 24hr. Open Apr.-Oct. Dorms €14. Cots in big tent €13. *Demi-pension* €22, *pension* €31. Cash only.) The rooms at the *chambres d'hôte* **Ty Va Zadou ❸,** overlooking the port, are filled with charming Breton hospitality. From the ferry, head left toward town. The stone house with light blue shutters is atop a hill next to the church. A pleasant proprietress oversees homey, carefully color-coordinated rooms, all with bath. Vacationers reserve up to a year in advance, so plan ahead. (☎61 76 91. Breakfast included. Reception 9am-10pm. Open Feb. to mid-Nov. Singles €40; doubles €60; 2-room family suite €80.) The grassy **Terrain d'Hérbergement de Plein Air ❶,** an open field on the beach near the lighthouse, is the sole legal campground on the island, but only allows tents. There's no permanent reception—a dues collector will come by. (☎61 75 70. Open mid-June to mid-Sept. €2.50 per person, €1 per child, €1.50 per tent. Cash only.)

From the port, bear left and follow signs to the **8 à Huit** supermarket, near the island's highest point. (Open Tu-Sa 9am-12:30pm and 2:30-7:30pm, Su 10am-12:30pm.) Dining options on the island are rather limited, especially when the supermarket is closed. A few restaurants and *crêperies* greet voyagers coming off the ferry at the port. With a terrace facing the sea, **La Cassonade ❶,** offers elegant service and budget prices. The house specialty, *Ilienne* (€8), is a gourmet treat—a *galette* with scallops and leek puree. (☎61 75 25. *Galettes* and *crêpes* €2.40-8. Open daily Apr.-Sept. and school vacations 9am-10pm. MC/V.) Relaxed **Kastell Gwenn ❷,** in the town center, serves generously sized pizzas. (☎61 76 34. Pizza €7-14. Open M-W and F-Sa 9am-8:30pm, Th 9am-noon, Su 9am-1pm. AmEx/MC/V.)

SIGHTS AND HIKING. The best way to see Ile de Batz is to take the *sentier côtier*, 14km of easy-to-follow **trails** that line the coast, running past the rugged *côte sauvage* along small, sandy beaches, over massive rocks, and past inland lakes. The 4hr. hike is not difficult. Find the trails from any point on the island by taking the nearest road to the coast, or by following signs from the port. The tourist office's guidebook has maps for easy 2hr. hikes on either side of the island.

At the southeast tip of the island, signs lead to the tranquil **Jardin Georges Delaselle,** a horticultural masterpiece featuring exotic plants from every continent except Antarctica. The garden is arranged around several different *paysages* (landscapes)—including a cactus garden, a palm grove, and the **Nécropole,** a grassy lawn dotted with Bronze-Age tombs—and provides excellent views of Roscoff from under its shaded canopy of trees. (☎61 75 65. Open July-Aug. daily 1-6:30pm; Apr.-June and Sept.-Oct. M and W-Su 2-6pm. €4.30, students and seniors €3.50, ages 10-16 €2, under 10 free. 1hr. guided visits Su 3pm; €7. 2hr. guided visits July-Aug. Tu 10am; €8.) For a great view of the island and Roscoff, climb the 198 steps of the **lighthouse,** which was built between 1832 and 1836 out of native granite. (Open daily July-Aug. 1-5:30pm; early Sept. and late June M-Tu and Th-Su 2-5pm; closed in poor weather. €2, under 18 €1.) Slightly inland, just before the garden, stand the ruins of the 12th-century Eglise St-Paul, renamed the **Chapelle Ste-Anne** after the patron saint of the island's sailors. During the **Fête de Ste-Anne,** the year's largest celebration, a parade proceeds from the town church to the chapel's ruins, where an open-air mass is held before a huge bonfire on the dunes (last Sa in July).

BREST ☎02 98

Brest (BREHST; pop. 153,000) became a wasteland in 1944 when Allied bombers drove out the occupying German fleet. Reconstructed in a modern style, the city may not be picturesque, but it does boast a seaside locale and a lively urban atmosphere. Tourists and locals alike throng to its enormous Océanopolis aquarium, and ferries leave regularly for daytrips to nearby Ile d'Ouessant.

TRANSPORTATION. The **train station** is at pl. du 19ème Régiment d'Infanterie. (Ticket office open M-F 5:20am-7:30pm, Sa 6am-6:30pm, Su 8am-7:50pm.) **Trains** go to Morlaix (30min., 13-20 per day, €9-12); Paris (4½hr., 10 per day, €65); Quimper (30min., 6 per day, €10); Rennes (2¼hr., 10 per day, €30-33). Penn-ar-Bed **buses** leave from the gare routière next to the train station. (☎44 46 73; http://infotransports.cg29.fr. Open M-F 6:50am-12:30pm and 1-7pm, Sa 8:45am-1:15pm and 2:30-7pm, Su 1:30-2:30pm and 5:15-7pm.) Buses run to Quimper (1¼hr.; M-Sa 5 per day, Su 2 per day; €6), Roscoff (1½hr., 5 per day, €2), and smaller towns in the region for €2. Penn-ar-Bed bus tickets are valid for 1hr. on the Bibus system (below). For information on **ferries** to Ile d'Ouessant, see p. 261. **Local buses** are operated by Bibus, 33 av. Georges Clemenceau. (☎80 30 30; www.bibus.fr. Open M-F 8:15am-6:15pm, Sa 9am-5pm. Regular service daily Sept.-June 6am-8pm; night lines hourly M-Th and Su 9-11pm, F-Sa 9pm-midnight. Service significantly reduced July-Aug.; check schedules and maps available at the bus and tourist offices.) Buy tickets (€1.20) and 24hr. passes (valid midnight-midnight; Sept.-June €3.20, July-Aug. €2) on board; get *carnets* of 10 tickets (€8.90) or weekly passes (valid M-Su; €9.15) at the office. For a **taxi,** call ☎42 11 11; there's a stand at the train station.

ORIENTATION AND PRACTICAL INFORMATION. To the right of the train station, av. Georges Clemenceau leads to the central **place de la Liberté,** an open square with fountains in front of the *hôtel de ville.* This is both the center of the city and the main terminal for its bus system. **Rue de Siam,** running south from the *place* to the sea, is the most vibrant street in the city, with boutiques lining either side and water running around stone blocks in the median. **Rue Jean Jaurès,** north of the *place*, is also prime shopping territory, but be careful at night. Ferries leave for nearby isles from **Port du Commerce.**

The friendly staff at the **tourist office,** pl. de la Liberté, offers a visitors' handbook, free maps, info on sights and tours, free hotel and ferry reservations; it also helps plan trips to Ile d'Ouessant and offers reduced-price bike rentals. (☎44 24 96; www.brest-metropole-tourisme.fr. Open July-Aug. M-Sa 9:30am-7pm, Su 10am-noon; Sept.-June M-Sa 9:30am-6pm.) The **Bureau Information Jeunesse (BIJ),** 4 rue Augustin Morvan, off pl. de la Liberté, has free Internet access and info on jobs and internships. (☎43 01 08; www.bij-brest.org. Open July and late Aug. M-F 10am-noon and 1:30-4:30pm; Sept.-June M-Tu 1:30-6pm, W-F 9:30am-noon and 1:30-6pm, Sa 9:30am-noon.) Other services include: **laundromats** at 8 pl. de la Liberté (open daily 8am-8pm) and 7 rue de Siam (open daily 8am-9:30pm); **police** at 15 rue Colbert (☎43 77 77); a **hospital,** 2 av. Foch (☎22 33 33); a **pharmacy,** 29 av. Clemenceau, off pl. de la Liberté (☎44 19 47; open M-F and Su 8am-10pm, Sa 8am-5pm); **Internet** access at the **BIJ** for free (see above), at **@cces.cibles,** 31 av. Georges Clemenceau (☎46 76 10, www.accescibles.fr; €4 per hr. for computer or Wi-Fi; open M-Sa 11am-1am, Su 2-11pm), and at **dialogues,** pl. Roull, a **bookstore** with an English-language section and free Wi-Fi with entrances on rue de Siam and rue Louis Pasteur. (☎44 88 68; www.librairiedialogues.fr. Open M-Sa 9:30am-7:30pm.) The **post office,** 90 rue de Siam, on espl. Général Leclerc, has **currency exchange,** fax, and photocopier. (☎33 73 06. Open M-F 8am-7pm, Sa 8am-noon.) **Postal Code:** 29200.

ACCOMMODATIONS AND CAMPING. The **Auberge de Jeunesse (HI) ❶,** 5 rue Kerbriant, is 4km from the train station, near Océanopolis and next to the artificial beach in Le Moulin Blanc. From pl. de la Liberté, take bus #3 (dir.: Océanopolis; M-Sa 6:30am-8:30pm, Su 9:45am-8:30pm) or night bus #n25 or #n27, to "Palaren." From the bus stop, turn right, walk under the overpass, and take the second right. Walk up the small hill and turn left to reach the hostel. Palm trees, a luxuriant garden, and a nearby beach add a tropical feel to this site, which features sleek and spacious four-bed rooms with modern furnishings. Facilities include an enormous common room looking out onto the garden, a grand stone fireplace, piano, foosball, ping pong, pool tables, and a separate TV room. A friendly and experienced staff gives a brief tour to each new guest and provides helpful info on Brest, including discounts on ferries to Ile d'Ouessant. Bicycle garage, luggage storage, kitchen, and laundry are also available. (☎41 90 41; www.aj-brest.org. Breakfast included. Reception July-Aug. 7:30-10am and 5pm-midnight; Sept.-June 7:30am-10am and 5-11pm. Lockout 10am-5pm. Curfew July-Aug. midnight; Sept.-June 11pm. Key deposit for late entry. Dorms €16, *demi-pension* €24. MC/V.) Central, quiet, and spotless, the **Hôtel Astoria ❷,** 9 rue Traverse, offers compact, modern rooms with TV and classy accents like armchairs. (☎80 19 10; www.hotel-astoria-brest.com. Breakfast €7. Showers €4. Reception daily 7am-11pm. Reserve a week ahead, especially July-Aug. Singles and doubles €28, with shower and toilet €44-49, with bath €52-54. AmEx/MC/V.) Nearer to the train station, **Kelig Hôtel ❸,** 12 rue de Lyon, has 27 generously-sized rooms with TV, dark wooden wardrobes, and comfortable beds. (☎80 47 21; lucas.pascale@wanadoo.fr. Breakfast €6-7. Laundry €8. Reception M-F 7am-9:30pm, Sa 8am-7pm, Su 8am-12:30pm. Singles with shower and toilet €32-40, with tub and toilet €40; doubles €37-48/45; triples €47-53/53. MC/V.) To get to **Camping du Goulet ❶,** 7km from downtown in Ste-Anne du Portzic, take bus #28 (dir.: Plouzané) to "Cosquer" (20-25min.). At night, take bus #n26 (dir.: Plouzané), making sure to go via Technopôle (M-Th and Su 1 per night, F-Sa 3 per night.). Amid plenty of greenery, this campground seems more like a luxury resort with its pool and waterslides, game room, bar, and clean facilities. (☎45 86 84. Reception July-Aug. 8am-8pm; Sept.-June 9:30am-noon and 2:30-7pm. 2 adults and car €11-15, €2.50-4 per extra adult, €2 per child under 7, €1.30 per extra car. Electricity €2.50-3. Laundry €3, dry €1.50. AmEx/MC/V.)

FOOD. Markets are held every day in various locations, such as the traditional and organic markets on **rue du Moulin à Poudre** (open Tu 4-8pm, Sa 8:30am-12:30pm), the enormous market on **place St-Louis** (open Su 8:30am-12:30pm), and a slightly pricey indoor market at **Les Halles St-Louis,** one block from rue de Siam (open M-Sa 7am-1pm and 4-7:30pm, Su 7am-1pm). *Pâtisseries* and kebab counters can be found on and around **rue Jean Jaurès** and **rue de Siam;** more filling meals are at the end of rue de Siam near the port. A handful of restaurants and

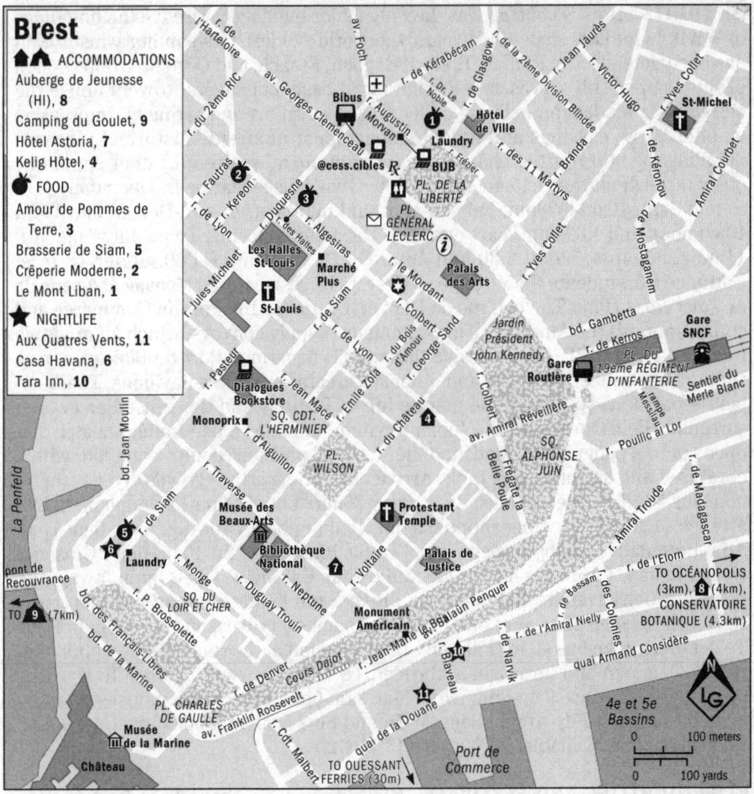

bars cluster to the southeast at **Port du Commerce.** For groceries, head to **Marché Plus,** 59 rue Louis Pasteur, just off rue de Siam (open M-Sa 7am-9pm, Su 9am-1pm), or the basement of **Monoprix,** 49 rue de Siam (open M-Sa 8am-8pm).

Couples *rendez-vous* at the intimate **Le Mont Liban ❸,** 8 pl. de la Liberté, to chat over catchy Arabic music and splurge on two-person *mezzes* (€40-52), or assortments of 15 different Middle-Eastern delicacies. Lots of vegetarian dishes. (☎80 12 76. Lunch *menus* €8.50-16. Open M-F noon-2pm and 7:30-10pm, Sa 7:30-11pm. MC/V.) Around the corner from pl. Liberté, locals both young and old frequent the casual **Crêperie Moderne ❶,** 34 rue Algésiras, to enjoy classic *galettes* and *crêpes* (€1.50-10). Double your portion for only a few extra centimes. (☎44 44 35. Open M-Sa 10:30am-2:30pm and 6:30-10:30pm. MC/V.) **Amour de Pomme de Terre ❸,** 23 rue des Halles St-Louis, hidden behind the indoor market, is a slightly pricey, spuds-heavy establishment with a down-to-earth feel. Potato lovers will revel in the abundance of their favorite vegetable, although true vegetarians will find few options. (☎43 48 51. Lunch *menus* €7-14. *Plats* €15-28. Open M noon-2pm and 7-10pm, Tu-Th noon-2pm and 7:30-10:30pm, F noon-2pm and 7:30-11pm, Sa noon-2pm and 7-11:30pm, Su noon-2pm and 7:30-10pm. MC/V.) Near the port, **Brasserie de Siam ❸,** 12 rue de Siam, serves seafood dishes, pizzas, and salads amid colorful—if loud—modern décor. (☎46 05 52. *Menus* €7.50-13. *Plats* €7.90-18. Open M-Th and Su noon-3pm and 7-11pm, F-Sa noon-3pm and 7pm-midnight. MC/V.)

SIGHTS. Brest's **château** was the only major building to survive the bombings of WWII. In its 1700 strife-filled years, the world's oldest active military institution has been defended by Roman, Breton, English, French, and German troops. Much of the fortress still serves as a French naval base, but several towers house the **Musée de la Marine,** an eclectic collection of naval art and artifacts. Impressive wooden prow carvings and model ships appear alongside historical placards detailing the story of the château's construction, all scattered rather spontaneously throughout the château. (☎22 12 39; www.musee-marine.fr. Open daily Apr. to mid-Sept. 10am-6:30pm; Feb. to Mar. and mid-Sept. to mid-Dec. M and W-Su 10am-noon and 1:30-6pm. Last entrance 1hr. before closing. Tours July-Aug. M-F 11am, 2:30, 4pm; Sa-Su 2:30 and 4pm. €6.10, students €4.60, under 18 free. Entrance €5, students €3.50, under 18 free.) The rose-colored **Monument Américain** or *Tour Rose* (Pink Tower), rue de Denver, overlooks the Port du Commerce and commemorates the American Navy's immense supply convoys, which entered this port in 1917 and 1918. The massive **Océanopolis** aquarium, Port de Plaisance, presents a huge collection of fish and other sea creatures in three pavilions. The "temperate pavilion" spotlights the marine life of Brittany and the Iroise Sea (which surrounds Ile d'Ouessant), the "polar pavilion" contains a panoramic theater that opens onto a penguin playland, and the "tropical pavilion" comes complete with a coral reef and sizable shark tank. Arrive early to beat the crowds. To get there, take bus #3 (dir.: Océanopolis; daily every 30min. until 7:30pm) from pl. de la Liberté. (☎34 40 40; www.oceanopolis.com. Open mid-July to Aug. daily 9am-7pm; Apr.-June daily 9am-6pm; Sept.-Mar. Tu-Sa 10am-5pm, Su 10am-6pm. Closed 2 weeks in Jan. €16, ages 4-17 €11. Audio tour €4. MC/V.) Just 5min. away, the beautiful **Conservatoire Botanique de Brest,** a public garden and conservatory, stretches through 2km of exotic plant life, bamboo groves, and trickling brooks. To get there, take bus #3 to "Palaren," then head left at the roundabout, uphill onto rte. de Quimper, and turn right at the sign. (☎02 46 00; www.cbnbrest.fr. Gardens open daily May-Oct. 9am-8pm; Nov.-Mar 9am-6pm. Free. Greenhouses open by guided tour only July to mid-Sept. M-Th and Su 2-5:30pm; Sept.-June Su 4:30pm. English booklet available. €3.50, ages 10-16 €2.)

NIGHTLIFE AND FESTIVALS. Nightlife centers around the **Port de Commerce,** the near side of the **pont de Recouvrance,** and the streets near **place de la Liberté.** Avoid the neighborhoods on the other side of the pont de Recouvrance after dark. The young crowd in **Casa Havana,** 2 rue de Siam, munches tapas (€2.90) and desserts (€3.10) amid lively Latin music and bright red walls. There's a long list of cocktails—including plenty of non-alcoholic options—and a non-smoking room upstairs. (☎80 42 87. Beer €1.70-4.70. Mixed drinks €5-7. Free salsa lessons M and Th at 7:30 and 9pm. Open daily 3pm-1am. AmEx/MC/V.) A varied crowd of locals packs the nearby **Aux Quatres Vents,** 18 quai de la Douane, a nautical port-side bar with inexpensive drinks, intricate model ships, a real boat hanging from the ceiling, and tables covered with maps. (☎44 42 84. Beer €2.20-4.50. Grog €3. Open M-F 9am-1am, Sa 10am-1am, Su 2pm-1am. AmEx/MC/V.) The aggressively Celtic-themed **Tara Inn,** 1 rue Blaveau, near the Port du Commerce, features local musicians on Thursday nights, authentic bluegrass the last Saturday of every month, and Breton music the first Sunday of every month. (☎80 36 07. *Kir* €2.20. Beer €2.20-5.40. Open M-F 11am-1am, Sa-Su 3pm-1am. MC/V.)

On Thursdays in summer, the popular **Jeudis du Port** concerts enliven the Port with the sounds of Breton music, rock, and jazz. (Port du Commerce. Mid-July to late Aug. Th 7pm-1am. Free.) Every four years, Brest hosts a major **Fête Maritime Internationale** (☎32 20 08; www.brest2008.fr), assembling antiquated boats from around the world into a single unique fleet. From July 11 to 17, 2008, visitors can go aboard the larger vessels at anchor, sail amidst the flotilla, or stay on firm ground for musical performances and shipbuilding demonstrations on the *quais.*

ILE D'OUESSANT ☎02 98

The westernmost point in metropolitan France, wind-swept Ile d'Ouessant (EEL dwess-AHN; "Enez Eussa" in Breton; pop. 950), an island settlement of hardy Breton villagers, is a peaceful refuge for hikers, cyclists, and nature-lovers. An hour's boat ride from the nearest point on the mainland, the island is a wide-open expanse of green and golden pasture, mysterious rock formations, blue-green waters, and grazing sheep and cattle.

TRANSPORTATION. Penn-ar-Bed **ferries** run from Brest to Ouessant. (3hr.; at least 1 per day, more Apr.-Sept.) They also serve the islands of Molène and Sein. Reservations are required at least a day in advance; reserve a week ahead July to August. The company also rents **bikes.** (☎80 80 80; www.pennarbed.fr. Round-trip €33-34, ages 4-16 €18-20, ages 1-4 €2. 15% student discount. Bikes €12, under 18 €5.60.) Boats dock at Port du Stiff, 3.5km from Lampaul, the island's main town.

Several **bus** companies, including Ouessant Voyages (☎06 81 04 31 04) await the boats' arrival at the port and take you to the central church (5-10min.; €2, round-trip €3.50). Get off the boat early to grab a seat and be punctual meeting the return bus; on foot it's a 45min. stroll to town. Bus companies also offer a 2½hr. French-language guided visit of most of the island with frequent stops (€12 round-trip). **Biking** is the best way to get around the island, as distances between landmarks are long and the roads are well paved; a multi-speed bike makes things easier, as there are several hills. Three companies rent bikes for identical prices at the port and in Lampaul. (1-speed bike €7 per ½-day, €10 per day, €37 per week; mountain bike €10/14/50. Helmets available.) Reserve in advance at the Brest tourist office to get a mountain bike for the price of a 1-speed bike.

PRACTICAL INFORMATION. Lampaul's **tourist office,** near the church in the town center, sells a pedestrian guide (€2.50; see **Sights and Festivals,** p. 262); they also have a free island map showing bike-friendly roads, which is useful since cycling is forbidden on foot paths. (☎48 85 83; www.ot-ouessant.fr. Open July-Aug. M-Sa 9am-7pm, Su 10am-noon; Sept.-June 10am-noon and 1:30-6pm, Su 10am-noon.) **Public restrooms** are available by the tourist office, but bring your own toilet paper. **Police** (☎48 81 61) only operate on the island in July and August. A **pharmacy** is located down the hill from the church and around the corner to the left. (☎48 81 59. Open M-Sa 9am-12:30pm and 5-7pm.) The **post office** is to the left of the church and 30m downhill, across from the 8 à Huit; it has **currency exchange.** (☎48 81 77. Open July-Aug. M-F 9am-noon and 2-5pm, Sa 9am-noon; Sept.-June M-F 9am-noon and 2-4:30pm, Sa 9am-noon.) **Postal Code:** 29242.

ACCOMMODATIONS AND CAMPING. Tiny Lampaul is home to almost all of the island's restaurants and lodgings. Reserve ahead in the summer. The cheerful and clean **Auberge de Jeunesse d'Ouessant ❶** is 5min. from the tourist office and the center of Lampaul. Take the stairs to the right of the SPAR supermarket across from the church and turn right on the first road (not at the top of the stairs). Follow the road as it bears left; the hostel is ahead on the right. The hostel offers 43 beds in basic two-, four-, five-, and six-person rooms, a communal kitchen, and a dining area with views of the countryside. (☎48 84 53; ajouessant@club-internet.fr. Breakfast included. Sheets €4.10, students and under 26 €3.70. Reception 8am-noon; phone ahead for late arrival. Dorms €17, students and under 26 €15; *demi-pension* €29/26; *pension complète* €41/37; singles €30.) **Le Fromveur ❹,** in the

BRITTANY

center of town, has simple pastel rooms with TV, shower, and toilet, as well as a glass-walled TV and exercise room upstairs. The popular restaurant (*menus* €13-32) below serves the local catch of the day. (☎48 81 30; fax 48 85 97. Breakfast included. Reception 8:30am-10pm. Open Feb. to mid-Nov. Singles and doubles €46-52; quads €93. *Demi-pension* €49-56 per person. MC/V.) **Camping Municipal ❶**, located 2km from the port along the main road, is on the left 300m before the church in Lampaul. A low stone wall separates the site from softly rolling hills of the countryside. The bus from the port stops here; ask the driver. (☎48 84 65. Showers €1.65. Laundry €5.70. Reception July-Aug. 7am-11pm; Apr.-June and Sept. 9am-noon; hours vary, so call ahead. Open Apr.-Sept. Night guard 11pm-7am. €2.85 per adult, €1.30 per child under 7, €2.85 per tent. Cash only.)

FOOD. A **SPAR** supermarket is next door to the tourist office (open M-Sa 8:30am-7:30pm, Su 9am-12:30pm) and a **8 à Huit** supermarket lies just downhill (open July-Aug. M-Sa 8:30am-7:30pm, Su 9:30am-12:30pm; Sept.-June M and W-Sa 8:30am-7:30pm, Tu 9:30am-12:30pm, Su 9:30am-12:30pm); they have the island's only **ATMs.** There is also a local grocery store, **Le Marché des Iles,** on the road to the *bourg*, 50m before the campground. (Open M-Sa 8:30am-8pm, Su 9am-1pm and 5-7pm.) For a wallet-friendly sit-down meal, try **Crêperie Ti A Dreuz ❶**, just past the 8 à Huit on the left, which serves filling *galettes* and *crêpes* (€1.60-6.70), including some vegetarian options. Two sunny, homey rooms with traditional decorations look onto a rear garden. (☎48 83 01. Open July-Aug. daily 11:30am-3:30pm and 7-11pm; Apr.-June and Sept. daily noon-2pm and 7-9pm; Oct.-Mar. Tu-Su noon-2pm and 7-9pm. MC/V.) **Ty Korn ❸**, across from the church in Lampaul, offers a variety of marine delights in a small room decorated to feel like the deck of a ship. (☎48 87 33. Fish and meat *plats* €13-24. Lunch *menu* €15. Dinner *menu* €29. Open Tu-Sa noon-1:30pm and 7:30-9:30pm, Su 12:15-1:30pm. MC/V.)

SIGHTS AND FESTIVALS. Biking is forbidden on footpaths and, for safety reasons, along the coast. Cyclists should stick to the relatively flat roads (some paved, others less so) that lead to all major sights. The tourist office's booklet of coastline hiking paths (€2.50) is helpful and includes details of all of the ruins and rocks along each of the four 1½-3hr. coastline routes. If you only have time to choose one path, take the 12km (3hr.) northwest trail or the paved road (45min.) to the **Pointe de Pern,** the westernmost point in continental Europe. Curious rock formations march into the sea toward a lighthouse standing alone in the water. Off of the main road leading to the Pointe de Pern, side roads lead to Ouessant's two museums. The **Ecomusée and Maison du Niou,** 1km northwest of Lampaul, may be interesting to budding archaeologists, but perhaps no one else. Covering the island's culture and history, it displays a few local artifacts in a traditional *ouessantine* home. (☎48 86 37. Open daily Apr.-Sept. 10:30am-6:30pm; Jan. and Oct. 1:30-5pm; Nov.-Dec. 1:30-4pm; Feb. to mid-Mar. 10:30am-5:30pm; mid-Mar. to Apr. 1:30-5:30pm. €3.50, ages 8-14 €2.20.) The **Musée des Phares et Balises,** in the striped **Phare du Créac'h,** Europe's most powerful lighthouse, explores the history of lighthouses and maritime signaling. The evolution of lighthouses is illustrated by models ranging from Alexandria to the present day, but the most impressive artifacts are giant lighthouse lenses that send flashing signals across the museum's cavernous interior. Behind the museum, pinnacles of stone stand against the crashing waves, with a few wet paths winding down towards the ocean for an even more breathtaking seascape. (☎48 80 70. Open daily Apr.-Sept. 10:30am-6:30pm; Feb. 10:30am-6pm; Jan., Mar., and Oct. 1:30-5:30pm; Nov. to mid-Dec. 1:30-5pm. Last entry 30min. before closing. €4.30, ages 8-14 €2.80.) A joint ticket allows entry to both museums (€7, ages 8-14 €4.30.) In late August, Ouessant hosts the

Salon International du Livre Insulaire (☎06 81 51 12 87; www.livre-insulaire.fr), four days of literary conferences, exhibits, and readings of books with an island theme.

QUIMPER ☎02 98

The quintessential Breton city, Quimper (kam-PAIR; pop. 63,000) is filled with local tradition, from its hand-painted *faïence* (earthenware) to its unique 13th-century cathedral. Ubiquitous placards (in Breton as well as French) mark sights of historical interest, making a stroll along the flower-lined footbridges over the Odet River both charming and educational. Quimper renews its strong connection with Breton culture each year in August at the week-long Festival de Cornouaille, when the town explodes in celebration—complete with traditional garb, concerts, and dancing in the large town square.

TRANSPORTATION

Trains: Pl. Louis Armand, off av. de la Gare. Open M 5am-7:50pm, Tu-Th 6am-7:50pm, F 6am-8:35pm, Sa 6:10am-7:10pm, Su 7:20am-8:35pm. To **Brest** (1¼hr.; M-F 6 per day, Sa-Su 4 per day; €10); **Nantes** (2¾hr.; M-F 6 per day, Sa-Su 4 per day; €31); **Paris** (4¾hr., 5 TGV per day, €86); **Quiberon** (2hr., 4 per day, €18) via **Auray; Rennes** (2½hr., 14 per day, €30-36).

Buses: Next to the train station (☎90 88 89; http://infotransports.cg29.fr). To **Brest** (1½hr.; M-Sa 4-6 per day, Su 2 per day; €6), **Pont-Aven** (1¼hr.; M-Sa 4-7 per day, Su 2-3 per day; €2), and **Roscoff** (2½hr., July-Aug. 1 per day, €2).

Public Transportation: QUB (Quartabus), 2 quai Odet (☎95 26 27), across the river from pl. de la Résistance. The office has schedules and a confusing map of the bus lines. Open M-F 9am-12:15pm and 1:30-6:30pm, Sa 9am-noon and 1:30-5:30pm. Buses run M-Sa 6:15am-8:30pm, Su 1:30-8pm (3 lines only). Fewer buses July-Aug. Tickets €1, *carnet* of 10 €9, day pass €3.

Taxis: Radio-Taxi Quimperois (☎90 21 21), in front of the train station.

Car Rental: Avis (☎90 31 34), next to the train station. Open M-Th 8am-noon and 2-7pm, F 8am-noon and 1:30-7pm, Sa 8am-noon and 1-6pm, Su 1:30-6pm. **Hertz,** 19 av. de la Gare (☎53 12 34), across the street from the train station. Open M-F 8am-noon and 2-7pm, Sa 8am-noon and 2-6pm.

Bike Rental: Torch VTT, 58 rue de la Providence (☎53 84 41). €15 per day; €500 or passport deposit. Open Tu-F 9:30am-12:30pm and 2:30-7pm, Sa 9:30am-12:30pm and 2:30-3:30pm. MC/V.

ORIENTATION AND PRACTICAL INFORMATION

In the heart of the Cornouaille region, Quimper is separated from the sea by miles of rich farmland. To reach the center of town from the train station, turn right onto av. de la Gare, bearing left as the road forks, and continue onto bd. Dupleix. Keeping the river on your right, follow it to **place de la Résistance** (10-15min.). The tourist office is on the left at the back of the parking lot; the *vieille ville* is across the river to the right.

Tourist Office: 7 rue de la Déesse, at pl. de la Résistance (☎53 04 05; www.quimper-tourisme.com). Free map; larger, more detailed map €1. Free hotel reservations. Tours of the city in English and French (1½hr.; July-Aug. several per week; €5.20, students and under 26 €2.60; call to reserve). Open July-Aug. M-Sa 9am-7pm, Su 10am-1pm and 3-5:45pm; June and early Sept. M-Sa 9:30am-12:30pm and 1:30-6:30pm, Su 10am-12:45pm; Oct.-May and late Sept. M-Sa 9:30am-12:30pm and 1:30-6:30pm.

Bookstore: Librairie de Mousterlin, 19 rue du Frout (☎64 37 94; www.librarie-de-mousterlin.fr). Small English section; mostly classics. Open M-Sa 10am-7pm.

Laundromats: Point Laverie, 47 rue de Pont l'Abbé, 5min. from the hostel. Open daily 8am-10pm. **Laverie de la Gare,** 6 av. de la Gare. Open daily 8am-8pm. **Lavomatique,** 9 rue de Locronan. Open daily 7am-9pm.

Public restrooms: At the tourist office (free), les Halles (€0.20), and the bus station (€0.50).

Police: 3 rue Theodore Le Hars (☎65 60 00).

Hospital: Hôpital de Cornouaille, 14 av. Thépot (☎52 60 60).

Pharmacy: 24 pl. St-Corentin (☎95 00 20), across from the cathedral. Open M-Sa 8:45am-7:30pm.

Internet Access: Available at **C.com** (see **Food,** p. 266). Also at **Eixxos,** 10 bd. Dupleix (☎64 40 56). €2.50 per 30min., €4 per hr. Open M-Sa 11am-10pm, Su 3-10pm.

Post Office: 37 bd. A. de Kerguelen (☎64 28 25). **Currency exchange.** Open M-F 8am-6:30pm, Sa 8am-noon. Branches on chemin des Justices (by the hostel) and on the corner of rue Chapeau Rouge and rue Falkirk. **Postal Code:** 29000.

ACCOMMODATIONS AND CAMPING

The tourist office has info on local *chambres d'hôte.* For July and August, make reservations as early as possible—at least a couple of weeks ahead if you're arriving for the Festival de Cornouaille.

Auberge de Jeunesse de Quimper (HI), 6 av. des Oiseaux (☎64 97 97; quimper@fuaj.org). Cross the river from pl. de la Résistance and turn left on quai de l'Odet. Turn right onto rue de Pont-l'Abbé and continue through the roundabout; the hostel is just past Lycée Chaptal on the left (20-25min.). By bus, take #1 (M-F; bus A Su) from pl. de la Résistance (dir.: Kermoysan) to "Chaptal" (last bus 7:30pm). A no-frills establishment with simple but sturdy dorm-style furniture and a friendly, young, English-speaking staff. Communal kitchen, dining room, and common room with TV, foosball, and games make meeting other travelers easy. Bike garage and kitchen. Accepts Pass Bretagne (see p. 239). Breakfast €3.50. Reception 8-11am and 5-8pm; call if arriving later. Lockout 11am-5pm; code for late entry. Open Apr.-Sept. 8- to 14-bed dorms €12; 1 single €14. Cash only. ❶

Hôtel le Derby, 13 av. de la Gare (☎52 06 91; fax 53 39 04), across from the station. Owners let modern rooms above a cheerful neighborhood bar for some of the lowest prices in town. All rooms come with shower, toilet, and TV. Breakfast €5.60. Reception M and Su 7am-8pm, Tu-Sa 7am-11pm. May-Sept. singles €31; doubles €41; triples €48. Nov.-Apr. €28/38/45. MC/V. ❷

Camping Municipal, 4 av. des Oiseaux (☎55 61 09; www.mairie-quimper.fr), next to the hostel (see directions above). Secluded, forested area with trees and small hedges. Reception June-Sept. M 1-7pm, Tu and Th 8-11am and 3-8pm, W 9am-noon, F 9-11am and 3-8pm, Sa 8am-noon and 3-8pm, Su 9-11am; Oct.-May M-Tu and Th 9-11:30am and 3:30-7:30pm, F 9:30-10:30am and 3:30-7:30pm, Sa 9:30-11:30am and 4:30-6:30pm. €3.30 per adult, €1.67 per child under 7, €1.67 per car, €1.42 per caravan, €0.73 per tent. Electricity €2.90. Cash only. ❶

BRITTANY

FOOD

The lively covered market at **Les Halles,** on **rue St-François,** has bargains on produce, seafood, meats, and cheeses—get there early, as some vendors shut down in the afternoon. (Open daily 9am-7pm.) An **open market** is also held twice a week outside Les Halles (open W and Sa 7am-9pm) and an organic market north of the

city center in Kerfeunteun (open F from 4pm.) A **Monoprix** is across the river from the tourist office on quai du Steir. (Open M-Sa 9am-7pm.) There is a **Shopi** grocery downstairs at 20 rue Astor. (Open M-Sa 8am-8pm, Su 9:30am-12:30pm.) Nearer to the hostel, there's a **Proxi** on quai de l'Odet. (Open M-Sa 7:30am-8pm, Su 8:30am-12:30pm; longer hours July-Aug.)

C.com, 9 quai du Port au Vin (☎95 81 62), across from Les Halles. Bright colors, delicious smells, and plastic pastel furniture fill the 2 sunlit floors of this popular café. A young and stylish clientele comes for delicious muffins (€2), salads (from €7), and build-your-own sandwiches (around €4). Internet access €1 per 15min., €3 per hr. Free Wi-Fi. Open M-Sa 8am-7pm. MC/V. ❶

Gandhi, 13 bd. de Kerguélen (☎64 29 50), near the train station. One of the best of Quimper's many ethnic restaurants. Serves delicious curries and tandoori-grilled meats amid tastefully exotic décor, including a statue of Gandhi marching with a flag. Traditional Indian music plays in the background. Vegetarians will find a refreshingly wide selection. *Plats* €8.40-15. Lunch *menu* €8.70-14. Dinner *menu* €19. Open daily noon-2:30pm and 7-10:30pm. MC/V. ❸

Le Saint Co., 20 rue du Frout (☎95 11 47). On a quiet street around the corner from the cathedral, this comfortable bistro offers a tasty variety of steak and fish *plats* (€14-20) and salads (€7-9.) Lunch *menus* €13-17. Dinner *menus* €20-25. Open M-F noon-2pm and 7-10pm, Sa noon-2pm and 7-11pm. AmEx/MC/V. ❸

SIGHTS

The *Passeport Culturel* gets you into your choice of four sites from a list of six: the Musée des Beaux-Arts, Musée Départemental Breton, Faïenceries de Quimper HB-Henriot, Centre d'Art Contemporain, Musée de la Faïence, and the tourist office city tour (available at tourist office; €13). For a break from museums, head to **Mont Frugy,** a public wooded hillside next to the tourist office. A small clearing near the bottom of the hill offers an amazing view of the cathedral spires.

CATHÉDRALE ST-CORENTIN. The twin spires of **Cathédrale St-Corentin,** built between the 13th and 15th centuries, rise high above the center of the old quarter. Between the unique windowed spires, the stone figure of legendary *quimperois* king Gradlon the Great stands on horseback watching over the city. The surprisingly bright and colorful interior sports a beautiful pink tile ceiling with yellow ribs; the most curious feature, however, is the floor plan, which features a unique bend in the traditional cross-shaped footprint. *(Open May-Oct. M-Sa 8:30am-noon and 1:30-6:30pm, Su 1:30-6:30pm; Nov.-Apr. M-Sa 9am-noon and 1:30-6pm, Su 1:30-6pm. Mass M-F 9am; Sa 9am, 6:30pm; Su 8:45, 9, 10am, 6:30pm. Detailed explanation in English €1. Welcome desk offers tours on demand in English and French.)*

MUSÉE DÉPARTEMENTALE BRETON. In the former bishop's palace beside the cathedral, this museum offers unusually stylish exhibits on local history, archaeology, and ethnography, including a display of traditional Breton clothing and innovative temporary exhibits. *(1 rue du Roi Gradlon. ☎95 21 60; www.cg29.fr/culture/mdb.htm. Open June-Sept. daily 9am-6pm; Oct.-May Tu-Sa 9am-noon and 2-5pm, Su 2-5pm. €3.80, students and ages 18-26 €2.50, under 18 free.)*

FAÏENCERIES DE QUIMPER HB-HENRIOT. This factory is the production site for Quimper's world-renowned hand-painted earthenware. Guided half-hour tours in French and English take visitors inside the cavernous workshop to see artisans shaping and painting each piece. The adjoining boutique sells pricey but beautiful finished products. *(Rue Haute. ☎90 09 36; www.hb-henriot.com. Tours every 45min. July-Aug. M-Sa 9:30-11:45am and 2-5:15pm; Sept.-June M-F 9:30-11:15am and 2-4:15pm. Brochure available in English. Boutique open M-Sa 9:30am-7pm. €4, ages 8-14 €2.)*

MUSÉE DES BEAUX-ARTS. Across from the cathedral, this museum holds an excellent collection of paintings with Breton themes, as well as other European work. A permanent exhibit remembers *quimperois* poet-painter Max Jacob, a friend of Picasso and victim of the Holocaust. Each year, the museum hosts three large temporary exhibits. *(40 pl. St-Corentin. ☎95 45 20; http://musee-beauxarts.quimper.fr. Open July-Aug. daily 10am-7pm; Nov.-Mar. M and W-Sa 10am-noon and 2-6pm, Su 2-6pm; Apr.-June M and W-Su 10am-noon and 2-6pm. Wheelchair-accessible. €4.50, students and ages 13-26 €2.50.)*

NIGHTLIFE AND FESTIVALS

Catch some Breton culture at the **Festival de Cornouaille,** Quimper's annual summer gala. The week-long festival is held the third week in July, filling the town with lively Breton music from *biniou* (bagpipes) and the oboe-like *bombarde*. Dancers in traditional dress appear alongside musicians; over 3000 performers in Breton costume march the length of the city in the climactic grand parade on the final Sunday before the Queen of Cornouaille is crowned. (☎55 53 53; www.festival-cornouaille.com. Schedule and prices vary. Tickets required for some performances; €6-20.) **Semaines Musicales** brings various prominent orchestras and choirs to town during early to mid-August for performances in the Théâtre de Cornouaille, the cathedral, and smaller churches in town. Every year, the festival pays homage to a different selection of famous composers and musicians. (☎95 32 43; www.semaines-musicales-quimper.org. Tickets €21-23, ages 12-25 €6.)

An Poitín Still, 2 av. de la Liberation (☎90 02 77). The bright red walls, green tin ceiling, and boisterous, rowdy clientele will make your Coreff (€2.30) taste even better. Beer €2.30-5.40. Wild, impromptu Irish music performed live F 10pm. Open M-Sa 3pm-1am, Su 5pm-1am. AmEx/MC/V.

Café XXI, 38 pl. St-Corentin (☎95 92 34), across from the cathedral and next to Musée des Beaux-Arts. A metallic bar, polished wooden chairs and tables, and curving walls create a glittering and glamorous environment both day and night. Mixed drinks €6-6.50. Open July-Aug. daily 8:45am-1am; Sept.-June Tu-Sa 8:45am-10pm. AmEx/MC/V.

St-Andrew's Pub, 11 pl. du Stivel (☎53 34 49), just across the river from rue de Pont l'Abbé. Old-school comfort, a breezy riverside terrace, and a classy leather interior provide the perfect setting for a relaxed drink. Whiskey €4.90-7.30. Mixed drinks €7. Open daily 11am-1am. AmEx/MC/V.

DAYTRIP FROM QUIMPER

PONT-AVEN

Pont-Aven and Quimper are connected by Penn-ar-Bed buses (☎90 88 89; infotransports.cg29.fr. Line #14A, dir.: Quimper-Quimperlé; 1¼hr.; 3 per day; €2) via nearby towns.

The first major artist to paint Pont-Aven (POHNT-ah-vahn) was Paul Gauguin (1848-1903), who, fed up with mainstream Impressionism, came here in 1886 and inspired a movement that emphasized pure color, rejected perspective, and simplified figures. Today, this small Breton town is as vibrant an artists' colony as ever, with galleries on nearly every street exhibiting paintings of every style. *Biscuiteries* selling the town's famous *galettes*, *madeleines*, and *palets* (various types of butter cookies) are almost as prevalent; unlike the galleries, most of these shops offer free samples. To watch the cooks at work, visit **Biscuiterie de Pont-Aven,** 8 rue du Général de Gaulle, where an open window separates the baking studio from the shop. (☎09 14 20. Open daily July-Aug. 9am-7:30pm; Sept.-June 9:30am-12:30pm and 2:30-6:30pm.) For a refreshing break from civilization, venture into Pont-Aven's tranquil and beautiful natural surroundings. A free map at the tourist office details a number of hikes passing by spots that inspired Gauguin and others. From the town center, cross the bridge and take two quick rights to the **Promenade Xavier Grall,** a series of bridges bordered by greenery and gracefully drooping trees that hover over the swift Aven River. Farther upstream is the **Chaos de Pont-Aven,** a cluster of large, flat boulders around which the river roils and swirls—the perfect place to picnic. A pleasant stroll amid thriving farmland and tree-lined avenues leads to the **Chapelle de Trémalo.** (Open daily July-Aug. 10am-6pm; Sept.-June 10am-5:30pm.) The 16th-century Gothic church is an isolated retreat and houses the 17th-century wooden painted crucifix that inspired Gauguin's *Le Christ Jaune.* After seeing the environs, view the paintings they inspired at the **Musée de Pont-Aven,** pl. de l'Hôtel de Ville, up the street to the left when facing the tourist office. The museum showcases a small collection of works by Gauguin, Sérusier, and other adherents of the Pont-Aven school, as well as temporary exhibits of regional work. A 12min. film in French, shown every 45min., is a well-made introduction to the movement. (☎06 14 43; musee.pont-aven@wanadoo.fr. Open daily July-Aug. 10am-7pm; Apr.-June and Sept.-Oct. 10am-12:30pm and 2-6:30pm; Feb.-Mar. and Nov.-Dec. 10am-12:30pm and 2-6pm. €4, students €2.50, under 18 free.)

There are a few cafés and restaurants around the town center. Up rue E. Bernard (where the bus from Quimper arrives) is the **Ecomarché** supermarket. (Open daily 9am-7pm.) The **tourist office,** 5 pl. de l'Hôtel de Ville, a block from the bus stop on the city's main square, pl. Gauguin, offers a free handbook on local art galleries, a practical guide and a walking-tour map, an art history guidebook (€0.50), and tours in French of the town and museum. (Tours Tu, Th, Sa at 11am; 4-person min. Reserve ahead. €6, ages 12-25 €4; includes museum entry). The office also provides information on the **Fleurs d'Ajonc Folk Festival,** which takes place on the first Sunday in August. (☎06 04 70; www.pontaven.com. Open July-Aug. M-Sa 9:30am-7pm, Su 10am-1pm and 3-6pm; Sept.-June M-Sa 10am-12:30pm and 2-6pm.)

QUIBERON ☎02 97

Though it lacks significant museums, monuments, and history, the small peninsula of Quiberon (KEE-buh-rahn; pop. 7221), joined with Brittany by a slender thread of land, has more than its fair share of beaches and sunshine. Besides ample opportunities for sunbathing, surfing, kayaking, and sailing, the town also makes a good base for daytrips to the stunningly beautiful Belle-Ile-en-Mer and the mysterious *menhirs* of Carnac, or for a hike along the rugged coastline.

TRANSPORTATION AND PRACTICAL INFORMATION. Trains run from the Quiberon **train station** (open July-Aug. daily 8:35am-6:35pm; Sept.-June M-Sa 9:15am-12:25pm and 2:15-5:30pm) to Auray (45min., 6-10 per day, €2.80); connections run from Auray to Brest, Paris, Quimper, and Rennes. TIM **buses** (☎08 10 10 10 56; www.morbihan.fr) run to Auray (1¼hr., €6.30) and Carnac (45min., €4), departing from Quiberon's port and train station (all buses July-Aug. 1 per day; Sept.-June M-Sa 7-9 per day, Su 1-4 per day.). Explore the Côte Sauvage on **bikes,** tandems, or scooters from Cyclomar, 47 pl. Hoche, which also has an annex at the train station. (☎50 26 00. Bikes €8 per ½-day, €11 per day, €45 per week. Scooters €26-35 per ½-day, €38-49 per day. Cash, check, or ID deposit. Open July-Aug. daily 8am-10pm; Sept.-June Tu-Sa 8:30am-12:30pm and 2-5pm. Annex open July-Aug. daily 8:30am-noon, 2:30-3pm, and 4:45-7pm. MC/V.) For a **taxi,** call ☎06 07 09 01 27.

To find the **tourist office,** 14 rue de Verdun, cross the train station parking lot and turn left. Walk down rue de la Gare and bear right on rue de Verdun. The busy staff distributes a free city guide with a map and a handbook of six walking tours. (☎08 25 13 56 00; www.quiberon.com. Open mid-July to Aug. M-Sa 9am-1pm and 2-7pm, Su 10am-1pm; early July M-Sa 9am-1pm and 2-6:30pm, Su 10am-1pm; Sept.-June M-Sa 9am-1pm and 2-6pm. Other services include: a **laundromat** on rue de Port-Maria, near the beach (open daily 9am-8pm); **police,** 147 rue du Port de Pêche (☎50 07 39); a **hospital** at the **Centre Hospitalier Bretagne Atlantique** in Auray (☎01 41 41); a **pharmacy** at 12 rue de Verdun (☎50 07 79; open July-Aug. M-Sa 8:45am-12:45pm and 2-7:45pm; Apr.-June and Sept. M 2-7:30pm, Tu-Sa 9am-12:30pm and 2-7:30pm; Oct.-Mar. M 2-7:30pm, Tu-F 9am-12:30pm and 2-7:30pm, Sa 9am-12:30pm); **Internet** access, free with a drink at **Le Nelson,** 20 pl. Hoche, on the way to the beach from the tourist office (☎50 31 37; Wi-Fi and 1 computer; open daily noon-2am) and at **Quiberon.biz,** 10 rue Pasteur (☎06 27 55 39 04; Internet or Wi-Fi €1.50 per 15min.; €4 per hr., students €3; open July-Aug. daily 9am-9pm, Sept.-June closed Su). The **post office,** pl. de la Duchesse Anne, has **currency exchange.** (☎50 11 92. Open mid-July to Aug. M-F 8:30am-6pm, Sa 8:30am-noon; Sept. to mid-July M-F 8:30am-12:30pm and 2-5:30pm, Sa 8:30am-noon.) **Postal Code:** 56170.

ACCOMMODATIONS AND CAMPING. The **Auberge de Jeunesse (HI) "Les Filets Bleus" ❶,** 45 rue du Roch-Priol, is affordable and close to the town center and beach. From the station, cross the parking lot and turn left onto rue de la Gare. Turn left onto rue de Port-Haliguen at the church, right at the roundabout onto bd. Anatole France, and finally left onto rue du Roch-Priol (15min.). Three rustic and somewhat cramped 8- to 12-bed rooms open onto an outdoor picnic area. Camping and spots in a communal tent are also available. (☎50 15 54. Accepts Pass Bretagne, see p. 239. Kitchen. Breakfast €3.50. Reception July-Aug. M-Sa 9am-noon and 6-9pm, Su 6-9pm; Apr.-June and Sept. closes at 8pm. Reserve ahead for July-Aug. Open Apr.-Sept. Dorms €11. Cot in communal tent €7.70. Camping €6.10 per person.) On the waterfront, the central **Hôtel de l'Océan ❹,** 7 quai de l'Océan, offers well-furnished rooms, some facing the harbor, with colorful bedspreads and flowered wallpaper. A sunny bar with wicker chairs and *quai*-side views makes for a lovely place to people-watch. (☎50 07 58; www.hotel-delocean.com. Breakfast €7. Wi-Fi €1.50 per 15min. Reception 8am-9pm. Open mid-Apr. to mid-Nov. Aug. singles €42, with shower €54, with bath €60-65; doubles €50/62/68-73. Sept.-July €36/48/54-59/44/56/62-67. Extra bed €12. AmEx/MC/V.) The Quiberon Peninsula has a dozen campsites, and the tourist office provides information on all of them. A good choice is the three-star **Camping Bois d'Amour ❶,** rue St-Clément, just off plage du Goviro. The well-tended site has spacious, wooded grounds, a heated pool, a bar, a small restaurant, a TV room, and laundry. The staff organizes sports during the day and nightly events like karaoke. Cyclomar often has bikes to rent on-site. (☎50 13 52; fax 50 42 67. Reception daily July-Aug. 9am-noon and 2-8pm; Sept.-June 9am-12:15pm and 3-6:30pm. Gates closed 11pm-7am. Open Apr.-Sept. €6-17 per tent or caravan with car, €3-9 per adult, €2-4.50 per child under 10. Electricity €5. MC/V.)

FOOD. The traditional Quiberon cure for a sweet tooth is the lollipop-like *niniche*, available by the beach. For groceries, there's a **Marché Plus,** 2 rue de Verdun. (Open M-Sa 7am-9pm, Su 9am-1pm.) Produce markets appear on **place du Varquez,** behind the town hall (open Sa 6:30am-1pm), and on **Port Haliguen** (open mid-June to mid-Sept. W 6:30am-1pm). The jungle-themed **La Paillote ❷,** 30 rue de Verdun, with bamboo-backed chairs and stuffed tigers, dishes up large, reasonably priced pizzas fresh from the wood-fire oven in the corner. Ordering *La N'Importe Quoi* (The Whatever; €10) gives you a pizza smothered with whatever toppings the chef is in the mood to add. (☎29 51 32. Pizza €6-12. Open daily May-Nov. noon-2pm and 7-10pm; Oct.-Apr. closed W. Hours vary. MC/V over €15.) For a taste of the sea, try **La Criée ❹,** 11 quai de l'Océan, which gets fresh catches from the connected fish market. The *plateau gargantua*, an awesome array of oysters, crab, and other sea-creatures (€50), generously serves two. More modest fish dishes run €17-21. (☎30 53 09. Open Tu-Sa from 12:15pm for lunch and from 7:15pm for dinner, Su lunch only. MC/V.) Stylish but homey **Aux Armes de Bretagne ❷,** 54 rue de Port Haliguen, with well over 240 choices of *crêpes* (€2.50-8.50) and *galettes* (€2.50-12), is not for the indecisive. (☎50 01 20. Open Apr.-Sept. Tu noon-1:30pm, W-Su noon-1:30pm and 7-9pm. MC/V.) At the end of an alley near the tourist office, charming **Au SaFran ❸,** 20 rue Verdun, serves delicious meat and fish dishes smothered in incredibly rich sauces. (☎50 18 64; www.autourdequimberon.com/ausafran.html. Weekday lunch *menu* €11, dinner *menus* €16-29. Open July-Aug. daily noon-2pm and 7-10pm; Sept.-June Tu-Sa noon-2pm and 7-10pm, Su noon-2pm. Reservations recommended on weekends. MC/V.)

BEACHES. Heed signs marked *Baignades Interdites* (Swimming Forbidden)—plenty of people have been carried off by rip tides and drowned in these treacherous waters. Green flags mean safe supervised swimming; orange/yellow means dangerous swimming; red means swimming prohibited. For a safe beach near the center of town, follow sun-worshipping tourists, frolicking families, and carefree teenagers to **Grande Plage.** Meanwhile, smaller beaches on the east side of the peninsula offer more tranquil spots for sunbathing. The aptly-named **Côte Sauvage** stretches a wild, windy 10km along the western edge of Quiberon. The views from the road are amazing, but coastal footpaths give you an even better look at the waves and jagged rocks—be careful in the slippery tidal zone.

NIGHTLIFE AND FESTIVALS. The beaches don't empty until it's too dark to see the volleyball. One of the first bars to fill up is **Barantyno's,** 4 pl. Hoche, with colored lights and a trendy crowd. Friendly bartenders proudly show off the house special: *Mojito Royale* (€8), a mojito made with champagne. The décor changes frequently thanks to monthly theme nights. (☎50 18 87. Beer €2.50-5. Hard liquor €6-9. Mixed drinks €4.50-8. Open Apr. to mid-Nov. daily 1pm-2am; mid-Nov. to Dec. and Feb.-Mar. closed M-Tu. MC/V.) Later in the night, party-goers head to the tropical **Hacienda Café,** 4 rue du Phare, off pl. Hoche, where young *quiberonnais* drink and dance until the wee hours. Black lights and disco lights illuminate every surface, including the comfy couches and the dance floor. (☎30 51 76. Beer €3-5. Mixed drinks €7. Open May-Sept. daily 10pm-4am; Oct-Apr. F-Sa only.) Join the older crowd at the nightclub **Le Suroît,** 29 rue Port Maria. (Beer €5. Hard liquor €8. Mixed drinks €10. Open July-Aug. daily 11:30pm-5am; Sept.-June F-Sa only. AmEx/MC/V.) In early April, the **Semaine Océane** takes the town by storm with dance, music, and plays all along the waterfront; ask at the tourist office for more info.

DAYTRIPS FROM QUIBERON

BELLE-ILE-EN-MER

SMN, in Quiberon, sends ferries to Belle-Ile (45min.) from the gare maritime of Port Maria. (☎08 20 05 60 00; www.smn-navigation.fr. 5-13 per day; round-trip €26-27, express €29, under 25 €16/17-18, seniors €18/20. Bikes €16.) Renting a car or taking the bus-shuttles are the easiest ways to get around. Taol Mor Buses run from Le Palais to Belle-Ile's other main towns 4-7 times per day: Bangor (30min.), Locmaria (25min.), and Sauzon (20min.). Tickets are available on the bus or at Point Taol Mor, quai Bonelle in Le Palais. (☎31 32 32. €2.60, ages 4-12 €1.70; 2-day pass €11/7.) Cars Verts, at the gare maritime in Quiberon, runs one-day bus tours of the island at 11am and 12:15pm, returning by 4:30pm; to catch the tour, take the 9:30am ferry to the island. (☎31 81 88; www.cars-verts.com. Tours in French; English available with advance notice. €12, ages 4-12 €6, over 60 €11. AmEx/MC/V.)

This island's name—Beautiful Isle in the Sea—is a simple statement of fact. With its unique rock formations, crashing seas, and fields of green and gold, Belle-Ile-en-Mer (BEL-eel-ahn-mehr) is naturally breathtaking. A few scattered *menhirs* date man's presence on the island back to prehistoric times; since then, monks, sailors, pirates, and German POWs have all been temporary residents. Although the island can be seen as a daytrip (most conveniently from Quiberon), it is quite large (20km long) and deserving of an overnight stay.

Ferries from Quiberon dock in Le Palais, the island's biggest town, under the shadow of the massive **Citadelle Vauban.** Built in 1549 by Henri II and expanded under Louis XIV, the fortress was only captured twice—by the English during the Seven Years' War and by the Germans in WWII. Today, the walls protect a small museum of memorabilia from Belle-Ile's more important visitors and residents, such as Sarah Bernhardt and Claude Monet. It takes about 2hr. to explore the sprawling fortress; don't miss the great view of the port and the ocean from the ramparts. The arsenal, a large rectangular building, often holds concerts and temporary exhibits; on its top floor is a room filled with nautical artifacts. (☎31 84 17. Open daily July-Aug. 9am-7pm; Sept.-Oct. and Apr.-June. 9:30am-6pm; Nov.-Mar. 9:30am-noon and 2-5pm. €6.50, ages 7-16 €3.50, under 7 free.)

Belle-Ile's natural treasures lie scattered along the coast. **Plage de Donnant,** on the windy western coast, is the widest and most popular beach. Equally gorgeous is the secluded and algae-strewn **plage Port-Maria,** by the town of Locmaria on the southeastern shore, and the much larger powder-white **plage Grands Sables,** the longest beach on the island, southeast of Le Palais. Head 6km northwest from Le Palais to the postcard-worthy port-side town of **Sauzon.** Crisp pastel-hued houses with multicolored shutters line the port, facing mossy rock cliffs on the other side. Across the island, waves crash inside the thunderous **Grotte de l'Apothicairerie,** surrounded by sheer cliffs on three sides. While access to the grotto was recently restricted for safety reasons, the site still offers a spectacular panorama of the rocky coastline; just be careful to stay well back from the cliff edges, which are unguarded. The island's best-known coastal wonders, however, are the **Aiguilles de Port Coton,** pinnacles of stone memorialized by Monet in several paintings. Around their bases, the green water foams and churns against the rocks; the port owes its name to these bursting waves, which are whipped by the winds to be as white and fluffy as cotton. From late July to mid-August, **Lyrique-en-Mer** (☎31 59 59; www.belle-ile.net) brings classical concerts and opera to the island.

There is a **Super U** supermarket in Le Palais (open M-Sa 8am-12:30pm and 3:30-7pm, Su 8am-12:30pm) for picnic supplies; otherwise, there are mostly mediocre restaurants and *crêperies* in each of the island's four large towns.

The Palais **tourist office,** quai Bonnelle, is on the dock's left end. The staff distributes a guide to the island, which includes info on sailing and kayaking as well as lodging and restaurants, and a helpful map for exploring the island on foot or bike. A guide to hiking and biking trails is available in French for €8. (☎31 81 93; www.belle-ile.com. Open July-Aug. M-Sa 8:45am-7:30pm, Su 8:45am-1pm; Sept. and Apr.-June M-Sa 9am-12:30pm and 2-6pm, Su 10am-12:30pm; Oct.-Mar. M-Sa 9am-12:30pm and 2-6pm.) Several companies in Le Palais offer **bike rental,** including Cyclotour, quai Bonnelle, near the tourist office. (☎31 80 68. Bikes €8 per ½-day, €10 per day; check, ID, or passport deposit. Open daily July-Aug. 8:30am-7pm; Mar.-June and Sept.-Oct. 9am-noon and 2-7pm.) Bike trails are sometimes rocky, and bicycles share the road with cars. Coastal paths are reserved for pedestrians.

CARNAC

Sept. to June, TIM buses (☎08 10 10 10 56; www.morbihan.fr) run from Quiberon to Carnac 7 times per day (45min., €3.50); in July-Aug., the bus runs only once per day, making it easier to take the train from Quiberon to Plouharnel-Carnac (30min.; 6-10 per day; one-way €2.80, round-trip €5) and then the bus (line #1 or 18) from Plouharnel-Carnac to Carnac (7min., 12 per day, €2). 2 bus stops serve Carnac's 2 tourist offices: "Carnac-Ville," in the old town center and closer to the menhirs, and "Carnac-Plage," by the main tourist office and the beach. The 2 offices are about a 15min. walk apart; Tatoovu, a local shuttle, connects them. (5 min.; 7 per day 9:30am-7:30pm; tickets €1.10, carnet of 10 €10; buy tickets on bus.)

The fields of ancient megaliths in Carnac (kahr-NAK) are the largest and best-preserved prehistoric site of their kind in Europe. These lines of tall stones, erected by Neolithic man sometime between 5000 and 2200 BC, run for 4km along the edge of this summer vacation town. Though their original purpose is still unknown, today they make a great break from the beaches as a daytrip from Quiberon.

The entire site holds just under 2800 menhirs (the 18th-century term invented to describe these curious standing stones). The closest to town are the **Alignements du Ménec,** a 2km plot holding over 1000 stones up to 4m tall, running along lines neatly paralleling the adjacent highway. A few hundred meters east, the **Alignements de Kermario** holds another 1000 of Carnac's most impressive menhir specimens as well as a dolmen (stone-roofed communal tomb). Farther east, a trail leads from the main road to a small clearing holding the **Quadrilatère** (close-set rocks arranged to form a prehistoric rectangle) and the **Géant du Manio,** the largest menhir at Carnac. From October to March, visitors are allowed free access to all of

Carnac's sites; from April to September access is allowed only on guided tours to prevent soil erosion. Get tour info and tickets at the **Maison des Mégalithes,** rte. des Alignements, across from the Alignements du Ménec; to get there from the Carnac-Ville tourist office, take a right onto rue St-Cornély in front of the church, another right on rue de Courdiec, and then turn left at the menhirs onto rte. des Alignements (10min.). Be careful, as there is no sidewalk at some points. (☎02 97 52 89 99; http://carnac.monuments-nationaux.fr. Open daily July-Aug. 9am-8pm; May-June 9am-7pm; Sept.-Apr. 10am-5pm. 1hr. tours in French July-Aug. 3-8 per day, Apr.-June and Sept. 3 per week; in English July-Aug. W and F at 3pm. €4, ages 12-25 €3, under 12 free.) The Maison also has brochures in several languages and a 10min. film in French about the monuments. Behind the tourist office in the town center, the **Musée de Préhistoire,** 10 pl. de la Chapelle, provides good background information for a visit to the megaliths, with informative exhibits on cultural evolution from the Paleolithic Age to the Roman Empire. Highlights include stones bearing Megalithic carvings and a 6000-year-old human vertebra chipped by the arrow that ended its owner's life. (☎52 22 04; www.museedecarnac.com. Open July-Aug. daily 10am-6pm; Apr.-June and Sept. M and W-Su 10am-12:30pm and 2-6pm; Oct.-Mar. M and W-Su 10am-12:30pm and 2-5pm. €5, ages 6-18 €2.50. 1hr. guided tours of museum in French July-Aug. daily at 11am, 3pm, €2.50/1.70. Written guides available in 6 languages.) To return to modern times, head to the sandy, vacationer-filled **beach;** from the tourist office in the historic center, take av. de la Poste, which becomes av. de l'Atlantique, following signs to plages (15min.).

For picnic supplies, there are several supermarkets, including a **Proxi,** 15 rue Saint-Cornély, in the old city center (open Tu-Sa 8am-1pm and 3-7:30pm, Su 8:30am-1pm and 5-7:30pm) and a **Marché U,** 68 avenue des Druides, by the main tourist office (open M-Sa 8:30am-8pm, Su 8:30am-1pm and 5-8pm).

The "Carnac-Ville" and "Carnac-Plage" **tourist offices** offer transportation information, a visitors' guide, and a free map of the town. (☎02 97 52 13 52; www.ot-carnac.fr. Main office open July-Aug. M-Sa 9am-7pm, Su 3pm-7pm; Sept.-June M-Sa 9am-noon and 2-6:30pm. City center office open July-Aug. M-Sa 9:30am-1pm and 2-7pm, Su 10am-1pm; Apr.-June and Sept. M-Sa 8:30am-noon and 2-5:30pm).

VANNES

Vannes is connected by TIM buses (☎08 10 10 10 56; www.morbihan.fr) to Quiberon (2¼hr.; July-Aug. 1 per day; Sept.-June M-Sa 7-9 per day, Su 1-4 per day; €9.10) and other local towns. To get to the tourist office and city center from the train station, turn right on av. Favrel et Lincy, then left at the roundabout onto rue Victor Hugo. Take a right onto rue Joseph Le Brix, then a left onto rue Thiers; continue downhill to the tourist office on the right (15min.).

With carefully tended gardens sheltered by medieval ramparts, half-timbered houses overlooking cobblestone streets, and an architecturally eclectic cathedral, Vannes (VAHN; pop. 53,800) is as enticing now as when the Dukes of Brittany chose it as their capital. The city's major attractions can easily be enjoyed in a single day, and regular train service makes it a convenient and relaxing daytrip from Nantes, Quimper, or Rennes.

The city centers around the **Cathédrale St-Pierre,** on pl. St-Pierre, whose constant reconstructions and improvements since the 12th century have left it an architectural hodgepodge. The most curious feature is the circular **Chapelle du Saint-Sacrement,** which juts incongruously out of the left side of the building. In July and August, knowledgeable volunteers offer free tours of the cathedral in French; a free brochure available in several languages provides some history. (Open daily 9:30am-6:30pm except during services. Tours July-Aug. M-F 10am-6pm, Su 1-6pm.) Across from the cathedral is **La Cohue,** pl. St-Pierre, formerly the town's covered market and courtroom and now home to the **Musée des Beaux-**

Arts. The small permanent collection includes Romantic and Impressionist depictions of Brittany. However, the temporary exhibitions, which fill more than half of the museum's space, are the main attraction. (☎ 01 63 01. Open daily mid-June to Sept. 10am-6pm; Oct. to mid-June 1:30-6pm. €6, students €4, under 12 free. AmEx/MC/V.) The nearby **Château Gaillard,** rue Noé, holds anthropological artifacts from the Neolithic period through the Renaissance as well as temporary exhibits. Hidden away at the back of the second floor is the museum's real treasure: the **Cabinet des Pères du Désert,** a 17th-century wood-paneled room whose walls are covered with paintings of famous hermits. A single ticket, valid for several months, allows admission to both museums. (☎01 63 00. Open daily mid-June to Sept. 10am-6pm. €6, students €4, under 12 free. AmEx/MC/V.) Don't miss the comical Vannes et sa Femme (Vannes and his Wife) across from the entrance to the château; the medieval carved wooden figures, hanging from a half-timbered house, are an unofficial emblem of the city. Exit the city walls by the 17th-century **Porte St-Vincent** (the town's centerpiece) and turn left to visit the **Jardins des Remparts.** With the medieval ramparts and turrets in the background, these neatly arranged flower gardens by the Marle river make the perfect place for a picnic. Behind them and up the hill lies a larger park, the **Jardin de la Garenne,** with a large monument to Vannes residents who died at war. Every year, Vannes chooses a different period of its history to celebrate during the **Fêtes Historiques,** held on the weekend nearest July 14th. The small city comes alive with free street performances, concerts, and historical re-enactments.

The **tourist office,** 1 rue Thiers, has free maps and a glossy guide to the city, including a walking tour of the city center; the staff also offers a reservations service (€1) and information about attractions just outside the city. (☎08 25 13 56 10; www.toursime-vannes.com. **Internet** access €5 per 30min. Open July-Aug. M-Sa 9am-7pm, Su 10am-6pm; Sept.-June M-Sa 9:30am-12:30pm and 1:30-6pm.) There's a **Monoprix** supermarket on pl. Joseph Le Brix. (Open M-Sa 8:30am-8pm.)

NANTES ☎02 40

With a gargantuan château surrounded by neatly manicured lawns, restaurants packed with diners, and chic nightlife, Nantes (NAHNT; pop. 280,000) clearly knows how to live the good life. As the sixth largest city in France, Nantes has room on its expansive boulevards and in its quiet public gardens to welcome any visitor. Although relaxation may be the city's major attraction, its offerings also include an elegantly restored cathedral and an art museum housing cutting-edge modern exhibitions.

TRANSPORTATION

Flights: Aéroport Nantes Atlantique (☎84 80 00; www.nantes.aeroport.fr), 10km south of Nantes. **Air France** (☎08 20 32 08 20) flies daily to **Lyon, Marseille, Nice, Paris,** and **London.** A **Tan Air shuttle** (☎08 10 44 44 44; www.tan.fr) runs to the airport from pl. du Commerce and the south side of the train station (25min.; every hr. M-Sa 5:30am-9pm, Su 3:30-9pm; tickets €6, *carnet* of 4 €16.) Schedules available at info desk outside the train station, tourist office, or TAN info booth on pl. du Commerce.

Trains: Main entrance to the north at 27 bd. de Stalingrad, and a second entrance on rue de Lourmel. Ticket counters open M-Th 5:30am-9:30pm, F 5:30am-10:30pm, Sa 6am-9:30pm, Su 7am-10pm. **Luggage storage** at north side of station. (Open 6:15am-11pm. Backpack €4, larger luggage €6.50-8.50; 3 day max.) To: **Angers** (40min.; every 30min. 5am-9pm; €13, TGV €17); **Bordeaux** (4hr., 5 per day, €42); **La Rochelle** (1¾hr., 5 per day, €24); **Paris** (2-4hr., 1 per hr., €54-69); **Rennes** (1¾hr.; M-F 15 per day, Sa-Su 7 per day; €21).

Public Transportation: TAN, 4/6 allée Brancas (☎08 01 44 44 44), on pl. du Commerce. Office open M-Sa 7:30am-7:30pm. Runs buses and 3 tram lines daily 6am-1:30am. Ticket €1.30, 2-ride ticket €2.30, *carnet* of 10 €11, day pass €3.40.

Taxis: Allô Taxis Nantes Atlantique (☎69 22 22), at train station. 24hr.

Car Rental: A row of rental agencies sits near the south exit of the train station, including **Avis** (☎89 25 50). Open M-F 7am-10:30pm, Sa 8:30am-8:30pm, Su 10:45am-10:15pm. **Europcar** (☎47 19 38) is down the street. Open M-F 7:45am-10:15pm, Sa 8:30am-12:30pm and 2-6pm, Su 10:30am-12:30pm and 5-8:30pm.

Bike Rental: Check at the tourist office or the NGE office, 18 rue Scribe (☎02 51 84 94 51) for info on the **Ville à Velo** program, which rents bikes from the city's major parking lots (Graslin, Tour Bretagne, Cité des Congrès, Cathédrale, and Commerce), Ile de Versailles, and Camping du Petit Port. €1 per 2hr., €4 per day, €10 per week.

Canoe Rental: Available from companies on Ile de Versailles, including **Contre Courant** (☎06 62 28 60 48). Take tram line #2 (dir.: Orvault Grand Val) to "St-Mihiel" and cross the bridge to the island. €5 per hr., €14 per day; students €4/11. Open Apr.-Sept. Tu-F 10am-12:30pm and 2-7:30pm, Sa-Su 10am-7:30pm.

ORIENTATION AND PRACTICAL INFORMATION

Nantes's city center lies north of **cours Franklin Roosevelt,** a broad avenue running east-west through **place du Commerce,** the city's municipal transportation hub. Cours Franklin Roosevelt passes the **château** at pl. de la Duchesse Anne, where it becomes **cours John Kennedy** and continues to the **train station.** The wide **cours des 50 Otages** runs north from pl. du Commerce past the Tour Bretagne, a modest skyscraper; taking a right onto rue de la Barillerie leads to the city's lively pedestrian district around **place du Pilori.**

Tourist Office: 3 cours Olivier de Clisson (☎08 92 46 40 44; www.nantes-tourisme.com). Exit the train station at the north end and turn left onto cours John Kennedy. Continue to pl. du Commerce and turn left. Maps and info in English and French. 2hr. city tours in French with a variety of themes several times per week. Office open M-W and F-Sa 10am-6pm, Th 10:30am-6pm. Branch at 2 pl. St-Pierre, by the cathedral. Open Tu-W and F-Su 10am-1pm and 2-6pm, Th 10:30am-1pm and 2-6pm. City and cathedral tours €7, students €4.

Youth Center: Centre Régional d'Information Jeunesse (CRIJ; ☎02 51 72 94 50; www.infojeunesse-paysdelaloire.fr), on the ground fl. of the Tour de Bretagne. Free Internet access (30min. max.). Info on youth discounts, housing, and volunteer and employment opportunities. Open mid-July to mid-Aug. Tu-Th 10am-5:30pm, F 2-5:30pm; mid-Aug. to mid-July Tu-Th 10am-6:30pm, F-Sa 2-6:30pm.

English-Language Bookstore: Librairie L. Durance, 4 allée d'Orléans (☎48 09 14; www.librariedurance.fr). Open M 2-7pm, Tu-Sa 9:30am-7pm. MC/V.

Laundromats: 7 rue de l'Hôtel de Ville. Open daily 8:30am-8:30pm. Also at 11 rue Chaussée de la Madeleine. Open M 2:30-8pm, Tu-F 11am-8pm, Sa 3-7pm.

Police: 6 pl. Waldeck-Rousseau (☎37 21 21). Branch on cours Olivier Clossin, next to the tourist office.

Pharmacy: Pharmacie de la Gare, 2 allée du Commandant Charcot (☎74 14 04). Open M-F 9am-7:30pm, Sa 9am-1pm.

Hospital: Centre Hospitalier Universitaire, 1 pl. Alexis-Ricordeau (☎08 33 33; www.chu-nantes.fr).

Internet Access: Free at **CRIJ** (above). Also at **Cyberpl@net,** 18 rue de l'Arche Sèche (☎02 51 82 47 97; www.cyberplanet.fr), near Tour de Bretagne. €1 per 20min. Open M-Sa 10am-2am, Su 2-10pm. **K Point Com,** 15 allée Duguay Trouin (☎02 51 82 27

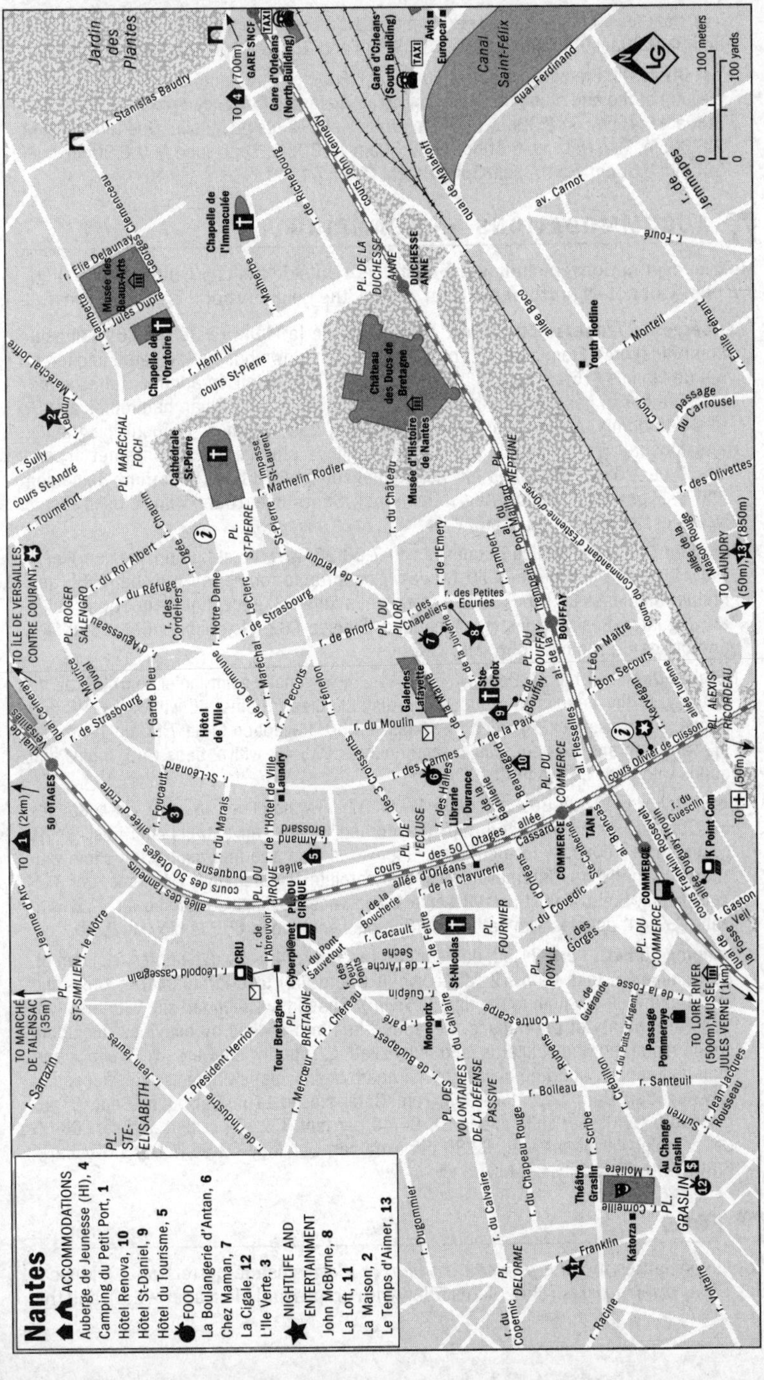
Nantes
ACCOMMODATIONS
Auberge de Jeunesse (HI), 4
Camping du Petit Port, 1
Hôtel Renova, 10
Hôtel St-Daniel, 9
Hôtel du Tourisme, 5
FOOD
La Boulangerie d'Antan, 6
Chez Maman, 7
La Cigale, 12
L'Ile Verte, 3
NIGHTLIFE AND ENTERTAINMENT
John McByrne, 8
La Loft, 11
La Maison, 2
Le Temps d'Aimer, 13
Jardin des Plantes
GARE SNCF
Gare d'Orléans (North Building)
Gare d'Orléans (South Building)
Avis
Europcar
Canal Saint-Félix
quai Ferdinand
100 meters
100 yards
Musée des Beaux-Arts
Chapelle de l'Immaculée
Chapelle de l'Oratoire
Château des Ducs de Bretagne
Musée d'Histoire de Nantes
Cathédrale St-Pierre
PL. MARÉCHAL FOCH
PL. ST-PIERRE
PL. DE LA DUCHESSE ANNE
DUCHESSE ANNE
Youth Hotline
PL. NEPTUNE
BOUFFAY
PL. DU BOUFFAY
Galeries Lafayette
Ste-Croix
Hôtel de Ville
Laundry
50 OTAGES
TO ÎLE DE VERSAILLES, CONTRE COURANT
TO LAUNDRY (50m), 13 (850m)
PL. ROGER SALENGRO
PL. DU CIRQUE
CRIJ
Cyberpl@net
Tour Bretagne
PL. BRETAGNE
St-Nicolas
PL. FOURNIER
PL. DE L'ECLUSE
Librairie L. Durance
COMMERCE
PL. DU COMMERCE
TAN
K Point Com
PL. ROYALE
Passage Pommeraye
Monoprix
TO LOIRE RIVER (500m), MUSÉE JULES VERNE (1km)
Théâtre Graslin
Au Change Graslin
PL. GRASLIN
Katorza
PL. DES VOLONTAIRES DE LA DÉFENSE PASSIVE
PL. DELORME
PL. ST-SIMILIEN
PL. STE-ELISABETH
TO MARCHÉ DE TALENSAC (35m)
PL. ALEXIS RICORDEAU
cours des 50 Otages
cours St-Pierre
cours St-André
cours John Kennedy
cours Olivier de Clisson
cours Franklin Roosevelt
quai de Malakoff
av. Carnot
allée Baco

71), near tourist office. €0.80 per 15min., €1.50 per 30min., €2.50 per hr. Open M-Th and Sa 9:30am-9:30pm, F 9:30am-12:30pm and 2:30-9:30pm, Su noon-9:30pm.

Post Office: Pl. Bretagne (☎02 51 10 57 25). From pl. du Cirque, take the stairs or the elevator at the end of rue de l'Abreuvoir to pl. Bretagne. **Currency exchange.** Open M-F 8:30am-6:45pm, Sa 8:30am-12:30pm. Branch at 3/5 rue du Moulin. Open July-Aug. M 2-6:30pm, Tu-F 9:30am-6:30pm, Sa 9:30am-12:30pm; Sept.-June M 2-6:30pm, Tu-F 9:30am-6:30pm, Sa 9:30am-5pm. **Postal Code:** 44000.

ACCOMMODATIONS AND CAMPING

Most budget options, including the hostel, are outside the city center. While there are plenty of hotels north of the train station, the neighborhood is rather seedy.

Auberge de Jeunesse "La Manu" (HI), 2 pl. de la Manu (☎29 29 20; nanteslamanu@fuaj.org). From north exit of station, go right down bd. de Stalingrad and left at rue de Manille (15min.); hostel is in a courtyard on the left. In a former tobacco factory, the hostel has–surprisingly enough–an industrial feel. Clean bathrooms and 3- to 6-bed dorms. Accepts Pass Bretagne (see p. 239). Kitchen, TV room, ping pong, and foosball. Tasty breakfast included. Luggage storage €1.50. Internet access €0.50 per 20min. Reception July-Aug. 8am-noon and 4-11pm; Sept.-June 8am-noon and 5-11pm. Lockout July-Aug. 10am-4pm; Sept.-June 10am-5pm. Closed last 2 weeks of Dec. Dorms €19. MC/V. ❶

Hôtel du Tourisme, 5 allée Duquesne (☎47 90 26; www.hotel-dutourisme.com), centrally located off cours des 50 Otages. Comfortable rooms, all with bath, TV, and phone. Breakfast €3.50. Free bike storage. Parking €2. Reception 7am-10pm; call if arriving later. Reservations recommended. Singles €33-41; doubles €41-46; triples and quads €51; quints €56. MC/V. ❸

Hôtel St-Daniel, 4 rue du Bouffay (☎47 41 25; www.hotel-saintdaniel.com), off pl. du Bouffay, in the heart of the pedestrian district. Clean rooms, all with bath, TV, and phone; some overlook a garden. Breakfast €3.50. Reception M-Sa 7:30am-10pm, Su 7:30am-2pm and 7-10pm. Singles and doubles €35-41, with 2 beds €46; triples and quads with bath €51. AmEx/MC/V. ❸

Hôtel Renova, 11 rue Beauregard (☎47 57 03; www.hotel-renova.com), off cours des 50 Otages. Behind a modern mosaic-adorned facade, an enthusiastic host greets guests to this centrally located hotel. Rooms range in size and quality; all come with shower or bath, free Internet access, and satellite TV. Breakfast €4. Reception M-F 7am-10pm, Sa-Su 7am-11pm. Reserve 1 week ahead. Singles with shower €32, with bath €39-44; doubles with bath €43-48; triples and quads €55. AmEx/MC/V. ❸

Camping du Petit Port, 21 bd. du Petit Port (☎74 47 94; www.nge-nantes.fr). From pl. du Commerce, take tram #2 (dir.: Orvault Grand Val) to "Morrhonnière." Cross the street and walk downhill to the right (15min.). Shaded, well-tended site with beautiful trees and plenty of park space. Reception has info on nearby activities, including canoe rental, bowling, billiards, and roller-skating. Laundry, showers, Wi-Fi, snack bar, mini golf course, and free access to the nearby municipal swimming pool. Reception July-Aug. 8am-9pm; Sept.-June 9am-7pm. Gates closed 11pm-7am. June-Sept. €3.25 per adult, €2.05 per child under 10, €4.40 per tent, €6.40 per tent and car, €8.60 per camping-car or caravan, €2.30 per extra car; Oct.-May €2.65/1.65/3.60/5.20/6.80/1.90. Electricity €3. MC/V. ❶

FOOD

Local specialties include *poisson au beurre blanc* (fish in butter sauce), Muscadet wine, *muscadines* (chocolates filled with grapes and Muscadet wine), and the trademark *Le Petit Beurre* cookies. There are plenty of reasonably priced eateries in the area between **place du Bouffay** and **place du Pilori**, from *crêpe* stands to sit-down spots. The city's biggest **market** is the indoor Marché de Talensac, north of the city. (Tu-Su mornings.) There's also a market on **rue de la Petite Hollande** Saturday mornings, and an organic market Wednesday mornings on place du Bouffay. The **Galeries Lafayette,** 2-20 rue de la Marne, have a supermarket on the bottom floor. (Open M-Sa 9am-8pm.) A **Monoprix** supermarket is at 2 rue de Calvaire, west of cours des 50 Otages. (Open M-Sa 9am-9pm.)

La Cigale, 4 pl. Graslin (☎02 51 84 94 94; www.lacigale.com). One of the most beautiful bistros in France. Fashioned in 1895 by *nantais* ceramist Emile Libaudière, the rooms are filled with decorated ceramic tiles, giant mirrors, and amusing sculptures in an explosion of artistic extravagance. Though it's worth visiting just for the décor (the site is an historical monument), the food is equally exquisite, with astonishingly reasonable prices. Breakfast €9.90. *Plats* €10-25. Lunch *menus* €13 and 24. Dinner *menus* €17 and 27. Desserts €6.50-8. Open daily 7:30am-12:30am. AmEx/MC/V. ❸

La Boulangerie d'Antan, 5/7 rue des Carmes (☎47 59 46). Decorated with rustic half-timbering, this bakery offers generous sandwiches (€2.45-3.65) and pastries (€1.50-2.50) to go. Perfect for a picnic on the château lawns, a few blocks to the east. Open M-Sa 7am-8pm. AmEx/MC/V over €15. ❶

Chez Maman, 2 rue de la Juiverie (☎02 51 72 20 63). In this restaurant-antique shop, nearly all the décor—ranging from giant Playmobil® figures to plastic lobsters and a large yellow dinosaur—is for sale. Generous salads and meat and fish *plats* €12-20. Lunch *menu* €9.80. Open Tu-Sa noon-2pm and 7-10:30pm. ❷

L'Ile Verte, 3 rue Foucault (☎48 01 26). This combined vegetarian café and bookstore serves a small selection of market-fresh organic salads and tarts. A large nature scene mural and flowered tablecloths maintain the fresh theme. Salads €4.20-8.80. *Plats* €8.80 (available to go). Desserts €4.20-5.10. Open M-Tu and Th-Sa 11:45am-2pm. Tea room open 2:30-6:30pm. Closed Aug. MC/V over €20. ❷

SIGHTS

TIP **DON'T PASS THIS UP.** Consider buying the comprehensive **Pass Nantes,** which offers unlimited rides on public transportation, admission to the château and all the city's museums, a guided tour, and discounts at several stores and recreational activities, such as canoe and bike rental. The pass is available at the tourist office, airport, youth hostel, and some hotels and campsites. €16 for 24hr. access, €27 for 48hr., €32 for 72hr.; under 12 free.

CHÂTEAU DES DUCS DE BRETAGNE. This fortress was built at the end of the 15th century by François II as an imposing ducal residence and a safeguard for the independence of the Breton duchy. It was subsequently used as a prison, an arsenal, and a German WWII barracks. Today, picnickers enjoy benches and neatly trimmed lawns sunken beside the castle moat, tourists wander the ramparts, and the massive walls guard only the Musée d'Histoire de Nantes, whose extensive collection and multimedia exhibits fill 32 rooms. The rooms are themselves historical treasures, and many contain elaborate graffiti carved by prisoners incarcerated here throughout history. An impressive interactive virtual balloon tour of the city allows you to travel back in time to 1752 and sail over Nantes to check out several different neighborhoods close up. The **Harnachement,** across the château courtyard from the museum, holds excellent temporary exhibits on the history of Brittany. *(4 pl. Marc-Elder. ☎08 11 46 46 44; www.chateau-nantes.fr. Château grounds open daily mid-May* *to mid-Sept. 9am-8pm; mid-Sept. to mid-May 10am-7pm. Free. Museum and exhibitions open mid-May to mid-Sept. daily 9:30am-7pm; mid-Sept. to mid-May M and W-Su 10am-6pm. Last entry 1hr. before closing. Museum and exhibitions each €5, ages 18-26 €3; both €8/4.80. Audio tours in Breton, English, and French; €3. Guided tours July-Aug. several times daily; Sept.-June on weekends and occasional weekdays. €4, ages 7-17 €2.40. Free baggage check required.)*

CATHÉDRALE ST-PIERRE. Built in stages from 1434 to 1891, St-Pierre has survived Revolutionary pillagers, WWII bombs, and a 1972 fire. Post-fire restoration has given this cathedral a clean, bright interior, with soaring Gothic vaults and 20th-century stained-glass windows. Bombs destroyed all but one of the originals; this lone survivor stands in the right transept above the tomb of François II, last Duke of Brittany. The tomb itself is an early 16th-century sculpted masterpiece. *(Cathedral open daily Apr.-Oct. 8am-7pm; Nov.-Mar. 8am-6pm. Cathedral crypt open Sa 10am-12:30pm and 3-5pm, Su 3-5pm; entry every 30min. Welcome desk open daily 10am-6pm. Free guided visits daily; check at welcome desk for times. Guided visits also provided by tourist office twice weekly in summer. €7, students €4.)*

MUSÉE DES BEAUX-ARTS. Nantes's art museum features a good collection of European masters from 13th-century Italian panels to Monet's water lilies. Temporary installations of modern works are housed on the first floor and in the **Chapelle de l'Oratoire,** around the corner from the museum off rue Henri IV. *(10 rue Georges Clemenceau. ☎02 51 17 45 00. Open M, W, F-Su 10am-6pm, Th 10am-8pm. Museum €3.50, students €2, under 18 free; after 4:30pm €2; Th 6-8pm and the 1st Su of each month free. Chapelle de l'Oratoire free. Tours of temporary exhibitions or museum collections July-Aug. W-Th and Su 3pm; Sept.-June W and Su 3pm. €4, students €2.40.)*

OTHER SIGHTS. Outside the center of town on a hill overlooking the Loire, the small **Musée Jules Verne** honors the science fiction author's life through sketches and artifacts, as well as first editions of his novels and posters from the movies they inspired. *(3 rue de l'Hermitage. ☎69 72 52; www.julesverne.nantes.fr. Take tram #1, dir.: Mitterand, to "Gare Maritime," then cross the tram tracks and take a right at the roundabout onto quai E. Renaud. Bear right and uphill on rue de l'Hermitage; the museum will be on your left. Open M and W-Sa 10am-noon and 2-6pm, Su 2-6pm. €3, ages 18-26 €1.50, under 18 and 4th Su of month free. Free tours in French July-Aug. daily 3:30pm; Sept.-June Su only.)* The **Jardin des Plantes,** across from the train station's north entrance, is a relaxing public garden with fountains and fishponds, many species of trees, and a playground with free lawn chairs. North of the city, the **Ile de Versailles** contains a park with Japanese-inspired gardens and a small area for children. Bridges connect the island to both banks of the Erdre. *(Jardin des Plantes and Ile de Versailles open daily mid-Mar. to mid.-Oct. 8:30am-7:45pm; shorter hours in winter.)* The **Passage Pommeraye,** a covered shopping arcade built on three levels connected by a monumental staircase, is a good example of the city's style of 19th-century masonry and wrought-iron balconies.

NIGHTLIFE AND FESTIVALS

From January 30 to February 3, 2008, Nantes will hold its 14th-annual **La Folle Journée,** a classical music festival with short, reasonably priced concerts. This year's theme will be the composer Schubert and the music of his era. (☎02 51 88 20 00). Pick up the guide *Aux Heures d'Eté* at the tourist office for a listing of summer events from mid-July to mid-August (☎02 51 82 37 70; www.auxheuresete.com). International filmmakers and photographers from Asia, Africa, and South America walk the red carpet at the increasingly popular **Festival des Trois Continents** (info ☎69 74 14) in late November and early December.

Katorza, 3 rue Corneille (☎08 92 68 06 60; www.katorza.fr), shows lesser-known international films in their original language (€7.20, students €5.70).

Nearby **rue Scribe** is full of late-night bars and cafés. A funky favorite, **quartier St-Croix,** near pl. du Bouffay, has bars and cafés on every block. Discos await adventurous travelers farther from the *vieille ville.*

John McByrne, 21 rue des Petites Ecuries (☎89 64 46). With a festive red-and-green facade and a fittingly jolly crowd, this Irish pub is popular among Nantes's expat crowd and its locals. Packed on weekends; gear up for a loud and boisterous drink. Beer €2.40-3.20 per ½-pint, €4.60-6 per pint. Guinness €5.70. Irish coffee €6.50. Live Irish music Su 10pm. Open M-Sa 2pm-2am, Su 3pm-2am. AmEx/MC/V.

Le Loft, 9 rue Franklin (☎48 29 00; www.leloft.net). On the weekend, multicolored lights, an eclectic mix of dance music, and a crowd that's dressed to impress liven up this chic nightclub. Mixed drinks €6.50. Open W 10pm-4am, Th-Sa 10pm-6am.

La Maison, 4 rue Lebrun (☎37 04 12; www.lamaisonet.com), off rue Maréchal Joffre. Hidden at the back of an alley, this bar's unique décor draws crowds of all ages. The 4 rooms are each furnished like part of a house, from the orange "kitchen" area, equipped with dishwasher, to the blue-tiled "bathroom." Free Wi-Fi and Internet access. Beer €2.50-5.90. Mixed drinks €7-9. Open daily 3pm-2am. AmEx/MC/V.

Le Temps d'Aimer, 14 rue Alexandre Fourny (☎89 48 60; www.letandem.com). Nantes's favorite gay discotheque. From the tourist office, take a left on cours Clossin over the river, where it becomes bd. des Martyrs. Continue and take a right onto rue de la Porte Gelée, which becomes rue Fourny. Alternately, take tram #2 from pl. du Commerce to "Wattignies." Walk up the street toward pl. du Commerce and turn left on rue de la Porte Gelée. Beer €7. Liquor €10. Mixed drinks 12. Cover €2; obligatory coat check €2. Open daily midnight-7am.

NORMANDY (NORMANDIE)

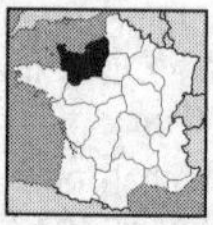

Normandy's history has always been tied to the sea; as early as AD 911, the Viking raider Rollo sailed in from Norway and established himself as the first Duke of Normandy. His descendant William the Bastard confirmed Normandy's naval power when he conquered England in 1066, earning himself a more flattering nickname: William the Conqueror. The English, eager to conquer the closest chunk of France, repeatedly sent their fleets to Normandy during the Hundred Years' War, and in 1431 they captured and burned Joan of Arc in Rouen. By 1450, however, Normandy was safely back in French hands. The English didn't attempt another invasion until June 6, 1944 (better known as D-Day), when they returned—this time in the name of France—with North American allies to reclaim Normandy from the Germans.

Today, Normandy still holds on to its maritime character and the traces of its tumultuous past with quaint harbors, fresh seafood, and medieval monuments scarred by warfare. The region also abounds in natural beauty, with exquisite coastal rock formations, stunning seascapes, and rolling countryside dotted with cows. In the larger cities, the atmosphere is livelier; the designer boutiques of Rouen are buzzing by day and the clubs of Caen are hopping by night. Be sure to take time from the sights to sample Norman culinary specialties—Camembert cheese, apple tarts, fresh seafood, and *bénédictine liqueur.*

HIGHLIGHTS OF NORMANDY

LAND on the haunting **D-Day beaches** (p. 303), just as the Allies did in 1944, then visit the **Caen Memorial** (p. 299), France's best WWII museum.

IMAGINE monastic life at the magnificent abbey of **Mont-St-Michel** (p. 312).

PEER over the breathtaking chalk cliffs of **Etretat** (p. 291), or amble around the sleepy harbor town of **Fécamp** (p. 292).

HAUTE-NORMANDIE

ROUEN ☎02 35

Ever since the Viking leader Rollo made it the capital of his new Duchy of Normandy, Rouen (roo-AHN; pop. 106,600) has been the gem of this province. Perhaps best known as the place where Joan of Arc met her fiery end in 1431, Rouen is also famous for its Gothic cathedral, which was immortalized by Monet in his numerous paintings of its facade. Because today's Rouen also houses a hip young population and bustling designer boutiques, it is an attractive stop for both scholarly and fun-loving travelers.

TRANSPORTATION

Trains: rue Jeanne d'Arc, at pl. Bernard Tissot. Main office open M-Sa 8am-6:30pm; smaller office open M-F 5:30am-10pm, Sa 6:30am-10pm, Su 6:45am-10:30pm; ticket

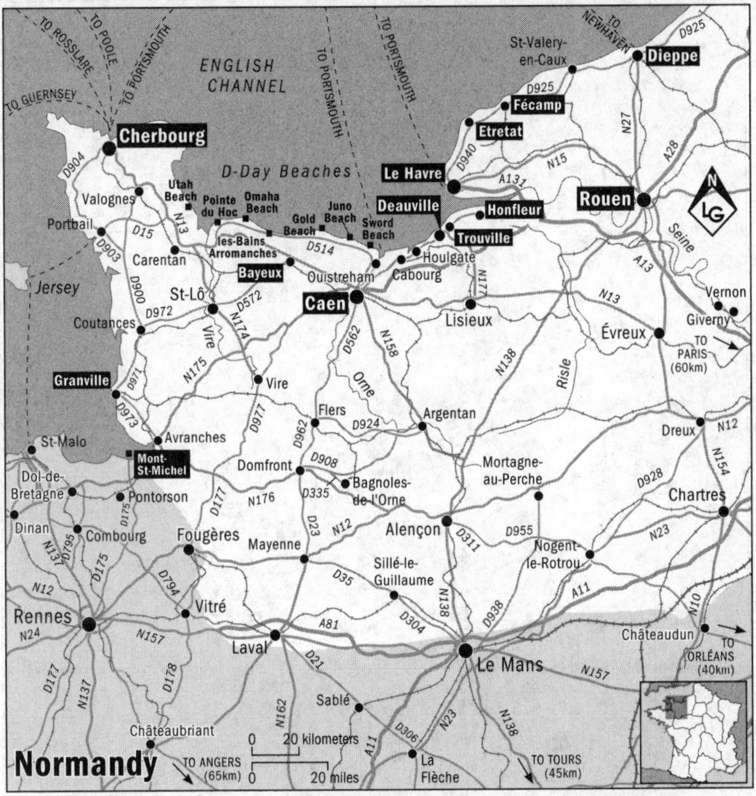

office open M-F 5:10am-9pm, Sa 5:50am-9pm, Su 6:10am-10:30pm. Trains go to: **Caen** (1½-2hr., 5-9 per day, €22); **Dieppe** (1hr., 6-13 per day, €9.70); **Le Havre** (1hr., 10-20 per day, €12.70); **Lille** (2¾-3½hr., 1-3 per day, €30); **Paris** (1-1½hr., every hour, €19).

Buses: VTNI/TVS has a station at 11 rue des Charrettes (☎08 00 25 07 60 27), open M-Sa 8am-6pm. Buses run to **Le Havre** (2½hr.; M-F 7 per day, Sa 6 per day, Su 2 per day) and various towns in the area, all destinations €2.

Public Transportation: TCAR, 9bis rue Jeanne d'Arc (☎52 52 52; www.tcar.fr), operates a subway and municipal buses. Open M-Sa 7am-7pm. Most buses run 6am-10pm. Night bus runs Sept.-June M-Th and Su 11pm-1am, F-Sa 11pm-3:30am. Subway open 5am-11pm. 1hr. ticket €1.40; 1-day pass €3.70, 2-day €5.40, 3-day €7; *carnet* of 10 €10.50.

Taxis: Radio Taxis, 8 av. Jean Rondeaux (☎88 50 50), across the Seine. Stands at the train and bus stations, as well as at the Palais de Justice on rue Jeanne d'Arc. 24hr.

Car Rental: AVIS, (☎88 60 94) at the train station. Open M-F 9am-noon and 2-6pm, Sa 9am-noon and 2-5pm.

Bike Rental: Rouen Cycles, 45 rue St-Eloi (☎71 34 30), between pl. du Vieux Marché and the Seine. Bike rental €20 per day, €30 per weekend, €50 per week. Reservations highly recommended. Open Tu-Sa 9am-noon and 2-7pm. MC/V.

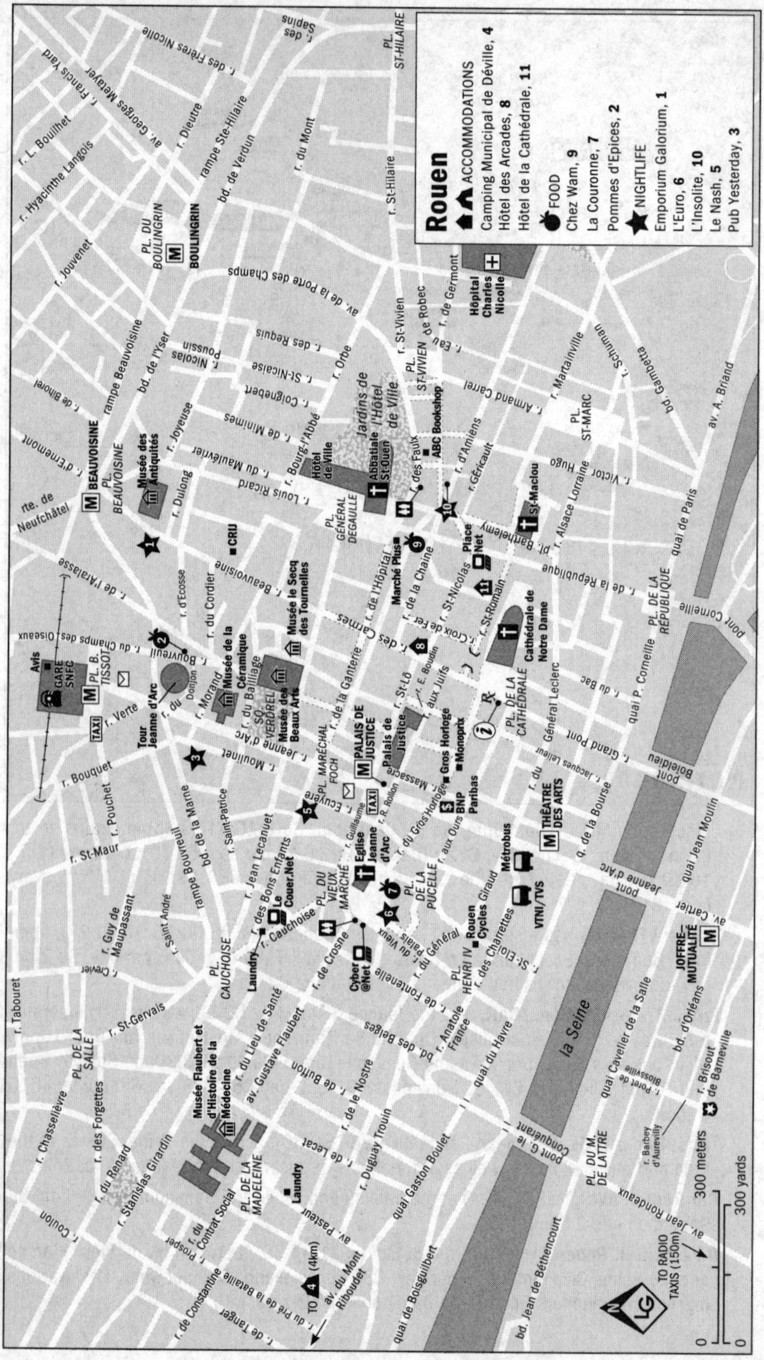
Rouen
ACCOMMODATIONS
Camping Municipal de Déville, 4
Hôtel des Arcades, 8
Hôtel de la Cathédrale, 11
FOOD
Chez Wam, 9
La Couronne, 7
Pommes d'Epices, 2
NIGHTLIFE
Emporium Galorium, 1
L'Euro, 6
L'Insolite, 10
Le Nash, 5
Pub Yesterday, 3
la Seine
300 meters
300 yards
TO RADIO TAXIS (150m)

ORIENTATION AND PRACTICAL INFORMATION

To get to the city center from the station, exit straight and follow **rue Jeanne d'Arc,** the city's main thoroughfare, for several blocks. When it crosses the cobblestone **rue du Gros Horloge,** you're in the heart of town; a left leads to **place de la Cathédrale** and the tourist office, while a right leads to **place du Vieux Marché,** where Joan was burned at the stake. If you continue down rue Jeanne d'Arc instead, you'll reach the Seine and (on the right) the bus station.

Tourist Office: 25 pl. de la Cathédrale (☎02 32 08 32 40; www.rouentourisme.com). In the oldest Renaissance building in Rouen. Free English map. **Currency exchange** with €2.50 commission. The French-language guide *Le Viking,* published once a year in Sept., describes favorite local hotspots. Audio tour of the city available in French, English, German, and Japanese for €5. Open May-Sept. M-Sa 9am-7pm, Su 9:30am-12:30pm and 2-6pm; Oct.-Apr. M-Sa 9:30am-12:30pm and 1:30-6pm.

Banks: Banks abound along rue Jeanne d'Arc, including **BNP Paribas,** 40 rue Jeanne d'Arc (☎08 20 82 43 00). Open Tu-F 8:45am-noon and 1:30-5:45pm, Sa 8:45am-1:30pm. There are **ATMs** across from the train station and throughout Rouen.

English-Language Bookstore: ABC Bookshop, 11 rue des Faulx (☎71 08 67), to the right past the Eglise St-Ouen. Open Tu-Sa 10am-6pm. Closes early in late July, and completely in early Aug. MC/V.

Youth Information: Centre Régional Information Jeunesse (CRIJ), 84 rue Beauvoisine (☎02 32 10 49 49; www.crij-haute-normandie.org). Provides information for youths interested in working, volunteering, or living in the region for a month or more. Open Tu-F 10am-6pm; closed for 3 weeks in July or Aug.

Laundromat: 56 rue Cauchoise near pl. du Vieux Marché (open daily 7am-9pm) and av. Pasteur near pl. de la Madeleine (open daily 7am-10pm). Wash €3-9, dry €1 per 8-12min.

Public Toilets: Rue des Faulx by the Abbatiale (€0.20) and pl. du Vieux Marché (open Tu-Sa; 8-11:45am and 1:30-6pm; free).

Police: 9 rue Brisout de Barneville, across Seine from *centre ville* (☎02 32 81 25 00).

Pharmacy: Grande Pharmacie du Centre, 29 pl. de la Cathédrale (☎71 33 17). Open M 10am-7:30pm, Tu-F 9am-7:30pm, Sa 9am-7pm.

Hospital: Hôpital Charles Nicolle, 1 rue de Germont (☎02 32 88 89 90), near pl. St-Vivien.

Internet Access: Cyber@Net, 47 pl. du Vieux Marché (☎07 73 02; www.cybernetrouen.fr). €2 per 20 min., €4 per hr. Open daily 10am-10pm. **Place Net,** 37 rue de la République (☎02 32 76 02 22; www.place-net.fr), near Eglise St-Maclou. €1 per 15 min. Open M noon-7pm, Tu-Sa 10am-midnight. **Le Coeur.Net,** 54 rue Cauchoise (☎02 35 15 45 42; www.coeur-net.fr.st). €4 per hr. Open M-Sa 10am-10pm, Su 2-10pm.

Post Office: 45bis rue Jeanne d'Arc (☎15 66 98). Offers **currency exchange.** Open M-F 8am-7pm, Sa 8:30am-12:30pm. Branch at 112 rue Jeanne d'Arc (☎02 32 10 55 60), to the left of the train station. Open M-W and F 8:45am-6pm, Th 9:15am-6pm, Sa 9am-noon. **Postal Code:** 76000.

ACCOMMODATIONS AND CAMPING

Rouen offers a variety of options, ranging from unique and intimate to standard but convenient chains, but none are genuinely cheap. If you're planning on spending a weekend in Rouen and reserving ahead, ask about the *"Rouen, vos Weekends"* deal—some hotels will give you two nights for the price of one.

Hôtel de la Cathédrale, 12 rue St-Romain (☎71 57 95; www.hotel-de-la-cathedrale.fr). Prime location by the Cathédrale with 26 adorable rooms, each featuring a different color scheme. Petite courtyard with mosaic-topped tables. Bar, elevator, and tea room (open 11am-7pm). Buffet breakfast €7.50. Internet access. Singles €52-72; doubles €62-89. Extra bed €15. MC/V. ❹

Hôtel des Arcades, 52 rue de Carmes (☎70 10 30; www.hotel-des-arcades.fr). Clean rooms in the center of town. Breakfast €6.50. Public shower €3. TV €4.50. Reception M-F 7am-10pm, Sa-Su 7:30am-10pm. Singles €29-36, with shower €40-46; doubles €30-37/41-47; triple with shower €53. Extra bed €6. AmEx/MC/V. ❷

Camping Municipal de Déville, 12 rue Jules Ferry in Déville (☎74 07 59), 4km from Rouen. Take the subway from the train station (dir: Technopole or Georges Braque) to Théâtre des Arts. Transfer to the TEOR T2 bus line (on the same ticket) towards Mairie V. Schoelcher/Notre Dame de Bondeville. Get off at Mairie de Deville and continue on foot down route de Dieppe 1 block, then turn left on rue Jules Ferry. Welcoming grassy lawn surrounded by 66 plots. Reception June-Sept. M-F 8am-1pm and 2-8pm, Sa-Su 9am-noon and 2-8pm; May M-Sa 9:30-11:30am and 5-6:30pm, Su 10am-noon; Oct.-Apr. M-F 9:30-11am and 4:30-6:30pm. Gates close 10pm. Closed one month around December. €4.20 per adult, €2.80 per child under 7, €1.60 per tent, €2.90 per RV. Electricity €2.15. Showers free. Cash only. ❶

FOOD

Outdoor cafés and *brasseries* crowd around **place du Vieux Marché,** which hosts a market with flowers, fish, fruit, and cheese (Tu-Su 8am-12:30pm). There are also eateries near the **Gros Horloge** and the **Cathédrale de Notre Dame.** For self-serve options, try the food section in the back of the **Monoprix** department store on rue du Gros Horloge (open M-Sa 8:30am-9pm), **Marché U** on pl. du Vieux Marché (open M-Sa 8:30am-8:30pm), or **Marché Plus,** 11 pl. du Général de Gaulle (open M-Sa 7am-9pm).

Pommes d'Epices, 66 rue Bouvreuil (☎71 73 57), right across from the Tour de Jean d'Arc. This quiet restaurant with country décor offers elegant and inexpensive lunches. Various *tartes* (€6.50) come with a fresh side salad. For dessert, try *Pomme d'Epices* (warm, syrupy apple chunks served over gingerbread). Lunch *plats* €7-13. *Menus* €14-25. Open M-W noon-1:45pm, Th-F noon-1:45pm and 7-10pm. Reservations recommended. MC/V. ❸

La Couronne, 31 pl. du Vieux Marché (☎71 40 90; www.lacouronne.com.fr). The food and elegant atmosphere of this sophisticated splurge embody French tradition. Housed in the oldest *auberge* in France, this intimate restaurant offers meat dishes and an excellent cheese tray (€15) but specializes in seafood. *Plats* €32-64. Lunch *menu* €25. Dinner *menu* €32-48. Open daily noon-2pm and 7-10pm. AmEx/MC/V. ❺

Chez Wam, 67 rue de la République (☎15 97 51), near the Abbatiale St-Ouen. The kebab-frites (gyro with fries) makes for a filling meal, and this joint serves the best around, complete with crispy fries (rare in France) and a wide variety of sauces. Don't be surprised if there's no one at the grill on a nice day—the cook is often taking a breather outside, but he'll show up in a second or two when he sees a customer examining the menu. *Kebab-frites* €3.50-4. Open daily 11am-2am. AmEx/MC/V. ❶

SIGHTS

Sights in Rouen fall into two basic categories: museums and churches. Each attraction has its own special charm—for instance, Notre Dame's mismatched towers and St-Ouen's sloping gardens—and captures both the casual observer and the avid lover of art, architecture, or history.

CATHÉDRALE DE NOTRE DAME. From the delicate stonework of its restored facade to the massive cast-iron spire, this Gothic masterpiece soars skyward in a rising crescendo of architectural extravagance. Almost completely destroyed by

Allied bombing during WWII, the Cathedral lost much of its stained glass and is currently undergoing restoration to recover its former glory. Its mismatched towers each represent different styles of the Gothic period—on the left is the 12th-century **Tour St-Romaine,** and on the right stands the 16th-century **Tour de Beurre** (Tower of Butter), which was funded by cholesterol-loving parishioners who preferred to pay a dispensation rather than go without the delicious ingredient during Lent. Don't miss the tombs of Richard the Lion-Hearted and Rollo, the first duke of Normandy, inside. The cathedral is especially impressive at night, when it is illuminated to striking effect. *(Pl. de la Cathédrale. Open Apr.-Oct. M 2-7pm, Tu-Sa 7:30am-7pm, Su 8am-6pm; Nov.-Mar. M 2-7pm, Tu-Sa 7:30am-noon and 2-6pm, Su 8am-6pm. Mass Tu-Sa 8 and 10am, Su 8:30, 10:30am, noon. Tours in French daily June-Sept. 2:30pm; Oct.-May Sa-Su 2:30pm. Free.)*

MUSÉE DES BEAUX ARTS. This magnificent museum presents a broad collection of European (mostly French) art, dating from the present day back to the 15th century. Caravaggio's *Flagellation of Christ* stands in a rotunda on the second floor, and the Impressionist collection proudly displays one of Monet's paintings of the Rouen cathedral. Special exhibits rotate periodically. *(Esplanade Marcel Duchamp, on sq. Verdrel. ☎71 28 40; www.rouen-musees.com. Open M and W-Su 10am-6pm; south wing closed 1-2pm. €3, groups and students ages 18-25 €2, under 18 free. Extra fee for some special exhibits.)*

MUSÉE FLAUBERT ET D'HISTOIRE DE LA MÉDECINE. Formerly a hospital, and later the childhood home of French novelist Gustave Flaubert, this eclectic little museum packs in a formidable number of (occasionally gruesome) objects loosely related to the history of medicine and to Flaubert himself. Among the objects preserved here are plaster moldings of the heads of Raphael and the Marquis de Sade, a pregnant mannequin used to teach midwives how to deliver babies, and a stuffed parrot that inspired Flaubert's short story Le Coeur Simple (The Simple Heart). Ring the bell if the door's locked when you arrive—if the museum is open, you'll be let in. *(51 rue de Lecat, next to the Préfecture. ☎15 59 95; www.chu-rouen.fr. Open Tu 10am-6pm, W-Sa 10am-noon and 2-6pm. €3, ages 18-25 €1.50, under 18 free.)*

GROS HORLOGE. An ornately gilded 16th-century timepiece, the *Gros Horloge* (Great Clock), is built into a carved stone bridge that spans rue du Gros Horloge. While a rotating disk depicting Greco-Roman divinities marks the days, a ball at the top tracks the phases of the moon. A small door underneath the bridge leads to a

PARDON ME, ST-ROMAIN

Every year since 1156, on the morning of Ascension Day, a prisoner is brought before Rouen's parliament. Without a judge, jury, or any sort of a trial, he is set free. By this annual act of mercy, Rouen celebrates the most famous miracle of its patron saint, St-Romain: his defeat of a dragon with the help of a convict.

While serving as Bishop of Rouen in the seventh century, St-Romain lived a life of quiet piety; it was not until well after his death in 641 that his fame as a dragon-slayer began to spread. When the saint's remains were moved inside Rouen's walls in the 10th century, they were interred in a flood-prone part of town that subsequently stopped flooding. With this new miracle attributed to St-Romain's intervention, the old legend of his run-in with a dragon recaptured popular imagination.

As the story goes, one day a dragon emerged from the Seine and sent a flood over Rouen. St-Romain tried to recruit villagers to stop the beast, but only one man—a prisoner—answered his plea. The two entered the dragon's cave, St-Romain made the sign of the cross, and the beast collapsed.

In order to honor their legendary patron saint and the lone convict who aided him, the people of Rouen began to annually pardon a prisoner. Improbable as it may seem, this millennium-old tradition continues to this day.

ticket office for self-guided audio tours of the clock tower, which houses exhibits. A trip up the winding staircase to the bell tower is rewarded by an unparalleled view of the cathedral spires and the city below. *(☎02 32 08 01 90; groshorloge@rouen.fr. Open Apr.-Oct. Tu-Su 10am-6pm; Nov.-Mar. T-Su 2-5pm. Adults €6, students 18-25 €3. MC/V.)*

ABBATIALE ST-OUEN. Once an eighth-century Benedictine abbey, this cathedral has since seen many additions—most recently a 19th-century facade. After checking out the cavernous and oddly bare interior, enjoy the view of the exterior from the sloping grounds of the **Jardins de l'Hôtel de Ville,** which provide a picturesque environment for anyone seeking a relaxing afternoon stroll or a lazy game of *pétanque*. *(Next to the Hôtel de Ville, at pl. du Général de Gaulle. Open Apr.-Oct. M and W-Su 10am-noon and 2-5:30pm; Nov.-Mar. Sa-Su 10am-noon and 2-5pm.)*

OTHER SIGHTS. For those interested in the history of Rouen's most famous heretic, the **Tour Jeanne d'Arc** offers little besides the memory of what it once was: Joan's last prison before her execution. *(Entrance on rue Bouvreuil. Open Apr.-Sept. M and W-Sa 10am-12:30pm and 2-6pm, Su 2-6:30pm; Oct.-Mar. M and W-Sa 10am-12:30pm and 2-5pm, Su 2-5:30pm. €1.50, students and under 18 free.)* A cross marks the spot where Joan burned in pl. du Vieux Marché, next to the **Eglise Jeanne d'Arc.** This simple church features a scaled roof, plain interior, stained glass, and long canopy stretching out into the square. *(Open M-Th and Sa 10am-12:30pm and 2-6pm. Closed during mass. Mass M-Tu and Th-F 6:30pm, W 12:15pm, Su 11am.)*

NIGHTLIFE

Emporium Galorium, 151 rue Beauvoisine (☎71 76 95; www.emporium-galorium.com). Hip drinks and regular live concerts (Th-Sa) make this cavernous spot one of the loudest and most raucous in Rouen. W €1 shot nights hard to pass up. Beer €3. Mixed drinks €5. Open Tu-W 8pm-2am, Th-Sa 8pm-3am.

Le Nash, 97 rue Ecuyère (☎98 25 24). Wide-ranging DJ selections (Th-Sa nights), red walls, and zebra-striped upholstery set the scene for a loud, youthful crowd dressed to impress. Beer €3.50-5. Mixed drinks €7. Tapas €3.50-5. Open M-Sa 6pm-2am. MC/V.

L'Euro, pl. du Vieux Marché (☎07 55 66). Three hip floors in an ancient *auberge*, each with their own ambience. Pumping music, cozy nooks, and low stools set the mood. Beer and wine €4. Mixed drinks €7.50-11. Open daily 3pm-2am. AmEx/MC/V.

Pub Yesterday, 3 rue Moulinet (☎70 43 98). Non-stop Irish music is the perfect sound track to a swig of Guinness served by hilarious owner Fabrice. Odd objects, including 2 old-fashioned bicycles and a piano, hang from the ceiling. Beer €3.50. Whiskey €5-7.60. Open M-Sa 5pm-2am. MC/V.

L'Insolite, 58 rue d'Amiens (☎88 62 53). Cozy gay bar invites visitors into an intimate and classy spot with dim red lighting. Beer €2.80. Mixed drinks €5. MC/V.

DIEPPE ☎02

The small picturesque seaport town of Dieppe (dee-EPP; pop. 34,700) was settled and named in AD 907 by the Vikings, who first realized how deep, or "djepp," its river is. The town never forgot the seafaring ways of its earliest founders and became an important channel port after the Norman invasion of England in 1066. Dieppe's turbulent history has also witnessed several setbacks, most famously during WWII when Allied Canadian troops suffered a devastating loss in 1942 to occupying Germans in Operation Jubilee. Today's visitors, many of whom speak English, enjoy the long gravel beach, hilltop castle, seafood restaurants, seagulls, and salt breeze of this distinctly maritime town.

TRANSPORTATION. The **train station,** bd. Georges Clemenceau (ticket office open M-F 5:35am-7:40pm, Sa 6:15am-7:23pm, Su 7:30am-8:20pm), has service to Paris (2½hr., every 1½hr., €25) via Rouen (45min., €9.70). **Stradibus,** 56 quai Duquesne (☎32 14 03 03), serves Dieppe and its outskirts (tickets €1.15, *carnet* of 10 €7.50, weekly pass €7.70). **Voyages Denis/Cars Denis buses,** 10 quai Duquesne (☎35 06 86 86), stop at the tourist office on Pont Ango and serve surrounding towns (€2) and also offer trips to most of Europe. **Transmanche Ferries** (☎08 00 65 01 00; www.transmancheferries.com) sail from their own dock, 1km past the Pont Ango, to New Haven (4hr.; July-Oct. €25-28, Nov.-June €18-25). Rent **bikes** at **Vélo Service,** across from the tourist office on the Pont Ango. (☎06 24 56 06 27. €1 per hr., €3.50 per ½-day, €5.50 per day, €10 per weekend, €15 per week. Tandems €2 per hr., €7 per ½-day, €11 per day. Open M-F 9:30am-6pm, Sa-Su 9am-7:30pm.)

ORIENTATION AND PRACTICAL INFORMATION. To reach the city center from the train station, walk straight along quai Berigny a few hundred feet until it becomes quai Duquesne. The **tourist office,** located on the Pont Ango, provides a free city guide and map, guided tours of the city in French on a tramcar (*Petit Train;* 1hr; €6, under 10 €4), and info on available accommodations and summer events. (☎32 14 40 06; www.dieppetourism.com. Open July-Aug. M-Sa 9am-7pm, Su 10am-1pm and 3-6pm; May-June and Sept. M-Sa 9am-1pm and 2-7pm, Su 10am-1pm and 3-6pm; Oct.-Apr. M-Sa 9am-noon and 2-6pm.) Find **ATMs** on the quai Henri IV and outside the banks throughout the town. Self-service **laundry** is available at **Lav-O-Clair,** at the end of rue Notre-Dame on pl. Nationale. (☎06 08 01 16 80. Open daily 7am-9pm. Wash €5-7, dry €1 per 12min.) Other services include: **public toilets** on pl. Carnot by the post office (free) and on the beachfront (€0.40); **police** to the left of the train station on bd. Georges Clemenceau (☎32 14 49 00); many **pharmacies,** including one on quai Duquesne (☎35 84 14 06; open M-F 9am-12:15pm and 2-7:30pm, Sa 9am-12:15pm); a **hospital** on av. Pasteur (☎32 14 76 76). **Internet** access at **@rt au bar,** 19 rue de Sygogne. (☎35 40 48 35; artaubar@wanadoo.fr. €1 per 15min., discounts for buying 5hr. or more. Open M-Sa 10am-7:30pm.) The **post office** is on bd. Maréchal Joffre. (☎35 06 99 20. Open M-F 8am-6pm, Sa 8am-12:30pm.) **Postal Code:** 76200.

ACCOMMODATIONS AND FOOD. Be willing to pay a little more than usual to stay in Dieppe, especially if you want a view of the sea; there's a lack of budget accommodations in the city, although one option is to stay in a chain hotel. To keep it cheap, try **Le Relais Gambetta ❷,** 95 rue Gambetta, across from the Gambetta stop on Stradibus line 2. This somewhat worn establishment is occupied mostly by students and, during the school year, school groups from England. (☎02 35 84 12 91. Breakfast €5. Pets surcharge €5. Rooms €30-33; pension €45, for 2 people €80; demi-pension €40, for 2 people 58. Extra bed €9.50. Cash only.)

There is a **market** in the *vieille ville* all day on Saturday, where vendors sell assorted fresh produce and other goods; Tuesday and Thursday mornings see a smaller version, with fruits and vegetables only. For groceries, head to **Shopi,** 59 rue de la Barre (open M-Sa 8am-8pm, Su 9am-1pm), or **Marché Plus,** 22 quai Duquesne (open M-Sa 7am-9pm, Su 9am-1pm). In **Le Pollet,** the fishing quarters, restaurants cook up the freshest catch of the day. The **quai Henri IV** offers a variety of restaurants, most of which specialize in seafood, especially Dieppe's famous mussels (see *Musseling Through Dieppe*, p. 288). If you'd like to gorge on this regional specialty, visit **Le Festival ❷,** 11 quai Henri IV, on a weeknight, when they offer "*moules marinère à volonté*" (all-you-can-eat mussels cooked with white wine), which come with fries and a dessert for €9.90. (☎35 40 24 29. English spoken. *Menus* €10-26. Open 11am-3pm and 7-11pm. MC/V.) For a *croque-monsieur* (grilled ham and cheese sandwich, €4.40) or a cool drink during the day, head to the oldest café in

MUSSEL-ING THROUGH DIEPPE

The restaurants along Dieppe's Quai de Henry IV each have their own unique personality, but they all serve one delicious Norman culinary staple: *la marmite à moules*, a pot of mussels.

In Dieppe, mussels are collected *aux bouchots*, using ropes wrapped around giant wooden *bouchots* (pillars) the size of tree trunks. These are then planted in a seabed location where they will be underwater at high tide and exposed at low tide. Newborn mussels floating in the sea clamp onto the ropes. When they grow big enough to eat, they are scraped from each pillar and swung on board amphibious metal boats designed specifically for mussel harvesting.

All their exposure to fresh air during low tide yields *moules* with a distinctive flavor unique to the region. In Normandy, mussels are often prepared as *moules marinière*, with white wine, onions, and garlic, or in cream or curry sauce. Another popular preparation with onions, white wine, and *crème fraîche* is called *Dieppoise*. Most dishes are served *avec frites* (with fries).

Wash your mussels down with some *calvados* (hard apple cider), and finish up with a *tarte Normande* (apple tart) for a tasty Norman meal.

town, the classy **Café de Tribunaux ❶**, 1 pl. du Puits-Sale. (☎32 14 44 65. Open daily 8am-8pm.)

SIGHTS. Take some time to relax on Dieppe's gravel **beach,** which spans over a mile from the harbor to the sheer white *falaises* (cliffs). Atop the cliffs sits the 15th-century **château,** now a museum of artistic works relating to Dieppe and its maritime history. Several rooms celebrate the *dieppois* tradition of ivory carving; intricate models of ships—including billowing sails and rigging—are on display. There are also charming Impressionist paintings of Dieppe and Baroque still-lifes full of fish. (☎35 06 61 99. Open June-Sept. daily 10am-noon and 2-6pm; Oct.-May M and W-Sa 10am-noon and 2-5pm, Su 10am-noon and 2-6pm. Last ticket sold ½hr. before closing. Adults €3, students €2, ages 12-18 €1.50, under 12 free.) From the château, take a short walk to the edge of the cliffs and enjoy the view of Dieppe and the Channel.

The small **memorial to the Canadian raid of 1942,** in a restored theater on pl. Saint-Saëns, holds authentic army uniforms, a video with testimonials about the failed raid, and a touching display of black-and-white photos of survivors from the first major Allied offensive against the Nazis in France. (☎35 40 36 65. Open daily 2-6:30pm; closed Tu June-Sept. and weekends and holidays Apr.-May and Oct.-Nov. €2.30, veterans and under 16 free.) The **Cité de la Mer,** 37 rue de l'asile Thomas, explores the maritime culture of Normandy, from the history of shipbuilding and fishing in Dieppe to the flora and fauna of the regional cliffs. Children will enjoy observing the two-room aquarium, navigating motorized mini-boats around the small pool, or building a Lego ship. (☎35 06 93 20; www.estrancitedelamer.free.fr. Open daily 10am-noon and 2-6pm. €5.50, students €4.50, ages 4-16 €3.50.)

If the weather's nice, rent a boat and fishing equipment from one of the stores in Le Pollet (ask tourist office for more info). For the slightly less adventurous, **Promenades en mer** offers half-hour boat tours around Dieppe's cliffs, leaving from a dock next to the tourist office. (☎32 90 11 91 or 06 09 52 37 38; www.bateau-ville-de-dieppe.com. Call in advance. €7, ages 4-12 €5.50.)

NIGHTLIFE AND FESTIVALS. Nightlife is almost non-existent on weekdays and limited on weekends. **L'Epsom,** 11 bd. de Verdun, is a fairly popular spot with a low-key atmosphere, red upholstered lounge, and a live band on Fridays. (☎35 84 12 27. Tea €3.50-9.50. Dessert €5.50. Mixed drinks €7-9. Tapas €3.20-9.50. Open M-Tu and Su noon-1am, Th-Sa noon-2am. AmEx/MC/V.) For dancing, mingling, or reclining in oversized armchairs, try the naval themed but luxurious **L'Abordage,** 3 bd. de Verdun, in the same building as the casino. This bar becomes a discotheque on Friday and Saturday nights. (☎32 14 48 00. Beer €6. Mixed drinks €7-9. Open M-Th and Su 9pm-3am, F and Sa 9pm-5am. Sept.-May ballroom dancing with live orchestra 3-7pm. AmEx/MC/V.) Every other September (next in 2008), windy Dieppe hosts the **Festival International de Cerf-Volant** (International Kite Festival), living up to its name as the kite capital of the world.

LE HAVRE ☎02 35

The largest transatlantic port in France, Le Havre (luh AH-vruh; pop. 193,000) wasn't built as a tourist destination, so there's not much for a traveler to do or see in the city. Nevertheless, among the postwar concrete architecture, there are a few bright spots—in particular, a good museum, a lively university, broad tree-lined boulevards, and some peaceful public parks. Moreover, Le Havre's cheaper accommodations make it an affordable base for daytrips throughout Normandy.

TRANSPORTATION. The train station is on cours de la République at the intersection with bd. de Strasbourg. (Open M-Th 5am-midnight, F 5am-2:30am, Sa 5am-11pm, Su 7:15am-2:30am. Ticket office open M-F 5:25am-7:40pm, Sa 5:40am-7:30pm, Su 7:30am-9:15pm.) **Trains** run to Fécamp (1hr., 6-12 per day, €7.40), Paris (2½-3hr., 8 per day, €28), and Rouen (1hr., 8-20 per day, €13). **Buses** are a convenient and cheap way to make daytrips along the Norman coastline; they leave from the *gare routière* (☎22 34 00; info office open M-Sa 7am-7pm), which is connected to the train station. Bus Verts (☎08 10 21 42 14; www.busverts14.fr) run to Caen via Honfleur (30min.; 4-10 per day; €4, under 26 €3.40), then Deauville (1hr., 4-7 per day, €6). See p. 296 for Caen-Le Havre express info. Keolis (☎28 19 88) runs two lines to Fécamp (1½hr., 9-19 per day, €2), one of which goes via Etretat (1hr., 5-6 per day, €2). LD Lines sends **ferries** (€25) to Portsmouth (daily 5pm) and New Haven (daily 8pm), England, from the station at terminal de la Citadelle. (☎19 78 78; www.ldlines.com. Ticket/info office open daily 8am-7pm.) **Taxis** wait at the train station and across from the Hôtel de Ville (☎25 81 81). Vélocéan bicycles can be rented at the bus station or tourist office. (€2 per 2hr., €3 per ½-day, €5 per day, €8 per weekend, €25 per week. Tandems available. Check and ID deposit.)

LE HAZARD. Be extra cautious at night near the train station and harbor.

ORIENTATION AND PRACTICAL INFORMATION. From the train station, take bd. de Strasbourg to pl. de l'Hôtel de Ville, in the center of the city (10min.). On the opposite side of the *place*, av. Foch continues for another 10min. to the beach. Take a left onto bd. Clemenceau to reach the **tourist office,** 186 bd. Clemenceau. The office offers info on nautical activities—sailing, windsurfing, and kayaking—hotels and restaurants, a monthly calendar of events, and a free map. (☎02 32 74 04 04; www.lehavretourisme.com. Open mid-Apr. to Oct. M-Sa 9am-6:45pm, Su 10am-12:30pm and 2:30-5:45pm; Nov. to mid-Apr. M-F 9am-6:15pm, Sa 9am-12:30pm and 2-6:15pm, Su 10am-1pm.)

Services in Le Havre include: **ATMs** near the Hôtel de Ville on bd. de Strasbourg and near the station on cours de la République; a **laundromat,** 85 rue Casimir Delavigne (open daily 7am-9pm); **public restrooms,** pl. de l'Hôtel de Ville (€0.30); **police,** 5 rue Jules Lecesne (☎19 20 20); a **pharmacy,** 35 cours de la République (☎25 18 74; open M-F 9am-12:30pm and 2:30-9pm, Sa 9am-7pm); and a **hospital,** 55bis rue Gustave Flaubert (☎02 32 73 32 15). **Internet** access is available at **Cybermetro,** 19-21 cours de la République, across from the train station. (€2.30 per 30min., €3.50 per hr. Open M-F 9am-2am, Sa-Su 1pm-2am.) The **post office** is at 172 bd. Strasbourg. (☎19 55 00. Open M-F 8:30am-6pm, Sa 9am-noon.) **Postal Code:** 76600.

ACCOMMODATIONS AND FOOD. There are plenty of two-star chain hotels by the train station, but better deals can be found elsewhere. Reasonably priced **Hôtel d'Yport ❷,** 27 cours de la République, tucked away on a small but inviting courtyard, pleasantly surprises budget travelers with its marble-tiled bathrooms. From the train station, cross cours de la République and turn right; you'll see the sign for the hotel, which is down a narrow street on the left, a block and a half ahead. (☎25 21 08; fax 24 06 34. Breakfast €6. Shower €5. Reception 24hr. Singles €25, with shower and toilet €30-35; doubles €30/35-45. MC/V.) The **Hôtel Celtic ❸,** 106 rue Voltaire, is close to the Bassin du Commerce and across the street from the Volcan. All rooms have shower, TV, and double bed; most have a toilet. (☎42 39 77; www.hotelceltic.com. Breakfast €6.50. Free Wi-Fi. Reception noon-10pm. Singles and doubles €36; singles with toilet €42-51; doubles with toilet €46-53. Extra bed €12. AmEx/MC/V.)

For groceries, there's a **Super U,** 5 rue de l'Abbé Périer, off av. Foch (a continuation of bd. de Strasbourg) just before the beach (open M-Sa 8:30am-8:30pm), and a **Marché Plus,** 156-158 rue de Paris, near the Volcan (open June-Sept. M-Sa 7am-9pm, Su 8:30am-noon; Oct.-May M-Sa 7am-9pm). The freshest food can be found at the morning market on **place Thiers,** by the Hôtel de Ville (M, W, F 7:30am-1:30pm), or the all-day market on **cours République** (Tu, Th, Sa 7:30am-7pm). There are a few restaurants near the Volcan, by **place de l'Hôtel de Ville** and on the streets surrounding the **quai Lamblardie.** A top option is the **Côté Jardin ❶,** 9 pl. de l'Hôtel de Ville. The attentive waitstaff serves designer salads (€9.40), desserts (€3.20-4.90), and a variety of *tartes* (€8.80) with side salads. (☎43 43 04. Open M 11:45am-2:30pm, Tu-Sa 11:45am-6:30pm. MC/V.) For a break from French fare, a good choice is **Le Mandarin ❸,** 22 rue de Paris, near quai Southampton and the ferry terminal. The overwhelming selection of well-prepared Asian dishes includes chicken, pork, beef, shrimp, and even frog legs. (☎42 28 81. *Plats* €6-11. *Menus* €13-19. Open Tu-Su noon-3:30pm and 7-10:30pm. MC/V.)

SIGHTS AND ENTERTAINMENT. Known for its Impressionist works, the **Musée Malraux,** 2 bd. Clemenceau, displays a small collection of paintings by Dufy, Monet, and a host of local artists. The second floor houses works by Eugène Boudin depicting Norman seascapes and cows; Boudin was a local artist responsible for introducing Monet to *plein air* (outdoor) painting. Special exhibits rotate every three months. (☎19 62 62. Open M and W-F 11am-6pm, Sa-Su 11am-7pm. €5, students €3, under 18 free.) The shaded gardens, modern gazebo, and stone bridge of the **Square St-Roch,** off av. Foch, provide a refreshingly lush and peaceful oasis, while multiple fountains lend character to the wide-open **place de l'Hôtel de Ville.** Auguste Perret, the 20th-century French architect known for his concrete constructions, made an unusual addition to Le Havre's skyline with the **Eglise St-Joseph,** which looks—both inside and out—like a futuristic rocket ship made of cement Legos. Likely inspired by Perret's modernism, **Le Volcan** (The Volcano), so named for its extraordinary resemblance to a smooth, white, sunken cinder-cone, adds to the unusual architecture of Le Havre. Although its weird design may be off-putting, it is nevertheless a state-of-the-art venue for renowned orchestral works and plays, as well as a cinema that screens international new releases, classics, and notable independent films. (☎19 10 10, cinema 19 10 11; www.levolcan.com. Info and ticket office open Tu-Sa 2-7pm. Closed July 20-Aug. 31.)

DAYTRIP FROM LE HAVRE

DEAUVILLE AND TROUVILLE

Bus Verts (☎08 01 21 42 14) sends buses to the train station in Deauville from Le Havre (1¼hr., €13). Voyages Fournier (☎02 31 88 16 73) runs shuttles from pl. du Maréchal Foch, next to the Trouville casino, between the 2 towns (€1.80). For a taxi, call ☎02 31 88 35 33 or 02 31 87 11 11.

Deauville (DOH-veel) and Trouville (TROO-veel)—stylish twin towns on the Norman coast—promise travelers fine sand, glittering casinos, and a sore wallet. A beachside stroll along the boardwalk in Trouville affords a view of volleyball courts and the spectacular houses that inspired novelist Gustave Flaubert. In Deauville, where each boardwalk changing room bears the name of a famous movie star, you're more likely to see bikinis than beach pails. Joined by the Pont des Belges over the river, La Touques, these sister cities have distinctive identities.

The **Casino Barrière de Trouville** (☎02 31 87 75 00), pl. du Maréchal Foch, has an adjoining cinema, while its twin **Casino Barrière de Deauville** has a nightclub and nightly shows (☎02 31 14 31 14; both casinos open M-Th and Su 10am-2am, F 10am-3am, Sa 10am-4am; stays open 1hr. later in summer). Residents of Deauville satisfy their love of horses at two *hippodromes* (racecourses): **Clairefontaine,** dedicated only to racing (☎02 31 14 69 00; www.hippodrome-deauville-clairefontaine.com; races and guided tours on certain days July-Aug. and Oct.; €3), and **La Touques,** which hosts the occasional polo game as well (☎02 31 14 20 00; www.france-galop.com; races on certain days Mar., July-Aug., and Oct.-Dec.; M-Sa €3, Su €4, students and seniors €2, under 18 free). Plan ahead, as the courses are only open a few times a month on race days.

A **market** on the quai across from the tourist office in Trouville sells fresh local fish and produce, as well as clothing. (Open W and Su 8am-1:30pm.) For groceries, there's a **Monoprix** in Trouville on the corner where bd. Fernand Moureaux meets rue Victor Hugo. (Open M-Sa 9:30am-7:30pm.) Many of the beachfront restaurants offer a perfect view of the horizon at sunset; join the locals as they flock to the terraces to dine during the last light of day. In Trouville, pizzerias, *crêperies*, and a slew of seafood restaurants featuring Norman mussels line the pedestrian **rue des Bains** and **boulevard Fernand Moureaux.** In Deauville, **Mamy Crêpes ❶,** 57 rue Désiré le Hoc, near the tourist office, a small lunch counter marked by a wooden grandma outside, serves filling sandwiches at affordable prices (€3-4), and also offers a range of quiches (€3), dessert *crêpes* (€2.20-3), and *tartes*. (☎02 31 14 96 44. Open daily in summer 9am-midnight; in winter 9am-10pm. MC/V.)

To get to the **Trouville tourist office** from the train and bus station, turn right and cross the Pont des Belges, then walk left on bd. Fernand Moureaux for one block. (☎02 31 14 60 70; www.trouvillesurmer.org. Open July-Aug. M-Sa 9:30am-7pm, Su 10am-4pm; Apr.-June and Sept.-Oct. M-Sa 9:30am-noon and 2-6:30pm, Su 10am-1pm; Nov.-Mar. M-Sa 9:30am-noon and 1:30-6pm, Su 10am-1pm.) To get to the **Deauville tourist office** from the train station, turn left. At the second roundabout, take the right fork onto rue Désiré le Hoc and follow it through pl. Morny (around the fountain) to pl. de la Mairie. (☎02 31 14 40 00; www.deauville.org. Open July to early Sept. M-Sa 9am-7pm, Su 10am-1pm and 3-6pm; mid-Sept. to Oct. and late Feb. to Mar. M-Sa 9am-12:30pm and 2-6:30pm, Su 10am-1pm and 2-5pm; Nov. to mid-Feb. M-F 9am-12:30pm and 2-6pm, Sa 9am-12:30pm and 2-8:30pm, Su 10am-1pm and 2-5pm; Apr.-June M-F 9am-12:30pm and 2-6:30pm, Sa 9am-6:30pm, Su 10am-1pm and 2-5pm.) Cycles Jamme, 11 av. de la République, offers **bike** rentals down the street from the train station. (☎02 31 88 40 22. €4.50 per hr., €10 per ½-day, €16 per day, €40 per week. Scooters also available. Check deposit. Open M-Tu and Th-Sa 9am-12:15pm and 2-6:30pm.)

ETRETAT ☎02 35

The former fishing village Etretat (EH-truh-tah; pop. 1640), an easy daytrip northeast of Le Havre, has captivated artists, writers, and tourists since the 19th century. When you reach the shore, it's easy to see why. Soaring chalk *falaises* (cliffs) and panoramic seascapes make this one of the most breathtaking spots along the Channel coast. To the west of the pebble beach, the **Aiguille** (Needle) rises up out of the sea beside the great arch of the **Falaise d'Aval.** To the east, the tiny reconstructed **Chapelle Notre Dame de la Garde** sits atop the **Falaise d'Amont,** whose base—as first noted by Guy de Maupassant—curiously resembles an elephant dipping its trunk in the sea. Paths from the beach up to the top of either cliff—sometimes coming within feet of a sheer drop to the ocean below—lead climbers to intense seascape views. Crooked streets crammed with eateries, small shops, and summer visitors wind from av. Georges V, where buses enter town, to the beach. In the other direction, just outside the town center at 15 rue de Maupassant, is **Le Clos Arsène Lupin,** formerly the home of crime novelist Maurice Leblanc and now reinvented as the home of his most famous character, the "gentleman burglar" Arsène Lupin. Visitors solve a mystery with a 45min. interactive audio tour of the antique home. (☎10 59 53. Open Apr.-Sept. daily 10am-5:45pm; Oct. to mid-Dec. and Feb.-Mar. F-Su noon-5pm. Tour in English or French. €6.50, ages 6-16 €4.)

Etretat has plenty of hotels, but not many that cater to budget travelers, especially near the beachfront; you may be able to find cheap rooms even at pricier hotels if you reserve well in advance. Rooms at **Hôtel de la Poste ❸,** 6 av. Georges V, atop a bar, provide some of the best options but are still more expensive than staying in Le Havre and taking a round-trip bus. The 17 simple rooms are clean, brightly decorated and come with shower and TV. (☎27 01 34; fax 27 76 28. Buffet breakfast €7. Reception 8am-8pm. Singles €35; doubles €39-50; quads €65. MC/V.) **Camping le Grandval ❶,** is in a quiet spot bordered by a steep slope of dense forest, a 15min. walk from the tourist office down rue Guy de Maupassant. Some buses from Le Havre and Fécamp stop opposite the site. (☎27 07 67. Laundry available. Reception 9am-noon and 3-7pm. Gates closed 10pm-7:30am. Check-out noon. Open mid-Apr. to mid-Oct. €3.10 per adult, €1.90 per child age 4-10, €3.10 per car with tent, €3.90 per car with RV. Electricity €4.50-5.40. Showers free. MC/V.)

Tourists wandering through town will have no trouble finding restaurants on the way to the beach, although skirting down side streets will reward you with a more authentic experience. Follow signs all over town to **Crêperie Lann-Bihoue ❶,** 45 rue Notre Dame, for a mouth-watering *menu* including a lunch *crêpe* and a dessert *crêpe* for €9. (☎27 04 65. *Crêpes* €2.50-9. Open Jan.-Nov. M and Th-Su noon-2:30pm and 7-9:30pm; hours may vary.)

Keolis (☎28 19 88) runs **buses** to Fécamp (35min., 12 per day, €2) and Le Havre (1hr., 7 per day, €2). Taxis wait by the bus stop (☎06 12 16 48 27). The **tourist office,** pl. Maurice Guillard, behind the bus stop, provides free maps and a guide to hotels and restaurants in town. (☎27 05 21; www.etretat.net. Open daily mid-June to mid-Sept. 9am-7pm; mid-Sept. to mid-June 10am-noon and 2-6pm.) To reach the water from the tourist office, take rue Monge, which becomes bd. Président René Coty. Find **Public restrooms** on rue Monge by the bus station, and at the beach (€0.30). There's an **ATM** near the water at 3 bd. Président René Coty. **Postal Code:** 76790.

FÉCAMP ☎02 35

Though it lacks Etretat's breathtaking beauty, Fécamp (FAY-kohn; pop. 22,000), with its quiet harbor, broad beach framed by cliffs, and green slope dotted with cottages, is a pleasant daytrip from Le Havre or Rouen. Its days as a tourist attraction began in the sixth century, when some drops of *précieux-sang* (Christ's blood) allegedly washed ashore in the trunk of a fig tree. The relic was later housed in the imposing **Eglise Abbatiale de la Trinité** (Abbey Church of the Trinity), pl. Général Leclerc, built by Richard II of Normandy in 1106 to prove his Christian piety. Today, Fécamp's main attraction is the magnificent **Palais Bénédictine,** 110 rue Alexandre Le Grand, home of the famous *bénédictine liqueur.* The *palais* is part art museum—with a fantastic collection of medieval and Renaissance work—part distillery, all housed in a fairytale-like castle. Best of all, the tour includes a free taste of the famous *liqueur* (see *History, on the Rocks,* right), originally a monastic healing elixir. (☎10 26 10; www.benedictine.fr. Open daily July-Aug. 10am-7pm; Sept. to mid-Oct. and Apr.-June 10am-1pm and 2-6:30pm; mid-Oct. to early Jan. and mid-Feb. to Mar. 10:30am-12:45pm and 2-6pm. Last entry 1hr. before closing. €6, ages 12-18 €2, under 12 free. Family of 2 adults and at least 1 child €13. AmEx/MC/V.)

Fécamp's lodgings unfortunately don't come any cheaper than the **Hôtel Vent d'Ouest ❸,** 3 av. Gambetta, opposite the bus stop and up the steps from the train station. Spotless, maritime-themed rooms come with bath, TV, and phone. (☎28 04 04; www.hotelventdouest.fm.fr. Breakfast €5. Reception 7am-11pm. May-Sept. singles €40; doubles €48; triples €55. Oct.-Apr. €34/40/46. AmEx/MC/V.) Though it costs as much as a cheap hostel elsewhere, **Camping Municipal de Reneville ❶,** chemin de Nesmond, is worth it for the neat, green hillside plots, all of which have a spectacular view of the ocean. From the train station or bus stop, turn right on av. Gambetta, which becomes quai Bérigny. Turn left onto rue du Président René Coty, right on rue Georges Cuvier, and left on steep rue d'Yport. Finally, make a hairpin turn onto chemin de Nesmond. (☎28 20 97; www.campingdereneville.com. Laundry available. Reception 8:30am-1pm and 2-7:30pm. Gates open 7am-10pm. Open Apr.-Nov. July-Aug. €11-13 per 2 people and tent, €4.20-4.70 per additional adult, €2.10-2.35 per additional child under 8, €13-15 per RV. Prices lower Apr.-June and Sept.-Nov. Electricity €2.50. Showers free. AmEx/MC/V.)

There's a **Marché-Plus** supermarket at 83-85 quai Bérigny. (Open June-Sept. M 8:30am-1pm and 3:30-8:30pm, Tu-Sa 7am-9pm, Su 9am-1pm; Oct.-May Tu-Sa 7am-9pm, Su 9am-1pm.) Nearly identical seafood restaurants cluster around **place Nicolas Selle,** at the end of quai Bérigny one block from the ocean. With ample outdoor seating and elegant burgundy tablecloths inside, **L'Escalier ❸,** 101 quai Bérigny, offers a la carte delicacies (€11-16) and reasonably priced *menus.* (☎28 26 79. *Menus* €14-23. Open daily noon-3pm and 7-10pm. MC/V.) For a snack, swing by **Jean-Paul Martin ❶,** 6 pl. Nicolas Selle, where just €1-3 buys excellent baguettes and pastries. (☎28 21 99. Open Tu-Su 6:30am-8pm. MC/V.)

Fécamp is accessible by **train** from Le Havre (45min., 5-10 per day, €7.40), Paris (2½hr., 5-8 per day, €27), and Rouen (1¼hr., 6-9 per day, €13). The station is at bd. de la République. (Office open M-Sa 9:30am-noon and 1:20-6pm, Su noon-7:10pm.) Get there by **bus** on Kéolis, which stops at pl. St-Etienne across from the church on av. Gambetta. (☎28 19 88. Open M-F 8:30am-12:15pm and 1:30-5:15pm.) Buses

THE LOCAL STORY

HISTORY, ON THE ROCKS

Though Benedictine *liqueur*—used in regional desserts, featured with brandy, or served solo on the rocks—is ubiquitous throughout Normandy, the *liqueur's* equally intoxicating history is less well-known. Its story began in the Renaissance, when a Venetian monk created an elixir that combined 27 plants and spices from around the world. When King François I took a taste, it was love at first sip. The *liqueur* became popular in court and across the country, until the French Revolution threatened the drink's survival. A noble from the small town of Fécamp purchased the secret formula to protect it, but, in the chaos of escaping town, forgot it in his library.

Fortunately for us, the noble had an enterprising distant relative, Alexandre LeGrand. In 1863, LeGrand found the recipe and immediately set out to mass-produce Benedictine *liqueur.* Instead of a utilitarian distillery, LeGrand built the **Palais Bénédictine** (☎02 35 10 26 10; see left) in Fécamp not only to profit from the famed *liqueur,* but also to celebrate it and—with a stained glass window of himself—to celebrate his role in its survival. Today, visitors can tour the palace and peruse the art that LeGrand amassed as a *liqueur* magnate, before concluding their visit with a complimentary tasting.

run to Le Havre (1½hr., 8-15 per day, €2) and other towns in the region. There is a **taxi** stand (☎28 17 50) across the street from the bus stop on pl. St-Etienne at the top of av. Gambetta. To reach Fécamp's **tourist office,** on quai Sadi Carnot, from the train or bus stations, take a right and walk to the roundabout. Make another right, and the tourist office is a few hundred feet down, at the corner leading to the pier. The staff books rooms (free, €1.60 for out of town) and dispenses maps and nautical info. (☎28 51 01; www.fecamptourisme.com. Open July-Aug. daily 9am-6:30pm; Apr.-June M-F 9am-6pm, Sa-Su 10am-6:30pm; Sept.-Dec. and Jan.-Mar. M-F 9am-6pm, Sa 9:30am-12:30pm and 2-6pm, Su 9:30am-12:30pm.) There is an **ATM** at 27 quai Bérigny, by the train and bus stations. **Postal Code:** 76400.

BASSE-NORMANDIE

Since the mid-19th century, the Parisian elite have flocked to the resorts and thalassotherapy centers (seaside health spas) in the villages along the Côte Fleurie, the northeastern coast of Lower Normandy. These days, tourists come from around the world to admire views of the ocean and to shop for regional delicacies like *Camembert* cheese and *calvados* (apple brandy). Because some of the smaller beach towns between Le Havre and Caen aren't exciting enough to justify their tourist-town prices, hotels and hostels in either city make good budget bases; Bus Verts connections between Le Havre, Caen, Bayeux, and other coastal towns make daytrips a viable option. Travelers doing a lot of touring will find the *Carte Liberté* bus passes useful (p. 296).

HONFLEUR ☎02 31

Miraculously unharmed by WWII, the harbor town of Honfleur (on-FLER; pop. 6000), offers an old-fashioned, quirky charm that fosters an aged population and a close-knit community of artists who often set up their easels in the streets. Large numbers of middle-aged and elderly tourists flock to Honfleur in the sunny months, mostly to browse local art galleries and boutiques, sample regional *liqueurs*, and mill around the picturesque waterfront.

TRANSPORTATION AND PRACTICAL INFORMATION. **Bus Verts** (☎08 10 21 42 14) leave from the *gare routière* at the end of quai Lepaulmier; line #20 goes to Caen (2hr.; 9-15 per day; €7, under 26 €5.95) and Le Havre (30min.; 4-5 per day; €4, under 26 €3.40). (Office open Sept.-June M-F 9am-12:15pm and 2:15-6:15pm, Sa 9am-12:15pm; July-Aug. M-Sa 8:45am-12:15pm and 3:15-6:45pm.) For a **taxi,** call ☎06 08 60 17 98 (24hr.).

To get to the **tourist office,** take a right out of the bus station and follow quai Lepaulmier two blocks. The office offers a good map, with several walking tours (2.5-7km) of the town and its forests. (☎89 23 30; www.ot-honfleur.fr. Open July-Aug. M-Sa 10am-7pm, Su 10am-5pm; Easter-June and Sept. M-Sa 10am-12:30pm and 2-6:30pm, Su 10am-5pm; Oct. to mid-Apr. M-Sa 10am-12:30pm and 2-6pm.) **Tram tours** (40min.) leave weekends in May and daily June-Sept. from the bus stop. (☎89 28 41. €5.60, under 18 €4.10.) **Postal Code:** 14600.

ACCOMMODATIONS AND FOOD. Like most coastal towns, Honfleur is stuffed with extravagant hotels hoping to attract stuffed wallets. Fortunately, **Les Cascades ❸,** 17 pl. Thiers, across from the tourist office with entrances on cours des Fossés and rue de la Ville, offers relatively inexpensive rooms in an ideal location. Airy rooms have window boxes, and some come with skylights. At the elegant seafood restaurant below, *plats* cost €9.50-14 and *menus* run €13-30. (☎89

05 83. Breakfast €6. Open Feb.-Nov. Singles and doubles with shower €32-40, with shower and TV €45-56, with bath €50. AmEx/MC/V.) **Camping du Phare ❶,** 300m from the town center at the end of bd. Charles V, provides basic plots for tents and RVs. Arrive early in summer to get a shaded spot. (☎89 10 26. Laundry. Reception July-Aug. 8:30am-10pm. Gates closed 10pm-7am. €4.90 per person, €3 per child under 12, €6.50 per campsite. Electricity €4.05-5.75. Shower €1.20. Cash only.)

Many relatively pricey and indistinguishable restaurants and *brasseries* along the **quai Ste-Catherine** and on **place Hamelin** provide a taste of local seafood (*menus* €13-25). For cheaper fare, there is a **Champion** supermarket up rue de la République, near pl. Sorel. (Open July-Aug. M-F 8:30am-1pm and 2:30-7:30pm, Sa 8:30am-7:30pm, Su 9am-1pm; Sept.-June M-F 8:30am-12:30pm and 2:30-7:30pm, Sa 8:30am-7:30pm. MC/V.) Wednesday mornings (8am-1pm), there is a **Marché Bio** (organic produce market) on pl. Ste-Catherine, beside the church; the regular market is held there Saturday mornings (8am-1pm). Dozens of occasionally bizarre and always delicious flavors of ice cream make **Pom'Cannelle ❶,** 60 quai Ste-Catherine, worth the price. (☎89 55 25. 1 scoop €2, 2 scoops €3.80. Open in high season daily 9am-11pm; in low season 2-7pm; hours vary. MC/V.) One of the most affordable options near the water, **Le Bistrot à Crêpes ❶,** 1 quai de Passagers, serves *galettes* (€2.50-9.50), *crêpes* (€3-7.50), and fondue (€14-15). A window to the kitchen allows patrons to savor the smells and sounds of cooking. (☎89 74 96. Open daily noon-3pm and 6:30-10pm; hours vary. Cash only.)

SIGHTS. Honfleur's side streets hide architectural delights, small antique shops, specialized boutiques, and countless art studios. The *Pass Musées* gives access to four of Honfleur's museums and its bell tower. (€9.10, students €6.10, under 10 free.) The wooden **Eglise Ste-Catherine,** intended as a temporary construction after its predecessor was destroyed in the Hundred Years' War, dates back to the 15th century. Its peculiar second nave (built to accommodate the growing population of the town) makes it look rather like a mix between an overturned boat and a half-timbered barn. (Open daily Easter-Sept. 9am-6pm; Oct.-Easter 9am-5:30pm. Free.) The church's wooden **bell tower,** across the street, holds a small exhibit of religious art. (€2; included with admission to Musée Eugène Boudin.) Named after Honfleur's most famous artist, the **Musée Eugène Boudin,** pl. Erik Satie, off rue de l'Homme de Bois, emphasizes artists—especially Boudin—who were born or worked in Honfleur and houses a good collection of Impressionist work. (☎89 54 00. Museum and bell tower open mid-Mar. to Sept. M and W-Su 10am-noon and 2-6pm; Oct. to mid-Mar. M and W-F 2:30-5pm, Sa-Su 10am-noon and 2:30-5pm. €4.60, students and under 18 €2.90, under 10 free. Audio tours in French or English, €2. Prices fall in low season. Cash only.) **Maisons Satie,** 67 bd. Charles V, is an interactive museum housed in the birthplace of prolific composer, musician, and artist Erik Satie. After being greeted by a giant winged pear (Satie's trademark image), grapple through the odd mind of an eccentric artist accompanied by a sound track of his compositions. Among the absurdities are a self-playing piano, a robotic monkey butler, and a *laboratoire des émotions*, which allows visitors to generate harmonies by pedaling a musical contraption. (☎89 11 11. Open M and W-Su May-Sept. 10am-7pm; Oct.-Dec. and mid-Feb. to Apr. 11am-6pm. €5.30, students and seniors €3.80, under 10 free. 1hr. audio tour in English or French.) For a hike (sneakers recommended), head to the top of **Mont Joli** by taking rue du Puits up to the winding rampe du Mont Joli. The lookout point offers a beautiful view (especially at sunset) over Honfleur and the **Pont de Normandie,** a suspension bridge connecting Haute- and Basse-Normandie that boasts the tallest pylons in the world. After admiring the scene, take a right on the road at the top and follow it around to the **Chapelle de Notre Dame de Grâce,** a tiny gem with model boats hanging from the ceiling and votive plaques covering the walls. (Open daily

8:30am-5:15pm except during mass.) Kids will enjoy picnicking by the playground in the **public gardens,** down on the Jetée de l'Ouest. (Open daily June-Aug. 8am-9:30pm; Sept.-Oct. and May 8am-7pm; Nov.-Mar. 8am-6pm). Farther along is the broad green expanse of the **Jardin des Personalités** (Garden of Fame), featuring busts of celebrities with a Honfleur connection.

CAEN ☎02 31

At the end of WWII, three-quarters of Caen (KAI-ehn; pop. 114,000) had been destroyed and two-thirds of its citizens were homeless. The city has since been skillfully restored to its pre-war condition and is now part historical monument, part sizzling university city. It makes a good base from which to explore the D-Day beaches, and, with a handful of busy bars and outdoor *brasseries*, it's decidedly younger in tenor and cheaper in price than its neighbors along the Côte Fleurie.

TRANSPORTATION

Trains: Pl. de la Gare. Ticket office open 5am-8:30pm. To: **Cherbourg** (1hr., 7 per day, €18); **Paris** (2¼hr., 11 per day, €29); **Rennes** (3hr., 2 per day, €30); **Rouen** (1½hr., 5-9 per day, €22); **Tours** (3hr., M-F and Su 3 per day, €31).

Buses: Bus Verts (☎08 10 21 42 14), at the *gare routière* to the left of the train station (open Sept.-June M 6:30am-7pm, Tu-F 7:30am-7pm, Sa 8:30am-7pm; July-Aug. M-Sa 7:30am-7pm, Su 9am-3pm) and a kiosk at pl. Courtonne in the *centre-ville* (open M 7:30am-7pm, Tu-F 7:45am-7pm, Sa 9am-7pm). To **Bayeux** (1hr.; M-F 3 per day; €4, under 26 €3.40) and **Le Havre** (2½-3hr.; 3 per day; €10, under 26 €8.50). **Caen-Le Havre express** (1½hr., 2 per day, €14) stops in **Honfleur** (1hr., 2 per day, €9.80). The *Carte Liberté* gives unlimited rides in a given period (1 day €18, 3 days €27, 1 week €43). Schedules change slightly July-Aug.

Ferries: Brittany Ferries to **Portsmouth, England** from Ouistreham, 13km north of Caen. See **Getting There: By Boat,** p. 30. Bus Verts #1 links Ouistreham to Caen's *centre-ville* and train station (40min.; M-F 24 per day, Sa-Su; €2, students €1.70).

Public Transportation: Twisto, the local **bus** and **tram** system, supplies comprehensive schedules and maps at its information office, 15 rue de Geôle (☎15 55 55; twisto.fr), across the street from the château. Open July 15-Aug.15 M-F 9am-5pm; Aug.16-July 14 M-F 8am-6:30pm, Sa 10am-12:30pm and 1:30-5pm; hours vary by season. Smaller kiosk by the Théâtre de Caen open M-F 8am-12:30pm and 1:30-5pm. Tickets €1.20, *carnet* of 10 €9.90, 1-day pass €3.20, weekly pass €11.10.

Taxis: Abbeilles Taxis Caen, 52 pl. de la Gare (☎52 17 89). 24hr. Late-night taxi stand at bd. Maréchal Leclerc near rue St-Jean open daily 10pm-3am.

ORIENTATION AND PRACTICAL INFORMATION

Caen's train station and youth hostel are located quite far from the town center (1km and 3km, respectively). Ambitious travelers can walk from the station, but it's best to take the tram or bus to and from the hostel. Trams stop running just after midnight, so plan accordingly. The two tram lines, A and B, leave from the train station and cut through the city center; take either line to "St-Pierre" (5min.). The St-Pierre station is on the bd. des Alliés, which intersects **avenue du 6 Juin** and **rue St-Jean.** These two parallel streets run toward the city center and border the lively commercial districts between **rue St-Pierre** and **rue de l'Oratoire.**

Tourist Office: Pl. St-Pierre (☎27 14 14; www.tourisme.caen.fr), on rue St-Jean by the Eglise St-Pierre. Hotel booking, useful brochures, and free maps. *Sortir à Caen,* printed

every 3 months, lists concerts and events. City tours July-Aug. in English and French (1hr.; Tu-Sa 1-2 per day; €5-6, students €3.50-4.50, under 10 free). Nighttime tours with historical reenactments in French mid-July to Aug. (2hr.; €13, students and ages 10-18 €9, under 10 free; reservations required). Office open July-Aug. M-Sa 9am-7pm, Su 10am-1pm and 2-5pm; Sept. and Mar.-June M-Sa 9:30am-6:30pm, Su 10am-1pm; Oct.-Feb. M-Sa 9:30am-1pm and 2-6pm, Su 10am-1pm.

Youth Center: Centre Régional d'Information Jeunesse (CRIJ), 16 rue Neuve-St-Jean (☎27 80 80; www.crij-bn.org), off av. du 6 Juin. Info on events, jobs, lodging, and the EU. Photocopiers available. Open M 1-6pm, Tu-Th 10am-6pm, F 10am-5pm.

Laundromat: 17 rue de Prairies St-Gilles (☎06 07 85 58 87). Open daily 7am-9pm. Wash €4 per 8kg, dry €1 per 10min. Also at 16 rue Ecuyère (☎06 80 96 08 26). Open daily 7am-9pm. 33 rue de Geôle (☎06 60 55 75 60). Open daily 7am-9pm.

Public restrooms: Pl. Courtonne, by the Bus Verts kiosk. Free.

Police: 10 rue Thiboud de la Fresnaye (☎29 22 22), at the end of rue Daniel Huet.

Pharmacy: Pharmacie Danjou-Rousselot, 5 pl. Malherbe (☎30 78 00), at the intersection of rue Ecuyère and rue St-Pierre. Open M 9am-7:30pm, Tu-F 8:30am-7:30pm, Sa 9am-7:30pm. Also at 2 bd. des Alliés (☎27 70 10). Open M-Sa 8am-8pm.

Hospital: Centre Hospitalier Universitaire, av. Côte de Nacre (☎06 31 06).

Internet Access: L'Espace, 1 rue Basse (☎53 68 68). Cybercafé offering 50 computers and video and DVD rental. €0.80 per 10min., €1 per 15min., €4.50 per 1½hr. Open M-F 10am-10pm, Sa 10am-11pm, Su 10am-1pm and 3-9pm.

Post Office: Pl. Gambetta (☎39 35 78), past the theater on bd. Maréchal Leclerc. **Currency exchange.** Open M-F 8am-7pm, Sa 8:30am-12:30pm. **Postal Code:** 14000.

ACCOMMODATIONS

In Caen, you'll find a couple of well-situated and reasonably priced options, all of which fill up quickly in the summer.

Auberge de Jeunesse (HI): Résidence Robert Rème, 68 rue Eustache Restout (☎52 19 96; fax 84 29 49). Take bus #5 (dir.: Fleury Cimitière) to "Lycée Fresnel." Walk half a block in the direction the bus came from, then turn right on rue Restout; the hostel will be on your left. Or, take tram B to "Rostand-Fresnel," walk half a block to the roundabout, and turn right onto bd. Foucauld. Make another right on rue Restout–the hostel is on your left. Far from the center of town (3km), but the clean and spacious rooms are worth the trek. 4-person, single-sex dorms with toilet and shower. Facilities include: lockers, communal kitchen, cafeteria, and TV room. Photocopy €0.10 per page, fax €0.20 per page. Breakfast €2. Sheets €2.50. Laundry €3, dry €1.50. Free Wi-Fi. Reception 5-9pm. Check-out 10am. Open June-Sept. Dorms €11. Cash only. ❶

Hôtel de la Paix, 14 rue Neuve-St-Jean (☎86 18 99; fax 8 20 74), off av. du 6 Juin, near the château. Simple, clean rooms with TV and firm beds. Breakfast €5. Reception 24hr. Singles €26, with shower €29, with bath €32; doubles €29/35/37; triples €37/43/45; quads €53. Extra bed €8. AmEx/MC/V. ❷

Hôtel de l'Univers, 12 quai Vendeuvre (☎85 46 14; www.hotelunivers-caen.com), off the Bassin Saint-Pierre. Well-maintained rooms of various sizes all come with TV, telephone, and shower or bath; pricier ones offer a view of the harbor. Breakfast €6. Reception M-F 7:30am-10pm, Sa-Su 8:30am-10pm. Singles €35; doubles €40, with toilet €46-50, with bath €55; triples €60. MC/V. ❸

FOOD

Brasseries compete with Chinese and African restaurants in the **quartier Vaugueux** near the château, and there are plenty of cafés around bd. Maréchal Leclerc. Large markets are held at **place St-Sauveur** (open F 7:30am-1:30pm) and **place Courtonne** (open Su 7:30am-2:30pm); ask at the tourist office for info on smaller markets. A daily produce stand appears on pl. Courtonne, at the end of rue Basse. (Open daily 8am-7pm.) There's also a **Monoprix** supermarket at 45 bd. Maréchal Leclerc. (Open M-Sa 8:30am-8:50pm.)

Maître Corbeau, 8 rue Buquet (☎93 93 00; www.maitre-corbeau.com). Herds of people wait for dinner at the door of this cow-themed eatery, where every dish includes dairy. For a cheaper but still filling meal, skip the dinner crowds and have lunch here instead. *Plats* €7.80-14. Lunch *menu* €9.80. Dinner *menus* €18-23. Dessert €5.10. Open M and Sa 7-10:30pm, Tu-F 11:45am-1:30pm and 7-10:30pm. Closed late Aug. to early Sept. Reservations recommended. MC/V. ❸

Schmilblic, 53 rue Froide, off rue St-Pierre. This mom-and-pop lunch counter is a local favorite for its giant, fresh, made-to-order sandwiches (€3.20-5.05) and *crêpes* (€1-2.20). Cheap and delicious. Open M-F 10:30am-8pm. Cash only. ❶

La Vie Claire, 3-5 rue Basse (☎93 66 72). A vegetarian spot tucked away in the back of an organic food store, serving filling and fresh lunches. *Plats* €4.50-9. Dessert €3-4.50. Store open Tu-Sa 9am-7pm. Open for drinks Tu-W and F-Sa 11am-5pm. Kitchen open 11:45am-2pm. MC/V. ❶

SIGHTS

MÉMORIAL DE CAEN. Hands-down the best—albeit the most expensive—of Normandy's WWII museums, the Mémorial de Caen immerses visitors in a powerful exploration of the war, beginning with the "failure of peace" after WWI, then the battles of WWII, the tensions of the Cold War, and finally the modern prospects for peace. Engaging exhibits unfold with a blend of vintage footage, high-tech audio/visuals, historical artifacts, and contemporary art. Explore the Nobel Peace Prize exhibit in the converted bunker in the basement and the peace gardens designed by different world powers. Allow at least 2hr. to see the museum. Also offers package tours of D-Day beaches. *(Take bus #2 dir.: Mémorial/La Folie to "Memorial." ☎06 06 44; www.memorial-caen.fr. Open mid-Feb. to mid-Nov. daily 9am-7pm; mid-Nov. to early Feb. Tu-Su 9:30am-6pm. Last entry 1¼hr. before closing. €17; students, seniors, and ages 10-18 €16. Prices fall Oct.-Feb. AmEx/MC/V.)*

CHÂTEAU. The ruins of William the Conqueror's enormous château sprawl across a small hill above the center of town. The fortress, built in 1060 and expanded over the centuries, was besieged several times during the Hundred Years' War and served as military barracks in WWII. It now hosts museums in its buildings, picnickers on its vast lawns, and tourists on its ramparts, which are open to the public. The free anthropological **Musée de Normandie,** within the château grounds on the left, displays miniature models, jewelry, clothes, and tools tracing the cultural and agricultural evolution of people living on Norman soil from the beginning of civilization to the present day. *(☎30 47 60; www.musee-de-normandie.caen.fr. 5-6 temporary exhibits per year housed in the church and the Salle de l'Echequiers; €3, students and groups €2, under 18 free. Open June-Sept. daily 9:30am-6pm; Oct.-May M and W-Su 9:30am-6pm.)* To the right as you enter the château are the spacious, well-lit galleries of the free **Musée des Beaux-Arts,** which features a good collection of European art from the 16th century onward. *(☎30 47 70; www.ville-caen.fr/mba. Open M and W-Su 9:30am-6pm. Entrance fee for temporary exhibits.)*

ABBEYS, CHURCHES, AND GARDENS. Caen, the seat of William the Conqueror's duchy, owes its first-class Romanesque architecture chiefly to William's guilty conscience. After he incestuously married his distant cousin Mathilda despite the pope's condemnation, William tried to get back on the road to heaven by building several ecclesiastical structures—most notably Caen's twin abbeys. The **Abbaye-aux-Hommes,** at rue Albert-Sorel, has functioned as a boys' school and as a shelter for 10,000 of the town's inhabitants during WWII; today, it is the Hôtel de Ville. *(☎30 42 81. Open to tourists only for 1½hr. tours in French daily 9:30, 11am, 2:30, 4pm; more July-Aug.; meet in lobby. €2.20, students and seniors €1.10, under 18 free; Su free.)* Inside the late Romanesque and early Gothic architecture of the adjacent **Eglise St-Etienne** is William's tomb, which was pillaged and stripped of all its contents save the monarch's left femur during the Wars of Religion. *(Open M-Sa 8:30am-12:30pm and 1:30-7:30pm, Su 8:30am-12:30pm and 2:30-7:30pm except during services.)* On the other side of the city sits the smaller **Eglise de la Trinité** of the **Abbaye-aux-Dames,** off rue des Chânoines, which houses Mathilda's tomb; it is surrounded by embroidered banners depicting famous biblical and historical religious women. *(☎06 98 98. Church open daily until 5:30pm. Free 1hr. tours in French daily 2:30 and 4pm.)* The sheltered **Jardin des Plantes,** 5 pl. Blot, features wooden arches, baby palm trees, creatively pruned bushes, and its own greenhouse. *(Turn left on rue Bosnières from rue Geôle. ☎30 48 30 32. Open June-Aug. M-F 8am-sunset, Sa-Su 10am-sunset; Sept.-May M-F 8am-5:30pm, Sa-Su 10am-5:30pm. Greenhouse open daily 2-5pm. Free.)*

NIGHTLIFE

Bars and clubs line the **quai Vendeuvre** and populate the area between **Notre-Dame de Froiderue** and the **Abbaye aux Hommes.** To start the evening, university students down cheap drinks amid medieval décor at **Vertigo,** 14 rue Ecuyère, just past the intersection with rue St-Pierre. The bar closes early but stays packed to the last minute. (☎85 43 12. Beer €2.20-2.70. Mixed drinks €4-4.50. Happy hour 7-9pm. Open M-Sa 10am-1am, last service 12:30am. MC/V.) Meanwhile, **Le Semaphore,** 44 rue le Bras, gets lively (and crowded) from 1am on, with loud music, neon lights, and sleek leather bar stools to set the mood. (☎39 08 57. Beer €2.20-3.50. Mixed drinks €3-4.50. Some prices rise after midnight. Happy hour 7-9pm. Open M-Sa 7pm-4am. MC/V.) Head over to **L'Excuse,** 24 rue Vauquelin, to dance the night away. Unusual seating—kegs, for example—provides a break from dancing. (☎38 80 89. Beer €3.50. Mixed drinks €5. Open Tu-Sa midnight-4am. Doors close 3:30am. AmEx/MC/V.) For a more upscale atmosphere, **Farniente,** 13 rue Paul Doumer, is an ultra-modern lounge that screams "underground chic." (☎86 30 00. Beer €2.50-3. Mixed drinks €5-6. DJ nightly. Open Th-Sa 6pm-4am. AmEx/MC/V.)

BAYEUX ☎02 31

Bayeux (BAH-yuh; pop. 15,000) may be most famous for its 900-year-old tapestry narrating William the Conqueror's victory over England, but the lively city offers more than historical needlework. Narrowly escaping the devastation of WWII and surviving both Nazi occupation in 1940 and Allied liberation in 1944, Bayeux today retains its charming architecture and a resplendent cathedral. The city's old-world atmosphere, pleasant—if slightly touristy—pedestrian byways, and manifold D-Day tour operators cater to a map-toting middle-aged crowd, but Bayeux makes an equally appealing base for younger travelers looking to tour WWII sites.

TRANSPORTATION

Trains: pl. de la Gare. Ticket office open M-Th 6am-8:40pm, F 6am-9:40pm, Sa 6:30am-9:20pm, Su 8:30am-9:20pm. To **Caen** (20min., 11 per day, €5.40), **Cherbourg** (1hr., 6 per day, €15), and **Paris** (2½hr., 7 per day, €32).

Buses: Bus Verts, pl. de la Gare (office ☎92 02 92, company 08 10 21 42 14). Buy tickets on board or at the office. Open June-Aug. M-F 9:30am-1:15pm and 2:30-6:45pm, Sa 10:15am-1:15pm and 2:30-4:30pm; Sept.-May M-Sa 10am-noon. Buses head west to small towns and east to **Caen** (Line 30; 1hr.; M-F 2-3 per day; €4, under 26 €3.40). Full-day *Carte Liberté* €12. See p. 303 for transport to D-Day beaches.

Public Transportation: Bybus, pl. de la Gare (☎92 02 92), in the same office as Bus Verts. Runs local buses 7:30am-6pm. Open June-Aug. M-F 9:30am-1:15pm and 2:30-6:45pm, Sa 10:15am-1:15pm and 2:30-4:30pm; Sept.-May 10am-noon. Tickets 9-11:30am €0.95, 2-4pm €0.70; *carnet* of 10 €7.10, under 20 €6.50. Buy tickets on board, *carnets* at the office.

Taxis: Taxis du Bessin (☎92 92 40), train station. Prices rise 50% 7pm-7am and Su.

ORIENTATION AND PRACTICAL INFORMATION

To get to the center of town from the train station, bear right to reach bd. Sadi Carnot, then turn left and follow it to a roundabout. Go right at the roundabout up rue Larcher to reach the **Cathedral.** Past the Cathedral on rue de Nesmond (which becomes rue de la Maitrise), lies **Place Charles de Gaulle.** The river **L'Aure,** running through the city, is traversed by several *ponts.*

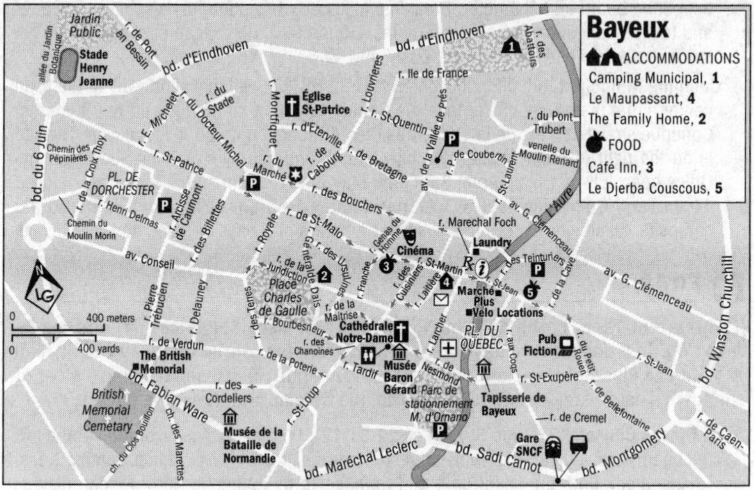

Tourist Office: Pont St-Jean (☎51 28 28; www.bayeux-bessin-tourism.com). From rue Larcher, make a right on rue St-Jean; the office is on the left (20min. from train station). English-speaking staff dispenses a city and regional guide and info on D-Day tours. Open July-Aug. M-Sa 9am-7pm, Su 9am-1pm and 2-6pm; Apr.-June and Sept.-Oct. daily 9:30am-12:30pm and 2-6pm; Nov.-Mar. M-Sa 9:30am-12:30pm and 2-5:30pm.

ATMs: Available around pl. St-Patrice, and up rue St-Martin (becomes rue St-Malo).

Laundromat: 10 rue Maréchal Foch (☎06 08 24 69 98). Wash €3.40-6.80, dry €0.40 per 5min. Open daily 7am-9pm.

Public restrooms: Near the cathedral on rue Leforestier.

Police: 2 pl. St-Patrice (☎92 02 42). Open M-F 8:30am-noon and 2-6pm, Sa 11am-noon.

Pharmacy: Pharmacie du Pont St-Jean, 1 rue St-Jean (☎92 07 63). Open M-F 8:30am-12:30pm and 1:30-7:30pm, Sa 8:30am-12:30pm and 1:30-7pm.

Hospital: 13 rue de Nesmond (☎51 51 51).

Internet Access: Pub Fiction, 14 rue Petit Rouen (☎10 17 41), close to rue St-Jean. 1 computer. €1 per 15min. Open M-Th 8:30pm-2am, F-Sa 8:30pm-3am.

Post Office: 14 rue Larcher (☎51 24 90). **Currency exchange, ATM,** and photocopies (€0.10 per page). Open M-F 8:15am-6:30pm, Sa 8:15am-noon. **Postal Code:** 14400.

ACCOMMODATIONS AND CAMPING

Demand for lodging often exceeds supply in Bayeux, especially during the summer months; it pays to call ahead, but don't expect to find anything terribly cheap. Caen is a cheaper base for the D-Day beaches. Plan with military precision if you want a room around June 6, the anniversary of D-Day.

Le Maupassant, 19 rue St-Martin (☎92 28 53; h.lemaupassant@orange.fr). Small, cheerful, clean rooms at the top of a wooden spiral staircase. On the ground fl., a **brasserie** ❶ serves salads (€7-9) and sandwiches (€3-5) on a pedestrian-filled street in the town center. Some rooms come with toilet; all have TV. Breakfast €5.80. Reception at bar 7:30am-9pm. Singles €29; doubles with shower €40; quads with bath €69. Extra bed €10. MC/V. ❷

The Family Home/Auberge de Jeunesse (HI), 39 rue Général de Dais (☎92 15 22). Dorms are in slight disrepair; nice breakfast room and stone courtyard with a British telephone booth add character. Breakfast included. Reception hours sporadic. Shower and toilet in hall and in some dorm rooms. Dorms €20. Help clean the kitchen and get lunch and a free bed for the night. Cash only. ❷

Camping Municipal, bd. d'Eindhoven (☎/fax 92 08 43), within a short walk of the town center. From the tourist office, take rue Genas Duhomme to the right off rue St-Martin. Continue straight on av. de la Vallée des Prés. Turn right onto bd. d'Eindhoven. The site is on the right (12min.). Volleyball, playground, and nearby swimming pool. Laundry. Office open July-Aug. 7am-9pm; Sept. and May-June 8-10am and 5-7pm. Gates closed 10pm-7am. Open May-Sept. €3.17 per adult, €1.68 per child under 7, €3.90 per campsite. Electricity €3.21. 10% discount for stays of 5 days or more. AmEx/MC/V. ❶

FOOD

There are markets in the morning (7am-1pm) on **place St-Patrice** (Sa) and **rue St-Jean** (W). Just down the pedestrian walkway from the tourist office on rue St-Jean is a **Marché Plus** supermarket. (Open M-Sa 7am-9pm, Su 8:30am-12:30pm.) Most of the town's eateries populate **rue St-Martin, rue St-Jean,** and their side streets.

Le Djerba Couscous, 67 rue St-Jean (☎22 51 12). With authentic decoration and a luxurious upstairs lounge, this Tunisian restaurant maintains a level of unassuming class. Take a break from the usual *pain* and *fromage* to try authentic North African dishes, including astonishingly filling (you guessed it) couscous. *Plats* €8.50-18. *Menus* €14-22. Open Tu-Su 6:30-10:30pm. MC/V. ❸

Café Inn, 67 rue St-Martin (☎21 11 37). A quiet corner perfect for a tea break or a snack. Offers salads (€5-7.30), sandwiches (€3.55-4.55), omelettes (€5), and pastries (€2.20-6.85). Open M-Sa 9am-7pm. MC/V. ❶

SIGHTS

TAPISSERIE DE BAYEUX. In 1066, Guillaume le Bâtard (William the Bastard) earned himself a more regal nickname by crossing the Channel with a large cavalry to defeat his distant cousin Harold, who, according to the Norman version of the tale, had stolen the English throne from William. After a grueling 10hr. battle in which Harold was dramatically killed by an archer, William triumphed in the last successful invasion of England—The Battle of Hastings—to become *le Conquérant* (the Conqueror). In 58 frames, this exquisite tapestry uses striking narrative techniques to illustrate the events leading up to and including the battle. A mere 50cm wide, but 70m long, the tapestry, now over 900 years old, hangs in all its glory at the **Centre Guillaume le Conquérant.** An edifying exhibit, including an annotated reprint of the tapestry and a film shown in English and French, precedes the viewing of the masterpiece itself. A well-paced audio tour, included in the entry ticket, is available in 14 languages. *(Rue de Nesmond. ☎51 25 50; www.tapisserie-bayeux.fr. Open daily May-Aug. 9am-7pm; Sept.-Oct. and mid-Mar. to Apr. 9am-6:30pm; Nov. to mid-Mar. 9:30am-12:30pm and 2-6pm. Last entrance 45min. before closing. €7.70, students and seniors €3.80.)*

CATHÉDRALE NOTRE DAME. The original home of the tapestry, Bayeux's Romanesque-style cathedral was consecrated in 1077. Its flamboyant, ornate central tower contrasts with the simpler twin towers at either side of the entrance. Dizzyingly intricate Gothic arches soar above the transept; beneath, the 11th-century crypt displays fading 15th-century frescoes. To the left of the entrance is the *salle capitulaire*, open only by guided tour. The room contains France's sole *chemin de Jerusalem*, a tile labyrinth in the floor that retraces Jesus's *via crucis*, the route he followed to Calvary. *(Rue de Bienvenue. ☎92 01 85. Open daily July-*

Sept. 8:30am-7pm; Apr.-June 8am-6pm; Oct.-Dec. 8:30am-6pm; Jan.-Mar. 9am-5pm. French tours of the vieille ville, *including access to the cathedral's labyrinth and treasury, offered by nearby Musée Baron Gérard daily July-Aug. 4pm. ☎92 14 21. €4, under 15 free.)*

LOCAL D-DAY SIGHTS. The events of the D-Day landing and the subsequent 76-day struggle for control of northern France are recounted in the **Musée de la Bataille de Normandie,** which was redesigned and reopened in June 2006. A stirring film in both English and French dramatizes the Battle of Normandy; a collection of war artifacts, from tanks to signposts to guns, accompanies the step-by-step illustration of each phase in the long battle. *(Bd. Fabian Ware. ☎51 46 90. Open daily May-Sept. 9:30am-6:30pm; Oct.-Apr. 10am-12:30pm and 2-6pm. Closed last 2 weeks of Jan. Last entrance 1hr. before closing. €6.50, students €3.80, under 10 free. English-language film every 2hr. MC/V.)* The rows of closely-set tombstones that line the **British Military Cemetery,** on the other side of the road from the museum, mark the graves of 4144 Commonwealth soldiers who died in the Battle of Normandy. The **British Memorial** across the street, which names the soldiers without graves, bears the Latin inscription "We, conquered by William, have freed the homeland of our conqueror."

D-DAY BEACHES

In 1943, German forces along the northern coasts of France fortified their defences. The Allies learned the difficulty of attacking a major port from the failed 1942 Dieppe raid, in which dozens of Canadians were either killed or taken prisoner. However, convinced that the only way to overthrow Hitler was to take his "Fortress Europe" by sea, and desperate to open a second front in order to relieve the pressure on the Russian Eastern front, Allied commanders decided that Normandy would be their beach-head for the liberation of France. Allied forces set the stage for the infiltration by flooding German intelligence services with false information and planting dummy tanks near Norway to confuse General Rommel and his troops. The action began in the pre-dawn hours of **June 6, 1944,** when 29,000 troops tumbled from the sky onto the coast between the Cotentin Peninsula and Orne. A few hours later, 130,000 more troops arrived by sea; by the end of June 850,000 had landed. The losses incurred on D-Day were devastating to both sides; the Allies alone lost 10,300 troops. The Allied victory was a key precursor to the August 25th liberation of Paris on, and later successes.

TRANSPORTATION AND ORIENTATION

Americans landed at the westernmost beaches, code-named Utah and Omaha; though you might find the occasional sunbather at these sites, they saw the bloodiest battles and consequently have changed the least since the invasion. **Voie de la Liberté** (Liberty Road) follows the US Army's advance to Bastogne, Belgium. British troops landed in the east at Gold and Sword, and Canadians landed at Juno. In the center, between Omaha and Gold, lies Arromanches, where the Allies hastily constructed one of two crucial offshore ports.

Bayeux makes the best base for the western and central beaches (Utah, Omaha, and Gold) and is home to companies offering guided tours; Caen has better access by bus to Juno and Sword. The best way to see the sights is undoubtedly by **car**—not only can you get farther and go at your own pace, but you'll also have the opportunity to stop at any of the myriad museums along the route. Even with a car, it is extremely difficult to get to all of the sights in a single day, as the beaches span over 50 miles. If driving is out of the question, get ready for a logistical nightmare involving erratic bus schedules. For a quick visit, it's best to focus on a single beach or a group of neighboring beaches; if you are careful with your bus connections, Juno and Sword Beaches can both be visited in one day, as can Utah and Omaha. **Bus Verts** is by far the cheapest way to get from sight to sight and offers many well-chosen routes, especially from July-August when service expands (see below). Numerous companies offer guided **minibus tours** of the major sights. These tours, typically geared toward visitors from a particular country involved in the D-Day invasion, are pricey but educational—quality ranges widely among different tour guides even within the same company, though, so it's a bit of a gamble. Call in advance to reserve. For the light-pocketed and physically fit, **biking** to the beaches is a viable option, though cyclists will only be able to visit a limited number of sites. Walking from beach to beach is practically impossible.

Bus Verts (☎08 10 21 42 14), offices in Bayeux and Caen. Provides no-frills bus service throughout Normandy. Special D-Day lines running once a day in July and Aug. leave from Caen and Bayeux and visit the 3 central beaches (**Omaha, Gold,** and **Juno**). Ask at office for complete listing of lines. Tickets €1.50-10 (under 26 €1.28-8.50), depending on distance. If you plan to do multiple D-Day sights by bus, consider buying a *carte liberté,* which allows unlimited rides for 1, 3, or 7 days (€12/22/32).

From Bayeux: Line #70 serves the area of **Omaha Beach,** with stops near **Pointe du Hoc** and the **American Cemetery** (M-Sa 2 per day). Line #74 serves **Gold** and **Juno Beaches,** with stops at **Arromanches, Ver-sur-Mer,** and **Courselles-sur-Mer** (M-Sa 3 per day). In July-Aug., line #75 runs from Bayeux to the sights on **Gold** and **Juno Beaches,** as well as **Sword Beach,** the easternmost beach by the port of **Ouistreham.**

From Caen: Line #1 serves **Sword Beach;** a transfer to line #3 will take you to **Juno;** another transfer to line #74 can take you on to **Gold;** you'll have trouble returning to Caen the same evening.

Normandy Sightseeing Tours (☎02 31 51 70 52; www.normandywebguide.com), based in Bayeux. ½- and full-day tours offering stops at the beaches, various museums, and lesser-known (and often completely unmarked) sights. Enthusiastic and incredibly knowledgeable English-speaking guides. 3hr. morning tours €40, students €35, under 10 €25; 4¾hr. afternoon tours €45/40/30; 9hr. full-day tours €75/65/45. Pick-up in Bayeux at the train station, at pl. du Québec, or at your hotel. MC/V.

Overlordtour (☎06 70 21 43 42; www.overlordtour.com). Anecdotes and historical photos add flair to tours in English and French. Personalized tours also available. ½-day tour €40, full-day tour €75. Tours depart from pl. du Québec in Bayeux.

Vélos Location, Impasse de l'Islet, or 5 rue Larcher (☎02 31 92 89 16). Bike rental ½-day €10, full-day €15, week €90; passport deposit.

WESTERN D-DAY SIGHTS

POINTE DU HOC. The US Ranger Force at Pointe du Hoc performed the most difficult landing at D-Day. These 225 specially trained Rangers scaled the sheer 30m bluffs on ropes and ladders under the rain of German gunfire and grenades, and successfully neutralized a key German naval battery. Expecting to be reinforced within 12hr., the surviving Rangers ended up defending the position alone against German counterattacks for two and a half days, despite having lost the majority of their supplies at sea during the landing. The ground is still pockmarked from the intense shelling that preceded the Rangers' landing, and shattered fragments of concrete bunkers cover the grassy terrain. *(☎02 31 51 90 70; www.cc-isigny-grandcamp-intercom.fr Info office open Apr.-Oct. daily 10am-1pm and 2-6pm; Nov.-Mar. M and F-Su 9am-1pm and 2-5pm. Grounds open daily 9am-6pm.)*

AMERICAN CEMETERY. On a cliff overlooking Omaha Beach in **Colleville-sur-Mer,** over 9000 American gravestones stretch in endless rows across a pristine 172-acre coastal reserve. A marble memorial with giant maps of the Allied advance and a 7m bronze statue, *The Spirit of American Youth Rising from the Waves*, face

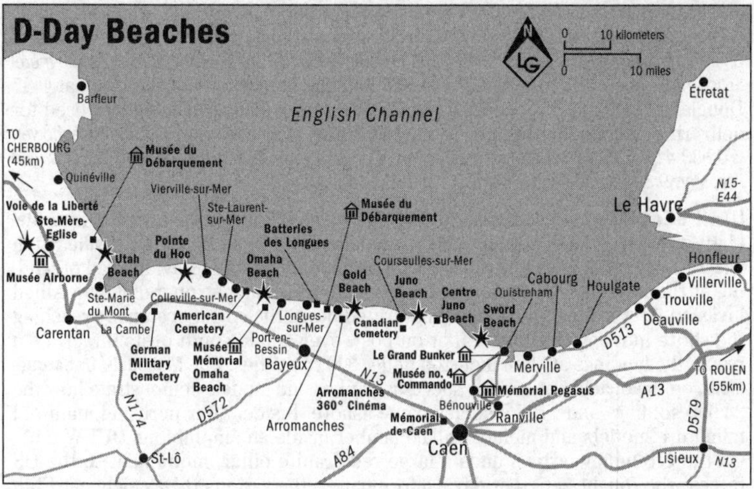

the graves. The **Garden of the Missing,** behind the statue, lists the names of 1557 soldiers whose remains were never recovered. The neat rows of white headstones, which hold only a fraction of those who died in France, are a moving reminder of the June 6 sacrifices. The newly-opened Visitors' Center has exhibits commemorating American losses and touch-screen computer catalogs for locating graves. *(☎02 31 51 62 00; www.abmc.gov. Open daily May-Sept. 9am-6pm; Oct.-Apr. 9am-5pm.)*

OMAHA BEACH. Often referred to as "bloody Omaha," this site near **Colleville-sur-Mer** saw perhaps the most famous—and by far the most disastrous—invasion. Preliminary Allied bombing did little damage here due to stormy weather and poor visibility; as a result, the German defenses were operating near full capacity. Bunkers (still visible on the hills above the beach) along the length of the coast mowed down hundreds of men and destroyed vehicles and equipment. The first waves of men, caught on the barbed wire and obstacles littering the beach, suffered 85% casualties. Little remains on the beach itself to mark the sacrifices made here, but up the road the **Musée Mémorial d'Omaha Beach,** av. de la Libération, presents uniforms, helmets, and equipment, as well as dioramas telling the story of the longest day of WWII. *(☎02 31 21 97 44; www.musee-memorial-omaha.com. Open daily July-Aug. 9:30am-7:30pm; mid-May to June and Sept. 7:30am-7pm; mid-Mar. to mid-May 9:30am-6:30pm; mid-Feb. to mid-Mar. 10am-12:30pm and 2:30-6pm.)*

GERMAN MILITARY CEMETERY. In **La Cambe,** not far from the American sights, are the often-overlooked graves of 21,300 German casualties, a reminder of the tragic costs of the war on both sides. *(☎02 31 22 70 76. Open Apr.-Oct. M-F 8am-7pm, Sa-Su 9am-7pm; Nov.-Mar. M-F 8am-5pm, Sa-Su 9am-5pm.)*

STE-MÈRE-EGLISE. During the invasion, many Allied paratroopers of the 82nd Airborne were accidentally dropped directly into this small town—including John Steele, who hung from the church steeple for two hours in the midst of a fierce firefight before being taken prisoner by the Germans. On the church for which this town is named, a model paratrooper still hangs from the roof, his parachute caught on a gable. Despite heavy casualties, the operation was a success after six hours of fighting, when the badly outnumbered paratroopers finally broke through heavy German defenses. Inside the church, a stained-glass window shows Mary and Jesus with paratroopers descending on either side. *(☎02 33 41 41 48; http://saintemereeglise50.cef.fr. Open daily except during services. The village is accessible by bus from Cherbourg. Tourist info for the town, 6 rue Eisenhower. ☎02 33 21 00 33; www.sainte-mere-eglise.info.)* The parachute-shaped **Musée Airborne** houses one of the original C-47 Douglas planes that dropped the paratroopers, as well as a Waco glider used for delivering equipment and a wide range of other war materiel. *(14 rue Eisenhower. ☎02 33 41 41 35; www.airborne-museum.org. Open daily Apr.-Sept. 9am-6:45pm; Oct.-Nov. and Feb.-Mar. 9:30am-noon and 2-6pm. €6, ages 6-14 €3. MC/V.)*

UTAH BEACH. Americans spearheaded the western flank of the invasion near **Ste-Marie-du-Mont** at Utah Beach, which runs along the coast below **Quinéville.** Utah was one of the luckiest and most successful operations of D-Day. Instead of landing at the intended location, a heavily fortified German strongpoint, the Allied invasion fleet lost its patrol boat and drifted down the coast, eventually reaching the shore in front of a far weaker outpost, over a mile south of its target. As a result, the landings at Utah incurred under 200 casualties. The **Musée du Débarquement,** on the beach, honors this success; its films and models demonstrate how the 23,000 soldiers and 1790 vehicles came ashore. Inside, after perusing manifold miniature models and memorabilia, clamber inside an amphibious DUKW tank. On the grounds nearby stands a large red granite pillar, monument to the US forces who fought here that day. Unfortunately, the various D-Day sights at Utah are not accessible by public transportation. *(☎02 33 71 53 35; www.utah-beach.com. Open daily June-Sept. 9:30am-7pm; Apr.-May and Oct. 10am-6pm; Nov. and Feb.-Mar. 10am-5:30pm. €5.50, students €4, ages 6-16 €2.50. MC/V.)*

EASTERN D-DAY SIGHTS

ARROMANCHES. This small town just west of **Gold Beach** was where the British built Port Winston (a.k.a. Mulberry B), the floating harbor that supplied the Allied forces until the Cherbourg port was repaired months later. The Allies sank retired ships as breakwaters and towed over 600,000 tons of concrete across the channel in order to build the port. Sixty years later, the hulking ruins of a harbor built in six days and designed to last only 18 months remain floating in a broken semicircle just off the coast. **Arromanches 360° Cinéma,** on the cliffs above the remains of the port, shows a well-made wordless 18min. film, *Le Prix de la Liberté* (The Price of Freedom). The circular screen around the entire viewing room allows visitors to vicariously fly planes over Pointe du Hoc, wait in pontoons just offshore, and storm the beaches as the troops did on June 6. *(Chemin du Calvaire. ☎02 31 22 30 30; www.arromanches360.com. Open daily June-Aug. 9:40am-6:40pm; early Sept. and mid- to late May 10:10am-6:10pm; mid-Sept. to Oct. and Apr. to mid-May 10:10am-5:40pm; Nov. and Mar. 10:10am-5:10pm; Dec. and Feb. 10:10am-4:40pm. Movies at 10 and 40min. past the hr. €4; students, seniors, and ages 10-18 €3.50; under 10 and veterans free. MC/V.)* **Musée du Débarquement,** on the beach, tells the history of the port. *(Pl. du 6 Juin. ☎02 31 22 34 31; www.normandy1944.com. Open June-Aug. daily 9am-7pm; May M-Sa 9am-7pm, Su 10am-7pm; Sept. M-Sa. 9am-6pm, Su 10am-6pm; Apr. M-Sa 9am-12:30pm and 1:30-6pm, Su 10am-12:30pm and 1:30-6pm; Oct. and Mar. M-Sa 9:30am-12:30pm and 1:30-5:30pm, Su 10am-12:30pm and 1:30-5:30pm; Nov. to mid-Dec. and Feb. daily 10am-12:30pm and 1:30-5pm. Guided 1¼hr. tours. €6.50, students and under 18 €4.50.)* **Gold Beach** can be seen from the nearby town of Asnelles; a lone German bunker, now blocked up, held the British forces at bay here for six hours before being silenced by a mortar.

JUNO BEACH. Approximately 14,000 Canadians—some on bicycles—along with 6000 Brits, invaded Norman soil at Juno Beach. The last time Canadians had set foot in France, in the 1942 Dieppe raid, they suffered disastrous losses and appalling casualties. Bent on revenge at Juno, Canadians pushed their attacks farther inland than any other Allied units. The **Centre Juno Beach,** located in **Courseulles-sur-Mer** and staffed by Canadian university students, tells the story of the war from the Canadian perspective. Nearby, a giant *Croix de Lorraine*, symbol of the "Free French," marks the spot where General de Gaulle first returned to French soil in 1944. *(Voie des Français Libres. ☎02 31 37 32 17; www.junobeach.org. Open daily Apr.-Sept. 9:30am-7pm; Oct. and Mar. 10am-6pm; Feb. and Nov.-Dec. 10am-1pm and 2-5pm. €6.50, students €5, under 8 free. With guided tour of park €9/7/free. MC/V over €15.)* The **Canadian Cemetery,** with just over 2000 tombs, is located at **Bény-sur-Mer-Reviers,** accessible by bus from Caen.

BATTERIE DE LONGUES. In tiny **Longues-sur-Mer,** 6km west of Arromanches, these heavily fortified bunkers are a somber reminder of the German presence. Naval bombardment on D-Day destroyed the town but left these bunkers and their guns mostly intact. Now the only remaining armed bunkers in the region, the Batterie de Longues are open for visitors to explore. *(☎02 31 21 46 87; www.bayeux-bessin-tourism.com Open Apr.-Oct. daily 10am-1pm and 2-6pm; Nov.-Mar. F-Su 10am-6pm. 1hr. tours in English and French 5 times daily Apr.-Oct. €4, under 10 free.)*

MÉMORIAL PEGASUS. On June 5, 1944, before any other Allied troops had arrived in Normandy, British paratroopers floated from the sky to capture the bridge code-named Pegasus between Benouville and Ranville. They achieved their goal within 10min. of landing and held the bridge until Scottish reinforcements arrived days later. This museum, also known as the Musée des Troupes Aéroportées Britanniques, is located at the site of the bridge and recounts the operations of the British Parachute Brigades behind enemy lines on D-Day. The museum grounds hold the actual bridge, as well as a full-scale model of the Horsa glider used to transport men and equipment. *(Av. du Major Howard, at the Pegasus Bridge between Benouville and Ranville. Take Bus Verts #1 from Caen to "Mairie" in Benouville. Take a right at the roundabout 200ft. away and cross the bridge; the museum is on the left. ☎02 31 78 19 44; www.normandy1944.com. Open daily Apr.-Sept. 9:30am-6:30pm; Oct.-Nov. and Feb.-Mar. 10am-1pm and 2-5pm. €6, students and under 18 €4.50.)*

OUISTREHAM. The British anchored the eastern flank of the invasion at **Sword Beach,** whose easternmost edge is now a popular beach town. The British success is memorialized by **Le Grand Bunker: Musée du Mur de l'Atlantique,** a former German bunker five stories high, which was the last part of the town to be captured, completely intact, when the garrison inside surrendered. The bunker's rooms have been recreated, complete with infirmary, communications room, weapons storage, and a working range-finding tower. The top of the tower is also open, accessible by iron rungs set in the concrete. *(Av. du 6 Juin. ☎02 31 97 28 69. Open daily Apr.-Sept. 9am-7pm; Feb.-Mar. and Oct. to mid-Nov. 10am-6pm. €6.50, ages 6-12 €4.50.)* Also in Ouistreham is the small **Musée no. 4 Commando,** which shows more artifacts from the war and models of soldiers in uniform. *(Pl. Alfred Thomas. ☎02 31 96 63 10. Open Mar.-Oct. 10:30am-6pm. €4.50, students €2.50.)*

CHERBOURG ☎02 33

Strategically located at the tip of the Cotentin peninsula, the port of Cherbourg (shehr-BOORGH; pop. 44,000) was a major Allied objective following the D-Day invasion; unfortunately, by the time the city was liberated, the Nazis had damaged its port so badly that it was non-functioning for six months. Now in working order, the port shuttles ferries to England and Ireland. Though the homey seaside city is short on noteworthy sights, it proudly holds a new aquarium and a *vieille ville* with enough bars, restaurants, and unusual boutiques to keep visitors busy.

TRANSPORTATION. Trains (ticket office open M-Sa 5:30am-7:55pm, Su 7:30am-8:45pm) run to Paris (3hr., 6 per day, €41) via Bayeux (1hr., 9 per day, €15) and Caen (1½hr., 11 per day, €18); you can also change trains at Lison to reach Rennes (3½hr., 3 per day, €32). VTNI/STN (☎44 32 22) sends **buses** to a variety of regional destinations; the station is across the street from the train station. (Open M-F 9am-12:30pm and 2-5:30pm.) **Ferries** leave from the **Gare Maritime Transmanche,** a 45min. walk from the town center along bd. Maritime. Brittany Ferries (☎08 25 82 88 28, www.brittanyferries.fr; office open June-Aug. daily 6am-9:30pm, reduced hours Sept.-May) go to Portsmouth and Poole (1-2hr.; 2-3 per day late May to Sept., every other day Oct. to mid-May). See **Getting There: By Boat,** p. 30. Irish Ferries make the overnight trip to Rosslare about every other day (☎23 44 44; www.irishferries.com; office open M-F 9am-noon and 2-6pm), as does Celtic Link, three times a week (☎43 23 87; www.celticlinkferries.com; office open M-Tu and Th-F 9am-1pm and 2-7pm, W 9am-1pm and 2-9:30pm, Su noon-5:30pm).

A local **bus** runs daily about seven times per day, in the early morning and late evening; at other times, walking or taking a taxi are the only options. Zéphir, 40 bd. Schuman, runs **city buses;** there is a stop in front of the STN office. (Buses run 6:30am-8pm. Tickets €1.10, *carnet* of 10 €9; night buses F-Sa €0.60.) Rent **bikes** and get info on nautical activities at Station Nautique, rue de Diablotin. (☎78 19 29; www.cherbourg-hague-nautisme.com. €7 per ½-day, €12 per day, €70 per week. Open July-Aug. daily 10am-6pm; Sept.-May M-Sa 9am-12:30pm and 1:30-6pm.) **Taxis** (☎53 36 38) wait at the train station and at the *gare maritime.*

ORIENTATION AND PRACTICAL INFORMATION. To reach the center of town and the **tourist office,** 2 quai Alexandre III, from the train station, turn right and cross av. Jean-Françoise. Continue to quai Alexander III, and walk along the *bassin.* The staff distributes excellent maps, a city guide, and a calendar of regional events, and leads hikes and bus tours on certain days in summer; reservations required. (☎93 52 02; www.ot-cherbourg-cotentin.fr. Open July-Aug. M-Sa 9am-6:30pm, Su 10am-12:30pm; June M-Sa 9am-12:30pm and 2-6:30pm; Sept.-May M-Sa 9am-12:30pm and 2-6pm.) The office has an annex at the *gare maritime.* (☎44 39 92. Open Apr.-Oct.; hours vary.) **Currency exchange** is available at 53 rue Maréchal Foch (☎20 08 27.) Other services include: a **laundromat,** 62 rue au Blé (open daily July-Sept. 7am-9pm; Oct.-June 7am-8pm); **public restrooms** on rue des Halles, just off pl. Général de Gaulle (open 9am-6:30pm); **police,** 2 rue du Val de Saire (☎88 76 76); **Pharmacie Goffin,** at 1 pl. du Général de Gaulle, off rue Maréchal Foch (☎20 41 29; open M-F 9am-12:30pm and 1:30-7:30pm, Sa 9am-12:30pm and 2-7pm); a **hospital,** 46 rue du Val de Saire (☎20 70 00); and **Internet** access at **Archesys,** 16 rue de l'Union (☎53 04 93; €0.50 per 6min., €5 per hr.; open Tu-F 11:30am-10pm, Sa 11:30am-midnight, Su 2-10pm), or at the hostel for guests. The **post office,** 1 rue de l'Ancien Quai, on pl. Divette, offers **currency exchange.** (☎08 87 01. Open M-F 8am-7pm, Sa 9am-noon.) There is a branch at 4 rue de Commerce. (☎10 12 50. Open Tu-F 8:45am-12:15pm and 1:30-6pm, Sa 9am-noon.) **Postal Code:** 50100.

ACCOMMODATION. The tourist office has lists of *chambres d'hôte* (€25-60) and campsites. The cheapest option is the modern **Auberge de Jeunesse (HI) ❶,** 55 rue de l'Abbaye. From the tourist office, turn left on quai de Caligny, then left on rue de Port, which becomes rue Tour Carrée and rue de la Paix. Bear left on rue de l'Union, which feeds into rue de l'Abbaye (10min.). From the train station, take bus #3 or 5 to Arsenal (last bus around 7:30pm), cross the street, and head back a half-block. Across town from the train station, this hostel has neat two- to five-person rooms, each with sink and shower. A kitchen, bar, TV, foosball table, and pool table are also on the premises. (☎78 15 15; cherbourg@fuaj.org. Breakfast included. Internet access €0.50 per 30min. Reception 9am-1pm and 6-11pm. Check-out 10am. Dorms €20. MC/V.) Run by an amiable, English-speaking staff, **Hôtel de la Gare ❸,** 10 pl. Jean-Jaurès, across the street from the station, is easy to find but far from the center of town. Basic rooms all have satellite TV and phone. (☎43 06 81; fax 43 12 20. Breakfast €6-7. Reception 8am-10pm. July-Aug. singles and doubles with shower €33-36, with shower and toilet €41-44; triples €53-62. Sept.-June €28-31/36-39/48-57. MC/V.)

FOOD. There is a market on place du Théâtre (8am-1pm; small market Tu and Sa, larger market Th). A huge Carrefour supermarket, quai de l'Entrepôt, is across the street from the station (open M-Th and Sa 8:30am-9pm, F 8:30am-9:30pm). Bars and kebab counters (€3.50-8) line rue de la Paix between the hostel and pl. de la République. Crêperie Ty-Billic ❶, 73 rue au Blé, is a tourist-free haven with a casual but elegant atmosphere and a wide selection. The ***menu*** is a full meal of two ***galettes,*** two ***crêpes,*** and a cider for €12-16; single ***galettes*** and ***crêpes*** run €2-8. (☎01 11 90. Open Tu-Sa 11am-2pm and 7-11pm. MC/V.) For a more upscale meal, try L'Antidote ❸, 41 rue au Blé, in a secluded stone courtyard surrounded by hanging paper lanterns. Indulge in delicious meat and fish ***plats*** (€8-14), exquisite desserts (€5), and a wide selection of wines. ***Menus*** €17-24. (☎78 01 28. Open Tu-Sa July-Aug. 10am-1am; Sept.-June 10am-2pm and 6-11pm. Lunch Tu-Sa noon-2pm; dinner Tu-Th 7-10pm, F-Sa 7-11pm. MC/V.)

SIGHTS AND ENTERTAINMENT. Cherbourg's newest and best attraction is **La Cité de la Mer,** located on a pier halfway between the tourist office and the ferry terminal. The site's 11m-tall aquarium—the tallest in Europe—holds 3500 creatures, while smaller tanks feature exotic underwater attractions like black seahorses and fluorescent blue jellyfish. A large touch tank has four different species of rays. The biggest attraction at the Cité, though, is the 128-meter **Le Redoutable,** the first French nuclear submarine ever built, now open to visitors from bow to stern on an audio tour (available in Dutch, English, French, and German). The main entrance to the Cité, housed inside a former ferry terminal, includes a post office, tourist office, restaurant, bar, and public restrooms. (☎20 26 69; www.citedelamer.com. Open daily July-Aug. 9:30am-7pm; May-June and Sept. 9:30am-6pm; Oct.-Dec. and Feb.-Mar. 10am-6pm. Last entry 1hr. before closing. Apr.-Sept. €15, ages 6-17 €11; Oct.-Mar. €13/9; under 6 free.) With intricate latticework, pillars carved in elaborate patterns, and dark, angular windows, the **Basilique de la Trinité,** 8 pl. Napoléon, off quai de Caligny, features a blend of architectural styles several centuries in the making. Above the altar stands a dramatic statue of the baptism of Christ. (☎53 10 63. Open daily 9am-6:30pm.)

The streets around **place Central** and **rue de la Paix** are filled with late-night eateries, pool houses, and bars that occasionally host live acts. Crowds congregate nightly to dance, imbibe creative cocktails, and discuss the rotating art exhibits housed at laid-back **Art's Café,** 69 rue au Blé. (☎53 55 11. Beer €2-2.20. Wine €2.10. Mixed drinks €4.30. Occasional live concerts and DJ F-Sa. Open June-Sept. M-Sa noon-2am; Oct-Apr. M-Th noon-1am, F-Sa noon-2am. MC/V.)

Every year during the first week in July, selected *places* and theaters around Cherbourg fill with professionals performing circus-like spectacles for **Charivarue: Festival dans l'Espace Publique** (☎88 43 73; www.charivarue.com). Around the first week in April, Cherbourg hosts the annual **Festival des Cinémas d'Irlande et de Grande Brétagne** (☎93 38 94) to celebrate films from across the Channel.

GRANVILLE ☎02 33

In 1439, the expatriate Lord Jean d'Argouges sold his family's fief—the rocky peninsula of Granville, acquired as a marriage dowry—to the English. It quickly became a fortified city and a base from which the English spent 30 years trying to overtake the famously impenetrable Mont-St-Michel. The seaside charms of Granville (grahn-VEEL; pop. 12,700) include a beautiful beach, a walled-in *haute-ville* with incredible views of the harbor, and relaxed nightlife. Though a popular base for daytrips to Mont-St-Michel and the Chausey Islands, Granville's distance from Paris keeps it less crowded and less expensive than might be expected.

TRANSPORTATION. The **train station,** pl. Pierre Sémard, off av. Maréchal Leclerc (ticket office open M 5:40am-12:30pm and 1-7pm, Tu-Th 8:20am-7pm, F 5:40am-12:30pm and 1-7:45pm, Sa 8:20am-7pm, Su 9:10am-noon and 1:10-8pm), has service to Cherbourg (3hr., 4 per day, €21) via Coutances (30min., 7 per day, €7) or Lison; connections also run from Coutances to Pontorson/Mont-St-Michel (1hr., 2-3 per day, €8.80), Rennes (2hr., 2 per day, €19), and Caen (2hr., 9 per day, €20). Manche Iles Express (☎08 25 13 30 50; www.manche-iles-express.com) at the gare maritime, sends **ferries** to Jersey (1hr.; Apr.-Sept. daily, Oct.-Apr. F-Su; €29-33, ages 4-16 €18-20; round-trip €38-43/23-26; prices rise July-Aug.). Compagnie des Iles Chausey (☎50 16 36) sails to the Chauseys (1hr.; daily May-Sept.; round-trip €21, ages 3-14 €13), as does Jolie-France. (☎50 31 81, in winter 49 62 32; jolie-france@wanadoo.fr; reservations required; Apr.-Sept. 1-5 departures daily, Oct.-Mar. several times per week; round-trip €20, ages 3-16 €13.)

ORIENTATION AND PRACTICAL INFORMATION. To reach the city center from the train station, turn right on av. Maréchal Leclerc (on the left as you exit the station), which becomes rue Couraye and ends at pl. de Gaulle in the town center. The **tourist office,** 4 cours Jonville, is around the corner on the right as soon as you reach pl. de Gaulle. The staff offers tours of the city in summer, a helpful city guide with a map, and the *Calendrier des manifestations*, a list of summer events. (☎91 30 03; www.ville-granville.fr. Tours in French July-Aug. Th-Sa 3pm, €2.50. Open in summer daily 9am-noon and 2-6pm; in winter M-Sa 9am-noon and 2-6pm; hours vary monthly.) Other services include: **ATMs** on av. Maréchal Leclerc; a **laundromat,** 10 rue St-Sauvier (open daily 7am-9pm; wash €3.20-4, dry €1 per 12min.); **public restrooms,** outside the train station and by the post office; **police** at rue du Port (☎91 27 50); a **hospital** at rue des Menneries (☎91 50 00); and a **pharmacy,** 2 rue Coraye (☎50 00 80; open M-F 9am-12:30pm and 2-7pm, Sa 9am-12:30pm and 2-7:15pm). Find **Internet** access at the post office or at the back of **La Citrouille** (see **Nightlife and Festivals**). The **post office,** 8 cours Jonville, has **currency exchange.** (☎91 12 30. Open M-F 9am-12:30pm and 1:30-6:30pm, Sa 9am-12:30pm.) **Postal Code:** 50400.

ACCOMMODATIONS. Hotels and the hostel are packed in summer. To get to the **Auberge de Jeunesse (HI) ❶,** bd. des Amiraux, from the train station, turn right onto av. Maréchal Leclerc and follow it downhill. Just before the town center, turn left onto rue St-Sauveur; turn right when the road forks and look for "Centre Nautisme" (nautical center) signs straight ahead, beyond the roundabout; the hostel is part of the Centre Nautisme complex. Comfortable dorms offer great ocean views. Pool tables, ping pong, a TV room, and a cafeteria sweeten the deal. Sailing (€23-42 per hr.), kayaking (single €11, double €15), wind-surfing (€20), and parasailing (€15) are also available through the Centre Nautisme. (☎91 22 62; www.crng.fr. Breakfast €2.95, nonmembers €3.90. Sheets free for members, nonmembers €4. Laundry available. Reception 9am-noon and 2-7pm. 4-bed dorms €14; 2-bed dorms €18; singles €23. AmEx/MC/V.) Family-run **Hôtel Michelet ❷,** 5 rue Jules Michelet, offers comfortable, modern rooms, some with balcony, in a calm location halfway up the hill near the beach. (☎50 06 55; fax 50 12 25. Breakfast €6. Reception M-Sa 7:30am-10pm, Su 7:30am-12:30pm and 6-10pm. Singles and doubles €27, with toilet €35, with toilet and shower €43, with toilet and tub €51. Extra bed €9. AmEx/MC/V.) **Hôtel Terminus ❷,** 5 pl. Pierre Sémard, across from the train station, features spacious, neatly furnished rooms in need of a little upkeep. All rooms have toilet and TV. (☎50 02 05; fax 50 73 35. Breakfast €6. Reception 8am-10:30pm. Singles and doubles €22-30, with shower €30-37, with bath €37; triples €40-47; quads €42-51. AmEx/MC/V.)

FOOD. There are markets on cours Jonville (Sa 9am-3pm) and on place du 11 Novembre 1918 (W 8am-1pm). For groceries, head to Marché Plus, 107 rue de Couraye. (Open M-Sa 7am-9pm, Su 9am-1pm.) Skip the pricey restaurants in town and opt for one of the small *crêperies* in the *haute-ville* near the Eglise de Notre-Dame. Kebab and ice cream stands cluster near the beach, and there are plenty of *boulangeries* and *pâtisseries* along rue Couraye. Try the savory *galettes* (€2.30-8.90) and specialty dessert *crêpes* (€2.10-7.80) at **La Gourmandise ❶,** 37 rue St-Jean, a quiet and romantic spot amid the cobblestone streets of the *haute-ville.* Flambéed right at the table, *la Granvillaise* (apples, apple sorbet, and Calvados) is a true Norman treat. (☎50 65 16. Open mid-June to mid-Sept. daily noon-3pm and 7-11pm; mid-Sept. to mid-June M-Sa noon-3pm and 7-9pm. MC/V.) Near the hostel, **Monte Pego ❷,** 13 rue St-Sauveur, serves steaming Italian pastas and freshly-prepared brick oven pizzas. (☎90 74 44. Desserts €5.90-6.40. Pasta and pizza €8-13. Open M-Sa noon-2:15pm and 7-10pm. MC/V.)

SIGHTS. The steep steps up to Granville's *haute-ville* may look daunting, but the lovely surprise at the top is definitely worth the exhausting climb. Ambling cobblestone streets and charming, old-fashioned architecture complement the *haute-ville*'s real draw: a stunning view of the water, beaches, and surrounding village below. Several stairways lead up to the *haute-ville;* the easiest to find is beside the casino on the beachfront. The staircase stretches from the casino to a German bunker guarding the harbor. In the center of the *haute-ville* stands the somber **Eglise Notre Dame du Cap-Lihou,** pl. du Parvis Notre Dame, where classical music concerts are held occasionally in the summer. Granville's most popular **beach** stretches northward from the *vieille ville* and features a swimming pool replenished by the tide. At high tide, though, the beach, swimming pool, and rocky tide pools are completely submerged. You'll also find quiet stretches of sand near the hostel on the opposite side of the peninsula. The **Musée Richard Anacréon,** which features modern art and a rare book collection including first editions of *Apollinaire, Cocteau,* and *Colette,* is anchored at the eastern edge of the *haute-ville,* at the top of the stairs from the casino on pl. de l'Isthme. (☎51 02 94. Open June-Sept. Tu-Su 11am-6pm; Oct.-Dec. and Feb.-May W-Su 2-6pm. €2.60, students and under 18 €1.40.) A coastal path leads from Granville's beach promenade to the stairs below the cliff top **Musée Christian Dior,** the childhood home of Granville's most famous son. The museum's exhibits change yearly, but impeccable taste and high fashion is always on display. In the elegant gardens, designed by Dior himself, you can smell perfumes and check out the teahouse, which features documentaries on fashion. A spectacular ocean view that inspired Dior opens from a rose-threaded white terrace. (☎61 48 21; www.musee-dior-granville.com. Open mid-May to late Sept. 10am-6:30pm. €5, students and seniors €4, under 12 free. Gardens open daily July-Aug. 9am-9pm; Sept.-June 9am-8pm. Free.) From May to September, boats leave daily for the **Chausey Islands,** a sparsely inhabited archipelago (for ferry info, see **Transportation and Practical Information,** p. 310). The idyllic natural beauty of the islands makes them a relaxing daytrip.

NIGHTLIFE AND FESTIVALS. Nightlife is low-key and stress-free in Granville. The best bet in town is the laid-back **La Citrouille,** 8 rue St-Sauveur, which plays lively tunes during the day and hosts occasional live concerts at night. Funky art-work, cheap drinks, a big-screen TV, and Internet access (€3 per hr.; free Wi-Fi) at its cyber café make this a good place to chill. (☎51 35 51. Wine €1.50. Beer €2.30. Hard liquor €4.70. Open July-Aug. daily 8:30am-1am; Sept.-June Tu-Sa 8:30am-1am. MC/V.) Mid-summer crowds come straight from the beach to the pool table at **Bar les Amiraux,** bd. des Amiraux, across from the hostel, with plenty of seating outside on the patio or inside in the vault-like nooks by the bar. (☎50 12 83; www.les-amiraux.com. Beer €2.20-3. Shots €2.80. Open July-Aug. M-Sa 1pm-2am, Su 3pm-2am; Sept.-June M-Th 1pm-1am, F-Sa 1pm-2am, Su 3pm-1am. MC/V.)

At the end of July, Granville hosts the **Grand Pardon de la Mer,** a spiritual celebration of all things maritime. Writers come for the **Journées des Livres,** a book fair held during the first week of August. In keeping with its many antique shops, Granville hosts a **Salon des Antiquitaires** in mid-August. A lively **Carnaval** takes place on the Sunday before Mardi Gras.

MONT-ST-MICHEL ☎02 33

It's little wonder that pilgrims in the Middle Ages considered Mont-St-Michel (mohn-SEHN-mee-shell; pop. 47) to be an image of paradise on earth, that the English expended such effort trying to capture it in the Hundred Years' War, or that it features so prominently on so many trips to France. From the moment the abbey comes into view across the causeway, it inspires visions of medieval grandeur and timeless majesty. A trip inside the millennium-old abbey, with or without a tour, is an indispensable part of the experience, but no less intoxicating are the views from its fortified walls. Expanses of sandy marshland seem to extend into the horizon, with the perfectly preserved Mont standing out in idyllic isolation.

TRANSPORTATION

Trains: Pl. de la Gare, Pontorson. Open M-Th and Sa 9:15-11:45am and 2:30-7:05pm, F 9:15-11:45am and 2:45-7:30pm, Su 1:30-7:10pm. To: **Caen** (2hr., 2 per day, €23); **Dinan** (1hr., 2-3 per day, €7.90); **Granville** (1hr.; M-F 3 per day, Sa-Su 2 per day; €8.80); **Paris** (4hr., 1-3 per day, €39) via Folligny; **St-Malo** (1½hr., 2-3 per day, €7.10) via Dol.

Buses: Les Courriers Bretons (☎19 70 70; www.lescourriersbretons.fr). Buses leave Mont-St-Michel from the entrance at Porte de l'Avancée and leave Pontorson from pl. de la Gare. Shuttles between Pontorson and the Mont run 7 times per day; more July-Aug. The 1st bus from Pontorson is at 8:45am, and the last bus from the Mont is around 7:30pm. €2; tickets on board. Its subsidiary **Illenoo** (illenoo.fr) runs to **Rennes** (1½hr.; M-Sa 6 per day, Su 1 per day; €3) and **St-Malo** (1¼hr., 2-3 per day, €2.50).

ORIENTATION AND PRACTICAL INFORMATION

Mont-St-Michel, on the border between Brittany and Normandy, is a small island connected to the mainland by a causeway. **Grande Rue** is its only major street. **Pontorson,** 9km due south down D976, has the closest train station and affordable hotels; there's also a supermarket and cheap cabins at the campground across the causeway, 1.8km from the Mont. There's no public transportation off the Mont after 8pm, so plan ahead if you're making a daytrip. Biking to or from Pontorson takes about 1hr. on terrain that is relatively flat but not always bike-friendly; the path next to the Couesnon River is the best route.

Tourist Office on Mont-St-Michel: (☎60 14 30; www.ot-montsaintmichel.com). Helpful multilingual staff in a tiny office to the left of the entrance has info on sites and lodging. A free *horaire des marées* (tide table) will tell you if the vista from the ramparts will be of ocean water or sandy flats. **Currency exchange.** Open July-Aug. daily 9am-7pm;

Sept. and Apr.-June M-Sa 9am-12:30pm and 2-6:30pm, Su 9am-noon and 2-6pm; Oct.-Dec. and Feb.-Mar. M-Sa 9am-noon and 2-6pm, Su 10am-noon and 2-5pm; Jan. M-Sa 9am-noon and 2-5:30pm, Su 10am-noon and 2-5pm.

Tourist Office in Pontorson: Pl. de l'Eglise (☎60 20 65; www.mont-saint-michel-baie.com). Offers maps and info on walking tours, accommodations, and the Mont. **Internet** access €4.50 per 30min., €8 per hr. Open July-Aug. M-F 9am-12:30pm and 2-6:30pm, Sa 10am-12:30pm and 3-6:30pm, Su 10am-noon; Sept.-June M-F 9am-noon and 2-6pm, Sa 10am-noon and 3-6pm.

Laundromat: In Pontorson (☎49 60 66), on rue St-Michel next to the Champion. Open daily 7am-9pm.

Public Restrooms: By the Mont tourist office (€0.40); at the Pontorson train station.

Police: In July-Aug., available on the Mont (☎60 14 42), left of the Porte de l'Avancée before you enter. **Police Municipale** ☎06 07 28 29 14. Also in Pontorson at 2 Chaussée de Ville Chérel (☎89 72 00).

Hospital: Emergency services are at 7 Chaussée de Ville Chérel in Pontorson (☎60 72 00) and in Avranches (☎89 40 00).

Internet Access: On the 2nd fl. of **Hôtel de la Croix-Blanche,** Grand Rue, on the Mont. (☎60 14 04). With a *télécarte*, 1 unit per min. Also at the **Pontorson tourist office.**

Post Office: Grande Rue (☎89 65 00), about 100m inside the walls. **Currency exchange.** Open July-Aug. M-Sa 9am-5:30pm, Su 9am-12:15pm and 1:15-5:30pm; Mar.-May and Sept. to mid-Nov. M-F 9am-noon and 2-5pm; June M-F 9am-5:30pm, Sa 9am-4pm. In **Pontorson,** 18 rue St-Michel (☎89 17 76), across from the tourist office. Open M-F 8:30am-noon and 2-5:30pm, Sa 8:30am-noon. **Postal Code:** 50170.

ACCOMMODATIONS AND CAMPING

Forget about staying on the Mont unless St-Michel himself is bankrolling the visit. Even 2km away at the other end of the causeway, hotels generally cost more than €40, though the campground there—which offers dorms—is affordable. Pontorson has cheap hotels, a hostel, and regular bus service, making it a good base for daytrips to the Mont. Granville and St-Malo are also possible bases, but there are fewer transportation options. There are also a number of campsites and *chambres d'hôte* in the vicinity (the tourist offices in Pontorson or on the Mont offer advice). Reserve ahead; tourists fill the hotels faster than the rising tide fills the bay.

Camping du Mont-St-Michel, 1.8km from the Mont on route du Mont-St-Michel (☎60 22 10; www.le-mont-saint-michel.com). Get off at "La Caserne," the stop before the Mont on the Courriers Bretons line from Pontorson. The closest affordable lodging to the Mont, with dorms and campsites a 4min. walk from the causeway. Excellent views of the Mont—especially at night. Next to a supermarket. Laundry €4.20, dry €1.70. Free Wi-Fi at adjoining Hôtel Motel Vert. Bike rental €5 per ½-day, €8.30 per ½-day, €17 per day. Reception 24hr. Check-out 2pm. Gates closed 11pm-6am. Open May to mid-Sept. Dorms €8.60. €6.30 per site, with electricity €9; €4.10 per adult; €2.40 per child. Mid-Sept. to mid-Nov. and early Feb. to Apr. €5.10/7.20/3.40/1.90. MC/V. ❶

Camping Haliotis, chemin des Soupirs and rue du Général Patton, Pontorson (☎68 11 59; fax 58 95 36), next to the hostel on rue du Général Patton. This 3-star site is a luxurious mini-resort, with cabins as well as campsites. Amenities include a heated pool, jacuzzi, sauna, tennis courts, volleyball, game room, bar, and playground. Breakfast €5. Laundry €3, dry €2. Free Wi-Fi. Bike rental €5 per ½-day, €9 per day. Reception 7:30am-10pm. Open Apr.-Nov., prices rise July-Aug. €4.50-6 per adult, €2-3.50 per child, €5-7 per tent and car or RV. Electricity €2.50-3. Cabins €25 and up. MC/V. ❶

Auberge de Jeunesse Centre Duguesclin (HI), rue du Général Patton, Pontorson (☎60 18 65; aj.pontorson@wanadoo.fr). At the train station, turn right onto the main road, then left

NORMANDY

A MOTHER'S LOVE, A MONT'S LEGACY

It's difficult to walk down the *Grand Rue* of Mont-St-Michel without noticing "Poulard" outside dozens of eateries. The name refers to Annette Poulard, a former Mont resident who opened an inn with her husband Victor when Mont-St-Michel, its days as a prison over, became a national monument in 1874.

Annette made a name for herself caring for exhausted pilgrims who had trekked over the quicksand on their journey to Mont-St-Michel. She would sit them down and serve them her specialty: an enormous, fluffy omelette. It wasn't long before Annette was bestowed with the affectionate title of *mère* (Mother). Today, her original chimney is preserved in the building that once housed Annette's inn—now the post office.

The legacy of fine omelettes continues at **La Mère Poulard,** though it's no longer a spot for impoverished pilgrims; *menus* here range from €35 to €65. Inside, visitors watch as chefs whip up the secret recipe and cook the omelettes over an open fire with ingredients like bacon, lobster, and salmon. The cost may be steep for this edible legacy, but the history—and the quality—is priceless.

Additional restaurant info at ☎02 33 89 68 68, or visit www.merepoulard.fr.

on rue Couesnon. Take the 3rd right on rue St-Michel. At the roundabout, take a left onto rue du Général Patton. The hostel is on the right past the campsite entrance. 4- to 6-person single-sex dorms in an enormous house with a huge but sparsely furnished lounge, kitchen, and dining area. Communal bathrooms; some rooms have showers and toilets. Breakfast €3.20. Reception July-Aug. 8am-10pm; Sept. and Apr.-June 8am-noon and 5-9pm. Open Apr.-Sept. Dorms €14. Cash only. ❶

Hôtel le Grillon, 37 rue du Couesnon, Pontorson (☎60 17 80), on right after rue St-Michel. Welcoming owners offer quiet, clean rooms behind a cheery *crêperie* (p. 314). All with shower; some with skylight. Breakfast €5. Reception daily 8am-midnight. Reservations recommended. Singles and doubles €29, with toilet €32. Extra bed €5. MC/V. ❷

Hôtel de l'Arrivée, 14 rue du Dr. Tizon, Pontorson (☎/fax 60 01 57), over a bar across from station. Polished wooden stairway leads to neat rooms. Breakfast €5.50. Reception July-Aug. daily 8am-10pm; Sept.-June Tu-Su 9am-10pm. Singles and doubles €22, with shower €29-30, with shower and toilet €37; triples €44; quads €67. MC/V. ❷

FOOD

If at all possible, plan a picnic lunch for the Mont, since food inside the walls is okay at best and sells at tourist-inflated prices; the causeway or the gardens above the town make beautiful lunch spots. Arrive prepared, as there are no grocery stores on the Mont; the nearest one is 2km away, at the entrance to the causeway (☎60 09 33). Pontorson has a market (W morning) on **rue Couesnon** and at **place de la Mairie,** as well as a **Champion** supermarket just outside of town, 2 rte. du Mont-St-Michel. From the Pontorson train station parking lot, take a right on the main road, which becomes bd. Général de Gaulle. The Champion will be on your right at the edge of town (10min.). From the hostel and campsite, turn left, then left again at the roundabout. (Open daily M-Sa 7am-7:30pm, Su 9am-noon.) If you do wind up buying food on the Mont, be prepared to spend at least €16 for a lunch *menu;* alternatively, lunch counters sell unimpressive hot dogs, sandwiches and *crêpes* to tourists for €3-8. Head to **La Sirène ❶,** Grande rue, for fresh salads (€3.20-8.40), *galettes* (€2.50-8.60), and *crêpes* (€2.10-7.80) in a single half-timbered room above a gift shop. (☎60 08 60. Wi-Fi €4.50 per hr. Open daily 9am-9:30pm. AmEx/MC/V.) Pontorson's dining options are slim, but the welcoming **Le Grillon ❷,** 37 rue Couesnon, will make you feel at home. The friendly staff serves well-prepared dinner and dessert *crêpes* (€1.90-7.10), fresh salads (€2.50-6.60), and multi-course *menus* (lunch €9.50, dinner €16) in a relaxing environment. (☎60 17 80. Open M-W and F-Su noon-2:30pm and 7-9:30pm. MC/V.)

SIGHTS

Mont-St-Michel's **Grande Rue,** the main thoroughfare leading up to the abbey at the summit, is lined with tourist traps. None of the "museums" or gift shops on Grande Rue are worth the money or time; just keep climbing until you reach the abbey and the scenic viewpoints on the town's ramparts.

THE REAL DEAL. It isn't easy to avoid the throngs of tourists that blanket Mont-St-Michel during peak months. To experience the Mont's magnificence, avoid visiting during the crowded summer months, even if it means missing some tours and spectacles. If you must come then, don't take the main road to the top; instead, take the stairway on the right just after the Porte du Roy or enter through the little-used entrance by the police station to the left of the main entrance. These routes are less packed with tourists and still head directly to the abbey.

TIDES. From various overlooks, you can see the immense tidal basin surrounding the Mont. The tides here are the largest in Europe; when the Earth, Moon, and Sun are aligned, the water can rush some 15km from low tide to high tide in just 4½hr., moving as fast as a galloping horse and completely flooding the beaches along the causeway. These *grandes marées* (great tides) happen about twice a month, as predicted by schedules available at the tourist office. You must be inside the abbey 2hr. ahead of time in order to watch the rising tide.

HISTORY. Legend holds that the **Baie de St-Michel** was created by a giant wave that carved three islands: Tombelaine, Mont Dol (now both located far inland due to the gradual silting of the bay), and Mont Tomba (meaning "mound" or "tomb"). Tomba was so appealing that heaven wanted a piece of it. In AD 708, Archangel Michael supposedly appeared to St-Aubert, Bishop of Avranches, and asked him to build a place of worship on the island. The bishop proved rather unresponsive; Michael reportedly had to put a flaming finger through Aubert's skull before the bishop heeded his vision and erected the first small church on the Mont's summit. In the 10th century, a Benedictine abbey was established on the Mont, and the four crypts supporting the abbey church were built. To French pilgrims, the Mont soon became a spiritual destination as important as Rome and Jerusalem. In the 14th and 15th centuries, Mont-St-Michel was fortified against a 30-year English attack. When church property was appropriated wholesale in the French Revolution, the Benedictines were driven out of Mont-St-Michel; going from heaven to hell, the abbey became a penitentiary, housing around 700 political prisoners. Finally, in 1863 the abbey closed as a prison and Mont-St-Michel was classified as a national monument. Today, the abbey is again home to a small community of monks—no longer Benedictines, but rather Brothers and Sisters of Jerusalem.

ABBEY. Mont-St-Michel's winding Grande Rue ends at the abbey entrance. A wide stairway leads up to the ticket office in the former alms-house of the abbey; keep climbing to the welcome desk, which offers pamphlets for self-guided tours in several languages. These steps also lead to the **west terrace,** the entrance to the **abbey church.** This is a prime lookout for views of the bay, and the departure point for tours. *(Tours of abbey daily; 4 in English, 8 in French. Tours of crypts daily July-Aug.; Sept.-June Sa-Su. 1hr. Free.)* Spanning 80m in length, the **church** is a product of ingenious planning, considering the incredible constraints of its hilltop location. The entire edifice rests on only 200 sq. m of solid rock at floor level—the choir, both sides of the transept, and the entire nave are held up by pillared crypts below the church floor. The adjacent **cloister,** framed by a unique arrangement of columns, rests on the top floor of **La Merveille** (the Marvel), a 13th-century, three-story Gothic monastery. Also on the top floor is the **refectory,** where the monks took their meals in silence as the inspiring life stories of saints were read. Descending to the cathedral's crypts, you pass by the **Salle des Hôtes,** where noble guests were lodged. Directly under the abbey's choir is the **Crypte des Gros Piliers,** whose pillars measure 6m in circumference. Under the southern transept is the **Chapelle St-Martin,** used as a cistern when the abbey became a prison; next door, the abbey's ossuary (once filled with the bones of deceased monks) was converted into a supply depot. It holds a giant wheel, powered by two to four men walking inside it; this was once used to pull supplies up the side of the walls on a sled. The visit continues through the **Chapelle St-Etienne,** the chapel of the dead, where dead monks rotted down to bones before being moved to the ossuary. Longer tours in French, offered daily in July and August and on weekends throughout the year, allow access to the 10th-century **Crypte Notre-Dame-sous-Terre,** the oldest part of the abbey. The narrow abbey gardens, clinging to the side of the rock, surround the compound's exit. (*☎89 80 00. Open daily May-Aug. 9am-7pm; Sept.-Apr. 9:30am-6pm. Last entrance 1hr. before closing. €8, ages 18-25 €5; 1st Su of the month free. Mass daily 12:15pm; entry for service noon-12:15pm only. Extended tour in French July-Aug. 4 per day; weekends Sept.-June 2 per day. €12, ages 18-25 €8, ages 12-18 €3. Audio tour €4, €6 for 2 sets of headphones. MC/V.*)

ILLUMINATION. At night, the illuminated Mont is best seen from either the causeway entrance or from across the bay. In summer, a separate night entrance opens into the abbey, offering an unforgettable view of the pitch-black skies above the bay. *(July-Aug. M-Sa 7-11:30pm. Last entrance 10:30pm. Included with regular admission.)* The Mont also puts on sound-and-light shows after dark in July and August. Unfortunately, there is no public transportation off the Mont after sundown; if you aren't staying on the Mont overnight, you'll have to walk or rent a bike—make sure you have a flashlight or bike light.

THE NORTH

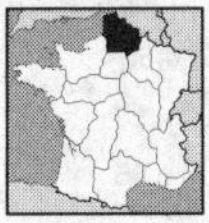

Every day thousands of tourists pass through the channel ports of the Côte d'Opale on their way to Britain, yet few manage more than a quick glimpse of the surrounding regions, leaving the northern regions of Flanders, Pas-de-Calais, and Picardy undiscovered. When you're fleeing the ferry ports, don't miss the area's hidden gems: the windmills and gabled homes of the once Flemish Flanders possess gingerbread charm. Lille (p. 317), a large and lively metropolis, has a strong Flemish flavor and a world-class art collection.

Pas-de-Calais's chalk cliffs loom along the Brit-accented coast; the village of Montreuil-sur-Mer (p. 324) seems to belong to a fairytale, while the busy channel port of Calais (p. 334) provides a dose of brash reality. Farther inland, cows and sheep graze near collapsed war bunkers on still-active mine fields in Arras (p. 324). Even after five decades of peace, relics from the two world wars haunt northern France. German-built observation towers still peer over dunes, testimonials to the resilience of this region, and scores of tombstones attest to the terrible tolls exacted at Arras, Cambrai, and the Somme.

In Picardy, seas of wheat extend in all directions, sprinkled in spring and summer with red poppies. A once royal and now Parisian retreat, this area is home to lush forests, France's largest Gothic cathedral, and dazzling châteaux.

HIGHLIGHTS OF FLANDERS AND PAS DE CALAIS

TAKE A DIP into culture at Lille's amazing modern art museum **La Piscine** (p. 323)—a public pool that has been transformed into a sleek exhibition space.

SOAK UP the bucolic village charm of tiny **Montreuil-sur-Mer** (p. 324), where Victor Hugo set much of his novel, *Les Misérables*.

STROLL through Amiens's cobblestone **Quartier St-Leu** (p. 340), where canals converge at flower-filled squares.

FLANDERS

LILLE ☎03 20

Lille (LEEL; pop. 220,000) is the boy or girlfriend who's fun to date, but just isn't the "One." Once the feared industrial colossus of the north, Lille has evolved into a lively metropolis, its stylish modern architecture melding with the older cobblestone cityscape. With Flemish facades crowding broad avenues and vibrantly diverse squares, Lille, the hometown of Charles de Gaulle, is colorful and lively, and the grand museums are not to be missed. The city's 100,000 students, who come here mainly for its cheaper-than-Paris prices, give it some of the best nightlife in the north. If you go to one city in France, go to Paris; however, if you end up in Lille, you'll probably have a good time.

TRANSPORTATION

Flights: Aéroport de Lille-Lesquin (☎49 68 68). **Allo Navette shuttles** leave from rue le Corbusier at Gare Lille Europe. (☎90 79 79; every hr. M-F 5am-10:30pm, Sa 5am-6:30pm, Su 10am-10:30pm; €4.60).

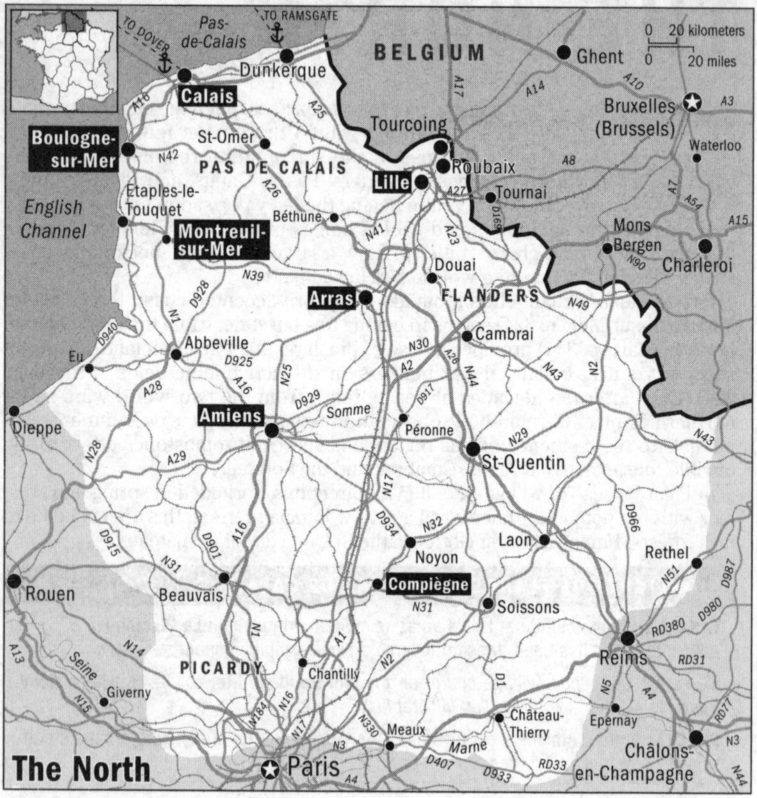

Trains: Lille has 2 stations:

Gare Lille Flandres, pl. de la Gare. Info desk open M-Sa 8am-8pm. Ticket office open M-F 5:30am-9pm, Sa 6am-9pm, Su 7:15am-9pm. **Currency exchange** open M-F 8am-7pm, Sa 10am-5pm, Su 10am-4pm. Luggage storage available. To: **Arras** (40min., 19 per day, €9.40); **Brussels** (1¾hr., 1-3 per day, €18-24); and **Paris** (1hr., 20 per day, €37-51.). AmEx/MC/V.

Gare Lille Europe, av. le Corbusier. M: Gare Lille Europe. Info office open M-Sa 5:45am-10pm, Su 7:30am-10pm. Station open daily 5:30am-12:15am. **Eurostar** (☎08 92 35 35 39) runs to **Brussels** (40min., 15 per day, €18-24) and **London** (1¾hr., 15 per day, €110-175). **TGVs** run to the south of France and **Paris** (1¼hr., 6 per day, €37-51).

Buses: Eurolines, office at 23 Parvis St-Maurice (☎78 18 88; www.eurolines.fr). Office open M-F 9:30am-6pm, Sa 10am-noon and 1:30-6pm. Buses from Gare Lille Europe to **Amsterdam** (5hr., 2 per day, €51); **Brussels** (1½hr., 3 per day, €22); **London** (5½hr., 1-4 per day, €61); and other European cities. MC/V.

Public Transportation: The **Transpole** bus terminal is next to the train station. The **Metro** and **trams** serve the town and its periphery daily 5:12am-12:12am. Tickets €1.25, *carnets* of 10 €11, day-pass €3.50. Office open M-F 7:30am-6pm.

Taxis: Taxi Union (☎06 06 06) or **Taxi Gare** (☎06 64 00). Both 24hr.

Bike Rental: Peugeot Cycles, 64 rue Léon Gambetta (☎54 83 39). €5 per day; €150 deposit. Open Tu-Sa 9am-12:30pm and 2-7pm. MC/V.

ORIENTATION AND PRACTICAL INFORMATION

Lille is like a spiderweb: streets disperse in all directions from the town's many squares. It's best to carry a map, especially when tackling *vieux* Lille. The newer part of town, with wide boulevards and 19th-century buildings, culminates in the **Marché de Wazemmes.** The city's largest shopping district is in the primarily pedestrian area off **place du Théâtre.** Lille, like any big city, can be unsafe, so be vigilant with your belongings and person at all times.

Tourist Office: Pl. Rihour (☎03 59 57 94 00; www.lilletourism.com), inside the Palais Rihour. M: Rihour. From Gare Lille Flandres, go straight on rue Faidherbe for 2 blocks. Turn left through pl. du Théâtre and pl. de Gaulle. Make a right at the Théâtre du Nord and walk into pl. Rihour; the office is ahead. Offers bus tours, bike tours, modern Segway tours, a tour conducted on your cell phone, and free maps. Useful guide book with 5 themed walking tours of the city €2. (**Let's Go walking tour of the city:** priceless. See "Lille By Foot," p. 322.) Tour schedules available at office. English and French tours €7.50-20. Larger map €0.50. **Currency exchange.** The Lille Metropole City Pass provides unlimited public transportation, admission to museums and monuments, a panoramic tour, and discounts. 1-day pass €18, 2-day €30, 3-day €45. Call the office for **pharmacie de garde.** Open M-Sa 9:30am-6:30pm, Su 10am-noon and 2-5pm.

Budget Travel: Voyage Wasteels, 25 pl. des Reignaux (☎06 87 66). Open M-F 9am-12:30pm and 1:30-6:30pm, Sa 9am-1pm.

English-Language Bookstore: V.O., 36 rue de Tournai. Large English-language book section. (☎14 33 96; lalibrairie.vo@wanadoo.fr). Open Tu-Sa noon-7pm.

Youth Center: Centre Régional Information Jeunesse (CRIJ), 2 rue Nicolas Leblanc (☎12 87 30), has info on work and long-term lodging and Internet access (€0.15 per 5min., €15 per 10hr.). Open Tu and Th 1-7pm, W 10am-6pm, F 1-6pm, Sa 10am-12:30pm. **CROUS,** 74 rue de Cambrai (☎88 66 33). Helps find housing, jobs, and study opportunities. Open M-Th 10am-noon and 1-4:30pm, F 10am-noon and 1-4pm.

Laundromat: Laverie, 2 rue Ovigneur. €3.60 per 5-6kg. Open daily 7am-8pm. **Lavotec,** 137 rue Solférino. €2.80 per 5-6kg, €5.60 per 10kg. Open daily 7am-9pm.

Police: Pl. Augustin Laurent (☎49 56 66), in the Hôtel de Ville. Call here for the **pharmacie de garde.**

Hospital: 2 av. Oscar Lambret (☎44 59 62). M: CHR-Oscar Lambret.

Internet Access: At the **CRIJ** (see **Youth Center,** above). Also at **Espace Web,** 14 rue Alexandre Desrousseaux. €3 per 1hr., students €2. 1hr. free per 3hr. bought. Open M-F 10am-8pm, Sa-Su 3-8pm. **Phone+.Net,** 27 pl. des Reignaux (☎40 96 07). €0.80 per 15min., €3 per 1hr. Open M-Th and Su 9am-midnight, F 9am-1am, Sa 9am-2am.

Post Office: 8 pl. de la République (☎36 10 23). M: République. **Currency exchange.** Open M-F 8am-7pm, Sa 8:30am-12:30pm. Branches on bd. Carnot, near pl. du Théâtre (open M-F 8am-5:30pm, Sa 8am-noon) and on the corner of rue Nationale and rue J. Roisin (open M 10am-6:30pm, Tu-F 9am-6:30pm, Sa 10am-1pm and 2-4pm). **Postal Code:** 59000.

ACCOMMODATIONS AND CAMPING

One- and two-star hotels in the €30-40 range cluster around **Gare Lille Flandres,** while more expensive accommodations dot **place du Théâtre** and **place de Gaulle.** Many of Lille's budget options are run-down or face noisy streets; to guarantee a comfortable stay, you may want to spring for one of the pricier options listed below. As most of these hotels serve a business clientele, try to reserve a month ahead and inquire about lower prices for the weekend.

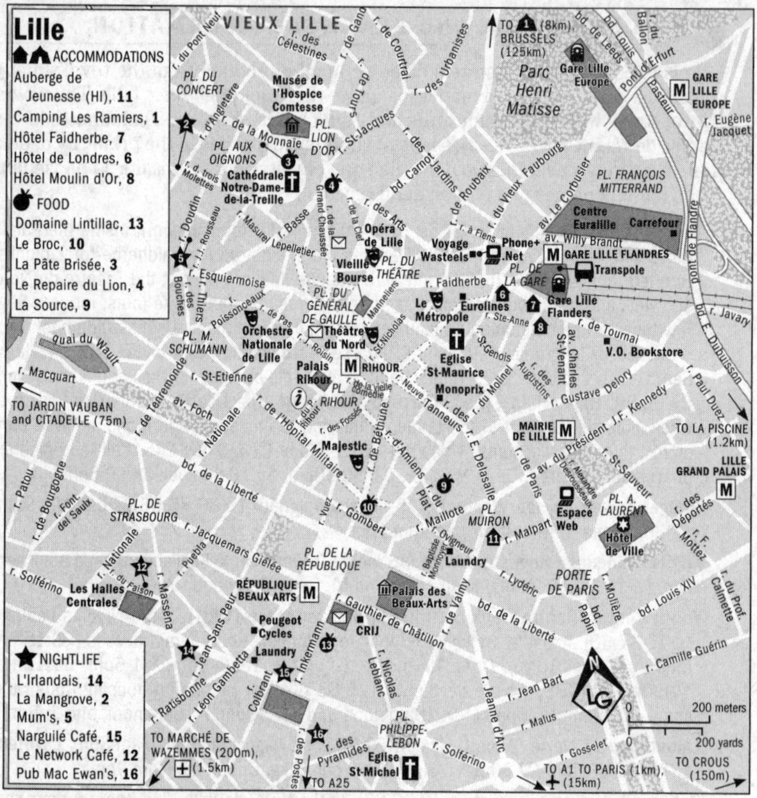

Auberge de Jeunesse (HI), 12 rue Malpart (☎57 08 94; lille@fuaj.org). M: Mairie de Lille. Take the left exit from Gare Lille Flandres, turn left onto rue de Tournai, and make a right at rue du Molinel. Head straight for 2 blocks and turn left onto rue de Paris; after 3 blocks, rue Malpart will be on your right. No-frills hostel with communal bedrooms amusingly named after Eastern European cities. Lots of international boarders. The hostel is not visually stimulating but perks include friendly reception and a quiet location. TV room, kitchen, and bar. Breakfast included. The hostel only supplies one key per room, meaning rooms are often left unlocked; take valuables with you when you leave the room. Luggage storage €1.50 per day. Free Internet access and Wi-Fi. Reception 3pm-midnight and 1am-11am. Check-out 10am. Lockout 11am-3pm. Open late Jan. to mid-Dec. 3- to 6-bed dorms €20. MC/V. ❶

Hôtel de Londres, 16 pl. de la Gare (☎12 09 10; fax 51 59 10). Close to the train station, this hotel boasts tidy rooms with smooth carpets, bright touches of color, and art prints of vegetables. Some rooms overlook the pretty but noisy pl. de la Gare; all have TV. Breakfast €6.10. Reception 24hr.; ring bell downstairs if glass door at the top of the stairs is closed. Check-out 11am. Singles with shower €46-54, with toilet €54-65; doubles with shower and toilet €67. AmEx/MC/V. ❹

Hôtel Faidherbe, 42 pl. de la Gare (☎06 27 93; fax 55 95 38). Modestly sized rooms are the best-dressed of Lille's budget options. Yellow and flowery, all but the least expensive have TV. Breakfast €5. Reception 24hr. Check-out 11am. Singles and doubles with shower or bathtub €32-38, with bath €46. Extra bed €10. AmEx/MC/V. ❸

Hôtel Moulin d'Or, 15 rue du Molinel (☎06 12 67; www.hotelmoulindor.com). The best option near the train station, this hotel isn't cheap, but it offers a level of comfort that usually costs much more. Rooms are decorated with large painted flowers on the wall, and all have bath, TV, hair dryer, and phone. Breakfast €7. Free Wi-Fi. Reception 7am-4pm and 5-9:30pm. Check-out 11am. Singles €55-65; doubles €75-80; triples €80-85. Ask about summer price reductions. MC/V. ❺

Camping Les Ramiers, 1 chemin des Ramiers (☎23 13 42), in Bondues. Take bus #36 (dir.: Comines Mairie) to "Bondues Centre;" continue on rue Césair Loridan. Turn right on chemin des Grands Obeaux and left onto chemin des Ramiers. Fences and gardens divide large sites. Reception July-Aug. 9am-9pm; Sept.-May 9am-4:30pm. Open mid-Apr. to Oct. €1.80 per person, €2.70 per site, €0.60 per car. Electricity €2.50-4. ❶

FOOD

Lille is known for *maroilles* cheese, *genièvre* (juniper berry *liqueur*), and, of course, *moules* (mussels). Find the cheese in any local market or *épicerie* around the central *places*, the *liqueur* in *brasseries* on rue Gambetta, and the mussels, well, everywhere. Crowded **rue Léon Gambetta** boasts a slew of cheap kebab joints and leads to the enormous **Marché de Wazemmes,** pl. de la Nouvelle Aventure (open Tu and Su 8am-2pm, F-Sa 8am-7pm). EuraLille, next to the Eurostar station, has an enormous **Carrefour** supermarket. (☎15 56 00. Open M-Sa 9am-10pm.) There is a **Monoprix** in the Centre Commerciale off rue les Tanneurs. (☎03 28 82 92 20. Open M-Sa 8:30am.)

La Pâte Brisée, 63-65 rue de la Monnaie (☎74 29 00). A cozy tea shop that serves quiches, salads, and dessert *tartes* from noon until night. For those with an indecisive or especially indulgent sweet tooth, the *assortiment des tartes sucrées* is the perfect way to end a meal (€8.10; includes drink). *Menus* €8-18. Open M-F noon-10:30pm, Sa-Su noon-11pm. MC/V. ❷

Le Broc, 17 pl. de Béthune (☎30 16 00). Serves hefty, delicious cheese-dominated dishes that run the gamut from fondues to *crêpes* and salads. Come hungry, pay little, and leave stuffed. Fondue €14-15 per person. *Plats* €7.40-16. Open Tu-Th noon-1:45pm and 7-10:30pm, F-Sa noon-1:45pm and 7-11pm. MC/V. ❸

Domaine Lintillac, 7 rue Inkermann (☎55 44 44). It's always duck season at this homey restaurant that specializes in fantastic *canard* dishes, and nothing else. Shady back terrace. With such a specific focus,

MAKING *SOUVENIRS*

Whether you are one of the people who stares at the strange paintings in a modern art museum and wonders, "How is this art? I could do this!" or part of the camp that gazes at complicated masterpiece and thinks, "Ah, I wish I could do this!" the **Palais des Beaux Arts de Lille** (p. 323) offers a unique opportunity for travelers to, well, "do this."

The museum hosts a series of art classes called "Les Ateliers Vacances," specifically designed for visitors to the city. Taught in the museum's beautiful sweeping galleries, class topics range from "the still life or the illusion of reality," which teaches students techniques for conveying daily life, to architectural studies using the museum's amazing *plans reliefs.*

The best part: you'll leave with an amazing souvenir–your own artwork, better than anything that can be found in any museum shop. The greatest challenge: fitting your lovingly created craft into your backpack.

Open to all ages and artistic abilities. Three-day periods in Feb., Apr., July, Aug., and late Dec. €22-40 for class and materials. Call ☎03 20 06 78 17 for more information. Reserve ahead, as the small classes fill fast. Most instruction is in French; ask for available English options.

BIKING TOUR | SCENIC DRIVE | **WALKING TOUR**

START: Musée de L'Hospice Comtesse

FINISH: Marché de Wazemmes

DISTANCE: 1.2km/¾ mi.

DURATION: 2-3hr.

WHEN TO GO: In the afternoon.

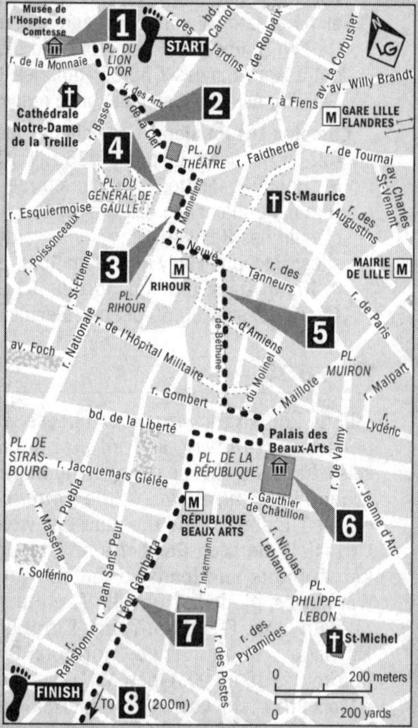

1. MUSÉE DE L'HOSPICE DE COMTESSE. This dark, atmospheric museum is less visited than most, but the former hospital and orphanage houses an intriguing collection of statues and period rooms. Look for the globe displaying the constellations as they were the day the Sun King was born. (32 rue de la Monnaie. Open M 2-6pm, W-Su 10am-12:30pm and 2-6pm.)

2. RUE DE LA CLEF. This quintessential *vieille ville* street is a charming cobbled walk, filled with offbeat boutiques and tiny cafés for shoppers and people-watchers.

3. PLACE DU GÉNÉRAL DE GAULLE. Traditionally known as the *Grand Place*, Lille's central hub is lined with gorgeous Flemish facades and numerous restaurants, cafés, pubs, and shops. Peruse the book markets in the ornate **Vieille Bourse,** a former stock exchange, and check to see if anything's playing at the **Théâtre du Nord.**

4. SALON DE THÉ DAGNIAUX. Grab some tasty Belgian waffles and homemade ice cream at this stylish tea room, which offers yummy Flemish flavors such as the cinnamon-cookie *speculoös*. (56 pl. de Général de Gaulle. Open M noon-7pm, Tu-Sa 11am-7pm.)

5. RUE DE BÉTHUNE. Pass by pl. Rihour and move down along this bustling counterpart to quiet rue de la Clef. The most popular boutiques, cinemas, and terrace restaurants crowd this lively center. Pop into **The Majestic** to check up on its regular screenings of classic old films.

6. PALAIS DES BEAUX ARTS. With one of the most extensive collections in France, this grand and well-designed museum houses a host of 15th- to 20th-century masters under its vaulted ceilings. Check out this month's featured temporary exhibit, and don't miss Monet's *Parliament de Londres* in the Impressionist wing. (Pl. de la République. Open M-W 2-6pm, Th-Su 10am-6pm. €5, students €3.50. Tours €4. Audio tours in English €5.)

7. RUE LEON GAMBETTA. The more modern section of town begins with this broad avenue and its slew of restaurants, cafés, and *pâtisseries*. Stop at one of the many *boulangeries* for a sandwich to snack on as you finish the tour.

8. MARCHÉ DE WAZEMMES. The tour ends with an indoor *charcuterie* and local produce market and a swirling—though slightly sketchy—flea market filling the outdoor *place*. Spend some time looking through the endless rows of clothing, regional products, and everything else under the sun, then buy some fresh fruit to savor during the walk back uptown.

it's no surprise that the quacky *plats* (€8.40-12) are so creative and delicious. Open Tu-Su noon-2pm and 7-10pm. MC/V. ❷

Le Repaire du Lion, 6 pl. Lion d'Or (☎74 20 36). This classic -style brick-and-wood *crêperie* boasts over 100 different *galettes* (€2.60-8.95), sweet *crêpes* (€2.40-6.50), and meal-sized salads (€6.20-6.50). Open M-Sa 11:45am-2:15pm and 7-11pm. MC/V. ❶

La Source, 13 rue du Plat (☎57 53 07). Downstairs a natural food store with vegetarian specialties like heavily spiced rice dishes; upstairs a relaxed restaurant serving creative vegetarian and other organic lunch *menus* (€8.50-15), all of which come with a 1.5L bottle of water and a large pitcher of hot tea. Restaurant open M-F noon-2pm; store open M-Th and Sa 8am-7pm, F 7am-9pm. AmEx/MC/V. ❷

SIGHTS

PALAIS DES BEAUX-ARTS. France's second largest art collection sits in this 19th-century mansion, surrounded by the gardens and fountain of pl. de la République. Sculptures and ceramics fill the museum's lower levels; upstairs, large hallways of mostly 15th- to 20th-century French and Flemish paintings culminate in displays of major *oeuvres.* It's possible to get happily lost in the enormous, colorful museum for hours on end. Rubens's bold and colossal *La Descente de Croix* is a must-see (and due to its size, you'll most likely see it whether you want to or not), while a calming set of Monet's oils are tucked away in a room of Impressionist works. Written guides to each room are available in English and French. *(Pl. de la République. M: République. ☎06 78 00. Open M 2-6pm, W-Su 10am-6pm. Admission €10, students €7. French tours €4; schedule at museum.)*

LA PISCINE. Still-lifes have replaced life guards in this museum, which is situated in a former municipal bath house and displays its eclectic art collection around a glittering, renovated indoor pool. Old shower stalls showing ceramics and textiles serve as nifty portals between the central hall's sculpture garden and alcoves of 19th- and 20th-century paintings. Look out for Claudel's marble bust of a bright-eyed *ingénue;* the quietly stunning statue won the hearts of the town's citizens, who pooled their money together to bring the piece to the museum. Every 15min., a short snippet of audio recorded from an indoor pool plays loudly throughout the building, a ghostly reminder of the funky museum's past. *(23 rue de L'Espérance. M: Gare Jean Lebas. Follow av. Jean Lebas; turn right on rue des Champs, and left on rue de l'Esperance. The museum is on the right. ☎69 23 60. Open Tu-Th 11am-6pm, F 11am-8pm, Sa-Su 1-6pm. €3.50, students of architecture and design €2.50; F all students free.)*

OTHER SIGHTS. The **Vieille Bourse,** the old stock exchange, built between 1652 and 1653, epitomizes the Flemish Renaissance baroque. Adorned in navy and gold trimmings, the dignified structure now plays host to regular book markets. *(Pl. du Général de Gaulle. Markets open Tu-Su 9:30am-7:30pm.)* The **Citadel** on the city's north side was redesigned in the 17th century by military genius Vauban using over three million blocks and is still used by the French military today. *(Open with tour in French Su 3pm. Reserve through the tourist office.)* The **Jardin Vauban,** an English garden designed in 1865, has a carousel, carnival games, and fields for Frisbee-playing.

NIGHTLIFE

Lille has thriving nightlife, with a spread of bars throughout the city that cater to all tastes. Around les Halles Centrales, college students fill the pubs on **rue Solférino** and **rue Masséna.** Across town, the *vieille ville* offers trendier clubs and a less raucous scene. Look for the free magazine **Going Out,** often displayed near the entrance of bars, which lists up-to-date nightlife information.

Pub Mac Ewan's, 8 pl. Sébastopol (☎42 04 42). Draws an energetic barley-loving crowd with its 140 beers (from €2). Open M-Th 11am-2am, F-Sa 11am-3am. MC/V.

Le Network Café, 15 rue Faisan (☎40 04 91; www.network-cafe.net). This hot spot admits only regulars on weekends, but weasel in during the week for nights worth of fun. With a packed dance floor and a laid-back lounge, this cavernous club encourages socializing–hence the name. Dress with style. Open Tu-Su 10:30pm-8am. MC/V.

La Mangrove, 36 rue d'Angleterre (☎51 88 89). This tropical-themed *rhumerie* (rum distillery) offers a lively dance floor, salsa nights, and DJs Th-Sa from 10pm, as well as live bands from time to time. Beer from €2.40. Mojitos €6. Happy hour 7-9pm; mixed drinks €5. Open M-Th 5pm-3am, F-Sa 3pm-3am, Su 6pm-3am. MC/V.

Mum's, 4 rue Doudin (☎06 61 87 68 76). A 2-story gay club whose pulsing dance beats draw crowds. Beer from €3. Mixed drinks €6. Open daily 9pm-3am. AmEx/MC/V.

Narguilé Café, 151 rue Solférino (☎63 91 05). With grey couches and plush pillows, this hookah bar offers a comfortable, aromatic setting for a late-night drink. Beer from €3.20. Mixed drinks from €7. Hookah €8. Open M-Th 4:30pm-1am, F 4:30pm-2am, Sa 2pm-2am, Su 4:30-11:30pm. MC/V.

L'Irlandais, 160-162 rue Solférino (☎57 04 74). A popular Irish pub with a jovial crowd. Small dance floor. Beer €3. Open daily 7pm-3am. MC/V.

ENTERTAINMENT AND FESTIVALS

For a dose of the performing arts, try the **Théâtre du Nord,** pl. Généràl de Gaulle, which puts on plays and concerts from September to June. (☎14 24 24; www.theatredunord.fr. Find schedules at the tourist office. Prices vary, most student tickets €8.50.) Or, visit the **Orchestre Nationale de Lille,** 3 pl. Mendes France. (☎12 82 40; www.onlille.com. Tickets €18-30, students €10.) The **Opéra de Lille,** 2 rue des Bons-Enfants, hosts concerts and musicals. (☎03 28 38 40 40; www.opera-lille.fr. Tickets from €8, students from €5.) The tourist office has information on **film festivals,** held at **Le Métropole,** rue des Ponts de Comines (☎08 92 68 00 73), and the **Majestic,** 54 rue de Béthune (☎03 28 52 40 40; student tickets €6). Many neighborhood and one-time festivals and events come to cosmopolitan Lille; the tourist office provides a detailed guide. Every year, the **Marché aux Fleurs** carpets the center of town at the end of April, while the huge flea market, **La Braderie,** occupies the city's central squares on the first weekend of September (10am to midnight).

PAS DE CALAIS

ARRAS ☎03 21

Arras (ah-RAH; pop. 44,000) features gabled townhouses and Flemish arcades, which lend the town a regal feel but can't hide its battle-plagued history. In WWI, the town suffered severe damage as the site of a long series of trench altercations, aptly named the Battle of Arras. Visit this scruffy survivor for its nearby war monuments, and you'll also discover its small-town appeal. Though Arras is over 100km from the ocean, its spirit remains close to the water: seafood specialties abound, and the sprawling outdoor cafés on the town's two squares seem like beach boardwalks—without the nearby waves.

TRANSPORTATION. Trains (info desk open M 6am-8pm, Tu-F 7am-8pm, Sa 8am-8pm, Su 8am-9pm) go from pl. Maréchal Foch to: Amiens (1hr., 12 per day,

€11); Lille (45min., 20 per day, €9-11); Lyon (3½hr., 3 per day, €77-78); Paris (50min., 12 per day, €28-41). **ARTIS,** which operates **local transportation,** has a **bus station** next to the train station. (☎51 40 30. Tickets for local buses €1. Open Sept.-June M-F 6:30am-12:30pm and 1:30-6:30pm, Sa 8am-noon; July-Aug. M-F 8am-noon and 2-6pm, Sa 8am-noon.) **Taxis** wait at the train station (☎23 27 74 or 23 69 69; 24hr.). **Avis car rental** is near the train station on 4 rue Gambetta. (☎51 69 03. Open M-F 8:30am-noon and 2-6pm, Sa 9am-noon and 4-6pm. AmEx/MC/V.)

ORIENTATION AND PRACTICAL INFORMATION. Arras is bounded by **boulevard du Général Faidherbe** to the east and **rue Gambetta** to the southwest. Both meet at the train station, pl. Maréchal Foch. The center of the town consists of three large squares, **Grande Place, place des Héros,** and **Petite Place.** The tourist office is in pl. des Héros. To get there from the station, walk across pl. Maréchal Foch onto rue Gambetta. Continue for five blocks, then turn right on rue Desiré Delansorne. The office is in the Hôtel de Ville.

The English-speaking staff at the **tourist office,** pl. des Héros, offers a free map and brochure with local hikes, as well as a reduced-price city pass to Arras's main sights (€15, students €8.50). The office leads many tours of nearby memorials—call ahead for themes and prices. Self-guided audio tours are offered in English, French, and Dutch (€6, students €3.20), while the free *Arras Pays* provides a comprehensive guide to current events around town. (☎51 26 95; www.ot-arras.fr. Open Apr. to mid-Sept. M-Sa 9am-6:30pm, Su 10am-1pm and 2:30-6:30pm; mid-Sept. to Mar. M 10am-noon and 2-6pm, Tu-Sa 9am-noon and 2-6pm, Su 10am-12:30pm and 2:30-6:30pm.) The town's other main square, Grand'Place, is across pl. des Héros from the tourist office. Other services include: **laundry** at **Superlav,** 17 pl. d'Ipswich, next to the Eglise St-Jean-Baptiste (wash €3.90 per 5-6kg, €5.90 per 10kg; dry €1 per 10min.; open daily 7am-8pm) and at **Laverie,** 3 rue des Visages around the corner from the tourist office (open daily July-Aug. 6am-9pm; Sept.-June 7am-8pm); **police** in the Hôtel de Ville (☎23 70 70); the hospital, bd. Georges Besnier (☎21 10 10; call for the **pharmacie de garde**); and the **post office,** 13 rue Gambetta, which offers currency exchange (☎22 94 94; open M-F 8am-7pm, Sa 8am-12:30pm). **Postal Code:** 62000.

ACCOMMODATIONS. The **Auberge de Jeunesse (HI) ❶,** 59 Grand'Place, offers tiny but colorfully decorated two- to 10-bed rooms in the middle of the action. The hostel also has a kitchen and TV room. (☎22 70 02; fax 07 46 15. Breakfast included. Reception 8-11am and 5-10pm. Closed Dec.-Jan. Dorms €18. MC/V.) Near the hostel, **Hôtel les Trois Luppars ❺,** 47 Grand'Place, occupies the oldest house in Arras, but guests can enjoy its ancient charms along with its modern conveniences, which include an elevator and a sauna. Large, white stucco rooms with wood paneling overlook the Grand'Place; smaller quarters face an enclosed courtyard. All rooms have bath, TV, and safe. (☎60 02 03; fax 24 24 80. Breakfast €8. Reception 6am-11pm. Check-out noon. Singles €50-65; doubles €65-70; triples €70; quads €75. AmEx/MC/V.) **Le Passe Temps ❸,** 1 pl. Maréchal Foch, across from the station, rents the cheapest hotel rooms in town above a *brasserie.* The well-worn rooms can get noisy, but even the least expensive have a large double bed, small desk, and TV. (☎50 04 04. Breakfast €6.10. Reception M-Sa 7am-midnight. Singles and doubles €32, with shower €36, with bath €40. MC/V.)

FOOD. There is a huge Monoprix supermarket across from the post office at 30 rue Gambetta (open M-Sa 8:30am-7:50pm), an open-air market on pl. des Héros (W and Sa 8am-1pm), and bakeries and specialty shops in the pedestrian shopping area between the post office and the Hôtel de Ville. Inexpensive cafés line pl. des Héros and the pedestrian area, elegant restaurants adorn the Grand'Place, and cheap *friteries* can be found on rue la Taillerie, the alley between the *places*. Seafood is prominently featured on most *menus* in town. La Planche du Boucher ❷, 36 bd. de Strasbourg, prepares large, colorful spreads of meats, fish, or vegetables atop thick wooden boards; these *planches* (from €11) are characteristic of French-Belgian cuisine. The €16 *menu* is a great value for diners with a sweet tooth, as it includes a *planche* and unlimited access to a delicious dessert buffet. (☎71 82 00. Open M noon-2pm, Tu-Sa noon-2pm and 7-10pm. AmEx/MC/V.) Tasty and trendy La Cave de l'Écu ❷, 54 Grand'Place, in a beautiful brick cellar decorated with all-things bird-related, offers elaborate salads (€8.80-15), *galettes*, and *crêpes* (€3-9.50), and (continuing with the bird theme) free-range chicken for €13. (☎50 00 39. *Menus* €17-23. Open daily noon-2:30pm and 7-10:30pm. AmEx/MC/V.) Le Bateau du Ch'ti ❷, 17 pl. des Héros, serves hearty seafood specialties and colossal salads in a dining room of maritime paraphernalia. Order any of the *moules* (mussels) platters in a generous half-size portion for €6. (☎23 20 38. Salads €8-14. *Plats* €8-16. Open mid-Apr. to mid.-Sept. M-F noon-2:30pm and 7-10pm, Sa-Su noon-2:30pm and 7-11pm; mid-Sept. to mid-Apr. M and Su noon-2:30pm, Tu-F and Sa noon-2:30pm and 7-10pm. MC/V.) *Crêped*-out travelers will rejoice at the unabashedly American-style Le Saint Germain Grill ❷, 14 Grand'Place. Its claim to having "best ribs in town" is right on—and not just because it has the only ribs in town. Chow down on the "classic ribs" (€13) while American film stars watch from posters on the walls. (☎51 45 45. Open daily noon-2pm and 7-10pm. AmEx/MC/V.)

SIGHTS. Arras's two great squares are framed by rows of nearly identical narrow houses with enormous windows. While the city offers a smattering of mediocre museums and attractions, most visitors are here either to visit the nearby war memorials or to enjoy the relaxing atmosphere. Amid shops, bars, and cafés, the ornate **Hôtel de Ville** is a faithful copy of the 15th-century original that reigned over pl. des Héros until its destruction in WWI. The best view of Arras is from its 75m **belfry;** an elevator takes you within 43 steps of the top. (Open May-Sept. M-Sa 9am-6:30pm, Su 10am-1pm and 2:30-6:30pm; Oct.-Apr. M 10am-noon and 2-6pm, Tu-Sa 9am-noon and 2-6pm, Su 10am-12:30pm and 2:30-6:30pm. €2.70, students €1.80.) Beneath the town hall, **Les Boves,** eerie labyrinthine tunnels, were bored into the site's soft chalk in the 10th century. The passageways were used at various times as chalk mines, wine cellars, and headquarters for Allied troops awaiting the Battle of Arras during WWI; now, each spring they are decorated with flowers as part of a temporary "Boves Garden" exhibit. The tourist office leads 40min. tours; inquire at the office. (☎51 26 95. Tours €4.70, students and under 18 €2.70.) A few blocks beyond the Hôtel de Ville, the 18th-century **Cathédrale** and **Abbaye St-Vaast** stand on the hill where St-Vaast used to pray. The abbey was founded in the seventh century, and the cathedral's Gothic interior contains massive Corinthian columns alongside Art Deco touches. Look for the seven stoic statues of saints taken from the Pantheon. (Open mid-May to mid-Oct. daily 10:30am-12:30pm and 2-6pm; mid-Oct. to mid-May M-Sa 2:30-5:30pm. Guided tours available through the tourist office mid-June to mid-Sept. Sa 3pm. €4.80, students and under 18 €3.20.) Inside the abbey, the **Musée des Beaux-Arts,** 22 rue Paul-Doumer, displays a small collection. The most interesting pieces are the gruesome skeletal sculpture of Guillaume Lefrançois and his worm-infested entrails on the first floor and Baglione's series of the eight muses at the top of the stairs. (☎71 26 43. Open M and W-Su 9:30am-noon and 2-5:30pm. Last admission 5pm. €4, students €2.) On the outskirts of the *vieille ville*, a number of military monuments and memorials dot the area around the **Vauban Citadel,** a site accessible only by tour on Sundays. (Map at the tourist office. Tours late July to Aug. 3:30pm. €4.80, students and under 18 €3.20.)

NIGHTLIFE AND FESTIVALS. Young blood courses through bars and cafés on **place des Héros, Grand'Place,** and the surrounding pedestrian roads. **Vertigo,** 12 rue la Taillerie, is a chic lounge with tempting red plush seating and a DJ spinning house every weekend. Early in the evening, the vibe is pretty relaxed, but the crowd grows energetic later. (☎23 18 00. Beer from €2.20. Mixed drinks from €8. Open M-Th noon-1am, F-Sa noon-2am, Su 2pm-1am. MC/V.) **Le Couleur Café,** 35 pl. des Héros, is a Caribbean-themed hangout, complete with sailors' rope on the wall. A mellow crowd of all ages fills the enormous terrace. (☎71 08 70. Beer from €2.30. Open Tu-Th 11am-1am, F 11am-2am, Sa 10am-2am, Su 4pm-1am. MC/V.)

For one weekend in July, the town dumps a few tons of sand in Grand'Place to create **Arras on the Beach.** The Riviera-inspired festival includes wild beach parties, sporting events, DJs, and live music. Locals play rugby or build sand castles on this bizarre makeshift shore. Contact tourist office for specific dates.

MEMORIALS NEAR ARRAS

Salient Tours offers Mercedes minibus tours of the scattered memorials surrounding the Arras region. Half-day tours cost €35 (students €30) and are the cheapest and most informative way of seeing all the memorials. Tours leave from the Arras train station (9:15am and 2:30pm), though you can arrange for pickup at your hotel for no additional fee. Reservations necessary. Tour guides are extremely knowledgeable about the sights' history, and have fascinating primary source documents available for examination. The Vimy and Somme memorials are covered in separate tours. Salient mainly visits the memorials below, though you can request to visit sites not covered (☎06 86 05 61 30; www.salienttours.com).

VIMY MEMORIAL

The Vimy Memorial is 3km from the town of Vimy, 12km northeast of Arras. From Arras, Vimy is 15min. by car along NI7. If you don't have a car and choose to go without the tour (the cheapest visiting option), catch a taxi in Arras (€20 each way). Walking along the highway to Vimy takes 50min. and can be dangerous.

In April 1917, Canadian troops successfully overtook German forces at the strategic Vimy Ridge, a feat that other Allied troops had tried and failed to accomplish. Today, the Vimy Memorial stands as a gift to the Canadian government honoring the more than 66,000 Canadian soldiers who were killed during WWI. The two pylons of the monument bear the names of 11,000 soldiers killed in the battle. Sculpted figures surround the edifice: the most poignant is that of a woman, *Canada Weeping for Her Children*, carved from a single 30-ton limestone block.

The surrounding park, criss-crossed by German and Canadian trenches, is morbidly beautiful; hills and craters carved out by shells and mines are now covered by grass and sheep. Explore the trenches, but be sure to stay on the marked paths, as there are still **active mines** in the fenced-off areas. Today, the town of Vimy employs several full-time mine defusers, who are kept busy with the area's frightening amount of remaining explosives. Huge herds of sheep graze the land so that people don't risk their lives mowing the grass. To the shock of curators, an enormous mine was recently discovered under the women's washroom in the visitor's center of the park—but don't head for the bushes yet; it has since been defused. A film at the monument's museum recounts the details of the excavation.

A free underground tour of the crumbling tunnels, given by Canadian students, starts at the kiosk near the trenches. Details hint at the realities of life on the front lines, with the original registration room and commander's desk, a maple leaf chiseled in the wall by a soldier, and a protruding shell that made it 5m into the ground but only halfway into the tunnels. The small museum near the monument recounts the battle and Canada's role in the war. (Monument ☎50 68 68. Open daily sunrise to sunset. Tunnels ☎48 98 97. Open May-Oct. daily 10am-6pm. Free tours in English and French every 45min. Reservations recommended; tours fill up fast. Museum ☎50 68 68. Open daily May-Oct. 10am-6pm; Nov.-Apr. 9am-5pm.)

BATTLE OF THE SOMME MEMORIALS

If you choose to go by car, pick up the useful brochure, The Visitors' Guide to the Battlefields of the Somme, *available at tourist offices throughout the* département; *however, the tour provides more information than you'll find at the memorials and is cheaper than renting a car. The following sights are listed in the order they are visited on the tour.*

When the French concentrated their forces in an attempt to halt the German advance, they left British and Commonwealth forces on the northern front, along the Somme *département*, just northeast of the tiny town of Albert. After sustaining heavy casualties at Verdun, the French asked their allies to create a northern diversion at the Somme to spread out the German forces. The Battle of the Somme, designed for just this purpose, began on July 1, 1916, and was one of the least successful battles of the war for the Allies. Anticipating such an attack, the entrenched German command had substantially fortified its position with a clever layered trench system. The battle, which the Allies expected to be a great success, quickly turned into a rout. The lines barely moved for six months, during which the Allied suffered heavy losses, until Germany voluntarily left the region for strategic reasons. All in all, over one million men were mobilized along the front, and 330,000 casualties were sustained, 58,000 on the first day alone. Memorials along the Somme commemorate various engagements along the line. Most take the form of cemeteries or monuments to those that were lost in the misguided attacks of 1916; some commemorate the more successful repulsion that finally came in 1918.

NEWFOUNDLAND PARK. Just outside Beaumont-Hamel, the Newfoundland Park and its enormous hilltop caribou statue facing the battlefield commemorates the loss of nearly an entire regiment of troops from the British colony of Newfoundland (which became part of Canada in 1949). An identical statue rests in Newfoundland, facing toward the Somme in reverence. The Allies planned to bombard the Germans for seven days with artillery, then explode a 17.5 ton underground mine to divert attention and send thousands of troops out of the trenches in a "surprise" attack. On July 1 (after the seven days), the Newfoundland regiment was ordered to walk carefully across 500m of barbed wire, only to discover the bombardment had failed completely—but by then it was too late. The Germans had hidden safely in fortified underground bunkers and, upon seeing the soldiers, opened fire; nearly 700 Allies died in the first half-hour of the attack, at the hands of only five or six German machine gunners. Tragically, only 78 men survived. The current park is maintained by the Canadian government, which offers free tours of the trench-marked land in English and French. You may want to slather on insect repellent before you arrive here; the fields are often swarmed with thousands of pesky (though non-biting) "Thunder bugs." *(☎03 22 76 70 86.)*

THIEPVAL VISITOR CENTER. Opened in September 2004, the Thiepval Visitor Center offers a great introduction to the multiple stages of the battle with a small museum, film, and narrative display leading to the monument outside. If you choose to visit the memorials by car, this is a good place to start and gain the background you would otherwise receive on the tour. *(☎03 22 74 60 47; fax 03 22 74 65 44. Open May-Oct. daily 10am-6pm; Nov.-Apr. 9am-6pm. Closed for 2 weeks over Christmas and New Year's. Free.)* The 45m Franco-British War Memorial, dedicated to the dead and missing of the Battle of the Somme, just outside Thiepval, is the largest British war memorial in the world. It bears the names of over 73,000 soldiers who were lost on the front from 1915 to 1918 and who have no known grave. *(Open sunrise to sunset.)*

ULSTER MEMORIAL TOWER. Completed in 1921, the memorial stands outside Thiepval. It commemorates the 36th Division troops from Northern Ireland, the only soldiers successful in taking their objectives on July 1—before being subjected to the full force of a German counterattack and losing 5500 men. The tower itself is a replica of Helen's Tower, a large, stoic landmark in Clandeboye, Ireland, that stands where the soldiers trained before the war. The memorial offers tours of the still mine-filled Thiepval Woods, which cannot be visited otherwise. If you're making a day of visiting the memorials, stop here for lunch. *(☎03 22 74 81 11. Memorial open Tu-Su 10am-6pm. Tour of woods Tu and Sa 11am and 3pm.)*

MUSÉE SOMME 1916. This museum is housed 2m below ground in a tunnel that sheltered the French and British during WWI and was used again in 1939 as a bomb shelter. The museum recreates the life of soldiers in the trenches in the July 1916 offensive front and displays photos, dioramas, and objects that narrate the battle of the Somme. *(☎03 22 75 16 17; www.somme-trench-museum.co.uk. Open daily June-Sept. 9am-6pm; Feb.-Dec. 9am-noon and 2-6pm. €4, students and under 18 €2.50. Guided tours available; reserve ahead.)*

NATIONAL MEMORIAL AND SOUTH AFRICAN MUSEUM. This museum and memorial, located at the Delville Woods commemorates South African soldiers in both WWI and WWII. Nearly 4000 South African men were killed in an attack on July 15, 1916. The surrounding woods were also destroyed, and the sole **tree** that survived the attack is as moving as the beautiful etched glass on display in the memorial museum. To find the tree, face the museum, walk behind it to the left, and look for a tree covered in crosses. *(☎03 22 85 02 17. Open daily Apr. to mid-Oct. 10am-5:45pm; mid-Oct. to Mar. 10am-3:45pm.)*

CHANNEL PORTS (CÔTE D'OPALE)

The sprawling channel ports of Pas-de-Calais may not make for the most scenic of vacation spots, but they provide delicious seafood and bring fun-seeking foreigners and happy honeymooners alike to France's northern coasts. Summer is the best time to capitalize on the coast's lively beaches; don't go out of the way to visit the area outside prime Coppertone season.

CHUNNELING TO BRITAIN. **Ferries** from Calais cross to Dover, while Boulogne services Dunkirk and Ramsgate. Calais is more heavily trafficked (though not necessarily a more enjoyable visit). **Eurostar trains** zip under the tunnel from London and Ashford, stopping outside Calais on their way to Brussels, Lille, and Paris. **Le Shuttle** carries cars through the Chunnel between Ashford and Calais. For details on operators, schedules, and fares, see **Getting There: By Boat** (p. 30) and **Getting There: By Train** (p. 32).

MONTREUIL-SUR-MER ☎03 21

Though its name is misleading (not a drop of salt water has been seen here since the 13th century, when the ocean began to recede considerably), tiny seaside Montreuil-sur-Mer (mahn-TRUHY soor mare; pop. 2430) is as idyllic as one might imagine. Victor Hugo chose to set a large portion of *Les Misérables* in this charming provincial town of winding cobblestone streets and tiny eateries, and the town continues to pay homage to the masterpiece with a mammoth annual performance of the story. Summer festivals stir the town up, but the surrounding countryside offers a constant sense of calm; Montreuil maintains a simple appeal, in part because it remains undiscovered by tourist hordes. With delicious cuisine, quirky nightlife, and expansive views from the city's fortified walls, Montreuil will delight the senses and encourage romance in even the most *misérable* of visitors.

TRANSPORTATION AND PRACTICAL INFORMATION. The **train station** is just outside the walls of the citadel. (☎06 05 09. Office open M-F 4:35am-8pm, Sa 5:45am-8pm, Su 9:20am-8pm.) **Trains** go to: Arras (1½hr., 7 per day, €13); Boulogne (30min., 7 per day, €6.80); Calais (1hr., 5 per day, €12); Lille (2hr.; M-F 5 per day, weekend service limited; €17). Rent a **bike** at **ETS Vignaux,** 73 rue Pierre Ledent; look for the sign that reads "Giant Bikes." (☎06 00 29. €10 per ½-day, €15 per day; €200 deposit. Open Tu-Sa 9am-noon and 2-7pm. AmEx/MC/V.)

To reach the **tourist office,** 21 rue Carnot, climb the stairs across from the station and turn right onto av. du 11 Novembre. Continue under the Porte de Boulogne and bear right on Parvis St-Firmin. Turn right at the sign for "Auberge de Jeunesse," onto rue des Bouchers, follow it to its end, and take a left on the footpath by the statue of Notre Dame; the office is straight ahead. An English-speaking staff distributes a free map and brochures in English and French. The walking tour guide for the city (€1) is well worth it if you are interested in the history of the buildings. Another free guide details the town's six churches. (☎06 04 27; www.tourisme-montreuillous.com. Open July-Aug. M-Sa 10am-6pm, Su 10am-12:30pm and 3-5pm; Apr.-June and Sept.-Oct. M-Sa 10am-12:30pm and 2-6pm, Su 10am-1pm; Nov.-Mar. M-Sa 10am-12:30pm and 2-5pm.) Other services include: **currency exchange** at Crédit du Nord, 37 pl. du Général du Gaulle (☎90 92 20; exchanges available Tu-F 8:45am-12:15pm, Sa 8:50-noon; bank open Tu-F 1:45-6pm); a **laundromat,** Laverie Montreuilloise, 44 rue Pierre Ledent (wash €3.50 per 6kg; open daily 8am-8pm); **police** at pl. Gambetta. (☎81 08 48); a **pharmacie de garde** listed in all pharmacy windows (or call the tourist office); a **hospital** in Rang du Fliers (☎89 45 45); and a **post office** on pl. Gambetta (☎06 70 00; open M-F 8:30am-noon and 1:30-5pm, Sa 8:30am-noon). **Postal Code:** 62170.

ACCOMMODATIONS AND FOOD. The cozy **B&B Madame Renard ❸,** 4 av. du 11 Novembre, up the stairs from the train station, rents large rooms in a three-story house with fireplaces in the common rooms and a secluded garden. The B&B is especially convenient for backpackers who don't want to lug their pack up the steep hill to the city. Reservations recommended; tell friendly Mme. Renard when you plan to arrive. (☎86 85 72. Breakfast included. Singles with sink and shared bath/shower €35, with private bath €40; doubles €45. Extra bed €10-15. Cash only.) The **Auberge de Jeunesse "La Hulotte Citadelle" (HI) ❶,** inside the citadel on rue Carnot past the tourist office, offers summer-camp-style accommodations in large 14-bunk rooms. Sweeping views are the payoff for an uphill hike to the hostel, which can be grueling when carrying luggage or a backpack. Once checked in, visitors can enjoy the citadel for free at their leisure. (☎06 10 83. Common kitchen. Reception 10am-noon and 2-6pm. Reservations recommended. Open Mar.-Oct. Closed during all performances of *Les Misérables*, late July to early Aug. Dorms €11. Cash only.) The often-packed **campground ❶,** 1 rue de l'Eglise, sits among lush green forests by the banks of the river Canche. A local *boulanger* (bread maker) pays the site a visit every morning at 8:45am with a fresh breakfast. (☎06 07 28. Reception 9-10am, noon-1pm, and 6-7pm; call ahead if arriving at other hours. Lockout 10pm-7am. Check-out noon. Closed Dec.-Jan. 1 or 2 people with car or tent €15; extra person €3.50. Electricity €3.50. AmEx/MC/V.)

Find many restaurants and a **Shopi** supermarket (open M-Sa 8:30am-7:30pm) at **place de Gaulle,** and bakeries and *chocolateries* sprinkled throughout the adjacent streets. A market floods **place de Gaulle** Saturdays from 8am-1pm. If you splurge on only one restaurant in this whole region, do it at **Le Jéroboam ❸,** 1 rue des Juifs, a classy restaurant named after the term for a 3L wine bottle. And sure enough, Le Jéroboam lives up to its promise, serving gourmet meals in a dining room decorated with wine barrels, crates, and corks. Meanwhile, its black-and-plum furnishings provide a touch of urban chic in the otherwise rustic town. *Plats* of creatively whipped up fresh vegetables and meats range from €14-48; the generous lunch *menu* (€16) and dinner *menus* (€25) are unbeatable deals. (☎86 65 80. Open July-Aug. M 7-9:15pm, Tu-Sa noon-1:45pm and 7-9:15pm; Sept.-June Tu-Sa noon-1:45pm and 7-9:15pm. MC/V.) The brick-walled **Taverne de l'Ecu de France ❷,** 5 porte de France, off pl. de Gaulle, offers regional specialties, including an array of *moules* (mussels platters; €10) and a dinner *menu* featuring cold meats and *frites* (fries). The huge summer salad (€11), covered in various meats and cheeses, is deliciously filling. (☎06 01 89. Open M-Tu and F-Su noon-2pm and 8:30-10pm. MC/V.) **L'Atelier du Goût ❶,** 9 rue Pierre-Ledent, boasts over 300 recipes for handmade chocolates, which customers savor in the *salon de thé*. (☎86 41 44. Chocolate €5 per 100g. Tea €3. Guided group tours of the *chocolaterie* available by appointment. Open Tu and Th-Su 8:30am-12:30pm and 2-7pm. MC/V.)

SIGHTS AND NIGHTLIFE. The 3km long **ramparts** overlook grassy hills, the verdant groves of the Canche valley, and distant villages; the *Promenade des Remparts* footpath follows their entire length. The crumbling 16th-century **citadel** in the *haute-ville* occupies the site of the old royal castle. Allegedly, Vauban (who designed or re-designed most of France's fortresses), was unimpressed with the safety features of the original and ordered renovations in the 17th century. (Open mid-Apr. to Nov. M and W-Su 10am-noon and 2-6pm; Mar. to mid-Apr. daily 10am-noon and 2-5pm. Closed Dec.-Feb. €2.50, under 18 €1.25.) Provincial cottages line **rue du Clape en Bas** and **Cavée St-Firmin. Club Canoë-Kayak,** 4 rue Moulin des Orphelins, across the canal from the station, offers **canoe** and **kayak excursions** of various skill levels on the Canche. (☎06 20 16; ckmontreuil@wanadoo.fr. Sessions from €10. Open May-Aug. daily 9:30am-5:30pm. Call for reservations.)

While several standard *brasserie*-bars surround **place du Gaulle,** Montreuil also offers a few unusual and funky nightlife options. Part *rhumerie*, part tapas bar, and part shrine to Che Guevara, the eclectically decorated **West Indies,** 25 rue Pierre Ledent, serves 180 types of rum (€4.50-45) and the popular Hemingway's Special mojito (€8) to an equally eclectic crowd of rugged locals and tourists who stumble in by chance. Tapas (€3.90-5.50) are

SCENTED FRENCH MEN

A strongly scented naked man has been following me throughout France, glaring at me on the street and waiting silently as I get off the bus. Yet unlike the numerous French men who use "*le catcall,*" this guy doesn't alarm me. To begin with, we are safely separated by a piece of glass—and by the third dimension.

The nude dude of whom I speak—a model in a prominent perfume company's advertisements—is on practically every billboard in northeastern France. And aside from the general health benefits of avoiding poison, it's also a good thing for this man's career that you can't drink perfume.

In 1991, health groups wishing to change France's alcohol-drenched reputation pressured France to pass the Evin Law, prohibiting models from appearing in alcohol ads. The fight began in 2005, when a woman wine maker, who happened to be attractive (but fully clothed, unlike my perfumed friend), appeared in an ad with a wine glass inches from her lips and a "come hither expression" in her eyes. Health campaigners cried foul, and the poster was revised, requiring the woman to hold the glass far from her newly frumpified body.

Curiously enough, when it comes to another alcohol you shouldn't drink—the one *mon homme nu* is hawking—there's not one advocacy group opposed to efforts, seductive or not, that encourage the French to smell delightful.

—Aliza Aufrichtig

served on the weekend. (☎81 95 92. Open M-F and Su 6pm-1am, Sa 6pm-2am. AmEx/MC/V) At the tiny **Crêperie et Artisinat,** rue du Clape en Bas, patrons listen to music ranging from the *"fantastique hommage à Jimmy Hendrix"* to Celtic folk and lots of jazz, while enjoying the cheapest *crêpes* and *galettes* around (€1.80-6.50). Earlier in the day (from 4pm), come to look in on local artists working in the adjoining *ateliers.* (☎06 23 71 17 28. Open daily mid-June to Sept. 4pm-midnight. Free concerts Th 9:30pm, Su 5pm. For concert schedule call the bar or pick one up at the tourist office. Cash only.)

FESTIVALS. Visiting festivals bring energy to Montreuil in the late summer. In late July and early August, the citadel hosts a *son-et-lumière* (light show) version of *Les Misérables*, featuring 300 actors in period costume, dance, song, horses, and fireworks. (Contact tourist office for info. €15, ages 5-12 €10.) The theater company **Les Malins Plaisirs** stages a series of operatic, theatrical, and musical performances in August. (☎98 12 26. Call or visit the tourist office for more info and to reserve tickets. €14-18, under 25 €9-14.) The **Day of the Street Painters** on August 15 draws hordes of artists to the ramparts and the *haute-ville* to paint landscapes of Montreuil, which are displayed in **place Verte** in the afternoon. Celebrate the fifth annual **Festival des Soupes, Bouillons, et Pains** (soup, stock, and bread) in late October at the citadel. (Contact the tourist office for specific dates; €5, includes bowl and unlimited soup and bread tastings.)

BOULOGNE-SUR-MER ☎03 21

The busy harbor of Boulogne-sur-Mer (buh-LOHN-YUH-suhr-mayr; pop. 45,000) is the city's lifeblood, but the Boulogne's most interesting diversions reside in its secluded *haute-ville* and by its white, sandy shores. The city appeals to beach bums and château enthusiasts alike, and the amazing aquarium is not to be missed by anyone. With a cool sea breeze, summer floral displays, and towering red-brick ramparts, Boulogne is the more aesthetically attractive of the two channel ports. As a local summer escape, Boulogne doesn't offer much in the low season.

TRANSPORTATION. Trains leave Gare Boulogne-Ville, bd. Voltaire, to: Calais (30min., 13 per day, €7.20); Lille (2hr., 11 per day, €21; TGV 1hr., 2-3 per day, €24); and Paris (2-3hr., 11 per day, €58). Buy tickets at the station. (Info office open M-Sa 8:45am-6:45pm. Ticket office open M 4:15am-7:30pm, Tu-Sa 5:15am-7:30pm, Su 6:15am-8:50pm.) BCD **buses** leave Gare Boulogne-Ville for Calais (40min., 4 per day, €7.20) and Dunkerque (1¼hr., 4 per day, €12). TCRB, with a station at 14 rue de la Lampe (☎83 51 51), sends local bus #10 from the train station and pl. de France to the *haute-ville* (get off at "Dernier Soy;" €1.10); most buses (€0.70-1.10) go through pl. de France. **Taxis** (☎91 25 00) wait at the train station.

ORIENTATION AND PRACTICAL INFORMATION. The Liane **river** separates the ferry terminal from everything else. To reach central **place de France** from the train station, turn right on bd. Voltaire, then left onto bd. Danou. Follow bd. Danou to the *place.* The tourist office is on quai Gambetta, past pl. de France and the roundabout. A right on quai Thurot leads to the **ferry port.** The streets between **place Frédéric Sauvage** and **place Dalton** form the town center, while the *vieille ville* is at the top of the hill, up rue de La Lampe, which becomes **Grand Rue.**

The **tourist office,** 24 quai Gambetta, has bus info, a reservations service, a free map, and an English-speaking staff. The *Guide Touristique*, in English and French, lists nearly every establishment in town. (☎10 88 10; www.tourisme-boulognesurmer.com. French port tours are offered Mar.-Sept.; check office for dates. €5.50, students €4, under 12 free. Open M-Sa 9:30am-12:30pm and 1:45-6:30pm, Su

TIP **ASSENT TO THE ASCENT.** Plan to visit all of your destinations in Boulogne-sur-Mer's fortified *vieille ville* consecutively. Unless you are an enthusiastic hiker, one trip up the very steep hill is trying; climbing it twice unnecessarily is masochistic. The walk from the train station is shorter than an ascent from the waterfront, but the gradient is much steeper.

10am-1pm and 3-6pm.) **Crédit Agricole,** 26 rue Nationale, has 24hr. **currency exchange** and an **ATM.** (☎08 10 81 06 96. Open Tu-W 8:45am-12:15pm and 1:30-5:30pm, Th 9:15am-12:15pm and 1:30-4:15pm, F 8:45am-12:15pm and 1:30-6:45pm, Sa 8:45am-12:15pm and 1:30-5pm.) Other services include: **laundromats** at 62 rue de Lille in the *haute-ville* (☎80 55 15; €4 per 6kg; open daily 7am-8pm) and 6 pl. Navarin (☎87 46 47; open daily 8am-8pm); **Internet** access at Forum, 57 rue Thiers (☎10 28 70; €4 per hr.; open M 2-7pm, Tu-Sa 10am-7pm) and at Syrius, 23 rue des Religeuses Anglaises (☎30 03 47; €3 per 1hr., €5 per 2hr.; open M-Sa 10am-8pm; cash only); **police** at 9 rue Perrochel (☎99 48 48; call for the **pharmacie de garde**); a **hospital** on allée Jacques Monod (☎99 33 33); and a **post office** on pl. Frédéric Sauvage (☎99 09 03; open M-F 8:30am-6pm, Sa 8:30am-12:30pm). **Postal Code:** 62200.

ACCOMMODATIONS AND FOOD. Many hotels in the €28-36 price range are near the ferry terminal; the tourist office has a list in the *Guide Touristique.* The **Auberge de Jeunesse (HI)** ❶, pl. Rouget de Lisle, across from the train station, gets crowded in the summer, but the tidy and well decorated two- to four-bed rooms offer visitors a haven of relative privacy. Each room has a bathroom, though they don't lock. Backpackers cram into the lively bar in summer. (☎99 15 30; fax 99 15 39. Breakfast included. Free Internet access. Reserve ahead in summer, especially for the weekend. Reception Mar.-Sept. daily 8am-midnight; Oct.-Dec. M-F 9am-11pm, Sa-Su 9am-noon and 5-11pm. Closed Jan. Check-out 11am. 24hr. code access. Dorms €21, ages 4-11 €12; €5 extra per person to ensure a private room. MC/V.) **Hôtel Alexandra** ❹, 93 rue Thiers, is located on a central pedestrian street midway between the train station and the ferry port. This classy, comfortable hotel offers clean and spacious rooms with beautiful bedspreads, all with shower and TV. (☎30 52 22; fax 30 20 03. Breakfast €6. Reception 7am-11pm. Check-out noon. June-Sept. Singles and doubles €55-60; triples €68; quads €75. Oct.-May €53/56-62/75. MC/V.)

Scads of restaurants, cafés, and bakeries cluster in the center of town. An excellent market is on **place Dalton.** (W and Sa 6am-1pm.) Daily fish markets surface along **place Gambetta.** A **Champion** supermarket, bd. Danou, is in the *Centre Commercial de la Liane.* (Open M-Sa 8:30am-8pm.) Small restaurants line the cobble **rue de Lille,** in the *haute-ville,* as well as **rue du Doyen** in the center of town. Big *brasseries* fill pl. Danton. **Restaurant de la Haute Ville** ❷, 60 rue de Lille, serves a *menu végétarien* (€13) and a delicious *île flottante* (€5) in a cute dining room or flower-strewn courtyard. (☎80 54 10. Open Tu-Su noon-10pm. MC/V.) **Le Doyen** ❸, 11 rue du Doyen, offers regional seafood dishes in an intimate dining room; the tangy *feuilleté* of *fruits de mer* (seafood platter; €5.80) is delicious and filling. (☎30 13 08. *Plats* €11-16. Open M-F noon-2pm and 7-9:30pm, Sa noon-2pm and 7-10pm. Reserve ahead for dinner. MC/V.) Grab a cheaper bite at **La Scala** ❷, 16 pl. Général de Bouillon, a French and Italian eatery with a basic (but gargantuan) pizza (€5) and a series of *menus* from €11. The outdoor terrace on the *place* is packed on sunny days. (☎80 49 49. Open daily noon-10:30pm. MC/V.)

SIGHTS AND NIGHTLIFE. Boulogne celebrates its main source of commerce and staple food item at the aquarium **Le Grand Nausicaä,** bd. Ste-Beuve. You'll find everything on the food chain, from plankton to frightening sharks, as you move through the aquarium's labyrinthine layout. Exhibits constantly remind visitors of the need to **respect the environment.** Oddly—and perhaps inappropriately—enough, seafood cafés exist through the aquarium, with signs reading, "*La mer vient à votre table,*" or literally, "the sea comes to your table". (☎30 99 99; www.nausicaa.fr. Open daily July-Aug. 9:30am-7:30pm; Sept.-June 9:30am-6:30pm. July-Aug. €17, students and ages 3-12 €11; Sept.-June €15/10. Closed for 3 weeks in Jan. Audio tours in Dutch, English, French, and German €3.) Down the boulevard is the **beach,** where **Le Yacht Club Boulonnaise,** 234 bd. Ste-Beuve, rents out windsurfers and catamarans. (☎31 80 67; www.ycboulogne.net. Windsurfers €20 per 1hr. Catamarans €35 per 1hr. Open M-Sa 9am-5pm. Closed Dec.-Feb.) Boulogne's *vieille ville* was built by the Romans; its ramparts, now grassy and tree-covered, offer expansive views of the town. The **Château-Musée,** rue de Bernet, occupies a 13th-century castle and contains an eclectic collection of worldly relics, including an Egyptian mummy and 550 Grecian urns. The collection contains France's second largest number of such relics, after the Louvre's cool 25,000. (☎10 02 20; chateaumusee@ville-boulogne-sur-mer-fr. Open M and W-Sa 10am-12:30pm and 2-5pm, Su 10am-12:30pm and 2:30-5:30pm. €1, under 18 free. Audio tours in Dutch, English, and French €2.) Nearby, on rue de Lille, the domed 19th-century **Basilique de Notre Dame** sits above a 12th-century crypt, the second largest in France. Father Haffreingue, an amateur architect, built this church following the Revolution, when the old one was destroyed. (☎99 75 98. Basilica open daily Apr.-Aug. 9am-noon and 2-6pm; Sept.-Mar. 10am-noon and 2-5pm. Free. Crypt open Tu-Su 2-6pm, €2, under 18 €1.)

Neon-lit pubs fill the pedestrian *centre-ville,* particularly at **place Dalton.** Around the corner, **O Sud,** 20bis rue du Doyen, serves tapas and cocktails in a stylish alcove with a dim orange glow and plush pillows. (☎83 97 05; www.restaurantosud.com. Tapas from €2.30; 3 for €6.50; available until 10:30pm. Mixed drinks €6.50. Open M-F and Su 11am-midnight, Sa 11am-1am. MC/V.) For cheap drinks in the *haute-ville,* head to **WoolPack Inn,** 14 pl. de la Résistance. (☎06 18 14 08 51. Open Tu-Su 5pm-2am. MC/V.) Down the hill by the port, the popular **Bar Hamiot,** 1 rue Faidherbe, serves inexpensive beer (bottles from €2) in a standard *brasserie* setting. (☎31 44 20. Open daily 6am-midnight. AmEx/MC/V.)

CALAIS ☎03 21

Calais (kah-LAY; pop. 80,000), with its slew of restaurants, bars, and clubs, caters to vacationers at all hours of the day. The port's expansive beach draws loads of locals and foreigners throughout the summer; with the Chunnel nearby, English can be heard everywhere. Brash and lively, though not aesthetically pleasing, this swath of shoreline promises a spirited nightlife when the weather is warm. Otherwise, the town features few remarkable attractions.

TRANSPORTATION AND PRACTICAL INFORMATION. Free **Balad'In buses** connect the ferry terminal, pl. d'Armes, and the station (every 30min., 24hr.). **Eurostar** stops outside the town at the Gare Calais-Fréthun, while most SNCF **trains** stop in town at the Gare Calais-Ville, bd. Jacquard. (Ticket office open M 5am-7:30pm, Tu-Sa 6am-7:30pm, Su 8:30am-7:30pm. Info office open M-Sa 9am-7pm. AmEx/MC/V.) **Trains** go to: Boulogne (30min., 11 per day, €7.20); Dunkerque (1hr., 2 per day, €7.70); Lille (1¼hr., 16 per day, €16); Paris (3¼hr., 6 per day, €30-60). BCD **buses** (☎83 51 51) stop at the station en route to Boulogne (40min.; M-F and Su 5 per day, Sa 2 per day; €7.20) and Dunkerque (40min.; M-F 6 per day, Sa 3 per day; €7.70). **OpaleBus,** 68 bd. Lafayette, operates **local buses.** (☎19 72 72. Info office open M-F 9am-noon and 1:30-6:30pm, Sa 9am-noon.) **Line #3** (dir.: Blériot/VVF) runs from the station to the beach, hostel, and campground (M-Sa 7am-7:45pm, Su 10:10am-7:40pm; €1.10). **Taxis** (☎97 13 14), line up outside the train station (24hr.).

The **tourist office,** 12 bd. Clemenceau, is near the station. Cross the street, turn left onto the bridge, and continue onto bd. Clemenceau; the office is on the right. The English-speaking staff offers free, poorly-printed maps, information on motorboat rental, and accommodations booking. In summer, *petit train* and guided walking tours leave from the office. (☎96 62 40; www.ot-calais.fr. *Petit train* July-Aug. daily 10:30, 11:30am, 2, 3, 4, 5, 6pm. €4, under 12 €2. Walking tours Th 3pm, €4. Office open June-Aug. M-Sa 10am-1pm and 2-6:30pm, Su 10am-1pm; Sept.-May M-Sa 10am-1pm and 2-6:30pm.) **Currency exchange** is located at the ferry and Hovercraft terminals, 5 bd. Clemenceau (open M-F 9:30am-12:30pm, Sa 10am-12:30pm) and at the post office. Other services include: **laundromat Lavorama,** 48 pl. d'Armes (wash €2.60 per 5kg; open daily 7am-9pm); **police** on pl. de Lorraine (☎19 13 17; call for the **pharmacie de garde**); a **hospital,** 11 quai du Commerce (☎46 33 33); and **Internet** access at **Cyber Espace** in passage Royale, 46 rue Royale (€0.50 per min., €3 per 1hr.) and at **Médiathèque Louis Aragon,** 16 rue du Pont Lottin. (☎19 01 40; €1 per hr.). The **post office** is on pl. d'Alsace. (☎85 52 85. Open M-F 8:30am-12:30pm and 1:30-6pm, Sa 8:30am-noon. Another branch on pl. du Rheims, off pl. d'Armes. Open M-F 8:30am-6pm, Sa 9am-noon.) **Postal Code:** 62100.

ACCOMMODATIONS AND FOOD. Calais's few budget hotels fill quickly in the summer; call two weeks ahead. The shiny, bright and meticulously clean **Centre Européen de Séjour/Auberge de Jeunesse (HI) ❷,** av. Maréchal de Lattre de Tassigny, is far from the train station but less than one block from the beach. From the station, turn left and follow rue Royale past pl. d'Armes. Cross the bridge and turn left onto av. Maréchal de Lattre de Tassigny; the hostel is down the street on the left. From the ferry, take a shuttle bus to pl. d'Armes. Cross the bridge and take a left at the roundabout onto bd. de Gaulle, turn right onto rue Alice Marie and bear left at the fork. The hostel is the third building on the left. Or, take bus #3 from the station to "Pluviose," one block away from the hostel. This beachside location offers spacious doubles and singles with glistening shared bathrooms. (☎34 70 20; www.auberge-jeunesse-calais.com. Pool table, bar, cafeteria, and library. Breakfast included. Reception 24hr. Check-out 10am. Singles €26; doubles €21. AmEx/MC/V.) **Hôtel Pacific ❸,** 40 rue du Duc de Guise, offers bright, sizable rooms, all with bath. (☎34 50 24; www.cofrase.com/hotel/pacific. Breakfast €6.50. Reception 7:30am-11pm. Check-out 11am. Reserve one month ahead in summer. Singles €35-45; doubles €53; triples €58; quads €68. AmEx/MC/V.) **Hotel Victoria ❸,** 8 rue du commandant Bonninque, an extension of rue de Thermes, close to the lighthouse, offers decent-sized, heavily-wallpapered rooms with TV. (☎34 38 32; fax 97 12 13. Breakfast €5. Reception 8am-11pm; code access after 11pm. Singles and doubles €28-39, with bathroom €42; triples and quads €41-44/48-50. AmEx/MC/V.) Beachfront **Camping Municipal de Calais ❶,** av. Raymond Poincairé, has small sites with little privacy and is packed with RVs. (☎97 89 79 or 06 60 46 19 93. Reception July-Aug. 7am-9pm; Apr.-June and Sept. 8am-noon and 2:30-8pm. Closed Oct. to mid-Apr. Gates closed 10:30pm-6am. Reservations required in July and Aug. and recommended otherwise. €3.50 per adult, €3 per child, €2.50 per site. Electricity €2.05.)

Calais cuisine is understandably seafood-centric; most restaurants offer regional seafood platters. Any *pâtisserie,* and especially those on bd. Jacquard, will have a *gâteau Calais,* composed of rich coffee buttercream, a crumbly cookie base, and a thick layer of icing (€1.50-2). Morning **markets** are held on pl. Crèvecoeur (Th and Sa 8:30am-12:30pm) and pl. d'Armes (W and Sa 8:30am-12:30pm). A **Match** supermarket is located at 50 pl. d'Armes. (☎34 33 79. Open M-Sa 9am-7:30pm; June-Sept. Su 9-11:45am.) Restaurants and *brasseries* line **rue Roy-**

ale and **boulevard Jacquard.** Cheaper-than-usual *glaciers* (ice-cream stands) dot the shore. An excellent, value-packed option is the cheery brick **Tonnerre de Brest ❷,** 16 pl. d'Armes, which offers an extensive selection of *crêpes* and *galettes* (€2.70-10) in a maritime-themed setting. The lunch *menu* (*galette, crêpe,* and wine, beer, or cider; €10) is a fabulous and filling deal. (☎96 95 35. *Menus* €10-18. Open July-Aug. daily 11:30am-2:30pm and 6-11pm; Sept.-June Tu-Su 11:30am-2:30pm and 6-11pm. MC/V.) **Histoire Ancienne ❸,** 20 rue Royale, serves vegetarian options and a tasty regional *toques d'Opale menu* (€25) in a classy dining room with black leather chairs and unique artwork. Diners should change out of beach wear before arriving. (☎34 11 20. Open M noon-2pm; Tu-Sa noon-2pm and 6-10pm. Reservations recommended for dinner. Closed 3 weeks in Aug. AmEx/MC/V.) A knight in full armor, along with an outgoing waitstaff, greet both French and British regulars all day to **Au Coq d'Or ❷,** 31 pl. d'Armes, a classy yet quirky restaurant serving regional cuisine. Beautiful fresh flowers grace each table. (☎34 79 05. *Plats* €10-23. Regional *menu* served M-F; €13. Open daily noon-10pm. MC/V.)

SIGHTS AND NIGHTLIFE. In the summer, head first to Calais's fantastic **beach,** the main reason anybody visits this town; follow rue Royale as it becomes rue de la Mer and continue until the end, then turn left along the shore away from the harbor. The beach becomes less crowded with hyper children and pick-up soccer games as you walk farther from rue de la Mer. The town's best off-shore sights are modest ones, such as Rodin's evocative sculpture, **The Burghers of Calais,** framed by the Hôtel de Ville's flowered lawn, near the striking sky-scraping clock tower. The statue depicts six burghers who surrendered the keys to Calais during the Hundred Years' War, offering their lives to England's King Edward III in exchange for those of the starving townspeople. Edward's French wife Philippa pleaded for mercy, and the burghers were spared. **Le Phare de Calais,** pl. Henri Barbuisse, a 58m lighthouse with a draining 271-step climb, has the best view in town (though the industrial Calais is not the most breathtaking sight to behold), and on a clear day, the Dover cliffs are visible from the top. A small museum in the base of the lighthouse explains the science and history of the structure. (☎34 33 34; www.pharedecalais.com. Open June-Sept. M-F 2-6:30pm, Sa-Su 10am-noon and 2-6:30pm; Oct.-May W 2-5:30pm, Sa-Su 10am-noon and 2-5:30pm. €4, ages 5-15 €2). Housed in an old German WWII naval bunker, the dank **Musée de la Seconde Guerre Mondiale,** in the Parc St-Pierre, thoroughly explains Calais's important naval role during the war with old uniforms, weapons, photographs, and newspapers. (☎34 21 57. Open daily May-Sept. 10am-6pm; Feb.-Apr. and Oct.-Nov. M and W-Su 11am-5pm. €6, students €5, families €14. Group rates available. Free audio tour in Dutch, English, French, and German.) The **Musée des Beaux Arts et de La Dentelle,** 25 is a bit of an ugly duckling; housed in a hideous building, the beautiful interior of the museum holds funky modern works of art and a unique collection of *dentelles* (lace) from all eras. (☎46 48 40. Open M and W-F 10am-noon and 2-5:30pm, Sa 10am-noon and 2-6:30pm, Su 2-6:30pm. Free.)

Come nightfall, a hearty spirit invigorates pubs on **rue Royale** and **rue de la Mer,** especially where they meet **place d'Armes.** Discotheques along rue Royale open late and have dancing until dawn. **La Bodega,** 45 rue Royale, is a cramped but merry bar where customers nurse their beers among large wooden kegs. Some weekends feature live music, ranging from blues to techno. (Beer from €2. Open daily mid-June to mid-Sept. 11am-2am; mid-Sept. to mid-June 5pm-1am. AmEx/MC/V.) **Last Night,** 10 rue de la Mer, a bar boasting 81 different mixed drinks, boasts flashy neon lights and tons of techno. (☎34 73 24. Beer from €2. Mixed drinks from €4. Open daily June to mid-Sept. 2pm-2am; mid-Sept. to May 2pm-1am. AmEx/MC/V.) Metallic **Le Bé...Keur,** 40 rue de Thermes, decorated in classy homoerotic art, offers a relaxed yet hip bar atmosphere for a gay and lesbian clientele of all ages, who often bring straight friends along. (☎03 27 85 90 64. Beer from €2.50. Open W-Th, Su, and the last M of the month 7pm-1am; F-Sa 7pm-2am. MC/V.)

PICARDY

AMIENS ☎03 22

At the heart of Amiens (ah-MEE-EHN; pop. 139,210) lies France's largest Gothic cathedral, over twice the size of Paris's Notre Dame. This impressive structure may be the city's claim to fame, but Amiens's particular charm comes from its more modest features: a colorful canal-lined pedestrian *quartier*, a quirky museum devoted to the work of Amiens native Jules Verne, and an array of compact pubs that draw animated, youthful clientele. Meanwhile, beneath its quaint facade, Amiens is a surprisingly modern commercial center. Small enough to fully explore on foot while enjoying its plentiful urban offerings, Amiens also has beautiful parks and nearby hiking trails that provide the perfect escape from city life.

TRANSPORTATION

Trains: Gare du Nord, pl. Alphonse Fiquet. Ticket office open 5am-9:20pm, Sa 5:15am-8:30pm, Su 6am-10:30pm. Info office open M-F 9am-7pm, Sa 9am-6pm. Trains go to: **Boulogne-sur-Mer** (1½hr., 8 per day, €18); **Calais** (2hr., 1 per day, €22); **Lille** (1½hr., 11 per day, €18); **Paris** (1¼hr., 23 per day, €19); **Rouen** (1¼hr., 3 per day, €17). AmEx/MC/V.

Buses: Gare Routière, rue de la Vallée (☎92 27 03), down the staircase that faces rue du Vivier. Buses depart for Beauvais, Mers-les-Bains, and other regional destinations. Tickets €1.50-14.

Public Transportation: Ametis, 10 pl. Alphonse Fiquet (☎71 40 00). Office open M-F 6:45am-7:15pm, Sa 8am-4:30pm. Buses run 5am-9pm. Buy individual tickets (€1.20) on board, and *carnets* of 10 (€9.90) or day passes (€3.40) at the office. All buses stop within a few blocks of the station.

Taxis: ☎91 30 03. 24hr.

Car Rental: Avis, 11 rue St-Martin aux Waides (☎91 31 21). Open M-F 8:30am-noon and 2-6pm, Sa 9am-noon and 4-6pm. AmEx/MC/V.

Bike Rental: Buscyclette, 3 rue des Corps Nuds Sans Teste (☎72 55 13). €1 per 1hr., €3.50 per ½-day, €5.50 per day; €100 deposit. Open daily 9am-12:30pm and 1:30-7pm.

PRACTICAL INFORMATION

Tourist Office: 6bis rue Dusevel (☎71 60 50; www.amiens.com/tourisme). From the train station, turn right onto bd. d'Alsace Lorraine and left onto rue Gloriette. Continue for 3 blocks, though pl. St-Michel and onto rue Cormont. Pass the cathedral and turn left onto rue Dusevel; the office is ahead on the left. English-speaking staff organizes tours, makes hotel reservations (€3), and offers excellent free maps of the town and suggested hiking circuits. Open Apr.-Sept. M-Sa 9:30am-6:30pm, Su 10am-noon and 2-5pm; Oct.-Mar. M-Sa 9:30am-6pm, Su 10am-noon and 2-5pm. Cathedral tours Apr. to mid-June Sa 11am, Su 3pm; mid-June to mid-Sept. M-F 10:30am and 4:30pm, Sa 10:30am, Su 4:30pm; Oct.-Apr. Su 3pm. City tours in French Sa 2:30pm. €5.50, students €4, under 12 €3. Call ahead for a bilingual guide; English, German, Italian, and Russian available.

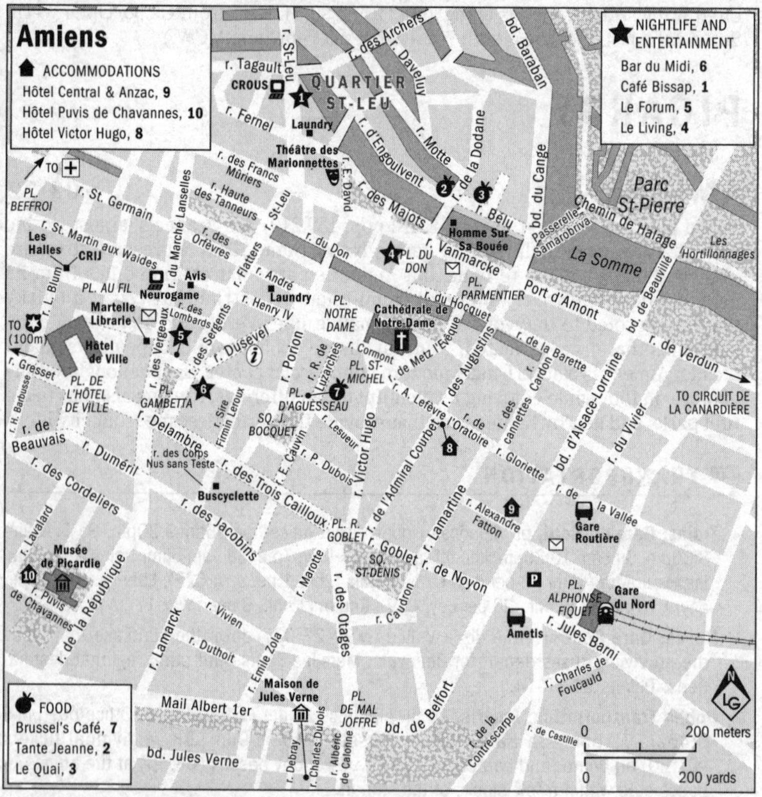

English-Language Bookstore: Martelle Libraire, 3, rue des Vergeaux (☎71 54 54). Small English section upstairs. Open M-Sa 10am-7pm. MC/V.

Youth Center: CROUS, 25 rue St-Leu (☎71 24 00; www.crous-amiens.fr). Offers assistance and info on lodging and work and study opportunities. Free Internet access. Open M-F 8:30am-5pm.

Laundromats: Net Express, 10 rue André (☎72 33 33). €3 per 7kg. Open daily 8am-6pm. **Laverie des Majots Salon Lavoir,** 15 rue des Majots (☎06 66 55 84 74). €3 per 7kg, €5.50 per 10kg. Open daily 8am-9pm.

Police: pl. Léon Gontier (☎22 25 50). Call here for the **pharmacie de garde.**

Hospital: Hôpital Nord, pl. Victor Pauchet (☎66 80 00). Take bus #10 (dir.: Collège César Frank) to "Hôpital Nord."

Internet Access: Free at **CROUS** (see **Youth Center,** above) and at the **Centre d'Information Jeunesse** (**CRIJ;** www.crij.amiens.com), in les Halles on rue de Metz near Pl. au Fil. Open M 1:30-6pm, Tu-Th 10:30am-6pm, F 10:30am-5pm, Sa 1:30-5pm. Also try **Neurogame,** 16 rue Chaudronniers (☎72 68 79). €3.50 per 1hr., €5 per 2hr. Open M-Sa 10am-midnight, Su 2-8pm.

Post Office: 7 rue des Vergeaux (☎97 04 04). Open M-F 8am-7pm, Sa 8am-12:30pm. Branches at 35 pl. Alphonse Fiquet (open M-F 8am-7pm, Sa 8am-noon) and 14 pl. Parmentier (open Tu-F 10am-1:30pm and 2:30-6pm, Sa 8am-5pm). **Postal Code:** 80000.

ACCOMMODATIONS

Hotels with the cheapest rooms (€30-40) cluster around the train station; options in the center of town tend to be pricier. Amiens has no hostel or campsite.

Hôtel Victor Hugo, 2 rue l'Oratoire (☎91 57 91; fax 92 74 02). Each of the rooms at this quiet, central location has its own décor, ranging from rich navy-and-crimson furnishings to simple, pretty pastel designs. All are a bargain, particularly those with street side views. Bath or shower and TV in every room. Breakfast €6.50. 24hr. reception; call if arriving after 11pm. Singles and doubles €41-65. MC/V. ❹

Hôtel Central and Anzac, 17 rue Alexandre Fatton (☎91 34 08; hotel-centraletanzac.com). A cheerful staff offers simple comforts at low prices, this hotel features small rooms with soft beds, large windows, and warmly-colored wallpaper. Note the bizarre stained glass in the entrance. Breakfast €5. Wi-Fi €10 per 3hr. Reception 24hr.; call if arriving 10:30pm-6:30am. Singles €26, with shower €29, with bath €41; doubles €33/40/45. AmEx/MC/V. ❷

Hôtel Puvis de Chavannes, 6 rue Puvis de Chavannes (☎91 82 96). Around the corner from the Musée Picardie. Rooms are small and basic, but reception is friendly, prices are low, and even the cheapest rooms have a TV. Breakfast €4.20. Shower €1.60. Reception 8am-8pm. Singles €24-28, with shower €32, with shower and toilet, €35; doubles €29-31/35/38. Extra bed €9. MC/V. ❷

FOOD

The place to be for a good meal and some of the best views in town, **quai Bélu** is packed with canal-front cafés and restaurants, and tourists as well. Cheap eateries and kebab stands cluster around the station and between the river and the cathedral; *brasseries* surround the **Hôtel de Ville.** A **Match** supermarket is in the mall to the right of the station (open M-Sa 8:30am-8pm); another is closer to the cathedral, at 29 rue Général LeClerc (open M-Sa 8:30am-7:30pm, Su 8:30-11:45am). Amiens's main market in **place Parmentier** sells vegetables from the *hortillonages* on Saturday morning (see **Sights,** below). Smaller markets are on pl. Beffroi. (Open W and Sa.)

Tante Jeanne, 1 rue de la Dodane (☎72 30 30; www.restaurant-tantejeanne.com). With a fantastic view of the cathedral from its outdoor patio, and a large, inviting statue of its namesake, this home-style restaurant serves up sweet *crêpes* and complicated, gourmet *galettes* (€7-16). Open daily noon-2pm and 7-10pm. MC/V. ❷

Le Quai, Quai Belu (☎72 10 80; www.restaurant-le-quai.com). The most popular place along the river, this classy purple restaurant specializes in extravagant seafood platters. *Plats* €11-24. Dinner *menus* from €16. Reserve ahead for a table next to the Somme. Open daily noon-2pm and 7-11pm. AmEx/MC/V. ❸

Brussel's Café, 1 pl. d'Aguesseau (☎91 46 69). A good value near the cathedral, this pub-like café serves a basic menu of sandwiches, omelettes, and salads. Surprisingly un-touristed. Seating available on a terrace by the verdant pl. Jules Bocquet. *Plats* €8-14. Open M-Sa 7:30am-11pm. MC/V. ❷

SIGHTS

CATHÉDRALE DE NOTRE-DAME. Though Amiens's signature monument is France's largest Gothic cathedral, it doesn't feel enormous from inside, until you realize that you've walked roughly the length of an Olympic-sized track and still haven't covered it all. The structure features soaring columns and majestic stained-glass windows, but its showcase of religious artwork and funerary monuments makes it feel like an intimate museum. The cathedral was built in the 13th century to house a relic of John the Baptist's head, which sits at the rear of the cathedral. Allied troops made the small, mournful *Weeping Angel* in the ambulatory behind the choir famous during WWI when they mailed home thousands of postcards of it. Try the labyrinth on the floor in the center of the cathedral that dates back to 1288; people used to complete the labyrinth on hands and knees as an acceptably holy alternative to the more difficult pilgrimage to Jerusalem. Nightly in the summer and at Christmas, the front portals are lit up to display their original color. *(☎80 03 41. Open Apr.-Oct. 8:30am-6:15 pm; Nov.-Mar. 8:30am-5pm. Towers are open to the public July-Aug. M and W-Su 2:30-5:15pm; Apr.-June and Sept. Sa-Su 2:30-5:15pm. €6.50, students €4.50, under 18 free. Tours of the towers conducted July-Aug. M and W-Su 11am; Apr.-June and Sept. M and W-F 3, 4:30pm; Oct.-Mar. M and W-Su 3:45pm. €3, under 18 free. Nightly illuminations June 10:45pm; July 10:30pm; Aug. 10pm; Sept. 9:45pm; Dec.-Jan. 7pm. 45min. Free. The tourist office holds tours in French; see* Practical Information, *p. 337, for details. The office also distributes audio tours at a desk just inside the cathedral. €4, 2 or more €3 each.)*

MAISON DE JULES VERNE. The *20,000 Leagues Under the Sea* author wrote most of his fantastical works in this extraordinary *maison*. The first floor shows Verne's home as it was in the late 19th century, complete with a ghostly audio of old *salon* parties, while the new upper floors encourage visitors to partake of the author's fictional adventures. A surprising life-size diorama of a ship echoes with the sound of roaring waves in the *voyage nautique* room on the second floor. Colorful old posters depict drawings of Verne's heroes and maps scattered throughout the museum trace their expeditions. Look for the large collection of nifty, old fashioned board games inspired by *Around the World in 80 Days*. *(2 rue Charles Dubois. ☎45 45 75; www.amiens.com/julesverne. Open M and W-F 10am-12:30pm and 2-6pm. €5, students €3.50, ages 8-18 €2.50, under 8 free, 2 adults and 2 children €12. Call ahead to reserve a guide.)*

QUARTIER ST-LEU. The most attractive area of Amiens lies just north of the cathedral, criss-crossed by branches of the Somme. Narrow, cobblestone streets border canals in this self-proclaimed "Little Venice of the North" (but don't get too excited—there are countless "Little Venices" in France). Nearby, *hortillonages* (market gardens) spread into the marshland. Walk along the path starting in the **Parc St-Pierre,** or tour the waterways on a traditional 10m *barque à cornets*, a small boat used by Hortillon gardeners in the early 1900s. Don't miss the creepy statue, "*Homme sur sa Bouée*" ("Man on the Buoy"), visible from the bridge on rue de la Dodane. *(☎92 12 18. Boat tours in French leave from 54 bd. Beauvillé Apr.-Oct.; call for hours. 45min. Adults €5.30, ages 11-16 €4.40, ages 3-10 €2.60. MC/V.)*

MUSÉE DE PICARDIE. This museum houses a little bit of everything, including a floor of archaeological pieces, works from the Roman age up to the 20th century, and a collection of mostly French paintings and sculptures. See eye-to-eye with many famous faces in the spectacular room of busts. A small display of modern art includes gems by Balthus and Masson; in the *rotonde des empereurs*, marble statues of Apollo, Diana, and Mars loom in a haunting alcove display. *(48 rue de la République. ☎97 14 00. Open Tu-Su 10am-12:30pm and 2-6pm. Wheelchair-accessible. €5, students €3 and ages 6-18 €2.50; special group rates. Ask for guides in English.)*

NIGHTLIFE AND FESTIVALS

The adorable **Théâtre de Marionnettes,** 31 rue Edouard David, off rue Vanmarcke, stages elaborate shows in the "*Chés Cabotans d'Amiens*" theater; swing by the lobby during the day to view various exhibitions of the marionettes for free. Check www.ches-cabotans-damiens.com for schedules, exhibition times, and prices. (☎22 30 90. Open Tu-Sa 10am-noon and 2-6pm, Su 2-6pm.) In November, the **Festival du Jazz** brings distinguished musicians from all over the world. The aptly named **Fête dans la Ville** fills the streets with concerts, street festivals, jugglers, and circus performers during the third week in June. The November **Festival International du Film** presents a slate of diverse dramas and documentaries (www.filmfestamiens.org).

Café Bissap, 50 rue Saint-Leu (☎72 51 50). Named for the African hibiscus flower drink, this *"rhumerie afrotropical"* serves rum from around the world, a selection of South African wine, and mixed drinks with an island flair. The massive snake skin, African instruments, and exotic plants on the ceiling shake from the dancing at the lively bar upstairs. Beer from €2.60. Rum from €4. Mixed drinks from €6.50. Open M-W 4pm-1am, Th-F 4pm-3am, Sa 6pm-3am, Su 6pm-1am.

Bar du Midi, 2 rue des Sergents (☎91 72 64). Cluttered with posters for old rock bands and local concerts, this merry, noisy bar serves cheap drinks to hip local youths who fill the joint from *midi* on. Beer from €2.20. Mixed drinks €5-5.50. Open M noon-1am, Tu-F 9am-1am, Sa 3pm-1am, Su 4pm-1am. MC/V.

Le Living, 3 rue des Bondes, off pl. du Don. A kitschy, closet-sized bar with metallic chairs, smooth beats, and an affable staff. Beer from €2.50. Mixed drinks from €6.50. Open M 7pm-1am, Tu-Sa 7pm-3am. MC/V.

Le Forum, 18 pl. Gambetta (☎92 44 45). More stylish than the average run-of-the-mill pub, this neon-lit bar has comfortable black leather booths that seat laid-back crowds from early afternoon till late. On sunny days, a mix of locals and tourists fill every director-style chair on the patio. Beer from €2.70. Open M-Sa 8am-1am. MC/V.

OUTDOOR ACTIVITIES

Aside from leisurely strolling through "Little Venice," Amiens offers several other exciting attractions to enjoy on a sunny—or for the hard core, even a rainy—day. Popular with bicyclists, joggers, and families, the **Circuit de la Canardière** begins in **Parc St-Pierre** and continues for a mainly flat 13.5km circuit along the Somme. To enter the trail, which is paved at first, walk across the small Passerelle Samarobriva footbridge from bd. du Cange. Take a right on chemin de Halage, which becomes the well-marked trail. Pick up a free map of the trail at the tourist office. Those who wish to rest in **Parc St-Pierre** will not be disappointed. The gardens, picturesque bridges and ample picnic space attract a plethora of couples, while the soccer fields, running trails, and volleyball and basketball courts are a draw for athletes of all ages. (Park open daily dawn to dusk.) Though Amiens is far from the beach, each summer from June to August, the city fills **pl. Jules Bocquet** and **pl. Gambetta** with sand, hammocks, beach chairs and mini waterfalls for what is called **Les Couleurs de l'Eté.** Do as the locals do and lay out for awhile.

COMPIÈGNE ☎03 44

In the Middle Ages, Compiègne (kohm-PEE-EHN; pop. 45,000) was a favorite summer haven among royalty. Louis XV and his lineage flocked to the Château de Compiègne, as did Napoleon I and Napoleon III. Today, the delicately beautiful hamlet is a retreat favored by Parisians, its royal pedigree still shamelessly apparent in its opulent landmarks and its acres of imperial gardens. The perfect destination for urbanites, Compiègne offers the conveniences and amusements of city life with the quiet, relaxing atmosphere of a small country town.

TRANSPORTATION AND PRACTICAL INFORMATION

Trains go to Paris (45-80min., 22 per day, €13) from pl. de la Gare, across the river from the town center. (Info office open M 9am-7:45pm, Tu-F 9am-8pm, Sa 9:50am-7:30pm. Ticket window open M-Sa 4:50am-9:10pm, Su 6:35am-10pm.) **Regional buses** run daily from the station to nearby towns. **Local TIC buses** travel throughout town. (☎40 76 00. Buses run M-Sa 6am-8pm, some until 10pm. Schedules and maps at the tourist office. Free.) For a **taxi,** call ☎83 24 24. The local **bike rental** company has no storefront but delivers for free to hotels. On summer weekends, it sets up on the Carrefour Royal; if you're only in town for a day, you can have the bike delivered to the tourist office. (☎06 07 54 99 26. €17 per day; ID deposit.)

The **tourist office** is in the Hôtel de Ville. Cross the station parking lot, turn right, cross the bridge, and follow rue Solférino to pl. de l'Hôtel de Ville. An English-speaking staff provides info on biking trails in the Compiègne forest, as well as a detailed forest map (€9.50). Themed city tours are offered most Sundays (3:30pm) from May to October; call ahead for the theme. (☎40 01 00; compiegne.tourisme.infos@wanadoo.fr. Tours €5. Open Easter-Oct. M-Sa 9:15am-12:15pm and 1:45-6:15pm, Su 10am-12:15pm and 2:15-5pm; Oct.-Holy Saturday M 1:45-5:15pm, Tu-Sa 9:15am-12:15pm and 1:45-5pm.) Other services include: a **laundromat** at **Blanc-Bleu,** 15 rue de Paris (☎36 63 48; wash €3.50 per 6kg; open daily 7am-9pm); **police** at 2 pl. de la Croix Blanch in the Quartier des Capucins (☎36 37 37; call for the **pharmacie de garde**); a **hospital,** 8 av. Henri Adnot (☎03 44 23 60 00); **Internet** access at **l'Evasion,** 5 rue St-Martin, near the Hôtel de Ville (☎40 21 34; €4 per 1hr., students €3.50; open Tu-Sa 11am-7pm); and a **post office** at 42 rue de Paris (☎36 31 80; open M-F 8:30am-6:30pm, Sa 8:30am-12:30pm). **Postal Code:** 60200.

ACCOMMODATIONS

Many moderately priced hotels surround the train station and **rue Solférino;** cheap options are hard to find, as there are no hostels or campsites in Compiègne. **Hôtel Vega ❷,** 4 rue du Général Leclerc, halfway between the train station and the central square, rents comfortable plain white rooms. (☎23 32 17. Breakfast €5. Reception M-F 7am-noon and 5:30-8pm, Sa 7am-noon. Check-out noon. Singles €29, with shower €32; doubles €33/35; triples €40. AmEx/MC/V.) Those looking for a little more luxury will enjoy the recently renovated **Armor Hôtel ❹,** 4 rue Solférino, which offers bright and spacious rooms, all with tiled bathroom, flat-screen TV, and minibar. (☎36 06 55; armorhotel@wanadoo.fr. Breakfast €8. Free Wi-Fi. Reception 7am-noon and 2-9pm; code access for later arrivals; inform reception in advance. Check-out noon. Singles €52; doubles €59. Extra bed €10. MC/V.) At the conveniently located **Hôtel de Flandre ❸,** 16 quai de la République, off pl. de la Gare, rooms are large but well-worn and sometimes smell like smoke. Some have balconies overlooking the river. (☎83 24 06 or 83 24 40; www.hoteldeflandre.com. Breakfast €8. Wi-Fi €2 per 2hr., €7 per 24hr. Reception 7am-midnight. Singles €28-36, with shower or bath €46-49; doubles €33-59; triples €61. MC/V.)

FOOD

Food, like everything else in Compiègne, is concentrated around **place de l'Hôtel de Ville,** toward rue des Domeliers and along both sides of the river Oise, near the train station. Restaurants also fill the pedestrian district between **rue Solférino** and **place du Marché.** There's a **Monoprix** supermarket at 33 rue Solférino. (☎40 04 52. Open M-Th and Sa 8:30am-8pm, F 8am-8:30pm. AmEx/MC/V.) Indulge in warm, classy comfort food at its best at the popular **Le Bouchon ❸,** 4 rue d'Austerlitz. Most of the meaty meals in this woody restaurant are served over a large bowl of beans. (☎20 02 03. Large dinner salads €10-13. Regional *plats* €7-15. Open daily noon-2pm and 7-10pm. MC/V.) In a city of fancier restaurants, the yellow and orange **La Friandine ❷,** 22 rue Jean Legendre, has a homey diner feel. Its stuffed *galettes* and dessert *crêpes* (€3.10-15) pack a serious punch. (☎40 04 06. Meal-sized salads €7.50-11. Open Tu-Su noon-2pm and 7-10:30pm. AmEx/MC/V.) **La Rotisserie du Chat qui Tourne ❷,** 17 rue Eugène Floquet, boasts elegance in both its atmosphere and cuisine. Simple dishes and vegetarian specialties are the most affordable options, but even veal brains can be ordered for a modest €13. (☎40 02 74. *Plats* €10-20. 2-course *menus* €15; 4-course €24, with wine €45. Open M and Th-Sa noon-2pm and 7-9:30pm, Tu and Su noon-2pm. AmEx/MC/V.) Sip a cup of coffee at the tiny, two-tabled **Le Chapitre ❶,** 6 rue des Lombard. Locals sit for hours at this used book/coffee shop while perusing the stacks of old volumes, so if you see an open table, snag it. (☎40 48 99. Coffee €1.20. Open Tu-Sa 9am-7pm.)

SIGHTS

The most famous landmark in town, the **Château de Compiègne** was formerly one of three royal residences for France's kings. Reconstructed in the 18th century at Louis XV's command, the château became a favorite retreat of Napoleon I and Napoleon III. A tour of the *grands appartements* reveals sumptuously restored living quarters, with lush bedrooms and a library that would make any book-worm drool. Look for the marble table upon which an admonished young noble carved the date of his punishment in 1868, and the leopard-carpeted *salle* in which Napoleon met his second wife. In addition to the gilded chambers and halls, the large complex contains the first Renault automobile in its **Musée de la Voiture,** pl. du Général de Gaulle, which showcases floors of royal chariots, classic cars, bicycles, and motorcycles. Unfortunately, the main showroom of classic cars will be closed for several years due to security reasons and is only visible from its entrance; the other showrooms are open for visitors. (☎38 47 02; chateau.compiegne@culture.gouv.fr. Open M and W-Su 10am-6pm. Last admission 5:15pm. The museum and usually the château are only accessible by painfully thorough French tours; call to ask about seeing the château without the tour. 1hr. tours every 20-30min. Reduced hours for the grands appartements tours Nov.-Feb. Wheelchair-accessible. Both tours €6.50, students and ages 18-25 €4.50, under 18 free; 1st Su of month free for all.) Behind the palace, the **Parc du Château** includes miles of breathtaking royal gardens designed by Berthault under Napoleon I. With shaded promenades, impeccably tended *jardins*, and open green expanses, the park's natural beauty rivals the opulence of its neighboring château. (Entrance to the right of the château. Open daily mid-Apr. to mid-Sept. 8am-6:45pm; mid-Sept. to Oct. and Mar. to mid-Apr. 8am-6pm; Nov.-Feb. 8am-5pm.)

Down rue du Dahomey from the château on pl. St-Jacques, the **Eglise St-Jacques** will be a relief for history buffs interested in more than miniature recreations. This 13th-century church is where Joan of Arc prayed the morning she was captured in 1430. To the right of the Eglise St-Jacques on pl. de l'Hôtel de Ville, the **Musée de la Figurine,** 28 pl. de l'Hôtel de Ville, displays over 100,000 historic and military figurines and offers a quirky diversion from Compiègne's grandeur. Hand-painted armies of ½ in. soldiers in full battle array shine with remarkable detail, while 8 in. giants sport tailored cloaks and hats. Look for the spectacular 4m by 4m scale representation of the Battle of Waterloo. (☎40 72 55. Open Mar.-Oct. Tu-Sa 9am-noon and 2-6pm, Su 2-6pm; Nov.-Feb. Tu-Sa 9am-noon and 2-5pm. Wheelchair-accessible. €2, students €1, under 18 free; 1st Su of month free for all.)

NIGHTLIFE AND FESTIVALS

At night, bars and pubs liven up the pedestrian district and the streets around **place de l'Hôtel de Ville,** especially near **rue des Lombards.** At hip hot spot **Le Must,** 17bis rue des Lombards, the uproarious **Jean-Baptiste** serves fancy cocktails along with fresh fruit and candy at a sleek metallic bar. The unofficial dress code is trendy. (☎86 36 28. Beer from €2.80. Mixed drinks €4-6. Open M-W 9:30pm-1am, Th-Sa 9:30pm-3am, Su 9:30pm-1am. MC/V.) **Le Cachot,** 2 rue des Lombards, has a neon-glowing dance floor and a cabana-like bar that caters to the mobs on weekends. (☎40 48 66. Mixed drinks from €4.50. Open daily June-Aug. 11pm-3am; Sept.-May 10pm-3am. AmEx/MC/V over €16.) Down the street, **Le St-Clair,** 8 rue des Lombards, is a more traditional café-pub with great outdoor seating, frequented by a slightly older crowd. (☎40 58 18. Beer from €2.90. Mixed drinks from €5.80. Open M-Tu and Su 11am-1am, W-Sa 11am-3am. Karaoke F-Sa 9pm-3am. MC/V.) The **Théâtre Impérial,** 3 rue Othenin, presents opera, ballet, and drama to the sophisticated masses. Originally scheduled to debut in 1871, the grand building, with its amazing acoustics, was finally finished in late 1991. (☎08 25 00 06 74; www.theatre-imperial.com. Info and ticket office open July-Aug. M-F 8:30am-12:30pm and 2-6pm; Sept.-June M-F 8:30am-12:30pm and 2-6pm, Sa 9am-noon and 2-5pm; also open 1½hr. before every show. MC/V.)

In April, the **Concours Complet International** takes place in the Hippodrome above the Parc du Château. This equestrian competition, one of the biggest in the world, is free for spectators. (☎40 18 50; www.cci-compiegne.com.) In mid-May, the annual **Foire aux Vins,** or wine fair, brings free wine tastings and exhibits to pl. St-Jacques. (Call tourist office for more information). Around Easter, an international exhibit of amazingly detailed decorated Easter eggs, the **Salon des Œufs Décorés,** hits the Salle Tainturier, rue de Clamart. (€6, under 12 free.)

HIKING

The misty trails of the **Forêt de Compiègne** provide a maze of peaceful hikes and winding bike routes, all eventually leading back to the château. Ask at the tourist office for a detailed map of these well-marked paths (€9.50). Many lengths and levels of difficulty are available; the most rewarding route, a 12km stroll through the center of the forest, culminates in the dazzling **Château de Pierrefonds,** in a tiny village of the same name. Bought by Napoleon I and marvelously restored by Viollet-le-Duc under Napoleon III, the medieval-style château is breathtaking. You can walk the ramparts, view the gallery, and visit the cavernous knight's hall to get a sense of royal medieval life. (☎42 72 72; www.monum.fr. Château open May-Aug. daily 9:30am-6pm; Sept.-Apr. Tu-Su 10am-1pm and 2-5:30pm. Last admission 45min. before closing. €6.10, students 18-25 €4.10, under 18 free.) Another route passes by the **Wagon de l'Armistice,** with a museum that recounts the famous history of the railway car in which the German army conceded defeat in WWI. The wagon witnessed the French—forced by Hitler—do the same in 1940. (☎85 14 18. Museum open daily Apr. to mid-Oct. 9am-12:30pm and 2-6pm; mid-Oct. to Mar. 9am-noon and 2-5:30pm. €3, ages 7-14 €1.50, under 7 free.)

CHAMPAGNE

Brothers, brothers, come quickly! I am drinking stars!
—*Dom Pérignon*

Synonymous with both sophisticated celebration and Dionysian revelry, the fizzy pop of a champagne cork always hits a seductive note. While champagne is reserved for special occasions in most of the world, in Champagne itself bubbly flows constantly, bringing with it glamour, luxury, and good times to one of France's wealthiest wine-growing regions.

According to European law, the word "champagne" may be applied only to wines made from grapes from this region and produced according to a rigorous, time-honored method. The process involves the blending of three varieties of grapes (pinot noir, pinot meunier, and chardonnay), two stages of fermentation, and frequent realignment of the bottles by *remueurs* (highly trained bottle-turners who can turn up to 50,000 bottles per day) to facilitate the removal of sediment. So fiercely guarded is the name that when Yves St-Laurent brought out a new perfume called "Champagne," the powerful *maisons* sued to force him to change it—and won. Though at first Dom Pérignon, a Benedictine monk, had to convince his compatriots to try the sweet nectar he is credited with inventing, few modern-day visitors need additional incentive to come to Champagne to see (and taste) the *méthode champénoise*. Travelers regularly visit the region's numerous *caves* (wine cellars)—at their best in lavish towns like Reims (see below) and Epernay (p. 353). Even local cuisine tends to center around the drink, as most regional dishes are drenched in some champagne-based sauce.

The grape-fed high life may buoy Champagne economically, but the smaller towns surrounding the vineyards also have distinct character. Come to the region for the giddy luxury of its namesake beverage and the boisterous *joie de vivre* of its signature towns, but don't miss out on the region's historical landmarks: the grand Cathédrale de Notre Dame in Reims (p. 320), traditional site of French coronations since its construction 1311, and the ornate 18th-century architecture of the self-satisfied champagne *maisons* of Epernay (p. 353).

HIGHLIGHTS OF CHAMPAGNE

MAKE THE MOST of your toast at Epernay's **Moët & Chandon** (p. 354), producers of the legendary Dom Pérignon.

QUENCH your thirst at the **Champagne Pommery** (p. 350) in Reims, home of the 75,000L wine cask that was a show-stopper at the 1904 World's Fair.

STROLL among the picturesque streets and half-timbered houses of beautifully preserved and cork-shaped **Troyes** (p. 356)—before actually popping a cork.

REIMS ☎03 26

Reims (RANSS; pop. 191,325) is the largest and best-known city in the Champagne region. It's fitting that Reims, with its reputation for celebration, is where France once transformed its princes into kings. The city has hosted the coronations of 26 French monarchs, and its ornate cathedral still houses a vial of the oil used to anoint Clovis, France's first king, in AD 486. Today, from the underground cham-

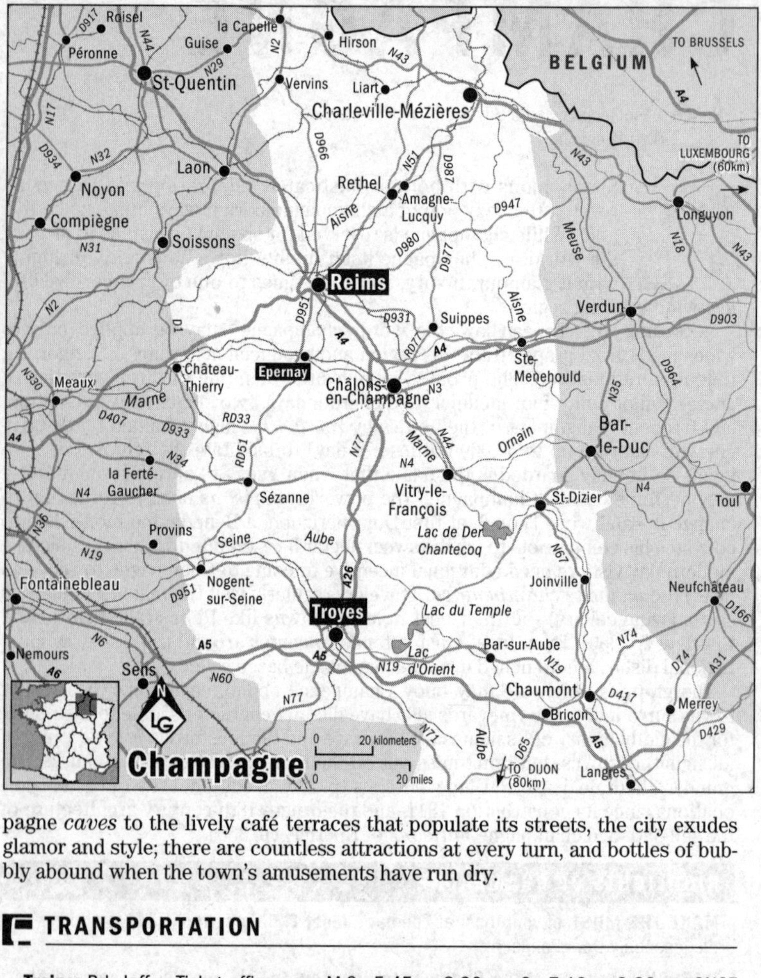

pagne *caves* to the lively café terraces that populate its streets, the city exudes glamor and style; there are countless attractions at every turn, and bottles of bubbly abound when the town's amusements have run dry.

TRANSPORTATION

Trains: Bd. Joffre. Ticket office open M-Sa 5:45am-8:20pm, Su 7:10am-9:20pm. SNCF office with info and reservations at pl. Myron T. Herrick. Open M-Sa 10am-7pm. To: **Epernay** (30min., 11 per day, €5.10) and **Paris** (1½hr., 11 per day, €23).

Public Transportation: Transport Urbains de Reims (TUR) buses stop at train station. Info office at 6 rue Chanzy (☎88 25 38). Open M-F 7:30am-7:30pm, Sa 10am-7pm. All buses run 6:35am-9:45pm; a few run until midnight. Buy individual tickets (€1) and day pass (€3) on bus, *carnet* of 10 (€8.60) from TUR office. Regional **buses** leave from the bus station for Troyes and Châlons-en-Champagne. Schedules at the tourist office. Many buses don't run in summer; check the dates listed at the bus stop.

Taxis: (☎47 05 05). 24hr.

Car Rental: Avis, cour de la Gare (☎47 10 08). Open M-F 8am-noon and 2-7pm, Sa 8am-noon and 2-6pm. AmEx/MC/V. **Europcar,** 76 bd. Lundy (☎88 79 03). Open M-F

8am-noon and 2-7pm, Sa 8am-noon and 2-5pm. AmEx/MC/V. **Hertz,** 26 bd Joffre (☎47 98 78). Open M-F 8am-noon and 2-7pm, Sa 8am-noon and 2-6pm. AmEx/MC/V.

Bike Rental: Centre International de Séjour, chaussée Bocquaine (☎40 52 60; www.cis-reims.com). €10 per ½-day, €15 per day, €25 per weekend; €80 or photocopy of credit card deposit. MC/V.

ORIENTATION AND PRACTICAL INFORMATION

In Reims, activity centers around **place Royale** and **place du Forum.** The major thoroughfare, **rue de Vesle,** begins at the river, becomes rue Carnot, and runs through pl. Royale, turning into rue Cérès and later av. Jean Jaurès. The tourist office is near pl. Royale. To get there from the train station, cross bd. Joffre upon exiting, continue onto rue Col. Driant, and bear left onto rue Thiers. Turn right onto cours J.B. Langlet and follow it until it becomes rue du Trésor; turn right on rue Guillaume de Machault and the office will be on your right.

TIP **STEER CLEAR.** Many of the roads in Reims's *centre-ville* are under serious construction until 2010. If you plan to drive in the city, be prepared for confusing detours. Bring an up-to-date road map to keep up with the changes, as one-way streets abound. The sidewalks are still open, so if you are on foot the only inconveniences will be aesthetic.

Tourist Office: 2 rue Guillaume de Machault (☎77 45 00; www.reims-tourisme.com), in a pint-sized ruin beside the cathedral. Free map, brochures in many languages, and free same-night accommodations service (with deposit). Ask for the student guide *Le Monocle* (French only). Audio tours of the town in 6 languages, including English; €5. Night-time walking tour of Reims in French Easter-May Sa 9pm; June Sa 9:30pm; July-Aug. F-Sa 9:30pm; Sept. to mid-Oct. F-Sa 9pm. Tour of Basilique St-Rémi in French July-Aug. F 2pm. Tour of cathedral in French July daily 3:30pm; Aug. daily 10:30am, 3:30pm; Easter-June Sa-Su 2:30pm. Tours €5.50, under 12 free. Office open mid-Apr. to mid-Oct. M-Sa 9am-7pm, Su 10am-6pm; mid-Oct. to mid-Apr. M-Sa 9am-6pm, Su 11am-6pm.

Budget Travel: Voyage Wasteels, 26 rue Libergier (☎79 88 03). ISICs and cheap flights. Open M-F 9am-6pm, Sa 10am-6pm.

Youth Centers: Centre Régional Information Jeunesse (CRIJ), 41 rue Talleyrand (☎79 84 79). Message board with flyers advertising seasonal work, including camp counselor positions and field work during the harvest. Free Internet access with a no-email policy (some travelers report that it is loosely enforced). Free Wi-Fi. **CROUS,** 34 bd. Henri Vasnier (☎50 59 00; www.crous-reims.fr). Comprehensive info on and assistance with housing and work or study opportunities in the area. Open M-F 8:30am-noon and 1:30-5pm, services for foreign students 9-11:30am and 2-4pm.

Laundry: Lavomatique, 49 rue Gambetta. Open daily 7:30am-9pm. €3 per 5.5kg. **Laverie Barbâtre,** 154 rue Barbâtre. €3.20 per 5kg. Open daily 7am-10pm.

Police: 40 bd. Louis Roederer (☎61 46 26), by the train station. Call here for the **pharmacie de garde.**

Hospital: 47 rue Cognac Jay (☎78 78 78).

Internet Access: Free at **CRIJ** (see **Youth Centers,** above). **Clique & Croque,** 27 rue de Vesle (☎86 93 92), set back from the street in Passage du Commerce. €4 for 1st hr., €3.60 for 2nd, €3 for 3rd. Open M-Sa 10am-12:30am, Su 2-8pm. Also at **Centre International de Séjour** and **Hôtel Azur** (see **Accommodations,** below).

Post Office: 2 rue Cérès (☎77 64 80), on pl. Royale. Open M-F 8:30am-6pm, Sa 8:30am-noon. **Currency exchange.** Branches at 2 rue Olivier Métra (☎50 58 01), near Porte Mars (open M-F 8am-7pm, Sa 8am-noon) and at 9 pl. Stalingrad (☎86 69 30), close to the hostel (open M-F 8:30am-noon and 1:30-6pm, Sa 8:30am-noon). **Postal Code:** 51100.

ACCOMMODATIONS

Pricier hotels cluster at the top of pl. Drouet d'Erlon toward bd. Général Leclerc, while somewhat inexpensive options can be found west of pl. Drouet d'Erlon, as well as in the region above the cathedral, near the *mairie*. It's wise to reserve ahead, especially in the summer.

Centre International de Séjour/Auberge de Jeunesse (HI), chaussée Bocquaine (☎40 52 60; fax 47 35 70), next to La Comédie-Espace André Malraux. Polished rooms house a mix of backpackers and visiting school groups in a park-side setting. When returning late at night, take chaussée Bocquaine instead of the wooded path next to the highway, as it can be unsafe. Kitchen, laundry, and Internet access. Breakfast €3.40. Internet €2.40 per 15min., €4.20 per 30min. Reception 24hr. Lockout 10pm-7am. Bunks in 4- to 5-bed dorms €16, with toilet and shower €19; singles €28/41; doubles €21/28; triples with shower €22. MC/V. ❶

Hôtel Azur, 9 rue des Ecrevées (☎47 43 39; hotelazurreims@free.fr). Minutes from the train station and close to the Hôtel de Ville. Very friendly owners welcome guests to simple, colorful, and florally-scented rooms along a quiet side street. All but the cheapest with shower or bath. Breakfast €6.50. Free Wi-Fi. Reception Apr.-Sept. daily 7am-9:30pm; Oct.-Mar. M-Sa 7am-9:30pm. Reserve ahead in summer and fall. Singles €35, with shower €40-48; doubles €42/50-60; triples €70. MC/V. ❸

Ardenn' Hôtel, 8 rue Caqué (☎47 42 38; www.ardennhotel.fr), near pl. Drouet d'Erlon. Within walking distance of the train station. Large, clean, and simple rooms, all with bath and TV; those on the top floor have an enormous skylight. Breakfast €5.50. Reception M-Sa 10am-midnight, Su 10am-noon and 4-midnight; call ahead if you're arriving later. Singles €31-41; doubles €47; triples and quads €59. Extra bed €6. MC/V. ❸

FOOD

At the heart of Reims's street life, **place Drouet d'Erlon,** you will also find its stomach; bakeries and sandwich shops compete for space with both cafés and classier restaurants. Slightly cheaper but comparable restaurants—minus the prime outdoor seating—can be found on some of the surrounding side streets. Kebab stands line **rue de Vesle,** while pastry shops line **rue Gambetta.** There's a **Monoprix** supermarket at 21 rue Chativesle, in espace d'Erlon (open M-Sa 9am-8pm; MC/V) and a smaller **Marché Plus** at 131 rue de Vesle (open M-Sa 7am-9pm, Su 9am-1pm; MC/V). The main **market** is on place du Boulingrin near Porte Mars. (Sa 6am-1pm.)

Louise, 15 rue Marx (☎78 00 61). A self-proclaimed "*crêperie* for the 21st century" (you'll have to come to discover what that means), which serves delicious *galettes* and *crêpes* in a stylish 2-story restaurant with hot-pink trimmings. Ambient dance beats are hip yet unobtrusive. *Crêpes* €2.30-5.90. *Galettes* €6.90-9. Fresh salads €6.50-8.80. Open M noon-2pm, Tu-Sa noon-10pm. MC/V. ❶

Le Coin des Crêpes, 123 av. de Laon (☎83 99 74). A classic street-corner *crêperie* away from the touristy bustle of the *centre-ville* and near the Musée de la Reddition. An extensive array of regional *galettes* with rich ingredients like Camembert and duck livers. *Galettes* and *crêpes* €2.50-14. Salads €5.80-8.60. Open Tu-Th noon-2pm and 7-10:30pm, F-Sa noon-2pm and 7-11pm. MC/V. ❷

Gust, 7 rue de l'Arbalète (☎40 23 20). A large modern sandwich shop with customizable salads and an array of pastries. The best–and most stylish–sandwich you'll get in

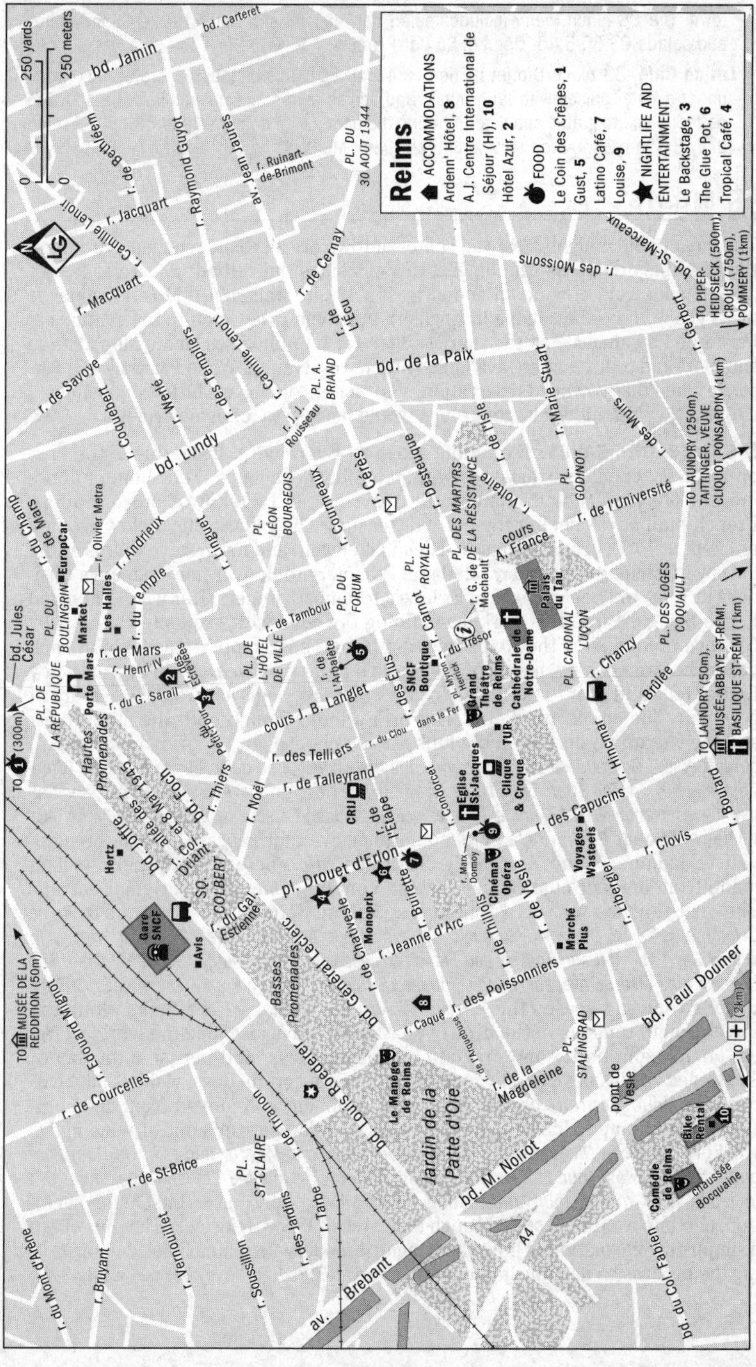
Reims
ACCOMMODATIONS
Ardenn' Hôtel, 8
A.J. Centre International de Séjour (HI), 10
Hôtel Azur, 2
FOOD
Le Coin des Crêpes, 1
Gust, 5
Latino Café, 7
Louise, 9
NIGHTLIFE AND ENTERTAINMENT
Le Backstage, 3
The Glue Pot, 6
Tropical Café, 4
0 250 yards
0 250 meters
bd. Carteret
bd. Jamin
r. de Bethléem
r. Raymond Guyot
av. Jean Jaurès
r. Ruinart-de-Brimont
PL. DU 30 AOUT 1944
r. Jacquart
r. Camille Lenoir
r. Macquart
r. de Cernay
r. de l'Écu
PL. A. BRIAND
bd. de la Paix
r. des Moissons
bd. St-Marceaux
r. Gerbert
TO PIPER-HEIDSIECK (500m), CROUS (750m), POMMERY (1km)
TO LAUNDRY (250m), TAITTINGER, VEUVE CLIQUOT PONSARDIN (1km)
r. des Murs
r. Marie Stuart
r. de l'Isle
r. de Savoye
r. Coquebert
r. Werlé
r. des Templiers
r. J.J. Rousseau
bd. Lundy
r. Cérès
r. Courmeaux
r. Desteuque
PL. DES MARTYRS DE LA RÉSISTANCE
r. Voltaire
PL. GODINOT
r. de l'Université
cours A. France
PL. LÉON BOURGEOIS
r. Linguet
r. Andrieux
r. Olivier Metra
r. du Champ de Mars
EuropCar
PL. DU BOULINGRIN
Market
Les Halles
r. du Temple
bd. Jules César
r. de Mars
r. Henri IV
r. des Écrevées
PL. DE LA RÉPUBLIQUE
Porte Mars
TO (300m)
Hautes Promenades
r. du G. Sarail
r. du Petit Four
PL. DE L'HÔTEL DE VILLE
r. de Tambour
PL. DU FORUM
PL. ROYALE
r. G. de Machault
Palais du Tau
PL. CARDINAL LUÇON
PL. DES LOGES COQUAULT
r. Chanzy
r. Brûlée
TO LAUNDRY (50m), MUSÉE-ABBAYE ST-RÉMI, BASILIQUE ST-RÉMI (1km)
Cathédrale de Notre-Dame
Grand Théâtre de Reims
pl. Myron Herrick
r. du Trésor
Boutique SNCF
r. Carnot
r. de l'Arbalète
cours J. B. Langlet
r. des Élus
r. du Clou dans le Fer
r. des Telliers
TUR
Clique & Croque
Eglise St-Jacques
r. de Talleyrand
r. Condorcet
r. Hincmar
r. des Capucins
Voyages Wasteels
r. Clovis
r. Boulard
r. Thiers
r. Noël
CRIJ
r. de l'Étape
bd. Foch
allée des 7 et 8 Mai 1945
bd. Joffre
r. Col. Driant
SQ. COLBERT
Hertz
pl. Drouet d'Erlon
r. Buirette
r. Marx Dormoy
Cinéma Opéra
r. de Vesle
r. Libergier
Marché Plus
r. de Thillois
r. du Gal. Estienne
Monoprix
r. de Chativesle
Gare SNCF
Avis
r. Jeanne d'Arc
Basses Promenades
bd. Général Leclerc
r. Caqué
r. des Poissonniers
bd. Paul Doumer
TO MUSÉE DE LA REDDITION (50m)
r. Edouard Mignot
r. de Courcelles
Le Manège de Reims
r. de l'Arquebuse
r. de la Magdeleine
PL. STALINGRAD
pont de Vesle
TO (2km)
r. de Trianon
bd. Louis Roederer
Jardin de la Patte d'Oie
bd. M. Noirot
Bike Rental
Comédie de Reims
chaussée Bocquaine
r. de St-Brice
PL. ST-CLAIRE
r. Tarbe
r. des Jardins
r. Soussillon
r. Vernouillet
r. Bruyant
r. du Mont d'Arène
av. Brebant
A4
bd. du Col. Fabien

CHAMPAGNE

town. The €8 lunch *menu* includes salad bar, quiche, and bottled water. Sandwiches and salads €3.80-5.40. Open M-Sa 8am-7pm. MC/V. ❶

Latino Café, 33 place Drouet d'Erlon (☎47 48 89). This brightly decorated restaurant under a hotel pulses with latin music and serves fajitas and quesadillas (€8-10). The perfect place to grab a snack after hitting the bars. Large dinner salads €8.50-12. Open daily 8:30am-3am; food service until 2:30am. MC/V. ❷

SIGHTS

The most popular sights near the center of town are all easily reached by foot. All the champagne *caves*—the biggest draw besides the cathedral—are at least a 25min. walk from downtown and at least a 10min. walk apart. Most champagne firms give tours (all available in English), but some *caves* require reservations at least one day ahead. Ask the tourist office for info on buses (many don't run in summer) and tours that are available without reservation. While **Pommery** and **Ponsardin** claim that you need reservation, solo visitors often have little trouble joining a tour if they ask nicely; larger groups would be wise to follow the rules.

CHAMPAGNE CAVES. Excluding a trip to Epernay (p. 353), this is the best opportunity you'll ever have to swim in bubbly decadence. Four hundred kilometers of *crayères* (Roman chalk quarries) and 200km of more modern French-built *caves* shelter the bottled treasure. The cellars, 30m below ground, are kept at 10°C; bring a sweater. The most elegant and impressive tour is at the massive **Champagne Pommery.** Madame Pommery took over her husband's business in 1858 and became one of France's foremost vintners. Her wealth allowed her to bring art into the workplace, lining the *cave* with exquisite carvings by Gustave Navlet. Now the *caves* host a different contemporary art exhibit each year. The firm also owns one of the world's largest *tonneaux* (vats), carved by Emile Gallé and sent to the 1904 World's Fair in St. Louis as a 75,000L gesture of goodwill. The *caves* are definitely worth a look, though both the modern art and the vat are on display in the lobby if you choose not to spring for a tour. *(5 pl. du Général Gouraud. ☎61 62 56; www.pommery.com. Open daily Apr. to mid-Nov. 10am-7pm; mid-Nov. to Mar. 10am-6pm. Last tour 1hr. before closing. Tours in English, French, and German by reservation. €10-17, under 12 free; includes tour and various tasting options. AmEx/MC/V.)* **Veuve Cliquot Ponsardin's** chic, comprehensive tour passes through the innovative Madame Cliquot's ornately-decorated *salon* before delving into cellars made from ancient chalk mines, which contain some of her original barrels. The visit finishes with a tasting in a stylish modern lounge. *(1 pl. des Droits de L'Homme. ☎89 53 90; www.veuve-clicquot.com. Open Apr.-Oct. M-Sa 10am-6pm; Nov.-Mar. closed Sa. 1½hr. tours in English and French by reservation only; Dutch, German, Italian, and Spanish may also be available. €7.50, under 16 free; includes tour and tasting. MC/V.)* **Taittinger's** tour showcases the *maison's* unique *caves*, which snake along the underground remains of the destroyed Abbaye St-Nicaise. See the world's largest champagne bottle and crystal champagne glass, and peruse a display of Taittinger bottles designed by modern artists. On certain days, visitors may witness the *dégorgement* process by which sediment is removed from aged bottles. In the tunnels, look for the statue of St-Jean, patron saint of wine cellar workers. *(9 pl. St-Nicaise. ☎85 84 33. Open daily mid-Mar. to mid-Nov. 9:30am-1pm and 2-5:30pm, last tour 1hr. before closing; mid-Nov. to mid-Mar. closed weekends. €7; includes short movie, tour, and tasting. AmEx/MC/V.)* For a more kitschy presentation, hop into a cart and spin through the caves of Piper-Heidsieck. The tour offers a simplistic explanation of how champagne is made, with mannequins demonstrating the process as an amusing recording narrates. *(51 bd. Henry Vasnier. ☎84 43 44;*

www.piper-heidsieck.com. Open daily Mar.-Dec. 9:30-11:45am and 2-5pm. 20min. tours in English, French, German, Dutch, Italian, Japanese, and Spanish. Limited wheelchair accessibility. €7.50-15, ages 13-18 €4.50, under 12 free; includes tour and choice of tasting. MC/V.)

CATHÉDRALE DE NOTRE DAME. Too lazy to quarry his own stone, the bishop who commissioned this colossal Gothic creation stole the protective walls of the surrounding city for building materials; fearing attack, the people appealed to the king, who famously declared "God will be the guard." The cathedral has since witnessed the crowning of 26 French kings, beginning with Clovis in AD 498. The current church's facade, begun in 1211, boasts 2307 opulent statues of angels, prophets, and saints. More recently, the building witnessed the reconciliation between President de Gaulle and German Chancellor Adenauer in 1962. While WWI bombing destroyed most of the original stained glass, the newest windows include spectacular sea-blue tableaux by Marc Chagall. Low-hanging chandeliers make the enormous church seem more intimate. *(☎47 55 34. Open daily 7:30am-7:30pm. The tourist office gives tours in French and provides audio tours in English and other languages. Tours €5.50, under 12 free; audio tours €5.)*

PALAIS DU TAU. Next to the cathedral, this former archbishop's residence-turned-museum got its name from its original floor plan, which resembled a "T." With relics from old coronation ceremonies, the Palais's exquisite collection offers an immersion into Reims's regal history. Don't miss the show-stoppers: Charles X's sumptuous 50 ft. robes and the massive statues and creepy gargoyles rescued from crumbling portions of the old cathedral's facade. The **Salle de Tau,** adorned in majestic tapestries, was where France's newly crowned kings celebrated their ascension to the throne with lavish feasting and partying. *(2 pl. du Cardinal Luçon. ☎47 81 79. Open Tu-Su May-Aug. 9:30am-6:30pm; Sept.-Apr. 9:30am-12:30pm and 2-5:30pm. €6.50, ages 18-25 €4.50, under 18 free. Call for information about guided tours.)*

MUSÉE DE LA REDDITION. Germany signed its surrender to the Allies on May 7, 1945, in a schoolroom across the railroad tracks from the *centre-ville*—now the small but fascinating Musée de la Reddition. A short film (in English, French, or German) with actual footage of the surrender, along with several galleries of photos and timelines, lead to the preserved room plastered with maps, which contains the 13 chairs in which the American, British,

GIVING BACK

OOH! PICK ME!

The Champagne region produces 300 million bottles of bubbly each year. It takes about 600 to 800 grapes to make one bottle of champagne. If you do the math, it would seem that about 240 billion grapes need to somehow make their way from the vines into the Champagne *maisons* (wineries) and into a store near you. And now you can help start the process.

According to the Mercier *maison,* the Champagne region employs about 100,000 workers each year for this magical grape transition: the *raisin* (grape) harvest. For visitors who want to take part in the highly regulated champagne-making process, September would be the time to hit France's most famous wine-drenched region. Though most Champagne *maisons* only offer paid picking jobs to EU residents, many allow Americans to volunteer in exchange for food, lodging, or both.

To score one of these hard laboring, but truly unique, jobs, contact the particular *maison de Champagne* yourself; tourist offices throughout the region offer contact information for *maisons* both large and small. Though it helps to speak French to secure a job, it's not necessary.

The best part is, when you see that 2008 vintage in the store a few years down the road, you'll know you had a hand in the historic and prestigious production process.

French, and German heads of state sat. The Soviets were out of town, which is why another more famous (but, the Musée would say, less important) surrender was signed on Stalin's soil several days later. Nothing here is sleek or showy, but as a historical time capsule, the place itself is powerful. *(12 rue Franklin Roosevelt, north of the train station. ☎47 84 19. Open M and W-Su 10am-noon and 2-6pm, Tu 2-6pm. €3, ages 15-18 €1.50, students and under 15 free. €3 pass includes 4 other museums in Reims.)*

OTHER SIGHTS. Near the Taittinger caves, the **Basilique St-Rémi** rises above a lavender garden. This Romanesque church was built around the tomb of St-Rémi, the bishop who baptized Clovis, France's first king. Almost entirely destroyed during WWI, it has since returned to its former glory. *(Pl. St-Rémi. Open daily in summer 8am-9pm; in winter 8am-5pm. Light show* (son-et-lumière) *July-Sept. Sa 9:30pm.)* Around the corner, the small **Musée-Abbaye St-Rémi** shelters an extensive collection of religious art, military uniforms, and artifacts from the Merovingian and Carolingian eras. Look for a mournful statue of Mercury's head, salvaged from a public edifice in AD 3. *(53 rue Simon. ☎85 23 36. Open M-F 2-6:30pm, Sa-Su 2-7pm. €3; 1st Su of the month free.)* Rising over pl. de la République on the other side of town, the **Porte Mars** is Reims's largest Roman arch, badly damaged by WWI fighting. The ancient monument is decorated with reliefs of Romulus and Remus, who gave the city its name.

TIP **BUBBLY FOR THE ROAD.** If you're out to purchase a souvenir bottle of champagne, don't assume that a famous brand is cheapest in its *maison's* boutique. Compare prices at local wine stores and supermarkets—you'll often discover the bottles featured in your **dégustation** for a few euro less than at the *cave*. If you're traveling by car, look for the small, independent *maisons* outside major towns. If the white, gold, and blue flag of the Champagne region is flying, the *maison* is open to visitors—and they'll usually offer you a free taste. Since these producers typically sell only to clients directly, they offer the best deals.

ENTERTAINMENT AND NIGHTLIFE

Reims offers a host of cultural activities befitting its cosmopolitan atmosphere. Follow the sidewalk covered with names of famous playwrights from around the world to the **Comédie de Reims,** 3 chaussée Bocquaine, a regional acting school and theater that stages performances and workshops. (☎48 49 00. Open Sept.-June M-F noon-7pm, Sa 1-7pm. Tickets to featured productions €10-13, students €5-7; prices for other events vary.) **Cinéma Opéra,** 3 rue Théodore Dubois, shows a range of international films in their original languages. (☎08 92 68 01 22. Tickets €5.80-7.30, under 16 €5.40; student discount with ID for weekday shows. Ticket office open daily 1:30-10pm.) The **Grand Théâtre de Reims,** 13 rue Chanzy, hosts operas and ballets. (☎50 03 92. Open Oct.-June Tu-Sa 2:30-6:30pm.) Throughout the year, less traditional **Le Manège de Reims,** 2 bd. du Général Leclerc, presents dance shows, performance art, and music on its stage, with *les dimanches des curiosités* (special themed performances) on most Sundays. (☎47 30 40. Tickets €5.50-20.) During the summer, Reims hosts the celebrated **Flâneries Musicales d'Été,** with over 80 concerts in six weeks. Esteemed classical musicians share the bill with smaller jazz groups and guitar soloists. (☎77 45 12; www.flaneriesreims.com. Late June to early Aug. Contact the tourist office for more info. Many performances free; some concerts €10-12, students and under 18 €8-10.)

At night, people fill the cafés and bars on **place Drouet d'Erlon** and **rue de Vesle.** Place Drouet d'Erlon is especially touristy, though the crowds are lively and last until late. **Tropical Café,** 89 pl. Drouet d'Erlon, features Afro-Caribbean décor and music, and a young lively crowd sipping on piña coladas. (☎61 35 72. Beer from

€3. Mixed drinks €7. 10% price increase after 10pm. Live music W-Sa. Open daily 11am-2:30am. AmEx/MC/V.) **The Glue Pot,** 49 pl. d'Erlon, is a popular English-style pub with food at all hours and comfy leather chairs on its outdoor terrace. (☎47 36 46. Beer from €2.80. Open daily noon-3am. 10% price increase after 10pm. MC/V.) For relaxed fun away from the town's main drag, check out **Le Backstage,** 13 rue de Sarrail, a small, local *brasserie* decorated in jazzy posters and filled at all hours with a mixed-age crowd sipping cheap beer. Beer from €2.30. Mixed drinks from €4. Open M-Th 7:30am-12:30am, F 7:30am-1:30am, Su 10am-1:30am. MC/V.

EPERNAY ☎03 26

Every town has its main street, but few could trump Epernay's avenue de Champagne. An endless cascade of opulent mansions, the boulevard holds the world's most celebrated champagne *maisons*, making Epernay (ay-pare-NAY; pop. 26,000) the region's showcase. Firms Moët & Chandon, Perrier-Jouet, and Mercier collectively store 700 million bottles of the sparkling spirit in 100km of tunnels beneath the town. At the heart of the *Route Touristique du Champagne*, Epernay also serves as an excellent base for exploring the surrounding vineyards, châteaux, and hills, which offer gorgeous natural diversions once the bubbly buzz has worn off. However, such plentiful luxury comes at a price: Epernay caters to scads of wealthy (and, eventually, intoxicated) tourists willing to spend, and thus offers few budget values for the thrifty traveler, although it's worth a day of splurging.

TRANSPORTATION

Trains leave from cour de la Gare, two blocks from central pl. de la République. (Ticket offices open M-Th 6am-7:20pm, F 6am-8pm, Sa 6:45am-7pm, Su 6:45am-9pm.) Trains run to Paris (1¼hr., 18 per day, €19), Reims (30min., 16 per day, €5.60), and Strasbourg (3½hr., 3 per day, €40). STDM **buses** (☎65 17 07) serve Paris, Reims, and small towns in Champagne; ask at the tourist office for a schedule and map. **Local buses** are run by **Sparnabus,** rue E. Duchâtel, at the *gare routière*. (☎55 55 50. Open M 2-6pm, Tu-F 9am-noon and 2-6pm, Sa 9am-noon. Tickets €1.10, *carnet* of 10 €8.) Rent **bikes** at **Fabien Royer,** 10 pl. Hugues Plomb. (☎55 29 61. 8 per ½-day, €14 per day, €23 per weekend, €65 per week. Open Tu-Sa 9am-noon and 2-7pm. MC/V.) **ABC Taxi** provides 24hr. service (☎06 30 81 69 58).

PRACTICAL INFORMATION

Be aware that there are two streets called **rue Gambetta**—one near the tourist office, and one across the water; be sure not to confuse them. To get to the **tourist office,** 7 av. de Champagne, from the station, walk straight ahead through pl. Mendès France, onto rue Gambetta or rue J. Moët; walk one block to **place de la République,** and turn left on av. de Champagne (5min.). The English-speaking staff provides free maps, a list of hotels, info on *caves*, suggestions for *routes champénoises*, and wine tastings (see **Maisons de Champagne,** p. 354). They also offer a list of local events and festivities in French. (☎53 33 00; www.ot-epernay.fr. Open Easter to mid-Oct. M-Sa 9:30am-12:30pm and 1:30-7pm, Su 11am-4pm; mid-Oct. to Holy Saturday M-Sa 9:30am-12:30pm and 1:30-5:30pm.) Other services include: a **laundromat,** 8 av. Jean Jaurès (open daily 7am-8pm); **police,** 7 rue Jean Chandon-Moët (☎56 96 60, call here for the **pharmacie de garde**); and a **hospital,** 137 rue de l'Hôpital (☎58 70 70). Access the **Internet** at **Cyberm@nia,** 11 pl. des Arcades. (€3 per 1hr.; €5 per 3hr. Open M 2pm-midnight, Tu-Sa 11am-midnight, Su 2-8pm.) The **post office,** pl. Hugues Plomb, has **currency exchange.** (☎53 31 65. Open M-F 8:30am-6:30pm, Sa 8:30am-noon.) **Postal Code:** 51200.

ACCOMMODATIONS AND CAMPING

Budget hotels in Epernay are scarce. A 10min. walk from train station, **Hôtel St-Pierre ❷,** 1 rue Jeanne d'Arc, past pl. d'Europe, is your best bet, offering three floors of spacious, antique-furnished rooms. (☎54 40 80; fax 57 88 68. Breakfast €6. Reception 7am-10pm. Reservations recommended. Singles and doubles €21-24, with shower €30-36. MC/V.) Near the station, **Hôtel de la Cloche ❸,** 3-5 pl. Mendès France, is a pricey but convenient option. The colorful, comfortable, and classy rooms—oh-so-surprisingly decorated with champagne advertisements—come with bath and TV. (☎55 15 15; hotel-de-la-cloche.c.prin@wanadoo.fr. Breakfast buffet €7.50. Reception 9am-10pm. Check-out noon. Singles and doubles with shower or bath €43-50; triples €53-58. AmEx/MC/V.) **Hotel le Progrès ❸,** 6 rue des Berceaux, offers minimally decorated but comfortable rooms in the center of town. All rooms come with shower or bath and toilet. (☎55 24 75; fax 55 72 83. Breakfast €7. Reception M 4:30-7pm, Tu-Sa 8am-noon and 3-7pm; call ahead if you plan to arrive when reception is closed. May-Sept. singles €37-42; doubles €37-52. Oct.-Apr. €35-40/35-49.) There's a **campground ❶** near the station (2km; dir.: Reims) at allée de Cumières, on the banks of the Marne. Small sites are divided by tall hedges for privacy. The site also has showers, laundry, volleyball, tennis, and ping pong. (☎55 32 14; camping.epernay@free.fr. Reception June-Aug. 7am-10pm; Sept. and Apr.-May 8am-8pm. Open mid-Apr. to Sept. €3.30 per adult, €1.50 per child, €2.50 per tent, €1.50 per car. Electricity €3. AmEx/MC/V over €15.)

FOOD

The pedestrian district around **place des Arcades** and **place Hugues Plomb** is dotted with delis and bakeries. There's a horde of pizza and kebab eateries near the tourist office on **rue Gambetta** and a **Marché Plus** supermarket at 17 pl. Hugues Plomb, near the post office. (☎51 89 89. Open M-Sa 7am-9pm, Su 9am-1pm.) **Halle St-Thibault,** near pl. de l'Europe, hosts a market. (W-Sa 8am-noon.) **La Cave à Champagne ❸,** 16 rue Gambetta, incorporates the adored local product into nearly all its dishes, from *foie gras à la champagne* to salmon in champagne butter. Packed with champagne lovers, this place offers novelty above all else, with champagne advertisements and regional flora. (☎55 50 70. *Menus* €17-40. Open M-Tu noon-2pm and 7-10pm, W 7-10pm, Th-Sa noon-2pm and 7-10pm, Su noon-2pm and 7-10pm. Reservations recommended. MC/V.) Across the water from the *centre-ville,* **L'Kenavo ❷,** 20 rue Jean Moulin, is the best and quirkiest *crêperie* around. Stuffed badgers and foxes look on as you dine in an Alsatian interior. You'll find a range of regional specialties and fairly pricey *galettes*, but the plate-sized dessert *crêpes* are near meals unto themselves. (☎51 00 25. *Galettes* €9.50-14. *Crêpes* €4.20-8.70. Open Tu-Su noon-1:30pm and 7:30-9pm. MC/V.) Epernay's plentiful ethnic restaurants serve some of the best value meals in town. At the cozy Moroccan restaurant **Les Palmeraies ❷,** 19 rue de Reims, flavorful meats and vegetables come atop heaps of couscous (€8-13). Get a generous half-sized portion for only €5. (☎32 54 42. Open daily noon-2:30pm and 7-10:30pm. MC/V.)

MAISONS DE CHAMPAGNE

The name says it all: **avenue de Champagne** is a long, broad strip of palatial *maisons de champagne* pouring bubbly for hordes of visitors from across the globe. The tours below are all offered in English or French; no reservations are required, though without reservations you may have to wait up to an hour for the next tour. All include a petite *dégustation* (ages 16+, 18+ at *Moët & Chandon*) and offer more extensive (and expensive) tastings as well. Without springing for a tour, the only thing visitors get to see at the *maisons* are liquor-lined boutiques and lush lobbies. *Caves* are maintained between 10 and 12°C; bring a sweater. Each firm's tour may give more or less the same explanation of the champagne-making process, but everything, from the dress of the guides to the design of the lobby, reflects the status and character of the producer.

For a cheap alternative to the big *maisons*, ask the tourist office about *l'esprit de champagne*, a free presentation and sampling given in the tourist office by several small companies. (Presentations offered June to mid-Oct. F-Sa 10:45am-noon and 3-6pm; July-Aug. Th-Sa 10:45am-noon and 3-6pm.) One of the younger participating *maisons*, **Esterlin,** 25 av. de Champagne, also offers a free tasting and a 10min. video history of the product at its *maison*. (☎59 71 52; www.champagne-esterlin.com. Open M-Sa 10am-noon and 2-5pm.)

MOËT & CHANDON. The granddaddy of them all, Moët & Chandon, the producer of legendary champagne Dom Pérignon, has been "turning nature into art" since 1743. The tour and tasting are worth every *cent*—and with a slogan like "Be Fabulous," what else would you expect? The mansion is full of the old-money opulence one would expect, from elegant carvings lining the inside of ancient *caves* to the stately mansion rooms decorated for Napoleon I, a close friend of the M&C family. The 1hr. tour details the process of champagne production and gives the history of champagne, highlighting M&C's superior standards at every turn. The polished *caves* are the most beautiful in town, filled with statues and an ornate cask given as a gift by Napoleon I, and the 5min. film is a thoroughly amusing bit of highbrow self-promotion. *(20 av. de Champagne. ☎51 20 20; www.moet.com. Open Apr. to mid-Nov. daily 9:30-11:30am and 2-4:30pm; mid-Nov. to Mar. M-F 9:30-11:30am and 2-4:30pm. Tours with several tasting options €11-23, ages 10-18 €6.70, under 10 free. AmEx/MC/V.)*

MERCIER. If Willy Wonka were to design a champagne *maison*, it would be the Mercier *maison;* in fact, the eccentric founder, Eugène Mercier is very similar to Roald Dahl's favorite chocolate maker. Less famous but equally swanky than nearby Moët, Mercier is the self-proclaimed maker of the "most popular champagne in France." The *maison* offers a 30min. tour beginning with a ride in a musical glass elevator that takes you past bubbly-sipping mannequins, then takes visitors on a ride in roller-coaster

THE LOCAL STORY

CHATTING WITH MOËT & CHANDON

Let's Go got the scoop on champagne caves by interviewing Cécile Titeux Doyer, the chief coordinator of tours at Moët & Chandon, a premier champagne maison.

LG: What appeals to you most about working at the *maison*?

A: I like to meet people from everywhere in the world. Thanks to the famous name of Moët & Chandon, we welcome about 80,000 visitors every year, and 80% are from foreign countries.

LG: How much champagne do you drink per week at M&C?

A: We try not to drink here while we're working, but sometimes we'll have a few glasses of champagne during lunch meetings. A few years ago, there was one guide who had a glass of champagne at the end of each tour, so he had about four or five a day.

LG: Has champagne lost any of its allure for you, now that you're surrounded by it all the time?

A: I have to say I love champagne. It's really my favorite drink. I've met a few people from other areas and countries who, after three or four months in our area, want a glass of champagne each time they have an *apéritif*. We quickly turn people into addicts!

LG: Do you have a favorite memory from working here?

A: The best moments are when the visitors leave, and we have the impression that, thanks to our personality, they've had a very good time.

style cars through its *caves*. The tour also details Mercier's wild rise from rags to riches. One of the wacky owner's 19th-century advertising schemes included sending a blimp-sized cask of champagne to the 1889 World's Fair exposition in Paris, brought him from rags to riches; the extravagant wooden vat, which took second place only to none other than the *Tour Eiffel* (p. 135), now sits in the *maison*'s central foyer. Always an innovator, Mercier offered *dégustations* in hot air balloons and was the first to feature electricity in his *caves*. *(70 av. de Champagne. ☎51 22 22; www.champagne-mercier.fr. Wheelchair-accessible. Open mid-Mar. to mid-Nov. daily 9:30-11:30am and 2-4:30pm; mid-Nov. to mid-Dec. and mid-Feb. to mid-Mar. M and Th-Su only. €7-15, ages 12-16 €3.50, under 12 free. MC/V.)*

DE CASTELLANE. Across the street from Mercier, de Castellane offers a less romantic tour than those of M&C and Mercier but gets into the nitty-gritty of champagne production. Whereas M&C and Mercier only allude to modern advancements in wine making, this tour walks visitors through the whole mechanical process, which is just as fascinating as the methods of old. Visitors during the week can observe factory workers unloading, corking, and labeling. Chance groups may get to witness the *dégorgement* (sediment-removal process) that takes place sporadically throughout each month. A ticket also buys admission to a rather dry museum of mannequins enacting the production process, a random yet thorough exhibit on label making, as well as access to a 237-step tower with sweeping views of the region. All are good way to kill time while waiting for the next tour, though not worth going out of your way to visit. *(57 rue de Verdun. ☎51 19 11. Open Apr. to late Dec. daily 10am-noon and 2-6pm; Mar. Sa-Su 10am-noon and 2-6pm. Last morning tour 11:15am; last evening tour 5:15pm. Tours in English, French, German, Danish, and Spanish; €7-25; include a variety of tasting options. AmEx/MC/V.)*

NIGHTLIFE

The quality of Epernay's nightlife ebbs and flows with the energy (and level of intoxication) of its generally older tourists; don't bank on a lively night out. However, Epernay is one of the few places where you can sip champagne in style at 9:30am without attracting stares. Try **place de la République, place Mendès France,** or **place Hugues Plomb** for youth-filled bars and pubs. **Le Central,** 15 pl. de la République, consists of a big, local eatery downstairs and a bar upstairs. The bar, with comfortable chairs surrounded by windows, attracts many tourists and locals who relax with friends over a drink. (☎59 19 93. Beer from €2.20. Mixed drinks from €6.50. Bar open Tu and Th-Su 8pm-1am. Food M-Tu and Th-Su noon-midnight. MC/V.) **Club St-Jean,** 12 rue Pierre Semard, is a small discotheque across from the train station with a DJ who spins French and international tunes. Students and tourists come and go, while most regulars are 30 and older. (☎55 26 42. Beer from €4. Mixed drinks from €8. Open M-Th 10:30pm-4am, F-Sa 10:30pm-5am. MC/V.) **The Garden Club,** 5 av. Foch, plays a techno-free sound track of music from the 70s to the present and attracts an older crowd. The club has a stylish terrace with a pool in the back where customers can daintily down drinks until 11pm. (☎54 20 30. Beer from €3.50 until 9pm; from €5.50 9pm-4am. Mixed drinks €5.50/8. Open M-Sa 5pm-4am, Su 7pm-4am. MC/V).

TROYES ☎03 25

Troyes (TRWAH; 60,900) is a stylish city that prides itself on living the good life. Cheap and delicious cuisine combine with massive amounts of bubbly to make this city a gastronomic delight, while both traditional and quirky museums entertain between meals. Yet despite its superficial sheen, the city boasts an extensive

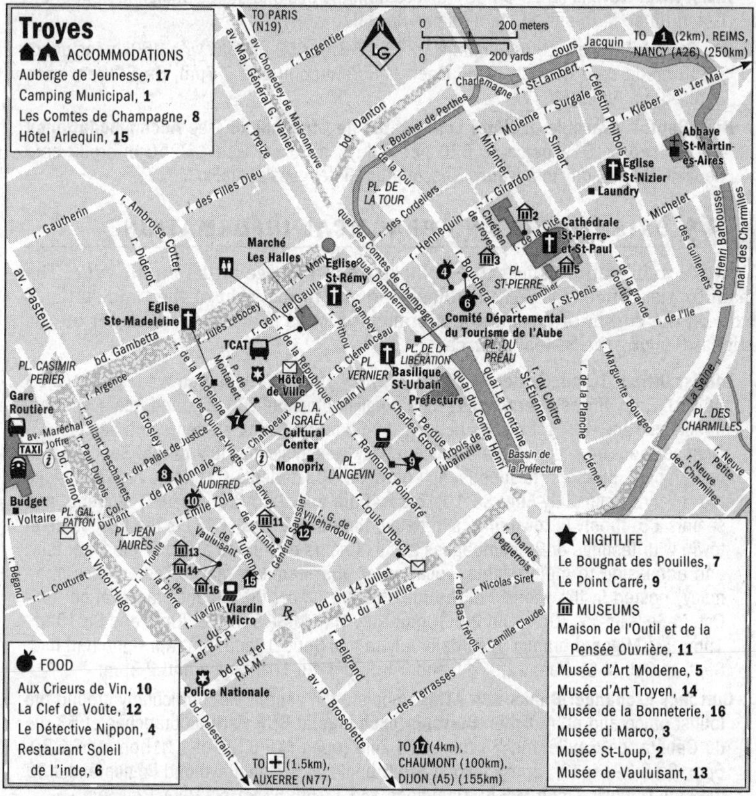

intellectual history: it was here that Chrétien de Troyes wrote *Parsifal*, Jewish scholar Rashi translated the Bible and the Talmud, and a local shoemaker's son—later named Pope Urbain IV—grew up. Today, Troyes benefits from a well-preserved *vieille ville* and a lively urban atmosphere—all contained within a city appropriately shaped like a *bouchon de champagne* (champagne cork).

TRANSPORTATION

Trains: At the intersection of av. Maréchal Joffre and rue du Ravelin (☎08 36 35 35 35). Ticket office open M-Sa 5:40am-8:40pm, Su 6:30am-8:40pm. Info office open M-Sa 9:30am-6:20pm. Routes marked "car" are serviced by buses. To **Mulhouse** (3-3½hr.; M-F 8 per day, Sa-Su 7; €38), **Lyon** (4-5hr.; M-F 12 per day, Sa-Su 9; €44, TGV via Paris €73-90), and TGV to **Paris** (1½hr.; M-F 16 per day, Sa-Su 13; €22).

Buses: Turn left out of the train station and enter the door on your left in the next building labeled *"gare routière."* **SDTM TransChampagne** (☎03 26 65 17 07) runs to **Reims** (2hr., M-Sa 2 per day, €22).

Public Transportation: TCAT (☎70 49 00; www.tcat.fr), in front of **Les Halles** market. Open M-F 8am-12:45pm and 1:30-7pm, Sa 1:30-6:30pm. Service every 12-23min. Tickets on the bus (€1.30, 3 for €3.30); Mini Turbo tickets at the office or in *tabacs* (12 for €11).

Taxis: Taxis Troyens (☎78 30 30), across from the bus and train stations, in front of the Grand Hôtel. M-Th and Su 4am-1am, F-Sa 24hr.

Car Rental: Budget, 10 rue Voltaire (☎73 27 37). €52 per day with 250km included; €650 credit card deposit. 21+. Open M-F 8am-noon and 2-7pm, Sa 8:30am-noon and 2-6pm. AmEx/MC/V.

Bike Rental: Available at **Hôtel Les Comtes de Champagne** (see **Accommodations**). €8 per ½-day, €12 per day, €20 per 2 days, €60 per week; €250 or credit card deposit. Book 1 day in advance. Discount for hotel guests. AmEx/MC/V.

ORIENTATION AND PRACTICAL INFORMATION

Troyes's train station is just three blocks from the edge of the *vieille ville*. The main tourist office is clearly visible ahead and to the right of the train station's exit, on the corner of bd. Carnot; a branch office is near the town center on rue Mignard, facing the St-Jean church.

Tourist Office: 16 bd. Carnot (☎82 62 70; www.ot-troyes.fr), and on rue Mignard (☎73 36 88). Both offices offer free city map, English brochure (€0.50), and free accommodations service with 1st night's deposit. Audio tours €5.50, students and seniors €3. Themed tours from the Mignard office; check weekly listing. July to mid-Sept. English and French; mid-Sept. to June French only. €5.50, students €3. Horse-drawn carriage tour every 45min. July-Aug. Sa 10:15-11:45am and 2:15-6:45pm; €7, students and seniors €5. If only in town for a short stay, the **Pass'Troyes** (€12) is the best value in town, with tastings of 2 champagnes at Aux Crieurs de Vin, an audio or personal tour, and admission to major sights. Location of **pharmacie de garde** (emergency pharmacy) posted in the window of the rue Mignard office. Bd. Carnot branch open Apr.-Oct. M-Sa 9am-12:30pm and 2-6:30pm; Nov.-Mar. M-Sa 9am-12:30pm and Su 10am-1pm. Rue Mignard branch open daily July to mid-Sept. 10am-7pm; Apr.-June and mid-Sept. to Oct. M-Sa 9am-12:30pm and 2-6:30pm, Su 10am-noon and 2-5pm.

Currency Exchange: Banks with **ATMs** populate the *centre-ville*, particularly around the tourist office and pl. A. Israël. **Currency exchange** at **BNP Paribas** branches at 53 rue du Général de Gaulle and 58 rue Emile Zola (open M-F 8:30am-12:15pm and 1:30-6pm, Sa 8:30am-12:15pm). Also at **SNVB** banks at 5-7 rue Raymond Poincaré and 39 rue Paul Dubois. (Open M-F 8:30am-noon and 1:15-5:55pm, Sa 9am-12:15pm.)

Laundromat: Laverie St-Nizier, 107 rue Rév. Père Lafra (☎06 14 66 11 29), near the cathedral. Wash €3.50 per 7kg, dry €0.50 per 6min. Open daily 7am-9pm.

Police: (☎42 34 21) near the Hôtel de Ville. **Police Nationale,** bd. 1ère R.A.M (☎43 51 00).

Hospital: 101 av. Anatole France (☎49 49 49).

Internet Access: Le Point Carré, 27 rue Raymond Poincaré (☎81 63 44). Look for the sign that reads "Cyber Café." €0.03 per min., €2 per hr. Free Wi-Fi with purchase of drink. Open daily 2pm-1:30am. **Viardin Micro,** 10 rue Viardin. €2 per hr. Open Tu 9:30am-noon and 2-7pm, W-Sa 9:30am-noon and 2pm-midnight.

Post Office: 38 rue Louis Ulbach (☎43 77 56). Open M-F 8am-7pm, Sa 9am-12:30pm. **Currency exchange.** Branch offices at 2 pl. Général Patton, a block to the right down bd. Carnot from the train station (☎45 29 00; open M-F 9am-noon and 2:30-6pm, Sa 9am-noon); 14 rue de la République (open Tu-F 10am-12:30pm and 1:45-5:30pm, Sa 9am-noon). **Postal Code:** 10000.

ACCOMMODATIONS AND CAMPING

Les Comtes de Champagne, 56 rue de la Monnaie (☎73 11 70; www.comtesdechampagne.com). This 16th-century mansion has large windows, a courtyard, and themed rooms decorated with stylish old magazine ads. Some have a rustic décor; others have dainty tables and pastel wallpaper. All rooms have TV, toilet, and telephone. Breakfast €6. Reception 7am-10pm. Reservations recommended. Singles €32; doubles from €38; triples from €61; quads from €67; rooms with kitchenette €66-€87. Some rooms fit 5-6. Extra bed €6. AmEx/MC/V. ❸

Hôtel Arlequin, 50 rue Turenne (☎83 12 70; www.hotelarlequin.com). Unless you're afraid of clowns, this circus-themed hotel is a welcoming home-away-from-home, with color-coordinated rooms, A/C, large windows, and high ceilings. Unbeatable suites for 3 or more guests. Breakfast €7.50. Wi-Fi. Reception M-Sa 8am-12:30pm and 2-10pm, Su 8am-12:30pm and 6:30-10pm. Singles and doubles with shower €40, with bath €54-58; triples with shower or bath €68; quads €78. Extra bed €5.50. AmEx/MC/V. ❸

Auberge de Jeunesse (HI), 10430 chemin Ste-Scholastique (☎82 00 65; www.fuaj.org/aj/troyes). Take local bus #8 from Les Halles (dir.: Château de Rosièrest) to "Liberté." Following the signs, continue down rue de la Liberté, take a left on rue Jules Ferry, and then a right on chemin Ste-Scholastique. This spacious converted abbey, open year-round and clean as a whistle, holds 104 beds. The only catch is that it's 5km from the center of town. Breakfast €3.50. Reception 8am-9pm. 5- and 6-person dorms with shower €14. MC/V. ❶

Camping Municipal de Troyes, 7 rue Salengro (☎81 02 64; www.troyescamping.net), on N77, 2km from town. Take bus #1 (dir.: Pont Ste-Marie) to this well-stocked 3-star site. Includes showers, toilets, TV, restaurant, and laundry, as well as a trampoline and playground. Reception 9am-10pm. Open Apr. to mid-Oct. €4.40 per adult, €3 per child, €5.90 per tent or car. MC/V. ❶

FOOD

The area from **rue Champeaux** south to **rue Emile Zola,** known as the **quartier St-Jean,** is the best place to enjoy a scenic and savory meal. Cafés, restaurants, *brasseries*, and *crêperies* line these pedestrian streets just west of pl. Alexandre Israël, which also form the center of *Troyenne* nightlife. A walk down **rue Général Saussier** or **rue Turrenne** leads to the smaller **quartier Vauluisant,** which boasts its own pedestrian avenue with delightful dining options. Inexpensive kebab joints line the less attractive **rue du Général de Gaulle** and **rue de la Cité.**

Les Halles, an indoor market on the corner of rue de la République and rue Général de Gaulle, offers fresh produce, meats, and baked goods from the Aube region, plus a lively outdoor flea market during the summer. Try the intense *andouillette de Troyes* (tripe sausage) or the rich and creamy *fromage de Troyes*. (Open M-Th 8am-12:45pm and 3:30-7pm, F-Sa 7am-7pm, Su 9am-12:30pm. Many stands accept MC/V.) Grab groceries at the **Monoprix** supermarket, upstairs at 71 rue Emile Zola (☎73 10 78; open M-Sa 8:30am-8pm), and picnic in pl. de la Libération, along the *Bassin de la Préfecture.*

Aux Crieurs de Vin, 4-6 pl. Jean Jaurès (☎40 01 01). As the name suggests, this eatery revolves around Troyes's favorite spirit, from the winery and tasting bar in the front, to the cellar-like dining area decorated with drinking advertisements. Waiters bring a chalkboard menu featuring a small selection of meat and cheese tastings (€5-10) and salads (€13). Meal with a glass of wine €13. 2 champagne samples free with purchase of the *Pass'Troyes* at the tourist office. Open Tu-Sa noon-2pm and 7:30-10pm. Bar open Tu-Sa 11am-midnight. MC/V. ❷

La Clef de Voûte, 33-35 rue Général Saussier (☎73 72 07). Though it's decorated with ski posters and snowshoes, this rustic restaurant offers a warm and inviting atmosphere. Cheese lovers will delight in the selection of *gratins* and fondues (€10-19); sausage fans should order the Andouillette AAAAA, approved by the Association Ami-

CHAMPAGNE

cale des Amateurs d'Andouillettes Authentiques (€5-15). Interested in lighter fare? Try one of the overflowing salads (€7-10). Open M 7:30-10pm, Tu-Th noon-2pm and 7:30-10pm, F-Sa noon-2pm and 7:30-10:30pm. AmEx/MC/V. ❷

Restaurant Soleil de l'Inde, 33 rue de la Cité (☎80 75 71). Popular with *Troyenne* youth, this stylish eatery offers an extensive Indian and Pakistani selection. The *Formule Rapide* (€9) includes naan, a meat dish, and a dessert. Plentiful number of vegetarian *plats* (all €7). Open Tu-Su noon-2:30pm and 7-10:30pm. MC/V. ❷

Le Détective Nippon, 21 rue de la Cité (☎46 19 48). Though its decorations—painted fans and paper lanterns—are painfully predictable, the food at this Japanese restaurant provides a worthwhile change from *Troyenne* fare. For hungry scholars, a filling student *menu* (€7) is offered M-F, except F dinner. *Menus* €8.80-14. Open M-Th noon-2pm and 7-10pm, F noon-2pm and 7-10:30pm, Sa 7-10:30pm. MC/V. ❷

SIGHTS AND OUTDOOR ACTIVITIES

CATHÉDRALE ST-PIERRE-ET-ST-PAUL. The sheer size of this Gothic cathedral is only slightly less stunning than its spectacularly intricate 13th- to 19th-century stained-glass designs, which illustrate everything from the Parable of Wise and Foolish Virgins to scenes from the life of Christ. A long history of fires and other disasters has claimed much of the original architecture, making the surviving windows all the more remarkable. Less conspicuous but equally impressive is the cathedral's 18th-century organ, which was declared one of France's most prestigious instruments in 1974 and is now frequently played at concerts. Call the church for concert listings. *(Pl. St-Pierre, down rue de la Cité. Enter via the small entrance to the right of the main doors. ☎76 98 18. Open Tu-Sa 10am-1pm and 2-6pm, Su 10am-noon and 2-5pm. Treasury open July-Aug. Tu-Sa 10am-noon and 3-5pm, Su 3-5pm. Treasury guides in French. Free. Info cards available on loan in English and German.)*

MUSÉE D'ART MODERNE. This well-designed museum is Troyes's cultural centerpiece, featuring over 2000 works of French art from 1850-1950, including pieces by Degas, Picasso, Rodin, and Seurat. A former bishop's palace, the expansive building and its grounds are almost as much of an attraction as the art itself—creative couches line the hallways and the open courtyards are ideal for a picnic. The museum contains a diverse collection of statues, masks, and paintings from Africa and Oceania—works that inspired their European counterparts. *(Pl. St-Pierre. ☎76 26 80. Open Tu-Su 10am-1pm and 2-6pm. €5, student and under 18 free; 1st Su of month free.*

MAISON DE L'OUTIL ET DE LA PENSÉE OUVRIÈRE. This collection of over 8000 tools and architectural models from the 18th and 19th centuries, contained in a delightful 16th-century Renaissance-style house, is the largest such display in the world. Elaborately arranged in bizarre geometric patterns, the instruments for working with wood, iron, leather, and stone will impress even those without an interest in "the tools and thoughts of the worker." *(7 rue de la Trinité. ☎73 28 26; www.maison-de-l-outil.com. Open M 1-6pm and Tu-Su 10am-6pm. €6.50, families €16, students under 25 free. English and German guidebooks available on loan. MC/V over €13.)*

EGLISE STE-MADELEINE. This 12th-century structure boasts an intricate display of stained glass, which includes a complete representation of Christ's family tree. The real sight to see, however, is the flamboyant Gothic *jubé* (gallery), made of carved stone, which sits in the middle of the church and divides the nave from the choir. Sift through your pockets for spare change: for €0.50, the attendant will shine a spotlight on the *jubé* to display the spectacular shadow effects. Well-labeled information panels in English, French, and German offer fascinating bits of trivia about the architecture. *(Rue de la Madeleine. ☎73 82 90. Open M-Sa 9:30am-12:30pm and 2-5:30pm, Su 2-5:30pm.)*

BASILIQUE ST-URBAIN. At night, this basilica's spear-like spires stand illuminated against the dark sky, but its flying buttresses are best seen in daylight. When Jacques Pantaléon became Pope Urbain IV, he commissioned the Gothic structure to be built—right upon the site of his father's old cobbler shop. The original 13th-century choir and transept remain, while stained-glass windows depicting Pantaléon's childhood were added as late as the 19th century. The choir has held Urban IV's remains since 1935. *(Pl. Vernier, off rue Georges Clemenceau. ☎73 13 37. Open M-Sa 9:30am-12:30pm and 2-5:30pm, Su 2-5:30pm.)*

OTHER SIGHTS. At the city's second largest museum, the **Musée St-Loup,** stuffed vultures lurk above a forest of taxidermal animals, the basement houses a geology exhibit, and portraits of old French royalty rest in luxury on the top floors, high above everything else. *(Rue de la Cité. ☎76 21 68; www.ville-troyes.fr. Open Tu-Su 9am-noon and 1-5pm. €4, students and under 18 free.)* The three-year-old **Musée di Marco** houses works by Angelo di Marco, who became famous for his hyper-realistic, pulpy style of comic book illustrations. The gallery features only a sampling of his drawings, but a movie about his life (in French only) showcases other pieces. *(Pl. de la Cathédrale. ☎40 18 27. Open Apr.-Sept. Tu-Su 10:30am-6:30pm; Oct.-Mar. W-Su 10:30am-6:30pm. €5, groups of 10 or more €4.)* The **Musée Vauluisant,** which houses both the **Musée d'Art Troyen** and the **Musée de la Bonneterie,** displays a collection of 16th- to 17th-century sculptures from the Troyes school and a 19th-century artisan's textile workshop. With old wood-patterned floors and winding stone stairwells, the building and the herb garden in the courtyard are as worthy of attention as the art. *(4 rue de Vauluisant. ☎73 05 85. Open Tu-Su 9am-noon and 1-5pm. €3, students and under 18 free.)*

OUTDOOR ACTIVITIES. Over 12,500 acres of freshwater lakes dot the region around Troyes. The sparkling Lake Orient welcomes sunbathers, swimmers, and windsurfers, while the wilder waters of Lake Temple are reserved for fishing and bird-watching. Those in search of adventure might favor Lake Amance, which is usually populated by speedboats and waterskiers. The **Comité Départemental du Tourisme de l'Aube,** 34 quai Dampierre, offers free brochures on local and regional outdoor activities, as well as campsites and cheap

(BAR)TENDING TO THE NEEDS OF OTHERS

Bartenders have always been connected with comfort and conversation (not to mention sexiness), but they aren't usually associated with community service. However, visitors to Troyes, in the Champagne region, will find that the two can be inextricably linked—in the **Kiwi Bar Project,** organized by the International Volunteer Program (IVP).

Since 1991, the IVP has been working with local groups to organize volunteer opportunities for visitors; their Kiwi Bar project employs participants in a local alcohol rehabilitation clinic. Volunteers are expected to not only provide assistance in the clinic but also to work as bartenders in the adjacent non-alcoholic bar, as well as (perhaps an extension of any bartender's responsibilities) chat with the clinic's patients. The bar also serves local university students, in addition to citizens of Troyes who come to visit.

There's nothing cooler than serving others, except maybe the chilled drinks you'll be mixing up.

This is just one of several opportunities available through IVP. Programs last from several weeks to over a year. Visit www.ivpsf.org for a complete list and description of programs as well as application materials.

summer-camp style lodgings in the area. *(☎42 50 00. Open M-F 9:30am-12:30pm and 1:30-6pm.)* The tourist office has bus schedules for the Troyes-Grands Lacs routes. In July and August, the **Courriers de l'Aube** takes travelers to Lake Orient three times daily. *(☎71 28 40. €5.60.)* There is also a scenic 42km bike-only path between Troyes and Port Dienville, along Lake Amance. In Dienville, camping is available at **Camping du Tertre** *(☎92 26 50)*.

ENTERTAINMENT AND FESTIVALS

Troyes may be small, but even the most jaded locals admit that it's a city *"qui bouge bien"* ("that's happening"). The most concentrated swath of nightlife is by **rue Champeaux** and **rue Molé** off pl. Alexandre Israël. Part bar, part cyber-café, the new and hip **Le Point Carré,** 27 rue Raymond Poincaré, caters to a crowd of young, laid-back regulars. Decorated with American film stills and lamps made of tree stumps and violins, the bar is funky yet relaxed. Customers sometimes use the piano and acoustic guitar for sporadic jam sessions. (☎81 63 44. Open daily 10am-1:30am. MC/V.) Festive during the school year and relaxed during vacations, **Le Bougnat des Pouilles,** 29 rue pl. de Montabert, off rue Champeaux, welcomes a mixed crowd of young and old until the wee hours. Enjoy a drink on the outdoor terrace or try to blend in with the dark, leopard-print-furnished interior. Concerts and themed nights 1-2 times per month; occasional displays of local artwork. (☎73 59 85. Beer from €2.20. Mixed drinks from €5. Open M-Sa 5pm-3am. MC/V.)

Summer in Troyes brings the **Ville en Musique,** a series of free performances ranging from modern French rock to classical organ tunes. (☎43 55 00. Stop by the cultural center for more info. Mid-June to mid-Aug.) A free sound-and-light *spectacle* guides visitors through the *centre-ville* streets on weekend nights at 10pm (mid-July to mid-Sept.; call tourist office for details). In October, Troyes hosts a weekend of concerts during the **Festival des Nuits de Champagne.** (☎72 11 65; www.nuitsdechampagne.com. Reservations ☎40 02 03. Prices vary with concert; call or check website for details.) Troyes's cultural center, the **Maison du Boulanger,** 42 rue Paillot de Montabert, has information on festivals, exhibits, and concerts. (☎43 55 00. Open M-F 9am-noon and 2-6pm, Sa 10am-noon and 2-5pm)

ALSACE, LORRAINE, AND FRANCHE-COMTÉ

An unfortunate history seems to be the only common thread linking the wildly distinct regions of Alsace, Lorraine, and Franche-Comté. Bordering Belgium, Switzerland, and—most importantly—Germany, these regions formed an eastern frontier that played top prize in numerous Franco-German wars—most recently, WWII. Today, this battle-ridden past has given way to a more tranquil state of affairs; travelers seeking a hip sojourn or historical vacation can visit the region's cosmopolitan cities, which possess a Germanic flair and an international feel.

Though Alsace and Lorraine are commonly referred to as "Alsace-Lorraine," the two regions are less similar than their hyphenated twin-ship leads most to believe. To the east, the cities of Alsace cluster on the west side of the Rhine, against the border of their former fatherland. German influence pervades daily life, from the half-timbered houses to the twang of the local dialect to the hearty, potato-heavy cuisine. Meanwhile, Lorraine unfolds to the west amid wheat fields and gentle plains. Its elegant, well-planned cities, featuring tree-lined boulevards and stately Baroque architecture, fail to forget their war-ridden past, which left the region's farmland useless for generations. In Nancy, the region's cultural capital, streets display turn-of-the-century Art Nouveau pieces.

Populated by cheerful farmers and dotted by vineyards that produce the regional *vin jaune* (yellow wine), Franche-Comté makes a great base for hiking in the summer and for cross-country skiing in the winter, while the city of Besançon is a student and hipster haven. With a tumultuous history giving way to rich diversity, and refined elegance coexisting with fearless fun, the northwestern coast of France promises to be a pleasant surprise.

HIGHLIGHTS OF ALSACE, LORRAINE, AND FRANCHE-COMTÉ

VISIT Ronchamp for a quiet moment at the **Chapelle de Notre Dame-du-Haut** (p. 401), a moving WWII memorial chapel and architectural marvel by Le Corbusier.

STOP on the Route du Vin to take in the rustic beauty (and intoxicating delights) of **Kaysersberg** (p. 387).

ADMIRE Art Nouveau at its best at the **Musée de l'Ecole de Nancy** (p. 368), where paintings and sculptures were inspired by the most famous muse of all: nature herself.

LORRAINE

NANCY ☎03 83

Nancy (nahn-SEE; pop. 106,000) first flourished when it played home to Duke Stanislas, whose passion for urban planning transformed the sprawling city into a model of 18th-century Classicism, complete with broad plazas, fountains, and streets, which are frequented by locals at any and all hours. At the turn of the 20th century, *Nanciens* created the Nancy School of Art Nouveau, which took its inspiration from the natural world. Today, this natural *joie de vivre* is most visible at night, in the glow of Nancy's beautiful cityscape.

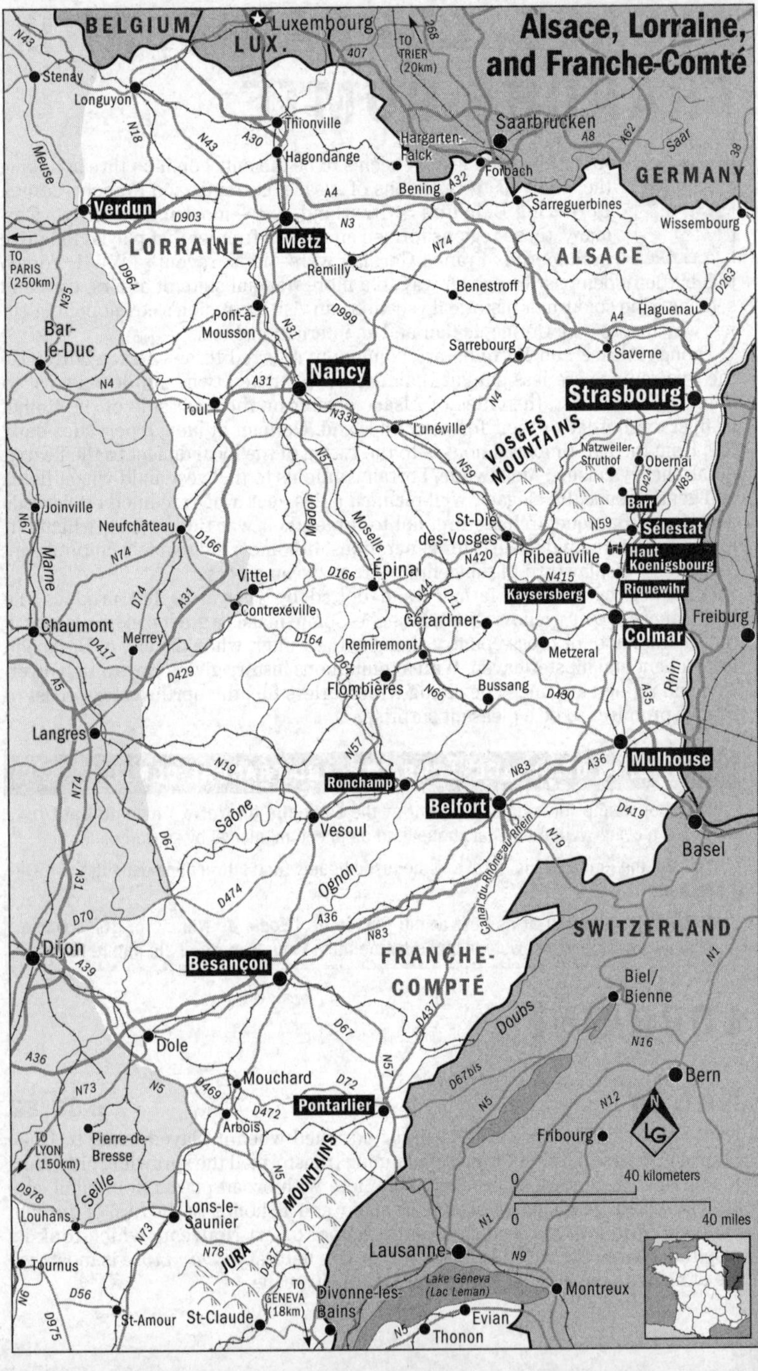
Alsace, Lorraine, and Franche-Comté
BELGIUM
LUX.
Luxembourg
TO TRIER (20km)
GERMANY
LORRAINE
ALSACE
FRANCHE-COMPTÉ
SWITZERLAND
VOSGES MOUNTAINS
JURA MOUNTAINS
Stenay
Longuyon
Thionville
Hagondange
Hargarten-Falck
Saarbrucken
Forbach
Bening
Sarreguerbines
Wissembourg
Verdun
Metz
TO PARIS (250km)
Remilly
Benestroff
Haguenau
Pont-à-Mousson
Bar-le-Duc
Sarrebourg
Saverne
Nancy
Strasbourg
Toul
Lunéville
Natzweiler-Struthof
Obernai
Barr
Sélestat
Haut Koenigsbourg
Ribeauville
Riquewihr
Kaysersberg
Colmar
Freiburg
Joinville
Neufchâteau
St-Dié des-Vosges
Épinal
Vittel
Contrexéville
Gérardmer
Chaumont
Merrey
Remiremont
Metzeral
Plombières
Bussang
Langres
Mulhouse
Ronchamp
Belfort
Basel
Vesoul
Dijon
Besançon
Biel/Bienne
Dole
Mouchard
Pontarlier
Arbois
Bern
Fribourg
TO LYON (150km)
Pierre-de-Bresse
Louhans
Lons-le-Saunier
Lausanne
Tournus
Montreux
TO GENEVA (18km)
Divonne-les-Bains
Lake Geneva (Lac Leman)
St-Amour
St-Claude
Evian
Thonon
Meuse
Marne
Moselle
Madon
Saône
Ognon
Doubs
Seille
Rhin
Saar
Canal-du-Rhône-au-Rhein
0
40 kilometers
0
40 miles

TRANSPORTATION

Flights: Aéroport de Metz-Nancy Lorraine (☎03 87 56 70 00), rte. de Vigny. Flights leave for **Clermont-Ferrand, Lyon, Marseille, Nice, Paris,** and **Toulouse.** Shuttles (☎03 87 78 57 57) run to the train station (35-40min., 6 per day, €4).

Trains: 3 pl. Thiers. Ticket office open M-F 5:40am-9pm, Sa-Su 6:30am-9pm. Info office open M-F 5:50am-9:35pm, Sa 6:45am-9:35pm, Su 6:45am-9:50pm. Trains go to **Metz** (40min., 9 per day, €5), **Paris** (1½-3½hr., 27 per day, €42), and **Strasbourg** (1¼hr., 20 per day, €23). Visit **SNCF,** 18 pl. St-Epvre, for info and reservations. Open M 12:30-6pm, Tu-F 9:30am-1pm and 2-6pm. AmEx/MC/V.

Buses: Rapides de Lorraine Buses, 52 bd. d'Austrasie (☎32 34 20). Depart from the train station. Open M-Sa 7am-7:30pm.

Public Transportation: STAN info office, 3 rue du Dr. Schmitt (☎30 08 08; www.reseau-stan.com). Additional info office at pl. de la République. Both open M-Sa 7am-7:30pm. Most buses stop at pl. de la République next to the train station and at Point Central on rue St-Georges. Buy individual tickets (€1.20) on board; find *carnets* of 10 (€8.70) or 3-day passes (€3.80) at the office. Buses 5:30am-8pm, some to midnight.

Taxis: Taxi Nancy, 2 bd. Joffre (☎37 65 37).

Car Rental: Avis (☎35 40 61) at the station. Open M-F 8am-1pm and 1:30-8pm, Su 6-8pm. **Europcar,** 18 rue de Serre (☎37 57 24). Open M-F 8am-noon and 1:30-8:30pm, Sa 8am-noon and 2-6pm. **National** (☎37 38 59), also at the station. Open M-F 8am-noon and 2-7pm, Sa 9am-noon.

Bike Rental: Michenon, 91 rue des Quatre Eglises (☎17 59 59). €13 for 1st day, €8.50 per extra day; €160 deposit. Open Tu-Sa 9am-noon and 2-7pm. MC/V.

ORIENTATION AND PRACTICAL INFORMATION

Newly renovated **place Stanislas** lies at the heart of the city. From the train station, walk straight ahead through **place Thiers** and turn left onto **rue Mazagran.** Continue until you see a stone archway on your right, and pass through that arch onto rue Stanislas. Continue for four blocks until you reach pl. Stanislas; the tourist office is in the Hôtel de Ville. The grid-like layout of the *centre-ville* is fairly easy to navigate, but be sure to carry a map when wandering through the small streets north of pl. Stanislas and west of the train station.

TIP **MAKE A PASS AT NANCY.** Pick up Le Pass Nancy (€13) at the tourist office for an audio tour, reduced admission price for all of Nancy's museums, reduced bike rental fee, round-trip ticket for bus/tram, and movie ticket.

Tourist Office: pl. Stanislas (☎35 22 41; www.ot-nancy.fr). Ask for the free city and bus maps. **Currency exchange.** English spoken. Open Apr.-Oct. M-Sa 9am-7pm, Su 10am-5pm; Nov.-Mar. M-Sa 9am-6pm, Su 10am-1pm.

Tours: Tourist office leads themed 1-2hr. tours of the city, Sa 2:30pm. €6, students €4, under 6 free. English tours available for groups by email reservation. **Audio tour** in English, German, and Japanese €5. **Minibus** tour of Art Nouveau sights in French. July-Sept. Sa 2:30 and 4pm, Su 11:30am; May-June and Oct. Sa 2:30 and 4pm. 1hr. €8, students and under 16 €4. Ask about **self-guided walking** tours of Art Nouveau sights. **Petit train** tours depart from pl. de la Carrière (☎03 89 73 74 24; www.petit-train.com). 5 per day May-Sept. 10am-4pm. 40min.; available in 10 languages. €6, ages 6-14 €4.

Budget Travel: Agence Wasteels, 1bis pl. Thiers. (☎35 91 99). Open M-F 9am-noon and 1-6pm, Sa 9am-noon.

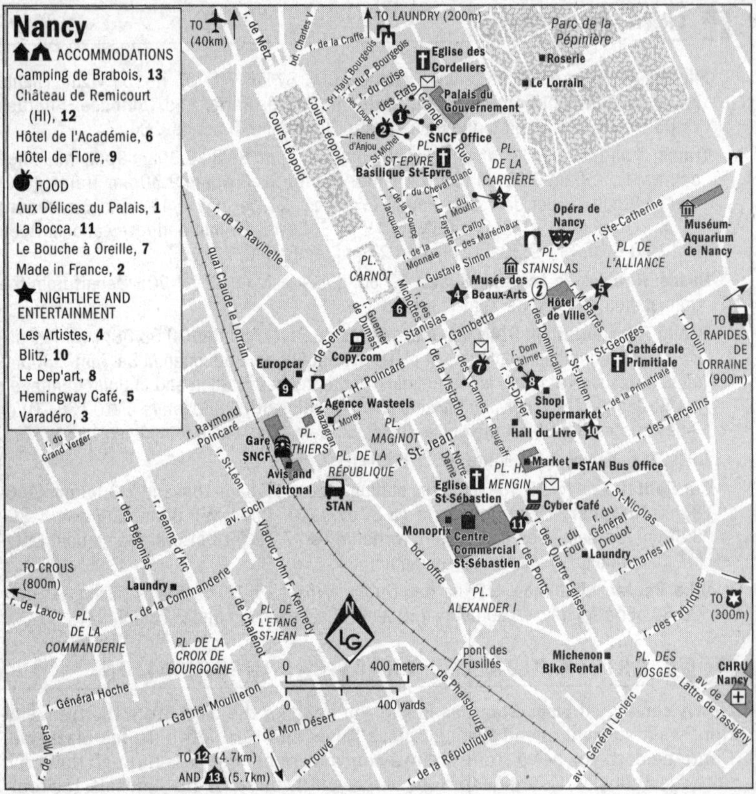

Youth Center: CROUS, 75 rue de Laxou, helps students find summer housing and opportunities for work and study. **Foreign Student Services** ☎91 88 26. Open M-F 2-5pm.

English-Language Bookstore: Hall du Livre, 38 rue St-Dizier (☎35 53 01). English book section. Open M-Sa 9am-8pm, Su 11am-7pm. MC/V.

Laundromat: Le Bateau Lavoir, 124 rue St-Dizier. Wash €3 per 6.5kg. Open daily 7:45am-9:30pm. **Laverie,** 5 rond-point M. Simon (wash €2.60 per 5kg, €3.20 per 7kg) and 30 rue de la Commanderie (wash €3.30 per 8kg). Both open daily 7am-9pm.

Police: 38 bd. Lobau (☎17 27 37), near the intersection with rue Charles III. Call here for the **pharmacie de garde.**

Hospital: CHRU Nancy, 29 av. du Maréchal de Lattre de Tassigny (☎18 09 13).

Internet Access: Copy.com, 3-5 rue Guerrier de Dumast (☎22 90 41). €2 per hr. Open M-Sa 9am-9pm, Su 2-8pm. **Cyber Café,** 11 rue des Quatre Eglises (☎35 47 34). €5.40 per hr., students €4.60. Open M and Sa 11am-9pm, Tu-F 9am-9pm, Su 2-8pm.

Post Office: 10 rue St-Dizier (☎39 75 20). Open M-F 8:30am-6:30pm, Sa 8:30am-noon. Branches at 66 rue St-Dizier (☎17 39 11; open M noon-6:30pm, Tu-F 8:30am-6:30pm, Sa 8:30am-5pm) and 75 Grande Rue (open M 1-5:30pm, Tu-F 9am-12:30pm and 2-5:30pm, Sa 9am-4pm). **Postal Code:** 54000.

Otel.com
Are you aiming for a budget vacation?
DO NOT DISTURB
US & CANADA
1-800-820-4171 OR 1-212-594-8045
EUROPE
00-800-468-35482 OR 44-207-099-2035

www.letsgo.com
LET'S GO
NEW ZEALAND
ON A BUDGET
You'd rather be traveling
LET'S GO
FRANCE
2008
ON A BUDGET
LET'S GO
MEXICO
ON A BUDGET
READY.
SET.
LET'S GO

ACCOMMODATIONS

There are several budget hotels around the train station, especially on **rue Jeanne d'Arc,** a 15min. walk from pl. Stanislas, on the opposite side of the train station from the *centre-ville.* The hostel offers the best prices but is far from the town.

Hôtel de L'Académie, 7 rue des Michottes (☎35 52 31). Despite an unappealing exterior, this hotel offers affordable, clean rooms with shower. Breakfast €3.50. Reception 7am-10pm; otherwise call ahead. Reservations recommended. Check-out 11am. Singles €20-28; doubles €28-39. Extra bed €6.50. AmEx/MC/V. ❷

Hôtel de Flore, 8 rue Raymond Poincaré (☎37 63 28; www.gardenflore.com), near the station. Jovial owners let bright but well-worn rooms that take the hotel's name ("hotel of flora") to heart. Some tiny, all with bath and TV. Breakfast €5. Reception M-F 7:30am-2am, Sa-Su noon-midnight. Reservations recommended in summer. Singles €30-35; doubles €40; triples €45. MC/V. ❸

Château de Remicourt (HI), 149 rue de Vandoeuvre (☎27 73 67; fax 41 41 35), in Villers-lès-Nancy. From the station, take bus #126 (dir.: Villers Clairlieu; 2-3 per hr.) to "St-Fiacre." Turn right on rue de la Grange des Moines, which turns into rue de Vandoeuvre. Simple, comfortable accommodations far from the *centre-ville.* Breakfast included. Reception M-Sa 9:30am-9pm, Su 5:30-9pm. Check-out 9:30am. 3- to 4-bed dorms €18; small doubles with sink €20. AmEx/MC/V. ❶

Camping de Brabois, av. Paul Muller (☎27 18 28; campeoles.brabois@wanadoo.fr), near the Centre d'Accueil. Take bus #126 or 122 (dir.: Villers Clairlieu) to "Camping." Showers, ball courts, and grocery store. Reception July-Aug. 8am-10pm; Sept.-Oct. and Apr.-June 8am-12:30pm and 2-9pm. Open Apr. to mid-Oct. July-Aug. 2 people with tent €12-14; extra adult €4.50-5.10, extra child €3-3.30. Sept.-Oct. and Apr.-June €11/4/free. Electricity €4. AmEx/MC/V over €15. ❶

FOOD

Nancy's signature *bergamote* is a bitter hard candy flavored by the same spice used in Earl Grey tea, and it's everywhere—all the *pâtisseries* on pl. Stanislas sell these overpriced suckers. The town is also famous for its ham-and-cheese *quiche lorraine.* The covered **marché central** is off rue St-Dizier in pl. Henri Mengin (open Tu-Th 7am-6pm, F-Sa 7am-6:30pm), a **Shopi** supermarket is at 26 rue St-Georges (☎35 08 35; open M-F 9am-8pm, Sa 9am-7:30pm; MC/V), and a larger **Monoprix** is in the Centre Commercial St-Sebastian off pl. Henri Mengin (☎17 78 71; open M-Sa 8:30am-8:30pm; MC/V). Restaurants spill from **rue des Maréchaux** onto **place Lafayette** and up **Grande Rue** to **place St-Epvre.** There are *crêpe* stands behind pl. Stanislas on **Terrace de la Pépinière** and cheap kebab joints along and around **rue Stanislas.**

Le Bouche à Oreille, 42 rue des Carmes (☎35 17 17). Enormous portions of cheese-based cuisine in a charming atmosphere. An extensive menu of fondues, *tartiflettes* (a skillet of cheese, potatoes, and meat), omelettes, and salads. Funky, antique-filled restaurant. Fondue €14-15 per person; 2-person min. Lunch *menu* €11. Dinner *menu* €17. Open M and Sa 7-10:30pm, Tu-F noon-1:30pm and 7-10:30pm. AmEx/MC/V. ❷

Aux Délices du Palais, 69 Grande Rue (☎30 44 19). A tiny, hip eatery serving creatively amped-up comfort food. Locals swivel on cow print stools while chowing down on lasagna with *roquefort* and chicken with mushrooms. Salads are small but sure to please, with toppings ranging from warm goat cheese to blini and gingerbread. *Plats* and salads €9. Open M-F noon-1:30pm and 7-9:30pm, Sa 7-9:30pm. Cash only. ❷

La Bocca, 33 rue des Ponts (☎32 74 47). A date-worthy Italian restaurant with heart-shaped velvet chairs and zebra-print lamp shades. Unlimited toppings for the popular make-your-own pizza (€8-9) range from mussels to pineapple—as long as you sign the disclaimer; proprietors take no responsibility for the possibly strange taste of your *"curieuse"* creation. Lunch *menu* €12. Dinner *menu* €18. Open M-F 11:30am-2:30pm and 7-11pm, Sa 11:30am-2:30pm and 7pm-midnight. MC/V. ❸

Made in France, 1 rue St-Epvre (☎37 33 36). A popular takeout joint. Prides itself on its fresh bread and vegetables. Rain or shine, day or night, lines of locals spill out the door. Smoothies €3. Sandwiches €2.60-5.60. Open M-Sa 11:30am-9pm. MC/V. ❶

SIGHTS

PLACE STANISLAS. Renovated for its 250th anniversary celebration in 2005, the stately square, now open only to pedestrians, is the city's cultural center. Its three Neoclassical pavilions were commissioned in 1737 by Stanislas Lesczynski, the former king of Poland, to honor his nephew, Louis XV. The finely molded **Portes d'Or** (Golden Gates) dazzle during the day and can be admired from the many cafés that line the *place*. From pl. Stanislas, pass through the five-arch **Arc de Triomphe** to find the tree-lined **place de la Carrière,** a former jousting ground with Baroque architecture and classical angel sculptures.

MUSÉE DE L'ECOLE DE NANCY. If nature could craft its own art, it would look something like the works in the Nancy School's tremendous museum. A trip through its lushly decorated rooms feels like a step into the wilderness: Emile Gallé's butterfly glassworks seem to belong in a fairytale forest. No visit is complete without a stroll through the splendid gardens. Ask to borrow the detailed English guide. *(36-38 rue du Sergent Blandan. Take bus #122, dir.: Villers Clairlieu, or #123, dir.: Vandoeuvre Cheminots, to "Painlevé." ☎40 14 86; www.ecole-de-nancy.com. Open W-Su 10:30am-6pm. €6, students €4, under 18 free; W students free; 1st Su of month 10am-1:30pm free for all. Tours in French F-Su 3pm, €1.60. Free audio tours in English, French, and German.)*

PARC DE LA PÉPINIÈRE. This park is one of the most popular and relaxing places in the city. Expanses of rigorously controlled flowers and trees give way to a sprawling zoo, outdoor café, and miniature golf. The aromatic **Roserie** displays vibrant flowers from around the world. Be sure to see Rodin's famous (and controversial) sculpture of **Claude Gellée (Le Lorrain),** which features Apollo among galloping horses. To the shock of its commissioners, Gallée looks less inspirational than confused, awkward, and distorted. The statue is located directly north of the main entrance. *(North of pl. de la Carrière, near pl. Stanislas. Open daily June-Aug. 6:30am-10:30pm; Sept.-Oct. and Apr.-May 6:30am-9pm; Nov.-Mar. 6:30am-8pm. Free.)*

MUSÉE DES BEAUX-ARTS. The collection of art in this Baroque building spans from 1380 to the present, with a strong focus on more modern works, and includes gems by Delacroix, Monet, Picasso, Rodin, and Rubens, as well as a fantastic exhibit of Art Nouveau Daum glasswork. *(3 pl. Stanislas. ☎85 30 72. Open M and W-Su 10am-6pm. €6, students €4, under 18 free; W students free; 1st Su of month 10am-1:30pm free for all. Tours in French €1.60. Free audio tours in English, French, and German.)*

OTHER SIGHTS. Unlike most French cities, Nancy doesn't even pretend that its churches are the most interesting sights. While its interior is classically plain, the **Cathédrale Primitiale** is notable for its 18th-century painted dome, which depicts a chaotic ensemble of saints, angels, and major Biblical figures. *(Rue St-Georges, past rue Montesquieu. Open daily 8am-7pm.)* North of pl. Stanislas, the 19th-century **Basilique St-Epvre** boasts brilliant windows from around the world. It also hosts free evening concerts of classical and organ music. *(Off Grande Rue at pl. St-Epvre. Open daily 8am-7pm.)* The recently renovated **Muséum-Aquarium de Nancy** holds hundreds of colorful fish, sea urchins, and other underwater dwellers in small tanks on the ground floor, organized by region, while the second floor contains a lackluster zoology museum filled with stuffed animals and a temporary exhibit hall. You may not want to visit during school hours, as you'll likely have to fight through schools of students to reach the schools of fishes. *(34 rue Ste-Catherine. ☎32 99 97; www.man.uhp-nancy.fr. Open daily 10am-noon and 2-6pm. €3.80, ages 12-18 €2.30; W students free.)*

ENTERTAINMENT AND NIGHTLIFE

In October, for the two-week **Jazz-Pulsations** festival, well-known international musicians perform in concert halls around Nancy. (☎35 40 86; www.nancyjazzpulsations.com. Tickets €50; prices higher at the door.) The **Opéra de Nancy et de Lorraine,** pl. Stanislas, presents a series of high-quality productions from February to July. (☎85 33 11. Tickets available Tu-Sa 1-7pm. €5-55, student discount available; 15min. before show tickets €5-41.) The theater also holds ballets and symphonies year-round. (☎85 09 01. Ticket office open M-F 10am-1pm and 2-6pm. Tickets €15-30, students €10-20.) In mid-May, the **Festival International de Chant Choral** brings 2000 singers from around the world. (☎27 56 56; www.chantchoral.org. Free.)

Soak up the evening beauty of the illuminated **place Stanislas** from one of its ritzy cafés, or grab a cheaper drink on **rue Stanislas** or **Grande Rue.** Check www.nancybynight.com for updates on bars, clubs, concerts, and theater events.

Blitz, 76 rue St-Julien (☎32 77 20). Smoky lounge style at its best. The red-velvet interior makes it hard to be anything but chill. Beer from €2.20. Mixed drinks from €5. Open M 5:30pm-2am, Tu-F 2pm-2am, Sa 2pm-2am. AmEx/MC/V.

Hemingway Café, 5 rue Maurice Barrès (☎30 04 04). This bookcase-lined bar attracts crowds of students salivating over the house mojitos. Beer from €2. Mixed drinks from €4. Happy hour nightly 6-9pm. Open M-Sa 2pm-2am. MC/V.

Varadéro, 27 Grande Rue (☎36 61 98). A Cuban-style bar with a live DJ, revolutionary vibe, and lots of 20-somethings ready to dance long into the night. Shots €1.50. Beer from €2. Mixed drinks €6. Open Tu-Sa 8pm-2am. MC/V.

Le Dep'art, 11 rue Dom Calmet (☎30 12 67). The dance floor at this spartan bar fills with young crowds on W student nights (beer €1) and during themed *soirées*. Beer from €2. Mixed drinks from €4.50. Open daily 5pm-2am. MC/V.

Les Artistes, 36 rue Stanislas (☎30 54 92). Students arrive here in the early afternoon to sip tea (€2.50) or the popular milkshake (€3.50) and don't leave till closing. Understandable given the 2 floors of comfy couches. Microbrew beer from €3.90. Mixed drinks from €4.60. Open M-Sa 8am-2am, Su 1pm-2am. MC/V.

METZ ☎03 87

The tranquil *vieille ville*, parks, and esplanades of Metz (MEHTSS; pop. 128,000), belie its turbulent past. One of the few cities in Lorraine that ceded to the Germans following the Franco-Prussian war in 1870, Metz bears the marks of its vacillating nationality. While many of the city's monuments are quintessentially French, German occupiers designed the town's massive (and now renovated) train station to to ship 25,000 troops into France per day. Now home to a hard-partying student population and a set of ultra-contemporary art exhibition halls, Metz—full of fountains, canals, and churches—is both a thriving metropolis and a walker's heaven.

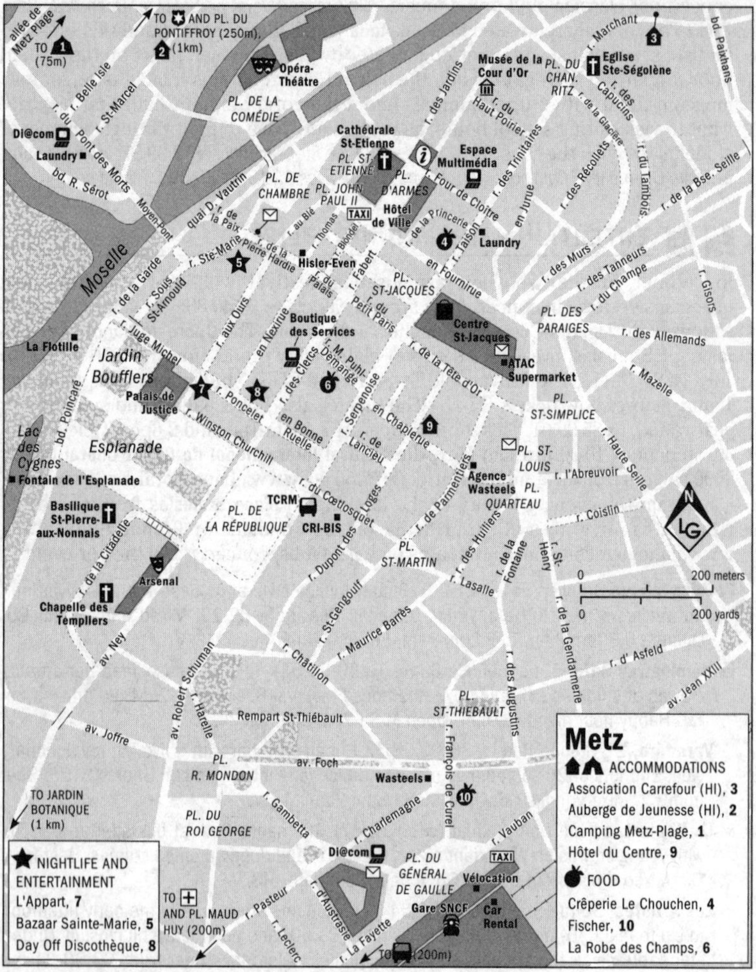

TRANSPORTATION

Trains: pl. du Général de Gaulle. Ticket window open M-F 5:55am-8:15pm, Sa 6:10am-8:15pm, Su 8:20am-8:55pm. Info office open M-Th and Sa 5:40am-9pm, F 5:40am-9:15pm, Su 6am-9:45pm. Trains go to: **Luxembourg** (1hr., every hr., €13); **Lyon** (5½hr., 4 per day, €50); **Nancy** (40min., 82 per day, €5); **Paris** (1½-3hr., 10 per day, €39-50); **Strasbourg** (1½hr., 10 per day, €21). AmEx/MC/V.

Buses: Les Rapides de Lorraine, 1 rue Louis Débonnaire, sends buses to small towns in the region (☎63 65 65 or 50 02 02; www.tim57.fr). Take the underpass to the right of the train station below the tracks, turn left, and continue straight; the ticket office is located in the Gare Routière. Ticket window open M-Tu and Th 7:30-11am and 2-5pm, F 7:30-11am and 2-4pm. **SNCF buses** travel to **Verdun** (1½hr., 4 per day, €6.20).

Public Transportation: TCRM, 1 av. Robert Schuman (☎76 31 11; www.republicain-lorrain.fr). Office open July-Aug. M-F 9:15am-12:30pm and 1:30-5:30pm; Sept.-June M-F 7:30am-6:30pm, Sa 9am-4:45pm. Most lines run M-F 6am-8pm, Sa-Su less often. Line #11 runs 10pm-midnight. Buy individual tickets (€1.20) on board; find *carnets* of 10 (€8.40) and day passes (€3) at the office.

Taxis: (☎56 91 92), at the train station. 24hr.

Car Rental: Avis (☎50 60 30), at the train station. Open M-F 8am-noon and 2-7pm, Su 5-8pm. **Europcar** (☎62 26 12). Open M-F 9am-noon and 3-7pm.

Bike Rental: Vélocation (☎57 88 24), at the train station. €4 per ½-day, €6 per day, €17 per week; €70 and photocopy of ID deposit. Open M-F 6am-8pm. Branch at rue d'Estrées (☎74 50 43). Open Mar.-Nov. daily 9am-6pm; Dec.-Feb. M-F 9am-6pm.

ORIENTATION AND PRACTICAL INFORMATION

The honey-colored *vieille ville* is mostly off-limits to cars. The cathedral dominates **place d'Armes,** and the tourist office is in the building situated between the cathedral and the Hôtel de Ville. To get to the tourist office from the station, take a right on rue Vauban, then left on rue des Augustins, which becomes rue de la Fontaine, pl. du Quarteau, and finally pl. St-Louis. At pl. St-Simplice, turn left onto rue de la Tête d'Or, which becomes rue du Petit Paris, and then make a right onto rue Fabert. The office is straight ahead. For a faster trip, take minibus line A or B to pl. d'Armes from the stop on the right of the train station (€0.70).

Tourist Office: 2 pl. d'Armes (☎55 53 76; www.tourisme.mairie-metz.fr). English-speaking staff reserves rooms (€1.50) and offers free maps. **Internet** access with *télécarte* €7.40 per 2½hr. **Currency exchange.** Open M-Sa 9am-7pm, Su 10am-5pm.

Tours: Tourist office leads 1hr. French tours of the **cathedral** (M-Sa 3pm) and the **city** (M-Sa May-Sept. 3, 4pm; Oct.-Apr. 4pm). €5 per tour, €7 for both; students and ages 12-25 €2.50/3.50; under 12 free. Dutch, English, German, Italian, or Spanish **audio tour** €7 with passport deposit. A 45min. **petit train** takes visitors through city and remote gardens. (☎73 03 08. English, French, German, Italian, and Spanish. Departs from the cathedral; ask tourist office for times. €5.50, under 18 €3.50.) Check at tourist office for info on themed tours and night tours.

Budget Travel: Agence Wasteels, 3 rue d'Austrasie (☎50 54 46). Open M-F 9am-noon and 2-6pm, Sa 9am-noon. Branch at 2 rue de Grand Cerf (☎18 44 34). Open M 2-6:30pm, Tu-F 9:30am-6:30pm, Sa 9:30am-5pm.

Youth Center: Centre de Renseignement et d'Information, Bureau Information Jeunesse (CRI-BIS), 1 rue de Coëtlosquet (☎69 04 50), on the 2nd fl. of an office building. Info on concerts, hiking, lodging, study, travel, and jobs. Free Internet access; reserve ahead by phone. Open M and F noon-5pm, Tu-Th 9am-5pm.

Laundromat: 22 rue du Pont des Morts (☎63 49 57). €3.80 per 7kg. Open daily 7am-8pm. Also at 23 rue Taison. €3.50 per 7kg. Open daily 7am-8pm.

English-Language Bookstore: Hisler-Even, 1 rue Ambroise Thomas (☎74 27 76). Small English section on the 1st fl. Open M-Sa 10am-7pm.

Police: 45 rue Belle Isle (☎16 17 17), near pl. de Pontiffroy. Call here for the **pharmacie de garde.**

Hospital: Centre Hospitalier Regional Metz-Thionville, 1 pl. Philippe de Vigneulles (☎55 31 31), near pl. Maud Huy.

Internet Access: At tourist office (see above). **Espace Multimédia,** 2 rue du Four du Cloître (☎36 56 56). Free. Open M 1-6pm and Tu-Sa 9am-6pm; 1st M of month closed. **Boutique des Services,** 9 rue des Clercs (☎75 97 13). €0.05 per min., €3 per hr. Open M 2-7pm, Tu-Sa 10am-7pm. **Di@com,** 20 rue Gambetta (☎63 08 85). €3 per hr.

Open M-Sa 10am-9pm, Su 11am-9pm. Branch at 34 rue du Pont des Morts (☎16 27 40). Open M-F 10:30am-9:30pm, Sa-Su 11am-9pm.

Post Office: 9 rue Gambetta (☎56 74 30). **Currency exchange.** Open M-F 8am-7pm and Sa 8:30am-12:30pm. Branches at Centre St-Jacques (☎37 99 00; open M-F 9am-7pm, Sa 9am-noon and 1:30-5pm); 1 rue de la Pierre Hardie (☎37 75 74; open M-F 9am-7pm, Sa 9am-5pm); and 39 pl. St-Louis (☎18 47 74; open M 2-6pm, Tu-F 9am-6pm, Sa 9am-noon). **Postal Code:** 57000.

ACCOMMODATIONS AND CAMPING

Relatively inexpensive hotels cluster around the train station, while pricier ones fill the pedestrian district. Metz attracts many business travelers, so reserve a few weeks ahead. For weekend stays, many hotels offer two nights with breakfast for the price of one; ask for the *Bon week-end en ville* promotion. (24hr. advance reservation required; offer depends on the availability of rooms at any given hotel.)

Hôtel du Centre, 14 rue Dupont des Loges (☎36 06 93; www.perso.wanadoo.fr/hotel-ducentre-metz). In the heart of the *vieille ville.* A 19th-century building with a winding lavender staircase. Well-decorated, classy rooms splashed with purple. All have bath and TV. Breakfast €6. Reception M-Sa 7am-10pm, Su 7:30am-9pm. Check-out 11am. Singles and doubles €56; triples €60; quads €68. Extra bed €8. AmEx/MC/V. ❹

Association Carrefour/Auberge de Jeunesse (HI), 6 rue Marchant (☎75 07 26; www.carrefour-metz.asso.fr). Take minibus A or B from the station to pl. d'Armes, head right on rue En Fournirue, and turn left on rue Taison, which becomes rue des Trinitaires, then rue Marchant. White floors, drapes, and bedspreads give these simple rooms a bright and fresh feel. A short walk from the center of town, this hostel is popular with large groups of travelers. Restaurant, laundry, and TV room. Breakfast included. Lockers available, €1 per day; inquire at reception. Internet access €1 per 15min., €3 per hr. Reception 24hr. 3- and 4-bed dorms €18; singles and doubles €22. AmEx/MC/V. ❶

Auberge de Jeunesse (HI), 1 allée de Metz Plage (☎30 44 02; www.ajmetz.free.fr), 15min. from the *vieille ville,* just off a major road. From the direction of the campsite, walk down rue Belle Isle. From the station, take bus #3 (dir.: Metz-Nord; last bus 8:30pm) or #11 (dir.: St-Eloy; last bus midnight) to "Pontiffroy." No-frills rooms with wooden bunks. Kitchen. Breakfast included. Free luggage storage. Reception 8-10am and 5-10pm. Reservations recommended. 2- to 6-bed dorms €19. AmEx/MC/V. ❶

Camping Metz-Plage, allée de Metz-Plage (☎68 26 48, off season 68 26 41; camping-metz@mairie-metz.fr), bordering the river. Enter from rue de la Piscine, behind the hospital on rue Belle Isle. A large grassy plot with views of the river and a great location minutes from the center of town but little privacy. Showers, grocery store, laundry, TV room, fishing, and a giant public pool next door. Reception 7am-noon and 2-10pm. Open May-Sept. €2.60 per adult, €1.20 per child, €2.50 per tent, €5-7.30 per car, €13-16 per trailer. Electricity free. Prices fall 10% May to mid-June and Sept. MC/V. ❶

FOOD

Local *pâtissiers* throw the region's yellow *mirabelles* (plums) into everything from tarts to preserves. Bakeries and other cheap eateries cluster in the pedestrian district on **rue Coislin** and near the hostel on **rue du Pont des Morts.** Restaurants line **place St-Jacques** and **rue Dupont des Loges.** The **Centre St-Jacques,** off pl. St-Jacques, has specialty stores, cheap eateries, and an **ATAC** supermarket in the basement. (☎74 02 90. Open M-Sa 8:30am-7:30pm. MC/V.) The biggest **markets** are near the cathedral (Th and Sa 7am-1pm). Cheap kebab stands occupy every corner of pl. St-Jacques and pepper many of the surrounding streets.

La Robe des Champs, 14 rue Marguerite Puhl-Demange (☎36 32 19). Don't let the pearl-draped chandeliers deceive you; this classy restaurant's signature baked potato *plats* (€8.50-19) are anything but dainty. Each delicious dish comes with 2 massive spuds and tons of fresh toppings, all neatly arranged on modern white plates. Open daily noon-2:45pm and 6:45-11pm. MC/V. ❸

Crêperie Le Chouchen, 10 rue Taison (☎18 50 50). Hidden down an alley, this *crêperie* serves fresh salads (€6-7.50) and an array of *crêpes* with regional ingredients (€2.50-9). The Lorraine *crêpe,* smothered in *mirabelles,* jam, ice cream, and *liqueur,* is a delicious immersion into the region's flavors. Open daily noon-2pm and 7-10pm. MC/V. ❷

Fischer, 6 rue François de Curel (☎36 85 97). Close to the train station, this sandwich shop layers its meats on the best bread in town–the fluffy baguettes turn standard sandwiches into standouts. Beats nearby competitors hands-down. Sandwiches €3.10-3.90. Salads €5-6. Open M-F 7am-6:30pm, Sa 7am-4:30pm; seating area closes 30min. before take-out window. MC/V. ❶

SIGHTS

CATHÉDRALE ST-ETIENNE. This golden 13th-century cathedral, the third-tallest cathedral in France at 42m, is known by locals as the "lantern of God." With over 6500 square meters of stained glass, ranging from the 13th to 20th centuries, it also boasts the largest collection of glass in the world. Don't miss Marc Chagall's modern windows in the western transept and the Chapelle de St-Sacrament near the welcome desk; his stunning designs feature jagged geometric fragments of brightly-hued stained glass. The Mutte Tower features 300 vertigo-inducing stairs, where intense claustrophobia is relieved only by the worthwhile view of the frightening precipice out the window; the fearful (or out of shape) should not attempt the climb. *(Pl. d'Armes. ☎75 54 61. Open daily June-Sept. 8am-7pm; Oct.-May 8am-6pm. Closed to tourists during services. Tours in French July-Aug. daily 10:30am, 2pm; Apr.-June by reservation only. €4, with crypt €6. Crypt and treasury open M-Sa 10am-noon and 2-6pm, Su 2-6pm. €1 each. Tours of Mutte Tower every hr. July-Aug. M-F and Su 3-6pm, Sa 9-10am and 3-6pm; Apr.-June Sa-Su 3:30-5:30pm. €7.)*

ESPLANADE AND GARDENS. At the other end of rue des Clercs from pl. d'Armes sits the Esplanade, a vast pavilion overlooking the sprawling lake and parks of the Moselle Valley. The pavilion has well-groomed flora and a colossal central fountain, but these features pale in comparison to the man-made **Lac aux Cynges,** in which the beautifully simple **fontain de l'Esplanade** shoots streams of water to lofty heights in artistic, mesmerizing patterns. In summer, the illuminated fountains spurt in time to music for **Les Eaux Musicales du Lac aux Cygnes.** *(Late June to early Sept. F-Su at nightfall. Free.)* Paddle or pedal your way around the nearby mouth of the Moselle with rentals from **La Flottille.** *(1 quai des Régates. ☎36 86 71. Paddle boats for 2 people €9.50 per 30min.; motorboats for 2 people €17 per 30min. Call ahead for hours. Cash only.)* One kilometer south of the Esplanade, swans preen at the **Jardin Botanique,** a botanist's heaven; foot paths are lined with trees and flower beds. *(☎55 54 00. Garden open daily 8am to sunset. Greenhouse open Apr.-Sept. M-F 9am-6:45pm, Sa-Su 9-11:30am and 2-6:45pm; Oct.-Mar. M-F 9am-4:45pm, Sa-Su 9-11:30am and 2-4:45pm.)*

OTHER SIGHTS. The **Arsenal,** 3 av. Ney, hosts contemporary art exhibits at its own minimalist gallery, as well as at two of Metz's nearby historical landmarks—the basilica and chapel. France's oldest church, Basilique St-Pierre-aux-Nonnains, was erected by the Romans in AD 380 to accommodate large baths and a sports arena; after it suffered a devastating fire in the fifth century, it was restored as a chapel in the sixth century. Little is left now except the church's sandy brick walls, which provide a striking contrast with the ever-changing and often bizarre modern art exhibits held inside. *(☎39 92 00; www.mairie-metz.fr/arsenal. Open mid-June to late Sept. M-Sa 1-6pm, Su 2-6pm; Oct. to mid-June Sa 1-6pm and Su 2-6pm.)* The **Chapelle des Templiers,** a pint-sized rotunda situated between the Arsenal and the basilica, fits fewer works of art but makes for a nice transition between the two larger spaces. *(Open mid-June to late Sept. M-Sa 1-6pm, Su 2-6pm. See Entertainment and Nightlife for more info about the Arsenal.)* Built over a swamp across town, **Place de la Comédie** served a less-than-comedic function during the Revolution: its main attraction was the *guillotine*, where 63 men were beheaded. Built in 1751, Metz's **Opéra-Théâtre** is the oldest functioning theater in France. *(4-5 pl. de la Comédie. ☎55 51 43; tickets 75 40 50. Ticket office open M-F 9am-12:30pm and 3-5pm. €10-39, students €5-13. MC/V.)*

ENTERTAINMENT AND NIGHTLIFE

The **Opéra-Théâtre** hosts various operas and ballets (see **Other Sights,** above, for ticket info). Concerts and guest lecturers regularly come to the modern performance hall at the **Arsenal** (see **Other Sights,** above). The hall is on the ground floor of the building, beneath the exhibition space and boutique. (☎39 92 00, reservations 74 16 16; www.mairie-metz.fr/arsenal. Ticket office open Tu-Su 1-6:30pm; exhibition gallery open Tu-Sa 1-6pm and Su 2-6pm. MC/V.) Bargain shoppers love Metz's twice-monthly **marché aux puces** (flea market), one of France's largest. (☎55 66 00; www.fim-metz.com. Open Sa 6am-noon.) In July, **Metz en Fête** brings free outdoor concerts and theater, and organ music in the cathedral. (Info at the tourist office or www.mairie-metz.fr.) These *soirées* culminate in the **Grandes Fêtes de la Mirabelle** at the end of August, a festival held in honor of the plum, which includes a huge street party. In December, Metz hosts the elaborate **Marché de Noël,** when over 100 market stalls open on pl. St-Louis and pl. de Gaulle.

Metz has a solid supply of lively bars and a few good clubs. At night, students pack the bars and cafés at **place St-Jacques. Place St-Louis** is another hot spot.

DO–Day Off Discothèque, 7 rue Poncelet (☎78 62 96). With a diverse dance sound track and frequent themed nights, this club draws loads of adults and students. Downstairs features couches perfect for an intimate chat, while a small bar upstairs echoes with tunes blaring from the lounge and dance floor. Beer from €3.50. Mixed drinks €8-10. Cover €10, includes 1 drink; often lower W-Th; women free before midnight. Open W-Sa 9pm-5am. AmEx/MC/V.

L'Appart, 2 rue Haute Pierre (☎18 59 26). A stylish gay bar—popular with both men and women—that goes wild with loud music and dancing (often atop the long metallic bar) late on weekend nights. Th karaoke. Beer from €2.70. Mixed drinks from €7.50. Open Tu-Su 8pm-2:30am. AmEx/MC/V.

Bazaar Sainte-Marie (BSM), 2bis-4 rue Ste-Marie (☎21 05 93). A quirky bar filled with worn sofas, colorful tapestries, and old carpets. Locals come to sit, smoke, chat or **make out for hours.** Perfect for laid-back types looking for an alternative to Metz's pubs and clubs. F-Sa DJ plays house, groove, and funk. Beer from €2. Mixed drinks from €5.80. Open M 2pm-2am, Tu-Th 10am-2am, F-Sa 10am-3am. MC/V.

VERDUN

☎03 29

The specter of war haunts the city of Verdun (vare-DUHN; pop. 22,000), which in WWI was the last eastern stronghold stopping the German advance on Paris. In 1914, the first German offensives pressed into Verdun, inaugurating four years of tense trench warfare that would devastate an entire generation. French and German forces held their ground as battle lines budged merely a few feet with each costly assault. In the 1916 Battle of Verdun, one of WWI's most horrific conflicts, each side lost nearly 400,000 men. Though Verdun's *centre-ville* is now a serene and scenic hub, with open terraces facing a calm yacht-filled river, eerie reminders of the events of almost a century ago remain on the outskirts of town, such as the ripples still in the ground from the brutal trench warfare. In 1987, the UN christened Verdun "World Capital of Peace, Freedom, and Human Rights." Besides WWI relics, the town offers little else to see.

TRANSPORTATION. **Trains** go to Metz (1½hr., 3 per day, €6) and Paris (3-3½hr., 4 per day, €32), from pl. Maurice Genevoix. (Ticket office open M 4:45-11:45am and 12:15-7pm, Tu-F 5:45am-12:45pm and 1:15-7pm, Sa 9:45am-12:15pm and 2:15-7pm, Su 12:30-7:30pm.) Regional **buses** run by **Les Rapides de la Meuse** (☎86 02 71) depart from the parking lot at the end of rue du 8 Mai to surrounding towns. **SNCF buses** leave from the train station for Metz (1½hr., 3 per day, €6). Rent **cars** from **AS Location,** 22 rue Louis Maury. (☎86 58 58. Open M-Tu and Th-F 8-11:30am and 2-6:15pm, W 9-11:30am and 2-6pm, Sa 9-11am and 4-6pm. AmEx/MC/V.) Rent **bikes** at **Flavenot Damien,** av. du Metz. (☎86 12 43. €10 per ½-day, €15 per day; passport deposit. Open Tu-F 9am-noon and 2-7pm, Sa 9am-noon and 2-6:30pm. AmEx/MC/V.)

ORIENTATION AND PRACTICAL INFORMATION. The **tourist office** is just across the bridge from downtown. To reach the office from the station, walk to the roundabout straight ahead and follow av. Garibaldi as it ends, curves to the right, and becomes rue Frères Boulhaut. Walk past the drawbridge to rue Chaussée, turn left, walk through Porte Chaussée, and cross the bridge (10min.). To reach downtown, do not cross the river, but continue straight past Porte Chaussée to the quai de Londres. English-speaking staff offers a free map of the city, info on the memorials, and daily 4hr. French tours of the battlefields and monuments—the best deal for those visiting these historical locations without a car. If you have a car, you may want to explore on your own; the tour provides little information besides what can be easily found in the English brochures at each location. (☎86 14 18; www.verdun-tourisme.com. Tours daily May-Sept. 2pm; €26, ages 8-16 €16, ages 4-7 €7.50, under 4 free. Open May-Sept. M-Sa 8:30am-6:30pm, Su 9am-5pm; Oct.-Nov. and Feb.-Mar. M-Sa 9am-noon and 1:30-5:30pm, Su 10am-1pm; Dec.-Jan. M-Sa 9am-noon and 1:30-5pm; Apr. M-Sa 9am-noon and 1:30-5:30pm, Su 9am-5pm. Tours can fill quickly; email or call ahead.) Other services include: a **laundromat** at 56 rue Raymond Poincaré (open daily 6:30am-9:30pm; €3 per 7kg); **police** at 2 rue Chaussée (☎86 00 17; call for the **pharmacie de garde**); a **hospital** at 2 rue d'Antohouard (☎18 83 31); **Internet** access at **Video Games,** 2 rue Saint-Sauveur, a 15min. walk from the town center (☎84 28 63; €3 per hr., €7 per 3hr.; open W-Th 11:30am-6:30pm, F 11:30am-2:30pm and 7pm-midnight, Sa 2-6pm and 7pm-midnight, Su 2-6pm). The **post office,** av. de la Victoire, has **currency exchange.** (☎83 45 58. Open M-F 8am-7pm, Sa 8am-noon.) **Postal Code:** 55100.

ACCOMMODATIONS. The **Auberge de Jeunesse (HI)** ❶, pl. Monseigneur Ginisty, beside the cathedral, offers renovated rooms in a quiet, converted seminary. From the station, head right on rue Louis Maury to rue de la Belle Vierge (10min.). A winding staircase leads to 4- and 6-bed rooms with wooden bunks and bathrooms. The two-story 11-bunk room offers views of the city below. (☎86 28 28; fax 86 28 82. Kitchen, bar, and foosball. Breakfast €3.50. Free luggage storage. Reception M-F 8am-noon and 5-11pm, Sa-Su 8-10am and 5-9pm. Check-in 5pm. Check-out 10am. Bunks €15. MC/V.) **Hôtel Montaulbain** ❷, 4 rue de la Vieille Prison, lets spacious, well decorated rooms on a quiet street near pl. Maréchal Foch. High ceilings and large beds lend a sense of luxury. Some rooms have antique furniture; all have bath. (☎86 00 47; fax 84 75 70. Breakfast €5.50. Reception 7am-10pm. Check-out 11am. Reservations recommended July-Aug. Singles €30, with toilet €34; doubles €34/40-42; triples €47; quads €50. Extra bed €10. MC/V.) **Hôtel Les Colombes**

LOCAL LEGEND

CONFECTIONS FOR CONCEPTION

Visitors to Verdun will find the town sprinkled with *dragées,* sugar-coated almonds painted in a rainbow of colors. These candies are everywhere, from gift shops to *chocolatier* storefronts. Their popularity stems from more than their delicious crunch; legend has it that they foster fertility.

The *dragée* was first concocted in 1220 by a Verdun apothecary who used honey as a glue to sugar-coat his almonds. Both almonds and honey were thought to possess healing powers, and the candy quickly assumed a medicinal role. In particular, *dragées* were fed to pregnant women to bolster their strength and their children's virility.

Four centuries later, when Louis XIV discovered the town's signature sweets, the King allegedly decreed them a mandatory part of his courtesans' diet, stopping at nothing to ensure a healthy lineage. The King made his ladies carry *dragées* with them at all times, tucked away in hidden hip-side pouches.

Modern science has since trumped the *dragées'* therapeutic mystique, but they haven't lost their charm. They are now served at weddings and baptisms to toast the health of newlyweds and newborns. In most locales, *dragées* are reserved for such celebrations; only in Verdun are they an everyday treat.

❷, 9 av. Garibaldi, one block from the train station, offers rooms with minimal decoration. The €60 room for two is surprisingly luxurious, with shower, bath, and celestial-themed décor. (☎86 05 46; fax 83 75 25. Breakfast €5.50. Reception 7am-9pm. Single with toilet but no shower access €26; doubles with toilet and shower €35-60; 3-to 4-person room €45. MC/V. **Camping Les Breuils ❶,** allée des Breuils, is 1km from town, past the Citadelle Souterraine on av. du 5ème RAP. Turn right onto av. Général Boichut, then take the first left. Caravans abound, but tall bushes offer some privacy. The site has a bar, grocery store, laundry, and pool. (☎86 15 31; www.camping-les-breuils.com. Reception July-Aug. 7:30am-10pm; Apr.-June and Sept. 8am-noon and 2-10pm. July-Aug. €5.50 per person; June €4.95; Apr.-May and Sept. €4.40. €4.50 per site. Electricity €4. MC/V.)

FOOD. Verdun's contribution to confection is the ***dragée,*** a sugar-coated almonds first engineered by a 13th-century apothecary; according to local legend, the sweet bonbons foster fertility. The treats can be found just about anywhere in town. The main covered market is on rue de Rû (open F 7:30am-12:30pm). Stock up at the Match supermarket a block away from the station on rond-point des Etats-Unis. (Open M-Sa 8:30am-7:30pm, Su 8:30am-12:30pm.) Verdun generally lacks quality restaurants and cafés; the best places can be found in the area along rue Chaussée and rue des Rouyers and by the canal on quai de Londres. Sea-side-themed Marie la Crêpe ❶, 54 rue des Royeurs, serves crispy ***galettes*** (€2.70-8.60) and sweet ***crêpes*** (€2.60-8.30) that will fill your stomach without emptying your wallet. Place mat doodlers can try for a spot on the wall among other talented patrons. (☎84 20 70. Open July-Sept. daily noon-10pm; Oct.-June Tu-Su noon-2pm and 6-9pm. Cash only.) Locals pack bright red Le Boucher du Quai ❶, 19 quai de Londres, for sandwiches (€3.50-4.70) and pasta (€7.20-8.20). Try the ***steak-frites*** and salad for €10. (☎86 72 01. Open for meals daily noon-2pm and 7-10pm. MC/V.)

SIGHTS. Towering over Verdun's pedestrian district, the soldier of the **Monument à la Victoire** exudes strength and persistence. The colossal sculpture stands on an old chapel, the remains of the **Eglise de la Magdeleine,** and the large pyramid-like stairs that lead up to it summon the grandeur of an ancient ziggurat. Inside the tiny chapel, three enormous volumes display records of the names of soldiers who fought here. (☎84 37 97. Open daily July-Aug. 9:30am-12:30pm and 1-6:30pm; Sept.-Oct. and Apr.-May 9:30am-noon and 2-5:30pm; June 9:30am-12:30pm and 2-6pm. Free.) The massive **Citadelle Souterraine,** down rue de Rû on av. du 5ème RAP, offers a reconstructed exhibit on trench warfare. This fortress once sheltered groups of 10,000 front-bound soldiers. The official *petit train* tour (the only means of entering) plunges visitors into the citadel's 4km of pitch-black underground galleries and depicts the underground lives of hungry soldiers and nervous generals through realistic, though unfortunately slightly corny, talking holograms. The citadel is a chilly 7°C; dress accordingly. (Tours in Dutch, English, French, German, Italian, and Spanish. Open daily July-Aug. 9am-6:30pm; Sept. and Apr.-June 9am-6pm; Oct.-Nov. 10am-noon and 2-6pm; Dec. 10am-noon and 2-5pm. 30min. tours in English or French every 5min. Wheelchair-accessible. €6, ages 5-15 €2.50. MC/V over €12.)

Verdun's pre-war constructions include the 10th- to 12th-century **Cathédrale Notre Dame,** rue de la Belle Vierge. Its crypt, unearthed during WWI bombings and renovated thereafter, features a set of beautiful modern stained-glass windows—yet what's most impressive about the Cathedral is that it managed to survive the war in the first place. *Les Heures Musicales*, a series of choir and organ concerts, fills the cathedral in June and July. (☎86 20 00; www.accv.fr. Concert times vary; call tourist office for details. Cathedral open daily Apr.-Sept. 8:45am-7pm; Oct.-Mar. 8:45am-6pm.) Built in 1200, the **Porte Chaussée,** quai de Londres, has served as a prison, a guard tower, and an exit for WWI troops. On rue Frères Boulhaut, a copy of Rodin's triumphant **La Défense** faces a parking lot; the Netherlands created the replica for the town after the Battle of Verdun. **Parc Municipal Japiot,** across from the tourist office, nurtures tall roses by the banks of the Meuse. (Open daily Apr.-Sept. 8:30am-8pm; Oct. and Mar. 9am-6pm; Nov.-Feb. 9am-5pm.)

NIGHTLIFE AND FESTIVALS. Stick around the quai de Londres and neighboring rue Chaussée for the best nightlife. The pubs around the river fill up most evenings, beginning before dark. L'Estaminet, 45 rue des Rouyers, has the feel of a German ***bierstube,*** serving bottled beer and its home brew amid a sound track of jazz and blues. (☎86 07 86. Beer from €2.50. Open M-Sa 2pm-3am. MC/V.) Locals pack Le Lapin Qui Fume, 31 rue des Gros Degrès, an endearingly gritty green-lit tavern with friendly service, loud music, and cheap beer. (☎86 15 84. Open Tu-Su 11am-2am. Beer from €1.80. Mixed drinks from €4. MC/V.) La Bidule, 1 rue des Gros Degrès, is a small discotheque that fills with 20- and 30-somethings after Verdun's bars have closed for the night. (☎86 02 86. Beer €5. Mixed drinks €7. Cover €7 for men; no cover for women. Open Th 11pm-4am, F-Sa 11pm-5am. AmEx/MC/V.)

Le Son et Lumière de la Bataille de Verdun recreates the battle, using over 300 actors and 1000 projectors, for a hushed crowd. (Info ☎84 50 00; www.connaissancedelameuse.com. June-July F-Sa night. Call Connaissance de la Meuse or the tourist office for tickets. June €15; July €18; ages 12-18 €9, under 12 free.) The sounds of **L'Eté Musicale** waft up the river from **quai de Londres** Saturday nights throughout July and August. (All types of music. Free concerts.)

DAYTRIP FROM VERDUN

WWI MEMORIALS

Many sites near Verdun commemorate the battle of 1916. The 4hr. bus tour conducted by the tourist office (p. 375) visits the first 4 memorials listed below, describing each in French. The office also offers a €13 pass (in addition to the price of the tour) to all of the mentioned monuments. Touring the entire 25km circuit requires a car.

After Alsace and parts of Lorraine were annexed by Germany in 1871, Verdun was thrust within 40km of the German border. France decided to build 38 forts to protect Verdun and the surrounding area. Yet after certain forts were destroyed by

German cannons, French General Joffre ordered the disarmament of all fortifications in 1915, redirecting his troops towards the offensive lines. The abandoned forts became the targets of German General von Falkenhayn's 1916 offensive. German troops first captured the immense concrete **Fort de Douaumont,** whose supported position, lookout, and 3km of passageways made it an invaluable acquisition. The French shelled it for the next eight months in an attempt to dislodge the German garrison. Finally, in October 1916, a fire broke out due to the shelling and the Germans fled; a detachment of French-led Moroccan troops then reclaimed the fort. Visitors to the dank fortress, with drippy, stalactite-covered ceilings, can still see the ruin resulting from the assault, which also tragically resulted in over 100,000 French deaths. Its walls have been warped and tattered; the dark and grimy conditions of its old toilets and disinfection room hint at their former squalor, while the shell firing room, bedrooms, and *boulangeries*, each only steps apart from each other, display the war's effect on daily life. Sporadically, the fort rings with a sonic recreation of a single exploding shell. These effects underscore the terrors of the 1916 battle more powerfully than Verdun's other monuments. (☎84 41 91. Open daily Apr.-Aug. 10am-6:30pm; Sept.-Oct. 10am-1pm and 2-5:30pm; Nov.-Dec. and Feb.-Mar. 10am-1pm and 2-5pm. €3, under 16 €1.50. Free informational brochures available in English, French, and German.)

The central and most moving monument is the **Ossuaire de Douaumont,** a vast crypt situated above an expansive cemetery. Aglow with the blood-orange hues from its stained-glass windows, the crypt's smooth granite walls bear the names of hundreds of dead soldiers who were never found. A small chapel in the middle of the crypt allows visitors a quiet moment to reflect, as the enormous halls are often filled with equally enormous crowds. Outside, small windows at the base of the monument's exterior reveal the ashes and bones of 130,000 unknown non-French soldiers. (☎84 54 81. Open daily May-Aug. 9am-6:30pm; Sept. 9am-noon and 2-6pm; Oct. and Mar. 9am-noon and 2-5:30pm; Nov. 9am-noon and 2-5pm; Apr. 9am-6pm. Brochures available in English. Historical film contains a few graphic scenes. Ossuary free. Film and tower €4, under 18 €3.) Nearby, the **Tranchée des Baïonettes** holds the bodies of members of France's 137th regiment, who died while taking cover from enemy fire. The precise events of the assault are not known, but some speculate that troops may have been buried alive. The only sign of the men was the points of their bayonets protruding from the ground; the tips of two guns can still be seen in the dirt.

The little town of Fleury was at the epicenter of the battle and changed hands 16 times during the war. The fighting left the town empty and the surrounding farmland unusable for generations. Stones have been placed where former houses used to sit, while white-painted plots of land signify the town's old streets. You can still see the remains of trenches in the rippled grass. Fleury's former railway station is now the **Memorial de Verdun** museum, which houses old weapons, uniforms, photographs, and a (perhaps surprisingly) fascinating exhibit on the development of medicine during the war. The basement recreates a devastated trench, with old helmets, shattered trees, remnants of artillery, and barbed wire. (☎84 35 34. Open daily Apr. to mid-Sept. 9am-6pm; mid-Sept. to Dec. and Feb.-Mar. 9am-noon and 2-6pm. €7, students and ages 11-16 €3.50, under 11 free. MC/V over €14.)

ALSACE

STRASBOURG ☎03 88

Clinging to the edge of Alsace, a few kilometers from the German border, Strasbourg (STRAHSS-boorg; pop. 270,000) is a French city with a truly international

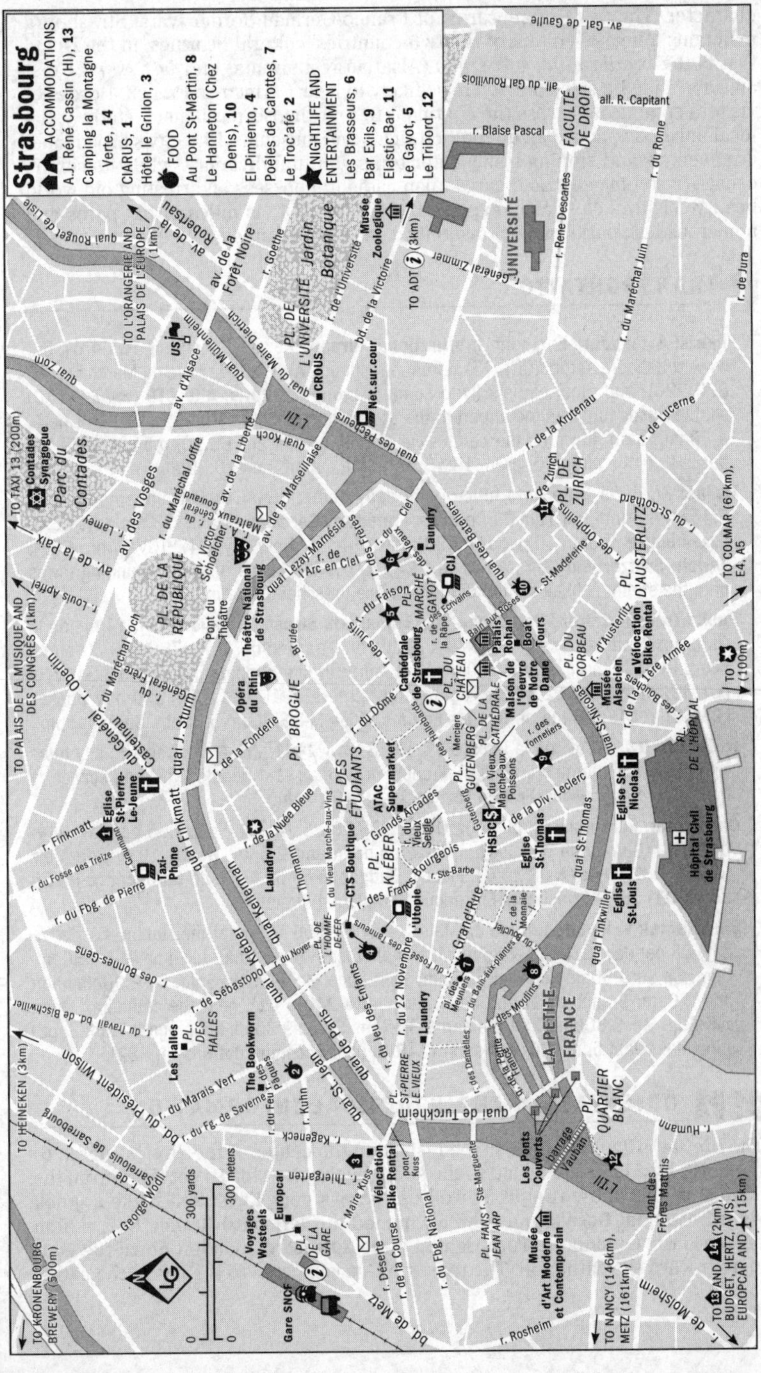
Strasbourg
ACCOMMODATIONS
A.J. Réné Cassin (HI), 13
Camping la Montagne Verte, 14
CIARUS, 1
Hôtel le Grillon, 3
FOOD
Au Pont St-Martin, 8
Le Hanneton (Chez Denis), 10
El Pimiento, 4
Poêles de Carottes, 7
Le Troc'afé, 2
NIGHTLIFE AND ENTERTAINMENT
Les Brasseurs, 6
Bar Exils, 9
Elastic Bar, 11
Le Gayot, 5
Le Tribord, 12
Gare SNCF
Cathédrale de Strasbourg
Palais Rohan
Musée Alsacien
Musée d'Art Moderne et Contemporain
Hôpital Civil de Strasbourg
LA PETITE FRANCE
PL. KLÉBER
PL. DE LA RÉPUBLIQUE
UNIVERSITÉ
300 meters
300 yards

character. The prize of centuries of Franco-German border wars, Strasbourg maintains a near-even mix of the two countries' cultural bearings; in the island that is the *vieille ville*, *winstubs* (Alsatian restaurants) and *pâtisseries* rest amicably side by side, and you're as likely to hear German as French. Hordes of visitors come from across the continent to tour the EU parliament, study at the local university, and soak up the rich sights and museums. The city's broad modern avenues and zipping trams cater to its youthful diversity, while its serene canals, pastel facades, and gargantuan cathedral possess an arresting old-world beauty. Visitors can easily explore the city by foot, as miles of flat paths and numerous lush parks make Strasbourg a pedestrian's dream.

TRANSPORTATION

Flights: Strasbourg-Entzheim International Airport, rte. de Strasbourg (☎64 67 67; www.strasbourg.aeroport.fr), 15km from Strasbourg. **Air France,** 7 rue du Marché (☎20 820 820), and other carriers fly to **London, Lyon,** and **Paris. Allô CTS** (☎77 70 70) shuttle **buses** run from the airport to the Strasbourg tram stop ("Baggarsee") on Line A, a 20min. tram ride from the *centre-ville* (12min.; 3 per hr.; €5.10, round-trip €9.50; buses from the airport 5:45am-10:45pm, to the airport 5am-10:30pm).

Trains: Pl. de la Gare. Info office open daily 4am-1:15am. Ticket office open M-Sa 5:45am-8:50pm, Su 7am-8:50pm. To: **Frankfurt, Germany** (2-4hr., 13 per day, €52); **Luxembourg** (2-3hr., 10 per day, €33); **Paris** (4hr., 24 per day, €47; TGV 2½hr., €63); **Zurich, Switzerland** (3hr., 4 per day, €40-47). **SNCF buses** run to surrounding towns from the station; check station or tourist office for schedules. AmEx/MC/V.

Public Transportation: Compagnie des Transports Strasbourgeois (CTS), 14 rue de la Gare aux Marchandises (☎77 70 11, bus and tram info 77 70 70; www.cts-strasbourg.fr). 4 tram lines run 4:30am-12:30am; 5th line opening in 2008. Find tickets (€1.30, round-trip €2.50) on board and *carnets* of 10 (€11.50) and day passes (€3.50) at **CTS,** 56 rue du Jeu des Enfants. Open M-F 8:30am-6:30pm, Sa 9am-5pm.

Taxis: Taxi 13, 30 av. de la Paix (☎36 13 13; www.taxi13.fr). Also gives 1hr. city tours with audio commentary in English, French, or German (1-4 people €33) and service to the *Route du Vin.* 24hr. **France Taxi** (☎22 19 19). 24hr.

Car Rental: Europcar, 16 pl. de la Gare (☎08 25 85 74 79). From €95 per day. 21+. Open M-F 8am-noon and 2-7pm, Sa 8am-noon and 2-5pm. **Hertz,** 10 bd. de Metz (☎32 57 62). **Avis** (☎08 20 61 17 00), **Budget** (☎64 69 40), and **Europcar** (☎08 25 00 41 01), all at Strasbourg-Entzheim International Airport.

Bike Rental: Vélocation, 4 rue du Maire-Kuss (☎23 56 75), near the station. €5 per ½-day, €8 per day; €100 check deposit and photocopy of ID. Open July-Aug. M-F 9:30am-5pm, Sa-Su 9:30am-noon and 2-7pm; Sept.-June M-F 9:30am-5pm, Sa 9:30am-noon and 2-6pm. Branch at 10 rue des Bouchers (☎24 05 61), near the cathedral. Open July-Aug. M-F 9:30am-12:30pm and 1:30-7pm, Sa-Su 9:30am-noon and 2-7pm; Sept.-June M-F 10am-5pm. MC/V. Also at **CIARUS** (see **Accommodations,** p. 382).

ORIENTATION AND PRACTICAL INFORMATION

The *vieille ville* is a lemon-shaped island in the center of the city, bordered to the north by a large canal and to the south by the river Ill. To get there from the train station, follow rue du Maire-Kuss across pont Kuss, and make a quick right onto **quai Desaix** and then an immediate left onto **Grande Rue,** which becomes rue Gutenberg. Turn right at **place Gutenberg,** then left down rue Mercière toward the cathedral. The tourist office is located to the left of the cathedral entrance. Continue quai Desaix, which becomes quai de Turkheim, to reach **La Petite France,** a neighborhood of old Alsatian houses, restaurants, and narrow canals.

Tourist Office: 17 pl. de la Cathédrale (☎52 28 28; www.ot-strasbourg.fr), near the cathedral. A small branch with maps but little else at pl. de la Gare (☎32 51 49). English-speaking staff makes hotel reservations (€2 plus 1st night's deposit). Free map; better map €1. The *Strasbourg Pass* (€12, ages 4-18 €5.70) quickly pays for itself, including a visit to 1 museum, ascent to the cathedral platform, boat tour of the city, bike rental for 1 day, and a view of the astronomical clock, along with other ½-price offers. Open daily 9am-7pm. **Bas-Rhine ADT,** 9 rue du Dome (☎15 45 88; www.tourisme67.com), has info on the *Route du Vin.* Open M-F 10am-noon and 2-5pm.

Tours: The tourist office organizes a variety of tours.

Walking Tour: Tours of the *vieille ville* and the cathedral in French, German, Italian, and Spanish. See office for schedule. €6.80, students and ages 12-18 €3.40. English audio tours €5.50.

Petit train Tour: Leave from pl. du Château. Gives a 50min. tour of downtown. Daily every 30min. May to mid-Sept. 9:30am-7pm; Apr. and mid-Sept. to mid-Oct. 10am-5:30pm; mid- to late Oct. 10am-5pm. €5.10, ages 4-12 €2.60.

Boat Tour: Departs from behind the landing-stage of the Palais Rohan. Daily Apr.-Oct. every 30min. 9:30am-9pm; Nov. and Jan.-Mar. 4 per day 10:30am-4pm; Dec. every 30min. 9:30am-5pm. Evening tours available May-Sept. 9:30, 10pm. €7.40, students and ages 3-18 €3.70. 15% family discount (includes 1 adult and 3children).

Budget Travel: Voyages Wasteels, 13 pl. de la Gare (☎23 00 83). Open M-F 9am-1pm and 2-6pm, Su 9am-noon.

Consulates: US, 15 av. d'Alsace (☎35 31 04; fax 24 06 95), next to pont John F. Kennedy. Open M-F 9:30am-noon and 2-5pm. Other nations' consulate information available at tourist office.

English-Language Bookstore: The Bookworm, 3 rue de Pâques (☎32 26 99), off rue du Faubourg de Saverne. Open Tu-F 9:30am-6:30pm, Sa 10am-6pm.

Youth Centers: CROUS, 1 quai du Maire-Dietrich (☎21 28 00; www.crous-strasbourg.fr). Info on employment, housing, and study opportunities. Open M-F 9:30am-noon and 1:30-6pm. **Centre d'Information Jeunesse (CIJ),** 7 rue des Ecrivains (☎37 33 33; www.cija.org), has info on jobs and housing. 1 computer with free Internet access; research only. Open M-Th 10am-noon and 1-6pm, F 10am-noon and 1-5pm.

Laundromat: Wash'n Dry, 15 rue des Veaux. Wash €7 per 16kg, dry €2 per 30min. Open daily 7am-9pm. **Lavomatique,** 29 Grand Rue. Wash €4 per 8kg. Open daily 7:30am-8pm.

LEAVING ON A JET TRAIN

Looking to travel to Strasbourg from the City of Light? Now you can—even closer to the speed of light. In April 2007, a French high-speed train shattered the world record for trains on rail. Clocking in at an astonishing 357mph, the V150, as the train is creatively nicknamed, exceeded the expectations of even the testers. This super-train reached top speeds and now shoots from Paris to Strasbourg in 2 hours and 20 minutes—nearly half the previous travel [redacted]

TGV Est began [redacted]ding through Alsace and [redacted]ine in June 2007—met with excitement at every stop. Strasbourg residents celebrated for a whole weekend when it came to town, and the party extended beyond the platform. One fancy restaurant, Le Crocodile, offered their very own TGV *menu: "Très Gastronomique Vôtre,"* with train-themed *plats* named after new stops on the line.

Citizens hope that the new fast track will electrify its burgeoning nightlife scene by attracting Parisians and tourists for convenient weekend getaways. Already an international hub[redacted]g will hopefully be the [redacted]pause en route to Lu[redacted] Germany, and Switzerland. And things are looking up: in a New York Times article, one student said of the city, "You can breathe here, literally." Leave the huffing and puffing to the TGV and catch your breath in Strasbourg.

Police: 11 rue de la Nuée Bleue (☎15 37 17) or **police nationale,** 34 rte. de l'Hôpital (☎03 90 23 17 17).

24hr. Pharmacy: Association SOS Pharmacie, ☎41 11 34.

Hospital: Hôpital Civil de Strasbourg, 1 pl. de l'Hôpital (☎11 67 68), south of the *vieille ville* across the canal.

Internet Access: L'Utopie, 21-23 rue du Fossée des Tanneurs (☎23 89 21). €1 per 15min., 3 per 1hr. Wi-Fi available. Open M-Sa 6:30am-11:30pm, Su 8am-10pm. **Net.sur.cour,** 18 quai des Pêcheurs (☎35 66 76). €1 per 30min. Open M-Sa 9:30am-8:30pm, Su 1:30-7:30pm. **Taxiphone,** 24 rue du Faubourg de Pierre (☎23 91 70). €2 per hr. Open daily 10am-11:30pm. Also at **CIJ, CIARUS,** and **Hôtel le Grillon** (see **Accommodations,** p. 382).

Post Office: 5 av. de la Marseillaise (☎52 35 50). Open M-F 8am-7pm, Sa 8am-noon. Branches at cathedral (open M-F 8am-6:30pm, Sa 9am-5pm); 1 rue de la Fonderie (open M-F 8am-6:30pm, Sa 8:30am-noon); and 1 pl. de la Gare (open M-F 8:30am-6:30pm, Sa 8:30am-noon), with **currency exchange** and **ATM. Postal Code:** 67000.

ACCOMMODATIONS AND CAMPING

There are relatively inexpensive, high-quality hotels all over the city, particularly around the train station. Make reservations early.

> TIP **PARLIAMENTARY PROCEDURE.** The EU parliament brings hordes of visitors to Strasbourg—especially when it is in session—and hotel prices increase accordingly. Room prices can decrease as much as €10 per night when the politicians are out of town. Go to http://www.europarl.europa.eu to find the schedule of sessions. Weekends are a safe bet for cheaper rooms.

Hôtel le Grillon, 2 rue Thiergarten (☎32 71 88; www.grillon.com), 1 block from the train station. A young staff, dark wood trimmings, and a ski-lodge feel make this the best choice in town. Large, clean hallway bathrooms, an Internet café (€1 per 15min.), and a hip bar. TV in all but the cheapest rooms. Breakfast €5.50. Reception 24hr. Check-out noon. Reservations recommended. Singles €33, with shower €43-58; doubles €40/50-65. Extra bed €13. MC/V. ❸

Centre International d'Accueil de Strasbourg (CIARUS), 7 rue Finkmatt (☎15 27 88; www.ciarus.com), 15min. from the train station. This big, bright, primary-colored hostel houses international boarders of all ages. Small, tidy rooms have metallic bunks, ample shelving, and bath. TV room, ping pong, cafeteria, bar, and laundry. W "Disco" night Th "make-your-own-*crêpes*" night. Breakfast included; lunch and dinner €5-7. Free Wi-Fi. Reception 24hr. Check-in 3:30pm. Check-out 9am. Reservations recommended. 6- to 8-bed dorms €21, €24 during parliamentary sessions; 3- to 4-bed dorms €25/28; 2-bed rooms €28/31; singles € 44/47; family rooms €21/24. MC/V. ❷

Auberge de Jeunesse René Cassin (HI), 9 rue de l'Auberge de Jeunesse (☎30 26 46; fax 30 35 16), 2km from the train station. Take bus #2 (dir.: Campus d'Illkirch) from the station to "Auberge de Jeunesse." Due to massive construction at the station, bus #2 may not stop there. In that case, take tram B or C (dir.: Elsau) to "Montagne Verte," then bus #2, 12, 13, 15, or 50 to "Auberge." Dark, clean, and small rooms with red and yellow bunks. Quiet, beautiful canal-side setting. TV room, kitchen, and bar. Breakfast included. Internet access €1.20 per 15min., €2.20 per 30min. Wi-Fi €5 per day, €10 per 3 days. Reception 7am-noon, 1-7:30pm, and 8:30-11pm. Code access after 1am. Open Feb.-Dec. 3- to 6-bed dorms €22; singles €36; doubles €49. MC/V. ❶

Camping la Montagne Verte, 2 rue Robert Forrer (☎30 25 46; fax 27 10 15), near the René Cassin hostel. Take bus #2 (dir.: Campus d'Illkirch) to "Nid de Cigognes." Turn right onto rue du Schokeloch and right again onto rue Robert Forrer. Spacious riverside campground with minimal privacy; each site is divided by only a small white fence. Tennis courts, basketball, laundry, and bar. Open mid-Mar. to Oct. and late Nov. to early Jan. Reception 7am-10pm. Closed to cars after 10pm. €4.80 per adult, €2 per child, €5.50 per site. Electricity €4.30. MC/V. ❶

FOOD

Local restaurants are known for *choucroute garnie* (sauerkraut with meats), but you can find delicious sausages at stands throughout the city. Other specialties include the ubiquitous *tarte flambée* (thin-crust pizza with a cream-sauce base; €5-8), and a vast array of wines from the *Route du Vin.* The streets around the cathedral are filled with reasonably priced restaurants, while pretty cafés line **rue du Vieux Seigle** and **rue du Vieux Marché aux Grains.** Less touristy restaurants can be found around **rue de la Krutenau.** In **La Petite France,** you'll find small **winstubs** (VIN-shtoob)—classic (and somewhat pricey) Alsatian taverns with a distinctly German flavor and characterized by timber exteriors, checkered tablecloths, and menus full of countless combinations of carbohydrates, melted cheese, and salted meats. Cheap kebab and sandwich joints cluster around the train station and on **Grand Rue.** Markets are held at **boulevard de la Marne** (Tu and Sa 7am-1pm), **place de Bordeaux** (Tu and Sa 7am-1pm), and **place Broglie** (W and F 7am-6pm). Supermarkets are scattered around the *vieille ville;* an **ATAC** is at 47 rue des Grandes Arcades, off pl. Kléber. (☎32 51 53. Open M-Sa 8:30am-8:30pm. MC/V.)

Le Hanneton (Chez Denis), 5 rue Ste-Madeleine (☎36 93 76). The place to go for a taste of the region. Pieffel Denis, the attentive host and chef at this relatively un-touristed *winstub,* prepares Alsatian favorites for friends, fans, and regulars. An enormous candelabra sits on each of the 7 tables, while dozens of traditionally Alsatian *sorcières* (witch dolls) hang overhead. Traditional favorite *choucroute à l'alsacienne* (€15) is a heaping pile of sauerkraut with 5 meaty toppings, and the potatoes with muenster cheese (€11) are wonderfully filling. *Tartes flambées* €6.50-7.50. Reservations recommended. Open Tu 7-11pm, W-Su noon-2pm and 7-11pm. MC/V. ❸

El Pimiento, 52 rue du Jeu des Enfants (☎21 94 52), by pl. Homme de Fer. At this chill, dimly-lit tapas restaurant, you may forget that Spain is a country away. Serves delectable Spanish treats like creative *ensalada de pimientos* (salad with roasted peppers and olive oil; €3), *chorizo* sausage (€3), and *arroz à la Espanola* (Spanish rice; €2.30). Tapas €2.30-6. Open M-Sa 11:30am-2:30pm and 6:30pm-midnight. AmEx/MC/V. ❷

Poêles de Carottes, 2 pl. des Meuniers (☎32 33 23; www.poelesdecarottes.com). An adorable canary-yellow restaurant on the outskirts of La Petite France. Healthful, delicious, and mostly-organic vegetarian options. Elaborate mixed drinks like the *Pétanquiste* (with apple and *pastis;* €4.75-6). Pizza €7-11. Huge salads €8.50-10. Vegetable *gratins* €8.50-11. Lunch *menu* €11. Open Tu-Sa noon-3pm and 7-10:30pm. MC/V. ❷

Au Pont St-Martin, 13-15 rue des Moulins (☎32 45 13). Super-touristy for a reason. A popular, consummately German *winstub* in La Petite France, featured on postcards of the area. The food is tasty, but it's the idyllic canal-side location that makes this large, bustling restaurant special. *Tartes flambées* €7-9. *Choucroute* €13. Beer from €2.70. Lunch *menu du jour* €8.90. Dinner *menus* €17. Open M-F 11:30am-2:30pm and 6-10:30pm, Sa-Su 11:30am-10:30pm. AmEx/MC/V. ❸

Le Troc'afé, 8 rue Faubourg de Saverne (☎23 23 29). A popular lunch spot that's all about atmosphere. Filled with enormous funky paintings, American movie posters in French translation, and old advertisements. It's like a cool-but-eccentric uncle's attic. Serves standard Alsatian fare and pastries. The perfect place to nurse a cup of coffee for hours. Beer from €2. *Plat du jour* €9. Open M-F 7:30am-9:30pm, Sa 11am-9:30pm. MC/V. ❷

SIGHTS

CATHÉDRALE DE STRASBOURG. In Strasbourg, nothing is as impressive as the majestic cathedral. Completed in 1439, this towering 142m structure took 260 years to build. As the story goes, German literary giant Goethe scaled its 332 steps regularly to cure his fear of heights. If you look to the southern transept of the cathedral's prized spire, the **Pilier des Anges,** you'll find a stunning depiction of the Last Judgment. Behind the spire, the massive **Horloge Astronomique** attests to the wizardry of 16th-century Swiss clock makers. At 12:30pm, tiny apostles march out of the face, and a rooster greets St-Peter. Beware of pickpockets around and within the cathedral. *(☎21 43 34. Cathedral open M-Sa 7-11:40am and 12:40-7pm, Su 12:45-6pm. Info desk open M-F 9:45-11:45am and 2-5pm. Tours in French July-Aug. M-F 3pm; in German July-Aug. M-F 2pm; €3. Tickets to Horloge film and performance available at 11:35am, film noon; €2, under 18 €0.50. Tickets available 9-11:30am and 11:45am-12:25pm. July-Aug. Arrive 30min. early. €0.80. Free film on cathedral every 11min. in southern wing. Tower open for climbing July-Aug. 8:30am-7pm; Apr.-June and Sept. 9am-6pm; Mar. and Oct. 9am-5:30pm; Nov.-Feb. 9am-4:30pm. €4.40, students and ages 5-18 €2.20.)*

LA PETITE FRANCE. The old tanners' district, in the southwest corner of the city center, is characterized by steep-roofed houses with carved, pastel-colored wooden facades—all surrounded by waterways. Locals flock to this relaxed neighborhood to chat in sidewalk cafés as accordion music and the gurgling of the river can be heard in the background. A host of restaurants and *winstubs* make this a perfect, though sometimes pricey, dining spot, and an ideal location for a date. The area is bordered by "covered bridges," which have kept their name despite the fact that they haven't had roofs since the 18th century. Four towers and the remains of the 14th-century city walls also surround the district, while farther west, the Vauban dam offers a **terrace** with an expansive view (open daily 9am-7:30pm).

PALAIS ROHAN. This magnificent 18th-century building houses three small museums. The **Musée des Arts Décoratifs,** once a residence for cardinals, was looted during the Revolution, then refurbished for Napoleon in 1805. The gold-encrusted ceilings and immense expanses of marble are stunning, but the highlight of the *appartements* tour is the more demure library, where majestic portraits and staid marble busts overlook shelves of books along the hall's perimeter. The museum offers an informative English guidebook. The impressively comprehensive **Musée Archéologique** illustrates the history of Alsace from 600,000 BC to AD 800 with old tools, relics, and an unsettling number of skeletons. *(Free French audio tour.)* It also displays samples from Alsace's collection—the largest in the world—of early and middle Neolithic tombs. Upstairs, the **Musée des Beaux-Arts** displays a solid collection of art from the 14th to the 19th centuries, including works by Botticelli, El Greco, Giotto, Goya, Raphaël, Rubens, and Van Dyck. *(2 pl. du Château. ☎52 50 00. Open M and W-Su 10am-6pm. Each museum €4, students €2; 1st Su of month free.)*

MUSÉE D'ART MODERNE ET CONTEMPORAIN. Opened in 1998, Adrien Fainsilber's glass and steel behemoth, which resembles a smaller version of Paris's Centre Pompidou, holds an impressive collection of late 19th- and 20th-century painting, including Impressionist, Abstract, Surrealist, and Cubist works. Highlights include gems by Dufy, Ernst, Gauguin, Kandinsky, Monet, and Picasso. The collection is distinctive for its creative arrangement; in a ground-floor foyer, a version of Rodin's stoic *Thinker* sits among violently colorful post-Millennium paintings. *(1 pl. Hans Jean Arp. ☎23 31 31. Open Tu-W and F-Sa 11am-7pm, Th noon-10pm, Su 10am-6pm. €5, students €2.50, under 18 free; 1st Su of month free.)*

L'ORANGERIE. Strasbourg's largest, most spectacular park, L'Orangerie was designed by the famed Le Nôtre in 1692 after he polished up Versailles. The park seems to have something for everyone: promenades, gardens, and pagodas are perfect for a leisurely stroll or a brisk jog, while a zoo and a miniature farm filled with traditional Alsatian storks provide diversions for children who may be less ecstatic about a long walk in the park. L'Orangerie also contains go-carts, a pond with waterfalls to be explored by rowboat, and Le Nôtre's original concrete-lined skateboard park. *(Take bus #6, dir.: Pl. des Sports, from pl. des Halles to "L'Orangerie." Free.)*

OTHER SIGHTS. The **Palais de l'Europe** houses the Council of Europe and the governing bodies of the European Union—the European Parliament—in a spectacular modern complex off av. de l'Europe, at the northwest edge of L'Orangerie. Across the canal from the Council, the Human Rights Building, designed by Richard Rogers in 1995, houses the European Court of Human Rights. Its shape is meant to simulate a ship following the curve of the river, while the building's facade is intended to evoke the scales of justice. *(The Council of Europe gives tours by reservation. ☎41 20 29.)* The **Musée Alsacien,** inside a quintessentially Alsatian half-timbered house, showcases everyday life in Alsace since the Middle Ages. The museum, which just celebrated its 100th birthday in 2007, is surprisingly enjoyable, as it transports visitors into a well-preserved 19th-century home. A model of a small synagogue showcases Jewish history in the area. *(23-25 quai St-Nicolas. ☎52 50 01. Open M and W-Su July-Sept. 10am-6pm; Oct.-June noon-6pm. €4, students €2, under 18 free; 1st Su of the month free.)* The **Kronenbourg brewery,** though no longer functional, gives visitors a taste of Germany, with tours including a short film in English, French, or German. You'll get a look at the different stages of brewing and a *dégustation*. *(68 rte. d'Oberhausbergen. Take tram to "Ducs d'Alsace." ☎27 41 59; siege.visites@kronenbourg-fr.com. Open May-Sept. and Dec. M-Sa; Oct.-Nov. and Jan.-June M-F; hours vary. By reservation only. €2.50.)* **Heineken** offers free tours of its brewery in English, French, and German, but only for groups and by advance reservation. *(4 rue St-Charles, Schiltigheim. ☎19 57 55. Call to schedule M-F 8am-noon and 1:30-4:30pm.)*

NIGHTLIFE

Strasbourg specializes in friendly bars rather than throbbing clubs. **Place Kléber** attracts a student scene, while **rue des Frères** and the tiny **place du Marché Gayot** fill up quickly after 10pm with a diverse, slightly older crowd. The area between **place d'Austerlitz** and **place de Zurich,** across the canal from the *vieille ville*, is lively until the wee hours. It is best to travel in groups at night.

Bar Exils, 28 rue de l'Ail (☎32 52 70), a few blocks from the cathedral. This casually hip bar starts buzzing in the evening and stays crowded until closing. Chatter and loud music fill the crimson-colored main room, while the small outdoor terrace and back billiards room offer a more subdued scene. Huge selection of beers from €2; after 10pm €2.50. Open M-F noon-4am, Sa-Su 2pm-4am. MC/V.

Le Tribord, Ponts Couverts (☎36 22 90), across the river from the Musée d'art Moderne. At pl. du Quartier Blanc, turn right onto the footpath by the canal in front of the Hôtel du Département. Follow the path to the waterside; the club is inside the first boat on the right. Forget a simple boat tour of the city—this popular new gay and lesbian club, inside a small boat just outside of Petite France, is lined with fuzzy, colorful couches to chat with friends and has a small dance floor in the center that fills up around midnight. Beer from €2.50. Mixed drinks from €4. Open Th-Sa 10pm-4am.

Les Brasseurs, 22 rue des Veaux (☎36 12 13; www.au-brasseur-strasbourg.com). An intimate, trendy microbrewery that serves 4 different home brews (on tap from €2, after 9:30pm €2.40; bottles from €4.10) and *tartes flambées* (€4.90-8.10) in a dark red and wood interior. The enormous, shiny brewing machines are visible from the bar. Students pack the pub's *cave* for its free concerts on weekend nights (F-Sa 9:30pm). Open daily 11:30am-1am; service ends 12:30am. Happy hour nightly 5-7pm. MC/V.

Elastic Bar, 27 rue des Orphelins (☎36 11 10). One of the city's most energetic scenes on weekend nights. Students and regulars shout over loud music in a bar that has taken grunge to heart, with graffiti, steel staircases, and metal stickers plastered on the wall. Beer from €2.60. Open M-W 6pm-3am, Th-Sa 6pm-4am. MC/V.

Le Gayot, 18 rue des Frères (☎36 31 88). This bar's classy and expansive terrace opens onto the lively pl. Marché Gayot and fills up early with 30-somethings who leisurely nurse their drinks. Mojitos €8.50. Beer €3.10. Mixed drinks from €6.10. Open June-Aug. daily 11am-2am; Sept.-May M-Sa 11am-1am. MC/V.

ENTERTAINMENT AND FESTIVALS

The **Orchestre Philharmonique de Strasbourg** performs at the Palais de la Musique et des Congrès, behind pl. de Bordeaux. (☎15 09 09. Performances Oct.-June. Student tickets ½-price or less.) The **Théâtre National de Strasbourg,** 1 av. de la Marseillaise, puts on performances September to June. (☎24 88 24; www.tns.fr. €16-23, students €14-16. MC/V.) The **Opéra du Rhin,** 19 pl. Broglie, features opera and ballet in its 19th-century hall. (☎75 48 00. Tickets €11-75, students under 26 ½-price; rush tickets from €10, students from €5.50.) Summer in Strasbourg centers on **place de la Cathédrale,** which becomes a stage every afternoon and evening for performers, including a troupe of musicians, flame-eaters, acrobats, and mimes. The cathedral hosts organ concerts throughout the summer. (Free concerts June-Sept. Su 5:30pm. Organ recitals F 8:30pm. €10, students €5.) A nightly *son-et-lumière* (light show) in July and August brings the austere facade of the cathedral to life with dazzling colors, accompanied by music (10pm-1am).

One of Strasbourg's most popular festivals is the annual **Festival de Musique de Strasbourg,** a two-week extravaganza in June that attracts some of Europe's best classical musicians. The **Festival de Jazz,** spanning the first two weeks of July, draws giants of the jazz world. (Tickets €22-48; student tickets available at reduced prices.) For info on these festivals, contact the helpful **Wolf Musique,** 24 rue de la Mésange (☎32 42 38; www.jazzdor.com). Clowns, musicians, and acrobats bombard Strasbourg's squares for the annual **Street Performance Festival,** which spans nine days in mid-August. Special performances are given nightly in pl. du Marché aux Poissons and pl. des Tripiers (5:30pm and 9pm; call the tourist office for details). **Musica,** a contemporary music festival held from mid-September to early October, includes an array of popular concerts, operas, and films. (☎23 47 23; www.festival-musica.org.)

ROUTE DU VIN (WINE ROUTE)

The vineyards of Alsace flourish in a 150km strip called the *Route du Vin* (root doo VEHN) which runs along the foothills of the Vosges mountains. The Romans were the first to ferment Alsatian grapes, but the Alsatians have perfected the process, now selling over 150 million bottles every year. Hordes of wine-loving and largely middle-aged tourists are drawn to the medieval villages along the *Route* by gorgeous houses and wineries giving free *dégustations*. Yet, with over 60 wine-producing towns, the *Route* offers an authentic Alsatian experience. Each town has a different attraction; some, such as Kaysersberg, combine wine-sipping with small-town charm, while others, like Barr, allow for grittier treks through massive vineyards.

Consider staying in Colmar (p. 392) or Sélestat (p. 389), larger towns that anchor the southern *Route*, and daytripping to the smaller (and pricier) towns. Buses run frequently from Colmar to surrounding towns, but transportation to northern towns is a little more difficult. You can explore the *Route* by car if you're willing to pay the steep rental fees in Strasbourg or Colmar. Biking, especially from Colmar, requires the stamina to endure lengthy, often hilly journeys, but the trails and turnoffs are well marked. Trains connect Sélestat, Molsheim, Barr, Colmar, and Mulhouse. The absence of good sidewalks makes walking unpleasant. The best source of info on regional *caves* is the **Centre d'Information du Vin d'Alsace,** 12 av. de la Foire aux Vins, at the Maison du Vin d'Alsace in Colmar. (☎20 16 20; fax 20 16 30. Open M-F 9am-noon and 2-5pm.) Tourist offices in Strasbourg (p. 386) or along the *Route* dispense helpful advice and hand out the *Alsace Wine Route* brochure.

KAYSERSBERG ☎03 89

If you only have time for one town on the *Route*, make it Kaysersberg (ky-suhrss-burg). Relatively un-touristed and tucked between green mountains, the town offers a complete immersion into rustic tranquility.

The ruined **château** on the hill is a 10min. climb from the tourist office and worth a visit, as its open peak provides stunning views over the surrounding vineyards and Kaysersberg's beige and pink facades. Overgrown vines create a romantic feel on the stony path up the hill, but steer clear of the poison ivy that rears its itchy head on parts of the walk. Before heading down to the central Hôtel de Ville, stop in at the **Musée Albert Schweitzer,** 126 rue du Général de Gaulle, located across the street from the Porte Haute bus stop. The small exhibit contains memorabilia tracing the life and achievements of the late Dr. Schweitzer, whose years of medical work in Lambaréné won him the 1952 Nobel Peace Prize. (☎47 36 55. Open daily Apr. to mid-Nov. 9am-noon and 2-6pm. €2, under 18 €1.) The glassblowing studio **Verrerie d'Art de Kaysersberg,** 30 rue du Général de Gaulle, offers free viewings of its workshops and explanations of its traditional glassblowing methods. (☎47 14 97. Open Feb.-Dec. Tu-W and F-Sa 10am-12:30pm and 2-6pm, Th 10am-12:30pm. Free brochures in English, French, and German.) Christmas season brings Kaysersberg's greatest *fête*, **Préludes de Noël,** with painting exhibitions, markets, and concerts for four weekends leading up to the big day (11am-8pm).

Compared with the other towns on the *Route*, Kaysersberg offers few wine *caves*, though the restaurants that line **rue du Général de Gaulle** and **rue des Forgerons** serve local Bacchanalian specialties. Nearly every eatery serves the popular *tarte flambée*, and if you don't mind eating on one of the city's many benches or grassy areas, you can take out one of the delicious *tartes* (€4-5.50) or an intensely large *wurst* baked in cheese (€2.40) from **Bretzel Chaud du Moulin ❶,** 60 pl. du 1er R.C.A. (☎03 80 47 39 23. Open Tu and Th-Su 10am-7pm.)

Kaysersberg has no train station, but Kunegel **buses** (☎24 65 65; www.l-k.fr) run to and from Colmar (35min.; July-Aug. 2-4 per day, Sept.-June 8 per day; €3). The stop in Colmar is in front of the train station; some buses also stop at the Unterlinden Théâtre. The Kaysersberg **tourist office,** 39 rue du Général de Gaulle, is in the Hôtel de Ville, down the street from the "Porte Haute" stop. (☎78 22 78; www.kaysersberg.com. Open mid-June to mid-Sept. M-Sa 9am-12:30pm and 2-6pm, Su 10am-12:30pm; mid-Sept. to mid-June M-Sa 9:30am-noon and 2-5:30pm. Free brochures in English, French, and German. Guided tours in French and German July-Aug. M and W-Th 8:30pm. €4.50, under 16 free.)

RIQUEWIHR ☎03 89

One of the most visited villages along the *Route* is the 16th-century walled hamlet of Riquewihr (rick-WUHRR). The town's quaint *vieille ville* is simple to navigate, with all of its highlights lining the central **rue du Général de Gaulle.** Old-fashioned cobblestone streets lend Riquewihr a sense of calm, which seems to persist even as summer tourists swarm to visit some of Alsace's biggest wine farms, as well as the overpriced gift shops that line the main streets.

The town's best sight is the **Tour des Voleurs** (Tower of Thieves), rue des Juifs, which served as a prison until the 18th century. The eerily enthralling torture chamber still holds its signature weapon: a rope-and-pulley *estrapade* that would hang prisoners by their wrists until their arms were disjointed. An audio tour in the chamber gives all the gruesome details in Dutch, English, French, or German. While the *estrapade* seems medievally distant, the last room of the museum, sponsored by several anti-torture political groups, alerts visitors to the continuing perils of torture in the modern world. (Open Apr.-Nov. daily 10:15am-12:30pm and 2-6:30pm. €2, under 10 free.) Riquewihr also has a **petit train** that tours the city walls and vineyards, leaving from the town hall. (☎73 74 24. 30min. Commentary in Danish, Dutch, English, French, German, Italian, Japanese, and Spanish. Every hr. 10am-6pm. €6, under 18 6-14 €4.) Markets take place every Friday on **rue des Trois Eglises** (open 8am-noon). In nearby **Ribeauvillé,** the **Foire aux Vins** (Wine Fair) comes to town at the end of July. On the first Sunday of September, the streets of Riquewihr are filled with classic Alsatian songs at the **Minstrel's Festival.**

Pauli Autocars (☎78 11 78; www.pauli.fr) runs **buses** from the train station in Colmar (30min.; Sept.-June 7 per day, July-Aug. 2 per day; €3.10). To reach the **tourist office,** 2 rue de la Première Armée, take the bus to "Poste" and walk through the gate of the Hôtel de Ville and up the hill; the tourist office is on the left and has free maps. The office also gives walking tours of the *vieille ville* in French. (☎49 08 40; www.ribeauville-riquewihr.com. Tours mid-July to Aug. M 6pm, F-Sa 9:30pm. Office open May-Sept. and Dec. M and W-Sa 9:30am-noon and 2-6pm, Tu 10am-noon and 2-6pm, Su 10am-1pm; Apr. and Oct. M and W-Sa 9:30am-noon and 2-6pm, Tu 10am-noon and 2-6pm; Nov. and Jan.-Mar. M-F 10am-noon and 2-5pm, every other Sa 10am-noon and 2-5pm.) Pitch a tent at the four-star **Camping Intercommunal ❶,** 1.5km from the town center. (☎47 90 08; campingriquewihr@wanadoo.fr. Open Apr.-Dec. Reception July-Aug. 8:30am-noon and 1-9pm; Apr.-June and Sept.-Dec. 8:30am-noon and 3:30-7pm. Apr.-Oct. €3.60 per adult, €1.70 per child, €4 per site; Nov.-Dec. €3.25/1.55/4. Electricity €3.50-4. Cash only.)

BARR ☎03 88

Of the *Route du Vin* towns, Barr (BAHRR), on the slopes of Mont Ste-Odile, seems most tied to its grapes: 2min. from the town center, you can sip a glass of white wine while strolling among the rows of vines where its grapes were nourished. With fewer crowds and touristy gift shops than other towns on the *Route*, Barr appears peacefully untouched.

To reach *caves* in the *vieille ville*, turn onto rue du Dr. Sultzer from pl. de l'Hôtel de Ville. Behind you sits the austere **Eglise Protestante,** which serves as the starting point for the **sentier viticole** (vineyard trail). The highlight of any trip to Barr, this path winds 2km through fields of glistening grapes, walkable alone or in tours led by local viticulturists (call tourist office). The tourist office leads free tours of Barr's wine caves, but most *maisons* expect you to buy something after the complimentary tasting. (☎08 52 50. Tours in French July-Aug. Tu 4pm. Call ahead. Free.) The local *vigniers* pull out their best bottles for the **Foire aux Vins,** or wine fair, in the second week of July, and the first weekend in October brings music, markets, and—of course— more wine for the **Fête des Vendanges.**

Trains to Barr run from Sélestat (25min., 10 per day, €3.20) and Strasbourg (50min., 14 per day, €6). Buy a return-trip ticket before you leave; the Barr train station does not sell tickets (open M-F 5:15am-8:10pm). The **tourist office,** pl. de l'Hôtel de Ville, has a English/French/German guide to the town. From the train station, turn right on rue de la Gare and left on av. des Vosges. Follow this past the roundabout, bearing left and avoiding what becomes rue de l'Hôpital de la Gare, and continue for several blocks onto rue St-Marc. Take a right, veer left through pl. du Marché aux Pommes de Terre and walk straight until the end of rue des Boulangers. Turn right onto rue des Bouchers; the tourist office is on the left. (☎08 66 65; www.pays-de-barr.com. Open July-Aug. M-Sa 9am-12:30pm and 2-6pm, Su 10am-noon and 2-6pm; Sept.-Oct. and Apr.-June M-Sa 9am-noon and 2-6pm, Su 2-6pm; Nov.-Mar. M-Sa 9am-noon and 2-6pm.)

SÉLESTAT ☎03 88

Halfway between Colmar and Strasbourg, Sélestat (SAY-leh-STAH; pop. 17,500) lacks the crowds of other stops on the *Route*, making it a peaceful change of pace from Alsace's more heavily touristed areas. Once part of the Holy Roman Empire and a center of Renaissance humanism, Sélestat is a relaxed hamlet with a few one-of-a-kind museums and quietly stunning churches. Still close to its past, the town has an infectious sense of tradition: every Tuesday morning since 1435, thousands of Alsatians have flooded the streets for Sélestat's weekly food and clothing market. Visitors to the tiny town could cover its gems in a weekend; those looking for affordable lodgings or exciting nightlife should explore Sélestat as a daytrip.

TRANSPORTATION AND PRACTICAL INFORMATION. From pl. de la Gare, **trains** run to Colmar (15min., 38 per day, €4) and Strasbourg (30min., 54 per day, €7.10). **Buses** run from the station to a number of surrounding towns (the tourist office provides a guide of bus companies and schedules). Several **taxi** companies (☎92 05 49; ☎92 10 00; or ☎08 94 46) with similar fares run 24hr. and are useful for daytrips to Haut Koenigsbourg.

The **tourist office,** bd. Général Leclerc, in the Commanderie St-Jean, is north of the town center. From the train station, walk straight on av. de la Gare and through pl. du Général de Gaulle to av. de la Liberté. Turn left onto bd. du Maréchal Foch, which becomes bd. du Général Leclerc after pl. Schaal. The office is a few blocks down, on the left. The staff doles out expert advice and guides in English, French, and German, as well as a free, poorly labeled map (more detailed map €1). The office also sells the *Pass Passion* (€3), which provides discounts at most major sites, and rents **bikes** from May to October. It runs various themed tours in French in July and August. (☎58 87 20; www.selestat-tourisme.com. Bikes €8 per ½-day, €13 per day, €55 per week; €150 deposit. Tours M-Th and Su; €5-7. Open July-Aug. M-Sa 9:30am-12:30pm and 1:30-6:45pm, Su 10:30am-3pm; Sept.-June M-Sa 9am-noon and 2-5:45pm; later hours during festivals.) Other services include: **police** at bd. du Général Leclerc (☎58 84 22; call here for the **pharmacie de garde**); a **hospital** at 23 av. Pasteur (☎57 55 55), behind the train station; and **Internet** access in a hip bar setting at **Bazook'Kafé,** 3 rue Ste-Foy, where flat-screen monitors, wireless keyboards, and large bowl chairs lend a sleek feel (☎03 90 57 20 66, www.bazook.net; €1.50 per 30min.; open M-Th 7am-1:30am, F-Sa 7am-3am, Su 2pm-1:30am). The **post office,** 7 rue de la Poste, near the Hôtel de Ville, has an **ATM.** (☎58 80 10. Open M-F 8am-noon and 1:30-6pm, Sa 8am-noon.) **Postal Code:** 67600.

ACCOMMODATIONS AND FOOD. **Hôtel de l'Ill ❷,** 13 rue des Bateliers, is on a peaceful residential street in the *vieille ville*. From the train station, take av. de la Gare, turn right on av. de Gaulle, and go halfway around pl. du Général de Gaulle, which becomes av. de la Liberté, rue du 4ème Zouaves, and finally rue du Président Poincaré. Make a left onto rue de l'Hôpital and follow it to pl. du Marché aux Choux; rue des Bateliers is on the right. The hotel has 15 cheerful pastel rooms, all with bath and TV. (☎92 91 09. Breakfast €5. Reception 7am-9pm. Check-out 10am. Singles €30; doubles €40; triples €50; quads €60. AmEx/MC/V.) To get to **Auberge des Alliés ❹**, 39 rue des Chevaliers, from the train station, follow the directions for the Hôtel d'Ill until you are on rue du Président Poincaré. Take a left on rue des Chevaliers; the hotel is two blocks down on the left. The simple, color-coordinated rooms are located above a bustling restaurant in the *vieille ville*. All rooms have bath and TV. (☎92 09 34; www.auberge-des-allies.com. Breakfast €7.50. *Menu du jour* €14. Free Wi-Fi. Reception 7am-10pm. Reservations recommended. Singles €48-50; doubles €55-65. AmEx/MC/V.) Small, shaded **Camping Les Cigognes ❶**, rue de la Première D.F.L., is on the southern edge of the *vieille ville*, near tennis courts, parks, and a lake. Though located on a grassy field, the site lies between low-rise buildings and has a distinctly suburban feel. (☎92 03 98. Reception July-Aug. 8:30-11am and 2:30-8:30pm; Sept. and Apr.-June 9-11am and 3-7pm. Open Apr.-Sept. July-Aug. €3.40 per adult, €2.75 per child under 10, €11 per site; Sept. and Apr.-June €1.70/1.35/8.50. Electricity free. Cash only.)

Culinary treats, from *boulangeries* to fine sit-down restaurants, line the cobblestone **rue des Chevaliers** and **rue des Clefs.** An enormous **market** fills the entire town center with breads, meats, and produce, as well as clothing, books, toys and countless other commodities that you may or may not need (Tu 8am-noon). Another market for regional specialties fills **place Albert Ehm** (Sa morning), and a third fills the **arsenal St-Hilaire,** rue des Chevaliers, with local artisans and produce (open Sa morning). For a distinctive meal on the outskirts of town, head to **A L'Improviste ❸**, 13 bd. du Général de Leclerc, which serves creative cuisine in an equally exotic dining room—with brightly colored walls, plenty of trees, and strange painted wooden shoe racks on the walls. From the *salade d'avocat au poulet caramalisée* (avocado and chicken salad; €7 for small, €13 for meal-sized) to the *magret de canard aux framboises* (duck breast with raspberries; €16), each original dish bursts with fresh flavor. (☎82 81 81. Open M-Tu 11:45am-2pm, W-Sa 11:45am-2pm and 7-10pm. MC/V.) In a colorful dining room on a peaceful side street, **Melina Crêperie ❷,** 14 rue de la Grande Boucherie, cooks crispy *galettes* and plate-sized *crêpes* overflowing with toppings. While the food isn't extraordinary, the nostalgic ambience can't be beat. Sit at a table made out of an old-fashioned sewing machine and enjoy the weekday lunch *menu* (€11), which features a dessert *crêpe* smothered in a combination of fruit, syrup, nuts, or jam. (☎58 48 36. *Galettes* and *crêpes* €2.50-7.10. Open Tu 7am-1:30pm and 6:45-9pm, Wed-Sa 11:45am-1:30pm and 6:45-9pm, Su 6:45-9pm. MC/V.) **JP Kamm ❶,** 15 rue des Clefs, is a casual local favorite, with a dazzling selection of pastries and ice cream in enormous display cases. Staring at the mouth-watering collection while dining will only make the (bitter) sweet final decision harder. (☎92 11 04. Pizzas and quiches €3.50-4.70. Salads from €4.50. Ice cream from €4.60; to go from €2.30. Open Tu and Th-F 8am-7pm, W 8:30am-7pm, Sa 8am-6pm, Su 8am-1pm. Terrace service Tu-F until 6:30pm, Sa until 5:30pm. MC/V.)

SIGHTS AND FESTIVALS. According to legend, Sélestat was founded by a giant. His thigh bone—a mere mammoth tusk, according to some skeptics—graces the town's **Bibliothèque Humaniste,** 1 rue de la Bibliothèque, entrance on pl. Gambetta. The austere one-room collection of beautifully printed books from Sélestat's 15th-century humanistic boom includes only five tables of text but spans from 13th-century annotated translations of Ovid to the 16th-century *Cosmographie Introductio*, the first book to mention America by name. The painstaking calligraphy and detailed ink prints are nothing short of marvelous. (☎58 07 20. Open July-Aug. M and W-F 9am-noon and 2-6pm, Sa 9am-noon and 2-5pm, Su 2-5pm; Sept.-June M and W-F 9am-noon and 2-6pm, Sa 9am-noon. €3.70, students and seniors €2.15. Audio tour in English; €1.65.) The **Eglise St-Georges,** rue de l'Eglise, at the north end of the *vieille ville*, houses Max Ingrand's startlingly modern 1960s stained glass, which, with their jagged, disjointed fragments, contrast starkly with the choir's detailed 14th-century Biblical tableaux. Built during the 13th and 14th centuries, the church sits on the site where Charlemagne spent Christmas in AD 775—as Sélestat's proud citizens never fail to mention. Surrounded by ivy-covered homes, the austere 12th-century **Eglise Ste-Foy,** pl. Marché aux Poissons, was constructed by Benedictine monks but later occupied by Jesuits. The church harbors an eclectic set of hard-to-spot artworks: a humble Roman *bas-relief* near the baptistry, two striking mosaics of the Ganges and Euphrates rivers on the church floor, and an exterior pair of grimacing lion statues, symbolic of the imperial Hohenstaufen family (a line of Germanic kings). Search for your zodiac sign; all 12 are randomly arranged in the mosaics on the floor. (Informative guides in French and German.) The **Maison de Pain,** 7 rue du Sel, located in the former seat of the bread makers' guild, provides a thorough history of bread-making from 12,500 BC to the present, accompanied by the spectacular aromas of fresh loaves baking in the ground-floor *pâtisserie.* Compare an old-fashioned *boulangerie* to a modern one—both in full size models—and then enter the real one downstairs to **twist your own pretzels** and ask the *maison*'s bakers about their art. (☎58 45 90; www.maisondupain-d-alsace.com. Open Jan. and Mar.-Nov. Tu-F 9:30am-12:30pm and 2-6pm, Sa 9am-12:30pm and 2-6pm, Su 9am-12:30pm and 2:30-6pm; Dec. daily 10am-7pm. Closed 2 weeks after Christmas and Jan. 15-Feb. €4.60, students €3.80, ages 12-18 €1.60, under 12 free. AmEx/MC/V.)

Bars and pubs cluster on **rue des Chevaliers;** for a livelier time, visit the *winstubs* of **rue du Président Poincaré,** along the southern wall of the *vieille ville.* The **Corso Fleuri,** or flower festival, made its debut in 1929 and is held on the second weekend in August. Street artists play music throughout the day as stilt-walkers strut through the town. The evening brings fireworks, a public ball, and the festival's most celebrated tradition: a cascade of floats decorated with over 500,000 dahlias. (☎58 85 75; www.ville-selestat.fr/corso. Call for ticket prices.) Founded in 1984, **Sélest'Art** is a biennial showcase of Alsatian and European art that will be on display next in 2009. (☎58 87 55; www.culture-alsace.org. Call for more details.) Home to the first recorded European Christmas tree, Sélestat decks itself in evergreen for the weeks leading to December 25.

DAYTRIP FROM SÉLESTAT: HAUT KOENIGSBOURG. On a rocky outcropping far above the *plaine d'Alsace*, this highly touristed **château** is an early 20th-century masterpiece of medieval restoration. When the people of Sélestat presented Germany's Kaiser Wilhelm II with the ruins of a 12th-century Hohenstaufen fortress demolished in the Thirty Years' War, he rebuilt the once-grand château on its original site. The castle he created delights streams of tourists with its dungeon, collection of medieval weaponry, hunting trophies, ornately carved green furnaces, and splendid architecture. The decadent *Salle des Fêtes* (Party Room) is particularly dazzling. On clear days you can make out Strasbourg's famous cathedral in the distance; on cloudier visits you can still gawk at the miles upon miles of villages and fields below. *(By car from Sélestat, take A35 to exit 17 via Kintzheim or 18 via St-Hippolyte, then take N59 via Lièpvre. A taxi is about €20 each way from Sélestat. The Sélestat tourist office runs several buses to and from the château July-Aug. daily; Sept.-Nov. Sa-Su. Inquire at the office for specific departure times; €4 round-trip. ☎82 50 60. Office open daily June-Aug. 9:30am-6:30pm; Sept. and Apr.-May 9:30am-5:30pm; Oct. and Mar. 9:45am-5pm; Nov.-Feb. 9:45am-noon and 1-5pm. Dungeon tours July-Aug. 10:45am, noon, 1:45, 3, 4:15pm; €1.50. Free brochures in English, French, and German. Audio tour €4. Free 1hr. tours of château in French July-Aug. every 20min.; free English tours available with prior arrangement. 10am-noon and 1:30-5pm; Sept. and Apr.-June 11am, 2:30, 4pm; Oct.-Mar. 11am, 2:30pm. Medieval musical €7.50, ages 18-25 €4.80, under 18 free; Oct.-Apr. 1st Su of month free.)*

COLMAR ☎03 89

The largest town on the *Route du Vin*, Colmar (kohl-mahrr; pop. 68,000) feels a bit like purgatory; though the city possesses its own charm, the enormous crowds are just waiting to get somewhere else. Hometown of Statue of Liberty sculptor Bartholdi—and now home to an amusing, smaller version of the lady—Colmar takes all the pride in the Statue of Liberty that New York never does. Though best used as a base for exploring smaller *Route* towns, Colmar itself hosts a smattering of worthwhile diversions, including a museum that holds the 16th-century Issenheim Altarpiece, arguably the most celebrated piece of Alsatian artwork. Otherwise, the pastel-colored *vieille ville* makes for scenic (if less than thrilling) visit.

TRANSPORTATION

Trains leave from pl. de la Gare for Lyon (4½-5½hr., 9 per day, €42), Paris (5¼hr., 2 per day, €52) via Mulhouse (20min., 42 per day, €7.10), and Strasbourg (30min., 12 per day, €10). Check the ticket office for info. (Ticket office open M-F 6:15am-8pm, Sa 8:30am-7pm, Su 8:30am-8:15pm. Station open daily 4am-1am.) Various **bus** companies on pl. de la Gare run to small towns on the *Route du Vin* (6am-7pm). **Trace,** on rue des Unterlinden, in a covered *galerie* to the right of the tourist office, circulates within the city (☎20 80 80; open M-F 8:45am-noon and 1:30-6pm; buses run 6am-8pm; tickets €1.05, *carnet* of 10 €7.50), and **Somnabus** provides infrequent night service (M-Sa 9pm-midnight). **Taxis,** pl. de la Gare (☎27 08 31) are available 24hr. Rent **bikes** from **Colmar à Bicyclette,** pl. Rapp, near av. de la République. (☎41 37 90. €3 per ½-day, €4.50 per day; €50 and ID deposit. Helmet only upon request. Open June-Sept. M-Tu and Th-F 8:30am-noon and 2-7pm, W 8:30am-8pm, Sa-Su 8:30am-noon and 1-8pm; Apr.-May and Oct. daily 9am-noon and 2-7pm. Cash only.)

PRACTICAL INFORMATION

To reach the **tourist office,** 4 rue des Unterlinden, from the train station, turn left on av. de la République in front of the large fountain and continue while it becomes rue Kléber and curves right through pl. du 18 Novembre into pl. Unterlinden. English- and German-speaking staff has small free maps, larger and more detailed maps (€3.50), cash-only **currency exchange,** and free same-night reservations service with a night's deposit. City tours are available in French and German, including the *vieille ville*, Bartholdi, and Judaic history tours. (☎20 68 92; www.ot-colmar.fr. Open July-Aug. M-Sa 9am-7pm, Su 10am-1pm; Apr.-June, Sept.-Oct., and Dec., M-Sa 9am-6pm, Su 10am-1pm; Jan.-Mar. and Nov. M-Sa 9am-noon and 2-6pm, Su 10am-1pm.) The **police** are located at 2 rue de la Cavelerie (☎29 47 00), and **Hôpital Pasteur** is at 39 av. de la Liberté (☎12 40 00). Check the tourist office window for the **pharmacie de garde.** A **laundromat,** 1 rue Ruest, is open daily 7am-9pm. (Wash €3.70 per 5-6kg.) **Internet** access is available at **Infr@ Réseau,** 12 rue du Rempart. (☎23 98 45. €2 per 30min., €3 per hr. Open M-Th 10am-8:30pm, F-Sa 10am-9pm, Su 2-8pm.) The **post office,** 36-38 av. de la République, across from the Champs de Mars, offers **currency exchange** and an **ATM.** (☎24 62 00. Open M-F 8am-6:30pm, Sa 8:30am-noon.) There is a branch at 21 rue du Nord. (Open M-F 8:30am-6:30pm, Sa 9am-noon.) **Postal Code:** 68000.

ACCOMMODATIONS AND CAMPING

To get to the **Auberge de Jeunesse (HI)** ❶, 2 rue Pasteur, take bus #4 (dir.: Europe) to "Pont Rouge." The hostel offers standard dorm accommodations at bargain prices. (☎80 57 39. Breakfast €4. Sheets €4. Reception Apr.-Sept. 7-10am and 5-10:30pm; Oct.-Mar. 7-10am and 5-11pm. Lockout 10am-5pm. Curfew Apr.-Sept. midnight; Oct.-Mar. 11pm. Reservations recommended June-Aug. Open mid-Jan. to mid-Dec. 6- to 8-bed dorms €12; singles €17; doubles €26. MC/V.) **Hôtel Primo ❷,** 5 rue des Ancêtres, about two blocks past the tourist office, lets cheap rooms in a relatively dark wing of a larger building. Rooms are clean yet spartan, but cheaper lodgings in town are hard to find. (☎24 22 24; www.hotel-primo.com. Breakfast €6. Internet €3 per 30min., €5 per hr. Reception 24hr. Check-out 11am. Singles €27, with shower and toilet €37; doubles €27/55. MC/V.) Conveniently located near the tourist office, **Hôtel Kempf ❸,** 1 av. de la République, is a friendly family-run hotel that rents rooms above a *brasserie*. (☎41 21 72. Breakfast €6. Reception 8am-midnight. Closed mid-Jan. to Feb. and 2 weeks in June. Singles and doubles with hall shower €38, with private shower €45; with bath €50-60; triples with bath €65. MC/V.) A few blocks from the train station and a 5min. walk from the *vieille ville*, **Hôtel Colbert ❸,** 2 rue des Trois-Epis, offers large and tidy rooms, all with A/C and bath; some have a small balcony. The hotel's proximity to the train station is a mixed blessing; many rooms face loud, frequently used tracks. (☎41 31 05. Breakfast €6. Reception 24hr. Singles €39; doubles €55; triples €65. AmEx/MC/V.) **Camping de l'Ill ❶,** rte. de Neuf-Brisach, is 2km from town on a river with a beautiful view of the Vosges. Take bus #1 (dir.: Horbourg-Wihr) to "Plage d'Ill." (☎41 15 94; www.camping-alsace.com. Reception 8am-noon and 2-8pm. Open mid-Mar. to mid-Dec. €3.25 per person, €1.95 per child, €3.60 per site. Electricity €3.20. MC/V over €15.)

FOOD

Colmar has a wealth of gastronomic goodies for the thrifty diner. There is a **Monoprix** supermarket at pl. Unterlinden (open M-Sa 8am-8pm; AmEx/MC/V) and **markets** on place St-Joseph (Sa morning) and at the intersection between rue des Ecoles and rue des Vignerons (Th morning). **La Pergola et sa Taverne ❷,** 28 rue des Marchands, is a cozy restaurant decorated with pink pigs. A mouth-watering menu features Alsatian specialties, including *roestis* (potato and cheese garnished casserole; from €12), *brouillards* (whipped-egg and potato dish; €8.50-17), and *tarte flambée* (€12) with Muenster cheese. (☎41 36 79. Open M-W and F-Su 11:30am-2:30pm and 6-10pm. MC/V.) **Djerba la Douce ❸,** 10 rue du Mouton, offers huge portions of Tunisian cuisine and, if you're lucky, the sound of the owner playing his drums. (☎24 17 12. Couscous €10-18. Grilled meats €10-17. Open M-Sa noon-2pm and 7-10pm. MC/V). At the charming **Le Croissant Doré ❷,** 28 rue des Marchands, on a cobbled pedestrian street, munch on delicious desserts (€2.80-3.10), quiches, and *tartes flambées* (€6.50-7) in one of the wicker chairs. While you wait, you can peruse the gossip magazines or old-fashioned advertisements on the wall. (☎23 70 81. Teas €2.50. Open Tu-Sa 8:15am-7pm, Su 10am-7pm. Cash only.) **La Cassolette ❸,** 70 Grand'Rue, prepares elaborate breakfast spreads and daily-changing lunch and dinner *plats* in a flower-strewn interior. Try the *choucroute* (sauerkraut; €15), a regional specialty. (☎23 66 30. Breakfast €5.10-6.30. Salads €13. 3-course weekday lunch *menu* €12. Open July-May M-Tu and Th-Sa 9am-2:30pm and 7-9:30pm, W 9am-2:30pm. MC/V.)

SIGHTS

A number of Colmar's sights are outdoors; the most interesting things the town has to offer are its traditional Alsatian houses. Flaunting a rainbow of Easter egg colors, these buildings cluster in the **quartier des Tanneurs** and **la petite Venise** (little Venice). On rue des Têtes, 105 grotesque stone heads stare out from the **Maison des**

Têtes, a must-see for its sheer absurdity. It also contains an elegant but expensive restaurant. The 13th- to 14th-century **Collégiale St-Martin,** pl. de la Cathédrale, boasts German stained glass and a multi-hued exterior that dazzles in the sunlight.

Converted from a 13th-century Dominican convent, the **Musée d'Unterlinden,** 1 rue des Unterlinden, holds largely religious art, including Mathias Grünewald's and Nikolaus Haguenauer's Issenheim Altarpiece (1500-1516), which depicts scenes from Christ's life in stunning iconographic detail. The rest of the collection is interesting for its wide variety, which includes a section of tiny 15th-century woodblock prints, a recreated wine cellar, and 20th-century art, all centered around a beautiful courtyard. (☎20 15 58; www.musee-unterlinden.com. Open May-Oct. daily 9am-6pm; Nov.-Apr. M and W-Su 9am-noon and 2-5pm. Last tickets sold 30min. before closing. €7, students and ages 12-17 €5, under 12 free. Free audio tours in English, French, and German. MC/V over €14.) From the museum, turn right onto quai de la Sinn and follow it until you reach the **Eglise des Dominicains,** pl. des Dominicans. As the church was originally built—predictably enough—by the Dominican order, the minimalist interior reflects the monks' strong attachment to spiritual austerity. Today, it's little more than a showroom for Martin Schongauer's exquisite *Virgin in the Rose Bower* (1473), a richly colored panel overwhelmed by an outrageously ornate neo-Gothic frame. On the walls, German-captioned paintings of Christ's ascent to the cross date to the German occupation of Alsace during the Franco-Prussian War. (Open June-Oct. M-Th and Su 10am-1pm and 3-6pm, F-Sa 10am-6pm; Apr.-May and Nov.-Dec. daily 10am-1pm and 3-6pm. Last tickets sold 15min. before closing. €1.50, students €1, ages 14-16 €0.50.) Take a right out of the church and follow the pedestrian road to rue des Serruriers, take a left, and then a right onto rue St-Martin. Turn right again onto a small pedestrian street, which will take you to rue des marchands and the **Musée Bartholdi,** 30 rue Marchands. This museum honors the noted French sculptor Frédéric Auguste Bartholdi (1834-1904), best known for a 47m statue of his mother entitled *Liberty Enlightening the World,* more often called the "Statue of Liberty." The giant plaster ear on display was a full-sized study for Ms. Liberty's left lobe, while the miniature lions in another room replicate the majestic *Lion de Belfort,* Bartholdi's most renowned sculpture still on French soil. ☎41 90 60. Open Mar.-Dec. M and W-Su 10am-noon and 2-6pm. €4.30, students €2.70, under 12 free.) Across town but worth a stop is the **Musée du Jouet et des Petits Trains,** 40 rue Vauban. Entering this "Museum of Games and Little Trains," visitors might think they've stumbled upon Santa's toy factory. The exhaustive collection includes many animated wonders, such as a life-sized diorama of Cinderella in her horse-drawn carriage and hundreds of Barbie dolls from throughout the ages. A 1000m network of button-activated model trains stands out in the collection, as does the fun marionette theater, where puppets perform four times a day. Look for the beheaded "Sleeping Pretty" doll. (☎41 93 10; www.museejouet.com. Open July-Aug. daily 10am-7pm; Sept. daily 10am-noon and 2-6pm; Oct.-June M and W-Su 10am-noon and 2-6pm; Dec. daily 10am-6pm. Marionette show 11am, 3, 4, 5pm. €4, students and ages 8-18 €3.)

ENTERTAINMENT AND FESTIVALS

Traditional pubs and bars dot the *vieille ville,* particularly around the cathedral and **Grand' Rue.** Locals and tourists alike head to **Les Dominicains,** pl. des Martyrs, a popular, wood-trimmed restaurant and bar with a large outdoor terrace in the center of town. (☎23 68 21. Beer from 2.50. Mixed drinks from €5. Open M-Sa 7am-midnight, Su 8am-10pm. AmEx/MC/V). The 10-day **Foire aux Vins d'Alsace** in mid-August is the region's largest wine fair. Tastings and exhibitions fill the daytime hours, while popular European bands hold concerts at 9pm. (☎03 90 50 50 50;

www.foire-colmar.com. Festival entrance 11:30am-1:30pm €1, 1:30-5pm €3, after 5pm €5. Concerts €20-43.) In the first two weeks of July, the more highbrow **Festival International de Colmar** features two dozen concerts by some of the best names in classical music, with an annual theme paying homage to one of the great composers. (Info ☎20 68 97, tickets 41 05 36; www.festival-colmar.com. Tickets €4.50-57, students €3-20.) The Collégiale St-Martin's organists play for the **Festival d'Orgue** (late July-Aug. Tu 8:45pm; concerts €10, students €7; €3 extra for opening concert), and the **Soirées Folkloriques** offers free folk music concerts and dancing Tuesday nights at 8:30pm in pl. de l'Ancienne Douane. (May to mid-Sept., except during the Festival International de Colmar. Call tourist office for details.)

MULHOUSE ☎03 89

Once a wealthy industrial powerhouse, Mulhouse (MOOHL-howss; pop. 118,000) is now a thriving cultural center. Unique for its set of museums devoted to modern technological marvels, Mulhouse provides a refreshing respite from the region's ubiquitous Gothic churches and 17th-century architecture. Not to worry, though—the small *vieille ville* will still fulfill any residual cravings for bustling boutiques. From its hip, young nightlife to its bustling city vibe, Mulhouse's throbbing heart may be a mechanical one, but this is one pacemaker that really gets going.

TRANSPORTATION

Trains (office open M-Sa 6am-8:30pm, Su 8am-8:30pm; AmEx/MC/V) run from 10 av. du Général Leclerc to Basel, Switzerland (20min., 28 per day, €6.20), Paris (4½hr., 18 per day, €51) via Belfort (45min., 16 per day, €8.10), and Strasbourg (1hr., 14 per day, €16). **Local buses** run from the train station and Porte Jeune, north of the pedestrian district. (☎66 77 77; www.solea.info. Most routes 5am-8pm; evening routes 8pm-midnight.) Buy tickets (€1.20, two rides €2.20, *carnet* of 10 €9.20, day pass €3.50) at the office in the SNCF station (open M-F 7:15am-12:15pm and 1:45-6:45pm) or at the Porte Jeune office (open M-F 7:30am-12:30pm and 1:30-6:30pm, Sa 9am-12:30pm), or buy individual tickets on the bus. If you are taking the tram (bus lines #1 and 2), buy your ticket from the machine on the platform. For a **taxi,** call Taxis Radio Mulhouse (☎45 80 00; 24hr.). **Car rental** is available at Hertz, 94 rue de Bâle. (☎65 15 04. Open M-F 8am-noon and 2-6:30pm, Sa 8am-noon and 3:30-6:30pm. MC/V.)

PRACTICAL INFORMATION

The **tourist office,** 9 av. Foch, is two blocks from the station. Cross any of the bridges and turn right on rue du 17 Novembre and left onto pedestrian-only av. Foch. The office is on your left. White signs from the station point out a circuitous route for drivers only, while yellow signs direct those on foot. The English- and German-speaking staff offers reservations service and free town maps. (☎35 48 48; www.tourisme-mulhouse.com. Open M-F 9am-noon and 2-6pm. Tours in French July-Aug. Tu and Sa 10:30am. €4, under 12 free.) The main office is farther from the station, in the Hôtel de Ville off pl. de la Réunion. (☎66 93 13. Open July-Aug. daily 10am-7pm; Sept.-June M-Sa 10am-6pm, Su 10am-noon and 2-6pm.) Other services include: a **laundromat** at 1bis rue des Halles (☎06 62 86 55 43; wash €4 per 7kg; open daily 7am-8pm); **police** at 12 rue Coehorn, off bd. de la Marseillaise (☎60 82 00; call for the **pharmacie de garde**); a **hospital** at 20 rue du Dr. Laënnec (☎64 64 64), behind the station; and **Internet** at **Brasserie Le Convivial,** 5 rue de la Sinne (☎46 11 06; €2.50 per hr.; open M-Tu and Th-F 7am-1:30am, W 5pm-1:30am, Su 9am-1:30am). The **post office,** 3 pl. de Gaulle, has **currency exchange** and an **ATM.** (☎56 94

11. Open M-F 8am-7pm, Sa 8am-noon.) There's a branch at pl. de la Réunion. (☎46 83 11. Open M 1-6pm, Tu-F 9am-6pm, Sa 9am-noon.) **Postal Code:** 68100.

ACCOMMODATIONS AND CAMPING

Dirt-cheap rooms in Mulhouse are scarce, but there are many comfortable and reasonably priced two-star accommodations. Rates often drop on weekends. The enormous dog for whom the **Hôtel St-Bernard ❸,** 3 rue des Fleurs, is named lazes in the lobby and welcomes guests. Halfway between the train station and the town center, this family-run hotel has small, bright rooms with shower and TV. Guests have free Internet access, a small library, and a safe. (☎45 82 32; stbr@evhr.net. Breakfast €7. Reception M-Sa 7am-9pm, Su 7am-1pm and 5-9pm. Singles €33; doubles €41-52. Extra bed €9. MC/V.) The recently refurbished **Auberge de Jeunesse (HI) ❶,** 37 rue d'Ilberg, offers basic but clean two-, four-, and six-bed rooms with co-ed bathrooms. From the train station, take bus #8 (dir.: Coteaux) to "Koechlin Dollfus." Transfer to the #2 bus (dir.: Coteaux) and get off at "Salle des Sports." You can also take bus #2 from Porte Jeune. (☎42 63 28; ajmulhouse@ifrance.com. Breakfast included. Kitchen and bar. Reception 8am-noon and 5-11pm. Lockout noon-5pm. Dorms €19. MC/V.) **Camping de l'Ill ❶,** rue Pierre de Coubertin, has an on-site grocery store. (☎06 20 66. Reception 8am-1pm and 3-9pm. Open Apr.-Oct. €4.70 per adult, €2.50 per child under 10, €4.70 per site. Electricity €3.50. MC/V.)

FOOD

The cheap kebab joints, gyro shops and *friteries* along **rue Wilson** and **avenue de Colmar** are packed with students looking to avoid Mulhouse's steep prices. A **Monoprix** supermarket is at the corner of rue du Sauvage and rue des Maréchaux. (Open M-Sa 8:15am-8pm. AmEx/MC/V.) Nearby, **Le Globe,** 27 rue du Sauvage, sells Alsatian *choucroute*, local sausages, and delicacies from *pâté* to handmade marzipan. (☎36 50 50. Open M 11:30am-7pm, Tu-Sa 8:45am-7pm. AmEx/MC/V.) In a timbered restaurant on pl. de la Réunion, the **Auberge au Vieux Mulhouse ❸,** 8 rue des Archives, cooks up *La Mulhousienne*, a pork and sauerkraut platter with spicy horseradish for €13. The spacious outdoor seating area, with a perfect view of the unique and gorgeous Hôtel de Ville, is ideal for people-watching. (☎45 84 18. *Plats* and salads €7-16. Weekday lunch *menu* €11. Open M-Th and Su 11am-10:30pm, F-Sa 11am-11pm. MC/V.) On a quiet street off the main drag, the unassuming facade of **Le Maharadjah ❸,** 8 rue des Tanneurs, conceals an intimate candlelit dining area populated with large elephant statues. Flavorful *plats*, including chicken *tikka masala* (€14) and vegetarian curried potatoes *alu saag* (€12) are enormous. (☎56 48 21; www.maharaja.fr. Vegetarian specialties €11-14. Meat *plats* €12-17. Weekday lunch *menu* €9. Reservations recommended. Open M 6:45-11:30pm, Tu-Su 11:45am-2pm and 6:45-11:30pm. AmEx/MC/V.)

SIGHTS

Mulhouse's historic district centers around **place de la Réunion** and the streets that run through it. The *place* is named for the occasions in 1798 and 1918 when French troops took the city from Germany and reclaimed it for France. Most museums are outside the *vieille ville* and accessible only by bus.

Housing a cornucopia of colossal trains, the theatrical **Cité du Train (Musée Français du Chemin de Fer)** celebrates France's longstanding love affair with the railway. Films detail the history of French trains since 1929, while potato-like mannequins narrate relevant scenes from cinema and literature. Peer into the perfectly restored compartments of an Orient Express train and walk into the small tunnel to gaze up at a train's complicated underbelly. Every hour, a massive 1949 steam engine (the last of its kind) chugs away (in place). (2 rue Alfred de Glehn. Take bus #20 from the train station to "Musées"; 2 per hr. On Su, use line M. ☎42 83 33. Open Apr.-Oct. daily 10am-6pm; Feb.-Mar. and Nov.-Dec. daily 10am-5pm; Jan.-Feb. M-F 1-5pm, Sa-Su 10am-5pm. Wheelchair-accessible. €10, students and ages 7-17 €7, under 7 free. Joint ticket to train and auto museums €18, students and under 18 €13. MC/V.) The 400 top-of-the-line automobiles on display at the enormous, though somewhat obscure, **Musée National de l'Automobile** once belonged to the brothers Schlumpf, whose staggering collection ranges from an 1878 steam-driven Jacquot à Vapeur to futuristic electric cars. Even those with little interest in the technical aspects of the vehicles will still be wowed by the cars' flashy aesthetics, and the *chefs d'oeuvres* (masterpieces) room is undeniably impressive. Look out for the famous *Bugatti Royale*, as well as cars owned by the likes of Charlie Chaplin and Emperor Bao Dai. (192 av. de Colmar. Take bus # 10 north to "Musée Auto" or tram #1 to "Musée de l'Automobile." ☎33 23 23; www.collection-schlumpf.com. Open Apr.-Oct. daily 10am-6pm; Feb.-Mar. and Nov.-Dec. daily 10am-5pm; Jan.-Feb. M-F 1-5pm, Sa-Su 10am-5pm. Wheelchair-accessible. €11, students and ages 7-18 €8, under 7 free. Free audio tours in English, German, Italian, and Spanish. MC/V.) The strange yet ultimately fascinating **Electropolis** examines energy using scale models, hands-on exhibits, and historical collections. Every facet of the museum is electrifying, from its hysterically hyperbolic introductory recording about "a day in the life with electricity" to a movie about ancient lightning gods from various cultures. The culminating exhibits is the 170-ton Grand Machine, a room-sized power generator that supplied the city with electricity from 1901-1947. (55 rue du Pâturage, next to the railway museum. ☎32 48 50; www.edf.electropolis.mulhouse.museum. Open Tu-Su 10am-6pm. Audio in English or German. Wheelchair-accessible. €8, students and ages 6-18 €4, under 6 free. MC/V.)

When construction of **Temple St-Etienne,** one of France's few Protestant Gothic cathedrals, began in 1859, St-Etienne demanded that its steeple rise higher than the original Catholic church. All that's left of the old 10th-century structure, demolished in 1851, are the 14th-century windows that now line the galleries. (☎66 49 06. Open May-Sept. M and W-F 10am-noon and 2-6pm, Sa 10am-noon and 2-5pm, Su 2-6pm. Free.) The **Musée de l'Impression sur Etoffes,** an homage to the printed textile industry that took root in Mulhouse in 1746, offers an obscure trip into the intricate world of hand-printing, dye-making, and mechanization. For €5, print a T-shirt using 200-year-old hand-carved blocks. (14 rue Jean-Jacques Henner. ☎46 83 00. Open Tu-Su 10am-noon and 2-6pm. €6, students €3, ages 12-18 €2, under 12 free.)

NIGHTLIFE AND FESTIVALS

Fun-loving Mulhouse is always busy in the center of town. **Rue Henriette** buzzes with pub chatter late into the night, and the area between **rue du Sauvage** and **place de la Réunion,** especially down **rue des Tondeurs,** boasts many nightlife options. Students and older locals flock to the crowded **O'Bryan Pub,** 5 pl. des Victoires, off rue du Sauvage. (☎56 25 58. Beer from €2.50, 4-beer tasting €6. Open M-Sa 10am-1:30am, Su 3pm-1:30am. MC/V.) On weekends at **La Salle des Coffres,** 74 rue du Sauvage, outside the *vieille ville,* a young crowd dances late into the night. A metallic staircase connects two floors outfitted in red. (☎56 34 98. Cover €9, includes 1 drink; students €6, without drink. Open Tu-Sa 10pm-4am.) **J.H.,** 1 rue Ste-Thérèse, off quai du Forst, a 12min. walk from the *vieille ville,* is the best (if only) gay club in town, welcoming both men and women. Use caution on the way home, as the walk can be dark and deserted. (☎32 00 08. Open daily 10pm-4am. MC/V.)

Throughout the year, but especially in summer, Mulhouse comes alive with concerts and festivals. Mid-June brings **Fête de la danse,** where locals take to the streets to salsa, tango, cha-cha and groove to music from around the world. Contact the tourist office for specific dates and times. The **Festival Automobile de Mulhouse** (☎42 47 73) brings together car lovers from around Europe in mid-July. This homage to the car includes drive-in movies, an auction, and a parade—all centered around the annual theme. **Bêtes de Scène,** also in mid-July, features four days of concerts by fringe rock bands, reggae groups, and underground DJs. (☎32 94 10; www.noumatrouff.com. Day passes €10-12; festival pass €20; some events free.) Every year, the city comes out for the **International Carnaval** party during the first weekend in March (info ☎42 10 35). The tourist office has a full calendar of events.

FRANCHE-COMTÉ

BELFORT ☎03 84

Called the "city of three sieges" because of a trio of failed Prussian attacks on the town in the 19th century, Belfort (BELL-fohr; pop. 52,000) celebrated its 700th birthday in 2006. Though the town houses the factories that produce TGV trains and Peugeot automobiles, the industrial development has not penetrated its *vieille ville,* which remains full of bustling shops—and hosts France's largest open-air rock festival every summer. The town now has little to offer besides a sprawling mountaintop citadel and the enormous lion statue below, but it is a great base for a trip to the surprisingly awesome concrete Chapelle Notre-Dame du Haut.

TRANSPORTATION AND PRACTICAL INFORMATION. Trains run to: Besançon (1½hr., 25 per day, €14); Mulhouse (30min., 16 per day, €8.10); Paris (2½hr., 17 per day, €46); Strasbourg (1½hr., 7 per day, €21). The train station is open daily 4:45am-11pm. Buy tickets at the ticket office. (Open M-F 5:30am-8pm, Sa 8:40am-6:30pm, Su 8:50am-8pm. AmEx/MC/V.) **CTRB,** 9 Faubourg des Ancêtres, runs **buses** around Belfort. (☎21 08 08; www.ctrb.fr. Office open M-F 9am-12:15pm and 1:45-6pm, Sa 9am-noon. Lines run 6am-8pm. Tickets €1.05, day pass €5.50.) For **taxis,** call **Radio Belfortains** (☎22 13 44; 24hr.). **Car rental** is available at **Avis,** 21 av. Wilson. (☎28 45 95. Open Sept.-June M-F 8am-noon and 2-7pm, Sa 8am-noon and 2-5pm; July-Aug. M-F 8am-noon and 2:30-6pm, Sa 10am-noon. AmEx/MC/V.)

To get from the station to the **tourist office,** 2bis rue Clemenceau, walk left down av. Wilson and keep right as it curves onto Faubourg de France. Turn left on Faubourg des Ancêtres and follow it to rue Clemenceau; the office, set back from the road, is to the right of the massive Caisse d'Epargne. The friendly staff distributes *Spectacles,* a free guide to restaurants and clubs, as well as free maps. Sold in the office, the *Pass Avantages* (€5) offers discounts to hundreds of stores and restaurants throughout town. The office also rents **bikes** year-round. (☎55 90 90; www.ot-belfort.fr. Bikes €4-5 per ½-day; €7 for 1st day, €5 thereafter; €42 per week. Open late June to Aug. M-F 9am-noon and 1:45-6:30pm, Sa 9am-noon and 1:45-6pm; Sept. to late June M-F 9am-noon and 1:45-6pm, Sa 9am-noon and 1:45-5:30pm.) Other services include: a **laundromat** at 60 Faubourg de Montbeliard (wash €5 per 7kg; open daily 7am-9pm); police at rue du Manège (☎58 50 00; call for the **pharmacie de garde**); a **hospital** at 14 rue de Mulhouse (☎57 40 00); **Internet** access at Belfort Information Jeunesse, 3 rue Jules Vallès (☎90 11 11; €1.50 per hr.; reserve ahead; open M 1:30-6pm, Tu-F 10am-noon and 1:30-6pm, Sa 2-5pm); and a **post office** with ATM, at 19 Faubourg des Ancêtres (☎57 67 67; open M-F 8am-7pm, Sa 8am-noon. AmEx/MC/V). **Postal Code:** 90000.

TIP **LET'S BE FRANCHE.** If traveling by train in Franche-Comté with more than one other person, consider using SNCF's *VISI'ter Pass* (€10), which can be used by its owner and up to 4 others. The first 3 people travel at half-price; the last two get round-trips for €1. Visit the SNCF Franche-Comté office or www.ter-sncf.com/franche_comte for more info. Pass valid July-Aug. daily; Sept.-June Sa-Su and holidays. Valid only for travel within Franche-Comté and for round-trips from Franche-Comté to Dijon and Epinal.

ACCOMMODATIONS AND FOOD. Belfort has a smattering of one- and two-star hotels but few truly budget places. The best option is the **Hôtel au Relais d'Alsace ❸**, 5 av. de la Laurencie. It would be hard to find a friendlier hotel in France than this one, which has a lobby decorated with a plethora of pictures and souvenirs left by past guests. Everything from the hand-pressed linens to the freshly-squeezed orange juice at breakfast speaks to the attentive care of owners Kim and Georges, who love to converse with travelers and offer useful advice about the town. The brightly-colored rooms have toilet, shower, TV, and phone. (☎22 15 55; www.arahotel.com. Breakfast €6. Reception M-Sa 7am-10pm; call ahead if arriving on Su. Singles €30-40; doubles €40; triples €45-55; quads €50-65. MC/V.) **Résidence Madrid (HI) ❶**, 6 rue Madrid, a cheap option 10min. from the station, caters to an international crowd and provides simple dorm-style rooms and singles, co-ed toilets, and clean showers. From the train station, turn left onto av. Wilson, left again on rue Michelet, then right onto rue Parisot, which becomes av. Général Leclerc. Rue Madrid is on the left. Be cautious on the street at night. (☎21 39 16; www.ufjt.org/adresse/belfort-madrid. Breakfast €2.80. Reception 24hr. Dorms €16. MC/V.) Find info on **camping** at the tourist office or on its website.

The local pastry is the *belflore*, a fluffy raspberry-almond meringue tart. Finding food is delightfully easy anywhere in the *vieille ville*, especially along **Faubourg de France,** which runs from the river to the train station. Cafés, *boulangeries* (bakeries), and restaurants cluster around **place d'Armes.** For a supermarket, try **Petit Casino,** by the hostel at 1 rue Léon Blum. (☎21 20 88. Open M-F 7am-12:30pm and 3-7pm, Sa 7am-12:30pm. AmEx/MC/V.) **Monoprix,** at the corner of bd. Carnot and av. Foch, is another option. (☎21 47 67. Open M-F 8:30am-8pm, Sa 8:30am-7:30pm. AmEx/MC/V). Find hearty *plats* and flavorful vegetarian options at **Gazelle d'Or ❸**, 4 rue des Quatre Vents, a quiet Moroccan eatery off pl. d'Armes that specializes in creative couscous dishes. (☎58 02 87. *Plats* €9-17. Open M-Sa noon-2pm and 7-10pm. MC/V.) **Aux Crêpes d'Antan ❷**, 13 rue du Quai, presents a formidable selection of *crêpes* and *galettes* (€2.80-11) filled with meats or sweets. Near the cathedral, this yellow-and-blue *provençal*-themed *crêperie* also has a small terrace. (☎22 82 54. Open daily noon-2:30pm and 7-10:30pm. MC/V.)

SIGHTS. Atop any list of Belfort's attractions—and atop the hill overlooking the town, on the winding road from pl. des Bourgeois—is its medieval **château,** which served as a military fortress during the Thirty Years' War but now shelters a scenic hodgepodge of historical attractions. A free 1hr. tour of the grounds recounts the state's turbulent history. (☎54 25 51. Open daily Apr.-Sept. 10am-6:30pm; Oct.-Mar. 10am-5pm. Tours in French daily July-Aug. every 30min. 10-11am and 2-5pm. Special themed tours July-Aug. Sa-Su; call ahead for schedule.) A passageway on one of the lower levels leads to the viewing platform of the enormous **Belfort Lion,** a monument to both the failure of the Prussians' 1870-1871 siege and the pride of the citizens of Belfort—though not necessarily in that order. Sculptor Frédéric-Auguste Bartholdi, the Alsatian native who also crafted the Statue of Liberty, carved the lion entirely out of pink Vosges sandstone. Photos—

and other representations—of the lion appear throughout the city, but don't do justice to the real thing. (Platform open daily June-Sept. 9am-7pm; Apr.-May 9am-noon and 2-7pm; Oct.-Mar. 10am-noon and 2-5pm. €5.65, students €4, under 18 free; includes the Musée d'Art et d'Histoire, Tour 46, and the Donation Jardot. Platform €0.90. MC/V.) Small and chic, the **Donation Maurice Jardot,** 8 rue de Mulhouse, surrounded by the floral abundance of **place Emile Lechten,** houses an impressive rotating collection by modern greats like Picasso, Braque, Léger, and Chagall. (☎90 40 70; www.mairie-belfort.fr. Open daily July-Aug. 10am-6pm; Apr.-June and Sept. 10am-noon and 2-6pm; Oct.-Mar. 10am-noon and 2-5pm. Wheelchair-accessible. €3.95, students €2.50, under 18 free. AmEx/MC/V.)

NIGHTLIFE AND FESTIVALS. The center of town, particularly along **Faubourg de Montbeliard** and its side streets, hosts several popular bars. Even on calm nights, locals flock to **Bistrot des Moines,** 22 rue Dreyfus Schmidt, a lively bar and restaurant with an extensive beer selection served from fun, artsy bar taps. Intimate round booths line the sides, while crowds congregate in the open center. (☎21 86 40. Beer from €2.20. Open M-F 10:30am-1am, Sa 10:30am-2am. MC/V.) **La Brasserie de Bruxelles,** 3 pl. des Armes, is a more relaxed option, with an outdoor terrace prime for people-watching in the heart of the *vieille ville.* (☎38 06 01. Beer from €2.30. Open M-F 8am-1am, Sa 8am-2am, Su 10am-1am. MC/V.)

The first Sunday of every month, except January and February, Belfort hosts an enormous flea market, the **Grand Marché aux Puces,** at numerous locations throughout the *vieille ville.* The tourist office opens a bureau at pl. d'Armes 8am-noon on the day of the market. In July and August, the château hosts free **jazz** (W 8:30pm) and free screenings of musical comedy **films** (F 9:45pm). Contact the tourist office for details. In the first weekend of July, 90,000 music fans from all over Europe descend upon Belfort for **Les Eurockéennes,** France's largest open-air rock festival. The 2007 lineup featured Amy Winehouse, Marilyn Manson, Queens of the Stone Age, The Hives, Arcade Fire, and nearly 60 other acts. Get tickets early. (Info ☎08 92 68 85 88, €0.34 per min.; www.eurockeennes.fr. Day pass €37; festival pass €85-95. Tickets sold at FNAC stores and at the tourist office.) At the beginning of June, over 2000 musicians from around the world hit town for the **Festival International de Musique Universitaire** (☎22 94 42; www.fimu.com), a three-day extravaganza offering over 200 free concerts ranging from classical and jazz to rock and world music. Reserve accommodations well in advance; rooms are next to impossible to find during the event. The tourist office has a free guide of other concerts and festivals during the summer. The last week of November brings the film festival **Entrevues,** which showcases both young directors and retrospectives. For info on all festivals, call the tourist office or **Cinéma d'Aujourd'hui** (☎22 94 44).

OUTDOOR ACTIVITIES. Belfort has 600km of hiking trails. The tourist office has pamphlets that list nearby hikes and biking trails. One popular route circles Bessoncourt, 4km to the east. The town is also the departure point for the daunting E5 trail from the Adriatic to the Atlantic. Follow one of the *petites randonnées* around the area for a fairly flat circuit (10-14km; 3-5hr.). North of town, three major long-distance trails, the GR5, GR7, and GR59, meet at the towering summit of the 1247m Ballon d'Alsace. The taxing 7km to Ballon's peak should be hiked only by the fit and biked only by the insane, but the panoramic views of the glacial Doller Valley and Rhine and Saône Valleys are nothing less than spectacular.

Lac du Malsaucy, west of Belfort, offers hiking, swimming, sunning, fishing, and outdoor performances. Small **boats, nautical bicycles,** and **mountain bikes** can be rented from the **Base de Loisirs du Malsaucy,** rue d'Evette (☎29 21 13). Nearby **Maison de l'Environnement** (☎29 18 12) has exhibits on everything from frogs to weather patterns. Throughout the summer, puppeteers, acrobats, comedians, and musicians perform here. Free outdoor movies are shown on Tuesdays at 10pm in late July and August. To get to the lake, take bus #17 from town. (See bus schedule for details.) For more info on **fishing** in and around Belfort, contact the **Fédération du Territoire de Belfort pour la Pêche** (☎23 39 49; www.unpf.fr/90).

DAYTRIP FROM BELFORT: RONCHAMP. A 20min. train ride west, in the tiny village of Ronchamp (rahn-SHAHN), stands Le Corbusier's famous 1954 **Chapelle Notre-Dame du Haut,** on the site of a disastrous 1944 German attack. The mushroom-shaped chapel, which draws architecture students and pilgrims from all over the world, was built as a testament to hope in the wake of WWII. Now, it proves that there's still hope for creative construction with concrete. Its beautiful sloping lines, receding walls, and sparsely decorated, candlelit interior "create a space of silence, prayer, peace, and interior joy." The asymmetrical pews and inscribed stained glass—instead of an illustration of Mary in the glass, her name is written—are truly unique. *To reach Ronchamp, take the SNCF train from the station in Belfort (15-20min., 4-6 per day, €4). Buy your return tickets in Belfort; the station in Ronchamp does not sell them. To reach the chapel from the train station, follow rue de la Gare left, turn left onto rue Le Corbusier, and left again onto rue de la Chapelle; then climb the steep, winding road for 1.5km. For those without a car, bike, or a desire for a moderately difficult hike, call Taxi Guy Bourgogne (☎20 65 66; 24hr.). The ride is about €6 each way from the train or bus stop. (☎20 65 13. Open daily Apr.-Sept. 9:30am-6:30pm; Oct. and Mar. 10am-5pm; Nov.-Feb. 10am-4pm. Wheelchair-accessible. €3, students €2, ages 5-12 free.)*

BESANÇON ☎03 81

The capital of rural Franche-Comté, Besançon ("bess-AHN-sahn"; pop. 123,000) boasts a wealth of museums, bargain restaurants, classy boutiques, and nightlife hot spots. The town's lively population of international students provides a constant infusion of energy and personality, and its gay scene is one of the best in France. Tucked in a horseshoe-shaped bend in the Doubs River, Besançon enjoys the beauty of the countryside and the sophistication of cities many times its size.

TRANSPORTATION

Trains: Gare de la Viotte, av. de la Paix. Ticket office open M-F 5:10am-9:30pm, Sa 5:40am-8pm, Su 6:25am-9:30pm. To: **Belfort** (1¼hr., 24 per day, €14); **Dijon** (1hr., 34 per day, €13); **Lyon** (2½hr., 8 per day, €25); **Paris** (2½hr., 9 per day, €49-60); **Strasbourg** (3hr., 9 per day, €30). **Gare de la Mouillère,** av. de Chardonnet, runs 1 train line to Morteau and Switzerland.

Buses: Monts Jura, in the train station. (☎08 25 00 22 44). Open M-F 8:30am-noon and 2:30-6:30pm, Sa 8:30am-noon. Take Bus 104 to **Pontarlier** (1hr., about 8 per day, €7.50).

Public Transportation: Ginko, 4 pl. du 8 Septembre (☎08 25 00 22 44; www.ginkobus.com). Open M-Sa 10am-7pm. Night buses run sporadically until midnight. Tickets €1.10, *carnet* of 10 €9.40, day pass €3.30. Buy individual tickets on bus, *carnets* at *tabacs,* and day passes on bus or at tourist office.

Taxis: ☎88 80 80. Min. charge €6. 24hr.

Bike Rental: Cycles Pro Shop, 18 av. Carnot (☎47 03 04). €8 per day; ID deposit. Open M-Sa 9:30am-noon and 2-7:30pm. MC/V.

ORIENTATION AND PRACTICAL INFORMATION

Most areas of interest in Besançon lie within the horseshoe-shaped turn of the Doubs River. To reach the tourist office, cross the train station's parking lot and head down the stairs. Follow av. de la Paix straight ahead and continue as it turns

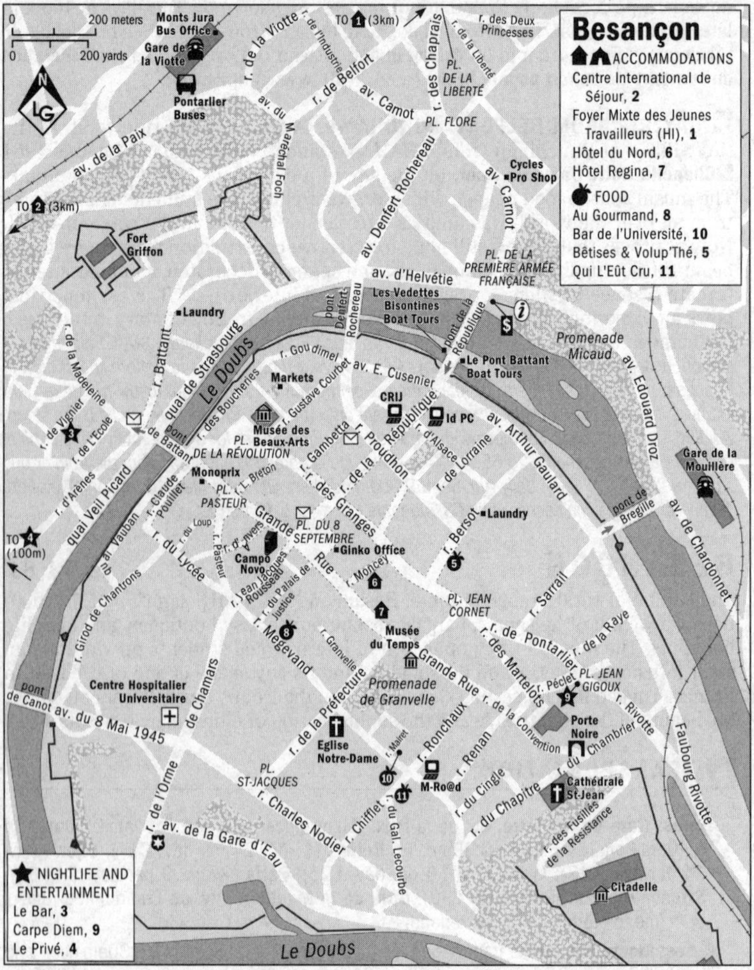

into av. Foch. Walk all the way down the hill, veering left at the river. Follow this road, av d'Helvétie, to pl. de la Première Armée Française at the second bridge. The office is in the park to the right, and the *vieille ville* is across the bridge. If you are heading to the tourist office on foot, ignore the signs pointing to it; they are designed for cars and will take you out of your way.

Tourist Office: 2 pl. de la 1ère Armée Française (☎80 92 55; www.besancon-tourisme.com). Provides student guide *La Besace,* a free map and city guide. Tours May-Sept. for individuals (in French; €6, students €4) and groups (in English, French, or German; by reservation). **Currency exchange.** Open June-Sept. M 9:30am-7pm, Tu-Sa 9:30am-7pm, Su 10am-5pm; Apr.-May and Oct. M 10am-6pm, Tu-Sa 9:30am-6pm, Su 10:30am-12:30pm; Nov.-Mar. M 10am-12:30pm and 1:30-5:30pm, Tu-Sa 9:30am-12:30pm and 1:30-5:30pm, Su 10:30am-12:30pm. MC/V over €15.

English-Language Bookstore: Campo Novo, 50 Grande Rue (☎65 07 70). Small selection of books in English. Open M 10am-7pm, Tu-Sa 9:30am-7pm. MC/V.

Youth Center: Centre Regional d'Information Jeunesse (CRIJ), 27 rue de la République (☎21 16 16; www.jeunes-fc.com). Info on internships, jobs, and apartments. HI cards. Free Internet access and Wi-Fi. Open July-Aug. M 1:30-6pm, Tu-F 10am-noon and 1:30-6pm; Sept.-June M and Sa 1:30-6pm, Tu-F 10am-noon and 1:30-6pm.

Laundromat: Laverie Automatique, 54 rue Bersot. Wash €3.50 per 5-6kg, €4 per 7kg, €6 per 10kg. Open daily 6am-9pm. Also **Salon Lavoire GTI,** 54 rue Battant. Wash €3.50 per 5kg, €4 per 7kg. Open daily 7am-7pm.

Police: 2 av. de la Gare d'Eau (☎21 11 22). Near pl. St-Jacques. Call here for the **pharmacie de garde.**

Hospital: Centre Hospitalier Universitaire, 2 pl. St-Jacques (☎66 81 66).

Internet Access: At **CRIJ** (see **Youth Center**). **Id PC,** 28 rue de la République (☎81 26 25) across from the CRIJ. €3 per hr. Open Tu-Sa 9:30am-noon and 2-7pm. **M-Ro@d,** 29 rue Ronchaux. €3 per hr. Open July-Aug. M-F 10am-noon and 2-5pm, Sa 10am-noon and 2-6pm; Sept.-June M-F 9am-7pm, Sa 10am-noon and 2-6pm. **Foyer des Jeunes Travailleurs** and **Hôtel du Nord** (see below), as well as **Bar de l'Université** (see **Food,** p. 404) have free access for guests.

Post Office: 23 rue Proudhon (☎65 55 82), off rue de la République. **Currency exchange** and **ATM**. Open M-F 8am-7pm, Sa 8:30am-12:30pm. Branches at pl. du 8 Septembre (open M 2-5pm, Tu-F 9:30am-noon and 1:30-5pm); and 1 rue Battant (☎25 23 22), with Cyberposte. Open M-F 9am-noon and 1:30-6:30pm, Sa 9am-12:30pm. **Postal Code:** 25000.

ACCOMMODATIONS

Besançon's hostels are a trek from the *vieille ville* (15-30min. by bus), but offer excellent facilities at a bargain. Both the Foyer and the Centre are easily accessible by daytime and nighttime bus lines, though the ride is longer at night. The hotels closer to the center of town aren't cheap and generally require reservations.

Foyer Mixte des Jeunes Travailleurs (HI), 48 rue des Cras (☎40 32 00; fax 40 32 01). Take bus #5 (or night line A) from pl. Liberté (dir.: Orchamps) to "Les Oiseaux," down the street from the hostel (3-5 per hr.; €1.05). To get to pl. Liberté from the train station, take a left on rue de la Viotte, then the 1st right on rue de l'Industrie. Turn left onto rue de Belfort, which leads to pl. de la Liberté. The stop is on rue de la Liberté. Populated by international students. Clean single rooms with private toilets and showers. Breakfast included before 8am. Cafeteria meal €7, Su €4. Free Internet access, ping pong, and foosball. Free live concerts twice per week. Reception 8:30am-8pm. Oct.-Mar. fewer rooms available. Singles €23, 2nd night €18. AmEx/MC/V. ❷

Hôtel du Nord, 8 rue Moncey (☎81 34 56; www.hotel_du_nord_besancon.com), on a charming street surrounded by tiny shops in the *vieille ville.* Some rooms have antique furnishings; others sport more modern décor. All are bright and tastefully decorated, with satellite TVs and sparkling bathrooms. Free Wi-Fi. Breakfast €4.80. Reception 24hr. Check-out noon. Reservations recommended. Singles and doubles with shower or bath €38-51; triples and quads with shower or bathtub €51-59. AmEx/MC/V. ❸

Centre International de Séjour, 3 av. des Montboucons (☎50 07 54; www.cis-besancon.com). Take bus #4 (dir.: Founottes or Temis) or bus #8 (dir.: Campus) from the Foch stop to "Intermarché." Walk back uphill and turn left on av. des Montboucons; the hostel is in the Pole Sportif complex on the left. Friendly staff and spartan but spacious rooms. Caters to international students. Social atmosphere with restaurant, TV room, and foosball. Breakfast €4.60. Reception 7am-1am. Check-in noon. Check-out 9am. Singles €20, with bath and TV €30; doubles €25/33; triples €27. MC/V. ❷

Hôtel Regina, 91 Grande Rue (☎81 50 22). In a courtyard set back from the center of town, this hotel offers large, color-coordinated rooms, many of which overlook a garden. Relaxing terrace furnished with wicker chairs. All rooms with bath. Breakfast €6. Reception 24hr. Singles €36-46; doubles €41-53; triples €58-63; quad €79. MC/V. ❸

FOOD

Besançon's dining options are plentiful and reasonably priced to accommodate the city's student population. **Rue Claude Pouillet, place de la Révolution,** and **rue des Granges** dish out tempting options at steep prices, while out-of-the-way eateries near the university cater to the student budget. Vegetarian-friendly restaurants abound. For a do-it-yourself meal, try one of the outdoor covered markets that set up shop near the Musée des Beaux-Arts, in the square between **rue Goudimel** and **rue Gustave Courbet.** (Open Tu and F 6am-12:30pm, Sa 6am-7pm.) Groceries are available at **Monoprix,** 12 Grande Rue. (☎65 36 36. Open M-Sa 8:30am-8pm. AmEx/MC/V.) Sharp cheddar-like *comté* cheese is Besançon's speciality. Wash it down with *vin jaune*, one of the more famous Arbois wines. *Charcuteries* (butchers) along **rue des Granges** sell *saucisse de Morteau*, a regional sausage specialty, while *chocolatiers* in the town center tempt with *boulets de la Citadelle*, also called *noisettines*, which are layered chocolate, nut, and sugar confections.

Au Gourmand, 5 rue Megevand (☎81 40 56). An astonishing array of meat-and-potato dishes at low prices. Cute cat-themed knick-knacks, retro clocks, and a collection of colorful *carafes* (pitchers) create the feel of dinner in a friend's kitchen—a very popular friend. Reservations recommended. Hearty salads €6-8. Rice and pasta dishes €6.50-7.80. Open Tu-F 11:30am-1:45pm and 6:45-8:30pm, Sa 6:45-8:30pm. MC/V. ❶

Bêtises & Volup'Thé, 28 rue Bersot (☎50 83 45). At once an enchanted garden, a fantasy tea party, and a heaven (complete with cotton clouds), this delightfully over-the-top eatery serves exotic teas (€2.50-3), extravagant salads (€8-12), and milkshakes in miniature planters (€4). You won't want to escape this pink and silver wonderland—especially after enjoying a salad with heart-shaped toppings from your plush purple velvet seat. Vegetarian *menu* €11. 3-course *menus* from €12. Open daily 9am-10pm. Kitchen open noon-2pm and 6-10pm. MC/V. ❷

Qui L'Eût Cru, 3 rue Chifflet (☎83 25 18). This elegant, new-age eatery is for the adventurous vegetarian. One *plat* per meal means your stomach is at the whim of the creative chef. Luckily, the artistic and delicious *plats du jour* (lunch €12, dinner €16) are vegetarian cooking at its finest. Open Tu-Sa 10am-3pm and 5:30-10pm. AmEx/MC/V. ❸

Bar de l'Université, 5 rue Mainet (☎81 68 17). Free Wi-Fi and large cheap sandwiches (€3-5) draw local students—laptops in hand—to this blue and yellow eatery. A café by day and popular student bar at night. Beer from €2. Open daily 9:30am-1am. MC/V. ❶

SIGHTS

Besançon's *vieille ville* is an expansive but walkable circuit; it takes 10min. to walk the length of the main Grande Rue—if you don't stop to peer in the windows of the enticing shops or at the remarkably well-preserved Renaissance buildings along the way.

MUSÉE DU TEMPS. Captain Hook would have hated this ticking homage to time, where hands-on exhibits cater to young time explorers, teaching the principles of physics that underlie mechanical and quartz-based clock-making. Elegant first-floor halls hold clocks dating back to Galileo's era, while whimsical upstairs rooms present high-tech devices, games, and experiments. After glancing at the glistening showcases of quartz, ascend to the observation deck to see Besançon's Renaissance buildings; with only the old, intricate roofs visible, the city seems frozen in the past. *(Palais Granvelle, 96 Grande Rue. ☎87 81 53; musee-du-temps@besancon.com. Free tour in French Su 3pm. Free English and German guides available at desk. Open Tu-Sa 9:15am-noon and 2-6pm, Su 10am-6pm. Wheelchair-accessible. M-F €5, Sa €2.50, Su free; students with ID free. Ticket includes entrance to the Musée des Beaux-Arts.)*

CITADELLE. A military masterpiece designed during the reign of Louis XIV by the Sun King's go-to architect, Vauban, this Renaissance-style citadel now holds several fascinating museums for children and adults alike. Getting there requires a steep, grueling trek from the town throughout most of the year, but a visit is worth every step. Summer visitors can take a free *navette* that runs between the *centre-ville* and the citadel (July-Aug. daily 9am-7pm, every 10-20min.). After passing through the park overlooking the city, a first priority should be the moving **Musée de la Résistance et de la Déportation.** This exhibition commemorates the 100 members of the French Resistance who were shot at the citadel in 1944 during the German occupation of Besançon. Blown-up photographs and relics of the dead leave nothing to the imagination. Twenty rooms hold a chronological display of the terrors of WWII. Free audio tours, in English and German, play survivors' recorded accounts as well as explanations of some of the items exhibited. Children under 10 are advised not to visit the museum. Most artifacts are in French, though extensive information cards in English and German are available in each room. The more lighthearted **Natural History Museum** features a number of smaller exhibits, including an Evolutionary Path that illustrates Darwin's theory by displaying plenty of "unfit" taxidermal animals. The insectarium next door is fascinating but not for the weak-stomached; a kitchen exhibit reveals the buggers that hide inside cupboards. An aquarium, climatorium, zoo, and noctarium make a significant attempt to be interactive; at the fish "petting pool," the grubby fingers of children harass dozens of fish crammed into a tiny tank. More conventional is the informative **Espace Vauban,** which chronicles the life of the citadel's famous creator with English-language informational cards. Those with the strength for further climbing can ascend the **Tour de la Reine** for a spectacular view of the city below. *(☎87 83 33; www.citadelle.com. Open July-Aug. daily 9am-7pm; Oct.-Mar. M and W-Su 10am-5pm; Apr.-June and Sept. daily 9am-6pm. Most sites wheelchair-accessible. In high season €7.80; in low season €7.20; 1½hr. before closing €6.50/6, 1hr. before closing €4; students €6.50/6; ages 4-14 €4.50/4. Includes entrance to every museum and facility. Be sure to buy your tickets at the entrance to the park near the parking lot before you ascend. Audio tour €2.20. Sound and light show July-Aug. F-Sa 10:30pm-midnight. €10, students €8, ages 6-13 €6.)*

MUSÉE DES BEAUX-ARTS ET D'ARCHÉOLOGIE. France's oldest museum, which began with Abbé Boisot's small collection of art in 1694, houses an exceptional anthology of more than 6000 works by Ingres, Matisse, Picasso, Renoir, and others. Its clever layout—an ascending ramp winding through intimate halls, not to mention chronologically through time—leads visitors from ancient Egyptian relics to modern oils for an impressively comprehensive tour. With half the number of tourists as museums half as interesting, this should be high on any visitor's list. *(1 pl. de la Révolution. ☎87 80 49. Open M and W-F 9:30am-noon and 2-6pm, Sa-Su 9:30am-6pm. Tours in French for groups only; reserve at tourist office. Wheelchair-accessible. €5, students with ID free; Su and holidays free. Includes entrance to Musée du Temps. AmEx/MC/V.)*

CATHÉDRALE ST-JEAN. Beneath the citadel, this graceful cathedral boasts the **Horloge Astronomique,** a 30,000-part 19th-century clock that would knock the springs out of any clock at the Musée du Temps. Its 57 faces provide information about all facets of the universe, such as the planets and eclipses. The clock is only shown in 10min. tour that culminates in the hourly awakening of the wooden religious figures at the top. The cathedral also features the modestly beautiful **Rose de St-Jean,** a circular white marble altar from the 11th-century. *(Cathedral ☎83 34 62. Open M and W-Su 9am-6pm except during Mass. Free. Horloge ☎81 12 76; www.monum.fr. Tours Apr.-Sept. M and W-Su 9:50, 10:50, 11:50am, 2:50, 3:50, 4:50, 5:50pm; Feb.-Mar. and Oct.-Dec. no tours W. Closed Jan. €3, under 18 free.)*

BOAT TRIPS. Les Vedettes Bisontines runs boat cruises on the Doubs and the citadel canals from pont de la République, near the tourist office. *(☎68 13 25; www.sautdudoubs.fr. Operates daily Apr.-Oct. 1¼hr.; 3-4 per day; €10, ages 4-12 €8.50.)* **Le Pont Battant,** on the other side of the bridge, offers similar cruises. *(☎68 05 34. Operates Apr.-Oct.; Nov.-Mar. for groups by reservation only. 1¼hr.; 4-5 per day; €10, under 18 €8. Days and tours vary; call ahead.)* The tourist office has information on several similar cruises down the Doubs as well.

ALSACE, LORRAINE, AND FRANCHE-COMTÉ

NIGHTLIFE

Besançon's international students pack bars and discotheques until the early morning on weekends and filter into pubs on calmer nights. Students overflow onto the streets between **rue Claude Pouillet** and **place Jouffroy d'Arbans.** Small, intimate *brasseries* proliferate in the pedestrian section of town.

Le Bar, 15 rue de Vignier (☎82 01 00); www.lebar.info. 2 radically different environments for a gay clientele. Decorated with homoerotic art, the upstairs bar is a casual pre-club spot until about 2am, when everyone heads over to discothèque Le Privé. Downstairs is another story: from the all-porn video room to lockable "pleasure rooms," the theme is sex—and everyone is exploring. Clientele is mostly male; some bring female friends. Beer €4. Mixed drinks from €4. Open M-Th 8pm-1am, F-Sa 9pm-2:30am, Su 9pm-2am. MC/V over €15.

Le Privé, 1 rue Antide Janvier (☎81 48 57). Follow rue d'Arênes past the Lycée Condé and turn left onto rue A. Janvier; club is on the right. Blasting a variety of French and American music from the 80s and sporting fluorescent green neon lights, this 25-year-old gay club feels like it never left the fabled "decade of greed." Nicely packed on the weekends, with an even mix of men and women. Cover Tu-Th €8, F €9, Sa €10; includes 1 drink. Open Tu-Th 11pm-4am, F-Sa 11pm-5am. MC/V.

Carpe Diem, 2 pl. Jean Gigoux (☎83 11 18). An outgoing owner runs this tiny watering hole according to his philosophy of *le rôle sociale du pub,* bringing together all ages and creeds for genial conversation and idea-swapping. Most solo patrons pore over novels or their own masterpieces beneath eclectic decorations that range from exotic instruments to Jameson Whiskey brand towels. Events, films, and concerts held regularly; some are organized, others improvised. Beer from €2. Open M-Th 9am-1am, F-Sa 9am-2am, Su 9am-11pm. MC/V over €16.

FESTIVALS

The tourist office publishes several comprehensive lists of events; make sure to get *Les Temps Chauds de l'Eté* guide for up-to-date summer information. In July and August, the city sponsors the **Temps Chauds de l'Eté** festival, with theater, music, dance, expositions, and films. (Many events are free. Call the tourist office for info.) **Jazz en Franche-Comté** brings a flurry of concerts in the second half of June, uniting jazz musicians from across France and abroad. (☎83 39 09; www.aspro-impro.fr. Tickets €10-18, students €5-12; some events free.)

Les Concerts de Granvelle bring a wide range of free musical acts to open-air Palais Granvelle on Friday nights in July and August. (Call tourist office for info.) The **Festival International de Musique** fills the air with classical concerts in mid-September. Orchestras from across Europe perform well-worn favorites as well as more recent compositions in 85 concerts, many of which are free. (☎82 08 72; www.festival-besancon.com. Tickets €12-45, students €5-20.)

JURA MOUNTAINS

The Jurassic Era derived its name from the Jura mountain range—an ancient ocean floor with an abundance of archaeological treasures. Travelers often overlook the mountains, flocking instead to the younger, pointier Alps to the south. Smoothed by the ravages of time, the Jura provide slightly easier but no less scenic hiking, biking, and skiing trails. Relatively un-touristed towns in the area provide convenient bases for exploration and have some of the lowest prices in France.

PONTARLIER ☎03 81

A storied tradition of absinthe production made Pontarlier ("Pon-TAR-lee-ay"; pop. 18,400) a psychedelic place to hallucinate until the infamous liquor was banned in 1915. Nearly 100 years later, the town still seems a bit hung over; a slow, relaxed atmosphere pervades, as locals spend most of their time sitting in cafés shooting the breeze. As France's second-highest town (837m), Pontarlier now serves as a base for hiking, horseback riding, skiing, and biking in the Jura, or for a trip to Switzerland, just 12km away.

TRANSPORTATION AND PRACTICAL INFORMATION. The train station is on pl. de Villingen-Schweningen. (Ticket office open M-F 4:50am-12:25pm and 1:30-8:40pm, Sa 4:50am-12:25pm and 1:25-8:30pm, Su 7:20am-12:30pm and 1:30-8:40pm.) **Trains** go to Dijon (1½hr., 7-9 per day, €19-22) and Paris (3½-4hr., 7-9 per day, €53-67). **Monts Jura buses** (☎39 88 80) leave from in front of the train station for Besançon (1hr., 5 per day, €7.50). Schedules are posted on the door of the **Ponta Bus office,** rue Remparts, next door to the post office. (Open M 3-6pm, Tu-F 9am-noon and 3-6pm.) The **tourist office** is at 14bis rue de la Gare. From the train station, take the road on the far left side of the roundabout, which is rue de la Gare. The office is a block down at the intersection with rue Marpaud. The staff has a free map of the *centre-ville*, info on hiking and other outdoor sports, and the free *Guide Pratique*, which lists cheap mountain lodgings. The office also rents GPS devices (€3 per ½-day) and offers several guides on outdoor activities in English, French, and German. (☎46 48 33; www.pontarlier.org. Open July-Aug. M-Sa 9am-7pm, Su 10am-noon; Sept.-June M-Sa 9am-12:30pm and 1:30-6pm. Guides available in English and German.) Other services include: a **laundromat** at 13 rue du Moulin Parnet (wash €3 per 5kg; open daily 7am-9pm); **police,** 19 Rocade Georges Pompidou (☎38 51 10; call here for the **pharmacie de garde**); a **hospital,** 2 Faubourg St-Etienne (☎38 54 54); and **Internet** access, available for a fee at the tourist office beginning in 2008. The **post office** is at 17 rue de la Gare. (☎38 49 44. Open M-F 8:30am-6:15pm, Sa 8:30am-12:15pm.) **Postal Code:** 25300.

ACCOMMODATIONS AND FOOD. The hostel, **Auberge de Pontarlier (FUAJ),** 2 rue Jouffroy, is currently undergoing intense renovation but should be up and running by early 2008. Meanwhile, colorful rooms, TV, and a central location above a bar make **Hôtel de France ❷,** 8 rue de la Gare, a good bargain. (☎39 05 20. Breakfast €5. Reception 7am-9:30pm; hours vary with bar downstairs. Singles with hall shower €22, with private shower €32; doubles €30; triples €37; quads €58. AmEx/MC/V.) The most scenic accommodations are at the three-star **Camping du Larmont ❶** on rue du Tolombief, which offers a gorgeous mountain view in all directions. From the station, turn right onto Rocade Georges Pompidou, cross the river, and bear left on rue de l'Industrie. Take the first right onto av. de Neuchâtel and follow the signs (20-25min.). Amenities include TV, ping-pong, a game room, and a bar. (☎46 23 33; lelarmont.pontarlier@wanadoo.fr. Reception July-Aug. daily 8am-10pm; Sept.-June M-Sa 9am-noon and 5-8pm, Su 9am-noon. July-Aug. €3.20 per adult, €2 per child, €7.50 per tent and car; Sept.-June €3.20/2/6.50. *Chalets* for 2 people July-Aug. €60 per day, €405 per week; Sept.-June €53/315. Extra person €5 per night. 6-person max. Electricity July-Aug. €4; Sept.-June €6. MC/V.)

Although it may not pack the hallucinogenic punch that once made it famous, a modern version of *absinthe Pontarlier* is available at most bars and cafés for €3-4. Buy groceries at the **Casino** supermarket, 75 rue de la République. (☎46 51 22. Open M-Sa 8:30am-12:30pm and 2-8pm, Su 9am-noon. AmEx/MC/V.) Outdoor markets appear Thursday and Saturday mornings at **place Jules Pagnier.** Good restaurants are concentrated around **rue de la République** or on **rue Jeanne d'Arc** and **rue Sainte-Anne.** The wood oven of **Le Gambetta ❶,** 15 rue Gambetta, off rue de la Gare, cooks 20 varieties of pizza. Mix-and-match your favorite toppings, choosing from a variety that includes ham, eggs, tuna, and potatoes. Shave €1.50 off the bill by ordering a "mini" pizza, barely smaller than the hefty regular portions. (☎46 67 17. Pizza from €6, design-your-own €9. Salads €6.50-7.50. Open W-Su noon-1:30pm and 7-9:30pm; closed much of Sept. MC/V.) In the wood dining room of **La Pinte Comtoise ❷,** 4 rue Jeanne d'Arc, sample the *menu régional* (€13), which features smoked *Haut Doubs* ham and local *saucisse de Morteau.* For vegetarians, a fondue of regional *comté* cheese (€12 per person; min. 2 people) provides a rare meat-free taste of Franche-Comté cuisine. (☎39 07 35. Open M and Th-Su noon-1:30pm and 7-9pm, Tu noon-1:30pm. MC/V.) **Le Grand Café Français ❶,** 36 rue de la République, is a popular lunch spot in the heart of town. Affordable *plats du jour* (€7.70) and *Flamenkuch,* a pizza-like dish with onions, ham, and cream or cheese (€7.80), bring in the masses, but service can be slow as a result. (☎39 00 72. Open June-Sept. M-Sa noon-2pm and 7-9:30pm; Oct.-May M-Sa noon-2pm. AmEx/MC/V.)

ELIXIR OF THE GREEN FAIRY

Though unassuming Pontarlier doesn't seem like an alcoholic hub, it was here that the notoriously hypnotic absinthe shed its medicinal role and became known for its inebriating effects.

Pierre Ordinaire, a French doctor exiled to Switzerland, first concocted absinthe in the late 1700s as an elixir for the sick. Fun-loving crowds soon got hold of the drink, relishing its mind-altering capabilities. Recognizing absinthe's commercial potential, Henri-Louis Pernod bought the recipe's rights, and in 1805 opened the Pontarlier distillery.

Pontarlier proved a fruitful site for absinthe production. Pernod cultivated wormwood, absinthe's controversial ingredient, in the nearby mountains, avoiding high Swiss taxes. French customers took to absinthe with enthusiasm, and Pernod's distillery reaped incredible returns. In its prime, it produced as many as 30,000L of absinthe per day.

After Pernod's success, a series of knock-off brands appeared in the region, and absinthe grew increasingly popular in France. By the late 1800s, France's absinthe consumption exceeded 13 million L per year. The drink was banned in 1915, but its prevalence owed much to sleepy Pontarlier. Today, Pernod-Ricard (spawn of the original Pernod Fils) makes a wormwood-free (a.k.a. non-hallucinogenic) absinthe imitation called *pastis.*

OUTDOOR ACTIVITIES AND SIGHTS. The pine-covered Jura mountains are home to 106km of **cross-country skiing** trails, which locals and visitors alike traverse in winter. The Jura are much colder than the Alps, so it's important to wear layers; prices are far cheaper, but the snow quality is less reliable. Nine trails on two slopes (**Le Larmont** and **Le Malmaison**) span every level of difficulty. Find a free outline of trails at the tourist office. (Daily pass for cross-country skiing €6, under 17 €3.50; downhill skiing €11, under 12 €8. MC/V.) **Le Larmont** (☎39 44 19; www.cc-larmont.fr.), the ski area nearest to Pontarlier, offers toboggan and snowshoe trails. Call the tourist office for ski conditions. **Sport et Neige,** 7 rue Mervil Zone des Grands Planchants, is the nearest store that rents ski equipment. (☎39 04 69; www.sportetneige.com. €9 per day, €45 per week; under 18 €7/40. Open M-Sa 9:30am-noon and 2-7pm. MC/V.) South of Pontarlier, at **Metablef Mont d'Or,** ski until the sun sets. (☎46 47 47. Lift tickets €19 per day, under 12 €15. MC/V.)

In the summer, skiing gives way to fishing, hiking, and mountain biking. There are two **mountain bike** departure points in Pontarlier, one to the north, just off rue Pompée, and one to the south, about 2km west of Forges. Hikers can try the **GR5,** an international 262km trail accessible from Larmont with an offshoot leading to the **Château de Joux et Musée d'Armes Anciennes.** The massive 1000-year-old castle houses an extensive series of dungeons and a collection of rare arms. It hosts music, theater, and merriment during the **Festival des Nuits de Joux,** held annually from late July to mid-August. (☎69 47 95, festival info ☎39 29 36; www.chateaudejoux.com. Open daily July-Aug. 9am-6pm; Apr.-June and Sept.-Oct. 9:45-11:45am and 2-4:30pm; Nov.-Mar. 10-11:30am and 2-4pm. €5.80, students €4.70, ages 6-14 €3. Shows €18, under 12 €11.) The tourist office sells a map (€3) with departure points for biking and hiking trails around town, including one near the train station at pl. St-Claude and one at Pont de la Fauconniere. The maps give easy-to-follow directions that help you make your way through the trails. More detailed maps can be found at **Librairie Rousseau,** 20 rue de la République. (☎39 10 28. Open M 2-7pm, Tu-Sa 9am-noon and 2-7pm. English books also available. MC/V.) **Le Poney Club,** rue du Toulombief, next to the campground, offers horseback riding for all skill levels. (☎46 71 67. €5 per 30min. For rides with a guide, call ahead.)

Though Pontarlier's greatest attractions lie in the surrounding mountains, you can learn about the intoxicating history of absinthe at **Musée Municipal de Pontarlier,** 2 pl. d'Arçon. The museum also holds a minor exhibit on local archaeology and a bizarre collection of 19th-century toilets and bedpans, but its real draw is the old handpainted posters advertising *La Fée Verte* (the green fairy) and other assorted absinthe-related drinking paraphernalia. (☎38 82 14. Open M and W-F 10am-noon and 2-6pm, Sa-Su 2-6pm. €3.40, students €1.75, under 12 free. Wheelchair-accessible). After you've learned the story of the scandalous serum, walk down the street and try some for yourself at the **Distillerie Les Fils d'Emile Pernot,** 44 rue de Besançon. Founded in 1890 by Emile Pernot to make Pontarlier's *"apéritif mythique,"* the distillery now produces tamer tonics, such as the scrumptious *liqueur du sapin* (pine liquor). Visit the functioning distillery for a tour and tasting of current hallucinogenic-free absinthe. (☎39 04 28. Open M-F 9am-noon and 2-6pm. Tour and tasting free; available in English, French, German, and Spanish.)

BURGUNDY (BOURGOGNE)

Siding with the English during the Hundred Years' War—or rather, siding against the French—the Burgundians betrayed young Joan of Arc and have never regretted it. With hilly pastures and rich green vineyards punctuated by bright-roofed villages, this largely agricultural area of France has long been saturated with a strong regional identity and an independent spirit.

The heartland of Roman Gaul in the first century BC, this fruitful region was finally conquered in the fifth century by the Burgundians, a Germanic tribe who proceeded to name the area after itself. By the Middle Ages, the duchy of Burgundy had grown fat off the land, building itself magnificent cathedrals and palaces, collecting priceless works of art, funding powerful monasteries, and creating a legacy of world-class winemaking. The ducal palace and sumptuous museums of Dijon, the regional capital, stand as vivid reminders of a time when Burgundian dukes wielded more power than the puny Parisian monarchy—though now, Paris reigns and Dijon has been reduced to mustard.

You can taste another source of regional pride by sampling the wines produced in this fertile area. Louis XIV called Burgundian wine "*le vin des rois, le roi des vins*" ("the wine of kings, the king of wines") and allowed little else in his glass. Today, a bicycle ride through the rolling hills of the Côte d'Or reveals some of the world's finest vineyards, which are haunted by connoisseurs in search of the perfect Pinot Noir or Chardonnay.

HIGHLIGHTS OF BURGUNDY

CONTEMPLATE monastic life at the impeccably restored 12th-century monastery **Abbaye de Fontenay** (p. 417).

DELIGHT in the city of **Dijon** (p. 410), whose Musée des Beaux Arts and Palais de Ducs commemorate its former power.

GET LOST in a wine stupor at one of the family-owned vineyards along the **Route des Grands Crus** (p. 418).

DIJON ☎03 80

While Dijon (DEE-jhon; pop. 150,000) is synonymous with the pungent mustard that has been produced here for centuries, the town hardly survives on Grey Poupon alone. Now simply the regional capital of Burgundy, the city was once the center of secular power for all of France, and its former grandeur lives on in its fine museums and splendid churches. Unlike the delectable Côte d'Or wineries nearby, which retain a rustic enchantment, Dijon is thoroughly modern. Though nothing spectacular, the town offers something for everyone—from *haute cuisine* to high culture, from pulsating clubs to peaceful *salons de thés* (tea shops).

TRANSPORTATION

Trains: Cours de la Gare, at the end of av. Maréchal Foch. Ticket office open daily 5am-11pm. Info office open M-F 9am-6:30pm, Sa 9am-6pm. To: **Beaune** (25min.; 26 per

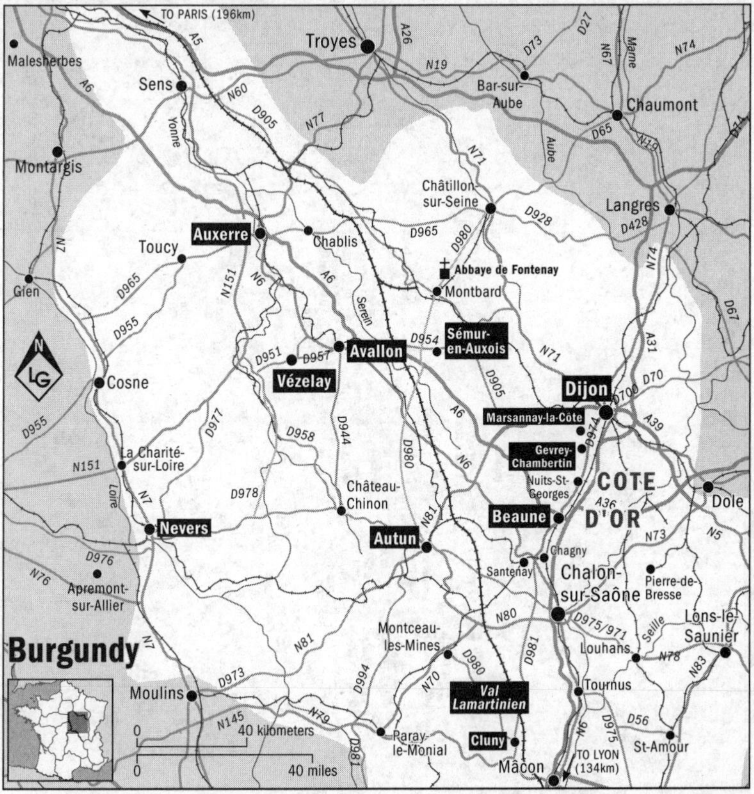

day, fewer Sa-Su; €6.40); **Clermont-Ferrand** (4-5hr.; 10-12 trains per day, 2 TGV; €44); **Lyon** (2-2½hr.; 14 per day, 4 TGV; €25); **Nice** (6-8hr., 6-8 per day, €88); **Paris** (1½-3hr.; 3-4 per day, 12-15 TGV; €52). **SOS Voyageurs** (☎43 16 34), in the train station, has travel information. Open July-Sept. M-F 8:30am-12:30pm and 2-6pm, Sa 8:30am-12:30pm; Oct.-June M-F 8:30am-6:30pm, Sa 8:30am-12:30pm.

Buses: TRANSCO, 21 cours de la Gare (☎42 11 00; www.cg21.fr), connected to the train station, left of the exit. Ticket and info office open M-F 6am-8pm, Sa 7am-2pm and 3-6pm, Su 10am-1pm and 4-8pm. Schedule posted outside the terminal. Tickets available on the bus. To **Beaune** (1¼hr., 6 per day, €6.30) via **Gevrey Chambertin** (10min., every hr. 6am-8pm, €1.80) and to various stops in the **Côte D'Or.**

Public Transportation: Divia (☎08 00 10 20 04; www.divia.fr), pl. Grangier. Office open M-F 7:30am-6:45pm, Sa 8:30am-6:30pm. Buses run 6am-9pm; limited night bus service until 12:30am. Tickets €0.95, day pass €3.10, *carnet* of 10 €7.40, 1-week pass €8.90. Buy individual tickets on board; *carnets* and passes are available at the office.

Taxis: Taxi Dijon (☎41 41 12). Outside the train station. 24hr.

Car Rental: Avis, National, Europcar, and Hertz share an office, 7bis cours de la Gare.

Avis (☎42 05 99). From €121 per day. Passport or ID deposit. 21+. Open M-F 8am-12:30pm and 1:30-9pm, Sa 8:30am-1pm and 1:30-5pm, Su 4-8pm. AmEx/MC/V.

Europcar (☎45 90 60). From €90 per day with 250km included. Under-25 surcharge €25. €600 deposit. 23+ weekdays, 25+ weekends. AmEx/MC/V.

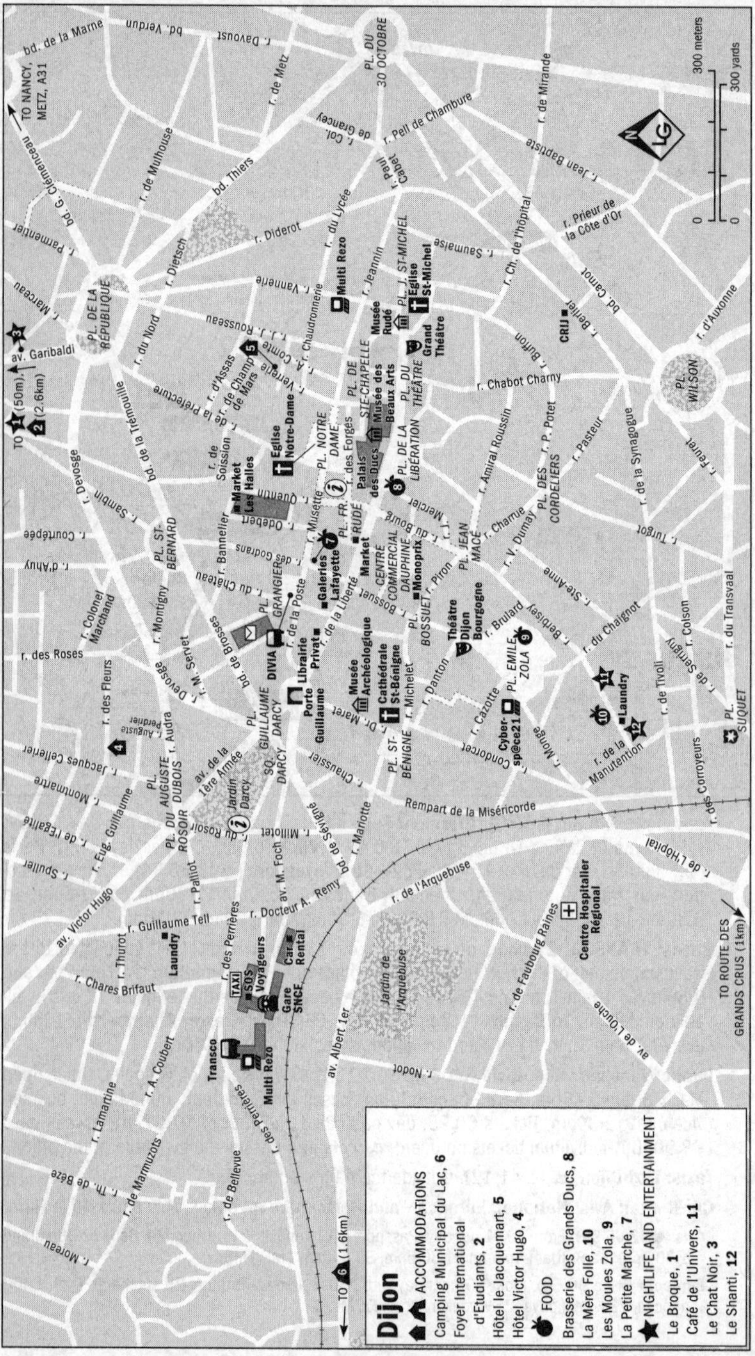
Dijon
ACCOMMODATIONS
Camping Municipal du Lac, 6
Foyer International d'Etudiants, 2
Hôtel le Jacquemart, 5
Hôtel Victor Hugo, 4
FOOD
Brasserie des Grands Ducs, 8
La Mère Folle, 10
Les Moules Zola, 9
La Petite Marche, 7
NIGHTLIFE AND ENTERTAINMENT
Le Broque, 1
Café de l'Univers, 11
Le Chat Noir, 3
Le Shanti, 12
300 meters
300 yards
TO NANCY, METZ, A31
TO ROUTE DES GRANDS CRUS (1km)
TO 6 (1.6km)
PL. DU 30 OCTOBRE
PL. DE LA RÉPUBLIQUE
PL. WILSON
PL. SUQUET
PL. DARCY
SQ. DARCY
Jardin Darcy
Porte Guillaume
PL. GRANGIER
PL. ST-BERNARD
PL. DU AUGUSTE DUBOIS
PL. DU ROSOIR
PL. NOTRE DAME
Eglise Notre-Dame
Market Les Halles
Galeries Lafayette
Market
Librairie Privat
DIVIA
Musée Archéologique
Cathédrale St-Bénigne
PL. ST-BÉNIGNE
PL. BOSSUET
Monoprix
CENTRE COMMERCIAL DAUPHINE
PL. FR. RUDE
Palais des Ducs
Musée des Beaux Arts
PL. DE LA LIBÉRATION
PL. DE STE-CHAPELLE
PL. DU THÉATRE
Grand Théatre
Musée Rudé
Eglise St-Michel
PL. J. ST-MICHEL
Multi Rezo
PL. JEAN MACÉ
PL. DES CORDELIERS
Théatre Dijon Bourgogne
PL. EMILE ZOLA
Cyber-sp@ce21
Laundry
CRIJ
Gare SNCF
SOS Voyageurs
TAXI
Car Rental
Transco
Centre Hospitalier Régional
Jardin de l'Arquebuse
Rempart de la Miséricorde
bd. Thiers
bd. de la Marne
bd. de la Trémouille
bd. de Brosses
bd. Carnot
bd. de Sévigné
av. Victor Hugo
av. Garibaldi
av. Albert 1er
av. Foch
av. de l'Ouche
r. de la Liberté
r. de l'Arquebuse
r. Chabot Charny

Hertz (☎53 14 00). From €44 per day with 200km included. Under-25 surcharge €34. Open M-F 8am-noon and 1:30-6:30pm, Sa 8am-noon and 2-5pm. AmEx/MC/V.

National (☎53 09 08). From €76 per day. Under-25 surcharge €24. Open M-F 8am-12:30pm and 2-6:30pm, Sa 9am-noon. AmEx/MC/V.

Bike Rental: Bikes are available for rent at the tourist office (see below).

ORIENTATION AND PRACTICAL INFORMATION

The main axis of the *vieille ville*, **rue de la Liberté,** runs roughly from **place Darcy** (recognizable by its big arch, Porte Guillaume) and the tourist office to **place St-Michel.** From the train station, walk ahead and follow **avenue Maréchal Foch. Place de la République** is the central roundabout for roads leading out of the city.

Tourist Office: Pl. Darcy (☎08 92 70 05 58, €0.34 per min.; www.dijon-tourism.com). Organizes themed city tours, some in English (daily July-Aug. €6, students €3, under 18 €1; reserve ahead), and vineyard tours (www.wineandvoyages.com; €55-65, reserve ahead). Offers a free detailed map of the city and a free accommodation service (☎44 11 59; www.reserver-dijon.fr). Also rents **bikes,** which you should reserve ahead (€12 per ½-day, €18 per day, €50 per 3 days; photocopy of passport and credit card deposit). Open daily May to mid-Oct. 9am-7pm; mid-Oct. to Apr. 10am-6pm. Branch at 34 rue des Forges. Open M-Sa 9am-12:30pm and 2:30-6pm.

Luggage storage: At the train station. July-Aug. M-F 8am-7:15pm; Sept.-June M-F 8am-7:15pm, Sa-Su 9am-12:30pm and 2-6pm. €4 per bag per 24hr., €2 per extra bag.

Bookstore: Librairie Privat, 17 rue de la Liberté (☎44 95 44). Small selection of books in English. Open M-Sa 9:30am-7pm.

Youth Center: Centre Régional d'Information Jeunesse de Bourgogne (CRIJ), 50 rue Berlier (☎44 18 35; www.crijbourgogne.com). Info on lodging, classes, grape-picking, summer jobs, and travel. Mostly in French. Open M 2-6pm, Tu-F 10am-6pm.

Laundromats: 36 rue Guillaume Tell (☎06 32 08 88 32). €4 per 7kg. Open daily 6am-9pm. Also 55 rue Berbisey. Wash €3.50 per 7kg, dry €2 per 28min. Open daily 7am-8:30pm.

Police: 2 pl. Suquet (☎44 55 00). Call here for the **pharmacie de garde.**

Medical Services: Centre Hospitalier Régional, 2 bd. Mar. de Lattre de Tassigny (☎29 30 31). **SOS Médecins** (☎59 80 80, €0.12 per min.). Doctors on call 24hr. **Médecin de garde** (☎40 28 28). **Dentiste de garde** (☎46 01 02).

Internet Access: Multi Rezo, 21 cours de la Gare (☎42 13 89). Open M-Sa 9am-midnight, Su 2-10pm. Also at 74 rue Vannerie (☎66 33 21). Open M-F 12:15-9pm, Su 2-9pm. Both €1 per 15min., €4 per hr. **Cybersp@ce 21,** 46 rue Mongue (☎30 57 43). €0.10 per min., €4 per hr. Open M-Sa 11am-midnight, Su 2pm-midnight.

Post Office: Pl. Grangier (☎50 62 19), near pl. Darcy. **Currency exchange.** Open M-Tu and Th-F 8am-7pm, W 9am-7pm, Sa 8am-noon. **Postal Code:** 21000.

ACCOMMODATIONS

Dijon's budget accommodations can be dark and impersonal, but its moderate hotels are universally pleasant. They are also very popular, so reserve ahead.

Hôtel Le Jacquemart, 32 rue Verrerie (☎60 09 60; www.hotel-lejacquemart.fr), centrally located on a side street near Eglise Notre Dame. A classy lobby and winding staircase leads to tidy rooms practically blooming with floral decorations. Breakfast €5.75. Reception 24hr. Reservations recommended. Singles €29, with shower or bath €43-53; doubles €32/48-63; triples €59-69; quads €72-74. AmEx/MC/V. ❷

Hôtel Victor Hugo, 23 rue des Fleurs (☎43 63 45). A great budget option, this hotel has impeccably neat and simple rooms, all equipped with TV, shower or bath, and toilet.

BURGUNDY

Some have great views of the back garden. Breakfast €6. Reception 24hr. Reservations recommended. Singles €31, with shower and toilet €35-39; doubles €39-49; quad €81. Extra bed €7. AmEx/MC/V. ❸

Foyer International d'Etudiants, 6 rue Maréchal Leclerc (☎71 70 00). A very long walk (30-40min.) or bus #3 from "Sévigné" (from the train station take a right on rue Remy and then a left on bd. de Sévigné. The stop will be on your right; dir.: St-Apollinaire la Fleuriée or Val Sully) to "Billardon" (20 min.), on rue Moulin. Rue M. Leclerc is a block ahead on the right; look for the building with the parking lot on the left. A colorless, dormitory-like hostel with an international crowd. Minimalist but spacious rooms with beds, desks, mini-fridges, sinks and closets. Common co-ed bathrooms, kitchen, laundry, ping-pong, tennis courts, piano, and TV rooms. Cafeteria open daily Oct. to early June. Reception 24hr. Singles €16; doubles €22. MC/V. ❶

Camping Municipal du Lac, 3 bd. Kir (☎43 54 72; www.campingdijon.com). Take bus #3 (dir.: Fontaine d'Ouche) from the station to "CHS La Chartreuse." From the stop, take an immediate right and follow the underpass straight to the campsite. This grassy site, within walking distance of a large lake, gets crowded in the summer. Wi-Fi, barbecue, and laundry. Reception July-Aug. 8am-8pm; Apr.-June and Sept.-Oct. 8am-12:30pm and 2:30-8pm. Gates closed 10pm-7am. Open Apr. to mid-Oct. Reservations recommended July-Aug. July-Aug. €3.50 per adult, €2 per child under 7, €6 per site; Sept.-Oct. and Apr.-June €2.50/1.50/2.15. Electricity €3/2.65. MC/V. ❶

FOOD

Dijon's reputation for *haute cuisine* is well deserved but, unfortunately, reflected in its high restaurant prices. **Rue Berbisey, rue Monge, rue Musette,** and **place Emile Zola** feature a variety of delicious restaurants that offer a meal for €10-15. Pedestrian **rue Amiral Boussin,** behind pl. de la Liberté, provides outdoor dining in a 17th-century setting. A colorful **market** takes place in the pedestrian area around **Les Halles,** extending to **place F. Rude** (open Tu and F mornings, Sa all day). Cheap kebab joints are located throughout the *centre-ville* (kebabs €3-5) but cluster around the train station. There's a **supermarket** in the basement of the **Galeries Lafayette,** 41 rue de la Liberté (open M-Sa 9:15am-8pm), and a **Monoprix** at 11 rue Piron, off pl. Jean Macé. (☎30 26 60. Open M-Sa 9am-8:45pm.) Popular picnic spots include the **Jardin Darcy** and the courtyard of the **Musée Archéologique** (see p. 415).

La Mère Folle, 102 rue Berbisey (☎50 19 76). A large painting of "the crazy mother" watches over as patrons enjoy traditional *bourguignonne* cuisine that's worth every euro. Try the rich and flavorful *poulet à la Gastro Gérard* (chicken in a white wine, *gruyère,* and mustard sauce; €13). For a taste of the exotic, the menu offers ostrich with escargots (€14) in addition to its popular standards. Gigantic salads €11. *Plats* €11-14. 2-course *menu* €15. Open M, Th, Su noon-2pm and 7-11pm, W 7-11pm, F noon-2pm and 7-11:30pm, Sa 7-11:30pm. MC/V. ❷

La Petite Marché, 27-29 rue Musette (☎30 15 10). Situated above a health food store, this restaurant features organic and vegetarian fare, like the fruit-filled *salade exotique* (€8.50), along with some meat dishes, such as the *steak haché (*€8). Everything is natural or almost natural, down to the leaf-shaped chairs. Salads €6.50-8.50. *Plat du jour* plus appetizer or dessert €11. *Tartes* €5.50. Open M-Sa 9am-2pm. MC/V. ❷

Les Moules Zola, 3 Place Emile Zola (☎58 93 26). As its name subtly suggests, this popular restaurant serves heaping bowls of mussels swimming in myriad sauces–such as the creamy regional mustard sauce or the spicy Spanish tomato sauce–with huge helpings of frites (€11-12). Those not in the mood for the restaurant's specialty can try one of the enormous seafood salads (€9.50). Open daily noon-2pm and 7-10pm. ❷

Brasserie des Grands Ducs, 96 rue de la Liberté (☎30 25 30). Features stained-glass depictions of the Ducs themselves and a sprawling terrace overlooking the *brasserie*'s namesake. The *quiche lorraine* (€4.85) or one of the various omelettes (€4-7) makes for a tasty lunch. Open M-Th and Su 6:30am-midnight, F-Sa 6:30am-2am. MC/V. ❶

SIGHTS

Dijon's major sights are all contained within a few blocks of one another in the *centre-ville*. The Palais des Ducs de Bourgogne is the city's most celebrated landmark due to its regal history, but other sights make for more entertaining diversions. In 2004, Dijon's mayor mandated **free admission** to all municipal museums; relish the bargain while you can before the city's 2008 elections.

MUSÉE DES BEAUX ARTS. With a collection of mostly 15th- to 20th-century European art, the museum's highlight is the **Tomb of the Dukes,** which showcases two ornate, gilded memorials for the 15th-century Valois dukes of Burgundy. The section dedicated to modern art includes a Cézanne and 20th-century technicolor paintings by Lapicque. Look for the amusing mouse-shaped smoking pipe in the glassware section. *(Pl. de la Libération. Enter by cours de Bar. ☎74 52 70; museedesbeauxarts@ville-dijon.fr. Open M and W-Su May-Oct. 9:30am-6pm; Nov.-Apr. 10am-5pm. Modern art wing closed 11:30am-1:45pm. Permanent collection free; temporary exhibitions €2, students €1. Audio tours in English, French, and German €3.90.)*

PALAIS DES DUCS DE BOURGOGNE. At the center of the *vieille ville* stands the most conspicuous vestige of ducal power, the 52m **Tour Philippe le Bon,** which towers over all buildings in the city. A climb up the 600-year-old tower's 316 steps is rewarded with a panoramic view of the *vieille ville*. *(Pl. de la Libération. ☎74 52 71. Tours Easter to mid-Nov. every 45min. daily 9am-noon and 1:45-5:30pm; mid-Nov. to Easter every hr. W 1:30-3:30pm, Sa-Su 9-11am and 1:30-3:30pm. €2.30, students €1.20.)*

MUSÉE ARCHÉOLOGIQUE. In the converted 11th-century Benedictine Abbey of St-Bénigne, view the evolution of the Côte d'Or's man-made art, from prehistoric jewelry and Gallo-Roman sculpture to 17th-century pottery. For those not interested in the content of the museum itself, the courtyard offers a shady place to relax. *(5 rue Dr. Maret. ☎30 88 54. Open M and W-Su 9am-12:30pm and 1:30-6pm. Free.)*

ÉGLISE NOTRE-DAME. Built over a span of only 20 years, this "miniature cathedral" has an amazingly

TOP TEN LIST

STREET SMARTS

Nearly every French city features the same national heroes on its street signs, making any town map a historical *Who's Who*. The usual suspects include:

1. Marquis de La Fayette: Short for Marie-Jean-Paul-Joseph Roche-Yves-Gilbert du Motier. Aristocrat who helped Americans win their Revolution.

2. Louis Pasteur: Enabled France's obsession with cream. Pioneered pasteurization.

3. Léon Gambetta: Had a vendetta. Statesman who opposed Napoleon III's imperialism.

4. Emile Zola: Promised to "live out loud"—and did. Novelist whose "J'Accuse" charged the government with anti-Semitism.

5. Jean Jaurès: These streets veer Left. WWI pacifist. Socialist defender of Dreyfus.

6. Joseph Joffre: a.k.a "Papa Joffre." WWI Commander in Chief. Used aggressive tactics and won.

7. Georges Clemenceau: WWI Premier and later Prime Minister. Wrote *The Grandeur* and *Misery of a Victory*, probably referring to his role in the Treaty of Versailles.

8. Ferdinand Foch: WWI Supreme Allied commander. Prophet. At Germany's surrender, he said: "This is not a peace. It is an armistice for 20 years."

9. Philippe Leclerc: Not your average clerk. WWII general who liberated Paris.

10. Charles de Gaulle: Man of numbers. 1st President of the 5th Republic. Earned fame in WWII as leader of the Resistance.

detailed and unified Gothic style. To the right of the altar, you'll find 13th-century stained glass, among the oldest surviving in France. According to legend, long ago one of the church's distinctive gargoyles fell on the head of the town's moneylender as she was leaving her own wedding service—giving new meaning to the phrase, "never a borrower or lender be." The **Horloge à Jacquemart** atop the church tower, one of the famous symbols of the city, was captured and brought to Dijon by Philippe le Hardi after a 1382 victory over the Flemish. As you leave the church via rue de la Chouette, remember to rub the well-worn *chouette* (owl) with your left hand for good luck. *(Pl. Notre Dame. ☎41 86 76; www.Notre-Dame-dijon.net. Information pamphlet available in Dutch, English, French, German, Italian, Spanish; worth the €0.50.)*

OTHER SIGHTS. Recognizable by its brightly colored Burgundian towers, the Gothic **Cathédrale St-Bénigne** was constructed in the sixth century over the tomb of its namesake. Four hundred years later, the powerful Abbey of Cluny had the church redone to make it the largest in Christendom. Don't miss the spectacular—and enormous—18th-century organ designed by Charles Joseph Riepp. *(Pl. St-Bénigne. ☎30 39 33. Open daily 9am-7pm. Crypt €1 with informative brochure.)* While the **Eglise St-Michel** has the dark, vaulted interior of a Gothic cathedral, its style changed mid-construction, resulting in a hybrid colonnaded Renaissance facade. The church suffered severe damage during the Revolution, and much of its stained glass and original sculptures were destroyed. *(Pl. St-Michel. ☎63 17 80.)* Though a visit to the unassuming two-roomed **Musée Rudé** will only take a few minutes, the mammoth 13x8m stone relief sculpture, *"Départ des Volontaires de 1792"* ("Departure of the Volunteers of 1792"; a.k.a *"La Marseillaise"*), makes the trip worthwhile. The piece is a copy of a part of Paris's Arc de Triomphe (p. 136), which Rudé was commissioned to sculpt after he won the *Légion d'Honneur* in 1833. Other statues (of a more normal proportion) by François Rudé line the floor of the museum. *(Pl. St-Michel, across from Eglise St-Michel. Open June-Oct. daily 9:30am-6pm. Free. Call tourist office for more information.)*

NIGHTLIFE AND FESTIVALS

In July, Dijon's **Estivade** brings dance, music, and theater to its streets and auditoriums. Pick up *l'Eté on Continue* at the tourist office for info. (☎74 53 33. Tickets up to €8.) The city devotes a week in late summer to the **Fêtes de la Vigne** and the **Folkloriades Internationales,** celebrations of grapes that feature over 20 foreign dance and music troupes. (☎30 37 95; www.fetesdelavigne.com. Tickets €10.)

The beautiful 18th-century **Grand Théâtre,** pl. du Théâtre, right next to St-Michel, presents operas from mid-October to mid-May. (Info ☎60 44 44; tickets ☎42 44 44 or www.fnac.com. Office open M-F 10am-6pm, Sa 10am-4pm. Tickets €15-48, students €5.50-10.) Check out the plays (both classic and contemporary) at the **Théâtre Dijon Bourgogne,** Théâtre du Parvis St-Jean; enter at rue Danton. (☎30 12 12; www.tdb-cdn.com. Performances Oct.-June. Info office open late Aug. to June M-F 1-7pm, Sa and performance nights 11am-4pm; July M-F 1-7pm. Performances M and W-Th 7:30pm, Tu and F 8:30pm, Sa 5pm. Tickets €20, students and under 26 €12.) **Rue Berbisey** is lined with bars and cafés, and *brasseries* stay open late around **Les Halles** and **place de la Libération.**

Le Broque, 4 rue de la Sablière (☎73 81 14), north of pl. de la République. A 2-story bar whose dance floor fills early and stays hopping late. With clients jiving on bar tops and belting along to songs, this stylish small club is refreshingly unpretentious. Beer from €2. Open daily 6pm-2am. MC/V.

Le Chat Noir, 20 ave. Garibaldi (☎73 39 57; www.lechatnoir.fr). This chic discotheque, adorned with stylish cats, starts late and doesn't stop. The cavernous ground floor plays techno and house, while a livelier basement blasts hits from decades past. Expect a line at the door. Theme nights Th-F; about 3 per month. Cover Sa before 1am €5, €10 thereafter; includes 1 drink. W-F women free. Beer €7-8. Mixed drinks from €8. Open W-Th 11:15pm-5am, F-Sa 11:15pm-6am. MC/V.

Le Shanti, 64 rue Berbisey (☎06 60 94 27 20). A *salon de thé*-cum-hookah bar for backpackers looking to put their feet up—literally—in private, pillow-furnished pods. To get his worldly patrons chatting, the outgoing owner offers free *"Thé au communitaire"* to those who share their stories at the bar. 30 flavors of exotic tea (large pot €3.50); 20 flavors of hookah (€7 for 1, €10 for 2). Open M and Su 8pm-2am, Tu-Sa 3pm-2am.

Café de l'Univers, 47 rue Berbisey. (☎30 98 27). The galaxy painted on the windows of this rock-and-roll bar only offers a taste of what lies within its depths. Décor includes an enormous Betty Boop and an egg machine. Caters to a slightly older clientele, but students fill the basement for weekly concerts. Beer from €2.50. Open daily 5pm-2am.

DAYTRIP FROM DIJON

ABBAYE DE FONTENAY

To get to Fontenay from Dijon, take the train to Montbard (45min., 4-5 per day, €11) and then a taxi to the Abbey (€21 round-trip). If there aren't any at the station, call ☎92 18 57 or 92 31 49. Most passengers who head to the taxi stand at Montbard are also visiting the Abbey—share a cab to cut costs.

If ever a single location could make a traveler yearn for the seclusion of monastic life, the Abbaye de Fontenay (ah-BAY du FOHN-tuh-nay) would be it. Converted into a paper mill in the 18th century but restored in the early 20th century, the Abbey now exists almost exactly as it did in the 12th century, though it is now surrounded by beautiful gardens. From the majestic Romanesque church—known for its Virgin of Fontenay statue—to the simple yet spacious dormitories that often hold art exhibitions, this out-of-the-way stop is worth the time, money, and effort it takes to get there. In May 2008, the Abbey will inaugurate a re-creation of the 12th-century forge, which was originally a joint effort of over 1500 students from 6 countries. The whole Abbey is now a **UNESCO World Heritage site.** Adjacent to the grounds is a museum that holds the enormous papal proclamation of the founding of Fontenay. (☎92 15 00; www.abbayedefontenay.com. Open daily Apr. to mid-Oct. 10am-5:30pm; Nov.-Mar. 10am-noon and 2-5pm. €8.90, students €4.20. Entrance fee includes 1hr. French tour. Most visitors choose to forgo the tour and instead use multilingual pamphlets from the information office.)

CÔTE D'OR ☎03 80

The 60km of well-tended slopes that run from Dijon to the tiny village of Santenay, 20km south of Beaune, have nurtured grapes since 500 BC. Limestone-laced soil, a perfect amount of rainfall, and ample sun exposure and drainage make the region a viticulturist's dream—not to mention some of the world's best real estate.

The Côte d'Or is divided into two regions, which by law can only bottle and sell wine produced from two kinds of grapes: the red Pinot Noir and the white Chardonnay. The **Côte de Nuits,** stretching south from Dijon through Nuits-St-Georges to the village of Corgoloin, is known for subtle, sophisticated reds. The **Côte de Beaune,** farther south, is known particularly for its white wines.

The most intimate way to see the vineyards near either Beaune or Dijon is to **bike** the **Route des Grands Crus.** Bike rental shops in both cities arrange tours of different lengths that can get you where you want to go. Renting a **car** in Dijon or Beaune (€55-90 per day) is the fastest way to the grapes, but not the best choice if you plan to not only taste—but also drink—the wine. TRANSCO **buses** (☎42 11 00)

BURGUNDY

run frequently from Dijon to Beaune (1hr.; M-Sa 7 per day, Su 3 per day; €6.30) and stop at all the great names in between, including Gevrey-Chambertin (30min., 19 per day, €1.80). Many buses are wheelchair-accessible. Call ahead or visit the Dijon or Beaune bus stations for schedules.

Lodging on the Côte is expensive: reserving a room at one of the many village *chambres d'hôtes* is usually the cheapest option, and Dijon is the cheapest base. The tourist offices in Beaune and Gevrey-Chambertin have comprehensive lists of bed and breakfasts. The Dijon and Beaune tourist offices also offer the *Bourgogne Hôtes* guide, which lists almost every hotel and campsite in the region.

ROUTE DES GRANDS CRUS

The city traffic on this flat, 60km road fades out a few kilometers outside Dijon, as the route winds through **Chenove, Marsannay-la-Côte, Couchey, Fixin, Brochon,** and **Gevrey-Chambertin,** each village more enchanting than the one before. The countryside's vast vineyards are speckled with church spires and fields of bright, colorful flowers. Family-owned *caves* (wine cellars) along the route offer free *dégustations*, but most will expect you to buy something. If you taste and bike, be careful.

MARSANNAY-LA-CÔTE. Only 20min. by bike from Dijon, Marsannay-la-Côte (MAHR-sah-nay lah KOHT), known as the "door to the Côte d'Or," is the only town on the Côte that produces rosé wines in addition to the traditional reds and whites. The tiny, peaceful village feels a world away from urban Dijon—and the Defense Association for the Quality of Life in Marsannay-la-Côte has been campaigning heavily to keep it that way. To sample the local specialties, try the **Château de Marsannay,** which hosts a tour of its grounds followed by an elaborate candlelit wine tasting in the deep *caves*. *Sommeliers* (wine stewards) take visitors through this personalized tasting of the château's wines—including a rosé and a *premier cru* red. (☎51 71 11. Open Apr.-Oct. daily 10am-noon and 2-6:30pm; Nov.-Mar. M-Sa 10am-noon and 2-6:30pm. 1hr. tour €10; includes *dégustation*. Wines for purchase from €6.) To reach the château from Dijon, follow signs for Marsannay-la-Côte and the Château, or take Divia **bus** #15 (dir.: Marsannay Château) to the last stop. The Marsannay-la-Côte **tourist office,** 41 rue de Mazy, has a list of wine makers in the region and houses a museum that offers a taste of the life of a wine maker in the 19th century. (☎52 27 73; www.ot-marsannay.com. Open June-Sept. M-Sa 9am-12:30pm and 2-6:30pm, Su 9am-1pm; Mar.-May and Oct. M-F 9:30am-12:30pm and 2-6pm, Sa 9am-12:30pm and 2-5:30pm; Nov.-Feb. M-F 9am-12:30pm and 2-6pm, Sa 9am-12:30pm and 2-5:30pm.)

GEVREY-CHAMBERTIN. Perhaps the finest vineyards in all of France surround Gevrey-Chambertin (jhay-VREE sham-BAYR-tehn), 11km south of Dijon. Nine of Burgundy's 33 *grands crus* ("best grown") are grown here. Meanwhile, the **Château de Gevrey-Chambertin** is the perfect place to unwind after a long bike ride. Its gracious proprietors will take you through their private, family-owned 10th-century château, which was built to protect the wine and villagers (in that order), and later handed over to the monks of Cluny in the 13th century. The monks turned the château's wine-making into a tradition, and workers still use their original methods. The house itself is filled with old fresco pieces and furniture dating back to the 17th century. Finish the ancient tour with an informative 3D animated video detailing the château's evolution through time. (☎51 84 85. Open daily 10am-noon and 2-6pm. Tour €5, ages 7-11 €2.50, under 7 free. Includes tasting. Tours in English by request.)

Lovers—and especially wine lovers—should not miss the romantic **Festival Musical des Grands Crus de Bourgogne,** held on weekends in September, which pairs tastings of precious just-harvested vintages with classical music. Student tickets to combined tastings and shows are as low as €8. Ask the tourist office for more info.

Getting to Gevrey-Chambertin from Dijon by bike takes about an hour; by foot, it's a 2½hr. hike. To get to the château from the bus stop, go left up the hill and left again. The Gevrey-Chambertin **tourist office,** 1 rue Gaston Roupnel, offers Internet access at €1 per 30min. (☎34 38 40. Open May-Sept. M-F 9am-12:30pm and 1:30-6pm, Sa 9am-12:30pm and 1:30-5:30pm, Su 10am-12:30pm and 1:30-4pm; October M-Sa 9am-12:30pm and 1:30-5:30pm; Nov.-Apr. M-Sa 9:30am-12:30pm and 1:30-5:30pm.) Bunk at **Marchands ❸,** 1 pl. du Monument aux Morts, a B&B with a country feel. (☎34 38 13; dmarc2000@aol.com. Reservations recommended in summer. Singles €30; doubles €40-45; triples €55-60; quads €70-75. MC/V.)

BEAUNE ☎03 80

The atmosphere in Beaune (BUHN; pop. 23,000) is decidedly bourgeois; while the cobblestone streets are accessible to all, prices at the boutiques, restaurants, and hotels are anything but. Budget travelers are best off spending an hour or two here drinking in the extensive presentations at the Musée du Vin before renting a bike and putting their newfound knowledge into practice on the *route du vin.*

TRANSPORTATION. Trains, av. de Lyonnais (info office open M-F 10am-noon and 2-7pm; ticket office open M-F 5:30am-8:30pm, Sa 5:45am-8pm, Su 6:15am-8:30pm), depart for Dijon (20-35min.; 26 per day, 3 TGV; €6.40-8.10), Lyon (1½-2hr., 10 per day, €21), and Paris (2-2½hr., 14 per day, €45-55). **TRANSCO buses** go to Dijon (1hr., 2-7 per day, €6.30) from several stops including the train station. (☎42 11 00. Schedule at tourist office.) **Allo Beaune Taxi** (☎06 09 42 36 80) has 24hr. service. **Cars** can be rented at **ADA,** 26 av. du 8 Septembre, half a block down from the train station. (☎22 72 90. 21+; 1 yr. with license required. From €55 per day with 250km included. Open M-F 8am-noon and 2-6pm, Sa 8am-noon and 2-4pm. MC/V.) The staff at **Bourgogne Randonnées,** 7 av. du 8 Septembre, near the station, rents **bikes,** offers free maps, free luggage storage, and great advice on suggested routes. (☎22 06 03; www.bourgogne-randonnees.com. €4 per hr., €17 per day, €32 per 2 days, €90 per week; credit card deposit. Open M-Sa 9am-noon and 1:30-7pm, Su 10am-noon and 2-7pm. MC/V.)

ORIENTATION AND PRACTICAL INFORMATION. Streets run in concentric rings around the **Collégiale Notre Dame.** Almost everything worth seeing lies within the circular ramparts enclosing Beaune's *vieille ville.* From the station, head straight on av. du 8 Septembre, which becomes rue du Château. Turn left onto rue Thiers and follow it as it becomes rue Poterne and then rempart Madeleine. Turn right onto **rue de l'Hôtel-Dieu,** which leads to the Hôtel-Dieu and the **tourist office,** 1 rue de l'Hôtel-Dieu (15min.). The staff provides maps and lists of *caves,* reserves rooms, offers tours of the *vieille ville* (daily July to mid-Sept. €9.90, ages 10-18 €8.40, under 10 free), and sells the *Pass Beaune,* which provides discounts to most of the town's major attractions. (☎26 21 30; www.ot-beaune.fr. Open late June to late Sept. M-Sa 9am-7pm, Su 9am-6pm; late Sept. to late June daily 10am-noon and 1-5pm.) The main branch is at the Porte Marie de Bourgogne, 6 bd. Perpreuil. (Open late June to late Sept. M-Sa 9am-7pm, Su 9am-12:30pm and 1:30-6pm; late Sept. to mid-Nov. and mid-Mar. to mid-June daily 9am-12:30pm and 1:30-6pm; mid-Nov. to Dec. and Jan. to late Mar. M-Sa 9am-12:30pm and 1:30-6pm, Su 10am-12:30pm and 1:30-5pm.) **Espace Jeunes,** 1 promenade des Buttes, has info on work, study, and sports, as well as free **Internet** access for the first 15min. of use; €1.50 for the next 30min. (☎24 55 32. Open M-Tu and Th-F 11:30am-6pm, W 1:30-6pm.) Other services include: a **laundromat,** 8 rue du Fbg. Madeleine (open daily 9:30am-12:15pm and 2-7pm); **police,** 5 av. du Général de Gaulle (☎25 09 25); a **hospital,** 120 av. Guigone de Salins, northeast of the town

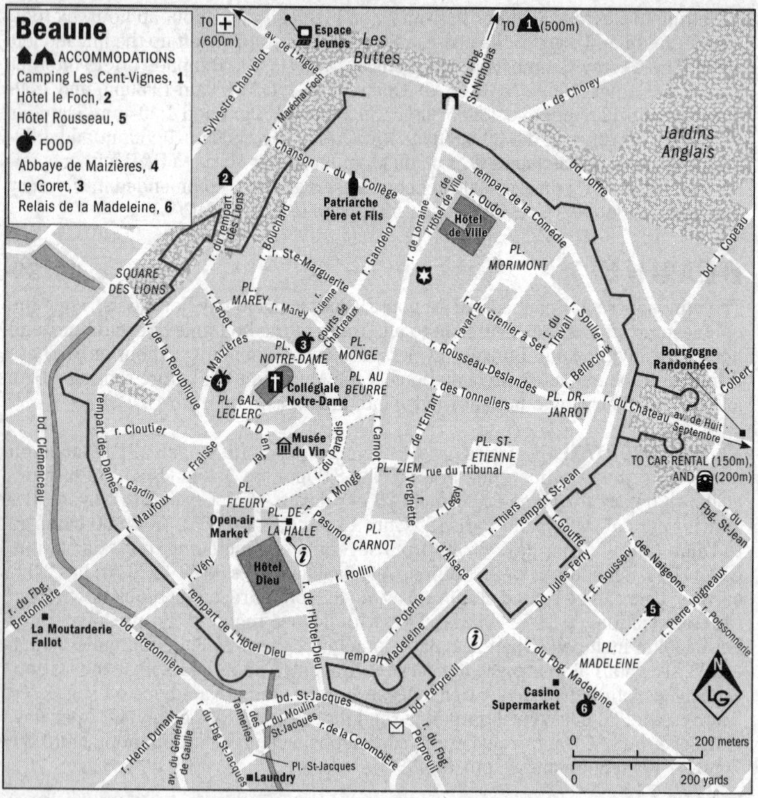

center (☎24 44 44); and a **post office,** bd. St-Jacques, which has **currency exchange** and **Internet** access for €7 per hr. (☎26 29 50. Open M and W-F 8am-6:30pm, Tu 8am-12:30pm and 1:30-6:30pm, Sa 8:30am-12:30pm). **Postal Code:** 21200.

ACCOMMODATIONS. Visitors swarm Beaune from April to November; reserve at least a week ahead and beware that there are no true budget hotels within the *vieille ville.* **Hôtel le Foch ❷,** 24 bd. Foch, not far from the town center, on the other side of the ramparts from the train station, offers bright blue rooms with enormous lace curtains, TV, and large sinks. (☎24 05 65. Breakfast €6. Reception 7am-9pm. Singles and doubles €25, with shower €33-38; triples €45; quads €48. MC/V.) Fifty-year-old **Hôtel Rousseau ❷,** 11 pl. Madeleine, has an antique ambience. Rooms feature floral wallpaper and wooden furnishings; some face a quiet interior courtyard. (☎22 13 59. Breakfast included. Shower €3. Reception 7:30am-11:30pm. Singles €28, with toilet €30, with bath €48; doubles €35, with toilet €41-45, with bath €55; triples with toilet €51, with bath €61. Cash or check only.) **Camping les Cent-Vignes ❶,** 10 rue Dubois, 500m from the town center, off rue du Faubourg St-Nicholas, is popular with both the rugged bikers of the *Route des Grands Crus* and those who want to relax in the *vieille ville.* To get there, begin at pl. Monge and walk away from the town center on rue Lorraine. Signs point the way as you walk down rue du Faubourg St-Nicholas and turn left on rue Dubois; the campsite is on your right. Gravel or grass sites are made private by hedges. Grocery store, laundry, restaurant, ping-pong, and tennis are available on-site. (☎22 03 91. Reception 8am-noon and 1-9:30pm. Open mid-Mar. to Oct. €3.50 per adult, €1.65 per child under 7, €4.50 per car. Electricity €3.25. MC/V.)

FOOD. The restaurants around **place Madeleine** and **place Carnot** serve the cheapest *menus*, but even here prices for regional wine can be high. There is a **Casino** supermarket at 28 rue du Faubourg Madeleine (☎26 25 25; open M-Sa 8:30am-7:30pm), and a **Petit Casino** along rue Carnot (open Tu-Sa 7:30am-12:30pm and 3-7:30pm, Su 9am-noon). An open-air **market** is on pl. de la Halle Wednesday and Saturday mornings. A cut above the rest, **Relais de la Madeleine ❷,** 44 pl. Madeleine, features large portions of specialties like pistachio duck *pâté*, pep-pered trout, and *mousse au chocolat*—all of which can be sampled as part of a four-course *menu* for €16. (☎22 07 47. *Menus* from €13. Open M-Tu and F-Su noon-2pm and 7-10pm, Th noon-2pm. AmEx/MC/V.) For a tasty dinner that takes you back in time, duck into the *cave*-like entrance of the 12th-century wine cellar at **Abbaye de Maizières ❸,** 19 rue Maizières, near the cathedral. (☎24 74 64; www.beaune-abbaye-maizieres.com. 3-course *menu* of regional specialties €18, 4 courses €26. Open M and F-Su noon-2pm and 7:30-9:30pm, W-Th 7:30-9:30pm. MC/V.) With some of the cheapest food in town, **Le Goret ❷,** 2 rue Maizières, is a small, friendly eatery that specializes in everything pig, from the regional ham and pork dishes to the expressive pig dolls that sit in the windows. (☎22 05 94. *Plats* and meal-sized salads €7-10. Specials €14-20. Open Tu-Sa 11am-2pm and 7pm-1am; kitchen open until 10pm. Bar open until 2am. MC/V.)

BURGUNDY

SIGHTS AND FESTIVALS. In 1443, Nicolas Rolin, chancellor to the Duke of Burgundy, built the **Hôtel Dieu,** 2 rue de L'Hôtel Dieu, as a hospital to help the city's poor recover from the ravages of famine following the Hundred Years' War. Patients were treated here until 1971, and today, the building is the town's best non-drinkable tourist attraction. In the courtyard, visitors ogle the multi-colored tiled rooftops; inside, they marvel at the majestic Salle des Pôvres, a room that once held several patients. The Hôtel's great treasures are its 16th-century tapes-tries—telling "the story of the human condition"—and The Last Judgment, a polyptych (a work consisting of connected carved panels) by Roger van der Wey-den. Most info placards are in English, French, and German. (☎24 45 00. Ticket office open daily late Mar. to mid-Nov. 9am-6:30pm; mid-Nov. to mid-Mar. 9-11:30am and 2-6:30pm. Ticket office closes 5:30pm. €5.60, students €4.80, ages 10-18 €2.80, under 10 free. With Musée du Vin €9.60/6.60/5.80/free. Tours in French July-Aug., 4 per day, €1.80. Call the Hôtel for times.) Inside the 15th-century **Hôtel des Ducs de Bourgogne,** the **Musée du Vin,** rue d'Enfer, off pl. Général Leclerc, offers a detailed analysis of the Côte's *terroire* (land), from the angle of sunlight, to the composition of the soil, to the location of individual vineyard plots and their char-acteristics. Winemaking instruments, third-century Gallo-Roman wine goblets, and even sheet music for drinking songs are on display. Detailed information is presented in French only, though each room has summary cards in English, Ger-man, Chinese, and Japanese. (☎22 08 19. Open Apr.-Nov. daily 9:30am-6pm; Dec.-Mar. W-Su 9:30am-5pm. €5.40, students €3.50.) At **La Moutarderie Fallot,** 31 Faubourg Bretonnière, Fallot Mustards presents an entertaining hands-on history of the famous yellow condiment. In a bizarre hour-long tour, professional guides, ani-mated films, and audio recordings explain the mustard-making process. Finish the visit by mixing your own mustard and comparing it to flavors of the Fallot brand. (☎26 21 33; www.fallot.com. Guided tours M-Sa 10, 11:30am. Extra afternoon visits July-Aug.; call the tourist office for times. €10, available at the tourist office.)

For three days in late November, Beaune's moderate level of wine intake swells to a spirit-soaked party during **La Fête de la Vente du Vin,** a celebration of the wine harvest. This family-oriented event promises live music, theatrical performances, and wine booths throughout the pedestrian district. The festival once encouraged drinking *"sans modération"* but has since shifted its focus from quantity to quality. In July, the **Festival International d'Opéra Baroque** hosts operas and concerts every weekend. (☎22 97 20; www.festivalbeaune.com. €12-80, students €10-68.)

DAYTRIPS FROM BEAUNE

These daytrips are accessible via nearby Mâcon, an unimpressive town that's surprisingly useful as a base for exploring. Trains and buses run from Beaune to rue Bigonnet in Mâcon (55min., 5 per day, €15). Check schedules at the station. (Ticket window open M-F 5:05am-7:50pm, Sa 5:40am-7:40pm, Su 6:10am-8pm.) Call ☎06 09 34 08 07 24hr. for a taxi. Car rental is available at Avis, 23 av. Edouard Herriot, in Mâcon (☎03 85 38 68 75).

TIP **PASS AWAY THE DAY.** To facilitate exploration of Mâcon, Cluny, and Cormatin, buy the one-day *pass balad* (€10), which provides unlimited bus travel (until 4pm) and discounts to most major museums and sights in the area. (☎03 85 45 86 10. Buy pass on any # 7 bus. Available mid-June to Oct.)

BURGUNDY

CLUNY

It can be challenging to reach Cluny, as it has no train station and infrequent buses; check schedules ahead. Transdev RSL bus #7 runs to Cluny from Mâcon (40min., 6 per day, €4.30). The schedule is at the Mâcon tourist office and the train station. Biking from Mâcon is possible for those up for the 23km trip; take the scenic, car-free Voie Verte path, a stretch of road that covers most of the rolling countryside near Cluny. The path begins at Charnay-les-Mâcon, a 15min. ride from Mâcon; purchase a Voie Verte *guide from the Mâcon, Cluny, or Cormatin tourist offices (€1.50).*

Founded in AD 910 by 12 monks, the Abbey of Cluny (KLOON-ee) became the most influential ecclesiastical organization in medieval Europe, controlling a vast network of daughter abbeys. At its height, Cluny and its omnipotent abbots escaped control of local bishops and secular powers and answered only to the Pope—nearly a dozen of whom came out of the abbey. A Romanesque building whose height rivaled that of most Gothic cathedrals, the abbey and its magnificent church were looted and used as a quarry during the Wars of Religion, as well as during the French Revolution and its aftermath. One-tenth of the complex remains today, giving guests a good idea of its former grandeur. Visitors are aided by several impressive models that reconstruct what Cluny is thought to have looked like as well as an excellent 3D video in French that creates the illusion of being inside the completed church. Guided tours take groups past the remaining transept, the ornately decorated Gothic **Pope Gelasius** facade, and numerous chapels. The central cloister is now home to the **Ecole Nationale Supérieure d'Arts et Métiers,** an engineering school whose students mostly live in the old monk's quarters. Tickets for the abbey are sold at the **Musée d'Art et d'Archéologie.** Entrance to the museum, which provides a good introduction to the Abbey, is included in the ticket price. To get to the museum from the tourist office, follow rue 11 Août 1944 to pl. de l'Abbaye. Turn left on pl. du Marché; the ticket office and museum are in the Palais Jean de Bourbon up the stairs on the right and past the school. This area, particularly rue d'Avril and rue Lamartine, is home to the best of the **medieval houses** which dot the city. (☎03 85 59 15 93; fax 03 85 59 82 00. Open daily May-Aug. 9:30am-6:30pm; Sept.-Apr. 9:30am-noon and 1:30-5pm. Abbey tours in French daily. English tours daily July-Aug.; Sept.-June by reservation. Call for schedule. €7, ages 18-25 €5, under 18 free. MC/V.)

To get from the Cluny bus stop to the **tourist office,** 6 rue Mercière, walk against traffic on rue Porte de Paris, turn right at pl. du Commerce, and continue for 5min. The office gives out a map and *Guide Pratique.* (☎03 85 59 05 34. Open July-Aug. daily 10am-6:45pm; May-June daily 10am-12:30pm and 2:30-6:45pm; Sept. and Apr. M-Sa 10am-12:30pm and 2:30-6:45pm; Oct. M 2-6:30pm, Tu-Sa 10am-12:30pm and 2:30-6pm; Jan.-Mar. M 2:30-5pm, Tu-Sa 10am-12:30pm and 2:30-5pm.)

VAL LAMARTINIEN

The Val Lamartinien area is accessible by the same routes as Cluny. The Transdev RSL bus # 7 from Cluny (20min., 8 per day 5:20am-7:54pm, €3) or Mâcon (1hr., 6 per day 8am-7:15pm, €6.40) stops next to the Château de Cormatin in Val Lamartinien.

The namesake of lush Val Lamartinien (vahl lah-MAR-tin-ee-en), Romantic poet Alphonse de Lamartine (1790-1869), drew his main inspiration from this bucolic paradise of gently rolling farmlands that lies at the base of forested hills. The fertile valley is filled with châteaux, most notably the privately owned **Château de Cormatin,** complete with a moat, aviary, maze, and beautiful formal gardens perfect for a stroll. Located in the north wing, the grand staircase was the height of sophisticated Italian style and engineering at the time of its construction (1605-1616); in an unadorned display of structure and form, it embodies the Renaissance neo-Platonic belief in the harmony of universal order. Tours immerse visitors in early 17th-century life, relating architectural and artistic elements of the building to their symbolism and practical functions at the time. (☎03 85 50 16 55. Open daily mid-July to mid-Aug. 10am-6:30pm; mid-Aug. to Sept. and June to mid-July 10am-noon and 2-6:30pm; Apr. and Oct. to mid-Nov. 10am-noon and 2-5:30pm. Tours in French with written English translations every 30min; tours in English available by reservation. €8.50, students ages 18-26 €5, ages 8-17 €4. Gardens only €4.)

Hard-core cyclists and casual peddlers alike won't want to miss the **Musée du Vélo,** Le Bois Dernier, the only museum of its kind in France. The first floor displays over 10,000 cycling-related objects—including posters, jerseys, and pins—while the second level houses over 150 bicycles, tracing the evolution of the bike from 1818. The museum is a 10min. walk from town; from the château, head toward Cluny for 1km; the museum is on the right. (☎03 85 50 16 00; www.museeduvelo.free.fr. Open daily June to mid-Sept. 10am-noon and 2-6:30pm; mid-Sept. to mid.-Nov. and Apr.-May 2-6:30pm. €4.50, students €3.20, under 13 €2.50.)

AUTUN ☎03 85

With a Roman amphitheater seemingly plopped in the midst of its surrounding fields, Autun (aw-TUHN; pop. 18,000) strikes a balance between its rich past and its thriving modern spirit. Founded around 15 BC by Emperor Augustus as a "sister and rival of Rome," the city is still oddly littered with stony remnants of the Empire. Today, history buffs rejoice in Autun's ancient offerings, while those dragged along for the ride enjoy relaxing in the city's tranquil atmosphere.

TRANSPORTATION AND PRACTICAL INFORMATION. **Trains** run from pl. de la Gare on av. de la République, but Autun is far from any major railway line and thus difficult to reach. Most trains to and from Autun require a change at Châlon-sur-Saône or Etang, and many involve tortuous connections. It is possible to get to Dijon almost directly by train with an SNCF bus or train connection at Chagny or Etang (1½-2hr.; M-Sa 7-8 per day, Su 4; via Chagny €14; via Etang €18). The train runs to and from Avallon (1½-2hr., 1-2 per day, €15). TGVs leave Gare Le Creusot for Paris (2-2½hr., 5 per day, €55-71). To get to Lyon, catch a bus to Châlon-sur-

Saône and take a train from there (3-4hr., 1-2 per day, €25). SNCF **buses** leave from outside the Autun station for Châlon-sur-Saône (2hr., 3 per day, €10). Check the station office for schedules. (Open M-F 7:05am-12:30pm and 12:50-7pm, Sa 9am-12:30pm and 2:30-6:30pm, Su noon-7:30pm.) For a **taxi,** call ☎52 04 83. (24hr.)

The main street, **avenue Charles de Gaulle,** runs from the train station to central **place du Champ du Mars.** Head left onto av. de la République from the station, and turn right on av. Charles de Gaulle. To get to the *vieille ville* from there, follow the signs from rue aux Cordeliers or rue St-Saulge. The **tourist office,** 2 av. Charles de Gaulle, off pl. du Champ de Mars, offers themed tours of the city, as well as nightly summer tours of the *vieille ville* in French. City brochures in English, French, and German cost €2. (☎86 80 38; www.autun-tourisme.com. City tours July-Aug. €6, under 12 €2.90. Night tours July-Aug. 10pm; €8, under 16 free. Call the office for tour schedules. Open May-Sept. daily 9am-7pm; Oct.-Apr. M-Sa 9am-12:30pm and 2-6pm.) There's also a branch at 5 pl. du Terreau, next to the cathedral. (☎52 56 03. Open daily June-Sept. 9am-7pm.) Other services include: **laundry** at **Salon Lavoir,** 1 rue Guerin (☎86 14 12; wash €3.40 per 5kg, dry €1 per 15min; open daily 6am-9pm); **police,** 29 av. Charles de Gaulle (☎86 01 80; call for the **pharmacie de garde**); a **hospital,** 7bis rue de Parpas (☎86 84 84); and **Internet** access at **Elge Inter@ctive,** 6 Grande rue Chauchien (☎86 13 07; €1 per 15min.; open M-F 9am-noon and 2-6:30pm). There is a **post office** with **currency exchange** at 8 rue Pernette. (☎86 58 10. Open M-F 8:30am-6:30pm, Sa 8:30am-noon.) **Postal Code:** 71400.

BURGUNDY

ACCOMMODATIONS AND FOOD. The city's two cheapest hotels are across from the train station. Reservations are recommended in summer. The gracious staff at **Hôtel de France ❷,** 18 av. de la République, lets modestly furnished rooms over a quiet restaurant and bar. The restaurant's hearty three-course lunch *menu* is a steal at €11. (☎52 14 00; www.hotel-de-france-autun.fr. Breakfast €4.90. Free parking. Reception M-Sa 8am-10pm, Su 8am-3pm. Call ahead if you plan to arrive Su night. Check-out 11am. Open Jan. and Mar.-Dec. Singles and doubles €23-25, with toilet €26, with shower €28-35, with bath €41; triples €35-41; quads €41-48; quints €56. MC/V.) Next door, the small but inviting rooms of the **Hôtel du Commerce & Touring ❷,** 20 av. de la République, have TVs and large bathrooms. Rooms with tubs are particularly spacious. (☎52 17 90. Breakfast €5. Reception M-Sa 7am-10pm, Su by reservation. Open Feb.-Dec. Singles and doubles €27, with shower €34-38, with bath €44; triples and quads €42. MC/V.) The **Camping Municipal de la Porte d'Arroux ❶,** an easy 20min. walk from town, offers three-star camping along the banks of Le Ternin river. From the train station, turn left on av. de la République, left on rue de Paris, and go under the Porte d'Arroux. Cross the bridge and veer right onto rte. de Saulieu; the campground is on the left. The grassy sites have some hedges for privacy. There's a restaurant (open June-Aug.), grocery store, common room with TV and Internet access (€8 per hr.), a playground, and a pond for fishing and swimming. Bike (€5 per ½-day, €10 per day; €100 deposit) and canoe (€5 per hr., €15 per ½-day, €20 per day; €20 deposit) rentals are available. (☎52 10 82; www.camping-autun.com. Office open daily June-Aug. 8am-noon and 4-9pm; Sept.-Oct. and Apr.-June 9-10:30am and 5-8pm. Check-out noon. Open Apr.-Oct. June-Aug. €3.20 per adult, €1.65 per child, €5.70 per tent, €1.80 per car; Apr.-May and Sept.-Oct. €2.90 per tent. Electricity €2.95. AmEx/MC/V.)

For a quick picnic on the ancient steps of the Théâtre Romain, grab supplies at ATAC supermarket, 46 av. Charles de Gaulle. Morning markets are held in place du Champ du Mars (open W and F 7am-noon). The steep trek to the upper city will leave travelers ready to refuel; thankfully, restaurants and pizzerias line the streets surrounding the cathedral. With its spacious terrace sitting in the shadow of the cathedral, **Le Lutrin ❷,** 1 Place du Terreau, offers larger salads (€5-13) and cheaper varieties of pizza (€7-9) than its numerous counterparts. Cool down outdoors with a beer while gazing at the church, or indoors at the attached Pub Le Lutrin. (☎52 48 44. Restaurant open May-Sept. daily noon-2pm and 7-10pm; Oct-Apr. M and W-Su noon-2pm and 7-10pm. Pub open May-Sept. M-Th 9am-2am and F-Sa 8:30am-3am; Oct.-Apr. W-Th 9am-2am, F-Sa 8:30am-3am. **Le Petit Rolin ❸,** 12 pl. St-Louis, near the cathedral, serves *crêpes* and salads for under €10, with romantic garden seating available at night. (☎86 15 55. Weekday lunch *menu* from €12. Dinner *menu* €18-26. Open Apr.-Oct. daily noon-3pm and 7-11:30pm; Nov.-Mar. W-Su noon-2:30pm and 7-10:30pm. MC/V.)

SIGHTS. The **Théâtre Romain,** northeast of the *vieille ville*, is delightfully un-restored. From the cathedral, take rue du Chanoine Triquet; bear right onto rue Bouteiller at Place D'Hallencourt. Turn right on rue du Faubourg St-Pancrace, left on Rue St-Branchez, and walk straight past the cemetery. The theater is on the left. Its remaining stones emerge from the grassy hillside, and picnickers relax where 12,000 enthralled spectators once sat. (☎52 52 52. Open M-Sa 8:30am-7pm. MC/V.) During the first two weekends in August, 600 locals bring chariot races and Roman games to life in the much-hyped **Augustodunum** show, held in the original theater. (☎86 80 13. Tickets sold at the tourist office. €14, ages 6-12 €5, under 6 free.) Visible from the back of the theater is the **Pierre de Couhard,** a 30m pyramid-shaped pile of stone bricks. Get a better view from rue du Vieux Colombier or rue St-Branchez, just below the *vieille ville*. The purpose of the pyramid remains unclear, although recent excavations unearthed a 1900-year-old plaque that cursed anyone who disturbed the eternal slumber of the man inside. To test your luck, follow chemin des Manies, a footpath off of chemin des Ragots, at the end of rue St-Branchez. At the top of the upper city, the **Cathédrale St-Lazare** rises above the Morvan countryside; the uphill walk from pl. du Champ de Mars feels like a pilgrimage. The elaborate **tympanum** (sculpted panel) above the church doors, which depicts the Last Judgement with expressive 12th-century figures, escaped the ravages of the Revolution. Before heading for a drink at one of the bars nearby, look to the right of the tympanum to see the sculpted fate of the drunkard with his barrel—you may opt for a *café au lait* instead. Information cards are available in Dutch, English, French, and German. (Open daily July-Aug. 8am-7pm and 9-11pm; Sept.-June 8am-7pm and 9-11pm. Capital room closes at 6:30pm.)

The **Musée Rolin,** 5 rue des Bancs, next to the cathedral, features the city's true archaeological treasures: beautiful mosaic floors harvested from ruins and 12th- to 15th-century statues and paintings taken from St-Lazare for safekeeping. Get a bird's eye view of the cathedral without having to climb; the museum houses an intricate model of the church. (☎52 09 76. Open Apr.-Sept. M and W-Su 9:30am-noon and 1:30-6pm; Oct.-Mar. Su 10am-noon and 2:30-5pm. €3.35, students €1.75.)

Several landmarks stand as reminders of Autun's former role as Roman Gaul's largest city. The easiest way to see these scattered sights is on the **petit train,** which leaves from pl. du Champ de Mars and from the tourist office annex near the cathedral. Tours are given in French, but the driver gives out English translations (50min.; late June-Aug. 7 per day 10am-6pm; €6, under 18 €3). To kill time before leaving Autun, check out the first-century **Temple de Janus,** in the fields behind the train station. The two remaining walls, which tower over pastures, offer a well-framed view of Autun's cathedral. From the train station, make a left on av. de la République, and another left onto rue du Faubourg d'Arroux. Continue ahead, cross the bridge, and turn left onto a footpath that goes to the ruins. This route to the temple will carry you through the double-decker **Porte d'Arroux,** one of the city's two remaining Roman gates. The arches once led the way to the **Via Agrippa,** the main trade road connecting Lyon and Boulogne and the source of

Autun's ancient wealth. Better preserved, the other gate, **Porte St-André,** is at the intersection of rue de la Croix Blanche and rue de Gaillon. Autun's ramparts and towers, including the **Tour des Ursulines** by the cathedral, are best seen from the hills above. To get there, take one of the paths off rue du Faubourg St-Blaise past the *vieille ville* and head toward the Pierre de Couhard. As part of the Morvan Valley, Autun provides easy access to over 2400km of marked mountain-biking trails. Ask the tourist office for the guide *Le Morvan à VTT* (€10) or call the **Morvan Park Authority** for more information (☎03 86 78 71 77).

NEVERS ☎03 86

A budding tourist destination in western Burgundy, Nevers (nay-VAYR; pop. 40,000) is a city of lush parks and medieval and Renaissance architecture. Ravaged by WWII bombings, Nevers has rebounded due to significant restorations. The perfect base for excursions to the picturesque châteaux that populate the region, Nevers also offers countless outdoor activities in its surrounding countryside.

TRANSPORTATION AND PRACTICAL INFORMATION. Trains travel to Bourges (45min., 11 per day, €7.80); Clermont-Ferrand (1½hr., 8 per day, €24); and Paris (2hr., 16 per day, €33), from the Nevers station on av. Général de Gaulle. (☎08 92 35 35 35. Ticket office open M 5:45am-8pm, Tu-F 6am-8pm, Sa 6am-7:30pm, Su 8am-9pm.) Local **buses** depart from rue de Charleville, to your left with your back to the train station's main entrance. (☎57 16 39. Open daily 6:45am-8:15pm. €1 to city center. Transit maps available at main office, 31 av. Pierre Bérégovoy.) For a **taxi,** call ☎59 58 00. **Le Bureau des Guides de la Loire,** on Quai des Eduens, rents **bikes** and **canoes,** complete with repair kit. (☎57 69 76; www.L-o-i-r-e.com. Bikes €12.50 per ½-day, €18 per day. Apr.-Sept. unguided canoe rentals €10 per 2hr. Call ahead to reserve guided trips, available for groups of 6 or more. Daytrip €23-45 per person, €42 per 2 days, €120 per week. Transport from destination included for canoes. Open Apr.-Sept. daily 9am-7pm.)

The town center is an easy walk from the station; av. Général de Gaulle runs into pl. Carnot, becoming rue Sabatier, where the **tourist office,** 4 rue Sabatier, offers free maps of Nevers, an English guide listing hotels and restaurants, directions for self-guided walking tours, accommodations booking (€2.30), and info on outdoor excursions. (☎68 46 00; www.nevers-tourisme.com. Open Apr.-Sept. M-Sa 9am-6:30pm, Su 10am-1pm and 2:30-5:30pm; Oct.-Mar. M-Sa 9am-noon and 2-6pm. Various tours offered; ask for schedule.) Other services include: **currency exchange** at **Crédit Municipal,** 8 pl. Carnot (☎71 66 86; open Tu-F 8:15-11:45am and 1:15-5:30pm, Sa 8:15am-12:30pm); **police** at 6bis av. Marceau (☎60 53 00); a **hospital,** appropriately enough, on bd. de l'Hôpital (☎93 70 00); a **pharmacie de garde** (☎60 53 00); and **Internet** access at **Forum Espace Culture,** 81 rue de Nièvre, a large bookstore. (☎59 93 40. €1 per 15min., €3 per hr. Open M 2-7pm, Tu-Sa 10am-7pm. MC/V). The **post office** is at 25bis av. Pierre Bérégovoy, and has **currency exchange** and **ATMs.** (☎59 87 00. Open M-F 8am-6:30pm, Sa 8am-noon.) **Postal Code:** 58019.

ACCOMMODATIONS AND FOOD. A 2min. walk from the center of town, **Hôtel de Verdun ❹,** 4 rue de Lourdes, overlooks the Parc Salengro and has clean, quiet, and spacious rooms (including one that is wheelchair-accessible) with tasteful décor. Some have large bathrooms. Helpful owners speak English. (☎61 30 07; www.hoteldeverdun-nevers.com. Buffet breakfast €6.30. Reception M-Sa 6:30am-9pm, Su 7am-noon. Singles and doubles with toilet and shower €38-43, with bath and toilet €41-46. Extra bed €10. AmEx/MC/V.) To get to the quiet **Hôtel Beauséjour ❷,** 5bis rue St-Gildard, exit the train station, walk left, and take a sharp right onto rue St-Gilard at the rotary. Clean and comfortable rooms and a personable owner make for a pleasant stay. (☎61 20 84; www.hotel-beausejour-nevers.com. Breakfast €6.20. Reception 7am-10pm. Singles and doubles with sink €28, with shower €33, with shower and toilet €36-47. Extra bed €10. MC.)

Although the *vieille ville* abounds with *brasseries*, cheaper and more interesting options can be found on and around pl. Carnot. The tourist office distributes a restaurant guide which lists reasonably priced *menus*. **Marché Carnot,** the covered **market** on av. du Général de Gaulle and rue St-Didier, is largest on Saturdays. (M-F 7am-12:40pm and 3-6:55pm, Sa 6:30am-7pm.) A **Champion** supermarket, 12 av. du Général de Gaulle, is a half-block from pl. Carnot. (Open M and W-Th 9am-7:30pm, Tu and F 9am-1pm, Sa 8:30am-7:30pm, Su 9am-noon. MC/V.) There is a **Monoprix** supermarket on rue Mitterand. (Open M-Sa 8:30am-7:30pm; Su 9am-noon. AmEx/MC/V.) The pleasant terrace and calming pastel decor of **Tandem Café ❷,** 7 pl. Guy Coquille, complement its menu of salads, *tartines*, and creative sundaes. The service lives up to the promise of "quality food as quickly as possible." (☎59 24 15. *Menus* €8-12. Open Tu-Sa 8am-8pm. MC/V.) Breton-inspired **Le Goémon Crêperie ❶,** 9 rue du 14 Juillet, serves omelettes (€4.50-6), enormous *galettes* (€3-9), and dessert *crêpes* (€2.50-6) with entertaining names like the "Popeye" (with spinach), in a timbered dining room just off pl. Carnot. (☎59 54 99. Lunch *menu* of appetizer, *galette*, and dessert €9.80. Open Tu-Sa noon-2pm and 7-10pm.)

SIGHTS. The most visible building in Nevers, **Cathédrale St-Cyr et Ste-Juliette,** off pl. Carnot on rue du Doyenné, is a true architectural oddity; after much of the original church was destroyed in a fire, a Gothic front half was added to the distinctly Romanesque rear. The cathedral was nearly reduced to rubble in WWII but has since been splendidly reconstructed and now features stunning, brightly-colored stained-glass windows created by modern artists. The large, intricate wooden clock in the back is worth a look—especially when the statue on top rings its bell. (☎36 41 04. Open Apr.-Sept. 9am-7:30pm; Oct.-Mar. 9am-6pm. Ask tourist office for schedule of tours.) Opposite the cathedral, fairy-tale turrets ornament the 15th-century **Palais Ducal,** once the seat of regional government. A small aquarium of local fish, a collection of historic paintings and engravings of Nevers, and displays of local porcelain reside within this modest museum, but the exquisite exterior is the real draw. (☎68 46 00. Open Apr.-Sept. M-Sa 9am-6:30pm, Su 10am-1pm and 2:30-5:30pm; Oct.-Mar. M-Sa 9am-noon and 2-6pm. Enter from tourist office. Free.) Near rue Mitterand, just off rue St-Etienne, the **Eglise St-Etienne** provides an example of unspoiled Romanesque architecture; though admittedly plain-looking, the church has not seen any major transformation since its construction in 1068.

OUTDOOR ACTIVITIES. Whether you choose to leave the city and explore the numerous activities on its outskirts or simply to enjoy the picnics, walks, and fishing made possible by its many parks, Nevers is sure to satisfy your more adventurous side. A walk through the rose-lined gardens of the **Promenade des Remparts,** which stretch from the Loire River to rue de la Porte du Croux, follows a segment of Nevers's 12th-century fortifications. In the center of the city, just off pl. Carnot, the paths of **Parc Roger Salengro**—where enormous trees shade picnic-ready lawns—wind through a playground, gazebo, and garden. The scenic **Sentier Ver-Vert** footpath stretches 3.5km along the rolling banks of the Loire, with informative signs in French along the way. To get there, follow rte. des Saulaies along the river west (dir.: Marzy) to Square Henri Virlogeux. Further west of the city along rte. D504 lies **Le Bec d'Allier,** the confluence of the Allier and the Loire, France's two most raging rivers. Hikers take advantage of the 1.5km nature trail that leads into the area around Le Bec, starting from the other side of the Loire in the town of Gimouille. To get there by car, exit Nevers by the Pont de la Loire on the N7 and take a right onto the D976 (dir.: Bourges); signs direct you to the parking lot and trails on the right, about 10min. down the road. By bike, follow the trail that runs beside the **Canal Latéral de la Loire** to Gimouille, where you will find a sign with information and a map. The tourist office provides maps and information on outdoor activities suited to Nevers's two rivers. **Le Bureau des Guides de la Loire** (p. 426) rents canoes, bikes, and camping gear, and offers guided canoe excursions down the Loire or Allier Rivers for an afternoon or overnight trip.

DAYTRIP FROM NEVERS: APREMONT-SUR-ALLIER

Apremont-sur-Allier, 16km southwest of Nevers, is accessible by bike or car. To get there, take rue St-Genest over the river and continue straight as it becomes D907. Veer right onto rue Louis Bonnet, and right again onto rte. du Bourges, or D976. Follow D76 until you cross the river again, and turn left onto rte. de Guerche, then left again onto rte. d'Apremont, which will take you into the village.

Set on the banks of the Allier River, the tranquil and unassuming village of Apremont-sur-Allier (AH-pruh-mohn suhr ah-lee-AY) seems to be in its own world. Apremont's focal point, **Le Parc Floral,** could easily be mistaken for the Garden of Eden. Butterflies weave through the sundry assortment of flowers and trees. Besides its trim lawn, which would put many golf course fairways to shame, the park also features three "follies" inspired by Russian artist Alexandre Serebriakoff: the Chinese Bridge, complete with a pagoda-style roof; the Turkish Pavillion, containing paintings evoking "the Ottoman Empire's splendors;" and the Belvedere, a gazebo containing Serebriakoff-style artwork. A fake but aesthetically-pleasing waterfall adds to the paradisiacal ambience. (☎02 48 77 55 06. Open daily Apr.-Aug. 10:30am-12:30pm and 2:30-6:30pm; Sept. M and W-Su 10:30am-12:30pm and 2-6:30pm. €7, ages 7-12 €4, under 7 free.)

BURGUNDY

AUXERRE ☎03 86

High above the banks of the Yonne River, Auxerre (OHG-zayr; pop. 40,000) has always thrived on its waterfront location. Starting in the first century, the town began to accumulate substantial wealth through trade; today, expensive yachts line the shores. Visitors can explore the river in rented mini-boats or walk up the hill to visit Auxerre's abbey, which formerly served as an important pilgrimage site and today holds the tunic and remains of sainted Bishop Germain (AD 378-448). Modern Auxerre also has pristine fishing areas, superb vineyards, and a lively *centre-ville* with timbered *ancien régime* houses.

TRANSPORTATION AND PRACTICAL INFORMATION. The train station is on rue Paul Doumer, across the river from the *centre-ville.* (Ticket office open M-F 5:15am-8:30pm, Sa 6:15am-8:30pm, Su 6:45am-9:30pm. Hub for regional bus routes and regional trains. AmEx/MC/V.) **Trains** run to Avallon (1hr.; M-F 6 per day, Sa-Su 3-4; €8.70); Dijon (2½hr., 12 per day, €23); Lyon via Dijon (3-5hr.; M-F 7-8 per day, Sa-Su 5; €41); Marseille via Laroche-Migennes (4hr. TGV, 5 per day, €70); Paris (2hr., 12 per day, €23). Allo Le Bus runs **local buses.** (☎94 95 00; www.auxerre.com. Schedules and maps at tourist office. Buses run M-Sa 7:30am-7:30pm. Buy tickets on the bus or at most *tabacs.* €1.10, *carnet* of 10 €9.) There is a **taxi** stand in front of the train station (☎46 78 78).

To get to the **tourist office,** 1-2 quai de la République, from the train station, veer left onto rue Jules Ferry, then turn right onto rue Gambetta and walk to the intersection at pl. Jean Jaurès. Cross pont Paul-Bert (the bridge on the left) and take a right onto quai de la République. The office is three blocks down on the left, after the Passerelle footbridge (12min.). The staff sells the *Auxerre Privilèges* passport (€2), which includes half-price admission to most attractions in town and half-price bike rentals; books accommodations (10% of the 1st night's cost is paid up front; 90% at the hotel); exchanges currency on weekends; hands out free maps; and organizes walking tours in English, French, Dutch, German, and Italian. (French tours June-Sept. daily; Oct.-May Sa-Su by reservation. English tours July-Aug. once per week; call the office for details. €4.50, students €3.) The office also rents **bikes** (€3 per hr., €5 per 2hr., €8 per 3hr., €13 per 7hr.; ID and €150 deposit) and **mini-boats** (Apr. to Sept. W-Su €12 per ½-hr., €19 per hr., €30 per 2hr.; ID and €150 deposit), which offer alternative ways to see the sights. (☎52 06 19; www.ot-auxerre.fr. Open mid-June to mid-Sept. M-Sa 9am-1pm and 2-7pm, Su 9:30am-1pm and 3-6:30pm; mid-Sept. to mid-June M-F 9:30am-12:30pm and 2-6pm, Sa 9:30am-12:30pm and 2-6:30pm, Su 10am-1pm.) There is another branch at rue des Fourbisseurs d'Epées. (☎51 03 26. Open mid-June to mid-Sept. Tu-Sa 10am-noon and 1-7pm; mid-Sept. to mid-Apr. M-F 10am-noon and 1:30-6pm, Sa 10am-noon and 1:30-6:30pm; mid-Apr. to mid-June Tu-Sa 10am-noon and 1:30-6:30pm.) Other services include: **laundry,** 17 rue Egleny (wash €3.20 per 5.5kg, dry €0.90 per 10min.; open daily 7am-9pm); **police,** 32 bd. Vaulabelle (☎51 85 00); a **hospital,** 2 bd. de Verdun (☎48 48 48); **Internet** access at **La Maison de la Jeunesse,** pl. de l'Arquebuse (☎72 18 18; free; open M-F 10am-noon and 2-6pm) and **Média 2,** 17 bd. Vauban (☎51 04 35; €1.25 per 15min., €4 per hr.; open M-Th 9am-noon and 2-7pm, F 9am-noon and 2-6pm); and a **post office** with **currency exchange** at pl. Charles-Surugue. (☎72 23 00. Open M-F 8:30am-6:30pm, Sa 8:30am-noon.) A second branch is at 110 rue du Pont. (☎72 07 20. Open M 1:30-6pm, Tu-F 9:30am-12:30pm and 1:30-6pm, Sa 9:30am-12:30pm and 1:30-5pm). **Postal Code:** 89000.

ACCOMMODATIONS AND FOOD. At **Hôtel le Seignelay ❷,** 2 rue du Pont, large windows and fragile antique furniture lend rooms a quirky sense of luxury. Some open onto a courtyard, which doubles as a delicious restaurant. All but the cheapest rooms come with shower or bath. (☎52 03 48; www.leseignelay.com. Buffet breakfast €6.50. 3- and 4-course *menus* from €15. Reception 24hr., except M mid-day. Buzz to be let in 9pm-7am. Reserve ahead June-Aug. Open Mar.-Jan. Singles €25, with shower or bath €38-42; doubles €30/48-53; triples €56-62; quads €65. AmEx/MC/V.) To get to the **Foyer des Jeunes Travailleurs (HI) ❶,** 16 bd. Vaulabelle, take rue Jules Ferry from the train station to rue Gambetta, turn right, and walk to pl. Jean Jaurès. Cross pont Bert and turn left on quai de la République; rue Vaulabelle is the first right. Walk down rue Vaulabelle for 10min., take a left at the alley after the Service Citroën, and continue through to the end of the parking lot. Turn right and enter the glass door on your left in between two handicapped parking spots. This out-of-the-way hostel has dim hallways leading to dorm-style rooms. (☎52 45 38. Hall showers and toilets. Breakfast included. Reception 9am-10pm. Singles €16. Cash only.) There is a **campsite ❶,** 8 rte. de Vaux, south of town on D163. (☎52 11 15; camping.mairie@auxerre.com. Reception 7am-10pm. Open Apr.-Sept. €2.90 per person, €2.55 per site. Electricity €2.35. MC/V.)

Markets are held on **place de l'Arquebuse** (Tu and F), in the **centre-ville** (W), and on **place Dégas** (Su morning). The **Monoprix** supermarket, 10 pl. Charles Surugue, in the heart of the old town, operates a cheap cafeteria with a €6 three-course lunch *menu*. (☎52 19 90. Store open M-Sa 8:30am-8pm. Cafeteria open M-Sa 11:30am-6pm; lunch service 11:30am-2pm.) Packed to the brim with locals and tourists alike, the casual dining room of **Au Grand Gousier ❷,** 45 rue de Paris, maintains a traditional French atmosphere, serving local favorites like the daunting *boudin* (blood sausage) for budget prices. (☎51 04 80. *Escargots* from €5.70. *Plats* from €9.50. Lunch *menu du jour* €11. Dinner *menu* €19. Open M-Tu noon-2pm and 7-9pm, W-Th noon-2pm, F-Sa noon-2pm and 7-10pm. MC/V.)

SIGHTS. The scenic **Passerelle footbridge,** to the right of pont Paul-Bert from the train station, is a good starting point for exploring Auxerre. The tourist office, across from the bridge, offers free guides in Dutch, English, French, German, and Italian to **The Thread of History,** a fading yellow line on the ground that weaves past every monument in the city. Newer bronze arrows embedded into the sidewalks now accompany the line, along with a character called **Cadet Roussel,** who points tourists in the right direction. The **Cathédrale St-Etienne,** built in 1215, is a must-see, featuring detailed stained glass. Its aged facade, which is now being restored, still displays statuettes that were decapitated by Huguenots when they occupied the city in 1567. The treasury on the south wall guards relics, manuscripts, and a moving 16th-century tableau of Christ painted by a student of Raphael. (Cathedral open Apr.-Oct. M-Sa 7:30am-6pm, Su 2-6pm; Nov.-May M-Sa 7:30am-5pm, Su 2-5pm. Crypt and treasury open June-Sept. M-Sa 9am-6pm, Su 2-6pm; Oct.-May M-Sa 10am-5pm. Crypt €2.80, under 12 free. Treasury €1.70, students free with entry to crypt. 50% off with *Auxerre Privilèges* passport. *Son-et-lumière*, sound and light show, with audio tours in English and German nightly June to mid-Aug. 10pm; mid-Aug. to Sept. 9:30pm. €5. Call ☎52 23 29 for details. AmEx/MC/V.)

The Gothic **Abbaye St-Germain,** 2 pl. St-Germain, commissioned around AD 500 by Clothilde, attracts pilgrims and tourists to the tomb of the former bishop of Auxerre. While the church contains a crypt with some of France's oldest frescoes, the Abbaye, which now houses a museum, better illuminates the history of the *centre ville*. Featuring St-Germain's preserved tunic, ancient coins, and monastic relics, the museum recreates Benedictine life. (☎18 05 50. Open daily June-Sept. 10am-12:30pm and 2-6:30pm; Oct.-May 10am-noon and 2-6pm. French tours of the crypt daily June-Sept. €2.10, €1.05 with passport; temporary exhibits €2.50/1.25. Students under 26 free for both.) Visitors wandering near pl. de l'Hôtel will notice the **Tour de l'Horloge,** a turreted 15th-century clock tower in white and gold, as well as the boldly painted statues of *Auxerrois* celebrities, such as Paul Doumer (13th president of France's Third Republic), that dot the area. The **Musée Leblanc-Duvernoy,** 9bis rue d'Egleny, set in an 18th-century mansion, has different art exhibits each summer, ranging from pottery that depicts the stories of saints to tapestries that illustrate Chinese history. (☎18 05 50. Open M and W-Su 2-6pm. €2.10, with passport €1.05; students under 26 free; 1st Su of month free.)

ENTERTAINMENT AND OUTDOOR ACTIVITIES. Concerts erupt in Auxerre throughout the summer, beginning with the *"Garçon, la note!"* series, which takes place throughout July and August in the city's terraces and cafés. (Free concerts M-F 9-11:30pm; call tourist office for details or visit for a comprehensive pamphlet.) Auxerre hosts a piano festival in September and a 5-day festival featuring international films and music in mid-October. (Inquire at the tourist office for details.) The **Théâtre of Auxerre,** 54 rue Joubert, is closed during the summer, but from September to May it presents a variety of musical and dramatic events (☎72 24 24). Laid-back pub-crawlers can find satisfaction in any of the bars that line **rue du Pont,** but none stay open much later than midnight. **Place des Cordeliers** is a better bet for a lively time, with a cluster of bars facing the open plaza, such as the self-dubbed "music café" **Le Subway,** on your right when facing the Cathedral. This hip, brightly colored pub keeps the youth of Auxerre up until the wee hours with local musicians and themed parties. (☎51 41 41. Wi-Fi. Open M-Sa 10am-3:30am and Su 10am-10pm. Call for information on upcoming events.)

Auxerre and the Yonne region contain some great fishing spots. Contact the **Fédération de Pêche de l'Yonne,** 9-11 rue du 24 Août, for info (☎51 03 44; www.peche-yonne.com). The **Société Mycologique Auxerroise,** 5 bd. Vauban (☎46 65 96), organizes mushroom-hunting expeditions in the spring and fall.

AVALLON ☎03 86

Though the oldest section of town contains picturesque 17th-century homes and specialty stores, Avallon (ah-vah-LOHN; pop. 8217) is no tourist's dream. Centered around its train and bus station, it lacks both compelling sights and charming hotels. Yet it offers a central base in the stunning Vallée de Cousin from which to take breathtaking daytrips by car or foot—or the less-reliable bus—around the surrounding Morvan countryside. Worthwhile sites nearby include small Burgundian towns, like Vézelay or Sémur-en-Auxois, as well as numerous relatively un-touristed vineyards and châteaux.

TRANSPORTATION AND PRACTICAL INFORMATION. **Trains** run to Autun (1¾hr.; 3-4 per day, Su 1 per day; €13); Auxerre (1½hr., 4-5 per day, €8.70); and Paris (2½-3hr., 4 per day, €28-50). SNCF **buses** run to Vézelay (25min.; July-Aug. M-F 9:20am, Sa-Su 10:45am; return daily 5:28pm; Sept.-June one bus F evening, returns M morning; €3.70). Routes marked "car" on SNCF's schedule are served by buses. (Station open M-F 5:30am-noon and 1:15-8pm, Sa 5:30am-12:15pm and 1:15-7:15pm, Su 8:45am-noon and 3:30-8pm.) TRANSCO **buses** (☎03 80 42 11 00) depart from the train station to Dijon (2hr.; M-Sa 3 per day, Su 5:05pm; €17) via Semur-en-Auxois (45min.; M-Sa 3 per day, Su 1; €6.80). Purchase tickets on the bus; times are posted at the train station. Find schedules at the tourist office. **Taxis** (☎34 04 52) are available 24hr. To rent **bikes,** stop by **M. Gueneau,** 26 rue de Paris. (☎34 28 11. €16 per day. Open Tu-Sa 8am-noon and 2-6pm. MC/V.)

To get to the **tourist office,** 6 rue Bocquillot, head straight from the train station on av. du Président Doumer and turn right onto rue Carnot. At the large intersection, turn left onto rue de Paris. Walk through pl. Vauban and head straight onto Grande Rue A. Briand, which passes through the Tour de l'Horloge and ends at the office on your right (15-20min.). The office offers an accommodations service (€2.50) and **Internet** access (€3 per 30min.), and sells €0.50 maps of the city. (☎34 14 19; www.avallonnais-tourisme.com. Open mid-June to Sept. daily 9:30am-1:30pm and 2:30-7pm; Oct.-Mar. M 2:30-6pm, Tu-Sa 10am-12:30pm and 2:30-6pm; Apr. to mid-June M-Sa 10am-12:30pm and 2:30-6pm; longer hours during holidays and festivals.) Other services include: **laundry** at 8 rue du Marché, off pl. du Général de Gaulle (open daily 7am-9pm); **police** at 2 av. Victor Hugo (☎31 09 50); a **hospital** at 1 rue de l'Hôpital (☎34 66 00); a **pharmacie de garde,** posted at Pharmacie Rauscent Maratier, 4 Grande Rue, and in the window of the tourist office; and a **post office,** 9 rue des Odebert. (☎34 91 05. Open M-F 8am-12:30pm and 1:30-6pm, Sa 8am-noon.) **Postal Code:** 89200.

ACCOMMODATIONS AND FOOD. Intricate wallpaper, elaborate quilts, and antique armoires entertain the eye at the snug **Hôtel St-Vincent ❸,** 3 rue de Paris, 10min. from the train station. Each room is outfitted with a TV and shower. (☎34 04 53. Breakfast €5.50. Reception M-Sa 8am-11pm at restaurant. Singles from €33; doubles from €40; triples €46; quads €60. MC/V.) A professional staff welcomes travelers to the stately **Les Capucins ❹,** 6 av. Paul Doumer. Turn left out of the train station and walk straight for 5min. The hotel will be on your left. All rooms are tastefully furnished with TV, desk, toilet, and shower or bath. Larger suites are particularly elegant, with spacious marble bathrooms; some rooms overlook a small backyard garden and feature bright, summery décor. Many rooms have A/C. The restaurant downstairs has full *menus* from €17. (☎34 06 52. Breakfast €6.50. Reception 8am-10pm. Reservations recommended. Singles and doubles €40-55; triples €61; quads €69. €40 rooms are not listed; ask if interested. AmEx/MC/V.) **Camping Municipal Sous-Roche ❶,** is a 2km walk downhill from the *centre-*

ville. Exit straight out of the train station on av. du Président Doumer, turn left on rue Carnot, and continue straight through the intersection at rue de Lyon. Follow the signs (which begin at the intersection) to "Camping" to reach this quiet campground located across the street from the murky Le Cousin river. (☎34 10 39. Reception 8am-noon and 3-8pm. Open mid-Mar. to mid-Oct. €3 per person, €1.50 per child under 7, €2 per site, €2 per car. Electricity €3. Cash only.)

Pick up groceries at the **Petit Casino** supermarket, 31 rue de Paris, a block away from the intersection at rue Carnot. (☎34 40 63. Open Tu-Sa 8am-12:30pm and 3-7:15pm, Su 8:45am-noon.) Morning markets are held Saturdays on **place du Marché** and Thursdays on **place du Général de Gaulle.** Head to **Relais des Gourmets ❷**, 45-47 rue de Paris, for saucy vegetarian and traditional *Burgundian* fare. The elegant dining room, outfitted with fresh flowers during the summer and full-grown indoor trees year-round, offers a two-course bistro *menu* with a classy, unlimited *hors d'oeuvres* buffet. (☎34 18 90. Buffet €14. Open daily 11:45am-2:30pm and 6:45-9:30pm. Gourmet *menus* available W-Su noon-2pm and 7:15-9:15pm. Reservations recommended. AmEx/MC/V.) At the top of town, **La Pizzeria de la Tour ❷,** 84 Grande Rue A. Briand, serves a variety of Italian and *Burgundian* dishes—from the escargot to the "Mafioso Pizza," adorned with spicy salami and red peppers—in a half-timbered 15th-century house behind the Tour de l'Horloge. For a cheap date, try the *formule cinéma* (€6.50), which includes a choice of any pizza and a ticket to the local movie theater. Pizza can be ordered to go—just say, "*A porter.*" (☎34 24 84. Large salads €4.50-7.50. Pizzas €7-9. Pastas €8.50-10. Open Tu-Sa 11:45am-2pm and 6:45-10:30pm. MC/V.) The central watering hole is the **Café de l'Europe ❶,** 7 pl. Vauban. Watch all of Avallon walk by from the porch of this big, bustling hangout. (☎34 04 45. Sandwiches from €3.30. Salads €5.30-6.80. Pizzas €6.70-8. Dinner *formule* including salad, *plat du jour*, wine, and coffee begins at €8. Open daily 7am-midnight. Bar open until 2am. MC/V over €16.)

SIGHTS. At the **Musée du Costume,** 6 rue Belgrand, off Grande Rue A. Briand, historical narrative meets fashion show with rooms full of 18th- to 20th-century *haute couture* on display. Manequins dressed in their finest sit in the extensive rooms of this mansion, which are still decorated as they were when the house belonged to the Governor of Burgundy in the 17th-century. (☎34 19 95. Open Easter-Nov. daily 10:30am-12:30pm and 1:30-5:30pm. Tours in French. €4, students and under 18 €2.50.) Those with more than a few hours to kill in Avallon should consider a walk through Avallon's surrounding countryside. The tourist office provides a free map of an 8km walk covering the area's highlights.

VÉZELAY ☎03 86

High above the Vallée de Cousin and seemingly frozen in time, Vézelay (VAY-zeh-lay; pop. 457) has distilled all the stereotypical perfections of a French village into its tiny *centre-ville.* From its hilltop perch, the town watches over dense forests, fields of golden wheat, and herds of cattle in distant pastures. The shops along the village's four main streets sell only local *Burgundian* produce and artisanal creations. Vézelay is one of France's most pristine villages, so budget travelers must contend with high prices and hordes of tourists in the summer, but these are not reasons to miss out on this perfect portrayal of the past.

TRANSPORTATION AND PRACTICAL INFORMATION. There's no train station in Vézelay; **trains** run from Paris to Sermizelles via Auxerre or Laroche-Migennes (2½hr., 3-4 per day, €27). From there, take **Allo Taxi Vézelay** for the 10km ride to Vézelay. ((☎32 31 88. Around €17. 24hr.) A cheaper option is to take the SNCF **bus,** which leaves the train station at Avallon for Vézelay. (July-Aug. M-F

9:20am, Sa-Su 10:45am, return daily 5:28pm; €3.70. Sept.-June bus leaves F night and returns M morning, €3.70.) A *navette* bus run by Les Cars de la Madeleine goes from Avallon to Vézelay on Saturdays. (☎33 50 38. Sa 11:30am. Info at tourist office.) **Taxis** from Avallon cost about €24. (☎34 04 52. 24hr.) Vézelay is also easily reached by bike—a great way to explore the nearby villages and countryside. Renting **bikes** at **A.B. Loisirs,** rte. du Camping in nearby St-Père, requires a 2km walk downhill along D957 toward Avallon. (☎33 38 38; www.abloisirs.com. €18 per ½-day, €25 per day. Open daily 9:30am-7pm.)

The **tourist office,** 12 rue St-Etienne, down the street from the church, has free maps and a helpful free *Guide Pratique* that lists all local establishments. The office also offers **Internet** access (€2 per 10min.), group tours by reservation, and individual tours July through August. Most are in French; some are in English and German. During the summer, local students give guided tours in various languages; call for more information. (☎33 23 69; www.vezelaytourisme.com. Open June-Sept. daily 10am-1pm and 2-6pm; Oct. and Apr. M-W and F-Su only; Nov.-Mar. M-W and F-Sa only.) For the **pharmacie de garde,** check the window of the Pharmacie de Vézelay at 25 rue St-Etienne. (☎33 24 85. Open M-Sa 9am-noon and 2-7pm.) The **post office,** 17 rue St-Etienne, has both an **ATM** and **currency exchange.** (☎33 26 35. Open M-F 9am-noon and 2-4pm, Sa 9am-noon.) **Postal Code:** 89450.

ACCOMMODATIONS AND FOOD. With more than 100,000 visitors passing through each summer, Vézelay's accommodations fill up rapidly. Book a month ahead, particularly in summer. Most have at least a few rooms with views of the surrounding Morvan countryside. Only a block away from the hilltop and the church, **Maison Les Glycines ❸,** rue St-Pierre, is a three-star hotel with tall windows, tiled floors, and simple but elegant furnishings; the larger rooms seem to belong to a rustic summer villa. In the artistic spirit of the town, each room is named for a French artist or writer. An attached *salon de thé* offers a wisteria-shaded outdoor dining area and food from €7.50. (☎32 35 30. Breakfast €6.50. Reservations required. Singles €30-52; doubles €52-64. Extra bed €15. AmEx/MC/V.) The **Auberge de Jeunesse (HI) ❶** shares space with **Camping de L'Ermitage ❶**. Both are a scenic 15min. stroll from downtown Vézelay. From rue St-Etienne, veer left downhill and bear right on rte. de l'Etang. Follow the signs; the hostel and campsite will be on your left. The hostel has dorm-style rooms with four to six beds and kitchen access. The campsite offers showers, bathrooms, electricity, and beautiful views of the Vallée de Cousin's farm fields. (☎33 24 18. Reception 5:30-7pm. Lockout 10am-5:30pm. Open Apr.-Jan. Dorms €7.50-9.50. Camping €3 per adult, €1.50 per child, €1 per tent. Electricity €2.50. Cash only.) The Fraternité Monastique de Jerusalem and the sisters of Ste-Madeleine run the **Centre Sainte Madeleine ❶,** rue St-Pierre, next to the church, and organize days of prayer, silence, and study. Most boarders are pilgrims, but the site is open to all. (☎33 22 14. Kitchen. Sheets €3. Reception closed noon-1:30pm. 12-bed dorms €8; doubles €11; singles €15. Cash only.)

Pick up groceries at the **Vival** supermarket, near the bottom of rue St-Etienne (open July-Aug. M-Sa 8:30am-2pm and 2:30-8pm, Su 9am-2pm and 2:30-8pm; Sept.-June M-Sa 8:30am-12:30pm and 3-7pm, Su 9am-12:30pm; MC/V) and picnic on the terrace behind the cathedral for the most expansive view in town. With its ruddy tile floor and smoky fireplace, the candlelit **Auberge de la Coquille ❷,** 81 rue St-Pierre, suits the local specialties it serves, including spicy escargot (12 for €12) and crumbling rounds of local *époisses* cheese (€3.50). The *menu bourguignon* (€10.90), which includes a ham-and-egg *galette*, a *crêpe* with honey, and a glass of red wine, provides the perfect fuel to finish the trek up the Vézelay hill. (☎33 35 57. 3- and 4-course *menus* from €13. Reservations recommended. Open daily June-Aug. noon-2pm and 7-9pm. MC/V.) At **Le Bouganville ❸,** 28 rue St-Etienne, vegetarians can dive into the four-course *menu du jardinier* (€20), which includes a salad, vegetables, cheese, and dessert, while carnivores can enjoy *noix de joue de porc au pain d'épices* (pork braised in a gingerbread sauce; €13) in a homey interior. (☎33 27 57. *Plats* from €11. Reservations recommended. Open Feb.-Nov. M and Th-Su noon-2pm and 7-9pm. MC/V.) At the foot of the hill, **La Dent Creuse ❷**, at the intersection of pl. du Champ de Foire and rue St-Etienne, offers a pizza *menu*, with options like the loaded *Bourguignonne* (tomatoes, cheese, cream, champignons, *escargots*, and eggs) and à la carte regional *plats* from €9.50, all of which visitors can enjoy on a panoramic terrace. (☎33 36 33. *Menus* €14-24. Open daily mid-Mar. to mid-Jan. noon-2pm and 7-10pm. MC/V.)

SIGHTS AND OUTDOOR ACTIVITIES. All roads in Vézelay converge at the famous hilltop **Basilique Ste-Madeleine.** An impressive representation of both the Romanesque and Gothic styles, the church has an intricately sculpted tympanum above the doors to its cavernous interior. (☎33 39 50. Open daily sunrise to sunset. Closed during mass. Tours in English with reservation; pamphlets in English €5.) **Concerts and performances** take place in the basilica and around town most summer nights; call the tourist office for info (tickets free-€25). The *caves* of local winery **Caves du Pèlerin,** 32 rue St-Etienne, offer guided tours and tastings. (☎33 30 84. French tours mid-Apr. to mid-Sept. Sa-Su 2:30-5pm. Tours in Dutch, English, German, and Spanish by reservation; reserve by at least the Th before your visit. €5, under 18 free. MC/V.) For a break from the old-world charm of Vézelay, step into **Musée Zervos**, rue St-Etienne, to view a sampling of modern art collected by French art critic Christian Zervos. Several Calder mobiles hang overhead, and works by Picasso, Ernst, Giacometti, and Kandinsky adorn the walls. (☎32 39 26. Open daily mid-Mar. to mid-Nov. 10am-6pm; last entry 5:20pm. €3, students €2, under 18 free.)

For a more adventurous way to return from Vézelay to Avallon, head downhill to St-Père (2km) and drop by the **Canoë-Kayak Club d'Avallon,** on rue des Graviers, across from the St-Père campsite. By canoe, raft, or kayak, you can take a half-day trip from St-Père to Sermizelles. Swimming ability is a must; insurance is highly recommended. (☎33 35 64. €26 per 2hr. trip for 2 people, €40 per ½-day for 2 people, €48 per day. Open daily 9:30am-5pm.) **A.B. Loisirs** (see **Transportation and Practical Information**) offers rafting (€33-41), *cave* explorations (guided tour ½-day €37), and horseback riding (€17 per hr, €34 per 2hr.).

SÉMUR-EN-AUXOIS ☎03 80

The crumbling towers that protect the *vieille ville* and seventh-century château of Sémur-en-Auxois (SAY-MOOR uhn ohk-SWAH; pop. 5000) have long defined its identity; the name of this 2000-year-old town stems from its Roman title, *Sene Muros*, meaning "old walls." Overlooking a bend in the Armençon River, the provincial town offers little other than stunning views of the walls and quirky specialty shops—which sell everything from ancient books to circus supplies. Nevertheless, with its rooted local community and old-fashioned accommodations, this summer tourist spot feels thoroughly unspoiled.

TRANSPORTATION AND PRACTICAL INFORMATION. TRANSCO (☎42 11 00) runs Rapides de Côte d'Or **buses** (☎78 93 33) from Sémur to Avallon (40min.; M-Sa 8:25am, 1:44, 7:50pm, Su 12:46, 7:59pm; €7.20) and Dijon (1½hr.; M-Sa 7:10am, 1, 6pm, Su 6pm; €11). Schedules are at the tourist office and the stop at rue de la Liberté. For a **taxi,** call ☎96 60 18. Rent **bikes** at **R.D.X.,** 2 rue du Bourg Voisin. (☎97 01 91. €8 per ½-day, €13 per day. Open Tu-Sa June-Aug. 9am-noon and 2-7pm; Sept.-May 9:30am-noon and 2-6:30pm. MC/V.)

The **tourist office,** pl. Gaveau, where rue de la Liberté meets the gates of the *vieille ville*, has bus schedules, free maps, a list of hotels, and an SNCF info and reservation office. (☎97 05 96; www.ville-semur-en-auxois.fr. Open July-Aug. M-Sa 9:30am-1pm and 1:45-7pm, Su 10am-12:30pm and 3-6pm; Sept.-June Tu-Sa 9am-noon and 2-6pm. SNCF info office open Tu-F 9am-noon and 2-6pm, Sa 9am-noon and 2-5pm.) Other services include: a **laundromat** at the Centre Commercial Champion (open daily 8am-8pm); **police** *municipale* at rue de la Fontaignotte (☎97 01 11); a **hospital** (☎89 64 64; open 24hr.) on av. Pasteur, east of the Centre Commercial; a **pharmacie de garde** (location listed on every pharmacy's window); **Internet** access at the **Cyber KFE** inside the Hôtel du Commerce, 19 rue de la Liberté (☎96 64 40; €2 per 30min.; open M-F 7:30am-8pm, Sa 8am-8pm) and at **Bar le Carpe Diem,** (see **Food,** below). **ATMs** and **banks** can be found on pl. de l'Ancienne Comédie, which also has a **post office** with **currency exchange** (☎89 93 06; open M-F 9am-12:30pm and 1:30-5:30pm, Sa 8:30am-noon). **Postal Code:** 21140.

ACCOMMODATIONS AND FOOD. **Hôtel du Commerce ❸,** 19 rue de la Liberté, close to the *vieille ville*, offers spacious, simply decorated rooms with bath, TV, and access to a terrace bar. (☎96 64 40. Breakfast €5. Reception M-Sa 7am-8pm, Su by reservation only. Reservations recommended during summer. Singles and doubles €37-55; quads €60. Extra bed €10. MC/V.) **Camping Municipal du Lac de Pont ❶,** 3km south of Sémur, offers a three-star spot in the sun next to a scenic lake with tennis courts, a beach, bike rental, laundry, and a mini-mart. From pl. de l'Ancienne Comédie, follow signs to "*Hotel du Lac de Pont;*" the campsite is just beside the hotel. Note that the signs are narrow and sometimes hard to find. (☎97 01 26. Open May to mid-Sept. Reception 8am-noon and 4-7pm. €3.70 per adult, €1.90 per child, €1.60 per car, €1.80 per site. Electricity €2.50. MC/V.)

For groceries, stop at the **Petit Casino** supermarket, located across from the church. (☎96 61 21. Open Tu-Sa 8am-12:30pm and 3-7:30pm, Su 9am-12:30pm. MC/V.) A small weekly market opens along **rue Buffon** on Sunday mornings. Rue Buffon has a number of affordable dining options, but the cheerful **La Goulue ❷,** 15 rue Buffon, stands out with its colorful décor and enormous portions. Chock full of regional dishes, the menu offers a tasty *escargot*-topped *crêpe bourguignonne* for €15. (☎97 28 97. 3-course lunch *menu du marché* €11. *Crêpes* from €10. Desserts from €4. Open summer daily noon-2:30pm and 7-10pm; low season M-Tu and Th noon-2pm, F-Sa noon-2pm and 7-10pm, Su noon-2pm. MC/V.) In an elegant wood-trimmed dining room, **L'Oriflamme ❸,** 16 rue Févret, channels the *vieille ville*'s medieval spirit with hearty meat-heavy *menus* (from €20) and an abundance of fish dishes. (☎97 32 40. Open M-Tu and Th-F 7-9:30pm, Sa-Su noon-1:45pm and 7-9:45pm. Reservations recommended in summer. MC/V.) Though Sémur is far from the ocean, you can float happily away at the nautical-themed restaurant and bar **Carpe Diem ❶,** 4 rue du Vieux Marché. Diners delight in a wide variety of omelettes (served all day; €5) or sip beer (from €2), often accompanied by live jazz. (☎97 00 35. Internet access free with purchase of food or drink. *Plat du jour* €7.50. Open M and Su 11am-10pm, Tu-Sa 11am-1:45am.)

SIGHTS AND ENTERTAINMENT. The tourist office schedules walking tours of the city, offers free brochures with self-guided itineraries, and runs a 45min. *petit train* in the summer. (July-Aug. Tu-Su; call tourist office for times. €4.30, ages 4-12 €2.70.) Don't miss the beautiful stroll around the ramparts and the orchard-lined Armençon river, a 10min. walk from the center of town. Romantics can take a moonlit walk down to the seldom-touristed **Pont Pinard** for a breathtaking view of the illuminated *vieille ville.* (From rue du Rempart, walk away from Notre Dame and make a left onto rue du Fourneau, then follow the signs. 10min. *Vieille ville* illuminated nightly mid-June to Sept. 10pm-midnight.) In the medieval town, down rue Buffon, mossy gargoyles menace the central *place* from the 15th-century Gothic facade of the **Collégiale Notre Dame.** The interior lacks the polish of other Burgundy cathedrals, but its stained-glass memorial to fallen WWI soldiers makes a peek inside worthwhile. The unusual windows show two soldiers kneeling before Joan of Arc as buildings behind them burn down in vibrant flames. Outside, a 13th-century tympanum on the **porte des Bleds** faces rue Notre Dame. (☎97 05 96. Open daily 9am-noon and 2-6pm.) Behind the church lies a quiet **park** perfect for a picnic. Filled with sculptures, local archeology, ancient metal plaques, and oil paintings—not to mention a huge statue of France's greatest hero, Vincengetorix—the small yet thorough **Museé Municipal de Sémur-en-Auxois,** rue Jean-Jacques Collenot, has it all. The collection of enormous snail shells will put the *escargots* on your plate to shame. (☎97 24 25. Open Apr.-Sept. M and W-Su 2-6pm; Oct.-Mar. M and W-F 2-5pm. €3.30, students €1.65, first Su of month free.)

At around 300 seats, the **Théâtre Municipale,** 11 rue du Rempart, is France's smallest opera house. Visitors will enjoy the impressive acoustics and architecture *à l'italienne.* (Check the tourist office for the season's schedule and ticket prices.) At night, to find the popular bars and *brasseries,* walk **rue Buffon** or **rue de la Liberté.** Playing an eclectic set of tunes ranging from hip-hop to be-bop, the bar and *brasserie* **Le Domysyl,** 13 rue Buffon, draws a youthful late-night crowd in this otherwise sleepy town. Food service available until close. (☎96 69 05. Beer from €2. Open M-F 10am-8pm, Sa 10am-1:30am. MC/V.) Each year on weekends in late May and early June, Sémur hosts **Fêtes de la Bague,** which includes a medieval festival with artisan products, music, theater, fireworks, and even horse races through the town. (Call tourist office for specific dates.) Thursdays bring **Jeudis de l'Eté,** a series of free concerts and *spectacles,* such as circus performers, to the streets of the town. (July-Sept. Call tourist office for details.)

RHÔNE-ALPES

As the Alps-bound train leaves the rolling countryside and begins its long climb into the mountains, riders abandon their newspapers to watch a stunning transition: hills give way to craggy peaks, calm rivers to rushing torrents, and lazy cows to dashing mountain goats. In the high Alps, vast snowfields and glaciers look down on mountainsides blanketed with wildflowers. The region's stunning beauty draws not only those who want to admire it, but also those who want to experience it up-close: world-class athletes descend on the area each year to hike, bike, ski, and climb its majestic peaks. A trip to the region isn't complete without at least a glimpse of Mont Blanc, Western Europe's highest peak, but the gentler ranges of the Chartreuse and Vercors provide an equally rewarding visit, dotted with tiny glacial lakes. Summer and winter visitors will find the most dependable weather and, naturally, the biggest crowds.

The region offers ancient alongside ultra-modern attractions, natural next to man-made wonders. Lyon, France's third largest city, is the area's major hub. Gleaming train stations, shopping centers, and concert halls attest to its current importance, while Roman ruins and Renaissance mansions reveal that the city's significance is nothing new. In Annecy, human architectural achievements take a backseat to those of Mother Nature. The pristine turquoise Lac d'Annecy is fringed by mountains, making the city a paradise for hikers and sailors alike. Higher up in the mountains, there's no doubt that skiing is the main attraction, but the hotels in Chamonix and Val d'Isère are also packed in the summer with hikers and climbers who visit to scale the rugged mountains.

HIGHLIGHTS OF RHÔNE-ALPES

CHILL with *chamois* (the antelope's smaller cousin) as you take in the amazing scenery along the many trails in Val d'Isère's **Vanoise National Park** (p. 481), the Alps's premier wildlife preserve.

ADMIRE the lake in **Annecy** (p. 461), where the well-heeled and well-booted meet for refined relaxation or rugged recreation.

INDULGE in gourmet luxury in **Lyon** (p. 444), arguably France's finest culinary center

LYON ☎04

Ultra-modern, ultra-friendly, and undeniably gourmet, Lyon (lee-OHN; pop. 453,000) is more relaxed than Paris and claims a few more centuries of history. Its location at the confluence of the Rhône and Saône rivers and along the Roman road between Italy and the Atlantic made Lyon an easy choice for the capital of Roman Gaul. Lyon's position as a center for global commerce never faded, from the Renaissance when merchants moved in for the tax-free markets, to the 15th century when it was Europe's printing house, to the 16th-century, when it became a silk paradise. Today, Lyon has shed its longstanding reputation as a gritty industrial city and is characterized by beautiful parks, a modern financial sector, and a well-preserved Renaissance quarter. However, the bustling city is best known as the stomping ground of world-renowned chefs Paul Bocuse and Georges Blanc and as an incubator of new culinary genius.

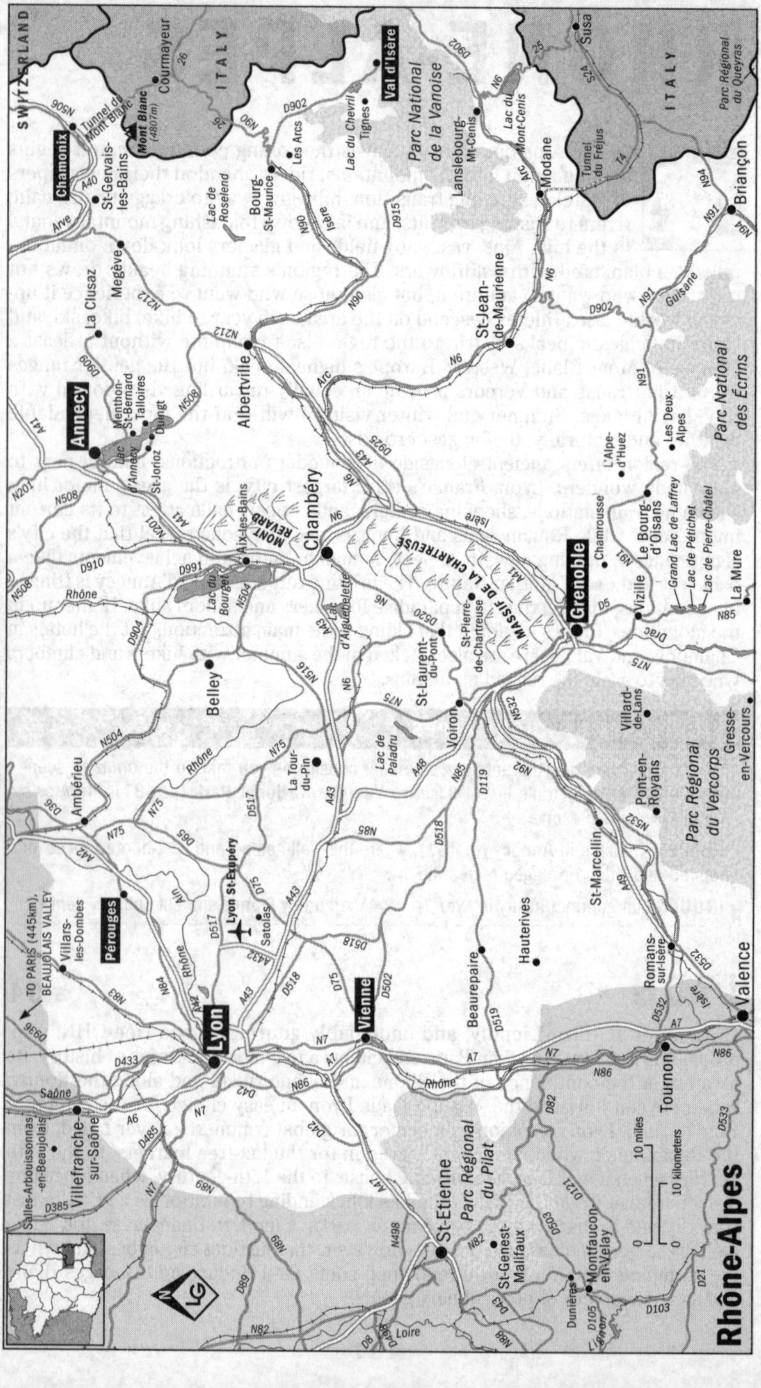

Rhône-Alpes
SWITZERLAND
ITALY
Chamonix
Tunnel du Mont Blanc
Mont Blanc (4807m)
Courmayeur
St-Gervais-les-Bains
Megève
La Clusaz
Annecy
Lac d'Annecy
Menthon-St-Bernard
Talloires
Duingt
St-Jorioz
Albertville
Bourg-St-Maurice
Les Arcs
Lac de Roselend
Tignes
Lac du Chevril
Val d'Isère
Parc National de la Vanoise
Lanslebourg-Mt-Cenis
Lac du Mont-Cenis
Modane
Tunnel du Fréjus
Susa
St-Jean-de-Maurienne
Parc Régional du Queyras
Briançon
Parc National des Écrins
Les Deux Alpes
L'Alpe-d'Huez
Le Bourg-d'Oisans
Grand Lac de Laffrey
Lac de Pétichet
Lac de Pierre-Châtel
La Mure
Vizille
Chamrousse
Grenoble
MASSIF DE LA CHARTREUSE
St-Pierre-de-Chartreuse
St-Laurent-du-Pont
Voiron
Lac de Paladru
Chambéry
MONT REVARD
Aix-les-Bains
Lac du Bourget
Lac d'Aiguebelette
Belley
La Tour-du-Pin
Ambérieu
Pérouges
Villars-les-Dombes
TO PARIS (445km), BEAUJOLAIS VALLEY
Lyon St-Exupéry
Satolas
Lyon
Vienne
Beaurepaire
Hauterives
St-Marcellin
Villard-de-Lans
Pont-en-Royans
Gresse-en-Vercors
Parc Régional du Vercorps
Romans-sur-Isère
Valence
Tournon
Salles-Arbouissonnas-en-Beaujolais
Villefranche-sur-Saône
St-Etienne
Parc Régional du Pilat
St-Genest-Malifaux
Montfaucon-en-Velay
Dunières
Rhône
Saône
Isère
Arve
Arc
Drac
Guisane
Loire
Lignon
10 miles
10 kilometers

INTERCITY TRANSPORTATION

Flights: Aéroport Lyon-Saint-Exupéry (☎08 26 80 08 26). The TGV, which stops at the airport, is cheaper and more convenient than the daily flights to Paris. **Satobuses/Navette Aéroport** (☎72 68 72 17) runs **shuttles** from the airport to Gare de la Part-Dieu, Gare de Perrache, and subway stops Grange-Blanche, Jean Macé, and Mermoz Pinel (every 20min., €8.60). **Air France,** 10 quai Jules Courmont, 2ème (☎08 20 32 08 20), has 10 daily flights to Paris's Orly and Charles de Gaulle airports (from €118). Open M-Sa 9am-6pm.

Trains: Trains passing through Lyon stop at **Gare de la Part-Dieu,** 5 pl. Béraudier (M: Part-Dieu), on the Rhône's east bank. Info desk open daily 5am-12:45am. Ticket windows open M-Th and Sa 5:15am-11pm, F and Su 5:15am-midnight. Trains terminating in Lyon go to **Gare de Perrache,** pl. Carnot (M: Perrache). Open daily 4:45am-12:30am. Ticket window open M 5am-10pm, Tu-Sa 5:30am-10pm, Su 7am-10pm. SNCF trains leave from both stations to: **Dijon** (2hr., every hr., €26); **Grenoble** (1½hr., every hr., €18); **Marseille** (1½hr., every hr., €44); **Nice** (6hr., 3 per day, €62); **Paris** (2hr., 17 per day, €60); **Strasbourg** (5½hr., 6 per day, €49); **Geneva, Switzerland** (3-4hr., 6 per day, €23). The **SNCF** office, 2 pl. Bellecour, is near the tourist office. Open M-F 9am-6:45pm, Sa 10am-6:30pm.

Buses: On the lowest level of Gare de Perrache and at Gorge de Loup in the 9ème (both ☎72 61 72 61). Domestic companies include **Philibert** (☎72 75 06 06), but it's usually cheaper and faster to take the train. **Eurolines** (☎72 56 95 30; www.eurolines.fr) travels out of France; office on the main floor of Perrache. Open M-Sa 9am-9pm.

Car Rental: National (☎78 53 46 89), Gare de la Part-Dieu. Open M-F 7am-10:30pm, Sa 8:30am-12:30pm and 2-6:30pm, Su 10am-noon and 3-6:30pm. AmEx/MC/V.

Bike Rental: Paths run along the banks of the Saône and the Rhône. **Holiday Bikes,** 56 rue Servient and 199 rue Vendôme, 3ème (☎78 60 11 10; www.holiday-bikes.com). M: Place Guichard. €12-14 per day, including helmet and lock; credit card deposit. Open M-Sa 9am-noon and 3-7pm. MC/V.

ORIENTATION

Lyon is easily navigable thanks to several very visible landmarks and two rivers, which separate the city into three sections. Lyon is also divided into nine **arrondissements.** Bounded by the Saône to the west and the Rhône to the east, the narrow **presqu'île** (peninsula) is the center of the city and home to the 1er, 2ème, and 4ème *arrondissements*. Here you will find Lyon's two major squares: **place Bellecour,** site of the tourist office and numerous bookstores, to the south, and **place des Terraux,** with the Hôtel de Ville and its giant statue of four horses, 15min. to the north. The 2ème includes the **Gare de Perrache,** pl. Bellecour, and major pedestrian shopping areas—**rue de la République** north of Bellecour and **rue Victor Hugo** to the south. North of the 2ème, the 1er is home to the city hall, giant opera house, Musée des Beaux-Arts, and the nocturnal Terraux neighborhood with its sidewalk cafés and student-packed bars. Farther north, the *presqu'île* widens into the 4ème and the famous Croix-Rousse hill, a residential neighborhood that once housed Lyon's silk industry. To the west of the Saône lies the oldest part of the city, **vieux Lyon** (5ème), with narrow cobblestone streets, cathedral, and Renaissance houses. From here you can walk up **Fourvière** hill to reach Roman ruins, the towering **Basilique de Notre-Dame de Fourvière,** and unbeatable views of the city below. Most of Lyon's permanent population, however, lives east of the Rhône in the 3ème and 6ème-8ème, home to **Gare de la Part-Dieu,** the enormous **Parc de la Tête d'Or,** and an ultra-modern commercial complex. The **Tour du Crédit Lyonnais,** a reddish-brown skyscraper shaped like a pencil, lies near the train station and mall and is Part-Dieu's most obvious landmark.

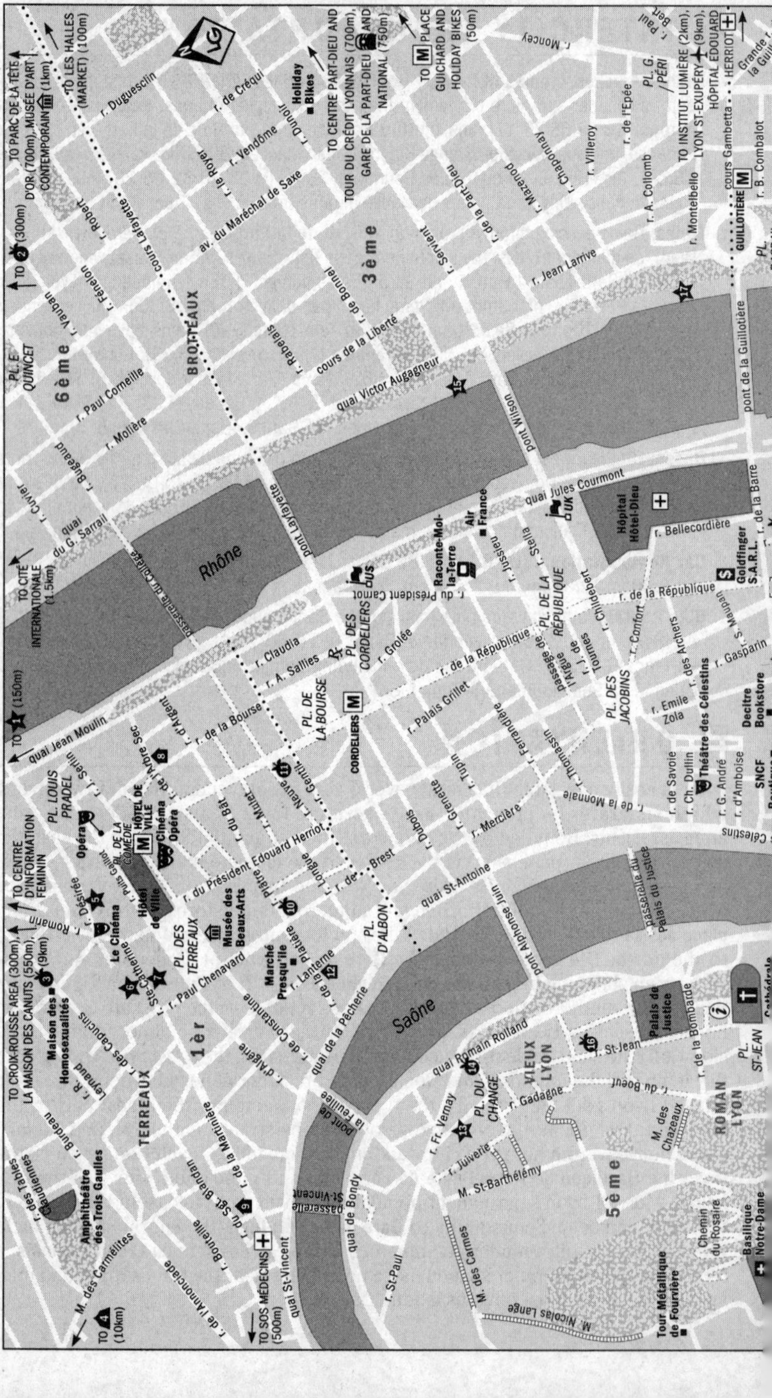
Rhône
Saône
6ème
3ème
1er
5ème
BROTTEAUX
TERREAUX
VIEUX LYON
ROMAN LYON
TO PARC DE LA TÊTE D'OR (700m), MUSÉE D'ART CONTEMPORAIN (1km)
TO LES HALLES (MARKET) (100m)
TO CENTRE PART-DIEU AND TOUR DU CRÉDIT LYONNAIS (700m), GARE DE LA PART-DIEU AND NATIONAL (750m)
TO PLACE GUICHARD AND HOLIDAY BIKES (50m)
TO INSTITUT LUMIÈRE (2km), LYON ST-EXUPÉRY (9km), HÔPITAL EDOUARD HERRIOT
TO CITÉ INTERNATIONALE (1.5km)
TO CENTRE D'INFORMATION FEMININ
TO CROIX-ROUSSE AREA (300m), LA MAISON DES CANUTS (550m), (9km)
TO SOS MÉDECINS (500m)
TO (10km)
TO (150m)
TO (300m)
Holiday Bikes
PL. E. QUINCET
PL. LOUIS PRADEL
PL. DE LA COMÉDIE
Hôtel de Ville
HÔTEL DE VILLE
Opéra
Cinéma Opéra
Le Cinéma
PL. DES TERREAUX
Musée des Beaux-Arts
Marché Presqu'île
PL. D'ALBON
PL. DE LA BOURSE
CORDELIERS
PL. DES CORDELIERS
Raconte-Moi-la-Terre
Air France
UK
PL. DE LA RÉPUBLIQUE
Hôpital Hôtel-Dieu
Goldfinger S.A.R.L.
PL. DES JACOBINS
Théâtre des Célestins
Decitre Bookstore
SNCF Boutique
PL. G. PÉRI
GUILLOTIÈRE
PL. RASPAIL
Maison des Homosexualités
Amphithéâtre des Trois Gaules
PL. DU CHANGE
Palais de Justice
PL. ST-JEAN
Tour Métallique de Fourvière
Basilique Notre-Dame
quai Jean Moulin
quai St-Antoine
quai de la Pêcherie
quai St-Vincent
quai de Bondy
quai Romain Rolland
quai Jules Courmont
quai Victor Augagneur
quai du G. Sarrail
pont Lafayette
pont Wilson
pont de la Guillotière
pont Alphonse Juin
pont de la Feuille
passerelle du Collège
passerelle du Palais du Justice
passerelle St-Vincent
cours Lafayette
cours de la Liberté
cours Gambetta
av. du Maréchal de Saxe
r. Duguesclin
r. de Créqui
r. Vendôme
r. Dunoir
r. Robert
r. Fénelon
r. Vauban
r. Paul Corneille
r. Molière
r. Bugeaud
r. Cuvier
r. Rabelais
r. de Bonnel
r. Servient
r. de la Part-Dieu
r. Mazenod
r. Chaponnay
r. Villeroy
r. de l'Epée
r. A. Collomb
r. Montebello
r. B. Combalot
r. Moncey
r. Paul Bert
r. Jean Larrive
Grande r. de la Guillotière
r. Claudia
r. A. Sallies
r. de la Bourse
r. d'Algérie
r. de la République
r. du Président Carnot
r. Grolée
r. Jussieu
r. Stella
r. Childebert
r. Bellecordière
r. de la Barre
r. Palais Grillet
r. Ferrandière
r. Thomassin
r. de la Monnaie
r. Mercière
r. Tupin
r. Dubois
r. Confort
r. des Archers
r. Gasparin
r. Emile Zola
r. de Savoie
r. Ch. Dullin
r. G. André
r. d'Amboise
r. du Président Edouard Herriot
r. Paul Chenavard
r. Longue
r. du Bât
r. Mulet
r. Neuve
r. de Brest
r. de la Platière
r. Lanterne
r. de Constantine
r. Romarin
r. Désirée
r. Puits Gaillot
r. Ste-Catherine
r. des Capucins
r. Leynaud
r. Burdeau
r. des Tables Claudiennes
M. des Carmélites
r. de l'Annonciade
r. Bouteille
r. du Sgt. Blandan
r. de la Martinière
r. St-Paul
r. Juiverie
r. Fr. Vernay
r. Gadagne
r. St-Jean
r. du Bœuf
r. de la Bombarde
M. des Chazeaux
Chemin du Rosaire
M. St-Barthélémy
M. des Carmes
M. Nicolas Lange
Célestins

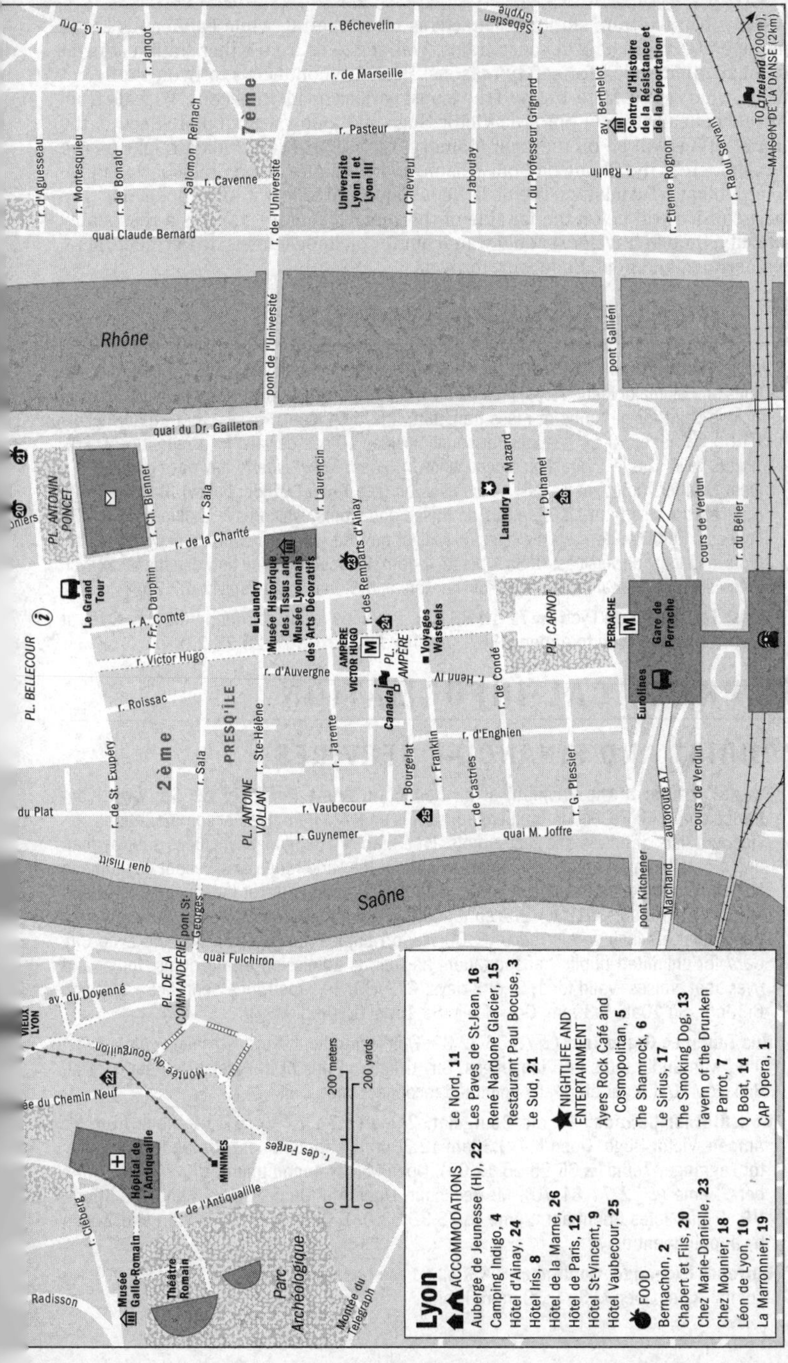
Lyon
ACCOMMODATIONS
Auberge de Jeunesse (HI), 22
Camping Indigo, 4
Hôtel d'Ainay, 24
Hôtel Iris, 8
Hôtel de la Marne, 26
Hôtel de Paris, 12
Hôtel St-Vincent, 9
Hôtel Vaubecour, 25
FOOD
Bernachon, 2
Chabert et Fils, 20
Chez Marie-Danielle, 23
Chez Mounier, 18
Léon de Lyon, 10
La Marronnier, 19
Le Nord, 11
Les Paves de St-Jean, 16
René Nardone Glacier, 15
Restaurant Paul Bocuse, 3
Le Sud, 21
NIGHTLIFE AND ENTERTAINMENT
Ayers Rock Café and Cosmopolitan, 5
The Shamrock, 6
Le Sirius, 17
The Smoking Dog, 13
Tavern of the Drunken Parrot, 7
Q Boat, 14
CAP Opera, 1
0
200 meters
200 yards
Rhône
Saône
PRESQU'ILE
2ème
7ème
PL. BELLECOUR
PL. ANTONIN PONCET
PL. ANTOINE VOLLAN
PL. AMPÈRE
PL. CARNOT
PL. DE LA COMMANDERIE
AMPÈRE VICTOR HUGO
PERRACHE
Gare de Perrache
Eurolines
Le Grand Tour
Laundry
Musée Historique des Tissus and Musée Lyonnais des Arts Décoratifs
Voyages Wasteels
Canada
Université Lyon II et Lyon III
Centre d'Histoire de la Résistance et de la Déportation
Hôpital de L'Antiquaille
MINIMES
VIEUX LYON
Musée Gallo-Romain
Théâtre Romain
Parc Archéologique
TO Ireland (200m); MAISON DE LA DANSE (2km)
quai Claude Bernard
quai du Dr. Gailleton
quai Tilsitt
quai Fulchiron
quai M. Joffre
pont de l'Université
pont Galliéni
pont Kitchener
pont St. Georges
autoroute A7
Marchand
cours de Verdun
r. de l'Université
r. Béchevelin
r. de Marseille
r. Pasteur
r. Cavenne
r. Salomon Reinach
r. Chevreul
r. Jaboulay
r. du Professeur Grignard
av. Berthelot
r. Raulin
r. Etienne Rognon
r. Raoul Servant
r. Sébastien Gryphe
r. G. Dru
r. Janqot
r. d'Aguesseau
r. Montesquieu
r. de Bonald
r. Ch. Bienner
r. Sala
r. de la Charité
r. Laurencin
r. des Remparts d'Ainay
r. Mazard
r. Duhamel
r. du Bélier
r. A. Comte
r. Fr. Dauphin
r. Victor Hugo
r. Roissac
r. d'Auvergne
r. Henri IV
r. de Condé
r. d'Enghien
r. Jarente
r. Ste-Hélène
r. Bourgelat
r. Franklin
r. de Castries
r. G. Plessier
r. Vaubecour
r. Guynemer
r. de St. Exupéry
du Plat
av. du Doyenné
Montée du Gourguillon
Montée du Chemin Neuf
r. des Farges
r. de l'Antiquaille
r. Cléberg
Radisson
Montée du Télégraph

RHÔNE-ALPES

Of Lyon's two train stations, **Perrache** is more central, while **Part-Dieu** is larger and operates more long-distance trains. Walking to or from either station at night is not recommended for safety reasons. Both are connected to Lyon's efficient **Metro,** which is the fastest way to the **tourist pavilion** on pl. Bellecour. To walk from Perrache, head straight onto rue Victor Hugo and follow it until pl. Bellecour; the tourist office will be on the right (15min.). From Part-Dieu, walk straight on rue Servient, cross the Rhône on Pont Wilson, and continue on rue Childebert to pl. de la République. Turn left on rue de la République and follow it to pl. Bellecour. The tourist office will be on the far side of the square (25min.). Lyon is a reasonably safe city, though travelers should watch out for pickpockets inside Perrache, at pl. des Terraux, and in pl. Bellecour's crowds.

LOCAL TRANSPORTATION

Public Transportation: TCL (☎08 20 42 70 00; www.tcl.fr) has info offices at both bus stations and all major Metro stops. *Plan de Poche* (pocket map) available from any TCL branch. Tickets valid for all forms of mass transport, including Metro, buses, and trams. Tickets €1.50, *carnet* of 10 €13; student discount includes 10 passes valid for 1 month (€10.80). Tickets valid 1hr. in 1 direction, connections included. *Ticket Liberté* day pass (€4.40) is a great deal for short-term visitors, as is *PassLyon* (see **Tourist Office,** below). The clean, efficient **Metro** runs 5am-12:20am, as do **buses** and **trams,** which have 2 different lines; T1 connects Part-Dieu to Perrache directly. A night *navette* (shuttle bus) runs between pl. Tarreaux and local universities; Th-Sa 1 per hr. 1-4am. **Funiculars** swing between the Vieux Lyon Metro stop, pl. St-Jean, and the top of Fourvière and St-Just until midnight. €2.20.

Taxis: Taxi Radio de Lyon (☎72 10 86 86). Perrache to airport during the day €40, at night €55; Part-Dieu to airport €36/50. 24hr. **Allô Taxi** ☎78 28 23 23.

PRACTICAL INFORMATION

TOURIST AND FINANCIAL SERVICES

Tourist Office: In the Pavilion, at pl. Bellecour, 2ème (☎72 77 69 69; www.lyon-france.com). M: Bellecour. Multilingual staff is eager to help. Free accommodations service and lists of hotels and restaurants. Free map in 7 languages includes subway map and a detailed map of the city center. Ask about the wide range of excellent city tours in French (English tours in summer). €9, students €5. Audio tours of the city in English and French; 1½hr. tours €10 for 2. Also for sale is a book describing walking tours through the 5 quarters included in the UNESCO World Heritage list (€5.35). Buy the *Lyon City Card* for unlimited public transportation, as well as admission to museums, tours, and river boat cruises. Valid for 1, 2, or 3 days; €19/29/39. Open June-Sept. M-Sa 9:30am-6:30pm, Su 10am-5:30pm; Oct.-May M-Sa 10am-5:30pm. MC/V.

Bus Tours: Le Grand Tour (☎78 56 32 39; lyon.legrandtour@voyages-naime.com). 1¼hr. tour, with audio tours in 6 languages. Buy tickets on bus or in hotels. Tour starts at pl. Bellecour. Get on or off at any point and reconnect later. Daily €17.

Consulates: Canada, 17 rue Bourgelat, 2ème (☎72 77 64 07), 1 block from M: Ampère-Victor Hugo. Open M-F 9:30am-12:30pm by appointment. **Ireland,** 58 rue Victor Lagrange, 7ème (☎06 85 23 12 03). Open M-F by appointment. **UK,** 24 rue Childebert, 2ème (☎72 77 81 70). M: Bellecour. Open M-F 9am-12:30pm and 2-5:30pm. **US,** 1 quai Jules Courmant, 2ème (☎78 38 33 03). Open M-F 10am-noon and 2-5pm by appointment only.

Currency Exchange: Goldfinger S.A.R.L., 81 rue de la République (☎72 40 06 00). No commission. Open M-Sa 9:30am-6:30pm.

LOCAL SERVICES

English-Language Bookstore: Decitre, 6 pl. Bellecour, 2ème (☎26 68 00 12; www.decitre.fr). Helpful English-speaking staff. Open M-Sa 9:30am-7pm. MC/V.

Budget Travel: Voyage Wasteels, 5 pl. Ampère, 2ème (☎78 42 09 02). M: Ampère Victor Hugo. Open M-F 9:30am-12:30pm and 2-6pm.

Women's Center: Centre d'Information Féminin, 18 pl. Tolozan, 1er (☎78 39 32 25; www.infofemmes.com). Open M-F 9am-1pm and 1:30-5pm.

GLBT Resources: Maison des Homosexualities, 19 rue des Capucins, 1er (☎78 27 10 10; www.aris-lyon.org). Call for events schedule.

Laundromat: 19 rue Ste-Hélène, north of pl. Ampère, 2ème. Wash €3.50 per 6kg. Open daily 7:30am-8:30pm. Also at 51 rue de la Charité, 2ème. Wash €3.10 per 7kg. Open daily 6am-9pm.

EMERGENCY AND COMMUNICATIONS

Police: 47 rue de la Charité (☎78 42 26 56). M: Perrache.

Crisis Lines: AIDS info service (☎78 27 80 80). **SOS Amitié** (☎78 29 88 88).

24hr. Pharmacy: Pharmacie Blanchet, 5 pl. des Cordeliers, 2ème (☎78 42 12 42). M: Cordeliers. Serves as the **pharmacie de garde.** Night fee €4.

Hospitals: All hospitals should have English-speaking doctors on call. **Hôpital Edouard Herriot,** 5 pl. Arsonval, 3ème. M: Grange Blanche. Best for emergencies, but far from the town center. More central is **Hôpital Hôtel-Dieu,** 1 pl. de l'Hôpital, 2ème. M: Bellecour. The central city hospital line (☎08 20 08 20 69) will tell you where to go. **SOS Médecins,** 10 pl. Dumas de Loire, 9ème (☎78 83 51 51), arranges home visits.

Internet Access: Free Wi-Fi at the Bellecour McDonald's. **Raconte Moi la Terre** (☎78 92 60 23), at the intersection of rue Grolee and rue Thomassin, 2ème. M: Cordeliers. €4 per hr. Open M noon-7:30pm, Tu-Sa 10am-7:30pm.

Post Office: Pl. Antonin Poncet, 2ème (☎72 40 65 22), next to pl. Bellecour. **Currency exchange** and **ATM.** Open M-F 8am-7pm, Sa 8:30am-12:30pm. **Postal Codes:** 69001-69009; last digit indicates *arrondissement.*

ACCOMMODATIONS AND CAMPING

France's second largest financial center (after Paris, *bien sûr*) is filled on most weeknights with businessmen who leave town on the weekends. September is the busiest season in Lyon; it's easier and cheaper to find a place in the summer, but it's still wise to reserve ahead. A room less than €30 is a rare find. Low-end hotels cluster east of **place Carnot** and prices rise toward **place Bellecour,** but there are inexpensive options just north of **place des Terraux.** The accommodations in *vieux Lyon,* aside from the hostel, tend to break budgets.

Auberge de Jeunesse (HI), 41-45 montée du Chemin Neuf, 5ème (☎15 05 50; fax 15 05 51). M: Vieux Lyon. Prime location in *vieux Lyon.* Grassy terrace offers breathtaking views, and a lively bar makes this the place to meet fellow backpackers. Some small rooms feature private baths. All baths are being renovated. Breakfast included. Laundry €4.05. Internet access €4.80 per hr. Reception 24hr. 6-night max. stay. Reservations (by fax only) recommended, especially in summer. Dorms €20. MC/V. ❷

Hôtel Iris, 36 rue de l'Arbre Sec (☎78 39 93 80; www.hoteliris.freesurf.fr). M: Hôtel de Ville. This convent-turned-hotel boasts a tranquil atmosphere in a prime location near Terreaux. Creatively decorated rooms demonstrate the artistic eye of its cheerful owner. Breakfast €5.50. Reception 8am-8:30pm. Reserve 2 weeks ahead in summer. Singles and doubles with sink €40-42, with bath €48-50. MC/V. ❸

Hôtel d'Ainay, 14 rue des Remparts d'Ainay, 2ème (☎78 42 43 42). M: Ampère-Victor Hugo. On bustling pl. Ampère, steps from the Metro. Spacious rooms with large windows, some with private baths. No communal showers. Breakfast €4.50. Reception 24hr. Singles €27, with shower €42; doubles €32/48. Extra bed €8. MC/V. ❷

Hôtel de la Marne, 78 rue de la Charité (☎78 37 07 46). M: Perrache. 2min. from Gare de Perrache. A recently renovated hotel with quiet, air-conditioned rooms with spacious bathrooms. The potpourri and abstract art in each room create a homey yet modern atmosphere. Breakfast €6. Reception 24hr. Singles €47; doubles €53-63. MC/V. ❹

Hôtel de Paris, 16 rue de la Platière, 1er (☎78 28 00 95; www.hoteldeparis-lyon.com), near pl. de Terraux. M: Hôtel de Ville. Small, no-frills rooms, many with balconies, in a good location. Clean, recently renovated bathrooms. The comfortable lobby is adorned with black-and-white Impressionist drawings of Lyon. Elevator. Breakfast €6.50. Reception 24hr. Singles €45-50; doubles €54-74; triples €84. MC/V. ❹

Hôtel St-Vincent, 9 rue Pareille, 1er (☎78 27 22 56; www.hotel-saintvincent.com), off quai St-Vincent. M: Hôtel de Ville. On a quiet street near the Saône. Comfortable rooms with white walls, wooden floors and sparkling clean bathrooms. Breakfast €5.50. Reception 24hr. Reserve ahead. Singles €50; doubles €60; triples €70. MC/V. ❸

Hôtel Vaubecour, 28 rue Vaubecour, 2ème (☎78 37 44 91; fax 78 42 90 17). M: Ampère-Victor Hugo. Quiet rooms with high ceilings on the 3rd fl. of an old building. The beds may not be the most comfortable, but the prices are hard to beat. Breakfast €4. Shower €2.50. Reception M-Sa 7am-10pm, Su 7am-12:30pm and 6:30-10pm; ring the bell to be let in. Reservations recommended June-Sept. Singles €28, with shower €37; double €35/45; triples €48-55; quads €70; quint €90. Extra bed €15. MC/V. ❷

Camping Indigo, 10km from Lyon (☎78 35 64 55; lyon@camping-indigo.com). From the Bellecour, M: line D to "Gare de Vaise." Then bus #89 (dir.: Dardilly) to "Gargantua." Quiet, shady site features a pool, TV, game room, volleyball, playground, and newly-added bar with terrace. July-Sept. €16 for 2 adults, tent, and car; €3.72 per extra adult, €2.88 per extra child. Winter €13/3.10/2.40. ❶

FOOD

The galaxy of Michelin stars adorning Lyon's restaurants confirms the city's status as the culinary capital of France—and perhaps even the western world. *Lyonnais* food is bizarre, elegant, and extremely (very often, surprisingly) appetizing; one delicacy consists of cow's tongue served with potatoes and a mustard sauce, while another local favorite features doughy dumplings slathered in rich, artery-clogging cream. It's hard to go wrong when it comes to cuisine here: while most dinner *menus* don't dip below €16, equally appealing options can be found during lunchtime. And if you're going to splurge on food, what better place to do so?

LYON: KING OF THE KITCHEN

Famous chef Jean-Paul Lacombe offers high-end cuisine at **Léon de Lyon ❺,** 1 rue Pléney, 1er. (☎72 10 11 12. *Menus* €59, €118, and €150. Open Tu-Sa noon-2pm and 7:30-10pm. AmEx/MC/V.) However, the pinnacle of the *lyonnais* food scene is **Restaurant Paul Bocuse ❺,** 4km out of town, where the *menus* (€120-195) probably cost more than your hotel room. (☎72 42 90 90; www.bocuse.fr. MC/V.) These restaurants occasionally have more accessible weekend buffet brunches hovering around €30-40; check outside or call. Meanwhile, *gourmands* need not sell their souls to enjoy Bocusian cuisine; the master has several **spin-off restaurants** in Lyon, themed around the four corners of the earth: *Le Nord, Le Sud, L'Est* and *L'Ouest.* Whether heading north, south, east, or west, reserve well in advance.

Le Sud, 11 pl. Antonin Poncet, 2ème (☎72 77 80 00). M: Bellecour. Specializing in *la cuisine du soleil,* and appropriately decorated with a huge metallic sun, Le Sud serves Mediterranean fare in a casual dining room. The seafood dishes are worth the splurge (from €15). Pasta dishes from €12. *Menus* €19-22. Open daily noon-2:30pm and 7-11pm, F-Sa noon-2:30pm and 7pm-midnight. AmEx/MC/V. ❸

Le Nord, 18 rue Neuve, 2ème (☎72 10 69 69). M: Cordeliers. Sample Bocuse's traditional food where suits come to lunch and suitors come to impress. Embroidered napkins and signature plates create an upscale atmosphere in the famed century-old *brasserie.* Try the *saucisson* for a true treat. *Menus* €20-28. Open daily noon-2:30pm and 7-11pm, F-Sa noon-2:30pm and 7pm-midnight. AmEx/MC/V. ❹

René Nardone Glacier, 26 quai de Bondy, 5ème (☎78 28 29 09.) M: Vieux Lyon. People pack the terrace to enjoy a huge selection of ice cream in a variety of quirky flavors. €2 per scoop. Ice cream dishes €4-9.50. Open daily 9am-1am. MC/V. ❶

Bernachon, 42 cours F. Roosevelt (☎78 52 23 65). M: Foch. Don't come to this grand *pâtisserie* for a cheap baguette. Specializes in expensive but extremely delicious desserts (from €1.20), as well as other sweet delights. Open Tu-Sa 8:30am-7pm. MC/V. ❶

OTHER FLEURS-DE-LYON

For a happy medium between *haute cuisine* and university canteens, try one of Lyon's many **bouchons,** descendants of the inns where travelers stopped to dine and have their horses *bouchonné* (rubbed down). These cozy restaurants serve delectable local dishes (€16-20) and can be found along **rue Mercière** and **rue des Marronniers** in the 2ème, as well as lining **rue St-Jean** in *vieux Lyon.* Cheaper Chinese fast-food restaurants and *brasseries* line the streets off **rue de la République** in the 2ème, and dozens of kebab joints surround the **Hôtel de Ville.**

Chez Mounier, 3 rue des Marronniers, 2ème (☎78 37 79 26). M: Bellecour. Top-notch cuisine and great prices make this restaurant a good choice. Lunch *menu* €8. 4-course *menus* €11-20. Open Tu-Sa noon-2pm and 7-11pm, Su noon-1:30pm. MC/V. ❷

Chabert et Fils, 11 rue des Marronniers, 2ème (☎78 37 01 94). M: Bellecour. A well-known, well-loved *bouchon,* 1 of 4 on rue des Marroniers run by the same family. *Museau de bœuf* (snout of cattle) is one of many *lyonnais* concoctions on the €18 *menu*. For dessert, try the exquisite, creamy *guignol* (€5.70), a rich, rum-soaked cake with a hint of orange. The lunch *menus* (€8-13) are the best way to enjoy Chabert. Dinner *menus* €18-34. Open daily noon-2pm and 7-11pm, F-Sa until 11:30pm. MC/V. ❸

Chez Marie-Danielle, 29 rue des Remparts d'Ainay (☎78 37 65 60). M: Ampère-Victor Hugo. Her collection of awards and newspaper clippings may be intimidating, but chef Marie-Danielle makes guests feel at home as she whips up superb *lyonnais* fare. Lunch *menu* €15. Dinner *menu* €22. Open M-F noon-2pm and 7:30-10pm. MC/V. ❸

Les Paves de St-Jean, 23 rue St-Jean, 6ème (☎78 42 24 13). M: Vieux Lyon. A worthwhile splurge. Offers excellent value and savory meat dishes. *Menus* €12-20. MC/V. ❸

La Marronnier, 5 rue des Marronniers, 2ème (☎78 37 30 09). M: Bellecour. Another local *bouchon.* Features filling French *plats,* like black pudding with apples and potatoes. Lunch *menu* €12. Dinner *menus* €15-20. Open M-Sa noon-2pm and 7-11pm. ❸

MARKETS

There are festive flower, food, and art markets on the **quais** of the Rhône and Saône (open Tu-Su 8am-1pm), and small **supermarkets** and **épiceries** close to most major squares, including Bellecour, St-Jean, and des Terreux. For a homemade *lyonnais* meal, head to the **Marché Presqu'ile** supermarket, 9 rue de la Platière, 1er. (☎72 98 24 00. Open M-Sa 9am-8:30pm. MC/V.) Lyon's university restaurants may not boast culinary masterpieces, but they are far cheaper than most other options.

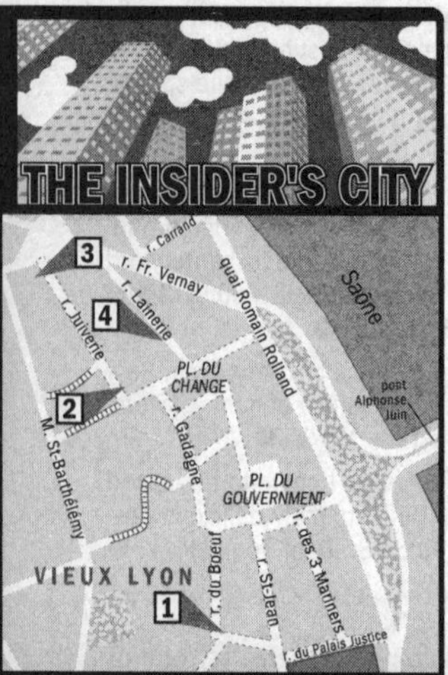

VIEUX LYON

Take a look beyond *vieux* Lyon's famous grand cathedral, charming *bouchons* (medieval restaurants), and dizzying network of *traboules* (tunnels) to find a hodge-podge of historical gems:

1. Check out the rose-colored tower behind 16 rue du Boeuf: its staircase spirals out of a flower-draped courtyard.
2. Rue Juiverie, or "Street of Jews," is named for the Jews expelled in 1394. The merchants and bankers who took their place left ornate friezes.
3. The two inner courtyards behind 8 rue Juiverie contain a centuries-old well and stunning 1536 gallery by the architect of Paris's Tuileries.
4. Finish the tour off at one of Lyon's oldest buildings, La Maison Claude Debourg, 14 rue Lainerie. The former magistrate's residence is an excellent example of the Flamboyant Gothic style.

SIGHTS

VIEUX LYON

Stacked against the Saône at the foot of the Fourvière hill, *vieux Lyon*'s narrow streets are home to lively cafés, hidden passageways, and magnificent medieval and Renaissance homes. The striking *hôtels particuliers*, with their delicate carvings and ornate turrets, sprang up between the 15th and 18th centuries when Lyon was the center of Europe's silk and printing industries. The regal homes around **rue St-Jean, rue du Bœuf,** and **rue Juiverie** have housed Lyon's elite for 400 years.

TRABOULES. The distinguishing features of *vieux Lyon* townhouses are their *traboules*, tunnels connecting parallel streets through a maze of colorful courtyards, often with vaulted ceilings and exquisite spiral staircases. Although their original purpose is still debated, the *traboules* were often used to transport silk safely from looms to storage rooms. During WWII, the passageways proved invaluable as escape routes for the Resistance. Many are open to the public at specific hours, especially in the morning. An informative 2hr. tour beginning at the tourist office is the ideal way to explore these hidden treasures; for those wanting to explore on their own, the tourist office also provides a list of open *traboules* and their addresses. However, inconsistent opening times make the guided tour more appealing. *(Tours in English and French every few days July-Aug. 2:30pm; Sept.-June irregular hours; contact tourist office. €9, students €5.)*

CATHÉDRALE ST-JEAN. St-Jean, a large but somewhat lackluster cathedral, dominates the southern end of *vieux Lyon*. Because the building took over 300 years to complete, its architecture features both Romanesque and Gothic elements. Look for the gradual shift in style where the rows of arches become more rounded. While many of the older stained-glass windows depict Bible stories, some of the newer ones installed to replace those destroyed during the Nazis' hasty retreat in 1944 are purely geometric. It's worth venturing inside to see the cathedral's impressive 14th-century **astronomical clock.** Every hour between noon and 4pm, automatons pop out of the top to a reenact the Annunciation. *(Open M-F 8am-noon and 2-7:30pm, Sa-Su 8am-noon and 2-7pm. Free.)*

FOURVIÈRE AND ROMAN LYON

Fourvière Hill, the nucleus of **Roman Lyon,** towers above the old city and is accessible via the rose-lined **Chemin de la Rosaire** (open daily 6am-9:30pm) and, for non-walkers, the **funicular** *(la ficelle)*, which leaves from M: Vieux Lyon.

BASILIQUE NOTRE DAME DE FOURVIÈRE. During the Franco-Prussian War, the people of Lyon and their archbishop prayed fervently to the Virgin Mary for protection; the thankful survivors erected this magnificent basilica in her honor. High upon a hill, the building's brilliant white exterior looms over Lyon and is visible from almost anywhere in the city. With octagonal turrets, the basilica bears some resemblance to a fortress, though many locals maintain that the building's unique architecture makes it look like *"un éléphant renversé"* (an upside-down elephant). Inside, colorful mosaics wrap around nearly the entire cathedral and depict the life of Mary, along with other religious scenes, such as Joan of Arc at Orléans. While many of France's cathedrals seem to blend together in travelers' memories, this one won't be easily forgotten. For amazing panoramic views of the city, ascend the **Tour de l'Observatoire,** or the nearby **esplanade Fourvière.** On clear days, scan for Mont Blanc, 200km east. *(Behind the Esplanade at the top of the hill. Chapel open daily 7am-7pm; basilica open daily 8am-7pm. Tower open by tour June-Sept. daily 2:30 and 4pm; Apr.-May W and Su 2:30 and 4pm. Elevator €2, under 15 €1.)*

MUSÉE GALLO-ROMAIN. Taking up five mostly underground floors, this surprisingly expansive museum educates and fascinates. History buffs and dunces alike will appreciate the vast collection of mosaics and statues, and such unique items as a bronze tablet inscribed with a speech by Lyon's favorite son, Emperor Claudius. Most artifacts are labeled in English and French. *(☎72 38 81 90; www.musees-gallo-romains.com. Open Tu-Su 10am-6pm. €3.80, students €2.30, under 18 free; Th free for all.)*

PARC ARCHÉOLOGIQUE. The Musée Gallo-Romain may provide a wonderful collection of artifacts, but this ancient park is the real thing. The Parc holds the well-restored 2000-year-old **Théâtre Romain** and the **Odéon,** both discovered when modern developers dug into the hill. Visitors are free to explore most of the hilltop ruins on their own. On summer evenings, relax and enjoy the **Nuits de Fourvière** (see **Festivals,** p. 450), which is hosted in both venues. *(Next to Minimes/Théâtre Roman funicular stop. Open daily mid-Apr. to mid-Sept. 7am-9pm; mid-Sept. to mid-Apr. 7am-7pm. Free.)*

LA PRESQU'ÎLE AND LES TERREAUX

Monumental squares, statues, and fountains are the trademarks of the *presqu'île*, the lively area between the Rhône and the Saône. Just to the west lies **place des Terreaux,** a large plaza covered with dozens of illuminated, geyser-like fountains. On the eastern edge of the square sits the imposing 17th-century facade of the **Hôtel de Ville,** while on the north side, opposite the **Musée des Beaux-Arts,** is the magnificent Fontaine Bartholdi, designed by the artist who created New York's Statue of Liberty (see p. 399). Lit in an alluring shade of crimson after dark, the **Opéra** building behind the Hôtel de Ville is a 19th-century Neoclassical edifice with what looks like an airplane hangar plopped on top of it.

MUSÉE DES BEAUX-ARTS. Lyon's excellent art museum takes visitors on a whirlwind tour through a diverse array of exhibits: an archaeological wing displays Egyptian sarcophagi and Roman busts; distinguished French, Dutch, and Spanish paintings, including works by Monet, Renoir and Picasso, line the third-floor walls; and an impressive sculpture collection graces the former chapel of this converted palace. Other highlights include a fascinating Islamic art display and an unbelievably large French, Greek, and Roman coin collection. Not into art? The museum is still worth visiting for the beautiful **garden** in its interior courtyard. This shady, flower-filled refuge is open to the public free of charge during museum hours. *(20 pl. des Terreaux. ☎04 72 10 17 40; www.mairie-lyon.fr. Open M and W-Su 10am-6pm. Sculptures and antiques closed 11:55am-2:15pm; paintings closed 1:05-2:15pm. €6, under 26 €4; students with ID free. MC/V.)*

MUSÉE HISTORIQUE DES TISSUS. While the rows of extravagant 18th-century dresses and 4000-year-old Egyptian tunics might not be considered chic today, those interested in clothing and textiles will enjoy this collection of fabrics and fashion from throughout history. Other highlights include scraps of Byzantine cloth and silk wall-hangings resembling stained-glass windows. Included in admission is the neighboring **Musée des Arts Décoratifs,** housed in an 18th-century hotel. The fully furnished rooms showcase a vast array of clocks, painted plates, silverware, and furniture from the Renaissance to the present. An upstairs room features a wrap-around mural of Lyon, painted in 1826. *(34 rue de la Charité, 2ème. M: Ampère Victor Hugo. ☎ 04 78 38 42 00. Tissus open Tu-Su 10am-5:30pm. Arts Décoratifs open Tu-Su 10am-noon and 2-5:30pm. €5, students €3.50, under 18 free.)*

LA CROIX-ROUSSE AND THE SILK INDUSTRY

Though mass silk manufacturing has left town, Lyon is proud of its former dominance of the industry in Europe. The city's Croix-Rousse district, a steep, uphill walk from pl. Terreaux, houses the vestiges of its silk-weaving days; it's here that Lyon's few remaining silk workers perform a different kind of delicate handiwork: reconstructing and replicating rare patterns for museum and château displays.

LA MAISON DES CANUTS. The silk industry of yesteryear lives on at this Croix-Rousse workshop, which provides the best introduction to Lyon's *canuts* (silk weavers). The workshop specializes in two methods of embroidery that are impossible to automate, and its weavers still use 19th-century looms. Friendly artisans demonstrate and explain their unbelievably complicated work and recount the evolution of the silk industry. Scarves and ties cost at least €32 in the gift shop, but you can take home a handkerchief for just €8.50. *(10-12 rue d'Ivry, 4ème. ☎ 78 28 62 04. Open Tu-Sa 10am-6:30pm. €5, students €2.50, under 12 free. Tours in French and English on demand daily 11am and 3:30pm and by request for groups of 10 or more.)*

PART-DIEU AND MODERN LYON

Lyon's newest train station and monstrous space-age mall form the core of the ultra-modern Part-Dieu district. Locals call the commercial **Tour du Crédit Lyonnais** *'Le Crayon'* (the pencil) for its resemblance to the writing utensil standing on end. Next to it, the seashell-shaped **Auditorium Maurice Ravel** hosts major cultural events.

CENTRE D'HISTOIRE DE LA RÉSISTANCE ET DE LA DÉPORTATION. Housed in a building where Nazis tortured detainees during the Occupation, this museum presents a sobering collection of documents, photos, and films about the Holocaust and Lyon's role in the Resistance. Audio tours lead visitors through displays of heartbreaking letters and inspiring biographies. *(14 av. Bertholet, 7ème. M: Jean Macé. ☎ 78 72 23 11. Open W-F 9am-5:30pm, Sa-Su 9:30am-6pm. €4, students €2, under 18 free; includes audio tour in 3 languages.)*

MUSÉE D'ART CONTEMPORAIN. This extensive, entertaining mecca of modern art resides in the futuristic **Cité International de Lyon,** a super-modern complex that also houses shops, theaters, and **Interpol's world headquarters.** The museum is known for its high-tech video displays; all of its exhibits are temporary—even the walls are built anew for each installation. *(Quai Charles de Gaulle, next to Parc de la Tête d'Or, 6ème. Take bus #4 from M: Foch. ☎ 72 69 17 17; www.moca-lyon.org. Open W-Su noon-7pm. €5, students €2, under 18 free.)*

INSTITUT LUMIÈRE. A must for film buffs, and interesting for ordinary movie-watchers (a.k.a. everyone else), the museum chronicles the exploits of the brothers Lumière, who invented the motion picture in 1895 (see **Life and Times,** p. 76). The museum is housed in their family's villa and exposes little-known facts—for example, that Louis created a forerunner to holograms in 1920. The Institut's complex also includes a movie theater, "Le Hangar du Premier-Film." *(25 rue du Premier-Film, 8ème. M: Monplaisir Lumière. ☎78 78 18 95; www.institut-lumiere.org. English audio tours €3. Open Tu-Su 11am-6:30pm. €6.50, students €5.50, groups of 4 or more €4.50.)*

PARC DE LA TÊTE D'OR. This massive park, one of the largest in Europe, is as diverse as the surrounding city. Its 259 acres offer a wide range of activities away from the hustle and bustle of Lyon: cyclists tour tree-lined bike paths, paddle boats dot the artificial lake, and African animals fill the free zoo. Visitors enjoy the tranquil 60,000-bush rose garden, while children delight in the park's merry-go-round and miniature golf course. The park's name (Park of the Golden Head) represents the element of mystery looming over its green expanses: legend has it that a golden head of Jesus lies buried somewhere on its grounds. *(M: Charpennes or Tram T1 from Perrache, dir.: IUT-Feyssine. ☎78 89 02 03. Open daily mid-Apr. to mid-Oct. 6:30am-10:30pm; mid-Oct. to mid-Apr. 6:30am-8:30pm.)*

ENTERTAINMENT AND SHOPPING

For info on summer entertainment and cinema, consult the weekly *Lyon Poche* and *Guides de l'été de Lyon* or the seasonal *Lyon Libertin* (€2), sold in many *tabacs*. For longer stays, pick up *Le Petit Paumé*, a comprehensive list of all the city's goings-on, available at l'EM Lyon, 23 av. de Collongue.

Lyon's major theater is the **Théâtre des Célestins,** 4 rue Charles Dullin, 2ème. (M: Hôtel de Ville. ☎72 77 40 40. Box office open Tu-Sa 12:15-6:45pm. Tickets €15-32, discounts for under 26.) The **Opéra,** pl. de la Comédie (M: Hôtel de Ville), has pricey tickets (€5-95), but the *Pass'Opéra Jeune* provides €10 tickets to certain shows for those under 26. (☎08 26 30 53 25; www.opera-lyon.com. Reservations office open Tu-Sa and M when there's a show noon-7pm.) The acclaimed **Orchestre National de Lyon** plays a full season from October to June. (☎78 95 95 95; www.auditoriumlyon.com. Tickets €15-45.) The **Maison de la Danse,** 8 av. Jean Mermoz, 8ème, M: Grange Blanche, keeps pace with the dance scene. (☎72 78 18 00; www.maisondeladanse.com. Tickets €10-45.) As the birthplace of cinema, Lyon is a superb place to see quality film. Both the **Cinéma Opéra,** 6 rue J. Serlin (☎78 28 80 08), and **Le Cinéma,** 18 impasse St-Polycarpe (☎78 39 09 72), specialize in black-and-white un-dubbed classics and international films, offering showings every night of the week. (€6.50, students €5.50, under 14 €3.50; W €5.50.)

Lyon's shopping scene will satisfy serious consumers and casual window-shoppers alike. The **Centre Commercial Part-Dieu,** across bd. Marius Vivier-Merle from Gare de la Part-Dieu, is your typical generic shopping mall, complete with chain clothing stores, food shops, a movie theater, bowling alley, and huge Galleries Lafayette. The 1er and 2ème *arrondissements*, particularly **rue de la République** and the charming **passage de l'Argue,** contain a regular mecca of upscale brand-name stores. Funky boutiques and poster stores cluster around **rue St-Jean** in *vieux Lyon*, and bookstores surround **place Bellecour.** Bargain-hunters will enjoy the massive **flea market** that sets up on Mondays on the *quais* east of the Saône.

NIGHTLIFE

Nightlife in Lyon is fast and furious. The vast array of riverboat clubs, student bars, Anglophone pubs, and gay establishments make going out in Lyon a constant adventure. There is a row of semi-exclusive joints off the Saône, on **quais Romain Rolland, de Bondy,** and **Pierre Scize** in *vieux Lyon* (5ème), but the city's best and most accessible late-night spots are the **riverboat dance clubs** by the east bank of the Rhône. Students buzz in and out of a series of tiny, intimate bars on **rue Ste-**

Catherine (1er) until 1am, when they head to the clubs. For a more mellow (but expensive) evening, head to the jazz and piano bars on the streets off **rue Mercerie.** When school is out of session, the scene is lively only on weekends. The tourist office guide provides a listing of spots that cater to Lyon's active gay community, and *Le Petit Paumé* offers superb tips. The most popular gay spots are in the 1er.

Ayers Rock Café, 2 rue Désirée (☎08 20 32 02 03). M: Hôtel de Ville. This Aussie bar (run, oddly enough, by a South African) is a cacophony of loud rock music and wild bartenders drumming on the hanging lights. Packed for rugby matches. Bouncers can be selective when the bar is crowded. Open daily 9pm-3am. Next door to Ayers and owned by the same group, the **Cosmopolitan,** 4 rue Désirée (☎08 20 32 02 03) serves New York-themed drinks, ranging from "Taxi Driver" to "Greenwich Village." Both bars are usually packed with students and offer €3 shots and mixed drinks from €7. Cosmo is slightly more chic than Ayers, with an atmosphere that is darker, a little less international, and a little more restrained. The best time to come to either is midnight-1am. Tu student nights, with Happy hour all night. Open M-Sa 8pm-3am. MC/V.

Le Sirius (☎78 71 78 71; www.lesirius.com), across from 4 quai Augagneur. M: Guillotière. Busiest riverboat on the Rhône. Cargo-ship-themed riverboat nightspot. A young, international crowd packs the bar for "serious" dancing to the beats of a wide variety of guest DJs on the lower-level dance floor. See website for concert listings. Open Tu-Sa 6pm-3am. MC/V.

The Shamrock, 15 rue Ste-Catherine (☎72 07 64 96). M: Hôtel de Ville. A happening but formulaic Irish pub with a smoky, wooden atmosphere and black lights. A young crowd knocks back pints (€5.20) to the beat of live concerts (nightly W-Su at 9pm). Open daily 6pm-1am. Happy hour 6-9pm. AmEx/MC/V.

Q Boat, across from 17 quai Augagneur (☎72 84 98 98). M: Guillotière. Plays electronic and house music on a swanky boat with 2 bars and a top-floor deck. Crowd tends to be chic young professionals. Dress well (black always goes); admission at bouncer's discretion. Open W-Sa 5pm-5am, Su 2pm-5am. AmEx/MC/V.

The Smoking Dog, 16 rue Lainerie (☎78 28 38 27). M: Vieux Lyon. The English-speaking bartenders serve €5 mixed drinks and €4.50 pints to loosen up patrons for Tu night's legendary "quiz night" (9pm). Guests can prep by browsing the bookshelves that cover every wall. Open daily 2pm-1am. MC/V.

Tavern of the Drunken Parrot, 18 rue Ste-Catherine (☎06 85 29 51 11). M: Hôtel de Ville. Get sloshed off extremely potent, homemade rum drinks (€2) in 28 flavors at this boisterous, nautically themed bar. Try the *citron* (lemon) or popular *piment* (hot pepper). Open daily 6pm-1am. MC/V.

CAP Opéra, 2 pl. Louis Pradel, 1er. A popular gay and lesbian bar, with red lights to match the Opéra next door. Black and purple décor and disco ball fit the festive mood. A mellow crowd gains momentum as the night progresses and spills out onto the lively stairs outside. Occasional *soirées à thème.* Open daily 9am-3am. Cash only.

FESTIVALS

During the summer, Lyon has a festival or special event nearly every week. **La Fête de la Musique** (June 21) and **Bastille Day** (July 14) naturally entail major partying. **Les Nuits de Fourvière** is a two-month summer festival held in the ancient *Théâtre Romain* in Lyon during June and July. Recent artists include The Strokes, Arcade Fire, Franz Ferdinand, and Sting, who perform alongside theater, dance, and film screenings. (☎72 32 00 00; www.nuitsdefourviere.fr. Tickets from €12, available at the Théâtre Romain or the FNAC on rue de la République.) The biennial **Festivals du Vieux Lyon,** 5 pl. du Petit Collège, 5ème, brings dancers and artists from around the world to showcase their talents in early and mid-December; odd-numbered years bring the **Contemporary Arts Festival,** while even-numbered years bring the

Dance Festival. (☎78 38 09 09. Tickets €15-36.) Every December 8, locals place candles in their windows and ascend with tapers to the basilica for the **Fête des Lumières,** an evening that honors the Virgin Mary.

DAYTRIPS FROM LYON

PÉROUGES

Trains run from Lyon (30min.; M-Sa 18 per day, Su 9 per day; €6) to Mexiemeux-Pérouges. From the station, turn left and follow the road around the curve to the roundabout; take a left and continue until the intersection at the Gendarmerie. Turn right, per the sign for Pérouges. Walk up the hill and turn right onto a dirt pedestrian road, which leads to the city gates (20min.). Arrive in the morning to avoid the tour groups.

The tiny, historic hilltop hamlet of Pérouges (pay-ROOJH) is such a source of pride for Europe that it was one of the official sights visited by the foreign leaders who attended the 1996 G-7 summit held in Lyon. It only takes a short time in the town to understand why the French government formally deemed it "one of the most beautiful villages in France." Pérouges's streets, called *galets*, are made with age-worn stones, collected from nearby rivers, whose shape and muted colors blend with the town's masonry. Exquisitely preserved, the houses, streets, and gardens are complemented by beautiful draping flora that invokes romantic visions of royalty. The town's culinary specialty is the *galette de Pérouges* (a large doughy pastry dripping in sugar and butter), which is served with **cerdon,** a magnificent wine. Whether they've come for the *galets* or the *galettes*, however, visitors quickly realize that there is virtually nothing to do in the tiny town. For a bit of area history, stop in at the small **Musée de Vieux Pérouges,** in the Maison des Princes, which showcases an assortment of historical documents, antiques donated by citizens, a sculpture garden, and a rotating contemporary art exhibit. The museum turret has a fabulous view of the rooftops below. (☎06 74 61 00 88. Open June-Oct. daily 10am-noon and 2-6pm. €4, under 10 free.) The **tourist office** is just outside the medieval city. (☎74 46 70 84. Open May-Aug. daily 10am-5pm; Sept.-Oct. and Mar.-Apr. Tu-F 10am-noon and 2-5pm, Sa-Su 2-5pm; Nov.-Feb. M-F 2-4:30pm.)

BEAUJOLAIS VALLEY

The most beautiful and authentic areas in the Beaujolais are difficult to access by public transportation; trains run between Mâcon and Lyon but stop mostly in uninteresting industrial towns like Villefranche. The best option is to rent a car in Lyon. Pick up the English tourist map highlighting points of interest and various wine routes, along with the helpful "Tours: Vistas of the Rhône Region," *which outlines 9 suggested driving itineraries. Venturing in by bike is more difficult but equally rewarding; rent a bike in Lyon from Holiday Bikes (☎78 60 11 10) and use one of the mid-point train stops on the Lyon-Mâcon line, such as Belleville-sur-Saône, as a starting point (bikes are welcome on the train). Take the scenic* Beaujolais Voie Verte, *a car-free path stretching from St-Jean d'Ardières near Belleville to Beaujeu, and offering 7 themed circuits (29-58km) along the way. Also available is the "Hikes through the Pays Beaujolais," with 16 shorter itineraries. Brochures with maps and descriptions of the area are available at the Lyon tourist office and at many hotels in the area. Ask for* Randonées en Pays Beaujolais.

Every mention of Beaujolais (BOH-jhoh-lay) induces a thirst for the cool, fruity wine that this region exports. Between the Loire and the Saône rivers, with Lyon at its foot and Mâcon at its head, the Beaujolais houses an important textile and lumber industry, but its claim to fame lies solely in its vineyards. The most touristed spot is **Le Hameau,** a wine museum in the town of Romaneche-Thorins that offers tastings, displays on winemaking, and a 3D movie about the Beaujolais tradition. (☎03 85 35 22 22; www.plaisirsenbeaujolais.com. Open daily Apr.-Oct.

9am-7pm; Nov.-Dec. and Feb.-Mar. 10am-6pm. Apr.-Oct. €16, Nov.-Dec. €13; under 16 free.) However, the real draw of the area lies outside of any city or museum. Endlessly rolling vineyards dotted with medieval châteaux, sleepy villages, and the occasional *dégustation* (tasting) await those who venture away from the main *autoroute*. Devoted wine enthusiasts should ask for a list of serious wine growers from the Lyon tourist office. A visit to the **Château de Corcelles,** not far from Belleville, makes for a lovely detour from the vineyards. Visitors can stroll through the inner courtyard, climb to the second-story chapel, and peer down into the dungeon of this 15th-century castle free of charge. Today, the château's main enterprise lies in the Beaujolais wine it produces from the surrounding countryside; bottles of the specialty spirit are available in the stable-turned-cellar filled with enormous casks. (☎74 66 00 24. Open M-Sa 10am-noon and 2:30-6:30pm.) Any tourist office in the area can provide directions to the castle, along with listings of other points of interest, ranging from **gardens** designed by Versailles's Le Notre to a flower-lined **cloister.**

VIENNE ☎04 74

In the days of the Roman Empire, Vienne (VYEHNN; pop. 30,000) was a Roman colony, a rare and coveted designation that entitled its inhabitants to all the privileges of Roman citizens. Today, Vienne is little more than a sleepy town on the banks of the Rhône, but the impressive vestiges of its glory days cluster in the town center and spread along a stretch of land across the river. In recent years, the town's name has become synonymous with the world-renowned Festival du Jazz à Vienne, a wine-soaked party that takes place in June.

TRANSPORTATION AND PRACTICAL INFORMATION. **Trains** leave from pl. de Pierre-Semard for both of Lyon's stations (20-30min., 45 per day, €5.60). The ticket booth is open M-Sa 5:15am-8pm, Su 5:15am-10pm. **Buses** are in front of the train station. Dubot **taxis** (☎57 69 21) congregate in front of the station.

Above and behind the train station is Mt. Pipet, which holds the Roman amphitheater. St-Romain-en-Gal and its treasure trove of ruins sit across the Rhône. To get to the **tourist office** from the station, walk straight on cours Brillier to the river; the office is on the left. The staff helps with train schedules and accommodations and offers a *guide pratique* with a tourist map, detailed city maps (€1), and themed walking tours of the city in French and English. (July-Aug. 2-3 per week 3:30pm; Sept.-June by reservation. €6.50, students €5.50. 2hr. audio tour in English €5.) **Internet** access (€7.50 per hr.) is also available. (☎53 80 30; www.vienne-tourisme.com. Open July-Aug. daily 9am-6pm; Sept.-June M-Sa 9am-noon and 1:30-6pm, Su 10am-noon and 2-5pm.) A **post office** in front of the train station has **currency exchange** and an **ATM.** (Open M-W 8:30am-noon and 1:30-6pm, Th 8:30am-noon and 2-6pm, F 8:30am-6pm, Sa 8:30am-noon.)

ACCOMMODATIONS AND FOOD. Most hotels in town start at around €50, but cheaper establishments are 8-10km outside of town; the tourist office provides a list and directions. The best bet is Vienne's hostel, located in the middle of the *centre-ville*. To reach the **Auberge de Jeunesse ❶,** 11 quai Rondet, 5min. from the tourist office, take a left along the river. Dorms overlook the Rhône. (☎53 21 97; mjcvienne.auberge@laposte.net. Breakfast €3.50. Sheets €2.80. Reception 5-9pm July to mid-Sept. daily; mid-Sept. to June M-F 5-9pm. Dorms €10. Cash only.)

Cafés and *brasseries* line **cours Brillier** toward the station, while **cours Romestang** has dozens of *pâtisseries* and *salons de thé*. A mid-sized **SPAR** supermarket is around the corner from the train station at 50 cours Romestang. (Open daily 7:30am-9pm. MC/V.) **La Medina ❷,** 71 rue de Bourgogne, a popular Moroccan restaurant, serves delicious and filling couscous (€11-16) in an intimate North African atmosphere. (☎53 51 35. Open M-Tu 7-10pm, W-Th noon-2pm and 7-10pm, F-Su noon-2pm and 7-11pm. MC/V.) Those craving Lyon-quality food should head to **Au P'tit Bouchon ❷**, 26 rue Voltaire, a small *brasserie* with a shady terrace and wooden tables topped with checkered cloths and packed with locals. (☎31 60 95. *Plats* €8.50-16. *Menus* €11-25. Open Tu-Sa noon-2pm and 7-10pm. MC/V.)

SIGHTS. Vienne's best sights represent what remains of its days as a Roman colony. The most spectacular of the city's Roman ruins is the well-preserved **Temple of Augustus and Livia,** in the heart of the pedestrian district. The temple dates from around 10 BC and was converted to a church during the Middle Ages. On the hillside, at the foot of Mt. Pipet, the steeply plunging **Théâtre Romain** is thought to have been one of the largest theaters in Roman antiquity; the well-restored amphitheater now hosts dozens of outdoor concerts. The flat-topped **Mont Pipet** looms over the amphitheater and offers spectacular views of the valley and its hillside ruins. The church and statue crowning its summit are dedicated to the Virgin Mary and have drawn pilgrims since the 19th century. From the theater, continue 15min. uphill on steep rue Pipet and take a left at the sign.

The oldest of the ruins is the **Gallo-Roman city,** across the river at **St-Roman-en-Gal,** accessible by a walkway from the *quai* or by the bridge at pl. du Jeu-de-Paume. Restored fountains gurgle amid the ancient streets, and elaborate gardens color the foundations of once palatial estates. The area contains the remains of some of the larger Roman homes, a forum, main streets, public bathrooms, baths, and underground storerooms. Analysis of amphorae (ancient storage jars) found here dated the Italian wine inside to around AD 124. The adjoining **museum** contains cutlery, amphorae, coins, and mosaics discovered in the city. (☎53 74 01. Open Tu-Su 10am-6pm. Museum and sites €3.80, students €2.30; Th free.)

Impressive churches fill the *centre-ville.* The facade of the **Cathédrale St-Maurice** is in decay, but the interior has an array of Romanesque capitals and stained glass. (Open daily 8:30am-6pm.) **Eglise St-Pierre,** pl. St-Pierre, was built on the ruins of a Gallo-Roman city in the fifth century AD and is now home to an archaeological museum with Roman artifacts. (☎85 20 35. Open Apr.-Oct. Tu-Su 9:30am-1pm and 2-6pm; Nov.-Mar. Tu-F 9:30am-12:30pm and 2-5pm, Sa-Su 2-6pm. €2.80.)

NIGHTLIFE AND FESTIVALS. Bars and cafés cluster on **rue du Musée, cours Romenstang,** and **rue Orfèvres. Cuba de Sol,** 3 rue du Musée, boasts a Cuban scene, with Che Guevara murals. (☎74 31 56 67. Open daily 7:30am-1am. MC/V.) **Boogaloo,** 1 rue des Carmes, features an Afro-Caribbean atmosphere and a huge variety of rum. (☎74 85 20 18. Open Tu-Sa 8am-3pm and 6pm-1am. Cash only).

From late June to mid-July, Vienne's famed **jazz festival** (www.jazzavienne.com) hosts world-renowned artists, usually at 8:30pm, in its ancient Roman **amphitheater.** Tickets are €27-30, but the *musique gratuite* (free music) that bookends the main shows makes the festival accessible to all; schedules are available at the box office, tourist office, or local supermarkets. From 11pm-2am, the free **Club de Minuit** sets up in the Théâtre de Vienne, behind the Cybèle gardens, packing awe-struck crowds into an intimate, cabaret-style venue. A makeshift stage at the **Jardins de Cybèle,** called the **Village du Jazz,** hosts free music, often featuring young bands and singers, every evening (4-8pm). **Le Châpiteau,** near the tourist office, offers free Jazz Mix performances from 11pm-4am. Tickets for the festival are available at the tourist office, the box office inside the amphitheater entrance (☎08 92 70 20 07), the Théâtre de Vienne (☎74 85 00 05), and at music stores across France. The amphitheater hosts pop, jazz, and classical artists all summer; the tourist office and the theater box office both have concert schedules.

GRENOBLE ☎04 76

A dynamic and diverse university town, Grenoble (gruh-NO-bluh; pop. 168,000) boasts great nightlife, charming sidewalk cafés, and shaggy hippies. Immigrant influxes in the 1920s and 50s gave Grenoble sizable Italian and North and West African populations, which contribute to its cosmopolitan atmosphere. Throughout the year, a thriving foreign exchange program fills the city with young scholars from all corners of the globe. The city is cherished not only by the students who call it home, but also by hikers, skiers, bikers, and aesthetes, who come for its snow-capped peaks and sapphire-blue rivers.

TRANSPORTATION

Flights: Aéroport de Grenoble St-Geoirs, St-Etienne de St-Geoirs (☎65 48 48), 41km from the city center. International flights only. British Airways and Easyjet fly to **London, England.** RyanAir flies to **Stockholm, Sweden.** Buses run between the bus station and the airport (€3.80). **Satobus** sends an hourly bus to **Aéroport Lyon St-Exupéry** from 5am-9pm (€20).

Trains: Gare Europole, pl. de la Gare. Ticket office open M-F 5am-8:45pm, Sa 5am-7:45pm, Su 6am-8:45pm. To: **Annecy** (1½hr., 18 per day, €17); **Lyon** (1½hr., 30 per day, €18); **Marseille** (4-5½hr., 15 per day, €37); **Nice** (5-6½hr., 5 per day, €57); **Paris** (3hr., 9 per day, €70). An **SNCF** office is on rue de la République, directly across from the tourist office. Open M-F 9am-6:30pm, Sa 10am-6pm.

Buses: To the left of the train station. Open M-Sa 6:15am-7pm, Su 7:15am-7pm. **VFD** (☎08 20 83 38 33; www.vfd.fr) runs to **Geneva, Switzerland** (3hr., 1 per day, €27) and **Nice** (7hr., 1 per day, €53). Frequent service to ski resorts and outdoor areas.

Public Transportation: Transports Agglomération Grenobloise (TAG) (☎20 66 66; www.semitag.com). Grenoble's extensive tram and bus network is useful only for transport to and from the *gare* and to the youth hostel, as the city center is pedestrian-friendly. Info desk in the tourist office open July-Aug. M-Sa 9am-6pm; Sept.-June M-F 8:30am-6:30pm, Sa 9am-6pm. Bus lines crisscross the city 6am-8:30pm, while 4 night lines run Th-Sa 9pm-midnight; 2 tram lines run daily 5am-midnight every 5-10min. Tickets €1.30, *carnet* of 10 €11; day pass €3.50, 5-day pass €12.

Taxis: (☎54 42 54). €68-72 to the airport. 24hr.

Car Rental: Rental agencies cluster around the train station. **Self Car,** 24 rue Emile Gueymard (☎50 96 96), across from the station. From €49 per day, €77 per weekend. Insurance included. 21+. Open M-F 7:30am-noon and 1:30-6pm, Sa 8am-noon. MC/V.

ORIENTATION AND PRACTICAL INFORMATION

The **Bastille** looms over the town from across the river. From the train station, the tourist office in the city center is a 15min. walk. Turn right onto **place de la Gare** and take the third left onto **avenue Alsace-Lorraine.** Follow the tram tracks through **rue Félix Poulat** and **rue Blanchard;** the tourist complex is on the left, before the tracks fork. The primarily pedestrian *vieille ville* stretches from the tourist office to the river, bounded by the **Jardin de Ville** and **Musée de Grenoble.** The winding streets intersect with many squares, making it tricky to navigate the city.

Tourist Office: 14 rue de la République (☎42 41 41; www.grenoble-isere.info). From the train station, tram lines A and B (dir.: Echirolles or Gières) run to "Hubert Dubedout-Maison du Tourisme." Hosts local bus office and post office. English-speaking staff provides maps, hotel info, and bus schedules. Tours of the *vieille ville* in English and French June-Aug. M-Tu and Th-Sa 10am, W 2:30pm; Sept.-May Sa 10am. €7.50, students and under 18 €5.50. Tours of the Bastille in English and French July-Aug. daily 3pm. €6,

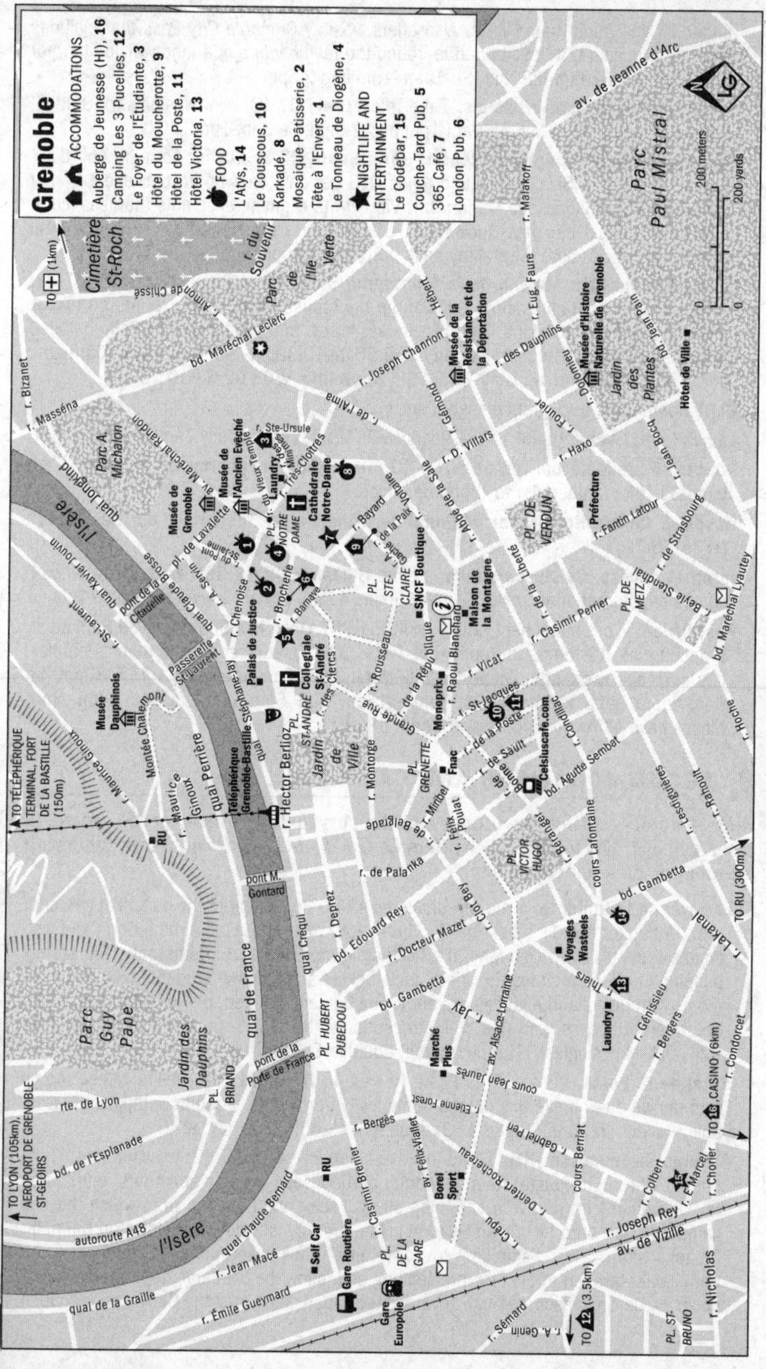
Grenoble
ACCOMMODATIONS
Auberge de Jeunesse (HI), 16
Camping Les 3 Pucelles, 12
Le Foyer de l'Étudiante, 3
Hôtel du Moucherotte, 9
Hôtel de la Poste, 11
Hôtel Victoria, 13
FOOD
L'Atys, 14
Le Couscous, 10
Karkadé, 8
Mosaique Pâtisserie, 2
Tête à l'Envers, 1
Le Tonneau de Diogène, 4
NIGHTLIFE AND ENTERTAINMENT
Le Codebar, 15
Couche-Tard Pub, 5
365 Café, 7
London Pub, 6
Cimetière St-Roch
Parc de l'Ile Verte
Parc A. Michalon
Parc Paul Mistral
Parc Guy Pape
Jardin des Dauphins
Jardin de Ville
Jardin des Plantes
l'Isère
TO LYON (105km), AEROPORT DE GRENOBLE ST-GEOIRS
TO TÉLÉPHÉRIQUE TERMINAL, FORT DE LA BASTILLE (150m)
TO RU (300m)
TO 12 (3.5km)
TO 16, CASINO (6km)
Musée Dauphinois
Musée de Grenoble
Musée de l'Ancien Evêché
Musée de la Résistance et de la Déportation
Musée d'Histoire Naturelle de Grenoble
Téléphérique Grenoble-Bastille
Palais de Justice
Collégiale St-André
Cathédrale Notre-Dame
SNCF Boutique
Maison de la Montagne
Monoprix
Fnac
Celsiuscafe.com
Préfecture
Hôtel de Ville
Voyages Wasteels
Laundry
Marché Plus
Borel Sport
Self Car
Gare Routière
Gare Europole
RU
PL. DE VERDUN
PL. VICTOR HUGO
PL. GRENETTE
PL. STE-CLAIRE
PL. ST-ANDRÉ
PL. NOTRE DAME
PL. HUBERT DUBEDOUT
PL. DE LA GARE
PL. DE METZ
PL. BRIAND
PL. ST-BRUNO
quai de France
quai Perrière
quai Créqui
quai Jongkind
quai Claude Brosse
quai Xavier Jouvin
quai Stéphane-Jay
quai Claude Bernard
quai de la Graille
pont de la Porte de France
pont M. Gontard
pont de la Citadelle
Passerelle St-Laurent
bd. Gambetta
bd. Edouard Rey
bd. Agutte Sembat
bd. Maréchal Leclerc
bd. Maréchal Lyautey
bd. Jean Pain
bd. de l'Esplanade
av. Félix-Viallet
av. Alsace-Lorraine
av. de Vizille
av. de Jeanne d'Arc
cours Jean Jaurès
cours Berriat
cours Lafontaine
autoroute A48
rte. de Lyon
Grande Rue
r. Hector Berlioz
r. de la République
r. Raoul Blanchard
r. Félix Poulat
r. Joseph Chanrion
r. de l'Alma
r. Casimir Perrier
r. Joseph Rey
r. Émile Gueymard
r. Jean Macé
0 200 meters
0 200 yards

under 18 €3. Audio tour €7.50. Also offers a 2-day *Grenoble City Pass* that includes entry to 1 museum, a *petit train* ride, round-trip *téléphérique* ride, and walking tour for €13. Open M-Sa 9am-6:30pm, Su 10am-1pm and 2-5pm.

Budget Travel: Voyages Wasteels, 7 rue Thiers (☎47 07 13; www.wasteels.fr). Student travel packages. Open M-F 9:30am-1pm and 2-6pm, Sa 9am-1pm. MC/V.

Ski and Climbing Equipment Rental: Borel Sport, 42 av. Alsace-Lorraine (☎46 47 46;fax 46 00 75). Skis, boots, and poles €13 per day. Snowboard package €17 per day. Cross-country package €8 per day. Via Ferrata climbing ensemble (harness, cord, and helmet) €10 per day. Snowshoes €7 per day. Open June-Aug. Tu-W and F-Su 10am-noon and 2-6pm; Sept.-May daily 9:30am-12:30pm and 2-7pm. MC/V.

Hiking Information: Maison de la Montagne, 3 rue Raoul Blanchard (☎44 67 03; www.grenoble-montagne.com). Across from the tourist office. Extensive info on hiking, mountaineering, and biking. Free brochures, maps, and expert advice. Sells detailed guides and topographic maps. Open M-F 9:30am-12:30pm and 1-6pm, Sa 10am-1pm and 2-5pm. **Weather:** ☎08 92 68 02 38. **Snow info:** ☎08 92 68 10 20.

GLBT Resources: www.grenoble-lgbt.com.

Laundromat: Lavomatique, 14 rue Thiers (☎96 28 03). Open daily 7am-10pm.

Police: 36 bd. Maréchal Leclerc (☎60 40 40). Call for the **pharmacie de garde.** Take bus #31 (dir.: Malpertuis) to "Hôtel de Police."

Hospital: Centre Hospitalier Régional de Grenoble, av. du Maquis du Grésivaudan (☎76 75 75).

Internet Access: Celsiuscafe.com, 11 rue Gutéal (☎46 43 36). Friendly owner welcomes an international crowd. €1 per 15min., €2.50 per hr. Open daily 9am-11pm.

Post Office: 7 bd. Maréchal Lyautey (☎43 51 39). Open M-F 8am-7pm, Sa 8am-noon. Branch office, 12 rue de la République (☎63 32 70), adjacent to the tourist complex, has **currency exchange.** Open mid-July to Aug. M-F 9am-noon and 1:45-5:30pm, Sa 9am-noon; Sept. to mid-July M 8am-5:45pm, Tu-F 8am-6pm, Sa 8am-noon. Both offices have **ATMs** outside. **Postal Code:** 38000.

ACCOMMODATIONS AND CAMPING

Budget hotels dotting downtown and the surrounding areas can be crowded; reserve ahead. The tourist office offers *Le Guide de l'Etudiant*, a free guide with information on long-term stays.

Le Foyer de l'Etudiante, 4 rue Ste-Ursule (☎42 00 84). Close to the historical center of town. A budget traveler's best bet for June-Sept., when it ceases to be a dorm and welcomes tourists. From Oct.-May, it's for female students and interns only. The stately building encloses a courtyard where backpackers and summer students mix. Spacious rooms with desks and high ceilings are a true bargain. Kitchen, piano, laundry (€2.20), free Internet access, and free Wi-Fi. Reception 24hr. June-Sept. singles €15; doubles €24. Oct.-May singles €280 per month; doubles €420. ❶

Hôtel de la Poste, 25 rue de la Poste (☎/fax 46 67 25). Large, well-furnished rooms with tall windows make this hotel a home away from home. 2 rooms with kitchen available. Reception 24hr. Singles €33; doubles €43-45. Cash only. ❸

Auberge de Jeunesse (HI), 10 av. du Grésivaudan. (☎09 33 52; www.fuaj.org). Take bus #1 (dir.: Pont Rouge) from the corner of rue Alsace-Lorraine and cours Jean Jaurès to "Quinzaine," in front of a shopping plaza. Facing the direction from which the bus came, turn left onto av. du Grésivaudan. The *auberge* is 3 buildings down on the right. Or, take tram A (dir.: Echirolles) to "la Rampe." Walk in the direction from which the tram came, turn left at the first intersection, and follow the "Auberge de Jeunesse" signs down av. de Grugliasco, through several intersections, and past the Casino supermarket

(15min.). Clean 3-year-old building features bar, patio, kitchen, and laundry (€3). Most of the 2- to 8-bed dorms have private shower and toilet. Breakfast included. Wi-Fi €2 per day. Reception 7:30am-11pm. 24hr. keycard access. Dorms €21. MC/V. ❷

Hôtel du Moucherotte, 1 rue Auguste Caché (☎54 61 40; fax 44 62 52). Though the furniture and baths are somewhat antiquated, a convenient location near the tourist office and spacious rooms with comfortable beds make up for any lack of style. Ring bell to be let in. Breakfast €5.50. Reception 8am-10:30pm. Singles with toilet €25, with shower €30, with bath €33; doubles €33/37/43; triples €37/43/37; quads €54. MC/V. ❷

Hôtel Victoria, 17 rue Thiers (☎46 06 36; fax 43 00 14). Halfway between the train station and town center. While the 11:30pm curfew isn't ideal for sampling Grenoble's nightlife, the peaceful, spacious rooms overlooking a courtyard provide a true refuge. All rooms have TV. Breakfast €7. Reception 7am-11:30pm. Closed Aug. and around Christmas. Singles €39, with shower €46; doubles €47/55; quads €74. MC/V. ❸

Camping Les 3 Pucelles, 58 rue des Allobroges (☎96 45 73; www.camping-trois-pucelles.com), 4km from town in Seyssins. From the train station, take tram A (dir.: Echirolles) to "Charvat," then take tram C (dir.: Seyssins Le Prisme) to "Mas des Iles." Turn left; it's a few blocks down. Small campsite in a quiet suburban neighborhood features private spots divided by tall hedges. Reception 8am-1pm and 3-9pm. Laundry €3. 1 person, tent, and car €9.50. Extra person €4. Electricity €2.50. Cash only. ❶

FOOD

The most lively of Grenoble's 17 markets can be found on **place St-André, place St-Bruno, place Ste-Claire,** and **place aux Herbes.** (Open Tu-Th 7am-1pm; pl. Ste-Claire Tu-Th 7am-1pm, F-Sa 3-7pm.) A **Monoprix** with a small food section is across from the tourist office. (Open daily 8:30am-8:45pm.) There is a large **Marché Plus** at 22 cours Jean Jaurès, near the "Alsace-Lorraine" tram stop. (☎12 91 44. Open M-Sa 7am-9pm, Su 9am-noon.) A **Casino** with a **cafeteria** is at 46 cours Jean Jaurès, up the street from the HI hostel. (Open M-Sa 8:30am-8pm. Cafeteria open daily 11am-9:30pm.) Grenoble boasts many affordable restaurants, some with student *menus.* **Restaurants Universitaires (RUs;** ☎57 44 00) sell meal tickets (€2.70) during the school year. Grenoble's three RUs are on 5 rue d'Arsonval (open M-F 11:30am-1:30pm and 6:30-7:45pm), 6 pl. Pasteur (open daily 11:45am-1:15pm and 6:30-7:45pm), and rue Maurice Gignoux (open daily noon-1:15pm and 6:30-7:50pm).

Grenoble's diverse population has brought an unbeatable array of ethnic cuisine to the city. Asian eateries abound between **place Notre Dame** and the river and on **rue Condorcet;** North African establishments congregate around **rue Chenoise** and **rue Lionne.** Cheap pizzerias and Italian joints line **quai Perrière** across the river. For more traditional fare, cafés and *brasseries* cluster around pl. Notre Dame and **place St-André** in the heart of the *vieille ville.* Regional restaurants cater to locals around **place de Gordes,** between pl. St-André and the Jardin de Ville.

Tête à l'Envers, 12 rue Chenoise (☎51 13 42). This 7-table gem offers a creative international melange. Menu changes daily, depending on what's fresh at the market and in the creative mind of the expert chef, who describes each delicious plate as he brings it out. *Plats du jour* €11. Lunch *menus* €15-17. Dessert platter €9.50. Open Tu-F noon-3pm and 7:30pm-1am, Sa 7:30pm-1am. Reservations recommended. MC/V. ❷

Le Couscous, 19 rue de la Poste. No surprises here: guests pack the terrace of this unassuming restaurant to fill up on generous portions of its namesake. *Plat du jour* €7.40. Couscous €6.50-17. Open M 7-11pm, Tu-Su noon-2pm and 7-11pm. MC/V. ❷

Mosaique Pâtisserie, 3 rue Chenoise (☎01 91 28). An African twist on a French staple. Come to this beautifully-tiled *pâtisserie* for honey- and almond-saturated Tunisian pastries (€1-2.50), bargain salads (€4-5), and couscous (€7-13). The specialty mint tea is a refreshing way to get your caffeine fix. Open daily 8am-10pm. MC/V. ❷

L'Atys, 1 rue des Bons Enfants (☎43 84 13; www.latys.com), off cours Berriat. Vegetarians should be sure not to miss this unique restaurant, which celebrates all non-meat cuisine. Delicious spiced, organic vegetarian and vegan choices. The walls of the green-themed dining room are decorated with silk paintings by the English-speaking owner. *Plats* €12. *Menus* €20-30. Open Tu-Sa 11am-2pm and 7-11pm. AmEx/MC/V. ❸

Le Tonneau de Diogène, 6 pl. Notre Dame (☎42 38 40). This café screams college. A budget-friendly menu, location underneath a bookstore (one of Grenoble's oldest) and walls covered with Nietzsche quotes keep students coming back. Salads €4.50-8.40. *Menu* €7.50. Open daily 11:30am-midnight. Closed mid-July to early Aug. MC/V. ❶

Karkadé, 6 rue Servan (☎44 02 78). Intimate Egyptian *salon de thé* serves flavorful *karkadé* (hibiscus flower) tea. Egyptian-themed books, African instruments, and a rotating art exhibit surround low, cushioned benches. Pastries €3. Teas €4. Open Tu 11am-3pm and 6-11pm, W-F 11am-3pm and 6:30-11pm, Sa 6:30-11pm. Cash only. ❶

SIGHTS

TÉLÉPHÉRIQUE GRENOBLE-BASTILLE. These spherical gondolas, the city's icons, depart every 10min. and head for the **Bastille,** a 16th-century fort sitting 475m above Grenoble. From the top, on a clear day, visitors can look north toward the Lyon valley and its two converging rivers, or east over the ridge of mountains to the distant peak of Mont Blanc. From the Bastille, follow signs to the **Grotte de Mandaran,** a long and exciting (a.k.a. barely lit) cave—bring a flashlight. History buffs can continue 1hr. up to **Mont-Jalla,** where a flower-studded memorial tells the story of the Alpine soldiers who have protected Grenoble for centuries. Starting in the **Jardins des Dauphins** and ending at the Bastille, the **Via Ferrata** gives alpine climbers the chance to scale the hill's rock face using cables and metal rungs; the route was the first urban climbing site constructed in the world. Rent equipment at **Borel Sport** (☎46 47 46). The **Parc Guy Pape** trail offers a pleasant way to bypass the *téléphérique;* its trails wind through flower-lined gardens, starting in the Jardin des Dauphins and ending at the Bastille (1hr.). Be cautious: the trail has several steep staircases, many of which pass through poorly lit tunnels. *(Quai Stéphane-Jay. ☎44 33 65. Open July-Aug. M 11am-12:15am, Tu-Su 9:15am-12:15am; June and Sept. M 11am-11:45pm, Tu-Sa 9:15am-11:45pm, Su 9:15am-7:25pm; Mar.-May and Oct. M 11am-7:25pm, Tu 11am-11:45pm, W-Sa 9:30am-11:45pm, Su 9:15am-7:25pm; Nov.-Feb. M-Tu 11am-6:30pm, W-Su 10:45am-6:30pm. Closed mid-Jan. €3.95, students €3.25.)*

MUSÉE DE GRENOBLE. Art lovers will swoon over one of France's most prestigious collections of fine art. Its masterpieces include larger-than-life canvases by Rubens, de la Tour, and Zurbarán, as well as an extraordinary 20th-century collection, with several works by Chagall and an entire room devoted to Matisse. The museum also includes local artists' depictions of the mountains, perfect for drumming up enthusiasm for the outdoor pursuits available just outside its doors. *(5 pl. de Lavalette. ☎63 44 44; www.museedegrenoble.fr. Open daily 10am-6:30pm. €5, students €2. English audio tour €3. Guided 1½hr. visits in French Sa-Su 3pm. €3.)*

VIEILLE VILLE. Built over 17 centuries, Grenoble's *vieille ville* is a motley but charming collection of old squares, fountains, and parks. Vestiges of the Roman ramparts are visible near the town's historic center, pl. St-André, now Grenoble's most popular student hangout. The 13th-century **Collégiale St-André** was the traditional burial place for Dauphins until 1349. Its soaring bell tower is made from volcanic rock. *(Open daily 8am-5pm.)* Across the street, the **Palais de Justice** boasts a flamboyant Gothic facade, a Renaissance-style right wing, and 19th-century heraldic shields of Grenoble over its door. The building was erected by Dauphin prince and future king Louis XI in 1453 to house the region's parliament. The **Café de la Table Ronde,** 7 pl. St-André, built in 1739, is the second-oldest coffee shop in France and has been frequented by many famous artists, writers, and politicians, from Léon Blum to Mussolini. It's not worth much more than a glance, but it's interesting nonetheless. *(☎44 51 41. Open M-Sa 9am-1am.)*

MUSÉE DAUPHINOIS. Transformed from convent to prison to Catholic school to historical site, this regional ethnographic museum merits a visit from anyone looking to learn about the traditions of the province. Situated on the north bank of the Isère, the beautiful 17th-century building houses four themed exhibits with surprisingly impressive multimedia and sound effects. The *Gens de l'Alpes* (People of the Alps) explores the history of the first pioneering settlers who carved out a livelihood in the mountains, while *La Grande Histoire du Ski* (The History of Skiing) traces the evolution of snow sports, featuring a vast collection of early and modern skis. These two permanent exhibits have English explanations, while the two temporary ones have signs only in French. *(30 rue Maurice Gignoux. Cross Pont St-Laurent and go up Montée Chalemont. ☎85 19 01; www.musee-dauphinois.fr. Open June-Sept. M and W-Su 10am-7pm; Oct.-May M and W-Su 10am-6pm. Free.)*

MUSÉE D'HISTOIRE NATURELLE DE GRENOBLE. While this museum appeals to all ages, children in particular love the interactive games and dioramas of alpine animals (including lynxes, bears, and birds) lining the stately wooden hall. The second floor presents exotic insects from around the world and a glittering array of gems. Many of the exhibits have English descriptions, but the beautiful displays need little explanation. *(1 rue Dolomieu. ☎44 05 35; www.museum-grenoble.fr. Open M-F 9:30am-noon and 1:30-5:30pm, Sa-Su 2-6pm. €2.20, ages 18-25 €1.50, under 18 free.)*

RHÔNE-ALPES

OTHER MUSEUMS. A number of free museums dot the city; consult the tourist office for a full list. The **Musée de la Résistance et de la Déportation,** 14 rue Hébert, highlights Grenoble's WWII resistance effort with innovative, theatrical exhibits. *(☎42 38 53. Open July-Aug. M and W-Su 10am-7pm, Tu 1:30-7pm; Sept.-June M and W-F 9am-6pm, Tu 1:30-6pm, Sa-Su 10am-6pm.)* The **Musée de l'Ancien Evêché,** 2 rue Très-Cloîtres, explores the history of the region from prehistoric times to the present in the old Bishops's Palace. *(☎03 15 25. Open M and W-Sa 9am-6pm, Tu 1:30-6pm, Su 10am-7pm.)*

NIGHTLIFE

Grenoble has all the funky cafés and raucous bars of a true college town; most are located in the area between pl. St-André and pl. Notre-Dame. Covers for clubs range from €8-10, and drinks are nearly as much. The **MC2,** Grenoble's **Maison de la Culture,** located at 4 rue Paul Claudel about 15min. from the *centre-ville,* organizes cultural events and performances. (☎00 79 00; www.mc2grenoble.fr. Open Sept.-June Tu-F 12:30-7pm, Sa 2-7pm.)

Couche-Tard Pub, 1 rue du Palais (☎04 75 44 18 79). A small bar whose walls are covered with customers' scribbled musings. An international 20-something crowd mixes it up on the neon-lit dance floor after downing large shots of flavored vodka (€1.60)—you may in fact want to *"couche tard"* (go to bed late). Beer €2.50. Mixed drinks €2.50. Happy hour M-W 7-11pm, Th-Sa 7-9pm. Open M-Sa 7pm-2am. AmEx/MC/V.

London Pub, 11 rue Brocherie (☎44 41 90). 2-floor international establishment features an odd combination of black lights and English paraphernalia, ranging from rugby balls to the Union Jack. At midnight, the crowded bar area becomes a dance floor. Shots €1.60. Happy hour daily 6-9pm; pints from €3. Open M-Sa 6pm-1am. AmEx/MC/V.

365 Café, 3 rue Bayard (☎51 73 18). A laid-back crowd of locals comes to this artfully decorated spot almost as many days a year as its name suggests. The delicious drink options and exotic atmosphere will keep you coming back too. Happy hour 6-8:30pm; drinks €2.50-4. Mixed drinks €5-13. Open Tu-Sa 3pm-1am. AmEx/MC/V.

Le Codebar, 9 rue Etienne Marcel (☎06 07 30 68 42; http://lecodebar.free.fr), off rue Jean Jaurès, 5min. from its intersection with av. Alsace-Lorraine. Gay and lesbian bar boasts a fun drink menu and theme nights. Mixed drinks €7. Open Tu-Su 6pm-1am.

ENTERTAINMENT AND FESTIVALS

Grenoble's main **theater** features plays and classical music performances; info and tickets are at the **billetterie** next to the theater on pl. St-André. (☎42 96 02. Open Tu-F 10am-noon and 1-6pm, Sa 1-6pm.) **FNAC Billetterie,** in a superstore on rue Felix Poulat across from the church, has info and tickets for most theater events. (www.fnac.com. Open M-Sa 10am-7pm.) For movie schedules, consult *Le Petit Bulletin,* free in cinemas and at the tourist office.

Given Grenoble's student-dominated vibe, it's not surprising that the city hosts many art, music, and dance festivals. July 14 kicks off the season with fireworks over the city *conseil.* From late July to early August, **Cabaret Frappe** celebrates international singers and songwriters from around the world, featuring free concerts at 7pm and €13 concerts at 9pm. (☎00 76 85; www.cabaret-frappe.com.) The **Festival du Court Métrage** celebrates short films in early July; contact the **Cinémathèque,** 4 rue Hector Berlioz (☎54 43 51). In late November, the **Festival 38ème Rugissants** (☎51 12 92) features African and South American music.

HIKING

Grenoble is surrounded by steep mountains, providing city-dwellers with a hiking paradise in their backyard. Trails with starting points accessible by TAG city buses crisscross the countryside. The free and invaluable trail map, *La Carte des Sentiers des Franges Vertes,* available at the Maison de la Montagne (p. 456), indicates which buses to take and highlights points of interest along paths that ramble through lush pastures, picturesque villages, and steep hillsides. Many excellent trails are accessible from the top of the *téléphérique.* The #31 bus takes nature lovers to the trailhead of a peaceful stroll through typical Alpine countryside. More isolated hikes are accessible only by car or infrequent buses; while getting to these trails can be challenging, their breathtaking beauty is worth the hassle. These hikes have well-marked trails, but taking an IGN hiking map of the trails you plan to follow is highly recommended (available at local bookstores; €9.50). All bus schedules and maps are available at the TAG info desk in the tourist office.

TOURBIÈRE AND COL DE L'ARC. Bus #10 takes hikers to a trail through the forest and along the Pissarde river, passing a waterfall and looping around through the **Tourbière,** a semi-marshland on a plateau beneath steep, white cliffs. Take bus #1 to Pont Rouge and change to bus #10, getting off at "Claix Mairie" (40min., every 20min., €1.20). Follow yellow and green signs along a paved road to the town of Allières, where a right onto rue du Pré du Merle leads to the dirt trailhead. A steep, rocky path follows the river and cuts through the town of Savoyères; a paved and dirt road leads to the Tourbière (4hr. round-trip, 8km). The path can also be used as a starting point for the full-day hike leading to the summit of **Col de l'Arc;** consult the Maison de la Montagne and before attempting the strenuous climb.

LE MOUCHEROTTE. For those looking to get their feet wet in the Alps, **Le Moucherotte** (4hr. round-trip, 8.4km, 731m vertical) is a relatively short hike that still delivers with beautiful views. Take VFD bus #5100 (dir.: Lansen) to "St-Nizier du Moucherotte" (40min., 1-3 per day, €2.90) and turn right from the bus stop toward the church a block or two away. Follow the road to the left of the church and cemetery to the trailhead of the **GR9,** across the street from the panoramic viewpoint. This route leads to the summit and is marked by red and white lines on trees and rocks lining the path. A red and white "X" indicates that you are leaving the trail. Bring a camera; Le Moucherotte offers incredible vantages of Mont Blanc and the other snow-capped *Hautes Alpes*. Descend by the same route.

CHAMECHAUDE. To the north of Grenoble, in the heart of the Chartreuse park, a steep, rocky trail reaches the summit of **Chamechaude** (6-7hr. round-trip, 14.2km, 1068m vertical) and makes a good daytrip for experienced hikers. The white-rock cliff at the top affords hikers panoramic views of rugged peaks, jagged cliffs, and village-dotted countryside. Take VFD bus #7140 to "Le Sappey-en-Chartreuse" (30min., 2-3 per day, €2.90). The bus stops after the church; follow the street to the right downhill. The trailhead is marked with yellow signs on the left. The first section of the hike follows **GR9 "Tour de Chartreuse,"** marked with red and white lines on tree trunks and rocks. At Habert Chamechaude, take **trail B** on the left toward Chamechaude. This trail is marked with yellow paint. The final 15m require a climb up a near-vertical rockface using a wire cable for assistance; it can be dangerous, especially when wet, so exercise caution. Descend along the same route.

SKIING

Rent equipment in town to avoid high prices at the resorts.

OISANS. The biggest ski areas are to the east in Oisans. The **Alpe d'Huez,** rising above one of the most challenging legs of the Tour de France, boasts a 3330m vertical drop and sunny, south-facing slopes; 250km of trails span all difficulty levels. (Tourist office ☎11 44 44; www.alpedhuez.com. Ski area ☎80 30 30. Lift tickets €38 per day, €192 per week.) Popular with advanced skiers, **Les Deux Alpes** has the largest skiable glacier in Europe, limited summer skiing, and a slope-side youth hostel. Its lift system, including two gondolas, runs up the 2000m vertical slope. (Tourist office ☎79 22 00; www.2alps.com. Ski area ☎79 75 01. Youth hostel ☎79 22 80. Lift tickets in winter €35 per day, €172-192 per week; in summer €30/143.)

BELLEDONNE. The Belledonne region, northeast of Grenoble, lacks the towering heights and ideal conditions of the Oisans but has lower prices. **Chamrousse** is its biggest and most popular ski area, offering a lively atmosphere and a youth hostel. If conditions are right, there's plenty of good alpine and cross-country skiing at a great value, especially for beginners. (Tourist office ☎89 92 65; fax 89 98 06. Youth hostel ☎89 91 31; fax 89 96 66. Lift tickets €26 per day, €149 per week.) Only 30min. from Grenoble, the resort makes for an ideal daytrip in the summer (6 buses per day, €3.80). Chamrousse maintains four **mountain bike** routes of varying difficulty in addition to a 230km network of **hiking** trails.

VERCORS. The neighboring slopes of the Vercors region, south of Grenoble, are popular with locals. In traditional villages with small ski resorts like **Gresse-en-Vercors,** vertical drops are around 1000m. Rock-bottom prices make the area a stress-free option for beginners or those looking to escape the hassles of the major resorts. The drive from Grenoble takes 40min. (Tourist office ☎34 33 40. Lift tickets €16 per day, €82 per week.)

ANNECY ☎04 50

Far from the noisy thoroughfares and high-rises of downtown, the *vieille ville* of Annecy (AHN-ssee; pop. 53,000) boasts narrow cobblestone streets, winding canals, and turreted castles, making it seem more like a fairytale than a modern city. Annecy provides a change of pace from the rugged Alpine countryside around it: life revolves more around the lake shore than the snow-capped peaks in the distance. As the sun rises over Lac d'Annecy, one of the purest bodies of water in Europe, the lake drifts into shades of deep azure, providing a stunning sight for both the windsurfers below and the paragliders above.

TRANSPORTATION

Trains: Pl. de la Gare. Open daily 4:30am-9pm. Ticket window open daily 7:40am-7:30pm. To: **Chamonix** (2½hr., 7 per day, €20); **Grenoble** (1½hr., 8 per day, €16); **Lyon** (2½hr., 8 per day, €22); **Nice** via Lyon (7-9hr., 6 per day, €86); **Paris** (4hr., 7 per day, €85).

Buses: Adjacent to the train station. Office open M-F 7:45-11am and 2-7:15pm, Sa 7:45-11am. **Autocars Frossard** (☎45 73 90) runs to **Geneva, Switzerland** (1¼hr., 2-3 per day, €10).

Public Transportation: SIBRA (☎10 04 04; www.sibra.fr). Info booth across from the train station at the southwest corner of rue de la Gare. Open M-F 7:30am-7pm, Sa 9am-noon and 2-5pm. Extensive service throughout the city; info booth provides schedules. A *Ligne d'Eté* bus runs July-Aug. from the train station and stops at the hostel, campground, and summit of Semnoz (dir.: Semnoz; July-Aug. 6 per day 9am-6:15pm, June and Sept. Sa-Su 6 per day 9am-6:15pm). €1; *carnet* of 10 €8.55, students €5.90.

Taxis: At the station (☎45 05 67). €10 to the hostel, €12 at night. 24hr.

Bike and In-line Skate Rental:

Roul' ma Poule, 4 rue des Marquisats (☎27 86 83; roulmapoule.com), next to the port. Bikes €8-10 per ½-day, €12-15 per day; includes helmet and lock. In-line skates €8 per ½-day, €12 per day. Open daily 9am-7pm. MC/V.

Golf Miniature de l'Imperial, 2 av. du Petit Port (☎66 04 99; www.roller-golf.annecy.com), beside plage d'Albigny. Ask about a 20% reduction if you're staying at the Auberge de Jeunesse. Bikes €5 per hr., €14 per day. In-line skates €8 per ½-day, €11 per day. Open daily 9am-10pm.

ORIENTATION AND PRACTICAL INFORMATION

Most activity centers around the lake southeast of the train station and the bustling *vieille ville* just off its shore. A canal runs east-west through the *vieille ville*, which is bounded by the elevated château on one side and by the tourist office in the main shopping area on the other. To reach the tourist office from the train station, walk one block down rue de la Gare and turn left onto rue Vaugelas, following it for four blocks. The office is straight ahead in the Bonlieu shopping mall.

Tourist Office: 1 rue Jean Jaurès (☎45 00 33 or 45 56 66; www.lac-annecy.com), in the Centre Bonlieu. Offers maps of the city, a practical guide, and a brochure outlining 5 self-guided walking tours of the city in English and French. The Lac d'Annecy map highlights hiking, climbing, and biking routes in the area. Hikers can purchase the *Walks and Treks* guide (€6.50), which details hiking paths around the lake, or an IGN map of the region (€9.50). Guided walking tours of the *vieille ville* also available (2hr.; July-Aug. tours in French M-Sa 3pm, in English Tu and F 4pm; €5.30, under 12 free). Open June-Aug. M-Sa 9am-6:30pm, Su 9am-12:30pm and 1:45-6:30pm; Sept.-May daily 9am-12:30pm and 1:45-6pm; late-Oct. to Feb. M-Sa 9am-12:30pm and 1:45-6pm.

Youth Center: Bureau Information Jeunesse (BIJ), 1 rue Jean Jaurès (☎33 87 40; infojeunes@ville-annecy.fr), in the Centre Bonlieu. Friendly staff offers advice and info on study options, housing, jobs, and recreational activities. Free Internet access, but expect a wait. Open M 3-6pm, Tu-Th 11am-6pm, F 11am-5pm, Sa 10am-noon.

Laundromat: Lav'Confort Express, 6 rue de la Gare, across the canal. Wash €4.30, dry €0.50 per 5min. Open daily 7am-9pm.

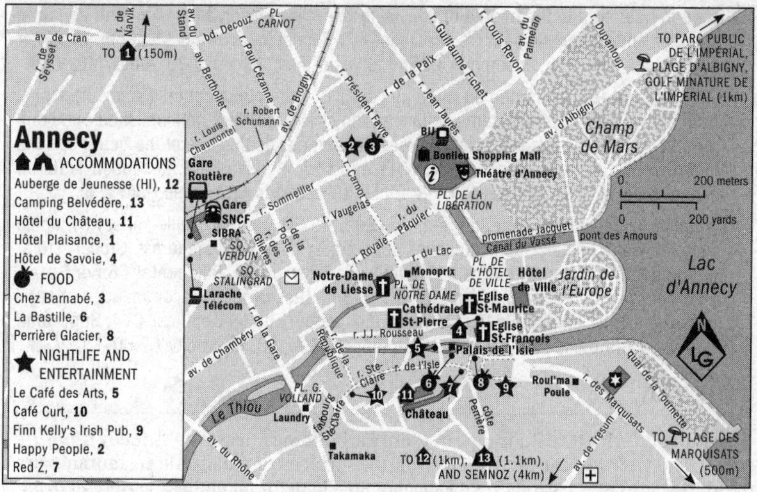

Police: 15 rue des Marquisats (☎52 32 00). Call here for the **pharmacie de garde.**

Hospital: 1 av. de Trésum (☎88 33 33).

Internet Access: Free at the **BIJ** (see **Youth Center,** above). **Larache Télécom,** 3 av. de L'Industrie (☎33 08 95), near the train station. €3 per hr. Open daily 9am-10pm.

Post Office: Entrance on rue des Glières (☎04 50 33 68 20), down the street from the train station. **Currency exchange** and **ATM.** Open M-F 8:30am-6:30pm, Sa 8am-noon. **Poste Restante:** 74011. **Postal Code:** 74000.

ACCOMMODATIONS AND CAMPING

Annecy's priciest hotels are in the *vieille ville* and by the lake, but prices drop along the city's outskirts. Reservations are recommended, especially in ski season and during the *Fête du Lac* at the beginning of August.

Auberge de Jeunesse "La Grande Jeanne" (HI), 4 rte. de Semnoz (☎45 33 19; annecy@fuaj.org). See **Public Transportation** (p. 462). Or, take bus #6 (dir.: Marquisats) from the station to "Hôpital," in front of the police station. Walk straight on av. de Tresum, away from the lake, and follow the signs to Semnoz. Take a left onto bd. de la Corniche and a right onto chemin du Belvédère for the ascent to the hostel (15min. by bus, 30min. by foot from train station). Makes up for its distance from the *centre-ville* with peaceful location near the Semnoz forest. Immaculate 4- and 5-bed dorms with modern furnishings, sinks, and showers. Single-sex rooms available. Game room, kitchen, TV room, bar, Internet access (€2 per 20min.), and laundry. Breakfast included. Reception 7am-11pm. Reservations recommended in summer via Internet at www.hihostels.com; pay ahead. Closed Dec. to mid-Jan. Dorms €18. MC/V. ❶

Hôtel Plaisance, 17 rue de Narvik (☎/fax 57 30 42), off av. de Cran, 7min. from the train station. Quiet, carpeted rooms with old yet comfortable 70s-style furnishings. TV salon and nice breakfast area. Breakfast €3.90. Showers €2. Reception 7am-midnight. Reservations recommended, especially during festivals. Singles and doubles €29, with shower €33, with bath €35; triples €44-56; quads €47. MC/V. ❷

Hôtel de Savoie, 1 pl. St-François (☎45 15 45; www.hoteldesavoie.fr). This convent-turned-hotel features small, colorful, and affordable rooms with wood floors. An impossible-to-beat spot in the middle of the *vieille ville.* Make reservations a month ahead in summer and during ski season. Breakfast €7. Reception 7:30am-11:30pm. In winter singles with sink €28, in summer €35; doubles with shower €65-90. AmEx/MC/V. ❷

Hôtel du Château, 16 rampe du Château (☎45 27 66; hotelduchateau@noos.fr). Uphill from the *vieille ville* on the same square as the château. Offers well-furnished and comfortable rooms with excellent views. Great location makes this one of the better options in the *vieille ville.* All rooms have TV, Wi-Fi, and bath. Breakfast €7. Reception 7:30am-10pm. Singles €49; doubles €60-68; triples €73; quads €83. AmEx/MC/V. ❹

Camping le Belvédère, 8 rte. de Semnoz (☎45 48 30; camping@ville-annecy.fr), uphill from the youth hostel. Open campsites dot a grassy hill next to the forest. Grocery store, phone booth, TV, and extensive hiking trails. Laundry €8.40. Bike rental €6 per ½-day, €10 per day. Reception 8:30am-2pm and 5-8pm. Reservations recommended in summer. Open early Apr. to mid-Oct. July-Aug. 1-2 people with tent and car €14; Sept.-June €11-12. Extra person €4.10-4.90, extra tent €1.70-2.50. Electricity €2.60. MC/V. ❶

FOOD

Reasonably priced restaurants in colorful buildings decorate Annecy's *vieille ville.* The views of the lake-front from the terraces of canal-side restaurants are hard to beat. Take a stroll down **Faubourg Ste-Claire** for an endless variety of *brasseries, glaciers, boulangeries,* and cafés. Lakeside picnics often make for the best meals, though; fill your basket with local specialties like *reblochon* cheese at the markets on **place Ste-Claire** (Tu, F, Su 8am-noon) and on **boulevard Taine** (Sa 8am-noon). A **Monoprix** supermarket fills most of pl. de Notre Dame. (☎45 23 60. Open M-Sa 8:30am-7:50pm. AmEx/MC/V.)

Chez Barnabé, 29 rue Sommeiller (☎45 90 62). Buffet-style to-go restaurant with a selection of hot dishes, a salad bar, and a massive selection of delicious cookies—the Snickers cookie is highly recommended. Salad bar €3.20-5.60. Pizzas €1.90. Sandwiches €2.30-3.50. *Plats* €2.10-5.30. Open M-Sa 10am-7pm. MC/V. ❶

La Bastille, 4 quai des Vieilles Prisons (☎45 09 37). A canal-side terrace and some of the best prices in the *vieille ville.* The perfect place to sample substantial servings of *savoyard* specialties. A wooden exterior, stone interior, and red-checkered tablecloths make for an unpretentious environment. *Plats* €9-14. *Menus* €14-19. Open M-Th 11am-2:30pm and 6-10:30pm, F-Sa 11am-2:30pm and 6-11pm. MC/V. ❸

Perrière Glacier, at the corner of quai Perrière and rue Perrière. While its prices are on par with the rest of the (countless) *glaciers* in town, Perrière's 56-flavor selection helps it stand out from the rest. In addition to the standard flavors and assortment of fruit sorbets, this *glacier* offers delicious alternatives, such as the "Don Vito" (vanilla, raspberry, and chocolate) and the colorful "Schtroumpfs" (a blue ice cream with **Smurfs** gummy candy). Single scoop €2. 5 scoops €6.50. Open daily 11am-midnight. ❶

SIGHTS

VIEILLE VILLE. Bring an extra roll of film (or an extra memory card) for a walk through Annecy's *vieille ville.* While the real attraction lies in its meandering alleyways and flower-lined canals, there are several stops along the way that should not be missed. The 13th-century **Palais de l'Isle** sits imposingly in the middle of the canal. Most recently, it served as a prison for WWII Resistance fighters, whose impassioned carvings mark the walls. A museum inside walks visitors through Annecy's history, but the château's main appeal is its beautiful exterior. *(☎33 87 30. Open June-Sept. daily 10:30am-6pm; Oct.-May M and W-Su 10am-noon and 2-5pm. €3.30, students €1.)* Beneath the towers of the castle on the other side of the canal,

quai Perrière, rue de l'Isle, and **Faubourg Ste-Claire** are some of Annecy's most charming streets, despite crowds of visitors. Straddling the town's narrowest canal, the large, bare **Eglise St-Maurice** is known for the 15th-century painting (on the left wall near the back) that marks the tomb of Philibert de Monthoux, an Annecy noble. The macabre mural of a decomposing corpse—finished two years before its patron's death—is thought to reflect de Monthoux's anxiety over the Hundred Years' War.

LE LAC. The lake is one of Europe's cleanest and purest; eight mountain streams and one underground source combine to fill the 14km long body of water. Beaches dot its perimeter, and it has two popular swimming spots. The grassy expanses of **plage d'Albigny,** 10min. up av. d'Albigny, draw tourists and locals in the summer, who dine in lakeside restaurants and windsurf, sail, and kayak on the waters. *(Open June-Aug. daily 10am-7:30pm; €3.50, students and under 12 €2. Sept.-May 24hr.; free.)* For €3.50, the young at heart can frolic in the **Parc Public de l'Impérial,** an aquatic wonderland next to plage d'Albigny with waterslides, sailing, tennis, swimming, and a casino. *(☎23 11 82. Open May-Sept. daily 11am-7:30pm.)* The smaller and more crowded **plage des Marquisats,** 1km south of the city down rue des Marquisats, permits swimming free of charge. The **Club de Voile Française,** on the lake, rents a selection of watercraft, while many companies rent out pedal boats on the south side of the Champ de Mars. *(€9 per 30min., €13 per hr.)* On the other side of Pont des Amours, speed boats take tours of the lake. *(€8 per 35min., €16 per hr. Cash only.)*

GARDENS. Graced by manicured hedges, fountains, and the occasional long-necked swan, the shaded **Jardin de l'Europe** is Annecy's pride and joy. At its northern side, the **Pont des Amours** (Lovers' Bridge) connects the European gardens to the **Champ de Mars,** a grassy esplanade frequented by picnickers, sunbathers, and soccer players. The gardens have won the national *Ville Fleurie* (Flower City) contest three times in the last decade.

CHÂTEAU. The unadorned 12th-century château, a short, steep climb from the *vieille ville*, rises over Annecy. Once a stronghold of Genevan Counts, the castle and its imposing parapets now contain archaeological exhibits. Rooms present medieval *savoyard* furniture, religious sculptures, and an exhibit on Alpine lakes. *(☎33 87 30. Open June-Sept. daily 10:30am-6pm; Oct.-May M and W-Su 10am-noon and 2-5pm. Château €4.80, students €1.80, under 12 free. Entrance to grounds free.)*

NIGHTLIFE

Relaxing bars line the canal in the *vieille ville*, creating a scene that tends to revolve more around mellow drinking than wild dancing.

Finn Kelly's Irish Pub, 10 Faubourg des Annonciades (☎51 29 40; www.finnkellys.com.). Play darts, shoot pool, and watch the game with a mix of locals and tourists. Plenty of beers on tap, with an emphasis on the Irish brew Beamish. Larger Anglophone crowd when rugby and soccer matches are shown on the big-screen TVs. Free Wi-Fi and free Internet access at 3 computers available with purchase of a drink. Beer €2.90-4.70. Open M-Sa 4:30pm-2am, F-Su 4:30pm-3am. MC/V.

Café Curt, 35 rue Ste-Claire. The lack of a telephone and fixed hours is an indication of the laid-back atmosphere at this small bar. Locals of all ages chat and people-watch while sipping some of Annecy's cheapest drinks. Known for its shooters (€2), which come in flavors from white chocolate to cotton candy. Wine €2-3.50. Kronenbourg €2. Cognac €5. Open daily June-Sept. depending on what the owners "feel like from day to day," roughly 10am-2am; Oct.-May 10am-1am.

Red Z, 14 rue Perrière (☎45 17 13). Americans might not appreciate the cleverly rhyming name (pronounced Red-Zed) of Annecy's flashiest, though slightly touristy, bar and discotheque, where 20-somethings congregate in a hip, dark interior. Live

DJs Th-Sa. Dancing picks up around 11pm and lasts into the morning. Beer €3-5. Mixed drinks €9-14. Open daily Apr.-Oct. 11am-3am; Nov.-Mar. 5pm-3am. MC/V.

Le Café des Arts, 4 passage de l'Isle (☎51 56 40). An eclectic crowd lounges on the terrace along the canal. Beer €2.30-4. Open daily 10am-1am.

Happy People, 48 rue Carnot (☎04 50 51 08 66). Lives up to its name. Wild nights are the norm at this gay- and lesbian-friendly disco, with a dark lounge in the back perfect for "romantic breaks" from the dance floor. Cover F-Sa €13; includes 1 drink. Open Tu-Su midnight-5am. MC/V.

ENTERTAINMENT AND FESTIVALS

The **Théâtre d'Annecy,** in the Bonlieu Mall across from the tourist office, hosts arts events and films, although tickets can be difficult to get at the last minute. (☎33 44 11. Tickets €20-25, students €17-22. MC/V.) Pick up festival schedules at the tourist office. The **Festival International du Film d'Animation** has become an Annecy mainstay, bringing animation professionals to town in early June. The biggest party is the **Fête du Lac,** a spectacular fireworks-and-water show that lights up the city every first Saturday in August. (☎33 65 65. Tickets €6-32. MC/V.) In early October, local traditions are celebrated during **La Retour des Alpages.**

HIKING

HIKES ON MOUNTAINS IN AND AROUND ANNECY

SEMNOZ FOREST. Annecy's Alpine forests shelter excellent hiking and biking trails. Dozens of circuits begin on Semnoz, a limestone mountain at the southern edge of the city. The Office National des Forêts (☎23 84 10) distributes a map of the area, *Sentiers Forestiers* (€3.10), outlining several routes that begin a 15min. walk from town. Relatively easy loops circle through Semnoz's forests; one 5hr. trail winds its way to the summit. One of the better hikes on the mountain is the **circuit de périmètre,** which begins at the Basilique de la Visitation, a 7min. walk from the hostel and campground. From town, take bus A to its terminus, "Visitation." With the basilica on your left, continue uphill on av. de la Visitation until it runs into rte. de la Petite Jeanne on the left. In front of you is the trailhead, labeled with a sign for "La Tambourne." From this point, there are several trails into La Forêt du Crêt du Maure. Follow the signs for the circuit de périmètre. This relatively gently graded trail, marked with blue blazes, follows a meandering circle through the Semnoz forest, past views of the city and glimpses of distant mountains. The loop terminates at a second trailhead just above the hostel and campgrounds. A short road above the campgrounds leads back to the start.

MASSIF DES ARAVIS. For those seeking an escape from the city into more rugged territory, the Massif des Aravis is the best bet. The mountain range is 25km from Annecy and boasts 150km of well-marked footpaths, stunning views, and mountain summits reaching up to 2753m. Annecy's tourist office can explain how to get to the area and sells necessary maps.

HIKES AROUND LAC D'ANNECY

A number of beautiful hikes of varying levels of difficulty can be found around the perimeter of **Lac d'Annecy.** Unfortunately, most of the advanced hikes are not easily accessible by public transportation. Those with cars should pick up information from the tourist office about hiking up the higher mountains on the southeastern edge of the lake, including La Tournette, the highest peak in the area. *Walks and Treks* (€6.50 at the tourist office) is an English guide with detailed directions for 15 hikes around the lake.

To cut your hike short, you can access some towns by bus and boat. Voyages Crolard **buses,** departing from the train station and stopping in front of the tourist office and near plage d'Albigny, circle the lake. (☎45 08 12; www.voyages-crolard.com. M-Sa 9 per day, Su fewer; €2.80-3.10.) The tourist office in Annecy can help clarify bus schedules, which tend to vary on the weekends. In summer, use Compagnie des Bateaux, which runs several **boat tours** around the lake. For a full tour, their best deal is the **Circuit Omnibus,** a 2hr. loop that makes stops at Veyrier, Menthon, Talloires, Doussard, Duingt, Saint-Joriez, and Sevrier. (☎51 08 40. 3 boats per day, leaving Annecy at 10:30am, 2:15, 4:45pm, with additional departures at 9:30am and 4pm in July and Aug. €14, under 12 €10.)

MONT VEYRIER AND MONT BARON. Unbelievable vantages of the lake can be found on the twin peaks of **Mont Veyrier** and **Mont Baron.** The easiest way to access this moderate hike (2½hr., 719m vertical) is to take Transdev Crolard's Rive Bus from the train station to Veyrier (dir.: Talloires; M-Sa 9 per day, Su 4 per day; €2). The tourist office, down the street from the bus stop in the direction of Annecy, provides a simple map and directions, but a more detailed IGN map is recommended. To reach the trailhead from the tourist office or bus stop, walk along the road away from Annecy until you reach the church. Head uphill to the right of the front steps. Go left at the roundabout, through pl. des Ecoliers, and then immediately left on chemin du Péril. Follow this to the trailhead at the entrance to the forest. At the fork in the trail soon after entering the forest, veer right and follow the trail until reaching the **Chapeau de Napoléon.** Turn left and follow the signs for **Col des Sauts.** The trail becomes flatter and winds through the forest, providing tantalizingly brief glimpses of the lake. It then renews its ascent up a series of switchbacks and some very rocky terrain that requires caution. After reaching Col des Sauts, follow the signs toward Mont Veyrier (15min.) and Mont Baron (25min.) on the trail marked with yellow and red lines. Dozens of spectacular viewpoints lie along the path as it follows a ridge to Veyrier. Descend by the same route.

MENTHON, TALLOIRE, AND LE ROC DE CHÈRE. A perfect way to combine sightseeing, hiking, and beach-hopping is to take Compagnie des Bateaux's morning boat to **Menthon,** where you can visit the town's castle before hopping on a trail that leads to **le Roc de Chère** and then into **Talloires** (2hr.), where another loop features a beautiful waterfall and panoramic views of the lake below. A boat from Talloires makes the return trip to Annecy, with stops at several other lakeside towns.

Menthon holds the opulent 12th-century **Château de Menthon.** The castle marks the birthplace of St-Bernard de Menthon, who made his name in the business of dog breeding. His wealthy descendants still live here, but the lower floors—including a walnut-paneled library with a Diderot Encyclopedia and a 14th-century bedroom—are open to the public. (☎60 12 05. Open July-Aug. daily noon-6pm; Sept. and May-June F-Su 2-6pm. €7, weekend tours with guides in period dress €8.)

To get to the **trailhead** from the port of Menthon, head uphill on rte. du Port until it reaches rue St-Bernard. Take a right and continue through the *centre-ville* and past the tourist office to pl. des Choseaux. Turn right on rte. des Bains and continue for 50m until you see the sign on the left for "Les Choseaux." Turn left on chemin du Crêt Martin, then bear onto chemin du Roc de Chère and follow the signs for the **Roc de Chère.** The road transitions to gravel and then to dirt as it enters the forest. Intersections with other major trails are marked with signs. Continue in the direction of "Liaison Talloires," marked by yellow arrows. The trail provides beautiful views of the lake as it descends and comes out of the forest near Talloires's port. Follow the road from the port along the lake shore as it turns left uphill and goes toward the tourist office. **La Cascade d'Angon** showcases waterfalls and incredible views of the lake. To get to the trailhead from the Talloire tourist office (☎60 70 64; open M-Sa 9am-7pm, Su 9am-12:30pm and 2:45-7pm), which provides a map and directions, take a right onto rte. du Crêt, a right through the roundabout, and a left onto rte. du Vivier. After 10min., the rocky trail marked with a sign for the Cascade d'Agnon branches off to the left. To reach the falls, go around a metal barrier on the right-hand branch of the fork in the trail. The path descends into the **Gorge du Nant d'Oy.** The trail dead-ends within 15 ft. of the largest waterfall. Be cautious; the trail near the falls can be slippery. Hikers can extend the trip another hour and complete a scenic loop back to the tourist office. From the fork where the trail to the falls begins, take the left branch toward **Verel** and **St-Germain.** Continue until the path forks again, and follow the sign for **Pirraz** to the left. After reaching a parking lot, cross the paved road on the right and take chemin de la Pirraz through the village. At the T-intersection, turn left onto rte. de Ponnay. As the road continues uphill, the lake comes into view. At the fork in the road, head left on chemin rural de Ponnay, which leads into the village. At the T-intersection, marked with a sign for Ponnay, turn left downhill and left again at the fork in the road. At the St-Germain church, follow the signs for Les Granges and Talloires to return to the *centre-ville.*

BIKING

Cyclists should be sure to check out the 30km *piste cyclable* (bike route) that hugs the level, western shore of the lake and goes through many visit-worthy towns. An entire circuit of the lake can be completed by cycling along the eastern shore's main road (D909a), but be prepared for hills and be vigilant of traffic. The tourist office has a free map of the lake that includes the bike route and some departure points for hikes. In addition, Semnoz has a variety of mountain biking trails, and Sibra runs a special bus (July-Aug. 6 per day) that caters to cyclists starting at the summit (see **Public Transportation,** p. 462).

SKIING

Cross-country skiers can hit the trails at nearby Semnoz, but Annecy's closest downhill **ski resorts** are in the **Massif des Aravis,** a large skiing area consisting of four stations and a total of 220km of trails with 96 lifts: **La Clusaz** (32km from Annecy, with 130km of trails and 56 lifts), **Saint-Jean-de-Sixt** (29km), **Manigod** (27km), and **Le Grand Bornand** (20km, with 90km of trails and 37 lifts). Transdev Crolard runs **buses** from the Annecy bus station to La Clusaz and Le Grand-Bornand (☎45 08 12; 1hr., 9 per day). The **Skibus** runs from December through April, linking Le Grand-Bornand, Saint-Jean-de-Sixt, and La Clusaz (late-Dec. to mid-Mar. 19 per day, reduced hours mid-Mar. to Apr.; €3.60, week-long pass €14). For those planning to ski for several days, the **Forfait Aravis** provides access to runs at all four stations and to a free shuttle bus between the four. The package also includes free access to the Skibus (2 days €59, under 15 €50; 7 days €174/129). Contact the **tourist offices** at any of the stations for info (La Clusaz: ☎32 65 00, www.laclusaz.com; Saint-Jean-de-Sixt: ☎02 70 14, www.saintjeandesixt.com; Manigod: ☎44 92 44, www.manigod.com; Le Grand-Bornand: ☎02 78 00, www.legrandbronand.com). The international youth hostel **La Clusaz ❶,** outside the resort on rte. du Col de la Croix Fry, has mostly quads with showers. (☎02 41 73; fax 02 65 85. Breakfast included. Reception 8am-noon and 5-9pm. Open mid-Dec. to mid-Apr. and mid-June to mid.-Sept. Mid-Dec. to mid-Apr. weekly stays only. *Demi-pension* €32, *pension complète* €38. V.)

OTHER OUTDOOR ACTIVITIES

With mountains above and the lake below, Annecy offers outdoors enthusiasts the best of both worlds: visitors can waterski one day and ascend sheer cliff faces the next. The **Bureau des Guides** (☎06 88 27 93 77; www.annecyguidesmontagne.com) and the staff at Anglophone **Takamaka,** 23 Faubourg Ste-Claire, run excursions for mountaineering activities, including **hiking, rock-climbing, canyoning,** and trips up the nearby **Via Ferrata.** Those inclined to stay at the water's edge should also consult Takamaka, which offers **kayaking, canoeing, water skiing, sailing,** and whitewater **rafting.** (☎45 60 61; www.takamaka.fr. Canyoning €49-69. Canoeing €15 per hr. Water skiing €29 per 15min. Climbing €390 per day for 2 people. Sign up the night before. Open July-Aug. M-Sa 9am-6:30pm, Su 1:30-6:30pm; Sept.-June M-F 9am-noon and 2-6pm. MC/V.) Takamaka also offers one of the best places in the world for **paragliding.** (Tandem paragliding €85, 5-day course €557.)

CHAMONIX ☎04 50

The train station is named "Chamonix-Mont Blanc" for more than practicality: the towering snow-capped mountain and the city in its shadow have an intimate connection. Chamonix (SHAH-moh-NEE; pop. 10,000) hosted the first Winter Olympics in 1924 and has yet to extinguish the torch. Today, athletes from around the world come here with mountains on their minds, determined to conquer the rugged peaks on skis, foot, rope, or bike. An aura of intensity hangs over Chamonix, but those who glance away from Western Europe's tallest peak will find a friendly town with authentic *chalets*, bustling pedestrian streets, hip bars and clubs, and an international population that speaks as much English as it does French.

The mountains around Chamonix are a challenge for hikers and skiers alike: steep grades, potential avalanches, and unpredictable weather make this entire region ill-suited for beginners. However, with adequate planning and equipment, expeditions into some of the highest altitudes in Europe are utterly (and literally) breathtaking. The low seasons, from October to November and May to late June, have fewer outdoor options; snow covers the mountains at elevations over 2000m while the lower altitudes are green, limiting hiking and skiing.

TRANSPORTATION

Trains: Pl. de la Gare (☎35 36). Ticket office open daily 6:40am-8:20pm. Most trains connect through St-Gervais on the Martigny line. From St-Gervais to: **Annecy** (1½hr., 8 per day, €13); **Geneva, Switzerland** (4½hr., 2 per day, €51); **Grenoble** (4hr., 1 per day, €26); **Lyon** (3½hr., 7 per day, €29); **Paris** (5-8hr., 6 per day, €75-95). There is an **SNCF** office in the SAT office at 13 av. Michel Croz (☎53 00 95). Open M-F 9am-noon and 2:30-6pm.

Buses: Société Alpes Transports (SAT), at the train station (☎53 01 15). Ticket office open July-Aug. M-F 7:30-11:30am and 1-6pm, Sa-Su 7:30am-noon and 1-6pm. Call for hours in low season. To **Courmayeur, Italy** (50min.; July-Aug. 6 per day, Sept.-June M-Sa 2 per day; €9.50) and **Geneva, Switzerland** (1½hr.; July-Aug. 3 per day; Sept.-Nov. and May-June M-Sa 1 per day; Dec.-Apr. M-F 4 per day, Sa-Su 5 per day; €35).

Public Transportation: The free **Mulet Navette** circles through town July-Aug. every 10min. 8:30am-6:30pm, with stops at the train station and Chamonix Sud; every 20min. May-June and Sept.-Dec. **Chamonix Bus** (☎53 05 55) runs to ski slopes and hiking trails. Follow signs from pl. de l'Eglise to the main bus stop. €1.50. A night bus makes the same circuit every hr. 8:30-11:30pm. €2. Chamonix hotels and *gîtes* dispense the **Carte d'Hôte,** which gives free travel on all buses.

Taxis: At the station (☎06 07 02 22 13). €12 to the Auberge de Jeunesse.

ORIENTATION AND PRACTICAL INFORMATION

At the intersection of **avenue Michel Croz, rue du Docteur Paccard,** and **rue Joseph Vallot,** each named for a conqueror of Mont Blanc's summit, lies the town center. The train station is south of the **Arve River.** Everything else is on the bank closer to the slopes. To get to the tourist office from the station, follow av. Michel Croz through town, turn left onto rue du Dr. Paccard, and take the first right to pl. de l'Eglise.

TOURIST, FINANCIAL, AND LOCAL SERVICES

Tourist Office: 85 pl. du Triangle de l'Amitié (☎53 00 24; www.chamonix.com). English-speaking staff has a list of accommodations, hiking map *Carte des Sentiers d'Eté* (€4), a hiking guidebook with map (€13) and info on local bus schedules and weather conditions. Wi-Fi. Open daily 8:30am-7pm. **Centrale de Reservation** (☎53 23 33; http://reservation.chamonix.com) books apartments or hotels for stays of 2 nights or more.

Laundromat: Cham'Laverie, 98 via d'Aoste (☎53 56 48), off av. de l'Aiguille du Midi. Wash, dry, and fold €11. Open July-Aug. M-Sa 9am-1pm and 2-7pm; late-Dec. to May M-Sa 9am-8pm. **Laverie Automatique,** 65 av. du Mont Blanc, in the Galerie Commerciale Alpina. Wash and dry €8.50. Open daily 8:30am-6pm.

English-Language Bookstore: Librairie Jean Landru, 74 rue Vallot (☎53 14 41). Small selection of popular English titles. Open daily July-Aug. 8am-7:30pm; Sept.-June 8:30am-12:30pm and 2:30-7pm. MC/V.

BIKING, HIKING, AND SKIING RESOURCES

Biking Information: Pick up the free, invaluable English map and guide to mountain biking itineraries at the tourist office or at mountain bike rental shops.

Bike and Ski Rental: Dozens of places rent skis, snowboards, bikes, and climbing equipment. Skis should not be more than €8-20 per day or €40-80 per week, depending on quality. Snowboards should not exceed €16 per day and €82 per week.

Hiking Information:

Office de Haute-Montagne (☎53 22 08; www.ohm-chamonix.com), on the top floor of the Maison de la Montagne, across from the tourist office. An expert staff helps plan your adventures given current weather conditions, provides printed material on *refuges* and cable cars, and sells detailed maps (€4-9.50). Extensive library of printed resources available, including route itineraries and recent travel-logs. Open July-Aug. daily 9am-noon and 3-6pm; Sept.-Oct. and Dec.-June M-Sa only; Nov. M-F only.

Club Alpin Français, 136 av. Michel Croz (☎53 16 03; www.clubalpin-chamonix.com). Best source of info on mountain *refuges* and road conditions. Bulletin board matches drivers, riders, and hiking partners. Hikers from far and wide convene in the office to plan the weekend's trips and excursions (F 7pm). Members only; email to inquire about membership. Open July-Aug. M-Tu and Th-Su 9am-noon, W 3:30pm-7pm; Sept.-June M-Tu and Th-Sa 3:30-7pm.

Hiking and Skiing Equipment: Outdoor outfitters abound in Chamonix's main shopping areas. **Snell Sports,** 104 rue Paccard (☎53 02 17; www.cham3s.com). Massive stock of skiing, climbing, and hiking gear and clothing. Rentals of everything from boots (€9 per day) and backpacks (€8 per day), to a "Mont Blanc" kit of boots, crampons, and ice axes (€18 per day). Open in high season 9am-12:30pm and 2:30-7:30pm; in low season 9am-noon and 2:30-7pm. AmEx/MC/V.

Mountain Rescue: PGHM Secours en Montagne, 69 rte. de la Mollard (☎53 16 89). 24hr. emergency service.

Skiing Lessons and Info: Ecole du Ski Français (☎53 22 57; www.esf-chamonix.com), on the 2nd fl. of the Maison de la Montagne. ½-day group lessons €56; ½-day private lesson for 1-6 people €155; guided group descent of Vallée Blanche for 1-4 people €260. Open Jan.-Apr. and Dec. daily 8:15am-7pm. MC/V. On the main floor, **Compagnie des Guides** (☎53 00 88; www.cieguides-chamonix.com) gives climbing lessons

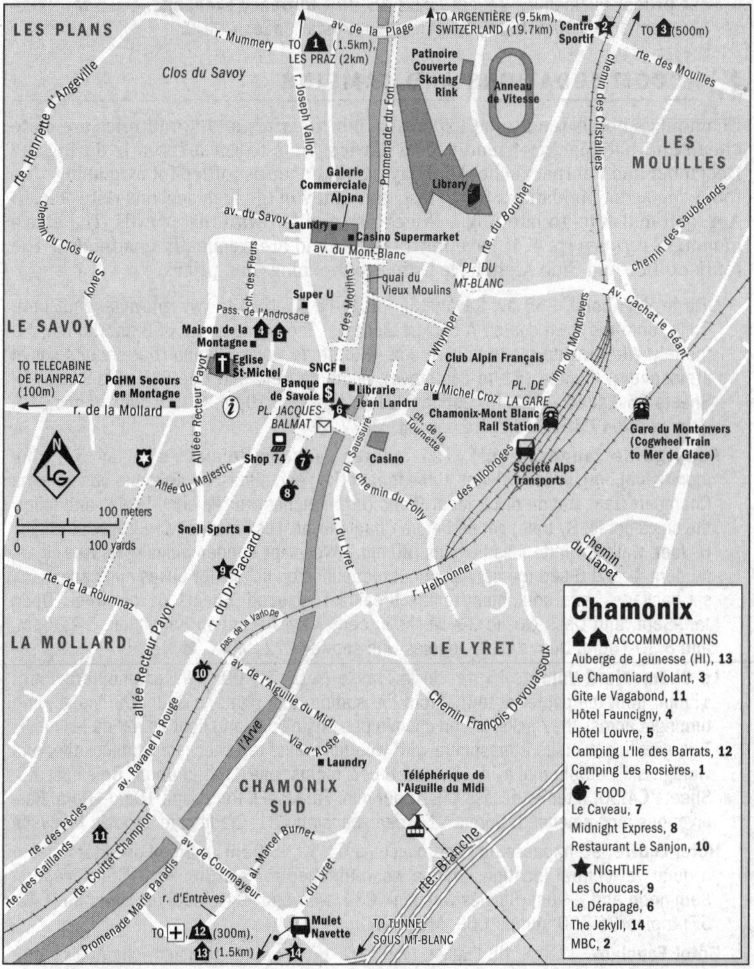

and leads guided summer hikes and winter ski trips. Morning climbing sessions €44. Group ski excursions €67 per person per day; min. 3 days. Register by 6pm the evening before. Open daily 8:30am-noon and 3:30-7:30pm. MC/V.

Weather Conditions: At the Maison de la Montagne, Club Alpin Français, and the tourist office. Call ☎08 92 68 02 74 for a French report of road and weather conditions.

EMERGENCY AND COMMUNICATIONS

Hospital: Centre Hospitalier, 509 rte. des Pèlerins (☎53 84 00). **Ambulance** (☎53 46 20).

Police: 48 rue de l'Hôtel de Ville (☎53 75 02).

Internet Access: Free Wi-Fi at the tourist office. **Shop 74,** 16 cours du Bartavel (☎90 73 17). €6 per hr. Free Wi-Fi with drink purchase. Open daily July-Aug. 10am-1pm and 3-7:30pm; Sept.-June 10am-7:30pm. MC/V.

Post Office: Pl. Jacques-Balmat (☎53 15 90). **Currency Exchange.** Open M-F 9am-12:30pm and 1:30-5:45pm, Sa 9am-noon. **Postal Code:** 74400.

ACCOMMODATIONS AND CAMPING

Chamonix's hotels tend to be expensive, but the *gîtes* and dormitories are quite cheap and backpacker-friendly. The hardest time to get a room is during the December and February school holidays. Call the tourist office for availability; the following accommodations fill up fast, especially in the high seasons (late Dec. to Apr. and mid-June to late Aug.). Prices rise and fall with the crowds. The area's mountain *refuges* (p. 474) have few facilities and are frequently unattended. The tourist office and Club Alpin have listings of openings and prices.

Gîte le Vagabond, 365 av. Ravanel le Rouge (☎53 15 43; www.gitevagabond.com), 7min. from the town center. A backpacker fave. The young group of Brits who run this friendly *gîte* provide rustic bunk rooms with stone walls. Popular bar creates social atmosphere. Kitchen (€1 to use stove), climbing wall, and free W-Fi. Breakfast €5. Sheets €5. Laundry €11. Reception 8-10am and 4:30-10pm. 4- to 6-bunk dorms €15, *demi-pension* €35. Credit card deposit. MC/V. ❶

Auberge de Jeunesse (HI), 127 montée Jacques Balmat (☎53 14 52; chamonix@fuaj.org), in Les Pèlerins at the foot of Glacier de Bossons. Take the bus from the Chamonix train station or pl. Mont Blanc (dir.: Pèlerins) to "Pèlerins Ecole" and follow the signs uphill. By train, get off before Chamonix at "Les Pèlerins" and follow the signs. By foot, walk down rte. des Pèlerins (30min.). Well-kept wooden building houses clean, modern 4- and 6-bed rooms. Ask about reductions on tickets for buses and cable cars, ski packages, and equipment rental. Breakfast included. Sheets €1 per week. Open Jan.-Sept. and Dec.; closed 2-3 weeks in early May. Reception 8am-noon, 5-7:30pm, and 8:30-10pm. Dorms €18; doubles with shower €22. MC/V. ❶

Le Chamoniard Volant, 45 rte. de la Frasse (☎53 14 09; www.chamoniard.com), 15min. from the center of town. From the station, turn right, go under the bridge, and turn right across the tracks, left on chemin des Cristalliers, and right on rte. de la Frasse. This *gîte* has a rustic atmosphere with wooden walls, red-checkered tablecloths, and vintage ski paraphernalia. 4-, 6-, and 8-bed rooms; one 15-bed dorm. Breakfast €5. Sheets €4.50. Internet access €0.10 per min. Free Wi-Fi. Reception 10am-10pm. Reservations recommended. Dorms €14, *demi-pension* €31. Credit card deposit. MC/V. ❶

Hôtel Louvre, 95 impasse de l'Androsace (☎04 50 53 00 51). Small one-star hotel in a quiet yet central location. Simple wood-trimmed rooms. Breakfast €6. Reception 8am-noon and 2-9pm. Singles with sink €34, with bath €48; doubles with bath €42-57; triples €54-60; quads €69. MC/V. ❸

Hôtel Faucigny, 118 pl. de l'Eglise (☎53 01 17; www.hotelfaucigny-chamonix.com). One of the best values in the center of Chamonix. Family-run hotel features comfortable, recently-renovated rooms in a hard-to-beat location near the tourist office. All rooms have shower and toilet. Free Wi-Fi. All but singles have TV. High season singles €45; doubles €77; triples €91; quads €110. Low season €42/68/82/98. MC/V. ❹

Camping L'Ile des Barrats, 185 chemin de l'Ile des Barrats (☎53 51 44), off rte. des Pèlerins. With your back to the cable car, turn left, pass the roundabout, and continue for 5min.; Barrats is on the right. A crowded grassy campground with great views of the surrounding mountains and amiable crowds. Small sites are separated by waist-high hedges. Luggage storage €1 per bag per day. Laundry (wash €5, dry €3). Reception July-Aug. 8am-noon and 2-8pm; Sept. and May-June 9am-noon and 4-7pm. Open May-Sept. €6.30 per person, €5.20 per tent, €2.40 per car. Electricity €3.30. Cash only. ❶

Camping Les Rosières, 121 clos des Rosières (☎53 10 42; www.campinglesrosieres.com), off rte. de Praz, close to les Praz. Follow rue Vallot for 1.2km or take a bus

RHÔNE-ALPES

to "Les Nants." Small, undivided sites with stunning views. Reception 8:30am-12:30pm and 2-8pm. Open June to Sept. 2 people, tent, and car €20. Electricity €3.10-3.30. ❶

FOOD

Tourist-driven Chamonix has a wider gamut of restaurants than one might expect. After a hard day on the slopes, it's easy to find a decent, hearty meal in one of the many bars and ski lodges in town. For a more traditional meal, however, head to one of the local bistros, where regional fare like fondue and *raclette* share menu space with international ski staples. Most *menus* tend to start around €14-16. There's a **Super U** supermarket at 117 rue Joseph Vallot (☎53 12 50; open M-Sa 8:15am-7:30pm, Su 8:30am-noon; AmEx/MC/V), and a **Casino** supermarket at 17 av. du Mont Blanc, inside the Galerie Commerciale Alpina (☎53 11 85; open July-Aug. M-Sa 8:30am-6:30pm, Su 8:30am-12:30pm; Sept.-June M-Sa 8:30am-6:30pm; MC/V). A morning market is held on **place du Mont Blanc** (Sa 7:30am-1pm).

Le Caveau, 13 rue du Dr. Paccard (☎55 86 18). This 300-year-old former wine cellar provides a romantic setting, but the laid-back, English-speaking staff prevents the atmosphere from getting too stuffy. Serves tasty brick-oven pizzas, *savoyard* specialties, and international and vegetarian dishes. Try the best-seller and house specialty: Swedish meatballs (€14). The garlic bread is widely considered the best in town. Open daily Jan.-Sept. and Dec. 6:30am-2am; Oct.-Nov. 6:30am-1am. MC/V. ❸

Midnight Express, 23 rue Dr. Paccard (☎53 44 10), near the post office. This burger joint has become a Chamonix mainstay. Cheap meals and late hours caters to backpackers and clubbers alike. Try the enormous Double American Midnight burger (€7.50). Burgers with fries €3.80-7.50. Open daily 11:30am-2am. Cash only. ❶

Restaurant Le Sanjon, 5 av. Ravanel le Rouge (☎53 56 44). The best bet for enjoying *savoyard* delicacies. Rustic atmosphere complements its specialty meat, cheese, and potato dishes. *Plats* €14-29. *Menus* €18-24. Open daily 11:30am-10:30pm. ❸

NIGHTLIFE

Chamonix's nightclubs and pubs are especially popular in winter, when people party hard with whatever energy they have left in their ski-weary bodies. Pubs are open year-round, although they are usually empty during the low season and not quite as rowdy during the summer months.

MBC*:* Micro Brasserie de Chamonix, 350 rte. du Bouchet (☎53 61 59). A 10min. walk from the center of town. Though a bit out of the way, this Canadian-owned micro-brewery stays packed with a laid-back crowd who comes for the tasty international fare, the 5 home-brewed beers on tap, and live music. Colorful lamps and a wooden canoe serve as décor. Pints €5. 1.5L pitchers €14. *Plats* €11-17. ½-price wings night M. Live music several times per week, more frequently in winter. Open daily 4pm-2am. MC/V.

The Jekyll, 71 rte. des Pèlerins (☎55 99 70). In an old stone barn, this Anglophone pub draws a crowd with its huge portions of hearty Irish food and big-screen TVs showing sporting events. *Plats* €13-21. Happy hour daily June-Aug. 6-7pm and 11am-midnight; Dec.-May 4-5pm and 11pm-midnight. Boot hour (for those still in ski gear) Dec.-May daily 6-7pm. Pub open daily June-Aug. 6pm-2am; Dec.-May 4pm-2am. MC/V.

Le Dérapage, 17 pl. Balmat (☎53 36 41), across from the post office. Run by British brothers, this laid-back bar gets busy late, especially on Quiz Night (Tu), Curry Night (Th), and weekends, when live music or DJs heat things up. 12 kinds of home-flavored vodkas line the walls behind the bar, many of which are blended daily from fresh fruit. Melon and strawberry are favorites. Shots €3-4. Wine €3-3.50. Happy hour 4-9pm. Open July to mid-Sept. Th-Sa 10pm-2am; mid-Sept. to June daily 4pm-2am. MC/V.

Les Choucas, 206 rue du Dr. Paccard (☎53 03 23). Show up late for a mix of alpine rusticity and a boisterous modern vibe in this revamped *chalet.* Cow-skin lounges and 4 big-screen TVs showing extreme skiing provide the backdrop for a strobe-lit dance floor. Beer €3.10-5.10. Mixed drinks €8-12. Live DJ. Concerts W. Regular *soirées spéciales.* Open daily late June to mid-Sept. 3pm-4am; mid-Dec. to mid-Apr. 5pm-4am. MC/V.

TÉLÉPHÉRIQUES

Hikers and skiers will probably need to take a *téléphérique* (cable car) during their stay in Chamonix, and others will want to take the ride just for the views. The tourist office and Office de Haute-Montagne provide a list of the lifts that are open; many close from early May to late June. Those who desire a spectacular trip should consider taking the **Aiguille du Midi,** which offers the best views of Europe's highest peak and the valley below. Be prepared for cold weather, as snowstorms can strike even in August. (☎08 92 68 00 67. Open daily July-Aug. 7:45am-5:30pm; Sept.-June 8am-5pm. Closed Nov. and part of May. From Chamonix to mid-point stop Plan de l'Aiguille €10, under 15 €8; round-trip €12/9.60. Aiguille du Midi summit €34/28; round-trip €37/30. AmEx/MC/V.)

From the Aiguille du Midi summit, many day-trippers continue on to **Helbronner,** a slightly rickety four-person gondola that runs into the glacial heart of the Alps and provides views of Matterhorn and Mont Blanc. The 25min. ride allows visitors to stride along the French-Italian border and eat a picnic lunch on the Glacier Géant. (May-Sept. Round-trip from Chamonix, including the Aiguille du Midi, €54; under 11 €44. AmEx/MC/V.) From Helbronner, a final *téléphérique* descends into Italy to **La Palud,** near the resort town of **Courmayeur.** Bring a passport and cash—the Italian side doesn't accept credit cards for the cable car. (Open July-Aug. 8am-5:30pm; Sept.-Oct. and June 8:30am-1pm and 2-4:20pm. Complete circuit from Chamonix €87, under 15 €70.) Verify at the tourist office that the entire *téléphérique* route is in operation before setting out.

Several *téléphériques* run year-round to the opposite side of the valley (away from Mont Blanc), which is known for popular hiking trails, panoramic restaurants, and paragliding take-off points. Gondolas to **Le Brévent** (2525m), stopping at the mid-station Planpraz, leave from the corner of rte. Henriette and La Mollard, up the street from the tourist office. (☎53 13 18. Open daily July-Aug. 8am-6pm; Sept.-June 9am-5pm. To Brévent €15, round-trip €21; to Planpraz €10, round-trip €12. MC/V.) Another great option is **La Flégère,** 2km east of the city in Les Praz, on rue Joseph Vallot. The car stops at its namesake plateau on the way to **l'Index** (2595m), a starting point for many ice climbs in the area. (☎53 18 58. Open daily July-Aug. 7:40am-5:50pm; Sept. and June 8:40am-4:50pm. €15, round-trip €18.)

A special train called the **Montnevers Railway** runs up to the **Mer de Glace,** France's largest glacier (97km long). It departs from a small cabin next to the train station. (☎53 12 54. Daily July-Aug. every 20min. 8am-6pm; Sept. and May-June every 30min. 8:30am-5pm; Nov. to Apr. every hr. 10am-5pm. Round-trip €16. MC/V.) From the top of the train at the Mer de Glace, a cable car runs to an **ice cave** that is carved anew each year—the glacier slides 30m per year, so last year's cave is farther down the wall of ice. (Car descent and return €4.40; cave admittance €3.40.) A **Forfait Global** pass includes a round-trip train and cable-car ride, along with admission to the cave (€20, under 11 €16). Alternatively, those up for a workout may consider hiking to and/or from the glacier (see **Hiking,** p. 475).

SKIING

Chamonix is surrounded by skiable mountains. The **south-facing side** of the valley opposite Mont Blanc, drenched in sunlight during the morning, offers terrain for

RHÔNE-ALPES

all abilities and has exceptional views to boot. Extreme skiers head over to the death-defying **north face,** which has mostly advanced, off-piste, and glacial terrain. Those aiming to ski for only one or two days should buy separate daily lift tickets at the different ski areas—one area is more than enough for each day. Those planning to stay longer might consider buying the **Chamonix Le Pass** or the **Mont-Blanc Unlimited pass,** available at the tourist office or major *téléphériques* (Brévent, Flégère, and Aiguille du Midi). *Chamonix Le Pass* is the cheaper option and gives unlimited access to ski areas in the Chamonix Valley, excluding Les Houches (7 days €209, ages 4-15 €167; passport photo required). *Mont-Blanc Unlimited* provides unlimited access to all of the areas covered by *Chamonix Le Pass,* plus the Aiguille du Midi and Helbronner cable car, the Montnevers train, the Logna-Grands Montets cable car, the Les Houches area, and one day in Courmayeur-Val-Veny, Italy (7 days €255, ages 4-15 €204; passport photo required). *Chamonix Le Pass* and *Mont-Blanc Unlimited* pass-holders also have free access to the local buses that connect the valley's string of resort villages; the trains of the Mont Blanc tramway make a stop at Bellevue, a point of entry to Les Houches. Extremely long lift lines at the base make early starts essential, but the crowds tend to thin out at the lifts higher up.

SKIING NORTH OF CHAMONIX

On the northern side of the Chamonix valley, advanced trails, vertical drops, and never-ending glaciers help to fuel Chamonix's reputation as a paradise for extreme skiers. **Les Grands Montets** (☎54 00 71; 3300m), 8km from Chamonix in Argentière, is the grande dame of Chamonix's ski spots, boasting some of the most difficult piste and off-piste terrain in the area. While skiers predominate, the resort also caters to snowboarders with a remodeled half-pipe (day pass €37). Directly above Chamonix, the infamous **Vallée Blanche** requires a hearty dose of courage and insanity. From the top of the Aiguille du Midi *téléphérique,* the ungroomed, unmarked, un-patrolled 20km trail runs down a glacier to Chamonix. Despite their appearance from below, glaciers are more ice field than snowfield, and their constantly moving snow bridges make the terrain quite dangerous. The best bet is to ski with a guide who knows the area. Try the **Compagnie des Guides** (p. 470; from €67 per person). English-speaking guides tailor the itinerary to you and make all the necessary arrangements, from equipment rental to lift reservations. *Let's Go* does not recommend skiing this area alone, but if you find yourself without a guide, always check conditions before venturing out and log your route with the **ski patrol** or the **Office de Haute Montagne.**

SKIING SOUTH OF CHAMONIX

At the end of the valley, near the Swiss border, **Le Tour-Col de Balme** (☎54 00 58), above the village of **Le Tour,** is the first of Chamonix's ski areas. Its sunny trails are most suitable for beginning to intermediate skiers, but a new gondola to the town of Vallorcine gives experts the chance to make tracks through pine forests (day pass €37). The **Brévent** and **Flégère** *téléphériques* closer to town have more dramatic runs for the non-expert. Connected by a cable car, Brévent and Flégère together constitute Chamonix's largest ski area; located steps from the tourist office, the Brévent *téléphérique* is particularly convenient. Note that the terrain at the top of the Brévent gondola is advanced; less-confident skiers should get off at the middle stop **Planpraz,** the starting point for several easier trails (day pass €37).

HIKING

Chamonix has 350km of marked hiking trails, with terrain ranging from forests to wind-swept glaciers. The *Carte des Sentiers d'Eté* map, available at the tourist office, lists all the mountain *refuges* and gives departure points and estimated lengths for all trails (€4). Climbers should buy the **IGN topographic map,** available

RHÔNE-ALPES

at the **Office de Haute Montagne** and local bookstores (€9.50). Grades are often steep, but using cable cars for either the trip up or back saves time and energy and takes hikers straight to the most scenic trails. Most hikes can be extended by avoiding the cable cars, but be prepared for steep trails on narrow switchbacks and ski runs. Walkers who would rather just look at the mountains can meander the trail that follows the **Arve River** through the valley; it begins next to the sports center. While there are hundreds of routes in the mountains, the following are well-known intermediate-level hikes that are easily accessible from Chamonix.

HIKES NORTH OF CHAMONIX

On the northern side of the valley, a vast network of trails wind near the ski pistes, offering unparalleled views of Mont Blanc and its offshoot glaciers on the opposite side. The lower-altitude **Chalet Floria** (45-50min.) trail is the perfect introduction to the mountains around Chamonix. Heading out of town toward Les Praz, turn left on rue Mummery, go right through the roundabout, and follow the signs to an uphill track that eventually becomes a narrow trail. The walk ends at a quaint *chalet*-turned-restaurant with red umbrellas, colorful flowers, and views of Mont Blanc. The owners allow picnics with the purchase of a drink (€3), but the price is really for the gorgeous setting. A good way to extend this hike is to ramble along the relatively flat **Petit Balcon Sud,** which winds through the forest and overlooks the valley below. The trail runs from above the town of Servoz to the west, through Chamonix, and all the way to Argentière, and is accessible from nearly all of Chamonix's surrounding villages; you can get on and off as you please. To access the trail from Chamonix, take the paved Chemin de la Pierre Ruskin to the left of the Brévent *téléphérique.* Signs lead to the Petit Balcon.

Another great starting point for hikes is the **Flégère téléphérique** station in les Praz. Ascend to the mid-station by either taking the cable car or climbing the ski slopes on the trail that starts behind the nearby golf course (2½hr.). From the station, a number of hikes lead along or farther up the craggy range. While the glacier is heavily touristed, a trip to **Lac Blanc** makes for a scenic afternoon. From the top of the Flégère cable car, follow signs on a breathless 2hr. ascent to Lac Blanc, whose turquoise alpine waters stay frozen through June. Hikers can picnic, sun themselves on rocks, and watch ice climbers descend a steep bowl. Those with money to spare can spend the night at **Refuge du Lac Blanc ❷,** which offers rooms with breakfast and dinner for €47. (☎53 49 14. Reservations required.)

West from la Flégère, the **Grand Balcon Sud** (yes, this trail is actually on the north side of the valley) is a spectacular, wildflower-adorned trail that traverses its way gently to **Planpraz,** the mid-station of the Brévent *téléphérique* (2hr.). From there, you can hike or ride back to town, or embark on the steep, gorgeous ascent to the **Col de Brévent** (2368m), the top of the Brévent lift (2hr.). Alternatively, take the steep trail from the "Planpraz" stop of the Brévent *téléphérique* to two pristine mountain lakes and views of the peaks beyond. From Planpraz, follow signs to Lac Cornu and Lacs Noirs along a narrow, rocky trail. The brilliant blue waters of **Lac Cornu** await after a 2hr. ascent, while a short, 45min. climb affords hikers a view of **Lacs Noirs.** Descend via the same route.

HIKES SOUTH OF CHAMONIX

Those itching to see glaciers up close should stick to trails on the southern (Mont Blanc) side of the valley. A number of picturesque trails surround the **Mer de Glace,** the largest glacier in France. One great 2½hr. trip through forests and boulder fields begins 900m beyond the Montnevers train station. Climb under the telesiège de Planards until signs appear to Rochets des Mottets. Follow the signs along a wide, moderately graded trail. After reaching the Rochets cabin (1½hr.), turn right onto the steeper trail, which climbs to the Montnevers train station (1hr.).

The train whisks tired hikers back to Chamonix, while daytrippers can extend the hike by heading under the tracks toward the glacier's **Hôtel Montnevers ❸** (☎53 87 70; breakfast and dinner included; open mid-June to mid-Sept.; dorms €37) and then following the sign toward the **Refuge du Plan de l'Aiguille ❶**, which takes 2½hr. to reach from the Mer de Glace (☎06 65 64 27 53, plandelaiguille.free.fr; open mid-June to late-Sept.; rooms €13, *demi-pension* €33). The spectacular, wild-flower-studded trail that winds gently toward the *refuge* is the **Grand Balcon Nord,** one of the many mountain traverses that was planned and constructed in the 1920s by famous Alpinist Joseph Vallot and his mountain-loving friends. The Balcon Nord may not be passable until late June; ask at the Office de Haute Montagne for up-to-date reports. After reaching the *refuge*, ascend a short trail to the midpoint stop of the Aiguille du Midi cable and ride down, or descend from the *refuge* along the steep left- or right-hand trails, both of which lead back to Chamonix (2½hr.).

Experienced mountain climbers, of course, come to Chamonix to ascend **Mont Blanc** (4810m), a two- or three-day climb. Don't try it solo. Climbers can be caught by vicious blizzards, even in August. The Maison de la Montagne, Compagnie des Guides, and Club Alpin Français all have info on this most classic of Alpine climbs (see **Biking, Hiking, and Skiing Resources,** p. 470).

VAL D'ISÈRE ☎04 79

Although Val d'Isère (VAL dee-ZAYR; pop. 1700) is less accessible than other Alpine ski towns, its unparalleled hiking, almost year-round skiing, and other top-notch outdoor options still attract visitors from all over the world. Travelers to this world-class ski resort worship its snow, the surrounding *hautes montagnes*, and native Jean-Claude Killy, who walked away with the gold in every men's downhill event in the 1968 Grenoble Olympics. As an area spokesman, Killy brought the Winter Olympics to Val d'Isère in 1992, permanently transforming the town's main street into a tourist-laden strip of expensive hotels, restaurants, and ski boutiques. The tradition will continue in 2009, when the town hosts the alpine skiing World Championship. When Val d'Isère "opens" for the summer (in late June), the turquoise Isère River emerges spectacularly from under melting snow, rushing past the rustic wood-and-stone *chalets* that line the narrow valley. Prices drop, and bikers, hikers, and climbers fill the hotels. The town's second high season "opening" occurs in early December; it can be eerily quiet during the low season. Expect to hear quite a bit of English in Val d'Isère, which is one of the biggest summertime skiing destinations for Brits and other Anglophones.

TRANSPORTATION

Trains: Pl. de la Gare in **Bourg-St-Maurice.** Ticket office open daily 5:10am-9:30pm. To: **Annecy** (3-4hr., 5 per day, €26); **Grenoble** (3hr., 4 per day, €20); **Lyon** (3-4hr., 5-6 per day, €31); **Paris** (5-6hr., 6 per day, €75-95). **SNCF** office (☎06 03 55) is in the Val d'Isère bus station. Open M-F 9:30am-12:30pm and 2:30-6:30pm.

Buses: Autocars Martin (☎06 00 42), at the Val Village bus station, 150m down the main drag from the tourist office. Open July-Aug. and Dec.-Apr. M 9-10:15am and 1-8pm, Th-F 9-11am and 1:30-8pm, Sa 6:45-10am and 12:45-7:30pm. **Main office** at pl. de la Gare in Bourg-St-Maurice (☎07 04 49; www.altibus.com). Open M-F 8am-noon and 2-6:30pm. During ski season (Dec.-Mar.), buses leave from Bourg-St-Maurice for: **Geneva, Switzerland** (4-4½hr.; Jan.-May and Dec. M-F 3 per day, Su 4 per day; €52) and **Lyon** (4hr.; Jan.-May and Dec. M-F 2 per day, Sa 4 per day, Su 3 per day; €56). Buses run year-round from Bourg-St-Maurice to **Tignes** and **Val Village** (45min.; M-F and Su 3 per day, Sa 7 per day; €13).

Public Transportation: Val d'Isère runs free **navettes** (shuttle buses) around town during ski season and again in July and Aug. **Train Rouge** runs between La Daille, Val Village, and Le Fornet (Jan.-Apr. and Dec. every 5min. 8:30am-5:30pm, every 20min. 5:30pm-2am; July-Aug. every 30min. 9am-7:30pm), while **Train Vert** runs from the Val Village tourist office up to the Manchet Sports complex and the entrance to the Vanoise national park (July-Aug. every 15min. 8:15am-7pm; Jan.-Apr. and Dec. every 30min. 10am-8pm). Both shave time off trips to the *refuges.*

Taxis: ABC (☎06 18 19 20 00). **Altitude Espace Taxi** (☎06 07 41 11 53). €50 to the train station in Bourg-St-Maurice. €15 from Val to the hostel.

ORIENTATION AND PRACTICAL INFORMATION

The Val d'Isère mega-resort is made up of three villages in a line along the Isère river: **La Daille** lies at the valley's entrance; **Val Village,** uphill from La Daille, is in the middle and is home to most accommodations, restaurants, and the **tourist office;** and an ascent from Val Village leads to **Le Fornet**, a tiny but welcoming slice of wilderness. Unless otherwise stated, listings below are in Val Village, the most substantial of the three towns. Street names are neither used nor clearly indicated, but the town is navigable with the tourist office's invaluable Practical Guide map.

Tourist Office: (☎06 06 60; www.valdisere.com). From the bus station, walk 5min. along the main road in the direction of Le Fornet. The office is on the left at the roundabout. Distributes excellent practical guide with map and list of hotels and restaurants in 6 languages. Has a hiking desk, which can help to plan summer and winter outdoor excursions. **Internet** access (€9 per hr.). Open July-Aug. daily 8:30am-7:30pm; Sept.-Nov. and May-June M-F 9am-noon and 2-6pm, Sa-Su 10am-noon and 3-6pm; Jan.-Apr. and Dec. M-F and Su 8:30am-7:30pm, Sa 8:30am-8pm.

Laundromats: Laverie Automatique (☎06 08 26 92 86), above the Spar supermarket, to the right of the roundabout from the bus station. Open daily 7am-9pm.

Weather, Ski, and Road Info: Call the tourist office or listen to French-language **Radio Val** (96.1FM; ☎06 18 66). **Weather forecast:** ☎08 92 68 02 73. **Ski Lifts:** ☎06 00 35. **Ski Patrol:** ☎06 02 10.

Police: (☎06 03 41), 600m past the tourist office in the direction of Le Fornet.

Hospital: (☎41 79 79), in Bourg-St-Maurice.

Post Office: (☎06 06 99), across from the tourist office on a side street. **ATM** outside. **Currency exchange.** Open July-Aug. M and W-F 8:30am-1pm and 2-4pm, Tu 8:30am-12:30pm and 2-4pm, Sa 8:30-11:30am. Winter hours vary. **Postal Code:** 73150.

ACCOMMODATIONS AND CAMPING

The world-class slopes surrounding the town don't make it easy to find a room in winter, let alone at budget prices. A less-expensive option for groups is to rent an apartment in one of the many *chalets* in town. **Val Location,** at the tourist office, does the booking. **Val Hôtel** (☎06 18 90; valhotel@valdisere.com) can help visitors find hotel deals during the ski season. The hotels that remain open in the low season maintain reasonable prices. The cheapest beds are at the *refuges*, **Le Prariond** and **Le Fond Des Fours,** each a 2hr. hike from downtown (see **Hiking,** p. 481), and at cheaper **gîtes** in Le Fornet, which offer an alternative to downtown hotels. The tourist office has a complete list.

Chalet Turia (☎06 06 26; fax 06 16 65), 2.5km from the tourist office, in Le Fornet. Accessible by the Train Rouge or by foot (see **Hiking,** p. 481). Across the bridge 20m off the right side of the main road as it enters town. An unbelievably friendly couple provides gorgeous wood-trimmed studios for 2, 4, or 10 people in a *chalet* overlooking the Isère. All come equipped with bathroom, kitchen, TV, heated floors, and splendid views. About as cheap as it gets in the area and one of France's best bargains. Apr.-Nov. €25 per person. Dec.-Mar. weekly rentals only. Dec. and Feb.-Mar. doubles €350; triples and quads €560; 10-person rooms €1750. Jan. €350/460/1600. ❷

Hôtel les Crêtes Blanches (☎06 05 45; www.cretes-blanches.com). Turn right at the roundabout above the bus station. English-speaking staff offers simple, wood-paneled rooms with large windows and TV. Perfect location near the bus stop, chair lifts, and Val Village's shops, restaurants, and nightlife. Breakfast €7. Reception 8am-8pm. Open July-Aug. and Dec.-May. July-Aug. singles €50-54; doubles €60-66; triples €72-78. Dec.-May €68-194/90-216/117-270. MC/V. ❹

Le Relais du Ski (☎06 02 06; www.valdisere.com/lerelaisduski), 500m up from the tourist office, on the left. Offers clean rooms with recently-renovated bathrooms. Breakfast €8. Reception 24hr. July-Nov. singles €51-65; doubles €58-72; triples €60-81; quads €76-88. Dec. to mid-May. €60-76/70-86/80-96/88-116. AmEx/MC/V. ❹

Hôtel Sakura (☎06 04 08; www.sakura7.com). Turn right at the roundabout above the bus station. Spacious apartment-style rooms with bath, free Wi-Fi, TV, and kitchen. English-speaking owner builds all the furniture himself. Reception 8am-8pm. Open July-Aug. and Dec.-May. July-Aug. singles and doubles from €45; triples and quads from €70; quints from €100. Jan.-May and Dec. €60-125/80-210/100-240. MC/V. ❹

Camping les Richardes (☎06 26 60; campinglesrichardes.free.fr), 1km from the tourist office. Take the Train Rouge to "Les Richardes." A fence surrounds this open, undivided field in a beautiful valley near the *centre-ville*. Reception June-Sept. 7:30am-12:30pm and 2-8pm. Open mid-June to mid-Sept. €3 per person, €1.60 per tent, €1.50 per car. Showers €1 per 5min. Electricity €1.90-3.80. MC/V over €15. ❶

FOOD

Restaurants in Val d'Isère tend to be pricey. Most specialize in cheesy regional dishes such as fondue and the meat-and-potatoes-heavy *tartiflette* and *raclette*, while the less expensive pizzerias around Val Village's bus station offer more standard fare. In the low season, only a few *brasseries* and restaurants remain open; ask at the tourist office for a list. A **Spar** supermarket is to the right of the roundabout from the bus station. (☎06 02 66. Open daily 8am-1pm and 3:30-8pm. MC/V.)

L'Arolay (☎06 11 68). The only restaurant in Le Fornet. Beautiful terrace overlooking the Isère makes this the best place to enjoy traditional *savoyard* cuisine. Wood-trimmed interior is adorned with mounted trophies and festive strings of lights. Fondue €17-22. *Tartiflette* €15. *Raclette* €23. *Plats* €16-24. Open July-Aug. and Dec.-Apr. daily 10am-10pm. MC/V. ❸

Le Bananas (☎06 04 23), to the right of the roundabout near the base of the *téléphériques*. Ski instructors and famished skiers pack the interior of this rockin' *chalet* for Tex-Mex and beers. Fajitas €23. *Menus* from €18. Happy hour Jan.-Apr. and Dec. 7-9pm. Open daily July-Aug. and Dec.-Apr. noon-3pm and 5pm-1am. AmEx/MC/V. ❸

La Casserole (☎41 15 71), behind the bus station. Enjoy savory specialties like *raclette* (€25) in a rustic *chalet* with animal skins hanging on the walls. Salads €16-19. *Plats* €16-27. Winter open daily noon-2:30pm and 7-10:30pm; summer Tu and Su noon-2pm, W-Sa noon-2pm and 7-9pm. AmEx/MC/V. ❸

Chevallot (☎06 29 36), 20m uphill from the bus station. This *boulangerie, pâtisserie,* and *salon de thé* offers lighter, cheaper fare. Serves gourmet treats such as *tourte au beaufort* (cheese tart), *quiche lorraine, tartiflette,* and sandwiches (€2.30-6.50). Don't miss the mouth-watering pastries, *fondant chocolat* (€3). Open daily July-Aug. and Dec.-Apr. 6:30am-8pm; Oct.-Nov. and May-June 7am-1pm and 3-7pm. MC/V. ❶

LOST IN TRANSLATION

Hollywood movies and American television may have captivated an enthusiastic market in France, but there's often little rhyme or reason regulating the translation of their titles:

Lolita in Spite of Myself (Mean Girls): Nabokov and Lindsay Lohan: the perfect pop culture union.

The Counter Attack of the Blondes (Legally Blond): Perhaps a little aggressive for a movie about Reese Witherspoon and handbags.

The Little Champions (Mighty Ducks): From the Flying V to the quack chant, the *canard* is the heart and soul of this film.

Rambo (Rambo): Some words just transcend linguistic and cultural barriers.

The Man who would Murmur at the Ears of Horses (The Horse Whisperer): Just in case there was any ambiguity in the original title.

A Day with No End (Groundhog Day): If you don't get the Groundhog Day reference, this is going to be a long movie.

La Grande Evasion (The Great Escape): If they didn't translate this literally, Steve McQueen probably would've just taken everyone down.

The Big Lebowski (The Big Lebowski): The French recognize that The Dude does not appreciate name changes.

Lost in Translation (Lost in Translation): Apparently this one wasn't.

-Vinnie Chiappini

NIGHTLIFE

Typical *après-ski* bars line the streets of Val Village, but most of the late-night action revolves around the roundabout above the Val Village bus station, Val d'Isère's unofficial nightlife strip. Locals and tourists jam to the beats of live DJs at the **Lodge Bar,** to the right of the roundabout from the bus station. The attached restaurant, only open during the winter, is famous for its fondue, which is widely considered the best in town. (☎06 02 01. Beer €3-5. *Soirées à thème* Sa. Happy hour daily 4:30-7:30pm. Open daily July-Aug. 6pm-2am; Nov.-Apr. 4:30pm-2am. MC/V.) Up the street, the discotheque **Dick's Tea Bar** (☎06 14 87) offers a great late-night option with its periodic theme nights; a touristy crowd packs the dance floor of this Val mainstay. Across from the bus station, rugby-themed **Le "XV"** is a popular *après-ski* spot—and with its outdoor terrace, a great *après-hike* spot as well. A diverse, often mostly-Anglophone crowd enjoys a mellow atmosphere, with big-screen TVs playing sporting events. (☎41 90 55. Beer €2.90. Mixed drinks €6. Open July-Aug. and mid-Nov. to early May 9am-1:30am.) **Le Bananas** (see above) also stays busy long into the night. A **Ciné Alps Val** movie theater across from the bus station regularly shows American movies in their original versions. (☎08 92 68 73 33; www.cinealps.fr. Shows daily at 2:30, 6, 9pm. €9, under 12 €7.50.)

OUTDOOR ACTIVITIES

SKIING

Skiing is more than the obsession in Val d'Isère—it's the way of life. Over 100 lifts, several of them originating in Val d'Isère and Tignes, provide access to 300km of trails. One can ski for a day without returning to the same base area, and for a week without repeating a run. Lift tickets are valid on the entire Espace Killy, which includes all lifts and runs from Val d'Isère to Tignes, a ski station 7km away. The mountains can generally be skied from late November to early May, with optimum conditions in midwinter. (Lift tickets available at slope-side ticket offices or www.stvi-valdisere.com. €42 per day, 6 days €203; discounts for ages 5-13 and over 65.) A number of ski schools offer group and private lessons, the largest of which is the **Ecole du Ski Français** (☎06 02 34; www.esfvaldisere.com).

BELLEVARDE, PISSAILLAS, AND TIGNES. Most good beginner runs start at higher altitudes, around the Marmottes and Borsat lifts on the south side of

Bellevarde (take the Bellevarde lift up) and in the scenic **Pissaillas** area (take the Solaise cable car, then the Glacier and Leissier lifts). Intermediate and advanced skiers frequent the slopes surrounding **Tignes,** while the north side of Bellevarde is known for expert runs. There's a giant **snow park** between Val and Tignes; a classic snowboard run starts at the top of the Mont Blanc lift and whirls its way down to La Daille, where a Funival car whisks boarders back to Bellevarde's summit. From late June to mid-July, **Pissaillas** and **La Grande Motte** in Tignes offer **summer skiing.**

OFF-PISTE SKIING. Val d'Isère locals are most proud of the area's off-piste offerings; limitless opportunities for back-country skiing await thrill-seekers, but these trails are generally quite dangerous, and access is often prohibited. To experience the fresh tracks of Val d'Isère's off-piste trails, inquire at the Ecole du Ski Français or hire one of the many independent guides in the area (ask the tourist office for a complete list). With or without a guide, always check weather conditions, leave an itinerary with the ski patrol, and never go alone.

HIKING

With expansive alpine meadows, plunging gorges, snow-covered glaciers, and free-ranging *chamois* (the antelope's smaller cousin), the mountains surrounding the Val offer some of the most spectacular hiking in the Alps. The trails are dotted with **refuges,** most of which offer full board in July and August; with proper planning, backpackers can stay in the mountains for days by hiking from *refuge* to *refuge.* The Val serves as an entry-point for hikes in the **Vanoise National Park,** which extends to the Italian border and is France's premier wildlife reserve. Before setting out for any trip, call ahead to make sure *refuges* and trails are open, check the weather report, and bring warm clothing—snowstorms can strike even in summer. Ask for *L'Estive* at the tourist office, which lists *refuges.* Many of the more advanced routes are suitable only for those with proper equipment and experience. Trails around Val are well marked with blazes and signs, but hikers should buy an **IGN map** (€9.50) and the detailed *Val d'Isère Les Sentiers de l'Eté* (€10), which describes over 50 routes spanning 100km, at the tourist office. The book also details several Vanoise hikes originating in Tignes, with trailheads at both the upper town and the hostel.

LE FORNET. Until the construction of modern ski areas in the 1960s, **Le Fornet** (1950m) was the highest continuously inhabited village in the French Alps. The easy trail leading up the valley starts from the church in Val Village (50min., 100m vertical). Following the signs for Le Fornet, walk though *vieux* Val to a pedestrian road that briefly joins up with the **GR5** before forking again toward Le Fornet.

REFUGE DE PRARIOND AND COL DE LA GALISE. The stunning **Refuge de Prariond** hike (1¼hr., 3km, 300m vertical) leads into the heart of the Vanoise and is a must for animal-lovers: sure-footed *bouquetins* (ibex), *chamois* (wild goats), and furry marmots roam the areas around the trail. The hike starts at pont St-Charles, a 30min. walk from Le Fornet along the main road going away from Val Village. The Train Rouge extends its route to Pont St-Charles four times a day; check at the tourist office for a schedule. From the parking lot near the bridge, a marked trail makes most of its ascent within the first kilometer. Upon reaching the **Gorges du Malpasset,** the trail plateaus and continues along the steep hillside above the Isère, allowing hikers to enjoy spectacular views of the surrounding mountains, through an alpine meadow to the **Refuge de Prariond.** (☎06 06 02; www.prariond.com. Staffed late Mar. to early-May and mid-June to mid-Sept. During un-staffed months, wood, gas, utensils, and a tin box are provided with payment. Breakfast €7. Reservations recommended. Shower €2.50. Sleepsacks €2.50. Beds €13, students €9; *demi-pension* €34/30.) The trail is fairly easy but passes through several small streams; be cautious when walking on the wet rocks. From the *refuge,* signs point to a more difficult trail that ascends to the **Col de la Galise** (2hr., 710m vertical), a small summit that straddles the French-Italian border. On a clear day, hikers can see deep into the heart of the glacial mountain ranges.

REFUGE DU FOND DES FOURS AND THE GR5. The intermediate **Refuge du Fond des Fours** (1¾hr., 560m vertical) hike starts at the Manchet entrance to the Vanoise; take the free Train Vert shuttle to Le Manchet (see **Public Transportation,** p. 478) and continue up the road to the park entrance, past the base of the chair lift and a cluster of old stone farmhouses. From just inside the entrance, follow the trail on the left marked *"Refuge du Fond des Fours."* The trail rises gradually through a valley before reaching steeper terrain, where it follows a series of switchbacks upward. After descending briefly into a small valley, it goes up another fairly steep rise to the *refuge*, in a high valley across from the **Méan Martin** glacier and alpine lakes. (Refuge ☎06 16 90. Staffed mid-Mar. to mid-May and mid-June to mid-Sept. Showers €3. Sleepsacks €3.25. Beds €13, students €8.80; *demi-pension* €35/32.) To return to Val, descend via the same path. Another option is to cross the **Col des Fours** pass and head back to town via the **GR5,** a 7hr. loop that crosses difficult terrain. Continue along the trail to the *refuge*, then turn left onto the path that ascends the line between the 3135m **Pelaou Blanc** and the 3072m **Pointe des Fours** (1¼hr., 450m vertical). Where the trail ends, turn left on the red-and-white marked **GR5** for a scenic descent on the **Col d'Iseran,** a popular leg of the Tour de France (3hr., 6km, 900m vertical). Acquire a good map before starting out.

LAC DU SANTEL. The full-day **Lac du Santel** advanced trek starts at the Fornet *téléphérique* (7hr. round-trip, 12.25km, 940m vertical). From the station, descend slightly and turn right at the trail marker for the **Balcon des Barmettes.** At the Balcon, head right on Trail #36, the **Bailletta,** which climbs steeply for 800m to the small **Lac de la Bailletta** (2½hr.), reaches a pass, and then descends gradually to the larger **Lac de la Sassière.** This man-made lake is packed with trout, and the surrounding area is inhabited by *chamois*, ibex, and marmots.

OTHER OUTDOOR ACTIVITIES

The **Bureau des Guides** (☎06 05 53) teaches ice climbing (morning session €76) and rock-climbing (afternoon session €28) and leads full-day canyoning trips (€64). Nature expeditions are offered for all levels. Advanced climbers should verify routes with guides before setting out. Beginners should check out the **Via Ferrata** (morning and afternoon sessions €46) in La Daille. This 3hr. climb (360m vertical) uses metal footholds and ropes and hugs the side of the mountain facing the valley; there is also a more demanding 4-6hr. climb that requires a guide. Make all reservations with the **Bureau des Guides** the night before. (Info desk on the lower-level of Killy Sports, next to the tourist office. Open daily 6am-7:30pm.)

For a relaxing trip to the summit of Val d'Isère, take a *téléphérique* over peaks, glaciers, and valleys to the top of the mountain. In the summer, a chair lift runs to Solaise, a small summit surrounded by a fish-packed lake and easy hiking trails, and to the higher Bellevarde, site of the 1992 Olympic downhill ski race. (*Téléphérique* to Solaise and Bellevarde Jan.-Apr., Dec., and July-Aug. In summer round-trip €6.50; in winter with ski pass only.)

MASSIF CENTRAL

Many claustrophobic travelers escape from Paris to the coastal regions of Provence and the Riviera—only to find that the rest of Paris has done the same—but the lucky few who penetrate the Massif Central, in the very heart of the country, find rugged, unadulterated beauty. A beautiful and sometimes bizarre landscape, the area features a forested chain of extinct volcanoes studded with giant lava needles. Although quiet, the Auvergne's lush countryside and wealth of outdoor adventures more than compensate for its lack of nightlife. The towering Puy-de-Dôme (p. 489) offers prime views of the volcanic park, though the real hiking (and skiing) mecca is Le Mont-Dore (p. 490), nestled in the shadow of a string of dormant volcanoes. The Massif's varied terrain also caters to less adventurous travelers. In Le Puy-en-Velay (p. 494), pumice-paved streets wind among Renaissance houses and statue-topped volcanic needles. The mineral waters of Le Mont-Dore (p. 490) and Vichy (p. 498), better known today as the former capital of Nazi-controlled France during WWII, attract both *curistes* (those who believe in the healing powers of the springs) and the curious. Whether you come seeking relaxation or recreation, the Massif Central is sure to deliver in a big way.

HIGHLIGHTS OF THE MASSIF CENTRAL

CLIMB to the top of Le Mont-Dore's **Puy de Sancy** (p. 492) for a 360° view of the mountain chains around it.

FEEL a little bit closer to heaven at the chapel of **St-Michel d'Aiguille** (p. 497), which sits atop a lava needle in Le Puy-en-Velay.

BE INSPIRED at Clermont-Ferrand's **Cathédrale Notre-Dame de l'Assomption** (p. 488), where 13th-century workers used volcanic rock to build the spire sky-high.

CLERMONT-FERRAND ☎04 73

During the Middle Ages, Clermont-Ferrand (CLARE-mohn fur-RAHN; pop. 141,000) existed as two separate cities, Clermont and Montferrand. The two were economic and political rivals until Louis XIII merged them in 1630. Clermont got a better deal: the allegedly "combined" city's walls excluded Montferrand. Now the outcast city is nearly forgotten, while its illustrious twin has become a bustling urban center. During the 20th century, red-roofed Clermont became synonymous with Michelin tires (rubber was first used in bike tires here) and the revered *Red* and *Green Guides*, thanks to brothers André and Edouard Michelin. Today, Clermont-Ferrand is a true college town, home to two major universities, nearly 35,000 students, and the comic shops, kebab stands, and tattoo parlors that so often accompany them. While the city itself provides ample entertainment for a short stay, it also makes a perfect base for trips to the surrounding mountains.

TRANSPORTATION

Trains: Av. de l'Union Soviétique (☎90 22 90). Ticket booths open M-Th 5:20am-8:20pm, F 5:20am-9:20p.m, Sa 6am-7:40pm, Su 7am-9:50pm. To: **Le Puy** (2hr., 4 per day, €21); **Lyon** (2½hr., 8 per day, €29); **Paris** (3½hr., 8 per day, €50).

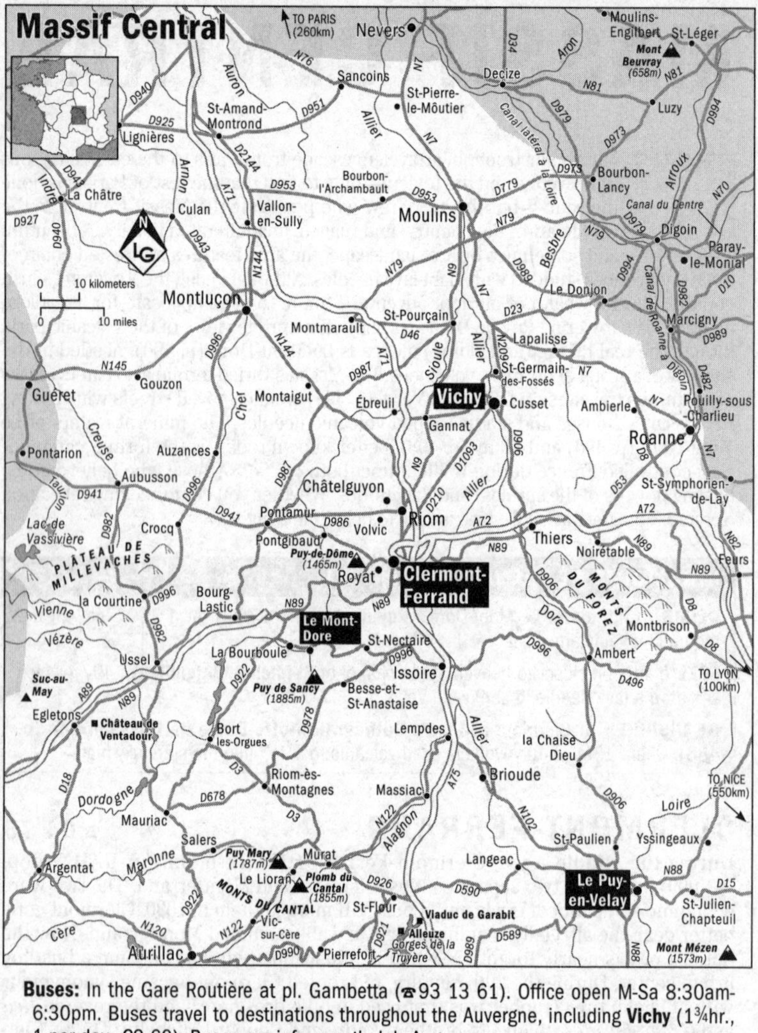

Buses: In the Gare Routière at pl. Gambetta (☎93 13 61). Office open M-Sa 8:30am-6:30pm. Buses travel to destinations throughout the Auvergne, including **Vichy** (1¾hr., 1 per day, €9.60). Buses run infrequently July-Aug.

Public Transportation: 24 bd. Charles de Gaulle (☎28 80 00; www.t2c.fr). Buses cover the city 5am-10pm. Individual ticket €1.30, day pass €4.20; available from vending machines at pl. de Jaude, across from the train station, and throughout the city.

Taxis: Taxi 63 (☎31 53 15). **Taxis Radio** (☎19 53 53). Both 24hr.

Car Rental: Avis, rue Pierre Semard (☎91 72 94), on the other side of the train tracks and accessible via an underground tunnel. Open M 9:30am-1pm and 2-6:15pm, Tu-F 9am-1pm and 2-6:15pm.

Bike Rental: MooviCité, 20 pl. Renoux and 43 av. de l'Union Soviétique (both ☎08 10 63 00 63). Open M-F 7am-7pm, Sa 8am-7pm. €3 per day, €10 per week. Electric bikes €5 per day, €16 per week. Discounts for students, under 25, and over 65. Cash only.

ORIENTATION AND PRACTICAL INFORMATION

Clermont-Ferrand's *centre-ville* is in Clermont, between **place Delille** and **place de Jaude.** Pick up a map at the information desk in the train station, which is a 20min. walk from the city center. Buses #2, 4, and 14 run from the station to pl. de Jaude. Several restaurants, a theater, and the monstrous shopping complex **Centre Jaude** surround the *place*, while clothing boutiques, the famous cathedral, and a plethora of bookstores line the streets of the *vieille ville.* From the station, turn left onto av. de l'Union Soviétique, left again onto bd. Fleury, and take a quick right onto av. Carnot. Continue on this road through several name changes to pl. de Jaude.

Tourist Office: Pl. de la Victoire (☎98 65 00; www.clermont-fd.com). From the train station, turn left onto av. de l'Union Soviétique. Follow the above directions to pl. Jaude, but after 10min. on av. Carnot, turn right onto rue St-Gènes (20min.). The office has great maps, bus schedules, hiking routes, an English and French self-guided walking tour, and a 2hr. English and French guided walking tours of Clermont (July-Aug. M, W, F 3pm and Tu and Th 8:30pm; early to mid-Sept. M, W, F 3pm) and Montferrand (July to mid-Sept. Tu, Th, Sa 3pm; €5.70, students €3.10). Office open May-Sept. M-F 9am-7pm, Sa-Su 10am-7pm; Oct.-Apr. M-F 9am-6pm, Sa 10am-1pm and 2-6pm, Su 9:30am-12:30pm and 2-6pm.

Budget Travel: Voyages Wasteels, 11a av. des Etats-Unis (☎19 07 95). Open M-Th 9:30am-noon and 2-6:30pm, F 9am-noon and 2-6:30pm, Sa 9am-noon and 2-5pm.

Youth Center: Espace Info Jeunes, 5 rue St-Genès (☎92 30 50; www.espaceinfojeunes.net). Helpful staff provides info on jobs, travel, lodging, and schools. Free Wi-Fi. Open M-F 10am-6pm, Sa 10am-1pm.

Laundromat: 57 rue du Port. Open daily 7am-11pm. Also at 6 pl. Hippolyte Renoux. Wash €4 per 7kg. Open daily 7am-8pm. Cash only.

Police: 2 rue Pélissier (☎98 42 42).

Poison Control: ☎04 72 11 69 11.

24hr. Pharmacy: Pharmacie Ducher, 1 pl. Delille (☎91 31 77). Night fee €6 (10pm-7am). AmEx/MC/V.

Medical Services: Hôpital Gabriel-Montpied, 58 rue Montalembert (☎75 07 50). **SOS Médecins,** 28 av. Léon Blum (☎42 22 22). Open 24hr.

Internet Access: Cyber Frag, 3 rue de la Boucherie (☎91 51 64), in the *vieille ville.* €1.50 per 30min. Open daily 11am-11pm.

Post Office: 1 rue Busset (☎30 65 42). **Currency exchange** and **ATM.** Open M-Sa 9am-7pm. Branch at 2 pl. Gaillard (☎31 70 00). Open M-F 9am-7pm, Sa 8:30am-12:30pm. **Postal Code:** 63000.

ACCOMMODATIONS AND CAMPING

Most inexpensive hotels are located just outside of the center of town or about halfway between the train station and the *vieille ville.* Several older, less attractive hotels cluster near the train station.

Hôtel Ravel, 8 rue de Maringues (☎91 51 33; hotelravel63@wanadoo.fr). An intricate mosaic decorates this hotel, conveniently located in a tranquil neighborhood between the station and city center. Clean, carpeted rooms with comfortable beds, bath, and TV. Breakfast €6. Singles €39; doubles €47; triples €58; quads €70. MC/V. ❸

Foyer Hôme Dome, 12 pl. de Regensburg (☎29 40 70; www.ethic-etapes.fr). From the intersection of av. Carnot and av. d'Italie, near the station, take bus #13 (dir.: Perignat) to "Regensburg." Or, from pl. de Jaude, follow rue Jaude to pl. Gallieni, cross onto rue des Salins, and take the 4th right onto rue de L'Etang. Recently renovated high-rise

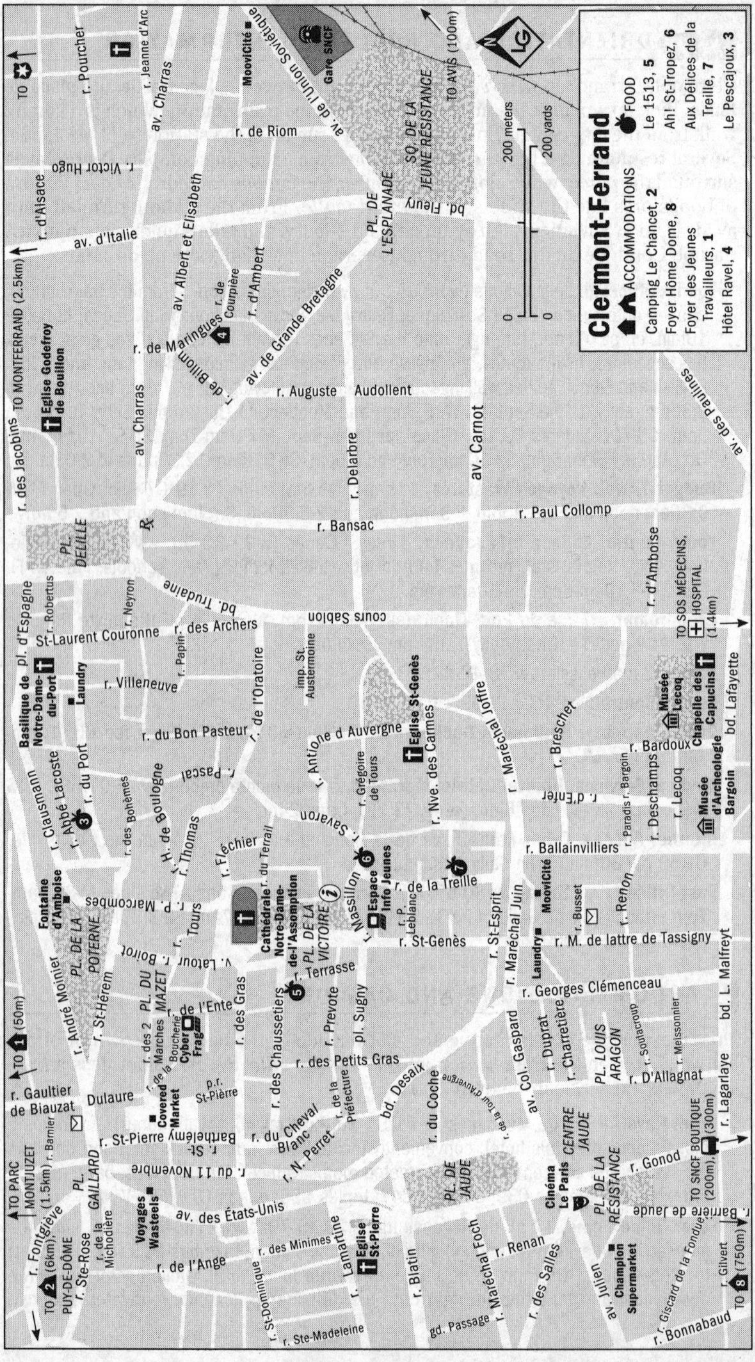
Clermont-Ferrand
ACCOMMODATIONS
Camping Le Chancet, 2
Foyer Hôme Dome, 8
Foyer des Jeunes Travailleurs, 1
Hôtel Ravel, 4
FOOD
Le 1513, 5
Ah! St-Tropez, 6
Aux Délices de la Treille, 7
Le Pescajoux, 3
200 meters
200 yards
Gare SNCF
MooviCité
av. de l'Union Soviétique
SQ. DE LA JEUNE RÉSISTANCE
TO AVIS (100m)
PL. DE L'ESPLANADE
bd. Fleury
av. Charras
r. de Riom
r. Pourcher
r. Jeanne d'Arc
r. Victor Hugo
r. d'Alsace
av. d'Italie
TO MONTFERRAND (2.5km)
Eglise Godefroy de Bouillon
r. des Jacobins
av. Albert et Elisabeth
r. d'Ambert
r. de Courpière
r. de Maringues
r. de Billom
av. de Grande Bretagne
r. Auguste Audollent
r. Delarbre
av. Carnot
av. des Paulines
r. Paul Collomp
r. Bansac
PL. DELILLE
bd. Trudaine
cours Sablon
r. d'Amboise
TO SOS MÉDECINS, HOSPITAL (1.4km)
pl. d'Espagne
r. Robertus
r. Neyron
St-Laurent Couronne
r. des Archers
r. Papin
r. de l'Oratoire
imp. St. Austermoine
Basilique de Notre-Dame-du-Port
Laundry
r. Villeneuve
r. du Bon Pasteur
r. Antoine d Auvergne
Eglise St-Genès
r. Maréchal Joffre
r. Breschet
Musée Lecoq
Chapelle des Capucins
bd. Lafayette
r. Bardoux
r. Clausmann
r. Abbé Lacoste
r. du Port
r. des Bohèmes
r. H. de Boulogne
r. Pascal
r. Grégoire de Tours
r. Nve. des Carmes
r. d'Enfer
r. Paradis
r. Bargoin
r. Deschamps
r. Lecoq
Musée d'Archeologie Bargoin
r. Thomas
r. Fléchier
r. Savaron
r. Ballainvilliers
Fontaine d'Amboise
r. du Terrail
Massillon
Espace Info Jeunes
r. de la Treille
MooviCité
r. Busset
r. Renon
r. P. Marcombes
Tours
Cathédrale Notre-Dame-de-l'Assomption
PL. DE LA VICTOIRE
r. P. Leblanc
r. St-Esprit
r. Maréchal Juin
r. St-Genès
r. M. de lattre de Tassigny
PL. DE LA POTERNE
r. André Moinier
r. St-Hérem
r. Boirot
v. Latour
PL. DU MAZET
r. de l'Ente
r. Terrasse
Laundry
r. Georges Clémenceau
TO 1 (50m)
r. des 2 Marchés
r. de la Boucherie
Cyber Frag
r. des Gras
r. des Chaussetiers
r. Prevote
pl. Sugny
r. Duprat
r. Charretière
PL. LOUIS ARAGON
r. Soulacroup
r. Meissonnier
r. Gaultier de Biauzat
Dulaure
Covered Market
p.r. St-Pierre
r. des Petits Gras
r. de la Préfecture
bd. Desaix
r. du Coche
r. de la Tour d'Auvergne
av. Col. Gaspard
r. D'Allagnat
bd. L. Malfreyt
r. Lagarlaye
TO PARC MONTJUZET (1.5km)
r. Barnier
r. St-Pierre
r. St-Barthelemy
r. du Cheval Blanc
r. N. Perret
PL. DE JAUDE
CENTRE JAUDE
TO SNCF BOUTIQUE (200m), (300m)
PL. GAILLARD
r. du 11 Novembre
Voyages Wasteels
av. des États-Unis
Cinéma Le Paris
PL. DE LA RÉSISTANCE
r. Gonod
Barrière de Jaude
r. Fontgiève
TO 2 (6km) PUY-DE-DÔME
r. Ste-Rose
r. de la Michodière
r. de l'Ange
r. des Minimes
r. Lamartine
Eglise St-Pierre
r. St-Dominique
r. Ste-Madeleine
r. Blatin
r. Maréchal Foch
r. Renan
gd. Passage
r. des Salles
av. Julien
Champion Supermarket
r. Giscard de la Fondue
r. Gilvert
TO 8 (750m)
r. Bonnabaud

building near a relatively quiet residential area. Staff offers simple but modern rooms with toilet and shower. Restaurant, kitchen, laundry facilities, and computer lab without Internet. Breakfast included. 2-night min. stay. Reception 24hr. Singles and doubles €19 per person, €17 for stays over 3 nights. MC/V. ❶

Foyer des Jeunes Travailleurs (Corum Saint Jean), 17 rue Gaultier de Biauzat (☎31 57 00; www.corumsaintjean.fr). Although the simple and private dorm-style rooms in this aging building leave something to be desired, the Foyer boasts a prime location near the *vieille ville* and an array of amenities. Bar, cafeteria-style restaurant, climbing wall, free Internet access, and laundry (€3). Some rooms with private showers. Breakfast included. Reception 24hr. Singles and doubles €19-27 per person. MC/V. ❷

Camping Le Chancet, av. Jean-Baptiste Marrou (☎61 30 73), 6km outside Clermont, on N89 (dir.: Bordeaux). From the station, take bus #4C (dir.: Ceyrat) to "Préguille." 3 stars. Rows of bushes separate spots. Heated pool, mini golf, and organized biking and hiking excursions in summer. Laundry. Reception 9am-10pm. June-Aug. €3.10 per adult, €2.10 per child under 10, €5.60 per site; Apr.-May and Sept. €2.80/1.80/4.20; Jan.-Mar. and Oct.-Dec. €2.65/1.80/3.35. Electricity €3.60. AmEx/MC/V. ❶

FOOD

Clermont-Ferrand's Michelin brothers may have created the most influential French restaurant guide, but their own hometown is not generally known for its cuisine. Unassuming college hangouts are tucked along side streets in the city center, fast-food joints cluster on av. des Etats-Unis, and a few *brasseries* surround the tourist office and cathedral. A **Champion** supermarket takes up much of rue Giscard de la Tour Fondue, just past pl. de Jaude. (Open M-Sa 8:30am-8:30pm, Su 9am-12:30pm. MC/V.) Just off pl. Gaillard, the **Marché Couvert/Espace St-Pierre** stocks local produce, cheese, and meats. (Open M 7am-7pm, Tu-Sa 7am-7:30pm.)

Le Pescajoux, 13 rue du Port (☎92 12 26). Relaxed dining room decorated with artist-owner's sculptures and abstract works. One of the largest *crêpe* and *galette* menus you'll ever see—with over 100 variations ranging from basic *chocolat* (€3.50), to the more intimidating "Popeye" with fresh spinach (€7.50), to the "XXL" (750g of steak, eggs, and cheese; €14). Open Tu-F noon-2pm and 7:30-11:30pm, Sa 7:30-11:30pm. AmEx/MC/V. ❶

Ah! St-Tropez, 10 rue Massillon (☎90 44 64), near pl. de Victoire. Set in a yellow dining room with vibrant murals. Serves tasty gourmet *menus* (lunch €13, dinner €16-24) of—illogically enough—entirely *provençal* cuisine, which makes you wish you were in the Riviera. Try the *Tian,* a *gratin* of spinach, onion, tomato, and cucumber. Open Tu-Th noon-2pm and 7:30-10pm, F-Sa 7:30-11:30pm. MC/V. ❸

Aux Délices de la Treille, 33 rue de la Treille (☎91 26 90). Quirky and colorful restaurant on a narrow medieval street. Serves delicious regional *menus* (€11-22). Toes the delicate line between cool and just plain eccentric. Doubles as a gallery for charismatic owner Yannick, who happily chats with customers and shows off his artwork. Open daily 11am-3pm and 6:30pm-midnight. Cash only. ❸

Le 1513, 3 rue des Chaussetiers (☎92 37 46). Tucked inside one of Clermont-Ferrand's best-preserved medieval hotels. Intimate atmosphere with 2 private courtyards and small stone-walled dining rooms with low ceilings. A wide variety of *galettes* (€2.50-12), enormous desserts (€2.50-9), and tasty salads (€2.50-11). *Menu* €14. Open M-F noon-2pm and 6pm-12:30am, Sa-Su noon-12:30am. MC/V. ❷

SIGHTS

Clermont's *vieille ville*, called the **Ville Noire** (Black City) for its many black-stoned buildings, features architecture from the Middle Ages, the Belle Epoque, and modern times. Tiny **Montferrand** doesn't boast much in the way of attractions, but it does feature some well-preserved half-timbered houses, medieval mansions, and a church built of volcanic rock. The best way to visit Montferrand (a 40min. walk up av. de la République) is to take the Clermont tourist office's French walking tour, which leaves from pl. Louis Deteix (2hr. Tu, Th, Sa 3pm; €5.70, students €3.10). Take tram line A (dir.: Champratel) to "Montferrand." Clermont-Ferrand's museums touch on archaeology, medieval art, and natural history; a combined €6.50 ticket allows entry into any two of the city's four museums. Most museums are free for students and those under 18 and free for everyone on the first Sunday of the month. The best sights, however, lie in the surrounding mountains.

CATHÉDRALE NOTRE-DAME-DE-L'ASSOMPTION. First built in AD 450 but completely reconstructed in Gothic style between 1248 and 1295, this magnificent cathedral rises high above the surrounding buildings and remains a presence wherever you are in the city. Tiny bubbles in the black volcanic stone used in construction made it much lighter, allowing the church's spires to soar to a height of 100m. The combination of the cathedral's gargoyle-covered Gothic exterior, towering height, and jet-black color make the building seem more like an evil citadel than a house of God. Climb up the 252-step tower for unrivaled views of Clermont-Ferrand and a closer look at the gargoyles and flying buttresses. *(Pl. de la Victoire. www.catholique-clermont.cef.fr. Open M-Sa 8am-noon and 2-6pm, Su 9:30am-noon and 3-7pm. Tower open M-Sa 10am-noon and 2-6pm, Su 3-6pm. €1.50. Info available in 12 languages.)*

BASILIQUE DE NOTRE DAME-DU-PORT. This 12th-century church, dedicated to the Virgin Mary, was built in Auvergnat Romanesque style. Allegedly, Pope Urban II started the First Crusade near this site. In May, pilgrims come to see the **Black Virgin** icon. Annoyingly, the basilica is closed for renovation until October 2008. *(Pl. Notre Dame-du-Port. ☎91 32 94. Open daily 8am-7pm. French Tours July-Aug. W, F 3pm.)*

PARC DE MONTJUZET. This immaculately groomed park covers a hill located high above Clermont, offering panoramic views of the city and its surrounding mountains, including Puy-de-Dôme, which are only bested by those from the cathedrals's tower. The hillside Mediterranean garden—one of the park's highlights—seems to be taken straight out of a Van Gogh landscape. The rest of the park features shaded paths, contemporary sculptures, and various playgrounds, making it a perfect spot for people of all ages to enjoy a picnic or afternoon stroll. *(Northwest of the main city. Main entrance and parking on rue du Parc Monjuzet; secondary pedestrian entrance closer to the vieille ville on rue des Aubepines. A 15min. walk from the cathedral; ask at the tourist office for directions. ☎42 63 63. Open 7am-8pm.)*

MUSÉE D'ARCHÉOLOGIE BARGOIN. Prehistoric skeletons and tools and North African textiles take a back seat to this small museum's rich collection of Gallo-Roman artifacts. What the array of artifacts lacks in size it makes up for in variety; figurines, glassware, mosaics, sculptures, and relics of Le Puy de Dome's Temple of Mercury are just some of the items on display. *(45 rue Ballainvilliers. ☎42 69 70. Open Tu-Sa 10am-noon and 1-5pm, Su 2-7pm. €4.20, students €2.70, under 18 free.)*

ENTERTAINMENT AND FESTIVALS

Pool tables and cheap beer are the main attractions at most bars across from the train station. Check out the excellent *Guide de l'Etudiant Clermont-Ferrand* (available at the tourist office) for complete bar listings and more information.

From January 1 to February 9, 2008, over 3000 filmmakers and over 130,000 guests will gather for Clermont-Ferrand's annual **Festival International du Court Métrage,** considered the Cannes of short film. Contact La Jetée, 6 pl. Michel de l'Hospital, for more info. (☎91 65 73; www.clermont-filmfest.com. 5- to 6-film pass €2.50.)

Throughout July, the annual **Contre-Plongées de l'Eté** (☎42 69 89) provides open-air film screenings and live concerts in parks and squares around the city.

DAYTRIP FROM CLERMONT FERRAND

PUY-DE-DÔME

Although Puy-de-Dôme is only 12km from Clermont-Ferrand, getting there takes some planning. A shuttle circulates 3 times per day from the Clermont train station to the summit and 4 times per day to the nearby Vulcania natural area. (☎08 00 50 05 24. 35min.; July-Aug. daily, May-June and Sept. Sa-Su and holidays; round-trip €5, €2.50 for students and under 16. Includes connecting shuttles to Vulcania.) Cyclists allowed on mountain June-Aug. W and Su 7-9am; July-Aug. daily 10am-6pm; Sept.-Oct. and May-June Sa-Su and holidays. Drivers must pay a €6 toll, leave their cars at the base, and take a bus to the top (last bus descends 6pm, round-trip €4). Limited free parking at base and summit.

Clermont-Ferrand's greatest attraction may be its proximity to an area of extinct volcanoes, crater lakes, and mountains. Puy-de-Dôme (PWEE duh dohm), the mountain dominating the middle of this region, is part of the **Parc Naturel Régional des Volcans d'Auvergne,** west of Clermont-Ferrand (☎65 64 00). Hikers, bikers, and skiers alike enjoy the unspoiled terrain of one of France's largest parks. A booklet available at the Clermont-Ferrand tourist office indicates hiking paths in the area. There are three main sections in the protected area: the **Mont-Dore,** the **Monts du Cantal,** and the **Monts Dômes,** the best base for exploring the mountains.

On a clear day, the sweeping view from flat-topped **Puy-de-Dôme** (1465m) encompasses the rest of the **Chaîne des Puys,** a lush ridge of extinct volcanoes. The scenery in late autumn can be particularly spectacular, as a sea of clouds often obscures the plains below so that only isolated peaks protrude into the sky. The ruins of the Roman **Temple de Mercure,** from the first and second centuries, sit on the summit. **Paragliding** (*parapent* in French) is quite popular on the summit. (Puy-de-Dôme open July-Aug. daily 10am-9pm; Sept.-June hours depend on daylight. Flights daily 10am-sunset, depending on weather. Contact the Puy-de-Dome paragliding director, ☎06 08 32 08 46, for information on hours and weather conditions. €70. Cash only.) Call ahead (☎62 12 18) to see if the road to the top is open.

For the adventurous, hiking to Puy-de-Dôme is a worthwhile trek. Hikers can take the *navette* to the base of the mountain and make the 45min. ascent up the chemin des Muletiers, a path that climbs

MASSIF SPENDER

If you thought the spectacular views from the summit of Puy-de-Dome couldn't get any better, think again. Paragliding is the newest way to enjoy breathtaking panoramas of the Massif Central. When weather permits, the truly brave and *faux courageux* strap in with an instructor for a 15-20min. tandem flight around Puy-de-Dome and the surrounding mountains. Securely fastened into a seat-like harness below the glider's canopy, which looks and works like an airplane wing, pilots take off with a running start; the cells comprising the canopy take in and trap air, lifting the glider airborne as it moves forward.

Scared of heights? Instructors swear that vertigo is not a problem for paragliders, who are strapped in so securely they can take photos in flight—and there is definitely plenty to be photographed. The Massif's weird lava formations and plush pine forests provide some of France's most beautiful and unique scenery.

Ready to fly? Come between March and October from 10am to 9pm. All safety equipment is provided, including gloves, a windbreaker, and a mandatory helmet, and most instructors speak English, or at least 'the important words,' as one jokes. Transportation from the landing site at the base of Puy-de-Dome back to the summit is also provided.

☎04 73 62 15 15; www.archipel-volcans.com. Standard flight €70. Cash only.

350m vertically before reaching the summit. Though tiring, the hike is reasonable for most. If you miss the *navette*, a longer hike is necessary: take bus #14 to "Royat" from the stop at pl. Allard. From there, take D68 to reach the first yellow markers that guide the rest of the wide, graveled, 3hr. hike along the PR Chamina to the summit. The hike from Royat is approximately 10km, mostly uphill, and largely upon a regular road. Buy the IGN *Chaîne des Puys* map and listen to the weather forecast for the day; conditions change rapidly, affecting access to the summit, guided tours, and paragliding.

LE MONT-DORE ☎04 73

In an isolated valley where the Dordogne river is little more than a trickle, Le Mont-Dore (luh MOHN dohr; pop. 1700) sits at the foot of the largest volcano in a dormant range. Puy de Sancy, the highest peak in Central France, is only 3.5km from the *centre-ville*, making the town a premier ski resort in the winter and a hiking mecca year-round—and thus a paradise for outdoor enthusiasts. As expected, the town itself brims with mountain *chalets* and rustic, timbered lodges; however, it also enjoys an atmosphere of natural luxury. For centuries, its famous *thermes* have attracted summer *curistes* seeking rejuvenation in the warm, mineral-rich hot springs waters that seep through cracks in the lava. Visitors find an interesting melange of these two worlds in the *centre-ville*, where ski and mountain bike rental shops sit next to wine *caves* and lace boutiques.

TRANSPORTATION. **Trains** and SNCF **buses** run from pl. de la Gare. (☎65 00 02. Ticket office open M-F 5:25am-7:45pm, Sa 5:25am-7:30pm, Su 9:30am-7:30pm.) Destinations include Clermont-Ferrand (2hr., 2-3 per day, €12) and Paris (6hr., 2 per day, €57). For a **taxi,** call Taxi Thierry Barlaud (☎65 09 32) or Taxi Sepchat (☎06 88 19 82 66). Rent **bikes** and **skis** at **Bessac Sports,** rue de Maréchal Juin, near the top of the hill. (☎65 02 25. Bikes €12 per ½-day, €18 per day. Ski packages €13-27 per day. Snowboard packages €16-21. ID deposit. Hiking equipment also available. Open daily May-Sept. 9am-noon and 2-7pm; early to mid-Dec. and mid-Jan. to Apr. 9am-noon and 1:30-7pm; mid-Dec. to mid-Jan. 8:30am-7pm. MC/V.)

ORIENTATION AND PRACTICAL INFORMATION. The narrow town of Le Mont-Dore is bounded by two major streets: **avenue de la Libération** on the west side of the Dordogne River, and **route de Clermont** on the east. To get to the tourist office from the station, head up av. Michel Bertrand, through pl. Charles de Gaulle, and onto rue Meynadier. Turn right onto allée Georges Lagaye; the office is across the iceskating rink.

The English-speaking staff at the **tourist office,** av. de la Libération, offers a city guide, hiking trail map (€7), and hiking guidebooks (€7-15) and helps with accommodations booking. (☎65 20 21. Open July-Aug. M-Sa 9am-7pm, Su 10am-noon and 2-6pm; May-June and Sept. M-Sa 9am-12:30pm and 2-6pm, Su 10am-noon and 2-6pm; Oct. M-Sa 9am-noon and 2-6pm.) Other services include: a **laundromat,** pl. de la République (open daily 9am-8pm); **police,** av. M. Bertrand (☎65 01 70); a **pharmacie de garde,** which alternates between Pharmacie du Parc, 17 rue Meynadier (☎65 02 86; open M-Sa 9am-noon and 2:30-7pm) and Pharmacie de l'Etablissement, 3 pl. du Panthéon (☎65 05 21; open M-Sa 9am-12:30pm and 2:30-7:30pm); and a **hospital,** 2 rue du Capitaine-Chazotte (☎65 33 33), off pl. Charles de Gaulle. The **post office,** pl. Charles de Gaulle, exchanges currency and has an ATM. (☎65 37 10. Open M-F 8:30am-noon and 2-5:30pm, Sa 8:30am-noon.) **Postal Code:** 63240.

ACCOMMODATIONS AND CAMPING. Le Mont-Dore has over a dozen hotels, and rooms start around €20, making it relatively easy to find an affordable bed in town. Even so, reservations are usually recommended during summer and peak skiing season. The wood-paneled rooms in **Hôtel Artense ❷,** 19 av. de la Libération, near the tourist office, may not reproduce the charm of a real mountain *chalet*, but they provide a clean and comfortable place to stay for a great price. (☎65 03 43; www.artense-hotel.com. Breakfast €5. Reception 8am-7pm. Closed Nov. Singles and doubles €20-40; triples with bath €40-45; quads €43-53. MC/V.) A rustic but modern ambience characterizes **Castel Medicis ❸,** 5 rue Duchatel, at the top of the main part of town, where clean, bright rooms have light-colored wooden floors and furniture. (☎65 30 50; www.castel-medicis.com. Breakfast included. Reception 8am-8pm. Check-in after 2pm. Singles €34; doubles €38. Extra bed €10. MC/V.) **Auberge de Jeunesse "Le Grand Volcan" (HI) ❶,** rte. du Sancy, is a 3km walk uphill from town. From the station, climb av. Guyot-Dessaigne, which becomes av. des Belges. Continue on D983 (through several name changes) into the countryside. The hostel is on the right, after the chair lifts. Take a taxi from town (€10) or one of the *navettes* that run to the hostel from the train station and the tourist office four times per day (last bus 5:55pm; €2.30). The hostel boasts a cozy ski-lodge atmosphere and tiny but clean one- to seven-bed rooms. Its location at the foot of Puy de Sancy, just steps from skiing and hiking trails, makes up for any lack of luxury. (☎65 03 53; fax 65 26 39. Outdoor kitchen, bar, pool table. Breakfast included. Internet access €4 per hr. Ski and snowboard packages from €34. Reception 8am-noon and 6-8pm. Dorms €19. Cash only.) The most convenient of the four campsites in Le Mont-Dore is **Des Crouzets ❶,** av. des Crouzets, across from the train station. In a hollow on the Dordogne, this poorly landscaped site is well-kept but lacks trees or hedges for privacy. (☎/fax 65 21 60. Reception M-Sa 9am-noon and 3-6:30pm, Su 9:30am-noon and 4-6pm. Open mid-Dec. to mid.-Oct. €2.90-3 per person, €3-3.10 per site. Electricity €3.50-3.90.)

FOOD. Le Mont-Dore's setting makes it an ideal spot for mountaintop picnics; you can find St-Nectaire cheese, links of flavored dry sausage, and other regional products at one of the specialty shops between **place de la République** and **place du Panthéon.** Another option is the **Spar** supermarket on rue du Cap-Chazzotte. (Open M-Sa 7am-12:30pm and 3-7:30pm, Su 7am-noon and 4-7pm.) Restaurants take a back seat to outdoor pursuits in Le Mont-Dore. However, after a long day on the slopes or trails, small spots serving regional dishes like *truffade*—potatoes with melted cheese—or its creamed cousin *aligot* are ideal. Many restaurants in Le Mont-Dore are affiliated with a hotel and give discounts to guests. Most *menus* begin at €12; fancier ones run €14-16. **Café de Paris ❷,** 8 rue Jean Moulin, evokes the Jazz Age in a classy 1920s salon that hosts frequent concerts. During the day, customers enjoy filling local dishes (*truffade* €13) and omelettes (€6) while jazz plays in the background. (☎65 01 77. Open daily 8am-8pm. Kitchen open noon-3pm. Closed Nov. Cash only.) Meanwhile, bicycles, bathrobes and boxing gloves hang from the ceiling of **La Grignote ❸,** 35 pl. André, behind the church, creating a festive, endearingly overwhelming atmosphere. A quirky couple offers an huge menu of pizzas and seafood specialties. (☎65 09 89; www.lagrignote.com. Salads €7-13. Pizza €7-13. Seafood €13-15. *Menus* €16-24. Open July-Aug. daily noon-2pm and 7-9:30pm; Sept.-June Th-Sa noon-2pm and 7-9:30pm, Su noon-2pm. Cash only.) The slightly upscale **Le Bougnat ❸,** 23 rue Georges Clemenceau, serves regional fare in a rustic yet romantic atmosphere near the top of town. The delicious *aligot* goes for €14. (☎65 28 19. *Plats* €12-17. Open daily noon-1:30pm and 7-8:30pm. AmEx/MC/V.)

SIGHTS. Every morning during the thermal season (May-Oct.), *curistes* (spa-goers) seeking the healing power of Le Mont-Dore's springs descend upon the ornate **Etablissement Thermal,** 1 pl. du Panthéon—a tradition that has sustained the town for centuries. The eight springs used today were originally channeled by the

Romans, who discovered that the water did wonders for their horses' sinuses. Today, a French-language tour of the *thermes* takes visitors through the building's neo-Byzantine interior and ends with a dose of the celebrated *douche nasale gazeuse*, a tiny blast of carbon and helium that **evacuates sinuses** better than any sneeze. (☎65 05 10. Tours late Apr. to late Oct. M-Sa every hr. 2-5pm, €3.20.)

HIKING AND BIKING

Over 650km of trails run through the region's dormant volcanic mountains, spanning dense forests and grassy mountainsides, passing rushing waterfalls, and running along jagged rocks. Scaling the peaks is relatively easy—the summit of **Puy de Sancy** (1886m) awaits at the end of a moderate 1½hr. climb—and day-long rambles along the grassy ridges bordering the valley provide a view of the town below. Those embarking on an extended hike should review their route with the tourist office, which has maps and good advice. Leave an itinerary of multi-day routes with the *peloton de montagne* (mountain police; ☎65 04 06 or 65 24 38), on rue des Chasseurs or at the base of Puy de Sancy. Buying a map is a must; while a few of the most popular trails feature yellow signs indicating the distance and direction to nearby destinations, many less-traveled trails are left unmarked. The tourist office, bookstores, and newsstands around town sell the comprehensive *Massif du Sancy Carte de Randonnée* (€7), which includes all the hiking trails within a 20km radius of Puy de Sancy. Hikers should also consult weather reports—mist in the valley often signifies hail or snow in the peaks.

CABLE CARS. For all the views without all the exertion, the **téléphérique** (cable car) runs from the base by the hostel to a station just below Puy de Sancy; a 10min. climb up steep wooden stairs leads to the summit. (☎08 20 82 09 48. Every 10min. July-Aug. 9am-7pm; Sept. and May-June 9am-12:30pm and 1:30-5pm; Oct.-Nov. schedule varies; Dec.-Apr. 8:45am-4:45pm. One-way €5.50, round-trip €7.20; under 10 €4.10/5.60. MC/V.) Farther north, the **funicular** departs from near the tourist office to **Salon des Capucins,** a rocky outcropping high above town. (Every 20min. daily 9:30am-12:10pm and 2:10-6:40pm. One-way €3.30, round-trip €4.20; under 10 €2.65/3.30. MC/V.) Both can be used to access other hikes, or to save weary knees from a final descent. The following recommendations represent only a few possibilities; innumerable routes can be planned using your map. Distances and times given are for round-trip hikes from the trailhead.

LA GRANDE CASCADE. The hike to La Grande Cascade (1½hr., 4km, 222m vertical) starts from the center of town and packs in a variety of sights. The trail ends above the falls on the **Plateau de Durbise,** a huge grassy plain high over the town that provides incredible views of the whole Sancy range. The largest waterfall in the area—the trail's 30m high namesake—is well worth the hike even without the views. During the summer, large, flat rocks at the base of the falls provide an ideal setting for picnics or afternoon sunbathing, while ice-climbers converge on the spot during the winter months to scale the frozen falls. From the *thermes*, follow rue des Desportes a few meters to the right and climb the stairs of chemin de la Bane on the left; at the top of the stairs, turn right onto chemin de Melchi-Rose, which runs into rte. de Besse. After crossing the road, the trail winds up a narrow gorge. A quick climb up the metal stairway to the right leads to the top of the waterfall and the grassy field above. Descend via the same route.

PUY DE SANCY. The ascent to the top of Massif's highest peak, the Puy de Sancy (6.2km, 3hr., 555m vertical), is simply spectacular. A 360° view from the summit on clear days includes the entire region, and the views from the trail on the way up are nearly as good. Start the hike at the base of Puy de Sancy and ascend the mountain via Val de Courre, a picturesque cow pasture. The trail begins a few hundred meters to the right of *téléphérique* #2. Follow the wide rocky path in the center of the valley as it climbs up Puy Redon. The trail veers left and narrows significantly at the top of Redon. Hikers should be careful on this upper section of the trail, especially on wet days, as there are no guard rails at the steep drop-offs. The trail heads upward toward the now-visible summit and eventually leads to a series of wooden steps up to a platform at the top. Descend via the same route.

SANCY TO LA GRANDE CASCADE. Experienced hikers with lots of energy left after the climb up Sancy may want to consider a scenic 8.9km hike along a chain of peaks between Sancy and La Grande Cascade. The hike's level of difficulty is rewarded by amazing views, and because it is less-traveled, it is often more peaceful. Potential hikers should be warned that the largely unmarked trails are often little more than foot-wide dirt paths or muddy ditches where rainwater has eroded whatever trail had been there. Between Puy des Crebasses and Roc de Cuzeau, the trail is particularly rugged. From the top of Sancy, head down the path on the opposite side of the platform from where you came up. After 700m, the path branches into three trails at **Col de la Cabane.** Take the leftmost path 300m to **Pan de la Grange;** at the fork in the road, take the right-hand trail. Walk 2km along the ridge to **Puy de Crebasses.** When the path branches off again, stay left and continue 1.3km to **Roc de Cuzeau.** Go downhill and onto the **Plateau de Durbise.** Follow the path to the road on the opposite side. The 1.1km trail to La Grande Cascade begins to the left. Most of the trek lies along the GR4, but the trail branches off at many points. A good map is a must-have; find one at the tourist office.

CASCADE DE QUEUREUILH AND CASCADE DE ROSSIGNOLET. An easy, flat hike through a quiet forest leads to two beautiful waterfalls, Cascade de Queureuilh and Cascade de Rossignolet (5km, 1-2hr., 60m vertical). Queureuilh is arguably the more spectacular of the two, falling from a steep 30m cliff face. To reach them, follow the same staircase as that to La Grand Cascade, but turn left at the top onto chemin de Melchi-Rose, which runs into av. de Clermont. Turn left onto chemin de Montieyroux, then right onto rte. des Cascades. The trailhead is marked by signs and begins 300m up on the right at Prends-Toi-Garde.

BIKING THE VOLCANIC LAKES. Bikers should visit the calm volcanic lakes, such as **Lac Servière** (15km northeast off of D983), which pool in nearby craters. Most of the lakes have small pebble beaches suitable for windsurfing, sailing, and swimming. **Lac d'Aydat,** to the northeast, offers paddle boats and other amusements, as does **Lac Chambon,** 20km east of Mont-Dore via D996, near Murol. **Lac Pavin,** 25km southeast of town, has plenty of good fishing opportunities.

SKIING

Le Mont-Dore offers as spectacular a winter wonderland as any area outside the Alps. Skiers and snowboarders will encounter pleasantly smaller crowds (and shorter lift lines) than elsewhere in France. A network of ski trails covers much of the Massif du Sancy; skiers can also venture down the other side of the valley into ritzy Super-Besse on clear days. Ski-rental shops fill the main village; rental packages generally cost €10-26 per day. Lift tickets for the entire Mont-Dore and Super-Besse area cost €19 per half-day and €24 per day. At the base of Puy de Sancy lifts is a ski school (☎65 07 43). The area also features an extensive network of cross-country skiing trails; ask at the tourist office or call the central cross-country resort (☎21 54 32) for information.

DAYTRIP FROM LE MONT-DORE: LA BOURBOULE

A shuttle connects La Bourboule and Le Mont-Dore. Contact the tourist office in either town for more information.

The region surrounding Le Mont-Dore has a number of small, picturesque towns within easy driving or hiking distance. La Bourboule (lah bohr-BOOL), which can also be reached by a shuttle service from Le Mont-Dore, was established in 1875 upon the discovery of its thermal springs and became a widely popular destination in the 20s. The city, just 15min. from Le Mont-Dore, maintains its roaring twenties atmosphere with exquisite, over-the-top Art Nouveau architecture, glamorous plazas, and charming hotels and restaurants. The sister town to Le Mont-Dore, La Bourboule has a more tranquil atmosphere.

Information on thermal visits, shuttles from Le Mont-Dore, and lodging is available at the **tourist office,** pl. de la République. (☎04 73 65 57 71; www.sancy.com. Open July-Aug. M-Sa 9am-7pm, Su 10am-noon and 2-6pm; May-June M-Sa 9am-noon and 1:30-6pm, Su 10am-noon and 2-6pm; Sept. M-Sa 9am-noon and 1:30-5pm, Su 10am-noon and 2-5pm; Oct. M-Sa 9am-noon and 1:30-5pm; Nov.-Apr. M-Sa 9am-noon and 1:30-6pm.)

LE PUY-EN-VELAY ☎04 71

Jutting crags of volcanic rock pierce the sky near Le Puy-en-Velay (luh PWEE uhn vah-LAY; pop. 20,500). For centuries the city has served as the starting point for the 1600km Via Podiensis pilgrimage trail, which ends in Santiago de Compostela, Spain. The summer influx of pilgrims, many of them young—as well as tourists who come for Le Puy's famous *lentilles* (lentils) and *dentelles* (lace)—gives Le Puy a vitality uncommon among other cities its size.

TRANSPORTATION

Trains: Pl. Maréchal Leclerc. Ticket office open M-F 5:30am-7:10pm, Sa 6:10am-7:10pm, Su 10:05am-8:10pm. To **Clermont-Ferrand** (2hr., M-F 5-6 per day, €21) and **Lyon** (1½hr., M-F 9 per day, €21).

Buses: Pl. Maréchal Leclerc, next to the train station. Schedules and info available at the tourist office. Those traveling south should take the bus to **Langogne** (1hr., M-F 3 per day, €7.80) to catch a train. Buy tickets on board.

Public Transportation: S.A.E.M. TUDIP buses leave from pl. Michelet. Info, map, and tickets at the tourist office. Runs daily 7am-7:25pm. Buy tickets (€1.05) on board, or *carnets* of 10 (€7.20) at the office.

Taxis: Radio-Taxis, pl. du Breuil (☎05 42 43). 24hr.

ORIENTATION AND PRACTICAL INFORMATION

From the station, walk left along **avenue Charles Dupuy,** cross **square du Docteur Henri Coiffier,** and turn left onto **boulevard Maréchal Fayolle.** A 5min. walk leads to the adjacent squares **place Michelet** and **place du Breuil.** Turn right onto rue Porte-Aiguière to reach the tourist office in **place du Clauzel.** Restaurants and stores cluster around this *place;* the cathedral, hostel, and *vieille ville* are uphill to the right.

Tourist Office: 2 pl. du Clauzel (☎09 38 41; www.ot-lepuyenvelay.fr). Helpful staff provides accommodations service, limited Internet access, a good city map, and a brochure with 3 walking tours in English and French, all free. Guided walking tours of the city (€5) and cathedral July-Aug. daily 3:30pm; Sept.-June Sa 3pm. Visits to nearby geological sites and guided hiking trips also early July to early Sept. Prices and schedule vary; ask the office for *"Visites Guidées."* Open July-Aug. daily 8:30am-7:30pm; Sept. daily 8:30am-noon and 1:30pm-6:15pm; Oct.-Holy Sat. M-Sa 8:30am-noon and 1:30-6:15pm, Su 10am-noon; Easter-June daily 8:30am-noon and 1:30-6:15pm.

MASSIF CENTRAL

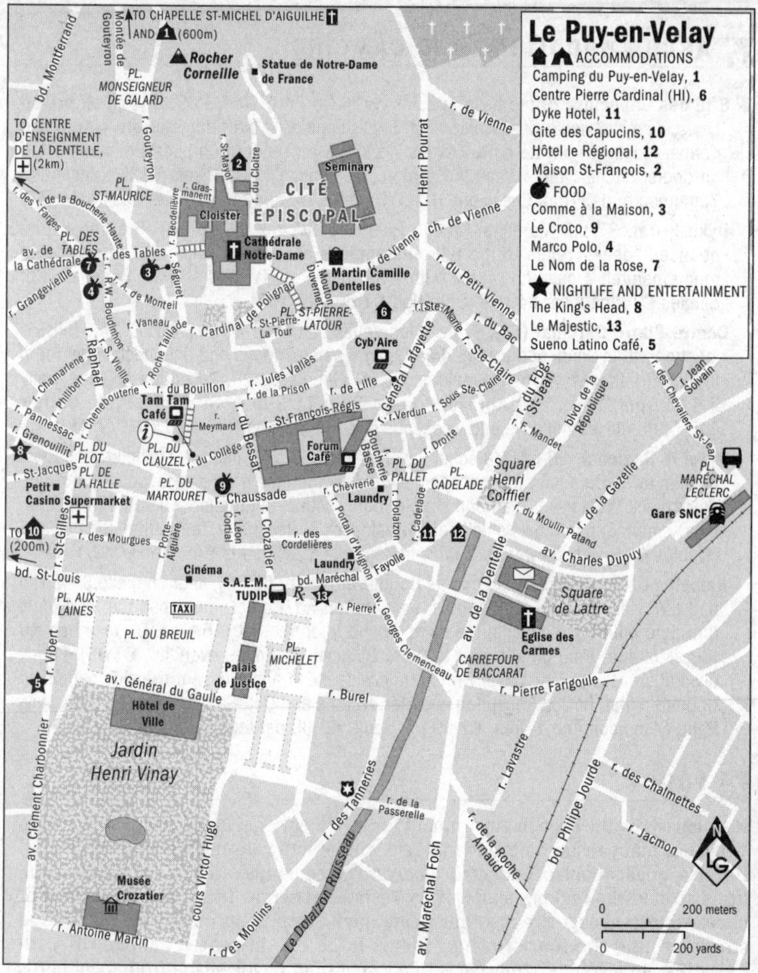

Laundromat: Lavo-Self, 12 rue Chèvrerie. €5.30 for 8kg. Open Tu-Sa 8am-noon and 1-7pm. **Lav'Flash,** 24 rue Portail d'Avignon. €3.70 for 7kg. Open M-Sa 8am-7:30pm, Su 9am-6:30pm.

Police: 1 rue de la Passerelle (☎04 04 22).

Medical Services: Centre Hospitalier Emile Roux, 12 bd. Dr. Chantemesse (☎04 32 10). Open 24hr. **Clinique Bon Secours,** 67bis av. M. Foch (☎09 87 00). **Ambulance** ☎09 87 60.

Internet Access: Free at the tourist office; 10min. limit. **Forum Café,** 5 rue Général Lafayette (☎04 04 98). €0.90 per 30min., €1.50 per hr. Open Tu-Sa 1-6pm. **Cyb'Aire,** 17 rue Général Lafayette (☎06 03 45). Internet and Wi-Fi €2.70 per hr. before 2pm, €3.50 per hr. after 2pm. Open M-Th 9am-9pm, F-Sa 9am-midnight, Su 3-7pm.

Post Office: 8 av. de la Dentelle (☎07 02 00). **Currency exchange** and **ATM.** Open M-F 8am-6:30pm, Sa 8:15am-12:15pm. **Postal Code:** 43000.

ACCOMMODATIONS AND CAMPING

Gîte des Capucins, 29 rue des Capucins (☎04 28 74 or 06 63 09 13 69), off bd. St-Louis, near the *vieille ville.* Welcoming, English-speaking staff. Immaculate 4- to 6-bed dorms, most with private bath. Fosters a social atmosphere with guests names posted on doors. Kitchen and a beautiful garden. Breakfast €4.60. Sheets €1.50. Reception 7am-noon and 5-7pm. Check-out 10am. Dorms €14; apartments €48. Cash only. ❶

Dyke Hotel, 37 bd. Maréchal-Fayolle (☎09 05 30; fax 02 58 66). The name, pronounced "deek," refers to the tall outcroppings of volcanic rock in Le Puy. Modern rooms painted a cheerful yellow, with wood paneling, TV, and shower. Breakfast €6. Singles €36; doubles €43-48. Extra bed €7.60. MC/V. ❸

Centre Pierre Cardinal (HI), 9 rue Jules Vallès (☎05 52 40; fax 05 61 24). Hillside location within 5min. of the cathedral. Clean 4-person dorms and one much larger room in former barracks. Kitchen. Breakfast €3.20. Sheets €3.20. Reception July-Aug. daily 2-11:30pm; Sept. and Apr.-June M-Sa 2pm-11:30pm, Su 10am-8pm. Curfew 11:30pm. Closed holidays and weekends Oct.-Mar. Dorms €10. AmEx/MC/V. ❶

Hôtel le Régional, 36 bd. Maréchal Fayolle (☎09 37 74), near pl. Michelet. Cheapest hotel in town. On a busy intersection a short walk from the train station; soundproof windows block the noise. Clean and simple rooms with TV and toilet separated from room by a screen. Situated over small café. Breakfast €5. Reception 7am-10pm. Singles and doubles €24, with shower from €28; triples from €29; quads €43. AmEx/MC/V. ❷

Camping du Puy-en-Velay, chemin de Bouthezard (☎09 55 09), near Chapelle St-Michel and the river. Walk up bd. St-Louis, continue on bd. Carnot, and when the road ends turn right onto av. d'Aiguille; the campground is on the left (15min.). Or, take bus #6 (dir.: Mondon) from pl. Michelet to "Parc Quincieu" (10min., every hr., €1.05). Poorly divided spots with little privacy in an otherwise clean and pleasant riverside campsite. Open mid-Mar. to Oct. Reception mid-Mar. to June and Oct. 8am-noon and 3-9pm; July-Sept. 8am-noon and 1-9pm. €2.80 per adult, €2.65 per tent. Electricity €3.10. ❶

FOOD

Recognized by the French government for its exceptional local cuisine, Le Puy-en-Velay has many restaurants and markets with mouthwatering regional specialties. Because quality-controlled *lentilles vertes* (green lentils) are grown in mass quantities around the region, nearly every restaurant serves them. Local varieties of cheeses and sausage are also must-eats; pick some up at one of the many food stores around the tourist office. Meals in Le Puy are often capped off with *Verveine*, an alcoholic *digestif* with a sweet mint flavor, made from local herbs and honey (€10-22 per bottle); the **distillery** outside of town on N88 gives tours and tastings. (☎03 04 11; www.verveine.com. Open July-Aug. daily 10am-noon and 1:30-6:30pm; Mar.-June and Sept.-Dec. Tu-Sa 10am-noon and 1:30-6:30pm; Jan.-Feb. Tu-Su 1:30-4:30pm. €5.80, students €4.20, under 12 €2.) A **Petit Casino** supermarket, 8 rue St-Gilles, sits near pl. du Plot. (Open Tu-Sa 7:30am-12:30pm and 2:30-7:30pm, Su 8am-12:15pm. MC/V.) On Saturdays (6am-noon), farmers set up fresh produce markets on almost every square. The markets on **place du Plot** and **place de la Halle** sell fresh fruit, cheese, mushrooms, and a few live chickens and rabbits; the adjacent **place du Clauzel** hosts an antique market and **place du Breuil** features clothing, shoes, and handbags. While most *menus* in the *vieille ville* hover around €15-30, inexpensive restaurants can be found on streets off **place du Breuil.**

Comme à la Maison, 7 rue Séguret (☎02 94 73). Serves superb gourmet *formules du jour* (€17-22) on a secluded stone patio in the garden. Inside are brightly colored walls reminiscent of a modern art gallery. Open daily noon-3pm and 7-11pm. Cash only. ❸

Le Croco, 5 rue Chaussade (☎02 40 13). Cheap eats served in a cheerful yellow interior. *Menus* (€13-19) include large plates of salad, meat, seafood, and baked potato. Check comes with gummy crocodiles. Open M-Sa noon-3pm and 7-10pm. MC/V. ❷

Le Nom de la Rose, 48 rue Raphael (☎05 90 04). Specializing in organic Mexican food, this small restaurant serves time-tested favorites like *chili con carne* as well as more unique house specialties like cactus leaf salad. Vegetarian *plats* €7.50-9.30. *Menus* €15-23. Open daily 12:15-2pm and 7-10:30pm. MC/V. ❸

Le Marco Polo, 46 rue Raphael (☎02 83 11). Serves large portions of delicious homemade pasta and regional fare. Cozy interior consists of 2 dining rooms with beige walls and paintings on potato sack canvases. *Plats* €10-13. *Menus* €17-18. Open Tu-Sa 11:30am-3pm and 7-11pm. ❸

SIGHTS

Le Puy's religious sights draw thousands each year; as a unit, they represent sections of the Bible's apocalyptic Book of Revelation. While most of Le Puy's attractions center on its numerous churches and statue-adorned rock formations, there is also much to see in the surrounding countryside; the tourist office sells *Le Puy-en-Velay et ses Environs à Pied* (€13), which lists 45 local hikes.

CHAPELLE ST-MICHEL D'AIGUILHE. Just outside the *vieille ville*, this ancient chapel sits atop an 80m spike of volcanic rock. Erected in the 10th century by Le Puy's bishop after he returned from a pilgrimage to Compostela, the church's polychromatic facade conceals an interior full of recently restored frescoes. *(☎09 50 03. Open daily May-Sept. 9am-6:30pm; Oct. to mid-Nov. and mid-Mar. to Apr. 9:30am-noon and 2-5:30pm; Feb. to mid-Mar. 2-5pm. €2.75, students €2.50, under 14 €1.25.)*

CATHÉDRALE NOTRE-DAME. Legend has it that in the fifth century the Virgin Mary healed a woman who came to pray at what is now the **Cité Episcopale,** a collection of religious buildings towering over the city from a rock known as *le puy.* The area became a pilgrimage site, and the current cathedral has attracted pilgrims and tourists for over 1000 years. The major attraction is the famous statue of **la Vierge Noir** (the Black Virgin), who sits serenely on a tabernacle flanked by two golden angels and encircled by 18 crimson lamps that hang from the ceiling. As part of the larger scene, it represents the New Jerusalem. Aside from the altar, the interior is less than spectacular and feels strangely divided by the stairwell and organ in the middle of the nave. The church is in the middle of a dense cluster of religious buildings, making it difficult to get a good look at the exterior. For a view of the beautiful polychromatic facade, walk up the steps on rue des Tables. To see the entire cathedral, including its dome and huge bell tower, a trip up the hill to the Statue of Notre-Dame is your best bet. *(☎05 98 74; www.cathedraldupuy.org. Open daily 6:30am-7:30pm. Tours in French early July to late Aug. Free.)*

STATUE DE NOTRE-DAME DE FRANCE. The pinnacle of the *vieille ville* is the **Rocher Corneille,** the 757m tall eroded core of a volcano. A 23m statue of the Virgin Mary cast from Russian cannons captured during the Crimean War crowns the summit and looks over the city. Notre-Dame earned national fame in 1942, when 20,000 young people came here to pray for the liberation of France. Marred inside by graffiti and painted an unattractive shade of red, the statue itself is more impressive from the bottom of the hill, but the site is worth visiting for its unbeatable views. A small staircase inside the statue leads to tiny windows, but the best vantage points are found around the base only 16m below. *(Open daily July-Aug. 9am-7:30pm; Sept. and May-June 9am-7pm; Oct. to mid-Mar. 10am-5pm; mid-Mar. to Apr. 9am-6pm. €3, students with ID and under 18 €1.50.)*

CLOISTER. Attached to the cathedral, the cloister has colorful terra-cotta mosaics and striped arches that reflect a Spanish Islamic influence. Beneath flame-red tiling and ornate arcades is the *bestiaire*, a series of grinning faces and mythical beasts carved into the stone around the courtyard; look for the centaurs that decorate one of its many capitals. Amid the Byzantine arches of the **salle capitulaire,** a vivid and well-preserved 13th-century fresco depicts the Crucifixion. The entry ticket also allows a peek at the second-level **Trésor d'Art Religieux,** a museum of 13th- to 18th-century sacred art containing impressive life-size wooden statues and a small collection of paintings, chalices, and crucifixes. *(☎05 45 52. Both open daily July-Aug. 9am-6:30pm; Sept. and May-June 9am-noon and 2-6:30pm; Oct.-Apr. 9am-noon and 2-5pm. Tours in French throughout the day, English available with reservation. €5, ages 18-25 €3.50. Free written explanation in 6 languages.)*

MUSÉE CROZATIER. This all-encompassing museum has a different theme on every floor: local craftsmanship, fine arts, archaeology, and natural history. Particularly impressive is an exhibit on Le Puy native Emile Reynaud, who invented the praxinoscope, the precursor to the film projector. The museum overlooks the beautifully manicured **Jardin Henri Vinay,** which has a small zoo, duck pond, and topiary peacock. *(☎06 62 40. Open May to mid-Sept. daily 10am-noon and 2-6pm; Oct.-Apr. M and W-Sa 10am-noon and 2-4pm, Su 2-4pm. €3.20, students and ages 18-25 €1.40, under 18 free. Map in English; all other info in French.)*

NIGHTLIFE AND FESTIVALS

Beginning with the **Fête de la Musique** in mid-June, Le Puy hosts a different festival each week, ranging from music to theater and culminating in the mid-September **Fête Renaissance du Roi de L'Oiseau** (☎09 38 41), a 400-year-old tradition with Renaissance activities galore. From mid- to late August, the world-renowned **Festival de la Chaise-Dieu** welcomes choral groups from all corners of the globe and features concerts in Le Puy and nearby Chaise-Dieu. (☎00 01 16; www.chaise-dieu.com. Tickets €10-77.) The tourist office gives out free copies of *Sortir*, a guide to the festival season, and can provide more specific info.

The **Municipal Theater,** pl. du Breuil, hosts plays and dance shows. (☎09 03 45.) For information on performances in towns around Le Puy, call the **Centre Culturel de Vals,** av. Charles Massot (☎05 90 12). A **cinema** is at 29 pl. du Breuil. (☎09 00 35. €6.50, students €5.50.)

The King's Head, pl. du Marché Couvert (☎02 50 35). An English pub with a chatty English owner. Prides itself on an excellent beer list (€3.50-9.50). Don't leave without trying a glass of John Martin's (€2.80). Open Tu-F 4pm-1am, Sa 10am-2am. Cash only.

Sueño Latino Café, 26 rue Vibert (☎02 61 56). In a new location near the Jardin Vinay, opened in 2007. Laid-back English-speaking owner serves beer and mixed drinks in a friendly environment, where locals chat amiably over Latin rhythms with mojitos in hand. Beer €2.50-4. Mixed drinks €4. Open Tu-Su 3pm-2am. Cash only.

Le Majestic, 8 bd. Maréchal Fayolle (☎19 06 30). A lively outdoor terrace and a sleek interior: contemporary art lines the walls, while low, colorful chairs give this nightspot creative flair. Open M-Th 8am-1am, F-Sa 8am-2am, Su 10am-1am.

VICHY ☎04 70

On June 22, 1940, the French government signed the armistice at Rethondes, surrendering to the German military and allowing Nazi occupation of France. The Nazis replaced Paris with Vichy (VEE-shee; pop. 27,000) as capital of France, choosing the town for its large hotels and modern telephone system. Under the

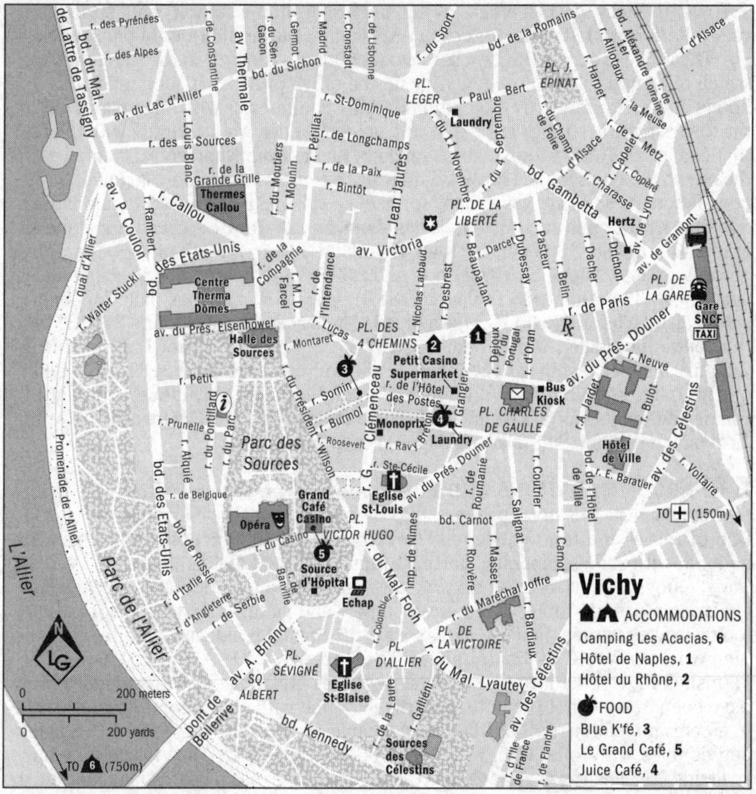

leadership of Maréchal Philippe Pétain, a WWI hero, Vichy remained the seat of the Nazi-controlled puppet regime from 1940 to 1944. Today, a tiny monument to the citizens deported from Vichy during the occupation stands in the shadow of a much larger WWI memorial, but the town is otherwise nearly devoid of vestiges of these dark years, creating an eerie historical gap. Instead, Vichy's lacy ironwork, leafy formal parks, and resplendent Belle Epoque architecture recall its pre-war days, when the town's mineral-rich hot springs, still popular with *curistes* world-wide, drew royalty, celebrities, and the fabulously wealthy.

TRANSPORTATION AND PRACTICAL INFORMATION. The **train station** is on pl. de la Gare. (Ticket desks open M 5:30am-8:20pm, Tu-Th 5:40am-8pm, F 5:40am-8:20pm, Sa 6:30am-8pm, Su 7:10am-8:30pm.) **Trains** run to Clermont-Ferrand (40min., 10 per day, €8.80), Nevers (1hr., 6 per day, €16), and Paris (3hr., 6 per day, €45). The **bus station** is next to the train station. (Office open M 9am-noon and 2-6pm, Tu-F 8:30-11:30am and 2-6pm; reduced hours July-Aug.) **Local buses** run from 6:30am-8pm (€1.10). Find schedules at the tourist office and at the **Bus Inter kiosk,** pl. Charles de Gaulle, near the post office (☎97 81 29; open M-Th 8:30-11:30am and 1-6pm, F 8:30-11:30am and 1-5pm). Buy tickets on board. Rent **cars** from **Hertz,** 5 av. de Lyon, a 2min. walk from the train station. (☎97 82 82. Open M-F 8am-noon and 2-6:30pm, Sa 8am-noon and 2-5pm. AmEx/MC/V.) For a **taxi,** call Vichy Taxis (☎98 69 69; 24hr.) from the free telephone at the train station taxi kiosk.

To get to Vichy's **tourist office,** 19 rue du Parc, from the station, walk straight on rue de Paris, turn left at the fork onto rue Clemenceau, and turn right onto rue Sornin. The office is across the **Parc des Sources** (10min.). Housed in the Hôtel du Parc, which once housed Pétain's government, the office provides a good map, a list of hotels and restaurants, free accommodations bookings, a written explanation of the town's natural springs in French, and guided French walking tours with themes that change daily. The tours, which range in theme from Napoleon III's impact on the city to the city's impact on WWII, may be the city's sole acknowledgment of the occupation. (☎98 71 94; www.vichy-tourisme.com. ☎98 23 83 for accommodations booking. Office open July-Aug. M-Sa 9am-7pm, Su 2:30-7pm; Sept. and Apr.-June M-F 10am-noon and 1:30-6pm, Sa 10am-noon and 2-6pm, Su 3-6pm; Oct.-Mar. M-F 10am-noon and 2-6pm, Sa 10am-noon and 2:30-5:30pm.) Other services include: a **laundromat,** 3 bd. Gambetta (☎06 64 75 34 31; €3.50 for 5kg; open daily 7am-9pm); **police,** 35 av. Victoria (☎30 17 28); **La Grande Pharmacie,** 48 rue de Paris (☎98 23 01); the **Centre Hospitalier,** 15 bd. Denière (☎97 33 33; open M-Sa 9am-12:15pm and 2-7:15pm); **Internet** access at cozy **Echap,** 12 rue Source de l'Hôpital (☎32 28 57; €0.07 per min.; open Tu-Sa noon-midnight, Su 2pm-midnight). The **post office** at pl. Charles de Gaulle has an **ATM** and **exchanges currency.** (☎30 10 75. Open M-F 8:30am-12:30pm and 1-6pm, Sa 8:30am-12:30pm.) **Postal Code:** 03200.

ACCOMMODATIONS AND FOOD. As Vichy first gained notoriety by pampering its guests, it's not surprising that the city has an above-average concentration of three- and four-star hotels. Nevertheless, budget accommodations also abound, with rooms generally starting around €25-30. **Hôtel du Rhône ❸,** 8 rue de Paris, enjoys a great location midway between the train station and the *thermes*. Quiet, comfortable rooms feature red carpets and vintage décor, and some overlook a private garden. (☎98 63 45; fax 98 77 40. Small breakfast €3, buffet €7. Singles with shower €29-35; doubles €37-58; triples €49-59. AmEx/MC/V.) The varnished plywood adorning the **Hôtel de Naples ❷,** 22 rue de Paris, might never have been in style, but the hotel gets the job done with clean, comfortable rooms in a central location. (☎97 91 33; hoteldenaples@orange.fr. Breakfast €6. Singles and doubles with toilet €26, with bath €36-39; triples €45. MC/V.) The four-star, riverside **Camping Les Acacias ❶,** rue Claude-Decloitre, has a bar, a small market, a pool, tennis courts, and laundry facilities, bordered by colorful flowerbeds. Sites are separated by perfectly trimmed hedges. Take bus #7 from the train station (dir.: La Tour d'Abrest) to "Charles de Gaulle," then bus #3 to Les Acacias; it's 3.5km on foot. (☎32 36 22; www.camping-acacias.com. Reception 8am-10pm. Open Apr. to mid-Oct. €4.90 per person, €5.80 per tent. Electricity €3. Prices lower Apr.-June and Sept.-Oct. MC/V.)

While Vichy's springs attract visitors who seek healing, its restaurants ensure that they're well fed. Inexpensive meals are difficult to find; *menus* hover around €20 in restaurants tucked behind the Opéra, but cheaper fare can be found in the small eateries along **rue de Paris.** Many of Vichy's restaurants are affiliated with hotels. To avoid paying top dollar at one of Vichy's restaurants, head to the **Monoprix** supermarket on the corner of rue Georges Clemenceau and rue Ravy Breton (open M-Sa 8:30am-8pm, Su 9:30am-12:30pm and 2:30-7pm; AmEx/MC/V), or the **Petit Casino** at the corner of pl. Charles de Gaulle or rue de l'Hôtel des Postes (both open M-Sa 8:30am-12:30pm and 2:30-7:30pm). The friendly British owner at **Juice Café ❶,** 16 rue Ravy Breton, whips up fruit-filled smoothies and milkshakes (€5-6), as well as pasta (with pesto or tomatoes; €7-8), in a tropical-themed room lined with popular English-language novels. (Open June-Aug. M and Su 2-8pm, Tu-Sa 10am-8pm; Sept.-May closed M. Cash only.) Those with big appetites will love the enormous buffet at **Le Grand Café ❸,** 7 rue du Casino. Attached to the casino itself, the restaurant is known for its wide variety of *crudités*, fruits, cheeses, *foie gras*, cold cuts, seafood, and scrumptious desserts featured in its €18 all-you-can-eat lunch buffet. (☎97 16 45; www.casinodugrandcafe.com. *Plats* €11-18. *Menus* €18-26. MC/V.) Lighter fare can be found at the **Bleu K'fé ❷**, 22 passage de l'Amirauté, which specializes in salads and vegetarian *plats*. In the middle of the *centre-ville*, this restaurant—whose décor lives up to its name—provides a quiet refuge. (☎98 56 04. *Plats* €7.80. 2-course *menu* including wine and coffee €11. Open Tu-Sa 9:30am-6:30pm, Su 11:30am-7:30pm. Closed Su mornings in winter. MC/V.)

SIGHTS AND ENTERTAINMENT. The only evidence of Vichy's dark years is a small memorial down the street from the tourist office commemorating the 1942 deportation of 6500 Jews to Auschwitz. Significant WWII buildings are not marked, and information about the period is difficult to find. The best way to see the Nazis' Vichy is to take the tourist office's French-language **tour** about Vichy during the occupation. (June and Sept. W 3:30pm; July-Aug. W 3:30pm, Sa 10:30am. Tours depart from the tourist office. €6, under 12 free.)

Vichy's real attraction springs from its *sources* (springs). Due to volcanic forces, the water circulates for hundreds—even thousands—of years deep underground, collecting dissolved mineral deposits before finally bubbling up to the surface. These deposits reputedly endow Vichy's water with certain healing effects for a number of ailments, ranging from common allergies to indigestion. Just one sip of Vichy's nectar, however, makes one wonder why people keep coming back for more—its putrid taste is nearly insufferable. The town's *sources*, each of which provides water with a distinct chemical makeup and alleged healing effect, are housed in covered fountains at various points throughout the city. Close to the *centre-ville*, **Célestins** bubbles up free of charge at the fountain on bd. Kennedy. It is said to be good for the skin and, according to a sign at the source, was proven to relieve arthritis, as confirmed by a 1992 Hôpital Cochimin (Paris) study. (Open Apr.-Sept. M-Sa 7:45am-8pm, Su 8am-8pm; Oct.-Mar. daily 8am-6pm.) The nearby **Hôpital** source, used to cure stomach and intestinal ailments, flows behind the Grand Casino. (Open M-Sa 6:30am-8:30pm, Su 7:45am-8:30pm.) All of Vichy's spring waters are on tap in the **Halle des Sources** at the edge of the **Parc des Sources.** (☎08 00 30 00 63. Open Mar.-Nov. M-Sa 6am-7:30pm, Su 7:45am-7:30pm.) Regulars bring their own glass—encased in a special woven carrying basket available for purchase at Vichy pharmacies for €8.50. Visitors may purchase a less classy plastic cup on site for €0.20. Two springs are actually located within the Halle des Sources: **Chomel** is the most popular among the hot-water sources, while **Grand Grille** is the most powerful, with only very small doses advised. Visitors can recover with older *curistes* in the Parc des Sources. Surrounded by a wrought-iron Art Nouveau promenade and flanked by the Opéra, the space exemplifies Vichy elegance.

Vichy's water is not the only attraction in town. The beautiful *vitraux* and frescoes of **Eglise St-Louis**, rue St-Cécile (☎96 51 20), merit at least a quick visit; the church was given as a gift to the town by Napoleon III in 1865. Manicured floral displays, swan-filled ponds, and thick trees shade the English-style gardens in the elegant riverside **Parc de l'Allier,** also commissioned by Napoleon III.

Take a risk at the **Grand Café Casino** in the Parc des Sources. (☎97 07 40. Open daily 10am-4am.) Operas and concerts fill the beautiful **Opéra,** 1 rue du Casino, with reduced prices for concerts available in the summer. (☎30 50 30. Box office open Tu-Sa 1:30-6:30pm, until curtain on performance nights; by phone only Tu-F 10am-12:30pm. Operas €30-60, under 25 €28-54; concerts €21-42/18-26. MC/V.)

DORDOGNE AND LIMOUSIN

A lack of large population centers, waterfronts, and well-known attractions has kept these regions from the fame they deserve. Most of their sights are relatively undiscovered, offering a welcome respite from the ceaseless crowds that storm the Loire châteaux. Dordogne and Limousin have long been artistic breeding grounds, producing painter Auguste Renoir, dramatist Jean Giraudoux, and novelist George Sand. Shops and museums throughout the regions proudly display local craftsmanship, particularly those in Limoges (p. 502), where some of the world's finest porcelain is made. The ambling waters of the Dordogne river cut through the regions' rolling hillsides, creating a spectacular backdrop for castles and hilltop cities. Named after the river, the Dordogne—where green countryside is splashed with yellow sunflowers, steep and chalky limestone cliffs, and ducks paddling down shady rivers—boasts exceptional historical remnants of the Neolithic, Roman, and medieval periods, including the most famous cave paintings in the world at Lascaux. Neighboring Limousin is home to vibrant cities, while the southern Lot Valley offers a jumble of French favorites: villages, vineyards, cliffs, and caves. Undiscovered but not uninteresting, Dordogne and Limousin offer diverse natural attractions without attracting naturally annoying tourist hordes.

HIGHLIGHTS OF DORDOGNE AND LIMOUSIN

BECOME BREATHLESS when you see the spectacular paintings at the caves of the **Vézère Valley** (p. 520)–no, seriously, human breath ruins the artwork.

GO NUTTY over Brive-la-Gaillarde's **Maison Denoix** (p. 510), the oldest liquor distillery in France, known for its signature walnut *liqueur.*

NEVER FORGET the ghost town of **Oradour-sur-Glane** (p. 508), untouched since Nazis systematically massacred its residents–it remains a moving testament to the human capacity for brutality.

LIMOUSIN

Home to relatively substantial cities Limoges and Brive-la-Gaillarde, the rural region of Limousin has just recently caught up with the rest of France—until the 1970s, thê majority of non-urban residents still spoke Occitan. Today, Limousin is home to beef farming, porcelain production, and sleepy villages that make excellent daytrips. Though its not the most exciting part of France, Limousin makes a nice change from the frenetic pace of most travelers' itineraries.

LIMOGES ☎05 55

For centuries, Limoges (LEE-moh-jhs; pop. 137,500) has manufactured porcelain and enamel for the French upper class. The trade and its proceeds have given Limoges a graceful beauty; wide boulevards, green parks, and monumental fountains fill the *centre-ville.* While the small artisan boutiques lining its older streets

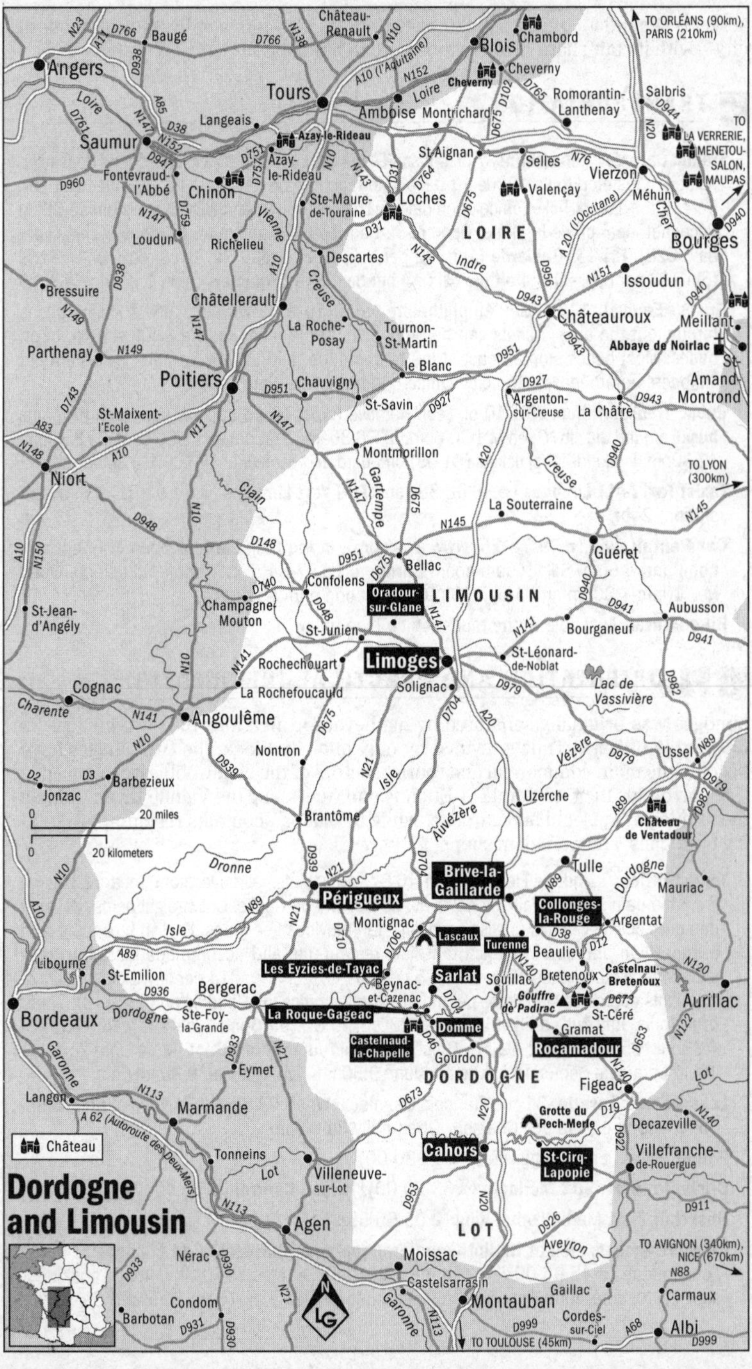

DORDOGNE AND LIMOUSIN

serve as reminders of its past, Limoges today is very much a diverse and modern city—with its fair share of anonymous urban buildings and graffiti.

TRANSPORTATION

Trains: Gare des Bénédictins, 7 pl. Maison-Dieu (☎11 12 00), off av. du Général de Gaulle, has been restored to its 1920s Art Deco splendor. Info booth open M-F 4:30am-10:30pm, Sa 4:30am-10pm. Ticket office open daily 5:15am-9:45pm. An **SNCF** office is on rue Othon Péconnet, near pl. de la Motte. Open M-Sa 9am-7pm. Trains run to: **Bordeaux** (3hr., 5 per day, €28); **Brive-la-Gaillarde** (1hr., 12 per day, €17); **Lyon** (6hr., 1 per day, €44); **Paris** (3hr., 13 per day, €48); **Poitiers** (2hr., 3 per day, €19); **Toulouse** (4hr., 6 per day, €38).

Buses: Equival, 14 rue de l'Amphithéâtre (☎10 10 03; www.equival87.fr), runs buses throughout the area. Tickets can be purchased at the office, at the SNCF station, or on buses. Most buses stop at least at the train station, and usually at more places around Limoges, before leaving the city. Office open M-F 9am-6pm.

Public Transportation: TCL, 10 pl. Léon Betoulle (☎32 46 46), across from town hall, runs **buses** around the city. Open M 1:30-6pm, Tu-F 8:30am-12:30pm and 1:30-6pm, Sa 8:30am-12:30pm. Find individual tickets (€1.05) on board and *carnets* of 10 (€9.10) at the station.

Taxis: Taxi AALT Limoges (☎38 38 38) and **Taxi Vert Limoges** (☎37 81 81) wait by the station. 24hr.

Car Rental: Avis (☎79 78 25; www.avis.com), in the train station. Open M-F 9:45am-noon and 4-6pm, Sa 9:45am-noon. **Europcar** (☎77 64 52), in the train station. Open M-F 10am-1:30pm and 4-6pm, Sa 9:30am-noon and 2-5:30pm.

Bike Rental: Available at the tourist office (see below).

ORIENTATION AND PRACTICAL INFORMATION

Limoges was originally separated by medieval fortifications into two villages: **la Cité** and **le Château.** Today, divided by only one city block, the two villages have become the main commercial and tourist sectors of the city. Cobblestone-paved le Cité surrounds the Cathédrale St-Etienne and runs along the Vienne River, holding the municipal museum and gardens, while le Château contains restaurants, clothing boutiques, and porcelain shops.

Tourist Office: 12 bd. de Fleurus (☎34 46 87; www.tourismelimoges.com), near pl. Wilson. From the train station, walk left down av. du Général de Gaulle. Cut straight across pl. Jourdan onto bd. de Fleurus. English-speaking staff provides free maps, English brochures, and a free *guide pratique* in French that lists restaurants and accommodations. **Currency exchange** at steep rates. Bike rental €5 per 2hr., €7 per 3hr., €14 per day. Guided tours of city sights offered several times per month. Contact office for schedule and prices. 1hr. *petit train* tours July-Aug. daily 11:30am, 2:30, 4, 5:30, 9:30pm; June and early Sept. 3, 4:30pm. €5, ages 3-12 €3.50. Office open mid-June to mid-Sept. M-Sa 9am-7pm, Su 10am-6pm; late Sept. and Apr. to mid-June 9:30am-7pm; Oct-Mar. 9:30am-6pm.

Laundromat: Laverie, 31 rue François Chenieux. Wash €3.80 per 7kg. Open daily 7am-9pm. Also at 14 rue des Charseix. Open daily 8am-9pm.

Police: 84 av. Emile Labussière (☎14 30 00).

Crisis Hotlines: SOS Médecin (☎33 20 00). **Poison Control** (☎96 40 80).

Hospital: 2 av. Martin Luther King (☎05 55 55).

Internet Access: Free at **Bibliothèque Francophone Multimédia de Limoges,** 2 rue L. Longequeue (☎45 96 00), next to the Hôtel de Ville. Free Wi-Fi. Often long lines. Must sign up for free library membership. Internet available W 10am-7pm and Sa 10am-

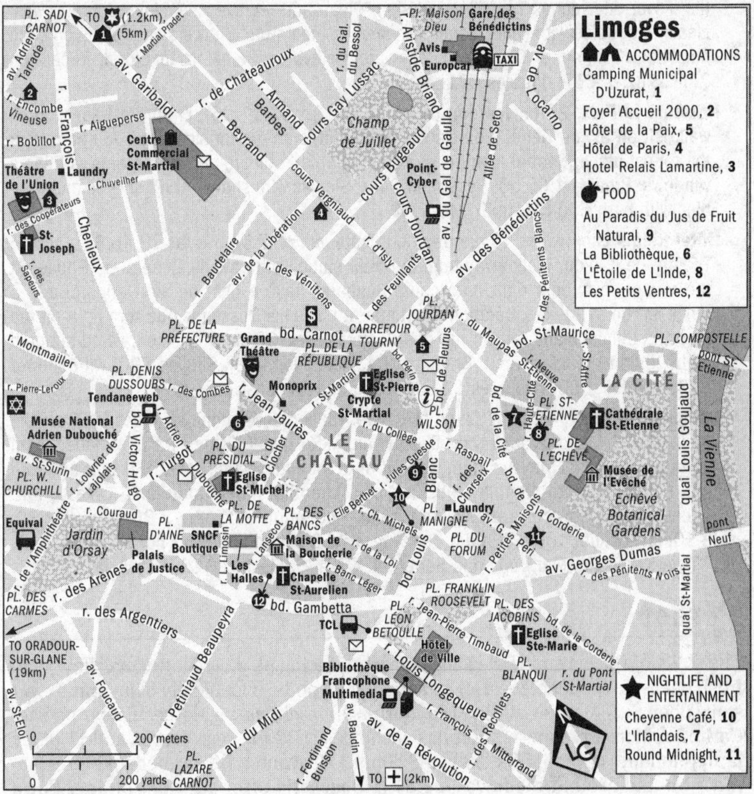

6pm; 1½hr. limit. **Tendanceweb.com,** 5 bd. Victor Hugo (☎10 93 61; www.tendanceweb.com). €2 per 30min., €7 per 2hr. Open M-Th 10am-4am, F-Sa 10am-6am, Su 2pm-4am. **Pointcyber,** 7 av. du Général de Gaulle (☎79 03 28), near the train station. €2 per 30min., €3.20 per hr. Open M-Sa 9:30am-midnight, Su 2pm-midnight.

Post Office: 39bis av. Garibaldi (☎79 81 00), part of the St-Martial shopping complex. **Currency exchange.** Open M 2-7pm, Tu-F 10am-7pm, Sa 10:30am-12:30pm and 1:30-6pm. **Postal Code:** 87000.

ACCOMMODATIONS AND CAMPING

Hôtel de Paris, 5 cours Vergniaud (☎77 56 96). From the train station, walk up av. du Général de Gaulle and turn right onto cours Bugeaud, then right onto cours Vergniaud. Hallways with Victorian wallpaper and light fixtures lead to rooms with double doors, tall windows, clean bathrooms, and balconies. Breakfast €5. Reception 7am-10pm. Singles €26-43; doubles €36-43; triples €51-54. MC/V. ❷

Foyer Accueil 2000, 20 rue Encombe Vineuse (☎77 63 97; fjt.accueil-2000@wanadoo.fr). From the train station, head to the right on Champ du Juillet, onto cours Gay Lussac. Turn right onto av. Garibaldi, then left onto rue Aigueperse. Make a right on rue Chénieux and a quick left on rue Encombe Vineuse. The hostel is on the right; look for the 'Foyer des Jeunes Travailleuses' sign. Clean and relatively spacious dorm-like singles and doubles with sinks; some with small refrigerators. Showers and toilets on each floor hall. Communal TV room, kitchen, and elevator. Breakfast included. Reception 24hr. Singles €17; doubles €21. ❶

Hôtel de la Paix, 25 pl. Jourdan (☎34 36 00; fax 32 37 06). From the train station, walk left on av. du Général de Gaulle. The hotel is on the far side of pl. Jourdan, near the tourist office. Central location overlooking a park. Clean, carpeted rooms with large windows. Breakfast €6.50. Reception 24hr. Singles with shower €39; singles and doubles with bath €50-62. AmEx/MC/V. ❸

Hôtel Relais Lamartine, 10 rue des Coopérateurs (☎77 53 39; fax 79 46 92), next to Théâtre de l'Union. Walk away from the train station onto av. du Général de Gaulle. At the roundabout, bear right onto cours Bugeaud. Take a right on av. Garibaldi and a quick left on av. de la Libération. Continue to pl. Denis Dussoubs and turn right on rue François Chinieux and left on rue des Coopérateurs (20min.). Crimson, wood-trimmed lobby. Bright breakfast area. Breakfast €4. Reception 24hr. Singles €20, with shower €22, with toilet €26; doubles €27-33. Extra bed €7. Cash only. ❷

Camping D'Uzurat, 40 av. d'Uzurat (☎38 49 43; contact@campinglimoges.fr). From the train station, take bus #20 (dir.: Beaubreuil; M-Sa 6am-8:30pm) to "L. Armand," 5km north of Limoges. From the stop, walk 50m to the intersection at av. d'Uzurat and turn left. Follow signs to campground. Part of a beautiful park surrounding Lake Uzurat. Access to tennis courts and hiking trails. Reception 8:15am-12:30pm and 2:30-8:10pm. Lockout 10pm-7:30am. July-Aug. €3.50 per adult, €1.50 per child age 2-14, €7 per campsite. Mar.-June and Sept.-Oct. €3/1/5. Electricity €3. MC/V. ❶

FOOD

The stalls of the central Halles **indoor market,** facing pl. de la Motte, overflow with fresh cheeses, produce, meat, fish, and baked goods. (Open daily 8am-1pm, fewer stalls open Su.) A larger market (Sa mornings) brightens pl. Marceau, near pl. Sadi Carnot. A **Monoprix** supermarket has entrances at 42 rue Jean Jaurès and 11 pl. de la République. (Open M-Sa 8:30am-8:30pm.) Charming, flower-bedecked restaurants on and around medieval **rue de la Boucherie** offer gourmet dining. For a cheaper meal, look to **rue Haute-Cité,** near the cathedral, for *crêperies* and *brasseries.* For an even greater variety of flavor, **rue Charles Michels** offers a bit of everything, from Chinese to Moroccan to Tex-Mex.

Au Paradis du Jus de Fruit Naturel, 5 rue Jules Guesde (☎11 98 46). At this tropical café, with its extensive menu of delicious fresh juices (€3-6), milkshakes, and exotic teas, you're sure to find the perfect pick-me-up. Open M-F 10am-noon and 2-7pm, Sa 10am-noon and 2-7:30pm. AmEx/MC/V. ❶

Les Petits Ventres, 20 rue de la Boucherie (☎34 22 90; www.les-petits-ventres.fr). In a converted 15th-century home, with a touch of medieval charm and a peaceful outdoor terrace. Known throughout Limoges for its traditional cuisine. *Plats* €15-25. *Menus* €22-36. Open Tu-Sa noon-2pm and 7:30-10:30pm. AmEx/MC/V. ❹

La Bibliothèque, 7 rue Turgot (☎11 00 47). Restaurant by day and busy bar by night. Lives up to its name (which means library) with chic mahogany stools and shelves of leather-bound books. Much more interesting to the crowd of 20-somethings that gather here, however, is the constant stream of music videos played on large-screen TVs. Big, tasty pizzas and salads €5-19. Open M-Th 7am-1am, F-Sa 7am-2am. MC/V. ❸

L'Etoile de L'Inde, 7 rue Haute-Cité (☎32 46 95). Serves Tandoori specialties in an elegantly French atmosphere, with white tablecloths and flowers. *Plats* €6-16. *Menu* €16. Open Tu-Su noon-2pm and 7:30-11pm. MC/V. ❸

SIGHTS

MUSÉE NATIONAL ADRIEN DUBOUCHÉ. Founded in the 19th century by a wealthy Cognac merchant, this beautiful national museum houses one of the largest ceramics collections in Europe. Amazingly diverse, it features ceramic pieces from antiquity through the modern era—and from all over the globe—including ornate sculptures, playful figurines, and colorful plates. Particular emphasis is given to French porcelain, especially pieces from Limoges. A first-floor room walks visitors through the stages of ceramics production. The large Chinese plate with a dragon in its center, dating from 1345, is one of the most valuable pieces of china in the world. *(8bis pl. Winston Churchill. ☎33 08 55; www.musee-adriendubouche.fr. Open M and W-Su July-Aug. 10am-5:40pm; Sept.-June 10am-12:25pm and 2-5:40pm. €4.50, students €3, under 18 free; 1st Su of month free for all. Free English audio tours.)*

MUSÉE MUNICIPAL DE L'EVÊCHÉ. Also known as the Musée de l'Email (enamel), this 18th-century bishop's palace contains the city's impressive collection of 12th-century enameled art. Its display of ceramics cannot compete with Dubouche, but its other miscellaneous art, including interesting Egyptian figurines and sarcophagi, as well as the free admission, make this museum a great place to visit. *(Place de la Cathédrale. ☎45 98 10. Open June-Sept. daily 10am-noon and 2-6pm; Oct.-May M and W-Su 10am-noon and 2-5pm. Free.)*

EVÊCHÉ BOTANICAL GARDENS. With a prime spot on a hillside overlooking the Vienne and the cathedral, this floral oasis is perfect for a mid-morning stroll. Its themed gardens are neatly arranged according to the color of the plants, and a promenade along the outer walls of the gardens reveals panoramic views of the valley surrounding Limoges. *(☎45 62 67. Open daily May-Sept. 8am-8:30pm; Mar.-Apr. and Oct. 8am-7pm; Nov.-Feb. 8am-5pm. Tours by appointment.)*

OTHER SIGHTS. The magnificent **Cathédrale St-Etienne** is one of the few examples of Gothic architecture south of the Loire; it was built on the site of a Roman temple and took over 600 years to complete. *(Pl. St-Etienne in la Cité. Open daily 2:30-5pm.)* For a slice of life as a butcher, visit the **Maison Traditionelle de la Boucherie,** 36 rue de la Boucherie. Guides lead English and French tours through the house. *(Open July-Sept. daily 10am-1pm and 2:30-7pm. Free.)* Across the street, the 15th-century Chapel St-Aurelien still lights candles to honor the patron saint of butchers. A short walk toward 71 bd. Gambetta reveals a plaque commemorating the birthplace of painter Auguste Renoir. While the majority of the city's porcelain boutiques are found on rue Louis Blanc, Limoges's famous ceramics also decorate several remarkable structures, including Les Halles, the nearby Pavilion de Verdurier, and the fountain in front of the Mairie. The Manufacture Bernardaud offers factory tours for those who want to learn more about porcelain production. *(27 av. Albert Thomas. ☎10 55 91. €4. Tours June-Sept. daily 9am-7pm; Oct.-May by reservation.)*

ENTERTAINMENT AND NIGHTLIFE

The **Grand Théâtre,** 48 rue Jean Jaurès, presents 60 ballet, orchestral, operatic, and choral productions each season, between September and early June. (Reservations ☎45 95 95. Box office open Jan.-June and Sept.-Dec. daily 10am-6pm. €5-35. MC/V.) The **Théâtre de l'Union,** 20 rue des Coopérateurs (☎79 90 00; www.theatre-union.fr; ticket office open Tu-Sa 1-7pm, Su 2-7pm), puts on performances from October to May. On weekdays, the five **Centres Culturels Municipaux** host concerts, theater productions, and films. Both the **Centre Culturel Jean-Moulin** (☎35 04 10) and the **Centre Culturel John Lennon** (☎06 24 83), which caters particularly to young people, are located at 76 rue des Sagnes.

At night, the streets of Limoges seem to empty out, though a handful of popular bars and clubs dot the streets. Many *brasseries* serve as social hangouts in the evening, but most nightlife centers around **rue Charles Michels,** known affectionately among locals as *"la rue de la soif"* ("the street of thirst"), and **cours Jourdan.** At the **Cheyenne Café,** 4 rue Charles Michels, get a glimpse of France's perception of the Wild West. Twenty-somethings enjoy hip-hop music blasting from the speakers—both anachronisms in this saloon-themed bar. (☎32 32 62. Beer €2-4. Open M-Sa 7:30pm-2am.) A more laid-back atmosphere prevails on the sidewalk terrace of **L'Irlandais,** 2 rue Haute-Cité, near the cathedral, which transforms from an Irish-themed restaurant to a popular bar at night. Live music provides the evening's sound track Friday and Saturday nights in summer. (☎32 46 47. Pints €4.50-6. Open Tu-F 5pm-2am, Sa-Su 3pm-2am.) Jazz fans (read: 30- and 40-somethings) flock to **Round Midnight,** 12 av. Gabriel Péri, a small bar just outside the Cité. This colorful club boasts an intimate atmosphere, with comfy leather chairs surrounding a small stage. (☎06 83 28 70 58; round.midnight@aliceadsl.fr. Piano bar 8pm. Concerts 9:30pm. Open W-Th and Su 7:30pm-1am, F-Sa 7:30pm-2am.)

FESTIVALS

Limoges sees a constant stream of festivals, outdoor movie showings, and street performances in summer. The **Fête de St-Jean,** also known as the **Fête des Ponts,** held at the end of June every year, brings diving, fireworks, water shows, dancing, and musical performances. The popular **Festival Urb'Aka** (☎32 08 42 or 45 63 85) heats up the last three days in June with street performances, fireworks, and concerts. At the end of September, the **Festival International des Théâtres Francophones** (☎10 90 10; www.lesfrancophonies.com) features thousands of Francophone performing artists from around the world.

DAYTRIP FROM LIMOGES

ORADOUR-SUR-GLANE

The tiny town of Oradour-sur-Glane (pop. 2000)—not to be confused with Haute-Vienne's 2 other Oradours—contains 2 distinct sections: the new town and its obliterated predecessor. Equival runs a daily bus (#12) from Limoges (train station, pl. des Charentes, pl. des Carmes, or pl. Winston Churchill) to the Centre de la Mémoire (old town) Sept.-June, and to both towns July-Aug. (30min., 4-6 per day, €3). Schedules at the Limoges tourist office and train station.

On June 10, 1944, in a heinous act of brutality, Nazi SS troops massacred all the residents of the farming village Oradour-sur-Glane (OH-rah-door suhr GLAHNN), without warning or provocation, in their relentless quest to rid the countryside of resistors. The Nazis entered the town at 2pm and corralled the women and children into the church and the men into six barns. At 4pm, a shot was fired, ordering the troops to begin the massacre. The women and children in the church were burned alive; the men were shot, then burned as well. By 7pm, 642 people, including 205 children, had been slaughtered. Most of the SS troops involved in the attack were tried in 1953, found guilty, and immediately freed due to the French government's general amnesty decree. Heinz Barth, commander of the unit, served part of a life sentence in a German jail until he was released as a result of ill health.

Today, the town remains in hauntingly untouched ruins. Houses with crumbling walls stand watch over the silently rotting remains. Telephone lines dangle eerily over deserted streets lined with rusted-out skeletons of 50-year-old cars. The village has been preserved in the hope that no one will forget the atrocities that occurred in Oradour and elsewhere under the Nazi regime. Visitors can walk freely along the main thoroughfare and peer into remnants of homes; signs indicate the name and profession of many former residents. Some homes contain the remains of sewing machines and bed frames, as well as hearths with the residents' names engraved. A small memorial between the cemetery and town displays bicycles, toys, and watches that were all stopped at the same moment by the heat of the fire. The incredible **Centre de la Mémoire** places the massacre and the Nazi regime in a social and historical context with artifacts, timelines, and an informative 12min. film, all with English subtitles. (☎43 04 30. Museum and town open daily mid-May to mid-Sept. 9am-7pm; mid-Sept. to Oct. and Mar. to mid-May 9am-6pm; Nov. to mid-Dec. and Feb. 9am-5pm. Museum €7; students, unemployed, war veterans, and ages 10-18 €5; under 10 free.)

BRIVE-LA-GAILLARDE ☎05 55

When the courageous citizens of Brive-la-Gaillarde (BREEVE lah gay-YAHRD; pop. 50,000) repelled English forces during the Hundred Years' War, they earned their town the nickname *la Gaillarde* ("the Bold"), an appellation reaffirmed in 1944 when Brive became the first French town to liberate itself from the Germans. Today, Brive's residents keep their fighting spirit through their support of the town's First Division rugby team, whose jerseys, flags, and bumper stickers dominate almost every street. Unpretentious and un-touristed, Brive has a vibrant atmosphere and peaceful *centre-ville;* the town also provides an inexpensive base for exploring the ancient villages of Limousin.

TRANSPORTATION AND PRACTICAL INFORMATION. Trains leave from av. Jean Jaurès for Bordeaux (2½hr., 4 per day, €26); Limoges (1hr., 12 per day, €15); Lyon (6-9hr., 4 per day); Sarlat (1hr. via Souillac, 3-4 per day, €13); Toulouse (2hr., 5 per day) via Montauban (2½hr., 5 per day). Buy tickets at station. (Ticket and info offices open M 4:15am-8:35pm, Tu-Sa 5:25am-8:35pm, Su 6:35am-9:35pm.) **Buses** stop at the train station and in pl. de Lattre de Tassigny, next to the central post office. STUB runs **public buses** in the city. (Tickets €1.10, *carnets* of 10 €7.20.) CFTA, pl. du 14 juillet, next to the tourist office, runs to surrounding areas, including Collonges-la-Rouge and Turenne. (☎17 919. Info desk open M-Sa 8:15am-12:15pm and 2-6:15pm.) For a **taxi,** call ☎24 24 24. (24hr.) **Rent cars** at **Avis,** 58 av. Jean Jaurès (☎24 51 00; open M-F 8am-noon and 2-6:30pm, Sa 9-11:30am and 2:30-5:30pm) and **Europcar,** 52 av. Jean Jaurès (☎74 14 41; open M-F 8am-noon and 2-6:30pm, Sa 8:30am-12:30pm and 2-6pm). **Bikes** can be rented at Sports Bike, 142 av. Georges Pompidou, a 20min. walk down av. Thiers. (☎17 00 84. €14 per day. Open Tu-Sa 9am-12:30pm and 3-7pm. AmEx/MC/V.)

To get to the **tourist office,** pl. du 14 Juillet, from the station, walk down av. Jean Jaurès to the end, then down rue de L'Hôtel de Ville toward the cathedral. Cut diagonally across pl. Charles de Gaulle. After the library, veer left onto rue Toulzac, which becomes av. de Paris, and cross the parking lot. The staff provides maps and brochures, an English audio tour of sights, bus schedules, and city tours in English and French for groups of five or more. (☎24 08 80; www.brive-tourisme.com. Call for schedule. Tours €4. Open July-Aug. M-Sa 9am-7pm, Su 10am-4pm; Sept. and Apr.-June M-Sa 9am-12:30pm and 1:30-6:30pm; Oct.-Mar. M-Sa 9am-noon and 2-6pm.) Other services include: a **laundromat,** 39 rue Dubois (☎17 08 67; €3 per 5kg, €3.70 per 7kg; open daily 6am-9:30pm); **police,** 4 bd. Anatole France (☎17 46 00); a **hospital** at bd. Docteur Verlhac (☎92 60 00); and free **Internet** access at the **Centre Culturel de Brive,** 31 av. Jean Jaurès (☎74 20 51; www.centreculturel-brive.com). The central **post office,** behind pl. de Lattre de Tassigny, **exchanges currency.** (☎18 33 10. Open M-F 8am-6:45pm, Sa 8am-noon.) **Postal Code:** 19100.

ACCOMMODATIONS AND FOOD. With silent meals and vesper services, the **Hotellerie des Grottes de St-Antoine ❷**, 41 rue Edmond Michelet, gives guests a peek at the monastic lifestyle. However, staying in the rooms in this Franciscan-run complex—located near the caves where Saint Anthony of Padua came to pray when he lived in Brive—is hardly like being cloistered. Completely renovated in 2007, the hostellerie welcomes travelers to its serene location, 15min. from the *centre-ville*, with comfortable, immaculate rooms. (☎24 10 60; www.fratgsa.org. Breakfast included. Free Internet access. Singles €17-23; doubles €26-38.). To get to the **Auberge de Jeunesse (HI) ❶**, 56 av. du Maréchal Bugeaud, from the station, walk the length of av. Jean Jaurès and turn onto bd. Maréchal Lyautey, which becomes bd. de Puyblanc. Bear left onto bd. Jules Ferry, then turn right on av. du Maréchal Bugeaud. Located in a quiet neighborhood, the hostel has clean hall bathrooms, a kitchen, a big-screen TV, a dining area, and small two- to four-bunk rooms. This typical no-frills hostel earns points for its great prices, cleanliness, and location just 5min. from the *centre-ville*. (☎24 34 00; brive@fuaj.org. Breakfast €3.50. Reception M-F 8am-noon and 2-10pm, Sa-Su 6-10pm. Dorms €13.) Located near the town center, **Hôtel Le Chêne Vert ❷**, 24 bd. Jules Ferry, lets clean, well-lit rooms, some with balconies. (☎24 10 07. Breakfast €6. Singles and doubles with sink and toilet €30, with bath €36-39; triples €42-50. AmEx/MC/V.)

Regional fare like *foie gras*, duck, walnuts, truffles, apples, and cheese are featured on most menus, and gourmet food shops fill the *centre-ville*. Brive's open-air markets, at **place Tassigny** and **place du 14 Juillet**, outside the tourist office, feature such items as clothing, shoes, jewelry, and local produce. (Tu, Th, Sa 8am-noon; Sa smaller market.) A friendly and unassuming neighborhood restaurant, family-run **Le Corrèze ❸**, 3 rue de Corrèze, prepares large servings of regional fare at great prices. The three-course *plat regional* (€16) is a worthwhile splurge. (☎24 14 07. 2-, 3- and 4-course *menus* €7/8.50/12-20. Open M-Sa noon-2pm and 7-10:15pm. MC/V.) Pricey but laid-back, Parisian-style bistro **Chez Francis ❸**, 61 av. de Paris, combines a polished atmosphere with a quirky attitude. While tables feature candles and signature plates, the walls and ceiling are covered with messages and caricatures drawn by satisfied customers. (☎74 41 72. *Plats* €9. *Menus* €15-23. Open Tu-Sa noon-1:30pm and 6:30-9:30pm. Reservations required. MC/V.) **La Saladière ❸**, 13 rue de l'Hôtel de Ville, is a vegetarian's paradise, filling its *plats* with such goodies as *cabecous* (goat cheese), tomatoes, and green beans. Carnivores will be pleased with the vast selection of meat dishes, including an Indian salad with tandoori chicken. (Salads €6.60-10. Lunch *menus* €8.20-10. Dinner *menus* €15-22. Open M-Sa noon-2pm and 7-10pm. MC/V.)

SIGHTS. Eclectic **Musée Labenche,** 26bis bd. Jules Ferry, is bound to satisfy visitors with all kinds of interests. Housed in the 16th-century **Hôtel de Labenche,** the museum's wide galleries house an impressively varied collection, featuring human skeletons, ancient coins, 17th-century English tapestries, prehistoric artifacts, old accordions, contemporary art, and medieval weapons. All signs are in French. *(☎18 17 70; www.musee-labenche.com. Open M and W-Su Apr.-Oct. 10am-6:30pm; Nov.-Mar. 1:30-6pm. €4.70, students €2.50, under 16 free; last Su of month free. Temporary exhibits free. Free English audio tours available.)* The oldest liquor distillery in France, **Maison Denoix,** 9 bd. Maréchal Lyautey, is most famous for *"La Suprême Denoix" eau de noix* (walnut *liqueur*). Since 1839, four generations of the Denoix family have produced this famous drink using an unchanged recipe and time-honored methods. Today, free 1hr. tours give an explanation of artisanal methods and a history of the distillery, ending with a fabulous *dégustation* (tasting). *(☎74 34 27; www.denoix.com. July-Aug. and Dec. M-Sa 9am-noon and 2:30-7pm; Sept.-Nov. and Jan.-June Tu-Sa 9am-noon and 2:30-7pm. Tours July-Aug. Tu-Sa 2:30pm.)*

Located in its namesake's former home, the **Centre National de la Résistance et de la Déportation Edmond Michelet,** 4 rue Champanatier, is a museum dedicated to the local hero, a Brive native and Resistance leader who survived internment at the Dachau concentration camp for over a year, then went on to become a minister under de Gaulle. The museum also displays photographs of women and children on their way to the gas chambers, heartbreaking last letters to loved ones, and mementos displaying Brive's role in the Resistance effort. *(☎74 06 08; www.centremichelet.org. Open M-Sa 10am-noon and 2-6pm. Free. Free audio tours available in English and French.)* A somber interior filled with enormous columns imbues the 12th-century **Eglise Collégiale St-Martin,** pl. Charles de Gaulle, with a solemn intensity. Its namesake was an iconoclastic Spaniard who introduced Christianity to the largely pagan Brive in the fourth century. Unreceptive town members beheaded Martin in AD 407, but when the following years saw devastating plagues and foreign invasions, citizens agreed to honor him with a local procession. According to legend, a great light appeared afterwards, and suffering ceased. The church, whose crypt now houses Martin's tomb, was built as a tribute to the saint.

NIGHTLIFE AND FESTIVALS. After dinner, the streets of Brive's *centre-ville* become relatively deserted, but pockets of nightlife can be found in tucked-away bars and *brasseries*. Framed rugby jerseys hang on the walls of **Bar Le Toulzac,** pl. du Civoire, the unofficial center for Brive's most enthusiastic fans. Easy to spot because of the huge posters of Brive's team outside, Le Toulzac is frequented not only by diehard supporters there to watch the game over a beer (€2-5), but also by those who want to enjoy the large terrace near the plaza's fountain. (Open July-Aug. M-Sa 7am-2am; Sept.-June M 1-9pm, Tu-Th 7am-9pm, F-Sa 7am-2am. Snacks available noon-2pm). A decidedly British vibe livens **Pub le Watson,** rue des Echevins, as its terrace fills with boisterous beer-drinkers. (☎17 07 87. Pints €4-5.50. Open M-Sa 4pm-2am. AmEx/MC/V.) At midnight, 20-somethings fill **La Charette,** a 25min. walk across the river at 33 av. Ribot, for the techno and disco beats. (☎87 65 73. Cover €10. Open Tu and Th-Sa until 5am. MC/V.)

Brive and its surrounding villages host a stream of musical and theatrical performances all summer. Only a few years old, the hugely popular **Brive-Plage** festival hits town during the last week of June, with man-made beaches that host rugby, soccer, and volleyball tournaments by day and concerts by night. In mid-August, **Orchestrades Universelles** attracts orchestras, bands, and choirs from around the world for a celebration of classical, traditional, and jazz music. Daily performances liven the streets and are free until 9pm on the last evening, when a spectacular gala celebrates 700 young musicians in l'Espace de Trois Provinces. (☎04 78 36 87 14; www.orchestrades.com. Tickets from €3.) In early November, pl. du 14 Juillet and Halle Georges Brassens become flooded with visitors for the presentation of the masterpieces of over 400 French authors for the renowned **Foire du Livre.** (☎18 18 41. Free.) Four times a year from December to February, the streets of Brive host **La Fois Grasses,** a market with the delicacies that make Brive famous: geese, ducks, *champignons* (mushrooms), truffles, chocolate, and *foie gras*.

DAYTRIPS FROM BRIVE

TURENNE

Timing your trip from Brive to Turenne can be tricky because buses run only 2 or 3 times a day; ask at the CFTA office, pl. du 14 Juillet, for schedules. Buses also stop at Collonges-la-Rouge, but the best option for those hoping to see both villages is to stop first in Turenne. The 8km trip from Turenne to Collonges can easily be made on a bike rented from the Turenne tourist office. Buses are the best way to get to Turenne, but you can also drive or bike. From

Brive, take av. Alsace-Lorraine (D38), and after 10km, at the roundabout, bear right onto D8, which leads to Turenne. Taxis run between Turenne and Collonges. (☎25 30 30. €19.)

Built dramatically into a steep hillside 15km south of Brive, Turenne (tuh-REHNN) carries a long legacy of power. In the 13th and 14th centuries, it served as the fortified seat of the region's viscount, who controlled more than 1200 villages in the surrounding territory. In the 17th century, with the Wars of Religion ravaging the country, Turenne became a bastion of Protestantism, almost never threatened. However, the town eventually proved too invincible for its own good. In 1738 Louis XV bought it from its indebted count and, in an assertion of royal power, had the castle largely dismantled. Today, Turenne remains nearly untouched by modernization and retains multiple vestiges of its long-lasting heyday. Perhaps the best part of Turenne is the wonderful uphill walk to the **château,** as narrow medieval streets cut between flower-draped houses and provide astonishing views. On the way to the summit, be sure to stop at **La Collegiale Notre Dame,** a modest and distinctly French church with a touching war memorial and elaborate gold tabernacle. At the château, visitors can tour the keep, wander through the small garden, or climb the narrow, uneven steps of the intact watchtower for an unparalleled view of the region. (Guide available in English. Open July-Aug. daily 10am-7pm; Sept.-Oct. and Apr.-June daily 10am-noon and 2-6pm; Nov.-Mar. Su 2-5pm. €3.50, ages 10-18 €2.30.)

At the base of town, Turenne's **tourist office** offers maps (€1-3.40), guided French city tours (June-Sept. W, F 10:30am, 5pm; €4; reservations recommended), English audio tours, and rents bikes for €10 per day. (☎85 94 38. Open July-Aug. daily 9:30am-12:30pm and 2:30-6:30pm; Apr.-June and Sept. Tu-Su 10am-12:30pm and 3-6pm.)

COLLONGES-LA-ROUGES

CFTA runs infrequent buses to the village on line #4 from Brive (M-F 2-3 per day, Sa 2 per day; fewer buses July-Aug.) From the main road, signs point to the town's tourist office (☎25 47 57 or 25 32 25), which provides maps (€1), extensive hiking guides (€1), and city tours in English and French. French tours July-Aug. 4 per day. English tours by reservation. Open July-Aug. daily 10am-1pm and 2-7pm; Apr.-June and Sept.-Oct. daily 10am-noon and 2-6pm; Nov.-Mar. M-Sa 10am-noon and 2-5pm.

Twenty kilometers southeast of Brive, peaceful Collonges-la-Rouge (koh-LONJH lah ROOJH) seems too good to be true: red sandstone buildings are covered with green vines, trellises brim with blooming flowers, and overhanging archways provide refreshing shade from the sun. There's little to do here but appreciate why this village has been ranked one of the most beautiful in France. Those visiting Collonges-la-Rouge should stop into the 12th-century **Eglise St-Pierre;** inside, dull red bricks contrast with the bold green and gold altar. The **Maison de la Sirène** houses a small museum of local history, while medieval figurines depicting Ulysses and a young siren are sculpted on the building's exterior.

ROCAMADOUR

While Rocamadour is in the Lot Valley, it is most easily accessible from Brive. Trains run from Brive, stopping at the Rocamadour station, 4km from town on rte. N140 (40min.; M-Sa 6 per day 8:30am-6:25pm, Su 3 per day; last return train 7:50pm; €12). The Brive train station provides schedules and tickets. From the Rocamadour station, a flat, winding road leads to the top of town (45min.). A hiking trail provides a more direct route: with your back to the station, head left down the street for 2min. until you see a wooden sign on the right side of the road indicating the trailhead. For a taxi call ☎05 65 50 14 82. €10.

Tiny Rocamadour (ROH-kah-mah-DOOR) is a stunning three-layered city, carved into large chalk cliffs overlooking a deep valley. The town was named for St-Amadour, whose perfectly preserved body was unearthed near the chapel in the 12th century. The saint was reputed to have been the biblical Zacchaeus, a thieving tax collector who mended his ways after dining with Jesus. A stop on the road to Santiago de Compostela, Rocamadour continues to see faithful pilgrims who come to pray in its chapels, but the town's holy sites and stunning views attract more tourists than religious devotees. The narrow streets winding upward through the town are crowded; those seeking tranquility should plan to arrive early or stay late.

At the top of the three-tiered city sits the 12th-century **château,** home to the chaplains of Rocamadour and closed to the public. Walk along the **ramparts** for great views. (€2; coins only.) Zig-zagging up a steep pathway to the château is the **Chemin de Croix,** which depicts the 14 stations of the cross. The middle section of the cliff is dominated by the **Cité Religieuse,** an enclosed courtyard that encompasses seven chapels, two of which can be visited without a guide. Its nucleus is the **Chapelle Notre Dame,** a silent place of prayer containing a model ship honoring shipwreck victims. Outside the entrance to the chapel is a fading—but nevertheless haunting—fresco depicting death personified, while high up on the cliff to the left of the entrance, wedged into the rock, is the legendary **sword in the stone**—which was allegedly wielded by Hector of Troy and used by Roland, an epic hero who served under Charlemagne. **La Basilique St-Sauveur,** adjacent to the chapel, attracts visitors to its gilt altar. (☎05 65 33 23 30. Open Apr.-Oct. M-Sa 9am-noon and 2-6pm.) Under Notre Dame and St-Sauveur lies the **Crypte St-Amadour,** where the saint's body rested undisturbed until a Protestant tried to set it ablaze during the Wars of Religion. Though apparently immune to the flames, the saint's body could not withstand the assailant's back-up plan: an axe.

The old medieval town—whose streets now host tourist-friendly *glaciers* and *sandwicheries*—occupies the lower level of the city. A long staircase leads up to the *cité religieuse*, and the château sits at the top of the cliff. Your best bet is to start from the château and move downward. Unless you are physically unable to make the trip, the two elevators that connect the three levels are not worth the steep prices. (☎05 65 33 62 44. Elevators operate daily July-Aug. 8am-8pm; Sept.-June 9am-6pm. €2, round-trip €3.)

Rocamadour's surrounding areas offer appealing, family-oriented attractions. The **Grotte des Merveilles,** beside the upper tourist office, is a cave of stalactites and remnants of prehistoric paintings. Guided tours (40min.) in English and French point out the paintings. (☎05 65 33 67 92. Open daily July-Aug. 9:30am-7pm; Apr.-June and Sept.-Nov. 10am-noon and 2-6pm. €6, under 18 €4.) Signs from the upper tourist office point the way (300m) to **La Féerie,** a fantastic model world, complete with realistic trains, cars, barges, and people who move around. Every detail, down to the last doorknob, was constructed by one man over 60,000 hours. The 1hr. show in French (English subtitles) tries—and fails—to construct a coherent story around the impressive demonstration of the models' bells and whistles. While the show may be corny, La Féerie is well worth a visit. (☎05 65 33 71 06; www.la-feerie.com. Apr.-Sept. 4-8 shows per day; Oct. 2 per day. Tickets sold daily mid-July to late Aug. 9am-noon and 2-7pm; late Aug. to early Nov. and Easter to mid-July 10am-noon and 2-6pm. €8, under 12 €5.) The **Rocher des Aigles** shares the plateau with the castle and hosts a 1hr. show with trained birds of prey. (☎05 65 33 65 45; www.rocherdesaigles.com. Open early to mid-July and mid- to late Aug. daily 1-7pm, 4 shows; mid-July to mid-Aug. daily 11am-7pm, 5 shows; Apr.-June and Sept. daily 1-6pm, 3 shows; Oct.-Nov. Tu-Su 2-5pm, 1 show. €8, ages 5-14 €4.50.) See Rocamadour at night to glimpse it at its most spectacular. After the afternoon crowd has poured out of the town, its buildings and cliffs are illuminated in soft, glowing light. A tour on the town's *petit train*, which leaves from Porte du Figuier, affords a good view and provides interesting historical commentary. (☎05 65 33 22 00. Open daily from 10am. Tours 30min. Night tours from 7:30pm. Call tourist office for schedule. €5, under 18 €2.50.)

Separate **tourist offices** (☎05 65 33 22 00; www.rocamadour.com) serve the cliff's top and bottom layers. Both have town guides, free accommodations booking, maps (€1), and currency exchange at terrible rates. The upper office is in l'Hospitalet, on rte. de Lacave, and the lower is in the old Hôtel de Ville. Neither has strict hours, but one of the two will be open daily July.-Aug. 10am-12:30pm and 1:30-6pm; Apr.-June and Sept.-Oct. 10am-noon and 2-6pm; Nov.-Mar. M-Sa 10am-noon and 2-5:30pm, Su 2-5:30pm. Other services include an **ATM** inside the **post office** near the lower tourist office. (☎05 65 33 62 21. Open July-Aug. M-F 10am-noon and 1:30-4:30pm, Sa 10am-noon; Sept.-June M-F 1:30-4:30pm.) **Postal Code:** 46500.

DORDOGNE

Dramatic cliffs and poplar thickets overlook the Dordogne River's lazy waters, which provided a natural boundary between French and English Aquitaine during the Hundred Years' War. In the summer, tourists on bikes and in cars and canoes descend on valley; in many places you'll probably hear more English than French. To the north, the terrain ranges from deep vales amid rolling hills to towering white cliffs above fields of tall grass. Renting a car is the wisest option, but biking the Dordogne is feasible if you are prepared for long distances and steep hills.

PÉRIGUEUX ☎05 53

High above the Isle River, the towering steeple and five massive cupolas of the Cathédrale St-Front—often a stop on the pilgrimage to Santiago de Compostela—dominate the skyline of Périgueux (PARE-ee-guh; pop. 65,000). Beneath the cathedral lies the quiet, colorful, and largely pedestrian town center, whose narrow streets are lined with myriad shops, cafés, and restaurants featuring the regional specialties—duck and walnuts. Travelers with cars might want to daytrip to the caves of the Vézère Valley from Périgueux rather than from Les Eyzies-de-Tayac.

TRANSPORTATION

Trains: rue Denis Papin. Info office (☎06 21 94) open M-F 4:15am-12:30am, Sa 5am-12:30am, Su 6am-11:30pm. Ticket booth open M-Th 5:40am-7:40pm, F 5:40am-8:25pm, Sa 7:10am-7:10pm, Su 7:20am-7:40pm. To: **Bordeaux** (1½hr., 12 per day, €18); **Brive-la-Gaillarde** (1hr., 6 per day, €11); **Limoges** (1hr., 12 per day, €14); **Lyon** (6-8hr., 2 per day, €51); **Paris** (4-6hr.; 13 per day; €57); **Sarlat** (1½hr., 5 per day, €13); **Toulouse** (4hr., 12 per day, €32) via **Agen, Brive,** or **Bordeaux.**

Buses: CFTA Centre-Ouest. Info at the *gare routière*, 19 rue Denis Papin (☎08 43 13). Open M-F 9am-noon and 2-5pm. Buses go to **Angoulême** (stops at the train station; 1½hr.; M, W, F 2 per day; Su 1 per day; €13) and **Sarlat** (1½hr.; M-Tu and Th-F 1 per day, W 3 per day; €7.70).

Taxis: Taxi Périgueux, pl. Bugeaud (☎09 09 09). €5.50 base; €1.24 per km during the day, €1.84 at night. 24hr.

Car Rental: Avis, 18 rue du Président Wilson (☎53 39 02). From €47 per day. 21+. Open M-F 8am-noon and 2-7pm, Sa 8am-noon and 2-6pm. AmEx/MC/V. **Hertz,** 1 av. Henri Barbusse (☎54 61 80), across from the train station. Open M-F 8am-noon and 2-7pm, Sa 8am-noon and 2-6pm. AmEx/MC/V.

ORIENTATION AND PRACTICAL INFORMATION

The *vieille ville* is bordered by **cours Tourny** and **cours Fénelon** to the north and south, **boulevard Georges Saumand** along the river, and **boulevard Michel de Montaigne** to the east and west. To reach the *vieille ville* and tourist office from the station, turn right on rue Denis Papin and left on rue des Mobiles-de-Coulmiers, which becomes rue du Président Wilson. After the Monoprix, turn right and walk one block. The office is on the left, beside the Mataguerre Tower (15min.).

Tourist Office: 26 pl. Francheville (☎53 10 63; www.tourisme-perigueux.fr). Free map and info on walking, *petit train,* and bike tours. 1½hr. walking tours are highly recommended and provide entry to otherwise inaccessible buildings, such as the Tour Mataguerre. Tours July-Aug. M 10:30am, 2:30, 3pm; Tu-Sa 10:30am, 2:30, 3, 9pm; Su 3pm. June and Sept. M-Sa 10:30am, 2:30, 3pm; Su 3pm. Oct.-May M-Sa 2:30pm, Su 3pm. €5, students €3.80. Bike tour July-Aug. Tu 10am. €5, students €3.80. Office open June-Sept. M-Sa 9am-6pm, Su 10am-1pm and 2-6pm; Oct.-May M-Sa 9am-1pm and 2-6pm. **Espace Tourisme Périgord,** 25 rue du Président Wilson (☎35 50 24), has excellent topographic maps and info on travel in the Dordogne, campgrounds, *gîtes,* and *chambres d'hôtes.* Open M-F 9am-12:30pm and 1:30-5pm.

Laundromat: Lav'matic, 20 rue Mobiles de Coulmiers, near rond-point Lanxade on the way to the train station. Wash €3-8, dry €1 per 9min. Open daily 8am-9pm.

Police: rue du 4 Septembre (☎06 44 44), near the post office.

Hospital: Centre Hospitalier, 80 av. Georges Pompidou (☎45 25 25).

Internet Access: Multimédia.com, 9 cours Fénelon (☎53 03 52), around the corner from the tourist office. Offers international calling and several computers. €1 per 15min., €3 per hr. Open M-Sa 10am-1:30pm and 2:30-9:30pm, Su 3-9pm.

Post Office: 1 rue du 4 Septembre (☎03 61 12). **Currency exchange.** Open M-F 8:30am-6:30pm, Sa 9am-noon. **Postal Code:** 24000.

ACCOMMODATIONS AND CAMPING

Les Charentes, 16 rue Denis Papin (☎53 37 13), across from the station. Clean, comfortable rooms with almost-endearing 1970s décor. A tiny hotel managed by a friendly couple eager to share Périgueux with its guests. Extensive organic vegetarian menu in the attached restaurant. Breakfast €5. Reception 7am-10pm. Closed late Dec. to early Jan. Reservations recommended in summer. Singles with shower €25, with TV €30, with toilet €35; doubles €30/35/40. Extra person €5. AmEx/MC/V. ❷

Les Barris, 2 rue Pierre Magne (☎53 04 05; www.hoteldesbarris.com). 5min. walk from the town

QUIET RIOT

During the first week of August, a hush falls over the town of Périgueux, but it is in no way a mournful one. Rather, it's for the annual **Mimos,** an international mime festival. The week-long festival transforms Périgueux into a whirlwind of silent performances and welcomes entertainers from three continents, including countries such as Canada, Great Britain, Korea, and Germany. Forget the stereotypical silent men donning black and white bodysuits; this mime festival features a much more diverse—even circus-oriented—array of performances. Shows take place throughout the city, in squares, parks, and concert halls, as mime companies and individuals compete for prizes awarded by the Mimos Jury.

Spectators watch as performers display their talents in everything from physical theater to acrobatics to juggling. Performances, which range from innocent, clownish gags and visual humor to sensual modern dance reenactments of ancient myths, cater to a universal crowd. Also noteworthy, and more somber, is the Korean mime spectacle depicting the separation of the Korean peninsula. Contemporary and engaging, the festival offers a unique deviation from the jazz and wine events so common in the southwest region.

Tickets available at Le Théâtre, Esplanade de Théâtre. ☎*05 53 53 18 71. Tickets €8-15.*

center. A riverside hotel commanding spectacular views of the cathedral and *vieille ville*. Comfortable, modern rooms with toilets and showers. Breakfast €6. Wi-Fi. Singles €44; doubles €49; triples €54; quads €59; quints €64. MC/V. ❹

Foyer des Jeunes Travailleurs Résidence Lakanal (HI), rue Thermes (☎06 81 40; fax 06 81 49). Turn right from the station onto rue Denis Papin and follow it as it becomes rue Chanzy. Turn left on av. Cavaignac, then right on rue Romaine. Cross the roundabout and take rue Mosaïque until it hits rue de Thermes, then turn right and walk along the train tracks; the hostel is at the end of the street (25min.). Although from the outside it appears slightly worn and run-down, this dormitory has several enjoyable indoor features, including a large cafeteria, a busy TV room, ping-pong tables, and a bar. 4-bunk dorms with small showers see few tourists until mid-summer. Reception M-F midnight-noon, 1:30-6:30pm, and 8pm-midnight; Sa-Su midnight-2:30pm and 6:30pm-midnight. Dorms with breakfast €16, with dinner €23. MC/V over €15. ❶

Camping Barnabé-Plage, 80 rue des Bains (☎53 41 45), 1.5km away in Boulazac. From cours Montaigne, take bus #8 (dir.: Cité Bel Air; M-F 1 per hr. 7am-7pm, Sa less frequent; €1.25) to "rue des Bains." It may be faster to walk; from Cathédrale St-Front, head downhill and cross Pont des Barris. Turn left after the bridge onto rue des Prés; the street ends at rue des Bains. Take a right and an immediate left on rue des Jardins to reach the entrance (25min). Shady, tranquil riverside site. Packed in summer. Reception 9am-midnight. €4 per person, €3.30 per tent, €2.40 per car. MC/V. ❶

FOOD

The labyrinth of narrow stone streets between **cours M. Montaigne** and **rue Taillefer** reveals enchanted *places* filled with small-town charm and restaurants serving regional culinary treasures, including *foie gras*, walnuts, fruit *liqueurs*, and *cèpe* and *girolle* mushrooms. A stroll down **rue Salinière** and **rue Limogeanne** reveals an assortment of *charcuteries* (butchers), *pâtisseries* (pastry shops), *boulangeries* (bakeries), and *sandwicheries*. There are small morning markets on **place du Coderc** and **place de l'Hôtel de Ville**, and a larger one on **place de la Clautre**, near the cathedral (open W and Sa 8am-1pm). The behemoth **Monoprix**, pl. Bugeaud, is impossible to miss (open M-Sa 8:30am-8pm; MC/V), and there's a **Marché Plus** at 55 rue du Président Wilson (open M-Sa 7am-9pm, Su 8am-1pm; MC/V).

Au Bien Bon, 15 rue des Places (☎09 69 91). Exceptional regional cuisine. Specialties include *magret* (duck steak; €14) and *cèpes* omelettes (€12). Tables outside this picturesque medieval building overlook a quiet pedestrian street. Lunch *menu* €14. Open M noon-1:30pm, Tu-F noon-1:30pm and 7:30-9:30pm, Sa 7:30-9:30pm. MC/V. ❷

Le Romarin, rue de la Clarté (☎53 27 84), near pl. du Coderc. Another excellent place to sample the Dordogne's cuisine. Small restaurant with a marble-topped bar and laid-back atmosphere. Filling salads (€8) and huge *tartines* (€8.50). *Menus* €13-20. Open May-Sept. daily 8am-10pm. Kitchen open noon-2pm and 7-10pm. ❸

L'Olivio, 14 rue de l'Aubergerie (☎09 63 88). Pizzeria in a restored medieval house. Salads from €5. Pizzas from €7. Open Tu-Sa noon-2:30pm and 7-10pm. MC/V. ❶

SIGHTS

Périgueux is divided into two distinct historical districts: the Medieval and Renaissance section to the northeast, and the Gallo-Roman city to the southwest.

MEDIEVAL AND RENAISSANCE PÉRIGUEUX. For travelers who have seen one too many Gothic cathedrals during their stay in France, Périgueux's **Cathédrale St-Front** offers a break from the ordinary. The massive church—built in the shape of a Greek cross—is crowned by five immense Byzantine cupolas next to a soaring belfry. The interior features beautiful chandeliers, an impressive organ, and a spectacular wooden altarpiece. In the 19th century, St-Front was restored by architect Paul Abadie, who used the cathedral as inspiration for his design of the Basilique Sacré-Cœur (p. 138) in Paris. *(Open daily 8am-noon and 2:30-7pm.)* Down rue St-Front from the cathedral, the **Musée du Périgord,** 22 cours Tourny, is home to one of France's most important collections of prehistoric artifacts, including fossils from Les Eyzies, 2m-long mammoth tusks, and an Egyptian mummy whose bare toe bones peek out from crusty coverings. It also holds a small collection of art from the medieval through modern periods. *(☎06 40 70. Open Apr.-Sept. M and W-F 10:30am-5:30pm, Sa-Su 1-6pm; Oct.-Mar. M and W-F 10am-5pm. €4, students €2, under 18 free.)* Walk back to the tourist office to find the medieval **Tour Mataguerre,** which derives its name from the Occitan (ancient Languedoc) language—"matar" meaning "to hold at bay," and "guerra" meaning "war."

GALLO-ROMAN PÉRIGUEUX. The few remains of Gallo-Roman Périgueux lie west of the *vieille ville*, down rue de la Cité from pl. Francheville. The ruins of impressive **Tour de Vésone,** built in the first century AD, were once part of a huge temple dedicated to the patron goddess and namesake of Vésone (the name of ancient Périgueux). Although only the crumbling shell of the tower remains, it was originally a "cella," the center of worship in Roman temples. About a quarter of the weighty structure was demolished, supposedly by the last fleeing demons of paganism, although it was more likely dismantled to create the city's defensive wall. *(Park grounds open daily Apr.-Sept. 7:30am-9pm; Oct.-Mar. 7:30am-6:30pm.)* Next door, the **Musée Gallo-Romain,** rue Claude Bernard, has built an intricate walkway over the excavated ruins of the Domus de Vésone, once the lavish home of a wealthy Roman merchant. The museum boasts a rich collection of Roman artifacts, murals, and stonework, while detailed displays describe Roman life and the design of ancient Périgueux. *(☎05 65 60. Tours in French daily July-Aug. €1. Audio tour in English €1. Open July-Sept. daily 10am-7pm; Apr.-July and Sept.-Oct. Tu-Su 10am-12:30pm and 2-6pm; Feb.-Mar. and Nov.-Dec. Tu-Su 10am-12:30pm and 2-5:30pm. €5.70, under 12 €3.70.)* Cross the bridge from the Tour de Vésone and turn left down rue Romaine to reach a cluster of architectural vestiges dating from the first century through the high Middle Ages. Flowers sprout through the crevices of the **Château Barrière,** a four-story late-Gothic castle. The Romanesque house next door is an example of the use of "spolia"—chunks of ruins incorporated decoratively into new buildings. The **Porte Normande** is a fragment of the wall that once surrounded the city to defend against the first Norman and barbarian attacks. On rue Romaine, the 11th-century **Eglise St-Etienne-de-la-Cité,** the city's cathedral until it was badly damaged during the Wars of Religion, features two simple but stately cupolas dotted with small Romanesque windows. *(Open daily 9:30am-noon and 2:30-6:30pm.)* A Roman **amphitheater** currently serves as a public park, with luxurious foliage and an inviting fountain. *(Open daily Apr.-Sept. 7:30am-9pm; Oct.-Mar. 7:30am-6:30pm.)*

NIGHTLIFE AND FESTIVALS

Macadam Jazz presents free outdoor concerts on Tuesday nights in July and August. Périgueux quiets down during the first week of August for **Mimos,** the world's leading international mime festival. The big events charge admission, but there are free performances and workshops all over town. (☎53 18 71. Ticketed events €10, students €8.)

Although the streets may be sleepy, Périgueux's *places* jump with activity in the evenings. **Place St-Silain** and **place St-Louis** are the centers of the city's nightlife, with music and outdoor cafés, while **place du Marché au Bois** hosts frequent concerts. Bars line the lively **rue de la Sagesse.**

The Star Inn, 17 rue des Drapeaux (☎08 56 83; www.thestarinnfrance.com). A classic Irish pub in a Renaissance house. Friendly English-speaking owners are happy to suggest activities and sights around the region. Outdoor seating available. Drinks from €2.50. Happy hour M-W 7-9pm. Open July-Aug. M-Tu and Th-Sa 7pm-2am, W noon-2am; Sept.-June daily 7pm-1am. MC/V over €15.

Le Mellow, 4 rue de la Sagesse (☎08 53 97.) Sophisticated and appropriately named. A cool place to unwind with a martini. Lounge plays upbeat electronic music and features a sleek cigar bar. Mixed drinks €5.50-6.50. Open Tu-Sa 4:30pm-2am. MC/V.

Zanzi Bar, 2 rue Condé (☎53 28 99). Serves jungle-inspired mixed drinks (from €4.50) and exotic tapas (€6). Live music on weekends. Open W-Su 6:45pm-2am. MC/V.

LES EYZIES-DE-TAYAC ☎05 53

With jutting limestone cliffs, lush green forests, and steep hillsides dotted with the medieval châteaux of the Lords of Tayac, Les Eyzies-de-Tayac (layz AY-zee duh TAY-ak; pop. 900) is the picture-perfect base for travel to the Vézère Valley's famous caves; many of them, with the exception of Lascaux, are less than 20min. from the town center by foot. The nearby Vézère River provides an idyllic setting for post-spelunking relaxation as it flows past Les Eyzies and into some of

France's most picturesque landscapes. The village itself abounds with prehistoric-themed hotels and rustic restaurants serving duck specialties and Bergerac wines.

TRANSPORTATION AND PRACTICAL INFORMATION. **Trains** (☎06 97 22; station open M-F 8am-6pm, Sa-Su 10am-6pm) run to Paris (4-6hr., 4 per day, €60) via Limoges (1¾hr., 4 per day, €30), Périgueux (30min., 6 per day, €6.80), and Sarlat (1hr.; 2 per day, change at Le Buisson; €7.50). Facing away from the station, turn right and walk 500m down av. de la Préhistoire to reach the town center (5min.). For a **taxi** to the caves, call **Taxi Tardieu.** (☎06 93 06. 24hr. €7 to Combarelle; €4.75 to Le Grand Roc.) The **tourist office,** pl. de la Mairie, rents bikes (€8 per ½-day, €14 per day; ID or €20 deposit) and offers lists of caves and B&Bs, **Internet** access (€1.60 per 15min.), and **currency exchange.** (☎06 97 05; www.leseyzies.com. Open July-Aug. M-Sa 9am-7pm, Su 10am-noon and 2-6pm; Apr.-June and Sept. M-Sa 9am-noon and 2-6pm, Su 10am-noon and 2-5pm; Oct.-Mar. M-Sa 9am-noon and 2-6pm.) Other services include: an **ATM** next to the tourist office; **police** (☎30 80 00), rue le Pigeonnier, in St-Cyprien; a **hospital** in Sarlat (☎31 75 75); a **laundromat** in the eastern end of town, at the beginning of rte. de Sarlat (open M-Sa 9am-noon and 2:30-7pm); and a **post office,** av. de la Préhistoire, past the tourist office, with **currency exchange** (☎06 94 11; open M-Tu and Th-F 8:30am-noon and 2-4pm, W 9:30am-noon and 2-4pm, Sa 9-11:30am). **Postal Code:** 24620.

ACCOMMODATIONS AND FOOD. Rooms in Les Eyzies-de-Tayac tend to be expensive. The tourist office has a list of B&Bs in the area (€29-37 for 1-2 people). Drivers will notice signs along the main roads advertising *fermes* (farms) with camping space (€3-8). Some village homes rent rooms for €25-48 during the summer; look for *"chambres"* signs, especially on the east end of town. The Demaison family runs an exceptional **chambres d'hôte ❷,** rte. de Sarlat, 3min. outside town, with twelve charming, immaculate rooms—all with toilet and bath—in a home on the edge of the forest. From the train station, walk through town and follow signs to Sarlat; the house is past the laundromat on the right. (☎06 91 43. Breakfast €5. Reservations required. Singles and doubles €25-36; triples and quads €48. Cash only.) In town, try **Hôtel des Falaises ❸,** 35 av. de la Préhistoire. Spotless, brightly colored rooms have plenty of space and come with bath; larger rooms have a balcony overlooking the garden. The hotel offers more private and homey lodgings in the annex of a large, half-timbered building down the road toward Font-de-Gaume. (☎06 97 35. Breakfast €5. Reception in the bar downstairs 8am-6pm. Doubles €38-42. MC/V.) To get to **Camping La Rivière ❶,** rte. de Périgueux, turn left from the tourist office on av. de la Préhistoire. Follow the road for 5min., cross the bridge, and turn left at the gas station. The site has a restaurant, bike rental, laundry, Internet access, kitchen, and pool. (☎06 97 14; www.lariviereleseyzies.com. Reception 9am-noon and 2-7pm. Open Apr. to mid-Nov. €3.10-4.95 per person, €5.30-7.90 per site. Electricity €3.50. MC/V.)

From April to October, a **market** runs the length of town. (Open M 9am-1pm.) **Halle des Eyzies,** just past the center of town on rte. de Sarlat, houses a number of expensive stalls hawking *foie gras*, Bergerac wine, and walnut products. The *gâteau aux noix* (walnut cake) is not to be passed up. (Open daily mid-June to mid-Sept. 9am-1pm and 2:30-7:30pm.) Get groceries at the large convenience store, **Relais de Mousquetaires,** rte. de Sarlat. (Open M-Sa 8:30am-12:30pm and 3-7pm.) Budget dining choices are few and far between. For regional specialties at good prices, head to **Le Chateaubriant ❸,** 29 av. de la Préhistoire. Sample *foie gras*, duck, and local *fromage de chèvre* (goat cheese) in the sleek dining room or terrace overlooking the park. The €11 *menu du jour* is a great value. (☎35 06 11. Omelettes with salad €9-11. Grilled meat platters €10-13. Open M-Tu and Th-Sa noon-2pm and 7-9pm. MC/V.) **La Milanaise ❸,** av. de la Préhistoire, serves delicious thin-crust pizzas with a wide range of toppings, including duck, *foie gras*, and even mango (though usually not all together), as well as salads full of *gésiers* (duck livers) and walnuts. (☎35 43 97. Salads €4-14. Pizza €6.80-13. *Plats* €8.60-15. *Menus* €16-25. Open daily 11am-2pm and 6:30-10pm. MC/V.) **La Grignotière** ❷, down the street from the tourist office, serves cheap drinks, well-prepared omelettes (€5-8) and sandwiches (€3.20-4.50), as well as a *menu* for only €11. (☎06 91 67. Open daily 8am-10pm. MC/V.)

SIGHTS. The **Musée L'Abri Pataud** is the site of a prehistoric *abri* (shelter), where reindeer hunters lived for over 20,000 years. The museum provides an informative and in-depth explanation of archaeological finds in the region and the types of dwellings built by these early humans. On display is a selection of the thousands of artifacts recovered from the adjacent excavation site. The 18,600-year-old remains of a teenage girl cradling her infant found on the site is the highlight of the *abri* and may represent a link between Neanderthal and Cro-Magnon man. (☎06 92 46; pataud@mnhn.fr. Open July-Aug. daily 10am-7pm; Apr.-June and Sept.-Nov. M-F and Su 10am-12:30pm and 2-6pm; mid-Nov. to Mar. M-Th 10am-12:30pm and 2-5:30pm. Hours subject to change; call ahead for details. Tours in French 1hr., call for times; reservations required for groups. Tours in English on demand. €5.70, ages 6-12 €3.70.) The **Musée National de Préhistoire,** in a château at the southeast corner of town overlooking the village, displays a collection of prehistoric discoveries from the many caves around Les Eyzies. The remains of a Neanderthal infant lie next to etchings of bison. English explanations are available at the entrance of each room. (☎06 45 65; www.musee-prehistoire-eyzies.fr. Open July-Aug. daily 9:30am-6:30pm; Sept. and June M and W-Su 9:30am-6pm; Oct.-May M and W-Su 9:30am-12:30pm and 2-5:30pm. €5, ages 18-25 €3.50, under 18 free; with 1hr. French tour €10/€8.50/€5. English tours by reservation.

DAYTRIPS FROM LES EYZIES: VÉZÈRE VALLEY CAVES

LASCAUX

The Lascaux caves are 2km up the road from Montignac, 23km northeast of Les Eyzies on D706. The train station nearest to Montignac is 10km away at Condat-le-Lardin. Trains run from Les Eyzies to Condat-le-Lardin via Niversac (45min., 1 per day, €16). Taxis (☎50 86 61 or 51 80 46) will pick you up from the station. Trans-Périgord (☎59 01 48) runs 2 buses per day Sept.-June from Périgueux and 3 from Sarlat; call or check at the stations for times and prices. Making the trip by bike is possible for those who can handle the endlessly rolling countryside and the steep climb from Montignac to Lascaux.

The world's most famous pre-historic cave paintings line the ceilings of Lascaux (lahss-KOH), nicknamed "the Sistine Chapel of prehistory." In 1940, four teenagers chasing after their runaway dog discovered a small hole near some tree roots. When they came back the next day to explore further, they stumbled into this ancient cave of wonders. Though they decided to keep it a secret, they could only stay quiet about their amazing discovery for three days—fortunately for the rest of the world. After welcoming hordes of visitors, Lascaux closed to the public in 1963 because the humidity from the millions of breaths of visitors bred algae and spurred the formation of microscopic mineral deposits on the paintings nature had preserved for 17,000 years. Today, visitors line up to see **Lascaux II,** which duplicates every inch of the original and offers one of the best guided English and French cave tours in the valley. Visitors shouldn't scoff at the fact that this isn't the original. Sculptors spent over a decade shaping the new caves' walls to exactly match the contours of the original, and the new paintings were crafted with the same techniques as the originals. Lascaux also reveals the surprising sophistication of the prehistoric artwork.

The ancient artists used perspective to give the paintings depth—a technique not used in Western art until the Renaissance—and frequently used one line to define the shape of two animals, giving the huge murals a fascinating unity.

In nearby **Thonac, Le Thot Espace Cro-Magnon,** a museum 6km from Lascaux on rte. D706, serves as a great introduction to Lascaux and prehistoric discoveries in the area, painting a picture of ancient life, from hunting to making cave art. Featuring the 10% of Lascaux's art not reproduced in Lascaux II, Le Thot also boats a small zoo full of descendants of the animals encountered by prehistoric man. (☎50 70 44; www.semitour.com. Open daily July-Oct. 10am-7pm; Apr.-June and Sept. 10am-6pm; Oct. to mid-Nov. 10am-noon and 2-6pm; mid-Nov. to Feb. Tu-Su 10am-12:30pm and 2-5:30pm. €5.70, ages 6-12 €3.70; discount with ticket to Lascaux II.)

Numerous **campgrounds** dot the Vézère Valley near Montignac; the tourist office has a complete list. Five minutes from the *centre-ville* and within walking distance of Lascaux, **Le Moulin du Bleufond** ❶ offers 83 shady spots and a pool. (☎51 83 95; www.bleufond.com. Open Apr.-Oct. July.-Aug. €5.10 per person, €6.10 per tent. Electricity €3. Prices fall Apr.-June and Sept. AmEx/MC/V.) The Montignac **tourist office,** pl. Bertran-de-Born (☎51 82 60; www.perigordnoir.com), shares a building with the Lascaux II ticket office. (☎51 96 23. Ticket office open in summer 9am until tickets sell out. Tickets sold at the cave entrance during the winter. €8.20, ages 6-12 €5.20, under 6 free. English and French 40min. cave tours July-Aug. 9am-7pm; Apr.-June and Sept.-Oct. 10am-noon and 2-6pm; Nov.-Jan. and Feb.-Mar. 10am-noon and 2-5:30pm. Reservations recommended 1 week ahead July-Aug. MC/V.) Free tours in English and French of Montignac's medieval section are available Thursdays at 8:30pm during July and August.

CAVES WITHIN WALKING DISTANCE OF LES-EYZIES

The **Grotte de Font-de-Gaume,** 1km east of Les Eyzies on D47 (dir.: Sarlat), is the last cave in the Aquitaine basin with multi-colored paintings still open to the public. Though the spectacular 15,000-year-old friezes, completed over the course of hundreds of years, have faded slightly, they are still visible and display the innovative artistic technique of the ancient painters, who incorporated the natural contours of the cave for depth. Locals discovered the paintings in the 1700s but did not realize their importance until two centuries later, by which time several murals had decayed or been defaced by graffiti. Consequently, the most brilliant colors have been preserved only in the cavern's deeper recesses. The scene of a black reindeer licking the nose of its kneeling red cousin demonstrates expressive use of detail, but the *voûte* (vault) where 12 bison stampede across the ceiling is the undisputed highlight. The cave can be chilly; bring an extra layer. Cave access is limited to 180 visitors per day; it is best to reserve four weeks ahead July-August and two weeks in advance September-June. Meanwhile, 50 same-day tickets go on sale at 9:30am; arrive early in summer. *(☎06 86 00; www.leseyzies.com/grottes-ornees. Open mid-May to mid-Sept. M-F and Su 9:30am-5:30pm; mid-Sept. to mid-May M-F and Su 9:30am-12:30pm and 2-5:30pm. Visit only by 1hr. tour; tours in French, in English based on demand; €6.50, ages 18-25 €4.50, under 18 free.)* The **Grotte des Combarelles,** 2km farther down, has lost its paintings to humidity, but the intricate etchings in the "Lascaux of engravings" are spectacular even without color. Over 600 surprisingly realistic carvings depict cave lions, donkeys, rhinos, and early humans. The six-person tours are wonderfully personalized; reserve far in advance for the summer and bring an extra layer. *(Tickets and reservations ☎06 86 00. Reservations required. Hours, prices, website, and tour information same as Font-de-Gaume.)*

NATURAL CAVES WITHIN WALKING DISTANCE OF LES-EYZIES

Many nearby caves have fascinating natural sights. A 1.5km walk northwest of Les Eyzies (15min.), the **Grotte du Grand Roc** is a geologic treasure chest. Halfway up the chalk cliffs, the cave commands a spectacular view of the valley and Tayac's church. While the tour of the cave is short and only features a small portion of the cave itself, the millions of stalactites, stalagmites, and *eccentriques*—small calcite accretions that grow neither straight down nor straight up—make the cave a delight. Among the most remarkable are naturally-occurring raised triangular basins on the limestone floor and two pieces of an eroded column that resemble a giant foot and the leg from which it was detached. *(☎06 92 70; www.grandroc.com. Open daily July-Aug. 9:30am-7pm; Apr.-June and Sept.-Oct. 10am-6pm; Feb.-Mar. and early Nov. 10am-12:30pm and 2-5pm. 30min. tour in French every 30min., or in both French and English according to demand. Written guides available in English. €7.50, under 18 €3.50.)*

CAVES ACCESSIBLE BY BIKE OR CAR

The three caves below make for a great daytrip by bike. If you choose to visit this way, it is easiest and most enjoyable to begin with Abri du Cap-Blanc, go to Roque St-Christophe next, and end with Rouffignac. Take D48 east out of Les Eyzies, D6 west to Roque, D6 (often also D706) to Rouffignac, and D32 back to Eyzies. Northeast of Les Eyzies on D706 (8km), the **Roque St-Christophe** is the most extensive cave dwelling ever discovered. Five floors of limestone terraces house 100 cave shelters 80m high and over 400m long. From 40,000 BC until AD 1580, when it was destroyed by a Catholic army attacking the Protestants who sought refuge here, this sanctuary served as a defensive fort and housed over 3000 people. Detailed pamphlets (available in English) guide visitors on a 45min. loop through the complex. Spectacular re-creations of the 11th-century kitchen, armory, and quarry, complete with functional replicas of machines used to move supplies to and from the fortress, show visitors what life was like during the Middle Ages. *(☎50 70 45; www.roque-st-christophe.com. Open daily July-Aug. 10am-8pm; Apr.-June and Sept. 10am-6:30pm; Feb.-Mar. and Oct. to mid-Nov. 10am-6pm; mid-Nov. to Jan. 2-5pm. Last entry 45min. before closing. €7, students €6, ages 12-16 €4, ages 5-11 €3.)* Only 12 indistinct figures, less detailed than those in Font-de-Gaume, are visible on the sculptured frieze **Abri du Cap-Blanc,** northeast of Eyzies on D48 (7km), but they are extremely well-preserved. Hunters etched horses, bison, and reindeer onto the thick limestone walls 15,000 years ago. The centerpiece is a 2m-long herd of shuffling animals. *(☎59 21 74; www.leseyzies.com/cap-blanc. Open daily July-Aug. 10am-7pm; Apr.-June and Sept.-Oct. 10am-noon and 2-6pm. Reservations required July-Aug. Visit only by 45min. French tour with English translations; €6.50, under 18 €3.70. Ask about student discounts.)* 15km northwest of Les Eyzies in Rouffignac on the road to Périgueux, **La Grotte de Rouffignac,** also called the *Grotte aux Cent Mammouths*, houses 250 pieces. Etchings of rhinos and horses are interspersed with striking paintings of shaggy mammoths. It's one of the longest caves in the area. The tour (via train) lasts an hour. *(☎05 41 71; www.grottederouffignac.fr. Open daily July-Aug. 9-11:30am and 2-6pm; late Mar. to June and Sept.-Oct. 10am-11:30am and 2-5pm. Closed Nov. to mid-Mar. Tours in French only. Tickets sold same-day, from 9am for morning visits; from noon for afternoon visits. Wheelchair-accessible. €6.20, under 18 €3.90.)*

SARLAT ☎05 53

Narrow, twisting alleyways open onto *places* lined with bustling *brasseries*, giving Sarlat (sar-LAH; pop. 11,000) both a medieval and modern atmosphere. The town was relatively unknown until 1962, when Minister of Culture André Malraux selected it for a massive restoration project. Three years later, a handsomely refurbished Sarlat emerged, its medieval buildings in immaculate condition, making it the perfect setting for films like *Cyrano de Bergerac* and *Manon des Sources*. Sarlat's sights are concentrated enough to explore in one day at a relaxing pace, leaving time for excursions to the nearby lower Dordogne and Lascaux (p. 520).

TRANSPORTATION. Trains (☎59 00 21; ticket office open M 5:10am-8:15pm, Tu-Th 5:30am-8:15pm, F 5:30am-10:30pm, Sa-Su 7am-8:15pm) run from av. de la Gare to Bordeaux (2½hr., 5-8 per day 5:30am-7:45pm, €23) and Périgueux (3hr., 3 per day M-Sa, €14), the latter via le Buisson. Trans-Périgord (☎02 20 85; www.cg24.fr) runs **buses** from the train station to Souillac, a stop on the Paris-Toulouse line (40min., 3 per day, €4.70) and Périgueux (1½hr.; €8.90) via Montignac. CFTA (☎05 55 59 01 48) runs a bus from pl. Pasteur to Périgueux via Montignac (1½hr.; Sept.-June M-F 6am, July-Aug. W 7:30am; €11). Sarlat Bus runs **local buses** on two routes; line A stops at the train station, while line B stops at the roundabout one block down rue Dubois. (☎59 01 48. Office open M-Sa 8:30am-noon and 2-6pm.) For a **taxi** call ☎59 06 27 or 59 02 43. **Car rental** is available from **Europcar** at pl. Tassigny; from the train station, walk down rue Dubois and across the roundabout. (☎30 30 40. Open M-F 8am-noon and 2-6:30pm, Sa 8a-noon and 2-6pm. AmEx/MC/V.) To rent **bikes,** call friendly and knowledgeable Englishman **Joel Caine** of MultiTravel, who offers free delivery and pickup (within a 10km radius of his shop next to Maisonneuve near Castelnaud), help with route-planning, guided rides, and transfers from one point to another for €1.50 per km. (☎06 08 94 42 01; www.multitravel.co.uk. €10 per ½-day, €15 per day. Locks and repair kits provided; helmets and maps €1 each. Seventh day free for week-long rentals. Call in advance to arrange guided tours. Open daily according to demand. Cash only.) **Vélo & Oxygen: Cycles Sarladais,** av. Aristide Briand, past av. de la Gare from the *centre-ville*, also offers bike rental. (☎28 51 87; cycles-sarladais.com. €8 per ½-day, €13 per day, €35 per 3 days, €63 per week. Open July-Aug. M-Sa 9am-noon and 2-7pm; Sept.-June Tu-Sa 9am-noon and 2-7pm. MC/V.)

ORIENTATION AND PRACTICAL INFORMATION. Sarlat's *centre-ville* is bounded by two main streets, which form a ring around it. To the north and west is **boulevard Nessman,** and to the south and east is **boulevard Voltaire. Rue de la République** runs north-south and bisect the town. The tourist office is in the centre-ville; to get there from the station, turn left as you exit, onto av. de la Gare. Take a right at the bottom of the hill onto av. Thiers, which becomes av. Général Leclerc, then rue de la République. Bear right on rue Lakanal; the tourist office will be visible to the left.

The staff at the **tourist office,** rue Tourny, offers accommodations booking (€2 inside Dordogne, €3 outside Dordogne), a comprehensive list of area campgrounds, city tours, and a city guide in English. (☎31 45 45; www.sarlat-tourisme.com, 1-3 French tours daily. English tours June-Sept. W 11am. €5, students and ages 12-18 €3, under 12 free. Open July-Aug. M-Sa 9am-7pm, Su 10am-noon and 2-6pm; May-June M-Sa 9am-1pm and 2-7pm, Su 9am-1pm and 2-5pm; Sept. M-Sa 9am-1pm and 2-7pm, Su 10am-noon and 2-6pm; Apr. M-Sa 9am-noon and 2-7pm, Su 9am-1pm and 2-5pm; Oct. M-Sa 9am-noon and 2-6pm, Su 10am-1pm; Dec. and Mar. M-Sa 9am-noon and 2-6pm; Jan.-Feb. M-Sa 9am-noon and 2-5pm.) An **ATM** is opposite the tourist office. Other services include: a **laundromat** at pl. Bouquerie (wash €4; open daily 6am-10pm); **police** (☎31 71 10) at pl. Salvador Allende and across from pl. de la Grande Rigaudie near the post office; a **hospital** (☎31 75 75) on rue Jean Leclaire; and **Internet** access at **Easy Planet,** 17 av. Gambetta, with print services, Wi-Fi access, video games, a snack bar, and a friendly, English-speaking staff. (☎29 23 48; www.easy-plant.net; €6 per hr.; open July-Aug. M-Sa 10am-10pm, Su noon-8pm; Sept.-June M-Sa 10am-7pm). The **post office,** pl. du 14 Juillet, offers **currency exchange.** (☎31 73 10. Open M-Sa 8:30am-5:30pm, Sa 8:30am-noon.) **Postal Code:** 24200.

ACCOMMODATIONS AND CAMPING. Sarlat's hotels are quite expensive; the best option is to book a room at one of the *chambre d'hôtes* (€25-50) close to the city center. The tourist office has a complete list that also includes *gîtes*, farms, and campgrounds in the surrounding countryside. An excellent and affordable option is **La Chambre d'Hôtes Le Versau ❷**, 49 Rte. de Pechs, in a quiet location on a hill overlooking Sarlat. With bookshelves in each room and breakfast served in a colorful garden, Le Versau feels just like home. The *chambre* is a 10min. walk up the steep chemin du Plantier. (☎31 02 63; www.versau-sarlat.com. Breakfast included. Reservations required. Singles €24-40; doubles €32-44; quads €49-54. Cash only.) For those who want to avoid a walk into the *centre-ville*, the pricier **Chambres d'Hôtes de Charme ❸,** 4 rue Magnanat, sits on a quiet street on the edge of the medieval city. Friendly owners rent three spacious rooms with high ceilings and beautiful wooden floors in a building classified as a historic monument. A walled garden allows guests to escape the city without ever leaving. (☎31 26 60 or 06 08 67 76 90; www.toulemon.com. Doubles July-Aug. €45; Sept.-June €38.) **Hôtel de la Mairie ❹,** 13 pl. de la Liberté, boasts one of Sarlat's best locations and features large, wood-trimmed rooms. (☎59 05 71. Breakfast €6. Singles and doubles €47-57; triples €62-73; quads €89. Extra bed €10. AmEx/MC/V.)

Maisonneuve ❶, a campground 11km from Sarlat and a few hundred meters from Castelnaud on D57, provides a beautiful and convenient base from which to explore Castelnaud, Domme, La Roque Gageac, and the Château des Milandes. The modern site offers a café, grocery store, mini golf, ping pong, pool, and idyllic riverside swimming hole. A *gîte* in a restored farmhouse featuring a kitchen, bath, and beds for 10 guests is also on the grounds. (☎29 51 29; www.campingmaisonneuve.com. Reception 9am-8pm. Open Apr.-Oct. July-Aug. €5.30 per adult; €3.60 per child under 7; €7.20 per site, includes vehicle. 10% reduction in June and Sept., 20% in May, 30% in Apr. and Oct. *Gîte* €10 all season. Electricity €3.60. MC/V.) **Le Montant ❶,** 4km from town off D57 toward Bergerac, provides another camping option. While not as conveniently located as Maisonneuve, the modern campsite has a bar, laundry, jacuzzi, pool, and mini golf. (☎59 18 50; www.camping-sarlat.com. Reception 9am-12:30pm and 1:30-8pm. Reservations recommended July-Aug. Open Apr.-Sept. July-Aug. €5 per adult, €3.50 per child, €7.60 per tent and car; Sept.-June €3.50/2.10/4. Electricity €2.80. AmEx/MC/V.)

FOOD. Most regional delicacies—*foie gras, confit de canard* (preserved duck), truffles, walnut oil, and Bergerac wine—can be purchased directly from their sources in the surrounding countryside or in the seemingly endless rows of shops in town. Sarlat's *pâtisseries* and *confisseries* (confectioners) sell decorated breads, walnut-and-chocolate tarts, *gâteaux aux noix* (walnut cakes), and chocolate-dipped meringue *boules* the size of grapefruits. A lively **market** packs the entire *vieille ville* on Saturday (8:30am-6pm), while a smaller market fills **place de la Liberté** each Wednesday (8:30am-1pm). **Eglise Ste-Marie,** next to pl. Marché Aux Oies, houses a covered market. (Mid-Apr. to mid-Nov. M-Th and Sa-Su 8:30am-2pm, F 8:30pm-8pm; mid-Nov. to mid-Apr. Tu-W and F-Sa 8:30am-1pm.) There's an enormous **HyperChampion** supermarket 15min. from the town center, along av. de Selves (open M-Sa 9am-8pm, Su 9am-12:30pm) and a **Petit Casino** at 32 rue de la République. (☎59 05 25. Open July-Aug. daily 7:30am-12:30pm and 2:30-7:30pm; Sept.-June M-Sa 7:30am-12:30pm and 2:30-7:30pm, Su 7:30am-12:30pm.)

DORDOGNE AND LIMOUSIN

A walk down any of the narrow streets of Sarlat's *vieille ville* reveals a variety of excellent, though slightly pricey, restaurants—each with its own distinct character. For a change of pace, consider **Chez le Gaulois ❷,** 3 rue Tourny, near the tourist office. Strings of sausages hang from the ceiling, hinting at the restaurant's emphasis on excellent cuts of meat served in generous portions. The assorted meat platters are a relatively cheap but filling way to sample the many varieties available. Cut by a butcher at a table in the back of the dining area, the meat comes on a wooden pig-shaped platter and is accompanied by a side salad and jar of pickles. (☎59 50 64. *Plats* €9.50-11. Open July-Aug. daily noon-2pm and 7-10pm; Sept.-

June Tu-Sa 11:30am-2:30pm and 6:30-9:30pm. V.) **Auberge des Lys D'Or ❷,** 17 rue Albéric Cahuet, offers fish and duck specialties in a pleasant dining room with stone walls and a timbered ceiling. The *formule* (€10), available until 8pm, is a good deal. Try the deliciously juicy *confit de canard.* (☎31 24 77. *Menus* €13-24. Open daily 11:30am-2pm and 6:30-10pm.) Although its golf theme doesn't extend much further than items like the 'Fairway' salad and 'Mulligan,' 'Dogleg,' and 'Bogey' cocktails (€6.50), **Bar Le Practice ❷,** 19 rue de la République, is one of the few good cheap eateries in Sarlat's *centre-ville.* Delicious meat dishes (€8-9) and omelettes (€5-8) satisfy without breaking the bank. (☎28 94 08. Open daily June-Sept. 8am-2am; Oct.-May 8am-1am. MC/V over €15.)

SIGHTS. Without a doubt, Sarlat is a city best explored by wandering the alleys and cobblestone streets of the *centre-ville.* The tourist office's walking tour provides a comprehensive introduction to the city's major and minor landmarks, but don't feel obliged to visit them all. The neo-Gothic **Cathédrale St-Sacerdos,** to your right as you exit the tourist office, however, is one sight that shouldn't be missed. Originally part of a Benedictine abbey, it was largely rebuilt in the 16th and 17th centuries. Small and sparsely decorated compared to the Gothic behemoths for which France is famous, the cathedral presents a warmer, less intimidating atmosphere. Multiple altars line the sides, and the varying architectural styles and general asymmetry testify to the various construction stages. The small chapel behind the altar is particularly beautiful and offers a serene spot to escape from the busy streets outside. The lovingly-landscaped **Jardin Public du Plantier,** just outside the town center on bd. Henri Arlet, also offers refuge from the downtown bustle. It features benches along flower-lined paths, which look out onto picture-perfect vistas of Sarlat's rooftops.

NIGHTLIFE AND FESTIVALS. Nearly every weekend during the summer, street performers and musicians converge on **place de la Liberté,** and pleased audiences fill the cafés. For an old-fashioned ambience and a late-night drink, **Le Pub,** just off pl. de la Liberté, can't be beat; it is Sarlat's only establishment that doesn't close before 2am. The bar features billiards and a wooden countertop with traditional brass railing. In July and August, Le Pub hosts concerts most nights for a mixed, mostly English-speaking crowd. Musicians perform occasionally on weekends during the low season. (☎59 57 98. Drinks €3-15. Fine cognacs €20-40. Open daily July-Aug. and vacation periods 7pm-5am; Sept.-June M-Th and Su 7pm-2am, F-Sa 7pm-5am. MC/V.) Young party-goers meet in the less-polished **Le Bataclan,** 31 rue de la République, an unpretentious bar and *brasserie* with delicious, cheap food. Noisy rock and a carefree crowd spill onto the streets from within. (☎28 54 34. Drinks €2.50-5. Open daily 8am-2am. MC/V.) **CinéRex,** av. Thiers, occasionally screens foreign films in their original languages. (☎08 92 68 69 24. Films €7.30. Discounts all day M and in the afternoon or evening Tu-F.) During the last two weeks of July and the first week of August, Sarlat hosts the **Festival des Jeux du Théâtre,** which features open-air performances, comedies, musicals, and panel discussions. (☎31 10 83. Tickets €15-25. 20% student discount with ID.) In early November, Sarlat hosts many of France's leading filmmakers in its annual **film festival.** Screenings are open to the public at the Cultural Center and Cine Rex.

DAYTRIPS FROM SARLAT

CASTELNAUD-LA-CHAPELLE AND CHÂTEAU DES MILANDES

These daytrips are not accessible by public transportation. To get to Castelnaud-la-Chapelle, 12km south of Sarlat on D57, follow rue Faure, which becomes rue de Cahors, then rue Gabriel Tarde. At the roundabout, head down av. de la Dordogne, then follow signs for D57 and Château de Castelnaud. D57 is hilly; bikers might prefer to take a slightly longer but much flatter route with less traffic. At the 2nd roundabout, turn left on D46 towards Vitrac. From Vitrac, follow the roadside signs to Castelnaud. The Château des Milandes is 5km from Castelnaud on D57.

Although the panoramic views of the Dordogne Valley alone make the trip worthwhile, **Castelnaud-la-Chapelle** (kah-stell-LOH lah shah-PELL) is exciting in its own right, transporting visitors to the medieval court. It has countless replicas and originals of medieval armor and weapons, as well as four French catapults. Actors in medieval garb show guests what life was like in the Middle Ages and hold demonstrations with the impressive full-size *trébuchets* (catapults) outside. (☎31 30 00; www.castelnaud.com. Open daily July-Aug. 9am-8pm; Sept. and Apr.-June 10am-7pm; Feb.-Mar. and Oct. to mid-Nov. 10am-6pm; mid-Nov. to Jan. 10am-5pm. Château and museum €7.20, ages 10-17 €3.60, under 10 free. July-Aug. 8 French tours per day; M-F 3 English tours per day, Sa 8 per day. Call in advance for low-season English tours and for schedule of demonstrations.) Halfway down the hill from the castle lies the **Eco-Musée de la Noix de Périgord,** a restored farmhouse that showcases the history and inner workings of the region's famous walnut industry. In the store, nut-lovers can purchase delicious homemade walnut products galore (€5-9), but true nut nuts should stop in the small museum as well. (☎59 69 63. Open Apr. to mid-Nov. daily 10am-7pm. €4, under 18 €3, under 10 free.)

The elegant Renaissance **Château des Milandes** (shah-TOH day mill-AHND) was built by François de Caumont in 1489 to satisfy his wife, who wanted a more stylish home than the outdated fortress of Castelnaud. Centuries later, cabaret singer Josephine Baker fell in love with the neglected château's pointed roofs and gables, purchased the property, and created a "world village" to house and care for the children she had adopted on her international tours. A museum devoted to her life now occupies the château, its luxurious rooms showcasing the cabaret star's authentic stage costumes, furniture, and glamour shots. In a seemingly random acknowledgement of its medieval origins, the château offers a **falconry show,** complete with handlers in costume. (☎59 31 21; www.milandes.com. Open daily July-Aug. 9:30am-7:30pm; Sept. and May-June 10am-6:30pm; Apr. and Oct. 10am-6:15pm. €7.80, students €6, handicapped and ages 5-10 €5.50, under 5 free. Audio tours in French. Apr.-Oct. 2-4 falconry shows daily; call for schedule.)

DOMME AND LA ROQUE GAGEAC

These daytrips are most easily accessible by car. From Sarlat, take av. de la Dordogne and head southwest at the roundabout on D57 toward Beynac, or south on the significantly less hilly D46 (dir.: Vitrac and Domme). Découverte et Loisirs minibuses run through the valley several times per week from Sarlat. (☎05 65 37 19 00; www.decouverte-loisirs.com. €30-40. Call for schedule.) For cyclists, Sarlat is the best starting point. It's about 4-10km between each village, and once along the Dordogne, the bike ride is fairly level, with small hills every few kilometers. Car rentals are available in Sarlat.

Domme (DOHMM), built by King Philip the **Bold** in 1281 as a defensive stronghold, can be reached by bike or car on a winding 2.5km ascent on D49 from Cénac, which is 10km from Sarlat on D46. Across from the Domme tourist office, a 45min. cave tour descends into the **Grottes de la Halle.** Discovered almost 100 years ago, this beautiful network of expansive caverns is filled with rows of breathtaking white stalactites and stalagmites reminiscent of organ pipes. An visit to this natural cathedral affords visitors a detailed explanation of the cave's geological features and a chance to admire the colorful and well-lit formations. (☎31 71 00. French cave tours with written English explanations. July-Aug. every 20-30min. 10:15am-7pm; Sept. and Apr.-June every 45min. 10:15am-noon and 2-6pm; Oct. and Feb.-Mar. every hr. 2-5pm. Call ahead for English tours. €6.50, students €5.50, ages 5-14 €4.)

Guided 1hr. tours in French explore the dilapidated **Porte des Tours.** Seventy Templar Knights were imprisoned here in 1307 and tortured for nearly 20 years by King Philip IV, who wanted the secret of their hidden treasure. The artistic graffiti they scratched into the walls with their teeth, hands, and fingernails remains a mysterious combination of Christian iconography and Muslim and Jewish motifs encountered by the Templars during the Crusades. (Accessible by tour only. July-Aug. 2-3 per day; Sept.-Dec. and Feb.-June by reservation. €6.50, students €5.50, ages 5-14 €4.) The Domme **tourist office** is at pl. de la Halle, in the stone building near the river's edge; it sells tickets for village tours. (☎29 17 01. Open daily July-Aug. 9am-12:30pm and 2-6pm; June and Sept. 10am-12:30pm and 2-5:30pm.)

Downstream, the picturesque village of **La Roque Gageac** (lah ROHK gah-jhay-AHK) overlooks the Dordogne river. While the town has few sites of its own, it offers a relaxing location for a picnic and serves as a good canoeing outpost. A 1hr. tour on a *gabare*, a traditional wooden boat, affords a perfect view of the châteaux along the Dordogne. **Norbert** (☎29 40 44; www.norbert.fr; tours daily Apr.-Oct. every hr. 10am-6pm; English-speaking audio tours available, €2; €8, under 18 €5) and **Caminade** (☎29 40 95; garbarrecaminade@wanadoo.fr; tours Easter-Oct. daily 10am-6pm, commentary in English and French; €8, under 18 €5.) have boats departing from La Roque Gageac. The 12th-century **Fort Troglodytique Aérien,** high above La Roque, commands a spectacular view of the Dordogne River Valley. Nestled securely into a cliff, it withstood all English assaults during the Hundred Years' War. (☎31 61 94. Open daily Apr. to mid-Nov. 10:30am-7pm; mid-Nov. to Mar. 11am-5pm. €5, students €4, ages 10-18 €2, ages 6-10 €1, under 6 free.)

Many campgrounds and companies along the river rent **canoes** and **kayaks.** At the Pont de Vitrac, near Domme, try **Canoës-Loisirs** (☎31 22 92; www.canoes-loisirs.com). **Canoë-Dordogne** (☎ 29 58 50; www.canoe-dordogne.fr) and **Canoë Vacances** (☎28 17 07; www.canoes-vacances.com) are located in La Roque Gageac. (Tourist offices have schedules and info. €11 per person per ½-day, €16 per day.)

LOT VALLEY

The fertile Lot Valley winds its way from Cahors to Cajarc, a strip of green that shelters its temperate river and vineyards between steep cliffs. Infrequent bus traffic makes it easiest to explore the many out-of-the-way wonders by car. Experiencing the natural beauty of the area at a walking pace is highly recommended—the Cahors tourist office sells hiking maps (€4.60) of the entire Lot Valley. Expect the distances to some sights to be at least 5km. Some travelers choose to hitchhike, though *Let's Go* does not advise it.

CAHORS ☎05 65

Nestled in the crook of the Lot River, Cahors (kah-OHR; pop. 20,000) is a staple in the St-Jacques de Compostela pilgrimage, as well as a convenient—though not picturesque—base for daytrips to the villages, vineyards, cliffs, and caves of the Lot Valley. The town itself offers an impressive 14th-century Valentré Bridge and a medieval quarter—both of which can be leisurely explored in an afternoon.

TRANSPORTATION AND PRACTICAL INFORMATION. Trains leave from av. Jean Jaurès (info booth open M and F 6am-6pm, Tu-Th and Sa-Su 8am-6pm) for: Brive-la-Gaillarde (1hr., 8-9 per day, €15-17); Limoges (2½hr., 6 per day, €26-29); Montauban (45min., 10 per day, €9.80-12); Toulouse (1½hr., 9 per day, €17). For a **taxi,** call Allo-Taxi, 742 chemin des Junies. (☎22 19 42. 24hr.) Rent **cars** at Avis, 26 av. Jean Jaurès, on pl. de la Gare. (☎30 13 10. Open M-F 8am-noon and 2-6pm, Sa 8am-noon. AmEx/MC/V.)

To get to the **tourist office,** pl. Mitterrand, from the station, bear right, cross the street, and head up rue Anatole France. At the end of the street, turn left on rue du Président Wilson, then right on **boulevard Gambetta,** the main thoroughfare separating the *vieille ville* from the rest of Cahors. The office is around the corner on the right (15min.). The staff reserves accommodations (€0.90) and gives tours of the *cité médiévale* and the *Pont Valentre* in French. (☎53 20 65; www.mairie-cahors.fr. Open July-Aug. M-Sa 9am-12:30pm and 1:30-6pm, Su 10am-1pm; Sept.-June M-Sa 9am-12:30pm and 1:30-6pm. Call ahead for tour times. €6.50, students and ages 12-18 €4, under 12 free.) **Internet** access is available at the **Bureau Information Jeunesse,** in the Foyer des Jeunes, 20 rue Frédéric Suisse, which also offers printing service, travel planning, and info on housing and summer jobs. (☎23 95 90. €2 per hr. Open M-Tu 1-6pm, W 9am-noon and 1-6pm, F 1-5pm.) You can also find Internet access at the youth center in **Les Docks,** 430 allées des Soupirs. (☎22 36 38. €2 per hr. Open Tu-F 2-6pm.) Other services include: **laundromats** at 208 rue Clemenceau (wash €3.60-7, dry €0.40 per 5min.; open daily 7am-9pm) and 265 rue Nationale (wash €3.40, dry €1 per 10min.; open daily 7:30am-9:30pm); **police** at pl. Bessières (☎23 17 17); and a **hospital** at 449 rue du Président Wilson (☎20 50 50). The **post office,** 257 rue Wilson, has **currency exchange.** (☎20 61 00. Open M-F 8:15am-6pm, Sa 8:30am-noon.) **Postal Code:** 46000.

ACCOMMODATIONS AND FOOD. To reach the **Foyer des Jeunes Travailleurs Frédéric Suisse (HI) ❶,** 20 rue Frédéric Suisse, from the station, bear right on rue Anatole France and left on rue Frédéric Suisse. Close to all the sights, this 17th-century mansion has bare co-ed dorms, more comfortable private rooms, and large multi-room suites—all with paneled wooden ceilings. Toilets and showers are in the hall. (☎35 64 71; fax 35 95 92. Breakfast €3.50. Sheets €2.90; pillow €0.50. Reception 9am-noon and 1:30-9pm. If the office is closed, pull the rope. 2- to 10-bunk dorms and singles €10. Cash only.) Near the station and a favorite with pilgrims, **Le Melchior ❸,** 397 av. Jean Jaurès, is the cheapest family-run hotel in town, with respectably clean—though somewhat dark—rooms, all with bath. Reserve early for bargain singles. (☎35 03 38; www.lemelchior.com. Breakfast €5.80. Reception daily 7am-10pm. Singles €35; doubles €43-50; triples and quads €60. Extra bed €8. MC/V.) A long but pretty hike from town leads to **Camping Rivière de Cabessut ❶,** rue de la Rivière, with a bar, laundry, pool, and mini golf, as well as large, shady sites with clean facilities. From pl. de la Libération, take the second left onto rue Pelegry; turn right over the bridge. Once across, turn left; walk along the water for 2km (35min.). Or take the free shuttle from the tourist office to "Stade" and walk 10min. along the river. (☎30 06 30; www.cabessut.com. Open Apr.-Sept. Reservations recommended in summer. Reception 8am-10pm. €4 per adult, €2.50 per child, €8 per site. Electricity €2. Cash only.)

Fresh produce, local wine, *Cabécou* cheese, and a friendly atmosphere are all to be found at the open-air **markets** on **place Chapou** (W and Sa 8am-noon) and **Les Halles** (Tu-Sa 8am-12:30pm and 3-7pm, Su 9am-noon). The first and third Saturdays of the month are particularly impressive. A **Casino** supermarket is on pl. Imbert, near the tourist office. (Open July-Aug. M-Sa 9am-12:30pm and 3-7:30pm, Su 9am-12:30pm; Sept.-June M-Sa 9am-12:30pm and 3-7:30pm.) Off the beaten path, **Le Mephisto ❷,** 10 av. Jean Jaurès, serves hearty food on a shady terrace. The boisterous owner ensures a warm welcome. (☎53 00 77. Salads €8. *Menus* €9-18. Open M-Sa 7am-9pm. MC/V.) **Le Lamparo ❸,** pl. de la Halle, serves pizzas (€7.60-9.50), heaping plates of pasta (€7-8.90), and traditional French meat dishes on a sprawling terrace in the *cité médiévale.* (☎35 25 93. *Menu* €12-22. Open M-Th 11:45am-2:15pm and 7-10:30pm, F-Sa 11:45am-2pm and 7-11:30pm. MC/V.)

SIGHTS AND FESTIVALS. The imposing 14th-century **Pont Valentré,** credited with staving off invaders during the 1580 Siege of Cahors, is by far the city's most impressive sight. Legend has it that its architect, dismayed by construction delays, sold his soul to the devil with the promise that he could have any wish before dawn fell. His first was that the bridge would be finished before the next day, and the second was that the devil would bring him water in a strainer, which he was unable to do. Thus, the demon lost his end of the deal and was turned to stone. Look carefully to see the devil clutching a corner of the central tower. Hike up the trail on the other side of the bridge for a spectacular view of the city. Across town and farther up the river, 12th-century **Cathédrale St-Etienne,** pl. Chapou, offers a juxtaposition of Roman and Gothic styles. The cathedral is topped by two recently uncovered cupolas and boasts wide, vividly restored medieval murals. St-Etienne also often hosts classical concerts. (☎35 27 80. Open daily 9am-7pm.) In addition to contemporary Cahors-themed temporary exhibits, **Musée Henri Martin,** 792 rue Emile Zola, displays some earlier modern art, including Neo-Impressionist interpretations of Cahors and the area by the Toulouse-born and locally renowned Henri Martin. (☎20 88 66. Open M and W-Sa 11am-6pm, Su 2-6pm. €3; students, seniors, and ages 7-18 €1.50; under 6 free; 1st Su of the month free.) The poignant **Musée de la Résistance, de la Déportation, et de la Libération du Lot,** located in the former barracks of a military base on pl. Bessieres, recounts Cahors's role in WWII. Each of three floors is dedicated to one of the themes mentioned in the title—do not miss the heart-wrenching display of detainees' drawings and poems on the second floor. Info is available in English, but a good grasp of French is required to fully appreciate the exhibits. (☎22 14 25. Open daily 2-6pm. Free.)

In mid-July, Cahors taps its toes to blues during the four-day **Cahors Blues Festival.** Afternoon and evening blues "appetizers" in cafés and bars are free, while on Wednesday and Friday, concerts on pl. Bessieres are €20. (☎20 87 83; www.cahorsbluesfestival.com. Buy tickets online.) The **Festival de Saint-Céré** features classical music in Cahors from late July to mid-August. (☎38 28 08; www.festival-saint-cere.com. Buy tickets by phone or last minute at the tourist office.)

ST-CIRQ-LAPOPIE ☎05 65

One of the most beautiful villages in France (as the sign outside town proudly proclaims), tiny St-Cirq-Lapopie (SEHN sehrk lah-poh-pee; pop. 207), 35km east of Cahors, atop a cliff ledge, has streets so steep that the roof of one 13th-century house begins where its neighbor's garden ends. St-Cirq was a young local martyr slaughtered in the Middle East during Crusades, while "Lapopie" signifies "nipple" in Old Celtic and was first used to describe the suggestive form of the cliff on which the village was founded. Scandalous connotations aside, gorgeous St-Cirq-Lapopie has been classified as a national historical monument; not a single new building ruins the skyline that Surrealist André Breton so deeply loved.

Though all existing archives of the village were burned during the Revolution, the cultural center **Maison de la Fourdonne** chronicles what can be pieced together of St-Cirq's rocky history, and also hosts plays and concerts every Tuesday evening. (☎/fax 31 21 51. Open Apr.-Nov. Tu-Su 2:30-7pm. Guided tours including museum Tu-Sa 11am or with reservation; €4. Museum €1.50, students €1. Evening shows June-Sept. Tu; €3-5.) Stairs located behind the tourist office lead up to the highest point of the village: the ruins of **Château Lapopie.** Condemned to destruction in 1580 by Henri de Navarre, the castle had proved impervious to sieges for centuries; today, it offers a stunning panorama of the valley.

The best beds in St-Cirq are at the *gîte d'étape* and cultural center **Maison de la Fourdonne ❶,** a restored 16th-century house with a stocked kitchenette and timbered common room containing an old (though non-functional) stone fireplace.

Pine-paneled three- to five-bed rooms all have baths; some have balconies. Arrived on a horse or donkey? No problem—special parking in the nearby field is available for €1. (☎/fax 31 21 51. Bring sheets. Reception early Apr. to early Nov. 10:30am-12:30pm and 2:30-7pm. Reservations highly recommended July-Aug. Closed mid-Nov. to mid-Mar. Dorms €13. Cash only.) **Auberge du Sombral ❹,** in front of the tourist office, offers elegant rooms with tasteful paintings, which justify the steep prices. (☎31 26 08; fax 30 26 37. Breakfast €8. Singles with shower €50; doubles with shower €70, with bath €78; triples €88. MC/V.) Between the town and the bus stop, the riverside **Camping de la Plage ❶** is close to a small beach, as well as kayak and canoe sites. High bushes provide privacy for campers in this crowded site. Free Wi-Fi at reception. (☎30 29 51; www.campingplage.com. €5 per person; July-Aug. €7 per site, Sept.-June €5. Electricity €4-5. MC/V.) For a good meal, try **L'Atelier ❸,** just before the village on the main road into town. Traditional meaty French *plats* are served in a shaded courtyard with a great view of the valley. While waiting for your meal, don't hesitate to doodle on your place mat—generations of drawings are pinned to the walls. (☎31 22 34. Open Feb.-Dec. M and Th-Su noon-2pm and 7-9:30pm, Tu noon-2pm; hours are "elastic." MC/V.)

To get to St-Cirq-Lapopie by car, follow D653 out of Cahors and turn right onto D662 when you reach Vers. SNCF **buses** run past St-Cirq-Lapopie from Cahors on the way to Figeac (line #16; 45min.; M-Sa 5 per day, Su 4 per day; €5.30). Get off at "Tour de Faure," walk in the direction from which the bus came, cross the bridge on the left, and hike uphill to town (30min.). The **tourist office,** pl. de Sombral, in the main square, offers brochures in English, walking tours in French, and a list of hotel vacancies. (☎31 29 06. Open July-Aug. M-F 10am-1pm and 2-7pm, Sa-Su 10am-1pm and 2-6pm; Apr.-May and Sept.-Oct. daily 10am-1pm and 2-6pm; Nov.-Mar. and June M-Sa 2-6pm.) **Kalapca Loisirs,** near the campsite, offers **kayak rental** and books two- to six-day trips with camping or *gîte* packages. (☎30 29 51; www.kalapca.com. Canoe €5 per hr. Kayak €7 per hr., €10-13 per ½-day. MC/V.)

POITOU-CHARENTES

After adopting Christianity in the fourth century, Poitou-Charentes emerged as an influential political and religious center. The eighth century saw Charles "the Hammer" Martel fend off Moorish attempts to conquer the region, only to have the British take over for 300 years, starting when Eleanor of Aquitaine ran off with England's Henry II in 1152. The 17th century witnessed Cardinal Richelieu's attack on the Protestant stronghold of La Rochelle, which relegated the town to a century of obscurity until trade with the "New World" (a.k.a. Canada) finally restored it to prosperity. Meanwhile, the rest of the region is by no means lacking history and character: Cognac (p. 544) brews its luxurious *liqueur*, while other towns take pride in their architecture, dating from ancient to medieval times, and otherwise quietly occupy themselves with fishing, sunbathing, and wine-making.

Poitou-Charentes could be France's best-kept secret. Distinctly influenced by its proximity to the Atlantic Ocean, it is a brilliant collage of coastal fishing towns, wetland preserves, and untouched islands. The diverse landscapes of Ile de Ré (p. 556) and Ile d'Yeu (p. 565), with pine forests, rolling meadows, and brilliantly white beaches, cater to curious cyclists, passionate history buffs, and topless tanners alike. Though rich in history, with medieval towns and countless châteaux, the region also offers distinctly modern diversions. Today, though still marked by the vestiges of its intriguing past, La Rochelle welcomes party animals and leisure-seekers alike, with roaring festivals and succulent seafood. Those looking for a lighter side of the region head to technologically advanced Futuroscope theme park (p. 537) and Angoulême (p. 539), the French capital of comic books.

HIGHLIGHTS OF POITOU-CHARENTES

STUFF YOURSELF with boatloads of seafood in coastal **La Rochelle** (p. 549), where locals aren't stingy with their *fruits de mer.* Walk it off with a hike around the wild countryside of nearby **Ile de Ré** (p. 556) or sleep it off with a nap one of Ré's sunny beaches.

MARVEL at the region's unique natural beauty as you set off in a canoe from picturesque **Coulon** (p. 560) into the wetlands preserve of the **Marais Poitevin** (p. 560).

INDULGE both your inner sophisticate and inner child with the liquor bouquets at distilleries in **Cognac** (p. 544), and the comic-spattered walls of **Angoulême** (p. 539).

POITIERS ☎05 49

The magnificent churches of Poitiers (PWAH-tee-ay; pop. 83,000) testify to the power Catholicism had over the city during the early Middle Ages. Though the Church left behind a rich history, today, these holy sites remain probably the only "magnificent" feature of the city. In 1432, Charles VII founded the Université de Poitiers, and students now make up over 25% of the population. The city bustles with youngsters during the year but deflates entirely in the summer, as increasingly fewer tourists pass by here on their way to Futuroscope. Though the city is a loud and polluted commercial metropolis, its lively nightlife and cultural events serve as redeeming qualities.

TRANSPORTATION

Trains: bd. du Grand Cerf. Ticket office open M-Th and Sa 6am-9pm, F 6am-10pm, Su 7am-10:20pm. To: **Bordeaux** (2hr., 15 per day, €33); **La Rochelle** (1½hr., 15 per day, €20-23); **Paris** (2hr., 20 per day, €48-61); **Tours** (1hr., 10 per day, €15-18).

Public Transportation: Vitalis, 9 av. de Northampton (☎44 66 88). Open M-F 8:30am-12:15pm and 2-5pm. Buses run throughout the city during the day; a night bus runs the same route infrequently 9pm-1:50am. Timetables are at the tourist office and train station. Buy individual tickets (valid for 1hr., €1.20) on board and *carnets* of 5 (€4.80, under 25 €4.30) at *tabacs* or at the office.

Taxis: Radio Taxis, 22 rue Carnot (☎88 12 34), wait outside the train station. €12 to hostel. €1.42 per km during the day, €2.06 at night. 24hr.

Car Rental: Avis, 133 bd. du Grand Cerf (☎58 13 00). Open M-F 8am-12:30pm and 1:30-7pm, Sa 1:30-5pm. AmEx/MC/V. **National,** 107 bd. du Grand Cerf (☎58 51 58). From €88; under-25 surcharge €24. Open M-F 8am-12:30pm and 2-5pm. AmEx/MC/V. **ADA,** 19 bd. du Grand Cerf (☎50 30 20). From €45. Open M-F 8am-noon and 2-7pm, Sa 8am-noon and 2-6:30pm. MC/V. **Europcar,** 48 bd. du Grand Cerf (☎58 25 34). From €62; under-25 surcharge €33. Open M-F 8am-7pm, Sa 8am-noon and 2-7pm. AmEx/MC/V.

Bike Rental: Atelier Cyclaman, 60bis bd. Pont Achard, 400m from the station. (☎88 13 25). €9.10 per ½-day, €14 per day; €150 deposit. Open Tu-F 9am-12:30pm and 3-7pm, Sa 9am-12:30pm and 2-7pm.

ORIENTATION AND PRACTICAL INFORMATION

Poitiers centers around **place Maréchal Leclerc, place Charles de Gaulle,** and the restaurant- and shop-filled streets in between. Buses run from the stop opposite the train station to the **Hôtel de Ville** in pl. Maréchal Leclerc. The *centre-ville* and the surrounding area is bordered by the Le Clain and La Boivre rivers.

> **LET'S NOT GO.** Though a bustling transport hub during the day, Poitiers's train station and the surrounding badly lit streets become a prostitution and drug-dealing center as soon as night falls; they are best avoided after dark.

Tourist Office: 45 pl. Charles de Gaulle (☎41 21 24; www.ot-poitiers.fr). The staff distributes free maps and lists of hotels and campgrounds. Ask for a free English-language walking guide, a guidebook with hiking and biking trail maps (€11), and *Laissez-vous conter Poitiers,* the calendar of cultural events organized by the office. City tours in French (1-2hr.) July-Sept. daily 11am and 3pm; themed tours throughout summer. €5.50, ages 11-25 €4, under 10 free. Free nocturnal tours July-Aug. Sa-Su 9pm. Open June 21-Sept. 21 M-Sa 10am-11pm, Su 10am-6pm and 7-10pm; Sept. 22-June 20 M-Sa 10am-6pm.

English-Language Bookstore: Librairie de l'Université, 70 rue Gambetta (☎41 02 05), off pl. M. Leclerc. Open M-Sa 9am-7:30pm. AmEx/MC/V.

Youth Center: Centre Regionale Information Jeunesse (CRIJ), 64 rue Gambetta (☎60 68 68), near pl. M. Leclerc. Helps with jobs, lodging, budget travel, and activity planning. Free Internet access for students. Open Tu-Sa 1-6pm.

Laundromat: Laverie, 180 Grande Rue. Wash €3.20 for 7.5kg, dry €0.50 per 5min. Open daily 8am-8pm.

Police: 38 rue de la Marne (☎60 60 00).

Hospital: 2 rue de la Miletrie (☎44 44 44), on the road to Limoges.

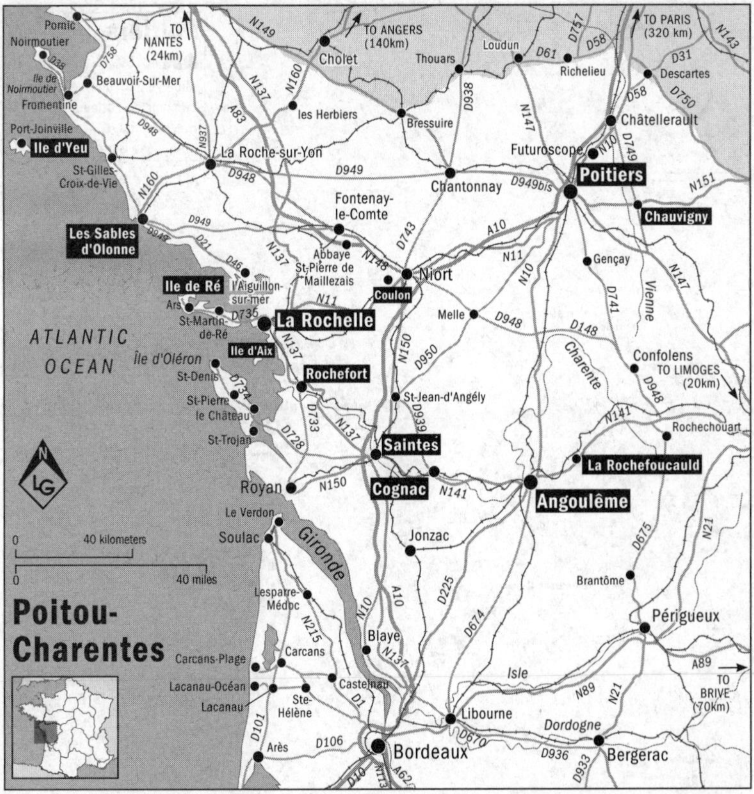

Internet Access: Free at **CRIJ** (see **Youth Center**). **Virtual 86,** (53 63 42) 21 rue Magenta. €2 per hr. Open M-Sa 10am-2am, Su noon-2am. **Cybercafé LRM,** 171 Grande Rue (☎39 51 87). €3 per hr., students and unemployed €1. Open M 10am-8pm, Tu-Th 10am-11pm, F-Sa 11am-8pm, Su 3-8pm. Cash only.

Post Office: 2 rue des Ecossais (☎55 52 36). **Currency exchange.** Open M-F 8:30am-7pm, Sa 8:30am-noon. **Postal Code:** 86000.

ACCOMMODATIONS AND CAMPING

The hostel and campgrounds are far from town, and most hotels in the city center are rather pricey. More reasonable alternatives can be found near the less pleasant area near the train station, but beware that nightfall heralds sketchiness—make sure not to travel alone after 10pm.

Hôtel Central, 35 pl. M. Leclerc (☎01 79 79; www.centralhotel86.com). Simple, clean rooms, with furniture dating to the 50s. Top-floor rooms have private balconies overlooking the town's liveliest square. Breakfast €6.50. Singles and doubles €38, with toilet and shower €45-55, with bath €48-60; triples €55-60. Extra bed €10. AmEx/MC/V. ❸

Auberge de Jeunesse (HI), 1 allée Tagault (☎30 09 70). Turn right at the train station and follow bd. du Pont Achard to av. de la Libération. At the fork, take a right onto rue

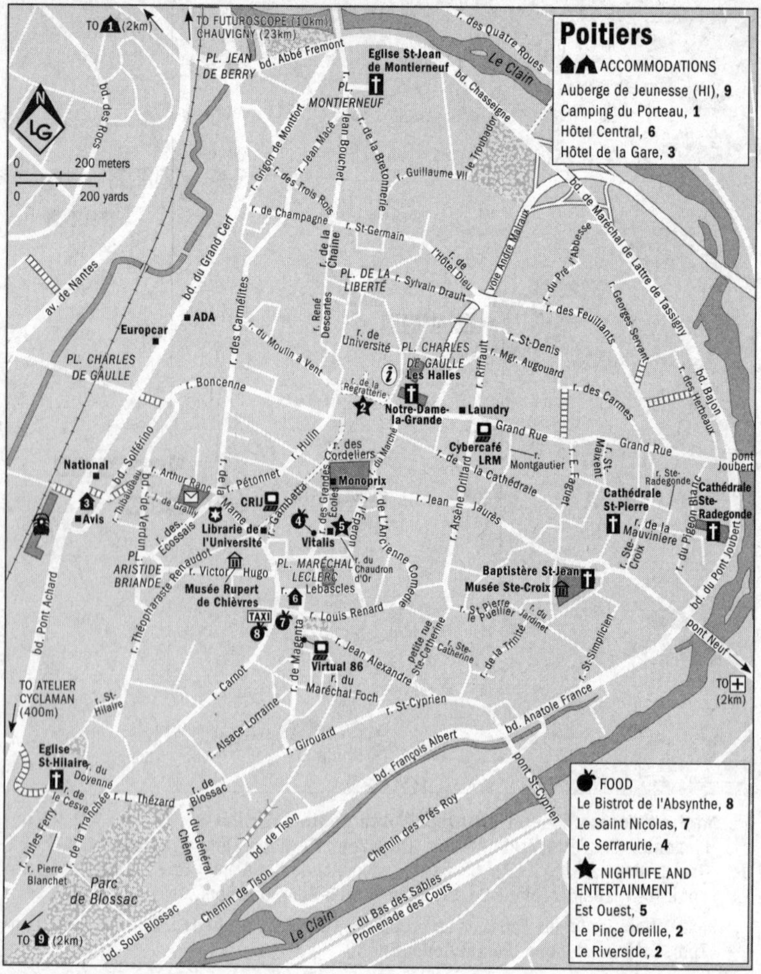

B. Pascal, another right onto rue de la Jeunesse, and a left onto allée Tagault. The hostel is ahead on the left (3km; 45min.). Or, take bus #7 (dir.: Pierre Loti) to "Bellejouanne" from the train station or the Hôtel de Ville near pl. Leclerc (10min. M-Sa every 30min. until 7:50pm, €1.20). Dining area, pool table, Internet access (€0.15 per min.) and bike rental (€3 per day). Bright, old-fashioned, and somewhat stuffy 4-bed rooms with sinks. Common bath in the hall. Breakfast €3.50. Reception M-F 7am-noon and 4-11pm, Sa-Su 7am-noon and 6-11pm. Bunks €15. Camping €9. AmEx/MC/V. ❶

Hôtel de la Gare, 131 bd. du Grand Cerf (☎58 56 30; fax 61 23 59), across the street from the train station. Some of the lowest prices in Poitiers. A good deal if all you want is a place to sleep. Friendly English-speaking owner rents dimly lit rooms that are a bit run-down, with old carpeting and some taped-up areas. Avoid venturing out alone in the surrounding area at night. Breakfast €5. Singles and doubles €24-28, with shower and TV €29-33; triples €38. Cash only. ❷

Camping du Porteau, rue du Porteau (☎41 44 88), 2km from town. Take bus #7 from the station (dir.: Centre de Gros) to "Porteau" (25min., M-F every 30min., €1.20). Small campsite, used mostly by caravans, with brand-new IKEA-style facilities. Reception July-Aug. 7am-10pm; late May-June and Sept. 7:30-11:30am and 2:30-7:30pm. €2.80 per adult, €1.80 per child, €6 per site. Electricity €3. MC/V. ❶

FOOD

In Poitiers, it's easy to find local specialties—from macaroons to goat cheese, from the wines of Haut-Poitou to lamb from nearby Montmorillon. The problem is finding a budget-friendly *menu;* most hover around €15-30. Many *brasseries* and hotel bars post adequate three-course *menus* for €12-13, and inexpensive pizzerias line the pedestrian streets between **place Leclerc** and **Notre-Dame-la-Grande,** as well as the more student-frequented areas north of the cathedral. Most restaurants fill quickly at noon, as their best deals are offered during lunch. There is a market at **Les Halles,** pl. Charles de Gaulle, which expands to epic proportions on Saturdays (Tu, Th, Sa 7am-1pm), and a **Monoprix** supermarket at Ilot des Cordeliers on rue des Grandes Ecoles (open M-F 9am-9pm, Sa 9am-8pm; AmEx/MC/V).

Le Saint Nicolas, 7 rue Carnot (☎41 44 48). Tucked away in a quiet alleyway. Prepares delicious French cuisine in what could easily be an intimate living room. Appetizers €7.90-14. *Plats* €12-20. *Menus* €17 and €21. Open M-Tu and Th-Sa noon-1:30pm and 7:30-10pm, Su 7:30-10pm. MC/V. ❸

Le Bistrot de l'Absynthe, 36 rue Carnot (☎37 28 44). Regulars enjoy upscale French favorites like *escargots* (€8), *foie gras de canard* (€11), and absinthe (€4.30). Lunch *menu* €9. Dinner *menus* €19-24. Open M-Sa noon-2pm and 7:30-10pm. MC/V. ❸

La Serrurerie, 28 rue des Grandes Ecoles (☎41 05 14). Poitiers's Notre Dame—not to be missed. This bistro is just as busy all day as a restaurant as it is at night as a bustling student bar. Generous portions and vegetarian options. Omelettes €6.80-8. *Plats* €6.50-15. Open M-F 8am-2am, Sa 9am-2am, Su 10am-2am. AmEx/MC/V. ❷

SIGHTS

Modern-day Poitiers is unfortunately noisy and polluted, with its once-beautiful buildings crumbling and choked with soot. However, the city remains a haven for church lovers; its religious monuments date from the fourth century and are unquestionably its most impressive attractions. (Open daily 9am-6pm; frequent random closings. Free.) Many hold concerts in July and August; check the *Guide des Manifestations* or *Concerts d'Orgues à Poitiers* (at the tourist office) for more info.

BAPTISTÈRE ST-JEAN. This fourth-century baptistry, sunk 2.5m into the ground, is one of the oldest Christian structures in France. Today, the Baptistère is a museum filled with Roman, Merovingian, and Carolingian sarcophagi, which were found during excavations in the 1950s beneath the church. The relics were kept by early Christians when Gauls destroyed Poitiers's Roman baths, arches, and amphitheater. St-Jean's interior contains a fourth-century baptismal pool that looks like a modern-day jacuzzi and is surrounded by remarkably well-preserved 12th-century frescoes. Informational English pamphlet (€0.50) available. *(Rue Jean Jaurès, near the cathedral. Open Apr.-Sept. M and W-Su 10:30am-12:30pm and 3-6pm; Oct.-Mar. M and W-Su 2:30-4:30pm. €1, under 12 and groups €0.50.)*

NOTRE-DAME-LA-GRANDE. Though small, this is one of France's most celebrated churches, known for its 12th-century Romanesque facade, on which storybook-like biblical scenes and history can be read. Though the crypt is not open to the public, some people choose to stick their arms through the bars of the small door on the right side (bring butter) and feel around for potential light switches (on the left)

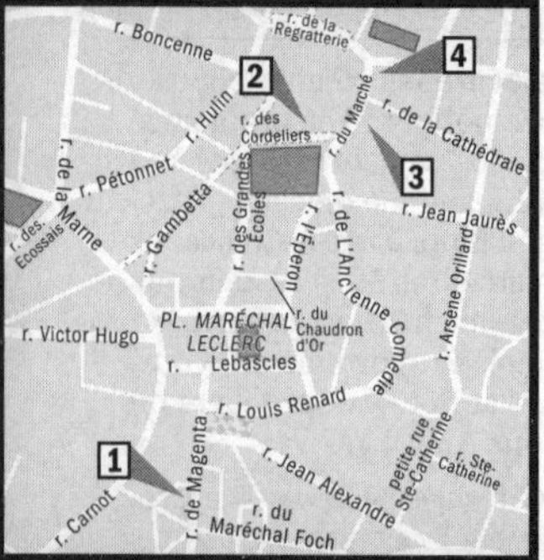

THE WRITING ON THE WALL

Poitiers brims with ancient creations, like elaborate churches and medieval houses, but also hides modern works, such as...graffiti. Discover this effervescent urban art form with an exclusive walking tour in the heart of the "student city."

1 Poitiers may be far from the beach, but in the small square off rue Magenta, you can lose yourself in the sun-baked tropical paradise depicted on a 20m wall.

2 Perfect the art of shutter-shopping. Check out the flowing sea of chocolate on Benoit Chocolaterie's storefront on rue des Cordeliers.

3 At the end of the street, take a left to face the gigantic lens of Phox's inked camera.

4 Turn right on Grand Rue to finish off your intro to the world of stenciling: the 2m head of Bob Marley will bid you goodbye.

in order to peek into its dank depths. Dim light filters through stained-glass windows, illuminating the church's meticulously painted columns. During the summer, **polychromies** (light shows) project representations of the original colors onto the facade, reviving the medieval splendor of the painted carvings; seven different light show themes rotate throughout the week. *(Pl. de Gaulle, off Grande Rue. Free 15min. projections daily mid-June to Aug. 10:30pm; early Sept. 9:30pm.)*

CATHÉDRALE ST-PIERRE. In 1160, the construction of the bright and high-arched St-Pierre was funded by Eleanor of Aquitaine and her husband King Henri II, who lived in the present Palais de Justice. The church's massive Cliquot organ (1787-1791) is one of only two that survived the Revolution. The **cryptic wooden carvings** that crown the stalls behind the choir, however, are the main attractions of the church. Deciphering them has been a challenge for centuries; answers to the riddles include a giant bat, a two-headed drowning dog, and half-man and half-tree figures. *(Pl. de la Cathédrale, off rue de la Cathédrale.)*

EGLISE STE-RADEGONDE. Legend has it that in AD 587, Christ appeared to Radegonde, a Thuringian princess and sister-in-law to Clovis, who then fled her violent husband Clothaire to found this church. Christ predicted her death and allegedly told her she was the most beautiful jewel in his crown, which explains why his statue is pointing to his head. Unfortunately, the crown was stolen in 2006, rendering the statue's gesture somewhat incomprehensible. Christ is said to have left a footprint in the stone floor before vanishing—a print that can still be seen today. This church is an important pilgrimage destination—traditionally, pilgrims and believers crawled under Radegonde's tomb in the crypt for good luck. *(Off rue de la Mauvinière, down the street from the cathedral.)*

MUSÉE STE-CROIX. This eclectic museum spans four millennia, its contemporary exterior housing everything from regional prehistoric artifacts to renderings of the plump naked ladies of the 18th century. In the basement is a Roman excavation site with the original walls and foundations of ancient homes. A stone representation of Minerva was found under one of the streets of modern-day Poitiers and is now on display with other Roman paraphernalia. The museum also holds a small sculpture from Rodin and works of his famous muse, Camille Claudel. *(3bis rue Jean-Jaurès. ☎41 07 53. Open June-Sept. M 1:15-6pm, Tu-F 10am-noon and 1:15-6pm, Sa-Su 10am-noon and 2-6pm; Oct.-May M 1:15-5pm, Tu 10am-5pm, W-F 10am-noon and 1:15-5pm, Sa-Su 2-6pm. Free guided tours in French Tu 6-7pm. €3.70, students and under 18 free; Tu and 1st Su of the month free. Admission includes entrance to the Musée Rupert de Chièvres.)*

OTHER SIGHTS. Often overlooked, the 11th-century Gothic **Eglise St-Jean de Montierneuf** was originally constructed by the Count of Poitiers to purge his sins—which must have been grave indeed to necessitate such a grand building. The church contains some of the most striking stained-glass windows in the city. *(To the right of Pl. Montier-Neuf from the city center.)* Behind skillfully sculpted wooden doors, the **Musée Rupert de Chièvres** displays a collection of Dutch, Flemish, French and Italian paintings—many by anonymous artists. The portrait of an ecstatic (read: orgasmic) Ste-Madeleine, by Louis Finson, is tucked away among less interesting pieces. *(9 rue Victor Hugo. ☎41 42 21. Open June-Sept. M 1:15-6pm, Tu and F 10am-noon and 1:15-6pm, Th 10am-noon and 1:15-9pm, Sa-Su 10am-noon and 2-6pm; Oct.-May M 1:15-5pm, Tu-F 10am-noon and 1:15-5pm, Sa-Su 2-6pm. €3.70; students and under 18 free; Tu, 1st Su of the month, and June-Sept. free. Admission includes entrance to the Musée St-Croix.)*

NIGHTLIFE AND FESTIVALS

The **Rencontres Internationales Henri Langlois** in early December draws film students from international schools for independent and mainstream screenings (€3 per film). From the end of June through August, free musical performances, ranging from period Renaissance to world music, echo through the cavernous Notre-Dame-La-Grande during **Les Nuits en Musique;** concerts begin at 9:30pm on Friday (contact tourist office for more info). Throughout these months, *passeurs d'images* (open-air cinemas) also show free films in different neighborhoods around town. (☎44 12 48. July 10:30pm; Aug. 10pm; Sept. 9:30pm.) In late September, a series of light show concerts illuminate the city during **Les Concerts Allumés,** a festival seeking to unite classical musical with imaginative lighting—in such unusual locations as churches and cathedrals. (Call ☎03 18 98 for more info. Tickets €3.50-12.) *Le guide des manifestations,* a free guide in English and French at the tourist office, lists the seasons' concerts and shows.

Nightlife in Poitiers is rowdy and lively during the school year, when students go to the pubs and restaurants along the side streets of **place Leclerc.** In summer, however, a lot of venues tend to close as students leave the town vacant for the occasional tourist. Ask for a photocopy of *Café-Concert: Bars avec Animations* at the tourist office for a complete list of all the bars and clubs in town.

Le Pince Oreille, 11 rue des Trois Rois (☎60 25 99; www.lepince-oreille.com). Draws a lively local crowd—mostly students from the nearby music conservatory—despite its distant location. Putting its stage to good use, Le Pince hosts a variety of jazz, rock and reggae bands, and "open" jam sessions—although you may want to think twice before taking on the conservatory students. Plush chairs, soft lighting, and a constant stream of cheap beer create a vibe that promotes music but not pretension. Beer €1.50. Mixed drinks €5-7. Concerts F-Sa, free jam sessions Tu-Th; both at 10:30pm. MC/V.

EstOuest, 10 rue l'Eperon (☎41 13 36). A crowded 2-story pub with young, homogenous clientele, last year's music, and pool tables near the heart of Poitiers's nightlife. Try the specialty Vodka Malabar (€2), made by plopping the popular French bubble gum into the alcohol for flavor. Karaoke F midnight. Beer from €2.10. Mixed drinks €5.50. Open M-F 11am-2am, Sa 3pm-2am. AmEx/MC/V.

Le Riverside, 18ter rue de la Regratterie (☎41 76 36). For those tired of loud student drinking holes, this classy gay bar is tucked away in a small courtyard near Notre-Dame. Beer €2.90. Homemade punch €2.10. Open M-Sa 11am-2am. MC/V.

DAYTRIPS FROM POITIERS

FUTUROSCOPE

10km north of Poitiers, near Chasseneuil. Take bus #9 during the week (30min.; M-F every 20min., Sa every 30min.; last bus 7:52pm; €1.20) or line E on Su (30min., Su 3 per day, last bus 6:43pm) from Poitiers's "Hôtel de Ville (Marne)" stop or across from the train station.

Schedules are subject to change. Get off at "Parc du Futuroscope" and follow directions to the park entrance. By car, follow A10 (dir.: Paris-Châtellerault) to exit 28. The park is also accessible by TGV from Bordeaux (2hr., 1-2 per day, €36) and Paris (1¾hr., 2-3 per day, €45). ☎ *49 30 08; www.futuroscope.com. Open daily 10am-nightfall, closed in Jan. €33, ages 5 to 16 €24, under 5 free. All main attractions included in the price except the video games on* Cyber Avenue *and the* Les Yeux Grands Fermé *attractions (€4).*

Futuroscope theme park is a fun, though somewhat overwhelming, collection of spectacular architecture, high-tech film theaters, virtual reality, and high-definition 3D simulation rides. *La Cité de Numérique* overflows with the latest XBox 360® games for visitors—more accurately, teenage boys—to play on plasma screens. Tremendous IMAX movies take visitors on sappily-narrated journeys to the bottom of the ocean to the tops of untouched mountains, and through the cosmos. Some of the attractions have moving seats, which coordinate with the on-screen adventures to throw you into the action. *Les Yeux Grands Fermés* offers tours in French led by blind guides through a pitch-black world, offering visitors the chance to get a glimpse of life without sight. (€4. A portion of the proceeds benefits an association for the visually impaired.) A free headset from the *Maison de Vienne* near the entrance provides the English translation for many films. Hotels and restaurants are in close proximity to the park for those who are enticed to stay longer (after the last bus departs) for the late-night laser show, with images projected onto water and synchronized with music and fireworks.

CHAUVIGNY

SNCF buses leave Poitiers for Chauvigny from outside the station (dir.: Châteauroux; 30min.; M-Sa 6 per day, Su 4:52 and 9:20pm; €4.40). Buy tickets at the SNCF train station in Poitiers. The bus will stop at pl. de la Poste in the center of modern-day Chauvigny. The cité médiévale, *encompassing all the castle ruins, lies up on the hill. To get there by foot, walk back on rue du Marché in the direction the bus came from, turning right onto rue du Petit Pont after the Hôtel de Ville. At the end of the street, turn right and take a left onto rue Poulizard, which will lead you to a set of stairs going into the cité. The tourist office is on rue St-Pierre, across the street from the ruins of the bishop's palace.* ☎ *46 39 01. Open July-Aug. daily 10am-1pm and 2-7pm; Sept. and June Tu-Su 10am-12:30pm and 2-6:30pm; Nov.-Mar. Tu-F 2-6:30pm, Sa 9am-noon; Apr.-May and Oct. Tu-Su 2-6pm, Sa 9am-noon. July-Aug. tours several times per week; €3.10. Call* ☎ *46 35 45 ahead for schedule and tours in English.*

Chauvigny (shoh-VEE-nyee), 23km from Poitiers on N151, boasts a *cité médiévale* that stands alone in Europe: a striking skyline of five 11th- to 13th-century fortresses lines its single outer wall. Among these lies the 12th-century **Collégiale St-Pierre,** a bright and perhaps excessively well-restored church—complete with modern light-switches—of soft colors and renowned column heads that are engraved with nightmarish figures such as lion-headed dragons, vultures eating naked men, a Babylonian prostitute, and a grinning Satan. Marrying the medieval with the modern, the **Espace d'Archéologie Industrielle** showcases its exhibits as well as its ingenious interior design in what remains of the Gouzon dungeon. Featuring displays about regional quarrying, porcelain-firing, milling, and steam-engine activity, the museum transports its visitors from level to level in a glass elevator, whose last stop brings them to a spectacular 360° view of the city and countryside below. All explanations are in French; the visit may be somewhat confusing for English speakers. (☎46 35 45. Open mid-June to Aug. M-F 10am-12:30pm and 2:30-6:30pm, Sa 2:30-6:30pm, Su 11am-6:30pm; May to mid-June and Sept.-Oct. daily 2-6pm. French tours available, call ahead for a schedule. €4.60, students €3.10, under 14 free. MC/V.) The imposing—though crumbling—walls of the old bishop's palace are now home to **Les Géants du Ciel,** a show that boasts 60 eagles, falcons, vultures, arctic owls, African storks, and other birds. The highlight is a bird show in which the flock swoops over the city, just above the heads of the audience. (☎46 47 48. Open daily

Apr.-June and Sept. 2-7pm; July-Aug. 10am-noon and 2-7pm. Shows daily Apr.-June 3 and 5pm; July-Aug. 11am, 3, 5pm; Sept. M-F 3pm, Sa-Su 3 and 5pm. €8.50, ages 4-10 €5.50.) A 30min. walk from pl. du Marché, **St-Pierre-les-Eglises** houses some of the oldest frescoes of Occidental Christianity, estimated to date from the eighth to tenth century. A large cemetery sits on its remote riverside site. To get there from pl. du Marché, walk down rue du Marché in the direction of Poitiers and take a left onto D749 at the roundabout. Continue straight past the bridge and through the next roundabout; the church is down a small road on the right. (Open July-Aug. daily; Sept.-June call tourist office for reservations.)

To play train conductor for a day, take a ride on **Vélo-Rails,** 10 rue de la Folie. These rail contraptions, powered by pedaling, take passengers on a demanding 17km loop around the Chauvigny valley, along the viaduct that traverses the Vienne River. Reservations must be made at least one day ahead. To get there from pl. de la Poste, walk down rue du Marché, cross the Vienne River, and continue straight as the road becomes rue de Poitiers. After reaching rue de la Verrerie, turn right, then left onto rue de la Folie. (☎41 08 28. Open daily July-Aug. 10am-7pm; departures 10:30am, 2:30, 7:30pm. Sept.-Oct. and Apr.-June 2-6pm; departures 2:30pm. 2hr.; €20 for 2 adults, €25 for 2 adults and 1 child.)

In July and August, the **Festival d'Eté** fills the city with (occasionally free) concerts, theater, and street performances. (€10; call the tourist office for more info.)

ANGOULÊME ☎05 45

Unmarred by tourist hordes, Angoulême (AHN-goo-lem; pop. 46,000) sits high upon a plateau overlooking the Charente River. Host to John Calvin (as in the man who invented Calvinism) in 1534, the city teems today with another kind of celebrity: comic book characters. The capital of French comic strip production, Angoulême has speckled the tortuous streets and medieval buildings of the *vieille ville* with impressive fantasy murals, designed by various famous cartoonists.

TRANSPORTATION

Trains: Pl. de la Gare. Info office open M-F 7am-1pm and 2:30-8:30pm, Sa-Su 2:30-8:30pm. Ticket windows open M-F 5:40am-8:50pm, Sa 6:40am-8pm, Su 7:40am-9:30pm. To: **Bordeaux** (1hr., 8 per day, €19-24); **Paris** (3hr., 6 per day, €56-62); **Poitiers** (45min.; 10 per day; €21, TGV €17); **Saintes** (1hr., 8 per day, €12).

Buses: Autobus Citram (☎95 95 99). Office open mid-July to mid-Aug. M-F 2-6:15pm; mid-Aug. to mid-July M-F 9:15am-12:15pm and 2-6:15pm. Buses go to **Cognac** (1hr., 8 per day, €7.45) and **La Rochelle** (3hr., 2 per day, €17). Buy tickets on board. **CFTA Périgord** (☎05 53 08 43 13) runs from the train station to **Périgueux** (1½hr.; 1 per day M-W, F, Su, and 2nd Th of the month; €12).

Public Transportation: STGA, pl. Bouillaud (☎65 25 25). Maps available. Open the 6th-27th of each month M-F 1:15-6pm, Sa 8:45am-12:15pm; the 1st-5th and 28th-31st of each month M-Sa 8:45am-12:15pm and 1:30-6pm. Buses run M-Sa 6am-8pm to many of the museums. Tickets €1.30, *carnets* of 10 €9.10, 1-week pass €11.

Taxis: Radio Taxi (☎95 55 55), in front of train station. Base €2.46; €1.38 per km during day, €2.04 after 7pm. €7-8 to Auberge de Jeunesse. 24hr.

Car Rental: Europcar, 15 pl. de la Gare (☎92 02 02). Cars can be returned to other locations throughout France. From €59 per day; under-25 surcharge €33. 21+. 10% student discount on vans only. Open M 8am-noon and 2:30-6:30pm, Tu-F 9am-noon and 2:30-6:30pm, Sa 9am-noon and 2:30-5pm. **ADA,** 19 pl. de la Gare (☎92 65 29), across from the station. From €45 per day. Open M-F 8am-noon and 2-7pm, Sa 8am-noon and 2-5pm.

ORIENTATION AND PRACTICAL INFORMATION

Angoulême's *vieille ville* sits encircled by ramparts just south of the Charente river and southwest of the train station. It is easy to get lost in its maze of steep streets, which are often on different planes of elevation; check the map outside of the train station before throwing yourself into comic book land.

Tourist Office: 7bis rue du Chat, pl. des Halles (☎95 16 84; www.angouleme-tourisme.com). From the train station, follow av. Gambetta right and uphill to pl. G. Perrot, continue straight up the rampe d'Aguesseau, and turn right onto steep bd. Pasteur. Keeping close to the rail overlooking the valley, pass the market building; the office will be directly across from it. Info on restaurants, hotel availability, museums, and outdoor activities (available only in French). The multilingual staff helps make hotel reservations in the area. Open July-Aug. M-F 9:30am-7pm, Sa 10am-7pm, Su 10am-1pm and 2-5pm; Sept.-June M-F 9am-12:30pm and 1:30-6pm, Sa 10am-noon and 2-5pm.

Tours: Day and night tours offered through the Hôtel de Ville's **Via Patrimoine** (☎38 70 79; www.patrimoine-charente.com). Office open M-F 9am-noon and 2-6pm. Enter the main gates of the Hôtel de Ville and cross the courtyard; the office is on the left. 2hr. daytrips (1hr. tour of the old Château Comtal, 1hr. tour of the *vieille ville*) leave July-Aug. daily 4pm; Sept.-Oct. and Apr.-June Sa-Su 3pm; Nov.-Mar. 3pm on select weekends. Those who want to tour only the *vieille ville* can join an hour later. Both tours €5, students and ages 12-18 €3.50, under 12 free; 1 tour €4/2.50/free. Tours with English-speaking guides are available; call ahead.

Budget Travel: Voyages Wasteels, 2 pl. Francis Louvel (☎92 21 45). Open M-F 10am-noon and 2-5pm, Sa 10am-12:30pm. **Jet tours,** 5bis rue de Goscinny (☎92 07 94). Open M-F 9:30am-12:30pm and 2-6:30pm, Sa 9:30am-12:30pm and 2-6pm.

Currency Exchange: At the **post office** (p. 540). For other monetary needs, the high-security **Banque de France** is at 1 rue de Général Leclerc (☎97 60 00), on pl. de l'Hôtel de Ville. Open M-F 8:40am-noon and 1:30-3:30pm.

Youth Center: Centre Information Jeunesse (CIJ), 1 bd. Berthelot (☎37 07 30; www.info-jeunesse16.com), inside the Espace Franquin building. Provides advice, info on jobs, housing, concert tickets, and free condoms. Internet €0.75 per 15min., €2 per hr. Open mid-July to Aug. Tu-F 10am-12:30pm and 2-6pm, Sa 2-6pm; Sept. to mid-July Tu-F 10am-6pm, Sa 2-6pm.

Laundromat: Lavomatique, 3 rue Ludovic Trarieux, in the heart of the *vieille ville*. Wash €3.20-7, dry €0.50 per 5min. Open daily 7am-9pm.

Police: Pl. du Champs de Mars (☎39 38 37), next to the post office. Call here for the **pharmacie de garde.**

Medical Services: Hôpital de Girac, rte. de Bordeaux (☎24 40 40). Take bus #1 (dir.: La Couronne Galands) or #8 (dir.: Nersac Les Epinettes) from the Hôtel de Ville or pl. du Champ de Mars to "Girac" and follow the signs.

Internet Access: The **Musée de la Bande Dessinée** (p. 542) has 10 Internet terminals that can be used free with a museum ticket or for €2 per hr. Internet also available at the **CIJ** (see **Youth Center,** above). Directly below the youth center, in the basement of the Espace Franquin building, the **Espace Culture Multimédia** (☎37 07 32) offers up to 2hr. free; longer sessions require €12 year-long pass. Open Tu-W 9am-noon and 2-6pm, Th-Sa 2-6pm.

Post Office: Pl. du Champs de Mars (☎66 66 00; fax 66 66 17). Branch office at pl. Francis Louvel, near the Palais de Justice (☎90 14 30). Both open M-F 8am-6:30pm, Sa 8:30am-noon. Both offer **currency exchange. Postal Code:** 16000.

ACCOMMODATIONS

Cheap hotels cluster near the intersection of av. Gambetta and the pedestrian district, which is in the southeastern corner of the *vieille ville.* Located across from the train station, **Hotel d'Orléans ❷,** 133 av. Gambetta, is surprisingly both classy and budget-friendly, with a comfortable lounge and bar area and clean, color-coordinated rooms at bargain prices. (☎95 07 53. Breakfast €5. Reception 6:30am-10pm. Singles and doubles €29, with shower, toilet, and TV €36; triples €43. Extra bed €6. MC/V.) The **Auberge de Jeunesse (HI) ❶,** on Ile de Bourgines in the Charente, is a hike from the town center. To get there on foot, turn right out of the train station onto av. Gambetta and take the first right onto rue Denis Papin, continue across the railroad tracks and veer left. Take a right onto rue de Paris, then a left onto rue Lamaud; walk past the church and turn right along the Charente until you reach a footbridge that leads onto the island. The hostel is on the left (30min.). To get there by bus, turn right onto av. Gambetta from the train station; the stop will be on the left-hand side, right after the intersection with bd. de la République. Take bus #7 (dir.: Le Treuil, last bus 8pm, €1.20) to "St-Antoine," then take a left along the water to reach the footbridge. Once across the bridge, take a left. Large and clean two-bed rooms host mainly short-term workers but fill with young international visitors during festivals. Kitchen and bike rental are available. (☎92 45 80; angouleme@fuaj.org. Breakfast €3.50. Lockout noon-5pm. Reception M-F 8:30am-noon and 5-9pm, Sa-Su by appointment only. Dorms €12. MC/V.)

FOOD

Pricey restaurants throughout the *vieille ville* feature the local specialty, *cagouilles à la charentaise* (garlic and parsley snails with sausage, smoked ham, and spices), while the flower-shaped *marguerite* chocolate—named for François I's sister, Marguerite de Valois—as well as *cornuelle* (a triangular cake), can both be found in all *pâtisseries.* Bars, cafés, and bakeries line **rue de St-Martial** and **rue Marengo,** but more inventive eateries crowd the narrow streets of the quadrant formed by Les Halles, pl. du Palet, Eglise St-André, and the Hôtel de Ville. The recently renovated market on **place des Halles,** down rue de Gaulle from the Hôtel de Ville, sells the town's freshest produce, perfect for a picnic on the banks of the Charente. (Open daily 7:30am-1pm.) There's a **Champion** supermarket, 19 rue Goscinny, by the Champ de Mars. (Open M-Sa 8:30am-7:30pm, Su 9-11:45am. MC/V.)

The lantern-lit interior—complete with red velvet couches and columns draped in richly colored fabrics—at **Chez Paul ❸,** 8 pl. Francis Louvel, is almost too luxurious. The dark indoors open onto a paradise-themed garden with sculptures of giraffes and storks standing in a long, quietly flowing fountain. This hidden gem offers excellently prepared and presented regional food. (☎90 04 61; www.chezpaul.com. *Plats* €8-25. Lunch *menus* €11-14. Dinner *menus* €25. Open daily 11am-3pm and 7pm-midnight. MC/V.) **Le Chat Noir ❶,** pl. des Halles, serves bruschetta (€6-8), sandwiches (€3-5), and sweet *crêpes* (€2-4) to tourists and locals alike, who come to people-watch from the shaded terrace. (☎95 26 27. Open M-Sa 7:30am-2am; service noon-2pm, bruschetta in the evening only. MC/V.)

SIGHTS

Childhood heroes such as Lucky Luke and Gaston Lagaffe greet passersby from windows and 22 murals all over the *vieille ville*—a stroll along the streets will get tourists well-acquainted with French comic-book celebrities. With its lovely views and painted pedestrian area, Angoulême is truly a city that knows how to dream.

MUSÉE DE LA BANDE DESSINÉE. Housed in the amazing building of the **Centre Nationale de la Bande Dessinée et de L'Image (CNBDI),** this museum is a tribute to Angoulême's leading role in the development of *la bande dessinée* (the comic strip). Enter the realm of comic books—literally, complete with giant cardboard characters and cartoon buildings—where exhibits feature French and international cartoons from the 19th and 20th centuries, including worldwide favorites like Tintin, Astérix, and Popeye. Free audio tours in a variety of languages enhance the pictorial displays. The Centre also holds a comic-book library and bookstore, as well as the art-house cinema **Salle Nemo,** which screens international indie films (€7, students €5); ask at the museum for times. *(121 rue de Bordeaux. From pl. du Champ de Mars and pl. de l'Hôtel de Ville, take bus #3 or 5 to "Nil-CNBDI" or walk along the ramparts, following the signs; 10min. ☎38 65 65; www.cnbdi.fr. Open July-Aug. Tu-W and F 10am-6pm, Th 10am-7pm, Sa-Su 2-6pm; Sept.-June Tu-W and F noon-6pm, Th noon-7pm, Sa-Su 2-6pm. €6, students €4.50.)*

MUSÉE DE LA RÉSISTANCE ET DE LA DÉPORTATION. Occupying the one-time residence of 16th-century religious reformer John Calvin, this museum chronicles Angoulême's experience under the Nazi occupation, in particular the actions of French Resistance fighters, many of whom were captured and tortured to death by the Nazis. On the ground floor, a letter from a young Resistance member to his mother on the eve of his execution is only a mere warm-up; horrifying photographs on the second floor document the life and death of the 1180 Jews deported from the Charente region to concentration camps. All exhibits are in French, with some English explanations. *(34 rue de Genève. ☎38 76 87. Open July-Aug. M-F 9am-noon and 2-6pm; Sept.-June 2-6pm or by appointment. €2.50, students €1.50, under 16 free.)*

CATHÉDRALE ST-PIERRE. The elegant 12th-century cathedral of Angoulême, with its story-telling facade, follows the formal Romanesque style, but for one main element: internal columns were omitted to create an uninterrupted view of the interior. The edifice exerted considerable architectural influence during the height of religious power, not only on other diocesan churches, but also on more distant buildings like the Loire's Fontevraud and Poitiers's Notre-Dame-la-Grande. In the northern wing lies a recently canonized 19th-century saint, who was murdered during a mission in Korea. *(Pl. St-Pierre. ☎95 20 38. Open daily 9am-6pm.)*

EGLISE ST-ANDRÉ. The 12th-century church, initially built in Romanesque style, was reworked in a Gothic design, leaving only the front vestibule of the original work. Today, it holds paintings from the 16th to 19th centuries, a massive altarpiece, and a superb Baroque oak pulpit. The facade was redone in the early 19th century and hides the magnitude of the church surprisingly well. *(8 rue Taillefer, near pl. Louvet in the* vieille ville. *Open daily 9am-7pm.)*

OTHER SIGHTS. Angoulême's ramparts and green riverside areas complement the quiet city's relaxed pace. At the bottom of av. du Président Wilson, beneath the park's meandering paths, *cascades* (waterfalls) flow in the **Jardin Vert,** a great place to unwind among unruly grass and trees. The fourth-century ramparts that surround the town provide a view of the red-roofed houses. To find out about hiking opportunities, call **Randonnée en Charentes,** 22 bd. de Bury. (☎38 94 48. Open M-F 9am-noon and 1:30-5:30pm, Sa 10am-noon.) For water-skiing, call **CAM's water skiing.** (☎92 76 22. 15min. session €26, ages 10-17 €23, under 9 €17. Open daily July-Aug. 1-8pm.) The tourist office has information on other outdoor activities.

NIGHTLIFE AND FESTIVALS

As the sun sets, locals move toward the cafés on **rue Massillon** and **place des Halles,** and **avenue Gambetta** comes alive with bars and restaurants. Hip 20-somethings spill out of **Cinq Sens,** 14 rue Massillon, where everything is "it"—from the liquor to the modern art on white-washed walls. (☎95 34 24. Beer €1.50-3. Hard liquor €2.50-8. Open Tu-Sa noon-2am. MC/V.) **Blues Rock Café,** 19 rue de Genève on pl. des Halles, lives up to its name with its décor (guitars nailed to the wall) but not its music (mostly pop). A mixed crowd flocks to the outdoor seating for drinks and good company. (☎94 05 98. Live music Th in summer. Beer €2.60. Open Apr.-Oct. daily 10am-2am; Nov.-Mar. M-Sa 10am-2am. AmEx/MC/V.)

Every year during the last weekend in January, the world-famous **Salon International de la Bande-Dessinée** breezes into town. Over 200,000 visitors spend four days meeting artists, discovering new installments, and admiring comic-strip exhibits throughout town. (☎97 86 50; www.bdangouleme.com. For tickets visit the tourist office or www.ticketnet.fr.) Just 10km from the city center, the **Festival Musiques Métisses,** 6 rue du Point-du-Jour, features live *chaud* music (music from south of the equator) each year in mid-June. (☎95 43 42. Tourist office sells tickets. Prices vary; €20-35 per night.) In a field just south of Angoulême, popular bands from all around the (Anglophone) world get together for the weekend-long **Garden Nef Party** festival. (☎25 97 00; www.dingo-lanef.com. €40-45 per night, camping included.) Call the tourist office after mid-June for information on **Jeudi Jeux de Rue,** an open-air theater festival with free outdoor performances and films Thursday evenings in July and August in the *vieille ville.* The popular **Circuit des Remparts,** 2 rue Fontgrave, revs its engine in mid-September, when antique cars hold free races and exhibitions in the town center. (☎94 95 67; www.circuit-des-remparts.com. €10.) In October and November, international pianists participate in two-week-long installments of **Piano en Valois.** (☎92 11 11. Concerts €12-28.) In mid-November, **Gastronomades,** a culinary celebration, offers free cooking lessons, food samples, and tastings (☎67 39 30) and **Ludoland,** a children's festival, presents the newest toys and video games. (☎21 29 02; www.ludoland.fr. €8 per day, under 18 €5.)

DAYTRIP FROM ANGOULÊME

LA ROCHEFOUCAULD

Get to La Rochefoucauld by train (30min.; M-Sa 3 per day, Su 2 per day; €5.20). From behind the train station, cross the parking lot to the roundabout on the right. Go halfway around the roundabout and continue straight for 4 blocks through the town center. The château is straight ahead (8min.). The tourist office is at 1 rue des Tanneurs (☎63 07 45. Open June-Sept. daily 10am-1pm and 3-7pm; Oct.-May M-Sa 9:30am-12:30pm and 2-6pm).

La Rochefoucauld (lah ROHSH-foo-koh) has been home to over 43 generations of the aristocratic Foucauld family, members of which included an archbishop and the founder of Caisse d'Epargne (one of France's major banks). The present **château,** known as the "pearl of Angoumois" and a favorite for wedding pictures, owes most of its elegance to Anne de Polignac, wife of Duke Francis II de Foucauld, who added a Renaissance wing and an elegant chapel to the medieval fortress in 1520. Indeed, the castle seems to have been plucked from the Loire Valley and plopped into the heart of Charente. The magnificent central spiral staircase, also built in 1520, is said to have been designed by Leonardo Da Vinci. On the top floor, colorful costumes, spanning over six centuries of styles are available to try on. *La Roche à Foucauld* (the rock of Foucauld)—the town's namesake, a stone upon which the original fortress was founded—can be explored by descending into the dark and damp caverns underneath the castle, through the second guardroom. (☎62 07 42. Open Apr.-Dec. M and W-Su 10am-7pm; Jan.-Mar. Su 2-7pm. €8, ages 4-12 €4.) Other highlights (at the foot of the castle) include a well-preserved 14th-century cloister, **Le Couvent des Carmes,** and a church with an impressive and deeply colored stained-glass window, which dates from 1266.

COGNAC ☎05 45

Cognac (COHN-nyack; pop. 20,000) was a sleepy village until the invention of double distillation in the 16th century changed its fate. French law states that only crops produced in the Cognac region may become the brandy that bears its name. Today, Cognac's main attractions are still its many distilleries, which offer tours and tastings; the town returns to its past drowsiness as soon as the *caves* close.

TRANSPORTATION AND PRACTICAL INFORMATION. Trains go to Angoulême (40min., 5 per day, €8.30) and Saintes (20min., 6 per day, €4.80). To get to the **tourist office,** 16 rue du 14 Juillet, follow av. du Maréchal Leclerc out of the station to the first roundabout and take a right, following signs to the town center. Turn right on rue Bayard and go across pl. Bayard onto rue du 14 Juillet (15min.). The office offers free maps, and lists of accommodation availability in Cognac and its surroundings, and tours of a local barrel-making factory(☎82 10 71; www.tourism-cognac.com. Open July-Aug. M-Sa 9am-7pm, Su 10am-4pm; Sept. and May-June M-Sa 9:30am-5:30pm; Oct.-Apr. M-Sa 10am-5pm.) The **CIC Banque,** 36 bd. Denfert-Rochereau, has **currency exchange** with a 3% commission (traveler's checks min. €6 fee) and **ATMs** outside. Find **Internet** access at the **Bureau Information Jeunesse (BIJ),** 53 rue Angoulême, which offers information on jobs, vacations, and housing. (☎82 62 00. Open M-F 10am-noon and 2-6pm. Internet €0.90 per 30min., €1.60 per hr.) (☎36 84 84. Open Tu-F 8:45am-12:30pm and 1:45-6pm, Sa 8:45am-12:30pm.) In an emergency, contact the **police,** 68 bd. Denfert Rochereau (☎82 38 48) or the **hospital,** rue Montesquieu (☎36 75 75). The **post office** is at 2 pl. Bayard. (☎36 31 70. Open M-F 8am-6pm, Sa 8am-noon.) **Postal Code:** 16100.

ACCOMMODATIONS AND FOOD. Spending the night in Cognac, which has no budget accommodations, will be a bit of a splurge for the backpacker. The one-story **Hotel de la Gare ❹,** directly across from the train station, offers immaculately clean, spacious rooms for the best prices in the city. All rooms come with TV, bath, and phone; some come with A/C. Ask about discounts for the Hennessy distillery. (☎82 04 15; www.oliveraie-cognac.com. Breakfast €6. Reservations recommended. Wheelchair-accessible. Singles €43; doubles €48; triples €57. Extra bed €8. MC/V.) In town, across the street from the tourist office, **Le Cheval Blanc ❹**, 6 pl. Bayard, features small but spotless rooms, with A/C, bath, and TV. (☎82 09 55; www.hotel-chevalblanc.fr. Extra rooms scheduled to be added in 2008. Breakfast €6.80. Free Wi-Fi. Reception M-Sa 7am-12:30pm and 3-10pm, Su 8am-12:30pm and 5-10pm. Singles €44; doubles €50; triples €56; quads €62. AmEx/MC/V.) Three-star **Cognac Camping ❶**, bd. de Châtenay, 2.5km from Cognac on rte. de Ste-Sévère, is a 30min. walk from town on D24, just past Parc François 1er. From mid-July to August, bus lines A-C run here from pl. François I (15min., 2 per day, €1); get off at "Camping." Shade-dappled and well-kept sites are accompanied by ample foliage, laundry (€3), and a pool. (☎32 13 32; www.campingdecognac.fr. Open May-Oct. July-Aug. 2 people €15; Sept.-Oct. and Apr.-June €12. 3 people €20/15. MC/V.)

Stock up on the basics at **Supermarket Eco,** pl. Bayard, near the tourist office. (Open M-Sa 8am-8pm, Su 9-11:45am. MC/V.) There is an indoor market at **place d'Armes** (open Tu-Su 8am-1pm), and a lively outdoor market all day in the city center on the second Saturday of each month. Sampling Cognac's famous brandy doesn't necessarily mean drinking it; restaurants around **place François I** serve pricey meat and dessert specialties drenched in the luxury *liqueur*. **Le Cellier ❸**, 4-6 rue du 14 Juillet, just off pl. François I, is a local favorite, packed with customers not for its services but for its generous portions of meat and fish. (☎82 25 46. *Plats* €9-15. Lunch *menus* €9.50-12. Dinner *menus* €16-25. Open July-Sept. M-F noon-2:30pm and 7-10pm, Sa 7-10pm; Oct.-June M-F noon-2:30pm and 7-10pm. MC/V.) The pizzeria-*crêperie* **Le Dugueslin ❷**, 9 rue du 14 Juillet, off pl. François 1er, attracts young visitors and locals with cheap, tasty fare. (☎82 46 22. Salads €2.50-7. Pizzas €7.40-12. *Menus* €6.50-12. Open daily noon-2:30pm and 7-10pm. MC/V.)

COGNAC DISTILLERIES. The joy of visiting Cognac comes from traveling from one *liqueur* producer to the next, touring the cellars, learning the history and methods of each house—and best of all, tasting the delicate differences between their "VS" (Very Special), "VSOP" (Very Special Old Pale), and "XO" (eXtra Old) cognacs. In the summer, most houses give tours in English; call ahead during the winter. The distilleries listed below, with the exception of Rémy Martin, are located in the city center. **Hennessy,** quai Richard Hennessy, is the industry's biggest player and has the best and longest presentation, which includes a short boat ride along the Charente River and a glimpse of the region's oldest vintages, from 1800. (☎35 72 72; www.hennessy.com. Reservations recommended. Tours in English and French every hr. daily June-Sept. 10am-6pm; Oct.-Dec. and Mar.-May 10am-5pm; Jan.-Feb. by reservation only. Tour with taste of 1 vintage €7, 2 vintages €9; students and under 12 free.) Highly—and almost uncomfortably—classy, **Rémy Martin,** rte. de Pons direction Merpins, lies 5km outside the center of Cognac. A 1½hr. luxury experience awaits those who make the trip to the domain of the world's most elite Cognac producer. After a train ride through the vineyard and presentations on the art of achieving the perfect *bouquet* (the marriage of a variety of subtle aromas), visitors sample two vintages in an elaborate tasting session that includes gourmet enhancers like chocolate, smoked salmon, and *foie gras*. More "individualized" and extensive—not to mention expensive—tours also exist, starting from €25. (☎35 76 66. Open for tours May-Sept. M-Sa. 3-4 tours per day, starting at 10am. Reservations required. Tours in English by request. Tasting and tour €14, ages 12-18 €7, under 12 free.) For the more culturally inclined, **Otard,** 127 bd. Denfert-Rochereau, is housed in the Château de Cognac, François I's birthplace. The 50min. tour, led by guides dressed in medieval costumes, begins with the building's history and ends with a visit to the damp castle cellar where the cognac is stored, and where visitors partake in a *dégustation* of two vintages. (☎36 88 86. Open daily 10am-7pm. Tours July-Aug. daily every 15min.; Apr.-June and Sept.-Oct. daily 11am, 2, 3:30, 5pm; Nov.-Dec. M-F 11am, 2, 4pm; Jan.-Mar. reservations required. €6.50, students and ages 12-18 €3.50, under 12 free, families €13.) The oldest of the major houses, **Martell,** pl. Edouard Martell, founded in 1715, offers a history-based tour, and movies accompanied by the most dramatic music since *Titanic.* It features a replica of an 18th-century exporting ship and a visit to the founder's perfectly renovated cottage. (☎36 33 33; www.martell.com. Open for tours Apr.-Oct. M-F 10am-5pm, Sa-Su noon-5pm. Tours in English daily; call for times. €6, ages 12-18 and students €3. Tastings up to €20.)

SIGHTS AND OUTDOOR ACTIVITIES. The **Musée des Arts du Cognac,** pl. de la Salle Verte, has an extremely detailed sensory exhibit dedicated to the famous spirit and everything you could possibly dream of learning about it—including films that feature scenes with the drink, past advertisements and marketing campaigns, and even a glass-blowing machine. Explanations in English are available. (☎32 07 25; www.musees-cognac.fr. Open July-Aug. daily 10am-6:30pm; Apr.-June and Sept.-Oct. M and W-Su 11am-6pm. €4.50, students €3. Admission includes entrance to the Musée d'Art et d'Histoire.) The **Musée d'Art et d'Histoire de Cognac,** 48 bd. Denfert-Rochereau, recounts the history of Cognac through regional clothing, ceramics, and 20th-century paintings, including the remarkable but chilling *Marguerite au Sabbat* by Pascal Adolphe Dagnan-Bouveret, tucked away behind a red curtain on the second floor. (☎32 07 25; www.musees-cognac.com. Entrance included with ticket to Musée des Arts du Cognac. Open daily July-Aug. 10am-6:30pm; Apr.-June and Sept.-Oct. M and W-Su 11am-6pm; Nov.-Mar. M and W-Su 2-5:30pm.) Visit **L'Espace Decouverte,** next to the Musée des Arts du Cognac, to explore the region's heritage and view a short but artistic presentation on the Charente. The museum also features temporary exhibits and free activities such as chocolate tastings. (☎36 03 65. Open July-Aug. daily 10am-6:30pm; June and Sept. Tu-Su 10am-6:30pm; Apr.-May and Oct. Tu-Su 10:30am-6pm; Mar. and Nov. Tu-Su 2-6pm. Free.) The Hennessy distillery hosts an annual **film festival;** contact the tourist office for specific dates. Free concerts liven up the *quais* for the annual **Fête du Cognac** in mid-July, around Bastille day every year (☎81 21 05; www.lafetedecognac.com). More open-air music follows with **Blues Passion** during the last weekend in July. (☎36 11 81; www.bluespassion.com. Tickets €30-32.)

Cognac's valley promises great **hiking** among vineyards, fields, and forests. The tourist office has four *Sentiers de Randonnées* maps (€2.30 each, €9.20 for all 4); off-trail discoveries include abbeys, châteaux, and a 13th-century crypt. The free *Passion-Vélo* guide gives information on the cycling paths in the area. **Base de Pleine Air** on the northern banks of Parc François Ier, offers canoe and kayak rentals. (☎82 46 24. Open July-Aug. afternoons only. Rentals €7 per hr., €10 per 2hr., €17 per ½-day.) Parks in Cognac include the classy **Jardin Public de l'Hôtel de Ville** around the museum (open daily May-Sept. 7am-9pm; Oct.-Apr. 7am-7pm), and the tree-lined **Parc François I,** northwest of the center on the banks of the Charente.

SAINTES ☎05 46

Founded by first-century Romans, Saintes (SEHNT; pop. 27,000) today houses ancient ruins, grand medieval churches, and lively markets. Over the years, massive renovations have made the town a pleasant and pedestrian-friendly escape from the bustling cities in the area.

TRANSPORTATION AND PRACTICAL INFORMATION. Trains (info and ticket office open M 5:30am-7:30pm, Tu-Th 7:30am-7:30pm, F 7:30am-8:15pm, Sa 8:20am-7pm, Su 8:25am-8:15pm) run from pl. Pierre Senard to: Bordeaux (1½hr., 5 per day, €18); Cognac (20min., 7 per day, €4.80); La Rochelle (1hr., 6 per day, €12); Niort (1hr., 2 per day, €11); Paris (2¼-4hr., 7 per day, €51-63); Poitiers

(1½hr., 8 per day, €21-29). **Taxis** wait at the station. (☎74 24 24. €2 base; €1.42 per km during the day, €1.98 after 7pm.) **Car rental** is available at **Rent-a-Car**, 45 av. de la Marne (☎91 87 80; from €30 per day; open M-F 8:30am-12:30pm and 3-6:30pm, Sa 9am-noon; MC/V) and **Europcar**, 41 av. de la Marne (☎05 46 92 56 10; from €45 per day, from €214 per week; under-25 surcharge €15; €600 deposit; 21+; open M-F 8am-noon and 2-7pm, Sa 8am-noon and 2-6pm).

To get to the **tourist office,** 62 cours National, in Villa Musso, take a sharp left out of the train station and follow av. de la Marne. Turn right onto av. Gambetta and follow it to the river. Cross the bridge at pont Palissy and continue straight on cours National. The office is on the right in a villa set back from the street (20min.). It offers free maps and informative brochures (available in multiple languages) and organizes French walking tours of the city and its main sights, including the cathedral's bell tower, which is not otherwise open to the public. (☎74 23 82; www.ot-saintes.fr. Tours available to groups of 20 or by reservation only; available to individuals June-Sept., €3-5.50. Open July-Aug. M-Sa 9am-1pm and 2-7pm, Su 10am-1pm and 2-6pm at the riverside booth by Pont Palissy; Sept. and Apr.-June 9:30am-1pm and 2-6pm, 1st and 3rd Su of Sept. 10am-1pm and 2-6pm; Oct.-Mar. M-Sa 9:30am-12:30pm and 1:30-5:30pm.) Other services include **laundry** at Laverie Reverseaux, 46 cours Reverseaux (☎06 86 91 07 91; wash, dry, and folding service €10; self-service wash €3.20-8, dry €1 per 10min.; services open M-Tu and Th-Sa 9am-1pm and 2:30-4pm, self-service daily 7am-9pm); **police** at 1 pl. du Bastion (☎90 30 40); a **hospital** at pl. du 11 Novembre (☎92 76 76); **Internet** access at **Cyberzone,** 2 rue Alsace-Lorraine, near the cathedral (☎74 02 88; €1 per 15min., €2 per hr.; open M 3-7pm, Tu-Sa 10am-7pm); and a **post office,** 6 cours National, which offers **currency exchange** (☎93 84 53; open M and W-F 8:30am-6pm, Tu 9am-6pm, Sa 8:30am-noon). **Postal Code:** 17100.

⌐⌐ ACCOMMODATIONS AND FOOD. Hotels tend to fill quickly during festival season from early to mid-July; rooms should be easy to find otherwise. The cheaper accommodations are on the train station side of the Charente. To get to Saintes's high-quality **☒Auberge de Jeunesse (HI) ❶,** 2 pl. Geoffrey Martel, next to the Abbaye-aux-Dames, from the train station, take a left on av. de la Marne a right on av. Gambetta, a left on rue du Pérat, and a right on rue St-Pallais. Turn left through the archway into the courtyard of the abbey. Go straight through the courtyard and down the steps at the back; the hostel is on the right (15min.). This clean, renovated building houses cozy brick-walled, cabin-like rooms, most of which are equipped with spotless bathrooms. (☎92 14 92; fax 92 97 82. Breakfast included. Internet access €1 per hr. Reserve months ahead. Reception June-Sept. 7am-noon and 5-11pm; Oct.-May until 10:30pm. 2- to 6-bed single-sex dorms with bath €18-19. MC/V.) **Camping Au Fil de L'Eau ❶,** 6 rue de Courbiac, is 1km from the town center. From the train station, follow directions to the hostel until av. Gambetta, then turn right onto quai de l'Yser after crossing the bridge. The campsite is 500m ahead on the right (25min.). This campsite offers a private pool (free for campers), mini golf (€4), and a large expanse of shady sites. (☎93 08 00. Reception July-Aug. 8am-10pm; Apr.-June and Sept.-Oct. 8am-noon and 2-8pm. Gates closed 10pm-7am. Laundry €5, dry €2. €4.40 per adult; €2.20 per child; €4.40 per site, parking included. Electricity €3.50. MC/V.)

Restaurants in Saintes showcase the region's seafood, escargot dishes, and *mojettes* (white beans). Start things off with **☒Pineau,** Cognac's sweeter relative. Saintes is blessed with plenty of family-run restaurants and bars, especially in the pedestrian district by **rue Victor Hugo.** The town also holds **markets** at **place du 11 Novembre,** off **cours Reverseaux** (open Tu and F), near Cathédrale St-Pierre (open W and Sa), and on **avenue de la Marne** and **avenue Gambetta** (open Th and Su), all 7am-1pm. On the first Monday of every month, cours National and av. Gambetta host **Le**

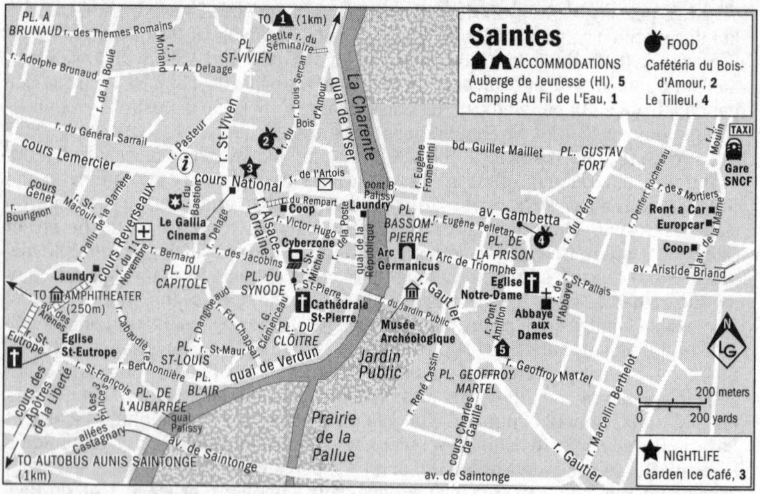

Grand Foire, an open-air market that sells everything, including clothes, sunglasses, and purses (opens at 8am). A huge **Leclerc** supermarket is on cours de Gaulle. (Open M-Th and Sa 8:30am-7:45pm, F 8:30am-8:15pm.) Smaller **Co-op** supermarkets can be found on rue Urbain Loyer, off cours National (open M-Sa 8:30am-12:30pm and 3-7:30pm), and at 162 av. Gambetta (open Tu-Sa 8am-12:45pm and 3:30-8pm, Su 3-6pm). In the shade of its namesake (a lime tree), **Le Tilleul ❸**, 72 av. Gambetta, on the main street, takes itself seriously, serving *plats du jour* like *faux-filet* (sirloin; €11) and *confit de canard* (duck preserved in fat; €15), as well as daily *menus* depending on the freshest produce—and the whim of the chef. (☎74 23 01. Lunch *menu* €12. Dinner *menus* €20-24. Open daily 8am-midnight; service noon-2:30pm and 7-10:30pm. MC/V.) In a true lunchroom atmosphere, **Cafétéria du Bois-d'Amour ❶**, 7 rue du Bois-d'Amour, serves the cheapest hot meals in town. (☎97 26 54. Appetizers €1-5.50. *Plats* €4.30-6.30. Open M-Sa 10:30am-3:30pm and 6:30-10pm. 5% student discount. MC/V.)

SIGHTS. From the center of town, the steps off cours Reverseaux wind through tree-lined fields down to the curious **St-Eutrope.** As the story goes, the church's patron saint was a Persian prince, who came to Saintes after having allegedly met Jesus in Palestine and converting to Christianity. Soon after he arrived, Eutrope successfully persuaded the daughter of the Governor of Gaul to convert and live an eternal life of solitude and contemplation—with him. The Governor, furious for what he saw as the corruption of his daughter, had St-Eutrope decapitated by the local butchers. His head now lies at the altar of the church, and the rest of his body in the magnificent Romanesque crypt underneath—in the same spot he was murdered. (Open daily 9am-7pm.) Not far from St-Eutrope lie the ruins of the sprawling **Roman amphitheater** that figures prominently on all of Saintes's postcards. Built in AD 40, it used to be able to seat up to 15,000 spectators. (☎97 73 85. €2, ages 10-18 €1, under 10 free. Guided tours M-Sa 3 and 4pm. €4, under 16 free. €3 audio tour in English and French. Open June-Sept. daily 10am-8pm; Oct.-May M-Sa 10am-5pm, Su 1:30-5pm.)

Built in AD 18 as a gateway into the city, the Roman **Arc Germanicus** rises above the right bank of the river in honor of Emperor Tiberius. Originally located at the entrance to a bridge that crossed the Charente, the arc was moved to its present location in 1843, when it began to lose stability due to the widening of the river. Farther down the river, on esplanade André Malraux, the two-roomed **Musée Archéologique** displays a modest collection of ancient Roman funeral monuments found in the area, as well as jewelry, pottery, and the reconstruction of a chariot, all dating back to the first century AD. However, an impressive (and free) Roman ruins exhibit outside outshines the one inside. (☎74 20 97. Open June-Sept. Tu-Sa 10am-6pm and Su 2-6pm; Oct.-May Tu-Sa 10am-5pm. €1.60, under 18 free.) Rue Arc de Triomphe leads to the often-renovated Romanesque **Abbaye-aux-Dames,** which now serves as a conservatory and cultural center, displaying frequent exhibits by local artists in its bright **Salle Capitulaire.** The bell tower of the connected **Eglise Notre Dame** dates from the 12th century and was partially funded by Eleanor of Aquitaine. The last abbess allegedly died in 1791 at the exact moment when the revolutionaries took the bells down from the tower. All explanations are written in French, though English headsets are available. Consult the *L'Abbaye aux Dames: Eté* pamphlet at the tourist office for information on the **Festival de Saintes** held here every July. (☎97 48 48. Exhibit and ramparts open daily Apr.-Sept. 10am-12:30pm and 2-7pm; Oct.-Mar. 2-6pm. Church free; abbey €2, under 16 free. Concerts €12-47. Tours in French early May to late Sept. 4 per day 2:30-5:30pm. €3.50. Audio tours €4, available in English and French.)

ENTERTAINMENT AND FESTIVALS. Late in the day, Saintes's cafés and pubs are great places to unwind. **Garden Ice Cafe,** 63 cours National, sports a snazzy interior, with leather couches and wall-sized mirrors, and a classy crowd. (☎93 19 64. Beer €2.70-3.20. Theme nights F-Sa. Open daily 7am-2am. MC/V.) **Le Gallia Cinema,** pl. du Théâtre, shows two to four movies a week, one usually in English, as well as live theater during the school year (€15-23). Movie times start between 6 and 10pm. (Open daily. €6, students €5.)

Festival-packed July starts off with **Les Oreilles en Eventail,** three days of free open-air concerts in the *vieille ville.* (☎92 34 26; www.ville-saintes.fr.) Following closely behind, in mid-July, the 10-day **Festival de la Paix** celebrates international folk music, food, and dance. (☎97 04 35; www.festival-de-la-paix.com. Some events free, others €12-27.) Around the same time, 10-day **Festival de Saintes** arrives, with over 35 classical music concerts held at the Abbaye aux Dames and other churches. (☎97 48 48; ww.abbayeauxdames.org. Tickets €12-48.)

LA ROCHELLE ☎05 46

One of France's best-protected seaports, La Rochelle (lah roh-SHELL; pop. 80,000) both thrived and suffered as a coveted Protestant prize in the Thirty Years' War. Today, its charming waterfront and relaxed outdoor cafés make it hard to imagine that this town was nearly starved into oblivion in 1627 by Cardinal Richelieu and Louis XIII—characters immortalized in Dumas's *The Three Musketeers*, an irate attack on the city's support of the English. Though the seaport's medieval architecture remains among vestiges of its turbulent past, La Rochelle now insists upon living the good life, with renowned museums, numerous festivals, pristine coastal islands, and excellent seafood restaurants.

TRANSPORTATION

Trains: Station on bd. Maréchal Joffre. Info office open M-Th and Sa 5am-11:15pm, F 5am-12:45am, Su 6:10am-11:45pm. To: **Bordeaux** (2½hr., 6 per day, €25); **Nantes** (2hr., 6 per day, €22); **Paris** (3-4hr., 9 per day, €58-72); **Poitiers** (1½hr., 12 per day, €20-23).

Buses: Océcars (☎00 95 21) sends buses from pl. de Verdun to **Royan** (2½hr., 3 per day, €13) and **Saintes** (4 per day, €13) via **Rochefort.** Buy tickets from driver or at the office. Info office open M-Th 8:30am-12:30pm and 1:30-6pm, F 8:30am-12:30pm and 1:30-5:30pm.

Ferries: Main office on pl. de Verdun (☎34 02 22; www.rtcr.fr). **Croisières Inter-Iles,** (☎44 49 70) sends boats to **Ile d'Aix** (1¼hr.; July-Aug. up to 5 per day, May-June and Sept. 2 per day; €25, ages 4-18 €17, under 4 €4); **Ile de Ré** (1hr., €16/10/4); and **Fort Boyard** (2hr. tour circles the privately-owned fort, €18/11/free). **Bus de Mer** (☎34 02 22) shuttles from the old port to Les Minimes (July-Aug. every 30min. 9am-11pm, Apr.-June and Sept. every hr. 10am-noon and 2-7pm; €1.50-2). **Le Passeur** (☎34 02 22) runs the same route as Bus de Mer (every 5-10min. June-Sept. 7:30am-midnight, Apr.-May 7:30am-10pm, Oct.-Mar. 7:30am-8pm; €0.60.)

Public Transportation: Autoplus (☎34 02 22). Open M-Sa 9:15am-12:15pm and 1:50-6pm. Maps and schedules available. Serves the campgrounds, hostel, and town center (every 20min. 7am-8pm, €1.20), and nearby towns. Tickets for rides within the city can be bought on board; buy tickets for longer trips at the pl. de Verdun office.

Taxis: 5 rue des Gonthières and pl. de Verdun (☎41 55 55). 24hr. €8-10 from train station to hostel. €2 flat rate; €1.42 per km during the day, €1.98 at night.

Car Rental: Several line av. Général de Gaulle, 100m from the train station. **ADA** (☎41 02 17; www.ada.fr). Open M-F 8am-noon and 2-7pm. MC/V. **Budget** (☎41 35 53; fax 41 55 26). Open M-F 8am-12:30pm and 1:35-6:30pm, Sa 9:30am-12:30pm and 1:45-5:45pm. AmEx/MC/V. **Hertz** (☎41 02 31). Open M-F 8am-noon and 2-7pm, Sa 8am-noon and 2-6pm. AmEx/MC/V. **Rent A Car** (☎27 27 27). Open M-F 8am-noon and 2-6:30pm, Sa 8am-noon and 2-6pm. For all expect to pay about €30 per day.

Bike Rental: Vélos Municipaux Autoplus (☎34 02 22), off quai Valin (open July-Aug. 9am-7pm; May-Sept. 9am-12:30pm and 1:30-7pm) or in pl. de Verdun, near the bus station (open M-Sa 9:15am-12:15pm and 1:50-6pm). 1st 2hr. free, €1 per additional hr.; ID deposit.

ORIENTATION AND PRACTICAL INFORMATION

The heart of La Rochelle spans the café-lined **quai Duperré** in the **vieux port** to the boutique-filled *vieille ville* inland. Opposite the *vieille ville*, to the south, is the more modern area of *la ville en bois* (wooden village), which, despite its name, is a complex of industrial buildings and museums, including the excellent **aquarium** and local university. Farther to the south is a little strip of beachfront, **Les Minimes.**

Tourist Office: Quartier du Gabut (☎41 14 68; www.larochelle-tourisme.com). 5min. walk from the station; head up av. du Général de Gaulle to pl. de la Motte Rouge, and turn left onto quai du Gabut. The office is on the left. Multilingual staff sells useful French brochure with maps and info, as well as a slightly abbreviated version in English (€0.20). Hotel reservations €2. Sign in window lists festivities and cultural events. 2hr. walking tours of the *vieille ville* July-Aug. daily 10:30am (€6, students €4). 1½hr. horse-and-carriage tours daily 2:30pm (€9, under 18 €6). 2hr. theatrical night tours July to mid-Sept. Th 8:30, 9, 9:30pm (€10.50, under 18 €7). Reservations required for carriage and night tours. Tours in French only. Open July-Aug. M-Sa 9am-8pm, Su 10:30am-5:30pm; June and Sept. M-Sa 9am-7pm, Su 10:30am-5:30pm; Oct.-May M-Sa 10am-12:30pm and 1:30-6pm, Su 10am-1pm.

Bank: Banque de France (☎51 48 00), on the corner of rue Réamur and rue Léance Vieljeux. Open M-F 8:30am-noon and 1:30-3:30pm. **Crédit Lyonnais,** 19 rue du Palais, has **ATMs.** 24hr. **BNP,** 1 rue de la Gross Horloge (☎08 20 82 00 01), in the *vieille ville,* also has ATMs. Open M-F 8:30am-noon and 1:30-5:30pm.

Youth Center: Centre Départemental d'Information Jeunesse (CDIJ), 2 rue des Gentilshommes (☎41 16 36). Apartment and job listings. Internet access €1 per 30min., €10 for 1 year (1hr. per day). Open M 2-6pm, Tu-F 10am-12:30pm and 1:30-6pm.

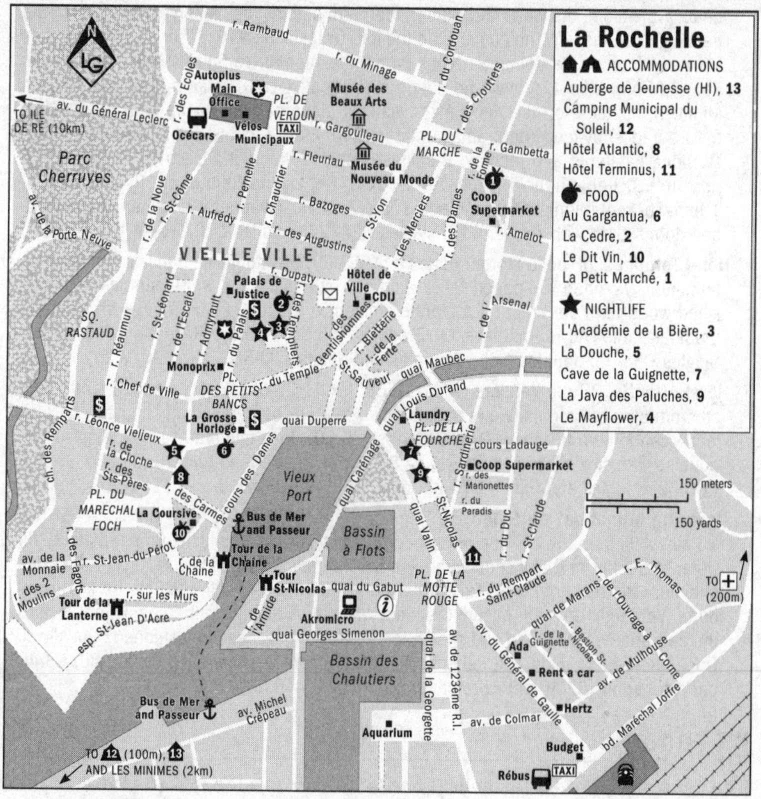

Laundromat: Laverie Automatique, 4bis quai Louis Durand. Wash €3.80 per 8kg, €6.90 per 16kg; dry €1 per 8min. €0.70 cheaper during W "Happy hour" 8:30am-12:30pm. Open daily 8:30am-8:30pm.

Police: 2 pl. de Verdun or 14 rue du Palais (☎51 36 36).

Hospital: rue du Dr. Schweitzer, 24hr. emergency entrance on bd. Joffre (☎45 50 50). English spoken.

Internet Access: Akromicro, 15 rue de l'Aimable Nanette (☎34 07 94; www.akromicro.com), in Le Gabut. €0.05 per min., €2 per hr. Open daily 10am-midnight.

Post Office: 52 av. Mulhouse (☎51 25 03), 50m from the train station. **Currency exchange.** Branch at 6 pl. de l'Hôtel de Ville (☎30 41 30). Both open M-F 8:30am-6:30pm, Sa 8am-noon. **Poste Restante:** 17087. **Postal Code:** 17000.

ACCOMMODATIONS AND CAMPING

Cheap beds in town are limited, especially during the festival-laden summer months. Make reservations as early as possible; for July and August book by June.

Centre International de Séjour, Auberge de Jeunesse (HI), av. des Minimes (☎44 43 11). From the train station, walk up av. de Gaulle, cross av. 123ème R.I. to the left and walk along quai Georges Simenon. Take a left and cross the bridge onto av. Michel Crépeau. Walk along the water for 20min., then turn onto av. des Minimes right before the parking lot on the left. The hostel is on the left. Or take bus #10, 17 or 19 (dir.: Port des Minimes) from av. de Colmar, 1 block from the station to "La Sole" (M-Sa every 20min. 7am-7:55pm; Su #42A every hr., last bus 6:30pm; €1.20). Take a right onto av. des Minimes; hostel is on the right. Avoid walking alone at night in the area. Well out of town but recently-renovated. Small, modern 2- to 6-bunk dorms and excellent facilities. TV room, cafeteria, and laundry. Breakfast included. Internet access (€1 base, €0.50 per 4min.). Reception July-Aug. 8am-10pm; Sept.-June 8am-noon, 2-7pm, and 9-10pm. Lockout midnight-6:30am and 10am-2pm. Reservations recommended. 4- to 6-bed dorms €18, with shower €19; singles €24/26; doubles €20/21. ❶

Hôtel Terminus, pl. de la Motte-Rouge (☎50 69 69; www.tourisme-francais.com/hotels/terminus). Victorian wallpaper, large windows with cascading white curtains, and polished wood furniture create a romantic ambience. Bright 1st-floor lounge and elegant breakfast area. All rooms have TV. Breakfast €6.50. Parking. Reception 7am-11pm. Singles €58-65; doubles €63-72; triples and quads €80-85. AmEx/MC/V. ❹

Hôtel Atlantic, 23 rue Verdière (☎41 16 68; fax 41 25 69). Heavy wooden furniture in comfortably-sized rooms. Views of sun-baked rooftops or a green inner courtyard. Excellent location near the *Vieux Port*. Breakfast €5.50. Open mid-Mar. to Nov. Singles and doubles with sink €32, with shower €48-56, with shower and toilet €60-68, with bath €60-62; doubles and triples €75-85; quads €85. MC/V. ❸

Camping Municipal du Soleil, av. Michel Crépeau (☎44 42 53; fax 52 25 18). A 10min. walk from the city center past Le Gabut, following av. Michel Crépeau along the water to the left at its junction with allée des Tamaris. Or catch bus #10 (dir.: Port des Minimes) to "Technoforum." Take a right and then the 2nd left onto rue de la Huguenotte. Veer right onto av. Michel Crépeau, which runs alongside the campsite. Close to the port and beach. Green and shady, this campsite provides old-fashioned bungalows. Open late June to mid-Sept. Reception 7:30am-11pm. 1 person and car €8.60; €3.40 per extra adult, €2.40 per extra child. Electricity €3.40. MC/V. ❶

FOOD

The fishy aroma of La Rochelle's *fruits de mer* (seafood) wafts through the streets; follow your nose to the covered market at **place du Marché** for fresh seafood (open daily 7am-1pm). A **Monoprix** supermarket is on rue de Palais, near the clock tower. (Open M-Sa July-Aug. 8:30am-9pm; Sept.-June 8:30am-8pm.) **Co-ops** operate at 41 rue Sardinerie (open M 3:30-8pm, Tu and Th-Sa 8:30am-1pm and 3:30-8pm, W 8:30am-1pm, Su 9am-1pm and 5-8pm) and on rue des Trois Fuseaux (open M 3:30-7:45pm, Tu-Sa 8:30am-12:45pm and 3:30-7:45pm, Su 9am-12:30pm). Copious restaurants line **rue St-Jean du Pérot** and **rue de la Chaîne,** and pack the waterfront, but they can be expensive.

La Petite Marché, 4 rue des Trois Fuseaux (☎34 30 30). Tucked behind the Vieux Marché. Students and the organically inclined alike delight in this tiny bistro's imaginative vegetarian meals. Recipes change often but include delicious dishes like honey-marinated carrots and lentil flour pancakes. Salads €4-10. *Plats* €8. Desserts €3. Open M-Sa 10am-3pm and 5:30-9:30pm. AmEx/MC/V. ❷

Le Dit Vin, 12 rue St-Jean-du-Pérot (☎27 50 23). The name "says" it all: the place is *divin* (divine). With its classy dark red décor, extensive wine selection (also alluded to in the name), and *menu* of house specialties, this bistro stands apart from the seafood racket in both style and value. Tasty appetizers from €6. *Plats* €13-24. Exceptional 3-course dinner *menu* €16. Open M-Sa 7pm-1am. MC/V. ❸

Au Gargantua, 4 rue Leonce Vieljeux (☎50 57 40). A small student-run takeout spot on the port, tucked between sprawling and expensive tourist attractions. Attracts broke students and sleepless clubbers, who come for its pasta with up to 6 different fresh sauces. Pasta €3.50-4.50. *Menu* with dessert and drink €6. Open M-Th and Su 11am-3am, F-Sa 11am-5am. MC/V. ❶

Le Cedre, 22 rue des Templiers (☎41 03 89). Lebanese sandwich shop with fresh vegetables and a shaded outdoor seating area where students come to eat after a night out. Its location and variety distinguish it from its counterparts. Wraps, kebabs, falafel, and burgers €2.20-6.50. *Formules* €5.30-8.50. Open daily 10:30am-3am. MC/V. ❶

SIGHTS

La Rochelle's flourishing commerce with "Nouvelle-France," or Canada, and the West Indies, endowed it with an impressive port fortified by walls and towers, three of which still stand. During WWII, the Germans also took advantage of these facilities, using the town as a submarine base. In fact, the Germans didn't let go of La Rochelle until the general surrender in May 1945, making it the last French city to be liberated. A unique blend of architecture and art—ranging from 17th-century graffiti to contemporary exhibitions—La Rochelle is a city full of hidden wonders. A mere €6.60 buys combined admission to the Musée du Nouveau Monde, Musée des Beaux Arts, and Musée d'Orbigny-Bernon. Joint tickets are available at the tourist office or at any of the three museums and are valid for one month.

AQUARIUM. This gigantic aquarium is home to a whopping 10,000 marine animals, and 500 different species, kept in habitats that simulate their natural environments—from the French Atlantic coast to the tropical rainforest, from the Indian Ocean to the Pacific. Audio tours offered in four languages (€3.50) provide surprisingly fascinating facts about the eating and sexual habits of the fish, which accompany the awe-inspiring tanks filled with sharks, translucent jellyfish, giant eels, and poisonous anemones. The aquarium makes for a perfect rainy day activity, but be prepared to deal with crowds of families with the same idea. Be sure not to step on a turtle in the tropical greenhouse, where they mosey about freely. *(Bassin des Grande Yacht, across the water from the tourist office. ☎34 00 00. Open daily July-Aug. 9am-11pm; Apr.-June and Sept. 9am-8pm; Oct.-Mar. 10am-8pm. Wheelchair-accessible. €12.50, students and under 18 €9.50.)*

TOUR ST-NICOLAS AND TOUR DE LA CHAÎNE. The port's 14th-century towers once guarded the town from attack and appear emblematically in paintings of the city's skyline. When hostile ships approached, guards would close off the harbor by raising a chain between the two towers. Now the 800-year-old chain lies along the dock, at the foot of the aptly-named **Tour de la Chaîne.** After Richelieu won the siege of La Rochelle, he had all of the city's fortifications destroyed except for these towers. **Tour St-Nicolas** impresses visitors with thick fortifications and a maze of dizzying staircases. According to local legend, Fairy Mesuline, the half-woman, half-eel ancestor of the mermaid, was flying above the city one night when her apron broke. The stones that magically spilled out formed St-Nicolas's present shape. Initially, the La Rochelle's citizens were planning to link the two towers with an arch, but these plans were abandoned when they discovered St-Nicolas had tilted in its foundations. The Tour de la Chaîne now houses a fascinating French timeline of the city's history and an exhibit on its past trade with Canada. *(☎34 11 81 or 41 74 13. Both towers open daily July-Aug. 10am-7pm; early to mid-Sept. and mid-May to June 10am-12:30pm and 2-6:30pm; mid-Sept. to mid-May Tu-Su 10am-12:30pm and 2-5:30pm. Last entrance 30min. before closing. €5, ages 18-25 €3.50, under 18 free. Combined ticket including Tour de la Lanterne, and ferry passage between the 2 towers €11, ages 18-25 €7; Oct.-Mar. and 1st Su of the month free.)*

OLD TOWN. The pedestrian *vieille ville*, dating from the 17th and 18th centuries, stretches beyond the townhouses of the harbor. Romantic arcades line its white meandering streets, due to the city's origins as a market town. The 14th-century **Grosse Horloge** (Great Clock Tower) is worth strolling by; its two-ton Gothic bell once tolled the raising of the chain between the port's two towers. The flamboyant Gothic facade of the Renaissance **Hôtel de Ville,** with a prominent statue of its builder, Henri IV, is also noteworthy. *(2hr. night tour July-Aug. M-Sa 10:30pm. €6, under 10 €4. 1½hr. horse-drawn tour July-Aug. M-Sa 2:30pm. €9, under 10 €6.)*

TOUR DE LA LANTERNE. Accessible from the Tour de la Chaîne by a low rampart, this 70m high tower is France's oldest lighthouse. Built in the 15th century around the foundations of a 12th-century tower, the tower has a morbid history: it acquired its second name, **Tour des Prêtres,** after 13 priests were thrown from the steeple during the Wars of Religion. The stone walls along its 162 steps are carved with three centuries' worth of intricate graffiti that provide remarkable historical documentation of shipwrecks and crews, recorded by the tower's French, British, Dutch, and Spanish detainees. One particularly impressive work depicts a 19th-century steam-engine with amazing detail. At the summit, only 1m of stone protects visitors from free-falls. On a sunny day, the view extends all the way to the Ile d'Oléron. *(☎41 56 04. Hours and prices same as Tour St-Nicolas and Tour de la Chaine.)*

MUSÉE DU NOUVEAU MONDE. This museum explores European perceptions of the New World during the Age of Exploration, and, more specifically, traces the history of La Rochelle's commerce with the Antilles. The striking *Mascarade Nuptiale* by Roza Jose Conrado, a painting of entertainers at the 18th-century Portuguese court, sums up the oddity of artifacts contained in this building, which originally belonged to the Fleuriau family, who made their fortune trading slaves and Caribbean sugar, spices, coffee. Curtis's 20th-century ethnographic *photogravures* (ancient predecessors to the photograph) on the top floor are also not to be missed. *(10 rue Fleuriau. ☎41 46 50. Open Apr.-Sept. M and W-Sa 10am-12:30pm and 2-6pm, Su 2:30-6pm. €3.50, students and under 18 free.)*

MUSÉE DES BEAUX ARTS. This museum houses mostly French works from the 17th century, which feature—surprise, surprise—naked women in front of utopian backgrounds. There's also a Fromentin series which appears on some of the town's postcards. Look for Paul Signac's 20th-century watercolor of the lively La Rochelle harbor. *(28 rue Gargoulleau. ☎41 64 65. Open M and W-Sa 2-6pm, Su 2:30-6pm. €3.50, students and under 18 free. English guidebook available at the desk.)* Downstairs, **L'Espace Art Contemporaine** contains more exciting temporary exhibits of modern art from local artists. *(☎34 76 55. Open M and W-Sa 2:30-6pm. Free.)*

NIGHTLIFE

The **cour du Temple,** a lively square just off rue des Templiers, offers a cool place to start off a hot summer night. The tourist office offers *Gay-Friendly La Rochelle,* a brochure listing gay- and lesbian-friendly nightlife. The streets leading to the clubs near the Tour de Lanterne are dark and isolated at night—exercise caution.

Cave de la Guignette, 8 rue St-Nicolas. No visit to La Rochelle is complete without a stop at this bar, in operation since 1933, when it lured local fishermen with barrels of wine. Now, the barrels serve as furniture for students, who sip cheap wine (from €1.30) before heading out to dinner. Try "la Guignette," white wine infused with fruit flavors (1L €8.50). Open M 4-8pm, Tu-W 10am-1pm and 4-8pm, Th-Sa 10am-1pm and 3-8pm. Cash only.

La Java des Paluches, 12 rue St-Nicolas (☎30 54 20). Welcomes a young laid-back crowd with Warhol-esque artwork, random kitchen furniture, low leather couches, and loud rock. Try their famous mojitos (€5.50) or any of their 50 different types of whiskeys—but good luck fighting your way to the bar. Beer €2.30. Open daily 7pm-2am.

L'Académie de la Bière, cours du Temple (☎42 43 78). Though the names implies a student crowd, a loyal older clientele drinks beers of all shades *(blondes, brunes, rousse)* in this rustic 2-story bar. Try a *"Girafe,"* a meter-high tube of beer (€22). Wine and hard liquor from €2. Open daily 10am-2am. MC/V.

Le Mayflower, 14bis Cour des Temples, (☎50 51 39) off rue des Templiers. A mixed crowd picks from the potent rum concoctions (€3.80) in a relaxed bar with loud rock music. Open M 8pm-2am, Tu-Sa 6:30pm-2am. V.

La Douche, 14 rue Leonce Vieljeux (☎ 41 24 79). This club promotes its "H2O concept" with real showers on the dance floor and cellophane on the ceiling. The live DJs love to play electro-house. €2 compulsory coat check. Beer €5. Cover €10; includes 1 drink. Open Th-Su midnight-5am.

ENTERTAINMENT AND FESTIVALS

La Coursive, 4 rue St-Jean-du-Perot, hosts concerts, plays, dance performances, and films. (☎51 54 00. Office open Sept.-June M-F 1-6:30pm.) In the summer, **quai Duperré** and **cours des Dames** are closed to cars and open to mimes, jugglers, and an outdoor market. (Open daily July-Sept. 8pm-midnight; May-June Su noon-8pm.)

La Rochelle's popular festivals attract art-loving and fun-seeking crowds. During the last week of June and the first week of July, the city becomes the Cannes of the Atlantic with its **Festival International du Film de La Rochelle.** Fans come to pull an all-nighter watching a wide range of movies. (☎01 48 06 16 66; www.festival-larochelle.org. All 100 films €80; students, under 25, and unemployed €60. 3 films €15/10. 1 film €6.) Without missing a beat, La Rochelle hosts **FrancoFolies,** a massive, nationally renowned six-day rock festival in mid-July that draws international Francophone performers. (☎50 55 57; www.francofolies.fr. Some afternoon performances €4, evening concerts €10-38.) To round out the month, the end of July brings a 10-day theater festival, **Théâtre en Eté** (☎06 66 79 60 65), on quai Simenon. During the second week of September, hundreds of boats in the Port des Minimes open to the public for the **Grand Pavois** (☎44 46 39; www.grand-pavois.com), a boat competition known as one of the biggest "boat salons" in Europe. The town has recently added the **Jazz entre les 2 Tours,** a week filled with jazz concerts in the beginning of October, to its repertoire. (☎27 11 19. www.larochelle-jazz-festival.com.) Capping the summer and fall seasons, runners pass through town in late November for an annual **marathon** (☎44 42 19; www.marathondelarochelle.com).

DAYTRIP FROM LA ROCHELLE

ROCHEFORT

Rochefort is accessible by Océcars, which shuttle between the gare routière *and La Rochelle (line #51; 1hr.; M-Sa 8 per day, Su 2 per day; €5.40) The tourist office on av. Sadi Carnot is very helpful. From the train station, follow the* centre-ville *signs. After the signs stop, veer left past the hospital and follow rue Thiers; turn right on rue Audry de Puyravault and continue past the post office. The tourist office will be on the left. (☎99 08 60. Open July-Aug. M-Sa 9:30am-7pm, Su 10am-6pm; Sept.-June daily 9:30am-12:30pm and 2-6pm.) The office offers the free* carte sésame *discount, valid at all the city's museums. After paying full price at one sight, receive a stamp valid for reduced admission at the rest of the museums.*

Modern Rochefort (ROHSH-fohr) was a sparsely populated marsh along the Charente River until Louis XIV claimed it for his own in the 17th century and transformed it into France's greatest dockyard. As a result, numerous fortifications were erected around the estuary, including on Ile d'Aix, Ile de Ré and Fort Boyard. In homage to their naval past, residents of Rochefort have begun the construction of an exact replica of **L'Hermione,** the vessel on which La Fayette sped to the aid of George Washington and the American colonies in 1780. Originally built in six months, this impressive wooden giant has required more than a decade of work to recreate. The ship is expected to be finished and sail to Boston in 2011. Guided tours of the work site demonstrate the craft of 18th-century blacksmiths and carpenters. (☎87 01 90. Open daily Apr.-Sept. 9am-7pm; Oct.-Mar. 10am-noon and 2-6pm. Tours July-Aug. 9am-7pm; Apr.-June and Sept. 11:30am, 2, 5pm; Oct.-Mar. M-F 2, 4pm, Sa-Su 11:30am, 2, 4pm. Entrance €6; students, retirees, and *carte sésame* €5; ages 8-16 €2.50; under 8 free. With tour €7.50/6.50/3.50.)

An avid imagination masterminded the **Maison Pierre Loti,** 141 rue Pierre Loti, which exhibits the exotic and bizarre collection accumulated by its creator, novelist and actor Loti. Eccentric to the extreme, this rich Rochefort resident transformed the rooms of his house into romanticized simulations of a Turkish lounge, an Islamic mosque, and a Gothic chamber—all of which he never visited. The museum can be seen by guided tour only. (☎99 16 88. Tours in French daily July to mid-Sept. daily every 30min. 10-11:30am and 2-6pm; Oct.-June M and W-Sa 10:30, 11:30am, 2, 3, 4pm; Su 2, 3, 4pm. €7.80, *carte sésame* €6.80, students and ages 8-18 €5.) The **Musée National de la Marine,** 1 pl. de la Galissonnière, next to L'Hermione, is housed inside the former naval commander's official residence. The museum is dedicated to Rochefort's nautical history, displaying a large collection of curious artifacts—from 17th-century ship models to carved coconuts made by prisoners on the ships. (☎99 86 57. Open daily May-Sept. 10am-8pm; Oct.-Mar. 1:30-6:30pm. €5, students €4.20, under 18 free.) The oddly futuristic 176m steel and iron **Pont Transbordeur,** 10 rue du Docteur Pujos, 2km farther down the Charente, was designed by engineering genius Ferdinand Arnodin, a student of the original architect of the Eiffel Tower, and constructed in 1900 with the same materials as the Tower. The Pont was built impressively high in order to facilitate the passage of high steam and sailboats.

If you really want to spend the night in Rochefort, the **Auberge de Jeunesse (HI) ❶,** 20 rue de la République, is just down the street in a spacious old house. Equipped with a small kitchen and green courtyard often available for camping, this clean hostel offers brightly colored 14-bed dorms and singles, some of which open onto a terrace. Bathrooms in the hall. Reservations recommended. (☎99 74 62. Breakfast €3.50. Dorms €15; singles €21; doubles €18. Camping €5.60 per tent. MC/V.) Rochefort locals recommend **Le Cap Nell ❸,** 1 quai Bellot, overlooking the small and often windy boat-filled harbor. The combined bistro-grill serves fresh seafood, along with duck (€5.50) and *steak flambé au Cognac* for €17. (☎87 31 77. *Menu* €17. Open July-Aug. daily noon-2pm and 7:30-10pm; Sept.-June M and Th-Su noon-2pm and 7:30-10pm, Tu noon-2pm. AmEx/MC/V.)

ILE DE RÉ ☎05 46

Ile de Ré (EEL-duh-ray; pop. 16,000, 250,000 in summer) was initially dubbed *"Ré La Blanche"* for its former salt trade, but the nickname could easily apply to its 70km of white-sand beaches. A sunny paradise just 10km from La Rochelle, the 30km-long island is connected by a bridge to the mainland. With ruinous monuments, a landscape of pine forests, farmland, vineyards, and ports—all connected by winding, well-paved bike paths—Ile de Ré is a one-stop shop for natural wonder. The population swells in summer, as crowds flood the main town of **St-Martin-de-Ré** and the beaches on the southern coast. Though this popular Parisian getaway is more touristed than nearby Ile d'Aix, easily accessible beaches and nature trails keep it charming and relatively calm even during high season.

TRANSPORTATION. To get to Ile de Ré, city **buses** are a viable means of transportation, but schedules change by season. Line #50 (from La Rochelle) goes as far as Sablanceaux (on the island). Make sure the bus is going to Sablanceaux: some buses on lines #1 and 21 stop before crossing the bridge. Visit the main office at pl. Verdun, La Rochelle, for schedules and information. In low season no buses go to Sablanceaux, and in early and late summer, buses (€1.20) operate only on certain days. For ventures beyond Sablanceaux, **Rébus** is a convenient way to travel between pl. de Verdun and the villages on Ré, including La Flotte (40min., 14 per day, €4.30); St-Martin (50min., 14 per day, €5.10); St-Clement (1½hr., 11 per day, €8.10); and Les Portes (1½hr., 11 per day, €8.60), at the northern tip of the island. (☎09 20 15. Info office at 36 av. Charles de Gaulle in St-Martin. Open M-F 9am-noon and 2-5:30pm.) **Croisières Inter-Iles,** 3 prom. des Coureauleurs, in la Rochelle, runs **ferries** to Sablanceaux. Ferries leave for the island at least four times a day in high season and once or twice a day in low season. (☎08 25 13 55 00; www.inter-iles.com. €16, ages 4-18 €10, under 4 €4. Schedules vary; check the island's transportation website, www.service-maritime-iledaix.com, for schedules) If you choose to **drive** across pont La Pallice, you'll pay steep tolls (June to mid-Sept. €17 round-trip; mid-Sept. to May €9. Motorcycles and scooters €2 year-round.) **Taxis** are available from the train station, but are expensive (€35-65). Alternatively, walk or **bike;** cycling from La Rochelle to Sablanceaux, the first beach on the island after the bridge, takes less than an hour. The ride to the island is a bit tough, but once on the island, the trails offer great coastal views. From pl. de Verdun in La Rochelle, head west on av. Maréchal Leclerc and follow road signs to Ile de Ré until the bike path appears on the left. Plenty of places on the island **rent bikes. Cycland** has branches in Rivedoux, La Flotte, St-Martin (first left off rue Sully on Impasse rue de Sully), Le Bois-Plage, Ars, Les Portes, St-Clément, and La Couarde. (☎09 08 66. €3.50-5 per hr., €6-9.50 per ½-day, €8-12 per day. ID deposit. Open daily July-Aug. 9am-1pm and 2-7pm; Sept.-June 9:30am-12:30pm and 2-7pm. MC/V.)

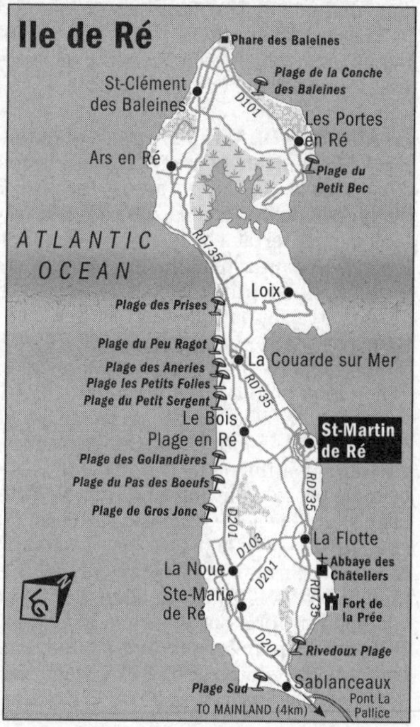

ORIENTATION AND PRACTICAL INFORMATION. The historical capital of the island, **St-Martin-de-Ré,** is the best starting place for exploring Ile de Ré. St-Martin's **tourist office,** on quai Nicolas Baudin, sells maps with biking trails (€1) but also offers a free guide booklet with a similar map in the back. Walking tours (1½hr.; mid-June to mid-Sept. W 10:30am; €5, under 18 €2) leave from the tourist office. Carriage tours (1¼hr.; by reservation only; mid-June to mid-Sept. Th 10am; €8.50, under 18 €5) leave from Parking Vauban. (☎09 20 06; www.saint-martin-de-re.fr. Themed tours also available. Open July-Aug. M-Sa 10am-7pm, Su 10am-1pm; Sept.-June M-Sa 10am-noon and 2-6pm.) Other services include: **police** (☎09 21 17); **St-Martin hospital** (☎09 20 01; emergency services and ambulances July-Aug.; Sept.-

June dial ☎15 or 18); **Pharmacie Du Port,** 7 rue de Sully (☎09 20 43; open July-Aug. M-Sa 9am-12:30pm and 2:30-7:30pm, Su 10am-12:30pm); and a **post office,** pl. de la République, which offers **currency exchange** (☎09 38 20; open M-F 9am-noon and 1:30-4pm, Sa 9am-noon). **Postal Code:** 17410.

ACCOMMODATIONS. Prices of hotels in Ré sky rocket in the summer to at least €55 a night; camping is highly recommended. St-Martin's **Hotel du Port ❺,** 29 quai de la Poitrinière, across the port from the tourist office, offers impeccable big-windowed rooms, with TV and recently renovated bathrooms, that overlook a quiet terrace or the lively port. (☎09 21 21; fax 09 06 85. Breakfast €7.30. Reception 8am-10pm. Singles and doubles €68-80; family suites for 3-5 people €78-155. Room prices vary according to season and view. Extra bed €15. AmEx/MC/V.) Straight out of a Martha Stewart magazine, **L'Hippocampe ❸,** 16 rue Château des Mauléons, in La Flotte, 4km east of St-Martin and 9km north of Sablanceaux, has harmonious pastel-colored rooms with light wooden furniture, which look onto a small inner garden. All but the cheapest rooms have shower and toilet. (☎09 60 68. Breakfast €5.80. Reception 8am-11pm. Reservations recommended 1 month ahead. Singles and doubles €49-69; triples €94. V.) Campsites are plentiful on Ile de Ré, but those between the bridge and St-Martin-de-Ré become crowded in July and August. Travelers seeking a lively camping experience should head to beachside **La Plage ❶,** 408 rte. du Chaume, near St-Clément. (☎29 42 62; www.la-plage.com. Reservations recommended months in advance. In summer, campers can stay only by the week. Open Apr.-Sept. 2 people with tent and car €17-25; extra adult €5.50-11.50, extra child €3.30-11.80. Electricity €5. MC/V.) Gorgeous and thickly forested **Camping Tamaris ❶,** 4 rue du Comte D'Hastrel, a popular site that could be mistaken for a large backyard, is in the center of Rivedoux. (☎09 81 28. Open Easter-Sept. 1-3 people €15, €5 per extra adult, €3 per extra child under 7. Electricity €4. Cash only.)

FOOD. Most towns have pizzerias and *crêperies* as well as morning markets, which are listed in Ré's free tourist packet. St-Martin's indoor market is off **rue Jean Jaurès,** by the port. (Open in high season daily 9am-1pm; in low season Tu-Su only.) Two supermarkets sit just east of St-Martin on the road to La Flotte: **Intermarché,** 4 av. des Corsaires (☎09 42 02; open M-Sa 8:30am-8pm, Su 9-11:45am) and **Super U,** 23 rue des Salières (☎09 42 80; open M-Sa 9am-7:30pm, Su 9-12:30pm). Tasty, albeit pricey, restaurants surround the port in St-Martin and overlook the fleet of fishing boats below. **Marco Polo ❷,** 6-8 quai de Bernonville, caters to tourists with more modest budgets with a selection of relatively cheap Italian food. (☎09 15 92. *Formules* €13-15. *Menu* €15. Open daily noon-3pm and 7-10:30pm. MC/V.)

SIGHTS. Between Sablanceaux and La Flotte are the romantic wind-whipped ruins of 13th-century **Abbaye des Châteliers.** Built in 1156, the abbey was destroyed during the Wars of Religion as Ré passed back and forth between Catholic and Protestant hands, only to be abandoned 400 years later. Many of its stones were taken to build the Fort de la Prée in 1625, and its remains—the walls of the nave and a gaping window frame—now stand in an isolated poppy field, visible from the bus from Sablanceaux to La Flotte. In La Flotte, the **Maison du Platin,** av. du Front de Mer, details the history of the island's fish and salt industries with photographs and costumed mannequins meant to represent Ré's earliest residents. A temporary exhibit on the ancestors of Quebec is planned for the summer of 2008. The museum offers walking tours in French of the old quarters, port, and nearby oyster farms. (☎09 61 39. €3.80, ages 6-18 €2.15, under 6 free. Open Apr.-Oct. M-F 10:30am-12:30pm and 2-6pm.) It also offers bike tours of the Abbaye. (1½hr.; €5, under 18 €2.60.) The mayor's office *(mairie)* organizes guided tours of the diamond-shaped **Fort de la Prée.** Schedules vary; call for information. (☎01 45 88 17 00 or 06 81 91 64 15. Open Apr.-Oct. daily 10am-12:30pm and 3-7pm. €4, ages 5-18 €2, under 5 free; guided visit €5/2/free.) Hour-long tours of the **écluses à poissons** (medieval fishing beds that are still functional today), 60 cours des Jailleres in Ste-Marie de Ré, teach visitors about the island's fishing traditions. The beds' stone walls, which lie along the coast's beaches between St-Clement and Sablanceaux, were erected to trap fish with the waning tides. The tour includes walking on shells; wear boots! (Times vary with tides. Call ☎37 47 50 for a schedule.)

St-Martin lays claim to a port built by Vauban and a citadel commissioned by Louis XIV in order to protect Ré from the invading English. Today, the **citadel** still serves as an active prison for around 400 inmates. The 15th- to 17th-century Renaissance gallery of the **Hôtel Clerjotte,** on av. Victor-Bouthilier, houses the **Musée Ernest Cognacq,** devoted to the island's history. The museum is closed for renovation, but when it re-opens in September 2008, it will house temporary exhibits—including one on Vauban—and a small *cabinet de curiosités* with artifacts from all over the world, carefully hand-labeled by their collector. (☎09 21 22. Open M-F 10am-noon and 2-5pm, Sa-Su 2-5pm. €4, students €2.50; 1st Su of the month free.) Just up the hill from the *quai* sits the imposing 15th-century **Eglise St-Martin,** marked by a tumultuous history. A haul up to the top of the bell tower at sunset is rewarded with a glowing panorama of the entire island. (Open daily July-Aug. 10am-11:30pm; Sept.-June 10am-sunset. Admission to church free. Bell tower €1.35, ages 11-15 €0.55, under 10 free. Guided tours €2.45/€1.65/free.) On the way up the island, stop by **Ars** to admire its 17 windmills, dismantled in the 19th century when an insect plague wiped out one of Ré's chief crops, cereals (sea salt is now the island's pride and joy). In **St-Clément-des-Baleines,** watch for the blinking red light of the **Phare des Baleines.** Built in 1854, the 57m high lighthouse is one of France's tallest. Climb its 257 stairs for a great view of the ocean. (☎29 18 23. Open daily July-Aug. 9:30am-7:30pm; Sept. 10am-6:30pm; Oct.-Mar. 10:30am-5:30pm; Apr.-June 10am-7pm. €2.50, ages 7-12 €1.30.)

BIKING AND BEACHES. It's easy, scenic, and affordable to rent a bike in any island town and pedal along the paths, coastal sidewalks, and wooded lanes spread out across the island. Although trails to St-Martin along the southern half of Ile de Ré are often packed, crowds thin out to the north. The *Guide des Itinéraires Cyclables* (€1), available from island tourist offices, describes five 10km- to 22km-paths. One of the island's best trails begins in Le Martray, just east of Ars, and runs along the northern coast through the island's salt marsh and bird preserve, home to herons and rare blue-throated thrushes. In winter, 20,000 birds use the sanctuary as a rest stop as they migrate from Siberia and Canada to Africa.

The island's major attractions are, of course, its splendid beaches. Put on some sunscreen—and nothing else—at the bathing suit-optional **plage du Petit Bec** in **Les Portes-en-Ré,** or head to the pine-fringed dunes of **plage de la Conche des Baleines,** near the lighthouse just off Gare Bec.

> **!** The beaches on the northern coast are large and uncrowded—for a reason. The sea off the north coast tends to be dangerous, and the shores rocky; for better swimming, try the sandy strip along the southern shore beginning at **La Couarde.**

ILE D'AIX ☎05 46

Smaller and less accessible than Ré, windy Ile d'Aix (EEL dex; pop. 200) is almost entirely free of the souvenir shops and fast-food stands that populate most beach towns in the region. Just 3km long and barely 600m wide, the island's tiny coves and rocky coastline are flooded with summer campers and school children, and its population grows ten-fold during the high season. The best beaches are along the southwest coast near the lighthouses, though **Sables Jaunes,** nestled between rocky cliffs on the northwest tip, is best sheltered from the wind.

Aix's most striking sight dates from the time the island hosted Napoleon in 1815 for three days before he surrendered to the English and was exiled to Ste-Hélène. The house in which he stayed was transformed into the **Musée Napoléonien** in 1928. Today, it contains a small but impressive collection of portraits and paraphernalia, including 40 clocks stopped at 5:49, the time of his death, and the rough draft of his letter of surrender to England. The **Musée Africain** next door, unaltered since the 1930s, presents a hodgepodge of Central African artifacts collected by Napoleon Gourgaud during five expeditions. Napoleon Bonaparte's stuffed dromedary (a camel-like animal) is also an interesting, if random, piece of the exhibit. (☎84 66 40. Both open daily July-Aug. 9:30am-1pm and 2-5:30pm; June and Sept.-Oct. daily 9:30am-12:30pm and 2-6pm; Nov.-Apr. M and W-Su 9:30am-noon and 2-5pm. One ticket provides admission to both museums. €4.50, ages 18-25 €3, under 18 free.) The **Fort Liedot,** commissioned and allegedly designed by Napoleon to help protect the arsenal in Rochefort, housed prisoners until the late 70s, including the Algerian president Ben Bella in 1968, and was later used as a children's summer camp. (Open for guided tours July-Aug. 1hr. tours in French available through the tourist office. Daily 11am and 6pm. €3.)

Ile d'Aix's only hotel, **Hôtel Napoleon ❹,** changed owners in September 2007; for information on new prices and amenities, contact the tourist office. Next to the port, quiet **Camping le Fort de la Rade ❶** offers a picturesque camping experience inside the battlements of a Vauban fort. (☎84 28 28; fax 84 00 44. Reception 9am-noon and 5-7pm. Pool facilities available. Open Apr.-Sept. July-Aug. €4.05 per adult, €3 per child; €8.50-13 per tent, depending on location. Apr.-June and Sept. €3.65/2.20/6.70. MC/V.) Aix's few restaurants tend to be pricey. The **bakery** on rue Gourgaud sells cheap sandwiches, and a little **grocery store** just across the street sells essentials. In the middle of the island, classy **Les Paillotes ❹,** rue Le Bois Joly, serves lamb and seafood in an elegant, shaded courtyard encircled by trimmed evergreens. (☎84 66 24. *Menus* €21-34. Open July-Aug. daily 9am-2am; Sept.-June M-F 9am-4pm, Sa-Su 7pm-2am; often closed M. MC/V.) The cheerful restaurant **Pressoir ❸,** down rue Le Bois Joly, sells a *formule* of fresh *moules frites* on the terrace for €12; it includes a drink. Communal tables add to the rustic feel, and the side room, with sketches of French celebrities, also serves as a bar. (☎84 09 37. *Menus* €20. Open daily 9am-1:45am. Reservations recommended. AmEx/MC/V.)

Aix is one of the only coastal islands with no highway to the mainland; only locals use cars on the island. Croisières Inter-Iles, 3 prom. des Coureauleurs, in La Rochelle (☎08 25 13 55 00), runs **boats** from La Rochelle to Ile d'Aix (€25, under 18 €17). Check the island's transportation website (www.service-maritime-ile-daix.com) for schedules. For a free map of the island, head to the **tourist office** at 6 rue Gourgaud, straight past the horse-drawn carriages. (☎83 01 82. Open daily July-Aug. 9am-5pm; Sept. and Apr.-June M 10am-noon, Th-Su 10am-noon and 2-5pm.) The horse-drawn carriages lead tours of the island in French. (☎84 69 73. 50min. €6.50, under 10 €5.50.) *Crêperies* and snack shops in town rent bikes (around €3.50 per hr., €8.50 per day; ID deposit). Pedestrians can walk around the island in a mere two hours, and some of the best spots are accessible only by foot.

COULON ☎05 49

The winding streets of tiny Coulon (koo-LOHN; pop. 2200) run alongside the canals of the Marais Poitevin, making the town an ideal launch for a boat ride into the marshland. Stretching from Niort to the Atlantic coast just north of La Rochelle, this "natural" wetland used to be flooded regularly at high tide—until monks in the ninth century decided to irrigate the area to protect their agriculture from salt water. Nicknamed *la Venise Verte* (the Green Venice) today for its serene canals, this tucked-away piece of France enchants and inspires painters, writers and poets alike. Visitors biking along the banks pass through a maze of narrow creeks, weeping willows, purple irises, and herds of cattle. By the Sèvre Niortaise river, trees form an overhanging canopy, while duckweeds carpet the water's surface, making the canals look like fleeting grassy paths.

TRANSPORTATION AND PRACTICAL INFORMATION. CASA Autocars **buses,** 11-13 chemin du Fief Binard (☎24 93 47), arrive from Niort's *gare routière* (next to the train station) and its central pl. de la Brèche (30min.; M-Tu and Th-F 5 per day, more on W, Sa, and during school vacations; €1.20). Take bus #20 (dir.: Coulon/Marais Poitevin). Once in Coulon, the best way to delve farther into the Marais is by **boat** or **bike.** Many hitch, but *Let's Go* does not recommend it. Though more expensive than bikes, **boats** are worth the extra money and are a unique way to experience the Marais. They can be rented at one of the 14 boat rental locations in eight towns along the river. Most travelers explore the area on their own, but a few places offer guides who instruct travelers in the marsh's history and secrets. Stirring the waters releases methane gas trapped below; especially dramatic guides might prod the water to light a fire right on the surface. In Coulon, **Le Trigale,** 6 rue de l'Eglise (☎35 14 14), supplies a private boat and boatsman, though few of the guides speak English. (1hr., 1-10 people €27-65.) The tight-budgeted and adventurous can rent a boat and navigate themselves (1-7hr.; €13-48; MC/V). Other vendors offer similar deals; places down the river are usually €1-2 cheaper.

Head to the **tourist office,** 31 rue Gabriel Auchier, for general info about hiking and bicycling tours and for a complete list of the area's *chambres d'hôtes* and campsites. The staff distributes biking, hiking and boating maps, as well as the free *Guide d'Accueil.* (☎35 99 29. Accommodation reservations service €1. Open daily July-Aug. 10am-12:30pm and 2-6:30pm; June 10am-12:30pm and 2-6pm; call for low-season hours.) Bike-, canoe-, and punt-rental locations are everywhere, especially along the river. Find an **ATM** at **Crédit Agricole,** pl. de l'Eglise. The **post office,** 17 rue Gabriel Auchier, next to the tourist office, offers **currency exchange** if notified a few days in advance. (☎/fax 35 90 11. Open M-W and F 9am-noon and 1:40-5pm, Th 10am-noon and 1:40-5pm, Sa 9-11:30am.)

ACCOMMODATIONS AND CAMPING. Hotels are expensive in Coulon, but many *chambres d'hôtes* are available from €45 for two people. **Le Central ❹,** 4 rue d'Autre-mont, is the cheapest hotel in town and offers spacious rooms that verge on apartments, with large modern bathrooms, tasteful décor, A/C, and TV. Prices vary according to season and view. (☎35 90 20; www.hotel-lecentral-coulon.com. Breakfast €8. Reception 8am-10pm. Closed Feb. Reservations recommended. Singles €48-59; doubles €55-69. AmEx/MC/V.) Located 3km south of Coulon, **Camping de La Garette (l'Ilôt du Chail) ❶,** is almost a small island—a tucked-away grove surrounded by three streams and accessible only by bridge. Lines of trees offer plenty of shade, while a pool, laundromat, and organized activities in July and August make this modest campground a true family affair. La Garette is just after Coulon on CASA bus #20. Get off at "La Garette-Centre des Loisirs." Continue walking in the direction of the bus, past the horse stables, until you reach the campsite. (☎35 00 33. Reception July-Aug. 8:30am-1pm and 2-8pm; June and mid-Sept. 9:30am-noon and 2:30-7:30pm; Apr.-May 10am-noon and 3-7pm. Open Apr. to mid-Sept. €3-3.50 per adult, €2-2.50 per child, €3-4 per site, €1.50 per car. Electricity €2.50. Bikes €4 per hr., €11 per day. Canoe rental available up the river. MC/V.) A hike through marshy forests starts next to the campsite and winds past the tall two-door houses (one for land, one for water) unique to the area. Three-star **Camping de la Venise Verte ❶**, 2km outside of town, is popular with caravans and long-term vacationers. Follow the river west from Coulon to reach the campground. Moderately sized sites are located on tired looking grass, with clean facilities, a private pool, and canoe and bike rental. (☎35 90 36; www.camping-laveniseverte.fr. Reception July-Aug. 8:30am-12:30pm and 2-8pm; Sept.-Oct. and Apr.-June 9:30am-12:30pm and 3-7pm. Open Apr.-Oct. and May to mid-Sept. 2 adults, tent, and electricity €22; mid-Sept. to Apr. €17-20. Extra adult €4-5.50. Car €3-4.50. 5- or 6-person bungalows €230-430 per week. Canoes €16 per 2hr. Bikes €9 per ½-day, €13 per day. MC/V.)

SIGHTS AND FESTIVALS. La Maison des Marais Mouillés, pl. de la Coutume, is worth a look for those who have mastered French. The *maraiscope*, an endearing presentation of the marshland's history, is the highlight of the museum, but it's only given in French. (☎35 81 04. Open daily July-Aug. 10am-7pm; Sept.-Oct. and Apr.-June 10am-noon and 2-6pm. €5.50, students €4.50, ages 6-16 €3. Guided tours for groups of 15 or more.) Every July, tourists flood the **Marché sur l'Eau,** the only market in France where customers row from one boat stand to the next to buy fresh produce. In the first week of July, for the **Fête du Miget,** citizens dress in authentic garb and lead a parade of traditional boats down the river. The **Rallye canoë-kayak** attracts 300 boats and 2000 spectators for a race down the Marais during the second-to-last weekend in June.

LES SABLES D'OLONNE ☎02 51

Les Sables d'Olonne (lay SAH-bluh duh-LOHN; pop. 15,5000) was once a port for the regional capital, Olonne (Celtic for "over waters"), but the city abandoned it when the harbor dried up. Les Sables ("the sands") is now a popular vacation spot for French teenagers and families alike. The favorable waters and weather make it a prime spot for watersports, fishing trips, and marshland hikes. An unusual mix of climates, this area combines Brittany's cold waters and the Riviera's sprawling sandy beaches—with perhaps a touch of tackiness.

TRANSPORTATION. The **train station** is on rue de la Bauduère. (Open M 5:20am-7:45pm, Tu-F 6:20am-7:45pm, Sa 8:40am-6:30pm, Su 10:30am-7:30pm.) Trains go to La Rochelle (2-3hr., 9 per day, €19) via La Roche-sur-Lyon, Nantes (1½hr., 12 per day, €16), and Paris (4hr., 6 per day, €64-78). The bus station is next door (office open M-F 8:30am-12:30pm and 2:30-6:30pm, Sa 9:30am-noon). Sovetours (☎95 18 71) sends **buses** to La Rochelle (3¼hr., 9am, €24) and Fromentine (2hr., 2-4 per day, €12). Compagnie Vendeenne, 11bis rue Bénatier, in La Chaume (☎08 25 13 90 85; www.compagnievendeenne.com), runs **ferries** to l'Ile d'Yeu (1½hr.; July-Aug. 2-5 departures weekly; round-trip €42, ages 4-18 €28, under 4 €6). **Local buses** run by TUSCO go to beaches. (☎32 95 95. Ask at the tourist office for a map and schedule. Buses run 7am-7:30pm. €1.20, *carnet* of 10 €8.50.) For **taxis,** call Radiotaxi Sablais (☎95 40 80, €1.30 per km). The **water taxi,** La Sablaise, crosses the small canal dividing Les Sables from La Chaume. (Leaves from quai Guiné. June-Aug. daily 6am-9pm; Oct.-Mar. daily 6am-8pm; Mar.-May and Sept. Sa-Su 6am-8pm. One-way €0.89.) **Car rental** can be found at Avis. (☎96 97 78. €69 per day. 21+. Under-25 surcharge €25. Open M-Sa 9am-noon and 2-6pm. AmEx/MC/V.) Holiday Bikes, 66 prom. Clemenceau, rents **bikes.** (☎32 64 15; www.holiday-bikes.com. Bikes €10-12 per day; scooters €39-43; motorbikes €105; €150/800/1600 deposit. Open June-Sept. daily 10am-8pm.)

PRACTICAL INFORMATION. To reach the tourist office, 1 promenade du Maréchal Joffre, from the train station, turn onto av. du Général de Gaulle going

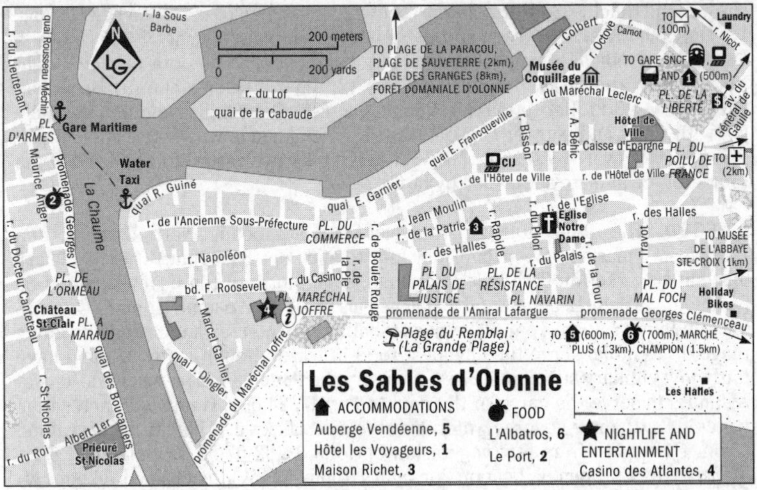

toward pl. de la Liberté, and continue straight through the park and past the fountain, onto rue de l'Hôtel de Ville. Take a left onto rue Travot and turn right when you reach the water. Walk along the beach to the casino, where the office is located (15min.). English-speaking staff provides free maps and itineraries. The office also books boat tours to Ile d'Yeu and other destinations; call the office for more information. (☎96 85 85; www.lessablesdolonne-tourisme.com. Open July-Aug. daily 9am-7pm; Sept.-June M-Th and Sa 9am-12:30pm and 1:30-6pm, F 10am-12:30pm and 1:30-6pm, Su 10:30am-noon and 3:30-5:30pm.) The **Centre d'Information Jeunesse (CIJ),** 34 rue de l'Hôtel de Ville, has services ranging from free Internet to apartment and cultural events listings. (☎33 76 29. Open M-Th 9am-noon and 2-6pm, F 9am-noon and 2-5pm.) Other services include: **laundry** at **Lavarie des Salines,** 5 rue Nicot (☎06 89 63 45 23; wash €4 per 7kg, €5.50 per 10kg; dry €0.50 per 15min., €1 less noon-3pm; open daily 7am-9pm) and **Castelnau,** 33 bd. de Castelnau (☎06 88 01 31 72; open daily 7am-9pm); **police** at 1 bd. Blaise Pascal (☎21 19 91); a hospital, 75 av. d'Aquitaine (☎21 85 85); and **Internet** access at **Mediafun 85,** 52 av. Général de Gaulle (☎96 86 30; €3 per hr.; open M 2:30-6:30pm, Tu-Sa 10am-noon and 2:30-6:30pm). The **post office,** 1 rue Haxo, **exchanges currency** and has a fax, photocopier, and **Western Union.** (☎21 82 82. Open M-F 8:30am-6pm, Sa 8:30am-noon.) **Postal Code:** 85100.

ACCOMMODATIONS. Lodgings in Les Sables are expensive, especially in the summer; most tourists camp outside of the city and commute to the beaches and shops during the day. **Hôtel les Voyageurs ❹,** 16 rue de la Bauduère, across from the train station and about 15min. from the beach, has bare rooms with tiny but clean bathrooms. The hotel is above a local *brasserie* with a magnificent wooden bar, which offers *menus* from €10-21. (☎95 11 49; http://voyageurshotel.free.fr. Breakfast €6.50. Reception July-Aug. daily 6:45am-9pm; Sept.-June M-F 6:45am-9pm. Ring bell if restaurant is closed. Closed last 2 weeks of Dec. Singles and doubles with shower and toilet €46-49; doubles with 2 beds €50-52; family room €26 per person. MC/V.) For a comparatively inexpensive hotel along the water, try the **Auberge Vendéenne ❸,** 36 rue Remparts, which offers simple, clean rooms that look onto an inner courtyard. (☎32 03 98; www.aubergevendenne.fr.st. Breakfast included. Reception 11am-2pm and 6-10pm. Singles €23-39; doubles €33-49, with shower and toilet €43-59; triples with shower and toilet €53-69. Extra bed €5. MC/V.) Only 50m from the beach and the town center, **Maison Richet ❹**, 25 rue de la Patrie, is a tropical escape, complete with palm trees, an outdoor terrace, bright blue rooms, and straw carpets. (☎32 04 12; www.maison-richet.fr. Breakfast €8.50. Free Wi-Fi. Reception 3:30-9pm. Open Feb.-Oct. Singles and doubles €45-55, with toilet and shower €55-65; triples €65-75; quads with toilet and shower €75-85. Prices vary by season. MC/V.) Les Sables's two **campsites** are listed at the tourist office and are accessible by bus.

FOOD. The 19th-century Art Nouveau **Les Halles,** behind Notre Dame de Bon Port, hosts a market. (Open daily mid-June to mid-Sept. 8am-1pm.) There's a **Champion** supermarket on 93 bd. de Castelnau, 500m north of the beach (open M-Sa 9am-8pm, Su 9am-12:30pm) and a **Marché Plus** on 87 av. Aristand Briand. (Open M-Sa 7am-9pm, Su 9am-1pm.) The near-identical *brasseries* and *crêperies* along plage du Remblai serve the cheapest food in town, though many of them have fairly low culinary standards. For a meal, try the **Porte de Pêche,** where dozens of restaurants serve the catch of the day. **Le Port ❷**, 24 quai Georges V, across the water in La Chaume near the water taxi stop, specializes in grilled fish and seafood (from €10) but offers few vegetarian options. (☎32 07 52. Appetizers €8-13. *Menus* €13-17. Open daily noon-2pm and 7-10pm. MC/V.) Beachside **L'Albatros ❸**, 8 pl. de Strasbourg, serves traditional seafood dishes, best enjoyed on the terrace. (☎32 03 80. *Plats* €7-15. *Menus* €16-32. Open daily 8am-3pm and 7-10pm. MC/V.)

SIGHTS AND ENTERTAINMENT. Les Sables boasts a few interesting sights hidden among the postcard racks and plastic beach toys, though they pale in comparison to the beach on a sunny day. The **Musée du Coquillage,** 8 rue du Maréchal Leclerc, near the Porte de Pêche, is one of a kind. Two hundred fifty glass cases display over 45,000 intricate, beautifully colored shells, corals, and crabs—even stuffed sharks—all personally collected by a local military soldier, who dropped out of the army to open the museum. Especially impressive are the yard-long Antiguan lobsters at the entrance, and the *crabe de cocotier*, whose long claws were once strong enough to tear apart coconuts. (☎23 50 00; museum-du-coquillage.com. Open May-Aug. daily 9am-8pm; Sept.-Apr. M-Sa 9:30am-12:30pm and 2-6:30pm, Su 2-6:30pm. €6, ages 4-11 €4.) The **Musée de l'Abbaye Ste-Croix,** rue de Verdun, occupies a wing of a restored 17th-century Benedictine abbey and presents an excellent collection of modern and contemporary art, as well as a smaller inventory of regional artifacts and folk crafts. Most notable are the works of writer/painter Victor Brauner and Gaston Chaissac's colorful paintings. Temporary exhibits showcase up-and-coming artists. (☎32 01 16; musee-lessables@wanadoo.fr. Open Tu-Su mid-June to Sept. 10am-noon and 2:30-6:30pm; Oct. to mid-June 2:30-5:30pm. €4.60, students and under 18 €2.30; 1st Su of month free.) **La Chaume,** the promontory across the channel from the center of town, has two monuments along its *quais:* the 15th-century **Château St-Clair,** where the **Tour d'Arundel,** the only lighthouse on the coast of the Vendée before the 18th century, is visible from a distance; and the restored **Prieuré St-Nicolas,** an 18th-century church and contemporary art gallery. Near the town center, the huge **Notre Dame de Bon Port,** pl. de l'Eglise, in front of Les Halles, features a rare blend of Gothic and Baroque styles. (Open M-Sa 9am-noon and 2:30-6:30pm, Su 9am-noon and 5:45-7:30pm. Mass Su 10:30am.) On Tuesdays and Thursdays during the summer, **Les Remblais,** the widest strip of the boardwalk, becomes a pedestrian walkway with organized concerts, outdoor theater, jugglers, clowns, and marionette shows (contact tourist office for more info). The nearby **Casino des Atlantes,** 3 bd. Franklin Roosevelt, is most notable for its neon lights and rattling slot machines. On most summer nights, the casino puts on free concerts or dance shows with dinner. (☎32 05 40. Open daily July-Aug. 10am-4am; Sept.-June 10am-3am. Restaurant open 7-10pm.)

BEACHES. **La Grande Plage,** otherwise known as Plage du Remblai, a beautiful 3km strip of sand on the outskirts of the *centre-ville*, is the largest and most crowded of Les Sables's shores, with souvenir shops and *crêperies* spilling out onto its banks. A popular surfing spot with great waves, **plage de Tanchet** is right beyond La Grande Plage, behind the Lac du Tanchet, when walking along the beach away from the tourist office; bus B also runs to Tanchet from the stop at Schwabac. For more solitude, take bus A to La Chaume's **plage de la Paracou** (*stop* at Le Large), known for its more dangerous, rocky waters. Following the coast north from Paracou, beachgoers will encounter two less crowded beaches with great surf and topless—and often bottomless—sunbathers. **Plage de Sauveterre,** nestling in a forest, is 4km north of Paracou, while **plage des Granges** is another kilometer farther. Adventurers may enjoy the **Forêt Domaniale d'Olonne** just east of here, where huge dunes span all the way from dry woodlands into the sea.

The tourist office distributes a free brochure in French with 10 hiking and biking trails, detailing jaunts that traverse its dunes, forests, and beaches. In July and August, the office also posts daily listings of local tennis tournaments, free concerts, and organized beach volleyball games, which welcome volunteers. Guided boat trips, canoeing, surfing, sailing, diving, and other watersports are also available. The closest hiking trail to Les Sables starts about 1km north of the train station. From the station, follow rue de la Bauduère until it intersects rue du Doctor Charcot; signs indicate the beginning of an 18km trail that winds through the Vendée countryside and its tiny villages to a beautiful church at Olonne-sur-Mer.

ILE D'YEU ☎02 51

Ile d'Yeu (eel DYUH; pop. 4800) has everything from dark pine tree forests to sandy beaches to mist-catching cliffs. Ferries unload French tourists who flood the island every summer; foreigners, however, rarely stumble upon Ile d'Yeu on their own. One out of a handful of islands splattered alongside France's Atlantic coast, Ile d'Yeu may not be the most popular or picturesque, but its rocky points, tucked-away beaches and rambling bike paths make it a paradise in its own right.

TRANSPORTATION AND PRACTICAL INFORMATION. Direct ferries run from Les Sables to Ile d'Yeu, but seaside village Fromentine is the easiest base from which to reach the island by **ferry.** Head to the Gare Maritime for Vedettes Inter-Iles Vendéenes (☎39 00 00; www.ile-yeu.com. 2-4 per day. Round-trip €25-30, students €28-32. Open M-Sa 9am-noon and 2-6pm, Su 9am-noon. MC/V.) Also at the Gare Maritime, find Yeu Continent Compagnie (☎08 25 85 30 00; www.compagnie-yeu-continent.fr. Office open M-F 9:30am-noon and 2-5pm, Sa 9:30-11:30am. Ferries 1hr.; 2-4 per day. Round-trip €31, seniors €25, ages 12-18 €21. MC/V.) **Taxis** on the island are available through Taxi Joinville (☎06 07 68 53 96), and public **buses** run to most destinations on the island. (☎37 13 93. Schedules vary by time. €1. Open M-F 8am-12:30pm and 1:30-6:30pm, Sa 9am-12:15pm.) Rent **cars** at Cantin, 1 quai de la Mairie, which stores bags and provides a map of suggested routes. (☎58 48 00. From €65 per day. 21+. Open June-Aug. daily 8:30am-7pm. MC/V.) **Biking** is the most efficient means by which to explore the numerous paths, and over a half-dozen bike rental shops pepper the docks near the Gare Maritime. La Roue Libre, 4 rue Calypso, rents **bikes** in many different sizes, as well as scooters. (☎59 20 70. Bikes €9 per day; mountain bikes €12. Open July-Aug. daily 8:30am-7:30pm; Apr.-June daily 9am-12:30pm and 2-7pm; Sept.-Mar. open for school holidays only. MC/V.) La Trottinette, next to the docks on rue de la Chaume, also rents bikes. (☎58 31 06. Bikes €8.50 per day. Scooter €39; €400 deposit; over 16 only. Open Apr.-Sept. daily 9am-7pm. MC/V.)

The **tourist office,** rue du Marché, distributes biking and hiking itineraries with directions to sights, as well as descriptions of them in English and French. The staff also provides information on hotel availability and transportation on and from the island. From the dock, turn right along the waterfront, left onto rue de l'Abbesse, and right onto rue de la République. (☎58 32 58; www.ile-yeu.fr. Open July-Aug. M-Sa 9am-7pm, Su 9:30am-1pm; Apr.-June and Sept. M-Sa 9am-12:30pm and 2-6pm, Su 9:30am-12:30pm; Oct.-Mar. M-Sa 9am-12:30pm and 2-5:30pm.) Police can be reached at ☎58 30 05, and the **hospital** is on Impasse du Puits Raimond (☎26 08 00). **Laundry** can be found at La Tornade Bleue, pl. Ketanou, near Hôtel L'Escale (wash €5 per 6kg.; dry €2 per 15min.; detergent €0.40; open daily 8am-8pm). **Internet** access is available on the right side of the port at **Oyanet Informatique,** 11 rue des Quais. (☎06 15 37 05 16; www.oyanet.com. €1 per 15min. Open M-Sa 10am-1pm and 2:30-7pm, Su 10am-1pm.)

ACCOMMODATIONS AND FOOD. Though accommodations on Ile d'Yeu are expensive, one is worth the price. The charming two-star **Hôtel L'Escale ❹,** 14 rue de la Croix du Port, is a 5min. walk from the quai at Port Joinville on a quiet street. Brand-new, renovated rooms—complete with flat-screen TVs—look out on a grassy courtyard filled with roses and folding chairs. Breakfast is served in a spacious, modern dining area with casual maritime décor. (☎58 50 28; www.yeu-escale.fr. Breakfast €7.30. Reception 7:30am-1pm and 5-8:30pm. Closed in Nov. Singles and doubles with bath, telephone, hair dryer, and TV €50-70; triples and quads €66-82. Prices vary by season. Extra bed €7.30. MC/V.) For a place to stay before the ferry leaves Fromentine, try the **Relais des Iles ❸,** 18 av. de l'Estacade, which offers unconsciously rustic rooms located behind the town bar. (☎68 52 11. Breakfast €5. Reception 8am-9pm. Singles with sink €30, with shower and toilet €45; doubles €40/50. Extra bed for children only €5. MC/V.) The island's crowded but jovial **Camping Municipal ❶,** 2km east of the port, is enclosed by a calm expanse of beach on one side and tennis courts on the other. (☎58 34 20. Reception M-Sa 9am-12:30pm and 2:30-7:30pm. €3.10-4.20 per tent, €6.40 per caravan, €2.50-3.10 per extra person, €3.50 per car. Electricity €2.) There are seven campsites in Fromentine; its tourist office, pl. de la Gare, has a list (☎68 51 83). Full of shady sites, the **Campeole de la Grande Côte ❶,** on the rte. de la Grande Côte, 1km from Fromentine and the beach, has a pool, bike and grill rental, laundry, a small restaurant, and a full calendar of activities. This popular campground gets crowded in the summer, so reserve early. (☎68 51 89; www.campeole.fr. Open May to mid-Sept. 2 people with car €13-20, €4.50-6.10 per extra person. Electricity €3.90. Reception M-Th 9am-noon and 1:30-5pm, F 9am-noon and 1:30-6pm, Sa-Su 10am-noon and 3-6pm.) Eating out on Ile d'Yeu is a rather expensive affair due to the touristy nature of the island, but fresh food is available from the outdoor market on **place de la Norvege,** by the docks. (Open daily 9am-1pm.) The **Casino** supermarket, 31 rue Calypso, is 2min. from the port past La Roue Libre. (Open July-Aug. M-F 9am-12:30pm and 3:30-7:30pm, Sa 9am-7:30pm, Su 9am-1pm; Sept.-June M-F 9am-12:30pm and 3:30-7:30pm, Sa 9am-7:30pm.)

OUTDOOR ACTIVITIES. Ile d'Yeu's tourist office skillfully lays out three easy **bike circuits** of the island, all originating from Port Joinville. The shortest, a 10km path, runs to the island's southern port and back in 2½hr. Its highlights are **Port Meule** and **Pointe du Châtelet,** a seascape vista crowned with a towering cross overlooking the withering ruins of the 14th-century **Vieux-Château.** The château, which was frequently attacked by the English, was used as a fortress in the 16th century until it was ultimately abandoned by Louis XIV, who demanded that it be demolished. This may have been the only one of his orders that wasn't carried out; the crumbling remains stand stubbornly on the craggy coast, accessible only by bike path. (Tours in French daily July-Aug. 11am-6pm; May to mid-June W-Th and Sa-Su noon-5:30pm; late June Tu-Su noon-5pm. €4, ages 7-18 €1.) Just past the Port Meule, a quiet harbor moored with bright blue-bottomed boats, rests the **Pierre Tremblante,** a sizable boulder that wavers if rubbed the right way. The longest route (5½hr.) circles the island, passing Renaissance churches, serene ports, and **plage des Conches.** One of the most popular bike routes (4½hr.) travels into the center of the island, stopping 2km southeast of Port Joinville at the 12th-century church in **St-Sauveur,** where stained-glass windows illuminate a cool, dark interior. Along this route lies the sparkling **plage des Sapins,** popular with windsurfers, where a pine tree forest peters out into soft sand. The route then curves around to the south coast, where cliffs rise in all directions. **Plage Anse des Soux,** nestled between looming cliffs, is the perfect place for a siesta or reclusive afternoon. The path then leads back to Joinville, but bikers can also continue past the town to the **Grand Phare,** a 20m-tall lighthouse on the island's highest hill, to get a view of the island from above. All coastal paths are reserved for pedestrians, while signs throughout the island direct bikers. As locals often say: "You never get lost on Ile d'Yeu; you just happen to meander."

AQUITAINE AND PAYS BASQUE

At the geographical edge of both France and Spain, Aquitaine and the Pays Basque are diverse in landscape and culture. The English held Aquitaine from the 12th to 15th centuries, and the Pays Basque was part of Basse-Navarre until its ruler, Henri IV, inherited the French throne in 1598. Today, a small Basque separatist minority still maintains that its homeland is independent of French and Spanish authority.

In Aquitaine, sprawling vineyards abound, especially near Bordeaux, while the pine forest of Les Landes opens to the windswept west coast, known for stunning beaches, wild waves, and great surfing. In Pays Basque, closer to the Spanish border, the clinking of cowbells mixes with the scent of seafood. An hour or two to the east, villages sit among the towering peaks, lush foliage, and roaring waterfalls of the Pyrénées. When locals aren't out enjoying the beach or mountain trails, they're relishing the regional cuisine. The Pays Basque cooks up some of France's best seafood, along with *jambon cru* (cured ham) and the ubiquitous *piperade* (omelette with green peppers, onions, and tomatoes). In Aquitaine, *Moulard* duck, *Roquefort* cheese, and *Armagnac*, a local brandy, are essentials. Aquitaine flavors its cuisine with the elusive *truffe noir* (black truffle), but its glory is its wine. The vineyards of Bordeaux produce some of the best vintages in the world.

HIGHLIGHTS OF AQUITAINE AND PAYS BASQUE

HANG GLIDE on Europe's tallest sand dune, the **Dune du Pilat** (p. 578).

HIT THE TRAILS and cross the border while you're at it. Starting from Cauterets, hike into Spain past towering waterfalls in the **Parc National des Pyrénées** (p. 602).

BE MERRY at the wineries of **St-Emilion** (p. 575), an idyllic village where grapes have been crushed since Roman times.

AQUITAINE

BORDEAUX ☎05

Though its name is synonymous with wine, the city of Bordeaux (bohr-DOH; pop. 235,000) has many highlights besides the rich and intoxicating drink. Punks and tourists—and everyone in between—gather on the elegant streets of the shop- and café-filled city center, while in the surrounding countryside, the legendary vineyards of St-Emilion, Médoc, Sauternes, and Graves draw international renown. Filled with history, drenched in culture, and animated with student nightlife, Bordeaux has more to offer than most tourists would expect.

TRANSPORTATION

Flights: Airport in **Mérignac** (☎56 34 50 50), 11km west of Bordeaux. A shuttle connects the airport to the Bordeaux St-Jean train station and pl. Gambetta (40min.; every

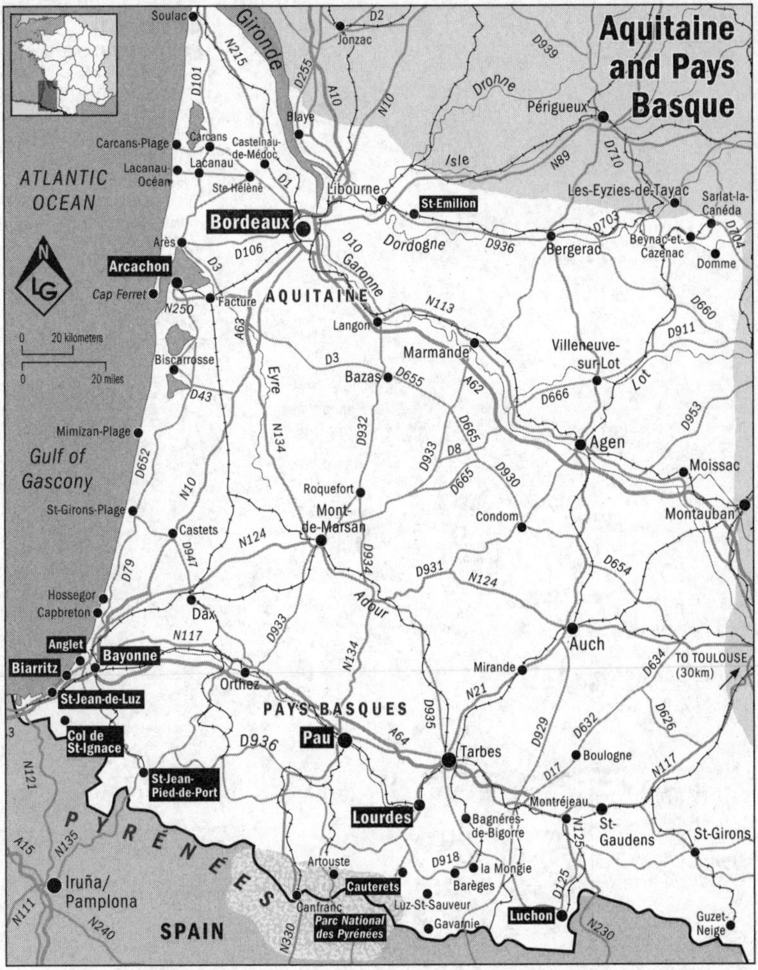

45min. 6:45am-9:45pm; €7, students, seniors, and under 26 €6). **Air France** office in Bordeaux, 37 allée de Tourny (☎08 20 82 08 20), makes reservations and provides schedules. Open M-F 9:30am-6:30pm, Sa 9:30am-1:15pm. AmEx/MC/V.

Trains: Gare St-Jean, rue Charles Domercq. Info office open M-Sa 9am-7pm. To: **Lyon** (8-10hr., 7 per day, €62-154); **Marseille** (6-7hr., 10 per day, €71-75); **Nantes** (4hr., 4 per day, €42); **Nice** (9-12hr., 2 per day, €103-110); **Paris** (3hr., 15-25 per day, €46-66); **Poitiers** (2-3hr., 10 per day, €36-39); **Rennes** (6hr., 2 per day, €54); **Toulouse** (2-3hr., 11 per day, €31-34).

Buses: Réseau Trans Gironde, pl. de Quinconces (☎56 43 68 43). Open daily 7am-7pm. Buses travel to over 50 small towns surrounding Bordeaux.

Public Transportation: The **TBC/Connex bus** and **tram** system (☎57 57 88 88; www.infotbc.com) serves the city and suburbs. Maps at the train station. Info offices at

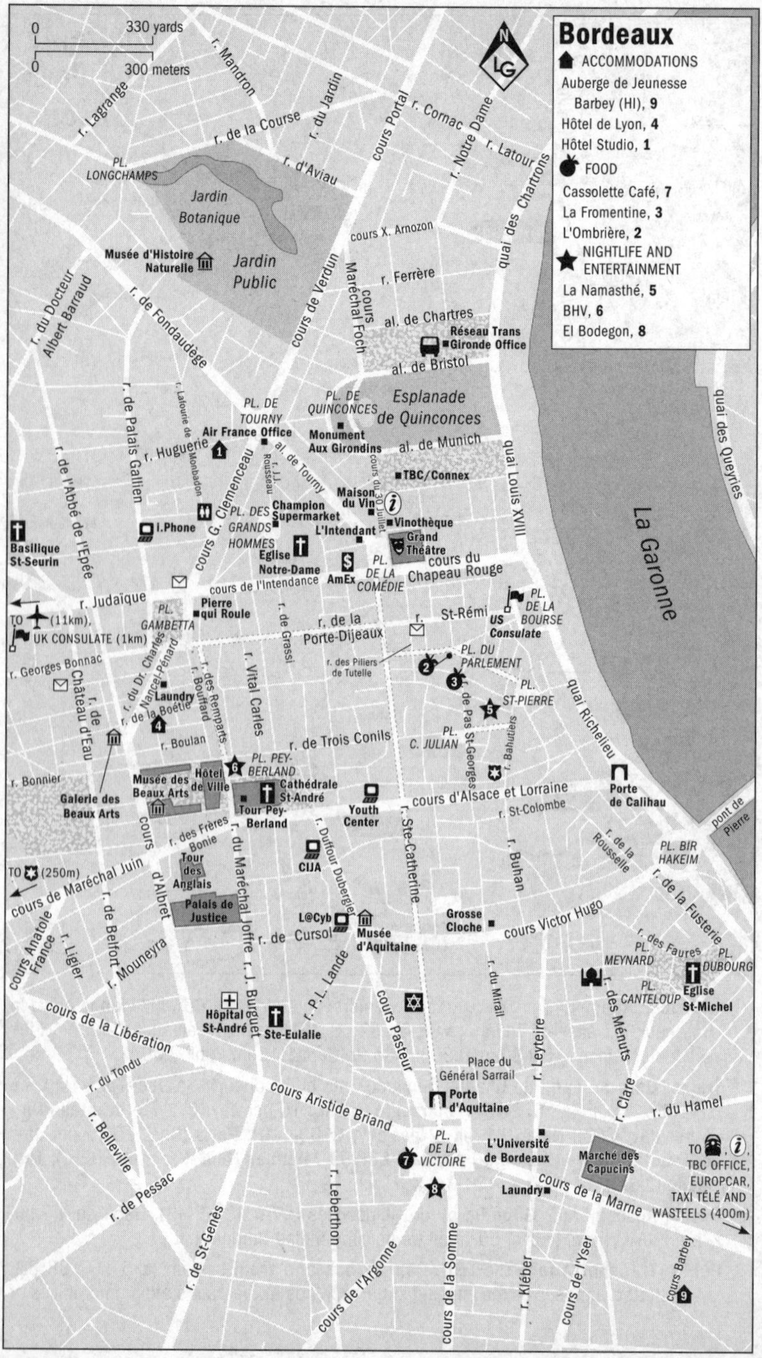
Bordeaux
ACCOMMODATIONS
Auberge de Jeunesse Barbey (HI), 9
Hôtel de Lyon, 4
Hôtel Studio, 1
FOOD
Cassolette Café, 7
La Fromentine, 3
L'Ombrière, 2
NIGHTLIFE AND ENTERTAINMENT
La Namasthé, 5
BHV, 6
El Bodegon, 8
0 330 yards
0 300 meters
N
LG
r. Lagrange
r. Mandron
r. de la Course
r. du Jardin
cours Portal
r. Cornac
r. Notre Dame
r. Latour
quai des Chartrons
PL. LONGCHAMPS
r. d'Aviau
Jardin Botanique
Jardin Public
Musée d'Histoire Naturelle
cours X. Arnozon
cours de Verdun
cours Maréchal Foch
r. Ferrère
al. de Chartres
Réseau Trans Gironde Office
al. de Bristol
r. du Docteur Albert Barraud
r. de Fondaudège
r. Lafaurie de Monbadon
r. de Palais Gallien
PL. DE TOURNY
PL. DE QUINCONCES
Esplanade de Quinconces
Monument Aux Girondins
al. de Munich
Air France Office
r. Huguerie
al. de Tourny
r. J.J. Rousseau
cours du 30 Juillet
TBC/Connex
quai Louis XVIII
quai des Queyries
La Garonne
r. de l'Abbé de l'Epée
cours G. Clemenceau
Maison du Vin
Champion Supermarket
PL. DES GRANDS HOMMES
Vinothèque
L'Intendant
Grand Théatre
i.Phone
Basilique St-Seurin
Eglise Notre-Dame
AmEx
PL. DE LA COMÉDIE
cours du Chapeau Rouge
cours de l'Intendance
r. Judaïque
TO (11km), UK CONSULATE (1km)
PL. GAMBETTA
Pierre qui Roule
r. de Grassi
r. de la Porte-Dijeaux
r. St-Rémi
PL. DE LA BOURSE
US Consulate
r. des Piliers de Tutelle
PL. DU PARLEMENT
r. Georges Bonnac
r. du Dr. Charles Nancel-Pénard
r. des Remparts
r. Bouffard
r. Vital Carles
r. de Château d'Eau
Laundry
r. de la Boétie
PL. ST-PIERRE
r. de Pas St-Georges
quai Richelieu
r. Boulan
r. de Trois Conils
PL. C. JULIAN
r. Bahutiers
PL. PEY-BERLAND
r. Bonnier
Musée des Beaux Arts
Hôtel de Ville
Cathédrale St-André
Galerie des Beaux Arts
Tour Pey-Berland
Youth Center
cours d'Alsace et Lorraine
Porte de Calihau
r. St-Colombe
pont de Pierre
PL. BIR HAKEIM
r. de la Rousselle
cours d'Albert
r. des Frères Bonie
r. du Maréchal Joffre
r. Duffour Dubergier
CIJA
r. Ste-Catherine
r. Buhan
TO (250m)
cours de Maréchal Juin
Tour des Anglais
Palais de Justice
r. de la Fusterie
cours Anatole France
r. de Belfort
r. Ligier
L@Cyb
r. de Cursol
Musée d'Aquitaine
Grosse Cloche
cours Victor Hugo
r. des Faures
PL. MEYNARD
PL. DUBOURG
r. Mouneyra
r. J. Burguet
r. P.L. Lande
r. du Mirail
PL. CANTELOUP
Eglise St-Michel
r. des Ménuts
cours de la Libération
Hôpital St-André
Ste-Eulalie
cours Pasteur
r. Leyteire
r. du Tondu
Place du Général Sarrail
Porte d'Aquitaine
r. Clare
r. du Hamel
cours Aristide Briand
r. Belleville
PL. DE LA VICTOIRE
L'Université de Bordeaux
Marché des Capucins
TO , , TBC OFFICE, EUROPCAR, TAXI TÉLÉ AND WASTEELS (400m)
r. de Pessac
r. Leberthon
Laundry
cours de la Marne
r. de St-Genès
cours de l'Argonne
cours de la Somme
r. Kléber
cours de l'Yser
cours Barbey

9 pl. Gambetta (open M-F 8am-7:30pm, Sa 9:45am-12:25pm and 2-6pm), at pl. de Quinconces (open M-F 7am-7:30pm, Sa 9:45am-12:25pm and 2-6pm), and at Gare St-Jean (open M-F 7am-7:30pm, Sa-Su 8:30am-3pm). 3 new **tram** lines A, B, and C run daily 5:30am-12:30am. The *Tickarte Bordeaux Découverte* provides unlimited city bus and tram use (1-day pass €4.10, 2-day €7.10, 3-day €9.20). Individual tickets €1.30.

Taxis: Taxi Télé (☎56 96 00 34), in front of the train station. €1.30 per km during the day, €1.96 after 7pm. €30-45 to the airport.

Car Rental: Europcar, cours des Arrivées (☎08 25 00 42 46), connected to the train station. From €118 per day, €282 per week; €650 deposit. 21+. Open M-F 7am-10pm, Sa 8am-7pm, Su 10am-7:30pm. AmEx/MC/V.

Bike Rental: Pierre Qui Roule, 32 pl. Gambetta (☎57 85 80 87; www.pierrequiroule.fr). Open M 2-7pm, Tu-Sa 10am-7pm. €7 per ½-day, €10 per day, €20 per weekend, €45 per week. Roller blades and pads €6 per ½-day, €9 per day. MC/V.

ORIENTATION AND PRACTICAL INFORMATION

Bordeaux's transportation hubs, **place Gambetta** and **place des Quinconces,** are in the *centre-ville,* while the bus depot is directly in front of Gare St-Jean. Tramway line C runs from the train station to pl. des Quinconces (10min.). To get to pl. Gambetta from the station, take line C to pl. de la Bourse and walk down rue St-Rémi, which becomes rue de la Porte Dijeaux. Bus #16 runs from the bus station to pl. de la Victoire and pl. Gambetta (every 10min. 5am-9pm, €1.30). To get to the *centre-ville* on foot, walk down the run-down but lively **cours de la Marne,** past Marché des Capucins and onto **place de la Victoire.** From here, turn right under the arch on the pedestrian rue Ste-Catherine, which continues into **vieux Bordeaux,** the hub of the city. To reach the tourist office, continue on rue Ste-Catherine for 15min., cross the wide cours de l'Intendance, and enter pl. de la Comédie as the street becomes cours du 30 Juillet. The tourist office is on the right, a block beyond the Grand Théâtre.

> **!** Bordeaux can be dangerous; there are many poorly lit, empty streets at night. Be aware of your surroundings and use caution, especially in the neighborhoods to the south of the city center, by the hostel, and around the train station.

Tourist Office: 12 cours du 30 Juillet (☎56 00 66 00; www.bordeaux-tourisme.com). Distributes free maps and brochures and makes hotel reservations for free. Open July-Aug. M-Sa 9am-7:30pm, Su 9:30am-6:30pm; May-June and Sept.-Oct. M-Sa 9am-7pm, Su 9:30am-6:30pm; Nov.-Apr. M-Sa 9am-6:30pm, Su 9:45am-4:30pm. Branch at train station (☎56 91 64 70) also makes hotel reservations. Open May-Oct. M-Sa 9am-noon and 1-6pm; Nov.-Apr. M-F 9:30am-12:30pm and 2-6pm.

Tours: Tourist office offers tours in English and French (☎56 00 66 24). **Walking** tours daily July-Sept. 10am and 3pm; Oct.-June 10am. €7.50, students and ages 12-18 €6.50, under 12 free. 2hr. **bus** tour W and Sa. Visit the tourist office for seasonal schedules. Also arranges bus tours to vineyards. Apr. to mid-Nov. daily 1:30pm; mid-Nov. to Mar. W and Sa 1:30pm. €29, students and seniors €25. Each day features a different vineyard; call in advance. AmEx/MC/V.

Budget Travel: Voyage Wasteels, 13 pl. de Casablanca (☎56 31 11 74), across from the train station. Open M-F 9am-1pm and 2-6pm, Sa 9:30am-12:30pm. MC/V.

Consulates: US, 10 pl. de la Bourse and 65 cours Alsace Lorraine (☎56 48 63 80; fax 56 51 61 97). Open only by appointment. **UK,** 353 bd. du Président Wilson (☎57 22 21 10; fax 56 08 33 12). Open M-F 9:30am-noon and 2-4:30pm. To reach other foreign consulates, contact the tourist office.

American Express: 11 cours de l'Intendance (☎00 63 33). Open M-F 9:30am-6pm. **Currency exchange.** For 24hr. refund assistance and lost traveler's checks or credit cards, call ☎01 47 77 72 00 or 08 00 90 86 00. ID required for all transactions.

Youth Center: Centre d'Information Jeunesse d'Aquitaine (CIJA), 5 rue Duffour Dubergier (☎56 56 00 56). Information about activities, jobs, long-term accommodation, and GLBT resources. Branch ½ block away, 125 cours d'Alsace Lorraine (☎56 56 00 56). Sells train tickets and provides free limited Internet access. Both open July-Aug. M-F 9:30am-5pm; Sept.-June M-Th 9:30am-6pm, F 9:30am-5pm.

Laundromat: 26 rue Docteur Charles Nancel-Penard. Wash €3.80, dry €0.50 per 6min. Open daily 7:30am-9:30pm. 10 rue Lafaure de Monbadon. Wash €3.80-7, dry €1.10. Open daily 7am-9pm. Rue Dupass St-Georges. Wash €3.50-7, dry €0.50 for 6min. Open daily 7am-9pm.

Police: 23 rue François de Sourdis (☎57 85 77 77).

Hospital: Hôpital St-André, 1 rue Jean Burguet (☎56 79 56 79).

Internet Access: Free at **CIJA** (see **Youth Center,** above), and free up to 15min. at CIJA branch on av. Alsace Lorraine. **L@Cyb,** 23 cours Pasteur (☎56 01 15 15), across from the Musée d'Aquitaine. €0.75 per 15min., €2 per hr. Open M-Sa 9:30am-2am, Su 2pm-2am. **i.Phone,** 24 rue Duplais Gallien (☎57 85 82 62), 3 blocks from pl. Gambetta. €0.50 per 15min. Open daily 10am-midnight.

Post Office: 52 rue Georges Bonnac (☎57 78 85 25), off pl. Gambetta. Open M-F 8:30am-6:30pm, Sa 8:30am-noon. Branch (☎57 14 32 00) with **currency exchange** at the corner of rue St-Rémi and rue des Piliers-de-Tutelle. Open M 2-6pm, Tu-F 10am-6pm, Sa 10am-12:30pm. **Postal Code:** 33000.

ACCOMMODATIONS

Bordeaux's main youth hostel is close to the train station, but that means it's in a run-down neighborhood where you won't want to be alone after dark. Great deals slightly farther from the station can be found in the *centre-ville,* on the streets around pl. Gambetta and cours d'Albret. Reserve a few days ahead in summer.

Hôtel Studio, 26 rue Huguerie (☎56 48 00 14; www.hotel-bordeaux.com). Walk 1 block down cours G. Clemenceau from pl. Gambetta, turn left on rue Lafaurie de Montbadon, and left again on rue Huguerie. A backpacker favorite. Tiny, relatively clean rooms have telephone, bath, and cable TV at the lowest prices in the city, and the friendly staff makes this hotel feel like home. Breakfast €5. Reception 7am-11pm. Reservations recommended. Singles €19-29; doubles €25-35. AmEx/MC/V. ❷

Auberge de Jeunesse Barbey (HI), 22 cours Barbey (☎56 33 00 70; fax 56 33 00 71). 4 blocks from Gare St-Jean, the popular hostel is in the run-down red-light district; travelers, especially those alone, should exercise caution at night. Shiny metal and bright colors characterize modern rooms where all furniture is securely nailed to the floor. Almost all rooms with shower, some with toilet. Also offers TV room, well-equipped kitchen, and foosball table. Breakfast included. Free Internet access. 3-day max. stay. Lockout 10am-4pm. Curfew 2am. 2- to 6-person dorm rooms €21. MC/V. ❷

Hôtel de Lyon, 31 rue des Remparts (☎56 81 34 38). Small, recently renovated rooms with bath, cable TV, and telephone. Reception 7am-11pm. Singles €27-32; doubles €32-39; triples €45-52; quads and quints €52-70. AmEx/MC/V. ❷

FOOD

Bordeaux boasts a range of local specialties. Try oysters straight from the Atlantic, *foie gras* from Les Landes, and beef braised in St-Emilion wine—all of which can be found on gourmet *menus.* Many restaurants cluster around **rue St-Rémi** and **place St-Pierre,** while small budget-friendly options line the narrow streets between

place du Parlement and **place C. Julian,** to the east of rue Ste-Catherine. *Bordelais* don't usually eat before 9pm in the summer; restaurants typically serve food until 11pm or midnight. Sample local fish, cheese, and produce at the **Marché des Capucins** (Tu-Su 6am-1pm), off cours de la Marne, and *bio* (organic) produce on **quai des Chartrons** (Th 5am-4pm), at **place Lucien Victor Meunier** (F 6:30am-1pm), and at **Caudéran place St-Armand** (Sa 6am-2pm). For pre-packaged goods, try **Marché Plus,** 268 rue Ste-Catherine (open M-Sa 7am-9pm, Su 9am-noon), or **Champion,** in the Marché des Grands Hommes (open M-Sa 9am-9pm).

L'Ombrière, 14 pl. du Parlement (☎56 44 82 86). This busy restaurant in the elegant district of town serves perfectly prepared French cuisine alongside a bubbling fountain. For lunch, try one of the meal-sized salads with baked goat cheese (€10) or *foie gras* on toast (€13). *Menus* €15-20. Open daily noon-2pm and 7-11pm. MC/V. ❷

La Fromentine, 4 rue du Pas St-Georges (☎56 79 24 10), near pl. du Parlement . Anything but your average *crêperie.* Two pots of fresh flowers herald the entrance to this bovine shrine, where the walls are covered with cows and the food is covered with cheese. Wide variety of salads €2.70-9.80. *Galettes* €5.80-7.80. *Menu* €10-15. Open M-F noon-2pm and 7-10pm, Sa 7-10pm. MC/V. ❷

Cassolette Café, 20 pl. de la Victoire (☎56 92 94 96; www.cassolettecafe.com). Bustling kitchen serves an array of local recipes in *cassolettes,* heavy clay skillets. Order a la carte or from a mix-and-match *menu* (€13). Open daily noon-midnight. MC/V. ❷

SIGHTS AND TASTES

Bordeaux is short on blockbuster sights but not on fun, quirky ways to pass the hours between glasses of wine. Admission to all Bordeaux museums is free the first Sunday of every month.

WINE TASTING. Those in town for only a day or two but desperate for the full wine experience should head to the **Maison du Vin/CIVB,** 3 cours du 30 Juillet, an immense building that houses industry offices and an extensive wine bar staffed by professionals who guide tastings. The 2hr. "Introduction to Bordeaux wines" course, available in English as well as French, teaches the art of oenophilia (the love of wines) through a comparative tasting of two reds and two whites. Tickets can be purchased across the street at the tourist office. (☎56 00 22 88; www.ecole.vins-bordeaux.fr/francais. Open M-F 9am-5:30pm. Wine-tasting course June-Sept. M-W and F-Sa 10am and 3pm. €22.) **L'Intendant,** a more intimate wine shop across the street at 2 allée de Tourny, offers an impressive selection of regional wines and is run by knowledgeable and helpful staff. (☎56 48 01 29. Open daily 10am-7:30pm. AmEx/MC/V.) Connoisseurs then venture across the square to buy their high-end bottles and crystal pitchers—not to mention obscure gadgets—at classy **Vinothèque,** 8 cours du 30 Juillet, a store specializing in all things *vin.* (☎52 32 05; www.la-vinotheque.com. Open M-Sa 10am-7:30pm. MC/V.)

CATHÉDRALE ST-ANDRÉ. Sculpted angels and apostles adorn the cathedral's facade, while large Gothic windows allow natural light to illuminate the interior. St-André has been home to a number of important royal weddings (a.k.a. alliances): that of Eleanor of Aquitaine and the future Louis VII in 1137, and that of Louis XIII and Princess Anne of Austria in 1615—whereupon Louis walked through the "royal portal" on the north side of the church, an entrance that has allegedly not been used since. *(Pl. Pey-Berland. ☎56 52 68 10. Open M 2-7pm, Tu-F 7:30am-6pm, Sa 9am-7pm, Su 9am-6pm.)* For a great view of the city, climb the 229 steps of the **Tour Pey-Berland,** which rises 66m into the sky and is topped with a golden statue of the Virgin Mary. For fear that the vibrations of the bells would make the cathedral collapse, masons built the tower 15m from the cathedral. *(☎56*

81 26 25. Open June-Sept. daily 10am-1:15pm and 2-6pm; Oct.-May Tu-Su 10am-12:30pm and 2-5:30pm. Last entry 30min. before closing. €5, seniors and ages 18-25 €3.50, under 18 free.)

MUSÉE DES BEAUX ARTS. Originally used as stables for the palace that is now the Hôtel de Ville, Bordeaux's art museum owns many great works by painters like Caravaggio, Matisse, Picasso, Renoir, Seurat, and Titian. However, the pieces have not been available to the public for years; the grandeur of the Hôtel's architecture is the highlight of the museum. The permanent collection is in the two buildings that frame the Hôtel de Ville, while the temporary exhibits are across the street in the **Galeries des Beaux Arts.** *(20 cours d'Albret, near the cathedral. ☎56 10 20 56. Open M and W-Su 11am-6pm. Permanent gallery free. Tickets for temporary exhibits €5, students €2.50.)*

EGLISE ST-MICHEL. Though the actual church is more often than not closed to the public, Bordeaux's best cityscape can be experienced from atop the St-Michel's 114m bell tower. At ground level, you're likely to see even more of the world: a lively flea market selling everything from African specialties to Syrian hookahs sprawls at the base of the tower (open daily 9am-1pm). Note that this area, like that of the train station, should not be frequented at night when alone. *(Tower open June-Sept. M and Sa-Su 2-7pm, Tu-F 10:30am-1pm. €2.50, under 12 free.)*

GRAND THÉÂTRE. The austere facade of this 18th-century opera house conceals a breathtakingly intricate Neoclassical interior. To see it, attend an opera, concert, ballet, or play, or take a daytime tour in English. *(Pl. de la Comédie. ☎56 00 85 95; www.opera-bordeaux.com. No shows in summer. Open M-Sa 11am-6pm. 1hr. tours organized through tourist office; frequency depends on theater's production schedule. Opera tickets €8-80, under 25 50% discount, over 65 10% discount. Student tickets 48hr. before any show €8.)*

NIGHTLIFE

With a student population of 70,000, Bordeaux abounds with bars and nightclubs. Ask for *Clubs and Concerts*, a free brochure at the tourist office. **Place de la Victoire** and **place Gambetta,** as well as most of the streets between **place des Quinconces** and **place C. Julian,** are mobbed during the school year and continue to serve as entertainment hot spots during the summer. Travelers should exercise caution when walking around the city at night.

El Bodegon, 14 pl. de la Victoire (☎56 94 74 02). Dominates nightlife in this popular *place.* DJ plays the latest club hits and plasma screens air the latest soccer match. Dances the line between bar and club. Teems with students and young backpackers. Also serves food noon-3pm. Beer €2.80. On W nights, crowds come for karaoke at 10:30pm. Theme nights such as foam parties every weekend. Happy hour 6-8pm. Open M-Sa 7am-2am, Su 2pm-2am. MC/V.

BHV (Bar de l'Hôtel de Ville), 4 rue de l'Hôtel de Ville (☎56 44 05 08). Flashing lights spin off mirrors in this small but fashionable and friendly gay bar. Welcomes both men and women, and fills up most nights. Beer €3.50. Mixed drinks €6. Sa theme nights July-Aug. Drag shows Sept.-June Su 10pm. Open daily 6pm-2am. MC/V.

Le Namasthé, 8 rue de la Devise (☎56 81 08 68). Gauze curtains, soft cushions, and a wide variety of exotic, non-alcoholic drinks greet guests in this teahouse. Tall *chichas* (a Spanish alcoholic drink; for 2-4 people €9) available in a dozen flavors to complete the relaxing experience. Reservations recommended for groups over 4. *Lassi* €5. Beer €5. Open in summer M-F 7pm-1:30am, Sa-Su 4pm-1:30am. Closed M in winter. MC/V.

DAYTRIPS FROM BORDEAUX: WINERIES AND VINEYARDS

Bordeaux's world-famous wines have been in relatively high demand since the Romans first conquered the area. However, the marriage of Eleanor of Aquitaine and England's King Henry II in 1152 changed the region's fate considerably. The Plantagenet king refused to be deprived of his *claret* (as the British call red Bordeaux wine), and thus bestowed special shipping rights on Bordeaux, opening it up to the seemingly unquenchable British market. At first the *Bordelais* simply shipped wines produced farther up the Garonne River, but the money flowing in sparked a local planting mania. Soon Bordeaux moved to ensure its monopoly over the market by refusing to ship wines produced elsewhere. Today, the region produces almost 800 million bottles per year.

TIP **MESSAGE ABOUT A BOTTLE.** Approximately 10,000 *châteaux*—the term used in Bordeaux for all wine establishments—dot the countryside of the Bordeaux region. This area is easiest to explore by car, as the vineyards spread over 120,000 hectares and most *châteaux* are only accessible by difficult-to-navigate local roads. Pick up a map of vineyard locations at the tourist office in Bordeaux, which also gives tours of the more popular *châteaux* in both English and French. (Tours Apr. to mid-Nov. daily 1:30pm; mid-Nov. to Mar. W and Sa 1:30pm. St-Emilion W and Su, Médoc Th and Sa, Graves and Sauternes F.) Some *châteaux* owners offer private tours to wine connoisseurs, but it's important to call ahead or ask the tourist office to call for you. Tours and tastings are often free, but at the end of the visit you're expected to buy a bottle or two.

ST-EMILION

Trains go to St-Emilion from Bordeaux (40min., 2 per day, €7.70). Watch carefully: St-Emilion is the 2nd stop, and the tiny station is poorly marked. The train schedule varies on the weekend; trains run very early in the morning and in the evening.

The famed viticulturists of St-Emilion (SEHNT-eh-meel-yohn), 35km northeast of Bordeaux, have been refining their technique since Roman times. Local wine-makers nourish 5400 acres, gently crushing the grapes to produce two and a half million liters of wine each year. The medieval village's cream-colored stone buildings, twisting narrow streets, and religious monuments are a pleasure to visit.

To take home a taste of St-Emilion at an affordable price, walk up the main rue Guadet to the *grand cru château* **Clos des Menuts,** on pl. du Chapitre des Jacobins, in the center of town. An aging, maze-like cellar displays vintages as old as 1922, whetting the appetite for the free *dégustation* available above ground. (☎57 74 45 77. Open daily Apr.-Nov. 10am-7pm; Dec.-Mar. 10am-6pm. Free entrance to cellars. Bottles from €6. MC/V.) The **Maison du Vin de St-Emilion,** pl. Pierre Meyrat, houses a free exhibit on wine-making with an *olfactif* (nasal) guessing game, offers a 1½hr. course on local wines in several languages, including English and French, and sells wine at wholesale prices. (☎57 55 50 55; www.vins-saint-emilion.com. Open daily Aug. 9:30am-7pm; Apr.-July and Sept.-Oct. 9:30am-12:30pm and 2:30-6:30-pm; Nov.-Mar. 10am-12:30pm and 2-6pm. Wine course daily mid-July to mid-Sept. 11am, €17. MC/V.) The **Eglise Monolithe,** carved by Benedictine monks over three centuries out of solid rock, is one of the largest and best preserved subterranean churches in all of Europe. Giant iron clamps keep the church's columns from collapsing under the weight of the heavy bell tower that was added in the 17th century. The damp underground **catacombs,** a burial place for infants and wealthy monks, and the adjacent cave of the hermit Emilion represent only a small part of the 70 acres of underground galleries in the region that have yet to be excavated. To visit the three monuments, you must take one of the guided tours, which depart from the tourist office. (45min. tours every hr. July-Aug. 10am-noon and 2-7pm; Apr.-June and Sept.-Oct. last tour at 6pm; Nov.-Mar. last tour at 5pm. English tours 11:30am, 2:30, 4:30pm. €6.30, students €4, ages 12-17 €3.10.)

GRANDS CRUS FOR TWO (EURO)

One of the priciest and most delectable treats awaiting visitors in France is the exquisite wine. St-Emilion, deep in the heart of Aquitaine's rich vineyards, is one of the most prestigious wine regions in the world; its grapes produce wines ranging from *grand cru* (the first level of prestige) all the way [redacted] *première grand cru classé A*, a distinction so exclusive that it's only given to a handful of *châteaux* (wine firms) every decade. Such luxury comes with a prohibitive price tag—except on three days of the year.

The second weekend in June, St-Emilion hosts **La Fête du St-Emilion,** a wine festival where visitors indulge in all they can drink for only €2. Overlooking the picturesque vineyards of the town, the festival not only features over 50 of St-Emilion's *grand crus* wines but also an art exhibition and occasional concerts. Festivalgoers are given an empty wine glass to be used for unlimited *dégustations* at the myriad booths lining the streets. Friendly vendors are happy to tal[redacted]th visitors about their wine's production and bouquet (smells due to aging). More than worth the paltry entrance fee, the *fête* gives budget travelers the chance to relish exclusive vintages without relinquishing their life savings. There's just one catch: the steep streets of St-Emilion are a bit daunting—especially after four glasses of *grand cru*.

The **tourist office,** on rue du Clocher in pl. des Créneaux, distributes the *Grandes Heures de St-Emilion*, a list of **classical concerts** and **wine tastings** hosted by nearby *châteaux*. To get to the office from the station, take a right on the main road; from town, walk 2km (20min.) up rue de la Porte Bouqueyre toward the tower. (☎57 55 28 28; www.saint-emilion-tourisme.com. Open daily July-Aug. 9:30am-8pm; mid- to late June and early to mid-Sept. 9:30am-7pm; Apr. to mid-June and mid-Sept. to Oct. 9:30am-12:30pm and 1:45-6:30pm; Nov.-Mar. 9:30am-12:30pm and 1:45-6pm.) The office gives tours in English or French and rents **bikes.** (Bikes €10 per ½-day, €14 per day; credit card deposit. Tours €6.30, students €4, ages 12-17 €3.10. MC/V.) To visit the vineyards of St-Emilion, pick up a list of contact information for local *châteaux;* some require appointments. The larger wine houses have tours ending in a tasting (generally €3-5 per person).

GRAVES AND MÉDOC REGIONS

To access vineyards in this region without a car, book one of the organized tours that departs from Bordeaux (€25-29), or take the Réseau Trans Gironde from the depot in pl. des Quinconces to Pauillac, a particularly renowned village. The bus leaves from pl. des Quinconces. (1hr.; M-Sa 8 per day, Su 2 per day; €12-15).

Though the vineyards of St-Emilion are best for a first visit, they are not the only worthwhile stop in the area. South of the Garonne, the **Graves** (grahv) region, so named for its gravel topsoil, is said to be the birthplace of Bordeaux viticulture. Graves's dry and semi-sweet wines were the drink of choice in Eleanor of Aquitaine's time, and though the reds of Médoc overtook their popularity in the 18th century, it was not due to a change in quality. Within Graves, at the southeastern end, is the **Sauternes** region, celebrated for its sweet white dessert wines. The **Médoc** (may-DOHK) area north of Bordeaux, between the Gironde Estuary and the ocean, gets its name from the Latin *medio-acquae*, meaning "between the waters." Within Médoc is the town of **Pauillac,** home to 3000 acres of vineyards, including some of the world's most famous *premier cru* reds: Lafite-Rothschild, Latour, and Mouton-Rothschild.

To get to the **tourist office,** take the bus to "Hôtel de Ville" and walk in the direction from which the bus came. The office, to your left on the banks of the estuary, provides maps, suggests hiking trails, and makes reservations for visits to local *châteaux*. (☎59 03 08; www.pauillac-medoc.com. Open July-Aug. M-Sa 9:30am-7pm, Su 10am-1pm and 2-6pm; June and Sept.-Oct. M-Sa 9:30am-12:30pm and 2-6:30pm, Su 10:30am-12:30pm and 3-6pm; Nov.-May M-Sa 9:30am-12:30pm and 2-6pm, Su 10:30am-12:30pm and 3-6pm.)

ARCACHON ☎05

Arcachon (ahr-kah-SHOHN; pop. 11,400) is one of the most beautiful in a chain of beach towns on the Côte d'Argent (Silver Coast), the thin strip of sand that runs along 200km of France's southern Atlantic seaboard. The Bassin d'Arcachon is known in particular for two sandy landmarks: the Dune du Pilat, Europe's highest sand dune, and the Banc d'Arguin, a 1000-acre sand bar in the form of a crescent. Created 150 years ago by French aristocrats suffering from poor lungs and boredom, Arcachon remains a classically posh southern French resort town, full of vacationing families in summer and empty except for loafing retirees in the low season. During the high season, the town offers guided tours of the surrounding wildlife parks, making it a perfect daytrip from Bordeaux.

TRANSPORTATION AND PRACTICAL INFORMATION. **Trains** go to Bordeaux (1hr.; 10-20 per day, last train 9:51pm; €9.40). The TGV goes to Paris (4hr., 1-3 per day, €71). Trains depart from the station on bd. du Gal Leclerc in Arcachon. (Ticket office open M-F 6am-9:30pm, Sa 8:30am-7:15pm, Su 8:50am-7:20pm.) City **bus** #1 runs from the train station to "Dune du Pilat," within 5min. of the dune. (☎08 10 20 17 14. 25min.; May-Sept. every hr., fewer in low season; €1) Locabeach 33, 326 bd. de la Plage, rents **bikes, scooters,** and **mopeds.** (☎56 83 39 64; www.locabeach.com. Bikes €7-10 per ½-day, €10-13 per day; deposit €160-200. Scooters and mopeds €39-59 per day; driver's license and €760-1200 deposit. Open daily July-Aug. 9am-8pm; Sept.-June 9am-12:30pm and 2-7pm. AmEx/MC/V.)

To reach Arcachon's **tourist office,** pl. Georges Pompidou, turn left from the train station and walk one block. (☎57 52 97 97; www.arcachon.com. Open July-Aug. daily 9am-7pm; Apr.-June and Sept. M-Sa 9am-6:30pm, Su 10am-1pm and 2-5pm; Oct.-Mar. M-Sa 9am-5pm.) Other services include: a **laundromat** on the corner of bd. du Général Leclerc and rue Molière (wash €5-8; dry €0.50 per 3min., €5 per 30min.; detergent €0.50; open daily July-Aug. 7am-10pm, Sept.-June 7am-8pm); **police** (☎57 72 29 30) on pl. de Verdun; and a **hospital** (☎57 52 90 00) on bd. Louis Lignon. The **post office,** 1 pl. Franklin Roosevelt, opposite the tourist office, has **currency exchange.** (☎57 52 53 88. Open M and W-Th 8:45am-6pm, Tu 8:45am-noon and 1-6pm, F 8:45am-7pm, Sa 8:45am-12:15pm.) **Postal Code:** 33120.

ACCOMMODATIONS AND FOOD. In the summer, rooms here start at €60 for a double, and even in the low season, prices begin at €45—don't expect to find any deals. Reservations are essential in the summer. Find the best value in town at **Le Bordeaux ❹,** 39 bd. du Général Leclerc, a two-star hotel located above a restaurant-bar 20m from the train station and a short walk from the beach. Though it might not offer the friendliest welcome, Le Bordeaux has modest rooms with lumpy beds, TV, and clean private bathrooms. (☎56 83 80 30; le.bordeaux@wanadoo.fr. Breakfast €6.50. Reserve 1 week in advance. July-Aug. singles €55; doubles €80. Sept.-June €45-50/75. AmEx/MC/V.) The **Auberge de Jeunesse (HI) ❶,** 87 av. de Bordeaux, is in Cap-Ferret. Take a ferry from Arcachon's Jetée Thiers on av. Gambetta. (☎57 72 28 28. Ferry July-Aug. daily at least 1 per hr. 9am-7pm, night shuttle at midnight; €7-8, under 18 €5-6, bikes €4; round-trip €11-13/7-8/6.) From the Cap-Ferret ferry pier, take av. de l'Océan and continue as it becomes rue des Bouvreuils after the roundabout (15min.). Turn left on av. de Bordeaux; the hostel is on your right. (☎56 60 64 62. Reception 8am-1pm and 6-9pm. Open July-Aug. No reservations. Camping available. Dorms €10.) In Arcachon, social and friendly **Camping Club d'Arcachon ❶,** 5 av. de la Galaxie, lies in the middle of a beautiful, hilly pine forest 2km from the beach and a 25min. walk from the *centre-ville*. Cut through the parc Mauresque and walk several minutes up allée Bouillaud; continue through the forest and turn right, following the signs. The three-star site has a pool, spa, billiards table, and bar-restaurant. (☎56 83 24 15; www.camping-arcachon.com. Laundry €5. Check-out noon. Closed mid-Nov. to mid-Dec. July-Aug. €6-7 per adult, €1 per child under 10, €10-13 per tent, €3-5 per car. Sept. to mid-Nov. and mid-Dec. to June €4-5/free/8-11/1-3. Electricity €4. MC/V.)

To save money, French tourists often buy bread from one of the many *boulangers artisanals* and produce from the **market** on **esplanade Pompidou.** (Open daily 8am-1pm.) Don't leave Arcachon without savoring some of the 15,000 tons of oysters gathered here each year. Cafés line **avenue Gambetta** and **boulevard de la Plage,** offering seafood and *moules frites* (mussels and fries; €10). **Le Commerce ❷,** 9 av. Gambetta, spills onto the street with wooden tables and famished tourists, providing a perfect seaside spot to enjoy shellfish. (☎56 83 05 17. Salads €9-13. Meat dishes €8-15. Fish dishes €10-11. *Menus* €15-24. Open daily 8am-1am. AmEx/MC/V.) A bit of a splurge, **Le Pavillon d'Arguin ❹,** 63 bd. du Général Leclerc, across the street from the tourist office, serves fresh and plentiful seafood platters, as well as continental specialties such as *millefeuille de foie gras canard* (€17), thin layers of duck *foie gras* served in melon and *liqueur.* (☎56 83 46 96. *Plats* €17-28. Open July-Aug. daily noon-2:30pm and 7-10:30pm; Sept.-June Tu-Su noon-2:30pm and 7-10:30pm. Reservations recommended Sa-Su. MC/V.)

SIGHTS AND ENTERTAINMENT. Rising from the edge of a pine forest 5km south of town, the 105m high **Dune du Pilat** (or Pyla) looks more like a section of the Sahara than a French beach; the wind races furiously across the face of the dune, creating an ocean of white sand unblemished by vegetation. Every year without fail, the dune moves a few centimeters east; the army barracks that were constructed at the summit in 1942 now litter the water's edge. At the edge of the dune, there is a protected area where wading is possible, although a fierce undertow makes deeper swims dangerous. Farther along the water, there are beaches for the clothed as well as the nude. From the bus stop "Dune du Pilat," head into the park and continue past the shops for about 500m to reach the staircase to the top. The **Sand Fly** offers **hang gliding** from the dune; ask at the tourist office.

Arcachon's bird sanctuaries and nature parks attract flocks of tourists. **UBA boats** take 2hr. excursions to the Dune du Pilat, the Cap-Ferret lighthouse, and the oyster beds around **L'Ile aux Oiseaux.** (July-Aug. 6 per day; June and Sept. 5 per day; Oct.-Apr. 3 per day. €14-18, under 18 €10-14.) The same company also offers trips to **Banc d'Arguin** from the Jetée Thiers pier. (☎08 25 16 33 16. 4½hr. July-Aug. daily 11am; Sept. and June W and Sa-Su 11am. €16, under 18 €11.)

In Arcachon itself, the **Ville d'Hiver** (Winter Village), a district of breathtakingly large turn-of-the-century villas, lies around the **Parc Mauresque.** In the 19th century, many members of France's aristocracy were suffering from a lung disease. When doctors diagnosed the Arcachon air as healthy, entrepreneurs jumped on the opportunity to make it big and designed the neighborhood's streets to hold as many mansions as possible. The village is accessible by a beautiful 30min. walk up the hill or by a *petit train.* (☎57 72 45 00. Departs from a stop in front of the *gare.* 35min. tours daily 11am, 3, 4, 5, 6pm. €4.50, under 18 €3.) The **St-Cécile Observatory,** a small, metal-enclosed staircase a few blocks from the park, offers a view of Arcachon—if you make it up the wobbly stairs. (Open daily 9am-7pm. Free.)

In the summer, when a younger crowd frolics in Arcachon, several beachfront **discotheques** on bd. de la Plage and bd. Mestrezat start getting rowdy as soon as night falls. The **Casino d'Arcachon,** 163 bd. de la Plage, features the usual suspects: slot machines, a bar, and table games like blackjack and roulette. The casino has a strict dress code: no flip-flops, sleeveless T-shirts, beach attire, or cameras. (☎56 83 41 44; www.partouche.com. 18+. Open July-Aug. M-Th and Su 10am-3am, F-Sa 10am-4am; Sept.-June 10am-5am; table games from 9:30pm. AmEx/MC/V.)

PAYS BASQUE

BIARRITZ ☎05 59

The town of Biarritz (BEE-ah-reetz; pop. 30,000) is synonymous with glitz—and not just because they rhyme. Once a minor whaling village, Biarritz became an aristocratic playground in the mid-19th century. Its natural beauty has drawn the likes of Napoleon III, Alphonse XIII of Spain, Nicholas II of Russia, and the Shah of Persia. While today Biarritz remains an opulent getaway for jet setters from around the world, its crowded beaches, jagged rocks, and glamorous clubs remain within the reach of budget travelers.

TRANSPORTATION

Flights: Aéroport de Parme, 7 esplanade de l'Europe (☎43 83 83). M-Sa take bus #6 (dir.: Bayonne Gare) from Hôtel de Ville (every 30min. 7am-7:20pm), Su take bus C (dir.: Aéroport; buses depart at irregular times). **Ryanair** (☎08 92 23 23 75) flies to **Dublin, Frankfurt, London,** and **Shannon** for €32-170.

Trains: Biarritz-la-Négresse (☎50 83 07), 3km from town. Information desk open daily 7:45am-7pm. To: **Bayonne** (10min., 29 per day; €2.20, TGV €4); **Bordeaux** (2hr., 14 per day, €29); **Paris** (5hr., 12 per day, €79); **Pau** (2hr., 3 per day, €17); **Toulouse** (4hr., 4 per day, €38). Additional SNCF ticket office at 13 av. Foch (☎50 83 34). Open M and W-Th 9:30am-noon and 2-6pm, Tu and F 9am-12:30pm and 1:30-6pm.

Buses: ATCRB (☎26 06 99) runs from the sq. d'Ixelles to **St-Jean-de-Luz** (35min., €3) and **Hendaye** (20min., €3). Buy tickets on the bus.

Public Transportation: STAB (☎52 59 52). Office with maps and schedules on rue Louis-Barthou (☎24 26 53). Open M-Sa 8:15am-noon and 1:30-6pm. Buses run to **Anglet** (M-Sa 6am-8:30pm bus #1, 2, or 6; Su 7:30am-8:30pm bus A, B, or C; 10min.) and **Bayonne** (M-Sa 6am-8:30pm bus #1, 2, or 6; Su 7:30am-8:30pm bus A, B, or C; 25-30min.). 1hr. tickets €1.20, *carnet* of 5 €4.75, *carnet* of 10 €9.50.

Taxis: Atlantic Taxi Radio (☎03 18 18). €2 base; €1.40 per km during the day, €1.80 per km at night. Approximately €12 from the taxi stand to either the train station or the airport; approximately €15 to Bayonne. Open 24hr.

Bike and Scooter Rental: Rent-a-Bike, 24 rue Peyroloubilh (☎24 94 47; www.sobilo-biarritz.com). Bikes and in-line skates €15 per day; €150 deposit. Scooters €31 per day; €1525 deposit or credit card number. Open daily July-Aug. 9am-8pm; Sept.-June 9am-7pm. €10 *Let's Go* discount. MC/V.

Surfboard Rental: Rip Curl Surf Shop, 2 av. Reine Victoria (☎24 38 40), 1 block from Grande Plage. €10 per ½-day, €15 per day, €85 per week; ID deposit. 1½hr. lesson €35, 3 lessons €90, 5 lessons €160. Open daily July-Aug. 10am-8pm; Sept.-June 10am-1pm and 3-7pm.

ORIENTATION AND PRACTICAL INFORMATION

Because the train station is 3km from the *centre-ville*, the STAB and ATCRB buses are the most practical means of reaching Biarritz, arriving near the tourist office from surrounding cities. Buses #2 (dir.: Sainsontan) and 9 (dir.: La Barre or St-Madeleine) run from the train station to the city center and the tourist office (every 20min. M-Sa 6:30am-9pm, €1.20). On Sundays, bus B (dir.: Sainsontan) travels the same route (every 30min. 8am-8pm, €1.20). To get there on foot, keep left as you walk out of Biarritz-la-Négresse. You'll find yourself on **allée du Moura,** which becomes **avenue du Président Kennedy.** Turn left onto **avenue du Maréchal Foch,** which continues to **place Clemenceau,** at the centre-ville (30min.).

Tourist Office: 1 sq. d'Ixelles (☎22 37 10; www.biarritz.fr), off av. Edouard VII. Friendly, English- and Spanish-speaking staff tracks down same-day hotel reservations or campsites for free. Pick up the free *Biarritzscope* for monthly events listings. Open July-Aug. daily 8am-8pm; Sept.-June M-F 9am-6pm, Sa-Su 10am-5pm.

Tours: The **Petit Train** (☎03 44 03), departing every 30min. from the Grande Plage (Casino) or the Rocher de la Vierge, offers 30min. guided bus-disguised-as-train rides of the Port des Pêcheurs, the Port Vieux, and the Perspective Côte des Basques. Open daily July-Aug. 9:30am-11pm; Apr. and Oct. 10:30am-1pm and 2-6pm; May-June and Sept. 10:30am-1:15pm and 2:15-6pm; hours depend on weather. €5, ages 3-12 €4.

Currency Exchange: Change Plus, 9 rue Mazagran (☎24 82 47). No commission. Open July-Aug. M-F 9am-7pm, Sa 9am-1pm; Sept.-June M-Sa 9am-noon and 2-6pm. Currency exchange also available at the **post office.**

Laundromat: La Gout de l'Eau, 4 av. Jaulerry, by the post office. Wash €4-7, dry €1 per 10min. Detergent €0.30. Open daily 7am-9pm.

Beach Information and Emergencies: Grande Plage ☎22 22 22. **Plage Marbella** ☎23 01 20. **Plage de la Milady** ☎23 63 93. **Plage Miramar** ☎24 34 98. **Plage du Port Vieux** ☎24 05 84. **Plage de la Côte des Basques** ☎24 92 70.

Police: 3 av. Joseph Petit (☎01 22 22).

Hospital: Hôpital de la Côte Basque, 13 av. Interne Jacques Loëb (☎44 35 35).

Internet Access: Sarl Quality Services, 60 av. Edouard VII (☎24 39 07). Internet access €4 per hr., €15 per 5hr. Fax €1.50 per pg. Open July-Aug. daily 8am-midnight; Sept.-June M-Sa 10am-8pm. Internet also available at the **post office.**

Post Office: 17 rue de la Poste (☎22 41 20). Open M-F 8:30am-6pm, Sa 8:30am-noon. **Currency exchange.** Open M-F 8:30am-6pm, Sa 8:30am-noon. **Postal Code:** 64200.

ACCOMMODATIONS AND CAMPING

For the budget traveler, bargains are hard to find in this upscale vacation town. To get the best deals, plan at least a month or two ahead for stays in July and August or enlist the help of the tourist office. The best-priced hotels are off rue Mazagran, around rue du Port-Vieux.

Hôtel la Marine, 1 rue Goélands (☎24 34 09). The best deal in central Biarritz. Run by an attentive and caring family. Spotless, comfortable, recently renovated rooms are decorated with maritime-themed wicker furniture. Some overlook the animated rue Mazagran. Breakfast in bed €5. Internet €2 per 30min. at computer in lobby; Wi-Fi €2 per day, available in all rooms; ethernet cable provided. Reception 8am-11pm; front door code allows after-hours access. July-Aug. singles €40-47; doubles €47-52; triples €75. Sept.-June €35-42/40-47/67. AmEx/MC/V. ❹

Auberge de Jeunesse (HI), 8 rue de Chiquito de Cambo (☎41 76 00; aubergejeune.biarritz@wanadoo.fr). A 15min. bus ride or 40min. walk from Biarritz. From the town center, take bus #2 (dir.: Gare SNCF) to Francis Jammes or #9 (dir.: Labourd) to Bois de Boulogne. When you get out, continue walking in the direction of the bus and turn right when you see a sign for the hostel; follow the road down the hill. At the bottom of the hill on the right, near a beautiful lake. Social hostel provides a well-stocked bar, a laid-back crowd, and great prices. Bright rooms with bunk beds decked out in red quilts have lockable cabinets and key card entry. Breakfast included. Laundry €3.50, dry €2.50. Internet €0.50 per 10min. Reception July-Aug. 8:30am-12:30pm and 6-10pm; Sept.-June 8:30-11:30am and 6-9pm. 2- to 4-bed dorms €18. AmEx/MC/V. ❶

Camping Biarritz, 28 rue d'Harcet (☎23 00 12; www.biarritz-camping.fr). A 10min. walk from Milady and a 30min. walk from town. Take bus #9 or follow signs down av. du Président J. F. Kennedy from the bus station. Quiet, unshaded plots separated by neat hedges. Restaurant, bar, laundry, jacuzzi, and pool. Internet €3 per 20min, €6 per hr. Wheelchair-accessible. Reception 8am-9pm. Reservations required July-Aug. Open early May to mid-Sept. Early July to late Aug. 2 people with tent €22, mobile homes €500-600 per week, electricity €3.50. May-June €15/€265-325/€2.80. MC/V. ❶

FOOD

In dining, as with everything in Biarritz, style trumps substance. A restaurant with a gorgeous view can charge for gourmet and deliver gruel. The restaurants around **Grande Plage** and **place St-Eugénie** tend to be expensive. Look on **rue Mazagran** and **place Clemenceau** for cheap *crêpes* and sandwiches. Several restaurants along rue du Port Vieux, near **Le Palmarium**, offer good meals at reasonable prices. The market on **rue des Halles** offers local produce and an abundance of specialties. (Open daily 7am-1pm.) Next door is a **Shopi** supermarket, 2 rue du Centre. (☎24 18 01. Open M-Sa 9am-12:40pm and 3-7:10pm, Su 9am-12:30pm. AmEx/MC/V.)

Casa Juan Pedro, Port des Pecheurs (☎24 00 86). Nestled in the rocky cove of the Port des Pecheurs, this outdoors-only seafood restaurant boasts a sensational view of the ocean.

THE LOCAL STORY

THE *MAIN* PRIDE OF BASQUE

A subject of fierce Basque pride, *la pelote Basque* (*pelota* in Spanish) infects Biarritz, Bayonne, and St-Jean-de-Luz in the summer, bringing not only a series of professional tournaments but also regular Thursday evening matches in Biarritz's Parc Mazon. Scholars trace the sport's origins to medieval French *jeux de paume* (palm games), and modern *pelote*, in its many forms, distantly resembles squash; the basic goal of the game is to prevent the other player from returning the ball.

According to the International Federation of Basque Pelota, *pelote* can be played in four types of court and with 14 specialties, or types of racket. In the most basic form, players smack the *pelote* (a small, relatively dead ball with a rubber core) against a *fronton* (a large wall) using their bare hands as racquets (*la pelote à la main nue*). A popular pastime at school recess, *pelote à la main nue* is nonetheless a serious sport; players develop massive calluses and risk debilitating hand injuries.

In the fastest and most famous version of *pelote, cesta punta*, players use large *xisteras* (long, curved, basket-like gloves) to send the ball whizzing around a three-sided court (the *jaï alaï*) at up to 300km per hr. The only thing fiercer than this game is the cultural pride of its Basque players.

Locals crowd the patio while dining on fresh fish dishes for good value. Try the *moules à la creme* (mussels in cream sauce; €8), *merlu à l'espagnol* (Spanish grilled merlin; €12), or the small tapas sandwiches (€1.40). Open daily July-Aug. noon-3pm and 7-11pm; Sept. and Apr.-June noon-2pm and 7:30-10pm. Closed in bad weather. MC/V. ❷

L'Atalaya, Plateau de l'Atalaye (☎22 33 34), located above the Rocher de la Vièrge and Musée de la Mer. This museum café stands out for its massive sandwiches (€3.80-4.40) and a view of the Rocher de la Vièrge. Paella €11. *Menu* €8.80. Open daily July-Aug. 9am-10pm; Sept.-June 9:30am-6pm. MC/V. ❶

Le Palmarium, 7 rue du Port Vieux (☎24 25 83). In a palm-lined courtyard, this local favorite serves a wide variety of meals at prices that won't break the bank. Options include pizzas (€6.50-10) and meat or fish dishes (€8-14), but the best choice is the *paella:* a house specialty that features as much rice, chicken and shellfish as you can eat for €13 (served 7-11pm). Open daily 10am-11pm. MC/V. ❷

SIGHTS AND BEACHES

Glittery beaches, Biarritz's main attraction, reel in sunbathers, surfers, and everyone in between. In summer, perfect bodies blanket the **Grande Plage,** while those seeking a slightly quieter beach experience head to the **Plage Miramar,** and Quiksilver-clad beach bums hit the waves at the **Plage de la Côte des Basques.**

The best way to soak in all that Biarritz has to offer is to stroll along the shoreline. Start at **Pointe St-Martin,** 10min. north of the center along Av. de L'imperatrice. This promontory not only provides the foundation for a lighthouse, **Le Phare de Biarritz,** but also offers a panoramic view of the city's coastline. From here, turn right on Av. de l'I'mperatrice, heading back toward the center of the city. You can't miss the **Hôtel du Palais,** crown jewel of Biarritz's luxury hotels, 500m down on your right. Constructed in 1845 by Emperor Napoleon III, the E-shaped palace now lets rooms starting at €260 per night. Those lacking royal wallets can soak up the atmosphere in the terrace café with a cup of coffee (€4.80), then continue along the walkway behind the Grande Plage past the **Casino Barrière.** Lying 200m past the casino, rock formations provide shelter for small fishing boats in the **Port des Pêcheurs.** Near the Port, **BAB Subaquatique,** organizes scuba excursions. (☎24 80 40. Open daily 8am-7pm. Guided dives. First dive €30. Open-water boat excursions for certified divers €42. Diving excursions to the *vieux port* and nighttime trips available for all experience levels. Cash and traveler's checks only.)

Continue down the coast, over the bridge, and through the iconic **Rocher de la Vierge,** a tooth-like rock with a statue of the Virgin Mary, to watch the sun set from a lookout point. Past the Rocher de la Vierge is **La Musée de la Mer,** which features an aquarium on the lower level and museum on the two upper levels. Drop by at 10:30am or 5pm to catch the feeding of the seals; otherwise, audio tours in English guide visitors through the exhibits, one of which includes the skull of a blue whale. (☎22 33 36; www.museedelamer.com. Open June-Sept. daily 9:30am-7pm; July-Aug. daily 9:30am-midnight; Nov.-Mar. Tu-Su 9:30am-12:30pm and 2-6pm. €7.50, students and under 16 €4.80, under 4 free.)

The 15min. trek to the **Musée du Chocolat,** 14 av. Beaurivage, is worth the effort for the exhibits on the history of chocolate—which include chocolate sculptures—and the free samples of rich hot chocolate. (☎24 23 72; www.planet-musee-chocolat.com. Guided tours in French for groups only. Wheelchair-accessible. Open M-Sa 10am-noon and 2-6pm. €6, students and ages 13-18 €5, ages 4-12 €3.50.) The boutique of chocolate maker **Henriet** sits next door and features a selection of Basque chocolates, like the *Rocher Biarritz*—almond and orange covered in chocolate. (☎41 54 69. Open daily 10am-12:30pm and 2:30-6:30pm.)

NIGHTLIFE AND FESTIVALS

The **Casino Barrière de Biarritz,** 1 av. Edouard VII, stands over the Grande Plage in all its Art Deco glory. In order to enter the red-carpeted ocean of slot machines (some now accept one-cent pieces) and craps tables, gamblers must come with 18+ ID. (☎22 77 77. Open July-Aug. M-Th and Su 10am-4am, F-Sa 10am-5am; Sept.-June M-Th and Su 10am-3am, F-Sa 10am-4am. Tables open 8pm-close.) Weekend evenings kick off at 11pm at the bars that cluster around **Hôtel la Marine** on rue Mazagran, especially at **Le Ventilo, La Marine,** or **La Tireuse.** At 2am, as bars close, young people form long lines outside Biarritz's clubs (*boîtes*). The small and swanky **Ibiza,** on Grande Plage, caters to a classy young crowd. (☎24 38 34. Mixed drinks €8. Cover €10.) Lively **Le Copa,** 24 av. Edouard VII, has a large tropical bar on its main floor and a dance club downstairs that plays Latin, techno, and hip-hop. (☎24 65 39. Mixed drinks €8-10. Cover €10. Bar open daily noon-4pm and 6pm-6am. Dance club open daily midnight-6am.) On weekend nights, many head for cheaper, wilder **San Sebastian,** just over the border in Spain, partying until the sun comes up and taking the first morning train back to Biarritz.

In July and August, *pelote* (see p. 582) and Basque dancing hit **Parc Mazon** Thursdays at 9pm. *Cesta punta* (or *jai-alai—pelote* played with the *xistera*, a curved basket) tournaments animate the **Fronton Euskal-Jai** in the **Parc des Sports d'Aguiléra.** For two weeks in mid-July, Biarritz hosts the international **Biarritz Masters Jai-Alai** tournament, and in mid-August the **Gant d'Or** takes over the town. Both festivals attract a large crowd of tourists and locals. The winning teams from each tournament compete for the **Trophée du Super Champion** in mid-September. (For these 3 events, call the tourist office ☎22 44 66. €10-20.) As a tribute to its other primary sport, Biarritz hosts surf competitions, including the **Roxy Jam** in mid-July and the **Junior Pro Competition** at the end of August. In September, **Le Temps d'Aimer** showcases music, ballet, and art. (Tickets at the tourist office. €10-35, students €10.) The **International Festival of Biarritz** (www.festivaldebiarritz.com) celebrates Latin American cinema and culture during the first week of October.

BAYONNE ☎05 59

Though only a few kilometers from the center of Biarritz, Bayonne (bay-OHN; pop. 42,000), the self-proclaimed chocolate capital of France, takes life at a slower pace than its fashionable neighbor. While parts of the city, particularly around St-Esprit, are dominated by X-rated shops and newer buildings, central Bayonne has much to offer. Visitors can wander along the banks of the Nive, admiring the many small bridges and shuttered half-timbered houses before heading to the nearest *chocolaterie.* Things pick up in the middle of July and August, as raucous tourists flock to Bayonne for festivals, bullfights, sports matches, and jazz concerts.

TRANSPORTATION

Trains: pl. de la Gare. Info office open M 5:35am-8:30pm, Tu-Sa 6:05am-8:30pm, Su 6:15am-8:30. To: **Biarritz** (10min.; 36 per day; €2.20, TGV €4); **Bordeaux** (2hr., 28 per day, €28); **Paris** (5hr., 10 TGV per day, €81); **San Sebastian, SPA** via **Hendaye** (30min., 15 per day, €8); **Toulouse** (4hr., 5 per day, €37). The *Passe Basque* gives travelers 1 weekend round-trip between Bayonne and San Sebastian (valid July-Sept.; €9.50, under 18 €5).

Public Transportation: STAB, Hôtel de Ville (☎52 59 52). Office open M-Sa 8:15am-noon and 1:30-6pm. Buses run every 20-30min. M-Sa 6:30am-8pm, Su 6:30am-7pm. Lines #1, 2, and 6 serve **Biarritz** M-Sa. Lines A and B serve Biarritz Su. Line #2 serves the Anglet tourist office, and line #7 serves Anglet's beaches and forest. 1hr. ticket €1.20, *carnet* of 5 €4.75, *carnet* of 10 €9.50.

Taxis: Taxi Bayonne (☎59 48 48) is stationed outside the train station and at pl. Charles de Gaulle. Open 24hr.

ORIENTATION AND PRACTICAL INFORMATION

Two rivers join to split Bayonne into three sections. **St-Esprit,** containing Bayonne's train station, cheap hotels, and internet cafés, is on the northern side of the Adour river. From here, the **pont St-Esprit**—usually lined with fishermen—connects to budget-friendly **Petit-Bayonne,** home of Bayonne's museums and smaller restaurants. Five bridges span the much narrower Nive to connect Petit-Bayonne to **Grand-Bayonne** on the west bank. This older part of town has a buzzing pedestrian zone, filled with a maze of side streets. The center of town is easily manageable on foot, and an excellent bus system makes Anglet and Biarritz easy to reach.

Tourist Office: pl. des Basques (☎46 01 46; www.bayonne-tourisme.com). From the train station, follow the signs to the *centre-ville.* Cross the main bridge to Petit-Bayonne. Continue through pl. du Réduit and cross pont Mayou to Grand-Bayonne. Take a right on rue Bernède and continue 300m; the street becomes av. Bonnat. The tourist office is on the left. Free city map, hotel reservations, and *Fêtes en Pays Basque* brochures. Organizes 2hr. walking tours of neighborhoods and old ramparts in French (10:30am or 3pm, depending on the day; in English for groups only, call ahead to reserve. €5, under 12 free). Open July-Aug. M-Sa 9am-7pm, Su 10am-1pm; Sept.-June M-F 9am-6:30pm, Sa 10am-6pm.

Budget Travel: Pascal Voyages, 8 al. Boufflers (☎25 48 48). Open M-F 8:30am-6:30pm, Sa 9am-noon.

Bank: BNP Paribas, 1 pl. de la Liberté (☎08 20 82 00 01). **ATMs** outside.

Laundromat: Atelier Lavopratic, 57 rue Bourgneuf (☎06 82 02 41 55). Wash €3.40, dry €0.40 per 5min. Ironing available. Owner will transfer laundry to dryer for you.

Police: 6 av. de Marhum (☎46 22 22).

Hospital: 13 av. Interne Jacques Loëb (☎44 35 35), St-Léon.

Internet: Taxiphone, 1 pl. St-Ursule (☎55 86 34). €0.60 per 15min. Open daily 11am-1:30pm and 3:30-10:30pm.

Post Office: 11 rue Jules Labat (☎46 33 60), Grand-Bayonne, in a beautiful art deco building. **Currency exchange.** Open M-W and F 8am-6pm, Th 8am-12:15pm and 1:45-

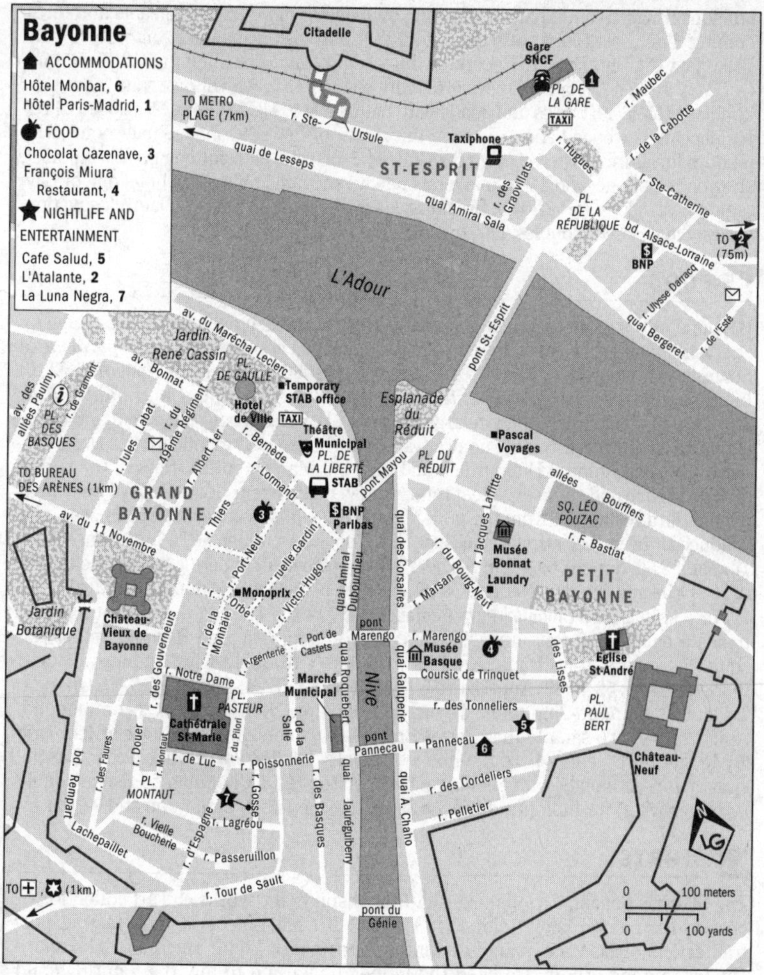

6pm, Sa 8:30am-noon. Branch office on the corner of bd. Alsace-Lorraine and rue de l'Este (☎50 32 90). Open M-F 8:30am-5:30pm, Sa 8:30am-noon. **Postal Code:** 64100.

ACCOMMODATIONS

Reasonably priced lodgings dot St-Esprit's train station area, but expect some noise at night. Hotels fill quickly in festival season, from the end of June to the beginning of October, so reserve ahead. The closest hostels are in Anglet (p. 587) and Biarritz (p. 579), each a 20min. bus ride away. **Hôtel Paris-Madrid ❷**, pl. de la Gare, is located to the left as you exit the train station, an 8min. walk from Petit-Bayonne. Don't let the plaster bunker-style exterior deter you; this is one of Bayonne's best bargains. Large windows make up for dim lightbulbs, and rooms are decorated with old wooden furniture. The fourth floor has personal balconies overlooking the busy pl. de la Gare. The gracious, English- and Spanish-speaking owners are more knowledgeable and forthcoming than most tourist offices. (☎55 13 98; sorbois@wanadoo.fr. In-room TV €1. Breakfast €4. Shower €1. Reception July-Aug. 24hr.; Sept.-June daily 6:15am-1am; Oct.-May M-Sa noon-6pm. Singles €19, with shower €27, with shower and toilet €34; doubles €24/28/49; triples and quads with bath €49-59. MC/V.) **Hôtel Monbar ❷,** 24 rue Panneceau, is wedged above a bar in the center of Petit-Bayonne. Small rooms with modern furniture, clustered around an indoor courtyard, all come equipped with toilet, shower, telephone, and TV to make this newly renovated nine-room hotel one of Bayonne's best values. (☎59 26 80. Breakfast €4.50. Reception opens 7:30am, closing time varies. Singles €32; doubles €32; triples €41; quads €51. MC/V.)

FOOD

Bayonne offers more than just chocolate. Most of the fish and meat dishes reflect a Spanish influence; menus abound with various tapas and *grillades à la plancha* (a Spanish style of grilling). The *café-brasseries* of **Petit-Bayonne** and **St-Esprit** offer €8-10 local specialties like *jambon de Bayonne* (dry-cured ham) and *poulet à la basquaise* (chicken wrapped in large peppers). For cheap eats, sandwich and *crêpe* shops are everywhere, though none are special. Three nearly identical cafés at the corner of the quai Admiral Dubourdieu and the pont Marengo offer views of the scenic quai de la Nive and serve excellent three-course lunch menus for €11. Try **Vivaldi** first; it's the third restaurant from the pont Marengo. Vendors sell meats, fish, cheese, and produce at the indoor **marché municipal,** quai Roquebert. (Open M-Th 7am-1pm, F 7am-1pm and 3:30-7pm, Sa 6am-2pm.) There is also a **Monoprix** supermarket on the corner of rue Orbe and rue Port Neuf. (☎59 00 33. Open M-Sa 8:30am-8pm. AmEx/MC/V.)

For a splurge, **François Miura Restaurant ❹,** 24 rue Marengo, stands out among upscale eateries in Bayonne. Patrons dine on sophisticated Basque dishes like squid marinated in pork juice and its own ink (€16) amid white stone walls and modern art. (☎59 49 89. Appetizers €14-19. *Plats* €18-21. *Menus* €19-30. Open M-Tu and Th-Sa noon-2pm and 8-10pm, Su noon-2pm. Reservations recommended. AmEx/MC/V.) To sample the best of Bayonne's sweets, head to **Chocolat Cazenave ❷,** 19 rue Port Neuf, where the house specialty is *chocolat mousseux*, a Basque spin on hot chocolate with chocolate foam on top (€5). Chocolate is also available (€16 per 250g) for bulk purchase. (☎59 03 16. Open daily 9am-noon and 2-7pm.)

SIGHTS

The **Musée Bonnat,** 5 rue Jacques Laffitte, displays the works and art collection of *bayonnais* painter Léon Bonnat (1833-1922). Bonnat, one of the most famous portrait artists of his time, painted haunting portraits of Victor Hugo and Alexandre Dumas, among others. He used the money he earned to buy the paintings and sculptures that occupy this museum—luckily for us, his taste was impeccable, and his collection includes works by Dégas, Goya, Rembrandt, and Van Dyck. (☎59 08 52. Open July-Aug. M-Tu and Th-Su 10am-6:30pm, W 10am-9:30pm; May-Oct. M and W-Su 10am-6:30pm; Nov.-Apr. daily 10am-12:30pm and 2-6pm. €5.50, students €3, under 18 free; Sept.-June 1st Su of the month and July-Aug. W 6:30-9:30pm free.)

The world's largest ethnographic museum devoted to the *Pays Basque*, the **Musée Basque,** 37 quai des Corsaires, includes everything Basque, from ancient shears that stripped Basque sheep of their wool to modern documentaries about the bombing of Guernica. Explanations are in Basque, French, and Spanish. (☎46 61 90; www.musee-basque.com. Open May-Oct. Tu-Su 10am-6:30pm, Nov.-Apr. Tu-Su 10am-12:30pm and 2-6pm. The tourist office leads guided visits in French through the museum; times vary. €5.50, students €3, under 18 free. Sept.-June 1st Su of the month and July-Aug. W 6:30-9:30pm free. Combined ticket for the Basque Museum and the Bonnat Museum

€9, students €4.50.) Turn right when you exit the Musée Basque, then left onto the pont Marengo, and walk straight until you see the **Cathedral St-Marie,** a UNESCO world heritage sight, on your left. (Open M-Sa 10-11:45am and 3-5:45pm, Su 3:30-6pm.) Savor the 85 ft. vault in this gothic cathedral before leaving for the **botanical gardens.** To reach them, turn left on rue Notre-Dame as you exit the cathedral, immediately turn right at rue des Gouverneurs, and then duck into the tunnel through the ramparts. The gardens flourish atop the battlements, with 1000 species of Japanese flora, including a miniature bamboo forest. (Open mid-Apr. to mid-Oct. Tu-Sa 9:30am-noon and 2-6pm.)

Those looking for a more secluded beach than the crowded plots of sand in Anglet or Biarritz should try the **Metro Plage** in Tarnos. Take bus #10 from the train station (30min., every 20min.-1hr. M-Sa 7:20am-7:25pm). Lifeguards are only on duty during July and August, but the beach is beautiful all year.

ENTERTAINMENT AND FESTIVALS

Nightlife is gentle in this town of long afternoons and short evenings. Students line **rue des Cordeliers** in Petit-Bayonne, enjoying cheap drinks in an atmosphere that is more conducive to conversation than dancing. Travelers seeking a more lively scene take the 10min. bus ride to Biarritz or head over the border to San Sebastian.

Café Salud, 63 rue Panneceau, serves good wine and mixed drinks to a young local crowd in a quiet bar distinguished by understated elegance. A mojito (€2.50) or a glass of *vin navarre* (€2) makes the perfect precursor to the slightly more raucous student scene one block over. (☎59 14 49. Open M-Sa 9am-2am. Wheelchair accessible. AmEx/MC/V.) Enter **La Luna Negra,** down narrow rue Gosse, through a red door to find a basement bar with a cornucopia of music styles on its cabaret-style stage. Weekends feature salsa, jazz, storytellers, and more. (☎25 78 05. Beer €2.50. Th blues. Most shows €9, students €7. Shows start 9-9:30pm. Open W-Sa 7pm-2am.) **L'Atalante,** 7 rue Denis Etcheverry, in St-Esprit, shows international films in their original language—with subtitles—and has an appealing bar. (☎55 76 63; www.cinema-atalante.org. Wheelchair-accessible. €6.20, students and under 18 €4.20. M-F screening at 6pm €5.60. Closed 2 weeks in early Aug.)

Even in an area rich with festivals, Bayonne stands out. During the **Fêtes Traditionelles** (usually beginning the first Wednesday of August, but on July 30 in 2008), locals enjoy five days of unrestrained hedonism, with concerts, bullfights, fireworks, and a chaotic cow race. The *fête* is one of the world's five biggest festivals, with over a million visitors (www.fetes-de-bayonne.com). From July to September, Bayonne holds several bullfights, or *corridas*, at the **Bureau des Arènes;** be aware that matadors actually kill the bull (☎46 61 00. Open M-F 10am-1pm and 4-7pm). Other festivals include the **Foire du Jambon** (Forum of Ham, three days before Easter), the **Journées du Chocolat** (Days of Chocolate, mid-May), and the **Marché Mediéval** (July 14). Visit www.bayonne-tourisme.com for specific dates. The orchestra **Harmonie Bayonnaise** gives jazz, pop, and traditional Basque concerts in the pl. de Gaulle gazebo. (July-Aug. Th 9:30pm. Free.) From September to June, the **Théâtre Municipale,** pl. de la Liberté, hosts various musical performances. (☎59 07 27. Ticket office open Tu-F 10am-2pm and 2:45-5:30pm, Sa 10am-1pm. €15-30, students €2 per 3 tickets.)

DAYTRIP FROM BAYONNE OR BIARRITZ

ANGLET

Anglet is best reached from Bayonne; while accessible from Biarritz, it is an inconvenient trip. From Bayonne, take the #7.1 or 7.2 STAB bus from Bayonne to Mairie Anglet Plages (20min., every 20-25min.). From Biarritz, take bus #2 from the train station and switch to bus #7.1 at 5 Cantons. On Su and holidays, take bus C from Bayonne or bus B from Biarritz; you'll have to walk from 5 Cantons if you take bus B.

King of the Côte Basque and the French surfing scene, Anglet (AHN-glay) boasts 4km of fine-grained white sand parcelled out into nine sparkling beaches. The waves are strongest at **Plage des Cavaliers,** where most of Anglet's surfing competitions are held (the surf is best at low tide), but swimmers all along the coast should be wary of the strong undertow. When in doubt, swim near a lifeguard (on all the beaches except Plage du Club, Plage des Dunes, and Plage de la Petite Madrague).

From the bus stop at Anglet Plages, turn left at the traffic circle and walk 100m towards the ocean, passing several beach-appropriate eateries (Tex-Mex, kebab joints, and *crêperies*). The road ends at av. des Dauphins; continue straight to reach **Plage des Sables d'Or** (lifeguards on duty mid-June to August), where public volleyball courts are available. You can rent surf and ski equipment at **Freestyle,** down the street (☎03 27 24; freestyle.surfacademy@wanadoo.com. Surfboards €12 per ½-day, €18 per day, €100 per week. Wetsuits €6-8/8-10/40-50. Skis and snowboards with boots €70-80 per week. 50% deposit required. Open daily June to mid-Oct. 9:30am-7pm; mid-Sept. to May 10am-12:30pm and 2:30-7pm).

For a non-beach outdoors experience, get off bus #7 a few stops earlier, at **Douanes.** From there, continue on the promenade de la Barre and follow signs to the **Centre Equestre.** The **Club Hippique** provides **riding lessons** and **horseback tours** of the Forêt du Chilberta. The stables are on rue du Petit Palais, off promenade de la Barre. (☎63 83 45; contact@chcotebasque.com. 1hr. lesson €20, forest-walk €18. Open July-Aug. M-F 9am-noon and 3-7pm, Sa 9am-noon and 3-6pm; Sept.-June M and F 3-7pm, Tu-W and Sa 9am-noon and 3-7pm. Reservations. MC/V.)

Along the coast, professional surf competitions are held throughout the summer and are free for spectators. Starting at the beginning of August, surfers from around the world gather at La Plage des Cavaliers to watch several of Anglet's featured surf competitions. In mid-August, pro and amateur surfers demonstrate their skills at the **Quicksilver Air Show,** a surfer favorite. The qualifying rounds take place during the day at the Sables d'Or. For five days in May, women take over the waves to compete in the longboard and bodyboard divisions of the **Kana Miss Cup.** In mid-September, the **Royal Single Trophée** comes to Marinella Beach, accompanied by concerts. 2008 dates are available at www.anglet-tourisme.com.

From the bus stop at Anglet Plages, turn left to reach the **Tourist Office Annex;** the annex has the same services as the main branch in town and is more convenient, as it is located near Anglet's beaches. (☎03 93 43. Open daily July-Aug. 10:30am-7:30pm, Apr.-June and Sept.-Oct. 10:30am-1pm and 3-6:30pm.)

ST-JEAN-DE-LUZ ☎05 59

St-Jean-de-Luz (SEHN-jhahn-d-looz; pop. 13,000) has everything: the red shutters and narrow sidestreets of Bayonne, a sheltered version of the sandy beaches of Biarritz, and a rich Basque tradition that takes over the streets in late summer's festivals. St-Jean has a storied past; its wealth comes from the plunder of whalers and pirates in the 17th century. Today, that wealth leaves in its wake fine examples of Basque architecture, from the bell-tower above Ravel's birthplace to the elaborate interior of the Eglise St-Jean-Baptiste. The town is pedestrian-friendly, as most sights fit in the 300m stretch between the train station and the beach. Budget travelers may want to visit St-Jean as a daytrip from more affordable Bayonne.

TRANSPORTATION

Trains: bd. du Commandant Passicot. Info office open M-Sa 7:45am-7:30pm, Su 10am-7:30pm. Trains go to: **Bayonne** (30min.; 10 per day; €4.20, TGV €6); **Biarritz** (15min.; 10 per day; €2.70, TGV €4.40); **Paris** (5½hr., 10 per day, €81); **Pau** (2hr., 7 per day, €18).

Buses: across from the train station. Office open M-F 9am-noon and 2-6pm. **ATCRB** (☎26 06 99) runs to **Bayonne** (1hr., 15 per day, €6) and **Biarritz** (40min., 17 per day, €3). Buy tickets on bus.

Taxis: at the train station (☎26 10 11).

Car Rental: Avis (☎26 76 66), at the train station. Can return at other locations, including Paris and Bayonne. From €326 per week; copy of credit card and driver's license as deposit. Under-25 surcharge €25 per day. Open M-F 8am-noon and 2-6pm, Sa 9am-noon and 2-6pm. AmEx/MC/V.

Bike Rental: Fun-Bike Location (☎26 75 76), at the train station. Bikes €12 per ½-day, €15 per day, €61 per week; €200 deposit. Scooters €35 per ½-day, €41 per day; €900 deposit. Open daily July-Aug. 10am-7pm; call in advance Sept.-June. MC/V.

ORIENTATION AND PRACTICAL INFORMATION

From the train and bus stations, the center of St-Jean-de-Luz is all that stands between you and the beach. To reach the tourist office, turn right when you exit the train station and left on av. Jauréguiberry at the traffic circle. Walk 100m; the office is on your right, at the intersection with bd. Victor Hugo. To reach the beach from the train station, turn left as you exit; at the traffic circle, follow av. de Verdun to pl. Foch. **Rue de la République** runs two blocks to **place Louis XIV,** the center of town. The beach is 50m ahead, and pedestrian **rue Gambetta** is to the right.

Tourist Office: 20 bd. Victor Hugo (☎26 03 16; www.st-jean-de-luz.com). Maps and info on accommodations and excursions. 2hr. town tours in French July-Aug. Tu and Th 10am; Sept.-June Tu 10am. €5, ages 12-18 and under €2.50, under 12 free. Open July-Aug. M-Sa 9am-7:30pm, Su 10am-1pm and 3-7pm; Sept.-June M-Sa 9am-12:30pm and 2-7pm, Su 10am-1pm.

Bank: Banque Inchauspé et Cie, 16 bd. Victor Hugo (☎26 24 71). Open Tu-W and F 8:40am-12:25pm and 2-5pm, Th 8:40am-12:25pm and 2-6pm, Sa 8:40am-noon. Several other banks and ATMs line bd. Victor Hugo.

Laundromat: Laverie du Port, 5 pl. Foch (☎85 17 69, cell 06 80 06 48 30). Two blocks from the train station; turn left out of the station and follow Av. de Verdun at the traffic circle. Wash €4.50-8, dry €0.50 per 5min. Full service; €11 per 7kg. Open daily 7am-9pm. Full service open Tu-F 9:30am-12:30pm and 2:30-7pm, Sa 9:30am-1pm.

Police: av. André Ithurralde (☎51 22 22).

Medical Services: Polyclinique, 7 rue Léonce Goyetche (☎51 63 63). Private hospital with 24hr. emergency services.

Internet Access: Internet World, 7 rue Tourasse (☎26 86 92). Internet access and Wi-Fi €1 per 10min. Fixed cards for sale €25 per 5hr., €45 per 10hr. Printing and photocopies €0.20. Open Sept.-June M-Sa 10am-6pm; July-Aug. daily 9am-midnight.

Post Office: 44 bd. Victor Hugo (☎51 66 54). Open M and W-F 8:45am-noon and 1:30-5:15pm, Tu 8:45am-noon and 2:10-5:15pm, Sa 8:45am-noon. **Postal Code:** 64500.

ACCOMMODATIONS AND CAMPING

Hotels are expensive and fill up rapidly in summer, particularly during festival season, so reserve early. For most budgets, it is best to commute from Bayonne (p. 583) or Biarritz (p. 579). The **Auberge de Jeunesse** in Biarritz and the **Hôtel Paris-Madrid** in Bayonne are particularly convenient, since they are near train stations.

Hôtel Verdun, 13 av. de Verdun (☎26 02 55), across from the train station. Unremarkable pastel-colored rooms have the lowest prices in town. Large bathrooms in good condition. Breakfast €5. Reception 8am-11pm. July-Sept. singles and doubles €40, with shower €50; triples and quads €60. Oct.-June €28/33/45. MC/V. ❸

Hôtel Bolivar, 18 rue Sopite (☎26 02 00; www.hotel-bolivar-stjeandeluz.com), on a central but quiet street near the beach. Spacious non-smoking rooms with wood trim, linoleum floors, TVs, and sparkling bathrooms fill the 3 floors above a comfortable, home-decorated common room. Breakfast €7. Reception 7:30am-9pm. Open May-Sept. July-Aug. singles with toilet €38, with toilet and shower €55; doubles €44/70; triples €75. May-June and Sept. prices €5-10 lower. AmEx/MC/V. ❸

Camping: There are 17 campsites in St-Jean-de-Luz and 13 more nearby. All are behind plage D'Erromardie. The tourist office has addresses and phone numbers. Take bd. Victor Hugo from the center of town, continue along the road as it turns into av. André Ithurralde, then veer left on chemin d'Erromardie (30min.). Or take an ATCRB bus (€1) headed to Biarritz or Bayonne and ask to get off near the *camping.* ❶

FOOD

St-Jean-de-Luz has the best Basque and Spanish specialties north of the border. The port's famous seafood awaits in every restaurant along **rue de la République** and on **place Louis XIV,** but expect to pay upwards of €13 per meal. Across from the train station, the restaurant under the **Hôtel Verdun** offers large meals at reasonable prices (€12 *menu* for lunch and dinner). There is a large market at **place des Halles.** (Open July to mid-Sept. daily 8am-1pm.) For groceries, stop at the **Shopi** supermarket, 87 rue Gambetta. (Open July-Aug. M-Sa 9am-8pm, Su 9am-8pm; Sept.-June M-Sa 9am-12:30pm and 3-7:15pm. AmEx/MC/V.)

Txantxangorri, 30 rue Chauvin Dragon (☎26 04 32). Offers a small menu of authentic Basque cuisine. Served in a traditional red-shuttered house, options here include some of the region's best dishes, such as the *gambas à la plancha* (grilled prawns, €13). The €11 lunch *menu,* which includes entrée, main dish, dessert, and coffee, is a great value. Open Tu-Sa noon-2:30pm and 7:30-10pm, Su 7:30-10pm. MC/V. ❷

Pil-Pil Enea, 3 rue Sallagoity (☎51 20 80). This tiny restaurant on St-Jean's side streets serves *merlu* (hake fish) and specialties from family recipes. Appetizers €10-18. *Menu* €27. Fish and meat dishes €15-18. Open M-Sa 12:15-2pm and 7:30-10pm. MC/V. ❹

Cosmopolitain, 5 pl. Foch (☎26 05 91). Serves bistro and Basque fare at a good value. Attracts a young crowd with its colorful chairs and large outdoor seating area. For lunch, try the generous *plat du jour* (€7.50) or poisson du jour (€9). Sandwiches and salads also available. Open daily July-Aug. noon-10pm; Sept.-June noon-8pm. AmEx/MC/V. ❷

Etchebaster Frères, 42 rue Gambetta (☎26 00 80). Cherry jam and cream-filled *gâteaux Basques* (€6.50-14) tempt passersby from the windows of this small bakery. The owner takes pride in his frosted *gâteaux des rois,* orange flour cakes (€6.50-14). Open July-Aug. Tu-Sa 8:30am-1pm and 3:30-7:30pm, Su 8am-1pm and 4-7pm; Sept.-June Tu-Su 8:30am-12:30pm and 3:30-7pm. MC/V. ❷

SIGHTS AND BEACHES

To see the coast of St-Jean-de-Luz at its most striking, turn right when you reach the beach. Follow **Promenade Jacques Thibaud** along the **Grande Plage.** As you continue to the **Sainte Barbe,** the *balade à pied* (footpath) leads you along the edge of St-Jean's cliffs. From the lookout points, gaze out over the river Nivell to Hendaye and the Spanish border. The Grande Plage is the perfect destination for daytrippers and provides some of the Basque region's best sailing and surfing. For information about boat rentals, contact the tourist office. Those seeking more secluded beaches can take the ACTRB bus (dir.: Biarritz or Bayonne) to Acotz, near several campgrounds, where there are two beaches popular with surfers. Before hitting the surf, head to **Billabong,** 16 rue Gambetta, for a full array of boards and wetsuits. (☎26 07 93. 2hr. lesson €40. Wetsuit €7 per ½-day, €12 per day; surfboard €10/15. ID deposit. Open July-Aug. daily 10am-11pm; Sept.-June M-F 10am-12:30pm and 2:30-7pm, Sa 10am-7:30pm, Su 11am-1pm and 3-7pm. AmEx/MC/V.)

In town, the spartan stone walls and wooden beams of the 15th-century **Eglise St-Jean-Baptiste,** rue Gambetta, offer a stark contrast to the nave and its elaborate painting and gold sculptures that preside over the altar. It was in this church that Louis XIV married the Spanish princess Maria-Teresa. (☎26 08 81. Open daily 10am-noon and 2-6pm. Mass Sa 7pm and Su 8:30am, 10:30am, and 6pm.) When you leave the church, turn right on rue Gambetta; the **Maison Louis XIV** is on the left at pl. Louis XIV. Owned by the same family for over 350 years, the elaborate royal furniture inside the house has been frozen in time as if awaiting the return of its famous boarder. The museum houses portraits of prominent royalty and even the royal sedan chair. (☎/fax 26 01 56. 30min. guided tour in French leaves every 30-60min. Written explanations in English and audio tours in French available upon request. Open July-Aug. M-Sa 10:30am-12:30pm and 2:30-6:30pm, Su 2:30-6:30pm; Sept. and June M-Sa 10:30am-noon and 2:30-5:30pm, Su 2:30-5:30pm. €5, students and ages 12-18 €3, under 12 free.)

From 1954 to 1956, St-Jean-de-Luz was France's primary tuna supplier. Fishing boats still leave from quai de l'Infante and quai Maréchal Leclerc, although they are not as fruitful as in the past. To get in on the seafaring fun, stop by the docks near Maison Louis XIV, where **Nivelle III** offers a 4hr. fishing trip from 8am to noon and an afternoon cruise along the Spanish coast from 2 to 4pm. Customers keep the fish they catch. (☎06 09 73 61 81. Trips May-Sept., more frequent July-Aug. Reservations required. Fishing trip €25, under 18 €13. Afternoon cruise €13/6.)

For the uncompromising devotee of Basque culture, the **Ecomusée Basque** is located 3km out of the city along the route of the ATCRB bus (dir.: Biarritz or Bayonne; get off at "Dubonnet"). The 1hr. audio tour includes free samples of sweet Basque *liqueur* (Izarra) and a documentary about the Basque method of making linen. Audio tour available in French, English, Spanish, and Basque. (☎51 06 06. Open July-Aug. daily 10:30am-6:30pm; Apr.-June and Sept.-Oct. M-Sa 10-11:15am and 2:30-5:30pm. Tours every 15min. €5.50, students €5, ages 5-12 €2.30.)

FESTIVALS

Summer in St-Jean-de-Luz is jammed with concerts, Basque festivals, and the much anticipated championship match of **cesta punta** (jai alai), featuring the fastest moving ball in any sport. (☎51 65 36; www.cestapunta.com. Qualifying series and finals July-Aug. Tu and F at 9pm. Tickets available at the tourist office; €6-19, under 12 free. MC/V accepted with phone reservations.) The biggest annual festival is the three-day **Fête de la St-Jean,** held on a weekend in late June, when singing and dancing fill the streets. Nearly continuous performances by amateurs and professionals animate the *fronton* (arena), while spectators sip on sangria and bite into barbecued Basque dishes. **Toro de Fuego** heats up summer nights in pl. Louis XIV with pyrotechnics, dancing, and bull costumes. (July-Aug. W and Su 10:30pm.) St-Jean celebrates tuna at the **Fête du Thon** (the first Sa in July beginning at 6pm). Locals gather around the center of town to eat tuna, dance, and toss confetti. Entrance is free, but meals at booths cost around €10. The homage to fish continues on the second Saturday of July with the all-you-can-eat **Nuit de la Sardine** at the Campos-Berri, next to the cesta punta stadium. (☎26 02 87; www.st-jean-de-luz.com.)

DAYTRIP FROM ST-JEAN-DE-LUZ

COL DE ST-IGNACE

Basque Bondissant (☎26 25 87) runs buses to Col de St-Ignace (dir.: Sare) from the green-rimmed bus terminal facing the train station in St-Jean-de-Luz (20min.; July-Aug. M-Sa 3 per day, Sept.-June M-Tu and Th-F 3 per day, W 2 per day; round-trip €17, ages 4-10 €12). Office open M-F 9am-noon and 1:45-6:30pm.

Ten kilometers southeast of St-Jean-de-Luz, the village of Col de St-Ignace (KOHL duh sehnt-ig-nahss) serves as a base for the Basque country's loveliest vantage point. Trains from Col de St- Ignace crawl at a snail's pace along an authentic 1924 *chemin de fer* (railroad) up the mountainside to the 905m summit of **La Rhune.** Each hair-raising turn reveals a postcard-perfect display of forests hovering above farmland, as *pottoks* (wild Basque ponies) return your stares and sheep bound down the mountainside. At the peak, chilly air and gusty winds prevail even in summer. Trains are operated by **Le Petit Train de la Rhune.** (☎54 20 26; www.rhune.com. Open mid-Mar. to early Nov. Trains run daily July-Aug. every 30min. 9am-5pm; Sept.-June regular departures at 10am and 3pm and irregular departures in between. Round-trip €13, ages 4-10 €11. MC/V.) La Rhune (*Larún* in Basque) is Spanish soil; shop owners slip easily between French and their native tongue. If you decide to walk down from La Rhune, take the well-marked trail to the left of the tracks to the village of **Ascain** instead of to St-Ignace, as loose rocks on the path to St-Ignace make for treacherous footing. Hike on D4 back to Col de St-Ignace (1½hr.; 3km) to catch a bus back.

ST-JEAN-PIED-DE-PORT ☎05 59

Tucked into the red Pyrenean hills, St-Jean-Pied-de-Port (SEHN-jahn-pee-ed-duh-pohr; pop. 1417) is the meeting place of three major trails—from Paris, Vezelay, and Puy. The town has been a resting place for pilgrims on the road to the tomb of St-James in Santiago de Compostela, Spain, since the 10th century. Today, St-Jean embodies rural Basque charm, with small white houses and red shutters, flower-lined stone-arch bridges, and a medieval citadel. Pilgrims have been replaced by backpackers from all corners of the world seeking to embark on one of many trails through the French and Spanish Pyrénées, which lie only a short distance outside the city walls. The GR10 and the GR65 trails, notoriously challenging for both hikers and cross-country skiers, lie nearby, making St-Jean the perfect intersection of backpacking paradise and peaceful small town.

TRANSPORTATION AND PRACTICAL INFORMATION. Trains leave for Bayonne (1¼hr; 5 per day, last train July-Aug. 6:30pm, Sept.-June 4:30pm; €8) from the station on av. Renaud. (☎37 02 00. Info office open M-Sa 6:30am-noon and 1-6:45pm, Su 9am-noon and 2-7pm.) Rent **bikes** at **Garazi Cycles,** 32bis au Jaï-Alaï. From the tourist office, turn right and keep left when the road splits; look for a shed on the right. (☎37 21 79. Bikes €10 per ½-day, €15 per day; passport or ID deposit. Scooters €18/30; €350 deposit. Motorcycles €35/50; €700 deposit. Open M-Sa 9am-noon and 2-6pm. July-Aug. service available Su by prior arrangement.)

From the station, turn left and then immediately right on av. Renaud, follow it uphill, and turn right at its end. Forty meters on the left, the **tourist office,** 14 av. de Gaulle, gives out maps of the town and sells hiking guides (€8) charting the 25 regional trails. (☎37 03 57; www.pyrenees-basques.com. Open July-Aug. M-Sa 9am-7pm, Su 10am-4pm; Sept.-June M-Sa 9am-noon and 2-6pm.) The **police** station (☎49 20 10) is on rue d'Ugange, and the **Clinique Luro** (☎37 00 55) in Ispoure handles **medical emergencies.** The **post office,** fittingly enough, is on rue de la Poste. (☎37 90 00. Open M-F 9am-noon and 2-5pm, Sa 9am-noon.) **Postal Code:** 64220.

ACCOMMODATIONS AND FOOD. St-Jean-Pied-de-Port is a paradise of budget accommodations. Hotels fill up quickly in the summer, but there is a glut of *gîtes* (rooms rented out in family homes, normally €8-12 a night), thanks to the city's position along the pilgrimage route to Santiago de Compostela, Spain. Many are clustered on rue de la Citadelle. Contact the **tourist office** (☎37 03 57) or the **Amis du Chemin** (☎37 05 09) to make reservations. One good option is Mme. Etchegoin's **gîte d'étape ❶**, 9 rte. d'Uhart. From the tourist office, turn left, cross the bridge, and take the first right. After you pass the city gates, the street becomes rte. d'Uhart; when the road splits, keep right, following the sign to Bayonne (5min.). Twelve spartan but comfortable bunks await in this 18th-century house, as do three attractive *chambres d'hôte* with handmade quilts, antique furnishings, and hardwood floors. Each room has one large bed and either a private shower or access to a communal one. (☎37 12 08. Open Mar.-Nov. Breakfast €4.50 with dorms, included with rooms. Sheets or sleeping bag €2. Reception 8am-10:30pm. Reserve ahead. Dorms €10; singles €32; doubles €38; triples €48.) Quiet and plain **Camping Municipal ❶** is 5min. from the center of town, on av. du Fronton. From the tourist office, turn left, then take an immediate left through the wall of the Citadelle on rue de l'Eglise. Turn right on rue d'Espagne, cross the river, and take your first left, on the unmarked rue de la Liberté. At the end of the block is a sign to the campground. (☎37 00 92. Open daily Apr.-Oct. 9-11am and 5-7pm. €2.50 per person, €2 per child, €2 per tent, €2 per car. Electricity €2.50. Bathrooms and showers free for campers, €2 for visitors.)

Farmers bring *ardigazna* (tangy, dry, sheep's-milk cheese) to the market on **place de Gaulle.** (Open M 9am-6pm.) In July and August, local fairs bring produce from nearby villages; ask for the dates at the tourist office. Bread, cheese, and wine are all available at any one of the small shops that line **rue d'Espagne.** For everyday food, try the **Relais de Mousquetaires** supermarket on the corner of rue d'Espagne and rue d'Uhart. (☎37 00 47. Open M, W, F-Sa 9:30am-12:30pm and 4-7pm; Tu and Th 9:30am-12:30pm.) None of the cheap restaurants in St-Jean-Pied-du-Port are spectacular, but there are several cafés and *crêperies* along **rue de Zuharpeta** that offer budget meals and refreshing sangria. For an excellent meal at a fair price, **Paxkal Oillarburu ❷**, 8 rue de l'Eglise, won't disappoint. From the tourist office, turn left and then left again at rue de l'Eglise to find this local favorite tucked behind the citadel wall. Basque specialties are served beneath wooden beams in a rustic but elegant atmosphere. (☎37 06 44. *Menu* €14. Open daily noon-2:30pm and 7-9:30pm. MC/V.) For a splurge, try the charming **Restaurant Etche Ona ❹**, on pl. Floquet. Expertly cooked and garnished with traditional Basque sauces, the duck, lamb, and rabbit (each €14) are superb. (☎37 01 14. *Plats* €14. *Menu* €28. Open July-Sept. daily 10am-2pm and 7:30-10pm; Oct.-June M-W and Sa-Su 10am-2pm and 7:30-10pm. MC/V.) A more affordable option, **Lizarra Ostatua ❷**, across the street on pl. Floquet, serves a variety of pizzas and an excellent paella dish. (☎37 00 99. Pizzas €7-9. Paella €10. *Plat du jour* €8.50-11. *Menus* €12-25. Open M-W and F-Su noon-2:30pm and 7-10:30pm. MC/V.)

SIGHTS. Though the Pyrénées are the main draw, the tiny center of St-Jean-Pied-de-Port is worth at least a brief visit. Bounded by the **porte d'Espagne** and **porte St-Jacques,** St-Jean's ancient *haute ville* consists of one narrow street, **rue de la Citadelle,** which is bordered by houses made from the regional crimson stone. To reach it, turn right when you leave the tourist office, right again on rue de France, and left on rue de la Citadelle. Continue up the hill to the **Citadelle de Vauban,** unquestionably St-Jean's greatest attraction. Originally built by Pierre de

Conty in the 1620s, the fortress was later reinforced by Vauban during the reign of Louis XIV and now towers over the town and surrounding farmland. In 1750, the citadel housed 2000 soldiers and protected Bayonne and Orthez from Spaniards lurking across the border. Although the stronghold's interior has since been converted into a middle school, visitors can still climb to the top to picnic on grassy ramparts and catch a breathtaking view of the town below and the surrounding mountains. Standing below the walls of the fortress is the **Prison des Evêques,** 41 rue de la Citadelle. Built in the 13th century, the small but beautiful building was used to discipline unruly soldiers during the 19th century and to torture French escapees during Nazi occupation. Today, the prison is a museum dedicated to St-Jacques's pilgrimage. (☎37 00 92. Open July-Aug. daily 10am-7pm; Easter-June and Sept.-Oct. M and W-Su 11am-12:30pm and 2:30-6:30pm. €3, under 10 free.)

HIKING. The most spectacular **hikes** from St-Jean-Pied-de-Port either require more than a day or are not accessible by public transportation. Nonetheless, one manageable 3hr. hike is worthwhile; striking views of Pau and the surrounding mountains on the second half of the hike are the reward for a less exciting walk along flat roads at the beginning. From the tourist office, turn right, staying left on Av. Jaï Alaï at the fork. Pass through the traffic circle and, following signs to Ispoure, turn left after the bridge over the river. Continue until you see the small church, the **Eglise d'Ispoure,** on your right. Turn right when the road ends and walk up the hill, passing the church, which should now be on your left. 50m past the church, turn left at the intersection marked by a stone cross. Continue to the second intersection and turn left, following the sign to Etchaine. After five minutes, keep left at the fork in the road marked by a row of four pine trees on the right. Walk up a steep hill with a stream to your right. At the next fork, continue upwards on the gravel road. You'll find yourself in the **Domaine Abotia** vineyard; turn around when you reach a four-way intersection and retrace your steps back to St-Jean. For a detailed map of the area, see hike #21 in the tourist office's guidebook.

The Spanish border is an 8-10hr. hike from St-Jean-Pied-de-Port along a clearly marked trail. The **GR65** leads through the Pyrénées toward the **Pass of Roncevaux** and, a paltry 800km later, to **Santiago de Compostela** and **St-James's tomb.** To get on the trail from the tourist office in St-Jean, turn left out of the office, then left immediately on tiny rue de l'Eglise and right on rue d'Espagne, following it out through the Porte de l'Eglise. At the first fork in the road, keep left on rue de St-Michel; at the second fork, turn right on rte. du Maréchal Harispe, following signs to Chemin de St-Jacques. The narrow road slopes up the mountainside, past family farms and into the Pyrénées, where sheep and horses wander. In France, red and white stripes on the telephone poles mark the GR65, but upon entrance into Spain, the trail markings become yellow arrows. The **Fontaine de Roland,** at the **col de Bentarte,** signals entry onto Spanish land. As a daytrip, it's possible to hike the first half of the route and then turn back; the restaurant at **Refuge auberge d'Orisson,** a third of the way to Roncevaux, provides a convenient destination. Before beginning any of these hikes, stop at **Amis du Chemin de St-Jacques de Pyrénées Atlantiques,** 39 rue de la Citadelle, in St-Jean, where the staff offers help, directions, maps, and lodging exclusively to hikers. (☎37 05 09. Open mid-Mar. to mid-Nov. daily 7:30am-12:30pm and 1:30-10:30pm. Shelter €7 per night, including breakfast.)

PAU ☎05 59

Once the seat of the kings of Navarre, Pau (PO; pop. 80,000) has transformed itself into a vibrant and youthful regional hub, where charming architecture and mountain vistas mix with the vivid colors and bustling sounds of a lively city. Just as remarkably, the château where King Henri IV was born and raised remains in near-perfect condition. As the capital of the Béarn region, Pau is also the center of *Béarnais* cuisine, home to more than 150 tempting restaurants.

TRANSPORTATION. The **train station,** on av. Gaston Lacoste, is at the base of the hill by the château. (Info and ticket office open M-Th and Sa 5:15am-8:30pm, F 5:15am-11:30pm, Su 7:15am-11:30pm.) **Trains** go to: Bayonne (1hr., 7 per day, €15); Biarritz (1½hr., 6-7 per day, €18); Bordeaux (2½hr.; 11 per day; €28, TGV €32); Lourdes (30min., 18 per day, €6.30); St-Jean-de-Luz (2½hr., 6 per day, €18). CITRAM runs **buses** to Agen (3hr., 1 per day, €26). Tickets are at the office on av. Thimonier. (☎27 22 22. Open M-F 9am-noon and 2-5pm.) Société TPR buses go to Lourdes (1¼hr.; M-Sa 5 per day, Su 2 per day; €4, under 6 free). The office is at 4 rue la Pouble. (☎27 45 98. Open M-F 9am-noon and 2-6pm.) STAP runs **local buses.** The office is on Chemin Larribau. (☎14 15 16. Tickets €1, day pass €2.50, *carnet* of 8 €5.50. First bus in any direction M-Sa 6:30am, Su 1:15pm; last bus in any direction M-Sa 8:20pm, Su 7:40pm.) Pau has little night transport; the **Noctambus** circulates on a few routes in the evening, running 2-4 buses from 8-11pm. The office is on the left side of rue Gachet. (☎27 69 78. Open M-F 8:30am-12:30pm and 1:30-6pm, Sa 9am-noon.) **Taxis** depart from the train station and the airport. (☎02 22 22. Base €2, €1.44 per km during the day, €1.88 at night. Approximately €30 from the train station to the airport.) **Romano Sport,** on the corner of rue Jean-Réveil and rue Castelnau, rents **mountain bikes** (€20 per day), in-line skates (€7 per day), skis (€20 per day, including boots), hiking boots, and mountain equipment. (☎98 48 56. ID deposit. Open daily 9am-noon and 3-7pm.)

ORIENTATION AND PRACTICAL INFORMATION. To get to the tourist office and town center from the station, ride the free funicular to bd. des Pyrénées (every 3min.; M-Sa 6:45am-12:10pm, 12:35-7:50pm, and 8:15-9:50pm; Su 1-7:50pm and 8:15-9pm), or climb the steep, zig-zagging path to the top of the hill. At the top, make sure to pick up a map at the **tourist office,** across the tree-lined pl. Royale from the funicular. (☎27 27 08; www.pau-pyrenees.com. Open July-Aug. M-Sa 9am-6pm, Su 9:30am-1pm and 2-6pm; Sept.-June M-Sa 9am-6pm, Su 9:30am-1pm.)

You can find a **laundromat** at the corner of rue Lespy and rue Emile Garet (☎82 73 60; wash €3, dry €0.30 per 4min., detergent €0.30; coins only; open daily 7am-10pm); a **police station** on rue O'Quin (☎98 22 22); and a **hospital** at 4 bd. Hauterive (☎92 48 48). Consult the tourist office or the signs posted on every pharmacy's door for the rotating **pharmacie de garde.** Access the **Internet** at **C Cyber,** 20 rue Lamothe, past the post office. (☎82 89 40. €0.80 per 10min., €4.80 per hr. Open M-Sa 10am-2am, Su 2pm-midnight.) The **post office,** on cours Bosquet at rue Gambetta, has **currency exchange,** Cyberposte, and copy and fax services. (☎98 98 98. Open M-F 8:30am-6:30pm, Sa 8:30am-noon.) **Postal Code:** 64000.

ACCOMMODATIONS. Low-priced, high quality accommodations are difficult to come by in Pau. On a street in a quieter section of town, **Hôtel Regina ❸,** 18 rue Gassion, offers clean linoleum-floored rooms with high ceilings and large windows, which are an especially good value for groups of two to four. (☎27 29 19. Breakfast €5. Reception 8am-11pm. Doubles and triples with full bath €32-55. MC/V.) Couples, larger families, or those willing to splurge should try two-star **Hôtel Central ❹,** 15 rue Léon Daran. The 28 large, spotless rooms are tended by an attentive owner and come with TV, shower, and clean bathroom. Saint-Exupéry, author of *Le Petit Prince,* stayed in room #7 before his rise to fame. The main floor features a billiard room and bar with cable TV. (☎27 72 75. Breakfast €6.50. Reception 7am-10:30pm. Reservations recommended. Singles €48-52; doubles €52-57, with 2 single beds €60. Extra bed €9. AmEx/MC/V.) **Hôtel de la Pomme d'Or ❷,** 11 rue Maréchal Foch, offers acceptable rooms in the center of town at the cheapest prices around—be prepared for peeling wallpaper and hard mattresses. Turn left from the tourist office onto rue Louis Barthou and left again on rue A. de Lassence. Walk through pl. Clemenceau and turn right onto rue Maréchal Foch. (☎11 23 23; fax 11 23 24. Breakfast €4. Reception 24hr. Singles €22-27, with shower and toilet €33; doubles €26-31; triples with shower €39-47; quads €43. Cash only.)

FOOD. The region famous for *béarnaise* sauce has no scarcity of specialties: *saumon* (salmon), *brochet* (pike), *oie* (goose), *canard* (duck), and *assiette béarnaise* (a platter of gizzards, duck hearts, and asparagus). The area around the château, including **rue Sully** and **rue du Château,** has elegant regional restaurants (*plats* €9, *menus* €16). Inexpensive pizzerias, kebab joints, and Vietnamese eateries can be found on **rue Léon Daran.** A sprawling **Super U** supermarket sits on the lower level of the Centre Bosquet megaplex on cours Bosquet. (Open M-Sa 9am-7:30pm. MC/V.) The equally enormous market at **Les Halles,** pl. de la République, is a maze of vegetable and cheese stalls. (Open M-Sa 6am-1pm.) The **Marché Biologique,** pl. du Foirail, sells organic produce. (Open W and Sa 8am-noon.) Hip **Ciel and Chocolat ❷,** 11 rue Maréchal Foch, serves chic food at reasonable prices. The €10 lunch *menu* includes a choice of appetizer or dessert (the profiteroles are delicious) and *plat*; try the *magret de canard au miel.* (☎27 44 15. Open M-W noon-2pm, Th-Sa noon-2pm and 7:30-10pm. MC/V.) For a filling dinner, try **L'Entrecôte ❷,** 26 rue Lamothe, a small pizzeria near the post office. Locals fight over tables to enjoy generous pizzas (€8-9) that come with a large assortment of toppings; the *pizza rocquefort* is a house speciality. The owner brings the hot pizzas directly from the oven to your plate. (☎27 45 75. Salads €8.50. Steaks €12-14. Open daily noon-2pm and 7pm-midnight. MC/V.) The beach chairs perched on the lawn at **L'Isle au Jasmin ❶,** 28 bd. des Pyrénées, tucked behind the château, overlook a captivating Pyrenean vista. The owner brews the coffee and blends the teas herself, using everything from dried mountain flowers to fresh wild berries. (☎27 34 82. Coffee €1.40. Teas by the pot €2.50. Cakes and *petits-fours* €1-2. Open daily 11am-8pm; closed in bad weather. Cash only.)

SIGHTS. After getting off the funicular, turn left along bd. de Pyrénées, taking in the mountains on your left and the city on your right. You'll come to the **Château d'Henri IV,** the birthplace of its namesake, the first of the Bourbon kings. Originally built as a medieval fortress, it was remodeled by Louis-Philippe and then by Napoleon III. Now a national museum, the castle displays a famous collection of Gobelin tapestries, as well as the enormous tortoise shell that served as Henri IV's crib. The château is accessible only through 1¼hr. guided tours in French, which depart every 15min. (☎82 38 02. English tours by appointment. Open daily mid-June to mid-Sept. 9:30am-12:15pm and 1:30-5:45pm; Apr. to mid-June and mid-Sept. to Oct. 9:30-11:45am and 2-5pm; Oct.-Mar. 9:30-11:45am and 2-4:15 pm. Last tour 1hr. before closing. €5, ages 18-25 €3.20, under 18 free.) The **Musée des Beaux Arts,** rue Mathieu Lalanne, contains an enormous tableau of Henri IV's birth. The rest of the museum houses a collection of modern art and 17th- to 19th-century European paintings. (☎27 33 02. English and French guides available if requested in advance. Open M and W-Su 10am-noon and 2-6pm. €3, students €1.50, under 18 free.)

NIGHTLIFE AND FESTIVALS. Cinéma le Méliès, 6 rue Bargoin, shows art films, some in English. (☎27 60 52; schedule available at www.pau-pyrenees.com. Movies 1:30-10:30pm. Closed 4 days in mid-Aug. Tickets €6, students €4.80, under 12 €3.) When night falls, don't miss **Le Garage,** 49 rue Emile Garet, on the corner of rue Langles past the Centre Bosquet, where local 20-somethings congregate. (☎83 75 17. Lunch and dinner *menus* available noon-2pm and 7-10pm. Pints and mixed drinks from €4. Salads €6-7. *Plats* €7-9. Open M-F noon-2am and Sa-Su

3pm-2am. MC/V.) Not only does the flower-lined **boulevard des Pyrénées** overlook expansive green mountains, but it also features great bars that cater to the young and beautiful, who overflow onto the sidewalk in the summer. The two-story **Galway,** 20 bd. des Pyrénées, draws a large Anglophone crowd with quality music and beer. (☎82 94 66. Pints from €4. Live music twice a month. Open daily July-Sept. 1pm-3am; Oct.-June 1pm-2am. MC/V.) For gay nightlife, try **La Station des Artistes,** 8 rue René Fournets, which offers lots of smoke and mirrors, as well as a transsexual show on Sundays at 11pm. (☎83 83 02. Open W-Su 9pm-2am. AmEx/MC/V.)

Summer in Pau brings a rash of festivals. In June, cars race around the town center during the Formula 3 **Grand Prix de Pau.** Bicycles replace cars in mid-July when the **Tour de France** passes through spectator-lined city streets. From mid-July to mid-August, the **Ciné Cité** hosts free concerts and outdoor films. Salsa, blues, and jazz bands perform at around 9pm and are quickly followed by either a recent film or an old classic. Contact the tourist office for schedules. At the same time, the city hosts a series of free matches of **Pelote Basque** every Monday and Thursday night at the distant outdoor *fronton* of the new Complexe de Pelote, 458 bd. du Fronton. (Ask at the tourist office for directions.) The Complexe de Pelote also hosts several types of indoor *pelote* all year long. (☎80 15 03; www.pilotak.fr.)

LOURDES ☎05 62

In 1858, 14-year-old Bernadette Soubirous reported seeing the first of 18 visions of the Virgin Mary in the Massabielle Grotto in Lourdes (lOOrd; pop. 16,300). Eventually, the Virgin Mary instructed her to have a chapel built on the spot. Today, over six million visitors from more than 100 countries come annually to this pilgrimage center, toting rosaries and praying for miracles as they march or are wheeled to the Blessing of the Sick. The sesquicentennial (150th) celebration of Bernadette's vision in 2008 will attract legions of pilgrims for a series of special events.

TRANSPORTATION

Trains (☎42 55 53; info office open daily July-Aug. 7:05am-9:30pm, Sept.-June 7:05am-6:30pm) leave from 33 av. de la Gare to Bayonne (2hr., 5 per day, €20); Bordeaux (3hr.; 7 per day; €32, TGV €36); Paris (6-7hr., 5 per day, TGV €84); Pau (30min., 16 per day, €6.60); Toulouse (2hr., 8 per day, €23). SNCF **buses** run from the station to Cauterets (55min., 6 per day, €6.50). The local **Citybus** (☎94 10 78) runs from all points in the city to the grotto, the Pic du Jer (from which the funicular departs), and Lac de Lourdes (Easter-Oct. daily every 15-30min. 7am-7pm, Sept.-June Tu, Th, Sa 7am-7pm; €1.20). **Taxis** (☎0 800 820 052) are at the train station and the grotto from Easter to October. Rent **bikes** at **Cycles Antonio Oliveria,** 14 av. Alexandre Marqui. (☎42 24 24. €10 per ½-day, €15 per day, €90 per week; €300 or photo ID deposit. Open Tu-Sa 9:30am-noon and 2-7pm. MC/V.)

ORIENTATION AND PRACTICAL INFORMATION

The train station is on the northern edge of town, 10min. from the town center. The religious heart of Lourdes is the **grotto,** located 15min. from the station. Follow av. de la Gare straight through the intersection, ignoring large white signs to La Grotte. After the intersection, when the road splits, keep left on bd. de la Grotte, and follow it as it snakes right at pl. Jeanne d'Arc. Follow the smaller green signs to La Grotte. Continue across the Gave River to reach the Esplanade des Processions, the Basilique St-Pius X, and the grotto.

To get from the station to the **tourist office,** pl. Peyramale, turn right on av. de la Gare, then bear left on the busy av. du Général Baron Maransin at the first intersection. Cross a bridge above bd. du Lapacca and proceed; the office is in a glass complex on the right (10min.). The staff distributes maps, info on religious ceremonies, a list of hotels, and brochures. (☎42 77 40; www.lourdes-infotourisme.com. Open July-Aug. M-Sa 9am-7pm, Su 10am-6pm; Sept. and Mar.-June M-Sa 9am-6:30pm, Su 10am-12:30pm; Oct.-Jan. M-Sa 9am-noon and 2-6pm.) Bernadette-related sights are managed by the **Sanctuaires de Notre Dame de Lourdes,** which has a **Forum d'Info** to the left as you approach the basilica. Glossy materials on religious sights and events are available in several languages. (☎42 78 78. Open daily 8:30am-12:15pm and 1:45-6:30pm; slightly shorter hours in the winter.) **Forum Lourdes/Bureau Information Jeunesse,** pl. du Champ Commun, a helpful **youth center** with **Internet** access, is in a red building behind Les Halles. (☎94 94 00. Internet access €3 per hr. Open M-F 9am-noon and 1:30-5:30pm.) Other services include: a **laundromat,** 42 pl. du Champ Commun (wash €4.20, dry €0.60 per 5min.; open daily 8am-8pm); **police,** 7 rue Baron Duprat (☎42 72 72); a **hospital,** 3 av. Alexandre Marqui (☎42 42 42), at the intersection of av. de la Gare, av. Marqui, and av. du Général Baron Maransin; **medical emergency services,** 2 av. Marqui (☎42 44 36); and **disabled services** at **Pavillon Handicapés,** bd. de la Grotte (☎42 79 92). The **post office** is at 31 av. du Général Baron Maransin and offers bills-only **currency exchange.** (☎42 72 00. Open M-Tu and Th-F 8:30am-noon and 1:30-6pm, W 9am-noon and 1:30-6pm, Sa 8:30am-noon.) **Postal Code:** 65100.

ACCOMMODATIONS AND CAMPING

Finding a decent room for €25 in Lourdes is relatively easy; hotels compete for the business of hordes of pilgrims. Similar hotels are grouped together—the cheap ones on **rue Basse** and the two-star establishments on **avenue de la Gare** and **avenue Maransin.** Though most budget hotels here are clean, they are often drab. In July and August, try to reserve at least a month ahead. The city's reputation as a healing center has induced many proprietors to improve wheelchair accessibility and construct facilities for the visually and hearing impaired. **Hôtel du Commerce ❷,** 11 rue Basse, next to a large pizzeria, faces the tourist office. The helpful owners take good care of the bright rooms, all of which come with telephones and sparkling bathrooms with toilet and shower. The back rooms look out onto the château. (☎94 59 23; hotel-commerce-et-navarre@wanadoo.fr. Breakfast €3. Singles €32; doubles €40; triples €50; quads €60. MC/V.) **Hôtel Lutétia ❷,** 19 av. de la Gare, is in an Art Nouveau building to the right as you exit the train station. Clean and comfortable, if austere, rooms all have telephones, and some have a TV. (☎94 22 85; www.lutetialourdes.com. Elevator and free parking. Singles €18, with toilet €25, with shower €32; doubles €25-64; triples €58. Students receive free upgrade to the next class of room. MC/V.) **Hôtel ❷ and Camping de la Poste ❶,** 26 rue de Langelle, is a small backyard campground 2min. beyond the post office (follow signs). It also lets eight small but clean rooms in an attached hotel. (☎94 40 35. Breakfast €5. Open Easter to mid-Oct. Doubles €26, with shower €28; triples €35/38; quads with shower €48. Camping €2.80 per person, €4 per site. Electricity €2.50. Shower €1.30. Cash or French check only.)

FOOD

Find groceries at the **Monoprix** supermarket, 9 pl. du Champ Commun. (☎94 63 44. Open M-Sa 8:30am-8pm, Su 8:30am-noon.) Produce, flowers, second-hand clothing, books, and cheap pizza are all sold at the **market** in Les Halles, pl. du Champ Commun. (Open M-F and Su 6:30am-1:30pm, Sa 5:30am-1:30pm.) On the central **boulevard de la Grotte,** similar restaurants charge similar prices (€9-12). Slightly cheaper *plats du jour* and *menus* can be found around the tourist office and on

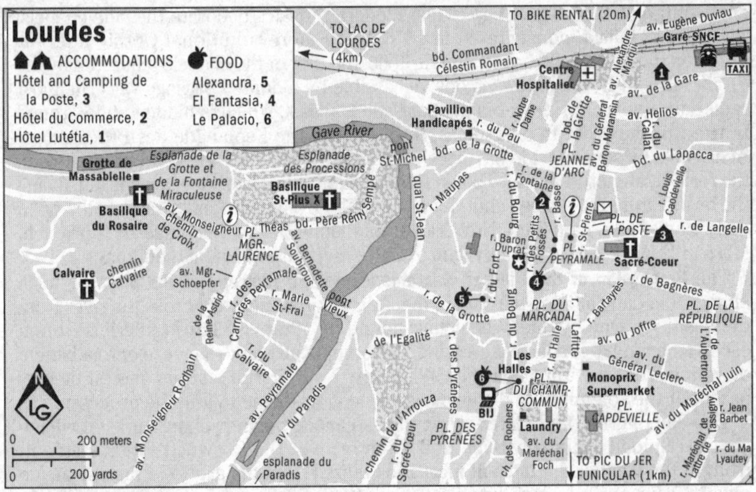

rue de la Fontaine. Somewhat swankier—though still touristy—restaurants, down the steps on both sides of the Gave, have the nicest views and breeze in town.

For a special meal at a reasonable price, try **Alexandra ❷**, 3 rue du Fort, just off bd. de la Grotte, with three-course lunch and dinner menus (€9/12). Stone, red plaster, cosiness, and elegance combine in this small restaurant, where *jambonneau de canard* (duck knuckle) is a specialty. (☎94 31 43. *Plats* €11-16. Open M-F noon-1:30pm and 7-9pm, Sa 7-9pm. AmEx/MC/V.) For French and Italian standards, **Le Palacio ❸**, 28 pl. du Champ Commun, with its white plastic awning and red columns, is a reliable option. The tagliatelle with smoked salmon (€10) fills you up for a low price. (☎94 00 59. Lunch *menu* €10. Dinner *menus* €15-26. Open M-Tu and Th-Su noon-2pm and 7-10pm. AmEx/MC/V.) **El Fantasia ❷**, 5 rue Basse, has a basic, wholesome Moroccan menu to relieve *brasserie*-tired palates. (☎94 15 58. *Tajines* €9.50. Open daily noon-2pm and 7-10pm. Cash only.)

SIGHTS

Lourdes offers both religious attractions and the natural beauty of the Pyrénées, although its sights draw more pilgrims than tourists. The **Lourdespass** (€30, ages 6-12 €15) can be purchased at the tourist office and provides access to four Bernadette-related museums, the Fortified Castle and its museum, the funicular to Pic du Jer, and the train that runs through town.

Visitors from around the world shuffle past the **Grotte de Massabielle,** a small, dark crevice in the mountainside at the edge of town; they touch its cold rock walls, whispering prayers and waiting to receive a blessing from the priest. Lines to touch the wall are longest 11:15am-3:30pm. Nearby, water from the spring where Bernadette washed her face is available for drinking, bathing, and bringing home in one of the numerous water bottles for sale (€1-3). The cave lies by the river on the right side of two superimposed churches, the Basilique du Rosaire and the upper basilica. (Site open daily 24hr. Wall open daily 11am-3:30pm and 4pm-6am. No shorts, tank tops, smoking, cell phones, or food.)

The **Basilique du Rosaire, La Crypte,** and the **upper basilica** were built triple-decker style above Bernadette's grotto. While these sights are important for religious reasons, they do not offer much aesthetically. The **Rosaire,** completed in 1889, houses a giant statue of the Virgin Mary, while modern mosaics decorate the side chapels. The **upper basilica,** consecrated in 1876, has a more traditional Gothic interior. Between the two sits **La Crypte,** built in 1866, the first of the chapels requested by the Virgin Mary in Bernadette's visions, accessible by a domed passageway. The most remarkable space for prayer is the **Basilique St-Pius X,** which is hidden underground in front of the other two basilicas, to the left of the Esplanade des Processions. Accessible by several wide passages, its stadium-sized concrete echo chamber is in the form of an upturned ship. When filled with singing, the space is inspiring, fusing the best features of a mega-church and an underground parking garage. (All 3 open daily Easter-Oct. 6am-7pm; Nov.-Easter 8am-6pm. Seven daily masses in French. Mass in English Apr.-Oct. daily 9am at St-Cosmas and St-Damian buildings.)

The **Procession of the Blessed Sacrament** and the **Blessing of the Sick** are huge affairs held daily at 5pm, starting in the Eglise St-Bernadette, across the river from the basilicas. One by one, wheelchair-bound or otherwise infirm pilgrims—often escorted by nuns—receive a blessing. Observers can stand, squeeze onto a bench, or watch from the upper basilica's balcony. Non-pilgrim visitors should be prepared for the solemnity of the event. Anyone is welcome to join the procession as a "one-day pilgrim" and march along the esplanade behind rolling ranks of wheelchairs. (Guided tours July-Sept. at 2:30pm meet at the Crowned Virgin statue in front of the basilica.) A **torch lit procession** blazes from the grotto to the esplanade nightly from April through late October at 9pm. Pilgrims from all over the world recite "Hail Mary" in six languages and proudly hold banners proclaiming church names and nationalities. In 2008, the sesquicentennial of Bernadette's vision, torch lit processions will continue on Fridays and Saturdays throughout the winter. The year will feature several other special events, including an English-language pilgrimage March 23-29. (For more information, consult the Forum Information of the Sanctuaires de Notre-Dame de Lourdes. ☎42 78 78; www.lourdes-france.org.)

OUTDOOR ACTIVITIES

Just outside of town, a **funicular** track climbs 1km up the **Pic du Jer,** the most interesting secular attraction that Lourdes has to offer. After the 8min. ride, a 10min. hike gives access to a summit observatory with a stunning view of the countryside and the town below. Energetic travelers can hike up the mountain using the map from the ticket booth (1½hr.). Beware of rapidly descending mountain bikers. Both funicular and hike are wheelchair-accessible. (To reach the depot, walk toward Les Halles from the tourist office, and continue straight for 1.5km to a sign for the funicular on the left. Bus #2 also runs from the tourist office to the depot. €2.20 round-trip. ☎94 00 41. Open July-Aug. 9am-8pm; mid-Nov. to late Mar. 10am-6pm. Last ride up 1hr. before closing, last ride down 15min. before closing. €9, ages 7-18 €6.50, under 6 free.)

At the large, peaceful **Lac de Lourdes,** 4km from the center of town, locals dive off the dock and eat ice cream in the neighboring café. (Buses D and #3 July-Aug. 4 per day 9:15am-5:45pm; Sept.-June Tu, Th, and Sa, less frequently. Times vary by month; check the schedule. By foot, take av. du Général Baron Maransin toward the train station and turn left onto bd. Romain. The street becomes av. Béguere and then av. Jean Prat. Take a left onto chemin du Lac to reach the water. 40min.)

CAUTERETS ☎05 62

Perched 930m in the air in a narrow valley between the near-vertical peaks of the gorgeously green Pyrénées mountains, tiny Cauterets (CO-tuh-ray; pop. 1300) lies on the edge of the *Parc National des Pyrénées Occidentales*. In the winter, skiers flock to the *Cirque du Lys*, and as the town thaws in spring, the melting snow draws wilderness lovers. Serious hikers will enjoy the sharply contrasting French and Spanish sides of the Pyrenees, accessible from Cauterets, while others can try the many dayhikes (1½-8hr.). Cauterets also attracts less athletic visitors—the town's famous *thermes* offer a relaxing array of restorative treatments.

TRANSPORTATION AND PRACTICAL INFORMATION. Cauterets is split by the Gave river and is small enough to cross on foot in 5min. It is accessible only by bus from Lourdes. SNCF **buses** (☎92 53 70; office open May-Sept. daily 9am-1pm and 3-6:30pm, Oct.-Apr. Tu-Sa 9am-1pm) run from pl. de la Gare to Lourdes (1hr., 8 per day, €6.50), where travelers can transfer to trains or other buses. Rent **bikes** at **Le Grenier,** 4 av. du Mamelon Vert. (☎92 55 71. €17-23 per ½-day, €22-32 per day. Open daily 9am-7pm. MC/V.) To rent **skis** or other mountain gear in Cauterets, visit **Starski,** 12 Av. Général Leclerc, near the tourist office. (☎92 55 99. Skis, boots, and poles €12 per day, €62 per 6 days. 10% student discount. Open daily Dec.-Apr. 8:30am-1pm and 2-7pm; May-Oct. 9am-12:30pm and 2:30-7pm.)

From the bus station, follow av. du Général Leclerc uphill to the **tourist office,** pl. Foch. The staff offers a map and a free *Guide Pratique.* (☎92 50 50; www.cauterets.com. Open July-Aug. M-Sa 9am-12:30pm and 2-7pm, Su 9am-noon and 3-6pm; Sept.-June M-Sa 9am-12:30pm and 2-6pm, Su 9am-noon.) The *Cauterets Spécial Rando Facile* (€5) is the best hike resource, but it is only available in French. The **police** station is on av. du Docteur Domer (☎92 51 13). In case of a **medical emergency,** call ☎92 14 00. Access the **Internet** at **Pizzeria Giovanni,** 5 rue de la Raillère (☎92 57 80; €3 per hr.; open daily 10am-2pm and 5-11pm) or in the basement of the **public library,** 2 esplanade des Oeufs (☎92 59 96; €5 per hr.; open W and Sa 3-6:45pm, Th-F 4:45-6:45pm; during school vacations W-Sa 3-6:45pm). Free **Wi-Fi** is available with the purchase of food or drink at **Skibar** (see **Food**). The **post office,** at the corner of rue Belfort and rue des Combattants, offers **currency exchange.** (☎92 53 93. Open M-F 9am-12:30pm and 2-4:30pm, Sa 9am-noon.) **Postal Code:** 65110.

ACCOMMODATIONS AND FOOD. **Hôtel le Chantilly ❸,** 10 rue de la Raillère, a street away from the center of town, is owned by a charming Irish couple who offer hiking advice. Rooms on the lower two floors are renovated, with large windows, shower, and toilet. (☎92 52 77; www.hotel-cauterets.com. Breakfast €6. Reception 7am-10pm. Closed Nov.-Dec. July-Sept. singles and doubles €34, with shower €38; triples from €42. Oct. and Jan.-June €30/34/38. MC/V.) **Hôtel Christian ❹,** 10 rue Richelieu, offers darts, *bocce*, and a Pyrenean view for somewhat steep prices, but a buffet breakfast is included. The gracious owner, whose family has run the hotel for generations, does all he can to make your stay pleasant. All rooms come with bath. (☎92 50 04; www.hotel-christian.fr. Reception 7:30am-10pm. Closed Oct.-Nov. July-Aug. singles €52; doubles €72; triples €91; quads €108. Sept.-June €49/66/86/102. AmEx/MC/V.) **Gîte d'Etape UCJG ❶,** 3 av. du Docteur Domer, seven minutes from the town center, is a practical accommodation for real mountaineers. From the Parc National office, cross the parking lot and street and turn left uphill on a footpath underneath the funicular depot. The *gîte* is five minutes down the street, just beyond the tennis courts. The *gîte*'s friendly hosts offer 60 beds in every possible setup, from traditional campsites to canvas barracks to small attic bedrooms. The inn is managed by a caring pastor who knows the area and enjoys introducing guests to one another. (☎92 52 95. Kitchen and shower facilities available. Reception 24hr. Open mid-June to mid-Sept. Dorms €8; tent €4; space in the *gîte*'s tent €6.50, in bungalow €8.50, in apartment €11. Cash only.)

Cauterets has few gourmet restaurants but plenty of hearty food. The local specialty is the *berlingot,* a hard sugar candy originally used by patients visiting the *thermes* to contribute to "the cure." Several small restaurants with outdoor seating line **rue Verdun.** The beautifully old-fashioned **Halles market,** near the tourist office on av. du Général Leclerc, has fresh cheese, meat, and sandwiches, as well as pre-cooked entrees and wine. (Open daily June-Sept. 8am-1pm and 4-7pm; Oct.-May M-Sa 9am-1pm and 4-7pm, Su 8am-1pm. Hours vary.) An **open-air market** selling food and clothing is held in the parking lot next to the casino. (Open mid-June to mid-Sept. Th-F 8:30am-1pm; Th food only.) Stock up on meats for hiking, homemade jams, and fresh pizzas, *tartes*, or quiches at **Au "Mille Pâtes ❶,"** 5 rue de la Raillère. (☎92 04 83. Open daily July-Aug. and Feb. 8am-12:30pm and 4-8pm; Jan., Mar.-Apr., June, Sept., Dec. Th-Tu 8am-12:30pm and 4-8pm. MC/V.) **En Sò de Bedaù ❷,** 11 rue de la Raillière, a wine bar and stone-lined basement restaurant, draws locals with a solid Pyrenean menu. The budget-conscious can choose the two-course *Menu Pitchoun* (ground beefsteak or filet of trout followed by dessert; €8), while others may decide to splurge on the *garbure* (€15), a filling Pyrenean stew combining pork, duck, white beans, potatoes, and carrots. (☎92 60 21. Open July-Aug. daily 6pm-2am; Sept.-June M-Tu and Th-Su 6pm-2am. MC/V.) *Crêpes* and every other kind of snack food imaginable, as well as pitchers of sangria, make **Le Ski Bar ❷,** pl. Foch, a popular spot with hikers. (☎92 53 85. Free Wi-Fi for customers. Snacks €3.50-6. *Plats* €6.50-11. Open July-Aug. daily 7:30am-midnight; Sept.-June M-Tu and Th-Su 7:30am-midnight. AmEx/MC/V over €15.) Forty flavors of candy, including caramel, licorice, and mountain berry, are prepared by hand and cranked through a candy-making machine to the delight of onlooking customers at **A la Reine Margot ❶,** pl. de la Mairie. The only *berlingot confiserie* that still uses all-natural ingredients, this local institution provides free samples and friendly conversation. (☎92 58 67. €1.60 per 100g. Delicious swirly lollipops €0.75-1.85. Open daily July-Aug. 9:30am-12:30pm and 1:30-11pm; Sept.-Oct. and Dec.-June 10am-12:30pm and 3-7:30pm. AmEx/MC/V.) **Chez Gillou ❶,** 3 rue de la Raillère, is a *pâtisserie* specializing in blueberry and almond cakes known respectively as *tourtes myrtilles* and *pastis des Pyrénées.* (☎92 56 58. Cakes €5.50. Open daily Feb.-Mar. and July-Aug. 7am-1pm and 3-7pm; Apr.-June, Sept., and Dec.-Jan. 7:30am-12:30pm and 3:30-7pm. AmEx/MC/V.)

SIGHTS AND ENTERTAINMENT. Cauterets's natural **sulfur springs** have been credited over the years with curing everything from sterility to consumption. Now accessible only through a spa-like complex on the edge of town, the water continues to draw legions of the sick, elderly, and over-stressed. Massages are available. For info on the *thermes*, contact **Thermes de César,** av. Docteur Domer. (☎92 51 60; www.thermesdecauterets.com. Aerobath-sauna-hydrojet pool €9.50 per 20min., hydromassage jet showers €11 per 20min. Open June-Sept. M-Sa 5-8pm; Oct.-May M-Sa 4-8pm and some Su. Hours vary.) The park area, Esplanade des Oeufs, includes a **cinema** and **casino.** The cinema plays French and foreign films (the latter are mostly popular American imports dubbed in French), while the casino features table games and a bar. (Both ☎92 52 14. Open June-Sept. M-Th and Su 10am-3am, F-Sa 10am-4am; Oct.-May M-Th and Su 11am-2am, F-Sa 11am-3am. Tables open 9:30pm. Movie showings W-Su 3:30 and 9pm.) The **patinoire** (skating rink) hosts skating nights, according to a variable schedule available at the tourist office. The rink itself can be reached through the parking lot of the train station. (☎92 58 48. €8, students and under 18 €5.50; skate rental €2.50.)

PARC NATIONAL DES PYRÉNÉES ☎05 62

Cauterets is the logical base from which to explore the Parc National des Pyrénées, which shelters endangered brown bears and lynxes and 200 threatened colonies of marmots, and encompasses 118 lakes and 160 unique plant species in its snowcapped mountains and lush valleys. Packed with sulfurous springs and unattainable peaks, the Pyrénées change dramatically with the seasons yet manage to maintain their allure year-round. To get a sense of the variety of the mountain range, hikers should explore both the lush French side and barren Spanish side (a 4- to 5-day round-trip hike from Cauterets). The park offers modest hiking opportunities as well; jaw-dropping views are just an hour away from civilization.

AT A GLANCE: PARC NATIONAL DES PYRÉNÉES

AREA: Narrow 100km-long swath along the Franco-Spanish border.

CLIMATE: Misty in France, arid in Spain.

GATEWAYS: Gavarnie; Luz-St-Sauveur; Ainsa, Spain.

DAYHIKES: Lac de Gaube (5-6hr. round-trip from Cauterets via Pont d'Espagne), Chemin des Cascades (4hr. round-trip from Cauterets).

LONG HIKES: Cirque de Gavarnie, through waterfalls and lush forests (2- to 3-day hike from Cauterets); or continue into Spain (4-5 days from Cauterets).

ACCOMMODATIONS: *Gîtes* (around €11) are available in towns along the GR10; 1-night camping permitted in areas at least 1hr. away from major highways.

PRACTICAL INFORMATION. Touch base with the helpful staff of the **Parc National Office,** Maison du Parc, pl. de la Gare, in Cauterets, before braving the wilderness. They provide info on the park and the 14 different trails beginning and ending in Cauterets. Trails in the park are designed for a range of abilities, from novices to expert backpackers. The **maps** at the Parc National Office are sufficient for most hikes starting from Cauterets. (Day-hike maps €6.40, topographical maps €9.) For the Cauterets region, use the Institut de Géographie Nationale Vignemale map #1647. Documentary films in French feature aerial views of the local mountains and inform hikers about the area. (☎92 52 56; www.parc-pyrenees.com. Open July-Aug. M-F 9:30am-noon and 2:30-7pm; Sept.-June M-F 9:30am-noon and 3-6pm. Hours may vary. Films Tu and F 5pm.) The **Bureau des Guides,** 8 rue Verdun, runs tours and guides for **rock-climbing, canyoning, hiking,** and **skiing.** Medium-difficulty tours are €15-40 per person; harder ones €55-150. (☎92 59 83, cell 06 88 71 90 77; www.lechendesmontagnes.com. Open daily 9am-7pm; ring bell and call cell if no one responds.) **Bordenave Excursions,** 8 pl. Clemenceau, runs shuttle buses from the Mairie in Cauterets in July and August and provides taxis the rest of the year. (☎92 53 68, cell 06 71 01 46 86. July-Aug. shuttles every 2hr. 8am-6pm. €6 round-trip, €4 one way. Taxi €14 one way. Office open daily 9am-noon and 4:30-7pm.)

TIP **HEADING FOR THE HILLS.** Natural wonders await hikers of all levels in the Pyrénées, but no one should go it alone. Before setting out, be sure to visit the Parc National office and tell the tourist office where you're headed; they will keep track of your information in case of emergency. These resources can ensure that your dayhike doesn't become a three-day–or three-week–fiasco.

Gîtes in the park, which average €11 per night, are generally located in towns along the GR10 and are marked on the maps as well as trail signs. Reserve at least two days ahead, especially in July and August, when the mountains teem with hikers. The Parc National Office in Cauterets will help plan an itinerary while the **Service des Gîtes Ruraux** (☎05 59 11 20 64) in Pau makes *gîte* reservations. Pick up a free listing of *gîtes* from the Parc office in case you need to find one while on the trails. As a general rule, camping is permitted anywhere in the wilderness for one night (7pm-9am), provided you are more than an hour's hike from the nearest highway. Long-term camping in one place is not allowed. Those looking to stay somewhere for a couple days should find a camp zone near a refuge.

Before setting out on any hike, listen to **Météo-Montagne** for a French **weather forecast** for nearby mountains (☎08 92 68 02 65; updated twice daily). For **Mountain Rescue,** call ☎92 71 82. Below, *Let's Go* recommends a number of hikes leaving directly from Cauterets, each also listed in the *Spécial Rando Facile,* available at the tourist office, and in the *Parc National* brochure. If you plan to take the hikes directly from Cauterets, use the **Chemin des Cascades** (see below) to reach the **Pont d'Espagne;** make sure to add an extra four hours round-trip to the given time.

HIKING

DAYHIKES

LE CHEMIN DES CASCADES. *(2½hr. Moderate.)* Deservedly popular, this steep, waterfall-laden climb begins in Cauterets on a staircase to the right of the casino and ends in the national park at Pont d'Espagne. From here, three additional hikes are possible: Lac de Gaube, Refuge Wallon, and Circuit des Lacs. *(Free trail maps are available in English and French at the Parc National office; follow red and white trail markers.)*

LAC ET REFUGE D'ESTOM. *(3¾hr. Easy.)* This stunning trail leads through a broad valley to a mountain lake. *(The trailhead is left of the Thermes de César.)* Follow signs to Chemin des Pères, the Fruitière, and Lac d'Estom. After two hours, you'll reach the **Fruitière.** The **Lac d'Estom** remains two hours further ahead. Once at the lake, the **Refuge Estom ❶,** offers an overnight stop if you want to continue onwards. *(☎92 07 18; call 8-9:30am and 7-10pm. Open June-Sept. Dorms €9, demi-pension €27.)*

LAC DE GAUBE. *(3hr. Moderate.)* A popular destination, this lake is one hour from Pont d'Espagne, making it a possible dayhike destination from Cauterets as well. *(Take the Chemin des Cascades to the Pont d'Espagne.)* Two more hours lead through a glacial valley to the 2km-high **Refuge des Oulettes ❶,** where food and lodging are available. *(☎92 62 97. Open June-Sept. Dorms €19, demi-pension €35. Cash only.)*

REFUGE WALLON/MARCADAU. *(6hr. Difficult.)* The journey to this refuge, less traveled than that to the Lac de Gaube, is a manageable dayhike from the Pont d'Espagne and allows access to a remarkable variety of Pyrenean vistas. Though the round-trip from Cauterets is not possible in one day, hikers can stay at the **refuge ❶.** *(☎92 64 28. Breakfast €5.90. Open June to late Sept. Dorms €16, demi-pension €37.)*

CIRCUIT DES LACS. *(8hr. round-trip. Difficult.)* The longest and most difficult of the dayhikes listed here, this remarkable trail will challenge your legs and reward your eyes. The trail turns off the Refuge Wallon/Marcadau route and heads steeply uphill; after about an hour, follow signs and yellow trail markers to Circuit des Lacs. The hike can be done from Cauterets if you take a bus or taxi to and from the Pont d'Espagne. *(Trailhead along the route to the Refuge Wallon/Marcadau. Check with the tourist or park office before taking this hike to make sure conditions are good.)*

COL DE RIOU AND PLATEAU DU LISEY. *(3¾hr. and 4hr. Moderate.)* These slightly more taxing hikes lead to two neighboring peaks, although they do not offer the same striking scenery as some of the other hikes. *(Ask at the tourist office or Parc National Office for more information.)*

OVERNIGHT HIKES

GR10. *(Difficult.)* The Parc National's major route, the GR10 meanders across the Pyrénées, connecting the Atlantic with the Mediterranean and looping through most large towns. Both major and minor hikes intersect with and run along it, including the Le Chemin des Cascades and Lac du Gaube trails mentioned above. Pick up one of the purple maps at the park office for €9. *(Near Cauterets, join the GR10 from one of the minor hikes that intersects it.)*

CIRCUIT DE GAVARNIE. *(2 days. Difficult.)* This round-trip hike from Cauterets to Gavarnie, which runs along the GR10, connects Cauterets to **Luz-St-Sauveur** over the mountain before going on to **Gavarnie,** another day's hike up the valley. The **Refuge des Oulettes** is the first shelter past the Lac de Gaube. Another option is to hike to Lac d'Estom (see above), and continue from there; the trails merge. The trek from Lac d'Estom is technically challenging and impossible in the winter. There are *refuges* between d'Estom and Jan Da Lo for those looking for an easier trip. From Gavarnie, hop on a horse offered by the *refuge.* *(☎92 49 10. 2hr. round-trip. €17.)* Then ride to the grandiose, snow-covered **Cirque de Gavarnie** and its misty waterfall. *(These towns are also accessible by SNCF bus. Cauterets to Luz 1hr., 6 per day, €6.20; Luz to Gavarnie 2 per day, €7. The Luz tourist office is at pl. du 8 Mai 45. ☎92 30 30.)*

INTO SPAIN AND BACK. *(5 days. Difficult.)* For a sense of the diversity of the Pyrénées, explore the Spanish and French sides of the range. Both the red rock of the Spanish side and the misty forests of the French side are accessible on a four-to five-day hike from Cauterets. A one- to two-day hike from Pont d'Espagne, possible only July-Sept. due to snow in winter, runs up and over the Spanish border. Descend the far side of the Pyrénées to the village of Torla and hop on a bus to the **refuge de Goriz.** *(☎34 974 34 12 01. Call ahead to reserve. Open year-round.)* A magnificent hike to the snow-capped peaks of **Brèche de Roland,** on the edge of the Cirque de Gavarnie, will start hikers' return to France the following day. Cut the hike short at four to five days and take a bus back from Gavarnie to Luz and then to Cauterets. *(Confer with the tourist office in Ainsa, Spain for reservations at the Spanish refuges before attempting this trek, and don't forget your passport. ☎34 974 50 07 67.)*

SKIING

A weekend's worth of skiing is available directly from Cauterets via the **Cirque du Lys** cable car, which leaves from near the train station. From the tourist office, turn right on av. Général Leclerc and right again on rue du Pont Neuf; the *télécabine* (lift) station is on the right. Cirque du Lys offers 36km of skiing on 21 slopes, including five green (easy) and two black (difficult) trails. (☎92 13 00; www.cauterets.com. Daypass €26, students €20, ages 6-10 €18.) The Cauterets tourist office has free *plans des pistes* (trail maps). Other resorts in the area are accessible by SNCF **bus** from Cauterets or Lourdes. **Luz-Ardiden** offers downhill and cross-country skiing. (☎92 30 30. €26 per day, students €16.) Farther away, **Barèges** offers 69 slopes. (☎92 68 86. €29 per day, during school vacations €30.)

LUCHON ☎05 61

Though it lacks the picturesque charm of Cauterets and the religious attraction of Lourdes, Luchon (loo-CHOHN; pop. 2900) nonetheless draws thousands of hikers and skiers each year, as well as a large elderly population seeking a cure at the town's sulfurous springs. Luchon's bounty of cheap food and lodging sweeten the deal. A *télécabine* (lift) ferries visitors from the town center to the nearby mountain, Superbagnères, a buzzing ski complex in winter. A few hikes depart directly from Luchon, but they do not approach the variety offered in Cauterets.

TRANSPORTATION AND PRACTICAL INFORMATION. The **train station,** av. de Toulouse, runs **trains** directly to Paris (11hr., 1 per day, €81) and Toulouse (2hr., 2 per day, €19). Trains and SNCF **buses** go to Montréjeau (50min., 7-8 per day, €6.15), which connects to Bayonne, Paris, St-Gaudens, Toulouse, and other cities. (☎05 62 00 71 63. Open M-F 8:15am-noon and 1:30-5pm, Sa 8am-noon and 1:30-7pm, Su 1:30-9:30pm.)

To reach the **tourist office,** 18 allée d'Etigny, from the station, turn left on av. de Toulouse and bear right at the fork to follow av. Maréchal Foch. At the statues of lions, cross the rotary and bear left, following signs to the *centre-ville.* Av. Maréchal Foch will become av. Carnot and finally the main **allée d'Etigny** (15min.). The office is one block down on the right and distributes information on nearby hikes, mountain bike trails, and ski slopes. (☎79 21 21; www.luchon.com. Open daily July-Aug. 9am-7pm; Sept.-June 9am-12:30pm and 1:30-7pm.) For ambitious outdoor excursions, check in at the **Bureau des Guides,** 66 allée d'Etigny, which has info on **biking, hiking, rock climbing, canyoning,** and **skiing.** (☎79 69 38, cell 06 18 69 46 36; info@bureau-des-guides-luchon.com. Guided hikes €14-74 per ½-day. Canyoning and climbing €28-54 per ½-day. Skiing excursions €60-150. Open May-Sept. daily 9am-noon and 3:30-7pm; Oct.-Apr. during *vacances scolaires.* MC/V.) Consider shopping around for **extreme sports** opportunities; at least half a dozen outdoor companies are within a few blocks of the tourist office. Other town services include a **laundromat,** 33 rue Lamartine (wash €6-8, dry €1 per 11min.; open daily 8am-11pm); **police,** at the Hôtel de Ville (☎94 68 81); a **medical center,** 5 cours de Quinconces (☎79 93 00); **Internet** access at **Espace Internet,** 3 Allée d'Etigny, across from the tourist office (☎84 71 97; open July-Aug. M-Sa 9:30am-8pm; Sept.-June M-F 9:30am-noon and 3-6pm, Sa 9:30am-noon; MC/V); and a **post office,** 26 allée d'Etigny, on the corner of allée d'Etigny and av. Gallieni (☎94 74 50; open M-F 8:45am-noon and 2-5:45pm, Sa 8:45am-noon). **Postal Code:** 31110.

ACCOMMODATIONS AND FOOD. Standard budget hotels with rooms for €25-30 abound in the town center. **Hôtel François 1er ❷,** 1 allée d'Etigny, is a good choice, and the price is hard to beat. Located above one of Luchon's cheapest *brasseries,* the small and clean rooms come with colorful curtains, shower, toilet, and telephone. Some rooms have TV. (☎79 03 93. Breakfast €4.50. Reception 7:30am-midnight. Singles €25; doubles €29; triples €39. MC/V.) An excellent—though slightly inconvenient—option is **Gîte Skioura ❶,** uphill from the tourist office on the way to Superbagnères (2km). Call ahead to be picked up. Otherwise, follow cours des Quinconces out of town and up the mountain. On weekday mornings, it's more convenient to catch the *car thermal* from the train station to the *thermes* and get off at the Beauregard camping stop (15min., every 30min., free). Keep walking uphill for 10min. Five large and extremely clean rooms house 35 beds, and there's a fireplace large enough to heat a castle, as well as a kitchen open to guests. In some rooms, cloth partitions between every two beds provide some privacy. (☎79 60 59; www.gite-skioura.com. Breakfast €4.50. Sheets €3. Reservations recommended. Dorms €16, *demi-pension* €36.)

The town **market** (open W and Sa 8am-1pm) is at pl. Rouy. A **Casino** supermarket is at 43 av. Maréchal Foch. (Open M-Sa 8:30am-12:30pm and 3-7:30pm, Su 9am-noon. MC/V.) For cheap and filling meals, head to **alleé d'Etigny,** where €8-12 *menus* are available at any of the *brasseries* that line the street, many of which become lively bars late at night. **Le Pub Gourmand ❷,** 6 av. Carnot, on the way from the train station to the tourist office, provides good food in massive quantities. This restaurant only lives up to half of its name: it will satisfy a gourmand, but its atmosphere is more elegant than pub-like. The pub features an all-you-can-eat buffet of cold *hors d'oeuvres* (with dessert €9.50), as well as traditional meat and fish dishes. (☎79 89 00. Buffet with *steak-frites* and dessert €11. *Plats* €10-14. Open Tu-Sa noon-2pm and 7-9pm, Su noon-2pm. Closed Nov. AmEx/MC/V.) The *pâtisserie* **Rino Marseglia ❶,** 9 av. Carnot, provides sweet and savory quiches and tarts, including the exquisite *tourte aux myrtilles* (blueberry tart). Most of the selection is under €2. (☎ 79 18 95. Open daily 6am-1pm and 3-8pm.)

SIGHTS AND HIKES. Enjoy a soak in the **thermes,** but be prepared for the sulfurous smell and medical atmosphere. The *thermes* are located in the lavish white marble building at the end of allée d'Etigny. For €14, you can buy unlimited afternoon access to the 30°C pool and the **Vaporarium,** a natural underground sauna. For this and other programs, inquire at **Vitaline,** the large modern building at the end of allée d'Etigny, next to the Greek temple-like bathhouse. (Reservations and info ☎ 94 52 52; www.thermes-luchon.fr. Open mid-Dec. to mid-Oct. Info office open daily 9am-noon and 2:30-7pm. Vaporarium open daily early July to early Sept. and mid-Dec. to late Mar. 3:30-8pm; late Mar. to early July and early Sept. to Oct. 3:30-7pm. Closed last Su of the month in spring. Tours of the *thermes* in French only June-Sept. Tu 2pm. €3.50, ages 14-18 €1.60.)

The tourist office has information about hiking paths and mountain bike trails that leave from Luchon. For a sunny afternoon hike, try the short walk to the small village of **Cazarilh** (3hr. round-trip). To reach the trailhead from the tourist office, turn left on allée d'Etigny, which quickly becomes av. Carnot. Walk through pl. Joffre to pl. Comminges and make a gentle left on rue Merée Boubée. When you reach the cemetery, turn right on cours de la Casseyde. Just after the edge of the cemetery, look for a red and white shack to your left; the trail begins there, and a hidden sign points the way to Cazarilh. From there, follow the yellow trail markers. A more strenuous, nearly day-long hike leads along the GR10 from Luchon to **Superbagnères** and back (5-6hr. round-trip). From the tourist office, turn left, then left again on rue Gambetta. Continue past the market on your right and turn right when rue Gambetta ends at rue Laity; the first left leads directly to the trailhead. Alternatively, the **Altiservice** runs a *télécabine* (lift) that transports hikers, bikers, and skiers to the top of Superbagnères. (☎ 79 97 00. €5.60, round-trip €8.60. Open daily July-Aug. 9:45am-12:15pm and 1:30-6pm; ski season daily 8:45am-6pm.) The tourist office has two free hiking and biking maps. Also check the Bureau des Guides (see **Practical Information**).

LANGUEDOC-ROUSSILLON

The southern area of Languedoc-Roussillon offers two distinct regions, both with their own independent cultures and both with enough reasonable accommodations and eateries to make this area a great opportunity for travelers to see the south of France on a budget. A region once independent of both France and Spain, the Languedoc had its own language, the *langue d'oc*. Languedoc (then called Occitania) stretched from the Rhône Valley to the Pyrenean foothills. Though it has been part of France since the 12th century, Languedoc preserves its rebellious spirit with frequent strikes and protests, and its *joie de vivre* shows up in impromptu street performances and large neighborhood parties.

Situated between the Mediterranean coast and the peaks of the Pyrénées, Roussillon inspired Matisse and Picasso and now attracts a mix of sunbathers and backpackers. At the southwest corner of France, the region was historically part of Catalonia, not France, and Perpignan (p. 626) was the capital of the Kings of Majorca. Many inhabitants of Roussillon identify more with Barcelona than with Paris and speak Catalan, which sounds like a hybrid of French and Spanish. Architecture, food, and nightlife all bear the zest of Spanish neighbors, and the natural attractions outside of Millau (p. 634) provide lively adventure sports.

HIGHLIGHTS OF LANGUEDOC-ROUSSILLON

ESCAPE the city with three peerless daytrips from Perpignan—to **Céret, Villefranche-de-Conflent,** and **Collioure**—and soak up all the cherries, art, and hiking you can take without spending a penny on transportation (p. 631).

GOGGLE at the largest Renaissance painting in the world in **Albi's cathedral** (p. 618).

PARTY in **Montpellier** (p. 640), taking advantage of great gay and straight **nightlife.**

TOULOUSE ☎05

Known as *la ville en rose* (the pink city), vibrant and zany Toulouse (TOO-looze; pop. 390,000) is the place to come when all French towns begin to look alike. Exuberant yet laid-back, clean yet gritty, Toulouse is a place that students don't want to leave after receiving their degree. During the school year, 100,000 scholars fill the cafés and *brasseries* in the narrow streets of this university town, where Thomas Aquinas introduced Aristotle to Latin theologians. At the center of the city sits the massive Capitole, whose eight grand columns symbolize the eight headstrong town councillors *(capitouls)* who defied counts and kings to govern the city until the Revolution. An abundance of museums and concert halls makes France's fourth largest city the Southwest's cultural capital. Family-owned art galleries, independent theaters, and a diverse music scene continue the city's free-thinking tradition. Whether it be the Garonne river or the grungy yet charming rue du Taur that makes your heart pound, it is hard to visit this city without falling in love.

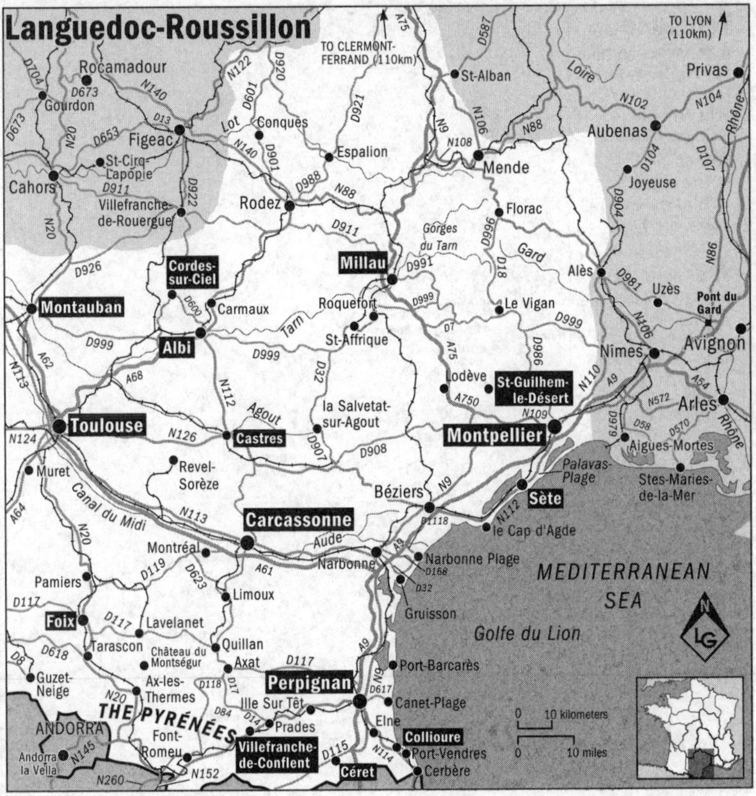

TRANSPORTATION

Flights: Aéroport Blagnac (☎08 25 38 00 00). **Air France** (☎08 02 80 28 02) flies to **London** (6 per day, round-trip from €330) and **Paris** (35 per day, round-trip from €110). **Navettes Aérocar** (☎34 60 64 00; www.navettevia-toulouse.com) serves the airport from the bus station and allée Jean Jaurès (30min.; every 20min.; €3.90).

Trains: Gare Matabiau, 64 bd. Pierre Sémard. To: **Bordeaux** (2-3hr., 14 per day, €33); **Carcassonne** (1hr., 15 per day, €13); **Lyon** (4½hr., 7 per day, €70); **Marseille** (4hr., 10 per day, €50); **Paris** (6hr., 12 per day, €90). Ticket office open daily 7am-9:10pm.

Buses: Gare Routière, 68-70 bd. Pierre Sémard, next to the train station (☎61 61 67 67). Open M-F 8am-7pm, Sa 9am-1pm and 2-6pm, Su 10am-4pm. To: **Albi** (1½hr., 4 per day, €13); **Carcassonne** (2¼hr., 1 per day, €12); **Foix** (2hr., 1 per day, €9.90); **Montauban** (1¼hr., 4 per day, €7.30). Buy tickets on the bus. **Eurolines** (☎61 26 40 04; www.eurolines.fr), with an office in the station, runs buses to most major cities in Europe. Open M-F 9:30am-12:30pm and 2-6:30pm, Sa 9:30am-12:30pm and 2-5pm.

Metro: Tisséo, 7 pl. Esquirol (☎61 41 70 70). Trains run M-F and Su 5:25am-midnight, Sa 5:25am-1pm; schedule varies. Maps at ticket booths and tourist office. Buy tickets inside the station. €1; €2.50 round-trip; *carnet* of 10 €11, ages 18-25 €6.70; 1-week pass €11 (max. 2 rides per day).

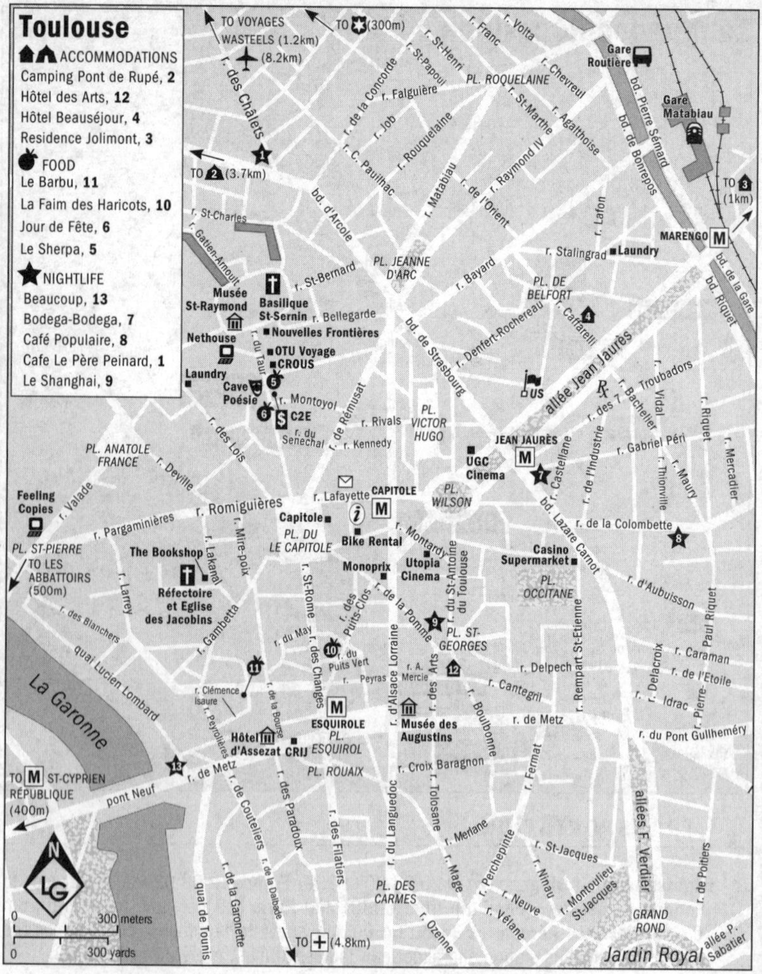

Taxis: Capitole Taxi (☎34 25 02 50). €25 from the train station to the airport. 24hr.

Bike Rental: In front of the tourist office. €1 per ½-day, €2 per day; €260 deposit. Open M-F 8am-6pm, Sa-Su 10am-6pm. MC/V.

ORIENTATION AND PRACTICAL INFORMATION

While residential Toulouse sprawls along both sides of the Garonne, the part of the city of interest to visitors, with its thriving student quarter, occupies a small section east of the river bounded by **rue de Metz** in the south, **boulevard de Strasbourg** to the north, and **boulevard Carnot** to the east. The center of town is the huge stone plaza known as the **Capitole.** The walk from the station to the main part of town takes less than 15min.

TIP **NOTHING TOU-LOUSE.** Those visiting Toulouse for more than a day or two should pick up a *Carte Privilège* at the tourist office. For a mere €13, cardholders get 30% discounts at museums and participating hotels. At most hotels, the card pays for itself in one night. As a final bonus, cardholders receive free *apéritifs* at many Toulouse restaurants. The tourist office has a list of participating museums, hotels, and restaurants.

Tourist Office: Donjon du Capitole, on rue Lafayette at pl. Charles de Gaulle (☎61 11 02 22; www.ot-toulouse.fr). From the station, take the Metro to Capitole or head straight down rue de Bayard, which runs perpendicular to the station's main exit. Veer left around pl. Jeanne d'Arc and continue on rue d'Alsace Lorraine; the park is on the right with the tourist office in the far right-hand corner. City tours in English (July-Aug. Th at 2:30pm, €9), French (M-F 2 per day), and Spanish (July-Aug. Th at 4:30pm). Pick up the helpful *Guide Pratique,* which lists hotels, restaurants, museums, transportation information, and cultural events. Office open June-Sept. M-Sa 9am-7pm, Su 10:30am-12:30pm and 2-5:15pm; Oct.-May M-Sa 9am-6pm, Su 10:30am-12:30pm and 2-5pm.

Budget Travel: Voyages Wasteels, 36 rue de Taur (☎61 12 18 88). Cheap airfares for students. Open M-F 10am-1pm and 2-6pm, Sa 10am-12:30pm and 2-5pm. **Nouvelles Frontières,** 2 pl. St-Sernin (☎61 21 74 14). Open M-F 9am-7pm, Sa 9am-6pm. AmEx/MC/V.

Consulates: US, 25 allée Jean Jaurès (☎34 41 36 50). Open M-F 9am-5pm; by appointment only.

Currency Exchange: C2E Capitole Echange, 30 rue du Taur (☎61 13 64 25). Open M-F 9am-12:30pm and 2-6pm, Sa 10am-noon and 2-5pm.

English-Language Bookstore: The Bookshop, 17 rue Lakanal (☎61 22 99 92). Novels, French history books, and guides. Open M 2-7pm, Tu-Sa 10am-7pm. AmEx/MC/V.

Youth Center: CRIJ (Centre Regional Information Jeunesse), 17 rue de Metz (☎61 21 20 20; www.crij.org). Info on travel, work, and study. Open daily July-Aug. 10am-1pm and 2-6pm; Sept.-June M-F 10am-6pm, Sa 10am-1pm and 2-5pm.

Laundromat: Le Centre des Lois, 44 rue des Lois. (☎06 81 41 17 60). Wash €4, including detergent; dry €0.50 per 5min. Open daily 7:30am-9pm. **Laverie Bayard,** 10 rue Stalingrad. Wash €2.90-3.30, dry €0.40 per 6min. Open daily 7am-9:30pm.

Police: Commissariat Central, bd. Embouchure (☎61 12 74 74).

Late-Night Pharmacy: 70-76 allée Jean Jaurès (☎61 62 38 05). Open M-Sa 8pm-8am, Su and holidays 8pm-9am.

Hospital: CHR de Rangueil, av. du Prof. Jean Poulhes (☎61 32 25 33).

Internet Access: Feeling Copies, 3 rue Valade. €1 per hr. Open M-F 9am-7pm. Also at **Nethouse,** 1 rue des 3 Renards (☎61 21 98 42). €3 per hr. Open M-Sa 9am-11pm, Su noon-8pm. Rue Taur has other establishments with similar prices.

Post Office: 9 rue Lafayette (☎34 45 70 82). **Currency exchange** and **Western Union.** Open M-F 8am-7pm, Sa 8am-noon. **Postal Code:** 31000, **Poste Restante:** 31049 Cédex.

ACCOMMODATIONS AND CAMPING

Toulouse has an innovative youth hostel that is a quick and easy Metro ride from the center of the city. Otherwise, cheap and attractive hotels are difficult to find in Toulouse, though there are a few good options.

Residence Jolimont, 2 av. Yves Brunaud (☎34 30 42 80; www.residence-jolimont.com). Metro: Jolimont. A member of the French league of youth hostels. Doubles as a long-term *résidence sociale,* helping 18- to 25-year-olds get on their feet. Large, clean, and plain double rooms include shower and toilet—for the best price in town. Free Internet access some mornings. Ping-pong, billiards, and basketball court. Breakfast M-F (€2). Dinner €7.80. Towel €1. Reception 24hr. Dorms €16. AmEx/MC/V. ❶

Hôtel des Arts, 1 bis rue Cantegril (☎61 23 36 21; fax 61 12 22 37). Metro: pl. Esquirol. Spacious, tastefully decorated rooms with high ceilings in a central location. Though showers and bathrooms do not live up to the standard set by the rooms, this hotel remains a top pick. Breakfast €6. Reception 7am-11pm. Reservations recommended 2 weeks ahead. Singles and doubles €35-42, with shower €44-50. MC/V. ❸

Hôtel Beauséjour, 4 rue Caffarelli (☎/fax 61 62 77 59), off allée Jean Jaurès, near the station. Despite less central location, clean, large, and bright rooms with new beds are a good value. Free Wi-Fi. Reception 7am-11pm. Singles and 1-bed doubles with shower €30, with shower and toilet €32; 2-bed doubles €37/39; triples €42/44. MC/V. ❷

Camping Pont de Rupé, 21 chemin du Pont de Rupé (☎61 70 07 35), at av. des Etats-Unis (N20 north). Take bus #59 (dir.: Fenouillet) from pl. Jeanne d'Arc. At stop, cross bridge; campsite is 200m down on the right. Snack bar and laundry. €13 for 1-2 people with a tent. €2.80 per additional person. MC/V. ❶

FOOD

What Toulouse lacks in cheap lodging, it makes up for with cheap food. Budget travelers should head directly to **rue du Taur** in the student quarter, where cheap eateries serve meals for €5-10. Chinese, Lebanese, and Mexican restaurants fill the storefronts on **rue des Filatiers** and **rue Paradoux.** On Tuesdays and Saturdays, **place du Capitole** becomes an open-air market selling organic food, as well as everything from shoes to sunglasses to purses (open 8am-3pm). Other food markets are held at **place Victor Hugo, place des Carmes,** and **place St-Cyprien.** (Open Tu-Su 6am-1pm.) There's a **Monoprix** supermarket at 39 rue Alsace-Lorraine (open M-Sa 9am-10pm; MC/V) and a **Casino** near pl. Occitane, downstairs in the Centre Commerciale St-Georges (open daily 8:30am-8:30pm; MC/V). Students who want a good, hot meal at a low price (€2.60) should head to the **restaurants universitaires,** scattered around Toulouse; contact the tourist office for locations. The *brasseries* that crowd busy **place Wilson** offer €8.50-15 *menus.*

Jour de Fête, 43 rue du Taur (☎61 23 36 48). A neighborhood favorite with local art on its walls, this student hangout serves a large *plat du jour* (€6.90) and features grilled steak and half-baked chicken. Salads (€6-7), tapas (selection of 4 €9.50), and *crêpes* (€3.50-5.90) also available. Open daily noon-midnight. Cash only. ❶

La Faim des Haricots, rue du Puits Vert, (☎61 22 49 25), between pl. Capitole and the student quarter. This vegetarian heaven offers a fresh, filling selection of pasta, *tartes,* and creative combinations of veggies. €10-13 *menus* let you pick 2-5 selections from the all-you-can-eat salad, *tarte,* soup, and dessert bars; the €15 *menu* adds an *apéritif* and coffee. Open M-Sa noon-2:30pm, Th-Sa noon-2:30pm and 7-10:30pm. MC/V. ❷

Le Sherpa, 46 rue du Taur (☎61 23 89 29), is that rare species: a sit-down *crêperie* that's not a rip-off. You can have 2 *crêpes* and still only pay €11. Add an egg to your *crêpe* (€0.20) and fill up while soaking in the hand-painted wall murals. Savory *crêpes* €3.50-6.50. Dessert *crêpes* €1.70-5. Open daily noon-midnight. Cash only. ❶

Le Barbu, 9 rue Clémence Isaure (☎61 21 96 62), offers massive portions of hearty food under brick arches, with boots hanging on the walls. At dinner, all main dishes come with delicious soup. The *boudin* is a specialty, but beware: blood sausage is the literal translation. *Plats* €11-16. Lunch *menus* €11. Open M-F noon-2pm and 8pm-midnight. Cash only. ❷

SIGHTS

Toulouse's best sights are not easily distilled into a list. Young people crowd the streets at all hours, creating the feeling of a large city in the concentrated downtown. Walking or biking is the best way to get around; exploration never goes unrewarded. Toulouse is famous for the **red-brick mansions** of the town's wealthy 15th- and 16th-century dye merchants and for its art, which ranges from masterpieces to local experiments. Most museums are free to students. Multi-sight passes are sold at all museums: €6 buys entry to any three museums, €9 to any six.

BASILIQUE ST-SERNIN. St-Sernin is the longest Romanesque structure in the world, but its most visible feature is an enormous brick steeple that rises in five ever-narrowing double-arched terraces, much like a massive wedding cake. St-Dominic, head of the Dominican order of friars, made this ornate church his base in the early 13th century, though in doing so he departed from the ascetic monastic traditions. At the end of the simple, elegant, and huge Romanesque nave lies the highlight of the visit: an impressive altar surrounded by vivid frescoes. Behind the left side of the altar is a crypt containing holy relics, from engraved silver chests to golden goblets—some from the time of Charlemagne. *(☎61 21 80 45. Church open daily July-Sept. 8:30am-6:30pm; Oct.-June 8:30am-noon and 2-6pm. Crypt open July-Sept. M-Sa 10am-5pm, Su 11:30am-5pm; Oct.-June M-Sa 10-11:30am and 2:30-5pm, Su 11:30-5pm. €2.)*

LE CAPITOLE. This mammoth brick palace faces a stone plaza, which is home to swanky restaurants, occasional political protests, and hundreds of students taking a break from their books on the stone benches. In short, it is the ideal spot for people-watching. The building was once home to the bourgeois *capitouls*, who unofficially ruled the city (which was technically controlled by counts) for many years. All people who marry in Toulouse must pass through its **Salle des Illustres.** Next door, **La Salle Henri Martin** has 10 post-Impressionist *tableaux* by Henri Martin, representing Toulouse in all four seasons. *(Salles open daily 10:30am-6:30pm. Free.)*

RÉFECTOIRE ET ÉGLISE DES JACOBINS. This 13th-century Gothic church is so beautiful that in 1368, Pope Urbain V decided it was worthy of St-Thomas Aquinas's remains. His ashes take center stage in a tomb lit from below. Be sure to notice the ceiling, whose vaults look like palm trees. The *réfectoire* houses temporary exhibits of world art. *(Rue Lakanal. Open daily 9am-7pm. Occasional summer piano concerts. Tickets at tourist office. Cloister and réfectoire exhibition €3, students with ID free.)*

MUSEUMS. The **Hôtel d'Assezat** has the *Fondation Bemberg*, which displays 35 Bonnards, a modest collection of Dufys, Gauguins, and Pissarros, as well as the occasional Matisse, Picasso, Braque, and Renoir. The rose-brick building also makes it worth a stop. From March 15-June 15 of 2008, the museum will host an exhibit of distinguished monochromatic painting, featuring Rubens, Boucher, and Doré, among others. Guided tours of the museum depart daily at 3:30pm. *(Pl. d'Assézat. Hôtel ☎61 12 06 89. Fondation ☎61 12 06 89. Open Tu-W and F-Su 10am-12:30pm and 1:30-6pm, Th 10am-12:30pm and 1:30-9pm. €4.60, students €2.75.)* The huge **Musée des Augustins** bristles with Romanesque and Gothic sculptures—including 15 howling gargoyles—in a redone Augustinian monastery. Look for the harrowing Rubens painting *"Christ entre les deux Larrons,"* inside the church in one of the insets to the left of the rose window. *(21 rue de Metz, off rue des Arts. ☎61 22 21 82. Free organ concerts W 8-8:30pm. Open M-Tu and Th-Su 10am-6pm, W 10am-9pm. €3, students with ID free. Temporary exhibitions €7, students €5.)* The **Musée St-Raymond** holds a decent collection of archaeological finds, including an impressive series of Roman portraits discovered in France and a detailed inquiry into life in ancient Toulouse. Artistic and anthropological finds are mixed; an ancient way-marker from Narbonne to Toulouse stands near the fragments of a beautiful mosaic. *(Pl. St-Sernin. ☎61 22 31 44. Open daily June-Aug. 10am-7pm; Sept.-May 10am-6pm. English text available. €3, students with ID free.)* Just across the river, **Les Abbatoirs,** old slaughterhouses converted into a vast art space, house intermittent exhibits of up-and-coming artists, as well as a collection of works from the late 20th century. Don't skip the basement, which contains the 8x13m curtain Picasso painted for the premier of Romain Rolland's play *"14 Juillet."* To reach the museum, take the Metro (dir.: Basso Cambo) to "St- Cyprien/République." When you exit, turn right off pl. St-Cyprien onto allée Charles de Fitte; the museum is two blocks down on your right. *(76 allée Charles-de-Fitte. ☎34 51 10 60. Open Tu-Su 11am-7pm. €6, students €3.)*

NIGHTLIFE

Café Populaire, 9 rue de la Colombette (☎61 63 07 00). A hot and smoky destination for a motley crowd of fun-loving but cash-strapped students. A tray with 13 glasses of beer costs €20, or a mere €13 M 9:30pm-12:45am. Every 13th of the month beer is €1 7-9pm. Happy hour with a variety of drink specials daily 7:30-8:30pm. Open M-F 11am-2am, Sa 2pm-4am. Cash only.

Bodega-Bodega, 1 rue Gabriel Péri (☎61 63 03 63), off bd. Lazare Carnot. A wildly popular destination for young crowds, this 2-fl. Spanish-themed club offers food by day and fun by night. When the clock strikes midnight, the atmosphere heats up with Latin music and plenty of dancing. €6 min. drink charge Th-Sa starting at 11:30pm. Beer €3. Margaritas €6. Tapas €5-10. Open M-F and Su 7pm-2am, Sa 7pm-6am. AmEx/MC/V.

Café Le Père Peinard, 1 rue des Chalets (☎61 63 81 82). A cozy place for a laid-back drink after a long day. Cheap beer (€2) and Sa night concerts (world music and traditional French songs, 9pm) make this a neighborhood favorite. Wine €1.50-2.20. Open M-F 6pm-2am, Sa 6pm-3am. MC/V.

Le Shanghai, 12 rue de la Pomme (☎61 23 37 80). The place for gay nightlife. A sleek club that also draws a straight crowd. Shiny black walls, mirrors, and red lighting abound. Mixed drinks €8. Cover €8. Open daily midnight-7am. Cash only.

Beaucoup, 9 pl. du Pont Neuf (☎61 12 39 29). This restaurant-by-day turns into a chill music bar when the sun goes down, drawing a trendy crowd with its hip lighting, outdoor seating, and funky tunes. Listen to resident "DJ Initial" mix F-Sa nights from 11pm. Beer from €2.50. Open W-Su 10am-2am, Sa and holidays 10am-dawn. MC/V.

ENTERTAINMENT AND FESTIVALS

Toulouse always has something going on, although things tend to be quieter in the summer, when the university isn't in session. **Cave Poésie,** 71 rue du Taur, hosts plays and performances. "Open stage" nights, when locals and amateur performers show off their talents, only happen when there is a full moon (begins 9:30-10pm, €2). Other plays, poetry readings, and concerts begin regularly at 7:30 and 10pm. Pick up a schedule outside the door or at the tourist office. (☎61 23 62 00. www.cave-poesie.fr.st. Tickets €12, students €8.) Most of Toulouse's **movie theaters** are located in and around pl. Wilson. **UGC,** 9 allée Roosevelt (☎08 92 70 00 00), plays mostly new American releases, some of them dubbed in French. At **Utopia Cinema,** 24 rue Montardy (☎61 23 21 22), everything is shown in its original language, including independent films from around the world.

From July to September, **Toulouse d'Eté** brings classical concerts, jazz, gospel, and ballet to the Jacobins courtyard and the Halle aux Grains at fantastic prices. Tickets are sold at concert halls (€10). Traditional music and dance groups parade through the streets on the last Sunday in June for the **Grand Fénétra** (☎06 86 55 20 24). In September, performers convene at 8:30pm for the **Festival International de Piano aux Jacobins,** which lasts 4-5 days. (☎61 22 40 05; www.pianojacobins.com. Tickets at the Bureau or tourist office. €15-32, students €6-9.)

DAYTRIPS FROM TOULOUSE

CASTRES

The train station, av. Albert I (open M 5:40am-7pm, Tu-F 6:10am-7pm, Sa 7:40am-noon and 1:40-7pm, Su 10:10am-noon and 1:45-8pm), has service to Toulouse (1hr., 12 per day, €13). Though trains from Albi eventually arrive in Castres (via St-Sulpice, 2hr.), buses are cheaper and more direct. They run from the bus station, pl. Soult (☎63 35 37 31), to Albi (45-55min., 8 per day, €6) and Toulouse (1½hr., 5 per day, €11).

When Castres (KAH-struh) acquired the bones of St-Vincent, the city became an essential pilgrimage stop for those en route to Santiago de Compostela. This prominence ended when the basilica was destroyed during the Wars of Religion. More recently, the city compensated by constructing three museums, each worth a brief pilgrimage—the **Musée Goya,** the **Centre National et Musée Jean Jaurès,** and the up-to-the-minute **Centre d'Art Contemporain.** Castres is worth a visit for these museums, but visitors should not expect breathtaking landscapes.

In front of the **Jardin de l'Evêché's** groomed shrubs, the **Musée Goya** occupies an ancient Episcopal palace. The museum houses a large collection of Spanish paintings, along with works by Catalan and Aragonese masters; the focus of the collection is four series of Goya engravings. Look for the gripping series *The Disasters of War,* in which Goya depicts the horrors of the Napoleonic wars through engravings. (☎63 71 59 27. Open July-Aug. daily 10am-6pm; Sept.-June Tu-Sa 9am-noon and 2-6pm, Su 10am-noon and 2-6pm. Tours offered in French July-Aug. 2-3 times each afternoon; ask at museum for exact schedule. Printed information in English. €2.30, students €1.15, under 18 free.) The small **Centre National et Musée Jean Jaurès,** 2 pl. Pélisson, caters to those interested in France's social history—or who wonder why every single town in the country seems to have an avenue Jean Jaurès. A brilliant scholar and professor of philosophy, Jaurès led the striking glassworkers of Carmaux in 1896 and vehemently supported Alfred Dreyfus, a Jewish officer framed as a traitor by the army and assassinated in 1914. The sleek building is packed with political cartoons, photographs, and newspaper articles that recount Jaurès's spirited life and rhetoric, as well as occasional small temporary art exhibits. (☎63 62 41 83. Open July-Aug. daily 10am-noon and 2-6pm; Apr.-June and Sept. Tu-Su 10am-noon and 2-6pm; Oct.-Mar. Tu-Sa 10am-noon and 2-5pm. €1.50, students €0.75.) The Musée Goya and Musée Jaurès sell a €4 ticket that allows admission to all three of Castres's museums, but it saves little money.

After enjoying what Castres has to offer indoors, don't miss a walk along the river Agout. The Agout was famous for its tanning properties, making Castres a magnet for tanners, whose houses lend the Agout its charm. For two weeks in mid-July, the **Extravadanses** festival celebrates Hispanic culture with concerts, exhibitions, and flamenco and ballet performances. Many events are free; tickets to others are at the tourist office or by calling the **Théâtre Municipale.** (☎63 71 56 58. Open M-F 10:30am-1pm and 2:30-6pm, Sa 10am-noon and 2-4pm.) The city also hosts a multicultural festival in mid-August with free concerts and dances.

When hunger strikes, try the market on **place de l'Albinque** (covered and open-air market Tu-Sa 7am-1pm, Su 7am-noon; organic market open Th 4-8pm). A **Monoprix** supermarket is on rue Sabatier at pl. Jean Jaurès. (Open M-Sa 8:30am-7:30pm. AmEx/MC/V.) For a sit-down meal, try **La Mandragore ❸,** behind pl. Jean Jaurès on rue Malpas. The restaurant serves regional cuisine like asparagus ravioli in cream sauce. (☎63 59 51 27. Lunch *menu* €13. Dinner *menus* €18-26. Open Tu-Sa noon-2pm and 7-9:30pm.) Traditional *nougatines castraises* (€7 for 125g) are the specialty of **Cormary ❶,** 13 rue Victor Hugo, which also sculpts chocolates, marzipan, and pastries into animal shapes. (☎63 59 27 09. Open M-Sa 6am-1pm and 1:30-7:30pm, Su 6am-1pm. AmEx/MC/V.)

Getting around Castres is easy, as all the sights are within a 5min. walk of one another. To get to the **tourist office,** 4 pl. de la République, from the train station, turn left onto av. Albert I and then, at Carrefour de la Gare, right onto bd. Henri Sizaire. At pl. Alsace-Lorraine, turn left along the gardens onto rue de l'Evêché; the office is a block down on the left (20min.). From the bus station, walk across pl.

Soult and continue straight on rue Villegoudou, cross the Pont Neuf, and turn left on rue de la Libération. Turn right at rue de l'Hôtel de Ville, then left on rue de l'Evêché; the office is on your right when you reach pl. de la République. (☎63 62 63 62; www.tourisme-castre.fr. Open July-Aug. M-Sa 9:30am-6:30pm, Su 10:30am-noon and 2:30-5pm; Sept.-June M-Sa 9:30am-12:30pm and 2-6pm, Su 2:30-4:30pm.)

MONTAUBAN

Accessible from Toulouse by train (25min., 30 per day, €8.20; info office open M-Sa 7am-7:30pm, Su 8am-8:30pm) and by bus (☎62 72 37 23; 1hr., 4 per day, €7.30). Trains are twice as fast and nearly 8 times as frequent—well worth the extra €0.90. Local buses are run by Transports Montalbanais, bd. Midi-Pyrénées. (☎63 63 60 60. 7:30am-7:15pm. €0.90, carnet of 10 €7.) Taxis (☎63 66 99 99) are often at the train station. €2.40 base; €1.36 per km during the day, €1.90 at night. Open daily 6am-midnight.

Montauban's (MOHN-toh-bahn) red brick buildings make it one of France's three *villes en rose* (pink cities), along with Toulouse and Albi. The city's ochre-tinted architecture dates back to 1144, when the Count of Toulouse incited local artisans to sack the wealthy abbey at Montauriol ("Golden Mountain") and use its stones to start construction of present-day Montauban. Never on good terms with mainstream Catholicism, Montauban was one of the last bastions of French Protestantism following the revocation of the Edict of Nantes in 1685. A quick trip from Toulouse, this town's main attraction is its large Musée Ingres. To get to the *centre-ville,* walk straight out of the train station onto av. de Mayenne and continue across the bridge (10min.). Immediately after the bridge, you'll find the **Musée Ingres,** 19 rue de l'Hôtel, on your right in the 17th-century bishop's palace. The museum honors 19th-century painter Jean-Auguste Dominique Ingres, who was born in Montauban. Look for the *Portrait de Caroline Gonse*, on the third floor, for an example of Ingres's mature work. This museum doesn't end with Ingres—in its large collection, it also features sculptures by Bourdelle, another well-known Montauban native. Don't miss the medieval hall in the lower basement, a remnant of the château built by the Black Prince Edward in 1362. (☎63 22 12 91. Open July-Aug. daily 10am-6pm; Sept.-June Tu-Su 10am-noon and 2-6pm; mid-Oct. to mid-Apr. Tu-Sa 10am-noon and 2-6pm, Su 2-6pm. Tours in French 2 times daily July-Aug. Museum July-Oct. €6, seniors €3, students free; Nov.-June €4/2/free. 1st Su of the month free. Tours €7, seniors €4.) If you turn right after exiting the Musée Ingres, **Notre Dame de l'Assomption** will be on your right. Four enormous sculptures of the Evangelists keep solemn watch in the church, and *Le Vœu de Louis XIII*, one of Ingres's most impressive religious works, dominates the left transept. Detailed murals decorate the smaller side chapels, and the entrance facade is the highest in Europe. (Open daily 10am-noon and 2-6pm.)

During the week-long **Alors Chante** festival, revelers play traditional French tunes at the Eurythmie, beginning the Tuesday preceding **Ascension** and finishing on that Sunday. (☎63 63 02 36. Tickets €20-32.) A **Jazz Festival** swings through during the third week of July. Big-name concerts, featuring artists such as Lucky Peterson, are ticketed events, but the week before the festival the streets of the *vieille ville* resound with free concerts, usually held at 8:30pm. (☎63 63 56 56; www.jazzmontauban.com. Tickets at tourist office. €20-45, students €15-40.)

To reach the **tourist office,** 4 rue du Collège, turn right out of the cathedral onto rue Notre Dame and left at bd. Midi-Pyrénées. When the road ends, veer left; the office is on the left. (☎63 63 60 60. Open July-Aug. M-Sa 9:30am-6:30pm, Su 10am-12:30pm; Sept.-June M-Sa 9:30am-12:30pm and 2-6:30pm.)

ALBI ☎05 63

The magnificent Cathédrale Ste-Cécile dominates the cobblestone streets of Albi (AL-bee; pop. 50,000), which twist down to the tree-lined Tarn River. The lights of

Paris and the Moulin Rouge lured away native son Henri de Toulouse-Lautrec, but not his paintings; the Toulouse-Lautrec museum alone would be worth a journey. Budget travelers be warned, however; this is not a town of bargains. To save, you might make Albi a daytrip from the easily accessible Toulouse, where more affordable food and lodging are available.

TRANSPORTATION AND PRACTICAL INFORMATION. **Trains** run from pl. Stalingrad to Castres (1½hr., 8 per day, €14) via St-Sulpice, and to Toulouse (1hr., 15 per day, €11). Check the info office for times. (Open M-F 5am-9pm, Sa-Su 6am-10pm.) **Buses** depart pl. Jean Jaurès (☎54 58 61) for Castres (1hr., M-Sa 8 per day, €6). Espace Albibus, 14 rue de l'Hôtel de Ville (☎38 43 43; open Tu-Sa 9am-noon and 2-5pm), runs **local buses** (€1). Albi Taxi Radio, 64 impasse Jean de la Fontaine (☎54 85 03), has **taxis** at the station (€6 from the station to the cathedral).

To reach the **tourist office** in Palais de la Berbie, at pl. Ste-Cécile, turn left from the station onto av. Maréchal Joffre, then left on av. du Général de Gaulle. Keep left at pl. Lapérouse and walk into the pedestrian *vieille ville* and onto rue de Verdusse. Walk straight ahead until you reach pl. Ste-Cécile; the office is ahead and to the left. The staff books rooms and offers city guides, tours in French (July-Sept. M-Sa noon, €4), and **currency exchange** on bank holidays. (☎49 48 80; www.albi-tourisme.com. Open July-Aug. M-Sa 9am-7pm, Su 10am-12:30pm and 2:30-6:30pm; May-June and Sept. M-Sa 9am-12:30pm and 2-6:30pm, Su 10am-12:30pm and 2:30-6:30pm; Oct.-Apr. M-Sa 9am-12:30pm and 2-6pm, Su 10am-12:30pm and 2:30-6pm.) Other services include: **ATMs** and **currency exchange** at **Crédit Agricole,** pl. du Vigan (☎08 10 04 45 89; open Tu-F 9am-noon and 1:45-5:30pm, Sa 9am-noon and 1:30-4pm); a **laundromat** at 10 rue Emile Grand, off Lices Georges Pompidou (☎54 51 14; open daily 7am-9pm); **police** at 23 rue Lices Georges Pompidou (☎49 22 81); a **hospital** on rue de la Berchère (☎47 47 47); and **Internet** access at **Ludi.com,** 62 rue Séré-de-Rivière (☎43 34 24; €4 per hr.; open M-Sa Sept.-June 11am-midnight; July-Aug. 2pm-midnight). The **post office,** pl. du Vigan, offers **currency exchange.** (☎48 15 50. Open M-F 8:30am-6:30pm, Sa 8:30am-12:15pm.) **Postal Code:** 81000.

ACCOMMODATIONS AND FOOD. Accommodation is pricey in Albi, but not less popular for it. Be sure to reserve ahead to secure a room, especially for summer weekends. For info on *gîtes d'étape* and rural camping, call **ATTER** (☎48 83 01; www.gites-tarn.com). **Hôtel Lapérouse ❸,** 21 pl. Lapérouse, halfway between the train station and the cathedral, offers well-furnished rooms with plenty of amenities, including toilet and shower, free Wi-Fi, and an attractive outdoor swimming pool. Ask the English-speaking owners for one of the cheaper, smaller rooms facing the street. (☎54 69 22; fax 38 0369. Breakfast €6. Reception 7am-10pm. Doubles €36-60. AmEx/MC/V.) The elegant **Hôtel Saint-Clair ❸,** 8 rue St-Clair, has large, immaculate rooms overlooking a small courtyard, as well as an annex across the street. The cheapest rooms are a great value, with the same attention to detail as the more expensive ones. The shaded outdoor patio features a *salon de thé.* (☎54 25 66; andrieu.michele.free.fr. Breakfast €7. Free Wi-Fi. Reception 8am-9pm. Singles and doubles with shower and toilet €38-60; triples €65; quads €68. MC/V.) **Hôtel La Régence-George V ❷,** 27 av. Maréchal Joffre, near the train station, has relatively cheap, homey, and basic singles, with hard beds and minimal décor. For double rooms, or rooms with more amenities, look elsewhere. (☎49 90 78; fax 49 90 78. Breakfast €6. Wi-Fi €2 per day. Reception 7:30am-10pm. Singles €29, with shower €35, with shower and toilet €43. MC/V.) Camp near the municipal pool at **Parc de Caussels ❶,** east of the town center, toward Millau on D999 (2km). Take bus #5 from pl. Jean Jaurès to "Camping" (M-Sa every hr. 7:30am-7pm), or walk (30min.), leaving town on rue de la République. Continue straight through the traffic circle, ignoring signs to the campground, and keep walking through a second traffic circle. Soon after, you will cross a small bridge; turn left on the path immediately after the bridge and walk up the hill to find the campground on the left. (☎60 37 06. Reception 7am-10pm. Open Apr. to mid-Oct. €9, €12 for 2 people with car. Extra person €3.50. Cash only.)

Near Albi, the region of **Gaillac** shelters *vignoble* estates that prepare some of the best wines in the southwest. There is a market at **place Lapérouse.** (Tu-Su 8am-noon.) An additional flea market is held at pl. du Forail (Sa 8am-noon). Stock up on groceries at **Casino,** 39 rue Lices Georges Pompidou. (Open M-Sa 9am-7:30pm. AmEx/MC/V.) Excellent regional food comes at a price. Wine cellar and restaurant **La Table du Sommelier ❷,** at 20 rue Porta, over the bridge, serves carefully prepared, modern cuisine. Choose *le plat du jour* or a pre-selected *tour,* including a dish and its complementary wine. The courtyard is the perfect place to enjoy one of the varieties of *vin* offered. *Dégustations* of up to six wines €9-18. (☎46 20 10. *Plats* €10. *Menus* €13-20. Open Tu-Sa 12:15-2pm and 7:15-11pm. MC/V.) Regional specialties like *foie gras,* duck salad, and creative grilled meats are presented at **La Tête de l'Art ❸,** 7 rue de la Piale. (☎38 44 75. *Plats* €17-49. *Menus* €14-29. Open M and Th-Su noon-2pm and 7:30-9:30pm. AmEx/MC/V.) **Le Tournesol ❷,** 11 rue de l'Ort en Salvy, a popular vegetarian restaurant behind pl. du Vigan, has vegan *pâté* (€6), as well as hummus, cheese, and heavenly homemade desserts. (☎38 38 14. *Plat du jour* €9. Desserts €5.20-5.60. Open Tu-Sa noon-2pm. AmEx/MC/V.)

SIGHTS. The pride of Albi is the red-brick **Cathédrale Ste-Cécile.** Inside, stained-glass windows, lavish gold and blue walls, and graphic frescoed depictions of hell combine to create an imposing manifestation of the Church's power. Built between the 13th and 15th centuries, this cathedral enforced "the one true religion." Carvings line the choir walls in intricate, lace-like patterns; don't miss the grapes carved by homesick Burgundian workers. The un-restored fresco covering the entire ceiling, painted in 1512, is the largest Italian Renaissance painting in the world. (☎43 23 43. Open daily June-Sept. 9am-6pm; Oct.-May 9am-noon and 2-6pm. Mass M-F 6:20pm, Su 11:15am. Free organ concerts mid-July to Aug. W 5pm, Su 4pm. Tours daily July to early Sept. 2:30pm; mid-July to Aug. 10am, 2:30pm. Choir €1.50. Treasury €3.50, ages 12-25 €2.50. Tours €5.20. English audio tour €5.)

The 13th-century **Palais de la Berbie,** the former bishop's palace, was constructed in a defensive style, reflecting the tense relations between the church and the ruling family. The fortress displayed the clergy's wealth and power; it was both the tribunal and prison for those charged of crimes by the church. Beautiful gardens and walkways, crafted after the building was converted into a residence, offer splendid vistas of the Tarn River. For the best views of the palace itself, cross the Tarn. (Gardens open daily July-Aug. 9am-7pm; Sept.-June 8am-noon and 2-6pm. Free.) The palace now contains the **Musée Toulouse-Lautrec.** The son of the Count of Toulouse and daughter of the Count's cousin (first-cousin marriage wasn't considered incestuous back then), **Henri de Toulouse-Lautrec** (1864-1901) moved to Paris to experience the high life of cafés, nightclubs, and brothels, capturing the pathos of late 19th-century city life in his sketches and paintings. The museum's impressive collection of his oil paintings and ink prints includes all 31 of the famous posters of Montmartre nightclubs. Works by Dégas, Dufy, Matisse, and Rodin are displayed on the fourth floor. Major renovations are under way, so expect some changes in 2008 and 2009. (☎49 48 70. Open June-Aug. daily 9am-6pm; Sept. daily 9am-noon and 2-6pm; Apr.-May daily 10am-noon and 2-6pm; Oct. M and W-Su 10am-noon and 2-5:30pm; Nov.-Feb. M and W-Su 10am-noon and 2-5pm. €5, students €2.50. Tourist office gives tours June-Sept. 11:15am and 4pm. €9, students €7.50, audio tour in English €3.)

NIGHTLIFE AND FESTIVALS. When the sun goes down, the crowds come out along place de l'Archevêché in front of the Palais de la Berbie and on Lices

Georges Pompidou near pl. du Vigan. Enormous and popular **Café Le Grand Pontie,** pl. du Vigan, doles out pizza, special house desserts, beer, and pitchers of local wine until late. Enjoy rock music near the neon, mirrored bar, or sit outside on pl. du Vigan. (☎54 16 34. Beer €3.10-3.60. Pizza €9.20. Pasta €9.20. Open daily 7am-2am. MC/V.) **L'Athanor Scène Nationale,** pl. de l'Amitié Entre les Peuples, off bd. Carnot and opposite Parc Rochegude, often screens foreign art films. (☎38 55 56. Open Tu-F 1-7pm, Sa 2-7pm. Movies M-Sa 6, 8:30pm; Su 3, 6, 8:30pm. €6.90, M and W students and seniors €4.70.)

For four days during the first week of July, a series of guitar concerts comes to Pl. St-Cécile and the Théâtre de Verdure for **La Pause Guitare.** (☎60 55 90; www.arpegesettremolos.com. Tickets €6-32, pass €115.) For a week in mid-July, **Les Scènes Estivales** animate the Théâtre de la Verdure and Théâtre de la Croix Blanche, bringing innovative theater to Albi. (☎54 99 70. Tickets €12-20, students €9-17.) On every Wednesday night in August, actors present a roving play, with parts all over Albi. (☎49 11 74. Shows start W 9:30pm next to the Cathedral. Free.)

DAYTRIP FROM ALBI: CORDES-SUR-CIEL. Situated on a hill and bounded by a crumbling wall with flowers between its stones, the center of this tiny city, 24km from Albi, is accessible only by a steep, cobblestone street. Archaeologist Charles Portal preserved much of the town's medieval architecture, and wherever you look, there are stone or half-timbered houses. The best thing to do in Cordes is wander around, resign yourself to an over-priced meal, and soak in the quaintness.

If you need more to do, try the **Musée de l'Art Moderne,** Maison du Grand Fauconnier, just off Grande Rue Raymond VII. Boasting a few works by Miró and Picasso, this small museum contains five rooms of modern artwork, all accessible by a key given out as a ticket. (☎56 14 79. Open daily June-Sept. 11am-12:30pm and 2-7pm; Nov.-Mar. 2-7pm; Apr.-May and Oct. 11am-12:30pm and 2-6:30pm. €3.50, students €2, under 12 free.) **Museé Charles Portal,** located in Portail Peint, 12 rue Raymond VII, chronicles the town's history with a varied collection of his finds. (Call ☎56 00 52. €2.30, ages 12-18 €1.10, under 12 free.) The **Musée de l'Art du Sucre,** a few steps farther down at 33 Grande Rue Raymond VII, sells all kinds of sweets and charges admission for a small but impressive exhibit on the use of sugar as an artistic medium. The museum also includes exotic fish, a model of Grande Rue Raymond VII, and an **80kg female nude sculpted from a massive block of chocolate.** (☎56 02 40. Open daily Feb.-Dec. 10am-12:30pm and 2-6pm. €3.) Across the street, **place de la Bride** once served as the town's defensive platform. Today, it provides a panoramic view of the countryside. Just past pl. de la Bride is the **Puits de la Halle,** a 114m-deep well constructed in 1222 by tunneling through an entire mountain; the oasis supplied Albi with water during sieges. Behind the well and to the left sits the **Eglise St-Michel,** whose tower marks the highest point in town.

For a few days around July 14th, fire-eaters play to a costumed crowd during the **Fête du Grand Fauconnier,** which offers plays, concerts, magic shows, banquets, and a medieval market. (☎56 49 13. €8, under 18 €3, free if costumed in medieval attire.) The **Festival Musique** sponsors classical music concerts during late July. (☎56 00 75. Tickets €25-30, students €10-15.)

A **market** takes place at the bottom of the hill next to the bus stop. (Open Sa 8am-noon.) **Buses,** which run on school schedules, provide the only feasible way of reaching Cordes by public transport. Catch the morning bus to school, and return on the bus after school. Consult the tourist office for exact times, or call Sudcar Rolland. (☎54 18 39. M-F 2 per day, 40min., €5.30; W bus returns in the early afternoon). The **tourist office,** Maison du Pays Cordais, 8 pl. Jeanne Ramel-Cals, offers guided tours and books rooms for free. From the bus stop in town, it's 50m ahead and to the left. (☎56 00 52; www.cordes-sur-ciel.org. 1½hr. tours July-Aug.; €4.60, students €3.50, under 18 €1.50. Open July-Aug. daily 9:30am-1pm and 2-6:30pm; Sept. and June M 2-6pm, Tu-Su 10:30am-12:30pm and 2-6pm; Oct. Tu-F and

Su 10:30am-12:30pm and 2-6pm, Sa 2-6pm. Nov.-Dec. and Feb.-May hours vary.) There is an annex (☎56 14 79) in the Musée de l'Art Moderne, on top of the hill. A **petit train** runs between the annex in the *haute-ville* and Cordes (daily 9:30am-12:50pm and 2-5:50pm every 20min.; €2.50, under 18 €1.50).

CARCASSONNE ☎04 68

Carcassonne (CAR-cah-sohnn; pop. 46,000) has two faces: *La Cité*—a fortress that, once upon a time, fell off the page of a fairytale and onto the bank of the Aube River—and Bastide St-Louise, the center of the contemporary city, where modern life exists under the shadow of the medieval fort. Gorgeous, dramatic, and perfectly preserved, Carcassonne has become one of France's largest tourist attractions for a reason. Experience the town late in the evening, when the streets are clear of crowds and the floodlit fortress echoes with free concerts. Up to 800,000 daytrippers flock to Carcassonne in July, when Bastille Day brings one of France's most spectacular firework displays.

TRANSPORTATION

Trains: Behind Jardin A. Chenier (☎71 79 14). Info office open daily 6am-7:30pm. To: **Lyon** (4hr., 5 per day, €65); **Marseille** (3hr., 4 per day, €42); **Montpellier** (1½hr., 10 per day, €21); **Nice** (6hr., 4 per day, €63); **Nîmes** (2hr., 10 per day, €28); **Perpignan** (2hr.; 10 per day, change at Narbonne; €18); **Toulouse** (1hr., 10 per day, €13).

Buses: Regional buses leave from bd. de Varsovie. From the train station, cross the canal and turn right on bd. Omer Sarrut, then left at the fork. Check schedules at the station. **Trans'Aude** (☎25 13 74) covers western Roussillon.

Public Transportation: In summer, a **navette** (shuttle) goes from the train station to the parking du Dome on bd. Camille Pelletan (in the lower city) to the citadel gates and continues to the Camping de la Cité. (☎47 82 22. Mid-June to mid-Sept. daily every 15min. 9:30am-12:30pm and 1:30-7:30pm, round-trip €1.50.) **Agglo'Bus,** bd. Camille Pelletan (☎47 82 22), runs **buses** through the city. To get from the station to the *cité* in the low season, follow directions below to pl. Gambetta and, after turning right, continue on bd. Camille Pelletan to the bus stop; take bus #2 (dir.: Montlegun) M-Sa every 40min.-1hr. 7:36am-7:05pm, €1.10. Pick up schedules at the tourist office.

Taxis: Radio Taxi Services (☎71 50 50). At the train station or across the canal by Jardin A. Chenier. €7 from station to *cité.* 24hr.

ORIENTATION AND PRACTICAL INFORMATION

The **Bastide St-Louis,** once known as the *basse-ville* (lower town), is Carcassonne's commercial center. Its main attractions are shops, hotels, bars, and the cathedral; from the **train station,** the **shuttle** runs to the citadel in the summer. To get from the train station to the *cité* on foot (25min.), walk down rue Maréchal Joffre, which turns into rue G. Clemenceau. Past the clearing of pl. Carnot, turn left on rue de Verdun past the **tourist office,** bear right when you reach pl. Gambetta, and turn left up rue du Pont Vieux. After the bridge, take a sharp right to reach rue Barbacane, which leads to the steep citadel entrance ramp.

Tourist Office: 28 rue de Verdun (☎10 24 30; www.carcassonne-tourisme.com), near the post office. Free map, English guide, and accommodations booking. French tours of Bastide St-Louis mid-June to mid-Oct. W-Th 9:30am; €5, under 18 €2. Audio tours €3. Regional excursions €35-40, under 18 €15. Open July-Aug. daily 9am-7pm; Sept.-June M-Sa 9am-6pm, Su 9am-1pm. Annexes in the *cité*'s Porte Narbonnaise (☎10 24 36) and near the station on Port du Canal (☎25 94 81).

Police: Comissariat, 4 bd. Barbès (☎ 11 26 00). Call here for the **pharmacie de garde.**

Medical Services: Centre Hospitalier, rte. de Ste-Hilaire (☎ 24 24 24).

Laundry: Hallwash, 63 rue Aimé Ramond, on the corner of rue Tomey. Wash €3.50 per 7kg, dry €0.50 per 5min. Open daily 7am-9pm.

Internet Access: Alerte Rouge, 73 rue de Verdun (☎ 25 20 39). €3 per hr. Wi-Fi free with 1 drink or €2 per hr. Open M-Sa 10am-11pm. **Call World,** 32 rue de la République (☎ 72 89 00). €3 per hr. Open M-Sa 10am-noon and 2-9pm, Su 3-9pm.

Post Office: 40 rue Jean Bringer (☎ 11 71 00). **Currency exchange.** Open M-F 8:15am-6:30pm, Sa 8:30am-12:30pm. **Poste Restante:** 11012. **Postal Code:** 11000.

ACCOMMODATIONS AND CAMPING

Carcassonne's Auberge de Jeunesse is a rare refuge of affordable comfort situated in the heart of the medieval city.

Auberge de Jeunesse (HI), rue de Vicomte Trencavel (☎ 25 23 16; carcassonne@fuaj.org). In summer, excursions (€20) are organized and concerts take place in the hostel's courtyard, which is a center of nighttime socializing. Lockers, shower, and sink in large, clean 4- to 6-bed rooms. Kitchen, snack bar, and bike rack complete the amenities. Bike rental €8 per day. Breakfast included. Laundry €5. Internet access €3 per hr. Reception 24hr. Room lockout 10am-3pm. Reservations recommended, especially for Bastille Day, which is booked months ahead. Bunks €19. MC/V. ❶

Notre-Dame de L'Abbaye, 103 rue Trivalle, offers plain accommodations at low rates, with only a 5min. walk to the *cité*. More expensive rooms are clean and well-finished. To reach the abbey, walk straight after crossing the Pont Vieux from the lower city. Breakfast included. Reception daily 8am-12:30pm and 2-6pm. Singles €20, with shower and toilet and without peeling wallpaper €36; doubles €34/45. AmEx/MC/V. ❸

Sidsmums Travelers Retreat, 11 chemin de la Croix d'Achille (☎26 94 49 or 06 16 86 85 00; www.sidsmums.com), 10km south of Carcassonne. Take the bus headed for Limoux from the *gare routière* (M-Sa 10:30am, 5:15, 6:15pm; €2.50) which passes through Preixan. Call ahead to get detailed directions or to catch a ride on one of the free daily lifts into town given by the owner. Escape the crowds by lodging in this quiet countryside retreat, but don't expect an easy commute into town. Spacious kitchen, newly erected wooden cabins with beds or bunks, comfy couches, and a bookshelf filled with books and games. Ask about hikes and daytrips to nearby castles and rivers. It is possible to stay as a volunteer, swapping lodging for 3hr. of work per day. Bike rental €8 per day. Internet access €3 per hr. Reception 24hr. Reservations recommended. Dorms €19-21; doubles €42-46. Cash only. ❷

Hôtel Astoria, 18 rue Tourtel (☎25 31 38; www.astoriacarcassonne.com), near the train station. Large rooms with big beds and tile floors. Plain doubles are fairly priced. Shower €4. Parking €3. Breakfast €6. Singles €29; doubles with shower €39, with toilet and shower €45-65; triples €59; quads €65. Prices €4-7 higher July-Aug. MC/V. ❷

Camping de la Cité, rte. de Ste-Hilaire (☎25 11 77; cpllacite@atciat.com). From the lower town, cross Pont Vieux and turn right across the garden down rue Dujardin Beaumetz; follow the footpath along the stream and past the sunflower field (45min.; from *cité* 30min.) until you reach a green fence, through which you can see the campground. Turn left and follow the path. Or take the *navette* (€1.50) that goes to the *cité* and continues to the campsite. Pool, snack bar, laundry, and grocery store. Karaoke, dancing, and bike excursions. Internet access €3 per 30min., €5 per hr. Reception July-Aug. 8am-8:30pm; mid-Mar. to June and Sept. to mid-Oct. 9am-noon and 2-7pm. July to late Aug. 1 person with tent €13, 2 people with tent €21, 2 people with car €24; mid-Mar. to June and late Aug. to early Oct. €9.30/15/17. Electricity €4. ❷

FOOD

The grassy, shady banks of the Aude, near the Pont Vieux, provide ideal picnic sites. If you do eat out, don't pass up Carcassonne's specialty, the rich and meaty white bean stew *cassoulet*. There is a fruit and veggie market every Tuesday and Thursday in **place Carnot,** and a larger version with dried fruit and olive vendors every Saturday (8am-noon). For a decent grocery selection, pop into the **Monoprix** supermarket, at the intersection of rue G. Clemenceau and rue de la République. (Open M-Sa 8:30am-8pm, Su 9am-noon. AmEx/MC/V.) Restaurants on **rue du Plô** offer €11-17 *menus;* save room for dessert at one of the outdoor *crêperies* on **place Marcou.** In the winter, restaurants in the *cité* tend to have limited hours.

Maison de la Blanquette de Limoux, pl. Marcou (☎71 66 09). Offers the best price on a *cassoulet menu* in the *cité*. Fill up on the region's famed *cassoulet castelnaudary,* a delicacy said to date back to a culinary experiment during the 100 Years' War. 3-course *menu,* including *cassoulet,* 0.25L wine, and an *apéritif* for €14. Sit outside and enjoy each rich spoonful with the knowledge that your neighbors at other restaurants in the *cité* are paying more for less. *Cassoulet* €11-13. Open July-Aug. daily 9am-midnight; Sept.-Nov. 15 and Apr.-June M and Th-Su 9am-midnight, Tu 9am-5pm. ❸

Blanche de Castille, 21 rue Cros Mayrevieille (☎25 17 80). This *salon de thé* serves what seems like the only iced coffee in France (€3.60). *Foie gras* with toast (€11.50) and tea (€2.90-3) arrive on a calm terrace. Ice cream €2.20-6.90. Sandwiches €3.70-4.70. Open July-Aug. daily 8:30am-8pm; June and Sept.-Oct. daily 9am-7pm; Feb.-May Th-Sa 10am-5pm. MC/V over €15. ❶

La Girouette, 8 pl. Marcou (☎47 29 68), on the far end of the square. One of the more affordable sit-down restaurants in the *cité,* it offers a large *menu* and pleasant outdoor seating. Paella €10. Pizza €8-12. *Cassoulet* €8-14. *Plats* €9-17. *Menus* €11-24. Open Feb.-Oct. daily 9am-2am. MC/V over €20. ❸

SIGHTS

On a steep hill along the bank of the Aube, Carcassonne's stone gray *cité* (pop. 120), capped with a melange of silver cones and flat medieval towers, is a breathtaking sight. The well-preserved walls and fortifications date to the first century. After centuries of unsuccessful sieges, Carcassonne finally came under French control in 1224. Thus began the *cité*'s architectural metamorphosis, a 600-year journey from Roman times to the Renaissance illustrated by the architecture of its 52 **watchtowers.** The outer ramparts were built by Louis IX and Phillip III. A *petit train* takes visitors around the ramparts with commentary in eight languages, including English and Spanish. (☎24 45 70. 20min.; May-Sept. daily 10am-noon and 2-6pm; €7, students €6.) A **calèche** (horse-drawn carriage) also crosses the bridge to the town. (☎71 54 57. 20min.; Apr.-Oct. daily 10am-6pm; €6, under 12 €4.) Both tours depart from the main entrance of the *cité,* at the Porte Narbonnaise.

Intended at the time of its construction in the 12th century to be a palace, the **Château Comtal,** 1 rue Viollet-le-Duc, was transformed into a citadel when Carcassonne submitted to royal control in 1226. In the 19th century, the castle went through a controversial restoration project, which capped the towers with cone-shaped roofs instead of preserving the medieval architecture. Join a guided tour to visit the château's inner walls, peruse its ramparts, and learn about the many and varied ways in which the fortress prepared a cruel death for attackers. The **Tour de la Justice's** treacherous staircase, which is a dead end, was a stairway to heaven for invaders who rushed upstairs only to find themselves trapped. Others, still less lucky, would be crushed by huge stones dropped through special openings. The **Cour du Midi** holds the remains of a Gallo-Roman villa, once home to the troubadours for which Carcassonne's court was famous. (☎11 70 77. 45min. tours in English, French, and Spanish. Mid-June to mid-Sept. frequent departures. Check the board at the entrance as times change daily. 1½hr. conference tours also available July-Aug. daily, Sept.-June Sa-Su; €4 extra. Audio tour in English, French, German, and Spanish €4, 2 for €6. Open daily Apr.-Sept. 10am-6:30pm, first tour 10:30am; Oct.-Mar. 9:30am-5pm, first tour 10:15am. €7.50, ages 18-25 €4.80.) The **Basilique St-Nazaire,** at the end of rue St-Louis, mixes Gothic and Romanesque styles and has a vast and open interior busy with colorful designs. From July to mid-September, the **Estivales d'Orgue de la Cité** brings organ concerts every Sunday at 5pm. (Open M-Sa 9-11:45am and 1:45-6:30pm, Su 9-10:45am and 2-4:30pm.)

Carcassonne's *cité* is filled with small museums, most of which are no more than tourist traps. One exception is the **Musée de l'Ecole,** 3 rue du Plô, in the old schoolhouse. In reconstructed classrooms, the museum displays life-size figures, photographs, and report cards from the late 1800s, when statesman Jules Ferry made primary education free, compulsory, and secular. (☎25 95 14. Open daily July-Aug. 10am-7pm; Sept.-June 10am-6pm. €4, students €3, under 12 free.)

The lower town—the **Bastide St-Louis**—was born when Louis IX, afraid enemy troops might find shelter close to his fortress, burned the houses that clung to the city's walls and relocated their residents. To make up for the loss, he gave the homeless townspeople their very own walled fortifications and church. Converted into a fortress after the Black Prince razed Carcassonne during the Hundred Years' War in 1355, the *basse ville*'s **Cathédrale St-Michel,** on rue Voltaire, still sports fortifications on its southern side. The church's back entrance opens onto a small but meticulously kept garden. (Open M-Sa 7am-noon and 2-7pm, Su 9am-1pm.)

NIGHTLIFE AND FESTIVALS

The evening is the best time for wandering Carcassonne's *cité* streets and relaxing in the cafés in **place Marcou.** Bars and cafés at **place Carnot,** in the lower city, are open until midnight or later. **Le Bar à Vins,** 6 rue du Plô, is the best bar in town. A fusion of glitter and electronica, this wine-bar-meets-beer-garden draws a mixed crowd of tourists and local youth. The excellent house mojito (€8) alone is worth a stop. (☎47 38 38. Tapas €6-12. Wine €2. Beer €2.80-5. Open daily Feb.-Nov. 9am-2am; hours vary Mar.-May and Oct. MC/V.) Grab a pint of Guinness (€6) at **O'Sheridans,** 13 rue Victor Hugo off pl. Carnot, a friendly Irish pub filled with French and Anglo crowds. (☎72 06 58. Live music Sept.-June every other Th at 10pm. Happy hour 6-8pm; whiskey half-price. Open daily 5pm-2am. MC/V.)

In July, the **Festival de la Cité** brings dance, opera, theater, and concerts to the Château Comtal and the amphitheater. (Info and reservations ☎11 59 15; www.festivaldecarcassonne.com. €30-68, most shows €15 for students.) The **Festival de la Bastide** showcases smaller bands as well as free comedy, music, and dance performances in the squares of the *cité* and the Bastide St-Louis. Pick up a schedule at the tourist office. On **Bastille Day,** deep red floodlights and smoke set the entire *cité* ablaze in remembrance of the villages burned by the inquisitorial jury headquartered here during the Tour de l'Inquisition. The fireworks display draws 700,000-800,000 visitors. The banks of the river provide a great view, but try to avoid getting trampled. For two weeks in mid-August, the *cité* returns to the Middle Ages for the **Spectacles Médiévaux,** *son-et-lumière* shows in French. Even non-French-speakers will enjoy the nightly 9:30pm show—a multimedia drama in the castle amphitheater that brings the 13th century to life (€2-5, under 7 free). For tickets, contact the tourist office. For the rest of the summer, at 3 and 4:45pm, the **Tournoi de Chevaliers,** an equestrian show, offers mock jousting and battles (€10, ages 7-18 €5, under 7 free). During the last week of August, the **Fiesta y Toros** brings horse shows, traditional dances, *abrivados,* and *corridas,* marking a celebration of Spanish culture. (☎72 37 40; www.carcassonetoros.com. *Corridas* €30.)

FOIX ☎05 61

The red tiled roofs and cobblestone streets of Foix (FWAH; pop. 9700) lie in the shadow of a massive medieval château. The counts who ruled from this magnificent fortress were not the only ones to leave their mark; nearby caves and grottoes hold paintings by the prehistoric peoples who settled the Ariège region. Today, the city is a base for hiking through the region's thick forests and kayaking down its twisting rivers. Consider renting a car here to visit surrounding areas; the prehistoric caves and serene Ariège passes are poorly served by public transportation.

TRANSPORTATION AND PRACTICAL INFORMATION. The train station (☎05 34 09 29 00), av. Pierre Sémard, is north of town off N20. (Info and ticket windows open M 5:40am-12:35pm and 2:15-9:10pm, Tu-F 6:55am-1:30pm and 2-9:10pm, Sa 9:55am-6:10pm, Su 2:25-10:20pm.) **Trains** go to Toulouse (1-1½hr., 20 per day, €13). Salt Autocars, 2 rue des Cheminots (☎48 61 51), runs **buses** to Toulouse

(2hr., 2 per day, €9). Rent **canoes** and **kayaks** from lakefront Base Nautique (☎65 44 19; €9 per ½-day) down the street from the campsite (see below).

To reach the **tourist office,** 29 rue Théophile Delcassé, turn right out of the train station, follow the street to the main road (N20), and take this highway to the first bridge on the right. Cross it, take the second left, and walk to the end of the street, about three blocks (10min). The office provides a free small map and tons of information on exploring the region. (☎65 12 12; www.ot-foix.fr. Open July-Aug. M-Sa 9am-7pm, Su 9:30am-12:30pm and 2-6pm; Sept.-June M-Sa 9am-noon and 2-6pm.) There is a **laundromat** at 22 rue de la Faurie. (☎01 72 15. Wash €4.60-6.50, dry €0.70 per 5min. Open daily 8am-8:30pm.) For **police,** 2 rue Lakanal, call ☎05 43 00. The **hospital** (☎03 30 30) is 5km out of town in St-Jean de Verges. For **Internet** access, drop by the **Bureau d'Information Jeunesse (BIJ),** rue Roger, across from the Mairie on pl. Parmentier. (☎02 86 10. €2.50 per hr. Open M 1-5pm, Tu 1-6pm, W and F 10am-noon and 1-5pm, Th 10am-noon and 1-6pm.) The **post office,** 4 rue Laffont, has **currency exchange.** (☎02 01 02. Open M-W and F 8:30am-6:30pm, Th 8:30am-noon and 2-6pm, Sa 8:30am-noon.) **Postal Code:** 09000.

LANGUEDOC-ROUSSILLON

ACCOMMODATIONS AND FOOD. The best option for budget travelers is the centrally located **Foyer Léo Lagrange ❶,** 16 rue Peyrevidal, around the corner from the tourist office. To get there, turn right onto cours Gabriel Fauré and right again onto rue Peyrevidal, just after the Halle Aux Grains; it will be on your right. A cross between a hotel and a hostel, it offers privacy and sociability in 18 clean 1- to 4-bed rooms, each equipped with a sink, desk, and private shower. (☎65 09 04; www.leolagrange-foix.com. Breakfast €5. Sheets €3. Free Internet. Reception 8am-11pm; call ahead if arriving late. Reservations accepted online. €14 per person. Cash only.) Classy **Hostellerie de la Barbacane du Château ❸,** 1 av. de Lérida, is just past the flowered roundabout, to the right on cours Gabriel Fauré, about 5min. from the tourist office. Elegant mahogany beds and sparkling bathrooms justify the price. A few rooms have excellent views of the château; call ahead to reserve these. (☎65 50 44; fax 02 74 33. Elevator. Breakfast €7. Reception Apr.-Dec. 7am-11pm. Singles and doubles €40, with bath €42, with view of château €50, with bath and TV €45-72. MC/V.) **Camping du Lac/Labarre ❷,** is a three-star lakeside site 3km up N20 toward Toulouse. Buses from Toulouse stop at the camp. From the train station, head left along N20 until signs for the campground appear on the left. (☎65 11 58; www.campingdulac.com. July-Aug. €21 for 2 people, car, tent, and electricity; Sept. and May-June €18; Oct.-Apr. €15.)

Foix's restaurants serve Ariège regional specialties. Try *truite à l'ariègeoise* (trout) or *cassoulet* (white-bean and duck stew). Restaurants with moderately priced local specialties line **rue de la Faurie.** For basic supplies, head to the **Casino** supermarket, rue Laffont. (Open M-Sa 8:30am-7:30pm, Su 8:30am-noon.) On Fridays and the first, third, and fifth Mondays of the month, open-air markets sprout up all over Foix, with meat and cheese at the **Halle aux Grains,** fruit and vegetables at **place St-Volusien,** and clothing along the **allées de Villote.** (Food 9am-12:30pm; clothes 9am-4pm.) For a taste of Ariège cuisine at unbeatable prices, try the casual **Le Jeu de l'Oie ❷,** 17 rue de la Faurie. The generous *plat du jour* (€6.90) is a great value, as is the three-course *menu* (€9.50); a two-course *menu* that includes a glass of wine (€8.60) is also a bargain. Dinner draws locals, who descend on this neighborhood favorite to feast on savory salads and grilled meat dishes. (☎02 69 39. Salads €3.50-8. *Plats* €7-13. Open July-Aug. Tu-Sa noon-3pm and 7-11pm; Sept.-June Tu-F noon-2:30pm and 7-10:30pm, Sa 7-10:30pm. MC/V.) Delicacies abound at **La Sainte Marthe ❹,** pl. Lazema, a small and worthwhile splurge. Individual *plats* range from the reasonably priced fish soup with garlic croutons (€7) to the decadent *magret de canard* (duck; €21) with *foie gras* and truffle sauce. (☎02 87 87. 3-course *menus* €23-40. Special house *cassoulet* €16. Open daily noon-2:30pm and 7:30-10pm. AmEx/D/MC/V.)

SIGHTS. Perched on a pedestal of jagged rock high above the city, the **Château de Foix** is worth visiting even if you don't plan to go inside; walk up the path around the château for a view of Foix among the Pyrenean foothills. To reach the château from the tourist office, turn right on Cours Gabriel Fauré, then right again just past the Mairie, on rue St-Jammes. Continue straight as the road becomes rue Lazema and rue des Chapeliers. Take a gentle left uphill on rue du Rocher. The château has three stunning towers, each built in a different century. The 15th-century round tower is tallest and a particularly impressive piece of fortress architecture. Inside the well-preserved castle, the regional **Musée de l'Ariège** displays a collection of armor, stone carvings, and artifacts from the Roman Empire to the Middle Ages. Don't miss a small collection of ornately carved medieval keys. After its glory days, the castle was used as a garrison and a prison: inside the round tower, graffiti written by desperate prisoners is still legible. After the tour, visitors haul themselves up the castle towers for an even better view. (☎05 34 09 83 83. Both open daily July-Aug. 9:45am-6:30pm; Sept. and June daily 9:45am-noon and 2-6pm; Oct.-May M and W-Su 10:30am-noon and 2-5:30pm. Free tours in French every hr., in English daily July-Aug. 1pm. €4.20, students €3.10.) Down the hill at pl. St-Volusien, the 14th-century **Abbaye Saint-Volusien** occupies the site of an ancient Roman church and still includes part of the Roman structure. Simple but imposing vaulted ceilings bridge the intricate rose- and beige-colored stone walls in this fine example of Gothic architecture. (Open daily 8am-8pm. Guided visits M-F 11am and 4-6pm, Sa 11am and 2-4pm.)

DAYTRIP FROM FOIX. The Ariège region boasts some of the most spectacular **caves** in France. At the **Grotte de Niaux,** lanterns illuminate pre-historic wall drawings of bison, horses, and ibex that date from around 12,000 BC. Reservations are required to enter the cave. Twenty kilometers south of Foix, the grotto is accessible only by car. Be sure to bring a warm jacket and appropriate footwear. (☎05 88 37. Open Apr.-Oct. daily; Nov.-Mar. Tu-Su. €9.40, students €7.50, under 18 €5.70.) An hour-long boat ride floats down the **Rivière Souterraine de Labouiche,** the longest navigable underground river in Europe. Six kilometers from town, the small metal boat cruises through galleries of stalactites and stalagmites, guided by wisecracking Anglophone guides. There is no public transportation to this site; a taxi from Foix costs about €12 each way (☎65 12 69). In summer, arrive as early as possible and at least before 3:30pm to avoid crowds. (☎65 04 11. Open July-Aug. daily 9:30am-5pm; Apr.-June and Sept. daily 10-11am and 2-5pm; Oct. to mid-Nov. Sa-Su 10-11am and 2-4:15pm. €8.50, students €7.50, under 18 €6.50.)

FESTIVALS. In August (1-15 in 2008) on Tu and Th-F at 10pm, an extravagant medieval spectacle, **L'Ariège au Fil du Temps,** enlivens the area around Foix's château. Villagers come out for a sound and light show about the history of Ariège, reenacting battles and shooting off more fireworks than some cities use on Bastille Day. (For info and tickets call Théâtre de l'Espinet ☎02 88 26. €8-23, under 18 €5-12.) The first weekend of July, the **Résistances** festival brings 100 art films—many of which premiere at Cannes—to Foix. (☎69 36 32; call the tourist office for more information.) At the end of July, **Trad'estiu** ("traditional summer") arrives in Foix. This festival of traditional music and dance features popular—and free—outdoor performances. (☎65 55 55; www.tradestiu.com.) The next weekend brings a **jazz festival,** with concerts nightly at 9:30pm and jazz playing from speakers around town. (☎01 18 30; www.jazzfoix.com. €25 per night, students €20; under 25 €10 coupon for ½-price tickets for each concert; week pass €130/80.)

PERPIGNAN ☎04 68

Perpignan (PEAR-peen-yohn; pop. 117,000) is a few kilometers from the Mediterranean, 27km from the Spanish border, and 30km from the foothills of the

Pyrénées. This is a town of contrasts, from the palm-lined and litter-strewn av. de Gaulle to the tiny streets of the *vieille ville* and the massive, open nave of the Cathédrale St-Jean. Yet Perpignan is also, and above all, a daytripper's paradise. Free week-long regional bus passes give access to the remarkable, and otherwise nearly unaffordable, towns of Céret, Villefranche-de-Conflent, and Collioure.

TRANSPORTATION

Flights: Aéroport de Perpignan-Rivesaltes (**PGF;** ☎52 60 70; aeroport@perpignan.cci.fr), 6km northwest of the town center, just outside of town along D117. **Ryanair** (www.ryanair.com) offers the cheapest flights to **London. Navette Aéroport** (☎55 68 00) runs shuttles from the SNCF train station and the *gare routière* to the airport. (15min.; M-F 4 per day, Sa-Su 5 per day. Shuttles are synchronized with flights, and the connection is usually guaranteed. Schedule changes frequently; check with tourist office. €4.50, ages 4-10 and groups €3).

Trains: Rue Courteline. Ticket window open M and Sa 5:10am-8:15pm, Tu-Th 5:40am-8:15pm, F 5:40am-10:05pm, Su 6:15am-10:05pm. To: **Carcassonne** (1½hr.; 3-7 per day, change at Narbonne; €17); **Lyon** (4-5½hr., 5 per day, €62); **Marseille** (4½-6hr.; 3 per day, change at Narbonne; €38); **Montpellier** (1½-2hr.; 8-11 per day, change at Narbonne; €21); **Paris** (5hr., 1-4 per day, €101); **Toulouse** (2½-3hr.; 2-7 per day, change at Narbonne; €26).

Buses: Regional buses depart the *gare routière,* near the train station (☎35 29 02); due to ongoing construction, this station is only temporary. Ask at tourist office or train station for more information. Office open M-Sa 7am-6:30pm. All buses **free** with **week-long regional bus pass.** To: **Céret** (45min.; M-Sa 10 per day, Su 4 per day; €4.40); **Collioure** (45-50min.; M-Sa 10 per day, Su 1 per day; €6.60); **Villefranche-de-Conflent** (1¼hr., 8 per day, €9.60).

> TIP **PASS FOR A PASS.** To obtain a free tourist pass for a week of **free regional bus rides,** bring your passport and photo to the tourist office.

Public Transportation: Compagnie Transports Perpignan Mediterranée (CTPM), 27 bd. Clemenceau (☎61 01 13). Office open M-F 7:30am-12:30pm and 1:30-6:30pm, Sa 9am-noon and 2:30-5pm. Runs **buses** throughout Perpignan and to Canet-Plage. 1st bus in any direction 6:30am, last bus around 8:30pm. Tickets within Perpignan €1.10, round-trip €2, *carnet* of 10 €7.80. Not covered by week-long regional bus pass.

Taxis: Accueil Perpignan Taxi (☎35 15 15), by the train station. 24hr. €2 per km, more at night and on weekends. €40 to the airport, €30 to Canet-Plage.

Car Rental: ADA, 30bis av. General de Gaulle (☎68 45 66), near train station. From €74 per day, 250km. 21+, with 1yr. driver's license. Open M-Sa 9am-noon and 2-6pm. **Europcar** (☎34 89 80), inside the train station. Cars can be returned elsewhere. From €315 per 5 days, 1750km. 21+. Under-25 surcharge €30 per day. Open M-F 8am-7pm, Sa 8am-noon and 2-6pm. AmEx/MC/V. **Hertz** (☎61 18 77), at the airport and near the train station; (☎51 37 40) also on 9 av. General de Gaulle. Cars can be returned elsewhere. From €168 for 3 days, 300km. 21+. Under-25 surcharge €34. Open daily 8am-7pm. AmEx/MC/V.

Bike Rental: Bouti Cycle, 20 av. Gilbert Brutus (☎85 02 71). €38 per 5 days, €54 per week. 5-day min. rental; €200 cash deposit. Open Tu-Sa 9am-12:30pm and 2:30-7pm. MC/V.

ORIENTATION AND PRACTICAL INFORMATION

Perpignan's train station was once referred to as "the center of the world" by off-center Salvador Dalí; it is almost constantly packed with weary travelers. The most lively part of the city is the labyrinth of small streets in the heart of the *vieille ville*, a 10min. walk from the station. The area makes a triangle whose three cor-

ners are marked by the regional tourist office, **place de Catalogne** toward the train station, and the **Palais des Rois de Majorque** to the south. Avoid **Quartier St-Jacques,** near the intersection of bd. Jean Bourrat and bd. Anatole France, at night.

Tourist Office: Palais des Congrès, pl. Armand Lanoux (☎66 30 30; www.perpignantourisme.com.) From the train station, follow av. de Gaulle to pl. de Catalogne, then take bd. Clemenceau to pl. de la Résistance. The *vieille ville* is directly across the canal. Veer left on cours Pamarole and continue along the Promenade des Plantanes until you see a large glass building on the right. Multilingual staff offers comprehensive tours in French. (1½-2hr.; new schedule appears at the beginning of each summer; €5, under 12 free) and English (mid-July to mid-Sept. 1 per week). The city can also be visited on a night tour, with music and dance shows (☎62 38 84; July-Aug. Tu 9pm; €8). Annex at pl. Arago. Main office open mid-June to mid-Sept. M-Sa 9am-7pm, Su 10am-4pm; mid-Sept. to mid-June M-Sa 9am-6pm, Su 10am-1pm. Annex open mid-June to mid-Sept. M-Sa 10am-7pm and mid-Sept. to mid-June M-Sa 10am-6pm.

Budget Travel: Cars Verts Voyages, 10 rue Jeanne d'Arc (☎51 19 47). Open in high season M-Sa 8:15am-noon and 2-6:30pm; in low season closed Sa. Organizes daytrips June-Sept. to: **Andorra** (€31), **Barcelona** (€37), and **Mt. Canigou** (€43).

Laundromat: Laverie Foch, 23 rue Maréchal Foch. Wash €2.90-6.50, dry €0.50 per 6min. Open daily 7am-8:30pm.

Police: Av. de Grande Brétagne (☎35 70 00).

24hr. Pharmacy: The rotating **pharmacie de garde** is listed on the door of every pharmacy and in the local newspaper *L'Indépendant* (€0.85, Su €1.30).

Hospital: Av. du Languedoc (☎61 66 33).

Internet Access: Cyber Espace, 45bis av. du Général Leclerc (☎35 36 29), facing the *gare routière.* €2 per 30min., €3 per hr.; 8-10am half-price. Open July-Aug. M-Sa noon-1am, Su 1-8pm; Sept.-June M-F 8am-1am, Sa noon-1am, Su 1-8pm. Or try one of the cheap (€2.10-3 per hr.) Internet cafes on av. de Gaulle.

Post Office: Quai de Barcelone (☎51 99 12). **Currency exchange.** Western Union. Open M-F 8:30am-7pm, Sa 8am-noon. **Postal Code:** 66000.

ACCOMMODATIONS AND CAMPING

The cheapest hotels are near the train station on av. du Général de Gaulle, although even they are not amazing bargains. A 10min. walk separates these hotels from the city center.

Avenir Hôtel, 11 rue de l'Avenir (☎34 20 30; www.avenirhotel.com), off av. Général de Gaulle. Sports colorful though stuffy rooms, terraces, and decorations painted by the owner. Beware of the communal shower's high price (€3.20 per day). Breakfast €4.50. Reception M-Sa 8am-11pm, Su 8am-noon and 6-11pm. Reservations recommended. Singles €18-24; doubles €22-24; singles and doubles with toilet €27, with shower €30, with bath €36; triples €39; quads €42. Extra bed €6. AmEx/MC/V. ❷

Auberge de Jeunesse La Pépinière (HI), allée Marc-Pierre (☎34 63 32), on the edge of town between the highway and the police station. From the train station, go down av. du Général de Gaulle and turn left on rue Valette. At the end, turn right on av. de Grande Brétagne, left on rue Claude Marty before the police station, and right on allée Marc-Pierre. Recently renovated rooms with bright yellow lockers make up for road noise and a hallway paint job that leaves much to be desired. The hostel's attractive outdoor terrace is a great picnic spot. Breakfast €3.50. Internet access €1 per 30min. Reception 7:30-10am and 5-11pm. Check-out 10am; strictly enforced. Lockout 10am-5pm. Closed mid-Nov. to late Feb. Dorms €15. Cash only. ❶

Hôtel le Berry, 6 av. de Gaulle (☎34 59 02). Offers clean and comfortable rooms at fair prices. A/C, TV, and proximity to the train station are this hotel's selling points. All rooms come with shower and toilet. Breakfast €5. Reception 9am-9pm. Singles €30-40; doubles €35-45; triples €45-50; quads €50-55. MC/V. ❸

Camping Le Catalan, rte. de Bompas (☎63 16 92). Take bus #15 (dir.: Bompas) to the "Lidl" stop, which is in view of the campsite (15min.; every 15min.-1hr. until 7pm but irregular schedule, check with tourist office or CTPM for exact times; €1.10). 94 spots with access to playground, laundry, and hot showers. Snack bar and pool open July-Aug. Wheelchair-accessible. Closed late Oct. to Mar. July-Aug. 2 people with car €18, extra person €5; Sept.-Oct. and Mar.-June €14/4. Electricity €3.50. MC/V. ❶

FOOD

Perpignan's food comes in a full range of prices. Local *charcuterie*, Catalan *pâté*, and *escargots* with garlic are specialties, as well as *touron* nougat in flavors like caramel or almond. **Place de la Loge, place Arago, place de la République,** and **place de Verdun** in the *vieille ville* stay lively at night, as restaurants dish out French and Spanish fare. Pricier options and candlelit tables line **quai Vauban** along the canal, while **avenue du Général de Gaulle,** leading into town from the train station, has as many kebab shops as it does Internet cafes. A variety of fresh produce can be found at the open-air markets on **place Cassanyes** (open daily 7am-1pm) and **place de la République** (open Tu-Su 7am-1pm). A huge **Casino** supermarket is on bd. Félix Mercader. (☎51 56 00. Open M-Sa 8:30am-8pm, Su 8:30am-12:30pm.)

Casa Sansa ❸, rue des Fabriques Couvertes, serves outstanding Catalan food under yellow awnings on a tiny street near the Castille. It's worth a trip just for the crusty country bread and garlic *aioli*. The trick is to order from the illustrated tapas menu (€3-7)—create a feast for only €10-15. More conventional meals are available at a higher price. (☎34 21 84. *Plats* €13-20. *Menu* €19. Open daily 11:30am-3pm and 6-11pm. AmEx/D/MC/V.) On a hot day, try the air-conditioned **Peace 'n' Love ❶**, 40 rue de la Fusterie, a vegetarian restaurant that will also satisfy meat-eaters on a budget. Everything costs €6.50, and most dishes are enough for a full meal. The spotless dining room has funky blue lighting. Try the cumin-spiced vegetable curry, which comes with bread instead of rice. (☎06 08 33 67 84. Desserts €3-5. Open M-W noon-2:30pm, Th-Sa noon-2:30pm and 7-10:30pm. Cash only.) **Spaghetteri'Aldo ❷**, rue des Variétés, offers filling pasta with fresh sauces (€8.50-12). The spaghetti bolognese (€8.50) or gnocchi gorgonzola (€9) won't disappoint. (☎61 11 47. Salads €8.50-9.50. Open Tu-Sa noon-3pm and 7-11pm. MC/V.)

SIGHTS

Along La Basse river, flower-lined *quais* beg for afternoon strolls; it's also worth setting aside time to wander the *vieille ville*. An uphill walk across the *vieille ville* brings you to the red-rock walls of Perpignan's 15th-century Spanish **citadel.** Concealed inside is the **Palais des Rois de Majorque,** where the kings of the Majorcan Dynasty (1272-1344) settled. The thick walls, sparse openings, and watchtower leave no doubt about their purpose. The **Ste-Croix chapel,** whose marble facade reveals French, Italian, and Moorish architectural influences, is a notable exception. The palace's courtyard serves as a concert hall throughout July, hosting plays and musical (mostly jazz) performances. (Enter from av. G. Brutus. Open daily June-Sept. 10am-6pm; Oct.-May 9am-5pm. Ticket sales end 45min. before closing. 1hr. French tours available July-Aug. every 30min.; Sept.-June 2 per day or by reservation. €4, students €2, under 12 free. Concert tickets €5-10; available at FNAC.)

Partly supported by a macabre pillar depicting the severed head of John the Baptist, the **Cathédrale St-Jean** is a paragon of Gothic architecture. Begun in 1324 and consecrated in 1509, the grandiose cathedral sports an 80m long nave, the third largest in the world. Stunning oil paintings, colorful stained glass, and crystal chandeliers are designed in Renaissance, Baroque, and 19th-century religious styles. (☎51 33 72. Open M 7:30am-noon and 3-7pm, Tu-Su 7:30am-7pm. Mass Su 8, 10:30am, 6:30pm.) Guarding the entrance to the city's center, **Le Castillet,** originally built in 1368 by the Spanish, was intended to repel French invaders. After the Treaty of the Pyrénées in 1659, the small castle was transformed into a prison and torture chamber for those who refused to acknowledge the victorious French crown. No longer a frontier pillar, the Castillet holds the **Casa Pairal,** a museum of Catalan domestic ware, religious relics, and, of course, farm equipment. Visit the reconstructions of old Catalan houses as well as the giant statues of the King and Queen of Majorca guarding the museum entrance. (☎35 42 05. Open M and W-Su May-Sept. 10am-6:30pm; Oct.-Apr. 11am-5:30pm. Guided tours in French twice a month in summer; call for exact dates. €4, students and under 15 €2.) Back in the *vieille ville*, the **Musée Hyacinthe Rigaud,** 16 rue de l'Ange, contains a collection of Gothic paintings by 13th-century Spanish and Catalan masters, as well as canvases by Ingres, Miró, Picasso, and Rigaud. The bottom floor houses temporary exhibits. (☎35 43 40. Open M and W-Su May-Sept. noon-7pm; Oct.-Apr. 11am-5:30pm. Wheelchair-accessible. €4, students and ages 15-18 €2, under 15 free.)

ENTERTAINMENT AND FESTIVALS

Perpignan is not known for its nightlife, but a few bars scattered in the tiny streets around the Castillet keep a small crowd entertained until the early morning. Don't let the more expensive bars around the Castillet keep you away from **L'Ubu,** 40 pl. Rigaud, a literary café with live jazz most nights. Grab a beer (€2.30) and listen to the music or take advantage of the free Internet access. (☎34 27 74; www.ubujazz.com. Open M-Sa 10am-2am. AmEx/MC/V.) The chic, the stylish, and the well-to-do frequent the plush seats and jazzy beats of the classy **Trois Soeurs,** 2 rue Fontfroide. (☎51 22 33. Beer €3. Mixed drinks €7-8. Live jazz Sept.-June W 7pm. Open Tu-Sa 10am-2am. AmEx/MC/V.) The clubs lining the beaches at nearby **Canet-Plage** (bus #1 from the train station, irregularly every 30min.-1hr. 6:30am-7:30pm) provide the wildest nightlife, but getting back to Perpignan means paying €20-25 for a taxi, except on Saturday nights, when a **bus service,** put in place to combat drunk driving, runs between Perpignan and the Canet clubs. (Buses leave from the Castillet at 11:45pm, 12:45, 2:10am; buses return from Canet-Plage 12:10, 1, 4, 5am. Make sure to check www.route-66.fr or call ☎06 09 49 89 27 for up-to-date schedules. €1 buys unlimited rides for the year.)

In July and August, beginning the first Thursday after Bastille Day, Perpignan hosts free musical performances and traditional Catalan dancing for the **Jeudis de Perpignan,** every Thursday from 7:30 to 11:30pm. (Call tourist office for info.) The **Procession de la Sanche** takes over the streets of the *vieille ville* on Good Friday, when a cross is paraded to the Eglise St-Jacques. A sacred fire permanently lit at Mt. Canigou is brought back to the Castillet in Perpignan on June 23 for the **Fête de St-Jean.** Known as the **Festa Major** (☎35 07 60), the two weeks surrounding the celebrated day are filled with traditional dancing, music concerts, and food tasting, culminating in a sound-and-light show. For two nights at the end of June, the entire town gets a little jollier for **La Fête des Vins,** when stands hand out wine samples between bd. Wilson and the cours Palmarole. Cheese, *foie gras*, and Catalan lamb are also available. (☎51 59 99. Empty glass at entrance €3.) Throughout July, the **Estivales de Perpignan** brings world-renowned theater and dance to town. (☎86 08 51. For tickets, visit www.estivales.com, or buy them at the Palmarium, next to the tourist office annex. Open daily mid-June to mid-Sept. 10am-6:30pm; Oct.-May 10am-5:30pm. Prices vary; student discounts available.) Perpignan's most important festival comes during the first two weeks in September, with **Visa Pour l'Image** (☎62 38 00; www.visapourlimage.com), a photojournalism festival that showcases the year's current events and brings a large share of foreigners.

DAYTRIPS FROM PERPIGNAN

VILLEFRANCHE-DE-CONFLENT

Trains (☎96 63 62) run from Perpignan to the Villefranche train station (1hr., 6-7 per day, €7.50). Couriers Catalans Buses (☎35 29 02) run from Perpignan directly to the gates of the ramparts around Villefranche (1hr.; M-F 5 per day, Sa 6 per day; €9.60, free with tourist pass). From the train station, located 200m before the town gates, cross the bridge and bear right along the highway to reach the town center. The walls that surround the city have 2 gates that lead to the parallel main streets. The left gate leads to rue St-Jacques; the right gate opens onto rue St-Jean.

Don't pass up a daytrip to the spectacular village-in-a-fortress Villefranche-de-Conflent (VEEL-frahnsh duh kahn-fluh), which lies deep in the Conflent mountains but is only a 1¼hr. free bus ride from Perpignan. The impenetrable Fort Liberia, a mere 734 underground steps above Villefranche, offers a stunning view of Mt. Canigou, and nearby stalagmite caves take visitors deep inside the mountains. Nature lovers will find canyons, valleys, and hiking trails only a short trip away on the *petit train jaune*, which goes deep into the heart of the Pyrénées.

Fort Liberia is what makes Villefranche worth the trip from Perpignan. Built into the mountainside high above the town, the fort takes the form of two overlapping hexagons, meant to prevent attacks from the front and back of the building. The stronghold was constructed in 1681 by Vauban in order to protect Villefranche and the rest of Catalonia from the Spanish army. The towers and narrow passageways make for an interesting tour, while the view of picturesque Villefranche amid sensational peaks, including Mt. Canigou, is breathtaking. The "Staircase of 1000 Steps" leads back down to the city; although there are actually only 734 steps, that is more than enough to discourage most from walking all the way up to the fort. To reach the fort, catch the *navette* (shuttle bus) from the train station or the parking lot at the town gates (10min.; July-Aug. every 30min., Sept.-June request at the St-Jacques info desk), or, better still, take the 30min. hike up along the road that begins on the side of the train station farther from town. Buy tickets at the tourist office on rue St-Jacques or at the fort entrance. (☎96 34 01. Open daily July-Aug. 9am-8pm; May-June and Sept. 10am-7pm; Mar.-Apr. 10am-6pm; Nov.-Feb. 10am-5pm. €5.80, including *navette* €8; students €5/7; ages 5-11 €2.80/4.10. *Navette* is free for visitors who arrive on the *petit train jaune*.)

After a sweaty climb down from Fort Liberia, cool off by going underground. The magnificent **Grandes Canalettes** contain water-carved galleries, stalactite-filled grottoes, underground lakes, and a bottomless pit. In July and August, a *son-et-lumière* show is held at an auditorium in the heart of the caves. (☎96 23 11; www.grotte-grandes-canalettes.com. Open mid-June to mid-Sept. daily 10am-6pm; mid-Sept. to Oct. and Apr. to mid-June daily 10am-5:30pm; Nov.-Mar. Su 2-5pm. €8, ages 5-12 €4; 2 caves €12/6. Visit to Les Canalettes next door only by guided tour; reservations required. *Son-et-lumière* daily July-Aug. 6:30pm. €11, under 18 €6, price includes guided tour. AmEx/MC/V.) Accessible through an entrance in the middle of rue St-Jacques, Villefranche's 11th-century **ramparts** include rock passageways in the remarkably well-preserved walls of the city, with occasional peepholes onto city alleys and mountainsides. (☎96 16 40. Open daily July-Aug. 10am-8pm; Sept. and June 10am-7pm; Oct.-Dec. and Feb.-May 10:30am-12:30pm and 2-5pm. Audio tour in Catalan, Dutch, English, French, Italian, or Spanish €3. For guided tours, call ahead; groups only. €4, students €3, under 10 free.) Running 63km through the Pyrénées, the **petit train jaune** departs from the train station and links Villefranche to Latour-de-Carol (3hr., 3-7 per day, €18). The train runs through mountain valleys on spectacular viaducts, stopping at 20 small towns. The train also carts **skiers** to the fashionable **Font-Romeu** (2hr., 3-8 per day, €10.30). Equipped with snow machines and chair lifts, this resort offers first-rate skiing. (☎30 60 61. Day pass €28. €4 student discount outside of *vacances scolaires*.) The *petit train jaune* does not take reservations, so arrive at the station at least 1hr. ahead (2hr. from mid-July to mid-Aug.) or in the early morning.

Celebrated throughout Catalonia around June 23, the **Fête des Feux de la St-Jean** lights up Villefranche. Runners carry a sacred flame from Canigou's summit to the Castillet in Perpignan, and locals celebrate by dancing the traditional *Sardane*, drinking wine, and leaping over bonfires. People dressed as giants appear in the village the first Sunday in April in recognition of **Easter.** Instead of Bastille Day, Villefranche-de-Conflent celebrates the **Fête de la St-Jacques** during the third weekend in July, with fireworks and traditional dancing.

The tourist office (☎96 22 96), post office, and *mairie* are all together at 1 pl. de l'Eglise. The tourist office provides free town maps. (All three open July-Aug. M-Sa 10am-noon and 2-6pm; May-June and Sept. M-F 10am-noon and 2-5pm, Sa 10am-noon; Oct.-Apr. M-Sa 10am-noon.)

CÉRET

Buses run from the train station and gare routière *in Perpignan to the center of Céret (45min., 8-11 per day, €4.40). Pick up a schedule at the* gare routière *office in Perpignan. Most buses stop outside Perpignan at a stop which, confusingly, is called either Pont or rue du 19 Mars. From the bus stop, turn back toward the traffic circle and follow the signs to Céret-centre. At the next traffic circle, marked by a large fountain, turn right, continuing to follow signs, onto rue Saint Férréol. Take this until it ends, turn left, and make the 2nd left (av. Clemenceau); the tourist office is on the corner (20min.). If your bus stops at "Céret-Centre," follow av. Clemenceau uphill toward the city center.*

Tucked into a valley in the foothills of the Pyrénées, Céret (suh-RAY) blossoms in the spring. Each season the President of France receives the first *cérises* (cherries) from the nearby orchards. The town holds more than fruit; known as the "Cubist Mecca," Céret was the beloved stomping ground of Chagall, Picasso, Manolo, and Herbin. As a result, it is home to one of the best modern art museums in France. At the same time, the town is far enough into the hills for spectacular hiking.

The **Musée d'Art Moderne,** 8 bd. Maréchal Joffre, is located uphill from the tourist office. The collections in this modern building are composed primarily of personal gifts to the museum by artists including Picasso, Matisse, Braque, Chagall, and Miró. Rotating every three months, the temporary exhibits are usually minor during the low season and superb from mid-June to mid-September. 2008 brings an exhibit on the ceramics of Chagall (Feb.-May), followed by an exhibit from July to September on the *Fauves Hongrois.* (☎87 27 76; www.musee-ceret.com. Open July to mid-Sept. daily 10am-7pm; May-June and late Sept. daily 10am-6pm; Oct.-Apr. M and W-Su 10am-6pm. Guided visits daily July-Aug. 10:30am and 3pm, Sept.-June or in English upon reservation; €3.50. Wheelchair-accessible. €5.50, students €3.50, under 12 free; €8/6 for temporary summer exhibits.) In the town center, the marble fountain of **place des Neuf-Jets** reminds visitors of the town's dual French and Spanish roots. Originally, the fountain's Castilian lion faced Spain. Now it faces France, symbolizing France's 1659 victory over Spain. According to legend, the **pont du Diable** (Bridge of the Devil), which links the town center to its outskirts, couldn't be successfully built until the devil agreed to aid in its construction. Satan demanded the right to the first soul to cross the bridge, but the villagers foiled him by sending a sacrificial black cat across it. However, the devil got the last laugh, taking revenge by loosening one stone from the bridge.

A quick **hike** (2½hr. round-trip from the center of Céret) takes visitors through cherry fields and into the hills, offering an expansive view of the town below. This hike is #3 in *Les Petits Guides Rando Pyrénées Roussillon*, but beware of the unclear French directions. From the tourist office, turn right onto bd. Maréchal Joffre and right again on rue St-Férréol. Continue to the first traffic circle, marked by a fountain, and follow the sign that reads "*toutes directions.*" Keep right, following signs to Perpignan and "Le Pont." After five minutes, you will see a stone footbridge to your right. This is the **Pont du Diable;** cross it and take a gentle left, on D615, following the sign to Llauro and Oms. Take this under the rail bridge and turn right on the unmarked road (Chemin de Vivès). When the road splits (about 2-3min.), keep left, walking uphill and around a corner to reach the trail; here, follow the wooden arrow that reads "Chemin St-Férréol." The trail winds through a cherry orchard for 10min. until it reaches a cement road marked "St-Férréol." After another five minutes, turn right through a dried-up creek bed onto a path that leads into the woods. After 20min. of climbing, you'll reach an iron cross and a gravel road. Cross the road and bear right up a small trail. Continue across a gravel road to the small **Ermitage St-Férréol,** the site of a festive meal during the Festa Major de Sant Férréol on September 18. To return, retrace your steps. The *Petit Guide* recommends another way back, but it takes you along a highway for 1km, and the directions are difficult to follow; the best bet is to return as you came.

From May 31-July 1, Céret celebrates the **Grande Fête de la Cérise** and the **Festival de Bandas** with two days of cherry markets and Catalonian music. Late in June, the **Querencias**—Festival de Musique de Céret—features musical and dance performances. (☎87 00 53. Tickets €20 for one night, €30 for both.) The most raucous *féria*, **Céret de Toros,** occurs every year for three days in the middle of July. During the boisterous festival, the town hosts two *corridas* (bullfights) and one *novillada* (a bull fight with an uncertified fighter). Music livens the streets well into the night. (☎87 47 47; www.ceret-de-toros.com. Tickets €35-86 for each *corrida*, €27-56 for the *novillada.*) For a week toward the end of July, the **Festival de la Sardane** commemorates traditional Catalan folk dancing with concerts and processions through town. The festival culminates in the *concours des Sardanes,* where *Sardane* groups compete against one another in the annual dance tournament and amateurs practice in the streets. (☎87 00 53. Viewers' fee €10-12.) On September 18, the **Festa Major de Sant Ferriol** (☎87 00 53) brings runners to town for 6.5 and 20km runs. The town also comes together for a celebratory feast at L'ermitage, the destination for the dayhike above.

The **tourist office,** 1 av. Georges Clemenceau (☎87 00 53; www.ot-ceret.fr) provides a free map with a walking tour of the *vieille ville* and *Les Petits Guides Rando Pyrénées Roussillon* guide with 1-5hr. hiking itineraries around Céret. (Open July-Sept. M-Sa 9am-1pm and 2-7pm, Su 10am-1pm; Oct.-June M-F 9am-noon and 2-5pm, Sa 9:30am-12:30pm.)

COLLIOURE ☎04 68

Located where the vineyards and orchards of the Pyrénées meet the blue-green waters of the Mediterranean, Collioure (KOH-lee-ohr; pop. 2930) is as breathtaking as its surroundings suggest. Once the prize of Greeks and Phoenicians, the town's rocky harbor became one of Matisse's favorite subjects, and artists like Dalí, Dérain, Dufy, and Picasso soon set up their easels here as well. Though the artistic *avant-garde* no longer populates the town, numerous art galleries are housed under the copper roofs. Outside the art world, tourists lie on the pebbly beaches or walk around the harbor buying ice cream and souvenirs.

TRANSPORTATION AND PRACTICAL INFORMATION. The train station (☎82 05 89), at the top of av. Aristide Maillol, sends trains to Perpignan (20min., 13 per day, €4.90). Trains also run to Barcelona, Spain (4-5hr., 3 per day, €23) via Port Bou (30min., 6 per day, €3.10). Ticket office and info desk open daily July-Aug. 6:30am-9pm; Sept.-June 9am-1pm and 2:40-5:45pm. **Buses** leave from the Carrefour du Christ, at the intersection of av. de Gaulle, rte. d'Argelès, and rue de la République. **Les Courriers Catalans** (☎35 29 02) travels to nearby towns and Perpignan (45min.; 5 per day; €6.60, free with regional bus pass). **X-Trem Bike,** 5 rue de la Tour d'Auvergne, has **bike** rentals. (July-Aug. ☎82 59 77, Sept.-June 06 23 01 93 01. Open daily 8:30am-12:30pm, 1:30-2:30pm, and 6-7pm. €10 per ½-day, €18 per day, €85 per week; €200 deposit. MC/V.) Departing from pl. 8 Mai 1945 across from the post office, a **petit train** offers a 45min. tour of the vineyards up to Fort St-Elme and Port-Vendres. (☎98 02 06; www.petit-train-touristique.com. Departures every hr. July-Aug. 10am-8pm; Sept.-Oct. and Apr.-June every hr. 10-11am and 2-6pm. €6.50, under 12 €4.50.) **Taxis** from Allo Almaya can be reached at ☎82 09 30.

To reach the **tourist office** from the train station, walk downhill on av. Aristide Maillol to pl. du Maréchal Leclerc. Continue along the canal, then take a left at pl. du 18 Juin. To reach the tourist office from the "Christ" bus stop, walk downhill along rue de la République and, after crossing the canal, turn right on av. Camille Pelletan and then left at pl. du 18 Juin. The staff provides free maps and a guide (€5.50) to 1-7hr. regional hikes. (☎82 15 47; www.collioure.com. Open July-Aug.

daily 9am-8pm; Sept. and June M and Sa 9am-noon and 2-6pm, Tu-F 9am-noon and 2-7pm, Sa 9am-noon; Oct.-May M-Sa 9am-noon and 2-6pm.) Other services include: **laundry,** 28 rue de la République (☎98 04 17; wash €4.20-8, dry €0.50 per 5min.; open daily 8am-9pm); **police,** also on rue de la République (☎82 09 53); a **pharmacy,** 7 rue de la République (open M-F 9am-12:30pm and 3-7:30pm, Sa 9am-12:30pm); **Internet** access at **Café Sola,** 2 av. de la République (☎82 55 02; €5 per hr., €7 per 2½hr., free Wi-Fi with purchase of food or drink; open daily 7am-2am); and a **post office,** on pl. 8 Mai 1945, which **exchanges currency** and has an **ATM** (☎98 36 00; open M-F 9am-noon and 1:30-5pm, Sa 9am-noon). **Postal Code:** 66190.

ACCOMMODATIONS AND FOOD. Collioure fills its hotels and beaches to the brim during July and August. Don't bother looking for cheap accommodations: in the summer, the cheapest rooms are €30-40. Your best bet is to daytrip from Perpignan. From the train station, follow av. Aristide Maillol to pl. du Maréchal Leclerc and turn right onto the bridge. At the small rotary, take a left onto av. Général de Gaulle, where **Hôtel Le St-Pierre ❸,** 16 av. Général de Gaulle, offers simple rooms with firm beds and white walls at some of Collioure's lowest prices. Some rooms have balconies and A/C. (☎82 19 50; hotel.saint-pierre@wanadoo.fr. Breakfast €5. Doubles with sink and toilet or shower €40, with toilet and shower €48-50; triples €50; quints €86. AmEx/MC/V.) The **Hostellerie des Templiers ❺,** av. Camille Pelletan, a block away from the tourist office, is more than a hotel—it's also a museum, and you will pay accordingly. Tiled stairways lead to hallways covered with over 2000 original paintings. The rooms come equipped with flat-screen TV, A/C, toilet, and shower. Two annexes offer cheaper rooms but fewer amenities. (☎98 31 10; info@hotel-templiers.com. Breakfast €6. Reception 8am-midnight. Closed early Jan. to early Feb. July-Sept. doubles €71-100 in main hotel, in annexes €60; Apr.-June and Oct. €62-86/55; Nov.-Dec. and Feb.-Mar. €52-62/43. AmEx/MC/V.) The cheapest way to spend the night in Collioure is to rent a *chambre d'hôte* (private room), though it won't be much cheaper than Hôtel St-Pierre. In the center of town, the **Chambres ❸,** 20 rue Pasteur, are arranged around a small, dark staircase; all are furnished with double beds and baths in need of renovation. (☎82 15 31. Singles €30; doubles €38, with shower €43, with bath €45; triples and quads €60-69. Cash only.) **Camping la Girelle ❷,** on plage de l'Ouille, is a scenic 25min. hike from the town center. From pl. du Maréchal Leclerc, walk uphill on av. du Miradou. Turn left on rte. du Plage de las Fourques and continue 15min. until you see the sign on your right. The campsite sits between a tree-topped incline and a smooth beach. BBQ, bar, grocery store, laundry, and hot showers are available. (☎81 25 56. Restaurant open July-Aug. Reception 9am-noon and 5-8pm. July-Aug. €24 per 2 people and tent; Sept. and Apr.-June €19. Extra person €7.50/6.50. Electricity €5/4. AmEx/MC/V.)

Local produce is sold at a market centered around place du Maréchal Leclerc and spilling out along the canal toward the Château Royal. (Open W and Su 9am-1pm.) Touristy *crêperies*, pizzerias, and cafés crowd rue St-Vincent near the port. For pre-packaged goods, head to the **Shopi** supermarket, 16 av. de la République. (☎82 26 04. Open July-Aug. daily 8:15am-8pm; Sept.-June M-Sa 8:15am-1pm and 2:30-7:30pm.) **Al Cantou Pizza ❶,** 19 rue Pasteur, offers delicious takeout wood-oven pizzas in small and large sizes. (☎82 27 79. Pizzas €4.50-9. Open M-W and F-Su 11am-2pm and 6-10pm. Cash only). Situated near the town's school, **Le Zouave ❸,** 14 rue du Dr. Coste, explodes with Spanish and Catalan flavor. (☎82 00 71. Tapas €3.50-8. Tapas assortment €12. Sangria €2.50. Tapas *menu* for 2 €32, includes 50cl of wine. Open M and Th-Su noon-2pm and 7-10pm. MC/V.)

SIGHTS AND FESTIVALS. The foundations of the **Eglise Notre Dame des Anges** lie deep in the Mediterranean. This architectural wonder includes richly decorated side chapels in addition to a monumental Baroque main altar. (Open daily 9am-noon and 2-6pm. Free.) Extending from pl. du 8 Mai 1945 to the port, the hulking white stone **Château Royal** first sheltered the Majorcan kings in the 13th century and was later fortified by both French and Spanish kings during unending border wars. Every architectural element—from the shape of the towers to the design of the ramparts—was designed to guarantee the utmost protection. The château is worth a visit for its spooky underground tunnels and spectacular view of the harbor. In summer, the main courtyard hosts plays and occasional dance performances. (☎82 06 43; www.cg66.fr. Open daily July-Aug. 10am-6:15pm; Sept.-June 9am-5pm. 1¼hr. tours in French available upon reservation. €4, students and ages 12-18 €2, under 12 free.) To retrace the steps of Matisse and Dérain, follow the **Chemin du Fauvisme.** Masterpiece reproductions are displayed exactly where they were originally painted. The *chemin* begins and ends in front of the tourist office, where the staff distributes free maps and sells a catalogue with detailed descriptions and images of every stop (€5.50; guided tours available in French July-Aug. Th 3pm). In the small ivy-covered Villa Pams on rte. de Port-Vendres, the **Musée d'Art Moderne** houses a modest collection of ceramics, as well as a few paintings by minor 20th-century artists. (☎82 10 19. Open July-Aug. daily 10am-noon and 2-6pm; Sept.-June M and W-Su 10am-noon and 2-6pm. €2, students €1, under 12 free.) Stop by **Les Anchois Roque,** 17 rte. d'Argelès, on the corner of av. du Général de Gaulle, for a taste of the harbor. Besides selling anchovies (€8.50 for 350g), the store allows visitors to watch the tiny fish being prepared and to taste a series of anchovies preserved in vinegar and flavored with Catalan sauce and *provençal* herbs. (☎82 04 99. Open M-F 8am-7pm. Free visit and *dégustation.* Store open M-F 8am-7pm, Sa-Su 8am-noon and 2-7pm.)

From August 14-18, the streets of Collioure fill with traditional dance and music for the **Festival de St-Vincent.** Midway through the folklore festival, on August 16, a **corrida** (bullfight) at the arena is followed by a fireworks display over the sea. Every Friday at 9pm in July and August, Collioure rocks to the sounds of **Vendredis du Jazz.** Jazz concerts take place in the castle and throughout the streets near the harbor. Contact the tourist office for all festival info.

OUTDOOR ACTIVITIES. A 15min. **hike** through the **Parc Pams,** behind the Musée d'Art Moderne, offers a good view of the 16th-century **Fort Saint Elme.** The Fort is privately owned and not open to visitors. To find the path from the tourist office, cross the canal to the château and walk around it to rue de la Démocratie. Turn left and continue as the road becomes rte. de Port-Vendres (3min.). Turn right into the parking lot of the **Hôtel le Bon Port** and follow the path up to the windmill (10min.). Continue for 20min. more to catch a panorama of Collioure's sail-filled port. The dirt path weaves through the mountains into neighboring towns. Hikers can get info from the tourist office on these and other magnificent trails nearby. For another short hike (1½hr. round-trip), try the walk to the **Ermitage de Consolation.** From the bus stop at Carrefour du Christ, follow the tiny rue du temple as it turns into rue de la Galérie and then Chemin de Consolation, leading you through quiet residential parts of town (20min.). At the sign that reads "Consolation," bear left and follow the path straight all the way until you reach the sign for the "Ermitage Bar Hôtel." The **Centre International de Plongée,** 15 rue de la Tour d'Auvergne, offers scuba lessons and rents underwater equipment. (☎82 07 16; www.cip-collioure.com. Beginners ages 8+ €39 for the first dive and lesson; 2nd lesson in ocean €45; 2 lessons €75. 8-session course July-Aug. €295; ages 14+ only. €23 per dive with scuba card, €30 per dive with scuba card and guide. Snorkeling €23. Open July-Sept. M-Sa 10am-noon and 3-6pm, Su 10:30am-noon and 5:30-7pm; Apr.-June and Oct.-Dec. M-Sa 10am-noon and 3-6pm. MC/V.)

MILLAU ☎05 65

In a small valley between the Tarn and Dourbie rivers, Millau (MEE-yoh; pop. 25,000) originally put itself on the map as a Roman industrial center acclaimed for its sturdy red pottery. Several centuries later, the town shifted its focus to fine leather production; today, it continues to export handmade gloves to elegant shops in Paris and New York. In summer months, the town becomes a vacation haven. Visitors come mainly for hiking trails, mountain sports, spectacular views, and the brand-new, tallest bridge in the world.

TRANSPORTATION. Infrequent **trains** go to: Béziers (2hr., 3 per day, €17), Montpellier (1¾-3hr., 3 per day, €16), and Paris (9hr., 1 per day, €64). Contact ticket desk for details. (☎60 34 02. Open M-F 5:25am-9pm, Sa 5:45am-9pm, Su 6:05am-9pm.) Both SNCF and La Populaire (☎61 01 01) connect Millau to Montpellier (2hr., 5-8 per day, €16-18), and S.A. Verdie Bel (☎05 62 18 84 54) runs to Toulouse (4hr., M-Sa 7am, €25). The information desk is inside the train station. (☎59 89 33. Open M-Tu and Th 8:30am-noon and 2:30-6:30pm, W and F 8:30am-12:30pm and 2:30-6:30pm, Sa 9am-noon.) For a **taxi,** call Laveissiere Roger, 610 rue de Naulas (☎06 85 74 05 07. €2.06 base; €0.75 per km, €1.12 at night). Europcar, 3 pl. Frédéric Bompaire, rents **cars.** (☎59 19 19; www.europcar.fr. From €220 per week, €736 per month. 21+. Open M-F 8:30am-noon and 2:30-7pm, Sa 9am-noon. AmEx/MC/V.)

ORIENTATION AND PRACTICAL INFORMATION. To get to the center of town, take a right out of the train station and walk one block down rue Georges Pompidou, turning left on rue du Barry, which becomes rue Droite at the *vieille ville*. The **tourist office** is on the left a few blocks down, at 1 pl. du Beffroi. The staff provides free city maps, has a list of hotels, and sells €9 regional maps and €8 guides with hike routes and times. (☎60 02 42; www.ot-millau.fr. Open July-Aug. M-Sa 9am-7pm, Su 9:30am-4pm; Sept.-June M-F 9am-12:30pm and 2-6:30pm, Sa 9am-6:30pm, Su 9:30am-4pm.) There is a **laundromat** at 12 av. Gambetta. (Wash €3.20-6.50, dry €0.50 per 5min.; detergent €0.50. Open daily 7am-9pm.) The **police** can be found at 14 rue de la Condamine (☎61 23 00). The location of the **pharmacie de garde** is posted outside every pharmacy, and the **hospital** is located at 265 bd. Achille Souques. (Info ☎59 30 00, emergency 59 31 35.) You can find **Internet** access at **Posanis,** 7 rue Droite, between the tourist office and pl. Maréchal Foch. (☎60 62 05. €3 per hr. Photocopies €0.15 per page. Open M-Sa July-Aug. 10am-10pm; Sept.-June 10am-12:30pm and 1:30-8pm.) The **post office,** 12 av. Alfred Merle, has **currency exchange, Western Union,** and **ATMs.** (☎59 20 50. Open M-F 8:30am-6:30pm, Sa 8:30am-noon.) **Postal Code:** 12100.

ACCOMMODATIONS AND CAMPING. The two-star **Hôtel du Commerce ❷,** 8 pl. de Mandarous, is a central option and has slightly sterile but affordable rooms with pearl-white baths. A few rooms have a view of the Beffroi and surrounding mountains. From the train station, walk straight on av. de Alfred Merle and turn right on bustling av. de la République. The hotel is at the end of this street on the third floor of an office building. (☎60 00 56; fax 60 96 50. Breakfast €5. Reception M-F 7am-1pm and 4-11pm, Sa-Su 8am-1pm and 5-11pm. Reservations recommended 1 week ahead. Singles and doubles €24, with toilet €27, with shower €36, with bath €38; triples €52-55; quads €64. Extra bed €10. MC/V.) At **Hôtel de la Capelle ❷,** 7 pl. de la Capella, a long corridor opens onto plain but sizable motel-style rooms with communal bathrooms and gorgeous views of the valley and mountains. From the train station, take av. Alfred Merle and turn right onto rue de la République. At pl. du Mandarous, veer left and walk along bd. de Bonald into the parking lot. The hotel is on the far left. (☎60 14 72; www.hotel-millau-capella.com. Breakfast €6. Doubles €28, with bath €36, with bath and toilet €42-45; triples €60-63. AmEx/MC/V.) Those who are willing to make the trek will not be disappointed by **Gîte de la Maladrerie ❶,** rue la Maladerie (main office at 25 av. Charles de Gaulle). This cottage offers homey and very clean two- to eight-bed rooms with views of the valley. Stop at the tourist office for a map, as the *gîte* is far from the center of town (30min.). From the train station, go down av. Alfred Merle and turn right onto rue Alsace Lorraine. Continue past pl. des Martyrs de la Résistance and Pont Lerouge, after which the road turns into av. du Pont Lerouge. At the traffic circle after the bridge, turn left onto av. du Languedoc; at the next traffic circle, make a gentle left onto av. Louis Balsan. The *gîte* is at the end of the road as it veers to the left. (Reservations ☎61 06 57, *gîte* ☎60 41 84. Kitchen available. Meals served for groups only. Sheets €2. Reception 6-9pm. Dorms €12 1st night, €11 thereafter. Cash only.) There are seven campsites across the Tarn River from the town center (15min.), most of which are filled in July and August. A 25min. walk from the town center, the four-star **Camping Les Rivages ❷,** av. de l'Aigoual, is the most luxurious site. Amenities include badminton courts, ping-pong tables, two pools, tennis courts, squash courts, a volleyball net, a basketball court, a playground, and a jacuzzi. To reach the campground from the center of town, take av. Gambetta to the pont du Cureplat, then follow the massive billboard signs. (☎61 01 07; www.campinglesrivages.com. Reception July-Aug. 8am-9pm; May-June and Sept. 8am-noon and 2-7pm. Gates open 8am-11pm. Reserve 2 months ahead for mobile homes July-Aug. Open May-Sept. July-Aug. 2 people and tent €26, 4-person bungalow or mobile home €55-90; May-June and Sept. €20/31-45. AmEx/MC/V.)

LANGUEDOC-ROUSSILLON

FOOD. There is a **Super U** on av. du Pont Lerouge, between the train station and the *gîte* Maladrerie (☎60 63 69; open M-Sa 8:30am-8pm, Su 8:30am-1pm; AmEx/MC/V), and the *centre-ville* is dotted with supermarkets. At **place Foche, place Emma Calvé,** and **place des Halles,** markets provide fresh meat and vegetables. (Open W and F 7am-noon.) Selling over 100 types of cheese, **Le Buron,** 18 rue Droite, is a *fromage*-lover's gold mine, specializing in regional *Roquefort.* (☎60 39 88. Open M 9am-noon and 3-7pm, Tu-Sa 8am-12:30pm and 3-7:30pm. AmEx/MC/V.)

More expensive than those along the coast, restaurants in Millau offer gourmet food produced with fresh local ingredients and an abundance of *Roquefort* cheese. In the heart of the *vieille ville,* **boulevard** and **rue de la Capelle** have a mixture of elegant restaurants and cheap pizzerias. **La Casse Croute ❶,** pl. Emma Cave, next to the tourist office, stands out from other sandwich shops with excellent bread and creative combinations. Try *La Chèvr'ô tartine* (€3.30), a large piece of country bread toasted and covered with goat cheese, marinated eggplant, honey, and toasted almonds. (☎59 45 36. Sandwiches €3.30-3.70, with a drink and pastry €5.80-6.50. Open daily July-Aug. 9am-9pm; Sept.-June 9am-7pm. Cash only.) **Le Chien à la Fenêtre ❷,** 10 rue Peyrollerie, serves elaborate *galettes* (€3.60-8) with generous portions of ingredients like salmon, cheese, or duck. Dessert *crêpes* (€2.30-5.50) come with bananas, chocolate, coconut, or ice cream. The open kitchen allows diners to watch their food being prepared. (☎60 49 22. Salads €8-9. Open M 7-10pm, Tu-Sa noon-2pm and 7-10pm. MC/V.) Nestled in a nook of Millau's *vieille ville,* **Au Bec Fin ❷,** 20-22 rue de la Capelle, prepares seafood platters and gourmet meals on a counter made out of wine barrels. (☎60 65 04. Salads €7.50-13. *Menu* €16. Open July-Sept. daily noon-2pm and 7-9:30pm; Oct.-June M-Tu and F-Su noon-2pm and 7-9:30pm. AmEx/MC/V.)

SIGHTS. Visit Roman pottery workshops at the archeological site of **Graufesenque,** on rte. Montpellier, 3km from the city. It's a long but scenic walk (45min.). To reach the site, follow the directions to the Gîte Maladrerie, but at the last moment don't veer to the left to reach the *gîte;* instead, follow the sign to Graufesenque and continue straight for 15min. Be careful: traffic is not heavy, but the road has no sidewalk. In the first century BC, the red ceramic bowls and vases produced here were exported from England to India. Remains of the pots have been found the world over and are used to date the conquests of the Roman army. (☎60 11 37. Open Tu-Su July-Aug. 10am-12:30pm and 2:30-7pm; Sept. and May-June 10am-noon and 2-6pm; Oct.-Apr. 10am-noon and 2-5pm. €4, ages 19-25 €2.70, under 18 free. Combined ticket to the Graufesenque and the Musée de Millau €6.) In the corner of pl. Maréchal Foch, the **Musée de Millau** displays local prehistoric artifacts and boasts a thorough exhibit on the process of making leather gloves—the film is graphic, so whether or not this appeals is a personal decision. (☎59 01 08. Open daily July-Aug. 10am-6pm; Sept.-June 10am-noon and 2-6pm. €5, ages 19-25 €3.70, under 18 free.) Across the street from the tourist office, on rue Droite, the ancient tower of the **Beffroi** rises above the *vieille ville.* Built in the 12th century as a medieval *donjon*, the belfry remained an active prison until just after the French Revolution. Today, visitors can wander through the small assortment of ancient jail cells and read the posted commentary in French, but they should take a moment to wonder whether €4 might be better spent on a sandwich next door at La Casse Croute. (☎59 01 08. Open daily July-Aug. 10am-noon and 2:30-6pm; mid-June to late June and Sept. 2:30-6pm. €2.70, under 18 free.)

LANGUEDOC-ROUSSILLON

NIGHTLIFE AND FESTIVALS. Bustling with tourists during the day, Millau does not offer much nightlife. Several café-bars sprinkled at the ends of **boulevard de Bonald** serve drinks in a calm, subdued atmosphere and cater to an older crowd. **Les Colonnes,** 8 pl. Maréchal Foch, hosts a middle-aged crowd during the day and draws some young local faces in the late evening with cheap beer, mixed drinks, hot music, and zebra-striped décor. A new restaurant serves food late into the night. (Beer €2-4. Mixed drinks €3-5. Open daily 6am-2am. Cash only.)

In the middle of July, the **Millau en Jazz** festival (☎60 75 41; www.millauenjazz.net) flows into the city's squares, streets, and concert halls with eight days of music. Pick up programs and tickets for big names (€17-20, 3 shows for €45) at the tourist office. For six days in the middle of August, thousands of *pétanque* players flock to Millau to compete in the town's annual **Mondial Pétanque** tournament (☎60 02 42; millau.petanque.mond.free.fr.). The international *boule* championship, free to viewers, includes male and female competitions.

OUTDOOR ACTIVITIES. The town's greatest asset is the beautiful **Parc Naturel Régional des Grands Causses,** stretching throughout the region and centering around Millau. Primitive humans first discovered this sunbathed region over 200,000 years ago and left behind various carved statues and cave paintings. Today, the 315,950-hectare park offers excellent mountain trails as well as an unlimited number of sporting activities. The tourist office sells hiking maps (€9), hiking guides (€8), and mountain-biking maps (€5), while the park's office, 71 bd. de l'Ayrolle, can answer questions, particularly for those setting off on long hikes. (☎61 35 50. Open M-F May-Sept. 9am-noon and 2-6pm; Oct.-Apr. 9am-noon and 2-5pm.) For a fairly easy dayhike from Millau (3hr. including walk to trailhead), stop by the tourist office for the *Corniches du Cade Discovery Footpath* guide (€2; in English and French). The guide gives directions for the walk as well as a catalogue of the flora you'll encounter along the way.

Taking advantage of the park's natural beauty, companies advertising every sporting activity imaginable fill Millau to the brim. However, as most companies don't provide transport, it is best to have access to a car. **Organisation Roc et Canyon,** 55 av. Jean Jaurès, stands out from the masses, offering paintball and providing transportation (€3) to their mountain sites. (☎61 17 77; www.roc-et-canyon.com. Paintball €26 per person. Rafting €28. Canoe trip €26-44. Mountain bike rentals €24 per day. Mountain biking excursions €30 per day. 50m bungee jump €34. Underground cave climb €32. Rock climbing €28. Reservations recommended. Base near campsites on rte. de Nant open daily mid-June to Sept. 9am-7pm; office at av. Jean Jaurès open Oct. to mid-June

9am-noon and 2-5pm. Cash only.) **Horizon Millau Vol Libre,** 6 pl. Lucién Grégoire, just off pl. Maréchal Foch, offers the same activities but specializes in hang gliding. (☎59 78 60; www.horizon-millau.com. Hang gliding €50-120, 5-session initiation course €350. Call 1-6 days ahead. Open July-Aug. daily 8am-noon and 2-6pm; Mar.-June and Sept. to mid-Nov. M-Sa 10am-noon and 2-5pm. Cash only.) **Antipodes,** 6 pl. des Halles, has similar activities but is the only outfit with a ropes course. (☎60 72 03, reservations ☎61 38 83; www.antipodes-millau.com. Ropes course €32-45. Hang gliding €70. Bungee jumping €35. Open Tu-Sa 9:30am-12:30pm and 2:30-7:30pm. AmEx/MC/V.)

MONTPELLIER ☎04 67

It's hard to find locals who were born in Montpellier (MAHN-pehl-yeh; pop. 225,000). A college town and cultural center, Languedoc-Roussillon's capital seduces visitors and then compels them to stay—permanently. Known as the most light-hearted place in the south, Montpellier prides itself on a diverse population of party-goers and some of the best gay nightlife in France. Amateur theatrical and musical performances sprout up in pl. de la Comédie, academics browse trendy bookstores, and tourists shop for funky flair in hip—but expensive—boutiques.

RE-FRÊCHE-ING LANGUEDOC-ROUSSILLON. In 2004, the socialist mayor of Montpellier, Georges Frêche, won the regional elections. He promptly set out on a campaign to revamp Languedoc-Roussillon and its institutions. To begin with, Frêche commissioned a new flag, a nondescript red and yellow flag (the region's colors), to replace the old one bearing Languedoc's cross and Roussillon's "Senyera" flag. Frêche also tried to create further unity by reviving the region's ninth-century name, "Septimanie" (nullifying the divisive duality of the current name). "Septimanie" didn't stick, but Frêche did succeed in moving Montpellier from the 25th to the eighth largest city in France, a huge achievement for Languedoc-Roussillon—or whatever you want to call it.

TRANSPORTATION

Flights: Planes take off from the **Aéroport Montpellier Méditerranée (MPL;** ☎20 85 00; www.montpellier.aeroport.fr), in nearby Mauguio. **Air France** flies to Paris 10 times per day. Info office outside the Polygone (☎08 20 82 08 20; www.airfrance.fr). **La Navette Aéroport** shuttles between the airport and the tramway stop at pl. de l'Europe (15min., 12 per day 5:45am-8:15pm, €4.90-5.40). Contact **Hérault Transport** (☎08 25 34 01 34) or visit the airport website for a bus schedule.

Trains: pl. Auguste Gibert (☎08 92 35 35 35). Office open M-F 6am-9pm, Sa-Su 6:30am-9pm. To: **Avignon** (1 hr., 13 per day, €14); **Marseille** (1¾hr., 11 per day, €26); **Nice** (4hr., 2 per day, €48); **Paris** (3½hr., 12 per day, €93); **Perpignan** (1½hr., 18 per day, €25); **Toulouse** (2½hr., 13 per day, €33).

Buses: 20 rue du Grand St-Jean. Exit the train station and turn left along the tram tracks; continue until you see the depot on your right (100m). **La Populaire** (☎58 75 95; www.cars-la-populaire.com; ticket office open M-Sa 9am-noon and 2:30-6:30pm) travels to **Millau** (2hr.; M-Sa 5 per day 8:45am-6:30pm, Su 11:05am and 6:30pm; €18).

Public Transportation: TAM, 6 rue Jules Ferry (☎22 87 87; www.tam-way.com). Open M-Sa 7am-7pm. Runs local **buses** and **trams** connecting the city center to its outskirts. Buses run 6am-9pm; fast, convenient trams run every 6-7min. 5am-1am. 1hr. tickets for trams and buses €1.30; 24hr. pass €3.20; weekly pass €13, students €8.30. Buy bus tickets from the driver and tram tickets from automated dispensers at the train stops. **L'Amigo** line connects the train station to 12 popular night clubs on the outskirts of town. Buses leave the station Th-Sa midnight, 1am; return 2:30, 3:30, 5am.

Taxis: TRAM, at the train station (☎58 10 10). €1.80 base; €1.40 per km during the day, €2.10 at night. €9-12 from station to hostel. €20-25 from station to airport. 24hr.

Car Rental: Ada, pl. Jules Ferry (☎92 78 77). To reach the car rental complex, enter train station, walk through to platform A and turn right. Continue along the platform until you see a squat white building on the right. From €89 and 100km per day, €229 and 500km per 5 days. Insurance included. 21+. License for 1 year required. Open M-Tu and Th-F 8am-1pm and 2-7pm, Sa and W 9am-1pm and 2-7pm. AmEx/MC/V. **Hertz, Avis, Europcar,** and **National** also share this location.

Bike Rental: TAM Vélo, 27 rue Maguelone (☎22 87 82). €1.50 per hr., €3 per ½-day, €6 per day; €150 and ID deposit. Open M-Sa 9am-7pm, Su 9am-12:30pm and 2-7pm. MC/V.

ORIENTATION AND PRACTICAL INFORMATION

Across from the train station, **rue Maguelone** leads to **place de la Comédie,** the city's lively central square. From there, the **tourist office** is visible to the right, at the entrance to Esplanade Charles de Gaulle. The *vieille ville* is bounded by **boulevard Pasteur** and **boulevard Louis Blanc** to the north, **esplanade Charles de Gaulle** and **boulevard Victor Hugo** to the east, and **boulevard Jeu de Paume** to the west. From pl. de la Comédie, **rue de la Loge** rises to the center of the *vieille ville*, **place Jean Jaurès.**

Tourist Office: 30 allée Jean de Lattre de Tassigny (☎60 60 60; www.ot-montpellier.fr). Free maps and same-night hotel reservation service. Distributes *Sortir à Montpellier* and *L'INDIC,* a student guide published in Sept. Wheelchair-accessible. Open July-Sept. M-F 9am-7:30pm, Sa 9:30am-6pm, Su 9:30am-1pm and 2:30-6pm; Oct.-June M-F 9am-6:30pm, Sa 10am-6pm, Su 10am-1pm and 2-5pm.

Tours: 2hr. city tours in English July-Sept. Sa; times vary, contact tourist office. Tours in French depart daily 5pm; July-Aug. themed tours depart at 10am. €6.50, students €5.50. A *petit train* (☎06 29 03 08 09) offers a tour of the *vieille ville,* leaving from pl. de la Comédie, near the Gaumont movie theater. June-Aug. every 45min. 11am-7pm; Apr.-May and Sept. 11am-6pm; Oct.-Mar. W and Sa-Su 2:30, 3:30, 4:30pm.

Budget Travel: Wasteels, 1 rue Cambacérès (☎66 45 79; www.wasteels.fr). Offers good plane, train, and bus ticket prices. Open M-F 9:30am-12:30pm and 2-6pm.

Currency Exchange: Banque Courtois, pl. de la Comédie (☎06 26 16). €6 commission. 1.2% commission on **traveler's checks** over €700; €8 commission if less. Open M-F 9:30am-noon and 1:45-4:30pm.

English-Language Bookstore: Book In Bar, 8 rue du Bras de Fer (☎66 22 90). Used books downstairs. Open M 1-7pm, Tu-Sa 10am-7pm. AmEx/MC/V.

GLBT Resources: Le Shopping du Village, 3 rue Fournarié, holds current copies of *IB News* and other regional and national gay magazines with info on restaurants, shops, and clubs. Open M 3-7pm, Tu-Sa noon-7pm.

Laundromat: Lavo Sud, 70 rue de l'Aiguillerie. Wash €3-6.80, dry €0.50 per 5min. Open daily 7am-9pm.

Police: pl. de la Comédie (☎04 99 74 26 74), next to the tourist office.

Hospital: 191 av. du Doyen Giraud (☎33 67 33). In an emergency, go to **Hôpital Lapeyronie,** 371 av. du Doyen Gaston Giraud (☎33 81 67).

Internet Access: Mostly located on or around rue de Verdun. **Cybercafé www,** 12bis rue Jules Ferry (☎06 59 52), across from the train station. €0.75 per 30min., €1.50 per hr. Fax, photocopier, and scanner. Open M-Sa 10am-10pm.

Post Office: pl. Rondelet (☎34 50 00). **Currency exchange** and **Western Union** services. Open M-F 8:30am-6:30pm, Sa 8:30am-noon. Branch at pl. du Marché aux Fleurs (☎60 03 67). Same hours as main branch. MC/V. **Postal Code:** 34000, for **Poste Restante** 34035.

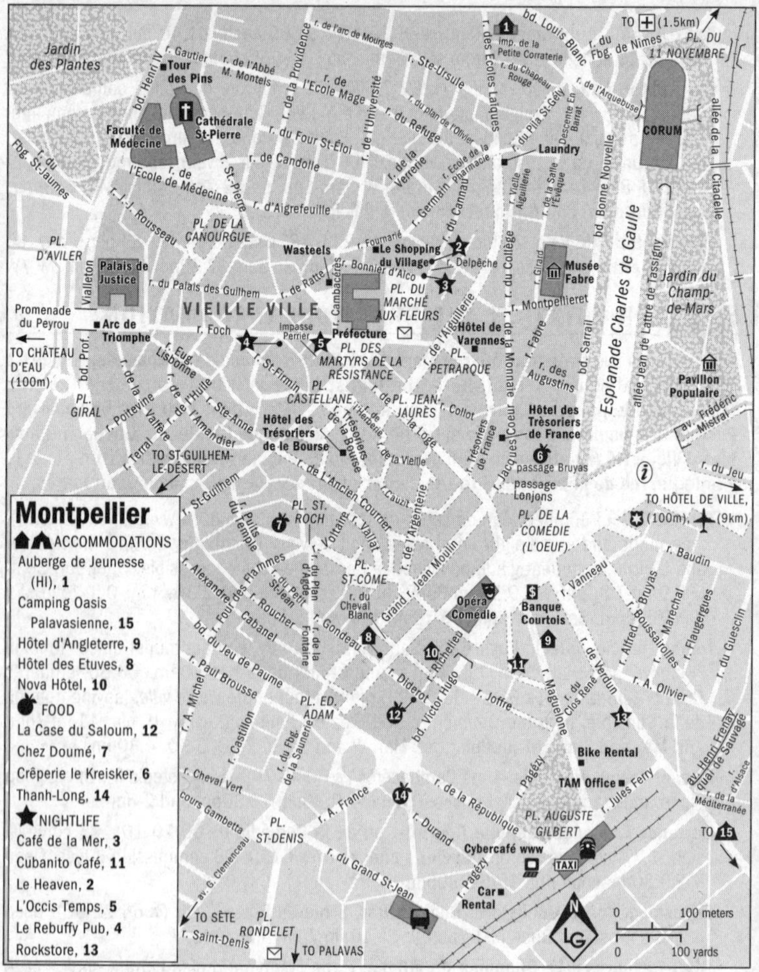

ACCOMMODATIONS AND CAMPING

Except for the campsite, all listings are in the city center. Search **rue Aristide Olivier, rue du Gal. Campredon** (off cours Gambetta and rue A. Michell), and **rue A. Broussonnet** (off pl. Albert I) for other reasonably priced hotels.

Hôtel des Etuves, 24 rue des Etuves (☎60 78 19; www.hoteldesetuves.fr). 13 plain, comfortable, small, clean rooms, all with toilet and shower, 7 with bath. Located on a quiet street near a major road. Breakfast €5. Reception M-Sa 6:30am-11pm, Su 6:30am-noon. Reservations recommended 1 week ahead. Singles €23, with TV €33, with bath €42; doubles with TV €37, with TV and bath €42. Cash only. ❷

Nova Hôtel, 8 rue Richelieu (☎60 79 85; hotelnova@free.fr). Stone staircase leads to large rooms in this family-run hotel. Breakfast €4.60. Reception M-Sa 7am-1am, Su 7am-11am and 7pm-1am. Reservations recommended in summer, especially in festival season. Singles €21, with shower €27, with toilet and TV €39-44; doubles €24/27-34/39-44; triples €40-56; quads €63. 5% discount with *Let's Go.* AmEx/MC/V. ❷

Auberge de Jeunesse (HI), 2 impasse de la Petite Corraterie (☎60 32 22; montpellier@fuaj.org). From the train station, take tram #1 to Louis-Blanc; walk opposite the direction of travel and take your first right onto Rue des Ecoles Laïques. Hostel is on the left. Good location and prices and a bright common area compensate for unappealing bathrooms. 90 beds in 2- to 10-person single-sex rooms. Pool table €2. Breakfast included. Lockers €1 for 24hr. Free Wi-Fi. Reception 8am-noon and 3pm-midnight. Lockout noon-3pm. Curfew 2am. Reserve ahead by Internet only. Dorms €15. MC/V. ❶

Hôtel d'Angleterre, 7 rue Maguelone (☎58 59 50; www.hotel-d-angleterre.com), off pl. de la Comédie. Convenient location between the train station and the Oeuf means some sunny rooms overlook the busy street where trams run late at night. Large rooms with queen beds, elevator, cable TV, and 24hr. bar justify slightly high prices. Breakfast €5.50. Reception 24hr. Singles and doubles with shower €45, with toilet €50; triples €53-61; quads €67. 10% discount with *Let's Go.* AmEx/MC/V. ❹

Camping Oasis Palavasienne, rte. de Palavas (☎15 11 61; oasis-palavasienne.com). Take tram #2 from the train station to "Saint-Cléophas" (dir.: Saint-Jean de Vedas). At "Saint-Cléophas," transfer to bus #32 and get off at "Oasis Palavasienne" in Lattes. At the traffic circle, turn left and walk under the bridge. The campground is 50m on the right (40min.). 4-star site includes sauna, gym, bar, and restaurant overlooking a beautiful swimming pool. In summer, site fills up with teenagers and students. Free shuttle takes campers to and from nearby beaches 9:30am and 2:30pm. Reception July-Aug. M-F 8:30am-12:30pm and 2-7:30pm, Sa-Su 8:15am-7:30pm; Sept.-June M-F 8:30am-12:30pm and 2-6pm, Sa-Su 8:15am-7:30pm. Mid-July to mid-Aug. €28; early to mid-July and mid-Aug. to Sept. €22; May-June €16. Extra person €5/4/3. AmEx/MC/V. ❷

FOOD

Montpellier has many reasonably priced restaurants. Standard French cuisine dominates the *vieille ville.* Find great bargains near **rue des Ecoles Laïques,** which has Greek, Egyptian, Moroccan, and Lebanese choices. The cheapest sandwich shops cluster on **rue Maguelone** and the streets which radiate into pl. de la Comédie. Morning markets set up daily at **Les Halles Castellane,** on rue de la Loge, and at **Plan Cabanes,** on cours Gambetta. The **INNO** supermarket, in the basement of the Polygone commercial center, past the tourist office from pl. de la Comédie, has some bargains. (Open M-Sa 8:30am-8:30pm. AmEx/MC/V.)

Crêperie le Kreisker, 3 passage Bruyas (☎60 82 50). Serves over 50 savory *crêpes* (€3.20-6.60), topped with ingredients like buttered snails, mushrooms, artichokes, and seafood, at excellent prices. Speedy and attentive staff also dishes out large salads (€5.80-6.60), 30 types of dessert *crêpes* (€1.90-5.70), and a stunning array of ice-cream flavors. Open M-Sa 11:30am-3pm and 6:30-11pm. AmEx/MC/V. ❷

Thanh-Long, 3 rue Durand (☎58 13 88), has excellent Vietnamese food at some of the lowest prices around. Get a main dish with rice and ¼L wine for €8. Vegetarian options include *tofu citronelle* (€6) and vermicelli (€6). Takeout available. Open daily noon-2pm and 7:30-10pm. Takeout M noon-10pm, Tu-Su 10am-10pm. AmEx/MC/V. ❶

La Case du Saloum, 18 rue Diderot (☎02 88 94). Hip and unassuming, this restaurant serves authentic Senegalese dishes, such as veal with peanut sauce (€7.80), in a small dining room and courtyard. Try the ginger punch (€3). *Plats* €8. Desserts €4. Open M-F 11am-3pm and 7:30-midnight, Sa 7:30pm-midnight. AmEx/MC/V. ❷

Chez Doumé, 5 rue des Teissiers (☎60 48 76), near Eglise St-Roch. In a charming side street with many restaurants, this bistro has crimson booths, colorful posters, and red-checkered table cloths, and serves typical French fare. *Plats* €12-14. Lunch *menu* €12.

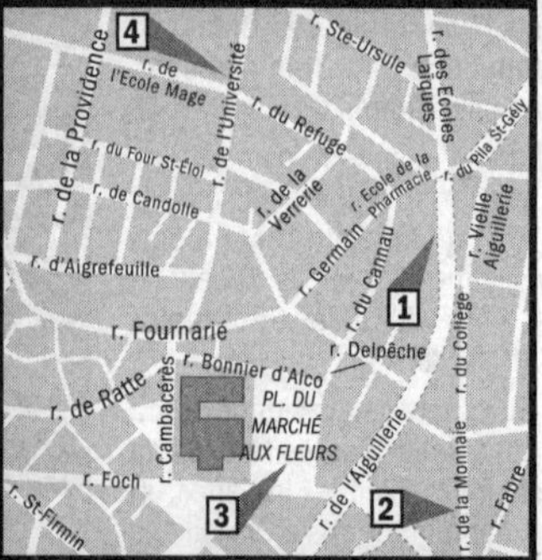

A NIGHT OUT

Straight or gay, a tour of Montpellier's gay-friendly nightlife is worthwhile. The establishments on this list also welcome women and straight men.

1. Start the evening off with meat grilled over a fire at gay-friendly **Le Vieux Four,** 59 rue de l'Aiguillerie.

2. Turn right out of Le Vieux Four and head to **Martin's Club,** 8 rue de la Monnaie, an upscale bar. Though the majority of the clientele is straight, the bar welcomes a small gay crowd.

3. Turn left out of Martin's Club to pl. du Marché aux Fleurs, home to two of Montpellier's best known gay bars, **Le Heaven** and **Le Café de la Mer** (see **Gay Nightlife,** p. 645).

4. From pl. du Marché aux Fleurs, turn right onto rue de l'Université and walk five blocks. Finish the night in style at **Pop-Art Café,** 43 rue de l'Université, which welcomes both gay and straight customers with massive, elaborate mixed drinks.

Dinner *menu* €15. Open M-F noon-2pm and 7:30-11pm, Sa 7:30-11pm. MC/V. ❷

SIGHTS

Built on a site where Molière performed from 1654-1655, the beautifully renovated **Musée Fabre,** 39 bd. Bonne Nouvelle, holds one of the largest collections of fine art outside of Paris. Focusing on 17th- to 19th-century painting, the museum features works by Courbet, Ingres, Poussin, and Delacroix. Winter and spring 2008 will bring a temporary Courbet exhibit. (☎14 83 00. Open Tu, Th-F, Su 10am-6pm; W 1-9pm; Sa 11am-6pm. €6, €7 including temporary exhibition; students €4/5.) The **Pavillon Populaire,** on the other side of the Esplanade Charles de Gaule, houses free rotating photography exhibitions. (☎66 13 46. Open Tu-Su 11am-7pm.)

The secret courtyards and intricate staircases of the 17th- and 18th-century *hôtels particuliers* hide behind grandiose oak doors. **Hôtel de Varennes,** 2 pl. Petrarque, once Montpellier's treasury, holds two small, free museums. The **Musée du Vieux Montpellier,** on the first floor, traces Montpellier's history through furniture, maps, ceramics, and other artifacts (☎66 02 94; open Tu-Sa 9:30am-noon and 1:30-5pm); the adorable second-floor **Musée Fougau** reconstructs 19th-century lifestyles in Montpellier (open W-Th 3-6pm). Occupying the **Hôtel des Trésoriers de France,** the **Musée Languedocien,** 7 rue Jacques Cœur, is an archaeological museum that contains everything from medieval artwork to 18th-century perfume bottles. (☎52 93 03. Open M-Sa mid-June to mid-Sept. 3-6pm; Sept. to mid-June 2:30-5:30pm. €6, students €3.) Visit the **Hôtel des Trésoriers de la Bourse,** 4 rue des Trésoriers de la Bourse, for its 16th-century architecture. The tourist office has a list of the city's best *hôtels* in its *Montpellier Discovery Guide,* available in English.

Montpellier's pedestrian streets, bookstores, and sprawling **place de la Comédie,** with its opening onto Esplanade Charles de Gaulle, provide some of the city's best entertainment. Countless outdoor cafés, many with water vapor dispensers to keep customers cool, also characterize the Montpellier atmosphere. Palm-lined **rue Foch,** off pl. des Martyrs in the northwest corner of the old city, leads to the **promenade du Peyrou,** which links the **Arc de Triomphe,** erected in 1691 to honor Louis XIV, to the **Château d'Eau,** the arched terminal of an aqueduct. Though locals claim it dates back to antiquity, it only just turned 500; walk up to it for a view over the western suburbs of Montpellier. While this area does not hold any truly exciting sights, it is a pleasant area to wander around. Boulevard Henri IV leads to the **Jardin des Plantes,** France's first botanical garden. (☎63 43 22. Open Tu-Su June-Sept. noon-8pm; Oct.-Mar. noon-6pm. Free.)

NIGHTLIFE

The most animated bars are scattered along **place Jean-Jaurès,** which is illuminated at night. At sundown, **rue de la Loge** fills with vendors, musicians, and stilt-walkers. The best discos, including **La Villa Rouge,** rte. de Palavas, in Lattes (☎06 50 54; open summer W-Su 11pm-6am; winter Th-Su 11pm-5am), lie on the outskirts of town; take L'Amigo buses (p. 640) from the train station to their doorsteps.

Cubanito Café, 13 rue de Verdun (☎92 65 82), near pl. de la Comédie. After 10pm, this revolution-themed bar overflows with 20-somethings who salsa to Latin beats (M and Su) or hip hop (Tu-Sa) while people watch from the terrace. Tapas served noon-9pm. Lunch *menu* with 4 tapas, a drink, and coffee €7.50. Pints €4.50-5.50. Mixed drinks €6.50. Open daily in summer noon-2am; in winter noon-1am. AmEx/MC/V.

Le Rebuffy Pub, 4 pl. Rebuffy (☎66 32 76). Packed with local regulars and international students, this cheerful pub is plastered to the ceiling with posters. With a yearly film festival, rotating art exhibits, and board games, there's always something to do and someone to meet. Beer €2.40-5.50. Open in summer M-F 9am-2am, Sa 11am-2am, Su 2pm-2am; in winter M-Sa 11am-1am, Su 2pm-1am. MC/V.

Rockstore, 20 rue de Verdun (☎06 80 00). With a model 1950s car sticking out of its facade, this bar is hard to miss. A young crowd bounces to pop-rock on the 1st fl. and gyrates to electro with an 80s flair above. Grunge bar in the evening and mega-disco by night, the bar hosts live rock concerts 1-6 times per week Sept.-June. Beer €3.70. Hard liquor €6.50. Concerts free-€25. Bar open M-Sa July-Sept. 6:30pm-6am; Oct.-June 6pm-5am. Disco opens 11:30pm. AmEx/MC/V.

L'Occis Temps, 2 impasse Perrier (☎54 59 96), near pl. des Martyrs de la Résistance. Montpellier's own brewery serves 3 homemade, all-natural beers (a pale ale, an amber ale, and a seasonal ale) inside a 13th-century cellar. Pints €5.50-5.80. Concerts F-Sa Sept.-June 9pm. Happy hour 7:30-9pm. Open Tu-Sa 3pm-2am, Su 6pm-1am. MC/V.

GAY NIGHTLIFE

Male-dominated gay nightlife abounds in Montpellier, centered in pl. du Marché aux Fleurs. There are no specifically lesbian bars, but women are not excluded from any of the bars listed here. Gay bars are hopping throughout the *vieille ville*.

Café de la Mer, 5 pl. du Marché aux Fleurs (☎60 79 65). A maritime-themed café-bar, the gay hub of Montpellier offers afternoon coffee (€1.50-2.50) as well as pre-party beer (€2.50). Open to all, but a majority of the clientele is male. Open in summer M-Sa 8am-2am, Su 3pm-2am; in winter M-Sa 8am-1am, Su 3pm-1am. MC/V.

Le Heaven, 1 rue Delpech (☎60 44 18). Techno and glittering disco balls make this a perfect dance floor to meet men; women are welcome, but only a few come. Every other Tu night, Le Heaven specifically welcomes lesbians. Beer €3-5. Liquor €6. Th night piano bar 11pm. Open daily 8pm-2am. AmEx/MC/V.

ENTERTAINMENT AND FESTIVALS

The **Corum,** on Esplanade Charles de Gaulle, and **Opéra Comédie,** 11 bd. Victor Hugo (☎60 19 99; www.orchestre-montpellier.com and www.opera-montpellier.com), host theatrical performances and concerts. (Corum Office open M-F 8am-7pm. Opera ticket office open M 2-6pm, Tu-Sa 11am-6pm. Philharmonic Orchestra €15-31, students and under 18 €12-26. Operas and plays €15-30/6.50-20. Prices vary.)

During the month of June, the open-air **Printemps des Comédiens,** featuring theatrical, circus, and dance performances, arrives in Montpellier. For details, contact the Opéra Comédie, pl. de la Comédie. (Info ☎63 66 67, reservations 63 66 66; www.printempsdescomediens.com. Tickets €5-28, under 25 and seniors €6-18.)

From late June to early July, the **Festival International Montpellier Danse** organizes performances, workshops, and films on local stages and screens. (☎60 83 60, reservations 08 00 60 07 40; www.montpellierdanse.com. Tickets €17-34.) The **Festival de Radio France et de Montpellier** offers over 100 musical performances during the rest of July. (Info and tickets ☎02 02 01; www.festivalradiofrancemontpellier.com. Most concerts free; others €30-50, students and seniors €15-40.) The **Festival International du Cinéma Méditerranéen** (☎04 99 13 73 73; www.cinemed.tm.fr) has been October's main event for more than two decades. Featuring over 250 films and related events, this festival draws close to 100,000 fans.

DAYTRIP FROM MONTPELLIER

ST-GUILHEM-LE-DÉSERT

With picturesque streets along a dramatic gorge, St-Guilhem-le-Désert (sehn GEEL-ehm-luh-day-zayr) has been popular among tourists since the 19th century. Despite its name, the village is far from a desert—it suffers from flooding by both water and people. When visitors flock to town in summer, local craftsmen open their tiny boutiques, selling anything from pottery to jams, jewelry, and candles. Despite the tourist frenzy, this hamlet, with its hiking trails and lovely river, is a pleasant—and very romantic—daytrip. However, due to limited public transportation from Montpellier, car-less travelers must choose between a short afternoon trip or a longer overnight stay.

St-Guilhem's main attraction is the **Abbaye de Gellone.** Founded early in the ninth century by Charlemagne's cousin Guillaume, the abbey celebrated its 1200th anniversary in 2004. A mix of Romanesque, Gothic, Baroque, and Classic architecture, the abbey has a been a stop for centuries for pilgrims on their way to Saint-Jacques de Compostelle. Unfortunately, part of the abbey looks bare because Gellone's unique eight-gallery vaulted cloister was sold around 1850 for a mere US$4000—it's now on display at The Cloisters in New York, after a stint as home decoration for American sculptor George Gray Barnard. (☎57 44 33. Op July-Aug. M-Sa 7:30am-6:30pm, Su 8am-6:30pm; Sept.-June M-Sa 7:15am-6pm, Su 8am-6pm. Free.) Near the abbey, the small **Musée Santonnier Paysagiste,** 15 rue Chapelle des Penitents, traces the town's past with tools, photos, life-size wax models, and an intricate miniature village accompanied by sound and light that mimics weather patterns. (☎57 77 07. Open daily 10am-7pm; in winter 10am-6pm. €4, students €3.) Tour the huge chambers of St-Guilhem's caves at **Grottes de Clamouse,** 3km from St-Guilhem on the rte. de St-Guilhem-le-Désert, overgrown with stalactites and stalagmites in a remarkable number of textures and gravity-defying forms. To get there, walk downhill from the tourist office and continue straight ahead; be cautious, as there is no sidewalk or shoulder on the side of the road (40min.). The visit includes a dramatic son-et-lumière (sound and light show). Make sure to stop at the tourist office in the village for a €1.30 discount on the price of entry. The bus that goes from Gignac to St-Guilhem stops at the grottes as well. (☎57 71 05; www.clamouse.com. Open daily July-Aug. 10am-7pm; Sept. and June 10am-6pm; Feb.-May and Oct. 10am-5pm; Nov.-Jan. call ahead, hours vary. 1hr. guided tour €8.50, students €7.20. Most tour guides speak some English.) For a day of swimming and picnicking, rent a canoe for the 12km descent to Pont du Diable (4-6hr.). **Rapido,** 2 rte. d'Aniane, on the way to the tourist office, rents kayaks and canoes and provides transportation for visitors willing to start at 10am. Call ahead to make sure transportation is available. Rental available at other times of the day for those with cars. (☎55 75 75. 2-person canoe €44. €2 discount with reservation. Open daily July-Aug. 10am-7pm; May-June and Sept. by reservation only. Cash only.)

If you plan to spend the night in St-Guilhem, what better than to sleep in a 13th-century home? The centrally located **Gite de la Tour ❶,** 38 rue de la Font du Portal, is just that. The simple attic rooms, with two to five dark-wood twin beds, have rustic charm. Clean communal showers and a kitchen are available. (☎57 34 00; gitedelatour@free.fr. Breakfast €5. Dinner €13. Sheets €2.50. Parking €2. Dorms €13; doubles €28. Cash only.) **Le Petit Jardin ❷,** rte. d'Aniane, on the way from the bus stop to the tourist office, is a convenient dining option, serving regional dishes on a shaded terrace with water misters for hot afternoons. (☎57 35 18. *Formules* €10-12. *Menus* €15-23. Open Apr.-Sept. daily noon-3pm and 7-10pm. Cash only.)

From the bus stop in the parking lot, walk uphill past Rapido to the **tourist office.** Staff provides free maps, a town guide in English, and advice on trekking, including two 3hr. circuits beginning in town. Tours of the village and the abbey are available upon reservation. (☎57 44 33; www.saint-guilhem-le-desert.com. Tours €4. Open daily July-Aug. 9:30am-7pm; Oct.-Mar. 9:30am-1pm and 2-5pm; Sept. and Apr.-June 9:30am-1pm and 2-6pm.) There's an **ATM** in the parking lot on the other side of the main road. Make sure to withdraw enough cash; few shops in St-Guilhem take credit cards. Hérault Transport (☎08 25 34 01 34) sends **buses** from the *gare routière* in Montpellier to Gignac, where you can switch buses to St-Guilhem (1½hr., 2 per day, total €5.40). Stop by the *gare routière* for a schedule. Buses depart in the early afternoon and return in the late afternoon; exact times vary.

> TIP **DON'T DÉSERT YOUR TICKET.** If you take the bus from Montpellier to St-Guilhem-le-Désert, you'll have to transfer at Gignac. Make sure to keep your receipt for the first leg of the journey—it will save you €1.30 when you switch buses.

SÈTE ☎04 67

Strategically situated between the Mediterranean and the Bassin Thau, Sète (SET; pop. 42,000) was founded in 1666 as a port town and is now France's largest Mediterranean fishing village. Its hybrid Italian-French culture, the result of an early 20th-century exodus from the Italian village of Gaet during the depression in Italy, produces unusual maritime festivals and the lovely *sètois* accent. Heavy machinery blots the otherwise picture-perfect shoreline, though there is a certain industrial beauty to the rusty ships and screeching gulls—the town gave birth to Paul Valéry, one of France's greatest modern poets. Nearby, the two local beaches and turquoise sea offer a sunny respite from the bustle of everyday life.

TRANSPORTATION AND PRACTICAL INFORMATION. The train station sends **trains** to: Montpellier (20min., 20-27 per day, €4.90) from quai M. Joffre. (Info office open M-F 5:50am-7:45pm, Sa-Su 6:40am-7:45pm.) Sétoise **buses** shuttle passengers throughout town until 6:30-8:45pm. (☎74 18 77; 1hr. ticket €1.) Bus #2 (every 20min. 7am-8pm) goes from the train station to the town center and tourist office; get off at "La Marine." To continue on to both beaches, get off at "Les Quilles." On foot, cross the bridge facing the station and take av. Victor Hugo. Cross the next bridge and turn right onto quai Rhin et Danube. Follow the river's edge and take the next bridge across to quai de la Résistance and the city center (15-20min.). Weary feet may be tempted by the **petit train,** which departs from quai Général Durand for a 30min. tour of the central city and harbor. (☎51 27 37. July-Aug. daily 11am and 2:30-10pm; Sept. and June daily 2:30-5:30pm; Apr.-May and Oct. Sa-Su 2:30-5:30pm. €5, under 12 €2.50.)

Sète's **tourist office,** 60 rue Mario Roustan, behind quai Général Durand, provides €1 maps, free city guides, and a tour of the city's *criée* (fish market; July-Aug. M-F 3:30, 4:45pm; €5). Audio tours of six different sections of the city (€5) are also available. (☎74 71 71. Office open July-Aug. daily 9:30am-7:30pm; Sept.-May M-F 9:30am-6pm, Sa-Su 10am-noon and 2:30-5pm. **Currency exchange** open M-F 9:30am-12:30pm and 2:30-5:30pm, Sa 9:30am-noon.) Other services include: a **pharmacy** at 6 av. Victor Hugo (☎74 62 59; open M-F 8:30am-12:15pm and 2-7:15pm, Sa 8:30am-12:15pm); **police** at Quai des Moulins (☎46 23 88); a **Centre Hospitalier** at Bd. Camille Blanc (☎46 57 57); and a **post office,** 5 bd. Casanova, a block from the tip of rue Gambetta, which has **ATMs** (☎46 64 21). **Postal Code:** 34200.

ACCOMMODATIONS AND FOOD. To stay the night, check out the **Auberge de Jeunesse ❷,** 1 rue Général Revest. From the tourist office, turn left and walk straight until you reach rue Paul Valéry. Turn left, then right onto rue de la Caurassane, and finally left uphill on rue General Revest (15min.). Stay in a plain and pleasant dorm room with four bunk beds and shared bathrooms. Most rooms have terraces overlooking the city and sea. (☎53 46 68; www.fuaj.org. Breakfast included. Dinner included mid-June to mid-Sept. Reception July-Aug. 8am-1pm and 6-10pm; Sept.-June 8am-noon and 6-10pm. Dorms mid-June to mid-Sept. €25; mid.-Sept. to mid-June €16. MC/V.)

During festivals and holidays, Sète's fusion culture becomes so thick you can taste it. *Frescati* can be found on every dessert menu. These sweet raisin biscuits are soaked in rum and topped with a layer of coffee cream and soft meringue. Invented in Sète, *tielle* was originally given to fishermen about to embark on long sea voyages. The round pie contains octopus, tomatoes, and spices in a flaky crust. Vendors on the canal offer them for €2-3. The restaurants lining **promenade J. B. Marty,** at the end of rue Mario Roustan near the *vieux port*, serve the catch of the day for €9-30. Cheaper pizzas, pastas, and seafood are the specialties of the eateries on **rue Gambetta** and its offshoots. Tourist-oriented but slightly less crowded and less expensive eateries are near the beaches. The **Monoprix** supermarket is located at 7 quai de la Résistance, between the train station and the tourist office. (☎74 39 38. Open in summer M-Sa 8am-8pm. AmEx/MC/V.) The daily market at **Les Halles,** just off rue Alsace-Lorraine, provides an abundance of fresh produce, local specialties, and fish. (Open 6am-1pm.)

SIGHTS. The **Société Nautique de Sète,** on Môle St-Louis, at the southern end of town, is one of France's oldest yacht clubs (☎74 98 97). All summer, yacht races, including the famed **Tour de France à la Voile,** sail by the Môle. The best place to watch is in front of café **L'AmeriKclub,** on promenade Maréchal Leclerc. **Plage de la Corniche,** in the southwest corner of town, starts off a 12km stretch of sandy beaches, accessible by bus #2, which stops a few blocks away from the beach at "Les Quilles" (departs from quai de la Résistance, the train station, and Pont de Pierre every 20min. M-F 7am-8pm, Sa 7am-7:30pm, Su 8:45am-6:30pm; €1). Pebbly beaches are available closer to the town center, along the way to Les Quilles. To reach any of the beaches, and see the best of Sète while you're at it, walk along the shoreline starting at Quai Général Durand. The tourist office has a full list of beach activities, including **scuba diving, jet skiing,** and **sailboat rentals. Sète Croisières** offers **boat rides** and **underwater viewing** of oyster and mussel beds along the coast. (Quai Général Durand. ☎46 00 46; www.sete-croisieres.com. 1hr. ocean ride; 6 per day; €10, ages 3-12 €5. 1hr. underwater viewing; 4 per day; €15/8.)

A walk to the *vieux port* and up the hill along rue Haute leads to the **maritime cemetery,** an oasis overlooking the sea that inspired Valéry's poem "Le Cimetière Marin." The poet is buried here. (Open daily July-Sept. 8am-7pm; Oct.-June 8am-6pm.) The **Musée Paul Valéry,** above the cemetery on rue François Desnoyer, retraces the history and culture of Sète since its 17th-century beginnings. One room is dedicated purely to the sport of water jousting; it displays ceramic models and modernistic paintings alongside jousting equipment. The modern museum also pays tribute to French poet Paul Valéry and hosts temporary exhibits. (☎46 20 98. Open daily July-Aug. 10am-noon and 2-6pm; Sept.-June M and W-Su 10am-noon and 2-6pm. July-Aug. €4.60, Sept.-June €3; students and ages 12-18 €1.50; 1st Su of each month free.) From the museum, take rue Haute to reach **Décanale Saint-Louis,** the oldest standing structure in town, with a terrace overlooking the sea. Built at the end of Louis XIV's reign, the church celebrated its 300th anniversary in 2002. (☎74 90 54. Open Tu-Sa 10am-noon and 2-6pm. Su mass 9:30am.) On the other side of the city, take bus #2 to **L'Espace Georges Brassens,** 67 bd. Camille Blanc, a multimedia museum that pays homage to the irreverent folk singer from Sète. Brassens's grave can be found in the nearby **cimetière le Py.** (☎53 32 77; www.villesete.fr/brassens. Open July-Aug. daily 10am-noon and 2-7pm; Sept.-June 10am-noon and 2-6pm; Oct.-May Tu-Su 10am-noon and 2-6pm. €5, students €2.)

NIGHTLIFE AND FESTIVALS. Every evening, the popular **Piano-Bar la Bodega,** 21 quai Noel Guignon, plays live music, from Brazilian jazz to hip-hop, and serves over 25 types of whiskey and 100 mixed drinks. (☎74 47 50; webfrance.fr/labodega.htm. Open daily 10pm-4am. MC/V.) **Le 747,** 21 quai Rhin et Danube, offers cramped dancing to Top 40 jams. (☎74 80 73. Beer €4-6; drink purchase required. Open Tu-Su midnight-5am. Cash only.) At pl. Edouard Herriot, **Casino de Sète** opens its slot machines early for the morning gamblers. (☎46 65 65. 18+; ID required. Roulette and blackjack open Tu-Sa at 9pm. Piano bar July-Aug. daily 10:30pm; Sept.-June F-Sa 10:30pm. Casino open M-F 10am-3am, Sa-Su 10am-4am.)

In the summer, Sète bubbles over with festivals. From August 22-28, locals celebrate **La Fête de St-Louis,** the town's biggest festival, with fireworks, concerts, dances, and street performances. The festival includes the animated **Tournois de Joutes Nautiques,** in which participants joust from oversized rowboats. Arrive 2-3hr. early to secure a spot on quai de la Résistance. On weekends from June 21-July 21, gladiators from various jousting societies stage exposition battles in preparation for the tournament; ask at the tourist office for a schedule. For four days around the first weekend in July, **La Fête de St-Pierre** brings solemn religious rites in the morning and loud festivities at night. On Sunday morning, during the **Bénédiction de la Mer,** fishermen invite crowds onto their decorated boats and toss flowers into the water to commemorate those lost at sea. In mid-July, Sète draws a few big names to its 5-day jazz festival, **Jazz à Sète.** (www.jazzasete.com. Tickets €25-39.) Later in the month, the **Festival de Chanson Française "Quand je pense à Fernande,"** named after one of Brassen's most famous songs, takes over, drawing musicians from all corners of France. (☎04 77 74 70 55. Tickets €26-31.) Finally, **Fiest'a Sète** brings Latin music to town in the first week of August (☎74 48 44).

PROVENCE

If Paris boasts world-class paintings, it's only because Provence inspired them. One of France's most diverse regions, Provence has Roman ruins, hilltop castles, fields of lavender, and basically everything else you might want to see. Fierce *mistral* winds cut through olive groves in the north, while pink flamingoes, black bulls, and white horses gallop freely in the marshy Camargue to the south. With 2600 years of tumultuous history, Marseille is France's second largest city and an energetic melting pot of French, African, and Middle Eastern cultures. The former stomping ground of medieval popes, Avignon combines a fun student vibe with a lively arts scene and world-renowned theater festival. Throughout the Lubéron and the Vaucluse, tiny towns brim with local legends and bold character. The countryside might look familiar, given that masterpieces by Cézanne, Matisse, and Van Gogh (to name a few) have sent images of Provence across the globe. Come summertime, Parisians head to Provence to "escape" the city while foreigners come to see if there's any truth behind all the hype. There is. It's what keeps visitors coming back year after year—for a dip in the jewel-green sea, a stroll through earthy vineyards, and a taste of *La Vie en Rose*.

HIGHLIGHTS OF PROVENCE

STROLL through the **Palais des Papes,** the monstrous Gothic palace built by the French popes in Avignon (p. 675) during their 39-year boycott of Rome.

WATCH an unforgettable opera or concert at the **Théâtre Antique** in Orange (p. 693) during the summer Chorégies. Just don't applaud too enthusiastically—the arena is home to one of only three Roman stage walls still intact.

LEAVE YOUR WHITES BEHIND as you wander the **Sentier des Ochres,** the fiery highlight of rust-colored Roussillon (p. 686).

MARSEILLE ☎04 91

Marseille (mahr-SAY; pop. 800,000) is like the *bouillabaisse* soup for which it is famous—there's a little bit of everything mixed in. A blend of color and commotion, the city buzzes—no, roars—with the sounds of traffic, construction, and endless partying. Although Marseille does inherit a typical French legacy, complete with Roman ruins, crumbling forts, and traditional 18th-century art workshops, a walk through its side streets is punctuated by the vibrant colors of West African fabrics hanging in market stalls, the sounds of Arabic music blaring from car stereos, and the smells of North African cuisine wafting out of hole-in-the-wall restaurants. A true immigrant city, Marseille offers a taste of both the ancient and modern cultures of the Mediterranean region.

TRANSPORTATION

Flights: Aéroport Marseille-Provence (☎04 42 14 14 14; www.marseille.aeroport.fr). **Air France** (☎08 20 82 08 20). Flights to: **Corsica, Lyon,** and **Paris.** Shuttle buses (☎08 91 02 40 25, €0.22 per min.) connect the airport to Gare St-Charles (every 20min.; from St-Charles 5:30am-9:50pm, from airport 6:10am-10:50pm; €8.50). Taxis from the *centre-ville* to the airport €40 during the day, €50 at night.

Trains: Gare St-Charles, pl. Victor Hugo (☎08 92 35 35 35). M: Gare St-Charles. Info and ticket counters open daily 5am-11:15pm. **SOS Voyageurs** (☎62 12 80) helps vis-

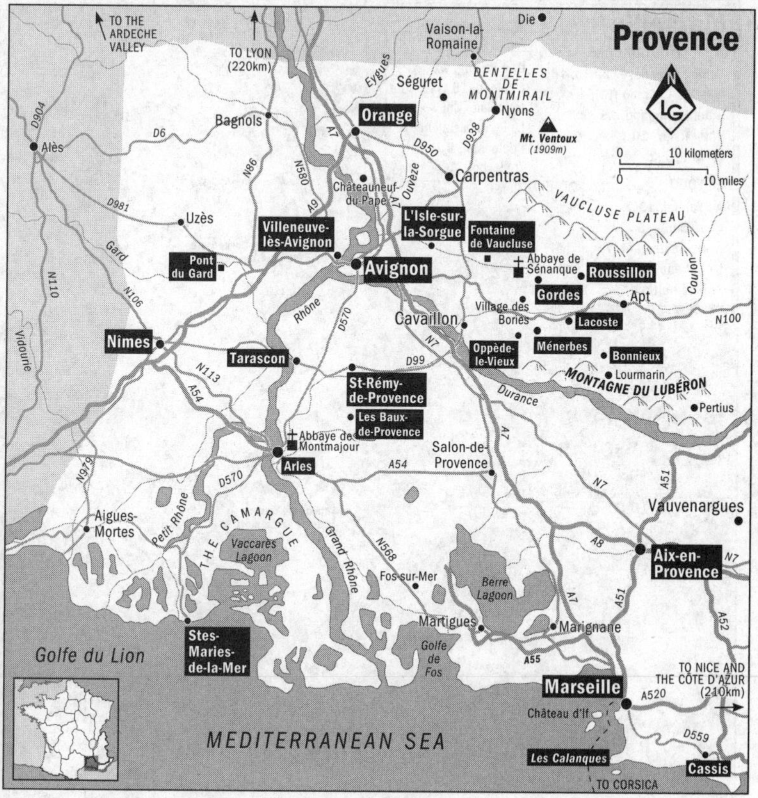

itors find lodgings and offers assistance to confused travelers, which is useful once the tourist office annex closes at 5pm. Open M-Sa 9am-7pm. Trains run to **Lyon** (1½hr., 21 per day, €55), **Nice** (2¾hr., 21 per day, €31), and **Paris** (3hr., 18 per day, €94).

Buses: Gare Routière, pl. Victor Hugo (☎08 91 02 402 5, €0.22 per min.), near the train station. M: Gare St-Charles. Ticket counters open M-F 6:15am-7:30pm, Sa 6:30am-6:30pm, Su 7:45am-noon and 12:45-6pm. Buy tickets at the window before boarding the bus. To **Aix-en-Provence** (every 10min. 6:30am-8:30pm, 2 per hr. 9-11:30pm; €4.60), **Cannes** (2¼-3hr.; 4 per day; €25, students €18), and **Nice** (2¾hr.; 1 per day; €26, students €18).

Ferries: SNCM, 61 bd. des Dames (☎08 25 88 80 88). M: Joliette. Phone line open M-Sa 8:30am-8pm. Office open M-F 8am-6pm, Sa 8:30am-noon and 2-5:30pm. To: **Algeria** (24hr., €92-250); **Corsica** (11½hr.; €35-53, students €20-40); **Sardinia, Italy** (14½hr., €59-69, students €50-65); **Tunisia** (24hr., €144). Prices vary according to season; high season June-Sept.

Public Transportation: RTM, 6 rue des Fabres (☎91 92 10; www.rtm.fr). Runs all Metro and bus lines. Tickets good for travel on buses and the Metro for 1hr. after validation (€1.70); sold at bus and Metro stations, or with exact change on board buses. Day pass (€4.50) and *Carte Liberté* (€6-12 for 5-10 trips) sold at tourist office and bus and Metro stations. **Metro** lines #1 and 2 stop at train station. Line #1 (blue) goes to the *vieux port* (dir.: Timone). Office open M-F 8:30am-6pm. Metro runs M-Th 5am-9pm, F-Su 5am-12:30am.

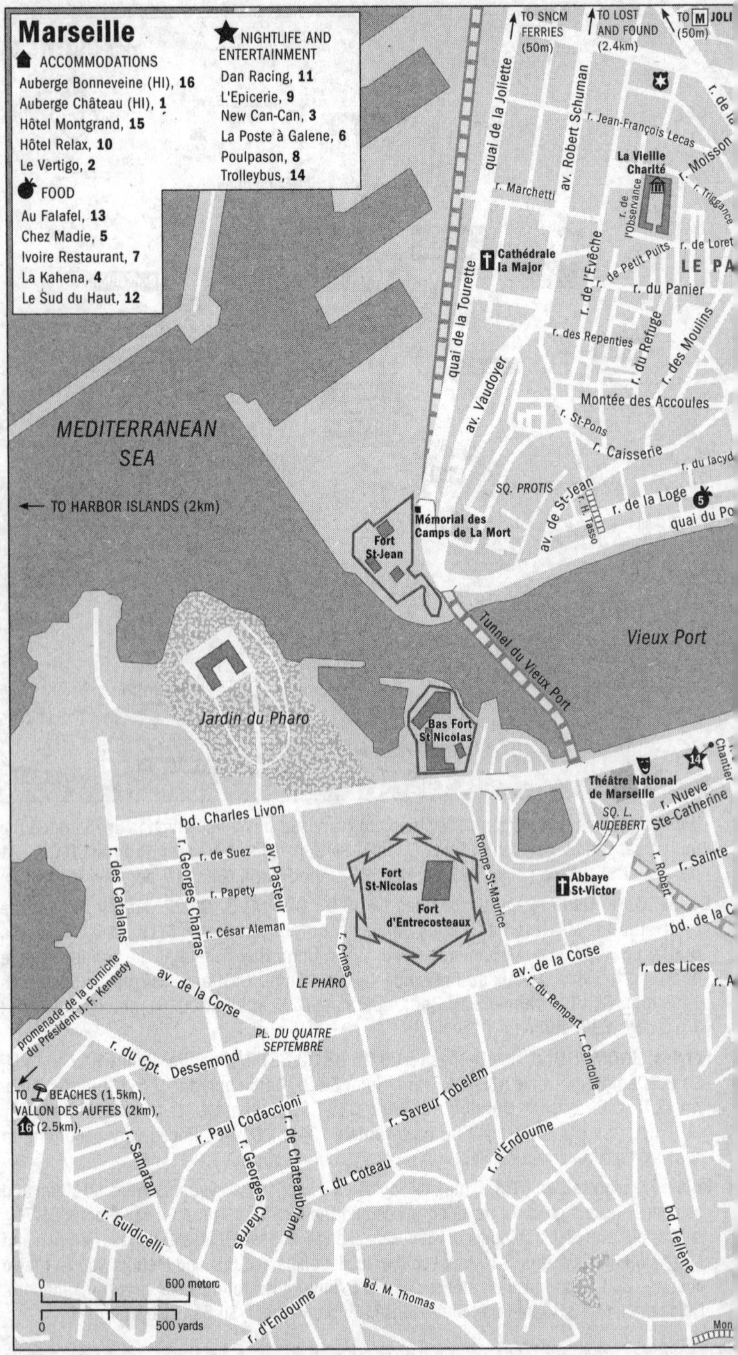
Marseille
ACCOMMODATIONS
Auberge Bonneveine (HI), 16
Auberge Château (HI), 1
Hôtel Montgrand, 15
Hôtel Relax, 10
Le Vertigo, 2
FOOD
Au Falafel, 13
Chez Madie, 5
Ivoire Restaurant, 7
La Kahena, 4
Le Sud du Haut, 12
NIGHTLIFE AND ENTERTAINMENT
Dan Racing, 11
L'Epicerie, 9
New Can-Can, 3
La Poste à Galene, 6
Poulpason, 8
Trolleybus, 14
TO SNCM FERRIES (50m)
TO LOST AND FOUND (2.4km)
MEDITERRANEAN SEA
TO HARBOR ISLANDS (2km)
quai de la Joliette
av. Robert Schuman
r. Jean-François Lecas
La Vieille Charité
r. Marchetti
r. de l'Observance
r. de Loret
Cathédrale la Major
quai de la Tourette
r. de l'Evêche
r. de Petit Puits
r. du Panier
r. des Repenties
r. du Refuge
r. des Moulins
av. Vaudoyer
Montée des Accoules
r. St-Pons
r. Caisserie
SQ. PROTIS
av. de St-Jean
r. de la Loge
quai du Po
Mémorial des Camps de La Mort
Fort St-Jean
Tunnel du Vieux Port
Vieux Port
Jardin du Pharo
Bas Fort St-Nicolas
Théâtre National de Marseille
SQ. L. AUDEBERT
r. Nueve Ste-Catherine
bd. Charles Livon
r. de Suez
r. Papety
r. César Aleman
r. des Catalans
r. Georges Charras
av. Pasteur
Fort St-Nicolas
Fort d'Entrecosteaux
Rompe St-Maurice
Abbaye St-Victor
r. Robert
r. Sainte
bd. de la C
av. de la Corse
r. des Lices
r. Crinas
LE PHARO
r. du Rempart
r. Candolle
promenade de la corniche du Président J. F. Kennedy
PL. DU QUATRE SEPTEMBRE
r. du Cpt. Dessemond
TO BEACHES (1.5km), VALLON DES AUFFES (2km), 16 (2.5km),
r. Saveur Tobelem
r. Paul Codaccioni
r. de Chateaubriand
r. Samatan
r. du Coteau
r. d'Endoume
bd. Tellène
r. Guldicelli
Bd. M. Thomas
0
500 meters
500 yards

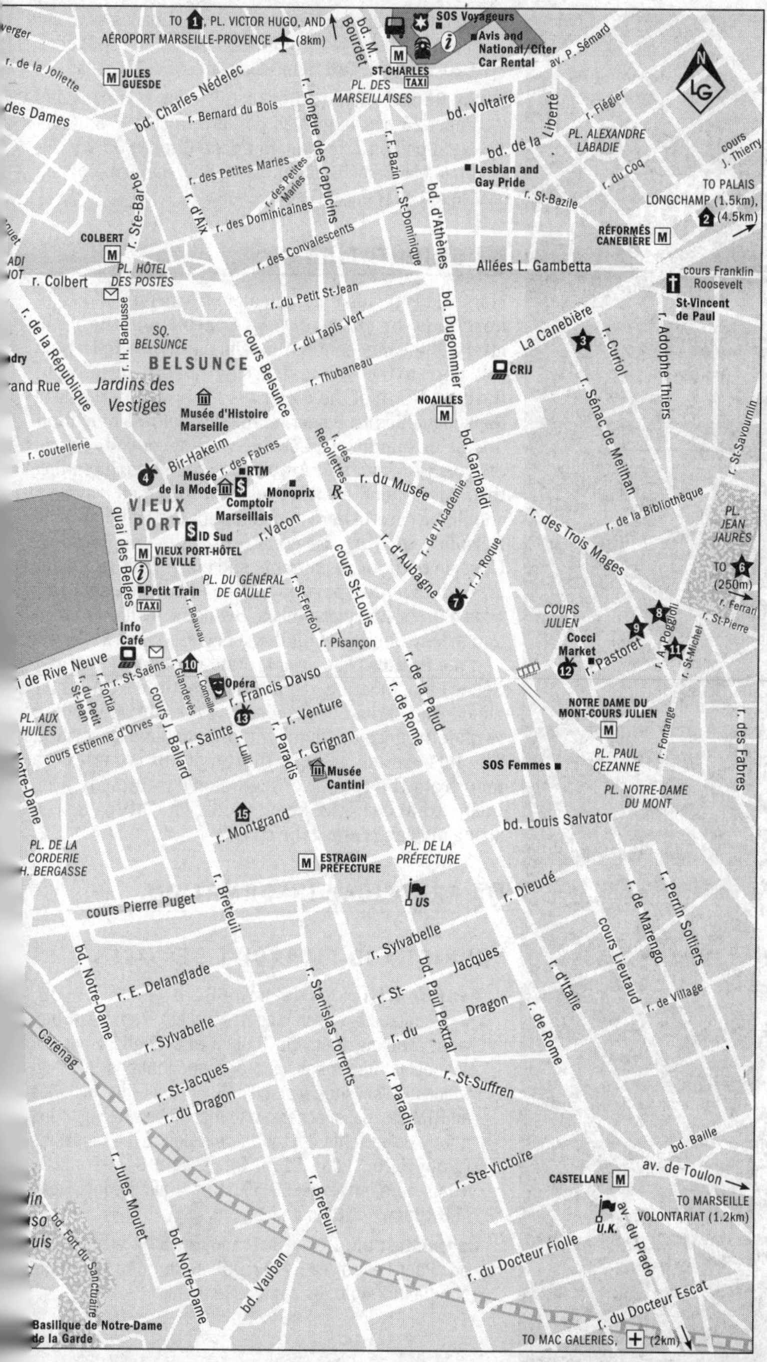
TO 1, PL. VICTOR HUGO, AND
AÉROPORT MARSEILLE-PROVENCE (8km)
SOS Voyageurs
Avis and National/Citer Car Rental
ST-CHARLES
PL. DES MARSEILLAISES
JULES GUESDE
bd. Charles Nédelec
r. Bernard du Bois
bd. Voltaire
bd. de la Liberté
PL. ALEXANDRE LABADIE
Lesbian and Gay Pride
TO PALAIS LONGCHAMP (1.5km), 2 (4.5km)
RÉFORMÉS CANEBIÈRE
Allées L. Gambetta
cours Franklin Roosevelt
St-Vincent de Paul
La Canebière
CRIJ
NOAILLES
BELSUNCE
Jardins des Vestiges
Musée d'Histoire Marseille
COLBERT
PL. HÔTEL DES POSTES
r. Colbert
r. de la République
cours Belsunce
bd. Dugommier
bd. Garibaldi
r. Curiol
r. Adolphe Thiers
r. Sénac de Meilhan
Musée de la Mode
RTM
Comptoir Marseillais
Monoprix
VIEUX PORT
ID Sud
VIEUX PORT-HÔTEL DE VILLE
Petit Train
TAXI
PL. DU GÉNÉRAL DE GAULLE
r. des Trois Mages
PL. JEAN JAURÈS
TO 6 (250m)
COURS JULIEN
Cocci Market
r. Pastoret
Info Café
Opéra
r. Francis Davso
cours St-Louis
r. de Rome
r. de la Palud
NOTRE DAME DU MONT-COURS JULIEN
PL. PAUL CEZANNE
SOS Femmes
PL. NOTRE-DAME DU MONT
Musée Cantini
bd. Louis Salvator
r. Montgrand
ESTRAGIN PRÉFECTURE
PL. DE LA PRÉFECTURE
US
PL. DE LA CORDERIE
cours Pierre Puget
r. Breteuil
bd. Notre-Dame
r. Paradis
r. Dieudé
r. Sylvabelle
bd. Paul Pextral
cours Lieutaud
r. Perrin Solliers
r. de Marengo
r. St-Suffren
r. Stanislas Torrents
r. Jules Moulet
CASTELLANE
av. de Toulon
TO MARSEILLE VOLONTARIAT (1.2km)
U.K.
av. du Prado
r. du Docteur Fiolle
r. du Docteur Escat
bd. Vauban
Basilique de Notre-Dame de la Garde
TO MAC GALERIES, (2km)

PROVENCE

PROVENCE: THE PROVINCE OF PÉTANQUE

Along any shady square in southern France, visitors are sure to find a friendly game of *pétanque*. The court is a large, sandy square, although you can play almost anywhere. This traditional game, also called *boules*, is much like Italian *bocce*, but the balls are smaller and the name is catchier. At the start of each game, an undersized, brightly colored ball is thrown into the middle of an inscribed circle; the goal is for each player to throw his metal ball so that it lands closest to the small ball, called the *cochonnet*. Although most of the serious players tend to be middle-aged or older, *pétanque* is easy enough to learn and unites generations.

A player's style reveals itself after a round or two. Grandsons and middle-aged men with slicked back hair adopt a more forceful style. They pitch balls at resting balls in order to knock them away from the *cochonnet* and often overthrow or send several balls flying, allowing another party to swoop in for victory.

More refined players, usually old men, throw with more finesse. These senior citizens know the slopes and curves of the playing field; they squat as close as possible to the ground to avoid a large bounce and launch their balls ever so softly. Onlookers are often amazed that these slowly-rolling balls reach their targets; when executed correctly, this method can

Taxis: Marseille Taxi (☎02 20 20). Taxi stands surround the *vieux port*. Taxis to hostels from Gare St-Charles €20-30. 24hr. **Taxi Blanc Bleu** (☎51 50 00). 24hr.

Car Rental: Avis (☎64 71 00; www.avis.fr). 21+. Under-25 surcharge €25 per day. Open M-F 6:30am-10:30pm, Sa 7am-8pm. **National/Citer** (☎05 90 86). Open M-F 8am-10:30pm, Sa-Su 8:30am-8pm. Both on the left as you exit Gare St-Charles.

ORIENTATION

Marseille is divided along major streets into 16 neighborhoods, or *quartiers*. **La Canebière** is the main artery of the city center, funneling into the *vieux port* (old port) to the west and turning into urban sprawl to the east. North of the *vieux port* and west of **rue de la République** lies **Le Panier,** Marseille's oldest neighborhood. Surrounding La Canebière are several *Maghreb*, or North African and Arabic, communities, including the market-filled **Belsunce quartier.** Although travelers should be careful here at night, both Le Panier and the Belsunce Quartier are great for daytime exploration. Upscale outdoor restaurants and chic nightlife cluster around the *vieux port* on **quai de Rive Neuve, cour Estienne d'Orves,** and **place Thiers.** Big-name fashion brands and pricey boutiques fill the shops along **rue St-Ferreol** and **rue Paradis.** The area around **rue Curiol** (near rue Sénac) is a meeting ground for prostitutes and their clients and should be avoided late at night. Marseille's two Metro lines are quick but provide limited service. The bus system is more thorough but complex—a map from the tourist office helps enormously. Use buses to access the beach and *Les Calanques*, a string of islands along the coast.

PRACTICAL INFORMATION

TOURIST AND FINANCIAL SERVICES

Tourist Office: 4 la Canebière (☎13 89 00; www.marseille-tourisme.com) M: Vieux Port. Staff provides walking tours (in French and English; ask for schedule), free maps, and accommodations booking. Office also sells the *Marseille City Pass*, which includes an RTM day pass, access to tourist office walking tours, a ferry ticket to Ile d'If, and admission to 14 museums (1-day €20, 2-day €27). Open M-Sa 9am-7pm, Su 10am-5pm. Annex (☎50 59 18) at train station. Open M-F 10am-12:30pm and 1-5pm.

Consulates: UK, 24 av. du Prado (☎15 72 10). **US,** 12 bd. Paul Peytral (☎54 92 00). Both open M-F 9am-noon and 2-4pm; by appointment only.

Currency Exchange: ID SUD, 3 pl. Général de Gaulle (☎13 09 00). Open M-F 9am-6pm, Sa 9am-5pm. **Comptoir Marseillais de Bourse,** 22 bd. de la Canebière (☎54 93 94). Open M-F 9am-6pm, Sa 9am-4pm. **ATMs** line rue Canebière.

Beyond Tourism: Marseille Volontariat, 4 rue Paul Casimir (☎79 70 72; www.marseille-volontariat.com) offers a range of volunteer opportunities by field of civic interest, including prison education, computer training, elderly care, and insurance disputes. Open M-Tu and Th 2:30-5pm, F 10am-12pm. See **Beyond Tourism,** p. 84.

LOCAL SERVICES

Youth Information: Centre Régional Information Jeunesse (CRIJ), 96 la Canebière (☎24 33 50; www.crijpa.com). M: Noailles. Info on short-term employment, recreation, vacation planning, long-term accommodation, and services for the disabled. Bulletin board advertises babysitters and other personal notices. Internet access €1 per hour. Free Wi-Fi at **Cyber-espace** (☎24 33 83), located in the CRIJ. Open Sept.-June M and W-F 10am-5pm, Tu 1-5pm; July-Aug. hours more limited.

GLBT Resources: Lesbian & Gay Pride, 8 bd. de la Libération (☎50 50 12; www.marseillepride.org).

Laundromat: Laverie, 8 rue Rudolf Pollack. Wash and dry €7.50. Open daily 9am-7pm.

EMERGENCY AND COMMUNICATIONS

Traveler Emergency: SOS Voyageurs, Gare St-Charles (☎62 12 80).

Police: 2 rue du Antoine Becker (☎39 80 00). Also in the train station (☎04 96 13 01 88).

Lost and Found: 41 bd. de Briançon (☎14 68 97). Open M-F 8am-2pm.

Crisis Line: SOS Femmes, 14 rue Théodore Turner (☎24 61 50). Rape victim assistance. 24hr.

Pharmacy: Pharmacie le Cours St-Louis, 5 cours St-Louis (☎54 04 58) M: Vieux Port. Open M-Sa 8:30am-7:30pm. Serves as one of 5 rotating **pharmacies de garde;** check pharmacy windows, the front page of *La Provence*, or with the police.

Hospital: Hôpital Timone, 246 rue St-Pierre (☎38 00 00). M: Timone.

SOS Médecins (☎52 91 52) and **SOS Dentist** (☎85 39 39). Doctors on call.

Poison Control: ☎75 25 25.

Internet Access: At the **CRIJ** (see above). **Info Café,** 1 quai Rive Neuve (☎33 74 98). M: Noailles. €3.80 per hr., students €3. Open M-Sa 9am-10pm, Su 2:30-7:30pm.

be devastatingly effective.

Pétanque is also a spectator sport. Once a game begins, it's not long before a large crowd gathers along the benches lining the makeshift court. Women, children, and small animals crowd the area to watch their loved ones compete. It's easy to be swept away by the action, rooting irrationally for a man you've never met, willing his *boule* to continue in the right path, rejoicing when he bests his opponents.

Though games are always friendly in spirit, things can get intense quickly as the serious players break out measuring tools (sticks, strings, or whatever else is handy) in order to discern who is closest to the *cochonnet*. Like any other sports enthusiasts, *pétanque* players brandish a wide range of sophisticated, non-essential tools which supposedly help them gain an edge. These include personalized balls (in a range of weights and diameters), and magnets attached to telescopic rods or long strings that allow players to retrieve their balls without bending over. In order to save their aging knees, this handy magnet on a stick appeals especially to the older crowd—the same people who proceed to bend down as close to the ground as possible in order to take their turn. An age-old tradition, *pétanque* promises something exciting with each new game.

CHARTERED CHOWDER

Say hello to the millennia-old *soupe d'or,* as hearty and unpretentious as Marseille itself: *bouillabaisse* (BOO-ya-bess). This fish stew was already a popular dish in Ancient Greece, when Marseille was founded. The Romans imagined that it put Vulcan to sleep so Venus could frolic with Mars. Originally the simple dish of fishermen, *bouillabaisse* became a delicacy for rich travelers brought in by the 19th century commercial expansion of Marseille. Today it is served both at home and as a refined dish in Marseille's best restaurants.

One of these is **Le Miramar,** whose chef Christian Buffa gives free *bouillabaisse* cooking lessons every month. Its flagship *bouillabaisse* conforms to the 1980 *Charte de la Bouillabaisse Marseillaise* (charter), as it includes over four of the 10 possible fish types (*rascasse, chapon,* monkfish, and so forth). Mr. Buffa presents the fish to guests before they are prepared, and his assistants turn down the heat when the stew boils–the name *bouillabaisse* comes from the provençal Occitan *bolh* (boil) and *abaissa* (lower). His final trick consists of adding a splash of *pastis* (an anise-flavored *apéritif*) to the soup.

Le Miramar, 12 quai du Port (☎91 10 40; www.bouillabaisse.com). Christian Buffa's monthly cooking lessons are for a maximum of 8 people. Get info and sign up at the tourist office (☎13 89 00).

Post Office: 1 pl. Hôtel des Postes (☎15 47 00). Take la Canebière toward the sea and turn right on rue Reine Elisabeth as it becomes pl. Hôtel des Postes. **Currency exchange.** Open M-W and F 8am-6:45pm, Th 9am-6:45pm, Sa 8am-12:15pm. Branch at 1 cours Jean Ballard (☎04 96 11 23 60), off quai des Belges. Open M-F 9:30am-12:30pm and 1:30-6pm. **Postal Code:** 13001.

ACCOMMODATIONS

Marseille has a range of hotel options, from pricey establishments in the *vieux port* to the less reputable but temptingly cheap places in the *quartier* Belsunce. Exercise caution when picking a budget hotel; the tourist office provides a **list of recommended accommodations.** Hotel prices are high in central Marseille—a good double costs €50. The HI hostels are located far from the city center, offering an escape from traffic and noise, but infrequent bus service makes them less accessible. On weekends and in the summer, reserve at least a week in advance.

Le Vertigo, 42 rue des petites Maries (☎91 07 11; www.hotelvertigo.fr). From the train station, make a sharp right after walking down the steps; le Vertigo is straight ahead (100m). This newcomer on the Marseille hostel scene combines the best features of a youth hostel and small hotel. While expensive for a hostel (€24 per night in 4-bed dorms), it's worth it: the young and dedicated English-speaking owners offer stylish hand-painted wooden furniture, comfortable beds, and spotless bathrooms. Breakfast €5. Beer €2.60. Bar open until midnight. Internet access €1 per 30min. Free Wi-Fi. Reception 24hr. Reserve ahead in summer. Doubles €50-60. MC/V. ❹

Hôtel Relax, 4 rue Corneille (☎33 15 87; www.hotelrelax.fr). M: Vieux Port. Around the corner from the *vieux port,* this charming hotel offers small, clean rooms with lots of amenities at fair prices. A/C, free Wi-Fi, soundproof windows, TV, shower, and toilet in all rooms. Breakfast €6. Doubles €50-55. Reception 6am-midnight. AmEx/MC/V. ❹

Hôtel Montgrand, 50 rue Montgrand (☎00 35 20; www.hotel-montgrand-marseille.com). M: Estragin-Préfecture. Proximity to the *vieux port* and bright, spotless rooms make this newly renovated hotel a great choice. A/C. Breakfast €5, but not worth it. Reserve ahead in Aug. Singles €41, with bath €45-49; family rooms €59. MC/V. ❸

Auberge de Jeunesse Bonneveine (HI), Impasse Bonfils (☎17 63 30; http://fuaj.org), off av. J. Vidal. Take Metro #2 to "Rond-Point du Prado" and transfer to bus #44; take it to "pl. Bonnefon." From the stop, walk back toward the traffic circle and turn left onto J. Vidal. Turn left onto Impasse Bonfils; the hostel is at the end of the street on the left. Main selling point is proximity to the beach (10min.). Plain concrete exterior and bare garden don't make a good first impression, but basic rooms are adequate. Group hikes (€10) or kayak trips (€40) to the Calanques organized in summer. Bar, restaurant, outdoor terrace, and pool table. Breakfast included. Laundry. Reception 7am-12:45pm, 1:30-8pm, and 8:45pm-1am. Guests under 18 must be accompanied by an adult or have a signed authorization from parents. Open mid-Jan. to mid-Dec. 3-night max. stay. Apr.-Aug. dorms €18; doubles €21. Sept.-Mar. €17/20. AmEx/MC/V. ❶

Auberge de Jeunesse Château de Bois-Luzy (HI), allée des Primevères (☎49 06 18). Take Metro #1 to "Chartreux," transfer to bus #8, and take it to "Félibres Lauriers." Continue up the hill 50m and turn onto a footpath along basketball courts. When you reach the end of the path (100m), climb the stairs and turn left; the hostel is on the left (5min. walk from bus stop, 1hr. total). This château provides 90 beds with panoramic views of the sea below, but it's only practical for those uninterested in central Marseille or willing to make a long commute. Kitchen without utensils. Mostly 3- to 6-bed dorms, with a few singles and doubles. Breakfast €3.50. Lunch and dinner €9.30, picnic €6. Luggage storage free 1st day, €2 per bag per day thereafter. Sheets €2.50. Reception 7:30-10am and 5-10:30pm. Lockout noon-5pm. Curfew July-Aug. 11:30pm, Sept.-June 10:30pm. 5-night max. stay. Dorms €11; singles €15; doubles €12. Cash only. ❶

FOOD

Marseille's restaurants reflect the city's cultural diversity. Options range from small African eateries and kebab stands along **cours St-Louis** and **rue d'Aubagne** to the *places provençals* on **rue St-Saens** and **rue Fortia.** The streets surrounding the *vieux port* are packed with restaurants serving the city's trademark *bouillabaisse* (a heavy stew comprised of various Mediterranean fish, broth, and a spicy red sauce called *rouille*, or "rust"). **Cours Julien** has a wonderful and eclectic collection of restaurants along side streets and beside fountains on the main pedestrian mall. There is a **Monoprix,** 36 la Canebière, a few blocks from the *vieux port.* (☎54 15 97. Open M-Sa 8:30am-9pm. AmEx/MC/V.) A daily fish market on **quai des Belges** (open 8am-1pm) supplies fresh ingredients for *bouillabaisse*, while vegetable and fruit markets on **cours Pierre Puget** (open M-F 8am-1pm) and at "Noailles" Metro stop on bd. de la Canebière (open M-Sa 9am-7pm) provide the fixings.

Ivoire Restaurant, 57 rue d'Aubagne (☎33 75 33). M: Noailles. Loyal patrons come to this excellent, no-frills restaurant for authentic West African cuisine and advice from Mama Africa, the exuberant owner. Specialties from the Côte d'Ivoire include *maffé* (€7.50), a meat dish with peanut sauce, and *jus de gingembre* (€3), a refreshingly spicy ginger drink and natural West African medicine—but be careful who you drink with, as it's also an aphrodisiac. *Plats* €7.50-11. Open daily 11am-2am. Cash only. ❷

Le Sud du Haut, 80 cours Julien (☎92 66 64). M: Cours Julien. Inviting décor, spacious outdoor seating, and creative *provençal* cuisine make this the ideal place for a leisurely meal. Changeable menu includes options like smoked salmon burritos, beautifully presented on a bed of greens (€8.50). The **lunch formule** (€11) is a great deal. *Entrées* €8-11. *Plats* €13-19. Open M-Sa noon-2:30pm and 8-10:30pm. MC/V. ❸

Au Falafel, 5 rue Lulli (☎54 08 55). M: Vieux Port. Warm pita bread is the best reason to visit this Israeli restaurant, which also offers first-class hummus, falafel, and schawarma. Try the *Assiette Israelienne Falafel* (€7); though it's listed as an appetizer, it will satisfy all but the hungriest travelers. Falafel sandwich €6. *Assiette Israelienne Schawarma* €10. Open M-Th and Su noon-midnight, F noon-4pm. AmEx/MC/V. ❷

La Kahena, 2 rue de la République (☎90 61 93). M: Vieux Port. Tasty couscous dishes (€8.50-15) with various additions, including fresh fish and traditional African ingredients, are served on hand-painted plates at this sunny Tunisian restaurant on the corner of the *vieux port.* Speedy service makes for a scrumptious, quick meal, and A/C sweetens the deal. Blue tile mosaics and the smell of warm spices create a North African feel. *Entrées* €4.50-5.50. Open daily noon-2:30pm and 7-10:30pm. MC/V. ❷

Chez Madie, 138 quai du Port (☎90 40 87). The place to visit for a real Marseille splurge. Beautiful views of the port and carefully prepared *provençal* cuisine create the perfect evening, particularly when the weather allows guests to sit on the terrace. Customers watch the port turn gold under the setting sun as they sample *émincé de gigot d'agneau* (lamb) with *tapenade* (olive puree). Free *apéritif* with *Let's Go.* Lunch *formule* €15. *Menus* €22-27. Open M-Sa noon-2:30pm and 8-10:30pm. AmEx/MC/V. ❸

SIGHTS

A walk through Marseille's streets tops any sights-oriented itinerary, as it provides glimpses of the influences of the African and Arabic communities amidst ancient Roman ruins and 17th-century forts. The *petit train*, which gives tours of the city, departs on two different circuits, to Le Panier and the Basilique, from quai Belges every 30min. (☎25 24 69. Open Apr.-Nov. 10am-12:30pm and 2-6pm. €5, under 18 €3.) Packed with tourists, this ride takes a direct route to the must-see monuments in the city. A hop-on hop-off bus is also available, leaving from quai du Port. (☎91 05 82. 1-day pass €17, students €14; 2-day €20/17. Leaves Apr.-Oct. every hr. 10am-1pm and 2:30-5:30pm; Nov.-Mar. 4 per day.) Check www.museum-paca.org for info on museums. Unless otherwise noted, all the museums listed below have the same hours (June-Sept. Tu-Su 11am-6pm; Oct.-May Tu-Su 10am-5pm).

BASILIQUE DE NOTRE DAME DE LA GARDE. A stunning view of the city, surrounding mountains, and island-studded bay make this a must for all travelers. Visit the windy perch in the evening, when crowds are small and the setting sun lends an unforgettable glow to the red roofs below. Climb the stairs to the intimate basilica to see gilded mosaics and touching *ex votos*, symbolic objects presented by the faithful in thanks for protection; the model ships hanging from the ceiling are the work of grateful shipwreck survivors. Towering nearly 230m above the city, the church's **statue of Madonna** is regarded by many as the symbol of Marseille. The east face of the church remains pocked with WWII bullet holes and shrapnel scars. *(Take bus #60, dir.: Notre Dame, or, from the tourist office, walk up rue Breteuil and turn left onto rue Grignon,*

MAMA (AFRICA) KNOWS BEST

At first glance, the **Ivoire Restaurant** (p[redacted]657) doesn't look like much—its kitschy interior houses an eclectic collection of African art. The exuberant personality of Ivoire's owner, a local celebrity known only as "Mama Africa," however, far outshines the simple décor.

Mama Africa, who moved to Marseille from the Côte d'Ivoire and started her own restaurant, comes complete with a back story of mystery and intrigue. She often claims that her father had 13 wives and lived to be 125 years old. Yet this woman's achievements are just as impressive as her father's alleged conquests. Since starting her own successful restaurant, she has earned the title "Mama Africa" by helping fellow immigrants to Marseille find homes and jobs and assimilate into the unique *Marseil-la*[redacted]ture. "When someone's hungry, I'm not going to say he can't eat," she says.

Regulars abound during lunch hours in the Ivoire Restaurant, where Mama Africa greets both locals and one-time visitors with a kiss on each cheek as she swoops from the kitchen to usher them to a table. A running conversation between the patrons and Mama Africa accompanies traditional African cuisine. Best of all, the food does not disappoint; meals here leave a lasting impression that rivals that of Mama Africa herself.

which becomes bd. de la Corderie. Turn left onto bd. André Aune to reach the basilica's huge staircase. ☎13 40 80. Open daily July-Aug. 7am-8pm; Sept.-June 7am-7pm. Free.)

HARBOR ISLANDS. The short ride to the islands takes you between the batteries of **Fort St-Jean**, whose original tower guarded a giant chain that blocked the harbor off in times of trouble, until King Aragon of Spain took the spire home as a trophy for his 14th-century victory. Resembling a child's sandcastle, the **Château d'If** guards the city from its rocky perch outside the harbor. The tiny island's most famous resident was the fictional Count of Monte Cristo. Nearby, **Ile Frioul** housed quarantined plague victims for two centuries, beginning in the 1600s. It was only marginally successful, as a 1720 outbreak killed half of the city's 80,000 citizens. In June, crowds enjoy open-air jazz concerts among the crumbling, starlit walls. All events depend on the weather and ferry schedules—check with the tourist office or *L'Espace Culture* (see **Practical Information,** p. 654) for details. Tiny inlets perfect for swimming, as well as a number of relaxing restaurants, make the islands a convenient escape from the city. *(Société des Armateurs Côtiers sends boats from quai des Belges to both islands. ☎46 54 65. Round-trip 1hr. Boats leave for the islands daily June-Aug. 6:45am-11:30pm; Sept.-May 6:45am-7:45pm. €10 for 1 island, €15 for both. Reserve ahead in the high season. Château ☎59 02 30. Château entry required for visit to Ile d'If. €5, ages 18-25 €3.50, under 18 free. Under 18 must be accompanied by an adult.)*

ABBAYE ST-VICTOR. Fortified against pirates and Saracen invaders, this medieval abbey's **crypt** is one of the oldest Christian sites in Europe; its construction in the fifth century brought the first traces of Christianity to the pagan *Marseillais*. The crypt holds the remains of two third-century martyrs, along with photos of their skeletons. Fascinating inscriptions and ancient rubble litter the space. The abbey hosts an annual choral concert festival from September to December. *(On rue Sainte at the end of quai de Rive Neuve. Follow the signs from the quai. ☎04 96 11 22 60, festival info 05 84 48. Open daily 9am-7pm. Crypt €2. Festival tickets €32, students €13.)*

MUSÉE CANTINI. This memorable museum, with its chic warehouse style, chronicles the region's artistic successes of the last century. Major Fauvist, Cubist and Surrealist collections, including works by Ernst, Kandinsky, Masson, Matisse, Miró, and Signac, are on display. Rotating temporary exhibits are often spread over two floors of the museum; a recent exposition featured Pière Bonnard. *(19 rue Grignan. M: Estragin-Préfecture. ☎54 77 75. €2, students €1, seniors and under 10 free.)*

PALAIS LONGCHAMP. The sweeping columns, majestic statues, and imposing stone facades of this palace, constructed in 1838, were meant to honor the completion of a canal that brought fresh water to the plague-ridden city. Today, the complex includes a museum, park, and observatory. The galleries of the **Musée de l'Histoire Naturelle** are filled with an assortment of stuffed wildlife and temporary exhibits recounting the history of subjects as diverse as dinosaurs, milk, and human speech. *(Take Metro #1 to "Cinq Avenues Longchamps." ☎14 59 50. Open Tu-Su 10am-5pm. €3, students €1.50, seniors and under 10 free.)*

MÉMORIAL DES CAMPS DE LA MORT. This memorial houses sobering exhibits on the death camps of World War II and the deportation of thousands of Jews from the *vieux port* in 1943. Contained in a blockhouse built by the Germans during their occupation of Marseille, the memorial has three levels. Glass panels on the first floor are engraved with quotes by Primo Levi, Elie Wiesel, and Anne Frank; on the second floor, photos display the details of Hitler's control of Marseille. A group of ashes provokes reflection on the third floor. *(Quai de la Tourette. M: Vieux Port. ☎90 73 15. Open Tu-Su June-Aug. 11am-6pm; Sept.-May 10am-5pm. Free.)*

LA VIEILLE CHARITÉ. A formidable example of the famous 17th-century work of local architect Pierre Puget, La Charité was constructed to house the beggars who

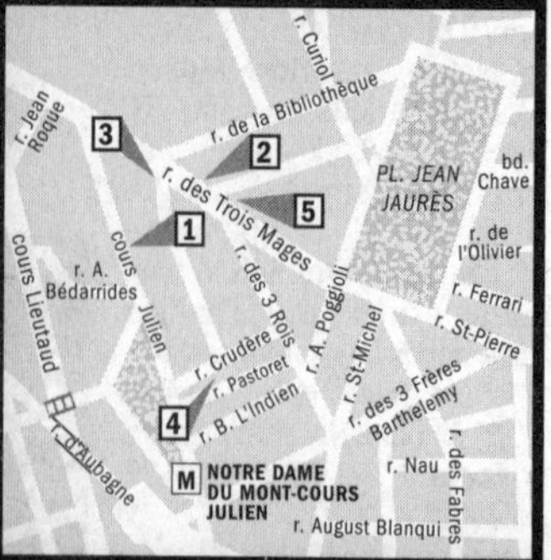

COURS JULIEN

An eclectic collection of murals, vintage music and clothing shops, bookstores, theaters, and countless cafés and restaurants make cours Julien the perfect place to stroll for a bargain. Many shops are closed on Sundays and Mondays.

1. Peruse dusty paperbacks at **Librairie du Cours Julien,** 51 cours Julien.

2. **Kaleidoscope,** 3 rue des Trois Mages, offers a variety of used records and CDs (€3-15).

3. **La Passerelle,** 26 rue des Trois Mages, features comic books and a snazzy bookstore café—and tiramisu for €3.

4. Street artists have turned **rue Pastoret** and **rue Crudère** into impromptu outdoor galleries with cartoonish, bright spray-paint murals.

5. **Black Music,** 12 rue des Trois Mages, has a large assortment of soul and hip hop.

crowded the entrances of Marseille's churches. Later, the building served as a hospice center for orphans; parents could leave their unwanted children in front of the church, where a wooden turnstile near the gate kept the nuns inside from seeing their faces. Now a national historical monument, it contains several of the city's museums. Egyptian, prehistoric, and anthropological collections are held in the **Musée des Arts Africains, Océaniens, et Amérindiens.** Temporary art exhibits are displayed beneath a soaring oval dome in the central Baroque chapel, and the **Musée d'Archéologie Méditerranée** houses the city's collection of Egyptian artifacts along with an assortment of ancient Greek pottery. *(2 rue de la Charité. M: Vieux Port or Joliette. ☎14 58 80. Temporary exhibits €5, permanent collections €2 each; students €2/1.)*

OTHER SIGHTS. The rotating exhibits at the **Musée de la Mode** feature international clothing designers from different fashion periods. *(Espace Mode Méditerranée, 11 la Canebière. M: Vieux Port-Hôtel de Ville. ☎04 96 17 06 00. €3, students €1.50, seniors free.)* At the nearby **Musée d'Histoire de Marseille,** Greek and Phoenician artifacts reveal Marseille's lively past. Don't miss the massive potter's oven, which dates to the first century BC. The museum ticket also provides access to the adjacent **Jardin des Vestiges,** marked by crumbling medieval foundations. Grab a sandwich in the **Centre Bourse** (above the museum) and picnic amongst ruins. *(Enter through the lowest level of the Centre Bourse mall. ☎90 42 22. Open M-Sa noon-7pm. English text available. €2, students €1, seniors and under 10 free.)* The **MAC, Galeries Contemporaines des Musées de Marseille,** features art from the 1960s to today, including works by César and Wegman. *(69 av. d'Haifa, off av. Hambourg. Bus #23 or 45. ☎25 01 07; dgac-mac@mairie.marseille.fr. Open Tu-Su June-Sept. 11am-6pm; Oct.-May 10am-5pm. €3, students €1.50.)*

BEACHES

From the Palais du Pharo to the av. du Prado, the **promenade de la corniche du Président J. F. Kennedy** runs along Marseille's most beautiful stretch of beaches. The picturesque views of the Mediterranean and nearby islands make the typically heavy traffic—human and automotive—bearable. Make a stop at **Vallon des Auffes,** a hidden cove where residents once spun fishing nets by hand from coconut fiber. Today the nets are synthetic, but little else has changed. Rows of brightly painted dories still dip and pull at their moorings as they have for years. Take bus #83 from the *vieux port* (dir.: Rond-Point du Prado) to "Vallon des Auffes." The bus continues on to Marseille's **public beaches.** Get off just after it rounds the statue of David and turns away from the coast (20-30min.). Or take bus #19 (dir.: Madrague) from M: Rond-Point du Prado. Both the north and south **plages du Prado** offer sandy stretches, clear water, and good views of Marseille's surrounding cliffs. On summer Sundays, a mass exodus occurs, as the entire city treks to the beaches here. **Supermarché Casino et Caféteria** is across from the statue of David. (Open M-Sa 8:30am-8pm. Cafeteria open daily 8:30am-9:45pm. MC/V.)

ENTERTAINMENT AND NIGHTLIFE

Late-night restaurants and a few nightclubs center around **place Thiers,** near the *vieux port.* On weekends, there's a rush for seats at the bar tables that spill out onto the sidewalk along **quai de Rive Neuve,** but a more eclectic crowd likes to unwind along **cours Julien.** Tourists should exercise caution at night, particularly on the dimly lit streets of the Panier and Belsunce *quartiers* and in the more far-flung areas of the city; night buses are scarce, taxis expensive, and the Metro closes early (M-Th and Su 9pm, F-Sa midnight). Gay nightlife abounds in Marseille; men and women often frequent the same establishments.

BARS AND CLUBS

Trolleybus, 24 quai de Rive Neuve (☎54 30 45; www.letrolley.com). M: Vieux Port-Hôtel de Ville. Known affectionately as "Le Trolley," this mega-club is a Marseille institution. 3 cave-like rooms playing pop-rock, techno, and soul-funk-salsa, each with its own décor, keep a hip crowd in the groove. The excellent DJs make sure every party is a hit. Beer from €4.50. Mixed drinks €4-7.50. Sa cover €10, includes 1 drink; free with *Let's Go*. Open July-Aug. W-Sa 11pm-6am; Sept.-June Th-Sa 11pm-6am. MC/V.

Poulpason, 2 rue André Poggioli (lepoulpason.free.fr). M: Cours Julien. Local and international DJs spin hip hop, funk, jazz, reggae, and electro-house at the Poulpason, where a giant eyelash-sporting octopus reaches out from the wall. Exposed pipes and flashing colored lights complete the experience. Mixed drinks €3-5. Cover on specially featured DJ nights €3-10. Open Tu and Th-Sa 11pm-4am. MC/V.

Dan Racing, 17 rue André Poggioli (☎06 09 17 04 07; www.dan-racing.tk). M: Cours Julien. Let your inner rock star run wild at this fun, casual bar, where a crowd of drunken revelers hop onstage for impromptu jam sessions every W. 20 guitars, 2 drum sets, and countless other instruments provide the makings for an ear-splitting insta-band. Auto-racing décor adds to the personality of this hilarious hangout. Beer €2.50. Wine €2. Champagne €4.50. Mixed drinks €2.50-3.50. Concerts Th-Sa 9pm; check website for upcoming concerts. Open W-Sa 9pm-2am. Cash only.

New Can-Can, 3 rue Sénac (☎48 59 76; www.newcancan.com). M: Noailles. Hosts a perpetual party for the city's gay community. Swanky discotheque with full-length mirrors, a small stage, and low-slung red leather couches. Check the website for the date of French Kiss, the monthly French-music-only night. All drinks €9. *Soirée Cabaret* Su nights. F cover €10 before midnight, €15 after. Open daily 11pm-dawn. AmEx/MC/V.

LIVE PERFORMANCES

L'Epicerie, 17 rue Pastoret (☎42 16 33). M: Notre-Dame du Mont. A creative showcase for budding artists, this funky new theater/gallery/café features everything from jazz and poetry performances to tango lessons. Open Tu-Sa 2-9pm, Su 3-8pm.

La Poste à Galene, 103 rue Ferrari (☎47 57 99). M: Cours Julien. A concert space that features popular local groups as well as English and American musicians. Pop, rock, heavy metal, techno, and everything else. Cover free-€19. Open M-Sa from 8:30pm on concert nights, 9:30pm otherwise; shows at 9:30pm.

PANIER AND BELSUNCE QUARTIERS

BIKING TOUR | SCENIC DRIVE | WALKING TOUR

START: Quai des Belges

FINISH: Bd. de la Canebière

DISTANCE: 2.7km/1¾ mi.

DURATION: 3-4hr.

WHEN TO GO: In the morning.

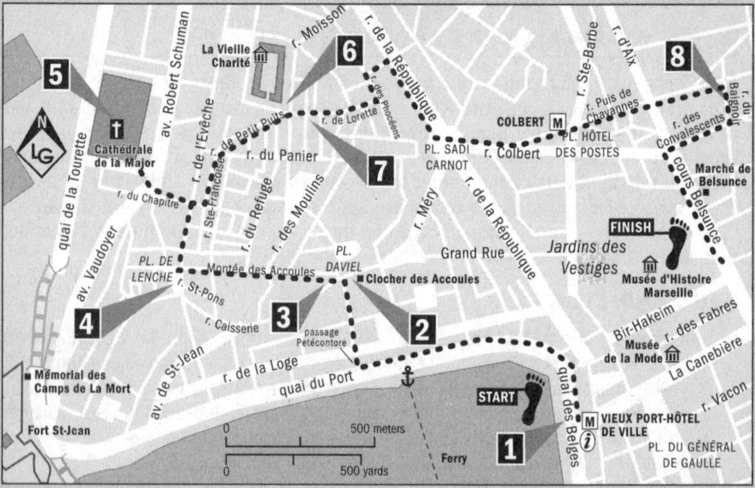

1. QUAI DES BELGES. Every morning the smell of seafood fills the air as fishmongers sell the day's catch along the *vieux port.* At noon, the city cleans up with firehoses.

2. L'EFFET CLOCHETTE. Follow quai du Port to passage Petécontore and head up the stairs. Grab a sandwich, coffee, or ice cream at this small and funky café.

3. CLOCHER DES ACCOULES. Take the staircase to the right of L'Effet Clochette to see the remains of one of Marseille's oldest churches. The towering 11th-century clock has become the symbol of the Panier district.

4. PLACE DE LENCHE. Continue up and left along the Montée des Accoules to pl. de Lenche. Though it's now filled with small cafés and *brasseries,* this square is presumed to be the site of the ancient Greek city center. It offers an excellent view, through modern buildings, of Notre-Dame-de-la-Garde and the *vieux port.*

5. CATHÉDRALE DE LA MAJOR. From pl. de Lenche, bear right on rue de l'Evêché, then left onto rue de Chapitre. The huge Roman-Byzantine cathedral appears suddenly on the coast. Built under the direction of Napoleon III, it contains beautiful mosaics.

6. VIEILLE CHARITÉ. Built between 1671 and 1749, the Vieille Charité was first an orphanage and a home for the poor. It now houses the Musée d'Archéologie, the Musée d'Arts Africain, Océanien, et Amérindien, and a small cinema.

7. ARTERRA. One of many shops on rue Petit Puits that perpetuates the 200-year-old Marseille tradition of *santon* making. This workshop demonstrates how *santons* (nativity figurines) are made, from the first mold to the finishing touches.

8. RUE DU BAIGNOIR. You'll glimpse the miniature Arc de Triomphe if you look left as you cross rue d'Aix on rue Puvis de Chavannes. Continue straight as the street changes to rue des Dominicaines, until you arrive at rue du Baignoir. The small shops in this neighborhood sell goods from North Africa, ranging from vibrant fabrics to fragrant incense.

FESTIVALS

From city-wide, month-long celebrations to local weekend *fêtes*, Marseille's festivals showcase the city's diverse culture. Ciné Plein-Air presents free outdoor movies from June to August at 9:30pm (☎91 07 99; www.cinetilt.org). Experience the International Documentary Film Festival in June at cinemas throughout Marseille. (☎04 95 04 44 90; www.fidmarseille.org. €6.) The Lesbian and Gay Pride March occurs in late June, while July's Festival Folklore du Château-Gombert highlights regional folkloric traditions. The Festival de Marseille, focused on dance, arrives during the first half of July, and late July brings Jazz des Cinq Continents, featuring jazz artists from all over the world. From September to December, visitors can enjoy the Festival de Musique, a jubilee of jazz, classical, and pop music at l'Abbaye de St-Victor. Pick up a Festival Guide from the tourist office or L'Espace Culture (see Practical Information, p. 654) for info.

PROVENCE

DAYTRIPS FROM MARSEILLE

LES CALANQUES

The G.A.C.M., 1 quai des Belges (☎55 50 09), operates 3-4hr. boat trips along Les Calanques to Cassis and back (mid-June to Sept. daily 9:30am, with a stop in Friou 2, 2:30pm; mid-July to Sept. W 9:30am and 2pm, Sa-Su 2pm; €25, ages 6-15 €18, ages 3-5 €13). Tickets are available at the tourist office. Raskas Kayak organizes kayak expeditions leaving from "Auberge de Jeunesse Marseille Bonneveinne," at the end of bus line #20. (☎73 27 16; www.raskas-kayak.com. 3hr.; 9am, 1, 5pm; €30.)

Centuries ago, glacial erosion, sea level fluctuations, and climatic change shaped the southern coasts of the *calanques* (kah-lahnk) into a string of magnificent rock formations. This region stretches from Marseille to Toulon and provides spectacular natural scenery. Plunging limestone cliffs shelter a fragile balance of terrestrial and marine animals and plants, including foxes and peregrine falcons. They also serve as Marseille's largest outdoor playground for scuba divers, mountain climbers, and cliff divers. If heights aren't your thing, get your thrills by going *au naturel* at one of the nude beaches along the coast. The *calanques* are very windy, so check the weather forecast before making plans; boat trips are sometimes cancelled.

Hiking is possible, though most of the 28km national trail between Marseille and Cassis (the GR98) is only recommended for those with considerable experience. Others can simply pick a *calanque*, admire the view, and get their feet wet. Before planning to go on foot, call ☎0 811 20 13 13, a multilingual automated system that provides info on fire risks and opening times for the *calanques* the following day (black means closed, red means open 6-11am, and green or orange means open all day); call after 7pm for the most up-to-date information. Forget about camping and abandon any fire-producing objects (lighters, cigarettes, etc.), all of which are forbidden; in summer, the *massif* is also closed to cars. The most spectacular—and most visited—*calanques* are those of **Sormiou** (bus #23), **Morgiou** (bus #22), and **Luminy** (bus #21). All buses leave from subway station "Rond-Point du Prado" and cost €1.70; for each, a 45-60min. walk from the bus stop leads to stunning views of the coast, distant Marseille, and the turquoise waters down below. The directionally challenged can join a small group led by a professional **guide** (Jan.-June and mid Sept. to Dec. F 2-5pm, Sa 9am-noon; €13; sign up at the tourist office).

CASSIS

Only 23km from Marseille, Cassis is accessible by bus and train. Buses leave from rue du Prado, past the Castellane Metro (40-60min., 9 per day 9:15am-7:30pm, €2.70.) Trains run at later hours (15-20min.; 24 per day from Marseille 6am-11:06pm, 26 per day from Cassis 5:17am-10:04pm; €4.70, students €3.60). For a taxi from the train station to town (€8-10), call ☎04 42 01 78 96. By bus, take the #2 shuttle (dir.: Gendarmerie, €0.80). From the stop, take a right onto av. du Professeur Leriche and then the second right at the roundabout onto av. de l'Arène. Walk 5min. towards the beach and find the tourist office to the right on quai des Moulins. (☎04 42 01 71 17. Open July-Aug. M-F 9am-7pm, Sa-Su 9:30am-12:30pm and 3-6pm; Sept.-June M-F 9:30am-12:30pm and 1:30-5:30pm, Sa 10am-12:30pm and 1:30pm-5pm, Su 10am-12:30pm.)

With slopes above and an emerald-green port below, Cassis (kah-seess) is a network of winding staircases, slender alleyways, and thick gardens. Wine enthusiasts will enjoy sampling delicate *rosés* from the 14 vineyards that surround the town.

To explore the renowned *calanques* of Cassis, pick up a map from the tourist office and follow the signs to **Port Miou** (30min., following the GR98-51 marked in red and white). The trail continues to the **Calanque de Port-Pin** (30min.). From there, scramble up the green-marked rocky trail and down towards the beach of the stunning **Calanque En Vau** (45min.). Though this last trail is steep, the view of limestone cliffs dropping thousands of feet into the water makes every step worth it. Still, the trail is probably best for experienced hikers or climbers. Avoid getting too close to the cliffside on days with strong winds, and bring water since there are no sources in the *massif*. Grabbing picnic supplies from the **Petit Casino,** 2 rue Victor Hugo, is also advisable for those mid-trail munchies. (☎04 42 01 70 56. Open M-Sa 8am-12:30pm and 3:30-7:30pm, Su 8am-12:30pm and 4-7pm. MC/V.)

Boats leaving from the Cassis port can take you to 3-9 *calanques*. (45-60min., every 30min. for 3 *calanques*, less frequently for more; departures Feb.-Oct. 9:30am-5pm or 6pm; €12-19. Buy tickets at the yellow stands in the port or on board. Cash only). Explore the crystalline water with a kayak at **Club Sports Loisirs Nautiques,** plage de la Grande Mer (☎04 42 01 80 01; culturel.cassis@wanadoo.fr; single kayak €40 per day, double €65), or see the cliffs on a boat tour (☎04 42 01 90 83; 1½hr.; Feb. to mid-Nov.; €11-16, under 10 €6.50-13; cash only). The *calanques* are known for great diving; for information, contact **Narval Plongée,** 11 av. de la Viguerie. (☎04 42 01 87 59; www.narval-plongee.com. €25-55; equipment rental €15. MC/V.) Food and wine connoisseurs will enjoy Cassis's festivals. In early September, dances and a parade, complete with costumes and horses, animate the **Fête du Vin.** On the last weekend of June, the **Fête des pêcheurs et de la mer** celebrates Cassis's original source of income: fish.

AIX-EN-PROVENCE ☎04 42

In Aix-en-Provence (ECKS-ahn-proh-vahnss; pop. 170,000) there seems to be a bubbling fountain at the end of every winding street. The *Aixois* are proud to share their *rues*, and rightly so: this is the city of Paul Cézanne, Victor Vasarely, and Emile Zola, where nearly every golden facade or dusty café has had a brush with greatness. Ambling through the picturesque streets, it's easy to understand the source of their inspiration. Aix lacks a symbol like the arenas of Nîmes and Arles or the papal palace of Avignon; its attractions are more diffuse. That doesn't deter tourists, however, who continue to arrive in droves. The best time to visit Aix is outside of July and August; fewer tourists crowd the streets, and a student population of more than 40,000 fuels hip, diverse nightlife.

TRANSPORTATION

Trains: At the end of av. Victor Hugo, off impasse Gustave Desplace. Ticket window open daily 6am-7:55pm. Reservations and info offices open M-Sa 9am-6pm. Almost every

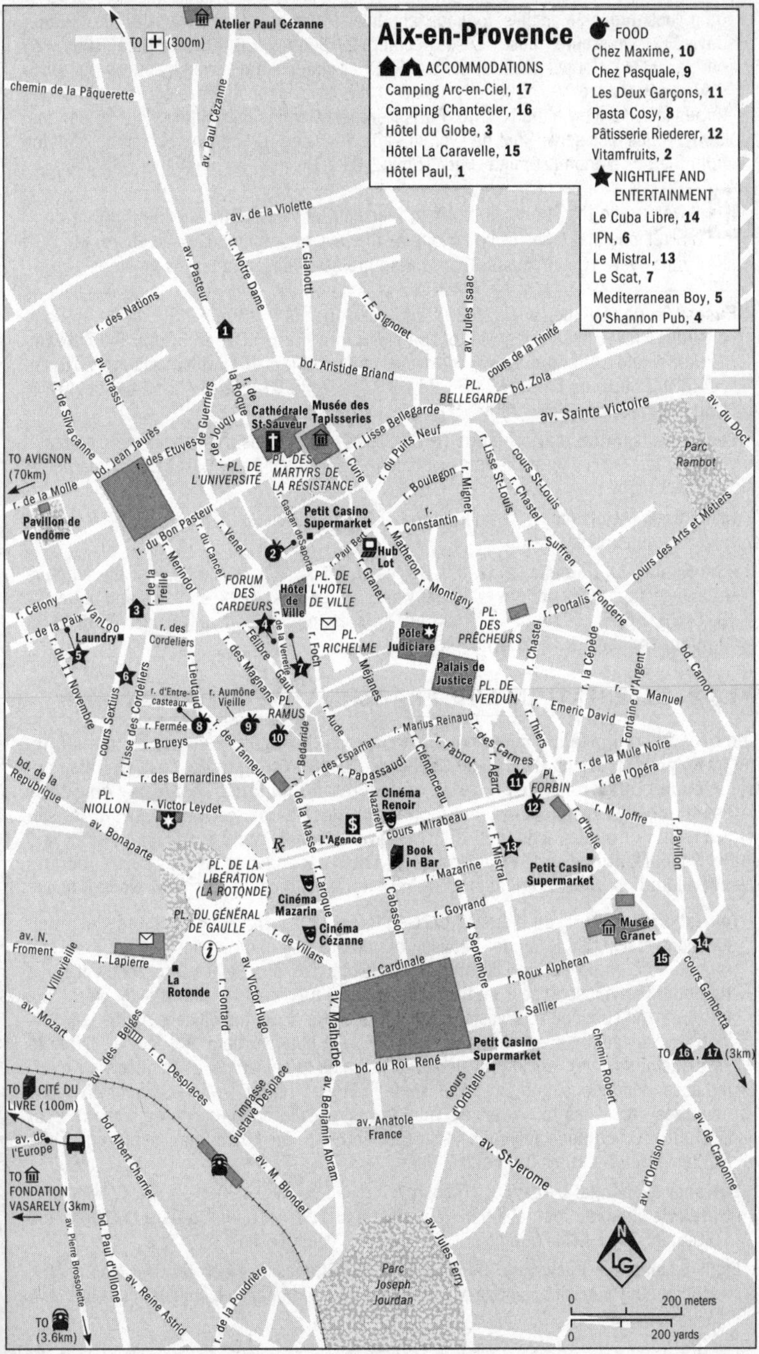
Aix-en-Provence
ACCOMMODATIONS
Camping Arc-en-Ciel, 17
Camping Chantecler, 16
Hôtel du Globe, 3
Hôtel La Caravelle, 15
Hôtel Paul, 1
FOOD
Chez Maxime, 10
Chez Pasquale, 9
Les Deux Garçons, 11
Pasta Cosy, 8
Pâtisserie Riederer, 12
Vitamfruits, 2
NIGHTLIFE AND ENTERTAINMENT
Le Cuba Libre, 14
IPN, 6
Le Mistral, 13
Le Scat, 7
Mediterranean Boy, 5
O'Shannon Pub, 4
Atelier Paul Cézanne
TO (300m)
chemin de la Pâquerette
av. Paul Cézanne
av. de la Violette
av. Pasteur
tr. Notre Dame
r. Gianotti
r. E. Signoret
av. Jules Isaac
cours de la Trinité
r. des Nations
av. Grassi
r. de Silvacanne
bd. Aristide Briand
PL. BELLEGARDE
bd. Zola
av. Sainte Victoire
av. du Doct
Parc Rambot
Cathédrale St-Sauveur
Musée des Tapisseries
r. Lisse Bellegarde
r. du Puits Neuf
TO AVIGNON (70km)
bd. Jean Jaurès
r. des Etuves
r. des Guerriers
r. de Jouqu
r. de la Roque
PL. DE L'UNIVERSITÉ
PL. DES MARTYRS DE LA RÉSISTANCE
r. Curie
r. Boulegon
r. Mignet
r. Lisse St-Louis
cours St-Louis
r. Chastel
cours des Arts et Métiers
r. de la Molle
Pavillon de Vendôme
r. du Bon Pasteur
r. Venel
r. Gaston de Saporta
Petit Casino Supermarket
r. Constantin
r. Suffren
r. Paul Bert
Hub Lot
r. Matheron
r. Merindol
r. du Cancel
r. de la Treille
FORUM DES CARDEURS
Hôtel de Ville
PL. DE L'HOTEL DE VILLE
r. Granet
r. Montigny
PL. DES PRÊCHEURS
r. Portalis
r. Fonderie
r. Célony
r. VanLoo
r. de la Paix
Laundry
r. des Cordeliers
r. Félibre Gaut
r. de la Verrerie
PL. RICHELME
r. Foch
Pôle Judiciare
r. Chastel
r. la Cépède
bd. Carnot
r. du 11 Novembre
cours Sextius
r. Lisse des Cordeliers
r. Lieutaud
r. des Magnans
Méjanes
Palais de Justice
PL. DE VERDUN
r. Fontaine d'Argent
r. Manuel
r. d'Entrecasteaux
r. Aumône Vieille
PL. RAMUS
r. Aude
r. Emeric David
r. Fermée
r. Brueys
r. des Tanneurs
r. Bedaride
r. Marius Reinaud
r. des Carmes
r. Thiers
r. de la Mule Noire
bd. de la République
r. des Bernardines
r. des Espariat
r. Papassaudi
r. Clémenceau
r. Fabrot
r. Agard
PL. FORBIN
r. de l'Opéra
PL. NIOLLON
r. Victor Leydet
r. de la Masse
r. Nazareth
Cinéma Renoir
r. M. Joffre
r. d'Italie
r. Pavillon
av. Bonaparte
L'Agence
cours Mirabeau
Book in Bar
r. F. Mistral
PL. DE LA LIBÉRATION (LA ROTONDE)
r. Mazarine
Petit Casino Supermarket
r. Laroque
Cinéma Mazarin
r. du 4 Septembre
r. Cabassol
r. Goyrand
PL. DU GÉNÉRAL DE GAULLE
Cinéma Cézanne
Musée Granet
av. N. Froment
r. Lapierre
r. de Villars
r. Villevieille
La Rotonde
r. Cardinale
r. Roux Alpheran
cours Gambetta
av. Mozart
r. Gontard
av. Victor Hugo
av. Malherbe
r. Sallier
av. des Belges
r. G. Desplaces
Petit Casino Supermarket
chemin Robert
TO 16, 17 (3km)
bd. du Roi René
cours d'Orbitelle
TO CITÉ DU LIVRE (100m)
impasse Gustave Desplace
av. Benjamin Abram
av. Anatole France
av. de l'Europe
bd. Albert Charrier
av. M. Blondel
av. St-Jerome
av. d'Oraison
av. de Craponne
TO FONDATION VASARELY (3km)
av. Pierre Brossolette
bd. Paul d'Ollone
av. Jules Ferry
Parc Joseph Jourdan
av. Reine Astrid
r. de la Poudrière
TO (3.6km)
N
LG
0
200 meters
0
200 yards

train goes through Marseille; look for schedules at the office. To **Cannes** (3½hr., 25 per day, €32), **Marseille** (mostly buses; 45min., 27 per day, €6.50), and **Nice** (3-4hr., 25 per day, €35). Routes marked "car" on SNCF's schedule are served by buses. The **Gare d'Aix-en-Provence TGV,** 20min. outside of the city, connects travelers to major cities throughout France via the TGV. To: **Paris Aéroport Charles de Gaulle** (3½hr., 5 per day, €90). Trains also serve Gare de Lyon in Paris. The Gare TGV can be reached by shuttles from the bus station (20min., every 15min., €3.70).

> **TIP** Don't take the "train" from Aix to Marseille or vice-versa; you'll end up on an SNCF bus that takes twice as long as the *navette* from the *Gare Routière,* which runs every 10min., costs €2 less than the SNCF bus, and makes no stops.

Buses: Av. de l'Europe (☎91 26 80). Info desk open M-F 7:30am-7:30pm, Sa 7:30am-6:30pm. Ticket desk open M-F 6:15am-7:30pm, Sa 6:30am-6:30pm, Su 7:30am-12:30pm and 1:30-6pm. Heavy commuter traffic to **Marseille,** with buses every 10min. (€4.60). **Phocéens Cars** (☎04 93 85 66 61) goes to **Cannes** (1¾hr.; 5 per day; €26, students €18) and **Nice** (2¼hr.; 5 per day; €26, students €18).

Public Transportation: Aix-en-Bus (☎26 37 28) runs buses throughout the city. Maps and *carnets* available at the tourist office M-Sa 8:30am-5pm. Ticket €1.10, *carnet* of 10 €7.70, day pass €3.70.

Taxis: Radio Aixois (☎27 71 11). Base €1.90; €1.40 per km during the day, €1.82 at night and on holidays. 24hr.

Bike Rental: La Rotonde, 2 av. des Belges (☎26 78 92), at the back of the furniture exchange store. €20 per day, €30 per weekend, €60 per week; students and under 12 €18/26/56; €160 deposit. Includes helmet, pump, and repair kit. Open M-Sa 9:30am-1pm and 2:30-6:30pm. MC/V.

ORIENTATION AND PRACTICAL INFORMATION

The broad and appealing **cours Mirabeau** sweeps through the center of town, linking **La Rotonde (place du Général de Gaulle)** with **place Forbin** to the east. On this central avenue, traffic rolls past a series of decorated fountains, separating countless cafés on one side from classy shops on the other. The pedestrian *vieille ville* sits within a ring of boulevards including **boulevard Carnot, cours Sextius,** and **boulevard du Roi René.** Boutiques and restaurants line the twisting side streets north of cours Mirabeau and create a magical atmosphere at night, particularly near **place Ramus.**

Tourist Office: 2 pl. du Général de Gaulle (☎16 11 61; www.aixenprovencetourism.com), facing La Rotonde, between av. des Belges and av. Victor Hugo. From the bus station, go up av. de l'Europe, turn left onto av. des Belges, and follow it to La Rotonde. The tourist office is on the right. From the train station, walk straight on av. Victor Hugo and continue as it veers to the left to La Rotonde; the office is on the left. Provides multilingual guides and maps and the *Visa pour Aix* card (€2; not available to students or seniors), which provides reduced rates to museums, assistance with booking accommodations, and city tours, some in English (€8, €4 with *Visa pour Aix*). Also organizes excursions to Provence's rural towns, a good option for those without a car (€28-56). Office open July-Aug. M-Sa 8:30am-9pm, Su 10am-8pm; Sept.-June M-Sa 8:30am-8pm, Su 10am-1pm and 2-6pm.

Currency Exchange: L'Agence, 15 cours Mirabeau (☎26 93 93 or 26 84 77). Accepts **traveler's checks.** Open M-F 9am-12:30pm and 1:30-6:30pm, Sa 9am-12:30pm and 1:30-5pm. 24hr. **ATMs** line cours Mirabeau and cours Sextius.

English-Language Bookstore: Book in Bar, 1 rue Cabassol (☎26 60 07). Also a café. Hosts monthly English-language readings and book signings, a bilingual book club, and musical performances. Monthly exhibitions feature local artists. Open M-Sa 9am-7pm. Also visit the **Cité du Livre** (see **Sights,** p. 669).

Laundromat: Laverie, 35 cours Sextius. Wash €3-6.20, dry €0.50 per 5min. Open Tu-Su 7am-8pm.

Police: 10 av. de l'Europe (☎93 97 00), near the Cité du Livre. Call here for the **pharmacie de garde.**

Crisis Lines: Call **SOS Médecins** (☎26 24 00) or **Médecins de Garde** (☎26 40 40) for 24hr. medical advice. **Service des Etrangers** (☎96 89 00) aids foreigners.

Poison Control: ☎04 91 75 25 25.

Hospital: Centre Hospitalier Général du Pays d'Aix, av. Tamaris (☎33 50 00; urgent care 33 90 28). **Ambulance** (☎21 37 37 or 21 14 15).

Internet Access: Hub Lot Cybercafé, 17 rue Paul Bert (☎21 37 31). €0.06 per min., €3.60 per hr. Wi-Fi available. Open M-Sa 10am-10pm.

Post Office: 2 rue Lapierre (☎16 01 50). Open M-F 8:30am-6:45pm, Sa 8:30am-noon. **Currency exchange.** Annex at 1 pl. de l'Hôtel de Ville (☎17 10 40) has the same services. Both open M and W-F 8am-6:30pm, Tu 8am-12:15pm and 1:30-6:30pm, Sa 8am-noon. **Postal Code:** 13100.

PROVENCE

ACCOMMODATIONS AND CAMPING

There are few inexpensive hotels near the city center, and during festival season all accommodations may be booked. Travelers hoping to find lodging in July should reserve as early as March or April, or hope for cancellations. The tourist office can reserve rooms and provide information on guest houses and nearby châteaux; visit www.aixenprovencetourism.com to make your own reservations. Campgrounds and basic chain hotels lie on the outskirts of Aix.

Hôtel Paul, 10 av. Pasteur (☎23 23 89; hotel.paul@wanadoo.fr). Clean, bright rooms with floral bedspreads at one of Aix's cheapest options. Guests can eat breakfast in the garden. Arrive before 6pm or forfeit your room. Breakfast €5. Singles and doubles with toilet and shower €40, with garden view €50; triples €62; quads €72. Cash only. ❸

Hôtel La Caravelle, 29 bd. du Roi René (☎21 53 05; www.lacaravelle-hotel.com). Cheery, recently renovated, and moderately sized rooms overlook a small, tangled garden. Large windows let in plenty of light. Some rooms with A/C; those without have fans. Breakfast €6.50. Reception 24hr. Singles with shared toilet €45; doubles €65, with garden view €70; quads €90, 1 wheelchair-accessible. AmEx/MC/V. ❹

Hôtel du Globe, 74 cours Sextius (☎26 03 58; www.hotelduglobe.com). These expensive rooms are spacious and well-lit, with colorful décor, pristine bathrooms, and TV. Some balconies. Sunny terrace on 5th fl. boasts a view of the Cathédrale St-Sauveur. Breakfast buffet €8.50. Parking €9. Reception 24hr. Singles €36, with shower €39; doubles with shower and toilet €65-69; triples €89; quads €95. Extra bed €9. June-Sept. add €4-6 to all rooms for A/C. AmEx/MC/V. ❸

Camping Arc-en-Ciel, rte. de Nice (☎26 14 28), 3km from the city center. Take bus #3 from "La Rotonde" to "Trois Sautets." The Roman *Pont des Trois Sautets,* immortalized by Cézanne, spans the river near this picturesque site. Swimming pool. Reception 8:30-11am and 3-8pm. €6.10 per person, €5.60 per site. Electricity €3.10. ❶

Camping Chantecler, Val St-André (☎26 12 98; www.campingchantecler.com), by rte. de Nice, is 3km from the city center. Take bus #3 (dir.: Val St-André) from "La Rotonde" to "Val St-André." Campsites on a quiet, wooded hill; several have views of Mont Ste-Victoire. Pool, restaurant, and bar. Reception 2-6pm. July-Aug. €14 per site, including one person; Apr.-June and Sept. €13; Oct.-Mar. €12. ❶

FOOD

Aix boasts a comprehensive selection of international and *provençal* cuisine, including many Italian and Vietnamese restaurants. The food may be good, but the candy is better. The city's staple *bonbon* is the *calisson d'Aix*, an iced almond-and-candied-melon treat. Other specialties include *merveilles de Provence* (pralines with kirsch and chocolate) and nougat candies. Stop by **Pâtisserie Riederer,** 67 cours Mirabeau, to sample *merveilles*. At dinnertime, tables crowd **rue de la Verrerie, place de L'Hôtel de Ville,** and **place Richelme.** For a place to see and be seen, nothing is better than one of the cafés lining **cours Mirabeau.** Markets with fruits, vegetables and regional products are on **place de la Mairie** (open Tu, Th, Sa 7am-1pm), **place de l'Hôtel de Ville,** and **place Richelme** (open daily 7am-1pm). Three **Petit Casinos** serve all your supermarket needs: 3 cours d'Orbitelle (open M-Sa 8am-1pm and 4-8pm); 16 rue d'Italie (open Tu-Sa 8am-8pm, Su 8am-1pm); and 5 rue Gaston de Saporta (open M-F 8:30am-1pm and 3-7:30pm, Sa 8:30am-7:30pm).

Pasta Cosy, 5 rue d'Entrecasteaux (☎38 02 28). With the subtitle "Noodles of the World," this restaurant is not shy about its taste for pasta of all shapes and nationalities. Pasta-filled banisters, cheese-graters-turned-lampshades, and a rolling pin coat rack make the theme clear. Go for the *fiochetti* (€15), with caramelized pears and a gorgonzola cream sauce. Noodles €13-25. Open M-Sa 7pm-midnight. MC/V. ❸

Vitamfruits, 2 rue Bedarride (☎06 03 08 17 33). For an afternoon snack, nothing beats a cheap nutella *crêpe* (€2) or fresh fruit drink (€3) from this small concession stand, which manages to stand out from the crowd. Try the peach-raspberry-lemon juice, blended before your eyes. Cheese *crêpe* €3. Open July-Aug. M-Sa 9am-8pm; Sept.-June M-Sa 10:30am-7:30pm, Su 10am-7pm. Cash only. ❶

Chez Pasquale, 7 rue Aumône Vieille (☎38 04 94). Grab a quick but carefully presented salad or panini at this cheap café. Escape the heat downstairs or enjoy the street life at tables outside. Paninis with green salad €4.50-8. Salads €6-8. Dinner prices €2 higher. Open M-Sa 11am-midnight, Su 7pm-midnight. Cash only. ❷

Chez Maxime, 12 pl. Ramus (☎26 28 51). Carefully crafted *provençal* dishes, well worth the steep prices, don a pinkish glow under Maxime's red canopy. Delicious fresh meats, an extensive wine menu, and the lavender *crème brûlée* (€6.70) make this place stand out. During lunch, an *entrée, plat,* dessert, and glass of wine are just €13. *Plats* €13-23. *Menus* €19-27. Open Tu-Sa 12:30-2pm and 6-10:30pm. AmEx/MC/V. ❹

Les Deux Garçons, 54 cours Mirabeau (☎26 00 51). The former watering hole of Cézanne and Zola, this upscale café charges a hefty price for its artistic pedigree and prime location on cours Mirabeau. Try the specialty *chocolat chaud* (€5). Coffee and a pastry €8.50. Lunch *formules* €15-20. Open daily 7am-2am. AmEx/MC/V. ❸

SIGHTS

Nearly every corner of Aix is marked by a timeworn mansion or elaborate facade, so wandering is the best way to savor the city's charm. Maps from the tourist office provide interesting facts on the city's various squares, markets, and fountains.

MUSÉE GRANET. The large and excellent collection here includes nearly 600 works, with an emphasis on the French school from the 17th to the 19th century. One room contains nine oil paintings by Aix's favorite son, Cézanne. *(Pl. Saint-Jean de Matte. ☎52 87 97; www.museegranet-aixenprovence.fr. Open Tu-Su June-Sept. 11am-7pm; Oct.-May noon-6pm. €4, students €2, under 18 free.)*

FONDATION VASARELY. This trippy black-and-white museum stands in stark contrast to the rolling green hills of the surrounding countryside. Designed in the

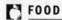

1970s by Hungarian-born artist Victor Vasarely, the father of optical illusion art, the building resembles a beehive from above and displays some of Vasarely's monumental work in eight huge hexagonal spaces. *(Av. Marcel-Pagnol, Jas-de-Bouffan. Take bus #4 from "Rotonde Poste," across from the tourist office, to "Vasarely." ☎ 20 01 09; www.fondationvasarely.fr. Open Apr.-Oct. M-Sa 10am-6pm; Nov.-Mar. Tu-Sa 10am-6pm. €7, students and ages 7-18 €4, under 7 free. Audio tours available in English, French, and German; €2.30.)*

CHEMIN DE CÉZANNE. Golden markers trace the footsteps of the artist on a self-guided 2hr. walking tour. Explore the haunts of Aix's favorite son, including his birthplace and favorite cafés. Each stop along the *chemin* has a reproduction of the work that he painted there, so you can compare his art to the actual landscapes that inspired him. To visit Cézanne's studio, the **Atelier Paul Cézanne,** where his overcoat and beret still hang in the corner, reserve a day ahead at the tourist office. In summer, music and projected images of Cezanne's art fill the garden at night. *(Atelier at 9 av. Paul Cézanne. Take bus #1 from "St-Christophe" to "la Rotonde," or walk 10min. uphill on av. Paul Cézanne. ☎ 21 06 53; www.atelier-cezanne.com. Open daily July-Aug. 10am-6pm; Apr.-June and Sept. 10am-noon and 2-6pm; Oct.-Mar. 10am-noon and 2-5pm. €5.50, students €2, under 13 free. Walking tour maps available at the tourist office.)*

PROVENCE

CATHÉDRALE ST-SAUVEUR. A mix of Roman, Romanesque, Gothic, and Baroque styles, this church is pure architectural whimsy. During the Revolution, angry *Aixois* chopped off the heads of the statues. They were re-capitated in the 19th century, albeit without necks. *(34 pl. des Martyrs de la Résistance, at pl. de l'Université. ☎ 23 45 65. Open daily 8am-noon and 2-6pm, except during funerals, Sa weddings, and Su services.)*

CITÉ DU LIVRE. Huge replicas of major French tomes mark the entry to this former match factory, now a cultural center. The **Bibliothèque Méjanes** is the second largest library in the region and contains ancient volumes from the personal collection of the Marquis de Méjanes, as well as British and American literature. *(Open Tu and Th-F noon-6pm, W and Sa 10am-6pm.)* World music is available for rent in the **Discotheque** section. Check the information desk for a schedule of films shown at the center's auditorium. *(8-10 rue des Allumettes, southeast of La Rotonde. From the tourist office, go down av. des Belges to a traffic circle, then turn right onto bd. Victor Coq, which ends at the entrance. ☎ 91 98 88. Borrowing from the Bibliothèque requires a €26 membership.)*

OTHER SIGHTS. A fine collection of 17th- and 18th-century tapestries is in the **Musée des Tapisseries,** the former seat of the clergy of Aix. Don't miss the series showing the misadventures of Don Quixote. *(Palais Archiépiscopal, 2nd fl., 28 pl. des Martyrs de la Résistance. ☎ 23 09 91 or 91 88 75. Open mid-May to mid-Oct. M and W-Su 10am-6pm; mid-Oct. to mid-May M and W-Su 10am-12:30pm and 1:30-5pm. €2, under 25 free. July-Aug. free tours in French and English F 3pm.)* Antique lovers may enjoy the 17th-century **Pavillon de Vendôme,** originally the lavish residence of a noble family. Today, it is a small museum housing paintings and furniture from the turn of the 18th century. The highlight of the Pavilion is the beautifully landscaped courtyard, lined with benches and trees. *(13 rue de la Molle and 32 rue Célony. ☎ 91 88 75. Museum same hours as Musée des Tapisseries. €2, under 25 free. Gardens open daily 9am-5:30pm. Free.)*

ENTERTAINMENT AND NIGHTLIFE

Crowds of students during the year and festival-goers in summer make partying a year-round pastime in Aix. Nightlife picks up on Tuesday and rocks the town until Saturday. Locals and visitors can be found in pubs until closing at 2am, when the party moves to Aix's clubs. **Rue de la Verrerie** has the highest concentration of bars and clubs, while lanterns sway in the breeze at cafés along the **Forum des Cardeurs,** behind the Hôtel de Ville. French and foreign films, all in the original language with French subtitles, screen at **Cinémas Mazarin,** 6 rue Laroque; **Cézanne,** 1 rue

Marcel Guillaume; and **Renoir,** 24 cours Mirabeau. (☎08 92 68 72 70; www.lescinemasaixois.com. €8; students, seniors, under 16, and the unemployed €7. MC/V.) Gay travelers have few options in Aix; many head to Marseille for nightlife.

IPN, 42 cours Sextius (www.ipn-aix.com). Head down the stairs and under the small red sign to party in this cave-like bar, a haven for foreign students–especially Americans, Brits, and Swedes. With live music most nights and soccer on TV during important matches, the intimate environment is perfect for a beer (€3-5) or a specialty wine cocktail (€5). Shots 1 for €2, 5 for €8. Open Tu-Sa 6pm-4am. Cash only.

Le Mistral, 3 rue F. Mistral (☎38 16 49). This neon-lit dance club has kept Aix's students hopping for 56 years with techno, R&B, and house. Expect pricey drinks, and don't arrive in shorts, jeans, or sandals. Cover €15. Open Tu-Sa 10:30pm-5am. MC/V.

Le Cuba Libre, 4 bd. Carnot (☎63 05 21). This vibrant bar with red accents brings a taste of island life to southern France with cigars and tropical mixed drinks, and salsa, hip hop, and rock spun by DJ Xcess. The specialty is its namesake, Le Cuba Libre (€6). Mixed drinks €6-12. Salsa lessons 9-11pm. Happy hour 6-9pm. Open M-Sa 5pm-2am. Cash only.

O'Shannon Pub, 30 rue de la Verrerie (☎23 31 63; www.oshannonaix.fr). Like any imitation Irish pub worth its green beer, O'Shannon comes complete with Guinness signs on wooden walls and barrels doubling as high tables. A perfect spot for getting the night started with friends, as tables are available both inside and out. Beer €3-5.50. Mixed drinks €5-9. Shots €2.50. Open M-Sa 10am-2am. AmEx/MC/V.

Le Scat, 11 rue Verrerie (☎23 00 23; lescatclub.aix.free.fr). A sophisticated crowd enjoys rock at free concerts in the funky basement, while a DJ mixes in another room. Things heat up at 2am. Beer €4.60. Mixed drinks €13. Open Tu-Sa 10pm-5:30am. Cash only.

Mediterranean Boy, 6 rue de la Paix (☎27 21 47; www.med-boy.com). Aix offers little in the way of gay nightlife apart from this tiny bar. Potted miniature palm trees out front and a rainbow flag indicate the theme. The crowd contains all age groups and some women. Beer €2.50. Open daily 9:30pm-2am. Cash only.

FESTIVALS

Aix shimmers year-round with festivals, concerts, and special events. The week-long **Cinestival** kicks things off in June, when screenings of hundreds of French and international films cost just €3.50 with the *Billet Scoop*, a free discount card available at the tourist office. Famous performers and rising stars descend on Aix for the **Festival d'Aix-en-Provence,** a series of operas and orchestral concerts that lasts from June to July. (Ticket office at 11 rue Gaston de Saporta. ☎17 34 34; www.festival-aix.com. Tickets from €8.) In July, the city puts on **Zik Zac Estival,** featuring hip hop, rap, and reggae groups for student crowds at the Théâtre de Verdure. (☎63 10 11. Tickets €15.) **Aix-en-Musique,** 3 pl. John Rewald (☎21 69 69), sponsors concerts year-round, including "Music on Saturday" programs for children. Check with the tourist office for a schedule of all festivals and special events.

AVIGNON ☎04 90

The heart of Avignon (ah-veen-YOHN; pop. 89,500) is a medieval maze replete with fashionable boutiques and old mansions. Looming above the Rhône river is Avignon's architectural jewel—the unparalleled Palais des Papes, a sprawling Gothic fortress known in its time as "the biggest and strongest house in the world." Some 700 years ago, political dissent in Italy led the homesick French Pope Clement V to move the papacy to Avignon. During this period, seven popes erected and expanded the palace, making the city a Rome away from Rome. While foreign visitors fill the city year-round, French tourists descend upon its flyer-filled streets *en masse* in July for its renowned theater festival. Travelers on a strict budget should be prepared for Avignon's tourist-targeted prices.

TRANSPORTATION

Flights: Aéroport Avignon Caumont (AVN; ☎81 51 51; www.avignon.aeroport.fr/fr), 8km from town. Air France flies to **Paris Orly** (4 per day), and Flybe goes to **Southampton** and **Exeter** in the UK (4 per week).

Trains:

Gare Avignon Centre, bd. St-Roch, porte de la République (☎27 81 89). Info and ticket desks open M 6am-9pm, Tu-Su 7am-9pm. To: **Arles** (20min., 25-30 per day, €8.80); **Lyon** (2hr., 7 per day, €31); **Marseille** (1¼hr., 18-22 per day, €28); **Montpellier** (1hr., 13 per day, €15); **Nice** (3-4hr., 5 per day, €52); **Nîmes** (30min., 13-15 per day, €8.10).

TGV departs from a 2nd train station outside of town, in the Quartier de Courtine. A *navette* **shuttle** bus (€1.10) runs every 15-30min. (5:30am-11:20pm) between the 2 train stations; it also stops in front of the post office on rue de la République. Fewer buses on Su. TGV ticket counters open M-Sa 5:30am-9:15pm, Su 6am-9:15pm. To: **Dijon** (3-4hr., 9 per day, €60); **Lyon** (1hr., 14 per day, €42); **Nice** (3hr., 7 per day, €49); **Paris** (3hr., 13 per day, €97).

Buses: Gare Routière, 5 av. Monclar (☎82 07 35). Turn right from the train station. Info desk open M-F 10:15am-1pm and 2-6pm. Buy tickets on bus. **CTM** goes to **Arles** (1hr., 5 per day, €7.10), **Les Baux** (July-Aug. only; 1hr., 5-6 per day, €7.20), and **Marseille** (2hr., 1 per day, €19).

Public Transportation: TCRA, av. de Lattre de Tassigny (☎04 32 74 18 32; www.tcra.fr). Office open M-F 8:30am-12:30pm and 1:30-6pm. Maps available at the tourist office. Tickets (€1.10) sold on the bus, *carnet* of 10 (€9.40) sold at the office.

Boat Shuttle: Navette Fluviale. Follow the signs to the right of Pont d'Avignon. Runs a free shuttle across the Rhône, providing great views of the famous *pont.* Every 15min. July-Aug. daily 11am-9pm; Sept. and Apr.-June daily 10am-12:30pm and 2-6:30pm; Oct.-Dec. and mid-Feb. to Mar. W 2-5:30pm, Sa-Su 10am-noon and 2-6:30pm.

Taxis: Radio Taxi, pl. Pie (☎82 20 20). €12 from the train station to the Auberge Bagatelle. 24hr.

Car Rental: Many offices located in both train stations. **National/Citer** is at the TGV station (☎27 30 07). From €270 for 5 days. Open daily 8am-10pm. AmEx/MC/V.

Bike Rental: Provence Bike, 52 bd. St-Roch (☎27 92 61; www.provence-bike.com), rents bikes and motorbikes at competitive prices. Bikes €9 per day, €39 per week. Mountain bikes €15/75. Scooters €19/155. Open M-Sa 9am-12:30pm and 3-7pm, Su by reservation. AmEx/MC/V. **Holiday Bikes Provence,** 20 bd. St-Roch (☎04 32 76 25 88; www.holiday-bikes.com). Bikes €8 per day, €25 per week. Scooters from €32 per day. Motorcycles from €58 per day. Cash only.

ORIENTATION AND PRACTICAL INFORMATION

Avignon's 14th-century ramparts enclose a delightful yet tourist-infested labyrinth of alleyways, squares, and tiny streets. To reach the tourist office from the train station, walk straight through **porte de la République** onto **cours Jean Jaurès.** The tourist office is 200m up the road on the right. Behind the tourist office, cours Jean Jaurès becomes **rue de la République** and leads directly to **place de l'Horloge,** Avignon's central square, below the looming Palais des Papes.

Tourist Office: 41 cours Jean Jaurès (☎04 32 74 32 74; www.avignon-tourisme.com). Staff provides maps and a sights pass. Open July M-Sa 9am-7pm, Su 10am-5pm; Aug.-Oct. and Apr.-June M-Sa 9am-5pm, Su 10am-5pm; Nov.-Mar. M-F 9am-6pm, Sa 9am-5pm, Su 10am-noon.

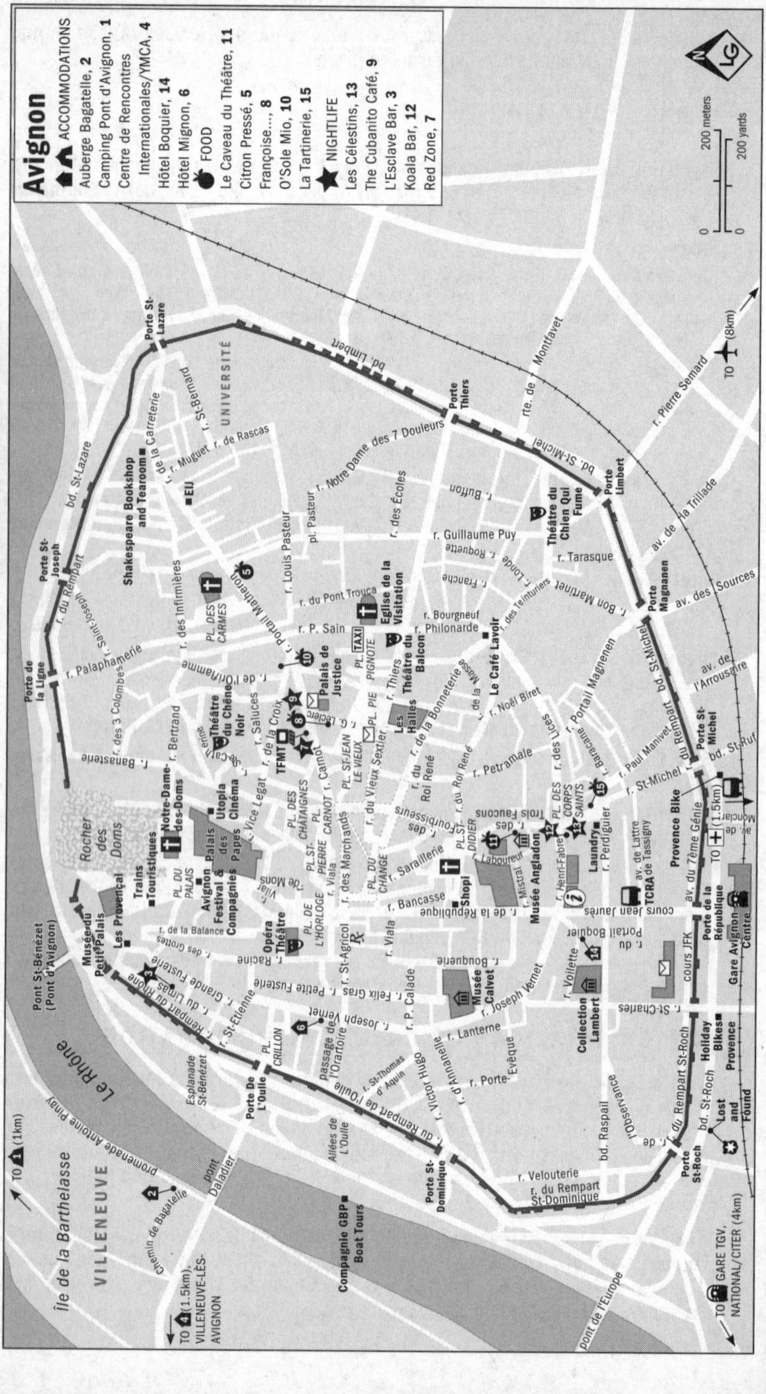
Avignon
ACCOMMODATIONS
Auberge Bagatelle, 2
Camping Pont d'Avignon, 1
Centre de Rencontres Internationales/YMCA, 4
Hôtel Boquier, 14
Hôtel Mignon, 6
FOOD
Le Caveau du Théâtre, 11
Citron Pressé, 5
Françoise..., 8
O'Sole Mio, 10
La Tartinerie, 15
NIGHTLIFE
Les Célestins, 13
The Cubanito Café, 9
L'Esclave Bar, 3
Koala Bar, 12
Red Zone, 7
200 meters
200 yards
Le Rhône
Île de la Barthelasse
VILLENEUVE
Rocher des Doms
UNIVERSITÉ
Palais des Papes
Notre-Dame-des-Doms
Musée du Petit Palais
Pont St-Bénézet (Pont d'Avignon)
Musée Calvet
Musée Angladon
Collection Lambert
Les Halles
Palais de Justice
Église de la Visitation
Théâtre du Chêne Noir
Théâtre du Balcon
Théâtre du Chien Qui Fume
Opéra Théâtre
Utopia Cinéma
Shakespeare Bookshop and Tearoom
Le Café Lavoir
Trains Touristiques
Les Provençal
Avignon Festival & Compagnies
Compagnie GBP Boat Tours
Provence Bike
Holiday Bikes Provence
Lost and Found
Laundry
TCRA
TFMT
Shopi
EIJ
Gare Avignon Centre
Porte de la République
Porte St-Michel
Porte Magnanen
Porte Limbert
Porte Thiers
Porte St-Lazare
Porte St-Joseph
Porte de la Ligne
Porte De L'Oulle
Porte St-Dominique
Porte St-Roch
pont Daladier
pont de l'Europe
TO GARE TGV, NATIONAL/CITER (4km)
TO (1.5km)
TO (8km)
TO (1km)
TO (1.5km), VILLENEUVE-LÈS-AVIGNON

Tours:

Walking Tours: Tourist office offers 2hr. walking tours W and F-Sa 10am. €7. Themed tours Apr.-Oct. €10-15, under 18 €7.

Train and Bus Tours: Les Trains Touristiques (☎06 11 35 06 66). 45min. tour of the *vieille ville*, ramparts, and the Rocher des Doms garden. Tours leave from the Palais des Papes daily every 20min. July-Aug. 10am-8pm; mid-Mar. to June and Sept.-Oct. 10am-7pm. €7, ages 10-18 €4. **Les Provençales,** 61 rue Grande Fusterie (☎14 70 00; www.provence-reservation.com), near Pont St-Benezet. Half-day excursions by bus June-Aug. €30, year-round by minibus €55-110. Bus tours leave from the company office; minibuses pick up customers where they choose. Same company also runs **Lavender Tours.** Tours visit lavender fields and the lavender museum in Coustellet June-Aug. €40 per half-day, €90 per day. Flight over lavender fields (mid-June to mid-July) from €240; min. 2 people.

Boat Tours: Compagnie G.B.P. (☎85 62 25; www.mireio.net) runs **Mireio Croisières** and **Bâteaux Bus,** which offer boat trips along the Rhône with a visit to Pont St-Benezet. 45min. July-Aug. 5 per day; Apr.-June and Sept. 2 per day. €7.50, with bridge entrance €8. 3 themed Dinner Cruises: the "Arles Cruise," the "Vineyard Cruise," and the "Kingdom Cruise." Include stops in Arles, Tarascon, and Châteauneuf-du-Pape. From €29, with dinner €45-62.

Lost and Found: 13 quai St-Lazare (☎04 32 76 01 73), at Municipal Police Office.

English-Language Bookstore and Book Exchange: Shakespeare Bookshop and Tearoom, 155 rue de la Carreterie (☎27 38 50), down rue Carnot toward the ramparts. Second-hand (€4-6) and new editions (from €4). English cream teas (3 scones and tea; €5). Open Tu-Sa 9:30am-noon and 2-6pm. MC/V.

Youth Information: Espace Info-Jeunes (EIJ), 102 rue de la Carreterie (☎14 04 05). Info on jobs, festivals, study, and housing. Open M-F 8:30am-noon and 1-5pm.

Laundromats: 66 pl. des Corps Saints. Wash €2.40 per 5kg, dry €1 per 16min. Open daily 7am-8pm. **Le Café Lavoir,** 101 rue de la Bonneterie (☎27 91 06; le-cafe-lavoir@wanadoo.fr). A funky café (coffee €1.50, juice €2.50) and laundromat, complete with a tiny art gallery. Wash €4-8, dry €1 per 10min. Open Tu-Sa 10am-6pm; during the Festival d'Avignon daily 10am-midnight.

Police: Bd. St-Roch (☎16 81 00), left of the train station. Call here for the **pharmacie de garde.**

Hospital: 305 rue Raoul Follereau (☎04 32 75 33 33), south of the town center near the TGV station. Open 24hr.

Internet Access: TFMT Cyber Café, 29 rue Carnot (☎04 32 76 02 41). Has some computers with English-language keyboards. €1 per 30min. Open daily 9:30am-midnight.

Post Office: Cours JFK (☎27 54 10), near porte de la République. **Currency exchange.** Western Union. Branch on pl. Pie (☎04 32 74 67 40). Both open M-F 8:30am-6:30pm, Sa 8:30am-noon. **Postal Code:** 84000.

ACCOMMODATIONS AND CAMPING

When the theater troupes hit town, lodging is generally unavailable no matter how many euro you are willing to spend; reserve up to six months in advance for July and August. The tourist office lists organizations that set up cheap housing during the festival; if hotels are full, festival-goers might consider staying in Arles, Nîmes, Orange, or Tarascon and commuting by train (€5.30-7.10).

Hôtel Mignon, 12 rue Joseph Vernet (☎82 17 30; www.hotel-mignon.com). *Provençal* fabrics adorn each comfortable, well-equipped room. Phone, TV, A/C, free Internet access and Wi-Fi, and a central location make this hotel a great deal despite small bathrooms. Breakfast included. Reception 7am-11pm. Singles €38-49, during festival €45-62; doubles €55-60/62-73; triples €66/80; quads €86/100. AmEx/MC/V. ❸

Centre de Rencontres Internationales/YMCA, 7bis chemin de la Justice, Villeneuve (☎25 46 20; www.ymca-avignon.com). Cross pont Daladier and continue past Ile Barthelasse, under the train bridge. At the roundabout, veer left onto chemin de la Justice; the foyer is uphill on your left (35min.). From the post office, take bus #10 (dir.: Les Angles-Grand Angles, M-Sa 2-3 per hr. 6:30am-8pm) to "Général Leclerc," or bus #11 (dir.: Villeneuve-Grand Terme, M-Sa 3 per hr. 6:30am-8pm) to "Pont d'Avignon." On Su, take bus #70 (dir.: Villeneuve-Grand Terme, 5 per day) to "Pont d'Avignon." Plain rooms with comfortable bunk beds are a great deal in July. Breakfast €5, dinner €12. Internet access €3 per hr. Reception 8:30am-6pm; July-Aug. F-Su reception at restaurant. July-Aug. singles €23, with shower and toilet €34; doubles €29/43; triples €34/52; quads €45/52. Sept.-June €19/27/23/35/27/42/36/42. MC/V. ❷

Hôtel Boquier, 6 rue du Portail Boquier (☎82 34 43; www.hotel-boquier.com), near the tourist office. Comfortable rooms, each with their own theme, in an 18th-century home. Private bath, phone, and TV. Breakfast €7. Reception 8am-9pm; owner prefers guests to check-in before 8pm. Reservations recommended. July-Aug. singles €50; doubles €54-64; triples €72; quads €88-90. Festival €58/65-72/85/90-105. Sept.-June €45/48-55/66/72-75. Extra bed €10. MC/V. ❹

Auberge Bagatelle, 25 promenade Antoine Pinay (☎86 30 39), on the edge of Ile de la Barthelasse. From the post office, take bus #10 or 11 to "Ile Piot." A 10min. walk to downtown Avignon, across pont Daladier. Incomparable view of city. You get what you pay for–cramped, barren dorms–at the cheapest option in Avignon. Laundry (wash €2.80 per 5kg), supermarket, 2 restaurants, and bike rental (€15 per 8hr., €18 per day; ID deposit). Sheets €2.50. Internet access €0.15 per min. Reception 7am-2pm and 5-10pm. Lockout 2-5pm. Dorms July-Aug. €13; Sept.-June €12. **Hotel** next door with worn but clean rooms. Singles and doubles €27, with shower €33; quads €50. Basic **camping** facilities in dense shade. Reception 8:30am-8:30pm. Reservations only accepted before May 15. €4.50 per person, €6.50 during festival. 2 people, car, and tent €16/18. Electricity €2.60/3. Water €1.50. MC/V. ❶

Camping Pont d'Avignon, 10 chemin de la Barthelasse (☎80 63 50; www.camping-avignon.com), on the edge of Ile de la Barthelasse. Showers, laundry, restaurant, pool, and tennis courts in a 4-star site that feels like a hotel. 300 shady sites in a quiet park. Also accessible by the Navette Fluviale (see p. 671); when you get off, take the road ahead to the left. Take another left at the main road; the campground will be on your left. Internet access €4 per hr. Reception July-Aug. 8am-10pm; Sept. and June 8:30am-8pm; Oct. and Mar.-May 8:30am-6:30pm. Open Mar.-Oct. 1 person and tent €15, 2 people and tent €22. Extra person €5.10. Electricity €2.60-3.10. MC/V. ❶

FOOD

There's a selection of creative restaurants on the chic **rue des Teinturiers.** The Vietnamese restaurants on side streets throughout the city are great budget options. A walk up **rue Carnot** and **rue de la Carreterie** reveals artisanal bakeries, cheap *sandwicheries*, and reasonably priced *brasseries.* The **Parc du Rocher des Doms,** overlooking the Rhône, provides picturesque picnic spots and has an outdoor café. **Les Halles,** the large indoor market on **place Pie,** promises endless amounts of regional produce, *chèvre* (goat cheese), meats, and wines. (Open Tu-F 6am-1:30pm, Sa-Su 6am-2pm.) For groceries, try the **Shopi** supermarket, 23 rue de la République, 100m from the tourist office. (Open M-Sa 7am-9pm, Su 9am-12:30pm. MC/V.)

Citron Pressé, 38 rue Carreterie (☎86 09 29). This tiny restaurant, fantastically cheap by Avignon's standards, serves basic French fare with some Lebanese and Indian touches. *Plats* €3-7. *Menu* with wine €12. Open M-Th noon-2:30pm, F-Sa noon-2pm and 7:30-11:30pm; during festival daily noon-2am. Cash only. ❷

La Tartinerie, 19 pl. de la Principale (☎82 34 19), serves filling, appealing *tartines* (€4.70-5.90) in many varieties. Try the three-cheese *tartine,* with mozzarella, *chèvre,* and *Fourme d'ambert* melted over pears on a slice of warm toast (€8). Open July daily 11am-midnight; Aug.-June M-Sa 11am-midnight. AmEx/MC/V. ❷

Françoise..., 6 rue Général Leclerc (☎04 32 76 24 77). Gourmet meals in an upscale cafeteria-like setting. Sandwiches and salads (€3-5), as well as full meals (€8-10). The owner welcomes diners with homey dishes, including apple-raspberry crumble (€3.50). Open M-Sa 11:30am-7pm; during festival daily 11am-11pm. AmEx/MC/V over €15. ❶

O'Sole Mio, 23 rue de la Croix (☎27 94 34). Offers first-rate pizzas (€9-11) and pastas (€9-13) at reasonable prices. *Plats* are enough for a meal. Sit on the terrace in summer and try the *gnocchi sorrentina* (€10). Open July daily 11am-2:30pm and 6:30pm-midnight; Aug.-June Tu-Su 11am-2:30pm and 6:30pm-midnight. AmEx/MC/V. ❷

Le Caveau du Théâtre, 16 rue des Trois Faucons (☎82 60 91; www.caveaudutheatre.com). This restaurant is a reliable stop for gourmet *provençal* cuisine. The menu changes every month. Lunch *formule* €11. Dinner *menus* €16-20. Open M-F noon-2pm and 7-10pm, Sa 7-10pm; during festival open daily. MC/V. ❸

PROVENCE

SIGHTS

TIP **PASS AND SCORE.** Most of Avignon's sights operate on a pass system. Pay full admission for entrance to any monument or museum, pick up your pass and get it stamped, and then get a reduced price at the rest of the sights you visit over the next 15 days (20-50% off sights; 30% off some guided tours and up to 20% off tourist excursions).

PALAIS DES PAPES. This golden *palais*, the largest Gothic palace in the world and a **UNESCO World Heritage Sight,** dominates the city. Begun in 1335 by the third pope of Avignon, Benoît XII, it was completed less than 20 years later by his successor, Clément VI. The papal palace is neatly divided into two sections, marked by the contrasting styles of their builders: the strict, spare grandeur of the Cistercian Benoît and the astonishing ostentation of the aristocratic Clément. Following the political unrest of the late 18th century, the castle was turned into a prison in 1790 and served as a barracks until 1906, when it was restored and opened to the public. Revel in the massive **Great Chapel,** whose single nave is 52m long, 15m wide, and 20m tall, typical of the palace's enormous rooms. Don't miss the *Cuisine Haute*, which lives up to its name with a massive chimney. Since 2004, the formerly bare rooms have become home to the **Musée de l'Œuvre,** a permanent display retracing the history of the papacy in Avignon. *(☎27 50 00; www.palais-des-papes.com. Open daily Aug. 9am-9pm; July and Sept. 9am-8pm; Oct. and Apr.-June 9am-7pm; Nov.-Mar. 9:30am-5:45pm. Last entrance 1hr. before closing. Free audio tour in 8 languages. Palace and exhibition €9.50, with pass €7.50. Palace and bridge €11.50, with pass €9.)*

PONT ST-BÉNÉZET. This 12th-century bridge is known to French children as the "Pont d'Avignon," immortalized in the song "Sur le pont d'Avignon." In 1177, Bénézet, a shepherd boy, was commanded by angels to build a bridge across the Rhône. Legend has it that when he announced his mission to the people of Avignon, they called him crazy. The Archbishop, also skeptical, pointed to a gigantic boulder and told Bénézet that he would have to place the first stone himself. Miraculously, the shepherd heaved the rock onto his shoulder and tossed it into the river. This holy shot put convinced the townspeople, who responded with shovels and mortar, finishing the bridge in 1184. Despite the divinely ordained location, the bridge has suffered from warfare and the once-turbulent Rhône. Now it extends only partway across the river. Farther down the river, **Pont Daladier** makes it all the way across, offering free views of the broken bridge. *(☎27 51 16. Open daily Aug. 9am-9pm; July and*

Sept. 9am-8pm; Apr.-June and Oct. 9am-7pm; Nov.-Mar. 9:30am-5:45pm. Free audio tour in 8 languages. July-Sept. €4, with pass €3.30; Oct.-June €3.50.)

MUSÉE DU PETIT PALAIS. Housed in a 600-year-old palace next to the Palais des Papes, this prestigious museum displays a large collection of medieval and Renaissance paintings, as well as Romanesque and Gothic sculptures. Look for Botticelli's *"La Vierge et l'Enfant"* in room XI. *(Palais des Archevêques, pl. du Palais des Papes. ☎86 44 58; musee.petitpalais@mairie-avignon.com. Open M and W-Su June-Sept. 10am-6pm; Oct.-May 9:30am-1pm and 2-5:30pm. €6, students or with pass €3.)*

COLLECTION LAMBERT. Drawing on work from the 1960s to the present, this museum presents three exhibits per year in an 18th-century *hôtel particulier.* Past artists include Sol LeWitt, Nan Goldin, and Basquiat. The museum displays two permanent pieces: a digitized message and a red neon room. *(5 rue Violette. ☎16 56 20; www.collectionlambert.com. Open July daily 11am-7pm; Aug.-June Tu-Su 11am-6pm. Guided tours July daily 3pm, Aug.-June F-Sa 4pm. €5.50, students or with pass €4.)*

PROVENCE

OTHER SIGHTS. On the hill above the Palais, the beautifully sculpted **Parc du Rocher des Doms** has views of Mont Ventoux, St-Bénézet, and the fortifications of Villeneuve; they are well worth the short climb. *(Open dawn-dusk.)* While you're at the Palais, stop in next door at the 12th-century **Cathédrale Notre Dame-des-Doms,** which contains the Gothic tomb of Pope John XXII. Thick columns support the arched ceiling, while intricate sculptures lace its rims. Sneak a peek at the murals in the chapels that sprout from its sides. *(Open daily July-Aug. 8am-6pm; Sept.-June 7am-7pm. Mass M and Sa 8am, Su 10am.)* The small but satisfying **Musée Angladon,** 5 rue Laboureur, houses an impressive permanent collection that includes works by Degas, Manet, and Picasso. Temporary summer exhibits add variety; an exhibit devoted to Odilon Redon will be on display from March 14 to June 15, 2008. *(☎82 29 03; www.angladon.com. Open May-Nov. Tu-Su 1-6pm; Dec.-Apr. W-Su 1-6pm. €6, with pass €4, students €3.)* **Musée Calvet** harbors everything from Bronze Age tools to 18th-century silverware, though its main focus is French artists from the 15th to 20th centuries. Works by Vernet, Claudel, and David are part of the permanent collection. *(65 rue Joseph Vernet. ☎86 33 84. Open June-Sept. M and W-Su 10am-6pm; Oct.-May M and W-Su 10am-1pm and 2-6pm. €6, with pass €3.)*

ENTERTAINMENT AND NIGHTLIFE

From October to June, opera, drama, and classical music performances take place in the **Opéra Théâtre,** 1 rue Racine (☎82 42 42). **Rue des Teinturiers** stays animated during shows in the **Théâtre du Chien qui Fume,** 75 rue des Teinturiers (☎85 25 87), the **Théâtre du Balcon,** 38 rue Guillaume Puy (☎85 00 80), and the **Théâtre du Chêne Noir,** 8bis rue Ste-Catherine (☎86 58 11). The popular **Utopia Cinéma,** 4 rue des Escaliers Ste-Anne, is an independent theater that screens a variety of documentaries and movies. (☎82 65 36; www.cinemas-utopia.org. €5.50, before 1pm €3.50; 10 showings €42.) When the festival rolls into town, Avignon explodes with incessant activity. Bars, shops, and restaurants stay open until early morning. Luckily, the rest of the year promises nighttime amusement that is only slightly tamer.

Koala Bar, 2 pl. des Corps Saints. Cheap beer, pink walls, and bubble-shaped chairs draw a talkative crowd amid French rock. Visit the quieter air-conditioned room upstairs for laid-back conversation. Beer €2.30. Mixed drinks €2-8. W-Su themed nights. Open M-Sa 7am-1:30am, Su 7pm-1:30am; during festival until 3am. Cash only.

Red Zone, 25 rue Carnot (☎27 02 44). Student bar and night club. Music ranges from salsa to R&B. Beer €3-3.50. Tu salsa lessons 9:30-11pm. Open July-Aug. daily 9pm-3am; Sept.-Dec. and May-June M-Sa 9pm-3am; Jan.-Apr. Tu-Sa 9pm-3am. MC/V.

L'Esclave Bar, 12 rue du Limas (☎85 14 91), by the Pont d'Avignon. Techno, house (Th), and 70s remixes keep a mixed, but mostly male, gay crowd dancing under neon lights. Beer €5. Mixed drinks €8. W "La Madame" drag show. Cover July-Aug. €5; includes drink. Open July-Aug. daily 11pm-5am; Sept.-June Tu-Su 11pm-5am. MC/V.

Les Célestins, 38 pl. des Corps Saints. Dramatically red café. Techno beats animate a fun-loving crowd. Beer from €2.20. Mixed drinks €3-5. Open Aug. daily 7am-1:30am; Sept.-June M-Th 7am-9pm, F-Sa 7am-1am; during festival daily 7am-3am. Cash only.

The Cubanito Café, 51 rue Carnot (☎86 98 04; www.cubanito.fr). This favorite among young tourists and locals features dancing to Cuban music in a rowdy atmosphere. Beer €2.30, after 9pm €3.30. Mixed drinks €5-8. DJ plays salsa nightly (9pm-1am) and gives occasional dance lessons. Open daily 5pm-1am. MC/V.

FESTIVALS

July is the definite highlight of Avignon's calendar—a wild, crazy, month-long theater binge. During the **Festival d'Avignon,** Shakespearean actors rub shoulders all night with Odyssey readers, African dancers, and Molière troupes. The official festival, known as the **IN,** is the most prestigious theatrical gathering in Europe and involves at least 20 different venues, from factories to cloisters to palaces. (Info and tickets ☎14 14 14; www.festival-avignon.com. Tickets free-€45. Reservations accepted after mid-June. Students and under 25 50% discount.) The cheaper and more experimental (although equally established) **Festival OFF** presents over 700 pieces, some in English, over the course of three weeks in July. The festival is run by **Avignon Festival & Compagnies,** on pl. du Palais (☎04 32 76 35 35; www.avignon-off.org). Tickets are free-€16 and can be purchased at the venue or the OFFice; holders of the Carte OFF (€13 at the OFFice or tourist office) receive a 30% discount on tickets. Programs are available at the tourist office. If you're low on cash, don't despair; tickets aren't necessary to get in on the action—free theater, parades, and extemporaneous performances overflow into the streets throughout the day and night. The Centre Franco-Américain de Provence sponsors the **Avignon Film Festival** in June at the Cinéma Vox. The festival showcases feature and short films directed by French and American aspirants. Meals, parties, and lectures make for good opportunities to schmooze with the next big thing. French and English subtitles are provided. (☎82 03 61; www.avignonfilmfest.com. Night showings €6, students €5; morning films €2; VIP badge with breakfast and lunch €50.)

DAYTRIP FROM AVIGNON

VILLENEUVE-LÈS-AVIGNON

From Avignon, take bus #11 from the Porte de l'Oulle or post office (every 20min. 7am-7:30pm; €1.10, 2 tickets €2.10) to "Villeneuve tourist office." On Sundays, bus #70 runs along the same route (5 per day). Alternatively, walk 25-30min. over the Pont Daladier bridge, just below Pont d'Avignon. Cross 2 bridges, turn right, and follow the signs to Villeneuve.

Villeneuve makes an easy and calm daytrip, and its huge monastery and fort provide plenty to explore. Founded in the 13th century to intimidate France's *provençal* neighbors, Villeneuve-lès-Avignon (VEE-nuhv-lays-ah-veen-YOHN) sits on a hill overlooking Avignon. The imposing towers offer panoramic views of Avignon, and the grand ruins of Fort St-André overlook the Rhône Valley. Meanwhile, the majestic 12th-century monastery dominates the center of town. Before venturing farther into town, stop by the Villeneuve tourist office for a map with a circuit that stops at all of Villeneuve's sights. The sights pass, available at any museum or sight in Avignon or Villeneuve, provides significant discounts after the first visit.

A small climb from the town center, **Chartreuse du Val de Bénédiction,** rue de la République, is one of the largest Carthusian monasteries in France and is full of beautiful Gothic arches. The solitary prison cells upstairs used to house monks who were exiled for practicing alchemy, keeping personal possessions, or associating with women. Abandoned in 1792, the Chartreuse has become home to the **Centre National des Ecritures du Spectacle,** which hosts artists and performances throughout the year. (☎15 24 24; www.chartreuse.org. Open daily Apr.-Sept. 9am-6:30pm; Oct.-Mar. 9:30am-5:30pm. Performances €25, students €13. Guided tours July-Aug. daily 5pm, free with admission. €6.50, students and with pass €4.50. Chartreuse/Fort St-André combo €8, with pass €6.) Info regarding regular and special events is available at the front desk.

A steep path leads to the Gothic **Fort St-André,** built by King Philip le Bel (the Fair) in the 14th century. The interior of this large, windowless citadel served as a prison after the Rhône river receded 100m, causing the fortress to lose its strategic value. Today it's perfect for exploration. The stone floors and walls still bear traces of the prisoners's desperate carvings. Wander around the fort's ground or mount the winding stairs for a sweeping panorama of Avignon. Be sure to follow the map that you receive with your ticket, and don't miss the small 12th-century Romanesque chapel. Boasting high windows and remnants of medieval frescoes, it hides at the top on the left. (☎25 45 35. Open daily mid-May to mid-Sept. 10am-1pm and 2-6pm; Apr. to mid-May and mid- to late Sept. 10am-1pm and 2-5:30pm; Oct.-Mar. 10am-1pm and 2-5pm. €5, pass-holders and students €3.50.) Within the fortress is the Benedictine **Abbaye St-André,** once home to as many as 90 monks in the 14th century. Although the original buildings were mostly destroyed during the Revolution, they have been replaced with Italian-style gardens with purple water lilies and olive trees. (Open Apr.-Sept. Tu-Su 10am-12:30pm and 2-6pm; Oct.-Mar. Tu-Su 10am-12:30pm and 2-5pm. Gardens €4, pass-holders €3.)

The **Musée Pierre de Luxembourg,** also on rue de la République, has a small collection of sacred art. The highlight is Enguerrand Quarton's *The Crowning of the Virgin*, which depicts the three-tiered Christian universe. (☎27 49 66. Open Apr.-Sept. Tu-Su 10am-12:30pm and 2-6:30pm; Oct.-Jan. and Mar. Tu-Su 10am-noon and 2-5pm. €3, pass-holders and students €2.) The Gothic **Tour Philippe le Bel,** at the intersection of av. Gabriel Péri and Montée de la Tour, is not for the faint of heart. Its spiral staircase can make your head spin, though the view from the tower's wind-swept platform is worth the climb. (☎04 32 70 08 57. Tower open Apr.-Sept. Tu-Su 10am-12:30pm and 2-6:30pm; Oct.-Nov. and Mar. Tu-Su 10am-noon and 2-5pm. €1.80, students and pass-holders €1.)

The **tourist office,** pl. Charles David, is located up av. Gabriel Peri. An English-speaking staff offers a free map with a walking tour. Guided tours of the *vieille ville* are given in July and August. (☎25 61 33; www.villeneuvelesavignon.fr/tourisme. 2hr. tours in French Tu and Th 5pm. €6.20, under 18 and pass-holders €4.20. Open July M-F 10am-7pm, Sa-Su 10am-1pm and 2:30-7pm; Aug. daily 9am-12:30pm and 2-6pm; Sept.-June M-Sa 9am-12:30pm and 2-6pm.)

THE LUBÉRON, THE VAUCLUSE, AND THE ALPILLES ☎04 90

This is French countryside *par excellence*—the kind you've seen in films and drooled over in pictures. Combed into neat rows of vineyards and studded with twisted olive trees, this part of rural Provence is all it's cracked up to be. If you're traveling by bus and train, don't miss Fontaine de la Vaucluse, with its cavernous *gouffre*, or Bonnieux, the only one of the gorgeous Lubéron hillside towns accessible by bus. By car, the lavender fields at the Abbaye de Sénanque, Roussillon's red cliffs, and the medieval mountain town of Oppède-le-Vieux are sure highlights. The Parc Naturel Régional du Lubéron has inspired artists from Petrarch to Picasso, and is perhaps what made Van Gogh wait as long as he did before cutting off his ear. Farther south, the hills of the Alpilles are a tranquil tourist retreat. Home to traces of Roman history, several famous artists and poets, and sunflower fields and apricot orchards, the small base towns of this region—Les Baux de Provence, St-Rémy, and Tarascon—provide access by public transportation and clear vistas, although they are less stunning than the villages of the Lubéron and the Vaucluse.

(DAY)TRIPPIN' IN THE LAND OF VAN GOGH. Avignon is the most practical hub for daytrips to nearby towns, and it is the only city from which public transport runs to the Lubéron and the Vaucluse. Arles is a possible, though less convenient, hub for daytrips in the Alpilles. Buses and trains are a cheap means of reaching some towns, but a car is hands-down the best means of transportation. Those with a more flexible schedule (and more energy) may consider biking between towns (usually 7-15km apart) to experience Provence at its finest, but if you choose this option, exercise caution. A few bike rental companies, including **Provence Vélos Location** (☎60 28 07) and **Mountain Bike Lubéron** (☎75 89 96), offer to drop off renters at cities that allow for strategic downhill coasting. However you choose to travel, good walking shoes are a must for the hilly, often unpaved roads.

PROVENCE

ACCESSIBLE BY PUBLIC TRANSPORTATION

Trains run to L'isle-sur-la-Sorgue (30min., 10 per day, €4.10) and Tarascon (12min., 20 per day, €2.90-5.20) from Avignon; Tarascon is also served by trains from Arles and Nîmes. **Buses** leave from Avignon's central bus terminal, by the train station. For all information on buses, your best bet is to call or visit the information office at Avignon's *gare routière*, 5 av. Monclar. (☎82 07 35. Info desk open M-F 10:15am-1pm and 2-6pm.) From Avignon or Arles, hop on the Rapides du Sud Est buses (☎04 32 76 00 40) to get to Les Baux de Provence (July-Aug. only; from Avignon 1½hr., 5-6 per day, €7.20; from Arles 35min., 4 per day, €5.90) and St-Rémy (from Avignon 45min.; July-Aug. 5 per day, Sept.-June 8 per day; €4.20; from Arles 50min., 3 per day, €5). Also leaving from Avignon, Transvaucluse buses (☎82 07 35) run to Fontaine de Vaucluse (1hr.; M-Sa 8 per day, Su 3 per day; €4.70), while CTM sends buses to Tarascon (45min., M-Sa 10 per day, €5.30). Bonnieux is accessible by bus (☎04 91 49 44 25) from Aix-en-Provence (1½hr., 2 per day) and Marseille (2hr., 2 per day).

TIP **PEDDLE LIKE A PRO IN PROVENCE.** Think twice before renting a bike in Provence. Roads are extremely hilly and often narrow, sometimes with sheer drops and no guardrail. If you do choose to bike through the countryside, plan a route along less traveled roads–visit the local tourist office for advice.

FONTAINE DE VAUCLUSE

At the base of 230m cliffs, with a shockingly clear emerald spring, Fontaine de Vaucluse (fawnh-TEHNN duh voh-CLOOZE; pop. 680) is a gem of a town blessed by usable bus service from Avignon and two first-rate accommodation options.

Fontaine is worth a visit for **Le Gouffre,** one of the largest river sources in the world. At its peak, Le Gouffre pours 70-90 cubic meters of water per second into the Sorgue. In 1985, divers finally reached the bottom of the source, pegging it at 308m. To reach Le Gouffre, continue straight from the bus stop until the traffic circle. Turn left along the river, past the tourist office, and continue on the path, lined by candy stands and trinket shops, until you see Le Gouffre ahead and to the right. In the summer, it looks like a massive hole in the cliff. Don't miss the mossy rocks nearby and great views of the cliffs above the water. In the town center, the 10m **Colonne** salutes Petrarch, who spent two decades composing sonnets in Fontaine. The opposite side of the river is scattered with several small museums, the best of which is the **Musée d'Histoire,** also known as the *Musée "L'Appel de la Liberté."* With a permanent collection of over 10,000 objects and documents, the museum presents fascinating details of the *années noires* (dark years; 1939-1945) under Vichy rule. Sleek exhibits include a slew of photos, propaganda posters, and a model classroom with a chalkboard, desks, and Vichy propaganda books. An allegory of the war's horror, Matisse's gouache painting *The Fall of Icarus* is the museum's most treasured piece. (☎20 24 00; musee-appel-liberte@cg84.fr. Open June-Sept. M and W-Su 10am-6pm; early Oct. and mid-Apr. to May M and W-Su 10am-noon and 2-6pm; mid-Oct. to early Nov. M and W-Su 10am-noon and 2-5pm; mid-Nov. to Dec. Sa-Su 10am-noon and 2-5pm; Mar. and early Apr. Sa-Su 10am-noon and 2-6pm. €3.50, students €1.50, under 12 free.) **Ecomusée du Gouffre** offers underground strolls through caverns that have been reconstructed for tourists. While the site is a bit artificial, the visit is surprisingly informative: guided tours are given by professional speleologists, whose passion for caves is contagious. (☎20 34 13. Open daily July-Aug. 10:30am-12:30pm and 2-7:30pm; Sept.-Nov. and Feb.-June 10am-noon and 2-6pm. 40min. tours in French with written English translation €5.50, under 18 €4.) Across from the tourist office is the **Moulin à Papier,** where visitors can peek at the art of paper-making; they use same pulp-pressing method as in the 15th century. (☎20 34 14. Open daily July-Aug. 9am-7:30pm; May-June and Sept. 9am-12:30pm and 2-7pm; Mar.-Apr. and Oct. 9am-12:30pm and 2-6:30pm; Feb. and Nov. 9am-12:30pm and 2-6pm; Dec.-Jan. 9:30am-12:30pm and 2-5:30pm. Free.)

PROVENCE

Surprisingly inexpensive lodgings can be found at **Hôtel Font de Lauro ❸,** 1.5km from Fontaine de Vaucluse, off the road to L'Isle-sur-la-Sorgue. Be on the lookout for the small sign. From the bus stop in Fontaine, walk opposite the direction of travel on the main road—the bus driver may stop at the hotel if you ask nicely, but it is not an official *arrêt.* A warm owner tends to guests in quiet, simple rooms with views of the Vaucluse landscape. A beautiful pool completes the bargain package. Satisfied clients have sent postcards from all over the world. (☎/fax 20 31 49. Breakfast €6. Gate closes at midnight. Reservations required. Open early Apr. to mid-Sept. Doubles with shower €28, with shower and toilet €39; triples with shower and toilet €51; quads with shower and toilet €68. MC/V.) The rural **Auberge de Jeunesse (HI) ❶,** chemin de la Vignasse, 1km from town (15min. walk), allows crowds of backpackers to enjoy the breathtaking outdoors in a spacious stone country house. From the bus stop, cross the bridge over the river and follow signs. (☎20 31 65; fontaine@fuaj.org. Kitchen. Breakfast €3.40. Laundry €3.50. Reception 8-10am and 5:30-9pm. Lockout 10am-5:30pm. Open Feb. to mid-Nov. Bunks €19. Camping €9.) For groceries, a **mini-market** is across the street from the post office. (Open July-Aug. M-Sa 8:30am-7:30pm; Sept.-June Tu-Su 8:30am-1pm. Cash only.)

Kayak Vert, located 500m from Fontaine on the road to L'Isle-sur-la-Sorgue, rents kayaks for the 8km trip down to L'Isle-sur-la-Sorgue. A minibus takes you back up to Fontaine. Guides are available for groups up to 16 (€80). The Sorgue is a Class I river, meaning it's suitable for all skill levels. (☎20 35 44; www.canoefrance.com. 2-person canoes €34; 1-person kayak €17, students with ID €14. Open mid-Apr. to Sept., weather permitting. Trips every hr. 9:30am-4pm; reserve 1 day ahead.) The **tourist office,** along chemin de la Fontaine toward Le Gouffre, has helpful hotel and campsite listings, as well as English information about activities in the area. (☎20 32 22; officetourisme.vaucluse@wanadoo.fr. Open daily 10am-noon and 2-6pm.) There is a **post office** with an **ATM** up the street from the Colonne, away from the river. (Open M-F 9am-noon and 2:30-4:30pm, Sa 9-11:30am.)

BONNIEUX

Though only slightly larger than its neighbors, Bonnieux (bohn-NYUH; pop. 1430) is the capital of the Lubéron and offers the views and narrow alleys that characterize this part of Provence. Flowers burst from balconies off the well-restored stone houses that cluster along the hillside. Part of Bonnieux's charm lies in its medieval church; the other part lies in the fact that it is accessible by public transport.

At the top of the village, the 12th-century **vieille église** can only be reached by climbing a steep 86-step staircase (open July-Aug.); if your limbs can make the hike, you shouldn't miss it. The walk is well worth it, rewarding perseverance not only with a beautiful old church but also with views of the countryside.

The town has many *maisons d'hôtes*, but the cheapest accommodation is the beautiful, shaded **Camping Municipal du Vallon ❶,** rte. Ménerbes D3, outside the city on the road to Lacoste. Walk downhill from the tourist office along rue Jean Baptiste Aurard and follow it to the right at pl. 4 Sept. Turn left on av. Clovis Hugues and follow the road out of town until you see a sign for the campground on the left. (☎/fax 75 86 14. Reception 8am-8pm. Open Apr.-Nov. 1-2 people with car €10, with tent €8.20. €2.70 per additional person. Electricity €2.80. Cash only.)

For a **taxi,** call Claude (☎06 81 75 87 13). Rent **bikes** and **motorbikes** at **Mountain Bike Lubéron,** rue Marceau, which offers free delivery within 15km of Bonnieux. (☎75 89 96 or 06 83 25 48 07. €9 per half-day, €15 per day, €75 per week. Motorbikes €35 per day. Open daily Mar.-Nov. 8:30am-noon and 1:30-6:30pm.) The **tourist office** for Ménerbes, Oppède-le-Vieux, and Bonnieux is in Bonnieux at pl. Carnot. (☎75 91 90. Open M-Sa 9am-12:30pm and 2-6pm.) A **post office** with an **ATM** is behind the *église neuve.* (Open M-F 9am-noon and 1:30-3:30pm, Sa 9am-noon.) **Postal Code:** 84580.

LES BAUX-DE-PROVENCE

Every summer, hordes of tourists descend on Les Baux-de-Provence (lay BO-duh-proh-vahnss; pop. 450) to explore its château, also called the *Cité Morte,* or dead city—an immense area of cliff top medieval ruins. Legend has it that Dante came to the village court and found inspiration for his *Inferno* in the twisted gorges of the Val de l'Enfer (Valley of Hell), so named for the tortuous cliffs below the castle. The Baux family line died out in the 14th century, and Louis XIII humiliated the town by destroying its castle and ramparts in 1632. The few residents left today are far outnumbered by the bus loads of visitors.

The ruined halls and towers of the mountaintop **Château des Baux** cover an area five times larger than the village and offer unparalleled views of the countryside below. A giant *trébuchet,* the largest, most powerful medieval siege engine, stands out on the plateau. Be careful of the gusting Mistral winds on the cliff. In July and August, visitors can try their hands at crossbow archery, with the help of a professional instructor, and enjoy a variety of shows centered on medieval warfare. (☎54 55 56; www.chateau-baux-provence.com. Open daily July-Aug. 9am-7:30pm; Sept.-Nov. 9am-6pm; Dec.-Feb. 9:30am-5pm; Mar.-June 9am-6:30pm. Detailed audio tour in 7 languages; 1½hr.; €7.50, students €5, under 17 free.)

Walk down the hill to the small, idiosyncratic **Fondation Louis Jou,** rue Frédéric Mistral. Look for a small glass sign up and to the right; the entrance to the museum itself is an unassuming door. The museum commemorates Les Baux's favorite son with major works by the print-maker himself as well as engravings by Dürer, Goya, and Rembrandt. Print-making workshops are organized within the Fondation. Often the Fondation seems closed when it is actually open; to make sure, turn back up the hill, walk 20m, and inquire at *La Boutique,* the small shop carved into the stone. (☎54 34 17; www.perso.wanadoo.fr/fondationlouisjou. Open July-Aug. W-Su 11am-1pm and 1:30-6pm; Feb.-June and Sept.-Dec. Th-Su 11am-1pm and 1:30-6pm. Call ahead; schedule changes frequently. €3, students €1.50.) Les Baux is also known for its limestone quarries, one of which has been converted into the impressive—and expensive—**Cathédrale d'Images.** Walk behind the tourist office, pass the parking lot, and continue down the hill to the left; turn right at the crossroads and follow the sign. As visitors stroll through the 4000 sq. m of cave galleries, a slide show projects 3000 images onto gigantic walls cut deep into the limestone. New shows come every year—2008 features Van Gogh's works. (☎54 38 65; www.cathedrale-images.com. Open daily Apr.-Sept. 10am-7pm; Oct. to early Jan. and Mar. 10am-6pm. Last entry 1hr. before closing. €7.50, ages 8-18 €3.50.)

Expensive restaurants and cafés abound in the stone tourist village, though there are more affordable sandwich, *crêpe*, and *panini* stands (€4-6). Most backpackers bring picnics to the *Cité Morte* for picturesque meals atop the hill (although you still have to pay for admission to the château).

Call **taxis** at ☎06 80 27 60 92. **Parking** costs €3-4 in the village or on the twisting mountain street. Park for free at the Cathédrale d'Images, 600m below the town; see directions above. The **tourist office,** Maison de Roy, immediately on the left at the entrance to town, offers a free map, as well as accommodations and transportation info. (☎54 34 39. Open Apr.-Sept. M-F 9:30am-12:30pm and 2-6pm, Sa-Su 10am-noon and 2-5pm; Oct.-Mar. M-F 9:30am-12:30pm and 2-5pm, Sa 10am-noon.)

L'ISLE-SUR-LA-SORGUE

L'Isle-sur-la-Sorgue (LEEL-suhr-lah-sohrg; pop. 21,000) is the first step from Avignon into the Vaucluse and draws visitors with its mossy water wheels and innumerable antique shops. Don't make this your first stop, however; nearby towns are more spectacular. Entangled in the green ribbon of its river, the tranquil *centre-ville* echoes with the rushing currents of water that twist around it. The river Sorgue splits into numerous channels to the east of the city, surrounding and running beneath the town center, aptly nicknamed "the Venice of Vaucluse."

L'Isle-sur-la-Sorgue has long depended on its narrow waterways for fish and industry; now it depends on them to draw tourists. The gardens along the river, particularly the **Jardin Public,** provide a convenient spot for a picnic, although there is a fair amount of noise. The town's main draw is more materialistic. The third largest center for antiques in Europe, L'Isle-sur-la-Sorgue counts over 300 **antique shops** housed in seven "antique dealers' villages" scattered throughout the city. Art collectors flock to the tiny village for a world-famous biannual **antique fair** that brings over 500 dealers at Easter and in mid-August.

The cheapest accommodations are located on the outskirts of L'Isle-sur-la-Sorgue but are only accessible by car. Consult the tourist office's guide to the region's hotels, B&Bs, and campgrounds. **Le Cours d'Eau ❷,** 15 Esplanade Robert Vasse, offers bright rooms with colorful tiled bathrooms at some of the lowest prices in town. All rooms have private baths. (☎04 40 38 01 18. Breakfast €5.50. Reception July-Aug. 8am-10pm; Sept.-June 8am-5pm. Singles €30; doubles €40-45; triples €55. AmEx/MC/V.) **La Gueulardière ❹,** 1 rte. d'Apt, on cours René Char, offers five large, well-kept rooms that open onto a garden restaurant. (☎38 10 52; fax 20 83 70. Breakfast €8. Reception 8am-3pm and 4:30-11pm. Open Feb. to mid-Dec. Doubles €55-56. Extra bed €8. MC/V.) The campsite at **La Sorguette ❶,** on rte. d'Apt (N100), 2km southeast of the town center, is well maintained and makes a good base for exploring the Vaucluse. On foot or by car, follow signs to Apt from the post office. The three-star campsite has showers, laundry, snack bar, free Internet access and Wi-Fi, *boules*, and volleyball. (☎38 05 71; www.camping-sorguette.com. Kayaks €13 per hr., €25 per half-day. Bicycles €17 per day, €88 per week. Reception 8:30am-12:30pm and 1:30-7pm. Open mid-Mar. to mid-Oct. 2 people with car €16-19; extra person €5.40-6.80. Electricity €3.60-4.70.)

Fruits and vegetables are sold every Thursday and Sunday at the **open-air market** in the town center. (Open 8am-1pm.) On the first Sunday of August, the only **floating market** in all of France brings merchants selling local products directly from their boats. (Open 9am-noon.) There is a Petit-Casino **supermarket** at 6 rue de la République. (Open July-Aug. M 7:30am-12:30pm, Tu-Sa 7:30am-12:30pm and 3:30-7:30pm, Su 8am-1pm and 4-7pm; Sept.-June Tu-Sa 7:30am-12:30pm and 3:30-7:30pm, Su 8am-1pm. MC/V.) Restaurants abound near Pont Gambetta, many with terraces overlooking the Sorgue. **Le Potager de Louise ❸**, 9 quai Rouget de L'Isle, has vegetarian options. The homemade *chèvre*-spinach lasagna (€14) is worth a try. (☎20 96 56. *Plats* €12-19. Open July-Aug. daily noon-3pm and 7-10pm; Sept.-June M-Th and Su noon-2pm, F-Sa noon-2pm and 7-9pm. AmEx/MC/V.)

Taxis can be reached at ☎38 27 84 or 06 08 09 19 49. **Tendil/Moto-Cycles,** on 10 av. de la Gare outside the train station, rents **bikes.** (☎38 19 12. €14 per day; passport deposit. Open Tu-F 9am-noon and 2-7pm, Sa 8am-noon and 2-6pm, Su 9am-noon. AmEx/MC/V.) For long-term rental, try family-run **Provence Vélos Location,** located in Carpentras, with a friendly, English-speaking staff who will drop off customers with their rental bikes in the village of their choice to avoid painful uphill climbs. (☎60 28 07; www.guideweb.com/provence-velos. Delivery €14.50, free with week rental of €69. 10% reduction for groups of 4 or more.)

The **tourist office,** next to the church on pl. de la Liberté, supplies free maps and comprehensive info on festivals, markets, lodging, and outdoor activities in and around town. (☎38 04 78; www.oti-delasorgue.fr. 2hr. town tours in French only July-Aug. Tu 10am-noon; €3. Open July-Aug. M-Sa 9am-12:30pm and 2:30-6pm, Su 9:30am-1pm; Sept.-June M-Sa 9am-12:30pm and 2:30-6pm, Su 9am-12:30pm.) For the **police station,** quai Jean Jaurès, call ☎20 81 20. The **Pharmacy Sprang,** 13 pl. F. Buisson, is behind the church. (☎38 00 20. Open M-Sa 8:30am-12:30pm and 2-7:30pm, Su 8:30am-12:30pm.) For medical needs, call the small **Hôpital St-Joseph** (☎21 34 00) or an **ambulance** (☎38 00 00). The **post office,** av. des Quatre Otages, across from the Jardin Public, provides **currency exchange** and an **ATM.** (☎21 28 44. Open M-F 8:30am-noon and 1:30-5:30pm, Sa 8:30am-noon.) **Postal Code:** 84800.

PROVENCE

ST-RÉMY-DE-PROVENCE

Lacking the natural and architectural beauty of Les Baux and the hillside villages of the Vaucluse and Lubéron, St-Rémy-de-Provence (SEHN reh-MEE duh-proh-vahnss; pop. 10,000) is mostly known as the temporary home of Van Gogh. Outside the maze of charming streets that makes up the *centre-ville* lies a small group of Roman ruins and the ancient city of Glanum, now a major archaeological site.

The **Musée Estrine,** in the 254-year-old Hôtel Estrine, 8 rue Estrine, is one of the small museums nestled in the heart of town. Two floors of the museum feature works by contemporary artists, and a third holds one of the best collections of works by early Cubist painter Albert Gleizes. A small rotating exhibit on the ground floor presents a collection of high-quality photographic reproductions of Van Gogh's masterpieces. Not surprisingly, the copies fail to elicit the angst and emotion evoked by the originals. (☎92 34 72. Open late Mar. to mid-Oct. Tu-Su 10am-1pm and 3-7pm; mid-Oct. to Nov. Tu-Su 10:30am-12:30pm and 2-6pm. €3.20, students and seniors €2.30.) **Glanum,** rte. des Baux de Provence, a settlement from the sixth century BC, lies 1km south of St-Rémy and is the best reason to visit the town. From the tourist office, walk away from the *centre-ville;* Glanum is on the left (15min.). If driving, park at St-Paul de Mausole, 50m before Glanum, to avoid the €2 parking fee. Discovered 80 years ago, the houses, temples, and wells unearthed here are still being studied. The on-site archaeological team believes that the vestiges of the city spread over a surface seven times larger than the area that has been unearthed. Glanum once prospered as a stop on the main road from Spain to Italy (the *Via Domitia*) and now provides insight into Provence's Gallo-Roman culture. (☎92 23 79. Open Apr.-Aug. daily 10am-6:30pm; Sept.-Mar. Tu-Su 10:30am-5pm. Last entry 30min. before closing. €6.50, ages 18-25 €4.50.) Across the street, the still-functioning **St-Paul de Mausole** psychiatric clinic, av. Van Gogh, is the therapeutic center where Van Gogh spent one year and produced over 100 drawings and 150 paintings. He painted his renowned *L'Oliveraie* on the olive tree-lined path that leads to the former monastery. Above the flowered 11th-century cloister, visitors can tour the rather bare rooms in which the artist spent the last year of his life. A small gallery now shows—and offers for sale—creative exhibits by current patients. (☎92 77 00. Open Apr.-Oct. daily 9:30am-6:45pm; Nov.-Mar. Tu-Su 9:30am-5pm. €4, students €3, under 12 free. Free parking.)

Near the statue of Nostradamus, you'll find a handful of good *brasseries* and a **SPAR** supermarket, 16 rue Carnot. (Open Tu-Sa 8:30am-12:30pm and 3:30-7:30pm, Su 8:30am-12:30pm.) Restaurants in St-Rémy are on the pricier side, but there's a market at **place de la République** every Wednesday and Saturday (open 8am-1pm; Sa market is much smaller and sells only fruits and vegetables). **Lou Planet ❷**, 7 pl. Favier, serves fresh *crêpes* and salads (€4-9) in a courtyard. The *légumes de saison et chèvre crêpe* (€7.50) gives a taste of the season's finest vegetables with fresh goat cheese. (☎92 19 81. Open daily Apr.-Sept. 11am-9:30pm. Cash only.)

Taxis are available at ☎06 09 52 71 54. To glimpse the vistas that inspired Van Gogh, take the walking tour *Circuit Van Gogh* (30min.), which retraces the artist's sources of inspiration throughout the town with a free, convenient map from the **tourist office,** pl. Jean Jaurès. From the bus stop, walk up av. Durand Maillane; the office will be on the left, in a parking lot next to the police station. The staff provides a free map; gives info on housing, restaurants, and local activities; and conducts group tours in French, English, German, and Spanish from late April to mid-September. (☎92 05 22; www.saintremy-de-provence.com. Open July-Aug. M-Sa 9am-noon and 2-7pm, Su 10am-noon; early Apr. to June and Sept.-Oct. M-Sa 9am-12:30pm and 2-6pm, Su 10am-noon; Nov. to early Apr. M-Sa 9am-noon and 2-6pm. Tours of old St-Rémy and Van Gogh sights €8, not including St-Paul entrance fee, Tu and Th-Sa 10am; only available upon reservation with min. 6 people.) There is a 24hr. **ATM** across from the tourist office. The **Pharmacie Cendres,** 4 bd. Mirabeau (☎04 32 60 16 43) has up-to-date info on the **pharmacie de garde,** as does the tourist office. Reach the **police** at ☎92 58 11. For health emergencies, an **ambulance** can be reached at ☎92 11 88. **Currency exchange** is available at the **post office,** rue Roger Salengro. (☎92 78 70. Open M-F 9am-noon and 2-5:30pm, Sa 9am-noon.) **Postal Code:** 13210.

PROVENCE

TARASCON

While Tarascon (TAH-rah-scohn; pop. 13,000) is not a pretty *provençal* town, a huge and well-preserved château, as well as good public transportation, might make it worth a visit. The town is linked to *provençal* folklore through its namesake, *la tarasque,* a **dragon** that once terrorized the village, hiding behind river rocks and gobbling up villagers. Legend has it that Ste-Marthe was walking along the Rhône, met the monster, and miraculously tamed him. For four days over the last weekend of June, during the **Fête de la Tarasque,** a dragon replica is paraded through town. Inaugurated in 1474, the *fête* has grown over the last 500 years and now features concerts, bullfights, horse shows, and dancing. Tarascon's proximity and frequent trains to Arles (17km), Avignon (23km), and Nîmes (24km), as well as less expensive lodgings, make it a good base from which to explore the countryside, especially when nearby neighbors are in the midst of festival madness.

Tarascon's major attraction is the imposing 15th-century **Château de Tarascon,** above a wedge of the Rhône. Under the reign of René I (1434-1480), the stronghold was transformed into a Renaissance palace complete with flamboyant Gothic carvings. From the 18th century until 1926, it was used as a prison. As a result, the château is well maintained but full of empty rooms; the star-painted ceiling in the Queen's chambers is still easily visible. Surrounded by a now-dry moat, it boasts a lovely *provençal* garden and arched ceilings. Prisoners' inscriptions, carved deep into stone, can be found on many of the walls. A climb to the 45m high roof reveals a picture-perfect view of the surrounding countryside and Tarascon's rival castle, the ruined Château de Beaucaire. (☎91 01 93. Open Apr.-Aug. daily 10am-6:30pm; Sept.-Mar. Tu-Su 10:30am-5pm. 1-1½hr. guided tours in French offered 4 times per day Apr.-Aug. €6.50, ages 18-25 €4.50, under 18 free.)

To reach the **Auberge de Jeunesse (HI) ❶,** 31 bd. Gambetta, from the train station, turn right on bd. du Viaduc, then go left at pl. Eimshorn and follow bd. Gambetta—you should see signs for the hostel ("FUAJ"). It has comfortable beds in 4- to 12-bed dorms, kitchen facilities, a secure bike area, and free parking. (☎91 04 08; tarascon@fuaj.org. Breakfast €3.50. Reception 8-10am and 5:30-10:30pm. Lockout 10am-5:30pm. Open daily mid-Mar. to mid-Oct. Dorms €15. Cash only.) **Hôtel du Viaduc ❸,** 9 rue du Viaduc, is on a quiet street by the elevated train tracks. From the train station, cross under the tracks and head left. The hotel has large, comfortable rooms (some newly renovated) and a terrace with a garden where visitors often eat breakfast. Popular with cyclists, the hotel maintains a locked bike area and free parking. (☎91 16 67; http://perso.wanadoo.fr/hotelduviaduc. Breakfast €5. Internet access €3 per 30min. Doubles Aug. €35, with shower €40, with toilet €46; June-July €30/36/42; Sept.-May €26/32/38. Family room €55/50/44. AmEx/MC/V.) **Camping Tartarin ❶,** bd. du Roy René, directly next to the château on the Rhône, is a simple site with a swimming pool, bar, snack stand, restaurant (*plat du jour* €8.50, pizzas €8-9.80), and free showers. Campers appreciate the quiet yet central location. (☎91 01 46; www.campingtartarin.fr. Reception 8:30am-12:30pm and 5-7pm; try the bar if you arrive after-hours but before 11pm. Open Apr.-Oct. July-Aug. €4.30 per person, €4.50 per tent, €2.20 per car; Apr.-June and Sept.-Oct. €3.70/4/2. Electricity €3. AmEx/MC/V.)

There's a **Petit Casino** supermarket on pl. du Marché. (☎91 04 48. Open M-Tu and Th-Sa 7:30am-12:30pm and 3:30-7:30pm, Su 8am-12:30pm.) **Bistrot des Anges ❷,** 20 pl. du Marché, serves up seasonal *provençal menus* (€10-17) and extraordinary chocolate cake (€4) on a sunny terrace. Work by local artists is displayed in the dining room. (☎91 05 11. Open M-Sa noon-2pm. MC/V.) The **Pâtissier la Tarasque,** 56 rue des Halles, near pl. Frédéric Mistral, offers melt-in-your-mouth treats, including *bésuquettes* (8 pieces €5.60), patented hazelnut truffles shaped like the **tarasque.** (☎91 01 17. Open Tu-Su 6:30am-1pm and 3-7:30pm. AmEx/MC/V.)

In a pinch, call **Accord Taxi** (☎06 08 40 75 31). The multilingual staff of the **tourist office,** 16 bd. Itam, provides free maps. From the train station, walk straight across pl. Colonel Berrurier, turn left along Cours Aristide Briand, and turn right at rue des Halles. Follow that until it ends and turn left on rue du Château. Turn right again immediately on rue de la Poissonnerie, then left on bd. Itam. The office is immediately on the left. (☎91 03 52; www.tarascon.org. Open July-Aug. M-Sa 9am-7pm; Sept. and June M-Sa 9am-12:30pm and 2-6pm; Oct.-May M-Sa 9am-12:30pm and 2-5:30pm.) There are no currency exchange bureaus in town, but several **24hr. ATMs** line cours Aristide Briand. For the **pharmacie de garde,** call the **police,** 3 bd. du Viaduc (☎91 52 90). The **post office** is to the left when exiting the train station. (☎91 52 00. Open M-F 8:30am-5:30pm, Sa 8:30am-noon.) **Postal Code:** 13150.

ACCESSIBLE BY CAR

Car rental companies in Avignon are concentrated in the Gare TGV. Helpful road maps are sold in the bookstore inside the *gare* (€4-6). N100 cuts through the middle of the Lubéron and branches off to the smaller villages, while D570 and D571 service Alpilles towns. Drivers should be cautious on the smaller roads and narrow passages, as they can be difficult to maneuver. Expect to pay €2-3 for parking.

ROUSSILLON

Radiant oranges, bright yellows, and earthy reds have made Roussillon (ROOSS-ee-yohn; pop. 1200) the most famous of the ochre villages. Its stunning natural park—a fiery incision in the otherwise green and tan wheat-filled countryside—can be seen from afar. An unforgettable destination, Roussillon is unfortunately only accessible by car. According to local legend, the intense red that colors Roussillon comes from the bleeding body of Dame Sermonde, who jumped from the *castruam* (the highest point in town) after her husband discovered her infidelity. More pragmatic minds have noticed that the village is built on the world's largest vein of natural ochre (tinted clay). Whatever the reason, every doorway, windowsill, and wall in Roussillon is tinted with warm and vibrant shades. Be warned, however: taking some of the colored sand as a souvenir is strictly prohibited and may result in a hefty fine. Ochre pigments can be purchased in local stores.

An exploration of the **Sentier des Ochres,** one of many outstanding trails in Roussillon, is a must; visitors can walk through a vast, dusty ochre deposit between wind-sculpted cliffs. The pigmented dust can leave its mark on clothing and shoes, so dress accordingly. (Open July-Aug. daily 9am-7:30pm; Sept. and Apr.-June M-Sa 9am-6pm, Su 9am-6:30pm; Oct. daily 9am-5:30pm; Mar. M-Sa 9:30am-5:30pm, Su 9:30am-6pm. Closed on rainy days for safety. €2.) The most devoted ochre fans may want to venture 2km east of town (turn right out of the tourist office and follow signs), where the **Conservatoire des Ocres et Pigments Appliqués,** rte. d'Apt, has restored a pigment-making factory and offers tours (€5, with ticket from le Sentier €3) and classes. Short-term 2hr. classes (€16, under 18 €7) range from photography to fabricating dyes from natural resources. (☎05 66 69; www.okhra.com. Open daily July-Aug. 9am-7pm; Sept.-June 9am-6pm. July-Aug. 30min. tour every hour except 1pm; first tour at 10am, last tour 1hr. before closing; less frequent Sept.-June. English tours daily July-Aug.; call ahead.) The villages of St-Saturnin, Gordes, Joucas, and Cavaillon, as well as the Monts de Vaucluse, can be seen from the **highest point** in Roussillon, beyond the church and marked as the *table d'orientation* on the map provided by the tourist office. Now in its 32nd season, the **Festival International de Quatuors à Cordes** brings the best of chamber music every year from late May to early September. (☎75 89 60; www.festival-quatuors-luberon.com. €23, students under 25 €18, ages 12-17 €8, under 12 free.)

A local market takes over **place Pasquier** every Thursday morning (open 8am-12:30pm). The **tourist office,** pl. de la Poste, has hotel listings and sells an English/French guide, which offers details on walking trails (€5). Information on an annual tribute to Samuel Beckett, who completed *Waiting for Godot* in Roussillon, is also available (call Mme. Joly at ☎05 73 82). Past summer events have included art exhibits, readings, and performances of the Irishman's most celebrated plays. (☎05 60 25; www.roussillon-provence.com. Open July-Aug. daily 9:30am-noon and 1:30-6:30pm; Sept.-June M-Sa 10am-noon and 2-5:30pm.) A **pharmacy** is located in pl. du Pasquier, just around the corner from the tourist office. (☎05 66 15. Open M-Sa 9am-noon and 2:30-7pm.) There's **currency exchange** and a 24hr. **ATM** at the **post office,** next door to the tourist office. (Open M, W, F 9am-noon, Tu and Th 9am-noon and 2-4:30pm, Sa 9-11:30am.) **Postal Code:** 84220.

GORDES

One of the most stunning of the hillside towns, cream-colored Gordes (GOHRD; pop. 2050) hangs on the side of a gorge, overlooking Provence's rural green and gold valleys. Inaccessible by public transport, Gordes attracts a large and wealthy crowd of tourists. Pack a picnic to enjoy a view of the vast valleys below the town.

Gordes and its surroundings are known for **bories,** stone huts and dwellings built by the skillful placement of stone upon stone without using mortar. Often seen in the middle of fields or lost in the tangled undergrowth of the hills, they predate the Roman Empire and were built and used by locals until the 18th century. The **Village des Bories,** just outside Gordes, is a unique hamlet of *bories*, inhabited until a little over 150 years ago. Be careful on the drive—the road has two-way traffic despite the fact that it is only wide enough for one car. The town of Gallic huts is complete with sheep-pens, barns, and a wine cistern. (☎72 02 48. Open daily 9am-sunset. €5.50, ages 10-17 €3.) A 4km twisting, narrow, and dangerous drive along a steep mountain road beyond Gordes leads to the **Sénanque Abbey,** an active Cistercian community surrounded by radiant fields of lavender. The abbey itself is a beautiful and simple piece of medieval architecture complemented by purple flowers and the surrounding mountains. Today, the abbey's shop sells prayer books, honey, lavender products, and *sénacole*, a *liqueur* produced by the monks. Despite recent efforts to curb tourist intrusions through reduced hours, mandatory guided tours, and restrictions on groups, visitors continue to flock to this postcard-perfect abbey. As it is a place of prayer, tourists are required to dress conservatively—no short shorts, bare shoulders or exposed midriffs are allowed. Mass is held daily in the Eglise Abbatiale. (☎72 05 72; www.senanque.fr. Visits by 1hr. French tour only; English info leaflets available; times vary by season. The tourist office in Gordes provides detailed schedules. €6, students €5, under 18 €2.50, clergy free.) In the town center, the **château,** used in the past as a barracks, a prison, and a stable, now houses the Hôtel de Ville, the tourist office, and a collection of 200 paintings and photo montages—mostly female nudes—in the **Musée Pol Mara.** Signed works by the modern Flemish artist (€3 for prints to €600 for paintings) can be purchased. (☎72 02 75. Open daily 10am-noon and 2-6pm. €4, ages 10-17 €3, under 10 free.) Held in early August, **Soirées d'Eté** is a festival that brings world-renowned artists to town for a diverse series of concerts, theatrical performances, and poetry readings. (☎72 05 35. Tickets €25-45.)

PROVENCE

A large **market** surrounds the château on Tuesday mornings (8am-1pm), selling everything from pottery and paintings to sausage and socks. As in most of Provence's stunning mountain villages, accommodations here are exorbitantly priced (€60-400). The **tourist office** has a list of *chambres d'hôte*, which are affordable for those traveling in small groups and make for a comfortable, homey stay.

Taxis, though expensive, are available at **Alizes Taxi** (☎06 07 11 77 68). The **tourist office** is in the château. (☎72 02 75; www.gordes-village.com. Open M-Sa 9am-noon and 2-6pm, Su 10am-noon and 2-6pm.) There's a 24hr. **ATM** in the square in front of the office. The **post office** is on the other side of the château and **exchanges currency.** (Open M-F 9am-noon and 2-4:30pm, Sa 9am-11:30pm.)

OPPÈDE-LE-VIEUX

If you rent a car in Provence, don't leave Oppède-le-Vieux (oh-PED-luh-vyuh; pop. 60) off your itinerary. Inaccessible by public transport, the tiny village clings to the mountainside above gardened terraces of lavender and olive groves, and below the stunning ruins of a château. Formerly a bustling market town, Oppède was slowly abandoned in the 16th century for more agriculturally advantageous regions. Early in the 20th century, the village was completely deserted following a violent earthquake that destroyed several houses, and only a few residents have returned. Oppède-le-Vieux has begun to restore the ancient ruins, some of which pre-date the 13th century.

The **walk** up the mountain through the old village and to the church and castle allows visitors to explore the town's remains undisturbed by modern-day infiltrations. Parking below the village (€2) is compulsory. From here, small hand-painted signs direct pedestrians toward the park promenade that leads to the village. Follow the signs up the terraced hillside, where you can soak in breathtaking views of the countryside and village. Take the steps next to the *mairie* to reach the 16th-century **Eglise Notre Dame d'Alidon** (open daily June-Sept. 10am-7pm; Oct. 10am-6pm; Apr.-May 10am-5pm) and the **château,** whose ruins are always open for wandering. Pay attention to warning signs around the castle: overhanging arches and cliff top towers have been known to drop loose stones on visitors.

L'Echaugette ❷, pl. de la Croix, one of the two restaurants in Oppède-le-Vieux, offers salads (€7-12) and delicious *poulet* specialties (€8-9) to hungry visitors. Ask the owners about the dwellings that lie on the path to the church. (☎76 83 68. *Plats* €8-10. Desserts €2.50-5. Open Apr.-Sept. M and W-Su 9am-10pm. Cash only.) To reach Oppède-le-Vieux from Avignon, take the A7 to the N100 and take the exit for Oppède, then continue through the modern town of Oppède, following signs to Oppède-le-Vieux. The town's **tourist office** is in nearby Bonnieux (p. 688).

MÉNERBES

Somewhere on the spectrum between the fairytale feel of Oppède-le-Vieux and the more happening vibe of Bonnieux, Ménerbes (may-NAYRB; pop. 995) sits on a precipice overlooking orange rooftops and a vast green valley. Closed to visitors, a caramel cobblestone church is high up at the edge of the village; its gardens offer 270° views of the surrounding countryside.

To indulge in *provençal* delicacies like *pieds paquets* (sheep's feet), *gardiane de taureau* (thick steaks drenched in red wine sauce), or *crespeu de légumes* (omelette with fresh produce), sit down at oak tables at **La Galoubet ❸,** 104 rue Marcellin Poncet, on the cliffside road that leads to the old church. (☎72 36 08. Lunch *plats* €7-13. Dinner *plats* €9-23. Dinner *menus* €18-30. Homemade desserts €5.30-8. Open July-Aug. daily noon-3pm and 7pm-11pm; Sept.-June M-Tu and Th-Su noon-2pm and 7-10pm.) Grab veggies and cheese at the small **épicerie** next door (open M-Sa 8am-12:30pm and 3:30-7:15pm, Su 8:30am-12:30pm), and head left up the road to the forested trails behind the town. The **post office** is 50m past the restaurant. (Open M-F 9am-noon and 2:30-4pm, Sa 9-11am.) **Postal Code:** 84560.

LACOSTE

Lying 6km from Bonnieux and inaccessible by public transport, Lacoste (lah-KOHST; pop. 417) makes up in quality for what it lacks in size. A steep drive or rigorous climb up a mountain ends at the *vieille ville* and manicured pedestrian passages. Free parking is available sporadically along the road; watch carefully to nab a spot. The white **castle ruins** above the tiny town was home to the Marquis de Sade, inventor of sadism, who brewed his dark stories here. Sadly for those intrigued by M. Sade, the castle is closed. To see the ruins, take the stairs on the right of the stone clock tower to the dirt road that winds around the abandoned castle and through the grassy knolls of the valley below. A few fruit, vegetable, and bric-a-brac stands arrive in Lacoste for the weekly **market** on Tuesdays (open 8am-noon).

ARLES ☎04 90

Every street in Arles (AHRL; pop. 35,000) seems to run into or out of the great Roman arena, and the alleys of the *vieille ville* harbor a surprising number of museums and monuments worth visiting. The capital of Roman Gaul, Arles was nearly destroyed by invasions in the Middle Ages. The town has since been a magnet for artists: Van Gogh lost two years and an ear here, and Picasso produced over 150 drawings in 35 days while pondering the town's bullfights (the 70 works he donated to the city now reside in the Musée Réattu). Today, the annual International Photography Festival fills the town's churches with exhibits. For the adventurous, the Alpilles hills and the Camargue marshlands are an easy daytrip away.

TRANSPORTATION

Trains: av. P. Talabot. Ticket office open M-F 5:50am-9:45pm, Sa 6:05am-8:45pm, Su 6:50am-9:30pm. To: **Avignon** (20min., 12-20 per day, €6.30); **Marseille** (50min., 18-27 per day, €15); **Montpellier** (1hr., 5-8 per day, €16); **Nîmes** (20min., 8-11 per day, €9.30).

Buses: Buses leave from the train station, on av. P. Talabot, and from bd. Georges Clemenceau. Consult tourist office inside the train station for schedules; Arles has no official station. Trains are the better option for trips to Avignon and Nîmes, as they cost little more and take half as long. **La Boutique des Transports** (☎08 10 00 08 16; www.laboutiquedestransports.com) runs buses to **Avignon** (1hr., 5-6 per day, €7.10), **Nîmes** (1hr., M-Sa 5 per day, €5.50), and **Tarascon** (20min., 10-15 per day, €2-3).

Public Transportation: LA STAR, 24 bd. Clemenceau (☎08 10 00 08 16; www.star-arles.fr). Tickets €0.80, day pass €2. Also runs the free Starlette shuttle, which loops around town and serves the tourist office (2 per hr. M-Sa 7am-7pm).

Taxis: ☎06 08 94 98 00.

Car Rental: ADA, 22 av. de Stalingrad (☎52 07 27; www.ada.fr), near the train station. From €59 per day with 100km. 21+. Open M-F 8am-noon and 2-6pm, Sa 8-10am and 5-7pm. AmEx/MC/V.

Bike Rental: Arles VAE, av. Talabot (☎04 90 43 33 14), in front of the train station. €5 per 4hr., €10 per day, €15 per 2 days. Open July-Aug. daily 9am-7pm; Sept.-June Tu-Sa 9am-noon and 2-6pm. MC/V.

PROVENCE

ORIENTATION AND PRACTICAL INFORMATION

The train station and bus hub are on the south bank of the Rhône, north of the *vieille ville.* The tourist office lies south of the old city center, between the commercial center and the residential areas farther south.

Tourist Office: Espl. Charles de Gaulle, bd. des Lices (☎18 41 20; www.arlestourisme.com). From the train station, turn left and walk to pl. Lamartine; after the Monoprix, turn left onto bd. Emile Courbes. At the big intersection by the southeast old city tower, turn right onto bd. des Lices. Excellent free maps and brochures. Accommodations service (€1 plus down payment). Bus schedules and info for visiting the region. Open daily Apr.-Sept. 9am-6:45pm; Oct.-Mar. 9am-4:45pm.

Tours: A *petit train* (☎04 93 41 31 09; perso.wanadoo.fr/lespetitstrainsdusud) leaves from the main tourist office and from Les Arènes every 35min. and tours the *vieille ville.* Apr.-Oct. daily 10am-7pm. 35min. €6, under 10 €3.

Currency Exchange: Arène Change, 22bis rond-point des Arènes (☎93 34 66). Open Apr.-Oct. M-Sa 9am-6pm. Several 24hr. **ATMs** surround pl. de la République.

Luggage Storage: Hôtel Acacias, 2 rue de la Cavalerie (☎96 37 88). €5 per day. Open daily 7:30am-10pm.

Laundromat: Laverie Miele, 12 rue Portagnel. Wash €3.50-7, dry €1 per 10min. Open daily 7am-9:30pm.

Ambulance: SMUR (☎49 29 22).

Police: on the corner of bd. des Lices and av. des Alyscamps (☎18 45 00). Call for the **pharmacie de garde.**

Poison Control: ☎04 91 74 66 66.

Hospital: Centre Hospitalier J. Imbert, quartier Fourchon (☎49 29 29).

Internet Access: Cyber Espace, 10 rue Gambetta (☎52 51 30). €1.50 per 30min., €3 per hr. Open daily 9am-12:30pm and 2-10pm.

Post Office: 5 bd. des Lices (☎18 41 10), between the tourist office and the police station. **Currency exchange.** Open M and Th-F 8:30am-6pm, Tu-W 8:30am-7pm, Sa 8:15am-noon. **Postal Code:** 13200.

ACCOMMODATIONS AND CAMPING

Arles has a few inexpensive hotels, especially in the area around **place Voltaire,** but for a little extra it's worthwhile to stay in one of the incredibly charming establish-

POLISHING UP PROVENCE

One NGO offers an opportunity to get up close and personal with provençal architectural history. **Le Sabranenque,** based in the small provençal town of St-Victor de la Coste, works to restore traditional rural architecture in southern France. Since the birth of the organization in 1967, it has relied heavily on volunteer labor.

Today, Le Sabranenque offers summer volunteer programs as well as programs that fit the needs of international travelers who would like to help with restoration projects as they explore the region. The programs are organized around morning work sessions and afternoon free time. From June to September, the organization offers two-week programs ($745 including room and board); in the fall and the spring, one-week programs are available, with daily afternoon excursions ($595).

Marc Simon, one of the directors, says that participants truly enjoy the work, which relies on the same techniques originally used to build the sites. "I think what people like best is the opportunity to see a provençal village from the inside," he says. Participants live in the restored houses in unfrequented villages and work in small groups. The organization picks up participants from the train station in Avignon.

For more information, visit www.sabranenque.com, or call ☎04 66 50 05 05.

ments near the center of the *vieille ville.* The tourist office provides guides to accommodations, *chambres d'hôtes,* and camping options. Reservations are crucial during the photo festival in July and should be made a month in advance.

Auberge de Jeunesse (HI), 20 av. Maréchal Foch (☎96 18 25; www.fuaj.org), 10min. from the city center and 20min. from the station. From the station, take bus #3 to "tourist office" (last bus 7pm). From there, walk behind the office onto bd. Emile Zola and make a left onto av. du Maréchal Foch; the hostel will be on the left, 50m down the street. Simple and clean 8-bed dorms, a large, social dining room, and a charming garden make this the best deal in Arles. Bar open until midnight. Breakfast included. Reception 7-10am and 5-11pm. Lockout 10am-5pm. Curfew July-Aug. midnight, Sept.-June 11pm. Reserve ahead online Apr.-June. Dorms €15. MC/V. ❶

Le Calendal, 5 rue Porte de Laure (☎96 11 89; www.lecalendal.com) in between Les Arènes and the Théâtre Antique. This hotel boasts charming *provençal* décor, amazing views, and a beautiful garden. The unbeatable location and spotless rooms make the big splurge worthwhile. Buffet breakfast €9. Reception M-F 7:30am-10pm, Sa-Su 7:30am-9pm. Reservations recommended 1 month ahead in summer. Singles and doubles €49-129; triples €99-129. AmEx/MC/V. ❹

Camping City, 67 rte. de Crau (☎93 08 86; www.camping-city.com). From the tourist office, take the Starlette bus to "Clemenceau." Then take bus #2 (dir.: Pont de Crau) to "Hermite" (€0.80). To walk, turn right on bd. Clemenceau and continue as it turns into bd. des Lices and av. Victor Hugo. Pass over the train tracks and keep left on rte. de Crau at the fork; the campground is 500m ahead on your left (20min.). Closest site to town, with pool, laundry, bar, and restaurant. Well-kept hedges create privacy. Bikes €10 per day. July-Aug. reception 8am-1am; Sept. and Apr.-June daily 8am-9pm. Open Apr.-Sept. €16 per person, car, and site; €17 per 2 people; €4.50 per extra adult, €3 per child under 7. Electricity €4. Cash only. ❶

FOOD

Arles's cuisine benefits from fresh seafood and hearty Camargue *taureau* (bull) meat. Restaurants with *cuisine régionale* are tucked into the small squares and narrow streets, particularly on **place du Forum** and around the **Arènes.** Regional produce fills the open-air markets on **boulevard Emile Combes** (open W 7am-1pm) and **boulevard des Lices** (open Sa 7am-1pm). For groceries, try **Monoprix,** pl. Lamartine,

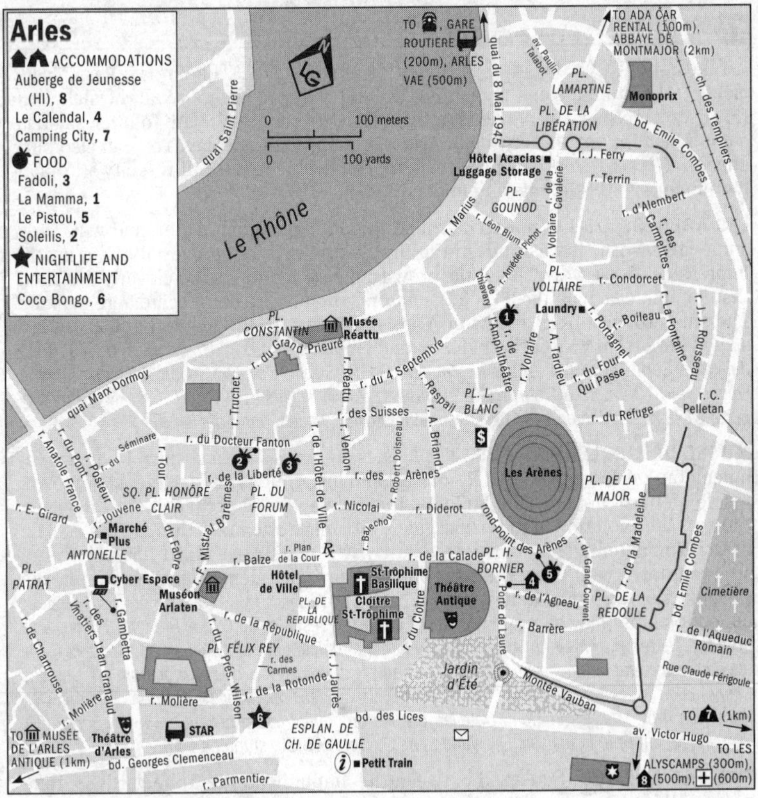

(☎93 62 74; open M-Th 8:30am-7:30pm, F-Sa 8:30am-8pm; AmEx/MC/V) or **Marché Plus,** 7 rue de la République (open M-Sa 7am-9pm, Su 9am-1pm; AmEx/MC/V).

Fadoli, 46 rue des Arènes (☎49 70 73). Behind forest-green shutters just off pl. du Forum, this sandwich counter serves more creative versions of the panini found at most cafés. Fresh basil and olive oil add kick. Sandwiches €3.50-6, takeout €2.70-5.50. Open July-Aug. daily 10am-midnight; Sept.-June Tu-Sa 11am-7pm. Cash only. ❶

Soleilis, 9 rue Docteur Fanton (☎93 30 76). After dinner, try a *boule* or 2 of excellent ice cream at a bargain price. Flavors range from chocolate and vanilla to bitter almond. Regular cone €1.20, 1 scoop with homemade waffle cone €2.20. Mountainous sundaes €6.50. Open July-Aug. M 2-6:30pm, Tu-Su 2-6:30pm and 8:30-10:30pm or later; Sept.-Oct. and Mar.-June daily 2-6:30pm. Cash only. ❶

La Mamma, 20 rue de l'Amphithéâtre (☎96 11 60). Just beyond the Roman arena and its touristed path, this homey restaurant serves up fresh pasta in a rustic atmosphere. Wine €2.30. Salads €9-10. Pizzas €8.20-9.20. Filling lasagna €9.90. Open Tu-Sa noon-2:30pm and 7-10:30pm, Su noon-2:30pm. MC/V. ❷

Le Pistou, 30bis rond-point des Arènes (☎43 86 09; www.lepistou.com). For a splurge, it's worth eating with a view of the Roman amphitheater. Pistou's Spanish-influenced gourmet cuisine matches its bullfighting-themed décor. *Plats* €13. *Plat* with dessert or *entrée* €18, with both €22. Open Apr.-Sept. M-F and Su 7-9:30pm. MC/V. ❸

SIGHTS

It takes about two days to see the city's major sights. The city's **Pass Monuments** (€14, students and under 18 €12) will give you access to all the sights on this list except the Abbaye de Montmajour. It pays for itself with four uses and is a good idea for anyone staying in Arles for more than one day. You can also purchase a *Circuit Romain* pass, which provides access to all the city's Roman monuments (€9, students and under 18 €7).

LES ARÈNES. Arles is centered around this Roman amphitheater, and while it is somewhat worn (it was built in the first century AD), the overall effect is still impressive. Don't worry about the crowds; the structure was so cleverly designed that it could evacuate the 20,000 spectators who used to congregate here in 5min. The small tower offers a view of Arles's rooftops. Bullfights and bull races are staged here from Easter through September. *(☎49 36 86, bullfights ☎96 03 70. Open daily May-Sept. 9am-6pm; Oct. and Mar.-Apr. 9am-5:30pm; Nov.-Feb. 10am-4:30pm. Tours in French daily 10am. €5.50, students and under 18 €4. Bullfights from €12/6. Weekly bull runs W 5pm; €7/3.50. Audio tours in English, French, German, Italian, and Spanish; €3.)*

MUSÉE DE L'ARLES ANTIQUE. The Arènes are Arles's most striking Roman monument, but the best-preserved Roman art and inscriptions are just outside of town. Inside an ultra-modern blue building, this awe-inspiring archaeological museum retraces the evolution of the Camargue from prehistoric times through the decline of the Roman empire in the sixth century AD. A 200-year effort has uncovered spectacularly well-preserved second-century mosaics, countless amphorae (ancient storage jars), statues, and pieces of jewelry, as well as the second largest collection of antique sarcophagi in the world. *(Presqu'île du Cirque Romain. 10min. walk from the center of town. With your back to the tourist office, turn left, walk on bd. Georges Clemenceau to the end, and follow the signs. Alternatively, take bus #1, dir.: Barriol, from bd. Georges Clemenceau to "Salvador Allende." ☎18 88 80; www.arles-antique.cg13.fr. Open daily Apr.-Oct. 9am-7pm; Nov.-Mar. 10am-5pm. Detailed English brochures and excellent tours July-Sept. daily 3pm in French, 5pm in English; Oct.-June tours Su 3pm. €5.50, students €4.)*

THÉÂTRE ANTIQUE. Squeezed between the amphitheater and the gardens, remnants of this ruined theater pale in comparison to the momentous *théâtre antique* in Orange. Only two columns of the stage wall stand among fascinating rubble, but enough remains for modern productions to take advantage of the magnificent acoustics and atmosphere. *(Rue de la Calade. For reservations call Théâtre de la Calade ☎93 05 23 or the tourist office. Open daily May-Sept. 9am-6pm; Oct. and Mar.-Apr. 9-11:30am and 2-5:30pm; Nov.-Feb. 10-11:30am and 2-4:30pm. €3, students and under 18 €2.20.)*

ALYSCAMPS. A twist on "Champs-Elysées" (Elysian Fields), Alyscamps held one of the most famous burial grounds from Roman times until the late Middle Ages. Consecrated by St-Trôphime, the first bishop of Arles, it now contains 80 generations of locals. Van Gogh and Gauguin enjoyed strolling through and painting the "romantic" alleys of unbreakable peace, which were mentioned in Dante's *Inferno*. Sadly, the most elaborate sarcophagi have been either destroyed or removed. *(10min. from town. From the tourist office, head east on bd. des Lices to its intersection with bd. Emile Courbes. Turn right to the roundabout, veer left on av. des Alyscamps, and cross the tracks. ☎49 36 87. Open daily May-Sept. 9am-6pm; Oct. and Mar.-Apr. 9-11:30am and 2-5pm; Nov.-Feb. 10-11:30am and 2-4:30pm. €3.50, students and under 18 €2.60.)*

ABBAYE DE MONTMAJOUR. The medieval Abbaye, with vast chambers of thick columns and pointed arches, lies 2km outside Arles. A courtyard reveals the magnificent proportions of the abbey's **Pons de l'Orme tower.** Founded in AD 948 by Benedictine monks, the abbey began as a small commune but slowly amassed a fortune from the gifts monks received for performing spiritual and burial rites. A **UNESCO World Heritage sight,** the abbey has welcomed visitors ever since Prosper Mérimee opened its doors in the late 20th century. *(Route de Fontvieille. From the Gare Routière in Arles, take bus #7 or 11; 10min.; M-Sa 18 per day, Su 6 per day; €2-3. ☎54 64 17; www.centredesmonumentsnationaux.fr. Open May.-Aug. daily 10am-6:30pm; Apr. and Sept. daily 10am-5pm; Oct.-Mar. Tu-Su 10am-5pm. Last entry 45min. before closing. July-Sept. guided tours in French by reservation. €6.50, ages 18-25 €4.50, under 18 free.)*

CLOÎTRE ST-TRÔPHIME. Named after Arles's first bishop, this small medieval cloister is a calm and shady oasis. Each carved column is topped by lions in brushwood, saints in stone leaves, and the occasional fluttering bird. The cloister is especially worth visiting from July to September, when the bare chambers of the Episcopal complex showcase an exhibit from the International Photography Festival. *(Pl. de la République. ☎49 36 36. Open daily May-Sept. 9am-6pm; Oct. and Mar.-Apr. 9am-5:30pm; Nov.-Feb. 10am-4:30pm. €3.50, students €2.60.)*

PROVENCE

MUSEON ARLATEN. Founded by turn-of-the-century poet Frédéric Mistral, who dedicated his life to safeguarding regional traditions, this museum features a collection of *provençal* objects. Museum guards don traditional 19th-century costumes, and visitors stroll through galleries of handicrafts, domestic furniture, jewelry, and a series of stunning dioramas depicting daily *provençal* life. Admission is only €1 because three-quarters of the museum is closed for renovation until 2009—when the whole museum will shut for a massive overhaul. *(29 rue de la République. ☎52 52 31. Open July-Aug. daily 9:30am-1pm and 2-6:30pm; June Tu-Su 9:30am-1pm and 2-6:30pm; Sept. daily 9:30am-12:30pm and 2-6pm; Apr.-May Tu-Su 9:30am-12:30pm and 2-6pm; Oct.-Mar. Tu-Su 9:30am-12:30pm and 2-5pm. €1; 1st Su and last W of month free.)*

MUSÉE RÉATTU. Once a stronghold of the knights of St-John, this museum now houses temporary exhibits as well as a collection of modern art that contrasts with the gargoyles and arched ceilings of the medieval building. At the heart of the museum, near exhibits of work by Henri Rousseau and Réattu, are the 57 drawings with which Picasso honored Arles in 1971. *(10 Rue du Grand Prieuré. ☎49 37 58. Open daily July-Sept. 10am-7pm; Oct. and Mar.-June 10am-12:30pm and 2-6:30pm; Nov.-Feb. 1-6pm. €4, students €3; during photography festival €6/4.50.)*

ENTERTAINMENT AND NIGHTLIFE

The **Théâtre d'Arles,** bd. Georges Clemenceau, hosts drama, dance, and concerts from October to June. (☎52 51 51; www.theatre-arles.com/accueil. Tickets €2.40-20.) Arles isn't a town for night owls, but the cafés along **boulevard Georges Clemenceau** attract a crowd with drinks and music. **Coco Bongo,** 14 bd. des Lices, is a large bar with a pleasant terrace. Tropical foliage adds to the atmosphere, and drinks come at reasonable prices. (☎43 55 27. Beer €2.50. Mixed drinks €5.50. Open July-Sept. daily 8am-1am; Oct.-June Tu-Su 8am-midnight. AmEx/MC/V.)

FESTIVALS

A major draw for tourists is the annual **Rencontres Internationales de la Photographie,** held in the first week of July. Undiscovered photographers court agents by roaming around town with portfolios under their arms, while established artists hold nightly slide shows (€8-12). When the festival crowd departs, the exhibits are left behind until mid-September (€3.50 per exhibit; all exhibits €28, students €22, under 16 free). For more info, contact **Rencontres d'Arles,** 10 rond-point des Arènes (☎96 76 06; www.rencontres-arles.com). During the festival, buy tickets in one of the many *billeteries* scattered throughout the city center, such as the one at

Espace Van Gogh. If you plan to stay in Arles during the festival, make sure to reserve a room two months in advance. The three-week **Fête d'Arles,** a tribute to the city's traditional culture, begins on the Solstice, with the lighting of a midsummer's fire on the last Friday in June. Other local festivals include the **Fête des Gardians** on May 1, which celebrates the brotherhood of herders of the Camargue's wild horses. Once every three years during the *fête*, the city elects the Queen of Arles and her six ladies, who then represent the city's language, customs and history at local events and international exchanges. Arles is also known for its **Ferias,** festivals organized around *corridas*. The two most important ones are the **Feria d'Arles,** held on Easter, and the **Feria du Riz,** during early September, in the Arènes. (Bureau des Arènes ☎08 91 70 03 70; www.arenes-arles.com. Tickets €17-90.) Those who stop in Arles in summer but outside the festival season can check out the weekly **Courses Camarguaises,** where men race with bulls, Pamplona-style. (July-Aug. W 5pm. €7, under 18 €3.50.) Held in mid-November, the **Marché de Noël** (Christmas market) draws large crowds in town. At the same time, the five-day **Provence Prestige** festival showcases *provençal* culture to 25,000 yearly visitors. Call the tourist office for more info, or check www.provenceprestige.com.

CAMARGUE

In contrast to the northern *provençal* hills, the Camargue is a humid delta lined with grasses and populated by all manner of wildlife. Pink flamingoes, black bulls, and the famous white horses roam freely across the flat expanse of marshland, protected by the confines of the national park. The Camargue is anchored in the north by Arles and in the south by Stes-Maries-de-la-Mer, the region's official capital and base for expeditions. Bring bug spray: the Camargue breeds mosquitoes.

STES-MARIES-DE-LA-MER ☎04 90

In AD 40 Mary Magdalene, Mary Salomé (mother of the Apostles John and James), and Mary Jacobé (Jesus's aunt) were cast out of Palestine and put to sea to die. According to legend, their ship washed ashore in Stes-Maries-de-la-Mer (sehnt-mah-RY-duh-lah-MEHR; pop. 2500, 25,000 in summer), where a dark, fortified church now houses their relics. Tourists flock like the resident flamingoes to Stes-Maries, mostly to use it as a base for exploration of the surrounding marshland. Don't come to Stes-Maries for architecture or beaches—most of the buildings are relatively new, and the stretches of sand are unremarkable.

TRANSPORTATION AND PRACTICAL INFORMATION. Buses leave from Arles (1hr.; M-Sa 5 per day, Su 4 per day; 7:50am-6:10pm; €5.20); contact Autocars Telleschi/Cartreize (☎04 42 28 40 22) for info. The bus stop in Stes-Maries-de-la-Mer is on pl. Mireille. Once here, rent **bikes** at **Le Vélo Santois,** 19 rue de la République, which provides free bike delivery within 10km. (☎97 74 56. €9 per ½-day, €15 per day, €61 per week; passport or ID deposit. Open daily July-Aug. 9am-7pm; Feb.-June and Sept.-Nov. 9am-6:30pm. Cash only.) A few minutes up the road at the town entrance, **Le Vélociste,** 8 pl. Mireille, offers similar prices for rentals, as well as day-long packages that include **horse rides** (€36) and **kayaking** (€30). The equestrian package includes 30km of biking and 2½hr. of horseback riding, and the kayak package includes 20km of biking and 7km of kayaking in two-person kayaks. (☎97 83 26; www.levelociste.com. Passport or ID deposit. Open mid-June to Aug. daily 9am-7pm; Sept. to mid-June M and W-Su 9am-12:30pm and 2-6:30pm. Closed Nov.-Feb. Cash only.) **Allô Taxi** is available at ☎97 94 49 or 06 18 63 08 59.

The town is wedged between conservation land to the north, sea to the south, and marshes to the east. Within the town, everything is less than a 10min. walk away. To explore the landscape around town, though, a bike, horse, or Jeep will be useful. To reach the **tourist office,** 5 av. Van Gogh, walk toward the ocean on rue de la République and make a right at the roundabout onto av. Van Gogh. The office is on the left. (☎97 82 55; www.saintesmaries.com. Open daily July-Aug. 9am-8pm; Sept. and Apr.-June 9am-7pm; Mar. and Oct. 9am-6pm; Nov.-Feb. 9am-5pm.) There is a 24hr. **ATM** outside the tourist office. A **pharmacy** is at 18 rue Victor Hugo. (☎97 83 02. Call for service when closed. Open M-Sa 9am-12:30pm and 3-8pm, Su 10am-12:30pm and 5-7pm.) The **police** are on av. Van Gogh (☎97 89 50), next to *les Arènes.* The **post office** is at 2 av. Gambetta and offers **currency exchange.** (☎97 96 00. Open M-F 9am-12:30pm and 1:30-5pm, Sa 8:30-11:30am.) **Postal Code:** 13732.

ACCOMMODATIONS AND FOOD. Rooms fill quickly in the summer, and there are no cheap accommodations. Budget travelers should visit Stes-Maries as a daytrip from Arles, but those determined to stay overnight can check out **Hôtel Méditerranée ❹,** 4 av. Frédéric Mistral. This quiet hotel has 14 pastel rooms, rustic furniture, and hand-painted motifs; three rooms have private terraces (☎97 82 09; www.mediterraneehotel.com. Breakfast on terrace €6. Parking €6. Reception 7am-10pm. Reserve 3-4 weeks ahead in summer. Closed part of Jan. July-Aug. doubles with shower €40, with shower and toilet €46-52; triples €65-68. Sept.-June €36/42-48/61-64. MC/V.) Ten kilometers north of Stes-Maries, in the heart of the Camargue, is the **Auberge de Jeunesse Hameau de Pioch Badet (HI) ❷.** To get there, take bus #20 to "Auberge de Jeunesse" (from Stes-Maries 10min., 7 per day, €1.70; from Arles 45min., €4.50). This camp-style hostel makes a great base for exploring the Camargue. The friendly owner, whose dog and cat wander the area, goes out of his way to help guests. (☎97 51 72. Horse tours €13 per hr., €54 per day. Bike rental €11 per day; passport deposit. Laundry €3. Reception 7:30-10:30am and 5-11pm. Lockout 10:30am-5pm. Curfew midnight, extended during festivals. Reserved primarily for groups Nov.-Jan. Obligatory *demi-pension* with bunk, breakfast, dinner, and sheets €32. Cash only.) Camp at **La Brise ❷,** rue Marcel-Carriere, a three-star site—crossed by watery ditches and dotted with trees—that has direct access to the beach. If coming from Arles, take the bus to the last stop, "La Brise." From Stes-Maries's center, face the ocean, walk left, and follow the beachside road until you reach the RV parking lot. Turn left along the fence, then continue around it to the right to reach the entrance of the campground (15min). The site has a large pool, supermarket, snack bar, laundry, and Internet access. In summer, the campsite organizes water polo, soccer games, karaoke nights, and scuba diving. (☎97 84 67; labrise@saintesmaries.com. Reception July-Aug. 8:30am-8:30pm; Sept.-June 9am-7pm. Lockout midnight. Internet access €7 per hr. July-Aug. 2 people with car €21, €7.30 per extra adult, €4.20 per extra child under 7; Apr.-June €19/6.80/3.90. Prices drop 30-40% in low season. MC/V.)

The Camargue's main crop is a sweet, fat-grained rice found in *gâteau de riz* (gelatinous rice cakes; €2), sold at *pâtisseries*, local restaurants, and on the shelves of supermarkets like **Petit Casino,** 6 rue Victor Hugo. (☎97 90 60. Open July-Aug. daily 8am-8pm; Sept.-June Tu-Su 8am-12:30pm and 3-7:30pm. V.) A market fills **place des Gitanes** on Mondays and Fridays (open 8am-12:30pm). Restaurants cluster near the waterfront and **rue Victor Hugo,** especially on **place Esprit Pioch,** and serve seafood, paella, *pavé du taureau* (bull), and refreshing sangria. *Moules-frites* (mussels with fries; €9-12) is a great option for a cheap and filling meal. Restaurants and snack bars with cheaper *menus* line **avenue Frédéric Mistral.** Most *menus* start around €12, but €9 will buy a good lunch. Sadly, restaurants in Stes-Maries are quite similar and not that special; the flip side of this homogeneity is that you can find a decent meal by the ocean almost anywhere.

SIGHTS. The only major sight in town, and Stes-Maries's focus, is the 12th-century **church,** which has a Romanesque interior, a windowless façade, and not much else. Climb the vertigo-inducing staircase for a view of the marshes and orange roofs that color the region. Exercise caution on the roof; it's easy to slip. (☎97 87 60. Church open daily 8am-12:30pm and 2-7pm. Roof and tower open daily July-Aug. 10am-8pm; Sept.-June 10am-noon and 2-5pm. €2, under 12 €1.50.)

OUTDOOR ACTIVITIES. Most organized visits to the Camargue leave from Stes-Maries; the tourist office has a complete list of tours in the region. The best way to see the Camargue is on **horseback.** Stables offering tours are scattered throughout the park and in Stes-Maries itself. White Camargue horses can go far into the marshes, wading through deep water to find a range of birds and bulls that you can't see by any other means. Most rides are appropriate for novices. Bring long pants and insect repellent. The **Association Camarguaise de Tourisme Equestre** has a list of stables that offer tours. (☎97 10 40; www.parc-camargue.fr. €13-16 per hr., €26-30 per 2hr., €35-40 per day; picnic usually included on daytrips.) Although most of the trails are open only to horseback riders and walkers, **bicycle touring** is another great way to see much of the area. Trail maps indicating length, level of difficulty, and dangerous spots are available from the Stes-Maries tourist office and from bike shops. Bring an ample supply of water. A 2hr. ride reveals some of the area, but a whole day is necessary to visit the wide, deserted white-sand beaches that line the trail. Aspiring botanists and zoologists should stop at the **Maison du Parc Naturel Régional de Camargue (PNRC),** 4km from Stes-Maries, at the "Pont de Gau" stop on bus #20, which runs between Ste-Maries and Arles. The staff distributes info on the region's unusual flora and fauna, has maps of the Camargue region, and gladly points out all possible walking or biking trails (2-30km). The office also presents panoramic views of the marshes. (☎97 86 32. Open Apr.-Sept. daily 10am-6pm; Oct.-Mar. M-Th and Sa-Su 9:30am-5pm. Free.) Next door, the **Parc Ornithologique de Pont de Gau** presents visitors with 60 hectares of the Camarguaise landscape, focusing specifically on regional birds. (☎97 82 62. Park open daily Apr.-Sept. 9am-sunset; Oct.-Mar. 10am-sunset. Office open daily Apr.-Sept. 9am-7pm; Oct.-Mar. 9am-6pm. Tours €9, under 10 €4.) Boats and Jeeps are also a good way to explore the marshes. **Le Camargue,** 5 rue des Launes, sends boats from Port Gardian deep into the Petit-Rhône for bird- and bull-watching. (☎97 84 72; www.bateau-camargue.com. 1½hr.; Mar.-Sept. 3 per day, Oct. 2 per day. July-Aug. 1st departure 10:45am, last departure 5:55pm; Sept. and mid-Mar. to Apr. 1st departure 10:30am, last departure 4:10pm. €10, under 18 €5.) For Jeep safaris, contact **Le Gitan,** 17 av. de la République, in Stes-Maries. The Jeeps hold 7-8 people. (☎97 89 33; legitansafari@libertysurf.fr. Trips depart May-Sept. 8, 10am, 2, 4, 6pm; Oct.-Mar. 10am, 2pm; Apr. 10am, 2, 4pm. 2hr. €40. Open Apr.-Nov. daily 9am-7pm.)

FESTIVALS. According to legend, the chief of the region's native Roma greeted the Stes-Maries when they arrived and asked that they baptize her people as Christians. The **Pèlerinage des Gitans** is a yearly event uniting Roma pilgrims from all over Europe (May 24-25, 2008). A costumed procession from the church to the sea bears statues of the saints and reenacts their landing. The two days are filled with prayers and attract a crowd of tourists. A pilgrimage on the weekend closest to October 20 hosts the **Maries** for local residents, with similar ceremonies. Around July 14th, the three-day **Féria du Cheval** brings horses from around the world for shows, competitions, and rodeos at the Stes-Maries arena. (Arènes in Stes-Maries ☎97 85 86. €31-75.) The last Sunday of July brings the **Festo Vierginenco,** a celebration of teenage girls' passage into adulthood; girls then dress for the first time in traditional women's clothing. In July and August, bullfights, bull games, and horse shows occur regularly at the modern arenas. Throughout the year, **Courses Camarguaises,** which do not end in the death of the bull, take place regularly at the *Arènes.* (☎97 85 86. Tickets €7-8.)

NÎMES ☎04 66

The fabric *de Nîmes* (of Nîmes), also known as denim, was first produced here. Now, the distinctly Spanish atmosphere draws foreign and French vacationers in the summer. In June and September, tourists flock to Nîmes (NEEM; pop. 135,000) for *férias*, festivals with bull runs, bullfights, and flamenco dancing. With affordable accommodations, a gorgeous garden, and a festive weekly market, Nîmes is a comfortable base for short excursions. The region's Roman ruins, especially the Pont du Gard aqueduct, are reasons to stay a night.

TRANSPORTATION

Trains: Bd. Talabot. Info office open M-Sa 6am-9pm, Su 6am-10pm. To: **Arles** (25min., 8 per day, €9.10); **Bordeaux** (5hr., 6 per day, €60); **Marseille** (1¼hr., 9 per day, €22); **Montpellier** (30min., 31-46 per day, €8); **Paris** (3hr., 15 per day, €93); **Toulouse** (3hr., 17 per day, €38).

Buses: Rue Ste-Félicité (☎29 52 00), behind the train station. Info office just inside the train station open M-F 7:30am-12:30pm and 2-6:30pm. **Lignes du Gard** (www.stdgard.com) runs to **Avignon** (1½hr.; M-Sa 5 per day, Su 3 per day; €8.30). **Cars de Camargue** serves **Arles** (M-F 5 per day, Sa 4 per day; €6.30).

Public Transportation: T.C.N. (☎08 20 22 30 30). Schedules available at the tourist office. Buses stop running at 9pm, and service is only frequent on most lines until 8pm. Tickets good for 1hr. Tickets €1, *carnet* of 5 €4. Buy single tickets on bus, *carnets* at the kiosks near the Station Esplanade. Validate on the bus.

Taxis: TRAN (☎29 40 11), in front of the train station. Base €2. 24hr.

Car Rental: At the train station. **Europcar** (☎29 07 94). From €129 per day. 21+. Under-25 surcharge €25 per day. Open M 8am-1pm and 2-7pm, Tu-Sa 8:30am-1pm and 2-7pm. AmEx/MC/V.

Bike Rental: Véloland, 4 rue de la République (☎36 01 80). €9 per ½-day, €15 per day, €60 per week. Open M 2-7pm, Tu-Sa 9:30am-12:30pm and 2:30-7pm. MC/V.

ORIENTATION AND PRACTICAL INFORMATION

Nîmes's shops, museums, and cafés cluster in the *vieille ville* between **boulevard Victor Hugo** and **boulevard Admiral Courbet.** To get there from the train station, follow av. Feuchères, veer left around the park, then head clockwise around the arena. To reach the tourist office, follow the signs and go straight on bd. Victor Hugo for five blocks until you reach the **Maison Carrée,** a Roman temple in the middle of pl. de la Comédie. The office is a few blocks down on rue Auguste.

Tourist Office: 6 rue Auguste (☎58 38 00; www.ot-nimes.fr). Offers maps, festival info, tours of the city (July-Sept. Tu, Th, Sa 10am; Oct.-June Sa 2:30pm; €5.50, students €4.50), and free accommodations service. Audio tours of the city €8, 2 tours €10. Provides free *Nîmescope,* which has event listings. Info on excursions to Pont du Gard, the Camargue, and nearby towns. Open July-Aug. M-W and F 8:30am-8pm, Th 8:30am-9pm, Sa 9am-7pm, Su 10am-6pm; Sept. and Easter-June M-F 8:30am-7pm, Sa 9am-7pm, Su 10am-6pm; Oct.-Easter M-F 8:30am-7pm, Sa 9am-7pm, Su 10am-5pm.

Tours: Le Petit Train (☎06 08 63 71 16). Gives a tour of Roman monuments and the *vieille ville,* leaving every hr. from esplanade Charles de Gaulle, in front of the Palais de Justice. Daily mid-July to mid-Aug. 10:30am-7:30pm; Sept.-Oct. and Apr.-June 10:30-11:30am and 2:30-5:30pm. €5, ages 2-11 €2.50.

Budget Travel: Nouvelles Frontières, 22 bd. Gambetta (☎67 38 94; fax 78 38 62). Open M-F 9:30am-7pm, Sa 9am-7:30pm.

Lost and Found: Rue de la Trésorerie (☎67 84 29).

Youth Center: BIJ, 8 rue de l'Horloge (☎27 76 86). Provides info on employment, education, and travel opportunities for students. Free Internet access by reservation; 1 walk-in kiosk is available for checking email. Open M-F 10am-6pm.

Laundry: Laverie, rue de Grand Couvent. Wash €3.50-7, dry €0.40 per 5min. Open daily 8am-9pm. **Laverie,** 14 rue Nationale, is a different establishment with the same (highly appropriate) name. Wash €3.40-6.80, dry €0.40. Open daily 7am-9pm.

Police: 3 rue du Colisée (☎02 56 00).

Pharmacy: Grand Pharmacie de L'Esplanade, 9 bd. de Prague (☎21 31 42). Open M-F 8:30am-8pm, Sa 8:30am-12:30pm and 2-7:30pm.

Hospital: Pl. du Professor Robert de Bré (☎68 68 68).

Internet Access: Cyber Café Aèdèmia, 4 bd. Gambetta (☎29 78 83). 10am-8pm and 10pm-midnight €2 per hr., 8-10pm €2 per 2hr. Open daily 10am-midnight.

Post Office: 1 bd. de Bruxelles (☎76 69 50), at the end of av. Feuchères. **Currency exchange.** Open M-F 8am-7pm, Sa 8am-12:30pm. Branch offices: 19 bd. Gambetta and 11 pl. Belle Croix. **Poste Restante:** 30006. **Postal Code:** 30000.

PROVENCE

ACCOMMODATIONS AND CAMPING

Auberge de Jeunesse (HI), 257 chemin de l'Auberge de la Jeunesse (☎68 03 20; fax 68 03 21). Take bus I (dir.: Alès) to "Stade" and walk 500m up the hill; helpful signs lead the way from the traffic circle to the Auberge. Unquestionably Nîmes's best option for single travelers, but it's an arduous uphill walk from the bus stop. Considerate staff greets travelers with a cold glass of water, a good introduction to the hostel's comfy 4- to 6-bed dorms and beautiful garden seating area. Some family rooms and camping available. Hostel minibus takes guests to the station (9am, €1.40). Laundry, refrigerator, bar, and kitchen. Key-card access. Breakfast €3.40. Lockers; bring your own lock or buy one (€3). Internet access €1 per 15min. Free Wi-Fi. Reception 7:30am-1am. Reserve ahead Mar.-Sept. Bunks €15. Camping €9, with tent rental €11. MC/V. ❶

Hôtel de l'Amphithéâtre, 4 rue des Arènes (☎67 28 51; perso.wanadoo.fr/hotel-amphitheatre). More central and upscale, in 2 17th- and 18th-century *hôtels.* Offers 15 elegant rooms named after French artists. Rooms have TV and bath; some have A/C. Breakfast €7. Reception 8am-10:30pm. Singles €41-45; doubles €53-81. MC/V. ❸

Hôtel Concorde, 3 rue des Chapeliers (☎67 91 03). Straightforward, clean, and in central Nîmes. Has some of the best prices around. An unbeatable deal for groups. Breakfast €4. Reception daily 9am-7pm. Singles €19, with toilet €24, with shower and TV €29, with all three €32; doubles €25/27/32/36; triples with shower and TV €41, with toilet and TV €44; quads with shower, toilet, and TV €49. AmEx/MC/V. ❷

Camping Domaine de La Bastide, rte. de Générac (☎ 62 05 82), 5km south of the train station. Take bus D (dir.: La Bastide, last bus 8pm) to its terminus. By car, drive toward Montpellier and get off at rte. de Générac. 3-star site with a restaurant and laundry facilities. €9.50 per person, €13 for 2 people, with electricity €13/17. MC/V over €15. ❶

FOOD

Nîmes specializes in *brandade de morue,* dried cod with olive oil packed in a turnover, pastry, or soufflé. A few good but pricey restaurants are hidden along alleys in the *vieille ville,* surrounded by unexciting tourist fare. Stock up on picnic food at the markets on **boulevard Jean-Jaurès** (open F 7am-1pm) and in **Les Halles** (open daily 6am-12:30pm). There's a **Monoprix,** 3 bd. Admiral Courbet, near Esplanade Charles de Gaulle (☎21 06 36; open M-Sa 8:30am-8:30pm, Su 9am-noon;

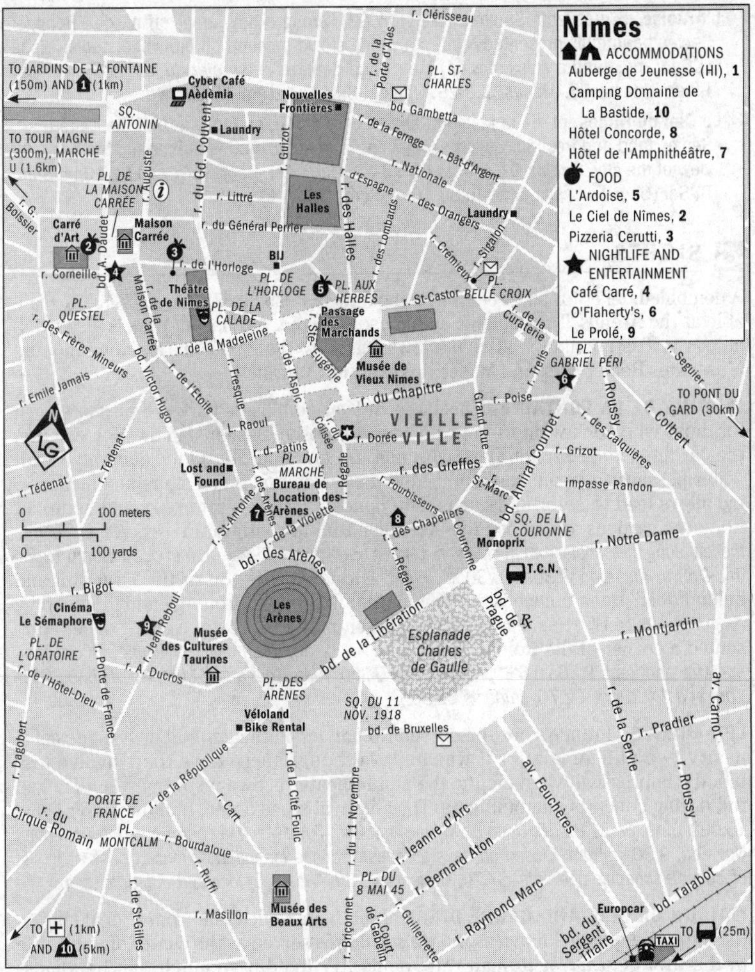

AmEx/MC/V), and a large **Marché U,** 19 rue d'Alès, just down the hill from the hostel at the traffic circle (☎28 80 80; open M-Th 8am-12:45pm and 3-8pm, F-Sa 8am-8pm). The terraced herb gardens, shady spots near the Tour-Magne, and ponds on the back slopes of the **Jardins de la Fontaine** are great places to picnic. *Caladons*, honey cookies with almonds, are Nîmes's favorite sweet. Cafés and bakeries line the squares; *brasseries* dominate **boulevard Victor Hugo, boulevard Admiral Courbet,** and the arena. Terraced **place du Marché,** with a crocodile fountain, reverberates with laughter late into the night, while dinner options line the quiet **rue l'étoile.**

Pizzeria Cerutti, 25 rue de l'Horloge (☎21 54 88). Serves hearty Italian fare at great prices and stays open late. Fresh salads (€4.90-9.50), pastas (€8-9), and pizzas (€7.70-8.20) with homemade sauces are cooked before your eyes in the large oven. Lunch *formules* €11-13. Open July-Aug. M-Tu and Th-Su noon-2pm and 7pm-midnight; Sept.-June Th-Su noon-2pm and 7pm-midnight. AmEx/MC/V. ❷

L'Ardoise, 5 rue Petits Souliers (☎21 06 02), along a tiny street off pl. de l'Horloge. Serves beautifully presented food to a young crowd perched on hip white stools. Tapas (€6 for three and a glass of wine) are a good deal, as is the *plat du jour* (€8) at lunch. Takeout pasta €5. *Menus* €23-29. Open M-Sa 11am-1am. MC/V. ❸

Le Ciel de Nîmes, pl. de la Maison Carré (☎36 71 70), on the 3rd fl. of the Carré d'Art. Serves food and fresh juice worth sampling. Take in the modern décor and the beautiful view of the city. Salads €12. *Plats* €9.80-17. Open Apr.-Sept. Tu-W and Su 10am-8pm, Th-Sa 10am-1am; Oct.-Mar. Tu-Su 10am-8pm. MC/V. ❸

SIGHTS

A combined ticket for all three Roman monuments (€9.80, students €7.40) is available at the Arènes, Tour Magne, and Maison Carrée. A museum pass is also available (€9.20, students €7.20) and allows access to the Musée d'Art Contemporain, Musée des Beaux Arts, and Musée des Cultures Taurines.

JARDINS DE LA FONTAINE. This large and varied hillside park is a pleasure even for those who don't want to stop and smell the roses. Designed in the 18th century, the Jardins exude French flair, with a grand and majestic *place* decorated with water passages, elegant sculptures, and *boules* courts. Steep stairs and meandering alleys lead to colorful gardens with ponds. Full of secret nooks and luxuriant flora, the gardens are among the most beautiful in southern France. *(Off pl. Foch to the left along the canals from the Maison. Garden open daily mid-Mar. to mid-Oct. 7:30am-10pm; mid-Oct. to mid-Mar. 7:30am-6:30pm. Free.)* Hidden at the top of the large hill and behind deep green foliage is the **Tour Magne.** Built in the Iron Age and modified by Augustus in 15 BC, this massive tower, essentially a blunt stone spike, once represented a corner of the Roman Empire. *(☎21 82 56. Open daily June-Aug. 9:30am-7pm; Apr.-May and Sept. 9:30am-6:30pm; Mar. and Oct. 9:30am-1pm and 2-6pm; Nov.-Feb. 9:30am-1pm and 2-4:30pm. €2.70, students €2.30.)*

LES ARÈNES. France's best-preserved Roman amphitheater still hosts spectacles nearly two millennia after it was built (although these days they involve less blood). Impressive when empty, the amphitheater is awe-inspiring when packed full during concerts and bullfights. The elliptical stone arena, built in AD 50, seats 15,000 fans. *(☎21 82 56. Open daily June-Aug. 9am-7pm; Mar.-May and Sept.-Oct. 9am-6pm; Nov.-Feb. 9:30am-5pm. Closed on days of férias or concerts; call in advance or ask at tourist office for a schedule of events. €7.70, students €5.80. Audio tour included with admission.)*

MAISON CARRÉE AND CARRÉ D'ART. Built using limestone from a local quarry, the imposing temple known as the **Maison Carrée** served as the center of public life in the first century of Roman rule. Louis XIV liked it so much that he almost ordered it to be brought to Versailles as a lawn ornament. Today, visitors can enjoy a 20min. 3D film inside the ancient monument, which retraces Nîmes's Roman roots. *(☎21 82 56. Open daily June-Aug. 9am-7:30pm; Apr.-May and Sept. 10am-7pm; Mar. and Oct. 10am-6:30pm; Nov.-Feb. 10am-1pm and 2-5pm. Film shows every 30min. €4.50, students €3.60.)* The Maison Carrée faces Norman Foster's ultra-modern glass cube, which houses the city's library and the **Carré d'Art.** The museum displays contemporary works—from monochromatic paintings to pop art—in a fresh, open setting, and hosts a wide variety of temporary exhibitions. *(☎76 35 03; info@carreartmusee.com. Open Tu-Su 10am-6pm. Last entry at 5:30pm. Guided tours Sa-Su 4:30pm; July-Aug. also Tu-F 4:30pm. €5, students €3.70.)*

MUSÉE DES CULTURES TAURINES. Vivid exhibits explain components of the bullfighting culture, from the types of regional bulls to the role of female *toreras.* Though the captions are in French, all visitors will understand the clothing and videos of the fatal *corridas.* *(6 rue Alexandre Ducros. ☎36 83 77. Open June-Oct. Tu-Su 10am-6pm, until 9pm on féria days and during the Jeudis de Nîmes. €5, students €3.70.)*

OTHER SIGHTS. The **Musée des Beaux Arts,** with marble pillars and mosaic floors, features paintings of the Dutch, Flemish, French, and Italian schools from the 15th to 18th centuries. *(Rue de la cité Foulc. ☎67 38 21. Open Tu-Su 10am-6pm. €5, students €3.70.)* Next to the cathedral, the **Musée du Vieux Nîmes,** in a 17th-century Episcopal palace, displays artifacts from the Middle Ages through the 19th century, as well as an exhibit on the history of blue jeans that honors Nîmes as the birthplace of denim. *(Pl. aux Herbes. ☎76 73 70. Open Tu-Su 10am-6pm. Free.)*

ENTERTAINMENT AND FESTIVALS

Cinéma Le Sémaphore, 25 rue Porte de France, plays films in their original languages. (☎67 83 11. €5.90, under 25 €5, noon shows €4.) Concerts, movies, plays, and operas take place at **Les Arènes** throughout the year. For info and reservations, contact the **Bureau de Location des Arènes,** 4 rue de la Violette. (For bullfights call ☎08 91 70 14 01. For concerts call ☎02 80 90; www.arenesdenimes.com. Open M-F 10am-6pm, Sa 10am-1pm.) The **Théâtre de Nîmes,** 1 pl. de la Calade, offers over 70 shows per year, from theater to dance to musical performances. (☎36 65 00. Oct.-June only. Tickets €15-30, students ½-price.) Students in Nîmes head for the **beach** in summer, where makeshift restaurant-bars open in June and entertain until early September. From July to August, **Lignes du Gard** (www.stdgard.com) runs buses from Nîmes *(gare routière)* to two beach hubs—Le Grau du Roi (1hr., 7 per day, round-trip €8.20) and La Grande Motte (1½hr., 8 per day, round-trip €9.60).

Outside festival season, nightlife in Nîmes is slow; bars are your best bet for a social scene. **Le Prolé,** 20 rue Jean Reboul, is a courtyard bar where young and old alike come to enjoy good company and good drinks. (☎21 67 23. Beer €2, during concerts €2.30. Jazz concerts July-Aug. F 8pm. Open M-Th and Sa 9am-10pm, F 9am-midnight. Cash only.) Locals fill the outside tables in summer at the **Café Carrée,** 1 pl. de la Maison Carrée, a lively bar by night. (☎67 50 05. Beer €2.50-6.20. Mixed drinks €5.90-7.50. Open daily 7am-2am. MC/V.) **O'Flaherty's,** 21 bd. Amiral Courbet, has live Irish, country, and rock shows on Thursdays. The dart-filled bar is popular with anglophone tourists. (☎67 21 63. Pints €5.20. *Menus* €12-18. Live music Sept.-June. Open M-F 11am-2am, Sa-Su 5pm-2am. AmEx/MC/V.)

To see the city's pride and glory, try to visit during one of the famous *férias* (bull fights): the **Féria des Vendanges** in mid-September, or the more boisterous **Féria de Pentecôte** (Pentecost; May 7-12, 2008). For five days, the streets resound with the clattering of hooves as bulls are herded to **Les Arènes** for *corridas,* where they face death at the hands of bullfighters. (☎08 91 70 14 01. Tickets €20-100. Reserve at least one month ahead.) The **Courses Camarguaises,** held throughout the summer, provide more humane entertainment. Fighters strip decorations from the bulls' horns, narrowly avoiding the lethal points, and then vault over barriers to safety. (Purchase tickets at the arena ticket office, 4 rue de la Violette. Cheap seats usually available on the day of the event. Tickets free-€15.) The summer is a party even when the bulls aren't in town, thanks to the weekly **Jeudis de Nîmes,** when craftsmen, painters, artists, and musicians fill every street corner. Ask the tourist office for a schedule of events (July-Aug. Th 6pm-midnight).

DAYTRIP FROM NÎMES

PONT DU GARD. The Pont du Gard, a **UNESCO World Heritage Sight,** is the centerpiece of a 50km Roman aqueduct that once supplied Nîmes with water. Its three

PROVENCE

levels of arches bridge the 275m wide valley of the Gardon River at a height of 48m. Built under the direction of Roman engineers in 19 BC to transport water from the springs near Uzès to Nîmes, the aqueduct, an architectural *coup de grace*, slopes at a crawling rate of 25cm per km, an average gradient of 0.34°. Ninety percent of the aqueduct is underground—it's a Roman feat of near-perfect construction.

Though a walk across the bridge is free, the welcome center (☎08 20 90 33 30; www.pontdugard.fr) houses a sleek multimedia museum (€7), shows a 25min. film in English and French about the construction of the bridge (€4, screening times available at the information desk), and has a children's learning center (€5). Guided tours of the bridge are available in several languages (€5). Day passes for all four activities are available for €12, students €11. Swimming in the river below the Pont du Gard offers a cool view of the bridge; stairs down to the rocky beach are on either side of the *pont*. Starting from Collias, you can also paddle 6km from the aqueduct toward Uzès. **Kayak Vert** rents canoes, kayaks, and bikes. The pleasant 2-3hr. paddle meanders down the river to the Pont du Gard. Call a day ahead to arrange for pickup from the Pont du Gard. (☎22 80 76. Kayak/canoe rental €19 per day. Bikes €15 per day. 10% discount for students and guests of the Nîmes Auberge de Jeunesse.) STDG (☎29 52 00) runs **buses** to the Pont du Gard from Nîmes (45min., 5 per day, €6.30) and Avignon (45min., 3 per day, €6.60).

ORANGE ☎04 90

Known for its massive and remarkably well-preserved Roman theater, Orange (ohr-RAHNJH; pop. 29,000) makes a perfect daytrip from Avignon. Though the *vieille ville* is not stunning, it is easily accessible by train, making a visit worthwhile even if you see nothing but the theater. The summer music and opera festival provides a compelling reason to spend the night in July and August.

TRANSPORTATION AND PRACTICAL INFORMATION. **Trains** run from the station (☎11 88 03) on av. Frédéric Mistral to: Avignon (20min.; M-Sa 19 per day, Su 13 per day; €5.20); Lyon (2½hr.; M-Sa 7 per day, Su 6 per day; €26); Marseille (1½hr., 7 per day, €21); Paris (3½hr., 2 TGV per day, €84). The ticket windows are open M-F 5:35am-8:20pm, Sa-Su 6am-8:20pm. TransVaucluse **buses** (☎34 15 59; ticket office in the *Arc de Triomphe;* open M-Tu and Th-F 8am-12:30pm and 3-5pm, W 8am-noon and 2:15-4:15pm) run from cours Pourtoules to Avignon (45-70min., M-Sa 14 per day, €5.80). For a **taxi,** call Taxi Monge, 306 av. Maréchal Foch. (☎51 00 00. €8 from station to Roman theater.) Rent **bicycles** at Bouti Cycle, 745 rte. de Caderousse, past the tourist office, down av. Charles de Gaulle away from the town center. (☎34 15 60. €12 per ½-day, €20 per day. Open M-Sa 9am-noon and 2-7pm.)

The **tourist office,** 5 cours A. Briand, is a straight shot from the train station (20min.); take av. Frédéric Mistral to get to the *centre-ville* and keep left as the road becomes rue de la République, then rue St-Martin. Continue straight; the office sits at the opposite side of the rotunda. The multilingual staff provides maps, daytrip ideas, and free hotel booking. (☎34 70 88; fax 34 99 62. Open July-Aug. M-Sa 9:30am-8pm, Su 10am-1pm and 2-7pm; Apr.-June and Sept. M-Sa 9:30am-7pm, Su 10am-1pm and 2-6:30pm; Oct.-Mar. M-Sa 10am-1pm and 2-5pm. Branch office, pl. des Frères Mounet, opposite Théâtre Antique. Open July-Aug. daily 10am-1pm and 2-6pm.) Other services include: a **laundromat,** 5 rue St-Florent, off bd. E. Daladier (wash €3.90 per 7kg, dry €1 per 15min.; open daily 7:30am-8pm); **police** at 427 bd. E. Daladier (☎51 55 55); **ambulances** (☎34 02 66); a **pharmacy,** 18 rue St-Martin (☎34 02 82; for the **pharmacie de garde,** check the list on the front door; open M 2-7:15pm, Tu-Sa 8:45am-12:15pm and 2-7:15pm); and the Louis Giorgi **hospital** at chemin Abrian, near av. H. Fabré (☎11 22 22). **Internet** access is available at **Atlas Télécom,** 22 rue V. Hugo. (☎11 04 60. €1 per 15min., €3 per hr. Open M-Th and Sa 10am-12:30pm and 3-10pm.)

There is a **post office** with **currency exchange** at 679 bd. E. Daladier, cours Pourtoules. (☎11 11 03. Open M-F 8am-6:30pm, Sa 8am-noon.) **Postal Code:** 84100.

ACCOMMODATIONS AND FOOD. Orange's hotels fill up fast in July and August for Les Chorièges and the Festival d'Avignon, and prices increase accordingly. **Hôtel St-Florent ❸**, 4 rue du Mazeau, near pl. aux Herbes, is worth a splurge. Spotless rooms are beautifully furnished in B&B style and benefit from a great location near the Roman theater. The *provençal* frescoes and paintings adorning the walls were made by the owner's wife and children. All rooms have A/C and free Wi-Fi. (☎34 18 53; www.hotelsaintflorent.com. Breakfast €6. Reception 7:30am-11pm. Open Mar. to mid-Jan. Singles with shower July-Aug. €40, with shower and toilet €53; triples and quads €80; larger rooms €58-77. Sept. to mid-Jan. and Mar.-June €35/45/70/50-65. Extra bed €8. AmEx/MC/V.) **Hôtel l'Herbier d'Orange ❷**, 8 pl. aux Herbes, rents comfortable, newly remodeled, sunlit rooms steps away from the Roman theater and the town center. Rooms facing south have A/C, and outdoor seating in the plaza makes breakfast pleasant. (☎34 09 23; fax 51 61 12. Breakfast €6. Parking €4. Reception 7am-11pm. Mar.-Sept. singles €32; doubles €37, with shower and toilet €50; triples with shower and toilet €55; quads with bath €67. Oct.-Feb. €25/30/45/50/62. AmEx/MC/V.)

The eateries on pl. aux Herbes and pl. de la République serve standard café fare, from goat cheese salads to steaming pizzas. Cheaper options are available on the streets surrounding the town center. For groceries, head to the **Petit Casino,** 16 rue de la République. (☎34 10 43. Open M-F 7:30am-12:30pm and 2:30-7:30pm, Sa 8am-12:30pm and 2:30-7:30pm. MC/V.) An open-air market selling produce fills the *vieille ville* on Thursday mornings. (Open 7am-1pm.) **Côté Jardin ❸**, 23 rue Victor Hugo, off rue St-Martin, serves tempting *plats du jour* (€8-14) and salads (€7.50) in a beautiful cave-like dining room and adorable courtyard garden. (☎30 28 36. Open M and Th-Su 11am-10:30pm. Cash only.) **The Festival Café ❸**, 5 pl. de la République, provides comfortable purple cushions for its outdoor seating, drawing summertime passersby. It serves hearty *menus* (€16-26), including salads (€10-12) and excellent *mousse au chocolat* for €6. (☎34 65 58. *Plats* €12-16. Open daily 7:30am-midnight. Kitchen open noon-3pm and 7-10:30pm. MC/V.)

SIGHTS. Built in the first century AD, Orange's breathtaking **Théâtre Antique** is the best-preserved Roman theater in Europe. Louis XIV is said to have called it the most beautiful wall in his kingdom. The theater originally held 10,000 spectators and was connected to a gymnasium complete with running tracks and sauna. Though the stage wall, 103m wide and 37m high, is one of only three remaining in the world, hundreds like it were once erected by the Romans. After the fall of Rome, this locus of pagan entertainment fell into disrepair. In the mid-19th century, engineers rediscovered its great acoustics and used the three remaining rows as a template for reconstructing the seating area. A free audio tour informs the visit, as does a film retracing the monument's history. A ticket to the theater provides access to the **Musée d'Art et d'Histoire,** across the street. The small museum traces the history of Orange, which was successively a Roman colony, a princedom linked to the Netherlands (1583-1702), and finally a French town. Fragments of its *cadastres*, the most complete Roman land register ever found, are displayed on the first floor. (☎51 17 60. Theater open daily June-Aug. 9am-7pm; Sept. and Apr.-May 9am-6pm; Oct. and Mar. 9:30am-12:30pm and 1:30-5:30pm; Nov.-Feb. 9:30am-12:30pm and 1:30-4:30pm. Museum opens 15min. after theater. Combined ticket €7.70, students €5.80.) Above the theater, amid the ragged remnants of the Prince of Orange's castle, **Colline St-Eutrope** (St-Eutrope Hill) offers a view of the yellow and orange city and its surroundings. To mount the hill, exit right out of the theater entrance. Orange's other major monument, the **Arc de Triomphe,** stands on the *Via Agrippa,* which once connected Arles to Lyon. From the tourist office, walk back into town on rue St-Martin, then turn left on rue Victor Hugo, which soon widens into av. de l'Arc de Triomphe. Though only a 5-10min. walk from the center of town, the arch's remarkably well-preserved facade draws fewer tourists than the theater—and the view here is free. Built during Augustus's time, the 19m stone structure depicts victories over the Gauls and is a tribute to those who founded the colony of Arausio.

NIGHTLIFE AND FESTIVALS. Most of Orange goes to bed early. Those who'd rather not should stop by **Academie de Billard,** 67 cours Pourtoule, 100m past the theater. A young crowd fills up booths in this American-style diner. (☎04 32 81 17 90. Beer €2.50. Sandwiches €3-4. *Crêpes* €1.50-7. Open M-Sa 10am-1:30am. Kitchen open 10am-11pm. MC/V.) Friday and Saturday nights draw locals looking to drink and dance to the **Café du Theatre,** 52 rue Caristie, across the street from the Roman theater. (☎34 12 39. Beer €2.50. Mixed drinks €4-7. Concerts F-Su 9pm-midnight. Open daily 7am-1:30am. Cash only.)

From early July to August, the Théâtre Antique regains its original function with the **Chorégies,** a series of world-class grand operas, choral productions, and symphonies. Info is available from the Maison des Chorégies, 18 pl. Sylvain, next to the theater. (☎34 24 24; www.choregies.com. Open June-Aug. M-Sa 10am-7pm; Feb.-May M-F 11am-1pm and 2-5pm. Tickets €18-200, students from €9.) Orange hosts two smaller festivals, both free: **Les Rencontres Théâtrales d'Orange** celebrates theater, and the **Orange se met au Jazz** is dedicated to jazz. Both take place from late June to July. In August, concerts, films, and shows take the stage. Call the **Service Culturel** in Palais des Princes on rue des Princes d'Orange to reserve free tickets in advance. (☎51 57 57. Open M-Th 8:30am-noon and 1:30-6pm, F 8:30am-noon.)

THE CÔTE D'AZUR

A sunny place for shady people.
—Somerset Maugham

Between Marseille and the Italian border, sun-drenched beaches and warm Mediterranean waters form a backdrop for this fabled playground of the rich and famous. Now one of the most touristed places in the world, the Côte d'Azur began as a Greco-Roman commercial base. Prosperous villages sprang up around 600 BC, only to be razed by barbarian invaders. Since then, the Riviera has been working toward its modern resort status.

When English and Russian aristocrats began the luxurious habit of wintering on the Côte to escape their abominable weather, Nice and its surrounding coastlines became the established vacation destination of the world's idle rich. In the 1920s, Coco Chanel popularized the *provençal* farmer's healthy tan. Parasols went down, hemlines went up, and sun-worship was born. Today, sunbathers bronze *au naturel* on pebbly beaches, high rollers drop millions in casinos, sleek yachts crowd lively harbors, and visitors from all over the world wander ancient coastal fortifications. At nightfall, the Riviera's most famed pastime begins: nonstop partying. In July and August, Europe's most extravagant—and often its most exclusive—nightclubs teem with the young and beautiful until the wee hours.

The Riviera has been the passion and the death of many artists, from F. Scott Fitzgerald to Picasso, as well as the luxury mecca of celebrities from Brigitte Bardot to Bono. Many towns along its eastern stretch boast a chapel, room, or wall decorated by Cocteau, Chagall, or Matisse. Idyllic villas behind scrubby vegetation on plunging cliffs are reminders that the Riviera is an international luxury mecca. However, it's anything but a lazy luxury—the Riviera boasts an unmatched cultural richness and spirit. Each May high society makes its yearly pilgrimage to the Cannes Film Festival and the Monte-Carlo Grand Prix, while Nice's raucous *Carnaval* in February and various summer jazz festivals are less exclusive and more budget-friendly. Despite the Côte's reputation for glitz and glamor, penny-pinchers can also soak up the spectacle, as well as plenty of sun, sea, and sand.

HIGHLIGHTS OF THE CÔTE D'AZUR

DANCE ALL NIGHT with the young and fashionable in **Cannes** (p. 740), the most accessible of the Riviera's glam towns.

TAN ALL DAY on the beaches of **Menton** (p. 729), the Riviera's hidden gem, surrounded by famous gardens, pristine waters, and a delightful *vieille ville*.

RAMBLE through the medieval streets of **St-Paul** (p. 718), where the ramparts provide a cultured respite from the fast life along the coast.

NICE ☎04

Sizzling Nice (NEESS; pop. 340,000), the former vacation haunt of dukes and tsarinas, continues to seduce tourists with nonstop parties, plentiful shopping, beautiful beaches, and first-rate museums. No matter the season, the maze of pedestrian streets buzzes with shoppers by day and lively bar- and club-hoppers by night, while an immense seaside promenade gives local joggers an occasion to

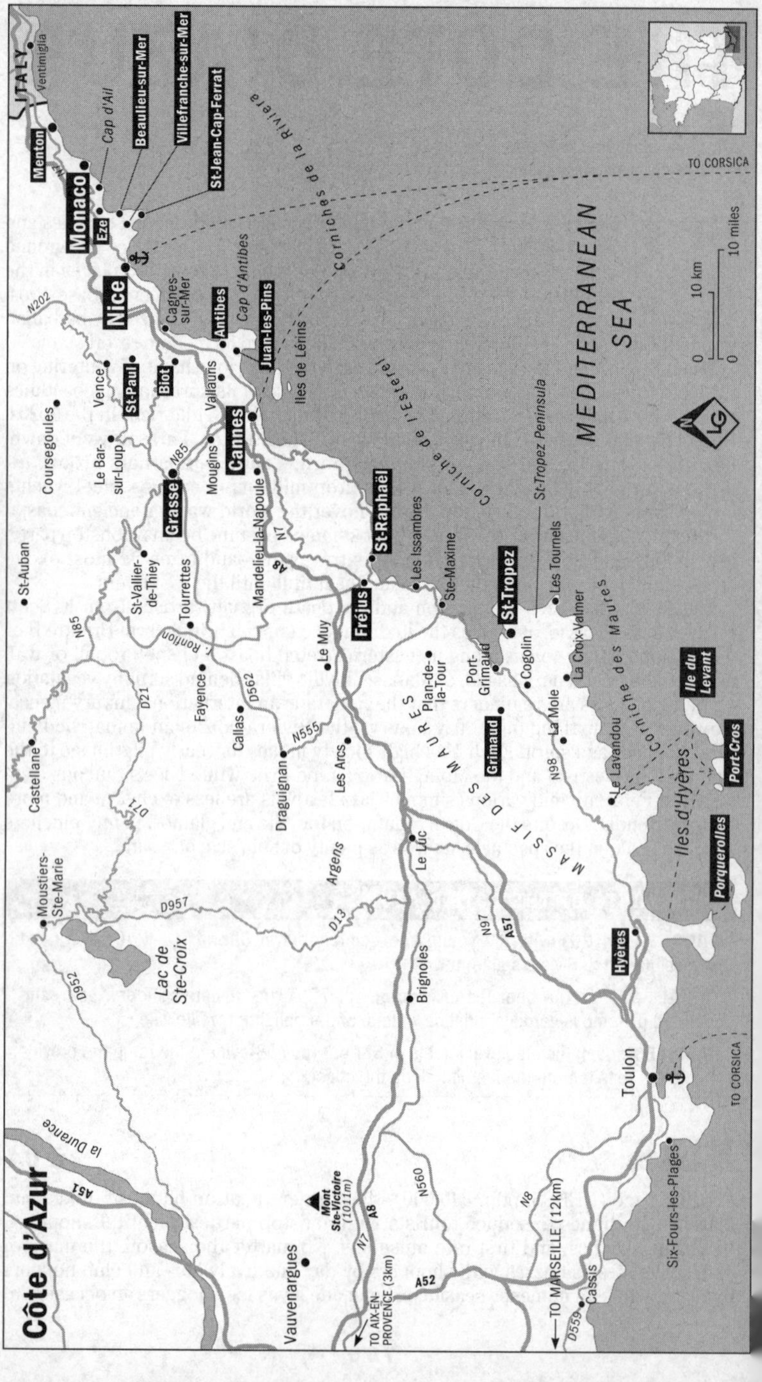

Côte d'Azur
ITALY
Ventimiglia
Menton
Cap d'Ail
Monaco
Eze
Beaulieu-sur-Mer
Villefranche-sur-Mer
St-Jean-Cap-Ferrat
Corniches de la Riviera
Nice
N202
Cagnes-sur-Mer
Antibes
Cap d'Antibes
Juan-les-Pins
Iles de Lérins
Vence
St-Paul
Biot
Vallauris
Coursegoules
Le Bar-sur-Loup
Cannes
Mougins
N85
Grasse
Mandelieu-la-Napoule
N7
A8
St-Raphaël
Corniche de l'Esterel
Les Issambres
Ste-Maxime
St-Tropez
St-Tropez Peninsula
Les Tournels
St-Auban
St-Vallier-de-Thiey
Tourrettes
Fréjus
Le Muy
Fayence
Callas
D562
D21
N555
Draguignan
Les Arcs
Plan-de-la-Tour
Port-Grimaud
Cogolin
Grimaud
La Croix-Valmer
La Mole
N98
Le Lavandou
Corniche des Maures
Ile du Levant
Port-Cros
Iles d'Hyères
Porquerolles
MASSIF DES MAURES
Castellane
D71
Le Luc
Argens
Moustiers-Ste-Marie
D957
D13
Lac de Ste-Croix
D952
Brignoles
N97
A57
Hyères
Toulon
TO CORSICA
MEDITERRANEAN SEA
0 10 km
0 10 miles
la Durance
A51
Mont Ste-Victoire (1011m)
N560
N8
Six-Fours-les-Plages
Vauvenargues
TO AIX-EN-PROVENCE (3km)
A52
TO MARSEILLE (12km)
Cassis
D559

exhibit their tans. Nice is a budget traveler's paradise; convenient transportation, budget lodgings, and reasonable restaurants make this city an inexpensive base for sampling the Côte d'Azur's pricier delights.

INTERCITY TRANSPORTATION

Flights: Aéroport Nice-Côte d'Azur (**NCE;** ☎08 20 42 33 33). **Air France,** 10 av. de Verdun (☎08 20 82 08 20). Open M-F 9am-6pm, Sa 10am-5pm. Flights to **Bastia** (€116, under 25 and couples €59) and **Paris** (€93, under 25 and couples €50). **EasyJet** flies to **London** (see **Getting There by Plane,** p. 26). Direct **buses** on the Ligne d'Azur (€4, every 15-20min. 8am-9pm) leave for the airport from the train station (#98) and the bus station (#99); before 8am bus #23 (€1.30, every 15-25min.) makes several stops, including the train station, on its way to the airport.

Trains: There are 2 primary train stations in town:

Gare SNCF Nice-Ville: Av. Thiers (☎93 14 82 12). Call M-F 9am-noon or 3-6pm for lost luggage, missed trains, and special assistance. Open daily 5am-12:30am. Same-day ticket office open daily 5:20am-11:20pm. Info and reservation center open M-Sa 8:30am-6:30pm, Su 9am-6pm. To: **Cannes** (40min., every 20min., €5.60); **Marseille** (2½hr., 16 per day, €27); **Monaco** (15min., every 10-30min., €3.10); **Paris** (5½hr., 6 per day, €94).

Gare du Sud: 4bis rue Alfred Binet. ☎97 03 80 80. 800m from Nice-Ville. Private outbound trains to **Digne-les-Bains** and **Plan-du-Var.**

Buses: 5 bd. Jean Jaurès (☎93 85 61 81). Info booth open M-F 8:30am-5:30pm, Sa 9am-4pm. To **Cannes** (2hr.; M-Sa every 20min. 6:10am-9:45pm, Su every 30min. 8:30am-9:40pm; €6) and **Monaco** (1hr.; M-Sa every 10-15min. 6:30am-8pm, Su every 20min. 6:30am-7:50pm; €1.30). Buy tickets on board.

Ferries: Corsica Ferries (☎92 00 42 93, reservations ☎08 25 09 50 95; www.corsica-ferries.com) and **SNCM** (☎93 13 66 66, reservations ☎93 13 66 99) send high-speed ferries from the port. Reserve ahead to avoid price increases. Take bus #1 or 2 (dir.: Port). To **Corsica** (€20-40, bikes €10, small cars €40-57). Be sure to check your terminal ahead of time, as the 2 terminals are on opposite sides of the port. A free shuttle runs between them. MC/V. See **Corsica** (p. 759) for more info.

ORIENTATION

The train station, **Gare Nice-Ville,** is surrounded by a rough-and-tumble neighborhood with cheap restaurants, budget hotels, Internet and phone shops, and X-rated video stores. As you exit the station, to the left is **avenue Jean Médecin,** the main artery toward *vieux* Nice. It is lined with snack stands, shops, and *brasseries.* The traffic-choked street almost meets the water at **place Masséna;** a left turn onto the pleasant **promenade du Paillon** leads to the bus station and to the large shops around Nice's main square, **place Garibaldi.** To the right of av. Jean Médecin is **boulevard Gambetta,** the other main water-bound thoroughfare. **Promenade des Anglais,** which becomes **quai des Etats-Unis** east of av. Jean Médecin, hugs the coast and is a people-watcher's paradise, as are the boutiques and pricey outdoor terraces of the restaurants to the west in the **rue Masséna** pedestrian zone. The ongoing construction of a new tramway system makes several of these areas difficult to access, even by foot. Come nightfall, the avenues fill with large crowds of tourists, party-goers, and street performers. Below and to the left of Jean Médecin lies the pulsating, ever-active **vieux Nice.** Continuing along past the old town, you'll find **Port Lympia,** a small harbor on **quai de Lunel** bordered by clubs and bars.

Unfortunately, Nice's big-city appeal also means big-city crime. Women should avoid walking alone at night, and everyone should exercise caution around the train station, on **avenue Jean Médecin,** in **vieux Nice,** and on the **promenade des Ang-**

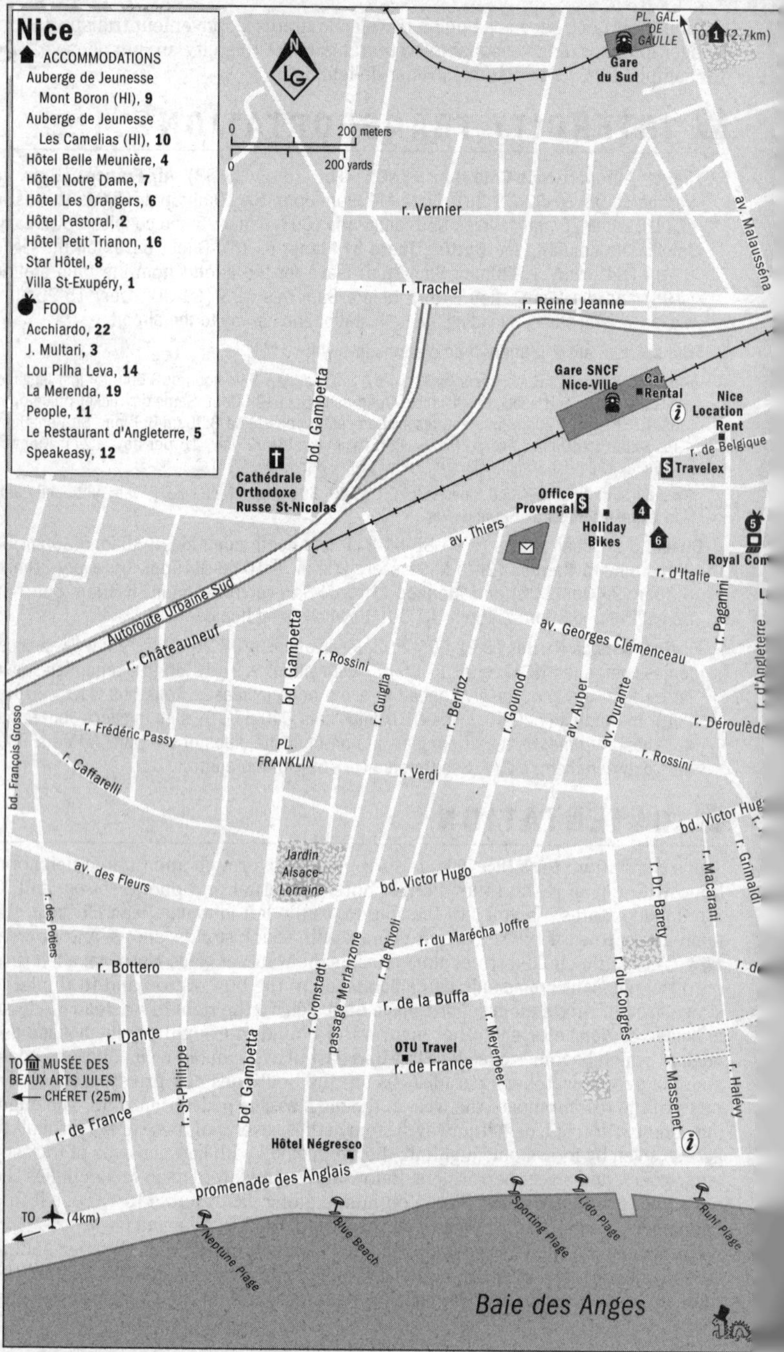
Nice
ACCOMMODATIONS
Auberge de Jeunesse Mont Boron (HI), 9
Auberge de Jeunesse Les Camelias (HI), 10
Hôtel Belle Meunière, 4
Hôtel Notre Dame, 7
Hôtel Les Orangers, 6
Hôtel Pastoral, 2
Hôtel Petit Trianon, 16
Star Hôtel, 8
Villa St-Exupéry, 1
FOOD
Acchiardo, 22
J. Multari, 3
Lou Pilha Leva, 14
La Merenda, 19
People, 11
Le Restaurant d'Angleterre, 5
Speakeasy, 12
0 200 meters
0 200 yards
PL. GAL. DE GAULLE
TO 1 (2.7km)
Gare du Sud
r. Vernier
r. Trachel
r. Reine Jeanne
av. Malausséna
Gare SNCF Nice-Ville
Car Rental
Nice Location Rent
r. de Belgique
Travelex
Office Provençal
Holiday Bikes
Cathédrale Orthodoxe Russe St-Nicolas
bd. Gambetta
av. Thiers
Royal Com
r. d'Italie
Autoroute Urbaine Sud
r. Châteauneuf
av. Georges Clémenceau
r. Rossini
r. Guiglia
r. Berlioz
r. Gounod
av. Auber
av. Durante
r. Paganini
r. d'Angleterre
r. Déroulède
r. Frédéric Passy
PL. FRANKLIN
r. Verdi
r. Caffarelli
bd. François Grosso
bd. Victor Hugo
av. des Fleurs
Jardin Alsace-Lorraine
r. Dr. Barety
r. Macarani
r. Grimaldi
r. des Potiers
r. du Maréchal Joffre
r. de Rivoli
passage Merlanzone
r. Cronstadt
r. Bottero
r. de la Buffa
r. du Congrès
r. Meyerbeer
r. Dante
OTU Travel
r. de France
TO MUSÉE DES BEAUX ARTS JULES CHÉRET (25m)
r. St-Philippe
r. Massenet
r. Halévy
Hôtel Négresco
promenade des Anglais
TO (4km)
Neptune Plage
Blue Beach
Sporting Plage
Lido Plage
Ruhl Plage
Baie des Anges

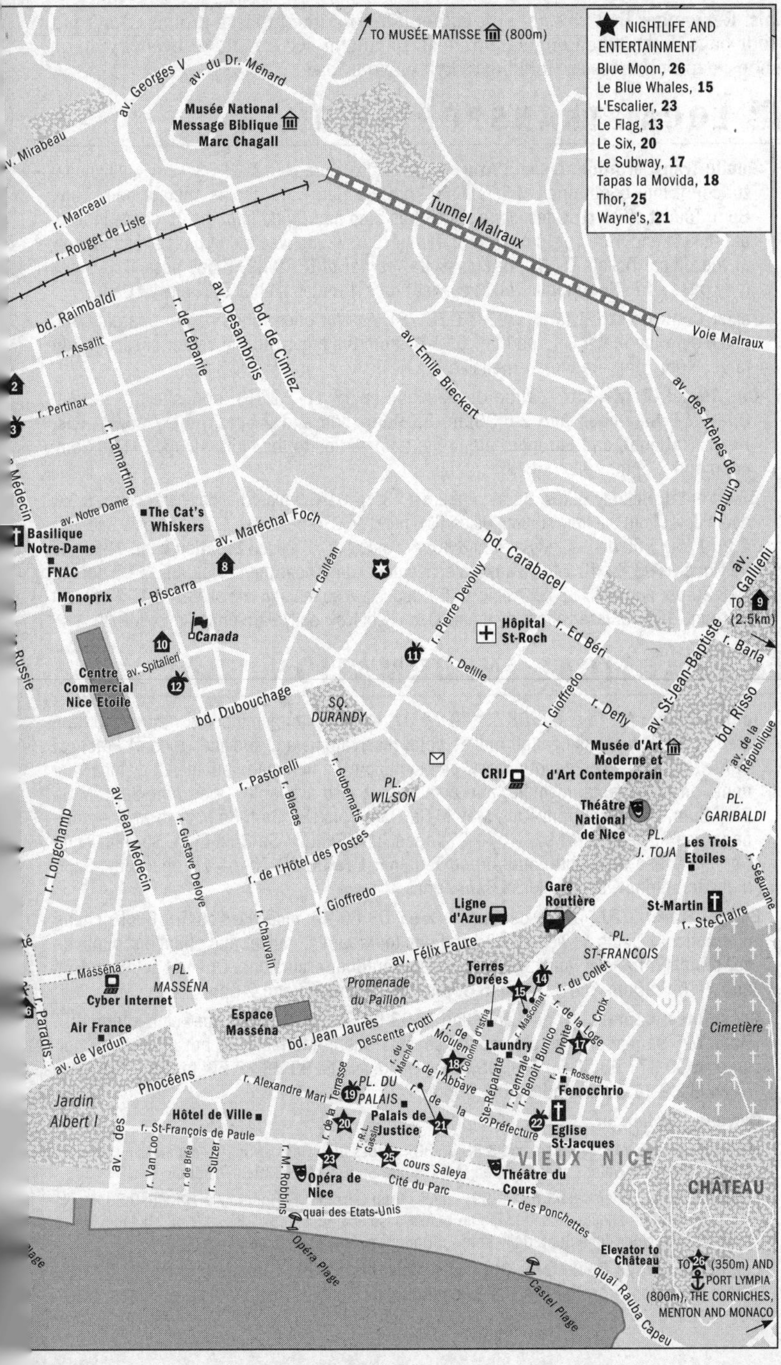
NIGHTLIFE AND ENTERTAINMENT
Blue Moon, 26
Le Blue Whales, 15
L'Escalier, 23
Le Flag, 13
Le Six, 20
Le Subway, 17
Tapas la Movida, 18
Thor, 25
Wayne's, 21
TO MUSÉE MATISSE (800m)
Musée National Message Biblique Marc Chagall
av. du Dr. Ménard
av. Georges V
av. Mirabeau
r. Marceau
r. Rouget de Lisle
Tunnel Malraux
Voie Malraux
bd. Raimbaldi
r. Assalit
r. Pertinax
r. de Lépanie
av. Desambrois
bd. de Cimiez
av. Emile Bieckert
av. des Arènes de Cimiez
r. Lamartine
av. Notre Dame
The Cat's Whiskers
av. Maréchal Foch
Basilique Notre-Dame
FNAC
Monoprix
r. Biscarra
Canada
Centre Commercial Nice Etoile
av. Spitalieri
r. Galléan
bd. Carabacel
r. Pierre Devoluy
Hôpital St-Roch
r. Ed Béri
av. Gallieni
TO 9 (2.5km)
r. Barla
r. Delille
bd. Dubouchage
SQ. DURANDY
r. Gioffredo
r. Defly
av. St-Jean-Baptiste
bd. Risso
av. de la République
Musée d'Art Moderne et d'Art Contemporain
CRIJ
PL. WILSON
r. Pastorelli
r. Blacas
r. Gubernatis
Théâtre National de Nice
PL. GARIBALDI
PL. J. TOJA
Les Trois Etoiles
r. Longchamp
av. Jean Médecin
r. Gustave Deloye
r. de l'Hôtel des Postes
r. Ségurane
St-Martin
Ligne d'Azur
Gare Routière
r. Gioffredo
r. Ste-Claire
r. Chauvain
PL. ST-FRANCOIS
av. Félix Faure
r. Masséna
PL. MASSÉNA
Cyber Internet
Promenade du Paillon
Terres Dorées
r. du Collet
Air France
Espace Masséna
bd. Jean Jaurès
Descente Crotti
r. de la Loge
Droite
Croix
Cimetière
r. Paradis
av. de Verdun
r. de Moulen
r. Colonna d'Istria
r. Mascoïnat
Laundry
r. Benoit Bunico
r. Rossetti
Fenocchrio
Jardin Albert I
Phocéens
r. Alexandre Mari
r. de la Terrasse
PL. DU PALAIS
r. du Marché
r. de l'Abbaye
r. de la Préfecture
Ste-Réparate
r. Centrale
Hôtel de Ville
Palais de Justice
Eglise St-Jacques
av. des
r. St-François de Paule
r. Van Loo
r. de Bréa
r. Sulzer
r. M. Robbins
T. R.L. Gassin
cours Saleya
VIEUX NICE
Opéra de Nice
Cité du Parc
Théâtre du Cours
CHÂTEAU
quai des Etats-Unis
r. des Ponchettes
Opéra Plage
Elevator to Château
Castel Plage
quai Rauba Capeu
TO 26 (350m) AND PORT LYMPIA (800m), THE CORNICHES, MENTON AND MONACO

lais. Remember that you are still vulnerable to crime in large groups. Don't put your bags down when enjoying a meal, buying an ice cream, or even trying on shoes; expert thieves are looking to lighten your load.

LOCAL TRANSPORTATION

Public Transportation: Ligne d'Azur, 10 av. Félix Faure (☎93 13 53 13; www.lignedazur.com). Info booth open M-F 7:15am-7pm, Sa 8am-6pm. Buses operate daily 7am-8pm. Tourist office provides *Ligne d'Azur* bus map and *Guide Infobus.* Purchase individual tickets and 1-day pass on board; *carnet,* 5-day, and week long pass available only at the office. Tickets €1.30, day pass €4, *carnet* of 8 €8.29, 5-day pass €13, week long pass €17. **Noctambus** (night service) runs 4 routes nightly 9:10pm-1:10am.

Taxis: Central Taxi Riviera (☎93 13 78 78). Ask for price range before boarding and make sure the meter is turned on. €20-30 from the airport to the center of Nice. Night fares (7pm-7am) are more expensive.

Car Rental: Rent-a-Car, 23 rue de Belgique (☎93 16 24 16), opposite the station. Open M-F 8am-noon and 2-6:30pm, Sa 9am-noon and 2-5pm. AmEx/MC/V. **Avis, Hertz, National,** and **Europcar** are in the train station to the right. All open M-Sa 8am-noon and 2-5pm. AmEx/MC/V.

Bike Rental: Holiday Bikes, 34 av. Auber (☎93 16 01 62; nice@holiday-bikes.com), a few doors down from the train station. Bikes €16 per day, €70 per week; €230 deposit. Scooters €35/175; €500 deposit. M-Sa 9am-6:30pm. AmEx/MC/V. **Nicea Location Rent,** 12 rue de Belgique (☎93 82 42 71; www.nicealocationrent.com), near the station. Bikes €5 per hr., €18-20 per day, €70-88 per week; €250 deposit. Also rents in-line skates. 5-10% student discount, 10% for reservations by email. Open Feb.-Nov. daily 9am-6pm. AmEx/MC/V.

PRACTICAL INFORMATION

Tourist Office: Av. Thiers (☎08 92 70 74 07; www.nicetourisme.com), next to the train station. English-speaking staff makes hotel reservations and provides *Nice: A Practical Guide* and maps. *Le Pitchoun* (www.pitchoun.com), a free guide published by local students on restaurants, nightlife, and activities, is also available. Open June-Sept. M-Sa 8am-8pm, Su 10am-5pm; Oct.-May M-Sa 8am-7pm, Su 9am-6pm. Also at 5 promenade des Anglais (☎08 92 70 74 07; open June-Sept. M-Sa 8am-8pm, Su 9am-7pm; Oct.-May M-Sa 9am-6pm) and Airport Terminal 1 (☎08 92 70 74 07; open June-Sept. daily 8am-9pm; Oct.-May M-Sa 8am-9pm.)

Budget Travel: OTU, 48 rue de France (☎97 03 60 90; nice.ville@otu.fr). Books cheap international flights as well as bike and bus tours within France, and offers discounts on car rentals. Arranges language courses and outdoor excursions. Open M 9:30am-1pm and 2:15-6:30pm, Tu-F 9:30am-6:30pm, Sa 10am-1pm and 2-5pm.

Consulates: Canada, 10 rue Lamartine (☎93 92 93 22; cancons.nce@club-internet.fr). Open M-F 9am-noon. The closest **UK** consulate is in Monaco, 33 bd. Princesse Charlotte (☎00 377 93 50 99 54). **US,** 7 av. Gustave V (☎93 88 89 55; fax 93 87 07 38). Open M-F 9-11:30am and 1:30-4:30pm.

Currency Exchange:

Office Provençal, 17 av. Thiers (☎93 88 56 80), across from Gare SNCF. 4% commission on euro-denominated traveler's checks. Open M-F 7:30am-8pm, Sa-Su 7:30am-7:30pm.

Travelex, 13 av. Thiers (☎93 88 59 99), across from Gare SNCF. Open daily 7:30am-6:30pm. No commission on checks issued by some banks; Visa 3%; AmEx 6%. Also at 2 pl. Magenta (☎93 88 49 88). Open June-Sept. daily 9am-7:30pm; Oct.-May M-Sa 10am-5pm.

English-Language Bookstore: The Cat's Whiskers, 30 rue Lamartine (☎93 80 02 66). Great selection, from bestsellers to cookbooks. Plenty of regional-interest titles, travel guides, and maps. Small used books section. Open M 2-6pm, Tu and Th-F 9am-noon and 2-7pm, W 9am-noon and 2-6pm, Sa 10am-12:30pm and 3-7pm. AmEx/MC/V.

Youth Center: Centre Régional d'Information Jeunesse (CRIJ), 19 rue Gioffredo (☎93 80 93 93; www.crijca.fr), near the Museum of Contemporary Art. Posts summer jobs for students and gives info on housing, study, and recreation. Free Internet access with student ID (30min. limit). Open M-F in summer 9am-6pm; in winter 10am-7pm.

Laundromat: 7 rue d'Italie (☎93 85 88 14), near Basilique Notre Dame. Wash €3.50, dry €1 per 18min. Open daily 7am-9pm. Also in *vieux* Nice, 11 rue de Pont Vieux (☎93 85 88 14). Wash €2.50, dry €1 per 16min. Open daily 7am-9pm.

Police: 1 av. Maréchal Foch (☎92 17 22 22), opposite end from bd. Jean Médecin.

24hr. Pharmacy: 7 rue Masséna (☎93 87 78 94).

Hospital: Hôpital St-Roch, 5 rue Pierre Dévoluy (☎92 03 33 75).

Internet Access: Free at **CRIJ** (see above). **Royal Com.** 23 rue d'Angleterre (☎97 20 10 79). €0.50 per 15min., €2 per hr. Open daily 7:30am-midnight. **Cyber Internet,** 9 rue Masséna. One of the best deals near the beach. €3.90 per hr. Open daily 10am-11pm.

Post Office: 23 av. Thiers (☎93 82 65 22), near the station. Open M-F 8am-7pm, Sa 8am-noon. **Postal Code:** 06033.

ACCOMMODATIONS

This budget-friendly city draws a constant crowd of international visitors, and hostels (in the city and on the outskirts) are often full. For economizing travelers, the city offers two clusters of hotels, near the train station and near the beach. Those by the station are poorly located but generally less expensive than the cluster closer to *vieux* Nice and the beach. Those traveling alone or planning to indulge in Nice's nightlife would be wise to stay near *vieux* Nice.

NEAR VIEUX NICE AND THE BEACH

Auberge de Jeunesse (HI) Les Camelias, 3 rue Spitalieri (☎93 62 15 54; nice-camelias@fuaj.org), near the Centre Commercial Nice Etoile. Recently built hostel located between train station and *vieux* Nice has a young crowd and clean bathrooms. Kitchen (open 3pm-10:30pm) and bar (beer €2; open until 11pm). Breakfast included. Lockers €1. Laundry €6. Internet access €3.50 per hr. Wi-Fi €3 per hr. Reception 24hr. Lockout 11am-3pm. Reserve online only at www.hihostels.com. Dorms €20. MC/V. ❶

Hôtel Petit Trianon, 11 rue Paradis (☎93 87 50 46; hotel.nice.lepetittrianon@wanadoo.fr), left off pl. Masséna. Colorful rooms in a central location for a great price. Kitchen. Breakfast €5. Free beach towel loan. Laundry €10 per 5kg. Free Internet access in the lobby. Free Wi-Fi. Reservations required and preferred by email. Mid-June to mid-Sept. singles €30, with bath €35; doubles €40-42/50-53; triples €60-75; quads €76-96. Mid-Sept. to mid-June €25/30/35-37/45-48/55-70/71-91. MC/V. ❷

Star Hôtel, 14 rue Biscarra (☎93 85 19 03; www.hotel-star.com), Quiet, charming hotel between the train station and *vieux* Nice with comfortable beds. TV, A/C, and soundproof windows. Breakfast €6. Open Dec.-Oct. June-Sept. singles €60; doubles with shower €70, with bath €75; triples with bath €87. Oct.-May €45/55/60/72. MC/V. ❹

NEAR THE TRAIN STATION

Hôtel Belle Meunière, 21 av. Durante (☎93 88 66 15; fax 93 82 51 76), opposite the train station. According to legend, one of Napoleon's generals gave this stunning mansion as a gift to his mistress. Today, it hosts a relaxed crowd in 4- to 5-bed co-ed dorms. Single beds, large windows, and free breakfast in the courtyard make this stop a favorite for budget travelers. Showers €2. Luggage storage available after check-out (€2).

Laundry washed, dried, and folded (€5.50). Parking available. Reception 7:30am-midnight; access code after hours. Dorms €18, with shower €22; doubles with shower from €50; triples from €60; quads from €80. MC/V. ❷

Hôtel Pastoral, 27 rue Assalit (☎93 85 17 22). From the train station, cross av. Jean Médecin and go down rue Assalit. Basic rooms at reasonable prices make it popular with students, although there's no common room to socialize. Mini-fridge. Breakfast €3. Reception 8am-8pm; later by arrangement. Reservations required. Singles with shower €23; doubles €32, with bath €42; triples €45; quads €55. Extra bed €8. MC/V. ❷

Hôtel Notre Dame, 22 rue de Russie (☎93 88 70 44; www.nicenotredame.com), at the corner of rue d'Italie, 1 block west of av. Jean Médecin. Coastal colors adorn the large rooms, each with shower, TV, Wi-Fi (€8 per hr., €30 per day), and phone. English-speaking owners serve breakfast in bed (from €4). Free luggage storage. Reception 7:30am-10:30pm. Inquire about budget singles (€26). Singles June-Sept. €46; doubles €53; triples €66; quads €77. Oct.-May €39/46/60/71. Extra bed €10. MC/V. ❹

Hôtel Les Orangers, 10bis av. Durante (☎93 87 51 41; fax 93 82 57 82), across from Hôtel Belle Meunière. Small, worn but clean co-ed dorms with showers and fridges. Owner loans beach mats and helps travelers find accommodations when hotel is full. Free luggage storage. Reception 7am-12:15am; key access after hours. Dorm lockout June-Aug. 10:30am-noon. Reservations recommended July-Aug. Open Dec.-Oct. Dorms €16; singles €25-35; doubles €42-45; triples €54-56; quads €64-66. MC/V. ❶

OUTSKIRTS

Villa Saint-Exupéry, 22 av. Gravier (toll free ☎0800 307 409; www.vsaint.com), 5km from the city center. Take bus #1, 2 or 23 to "Gravier," "Noisetiers B," or "Place St-Maurice" and walk 500m—or, if loaded down or lost, call for a free pickup at the stop. Renowned for its great value, social atmosphere, and Aussie staff, this 240-bed hostel attracts young travelers with outstanding amenities and €1 beer. Most rooms have a bathroom; some offer remarkable balcony views of Nice. Free Internet access (Wi-Fi and 12 desktops) and free breakfast in the common room, which turns into a lively bar at night. Dorms €22-24; singles €35-39; doubles €29-35; triples €27-31. MC/V. ❷

Auberge de Jeunesse (HI) Mont Boron, rte. Forestière du Mont-Alban (☎93 89 23 64; www.hihostels.com), 4km from the city center. From the bus station, take bus #14 (dir.: Mont Boron) to "l'Auberge." From the train station, take bus #17 and switch to #14 at "Ligne d'Azur." By foot, hike up from the port; ask for a map at the tourist office. Ultra-clean hostel draws a friendly crowd. Moderately sized 6-bed dorms have individual lockers. Breakfast included. Sheets €2.70. Laundry and kitchen available 5-9:30pm. Reception 7am-midnight. Lockout noon-5pm. Dorms €19. MC/V. ❶

FOOD

Nice offers the typical big-city repertoire of restaurants, from four-star establishments to basic *brasseries* to holes-in-the-wall. The city's pride and joy is its *niçois* cuisine, flavored with Mediterranean spices. Try the crusty *pan bagnat*, a loaf of bread topped with tuna, sardines, and vegetables; *pissaladière* pizza loaded with onions, anchovies, and olives; and *socca*, or *tourta de blea*, a thin tart with pine nuts. The *salade niçoise* combines tuna, olives, eggs, potatoes, tomatoes, and mustard dressing. Tomato, eggplant, and zucchini are baked to form *ratatouille*, and the local population enjoys zucchini flowers breaded and fried to form *beignets* (doughnuts). Ask the tourist office for a list of restaurants that serve traditional *niçois* dishes. Load up on groceries from the **Monoprix** supermarket, av. Jean Médecin, near the Centre Commercial Nice Etoile, toward the train station. (☎92 47 72 62. Open M-Sa 8:30am-9pm. AmEx/MC/V.) Fresh olives, cheeses, and fruits take over **cours Saleya** during the **morning market.** (Open Tu-Su 7am-1pm.)

Cours Saleya is also home to a **flower market.** Stop by just before it closes for bargain blossoms. (Open Tu-Su 7am-1pm.) A **produce market** springs up on **avenue Maché de la Libération.** (Open Tu-Su 7am-1pm.) Stay away from the unremarkable *brasseries* and pizzerias on rue Masséna and cours Saleya, as well as those along the promenade des Anglais, which trap tourists nightly. **Avenue Jean Médecin** features reasonably priced *brasseries*, *panini* vendors, and kebab stands.

La Merenda, 4 rue Bosio. Savor the work of a culinary master, Dominique Le Stanc, who turned his back on one of Nice's best-known restaurants to open this 12-table gem. Outstanding dishes like fried zucchini flowers, stockfish, and veal head. Try the *pâtés au pistou* (garlic basil pasta; €11). *Plats* €11-16. Open M-F noon-1:30pm and 7-9pm. Reserve in person for dinner; seatings at 7 and 9pm. Cash only. ❸

Lou Pilha Leva, 10-13 rue du Collet (☎93 13 99 08). Prime location in *vieux* Nice. Lively staff keeps things moving, dishing out plate after plate of *socca* (€2), *pissaladière* (€2), and *salade niçoise* (€7). The perfect spot for enjoying excellent and cheap—albeit greasy—grub. Open daily 8am-midnight. MC/V. ❶

People, 12 rue Pastorelli (☎93 85 08 43). A trendy setting for traditional cuisine, with stone walls and a stainless steel bar. Tasty dishes like *risotto aux truffes* (€13) and *magret de canard* with *foie gras* (filet of duck with *foie gras;* €18) fill enormous chalkboard menus. Plenty of ambience to go with the excellent wines. *Plats* €7.50-17. Lunch *menu* €13; dinner *menus* from €21. Open M noon-2:30pm, Tu-F noon-2:30pm and 5:30-11pm, Sa 5:30-11pm. AmEx/MC/V. ❸

Le Restaurant d'Angleterre, 25 rue d'Angleterre (☎93 88 64 49), near the train station. Frequented by a loyal crowd of locals who come for traditional French favorites. The €14 *menu* includes salad, *plat,* side dish, dessert, and *digestif.* Open Tu-Sa 11:45am-2pm and 6:45-9:55pm, Su 11:45am-2pm. AmEx/MC/V. ❷

Acchiardo, 38 rue Droite (☎93 85 51 16), in *vieux* Nice. Family-style tables are always filled with locals who come for simple Italian and French dishes. Try the *escalope maison* (veal in *provençal* sauce; €14). Regional specialties like *soupe au pistou* (vegetable soup with basil; €6) and *salade niçoise* (€7) stand out. Pasta €6-9. Meat dishes €11-13. Open July M-F 7-10pm; Sept.-June M-F noon-1:30pm and 7-10pm. ❷

Speakeasy, 7 rue Lamartine (☎93 85 59 50). Sample organic wine and beer or fresh carrot juice—the perfect *apéritif* to accompany delectable vegan options. Large specials (€8.50-9.20) and desserts satisfy even the staunchest carnivores. Testimonials of famous vegetarians from Gandhi to Brigitte Bardot adorn the facade. 2 courses and dessert €15. Open M-F noon-2:15pm and 7-9:15pm, Sa noon-2:15pm. Cash only. ❷

J. Multari, 58bis av. Jean Médecin (☎93 92 01 99). Excellent, cheap fare offered on marble counter tops and polished wood tables. Try a goat cheese, chicken, or ham sandwich (€3.30), pizza (€1.50), or *crêpe* with Corsican jam (€5). 4 other locations: 2 rue Alphonse Karr (☎93 87 45 90); 22 rue Gioffredo (☎93 80 00 31); 13 cours Saleya (☎93 62 31 33); and 8 bd. Jean Jaurès (☎93 62 10 39; takeout only). All open M-Sa 6am-8:15pm. Cash only. ❶

SIGHTS

One look at Nice's waves and you may be tempted to spend your entire stay stretched out on the sand. As the city with the second-most museums in France, however, Nice offers more than azure waters and topless sunbathers.

MUSÉE NATIONAL MESSAGE BIBLIQUE MARC CHAGALL. This extraordinary museum was founded by Chagall to showcase an assortment of biblically-themed pieces that he gave to the French State in 1966. Twelve canvases illustrating the first two books of the Hebrew Bible are arranged based on their colors (rather than the

FRENCH 101: A CRASH COURSE

Traveling through France, you will undoubtedly encounter many familiar words on signs and on menus. Though these cognates will seem to help in your struggle to comprehend *le monde francophone*, beware! Some can also lead you astray. Here are some *faux amis* (false cognates; literally, "false friends") to watch out for:

Blesser has nothing to do with spirituality (or sneezing). It means **to hurt,** not to bless.

Pain is anything but misery for the French: it's their word for **bread.**

Bras is not a supportive undergarment, it's an **arm.**

Rage is not just regular anger, it's **rabies.**

Rabais, it follows, is not the disease you can catch from a dog, but a **discount.**

A *sale* is not an event with a lot of *rabais;* it means **dirty.**

Draguer means **to hit on,** not to drag, unless you encounter an overly aggressive flirt.

Balancer is **to swing,** not to steady oneself.

A *peste* is slightly more serious than a bothersome creature. It is a **plague.**

Puéril is not grave danger, just **childhood.**

Preservatif is not something found in packaged food, but it can be found in other packages, so to speak. This is the French word for **condom.**

Crayon means **pencil,** not crayon, and *gomme* is not for

temporal development of the Bible), as the artist wished. The museum also includes an auditorium with stained-glass panels depicting the creation story. The auditorium hosts concerts; ask at the entrance for program information. *(Av. du Dr. Ménard. 15min. walk north of station, or take bus #15, dir.: Rimiez, to "Musée Chagall." ☎93 53 87 20; www.musee-chagall.fr. Open M and W-Su July-Sept. 10am-6pm; Oct.-June 10am-5pm. Last tickets sold 30min. before closing. €6.70, students 18-25 €5.20, under 18 free; 1st and 3rd Su of month free. MC/V.)*

MUSÉE MATISSE. A 17th-century Genoese villa is the setting for Matisse's three-dimensional works, including dozens of paper-cutting tableaux. The museum contains several of this Nice resident's early masterpieces, such as a painting of Ajaccio, where Matisse felt the first "shock of what became Fauvism." Furniture and other effects, like Matisse's painting table, lend a personal touch. *(164 av. des Arènes de Cimiez. Take bus #15, 17, 20, 22, or 25 to "Arènes." Free bus tickets between Musée Chagall and Musée Matisse; ask at either ticket counter. ☎93 81 08 08; www.musee-matisse-nice.org. Open M and W-Su 10am-6pm. Tours in English by reservation. Call for info on lectures. €4, students €2.50; 1st and 3rd Su of month free. Tours €4/1.50. MC/V.)*

VIEUX NICE. Hand-painted awnings, beautiful churches, and lively squares await at every turn in *vieux* Nice. Though filled with the inevitable slew of souvenir shops, *vieux* Nice remains the heart of the city. *(Tours of the old city start at the tourist office Sa 9:30am. €12.)* Bilingual street signs introduce you to *Niçard*, a subdialect of the Occitan language still spoken by half a million Frenchmen. **Rue Droite** has various handmade furniture stores and mosaic studios. At **Les Trois Etoiles,** 26 rue Pairoliere, you can fill a glass bottle with homemade vinegar, olive oil, or dessert *liqueur*. *(☎93 92 30 83. Open summer daily 10am-8pm; winter Tu-Su 10am-8pm. AmEx/MC/V.)* **Terres Dorées,** 8 rue du Pont Vieux, offers fresh-scented handmade soaps and bath products created using regional herbs. *(☎93 62 63 02. Open M-Sa July-Aug. 10am-7:30pm; Sept.-June 10am-noon and 2:30-7:30pm. MC/V.)* Line up at **Fenocchio,** on pl. Rosetti, Nice's best-loved ice cream shop; it offers over 54 flavors, including unusual choices like tomato basil, beer, thyme, black olive, and avocado. *(1 scoop in homemade cone €2, 2 scoops €3.50. Open daily 10:30am-2am. MC/V.)*

MUSÉE D'ART MODERNE ET D'ART CONTEMPORAIN. A monumental sculpture leaning against an impressive glass facade welcomes visitors to exhibits of French New Realists and American pop artists like Lichtenstein and Warhol. The minimalist galleries pay homage to avant-garde creations, including statues by Niki de St-Phalle and color pieces by Yves Klein. *(Promenade des Arts, at intersection of av. St-Jean Baptiste and Traverse Garibaldi. Take bus #5, dir.: St-Charles, to "Musée Promenade des Arts."* ☎ *93 62 61 62; www.mamac-nice.org. Open Tu-Su 10am-6pm. €7; 1st and 3rd Su of month free. Tours in English available July-Aug. by reservation; €4, students €2.50, under 18 free. Cash only.)*

MUSÉE DES BEAUX-ARTS. The former villa of Ukraine's Princess Kotschoubey has been converted into a celebration of French and Italian painting, with works by Dufy, Fragonard, Mossa, Picasso, Rodin, and Van Loo. Dufy captures his city's spontaneity with sensational paintings of the town at rest and play. The museum is also well known for its collection of lively Chéret works in bright pastels. *(33 av. Baumettes. Take bus #38 to "Musée Chéret" or #12 to "Grosso."* ☎ *92 15 28 28; www.musee-beaux-arts-nice.org. Open Tu-Su 10am-6pm. Tours 2:30pm Th and Sa in French, F in English. €4, students €2.50, under 18 free; 1st and 3rd Su of month free.)*

CATHÉDRALE ORTHODOXE RUSSE ST-NICOLAS. Also known as the Eglise Russe, this cathedral was commissioned by Empress Marie Feodorovna in memory of her first husband, Tsar Nicholas Alexandrovich. The cathedral stands on the site of the Tsar's villa, where he died in 1865. Following its dedication in 1912, the cathedral's ornate gold interior quickly became a haven for exiled Russian nobles. *(17 bd. du Tsarevitch, off bd. Gambetta.* ☎ *93 96 88 02. Open daily 9am-noon and 2:30-6pm, Su 2:30-5:50pm. Closed during Mass. €2.50, students €2.)*

LE CHÂTEAU. Le Château—the remains of an 11th-century fort—marks the city's birthplace. For years, Celto-Ligurian tribes called the hillside home, until they were ousted by the Romans in 154 BC. Centuries later, *provençal* counts built a castle and the Cathédrale Ste-Marie on top of the hill as a symbol of their authority over the developing village below. Louis XIV methodically destroyed the château and fortress in 1706; all that remains today is a green park, stone ruins, and **Nice's best view.** In summer, an outdoor theater hosts orchestral and vocal musicians. *(☎ 93 85 62 33. Info booth open July-Aug. Tu-F 9:30am-12:30pm and 1:30-6pm. Purchase tickets at FNAC in the Nice Etoile center. Park open daily June-Aug. 9am-8pm; Apr.-May 8am-7pm; Sept. 10am-7pm; Oct.-Mar. 8am-6pm. Free walk to the top. Elevator daily June-Aug. 9am-8pm; Apr.-Sept. 10am-7pm; Oct.-Mar. 10am-6pm. €0.70 up, round-trip €1.)*

JARDIN ALBERT I AND ESPACE MASSÉNA. Jardin Albert I, below pl. Masséna, is the city's oldest park. The outdoor **Théâtre de Verdure** presents concerts in summer (contact the tourist office for info). Unfortunately, the picturesque park is one of the most dan-

chewing, unless you like the taste of rubber—it is an **eraser.**

An *extincteur* is not some sort of bazooka. It is a **fire extinguisher.**

Fesses is not a colloquial term for 'coming clean'; it means **buttocks.**

As is not another way to say *fesses* or even an insult. This is a French compliment, meaning **ace** or **champion.**

Ranger is neither a woodsman nor a mighty morpher. This means **to tidy up.**

A *smoking* has little to do with tobacco (or any other substance). It is a **tuxedo** or **dinner suit.**

Raisins are juicy **grapes,** not the dried-up snack food. Try *raisins-secs* instead.

Prunes are **plums.** *Pruneaus* are the dried fruit.

Tampons are **stamps** (for documents), not the feminine care item. If you are looking for those, ask for a *tampon hygiénique* or *napkins.* To wipe your mouth, you would do better with a *serviette.*

The *patron* is the **boss,** not the customer.

A *glacier* does translate literally, meaning glacier, but you are more likely to see it around town on signs for **ice cream vendors;** *glace* does not mean glass, but a frozen treat.

If the French language seems full of deception, think again. *Deception* in French actually means **disappointment.**

—Jack Pararas

gerous spots in Nice after nightfall. Tourists should avoid crossing the park at night and instead stick to the pedestrian zones on pl. Masséna and av. de Verdun. *(Between av. Verdun and bd. Jaurès, off promenade des Anglais and quai des Etats-Unis. Box office open daily 10:30am-noon and 3:30-6:30pm. MC/V.)*

OTHER SIGHTS. Creatively named by the rich English community that commissioned it, the **promenade des Anglais,** a palm-lined seaside boulevard, is filled with ice-cream eating tourists and jogging locals. The stately **Hôtel Négresco** presents the best of *Belle Epoque* luxury with coffered ceilings, crystal chandeliers, and an extensive collection of valuable artwork. The seashore between bd. Gambetta and the Opéra alternates **private beaches** with crowded **public strands,** but a large section west of bd. Gambetta is public. Many travelers are surprised to find that the Baie des Anges is not lined with soft sand, but stretches of rock; bring a beach mat.

ENTERTAINMENT

The **Théâtre du Cours,** 5 rue Poissonnerie in *vieux* Nice, stages traditional drama. (☎93 80 12 67. €15, students €10. MC/V.) The **Théâtre National de Nice,** promenade des Arts, presents plays and concerts. (☎93 13 90 90; contact@theatredenice.org. Box office open June-July Tu-Sa 1-7pm; Aug.-May Tu-Sa 2-7pm; Su at 1pm for same-day tickets only. Tickets €10-30, students €7.50-28. MC/V.) The **Opéra de Nice,** 4-6 rue St-François de Paule, stages productions from September to May and hosts visiting orchestras and soloists year-round. (☎93 13 98 53 or 92 17 40 79. Ticket window open Tu-Sa 10am-5pm. €8-40. MC/V.) **FNAC,** 24 av. Jean Médecin, across from the Basilique Notre-Dame, sells tickets for most musical and theatrical events. (☎92 17 77 77; www.fnac.com. Open M-Sa 10am-7:30pm. AmEx/MC/V.)

NIGHTLIFE

In Nice, lazy days in the sun mean wild nights on the town. The bars and nightclubs around **rue Masséna, vieux Nice,** and **Port Lympia** cater to all musical tastes with house, jazz, and rock. As night falls, the **promenade des Anglais** fills with street performers and pedestrians. Local men have a reputation for harassing people on the promenade, around the train station, and in the Jardin Albert I at night; avoid empty streets, and do not walk alone. At night, tourists should be cautious on the beach. The dress code at bars and clubs is simple: look good, unless you are happy at a pub full of foreign backpackers. Almost all clubs and some bars will turn away people in shorts, sandals, sneakers, or baseball caps. Dressing with *classe* (style) is paramount. Still, Nice's dress code is not quite as strict as other places on the Riviera. A good pair of jeans and a nice shirt is often acceptable even at the most happening clubs. For gay nightlife, check out http://aglae.supersonique.net or ask at a local bar for a map listing all of the GLBT-friendly bars and clubs in town.

BARS

Wayne's, 15 rue de la Préfecture (☎93 13 46 99; www.waynes.fr). A laid-back crowd drinks at the bar while a rowdier crew dances to pop-rock rhythms on tables downstairs. Beer and mixed drinks €7. Karaoke with a live band Su. Live music or live DJ on other nights. Happy hour noon-9pm; all drinks €3.50. Open daily noon-2am.

Thor, 32 cours Saleya (☎93 62 49 90; www.thor-pub.com). This raucous Scandinavian pub is a favorite among Nice residents. The most popular décor is the svelte anglophone staff that pours pints and black shots of fiery *sma gra* (vodka with anise and Turkish pepper; €2.50) for a young, playful crowd. Choose between relaxed outdoor seating or head upstairs to jam with the band. Beer €3.50. Shots €2. Live music daily from 10pm. Happy hour 6-9pm. Open daily 6pm-2:30am. MC/V.

Tapas la Movida, 2bis rue de l'Abbaye (☎93 62 27 46). Hole-in-the-wall bar attracts a young, alternative crowd that enjoys live music and cheap drinks. Figure out how to crawl home before attempting the **bar-o-mètre** (€15), a meter-long box of shots. Live reggae, rock, and ska concerts M-F (€2). Theme parties F-Sa. Happy hour Su (shots €1). Open July-Aug. daily 9pm-12:30am; Sept.-June M-Sa 9pm-12:30am. Cash only.

Le Six, 6 rue Bosio (☎93 62 66 64). Halfway between a nightclub and a piano bar. Draws a mixed crowd that dances to Top 40 songs. Reasonably priced drinks and original décor, complete with an 18th-century ceiling. Look out for the occasional *soirées tapis* (kissing nights). Beer €7. Mixed drinks €5-10. Open Tu-Su 10pm-2am. MC/V.

Le Blue Whales, 1 rue Masscoinät (☎93 62 90 94). The only bar open after 2:30am on weekends without a cover charge. Attracts a large crowd of late-night party-goers. Grab a table and listen to live music downstairs or play pool upstairs. Beer €4.50. Mixed drinks €6-9. Prices double after 1am. Open daily until 4:30am. MC/V.

L'Escalier, 10 rue Bosio (☎93 92 64 39). DJs spin R&B, funk, house, and hip hop for a lively mix of locals late into the night. In early evening, a relaxed crowd shoots pool and sips gin fizz (€10), but the real party starts when the other bars close down around 2am and the pool tables give way to dancing. Beer €6-9. Mixed drinks €10-15. Cover €10 after 1am F-Sa; includes 1 drink. Open daily 10pm-5am. MC/V.

Le Flag, 6 rue Eugène Emanuel (☎93 87 29 67; www.le-flag.com). Grab a plush bean bag chair and join a youthful crowd of men and women at this chill gay lounge/café/art gallery. Try the lime-packed specialty cocktail *Les Flagrandélires* (€9). Things heat up for weekly Su parties. Happy hour 6:30-9pm (all drinks €3-5). Cover F-Sa €4-10. Open W-Th 7pm-12:30am, F-Sa 7pm-2am. AmEx/MC/V.

NIGHTCLUBS

Exorbitant covers and expensive drinks can make for pricey partying, but discounts are sometimes offered on Thursdays, Sundays, every day before midnight, and to well-dressed females. The scene in Nice is in constant flux: hotspots shift rapidly and *soirées itinérantes* are often held, so ask around to make sure you're hitting up the latest and greatest *boîtes de nuit.*

Blue Moon, 26 quai Lunel (☎93 26 54 79). White vinyl stools and blank tile walls provide the perfect setting for the young and the fashion-conscious to dance the night away. Cocktails are illuminated by glow stick stirrers. DJs spin club, funk, and house music. Mixed drinks €12. Cover €15; includes 1 drink. Open Th-Sa midnight-5am.

Le Subway, 19 rue Droite (☎93 80 56 27), in *vieux* Nice. Locals and tourists alike dance to pop-rock in vaulted rooms. The unpretentious, electric atmosphere comes at a more reasonable price than other clubs. Beer €3-5. Mixed drinks €7. Cover €8, includes 1 drink; women free after midnight. Open Th-Sa 11:30pm until dawn.

FESTIVALS

In mid-July, the **Nice Jazz Festival** attracts 55,000 visitors, who listen to 500 musicians in 75 concerts over an eight-day period. The olive trees of the suburb of Cimiez provide an unforgettable backdrop for over 120 hours of fabulous international music. (Arènes et Jardins de Cimiez. ☎08 20 80 04 00 or 08 92 70 75 07; www.nicejazzfest.com. Concerts 7pm-midnight. Tickets €33 per night; 3-day pass €84, 8-day €163. MC/V.) During the spring **Carnaval** (Feb. 16-Mar. 2, 2008), Nice gives Rio a run for its money as the promenade des Anglais and the quai des Etats-Unis host two weeks of parades, fireworks, and concerts. Confetti battles, masked balls, and floral processions fill the city with color by day, and endless partying by night. (Call the tourist office for info, or visit www.nicecarnaval.com. Tickets €10-30.)

DAYTRIP FROM NICE: ST-PAUL

If you visit one medieval village on the Côte D'Azur, make it St-Paul. This cliff top hamlet draws more than two million visitors each year to its ivy-covered, cobblestone streets. Though touristy, the village remains a pedestrian delight. A walk along the rambling streets yields incredible views of the countryside, while colorful artwork brightens the doorways of tiny galleries. An artist's paradise, St-Paul attracted a veritable colony of creation when Chagall, Léger, Matisse, Picasso, and several others came to the hilltop for inspiration. Many contemporary artists have followed in their footsteps, and more than 50 **galleries** display their wares. The somber 13th-century **Eglise Collégiale** is a period-appropriate dark, stark church. Its wide, vaulted interior is home to the mounted skull of St-Etienne. (Open daily 9am-8pm.) A quiet **cemetery** just outside the village walls at the southeast end is the resting place of Marc Chagall. As you descend the first steps, his gravestone is the second on the right. (Open daily July-Aug. 7:30am-8pm; Sept.-June 8am-5pm.)

Though the village is brimming with galleries, St-Paul's most impressive collection of art is in nearby **Fondation Maeght,** 1km from the town center. From the St-Paul bus stop, take chemin de St-Claire, to the left of the Chapelle Ste-Claire. Follow this path until it reaches a road, where blue signs will direct you to the foundation. The fantastic galleries, designed by Joseph Sert to showcase modern and contemporary art, are the perfect backdrop for a stunning collection of works by Arp, Calder, Chagall, Giacometti, Léger, and Miró. Highlights include Miró's whimsical garden labyrinth and the Giacometti courtyard. Temporary exhibits include Yan Pei Ming's paintings, on display until March 2008. (☎93 32 81 63; www.fondation-maeght.com. Open daily July-Oct. 10am-7pm; Nov.-June 10am-12:30pm and 2:30-6pm. €11, students €9, under 10 free. Camera permit €2.50. AmEx/MC/V.)

SAP (☎93 58 37 60) sends buses #400-410 to St-Paul from Nice (1hr.; 28 per day; €4.30). The last buses leave St-Paul for Nice at 7:20pm from the stop just outside the town entrance. The **tourist office,** 2 rue Grande, is inside the village walls just after the arched entryway. The knowledgeable staff dispenses free maps and info on galleries. Themed 1hr. tours are available in English by request. (Tours 10am-6pm. €8, under 12 free.) Rent balls for a round of *pétanque* (€3 per person per hr.), or schedule a game with an experienced tourist office liaison. (☎93 32 86 95; www.saint-pauldevence.com. Open daily June-Sept. 10am-7pm; Oct.-May 10am-6pm. €8, under 12 free.) The winner should be treated to lentils (€11) or tapas (€4) at **Chez Andréas,** rempart ouest, in the port. The well-designed *salon de thé* offers excellent *plats du jour* (€10), along with views of the ramparts and the sea. (☎93 32 98 32. Open daily noon-midnight. Cash only.)

CÔTE D'AZUR

THE CORNICHES ☎04 93

A panorama of rocky shores, beaches, and luxurious villas lines the coast between hectic Nice and high-rolling Monaco. More relaxing and less touristed than their glamorous neighbors, these tiny towns are a break from the bustle. While beaches are small and pebbly, and a few more stops on the train lead to larger, jaw-dropping Menton, short and inexpensive rides still make any town in the Corniches (kohr-NEESH) a sweet daytrip from Nice. The train offers an exceptional glimpse of the coast's towns, while buses maneuvering along the high roads of the Corniches provide views of the cliffs and sea below.

EZE

The medieval village of Eze (EHZ; pop. 2500) makes an excellent daytrip for its spectacular views of the coast, historic streets, and scenic hikes. On the top of the Corniches, **Eze-le-Village** is a tangle of arches and blooming jasmine. These houses, 429m above the sea, have been inhabited for over 25 centuries by everyone from

FINDING YOUR NICHE IN THE 'NICHES. Trains and buses between Nice and Monaco serve most of the Corniches. With about two departures per hour, **trains** from Nice to Monaco stop at **Villefranche-sur-Mer** (8min., €1.40), **Beaulieu-sur-Mer** (12min., €1.70), and **Eze-bord-de-Mer** (20min., €2.20). Several numbered RCA **buses** (☎85 64 44; www.rca.tm.fr) travel between Nice and Monaco. Bus #100 leaves Nice every 15min., stopping in **Villefranche-sur-Mer** (10min.), **Beaulieu-sur-Mer** (20min.), **Monaco-Ville** (40min.), and **Monte-Carlo** (45min.). **Eze-le-Village** can be reached by #82 (20min.; M-Sa 14 per day; Su 8:30, 10, 11:30am, 1:30, 3, 5pm), while #81 serves **St-Jean-Cap-Ferrat** (25min.; M-Sa 9:10am, 12:15pm). All tickets €1.30. The last buses from the Corniches to Nice (M-Sa) leave Eze-le-Village at 6:15pm, St-Jean-Cap-Ferrat at 7:50pm, Monte-Carlo at 8:30pm, Monaco-Ville at 8:35pm, and Villefranche-sur-Mer at 8:55pm.

the Moors to the Piedmontese. Now, only a few of Eze's residents live in the medieval village; most live below in **Col d'Eze** or even farther down in the seaside town of **Eze Bord-de-Mer** (also called **Eze-sur-Mer**). The rocky coast is popular with celebrities; Bono and Princess Antoinette Grimaldi of Monaco frequent nearby villas.

Centuries ago, Théodore de Banville complained that "to reach Eze one has to climb up from the sea or drop down from the sky." Today, roads make **Eze-le-Village** far more accessible. For a 1hr. hike to the top, follow **Chemin de Friedrich Nietzsche** (head down the road toward Monaco, and the trail will be on the left, 100m east of the train station). Before taking off, stop by one of the snack stands across from the train station and pick up water. This path is grueling but rewards hikers with increasingly spectacular and secluded vistas of the Corniches. Nietzsche certainly derived plenty of inspiration from the trail: it was here that he composed the third part of *Thus Spoke Zarathustra.* If you aren't in need of inspiration—or sweat stains—bus #112 connects Nice to Eze-le-Village (7 times per day). From May through October, daily municipal shuttle #83 also connects Eze-le-Village and Eze Bord-de-Mer (7 per day 9:30am-6:40pm, €1.30).

A favorite of photo-snapping tourists, Eze-le-Village recounts the Riviera's tumultuous past with a series of remains. The **Porte des Maures,** a doorway carved into the cliff-face, was the Moors' golden ticket into Eze during their 10th-century destruction of Provence. A surprise attack proved highly successful; they maintained control of the village for the following 70 years. Nearby, the **Chapelle de la Saint-Croix** is the oldest building in the village. The austere facade of the **Eglise Paroissial,** an 18th-century structure, conceals an elaborate Baroque interior adorned with *trompe-l'oeil* frescoes, large chandeliers, and Phoenecian crosses. (☎41 00 38. Open daily July-Aug. 9:30am-7:30pm; Sept.-June 9:30am-6pm.) The **Jardin d'Eze,** which offers fabulous views that stretch all the way from St-Tropez to the Italian coast, is centered on a Savoy fortress that was razed in 1706 by the armies of Louis XIV. The garden also displays the earth-goddess sculptures of Jean-Philippe Richard. Over 400 species of cacti and exotic plants dot the rocky hillside. (☎41 10 30. Open daily July-Aug. 9am-8pm; Sept.-June 9am-5pm or 7pm, depending on sunlight. €4, students €2.)

Eze-le-Village offers more than narrow streets and pretty vistas—the second largest factory of the **Parfumerie Fragonard,** built in 1968, clings to the hillside. Perfumes are sold at dramatically reduced, warehouse prices, and free 15min. tours in nine languages explain the elaborate perfume-, cosmetic-, and soap-making processes. (☎41 05 05; www.fragonard.com. Open daily Apr.-Oct. 8:15am-6:30pm; Nov.-Mar. 8:30am-noon and 2-6pm. AmEx/MC/V.) Another large perfume factory from Grasse has a location in Eze: the **Parfumerie Galimard** boutique, a small museum that offers free guided visits, is across from the tourist office. (☎41 10 70. Open daily 9am-6:30pm. AmEx/MC/V.)

If smelling good isn't your thing, try one of the 30 **trails** that crisscross the landscape, taking hikers to the seaside, the **Moyenne Corniche,** and the **Grand Corniche.** Routes range in length and difficulty; most take 1hr. and require sturdy shoes, water, and a map. One of the best leads to the Oppidum of Mont Bastide (560m), which offers superior vistas of Eze (1½hr., marked in yellow). The tourist office offers maps and info. For more details, contact **Eze Rando** (☎01 51 52). Some paths have fallen into disuse; check with the office or Eze Rando before you hit the trail.

Every other year in late July, Eze turns back the clock to the Middle Ages for **Eze d'Antan,** a three-day festival during which inhabitants dress up in period costumes and restaurants serve traditional medieval fare. Each year, the village focuses on a different theme: recent years' themes have included "Charms and Magic Spells of the Middle Ages" and "Saracen Invasions." For details call the tourist office. The next festival is expected to occur in summer 2008.

A **taxi** (☎06 09 84 17 84) from Eze Bord-de-Mer to Eze-le-Village costs €20. The **tourist office,** pl. de Gaulle, just outside the main part of the medieval city, is a few steps from the bus stop. (☎41 26 00; www.eze-riviera.com. Open daily Apr.-Oct. 9am-7pm; Nov.-Mar. 9am-6:30pm. Guided 1hr. tours of the medieval village and garden €6; 2-person min.) An annex next to the train station also provides info. (☎01 52 00. Open May-Oct. daily 10am-1pm and 3-6:30pm.)

VILLEFRANCHE-SUR-MER

The pastel houses of 700-year-old Villefranche-sur-Mer (VEEL-frahnsh suhr mehr; pop. 6650) have earned the town a reputation as one of the Riviera's most photogenic areas. The backdrop for dozens of films, including a James Bond installation, *Dirty Rotten Scoundrels*, and multiple Hitchcock movies, the town has lured the likes of Aldous Huxley and Katherine Mansfield to its shores. Today, Villefranche is a vacation spot for families and young people who come to enjoy the closest one gets to a sandy beach in the Corniches.

As you walk from the station on quai Courbet, a sign for the *vieille ville* directs you along 13th-century **rue Obscure,** the oldest street in Villefranche. The stone arches and shrunken doors served as an eerie backdrop for Jean Cocteau's 1959 film *La Testament d'Orphée.* Along the covered street, yellow lanterns throw long, creepy shadows, even midday. A right at the end of rue Obscure takes you to pl. de l'Eglise, a tiny square entirely occupied by the **Eglise St-Michel.** In addition to the clock tower, the church contains a wooden statue of Christ carved by a slave.

At the end of the *quai* stands the pink-and-yellow 14th-century **Chapelle St-Pierre,** decorated from floor to ceiling by Jean Cocteau. His simple trademark style fills the chapel with pastels, which are disrupted by the occasional burst of vivid green and yellow, as seen on exotic ceramic figures by the door. (☎76 90 70. Open Tu-Su June-Aug. 10am-noon and 4-8:30pm; Sept. to mid-Nov. 9:30am-noon and 2-6pm; mid-Dec. to Feb. 9:30am-noon and 2-5pm; Mar.-May 9:30am-noon and 3-7pm. Closed mid-Nov. to mid-Dec. €2.) Above the port is the rather dull 16th-century **Citadelle,** which houses three small museums. The most interesting is the **Musée Volti,** dedicated to Antoniucci Volti, who was known for creating curvaceous female forms in bronze, clay, canvas, and copper. (☎76 33 27; musees@villefranche-sur-mer.fr. Open July-Aug. M and W-Sa 10am-noon and 2:30-7pm, Su 2:30-7pm; June and Sept. M and W-Sa 9am-noon and 2:30-6pm, Su 2:30-6pm; Oct.-May W-Sa 9am-noon and 2-5:30pm, Su 1:30-6pm. Free.) On weekends, Jardin Binon, between the beach and the museum, provides excellent shopping at the **provençal food market** (open Sa 8am-1pm) and the **antiques market** (open Su 9am-4pm).

Though a day in the peaceful Corniches might leave you in no hurry to get back to Nice's wild shore, Villefranche isn't cheap. Family-owned **La Régence ❹,** 2 av. Maréchal Foch, has nine good-sized rooms on top of a *brasserie* along the main drag. All are well-kept, with comfortable beds and deep red carpets, and come with bath and phone. (☎/fax 01 70 91. Breakfast €6. Internet access €6 per 30min., €9 per hr. Reception 6am-2am. Singles and doubles from €49; triples €64. Cash only.) One awning down the street, the red-checked tables at **Loco Loco ❷** fill with hungry locals with delicious food at great prices. You can't go wrong with a heaping plate of *moules* (mussels; €11), the restaurant's specialty. (Open May-Sept. Tu-Su 11:30am-3pm and 7-11pm. Closed Oct.-Apr.)

To reach the **tourist office** from the train station, exit on quai 1 and head inland on av. Georges Clemenceau. At pl. Charles II d'Anjou, continue on to the right side of av. Sadi Carnot. The office is at the end of the street, on the edge of Jardin François Binon. It distributes a walking tour of town, helps plan excursions to nearby villages, and organizes guided tours. (☎01 73 68; www.villefranche-sur-mer.com. Open July-Aug. daily 9am-7pm; June and Sept. M-Sa 9am-noon and 2-6:30pm; Oct.-May M-Sa 9am-noon and 2-6pm. 1¾hr. walking tours of the Citadelle and *vieille ville* in English July-Aug. W 10am, in French Apr.-Sept. F 9:30am; €8.)

BEAULIEU-SUR-MER

Napoleon's creativity failed him when he named this seaside resort: he simply called it *beau lieu*—beautiful place. In the late 19th century, elite English and French visitors who shared Napoleon's sentiment flooded the town, building Belle Epoque villas, four-star hotels, and a classy casino. Today, the money has moved on to quieter mansions in nearby St-Jean-Cap-Ferrat, but Beaulieu (BOH-lyuh; pop. 3675) still attracts a few stars who dock their yachts in its 800-boat marina. A spectacular Greek villa turns this otherwise uninteresting town into a nice starting point for the lovely seaside walk to St-Jean-Cap-Ferrat and its beaches.

On a plateau overlooking the sparkling Baie des Fourmis, Renaissance man Theodore Reinach built his dream villa, **Kérylos,** which stands as a monument to the eccentricity of wealth and the sophistication of Ancient Greece. Completed in 1905, the mansion strives to imitate a Greek dwelling from the second century BC. Though modern comforts are hidden throughout, Reinach added artificially aged mosaics, gold-leaf cedar wood ceilings, and an enormous sundial to make the house seem as though it were plucked straight out of Athens. The millionaire and his wife ate on reclining woven Greek-style beds, took baths in enormous tubs made of Carrara marble, and showered in an open-air space that catches rainwater, just as the showers of ancient Greece did. A 1½hr. audio tour includes stops in the colonnade-filled courtyard, the mosaic bath house, and a mysterious antechamber. The gardens, encircled by statues, provide unforgettable views of the Mediterranean. (Open by tour only. Open July-Aug. daily 10am-7pm; Sept. to early Nov. and early Feb. to June daily 10am-6pm; early Nov. to early Feb. M-F 2-6pm, Sa-Su 10am-6pm. Last admission 30min. before closing. Audio tour in English, French, German, or Italian. €7.80, students €5.50, under 7 free. AmEx/MC/V.)

Those on a small budget should visit Beaulieu as a daytrip from Nice; however, if you're dead-set on sleeping here, your best option is **La Riviera ❺**, 6 rue Paul Doumer. Its 11 rooms have thick carpets, immaculate bathrooms, and a striking view of the surrounding cliffs. All have private shower, toilet, A/C, and phone. The hotel is strictly non-smoking. (☎01 04 92; www.hotel-riviera.fr. Breakfast €7. Reception 7:30am-noon and 4-8pm. Singles and doubles €56-62; triples €70, with bath €75. Sept.-Apr. prices drop €6-10. AmEx/MC/V.) To pack a picnic for the beach, stop by **place du Général du Gaulle** and pick up fresh produce at the **open-air market** (daily 7am-1pm). There is also a **Petit Casino** on 28 bd. Marini. (☎01 18 25. Open M-Sa 7:30am-12:30pm and 3:30-7:30pm. V.) Waterfront cafés and restaurants are expensive, while *brasseries* are unremarkable. For the best lunch deal in town, head to **La Pignatelle ❹**, 10 rue de Quinceenet, for its tasty *niçoise-provençal* lunch *menu*

CÔTE D'AZUR

(€14). This shaded restaurant, complete with fountain and chirping birds, serves local specialties at reasonable prices. (☎01 63 37. *Plats* €16-26. Open M-Tu and Th-Su noon-1:30pm and 7-9:45pm. AmEx/MC/V.) **Le Petit Paris ❸,** bd. Marinoni, just off pl. du Général de Gaulle, is one of the only *brasseries* that stands out. This purple street-side café draws crowds looking for fresh pizza (€6.50-8.50), tasty pasta (€8-10) and succulent meat dishes (€13-22), as well as a lunch *menu* (€14) based on the *plat du jour*. (☎01 69 91. Open M-F noon-2pm and 7-9:30pm. AmEx/MC/V.)

A promenade along the waterfront passes by the major hotels and the large Port de Plaisance, home to an impressive collection of private sailboats and yachts. Farther along the waterfront is plage des Fourmis, a perfect crescent of sand that draws an animated crowd of bathers. On the other side of the coast toward Eze and Monaco, a longer stretch of beach, the public plage Petite Afrique, offers more sand. The tourist office, pl. Georges Clemenceau, next to the train station, provides free maps of the village and a schedule of summer festivals. (☎01 02 21; www.ot-beaulieu-sur-mer.fr. Open July-Aug. M-Sa 9am-12:30pm and 2-7pm, Su 9am-12:30pm; Sept.-June M-Sa 9am-12:15pm and 2-6pm.)

ST-JEAN-CAP-FERRAT

For years, the quietly wealthy St-Jean-Cap-Ferrat (sehn JAHN cap feh-RAH; pop. 2100) has been a haven for the upper class. Yachts and beaches abound on the peninsula. The best thing this town has to offer budget travelers is the 30min. **seaside walk** from Beaulieu (in front of the casino). Lavish villas, rocky beaches, and once-beautiful docks provide endless photo opportunities. As you stroll along, glance back toward Beaulieu, where the mountain coastline drops into the sea. At the port, head toward the middle of the peninsula on av. Séméria, a winding road connecting St-Jean-Cap-Ferrat with the main coastal routes to Nice and Monaco.

The **Fondation Ephrussi de Rothschild,** off av. D. Semeria, between the tourist office and the Nice-Monaco road, is designed to look like an 18th-century château. Completed in 1912, the building holds the furniture and art collections of the Baroness de Rothschild. The upstairs rooms contain a collection of fine porcelain, tapestries, and paintings by two of the foremost artists of the 18th-century Rococo style: François Boucher and Jean-Honoré Fragonard. Exquisite gardens, with sea views on either side, form the shape of a boat's prow. From her perch on the villa's *loggia*, the offbeat Baroness liked to pretend that she was at the helm of a magnificent ship. To perpetuate her make-believe world, she required the gardeners to wear sailor costumes on the grounds. The villa can be accessed directly from Beaulieu. Follow the shore path toward St-Jean, turning right after the three-pronged tree before the pink villa that separates the path from the Mediterranean. From the top of this walled shore, turn left and follow the road uphill, turning right at the sign to the Fondation. (☎01 45 90; www.villa-ephrussi.com. Open July-Aug. daily 10am-7pm; Sept.-Oct. and mid-Feb. to June daily 10am-6pm; Nov. to mid-Feb. M-F 2-6pm, Sa-Su 10am-6pm. Gardens 10am-6:30pm. Last admission 30min. before closing. Upper floors of the mansion require an additional ticket for a guided tour available in 4 languages, including English, at 11:30am, 2:30, 3:30, 4:30pm; in summer also 5:30pm; €2. €9.50, students €7.)

St-Jean's beaches have earned it the nickname *presqu'île des rêves* (peninsula of dreams). But even its most popular, **plage Paloma,** is small and pebbly, and you'll want to pass up others, like the aptly named **plage Passable.** A few offer a more solitary sunbath: make a right off the end of av. Mermoz and go down the steps to the peaceful **Les Fossettes** and, farther on, **Les Fosses.** The **Ecole Française de Voile** at the Nouveau Port rents **sailboats, kayaks,** and **windsurfing** equipment. (☎76 10 08. Single kayaks €11 per hr., €19 per 2hr., €28 per 3hr.; double kayaks €14/25/36. Sailboats €38 per person per hr. Experienced skippers can rent boats for €36-38 per hr., €63-65 per 2hr. Open daily June-Aug. 9am-6pm; Sept.-May 9am-5pm.)

Three coastal sentiers (trails) border the peninsula, offering secluded sunbathing spots and sublime vistas. The easiest stretches are from Beaulieu to the Nouveau Port and can be completed in 30min. A tour of the Pointe de St-Hospice reveals an open view of the irregular eastern coastline (40min.), but the stunning chemin de la Carrière provides a taste of both coasts on a 1½hr. tour that stretches all the way down to the Pointe Malalongue. A tiny tourist office, 59 av. Denis Séméria, distributes free maps of the hikes. (☎76 08 90. Open July-Aug. M-Sa 9am-6pm, Su 9am-5:30pm; Sept.-June M-Sa 9am-5pm.)

MONACO ☎04

In 1297, François Grimaldi of Genoa established his family as rulers of Monaco (MOHN-ah-ko; pop. 7100) by overthrowing the town with a few henchmen disguised as monks (*monaco* in Italian). The tiny principality has since jealously guarded its independence and exclusivity. Monaco flaunts its wealth with ubiquitous surveillance cameras, high-speed luxury cars, multi-million-dollar yachts, and the famous casino in the capital, Monte-Carlo. Fashion-conscious residents and visiting celebrities give the impression that the Belle Epoque isn't over yet. The sheer spectacle of it all—not to mention the tabloid allure of Monaco's royal family—is worth the trip from Nice.

TO (OR FROM) MONACO, WITH LOVE. Monaco's country code is ☎377. To call Monaco from France, dial ☎00377, then the 8-digit Monaco number. To call France from Monaco, dial ☎0033 and drop the 1st zero of the French number. French phone cards will not work in Monaco's public phones, but cards purchased in Monaco will work throughout Europe. Cell phones send and receive calls anywhere in Monaco just as in France.

TRANSPORTATION

Trains: The new **Gare SNCF** has 4 points of access: galerie Prince Pierre (behind the old train station), pl. St-Dévote, bd. de Belgique (at the intersection of bd. du Jardin Exotique), and bd. Princesse Charlotte. Open daily 4am-1am. Info desk and ticket window open M-F 5:50am-8:30pm, Sa-Su 5:50am-8:05pm. To: **Antibes** (1hr., every 30min., €6.10); **Cannes** (1¼hr., every 30min., €7.70); **Menton** (11min., every 30min., €1.70); **Nice** (25min., every 30min., €3.10).

Buses: Buses leave from bd. des Moulins and av. Princesse Alice, near the tourist office. TAM and RCA (☎93 85 64 44). To **Nice** (45min.) and **Menton** (25min.). **Cap d'Ail, Eze-sur-Mer, Beaulieu-sur-Mer, Villefranche-sur-Mer,** and **St-Jean-Cap-Ferrat** via Nice route. Buses leave every 15min. (€1.30). Same-day return tickets to Monaco free.

Public Transportation: (☎97 70 22 22; www.cam.mc). 6 bus routes serve the principality (M-Sa every 11min. 7am-9pm, Su every 20min. 7:30am-9pm). Bus #4 links the Ste-Dévote train station to the casino; bus #2 connects the *vieille ville* and *Jardin Exotique* via pl. d'Armes and the casino; lines #5 and 6 connect Fontvielle with the rest of the city. Tickets €1.50, *carnet* of 4 €3.60, *carnet* of 8 €5.70. The €3.60 *carte touristique* offers unlimited travel on day of purchase. Buy tickets on board.

Taxis: ☎93 15 01 01. 11 taxi stands, including the Casino, pl. des Moulins, and the Ste-Dévote train station. Consult tourist office for complete list. €10 min. charge. 24hr.

Car Rental: Avis, 9 av. d'Ostende (☎93 30 17 53). Open M-Sa 8am-noon and 2-7pm, Su 9am-noon. AmEx/MC/V. **Europcar,** 47 av. de Grande-Bretagne (☎93 50 74 95; www.europcar.fr). Open M-Sa 8am-noon and 2-6pm. AmEx/MC/V. **Hertz,** 27 bd. Albert I (☎93 50 79 60). Open M-Sa 8:30am-noon and 2-6pm, Su 8:30am-1pm. AmEx/MC/V.

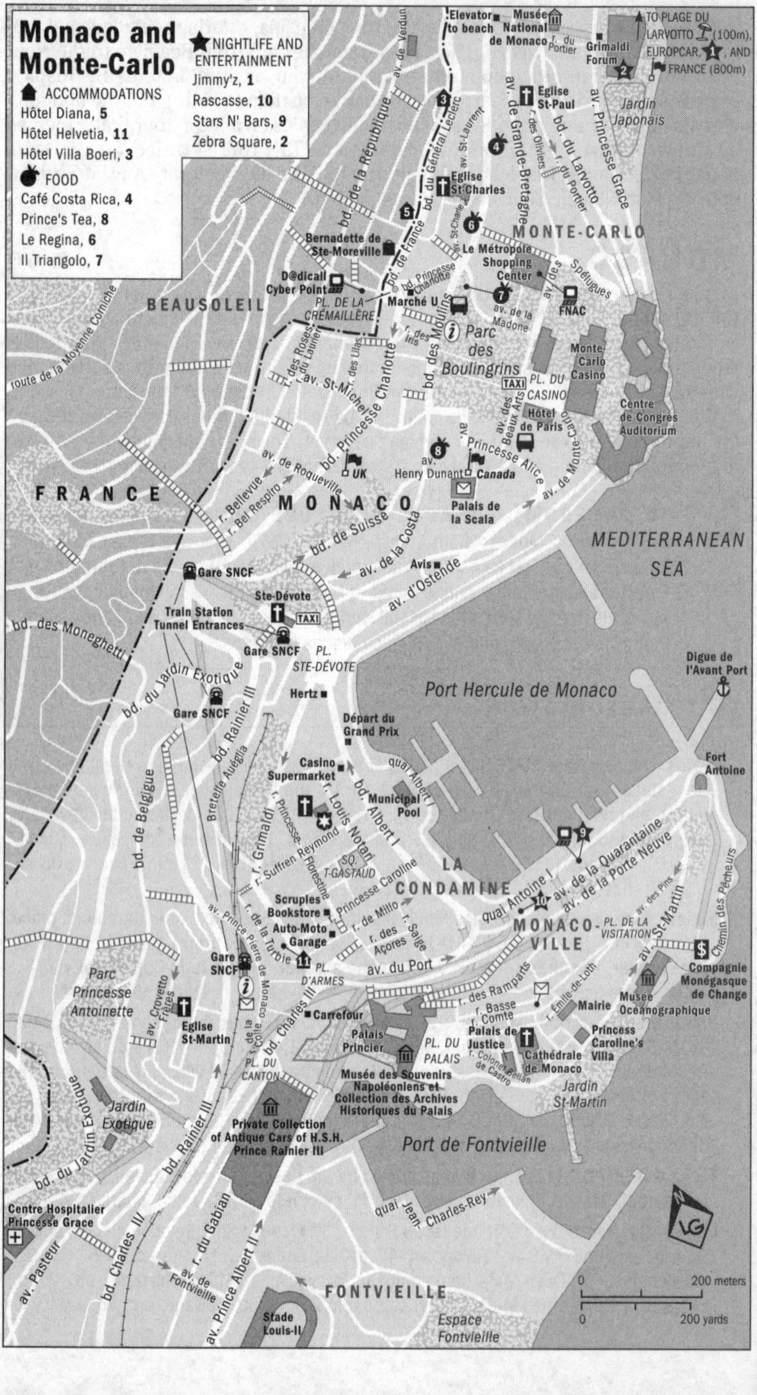
Monaco and Monte-Carlo
ACCOMMODATIONS
Hôtel Diana, 5
Hôtel Helvetia, 11
Hôtel Villa Boeri, 3
FOOD
Café Costa Rica, 4
Prince's Tea, 8
Le Regina, 6
Il Triangolo, 7
NIGHTLIFE AND ENTERTAINMENT
Jimmy'z, 1
Rascasse, 10
Stars N' Bars, 9
Zebra Square, 2
Elevator to beach
Musée National de Monaco
Grimaldi Forum
TO PLAGE DU LARVOTTO (100m), EUROPCAR, AND FRANCE (800m)
Jardin Japonais
Eglise St-Paul
Eglise St-Charles
MONTE-CARLO
Le Métropole Shopping Center
FNAC
Bernadette de Ste-Moreville
D@dicall Cyber Point
PL. DE LA CRÉMAILLÈRE
Marché U
Parc des Boulingrins
PL. DU CASINO
Monte-Carlo Casino
Centre de Congrès Auditorium
Hôtel de Paris
BEAUSOLEIL
FRANCE
MONACO
UK
Canada
Henry Dunant
Palais de la Scala
MEDITERRANEAN SEA
Avis
Gare SNCF
Ste-Dévote
Train Station Tunnel Entrances
PL. STE-DÉVOTE
Hertz
Port Hercule de Monaco
Digue de l'Avant Port
Départ du Grand Prix
Fort Antoine
Casino Supermarket
Municipal Pool
LA CONDAMINE
SQ. T-GASTAUD
Scruples Bookstore
Auto-Moto Garage
MONACO-VILLE
PL. DE LA VISITATION
Compagnie Monégasque de Change
PL. D'ARMES
Parc Princesse Antoinette
Eglise St-Martin
Carrefour
Palais Princier
PL. DU PALAIS
Palais de Justice
Mairie
Musée Océanographique
Princess Caroline's Villa
Cathédrale de Monaco
PL. DU CANTON
Musée des Souvenirs Napoléoniens et Collection des Archives Historiques du Palais
Jardin St-Martin
Jardin Exotique
Private Collection of Antique Cars of H.S.H. Prince Rainier III
Port de Fontvieille
Centre Hospitalier Princesse Grace
FONTVIEILLE
Stade Louis-II
Espace Fontvieille
0 200 meters
0 200 yards
route de la Moyenne Corniche
bd. des Moneghetti
bd. du Jardin Exotique
bd. de Belgique
bd. Rainier III
bd. de la République
bd. du Général Leclerc
bd. de France
bd. Princesse Charlotte
bd. des Moulins
av. de Grande-Bretagne
bd. du Larvotto
av. Princesse Grace
av. des Spélugues
av. Princesse Alice
av. de Monte-Carlo
av. de Roqueville
bd. de Suisse
av. de la Costa
av. d'Ostende
av. St-Michel
bd. Albert I
r. Grimaldi
r. Louis Notari
r. Princesse Caroline
quai Antoine I
av. de la Quarantaine
av. de la Porte Neuve
av. St-Martin
r. des Remparts
av. du Port
bd. Charles III
av. Prince Pierre de Monaco
r. du Gabian
av. Prince Albert II
av. Pasteur
quai Jean-Charles-Rey
av. de Fontvieille
Chemin des Pêcheurs

Scooter Rental: Auto-Moto Garage, 7 rue de Millo (☎93 50 10 80). €35 for 9am-7pm, €40 per 24hr., €245 per week; €150 credit card or check deposit. Open M-F 8am-noon and 2-7pm, Sa 8am-noon. AmEx/MC/V.

ORIENTATION AND PRACTICAL INFORMATION

This jam-packed principality can be divided into four neighborhoods (from southwest to northeast): **Fontvieille, Monaco-Ville, La Condamine,** and **Monte-Carlo/Larvotto.** Fontvieille is home to a small, quiet port. Monaco-Ville, the historical and legislative heart of the city, at the top of the enormous *rocher de Monaco* (rock of Monaco), is home to both the **Palais Princier** and the **Cathédrale de Monaco.** La Condamine, just below Monaco-Ville, along the main port, is the principality's busiest area. Monaco's glitziest section is concentrated in Monte-Carlo, which boasts the fabled tables of the **Monte-Carlo Casino** and the **Carré d'Or,** a cluster of thoroughfares lined with luxury boutiques. Monte-Carlo/Larvotto contains Monaco's only beach, **plage du Larvotto.** A 5min. walk uphill from the casino takes you across the border to **Beausoleil,** France, and to reasonably priced hotels and restaurants a stone's throw from the opulence on display at pl. du Casino.

Tourist Office: 2a bd. des Moulins (☎92 16 61 16), uphill from the casino. English-speaking staff provides city maps, events brochures, and same-day hotel reservations for free. Open M-Sa 9am-7pm, Su 10am-noon. Annexes in the train station at the av. Prince Pierre exit, in the chemin des Pêcheurs parking garage, outside the Jardin Exotique, and in the port (mid-June to Aug.).

Embassies and Consulates: Canada, 1 av. Henry Dunant (☎97 70 62 42); **France,** 1 Chemin du Ténao (☎92 16 54 60); **UK,** 33 bd. Princesse Charlotte (☎93 50 99 54). The nearest **US** consulate is in Nice (☎93 88 89 55).

Currency Exchange: Compagnie Monégasque de Change, av. de la Quarantaine (☎93 25 02 50), in the chemin des Pêcheurs parking garage; access at the end of the port or from Monaco-Ville near the Musée Océanographique. Offers MC/V **cash advances** (€50 min., 8% commission). Open M-Sa June-Sept. 10am-5pm; Oct.-May 10am-noon and 2-4pm; closed Nov. 5-Dec. 25.

English-Language Bookstore: Scruples, 9 rue Princesse Caroline (☎/fax 93 50 43 52). Open June-Aug. M and W-F 10am-7pm, Tu 10am-12:30pm and 2:30-7pm, Sa 10am-12:30pm and 2:30-6:30pm; Sept.-May M-F 9:30am-12:30pm and 2:30-7pm, Sa 9:30am-12:30pm and 2:30-6pm. AmEx/MC/V.

Police: 3 rue Louis Notari (☎93 15 30 15). 5 other stations throughout the principality.

24hr. Pharmacy: Monaco has a rotating schedule of **pharmacies de garde.** Call the police station or look in the daily *Monaco-Matin.* Emergency line for doctor or pharmacist ☎93 25 33 25.

Hospital: Centre Hospitalier Princesse Grace, av. Pasteur (☎97 98 99 00, emergency ☎97 98 97 69). Accessible by bus #5.

Internet Access: FNAC, Le Métropole Shopping Center, 17 av. des Spélugues (☎93 10 81 81). Free Internet access up to 20min. per person. Be prepared to wait. Open M-Sa 10am-5:30pm. **D@dicall Cyber Point,** 1 Impasse General Leclerc (☎93 57 42 14), on the right off bd. du Général Leclerc towards the Casino from Beausoleil. €3 per hr. Open 9:30am-9:30pm. **Stars N' Bars** (see **Nightlife,** p. 728) also has Internet access.

Post Office: Palais de la Scala (☎97 97 25 25). Branch office across from Hôtel Terminus at the av. Prince Pierre train station exit. 5 additional branches. All open M-F 8am-7pm, Sa 8am-noon. **Postal Code:** MC 98000 Monaco.

ACCOMMODATIONS

If you choose to stay near the casino, chances are you won't have much money left to gamble away. Your best bet is to sleep across the border in **Beausoleil,** where prices are nearly halved. The hotels aren't far from the casino and boast the best nightlife in the principality. The only other viable options are in **La Condamine,** or along **rue de la Turbie, rue Grimaldi,** and **avenue Prince Pierre,** by the train tracks.

Hôtel Villa Boeri, 29 bd. du Général Leclerc, in Beausoleil (☎93 78 38 10; fax 93 41 90 95), 10min. from the casino. Exit the train station at bd. Princesse Charlotte and keep left for 20min. Bd. de France changes to bd. du Général Leclerc. A variety of rooms, from singles with double bed and shower to deluxe doubles with huge bathtubs. All rooms have A/C, TV, and phone. English spoken. Breakfast €8. Reception 24hr. June-Aug. singles €59, with bath €63, in private pavilion €103; doubles €66/73/103 triples €75/81/103; quads €93/135. Sept.-May singles €49/53/93; doubles €56/63/93; triples €65/71/93; quads €83/125. AmEx/MC/V. ❹

Hôtel Helvetia, 1bis rue Grimaldi (☎93 30 21 71). Offers simple, comfortable rooms. Rooms do not have the same amenities as those in Beausoleil, but the hotel boasts a location in the Condamine. Breakfast €8.50. Singles €55-80; doubles €58-80. ❺

Hôtel Diana, 17 bd. du Général Leclerc (☎93 78 47 58; www.monte-carlo.mc/hotel-diana-beausoleil), in Beausoleil. On the shabby side, this hotel has rooms with large, firm beds, noisy A/C, TV, and phone. Balconies facing Monaco. Doubles have only 1 bed. Breakfast €6. Reception 6am-8pm. Reservations required. Singles 40-48; doubles €35, with shower €45, with bath €56-65; triples €67, with bath €70. AmEx/MC/V. ❹

FOOD

Not surprisingly, Monaco has little budget fare. Try behind pl. du Palais (**rue Comte Felix, rue Gastaldi,** and **rue Emile de Loth**) for reasonable prices. Fresh food awaits at the fruit and flower market on **place d'Armes** at the end of av. Prince Pierre (open daily 6am-1pm), the **Casino** supermarket at bd. Albert I (☎93 30 56 78; open July-Aug. M-Sa 8:30am-midnight, Su 9am-1pm; Sept.-June daily 8:30am-10pm; MC/V), or **Marché U** at 30 bd. Princesse Charlotte (☎93 50 68 60; open M-Sa 8:30am-7:15pm; MC/V). **Carrefour,** in Fontvieille's shopping plaza, has anything else you might need. (☎92 05 57 00. Open M-Th and Sa 8:30am-9:30pm, F 8:30am-10pm. MC/V.)

Café Costa Rica, 40 bd. des Moulins (☎93 25 44 45). Bright and bustling. Serves bruschetta, salads, and other Italian staples to hungry crowds. After 3pm the sunny interior transforms into a welcoming *salon de thé* and *crêperie.* Squeeze in at lunch for the fabulous *farfalle bersagliera* (€8) and other pasta dishes (€8-11). *Plats du jour* €10-11. Lunch noon-2:45pm. Open July-Aug. M-F 8am-7:30pm, Sa-Su 8am-3pm; Sept.-June daily 8am-7pm. Closed first 2 weeks of Aug. MC/V. ❷

Le Regina, 13-15 bd. des Moulins (☎93 50 05 05). Owner knows regulars by name. Serves delicious pizzas (€9-12), salads (€10-12), pasta (€10-12), and meat and fish dishes (€14-16). Open M-Sa 8am-9pm. MC/V. ❷

Prince's Tea, 26 av. de la Costa (☎93 50 63 91), near the tourist office. Offers princely treats at paupers' prices. Try the chocolate layered mousse (€2.50). Open July-Aug. M-Sa 7:30am-8pm; Sept.-June M-F 7:30am-8pm, Sa 8am-1pm and 3-8pm. MC/V. ❶

Il Triangolo, 1 av. de la Madone (☎93 30 67 30). Italian-speaking staff serves enormous pizzas (€10-16) and pasta dishes (€10-16) in corner terrace. Pizzas available at dinner only. Open M-F noon-2:30pm and 7pm-midnight, Sa-Su 7pm-midnight. MC/V. ❷

SIGHTS

MONTE-CARLO CASINO. This famous gambling house, where Richard Burton wooed Elizabeth Taylor and Mata Hari shot a Russian spy, shines along the rocky coast. The position is a hotbed for suicide, an end once sought by as many as four high-stakes losers in one week. High rollers, too, have their legendary habits: Cornelius Vanderbilt insisted on having his entire family present while he placed 40,000 francs on the table. While optimists tempt fate at **slot machines** (July-Aug. daily from noon; Sept.-June M-F from 2pm, Sa-Su from noon), **blackjack,** and **roulette** (daily from noon), the less intrepid can get a drink and check out the **Atrium du Casino** theater. The gorgeous interior rivals that of Monaco's palace and is well-worth the entrance fee. The casino frowns upon shorts, sneakers, sandals, and jeans, but a fancier **dress code** is not in effect until 8pm. Exclusive *salons privés* require coat and tie and charge an additional €20 cover. The **Café de Paris** next door opens for gambling at 10am with no cover. The 18+ rule is strictly enforced; bring a passport. *(☎92 16 20 00; www.casinomontecarlo.com. Cover €10. AmEx/MC/V.)*

PALAIS PRINCIER. Balanced on *le rocher*, the lavish palace is the occasional home of the tabloid-darling royal family. The stoic palace guard that nominally protects the entrance changes shift with great fanfare daily (11:55am), and only when the prince is away does the flag above the palace lower; it is then that doors open to tourists. Audio tours lead visitors by opulent silk walls, gilt furniture, and Venetian crystal chandeliers; for the gossip behind these you'll have to bring your own tabloid. Memorable stops include the courtyard's grand staircase, the hall of mirrors, the throne room, Princess Grace's official state portrait, and the chamber where the Duke of York died. *(☎93 25 18 31. Open daily May-Sept. 9:30am-6:30pm; Oct. 10am-5:30pm; Apr. 10:30am-6pm. Audio tour in 11 languages. €7, students €3.50. Cash only.)*

JARDIN EXOTIQUE. While Monaco is hardly a desert locale, many species of cacti imported from America in the 16th century thrive in this meticulously kept garden. Stone caves and tiny ponds covered with lily pads offer sweeping views of the principality. Unless you go the early to avoid the heat, you'll be thankful to venture 300 steps down into the cliffside; in addition to housing stunning stalagmites and stalactites, the damp grottoes stay cool at 65° Fahrenheit year-round. *(62 bd. du Jardin Exotique, up the public elevators on bd. de Belgique. Last stop on the #2 bus. ☎93 15 29 80; www.monte-carlo.mc/jardin exotique. Open daily mid-May to mid-Sept. 9am-7pm; mid-Sept. to mid-May 9am-6pm or until sundown. €6.80, students and ages 6-18 €3.50; under 6 free. MC/V.)*

CAR COLLECTION. If you thought the sweet rides parked in prime spots in front of the Casino were impressive, think again: the **Private Collection of Antique Cars of H.S.H. Prince Rainier III** puts them to shame. One hundred of the sexiest cars in the world acquired by the Prince himself are on display. Gawk at a restored 1924 Model T, the 1956 Rolls Royce Silver Cloud that carried Prince Rainier and Grace Kelly on their wedding day, and the car that captured the first *Grand Prix de Monaco* in 1929. *(Terrasses de Fontvieille, above the shopping center. ☎92 05 28 56. Open daily 10am-6pm. €6, students and ages 8-14 €3. Cash only.)*

MUSÉE OCÉANOGRAPHIQUE. An educational break from Monaco's excesses, this museum was founded by the prince-cum-marine biologist Albert I. The museum's main attraction is a 90-tank aquarium featuring Mediterranean and tropical sea life. An innovative system pumps 250,000L of seawater directly from the harbor each day to fill the tanks. Adults will enjoy the reconstructed coral reef, shark lagoon, and 1.9m green moray eel—the largest on display in the world—just as much as kids do. Exhibits on Albert I's expedition to Antarctica and Jacques Cousteau's pioneer scuba dives are also fascinating. *(Av. St-Martin. ☎93 15 36 00. Open daily July-Aug. 9:30am-7:30pm; Sept. and Apr.-June 9:30am-7pm; Oct.-Mar. 10am-6pm. €13, students and ages 6-18 €6.)*

CATHÉDRALE DE MONACO. Thirty-five generations of Grimaldis rest inside this white neo-Romanesque-Byzantine church, which hosted the 1956 wedding of the late Prince Rainier and Grace Kelly. The majestic interior includes an intricate marble floor, a quadruple organ, and an Episcopal throne constructed of white

Carrara marble. Princess Grace lies in a tomb behind the altar emblazoned with her Latin name, Patritia Gracia. Prince Albert Rainier III's tomb is just to the right of Princess Grace's. Citizens still adorn these two tombs with fresh flowers and hand-written notes. *(Pl. St-Martin, near the Palais. ☎93 30 87 70. Open daily Mar.-Oct. 8am-7pm; Nov.-Feb. 8am-6pm. Mass Sa 6pm, Su 10:30am. Free.)*

PLAGE DU LARVOTTO. Though Monaco's beaches can't compare to the rest of the Riviera's stretches of sand, residents and tourists fill this umbrella-speckled spot. Towering, ugly apartment buildings contrast with coastline cliff, making for a uniquely Monegascan background. *(Off av. Princesse Grace. The public elevator from the bd. des Moulins drops passengers off to the right of the beach.)*

OTHER SIGHTS. The dolls you played with as a kid were nothing like the fantastic wood-and-porcelain creations at the **Musée National de Monaco.** Housed in a pink villa designed by Charles Garnier, the collection of fragile 18th- and 19th-century dolls features several "automatons" that move and talk; it also displays some of Barbie's best dressed moments, featuring outfits by Chanel, Dior, and Givenchy. *(17 av. Princesse Grace. Elevator from pl. des Moulins drops pedestrians off next to the entrance. ☎93 30 91 26. Open daily 10am-6pm. Automaton demonstrations at 11am and every hr. 2:30-5:30pm. €6, students and ages 8-14 €3.50.)* History buffs will love the crowded cases at the **Musée des Souvenirs Napoléoniens et Collection des Archives Historiques du Palais,** to the left of the palace entrance. The jam-packed museum was assembled by Prince Louis II, the great-grandson of Napoleon's adopted daughter. The mezzanine level contains the general's legendary cocked hat and a locket with a strand of his hair. The rest of the collection, devoted to the history of Monaco, illustrates the principality's warfare-ridden history. *(Next to the Palais Princier entrance. ☎93 25 18 31. Open daily May-Sept. 9:30am-6pm; Apr. 10:30am-6pm; Oct. 10am-5:30pm; Jan.-Mar. and Dec. 10:30am-12:30pm and 2-5pm. €4, students €2. Price includes an audio tour available in 11 languages.)* If a big loss at the casino leaves you raging, practice your Zen at the **Jardin Japonais,** a tranquil seaside spot next to the Grimaldi Forum. Cherry trees, bamboo fountains, and a traditional tea house invite visitors to "purify mind and body." *(Open daily 9am-sunset. Free.)* Fashionistas who love big-name labels but not their big-time prices should check out **Second Hand Bernadette de Sainte Moreville** in Beausoleil, where racks stock (nearly) affordable secondhand Chanel, Dior, Armani, and Gucci threads from recent major collections. *(9 bd. Général Léclerc. ☎93 78 31 53. Open M-F 10:30am-1:30pm and 4-7:30pm, Sa 10:30am-1:30pm. Jeans €60-100, jackets €85-430, accessories €90-110, blouses €45-75. MC/V.)* Stroll through the seaside **Jardin St-Martin,** between the Musée Océanographique and pl. du Palais. The pleasant grounds offer excellent views of the coast amid flowering trees. *(Open daily 9am-7pm.)* Keep your eyes peeled for **Princess Caroline's villa,** a pink oasis just outside the gardens near the cathedral. It may be difficult to spot between the rows of trees, but the monk insignia on its gates should tip you off.

NIGHTLIFE

Monaco's nightlife is a little less wild and more sophisticated than that of most locales on the French coast. It has all the signature characteristics of the wealthy Riviera (high fashion, expensive drinks, exclusive private clubs) but remains low-key. The real center of attention is the famous high-stakes casino. Wherever you go in this glamorous principality, dress in your finest; jeans, sneakers, and flip flops should stay home. Bars are the best bet for most budget travelers, but a lounge by the sea could be worth the pricier drinks. In summer, seasonal bars in the Old Port stay open until at least 2am.

Rascasse, 1 quai Antoine I (☎93 25 56 90; www.larascasse.mc). Cozy bar with portside outdoor seating on the most famous corner of the Grand Prix. The young crowd from Stars n' Bars heads here late at night for dancing and expensive drinks. Live music and English pop-rock atmosphere downstairs. Upstairs a DJ lights up the party after 11pm with electro music. Beer €5-8. Mixed drinks €12-13. Happy hour M-F 6-9pm; drinks half-price. Open daily 10am-5am; upstairs F-Sa from 11pm. AmEx/MC/V.

Jimmy'z, 26 av. Princesse Grace (☎98 06 70 68), in the Sporting complex. A Monaco luxury hot spot for 30 years. Blaring music, multicolored lights, and the stylish crowd are fun to observe, but joining the party will cost you dearly. A grotto and brilliantly lit fountains provide a dazzling background for the pricey club. Beer €30. Mixed drinks €45. One-way cab ride to Monte Carlo €12. Open daily 11pm-5am. AmEx/MC/V.

Stars N' Bars, 6 quai Antoine I (☎97 97 95 95; www.starsnbars.com). Port-side restaurant by day and lively bar by night. A young crowd of locals and boat workers relaxes over pool and video games out on the port or inside the Grand Prix-themed bar. Pints €5.50. Mixed drinks €8-11. DJ spins nightly 10pm-1am. 18+. Happy hour M-F 5:30-7:30pm. Restaurant open July-Aug. daily 11am-midnight; Sept.-June Tu-Su 11am-midnight. Bar open 11am until the party moves to Rascasse. MC/V.

Zebra Square, 10 av. Princesse Grace (☎99 99 25 50; www.zebrasquare.com), on top of the Grimaldi Forum. Patrons in their late 20s and 30s prefer this groovy seaside lounge to the younger club downstairs. Ideal place to have a drink (€9-14) while gazing at the horizon. Open daily M-F until 2am, Sa-Su until 3am; DJs from 11pm.

FESTIVALS

At the end of January, Monaco kicks things off with the **Festival International du Cirque** (Jan. 17-27, 2008; ☎92 05 26 00), a circus exhibition, then follows with the **Flower-Arranging Competition.** (Mar. 25-Apr. 13, 2008; call the Garden Club of Monaco ☎93 30 02 04 for details.) But the real party starts at the end of May with the prestigious **Formula One-Grand Prix** (May 22-25, 2008), the jewel of the World Drivers's Championship. For four days, the roads surrounding the Old Port are transformed into a harrowing track where the world's best drivers test their skills. Sparkling yachts in the bay provide a perfect backdrop, as do throngs of cheering celebrities and tourists. If exhaust fumes, snazzy paint jobs, and bright jumpsuits aren't your thing, think twice about visiting Monaco during the race; tourist attractions close, waterfront access is limited, and hotel prices skyrocket. Every other year the competition is preceded by the **Historical Grand Prix** (May 10-11, 2008), which sets antique cars racing on the circuit.

MENTON ☎04

Often called the "Secret Riviera," Menton (mohn-TOHN; pop. 30,000) remains blissfully removed from the ice-cream stands of nearby tourist traps and the glare of extreme wealth. However, it still offers the picturesque beaches, lush gardens, and medieval alleys that have made the Riviera famous. In a micro-climate that keeps temperatures balmy, Menton is beautiful enough to make every visitor wish he could paint, especially when the setting sun turns the water a bright shade of pink. On France's eastern border, the town is flavored with hints of Italy; natives speak French with a decidedly Italian accent, and the local cuisine is spiced with more than the usual amount of zest.

TRANSPORTATION. **Trains** leave from pl. de la Gare (reservations available M-F 8:40-11:50am and 2-6:30pm, Sa 9:25-11:50am and 2-6:30pm, or from self-service machines) every 30min. from 5am to midnight to: Cannes (1¼hr., €8.30); Monaco (11min., €1.70); Nice (35min., €4.10); as well as Ventimiglia (10min., €4.40) and Genoa (2½-3hr., 11-14 per day, €15-19) in Italy. **Buses** depart from promenade Maréchal Leclerc; walk from the train station and take a left at the first major intersection. (☎93 35 93 60. Open M-F 8:30am-noon and 1:30-6pm, Sa 10am-noon. Buses operate 6:30am-7:30pm.) Rapides Côte d'Azur (☎93 85 64 64) runs buses every 15min. to Monaco (€2.20) and Nice (€5.10). Taxis can be found at five central taxi stands in the city. (☎92 10 47 02. Train station to hostel €8-10. Open daily 5am-11pm; reserve ahead by phone during off hours.) Rent **bikes** from Holiday Bikes, 4 espl. G. Pompidou (☎92 10 99 98; www.holiday-bikes.com). Scooters, motorcycles, and cars are also available. (Bikes from €13 per day, €60 per week; €230 deposit. Scooters from €30 per day; €500 deposit. Open M-F 9:30am-12:30pm and 3-6:30pm, Sa 9:30am-noon and 5-6:30pm. AmEx/MC/V.)

ORIENTATION AND PRACTICAL INFORMATION. Menton is divided into the *vieille ville* (old town), the new town, and the beach. **Avenue du Verdun** or **avenue Boyer** (depending on the side of the street) is the main thoroughfare of the new town and ends at the water. A left turn leads to shops and boutiques on **avenue Felix Faure,** to the crowded pedestrian **rue St-Michel,** and to the heart of the *vieille ville.* The palm-lined **promenade du Soleil** runs the length of the bay between the old and new towns, funneling into the quai de Monleon at the edge of the *vieux port.*

To reach the **tourist office,** 8 av. Boyer, from the train station, walk straight out of the station onto av. de la Gare, cross av. de Verdun, and turn right on av. Boyer. An English-speaking staff provides free maps and guidebooks, which are also available at the train station. (☎92 41 76 76; www.villedementon.com. Open July-Aug. M-Sa 9am-5pm; Sept.-June M-F 8:30am-12:30pm and 2-6pm.) Garden Tours are offered through the Service du Patrimoine, 24 rue St-Michel. (☎93 28 46 85. 2½hr. tours in French daily 10am and 2:30pm; €5-8. Call ahead for schedules.) Other services include: **police** (☎92 10 50 50), rue de la République; a **hospital,** La Palmosa, on rue Antoine Péglion (☎93 28 77 77, emergencies 93 28 72 40); **Internet** access at Le Café des Arts, 16 rue de la République (☎93 35 78 67; www.cafedesarts.com; €6 per hr.; open M-Sa 7:30am-10pm; MC/V); and the **post office,** cours George V, which offers currency exchange (☎93 28 64 87; open M-W and F 8am-6:30pm, Th 8am-6pm, Sa 8:30am-noon). Postal Code: 06500.

ACCOMMODATIONS AND CAMPING. The English-speaking owner greets guests like old friends at **Hôtel de Belgique ❸,** 1 av. de la Gare, ushering them into 20 spacious, attractively furnished rooms that come with TV and phone. (☎93 35 72 66; hoteldebelgique@wanadoo.fr. Breakfast €5. Reception 6am-2:30pm and 5:30-9:30pm. July-Aug. book 3 weeks in advance. Singles with toilet €31; doubles €39, with bath €49; triples €60; quads €72. Extra bed €12. MC/V.) **Hôtel Beauregard ❸,** 10 rue Albert I, has a serene breakfast patio and quiet rooms with TV near the train station. Turn right out of the train station and descend the steps behind Le Chou Chou *brasserie.* Turn right again; the hotel is 80m down the street, past the tennis courts. (☎93 28 63 63; beauregard.menton@wanadoo.fr. Breakfast €5. Reception 8am-9pm. Reserve ahead July-Aug. July-Aug. singles and doubles €34, with toilet and shower €42; triples with toilet and bath €55. Sept.-June €29/37/50. Extra bed €9. MC/V.) The **Auberge de Jeunesse (HI) ❶,** plateau St-Michel, compensates for its remote location with a friendly staff. Take bus #6 (8:40, 11:10am, 2, 5pm; €1.20) for the fabulous vistas and free breakfast (7:30-8:45am); if you choose to walk, beware that the hike is long and abandoned at night. Single-sex rooms are clean, each with eight sturdy wooden bunks and a small window. The bar (open daily 5-11pm) serves cheap drinks. (☎93 35 93 14; menton@fuaj.org. Laundry. Reception 7-10am and 5-10pm. Open Feb.-Oct. Dorms €19. Cash only.) Olive trees shade rows of tents at the isolated **Camping Municipal du Plateau St-Michel ❶,** rte. des Ciappes, 50 steps shy of the hostel. You get amazing views of Menton, even while brushing your teeth. An on-site restaurant-bar offers affordable pizzas (€8-9.50), pastas (€8-14), and meat dishes (€11-16), and features foosball and pool.

(☎93 35 81 23; fax 93 57 12 35. Laundry July-Sept. Reception M-Sa 8:30am-noon and 3-6:30pm, Su 8:30am-12:30pm and 5-6:30pm. €3.55 per person, €4 per small tent, €5 per large tent, €3.75 per car. Electricity €2.45. MC/V.)

FOOD. Menton prides itself on quality fruits and vegetables—not surprising for a city whose slogan is "my town is a garden." Sample *mentonnaise* produce at one of the town's three markets: the small **Marché Carëi,** av. Sospel (open daily 7am-12:30pm); **Marché Couvert** or **Les Halles,** quai de Monléon, off rue St-Michel (Tu-Su morning); and **Marché du Bastion,** near the Musée Jean Cocteau, quai Napoléon III (Sa morning). Waterfront restaurants dot the **promenade du Soleil,** but **place du Cap** and **rue St-Michel** in the *vieille ville* offer lively alternatives at rock-bottom prices. Street vendors bring an Italian flair, selling *paninis* and *glaces italiennes* (Italian ice cream). Pick up delicious homemade jam at **Maison Herbin et son Arche des Confitures ❶,** 2 rue du Vieux College. Combinations of Menton's famed citrus are produced daily in the small kitchen (€3-5). Stop by in the morning to watch the cooks at work. (☎93 57 20 29; www.confitures-herbin.com. Free guided visits of the kitchen with a tasting M, W, F 10:30am. Open June-Aug. daily 9:15am-12:30pm and 3:15-7pm; Sept.-May M-Sa 9:15am-12:30pm and 3:15-7pm. MC/V.) Settle into a squishy green booth at **Le Café des Arts ❷,** 16 rue de la République, where an English-speaking staff serves delicious salads (€8-8.50), pasta (€8-9), and reasonably priced *plats du jour*. (☎93 35 78 67. Open M-Sa 7:30am-10pm. MC/V.) Painted knights, faux stone walls, and cross-shaped menus pay homage to medieval Europe in eccentric **L'Occitan ❸,** 7 rue Marins, just off pl. aux Herves. Enjoy delicious *plats* like melon-mint soup and *carpaccio* of duck breast. (☎93 41 67 76; www.occitan.fr.st. Meat €11-18. Fish €12-16. *Foie gras* €11-20. *Menu* €16. Open Tu-Su noon-2pm and 7-10pm. MC/V.)

SIGHTS AND FESTIVALS. Plant lovers will appreciate Menton's gardens—the small town's pride and joy, originally planted in the late 18th century. Among the most exceptional is **Serre de la Madone,** 74 rte. de Gorbio, at the "Mer and Monts" stop on bus #7 (10min., €1.20). Designed by the American Lawrence Johnston, the garden is a designated *monument historique* and the most temperate garden in France. Look out for the enormous dragon tree imported from the Canary Islands. (☎93 57 73 90; www.serredelamadone.com. Open by guided tour only Feb.-Sept. Tu-Su at 9:30am and 3pm. €5, under 16 free.) June is Menton's official "month of gardens," when private gardens open to the public. Contact the Service du Patrimoine (p. 730) for reservations.

The *vieille ville* is reason enough to venture into Menton. Expansive, rocky beaches stretch along the coast from quai Napoléon III west to Monaco. If you want sand, head east of quai Napoléon to local favorite **plage des Sablettes.** Also on quai Napoléon is one of Menton's main attractions, the **Musée Jean Cocteau,** locally known as the Bastion. This fort was originally constructed by the Prince of Monaco in 1616 to ward off French invasions. (☎93 57 72 30. Open M and W-Su 10am-noon and 2-6pm. €3, students under 25 €2.25, under 18 free; 1st Su of the month free. Cash only.) The **Salle des Mariages,** in the Hôtel de Ville, is an unusual state marriage site. Jean Cocteau decorated this windowless room in the style of a colorful, pastel Greek temple and then added leopard rugs and burgundy velvet chairs for a Vegas-like effect. (☎92 10 50 00. Open M-F 8:30am-12:30pm and 2-5pm. €1.50, students €1.15, under 18 free.)

The tower of **Basilique St-Michel** rises majestically above the *vieille ville*. From rue St-Michel, take a left onto rue des Logettes, then ascend the steps of rue des Ecoles Pie. The Baroque facade hides glass drop chandeliers, a gold crown suspended above a gold-and-marble alter, and a gruesome secret: until 1850, Menton did not have a single cemetery, so paupers were buried in a common grave below the cathedral. (Open M-F and Su Sept.-May 10am-noon and 3-5:15pm; June-Aug. 10am-noon and 2-6:15pm. Mass Su 10:30am.) Climb 225m above the city to the

Monastère Annonciade, where a small terrace provides spectacular views of the city and sea below. To reach the monastery, head toward the bus station; the **Chemin de Rosaire** leads to the top. Though the hike is a heart-racing 30min. uphill, 15 chapels depicting the stations of the cross can help you count your way to the top. The chapels were built by Princess Isabelle of Monaco in gratitude to the Virgin of the Annonciade for curing her leprosy. Bus #4 leaves from the *gare routière* (8:30, 11:40am, 2:30, 6:35pm; €1.20) for the top. (☎93 35 76 92. Open daily 8am-noon and 2-6pm. Mass July-Aug. M-Sa 7:30am, Su 10am; Sept.-June M-Sa 11:15am, Su 10am.)

Every January, some 250,000 guests come to the **Fête du Citron** (Lemon Festival). What began in 1929 as a small flower and citrus exhibition is now a 15-day celebration, featuring a parade of floats covered with 120 tons of citrus. Themes have included "Astérix in the Land of the Lemon" and "Alice in Wonderland." Missed the festival? Console yourself with a *citronnade mentonnaise* in a local café.

ANTIBES ☎04 93

Antibes (ahn-TEEB; pop. 80,000 incl. Juan-les-Pins) provides a much-needed middle ground on the glitterati-controlled Riviera. Though blessed with beautiful beaches, a charming *vieille ville*, and a renowned Picasso museum, the city is less touristed than Nice and more relaxed than St-Tropez. Party-goers and sunbathers prefer neighboring Juan-les-Pins, but you'll need to venture to calmer and more budget-friendly Antibes to find sights other than sand and clubs. In between the twin towns is the unforgettable Cap d'Antibes, a peninsula of rocky beaches and luxurious villas, hidden off winding streets in scrubby forests.

TRANSPORTATION

Trains: pl. Pierre Semard. Ticket desk open daily 5:30am-10:45pm. Info desk open daily 9am-8pm. Station open daily 5:25am-12:05am. To: **Avignon** (1¾hr., 12 per day, €38); **Cannes** (15min., 23 per day, €2.30); **Marseille** (2¼hr., 12 per day, €25); **Monaco** (1hr., 5 per day, €6.10); **Nice** (15min., 25 per day, €3.60).

Buses: RCA (☎39 11 39) sends buses from pl. de Gaulle to **Cannes** (20min.), **Nice** (1hr.), and the **Nice airport** (30min.). Bus schedules are at the tourist office. All buses depart every 20min. and cost €1.30.

Public Transportation: Local buses leave from the *gare routière,* pl. Guynemer (☎34 37 60). On-site office provides transit maps. Office open July-Aug. M-F 8:30am-noon and 2:30-7:20pm, Sa 10am-12:30pm and 2:30-4:30pm; Sept.-June 7:30am-9pm. Tickets €1, *carnet* of 10 €8; 1-day pass €3, week pass €10; family ticket €5. Free **Minibus** connects travelers to various points in the city, including beaches, the train and bus stations, and the *vieille ville* (every 40min. 7:30am-7:30pm). Ask for a route map at the tourist office or look for *minibus gratuit* signs.

Taxis: Allô Taxi Antibes (☎67 67 67). At the train station. €15 from the train station to Juan-les-Pins. 24hr.

Car Rental: Europcar, 26 bd. Foch (☎34 79 79; www.europcar.fr). Cars can be returned at other Europcar depots. From €324 per week; €500 deposit. 21+. Open May-Sept. M-Sa 8am-noon and 2-7pm; Oct.-Apr. M-Sa 8am-noon and 2-6pm. AmEx/MC/V.

Bike Rental: Cycles Bike Shop, 7 bd. Dugommier (☎33 94 99). €12 per day; €500 deposit. Open M 2:30-6:30pm, Tu-Sa 8:30am-noon and 2:30-6:30pm. AmEx/MC/V.

ORIENTATION AND PRACTICAL INFORMATION

The city is far from compact; for most sights and accommodations, you'll want to take a bus. If you do walk, turn right from the train station onto av. Robert Soleau, which connects with **place de Gaulle** and farther down with the tourist office. From here, **rue de la République** (off the far left corner of pl. de Gaulle) passes the bus station and heads into **vieux Antibes,** along the eastern shore, south of the *vieux port*. **Boulevard du President Wilson** stretches from pl. de Gaulle across the peninsula, funneling into the center of Juan-les-Pins. Follow bd. Albert I from pl. de Gaulle and turn right at the water to reach a long stretch of beach and the beginning of **Cap d'Antibes** (15min.). The tip of the peninsula is 30min. from the base of the Cap.

Tourist Office: 11 pl. de Gaulle (☎04 97 23 11 11; www.antibesjuanlespins.com). Free maps; info on restaurants, camping, and festivals; and help with hotel reservations. Tours of the *vieille ville* M, W, F-Sa 10am-1:45pm (€8, ages 8-16 €3.50, under 8 free). Open July-Aug. daily 9am-7pm; Sept.-June M-F 9am-12:30pm and 1:30-6pm, Sa 9am-noon and 2-6pm. Branch at the train station (☎04 97 21 04 48). Open July-Aug. daily 9am-7pm; Sept.-June M-F 9am-12:30pm and 1:30-5pm.

Currency Exchange: Delta Change, 17 bd. Albert I (☎34 12 76). Open M-Sa July-Aug. 9am-12:30pm and 2-6:30pm; Sept.-June 9am-noon and 2-5pm. **Eurochange,** 4 rue G. Clemenceau (☎34 48 30). Open M-Sa Apr.-Oct. 9am-7pm; Nov.-Mar. 9am-6pm.

English-Language Bookstore: Heidi's English Bookshop, 24 rue Aubernon (☎34 74 11). An institution on the Riviera for 16 years and a resource for anglophones. Experienced staff suggests nightlife hot spots and provides a list of nearby English-speaking doctors. Sells budget-friendly used books. Open daily 10am-7pm. MC/V.

Laundromat: Lave Plus, 44 bd. du Président Wilson (☎06 61 86 06 19). Wash €4-8, dry €0.50 per 5min.; detergent €0.40. Wash, dry, and fold service €10 per 5kg, with ironing €20. Open daily 7am-8:30pm.

Police: 33 bd. du Président Wilson (☎04 92 90 78 00 or 04 92 90 53 12).

Pharmacy: 63 pl. nationale (☎34 01 63). Call the police or consult the local *Nice Matin* newspaper for the **pharmacie de garde.**

Hospital: Chemin des Quatres Chemins (☎04 92 91 77 77).

Internet Access: Xtreme Cyber, 8 bd. d'Aguillon (☎04 89 89 93 88; xtremecyber@club-internet.fr), at the Galérie du Port. €0.12 per min., €5 per hr. Happy hour 2-3pm; double your time for free. Open M-F 10am-8pm, Sa 10am-4pm. Internet also available at **The Crew House** hostel (see **Accommodations,** p. 733).

Post Office: pl. des Martyrs de la Résistance, off rue des Lices (☎04 92 90 61 00). Open M-F 8am-7pm, Sa 8am-noon. **Postal Code:** 06600.

ACCOMMODATIONS AND CAMPING

Antibes has a few affordable options; most lie between the new town and the *vieux port*. Interested in only a few of Antibes's attractions? You may want to daytrip from Nice or Cannes. Serious sightseers should stay in the *vieille ville*.

Stella's, 5 av. Paul Arène (☎34 12 14). From the station, cross av. Soleau and take av. de la Libération toward the port to the 3rd right after the roundabout (30min.). For 14 years, Stella has opened the top floor of her beautiful home—with a large common space and bright atrium—to backpackers and boat-handlers alike. 2 co-ed dorms provide a clean, quiet place to sleep. Laundry €8; no dryer. No reservations; call ahead M-F 10am-noon and 5-7pm. Open Mar. 15-Oct. 30. Dorms €27, €160 per week. ❷

The Crew House, 1 av. St-Roch (☎04 92 90 49 39; workstation_fr@yahoo.com), near Port Vauban. From the train station, walk down av. de la Libération; after the roundabout turn right onto av. St-Roch. The laid-back anglophones who congregate here make it a more social—and less peaceful—choice than Stella's. Internet €0.12 per min., €4.80 per hr. Luggage storage €1.50 per bag per day. Reception M-F 9am-7pm, Sa-Su 10am-6pm. Dorms Apr.-Oct. €20, €100 per week; Nov.-Mar. €15/75. MC/V. ❶

Nouvel Hôtel, 1 av. du 24 Août (☎34 44 07; fax 34 44 08). Compact, plain rooms with comfortable beds, individual safes, TVs, and clean bathrooms make this hotel a good option for budget travelers. Breakfast €4.60. Reception 6am-8pm. Singles €38, with shower €65; doubles €55-58/65; triples €84-100. MC/V. ❸

Camping Idéal, 991 rte. de Nice (☎74 27 07), RN7. For the cheapest deal in Antibes, grab one of 13 spots at this ideally located campsite. Family atmosphere. July-Aug. €15 per site; May-June and Sept. €12. Cash only. ❶

TIP **KEEP IT SHADY.** There are plenty of ways to beat the Riviera heat without an air-conditioned hotel room. Planning is everything—try to move around outside in the early morning or late evening to escape the hottest times of day, and look for museums, libraries, or movie theaters (all of which are generally air-conditioned) to pass the afternoon. Even a shady café and a cold drink can help battle the heat. At night you can dampen a pair of thin socks with cold water and put a pair of dry socks on top. The water will draw the heat out of your body, and the dry pair will keep your sheets from getting wet. Most importantly, stay hydrated, watch the booze, limit your bake time in the sun, and take advantage of the easiest escape from impending heat stroke: the majestic Mediterranean.

FOOD

Vieux Antibes offers many budget restaurants, most of which feature similar pizzas and grilled meats. Excellent *provençal* restaurants make for a great splurge. **Cours Masséna** hosts budget restaurants and the famous **marché Provençal,** one of the best and oldest on the Côte d'Azur. Tempting restaurants, bars, and cafés set up outdoor tables on **boulevard d'Aguillon.** For cheaper prices and great people-watching, head to lively **place Nationale** and **rue Aubernon.** The largest supermarket is **Intermarché,** 2 bd. Albert I. (☎34 19 10. Open M-Sa 8:15am-7:30pm.)

Le Brulot, 3 rue Frédéric Isnard (☎34 17 76), off av. G. Clemenceau. Specializes in wood-fired cuisine. Try the shrimp *au pastis* (€29), or choose from simple meat (€16-23) and fish (€13-29) options. Stop by the day before and reserve the excellent *bouillabaisse. Menu* €16-38. Open July and Sept. daily 7pm-midnight; Oct.-June M-W 7pm-midnight, Th-Su 1:30-2:30pm and 7pm-midnight. Closed Aug. AmEx/MC/V. ❹

Le Broc en Bouche, 8 rue des Palmiers (☎34 75 60), off rue Aubernon by the Hôtel de Ville. Serves gourmet food—like *artichoke carpaccio* (€13)—worthy of the glamorous locale. Wine-tasting offered in the *cave* below. *Plats* €11-24. Open July-Aug. M-Th 7:30-10pm, F-Sa 7:30-11:30pm; Sept.-June Tu-Sa noon-2pm and 7:30-10pm. MC/V. ❹

SIGHTS

Antibes was once home to Pablo Picasso, Graham Greene, and Max Ernst. The historical village and its highly artistic past left Antibes with a variety of museums that will appeal to art lovers and historians alike.

MUSÉE PICASSO. This museum displays a large collection of Picasso's paintings—mostly from the 1940s—and photos and video clips of the artist at work. Exhibits change every three months. The museum is expected to be closed for renovations until early 2008. *(Pl. Mariejol, in Château Grimaldi. ☎04 92 90 54 20. Call ahead for exact opening date, hours, and prices.)*

FORT CARRÉ. This 16th-century fort guards the entrance to **port Vauban,** the largest private marina on the Mediterranean. A magnificent view over the city, the port's 2400 yachts, and its new mega-yacht dock, affectionately called "Millionaire's Row," is worth the hike uphill. Inside the fort, a small exhibit showcases rare 19th-century swords and guns, as well as a famous statue of Napoleon on a horse. *(☎06 14 89 17 45. Fort accessible only by French or English guided tour every 30min. Open Tu-Su mid-June to mid-Sept. 10am-6pm; mid-Sept. to mid-June 10am-4:30pm. €3, students and seniors €1.50, under 18 free.)*

MUSÉE D'ARCHÉOLOGIE. Antiquity buffs will be thrilled to discover the Greek ceramics and Roman artifacts of ancient Antibes. Others can abstain. *(On the waterfront in the Bastion St-André-sur-les-Remparts. ☎34 00 39. 45min. Open July and Aug. Tu and F-Su 10am-noon and 2-6pm, W-Th 10am-noon and 2-8pm; Sept.-June Tu-Su 10am-noon and 2-6pm. French guided tours F 3pm. €3, students €1.50, under 18 free.)*

MUSÉE NAPOLÉONIEN AND HÔTEL DU CAP-EDEN-ROC. This museum is housed in an old battery tower built by Napoleon in 1794 before his *coup d'état.* Two galleries display a range of Bonapartist paraphernalia, including a bronze casting of the dictator's hand. *(Take bus #2A from "pl. Guynemer" to "Eden Roc." Every 40min. M-Sa 6:50am-7:30pm; €1. ☎61 45 32. Open Tu-Sa mid-June to mid-Sept. 10am-6pm; mid-Sept. to mid-June 10am-4:30pm. €3, students €1.50, under 18 free. Cash only.)* Next door, live the high life at the world-renowned hotel where the list of clientele reads like a *Who's Who: Celebrity Guide*—including everyone from the Kennedys to the Shah of Afghanistan. *(☎61 39 01. Beer €6-7. Hard liquor €15-35. Bellinis €24. AmEx/MC/V.)*

NOTRE DAME DU BON-PORT. Honoring Jesus's last struggle, the Twelve Stations of the Cross decorate the **Chemin du Calvaire** beginning at **Port de la Salis.** The stations lead up to the church's chapel, which overlooks the Garoupe beaches. According to legend, an old man once went to the church on a stormy night and the Virgin Mary appeared to him, drenched in seawater. Antibes locals have dressed up in nautical costumes every year since 1016 on the first Thursday in July to carry the Virgin statue to the shore and commemorate the divine apparition.

BEACHES. The two main public beaches in Antibes, **plage du Ponteil** and neighboring **plage de la Salis,** are crowded all summer. *(To reach them, turn right, toward Port Vauban, just after exiting the old town.)* The rugged, rocky beach on **Cap d'Antibes** has clear water perfect for snorkeling. *(Take bus #2A from the bus station to "Tour Gandolphe." Every 40min. M-Sa 6:50am-7:30pm; €1. Follow av. Mrs. L. D. Beaumont to the end. Turn left onto the pedestrian road, then right when a small door appears in the surrounding walls; take the dirt path to the isolated beach cove.)* Also on Cap d'Antibes, **plage Garoupe** put itself on the map in the 1920s when celebrities such as Cole Porter, F. Scott Fitzgerald, and Pablo Picasso began to frequent it. **Côte Plongée** provides **scuba diving.** *(On the beach below the Musée Napoléonien, at the corner of bd. Kennedy and bd. du Maréchal Juin. Take bus #2 from "pl. Guynemer" to "Eden Roc." Every 40min. 6:50am-7:30pm; €1.10. Walk along bd. Kennedy to the coast. Descend the stone steps and turn right. ☎06 72 74 34 94; www.coteplongee.com. Intro dive €45; dive from boat €33, at night €40, with guide €39. Snorkel rental €5. Open May-Oct. daily 9am-6pm. MC/V.)*

NIGHTLIFE AND FESTIVALS

Cinéma Casino, across from the bus station at 6 and 8 bd. du 24 Août, shows modern films in English. (☎34 04 37; www.cinefil.com. €7.50, students €6; M and Tu-F afternoons €6.) During the annual **Voiles d'Antibes Juan-les-Pins,** held the first week of June, traditional sailing ships from all over the world come to race the 23km of coastline between Antibes and Juan-les-Pins, accompanied by concerts every evening. During the first week in July, the **Festival d'Art Lyrique** brings world-class soloists and orchestras to the *vieux port.* (☎04 92 90 53 00. Tickets €15-50. MC/V.) Most clubbers head to **Juan-les-Pins** (see p. 737) at night, but the Antibes bars provide an alternative to the club scene. Although they are largely imitation pubs, they can get rowdy late at night. The bars and pubs along **boulevard d'Aguillon** hold Happy hours (usually around 6pm) for a fun-loving crowd.

La Gaffe, 6 bd. d'Aguillon (☎34 04 06). An energetic staff serves crowds of anglophones in this unpretentious bar. Squeeze in F-Sa nights to hear local, well-loved band "Blah-Blah" play rock hits. In summer, come for the **Wheel of Misfortune** every hour 6-11pm. Fills in after midnight when Le Blue Lady shuts down. Pints €6. Wine from €4.50. Karaoke Su 10:30pm draws a hilarious crowd. Open daily June-Aug. 11am-2am; Sept.-May 11am-12:30am. MC/V.

La Balade, 25B cours Masséna (☎34 93 00), in the basement of the covered *provençal* market. One of the world's few absinthe bars, La Balade serves countless types (mostly French) of the green anise-flavored liquor. A favorite of Baudelaire, Van Gogh, and the 19th-century avant-garde, the toxic drink is now illegal—what you'll find here is its mild cousin, so don't expect to be hit by divine inspiration. The faint-hearted can order *pastis* or simply check out the museum. Open M-Sa 11am-8pm. Cash only.

The Hop Store, 38 bd. d'Aguillon (☎34 15 33). Attracts a sedate pub crowd. Large outdoor seating area. Beer from €3.40. Live music on weekends. Happy hour 7-8pm. Open daily May to mid-Sept. 9am-2:30am; mid-Sept. to Apr. 3pm-12:30am. MC/V.

La Siesta, route du Bord de Mer (☎33 31 31; www.pearl-lasiesta.com). This seaside complex houses a casino and restaurant, as well as the huge open-air beach club Pearl. Come on weekends for DJs and shows or on Tu to take part in MP3 battles (teams compete for votes with playlists; register on website). Open June-Sept. daily 11:30pm-4am; Oct.-May F-Sa 11:30pm-4am. Cover €15. MC/V.

L'Endroit, 29 rue Aubernon (☎04 97 21 14 10). Plush couches and a chic modern aesthetic provide the perfect spot for locals to gather for a night out. Beer €3. Mixed drinks €7-10. Drink prices increase by €2 after 10pm. DJs spin house and lounge music nightly 9:30pm. Open Tu-Su June-Sept. 7pm-2:30am; Oct.-May 5pm-12:30am. MC.

Xtreme Café, 6 rue Aubernon (☎34 03 90). This trendy bar packs in a lively 20-something group. See-through balcony floor lets party-goers snoop on the scene below, but skirt-wearers beware: this is no one-way glass. Wine from €2. Beer €4.50. Mixed drinks €8-9. Open daily June-Sept. noon-2:30am; Oct.-May noon-12:30am. MC/V.

DAYTRIP FROM ANTIBES

BIOT

Biot's train station (☎08 92 35 35 35) is 1.5km from the town center; the best way to travel from Antibes is by bus (Sillages ☎04 92 28 58 68). Bus #10A connects Biot Village and the bus station in Antibes (25min.; M-Sa 11 per day, Su 8 per day; €1). To get to the tourist office from the station, head uphill and then take a right onto rue St-Sébastien; the tourist office is on the left. The last bus from Biot to Antibes departs at 6pm.

Just 3km from Antibes, the small town of Biot (bee-YOHT) hides a host of ceramic, pottery, and glass workshops *(verreries)* behind 15th-century vaults and fortified gates. Once home to the Greeks, Romans, Templars, and Malta knights, Biot is now one of Europe's glass capitals. Local artists design and sell pottery, basket weaving, and paintings; beyond their galleries, the narrow streets of **vieux Biot** are filled with traditional restaurants.

The source of much of Biot's modern-day renown, the **Verrerie de Biot,** chemin des Combes, continues to produce its founder's trademark "bubble glass." The Verrerie was created in 1956 by Eloi Monod, who married the daughter of the founder of the Poterie Provençal (see below). After watching his father-in-law create famous Biot pottery, he decided to reproduce it in a new medium: glass. His attempt resulted in the formation of accidental bubbles, for which his glass soon became famous. Visi-

CÔTE D'AZUR

tors can watch master glass-blowers form beautiful vases, goblets, and dishes in the workshop. Guided tours of the workshop and the Verrerie's Ecomusée explain the process of glass blowing. (Tours daily June-Aug. 11:30am, 4, 5:30pm; Sept.-May 4:30pm. €6.) Before leaving the Verrerie, be sure to stop by the **Galerie International du Verre,** considered the most prominent glass gallery in Europe. These unique, modern glass sculptures, created by 35 international artists, are expensive—no, seriously, as in over €100,000—but a trip through the gallery is free. (☎65 03 00; www.verrerie-biot.com. Open June-Sept. M-Sa 9:30am-8pm, Su 10am-1pm and 2:30-7:30pm; Oct.-May M-Sa 9:30am-6pm, Su 10:30am-1pm and 2:30-6:30pm. AmEx/MC/V.) The clay found in the fields surrounding Biot permits ceramicists to create enormous *jarres*, several of which are on display at the **Poterie Provençal,** 1689 rte. de la Mer, 5min. behind the train station. Founded in 1920, the *poterie* is the oldest in Provence. (☎65 63 30. Open M-Sa 8am-noon and 2-6pm, Su 2-6pm.) A free shuttle runs in July and August every 10min. from the parking lot at the entrance to the Verrerie, the Musée Fernand-Léger, and the Poterie Provençal. From October to May, bus #10a (also goes to Antibes; €1) stops several times between the village and the train station; ask the bus driver to let you off at your stop of choice. Follow the signs from the Poterie Provençal to the **Bonsai Arboretum de la Cote d'Azur,** 229 chemin du Val de Pome, a curious addition to Biot's art scene. The Okonek family maintains a collection of the trees in a peaceful Japanese garden. Trees of all ages, from newborns to an elaborate 105-year-old bonsai imported from China in 1986, line the arboretum's winding paths. (☎65 63 99. Open M and W-Su 10am-noon and 2-6pm. €4, students €2.)

Owned by a duo of friendly English speakers, **Crêperie du Vieux Village ❷,** 2 rue St-Sébastien, provides a large selection of sweet *crêpes* (€3.50-7; with ice cream €8) and omelettes (€7-11) in a 10-table dining room. The house *cidre* (hard cider) is a local favorite, especially on hot summer days. (☎65 72 73. Open M-W and F-Su July-Aug. noon-9pm; Sept.-June noon-3pm. Cash only.) Murals of French urban life during the Belle Epoque combine with colorful glass chandeliers to create a relaxed atmosphere in the spacious **Café de la Poste ❸,** rue St-Sébastien. You can eat inside in comfortable wicker chairs or across the street next to the small fountain in pl. de Gaulle. Choose from fresh tapas (€12-15), salads (€12-14), and fish (€17-26) and meat (€16-19) dishes. (☎65 19 32. Lunch *menu* €15. Open July-Aug. Tu-Su 7am-2am; Sept.-June Tu-Th and Su 7am-2pm, F-Sa 7am-8pm. MC/V.)

The **tourist office,** 46 rue St-Sébastien, is located in the heart of the village. (☎65 78 00; www.biot.fr. Open July-Aug. M-F 10am-7pm, Sa-Su 2:30-7pm; Sept.-June M-F 9am-noon and 2-6pm, Sa-Su 2-6pm.) There is a free guided tour of the *vieux village* in French (with accompanying translations in English and other languages) that leaves the tourist office Th at 3pm; otherwise ask for the self-guided tour map, available in many languages.

JUAN-LES-PINS ☎04 93

Under the Romans, Antibes was a major port and fishing base. To protect Antibes from the stench of the incoming seafood, nearby Juan-les-Pins (WAHN-lay-pehn; pop. 80,000 incl. Antibes) was constructed to store and ship the fish. It consisted mainly of houses for sailors and seafood factories until the 1920s, when it was revamped by robber baron Jay Gould. Hundreds of American tourists were drawn to Gould's seaside paradise, filling their days with sun and sand and their nights with swing. Decades later, not much has changed. Today, the sailors have returned to search for work among the thousands of yachts stationed in Antibes, and Juan-Les-Pins is flooded with vacationers seeking sun, sea, and sex (not necessarily in that order). In summer, ice-cream stands and boardwalk shops stay open late, and clubs blast music until the first rays of sun summon party-goers back to the beach.

TRANSPORTATION AND PRACTICAL INFORMATION. The train station is on av. l'Estérel where it joins av. du Maréchal Joffre. (Station open daily 6:40am-9pm. Ticket window open daily 8:50am-noon and 1:40-5pm.) **Trains** run to Antibes (5min., 25 per day, €1.20); Cannes (10min., 25 per day, €2); Monaco (1hr., 9 per day, €6.40); Nice (30min., 25 per day, €3.90). **Buses** (☎34 37 60) run from Sillages to pl. Guynemer in Antibes, where you can transfer to regional buses (#1A; 10min., every 30min. 6:55am-7:45pm, €1). #1 Abis Noctantibes shuttles between pl. de Gaulle in Antibes and Juan-les-Pins at night (July-Aug. 8pm-12:20am). The **petit train** (☎06 03 35 61 35) goes from rue de la République in Antibes, through the *vieille ville*, to Juan-les-Pins. Although touristy and more expensive, it serves as both a guided tour of Antibes and a means of transportation. (30min.; every hr. July-Aug. 10am-11pm, May-Oct. 10am-7pm. Round-trip €8, ages 3-10 €3.50. Buy tickets on train. Cash only.) **Taxis** usually wait at the Jardin de la Pinède and outside the train station. (☎04 92 93 07 07 or 08 25 56 07 07. From the station to Antibes €12-15.) To walk from pl. du Général de Gaulle in Antibes, head along bd. Wilson to the beach (25min.). Follow the beach to the right until you see the tourist office.

To reach the **tourist office,** 51 bd. Guillaumont, from the train station, walk along av. du Maréchal Joffre and turn right onto av. Guy de Maupassant; the office is 2min. away on the right, at the intersection of av. Admiral Courbet and av. Guillaumont. (☎04 97 23 11 10; www.antibes-juanlespins.com. Open July-Aug. daily 9am-7pm; Sept.-June M-F 9am-noon and 2-6pm, Sa 9am-noon.) Other services include: a **laundromat** on the corner of av. L'Estral and av. du Docteur Fabre (☎61 52 04; wash €3.90-9, dry €0.50 per 5min.; detergent €0.40; open daily 7am-9pm; cash only); **police** (☎97 21 75 60); a **pharmacy,** 1 av. Amiral Courbet (☎61 12 96); and **Internet** access at **Mediterr@net,** 3 av. du Docteur Fabre, across from the train station (☎61 04 03; €2.70 per hr.; open M-Sa 9am-9pm, Su 10am-9pm). A **post office** is on av. Joffre, across from the train station. (☎04 92 93 75 50. Open M and W-F 8am-noon and 1:45-6pm, Tu 8am-noon and 2:15-6pm, Sa 8am-noon.) **Postal Code:** 06160.

CÔTE D'AZUR

ACCOMMODATIONS AND FOOD. Animated beaches and incomparable nightlife make Juan-les-Pins a popular vacation spot; it's no wonder luxury hotels and upscale apartments abound, while budget lodging is hard to find. The closest campsites are two train stops away in Biot (ask the tourist office for more info); otherwise, reasonably priced restaurants will be your only consolation. Those planning a trip months in advance might beat the regulars at **Hôtel de la Gare ❷,** 6 rue du Printemps, a family-owned hotel with functional, clean rooms. (☎61 29 96. Breakfast €5. Doubles with shared bathroom and shower €29-36.) If the trains passing at night wake you up, head to **Hôtel Parisiana ❹,** 16 av. de L'Estérel, which has bright rooms with A/C, fridge, bath, TV, and attractive armoirs. (☎61 27 03; hotelparisiana@wanadoo.fr. Breakfast €5. Reception 7:30am-10pm. July-Aug. singles €48; doubles €62; triples €75; quads €82. Sept.-June €28-38/42-52/55-65/62-72. Extra bed €11. Prices lower for stays of more than 5 nights. MC/V.) First opened in 1920, the light yellow stucco **Hôtel Alexandra ❹,** rue Pauline, is one of the oldest hotels in Juan-les-Pins. Each spacious, tastefully decorated room comes with A/C, telephone, TV, and shower. The first floor is a restaurant, serving an authentic *provençal menu* that changes daily. (☎04 97 21 76 50; www.hotelalexandra.net. Breakfast €7. Reception 8am-10:30pm. July-Aug. reserve 1 month ahead. Open Mar.-Oct. July-Aug. singles €55; doubles €80-88; triples €88-92. May-June and Sept. €49/74-82/82-86. Mar.-Apr. and Oct. €45/70-78/78-82. AmEx/MC/V.)

The **Petit Casino** supermarket is on av. Admiral Courbet, across from the tourist office. (☎61 00 56. Open M-Tu and Th-Sa 8am-12:30pm and 3:30-7:30pm, W 8am-12:30pm, Su 8am-1pm. MC/V.) A **Casino** is on av. Dr. Dautheville. (Open M-Sa 8:30am-8pm, Su 9am-1pm.) To escape tourist-oriented beachside *brasseries* and pizzerias, head to **Autour de Lilly ❸,** 128 bd. Wilson. Local artists have decorated this unique restaurant with dazzling Baroque, East Asian, and Indian touches. The tasty *provençal* dishes, such as veal with couscous (€17), change daily. (☎04 92 93 02 76. *Plats* €8.50-19. Open Tu-Su 7pm-midnight. MC/V.) At **Ruban Bleu ❸,** promenade du Soleil, fill up on fresh fish and pizza at either the beachfront restaurant or boardwalk *brasserie*. The *brasserie* is less expensive but farther from the water. (☎61 31 02. At *brasserie* pizza €8-11; pasta €9-22; fish and meat dishes €14-25; *menus* €15. Restaurant prices €3-5 more. Open daily July-Aug. 7:30am-2am; Sept.-June 7:30am-10pm. AmEx/MC/V.) Farther from the water, **La Bamba ❸,** 18 rue Dautheville, serves pizzas (€9-12), pastas (€7.50-12), and a large selection of wood-fired meat and fish dishes (€12-24) to a large crowd. (☎61 32 64. *Menu* €19. Open daily July-Aug. 5:30pm-1am; Sept.-June noon-2pm and 7-11pm. AmEx/MC/V.) One of the more affordable beach clubs is **l'Oasis ❷,** bd. du Littoral, but a chair, mattress, and umbrella for the day (€11) will cost almost as much as a *plat du jour* (€13). A perfect ocean view and the luxury of eating on the sand may make it worthwhile. (☎67 41 54. *Menu* €17. Open daily noon-3pm and 7-11pm.)

NIGHTLIFE AND FESTIVALS. Sunset in Juan-les-Pins draws bronzed party-goers to the Casino area. A swanky crowd flocks to entirely white **Milk,** av. Gallice, for the dance floor and plush sofas. (☎67 22 74. Drinks €10-17. Cover €16; includes 1 drink. Open July-Aug. daily midnight-6am; Sept.-June F-Sa midnight-6am. AmEx/MC/V.) At **Whisky à Gogo,** 5 rue Jacques Leonetti, black lights and bubble columns frame a dance floor where a very young crowd grooves to house. (☎61 26 40. Drinks €9. Ladies free before 12:30am. 18+. Cover €16, students €8; includes 1 drink. Open June-Aug. daily midnight-5am; Apr.-May F-Sa midnight-5am; Sept. to mid-Oct. Th-Sa midnight-5am. AmEx/MC/V.) Mexican fiestas are held in **Le Village,** where the staff sets the bar on fire nightly—be careful when ordering a drink. (☎04 92 93 90 00. Ladies free M-Th midnight-12:30am. Cover €16; includes 1 drink. Open July-Aug. daily midnight-5am; Sept.-June F-Sa midnight-5am. MC/V.)

Most **discotheques** are open only on weekends in the low season. Fortunately, nearby **bars** pick up the slack and provide a great atmosphere of their own. Carrefour de la Nouvelle Orleans is home to two jointly owned, scarily similar, but hopping bars. With a large terrace in the middle of the action, **Ché Café** pays homage to Mr. Guevara with huge photos and camo-print chairs. A tempting lineup of rum shots (€9) includes banana, plantain, coconut, and guava flavors. (Beer €6. Mixed drinks €8-10. Open daily Aug. 3pm-5am; Apr.-Oct. 3pm-4am. MC/V.) Across the street at **Zapata's,** party-goers pack into the bar and crowd the outside tables to listen to salsa and drink margaritas. (Shots €6-7. Mixed drinks €8. Open daily Apr.-Oct. 5:30pm-4am. MC/V.) At the Brazilian-themed **Pam Pam Rhumerie,** 137 bd. Wilson, revelers squeeze in between large plants and tikis to sip exotic mixed drinks (€13) served in coconut-, monkey-, and tiki-hut-shaped glasses. This already hot bar starts smokin' when bikinied showgirls take the stage at 9:30pm. (☎61 11 05; www.pampam.fr. Open daily mid-Mar. to early Nov. 2pm-5am.) Fancy ice-cream mixed drinks (€9) attract a low-key group to **Le Crystal,** across from Pam Pam on av. Georges Galice. (☎61 62 51. Open daily 8am-2:30am. MC/V.) Escape the expensive, fake-Latin flavor at laid back local hangout **L'Esterel,** 12 av. de l'Esterel, across from rue Jonnard. (☎61 31 26. Beer €4.40. Mixed drinks €5-7. Shots €2-3 or 10 for €18-27. Live music every Tu, Happy hour W, and a special deal on a different drink every Th. Open daily 6pm-2:30am. Cash only.) If clubs haven't cleaned you out completely, head to gaudy **Eden Casino,** bd. Baudoin. (☎04 92 93 71 71. No T-shirts, jeans, or sneakers. 18+. Slot machines open daily 10am-5am.)

In mid-July, Juan-Les-Pins temporarily abandons its nightclub obsession for the 10-day **Festival International de Jazz (Jazz à Juan),** which draws a few big-name performers like B.B. King. (jazzajuan@antibes-juanlespins.com. Tickets available at tourist office. €20-62, students and under 18 €10-18. MC/V.)

BEACHES. The town's coast is punctuated by 35 beach clubs and countless restaurants and snack stands, meaning that public beaches are small and crowded. Juan-les-Pins's second-biggest playground (after the clubs, of course) is the waves, which are home to every watersport imaginable. The pontoon dock in front of Hôtel Meridien, 15 bd. Baudoin, on Garden Beach, is a good place to start; there, **Water Sports Services** offers waterskiing (€20), wake-boarding (€20), parasailing (€50-60), tubing (€20), and paddle-boat (€20) rental by the hour. (☎04 92 93 57 57. Open daily July-Aug. 7am-8pm; Apr.-June and Sept.-Oct. 8am-7pm. MC/V.)

CANNES ☎04 93

The name Cannes (KANN; pop. 67,000) conjures images of Catherine Deneuve sipping champagne by the pool, Marilyn Monroe posing red-lipped on the beach, and countless other starlets competing for camera time. But when Palmes d'Or turn back into palm trees after the city's renowned film festival, Cannes stashes the red carpet and becomes the most accessible of the Riviera's glam-towns. By comparison, Menton is old, Nice is a mess, Antibes is boring, and Juan-les-Pins lacks sophistication. Cannes draws an undeniably wealthy clientele to its palm-lined boardwalk, inviting sandy beach and innumerable boutiques, but many young, fun-loving travelers also come to soak up the sun, play in the waves, and party all night in Cannes's nonstop hot spots—at some of the lowest prices on the Côte.

TRANSPORTATION

Trains: 1 rue Jean-Jaurès. Station open daily 5:10am-1:15am. Ticket office open daily 5:30am-10:30pm. Info desk open M-Sa 8:30am-5:30pm. To: **Antibes** (15min., €2.30); **Marseille** (2hr., 6:30am-11pm, €24); **Monaco** (1hr., €7.50); **Nice** (40min., €5.50); **St-Raphaël** (25min., €5.70); and other coastal towns. TGV to **Paris** (5hr., €79-97) via **Marseille.**

Buses: Rapide Côte d'Azur, pl. de l'Hôtel de Ville (☎48 70 30). To **Nice** (1½hr., every 20min., €6) and **Nice airport** (1hr.; every 30min. M-Sa 7am-7pm, Su 8:30am-7pm; €13, under 25 €10). Buses to **Grasse** (50min., every 45min., €4) leave from the train station.

Public Transportation: Bus Azur, pl. de l'Hôtel de Ville (☎08 25 82 55 99). Info desk and tickets M-F 7am-7pm, Sa 8:30am-noon and 2-6:30pm. Tickets €1.40, *carnet* of 10 €9.40, weekly pass €11. Buy tickets on board. Don't forget to validate your ticket.

Taxis: Allô Taxis Cannes (☎04 92 99 27 27).

Bike and Scooter Rental: Holiday Bikes, 32 av. du Maréchal Juin (☎94 30 34). Bikes from €18 per day, €65 per week; €150 deposit. Scooters from €40/230; €750 deposit. Open M-Sa 9am-noon and 2-7pm, Su by appointment. AmEx/MC/V.

ORIENTATION AND PRACTICAL INFORMATION

The city's shopping hub is the *centre-ville*, between the train station and the sea; **rue d'Antibes** runs through its center, parallel to the sea. Heading right from the station on rue Jean-Jaurès, you come to the *vieille ville*, known as **le Suquet,** where flea-market-style shopping dominates **rue Meynadier** by day and upscale dining enlivens tiny **rue St-Antoine** by night. Stargazers should follow rue des Serbes down to seaside **boulevard de la Croisette.** The tourist office is on the left in the Palais des Festivals. At the adjacent *vieux port*, Cannes's beautiful beach stretches in both directions along the coast. Two kilometers east, the peninsular stretch of clubs known as **Palm Beach** draws sun-seekers and water sports enthusiasts alike.

Tourist Office: 1 bd. de la Croisette (☎04 92 99 84 22; www.cannes.fr). Books tickets for events and provides free maps. Open daily July-Aug. 9am-8pm; Sept.-June 9am-7pm. Branch at the train station (☎93 99 19 77). Open M-Sa 9am-7pm.

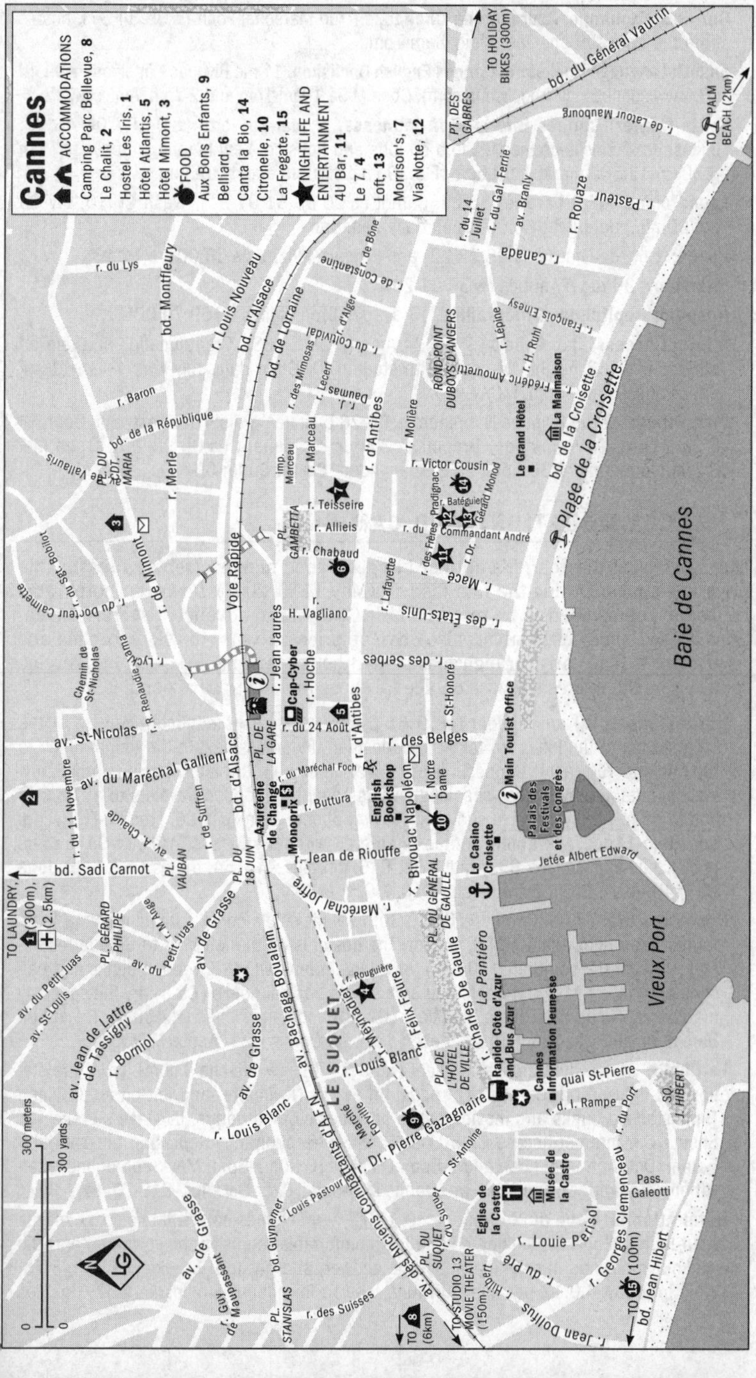
Cannes
ACCOMMODATIONS
Camping Parc Bellevue, 8
Le Chalit, 2
Hostel Les Iris, 1
Hôtel Atlantis, 5
Hôtel Mimont, 3
FOOD
Aux Bons Enfants, 9
Belliard, 6
Canta la Bio, 14
Citronelle, 10
La Fregate, 15
NIGHTLIFE AND ENTERTAINMENT
4U Bar, 11
Le 7, 4
Loft, 13
Morrison's, 7
Via Notte, 12
Baie de Cannes
Plage de la Croisette
bd. de la Croisette
Vieux Port
LE SUQUET
Main Tourist Office
Palais des Festivals et des Congrès
Le Casino Croisette
Jetée Albert Edward
Le Grand Hôtel
La Malmaison
Rapide Côte d'Azur and Bus Azur
Cannes Information Jeunesse
Eglise de la Castre
Musée de la Castre
English Bookshop
Monoprix
Azuréene de Change
Cap-Cyber
PL. DE LA GARE
Voie Rapide
r. d'Antibes
bd. d'Alsace
bd. de Lorraine
r. Jean Jaurès
r. Félix Faure
quai St-Pierre
La Pantiéro
av. de Grasse
bd. Sadi Carnot
TO LAUNDRY (300m), (2.5km)
TO HOLIDAY BIKES (300m)
TO PALM BEACH (2km)
TO STUDIO 13 MOVIE THEATER (150m)
TO 8 (6km)
TO 15 (100m)
300 meters
300 yards

Currency Exchange: Azuréene de Change, 17 rue Maréchal-Foch (☎39 34 37), across from the train station. Open daily 8am-7pm.

English-Language Bookstore: Cannes English Bookshop, 11 rue Bivouac Napoléon (☎99 40 08; www.cannesenglishbookshop.com). Open M-Sa 10am-1pm and 2-7pm. AmEx/MC/V.

Youth Center: Cannes Information Jeunesse, 5 quai St-Pierre (☎04 97 06 46 25; lekiosque625@ville-cannes.fr). Info on jobs and housing. Very helpful staff. Open M-Th 8:30am-12:30pm and 1:30-6pm, F 8:30am-12:30pm and 1:30-5pm.

Laundromat: Point Laverie, 56 bd. Carnot (☎06 09 51 97 91). Wash €6.10, dry €3 per 30min.; detergent €0.50. Open daily 7am-8pm.

Police: 1 av. de Grasse (☎06 22 22) and 2 quai St-Pierre (☎08 00 11 71 18).

Pharmacy: 36 rue d'Antibes (☎39 01 29).

Hospital: Hôpital des Broussailles, 13 av. des Broussailles (☎69 70 00).

Internet Access: Cap Cyber, 12 rue 24 Août (☎38 85 63). Great location and relaxed atmosphere. €3 per hr. Discount with student ID. Open daily July-Aug. 10am-11pm; Sept.-June 10am-10pm. MC/V.

Post Office: 22 rue Bivouac Napoléon (☎06 26 50), near Palais des Festivals. Open M-F 9am-7pm, Sa 9am-noon. Branch at 34 rue de Mimont (☎06 27 00). Open M-F 8:30am-noon and 1:30-5pm, Sa 8:30am-noon. **Postal Code:** 06400.

ACCOMMODATIONS AND CAMPING

During most of the year, it's not hard to get a good night's sleep at a reasonable price in Cannes. During the film festival (May 14-25, 2008), however, hotel rates triple and rooms need to be reserved at least a year in advance. Several conventions at the Palais des Festivals also drive up prices; be sure to ask before making reservations. Plan early for high season, particularly August. Frequent bus service to the campsite makes it a wise choice for those looking to save pennies.

Hôtel Mimont, 39 rue Mimont (☎39 51 64; www.canneshotelmimont.com). Exit the train station to the left, then take the pedestrian underpass next to the tourist office to rue Mimont. Turn right; Cannes's best budget hotel is on the left. Spacious rooms lovingly maintained by English-speaking owners eager to introduce travelers to all Cannes has to offer. All rooms have showers, TV, and phone. Breakfast €6. Free Wi-Fi. Reception 8am-11pm. Ask about *petites chambres* without showers for *Let's Go* readers (€30). July-Aug. singles €39, with toilet €46; doubles €46/54; triples €69. Sept.-June €34/40; 40/47; 60. Extra person €10. MC/V. ❸

Hostel Les Iris, 77 bd. Carnot (☎68 30 20; www.iris-solola.com). Turn right on rue Jean-Jaurès, then right again on bd. Carnot. The hostel is on the left next to Solada restaurant—look for the sombrero (10min.). Airy, large rooms with 2-6 wooden bunks and balconies. Terrace restaurant open until 3am serves tropical drinks (€5-8); try the specialty margaritas. Small café offers breakfast (€2.50) and sandwiches (€2.50-4). Reception 8am-midnight. Check-out 11am. Reserve ahead. Dorms €23. AmEx/MC/V. ❷

Le Chalit, 27 av. du Maréchal Gallieni (☎99 22 11; www.le-chalit.com). From the station, go right on bd. Carnot, right again on av. 11 Novembre, and left on av. Gallieni. Triple-stacked bunks and movie posters fill 2 basic 6-bed dorms. Luggage storage €3. Sheets €3. Internet access €2.50 per 15min. Reception May-Sept. 8:30am-1pm and 5-8pm; Oct.-Apr. 9am-noon and 7-8pm. Lockout 10:30am-5pm. May-Sept. online reservations required. Closed Nov.-Jan. Dorms May-Sept. €25; Oct.-Apr. €18-20. ❷

Hôtel Atlantis, 4 rue du 24 Août (☎39 18 72; www.cannes-hotel-atlantis.com), off rue Jean-Jaurès. English-speaking couple lets comfortable rooms in the town center. Attic workout room has mini-sauna, massage shower, and hot tub. Breakfast €5.75-8.75. Wi-Fi in lobby; €0.12 per min. July-Aug. reserve far ahead. Singles €45-57; doubles

€55-75; triples and quads €68-105. A/C €5 extra. Prices decrease with extended stay. 5% discount with *Let's Go.* AmEx/MC/V. ❸

Camping Parc Bellevue, 67 av. Maurice Chevalier (☎47 28 97), in La Bocca. Take bus #2 to "Les Aubépines" and walk straight for 500m, following signs for the campground. Mobile homes fill this quiet 3-star site, though tents are welcome. Impeccable showers, a large pool (open 9am-8pm), and a restaurant that occasionally hosts dance parties nestle among wooded trails. Laundry €3. Reception 8am-8pm. July-Aug. 1 person with tent €15, 2 people with tent €19; Apr.-June and Sept. €11/14. Electricity €3. ❶

FOOD

Though the city is dominated by high-end restaurants, good food for a reasonable price does exist in Cannes. There are **markets** on pl. Gambetta and pl. du Commandant Maria; the best one is the **Forville** market on rue Meynadier and rue Louis Blanc, as it has a large selection of fruit, vegetables, and fish. (All open daily in summer 6am-1pm; in winter Tu-Su 6am-1pm.) The **Monoprix** on the corner of rue Buttura and Jean Jaurès carries food, clothing, housewares, and just about everything else. (Open M-Sa 8:30am-8:30pm.) Good restaurants are in the pedestrian zone, particularly along **rue Meynadier.** The narrow, winding streets of **le Suquet** offer cozy corners for open-air dining, but the improved ambience adds to the bill.

La Fregate, 26 bd. Jean Hibert (☎39 45 39). This large bar/*brasserie*/café, situated by the beach, offers an extensive menu of Italian-inspired cuisine around the clock. Local youths enjoy pizza (€8.50-13), pasta (€7-13), grilled meats (€14-22), and large salads (€4.50-14) on a bright green-and-yellow terrace. On hot days, the restaurant refreshes its outdoor clients by sporadically spraying a fine mist of water on the terrace. Open daily June-Sept. 24hr.; Oct.-May 7am-2am. AmEx/MC/V. ❷

Aux Bons Enfants, 80 rue Meynadier. This 3rd-generation restaurant is worth the splurge. The chef constructs an excellent *provençal menu* (€20) every day based on what catches his eye at the morning market. Fridays bring *aioli* (garlic mayonnaise), a local favorite. Open May-July and Sept. M-Sa noon-2pm and 7:15-9:30pm; Oct.-Apr. M-F noon-2pm and 7-9pm, Sa noon-2pm. Closed Aug. Cash only. ❸

Canta la Bio, 6 rue Florian (☎39 49 40), near the Palais des Festivals. A rarity on the Riviera, this vegetarian restaurant serves cheap pasta and vegetable dishes (€11-20), like eggplant *gratin,* on a calm terrace. Open June-Sept. daily noon-11:30pm; Oct.-May M-Sa noon-11:30pm. MC/V. ❸

Belliard, 1 rue Chabaud (☎39 42 72). This 75-year-old bakery and *salon de thé* has been treating *Cannois* to scrumptious tarts and baked goods for years. A takeout gourmet plate (€9) includes a selection of 3 meat options, 7 *légumes* (vegetables), and a choice of a tasty quiche. Open M-Sa 7am-8pm. MC/V. ❷

Citronelle, 16 rue Bivouac Napoleon (☎06 63 97 73 08). Delicious sandwiches (€3.80-4.50), fresh salads (€3.80-4.50), and natural smoothies (€2-3.80) are prepared with market-fresh ingredients. Open M-Sa 10am-6pm. Cash only. ❶

SIGHTS AND ENTERTAINMENT

At the top of the Suquet, **L'Eglise de la Castre** and its courtyard provide an excellent view of the city below. The inhabitants of Cannes had to fundraise for 80 years to complete the costly structure; it was finally finished in the early 17th century. All that work paid off: the church houses ornate glass chandeliers and an impressive neo-Gothic organ. (Open daily June-Aug. 9am-noon and 3:15-7pm; Sept.-May 9am-noon and 2:15-6pm. Free.) The adjacent **Musée de la Castre** was formerly the private castle of the monks of Lérins; today, it displays collections of ancient relics from the Ameri-

TOP TEN LIST

MAKE A SCENE

Careers have been made—and ruined—at Cannes for the past 60 years. Movie stars gathering to bask in the limelight seem to never run out of ways to draw attention. Here are the best:

1. Self-promotion. In 2007, Jerry Seinfeld dressed as a bee.

[redacted] **ndifference.** When his 1992 film won two awards, Lars von Tier threw both in the trash.

[redacted] **nfamy.** Vincent Gallo earned renown in 2003 for *Brown Bunny*, considered to be the worst movie in Cannes's history.

[redacted] **nobbery.** In 2007, director Roman Polanski walked out of a news conference, calling the journalists' questions "empty."

[redacted] **Brevity.** Director Aki Kaurismaki accepted the Grand Jury priz[redacted]aying: "First, I would like to tha[redacted]myself. Second, I would like to thank the jury. Goodbye."

[redacted] **Modesty.** Actor Joaquin Phoenix left his own premiere, asking "Why would I watch? What, just to look at yourself?"

7. Nudity. Starlet Simone Silva began a tradition of exposure in 1954 with her mono-kini.

8. Passion. Actress Grace Kelly fell in love with the Prince of Monaco in 1955. Their lavish wedding was held at the next festival.

9. Controversy. In 2004, Michael Moore accepted the Palme d'Or for *Fahrenheit 9/11* wi[redacted]re Bush-bashing.

10. Idiocy. Interviewer: "Are you attending the Cannes film festival this year?" Christina Aguilera: "So, where's [it] being held?"

cas, Himalayas, and Pacific. A small exhibit by *provençal* artists recalls life in turn-of-the-century Cannes. The real treat of the museum is the 12th-century chapel, which houses musical instruments from all over the world. Don't miss climbing the tower to get a 360° view of Cannes. (☎38 55 26. Open Tu-Su June-Aug. 10am-1pm and 3-7pm; Apr.-May and Sept. 10am-1pm and 2-6pm; Oct.-Mar. 10am-1pm and 2-5pm. €3, students free.) When at the beach, take a break at **Centre d'Art/Malmaison,** 47 bd. de la Croisette, to the right of the Grand Hôtel, which houses temporary exhibits by contemporary artists. (☎04 97 06 44 90. Open July-Aug. M-Th and Sa-Su 11am-8pm, F 11am-10pm; Sept.-Nov. Tu-Su 10am-1pm and 2-6pm. Explanations in French only. €4, seniors €2, students free. MC/V.)

Cannes's three casinos provide countless opportunities to break the bank. The least exclusive, **Le Casino Croisette,** 1 espace Lucien Barrière, next to the Palais des Festivals, has slot machines, blackjack, and roulette. The Greek-inspired interior comes complete with faux-marble statues and an aquarium. (☎04 92 98 78 00. 18+. Slots open at 10am; table games daily 8pm-4am. No dress code for slots. No jeans, T-shirts, or gym shoes for gambling. Free entry.) The fashion-conscious city of Cannes is blessed with countless high-end boutiques, offering some of the coast's best window-shopping. **Boulevard de la Croisette** boasts names like Cartier, Chanel, and Dior. The less pricey **rue d'Antibes** mixes funky shops and chain stores with classy brand names. Head to **rue Meynadier,** a street market, for cheap knock-offs.

NIGHTLIFE

The elite nightspots that make Cannes famous are notoriously exclusive—those looking to get in should dress to kill. Cafés and bars near the waterfront stay open all night for just as much fun at half the price. Park yourself with a cold one and watch the nightly fashion show strut by, headed to private parties in the clubs and casinos. Nightlife thrives around **rue Dr. Gérard Monod.**

Morrison's, 10 rue Teisseire (☎04 92 98 16 17; www.morrisonspub.com). Head to Morrison's for casual, friendly company. Mahogany bookshelves and quotes by Irish playwrights cover the walls. Beer from €4.90. Irish whiskey €5.10-11. Live pop and rock W-Th and Su from 9:30pm. Women can drink as much beer and wine as they like for €6 on Su ladies' night. Happy hour 5-8pm. Open daily 5pm-2am.

4U Bar, 6 rue des Frères Bradignac (☎39 71 21; www.bar4u.com). Join a young, international, unpretentious crowd for drinks at gay-friendly 4U Bar. Fiberoptic lights and live house music create a relaxed lounge atmosphere. Vivacious bartenders clearly enjoy their work and keep the party going well into the night. Their specialty is the "cocktail4U," a mystery fruit drink. Beer from €3.20. Mixed drinks €8.50. Open July-Aug. daily 6pm-2:15am; Oct.-June M-Sa 6pm-2:15am. MC/V.

Le 7, 7 rue Rougières (☎39 10 36; www.discotheque-le7.com). Even Parisians concede to the fame of Le 7, known throughout France for outrageous nightly drag shows. Recently refurbished interior of white cushioned walls gives this bar an intimate feel. Mixed straight and gay clientele. Mixed drinks €9.50. Drag shows 2am. Cover F-Sa men €16; includes 1 drink. Open daily 11:30pm-8am. Reservations recommended. MC/V.

Loft, 13 rue du Dr. Gérard Monod (☎39 40 39). The quintessential hot spot for the young and beautiful to dance the night away. Dress your way in or pretend you know someone. Downstairs, the restaurant **Tantra** morphs into a club F-Sa, and tables serve as dance floors until the party moves upstairs. Live DJ. Mixed drinks €12. Open Sept.-May daily 10:30pm-2:30am; June-Aug. Th-Sa 10:30pm-2:30am. AmEx/MC/V.

Via Notte, 13 rue du Commandant André (☎04 92 98 62 82). A fashionable crowd sips drinks on the terrace before dancing livens up the otherwise plain interior around midnight. Open daily 5pm-2:30am. MC/V.

FESTIVALS

Stars and star-seekers descend with pomp and circumstance upon Cannes for the world-famous **Festival International du Film** (May 14-25, 2008). The festival is invite-only, though celebrity-spotting is always free. Beware, however, that prices will skyrocket. July 4 and 14 bring boisterous celebrations of American and French independence days—**Fête Américaine** and **Fête Nationale,** respectively—with spectacular fireworks over the bay. **Les Nuits Musicales du Suquet** are also celebrated in July, with open-air performances by professional musicians along le Suquet. (☎04 92 98 62 77. Tickets €30-40.).

TIP **REEL CANNES.** The world-famous Cannes Film Festival only happens once a year, but the city is never quite out of the influence of the silver screen; even budget travelers can participate in Cannes's connection with film. **Studio 13,** 23 av. du Dr. Picaud (☎06 29 90; www.mjcpicaud.com), puts together an intelligent, well-crafted program of movies from around the world in its intimate theater. All films, shown in their original languages (with French subtitles), are a mere €6, and only €4 for students (€5 for all on W). Showings M-Sa at 6 and 8:30pm, as well as F 2:30pm. Program available online, by phone, and from the Cannes Information Jeunesse office, across from pl. de l'Hôtel de Ville.

GRASSE ☎04 93

You'll know you're in Grasse (GRAHSS; pop. 45,000) when the smell of coconut tanning oil turns to jasmine and tea rose. With a unique climate ideal for growing heavily scented flowers, Grasse has been the capital of the world's perfume industry for over 200 years and houses France's three largest, oldest, and most distinguished *parfumeries*. Prepare to be spritzed with a barrage of flowery scents that will leave your nose delightfully overwhelmed. Outside the *parfumeries*, expansive vistas and tasty restaurants greet the other senses. Grasse's proximity to Cannes (15km) makes it a pleasant afternoon excursion.

TRANSPORTATION. A new **train station** makes traveling to Grasse from Antibes, Cannes, or Nice more convenient. (Ticket window open M-Sa 9am-6pm,

Su 9am-noon and 1-6pm; or use the automated machines.) Train route 4b runs 19 trains from Grasse to Antibes (€5.30); Cannes (€3.40); Nice (€7.90); Ventimiglia, Italy (€12). The **bus station,** pl. Notre Dame des Fleurs, has service to Cannes (50min.; M-Sa every 30min. 6am-8:35pm, Su every hr. 7:30am-7:30pm; €3.90) and Nice (1hr.; July-Aug. 14 per day, Sept.-June 23 per day; €6.30) through RCA bus lines #600 and 500, respectively. (☎36 08 43. Office open M-Th 7:30am-12:15pm and 1-4:45pm, F 7:30am-12:15pm and 1-4pm.) A free **navette** (shuttle bus) runs around the outskirts of town and connects the train station to the bus station and the rest of the village (M-Sa 7:15am-8pm). Call a **taxi** (☎36 37 07) to reach remote hotels.

ORIENTATION AND PRACTICAL INFORMATION. Most tourist destinations are concentrated in the pedestrian *vieille ville* and on the south-facing hillside. From the train or bus station, just above the *vieille ville,* walk left on av. Thiers past **Place aux Aires,** a lively square on the edge of the *vieille ville,* and continue onto **Boulevard de Jeu de Ballon** to the tourist office and its annex. Farther downhill, on your left, lies **place du 24 Août,** a large plateau with a valley view within easy reach of the Fragonard perfumery and several museums.

Next to the Palais des Congrès on cours Honoré Cresp, the **tourist office** hands out maps that lay out a 1½hr. self-guided walking tour of the city. For more information on the town's history, tours in English (1hr.; €2) are available in July and August Saturday at 2pm. (☎36 66 66; www.grasse.fr. Open July-Sept. M-Sa 9am-7pm, Su 9am-12:30pm and 2-6pm; Oct.-June M-Sa 9am-1pm and 2-6pm.) Other services include: **police,** 12 bd. Carnot (☎40 31 60); a **hospital,** chemin de Clavary (☎09 55 00); and a **pharmacy,** 26 pl. Aires (☎36 05 35). **Internet** access is expensive in Grasse. To log on, try to find a phone shop that also has computers, or check out **Le Petit Caboulot,** 8 pl. de la Foux. (☎40 16 01. Internet and Wi-Fi €7.65 per hr. Open M-Sa 8am-7pm.) The **post office** is in the garage under the bus station. (☎04 92 42 31 11. Open M-F 9am-noon and 2-5pm, Sa 9am-noon.) **Postal Code:** 06130.

ACCOMMODATIONS AND FOOD. Grasse has several budget hotels but lacks hostels and good camping options. **Hôtel des Palmiers ❸,** 17 av. Baudoin, has 11 plain rooms with fireplaces, showers, and TVs. Rooms facing the hillside have views of Cannes. (☎/fax 36 07 24. Breakfast €6. Reception 7am-10pm. July-Aug. reserve 2 weeks ahead. Singles €35-39; doubles €36-49; triples €44-61; quads €60-79, depending on view. AmEx/MC/V.) **Hôtel Napoléon ❷,** 6 av. Thiers, is one of the cheapest options in Grasse. (☎36 05 87. Breakfast €5. Reserve ahead. Singles €23-31; doubles €31-40. AmEx/MC/V.)

A morning **market** fills **place du Cours** (open W 7am-1pm). On Saturdays, the flower market on **place aux Aires** usually offers fruit and vegetable stands to go with the blossoms (open 7am-1pm). A **Monoprix** supermarket, rue Paul Goby, is near the bus station. (☎36 44 36. Open M-Sa 8:45am-7:30pm. AmEx/MC/V.) Dozens of *crêperies* and cafés occupy the *vieille ville.* Centered around cobblestone **place aux Aires,** Grasse's most affordable restaurants also have the best ambience. **Café des Musées ❷,** 1 rue Ossola, a small basement café, serves creative dishes like *l'assiette St-Marcellin* (roasted St-Marcellin cheese on bread with apples; €11) and a wide selection of homemade desserts (€5.50) in a bright, yellow-tiled interior. (☎04 92 60 99 00. Open July-Aug. daily 9am-7pm; Sept.-June M-Sa 9am-7pm. MC/V.) For a menu with a wider selection, stop by **L'Oasis ❸,** 23 pl. aux Aires, and escape the afternoon heat at shaded red tables. The kitchen quickly prepares pasta dishes (€9-12), mussels (€12), and a filling lunch *menu* (€15) based on the morning market's offerings. (☎36 00 95. Salads €9-16. Dinner *menus* €19-23. Open Feb.-Dec. Tu-Su noon-2:30pm and 7-10pm. Closed Jan. AmEx/MC/V.)

SIGHTS AND SMELLS. Even the directionally challenged will have no trouble finding their way to Grasse's three largest *parfumeries;* wafts of musky cologne

CÔTE D'AZUR

and *eau de toilette* lead visitors right to the factory doorsteps. The best *parfumerie*, **Fragonard,** 20 bd. Fragonard, gives free tours of its 225-year-old factory, still in use today. A museum on the top floor of the factory displays a large collection of perfume paraphernalia, including bottles ranging from ancient Egyptian to Calvin Klein. (☎36 44 65; www.fragonard.com. Open daily Feb.-Oct. 9am-6pm; Nov.-Jan. 9am-12:30pm and 2-6pm. Last tour 5:45pm.) **Molinard,** 60 bd. Victor Hugo, 5min. from the center of town, has a newer factory designed by Gustave Eiffel (of Parisian tower and Statue of Liberty fame). The *parfumerie*'s free tours take you past scented soap production, enormous perfume vats, and elaborate, aging bottle labels. If you don't find anything to suit your taste, concoct your own *eau de parfum* at the 1½hr. *Tarinologie* workshop for €40. (☎04 92 42 33 11; www.molinard.com. Open July-Aug. daily 9am-7pm; Sept. and May-June daily 9am-6:30pm; Oct. and Apr. daily 9am-12:30pm and 2-6pm; Nov.-Mar. M-Sa 9am-12:30pm and 2-6pm. Tours July 9:30am-6pm; Aug.-June. 9:30am-noon and 2-5:30pm. AmEx/MC/V.) Louis XIV's perfume and pomade maker founded the **Galimard** factory, 73 rte. de Cannes, in 1747 to keep the Sun King smelling divine. The factory offers 2hr. sessions with a **professional "nose,"** who will help you create a personal fragrance for €35 in the Studio des Fragrances. From the bus station, take bus #600 (dir.: Cannes) and make sure the driver knows you want to go to "La Blauquière" (€1.70). From the stop, walk downhill for 5min. (☎09 20 00; www.galimard.com. Open daily June-Sept. 9am-6:30pm; Oct.-May 9am-12:30pm and 2-6pm. Reservations required. AmEx/MC/V.)

A NOSE BY ANY OTHER NAME... The celebrities of the scent industry are known as "noses," the trade name for the master smellers who produce high fashion's most famous fragrances. The best noses train for 15 years, studying scents and chemistry before ever extracting an essence; by the time they're ready to mix a scent, students have memorized more than 3000 smells (the average person can only handle about 200). Noses can even distinguish the difference between *jasmin* grown in Grasse and that grown elsewhere! All French noses are trained at one of two French olfactory schools—one in Grasse and the other in Versailles. It can take up to 2 years for a nose to mix a new scent, and even the most prolific noses never produce more than 3-4 perfumes per year. Numbering 10 in all of France, noses are hot commodities and are required by contract to renounce alcohol, cigarettes, and spicy foods.

To make sense of all these scents, head to the superb **Musée International de la Parfumerie,** 8 pl. du Cours Honoré Cresp (☎04 97 05 58 00). Rotating exhibits showcase perfume production across the globe; look for the 3000-year-old mummy's hand and foot—apparently preserved by their perfume. In a 17th-century villa, the **Musée Jean-Honoré Fragonard,** 23 bd. Fragonard, features erotic canvases by the libertine painter and native son of Grasse, whose name was adopted by the *parfumerie* as a tribute in 1926. (☎36 01 61. Open daily July 10am-6:30pm; Aug.-June 10am-12:30pm and 1:30-6:30pm.) The **Musée Provençal du Costume et du Bijou,** next to the Fragonard factory, offers a small collection of 18th- and 19th-century clothing and jewelry. A highlight is the collection of intricate, ornamental crosses. (☎36 91 42. Open daily 10am-1pm and 2-6:30pm. Free.) At the highest point of the *vieille ville*, the Romanesque **Cathédrale Notre Dame-du-Puy** displays three works by Rubens, as well as Fragonard's only religious painting, *Lavement des Pieds*, commissioned especially for the Baroque chapel. While the paintings are magnificent, the church itself is less exciting. (☎36 11 02. Open M-Tu and Th-F 8:30-11:30am and 3-6pm, W 9:30-11:30am and 3-6pm, Sa 9:30-11:30am and 3-7pm, Su 8-11:30am.)

In the middle of May, **Expo-Rose** attracts rose growers from around the world for the largest exhibition of its kind. The *Grassois* pay tribute to their flowery source of income again in early August at the **Fête du Jasmin.** This fragrant festival features the election of a Miss Jasmin to preside over the festivities.

ST-RAPHAËL AND FRÉJUS

Situated along the Estérel Hills, the twin cities of St-Raphaël and Fréjus provide French families with sun, beaches and campsites every summer. Their configuration and limited nightlife, however, make them less attractive to independent travelers. The highly commercial beach town of St-Raphaël is nonetheless a good base for a visit to pricey St-Tropez. Those more keen on history than golden sand and ice cream stands will enjoy the nearby city of Fréjus, home to imposing Roman ruins. While both towns are relatively unappealing compared to the rest of the Riviera, they are also less exclusive—feel free to wear your flip-flops here.

ST-RAPHAËL ☎04 94

If St-Tropez limits its streets to the classy and glam, the young and brash St-Raphaël (SEHN rahf-aye-ell; pop. 32,000) welcomes everyone else with open arms. The town's most appealing area surrounds the beach, where one can find inexpensive food and miles of sand. Midway through the summer, the boardwalk turns into a carnival in the evenings, packed with gaming booths and flirting teenagers. If tacky isn't your cup of tea, skip St-Raphaël.

TRANSPORTATION AND PRACTICAL INFORMATION. St-Raphaël is a major stop on the coastal rail line, shuttling passengers among the Riviera's resort towns. **Trains** run from pl. de la Gare to Cannes (25min., every 30min., €5.90), Marseille (1¾hr., every hr., €24), and Nice (1hr., every 30min., €9.80). Ticket booths are open daily 6:30am-9pm. The info office is open daily 6:30am-10pm. **Buses** leave from behind the train station. Esterel Cars (☎53 78 46) serves Fréjus (25min., every hr. 7:30am-6:40pm, €1.10). Buses run later in July and August but are unreliable year-round. Sodetrav (☎95 24 82) goes to St-Tropez (1½hr., 11 per day 6:25am-9pm, €9.50). Beltrame (☎95 95 16) goes to Cannes via Trayas (1¼hr., 8 per day, €6.80) and to the airport in Nice (1¼hr., 4 per day, €21). Les Bateaux de St-Raphaël **ferries** (☎95 17 46; www.tmr-saintraphael.com), at the old port, go to St-Tropez (1hr.; 5 per day; €12, round-trip €21). Those at the hostel in Fréjus should ask about 10% discounts. **Taxis** (☎83 24 24) wait outside the train station.

The **tourist office,** opposite the train station on rue Waldeck Rousseau, books accommodations. (☎19 52 52; www.saint-raphael.com. Open July-Aug. daily 9am-7pm; Sept.-June M-Sa 9am-12:30pm and 2-6:30pm.) **Top Pressing,** 34 av. Général Leclerc, provides **laundry** services. (☎82 24 05. Open M-Tu and Th-F 8am-12:15pm and 1:30-6pm, W and Sa-Su 8am-12:15pm. Wash €4.70, dry €2-4. Cash only.) The **police** (☎95 24 24) is on rue de Châteaudun. **Cyber Bureau,** 123 rue Waldeck Rousseau, in the shopping center beside the train station, has six computers and Wi-Fi. (☎95 29 36. €2 per 15min., €6 per hr. Open M-F 9am-7pm, Sa 9am-1pm.) The **post office** is on av. Victor Hugo, behind the station. (☎19 52 00. Open M-F 8am-6:30pm, Sa 8am-noon.) **Postal Code:** 83700.

ACCOMMODATIONS AND FOOD. Package tourism runs rampant in St-Raphaël, making the independent traveler feel like the only person in the world who has not purchased a scuba excursion to go with the traditional room-and-breakfast combo. While accommodations are not cheap here, they are more convenient than those in Fréjus and far more budget-friendly than those in St-Tropez. The best deal in town, **Hôtel les Pyramides ❸,** 77 av. Paul Doumer, offers basic but well-kept and airy rooms near the waterfront. Exit left from the station, make a right onto av. Henri Vadon, and take the first left onto av. Paul Doumer. The spacious lounge and outdoor patio are great spots to relax after a day on the beach, which is only 100m away. All rooms have A/C, toilet, shower, and TV, and some have balconies. (☎04 98 11 10 10; www.hotellespyramides.fr. Breakfast €7. Reception 7am-9pm. Check-in July-Aug. 2pm; mid-Mar. to June and Sept. to mid-Nov. 1pm. Reservations required. Open mid-Mar. to mid-Nov. July-Aug. singles €35; doubles €46-65; triples €66; quads €74. Sept. to mid-Nov. and mid-Mar. to June €30/41-60/61/69. Extra bed €13. MC/V.) Bright rooms and a summery restaurant make a stay at **La Bonne Auberge ❸,** 54 rue de la Garonne, near the train tracks, a refreshing experience. Most rooms have a bathroom with shower; some share hallway toilets. (☎95 69 72. Breakfast €5. *Demi-pension* and *pension complète* available; ask for prices. Reception 7am-8pm. Open Feb.-Nov. Reservations required. Singles €26-36; doubles €36-50; triples and quads €38-50. MC/V.)

It's hard to come by interesting dining spots in a town where carnival stalls provide the entertainment. The most lively and affordable restaurants are near the *vieux port*, quai Albert I, while snack and ice-cream stands stretch down **cours Jean Bart** into Fréjus. The **Monoprix** supermarket is at 14 bd. de Félix Martin, by the train station. (☎19 82 82. Open M-Sa 8am-7:30pm. AmEx/MC/V.) Morning markets color **place Victor Hugo,** down the hill from the bus station, and **place de la République.** Find fresh fish at the *vieux port.* (All markets Tu-Su 7am-12:30pm.) Enjoy delicious thin-crust pizzas (€8-10) as well as meat and seafood dishes (€10-20) at local favorite **La Romana ❸,** 155 bd. de la Libération. This Italian wannabe, complete with Roman columns and bronze statues, is the best choice on the boardwalk. (☎51 53 36. *Menus* €16-22. Open July-Aug. daily noon-2:30pm and 7-11pm; Sept.-June M-Tu 7-11pm, W-Su noon-2:30pm and 7-11pm.) A white stone hearth is the focus of **Le Grillardin ❸,** 42 rue Thiers, which serves grilled meats (€13-18) and wood-fired pizzas (€6.50-12). The house specialty is the *marmite de pêcheur* (€18), a thick soup made from fish, olive oil, and cheese. (☎40 46 14. *Menus* €17 and €25. Open July-Sept. M, W, Su 7pm-1am; Tu and Th-Sa noon-2pm and 7pm-1am. Oct.-May M-Tu and Th-Su noon-2pm and 7-11pm. MC/V.)

BEACHES AND NIGHTLIFE. Thirty kilometers of public sand run along the coast from St-Raphaël west through Fréjus; in summer every inch that isn't covered with roasting bodies is taken up by ice-cream vendors or mini-carnival rides. Avoid the crowds; take a bus to more remote beaches, like the stunning one in Dramont (take bus #8, dir.: Trayas, from the *centre-ville*). At night, sunbaked clubbers head to **La Réserve,** promenade René Coty, one of the few clubs in St-Raphaël. (☎95 02 20; www.la-reserve.fr. Ladies free M-Th. Cover €13; includes 1 drink. Open July-Aug. daily 11:30pm-5am; Sept.-June Th-Sa 11pm-4:30am. AmEx/MC/V.) If a young crowd and techno music isn't your thing, trade the basement-level club for the beach-level restaurant-lounge, **Marine & blanc,** 1 promenade des Bains, across from the Casino on plage du Veillat. (☎19 22 45; www.marine-et-blanc.com. Mixed drinks €8. Open daily 11am-midnight. AmEx/MC/V.)

FRÉJUS

☎04 94

Founded by Julius Caesar in the first century BC, Fréjus (FRAY-jooss; pop. 52,000) remains of interest chiefly because of its Roman past. The town's crumbling ruins, situated among cafés, modern shops, and high-rise apartments, have earned it the nickname "Pompeii of Provence." A superb hostel and eclectic array of sights make Fréjus a welcome change from the beach party next door in St-Raphaël, although the city outside of the historical center is spread out and rather ugly.

TRANSPORTATION AND PRACTICAL INFORMATION. Fréjus's train station, rue Martin Bidoure (☎08 92 35 35 35), is little-used—St-Raphaël receives most **trains.** In summer, seven trains go daily from St-Raphaël to Cannes (30min., €6.10) and Nice (1hr., €9.70), six to Marseille (2hr., €20). **Buses** connect Fréjus to

St-Raphaël (M-Sa until 7:10pm, Su 6:05pm; later July-Aug.); ask for schedules at the tourist office. **Local buses** (€1.10) connect the *vieille ville* to the beach. The bus station, pl. Paul Vernet, is next to the tourist office. (☎53 78 46. Open M-F 8:30am-noon and 2-5:30pm, Sa 9am-noon.) For **taxis,** call ☎51 51 12.

Fréjus's 7km beach, a 20min. walk from the town center, is closer to St-Raphaël than to Fréjus, making a stay in Fréjus advisable only to those coming for the *vieille ville* and its surrounding sights. To reach the **tourist office,** 325 rue Jean Jaurès, from St-Raphaël, take bus #6 to pl. Paul Vernet (€1.10). The office conducts 2hr. guided tours Tuesday, Thursday, and Friday in July and August; contact the office for details. (☎51 83 83; www.ville-frejus.fr. Tours €5, students €3. Limited **Internet** access available. Office open July-Aug. M-Sa 10am-noon and 2:30-6:30pm, Su 10am-noon and 3-6pm; Sept.-June M-Sa 10am-noon and 2-6pm, Su 10am-noon and 3-6pm.) **Laundry** is at La Pastorale, 132 rue Grisolle. (☎06 08 88 49 70. Wash €4-5, dry €0.60 per 10min.) The **police** (☎51 90 00) are on rue de Triberg. There is a **pharmacy** at 62 rue Général de Gaulle (☎51 28 98). The **hospital,** Centre Hospitalier Intercommunal (☎40 21 21), 240 av. de St-Lambert, is on the corner of av. André Léotard. **SOS Médecins** can be reached at ☎62 06 76. The **post office,** av. Aristide Briand, is down the hill from the tourist office. (☎17 60 80. Open M-F 8am-6:30pm, Sa 8am-12:30pm; 3rd Th of every month closed 12:30-1:30pm.) **Postal Code:** 83600.

CÔTE D'AZUR

ACCOMMODATIONS AND FOOD. Fréjus is home to one of the best hostels on the Côte d'Azur: the **Auberge de Jeunesse de St-Raphaël-Fréjus (HI) ❷,** chemin du Counillier. From the Fréjus tourist office, take av. du 15ème Corps d'Armée. After passing two roundabouts, turn left on chemin de Counillier (30min.). Alternatively, bus #10 (€1.10) leaves from behind the bus station for the hostel at 6:30pm. From St-Raphaël, buses (1 per hr. 7:20am-7pm) head to "Les Chênes" (or "Paul Vernet," a farther but more frequent stop). From the "Les Chênes" stop, walk up av. Jean Calliès to chemin du Counillier; from the "Paul Vernet" stop, follow directions from the tourist office. There is a shuttle from the hostel to the beach and to the St-Raphaël train station daily at 8:55am (9:05am on Su), and bus #10 makes the reverse trip at 6:45pm from the St-Raphaël train station. This secluded hostel has immaculate showers and a 170-acre spread of parkland. Ask the knowledgeable staff about discounts on bike and canoe rentals, sailing lessons, and ferry tickets. (☎53 18 75; frejus-st-raphael@fuaj.org. Kitchen 6-9pm. Breakfast included. Laundry €3. Reception 8-11am and 5:30-10pm; phone during these hours for reservations. Lockout 11am-5:30pm. Curfew 11pm. Open Mar.-Oct. Dorms €18-20; quads with shower and toilet €20; doubles €23-26. Camping €13 per person with tent. Cash only.) **Hôtel La Riviera ❸,** 90 rue Grisolle, in the historic center, has functional rooms and its own *brasserie.* (☎51 31 46; fax 17 18 34. Breakfast €5. Lockout 10am-3pm. Reservations required in summer. Singles and doubles €30-40, with shower €45; triples €40-53; quads €53-60. MC/V.)

The *marché provençal* fills **rue de Fleury** and **place Formigé** on Wednesday and Saturday mornings with fruits, vegetables, and handmade trinkets. Bus #10 drops shoppers off directly. There's a **Casino** supermarket on the corner of av. du 15ème corps de l'Armée and av. André Léotard, at the second roundabout on the way to the hostel. (Open M-Sa 8:30am-8pm, Su 8:30am-12:30pm. MC/V.) Budget restaurants cluster around **place de la Liberté** and **place Paul Albert Février.** In the heart of the *vieille ville*, **Les Micocouliers ❸,** pl. Paul-Albert Février, serves classic regional dishes like *daube de boeuf à la provençale* (beef stew with *provençal*-style marinade; €13) and *soupe au poissons* (fish soup; €9) on shaded, yellow outdoor tables. (☎52 16 52. Pasta €7.80. *Menu provençal* €17. Open daily noon-2:30pm and 6:30-10pm. MC/V.) The husband and wife team at **Faubourg de Saigon ❷,** 126 rue St-François de Paule, off rue

Jean Jaurès, prepares excellent authentic Vietnamese dishes (€7-9) in a paper-lantern-filled interior. The almond chicken (€8.10) and *salade vietnamienne aux crevettes* (salad with shrimp; €6.50) are particularly good. A small glass of sake comes with the check. (☎53 65 80. *Menu* €16. Open M 6:30-10:30pm, Tu-Su 11am-2pm and 6:30-10:30pm. MC/V.)

SIGHTS. Fréjus's sights offer all things Roman and not much else. The **Episcopal Buildings** are the town's main highlight, resting on what is presumed to be the site of the ancient Roman town center. Today, the baptistry, cloister, and cathedral retain their central position at the heart of Fréjus's *vieille ville*. Worn, exposed walls and a floor of uneven stone slabs reveal 2000 years of building and rebuilding. An octagonal **baptistry,** constructed in the fifth century AD, is one of France's oldest buildings. The spectacular 12th- to 14th-century **cloister,** 58 Rue de Fleury, contains a wood ceiling decorated with over 1200 miniature paintings of medieval life and fantastical creatures. Next door, austere Gothic **cathedral doors** depict gruesome, devastating 10th-century Saracen raids on Fréjus. (☎51 26 30. Cloister open June-Sept. daily 9am-6:30pm; Oct.-May Tu-Su 9am-noon and 2-5pm. Doors and baptistry accessible only by 40min. guided tour in French; English info available. €5, students €3.50, under 18 free.)

Built in the first and second centuries AD to entertain 10,000 rowdy, homesick soldiers, the nearby **Roman Amphitheater,** rue Henri Vadon, lacks the embellishments of those in Arles or Nîmes, which were designed for more discerning patrician eyes; however, Christians and lions were slaughtered here just as frequently as in Rome. Today, stands are built into the ruins to accommodate concerts and bullfights. (☎51 34 31. Open May-Oct. M-Tu and Th-Sa 10am-1pm and 2:30-6:30pm; Nov.-Apr. M-F 10am-noon and 1:30-5:30pm, Sa 9:30am-12:30pm and 1:30-5:30pm. €2. Contact tourist office for concert and bullfight schedule.) The original wall of Fréjus's other ancient forum, the **Roman Theater,** remains intact; the rest now hosts concerts and plays. From the roundabout at the tourist office, walk 250m on rue Grande Bretagne. In July, the remains of the theater are turned into an outdoor performance space for **Les Nuits Auréliennes,** a week-long theater festival. (☎53 58 75. Open Apr.-Oct. M-Sa 10am-1pm and 2:30-6:30pm, Su 8am-7pm; Nov.-Mar. M-F 10am-noon and 1:30-5:30pm, Su 8am-5pm. €2.)

Outdoor enthusiasts shouldn't miss Fréjus's **Base Nature,** a 150-acre former military base on the beach reserved for all things extreme. Separate areas are designated for basketball, BMX biking, football, rugby, a skate park, and swimming. In October, the converted airplane hangar houses the **Roc d'Azur,** billed as the largest all-terrain biking competition in the world. From pl. Paul Vernet, take bus #9 (dir.: St-Raphaël, 15min., €1.10) to "Base Aeronavale." (☎51 91 10. Open daily June-Sept. 8am-9pm; Oct.-May 8am-6pm. Call for equipment rental prices.)

ST-TROPEZ ☎04 94

Luxe, calme, et volupté ("Luxury, calm, and pleasure") is what Matisse saw in St-Tropez (SEHN troh-pay; pop. 5400) and immortalized in his painting of the same name. Sixty-four years after he and other neo-Impressionists, including Paul Signac, first brought fame to the fishing hamlet, Brigitte Bardot's nude bathing scene in *Et Dieu Créa la Femme* (And God Created Woman) sealed the town's celebrity status. Ever since, the former village has bewitched everyone from Hollywood stars to daytripping backpackers. Fashionistas, yachtsmen, and ogling tourists rub elbows on the *vieux port* and in the narrow, shop-lined streets. Of course, this high-society playground's charm comes with a price: restaurants, bars, the boat ride there, and even campsites are sure to make a significant dent in your wallet.

TRANSPORTATION

Reaching the "Jewel of the Riviera" requires some effort, as it lies well off the rail line. Getting to the small beaches and villages outside of town is also a hassle. The fastest and cheapest way to travel is by **boat.**

Buses: Sodetrav buses, av. Général Leclerc (☎97 88 51), across from the ferry dock. To **St-Raphaël** (1½-2¼hr.; July-Aug. 14 per day, Sept.-June 10 per day; €11) and **Toulon** (2¼hr.; July-Aug. 15 per day, Sept.-June 9 per day; €19). Bus station open July-Aug. M-Sa 8:30am-8pm, Su 10:15am-1:30pm; Sept.-June M-F 10am-noon and 2-4pm, Sa 10am-noon.

Ferries: Les Bateaux de St-Raphaël (☎95 17 46; www.tmr-saintraphael.com), at the *vieux port,* sail to **St-Raphaël.** (1hr.; July-Aug. 5 per day, Sept.-June 4 per day; €12, round-trip same-day return €21. MC/V.)

Taxis: (☎97 05 27). From the Musée de l'Annonciade.

Bike Rental: Louis Mas, 3-5 rue Quarenta (☎97 00 60). Bikes €12 per day, €45 per week; €170 deposit. Mopeds €37-50; €915 deposit. Open mid-June to Aug. M-Sa 9am-7pm, Su 10am-1pm and 5-7pm; Easter to mid-June M-Sa 9am-12:30pm and 2-6:30pm. AmEx/MC/V.

ORIENTATION AND PRACTICAL INFORMATION

St-Tropez's glamorous life rises and falls with the seasons—warming up in May and June, sizzling from July to August, and winding down in September. Shops, museums, and nightlife have limited hours from September to June, but in July and August, St-Tropez is active all day. The town is condensed and pedestrian-friendly. Much of the action can be found along the *vieux port,* which is packed with cafés and restaurants that transform at night into bars and lounges.

Tourist Office: (☎97 45 21; www.saint-tropez.st) on the corner of quai Jean Jaurès and rue V. Laugier, facing the port. From the bus stop facing the port, go right and stay along the water until you see the office. Multilingual staff distributes schedules for the municipal *navette* (shuttle system; €1), free maps, and the *Manifestations* event guide. Open daily late June to early Sept. 9:30am-8pm; late Mar. to mid-June and mid-Sept. to early Oct. 9:30am-12:30pm and 2-7pm; mid-Oct. to mid-Mar. 9:30am-12:30pm and 2-6pm.

Currency Exchange: Master Change, 18 rue Gen. Allard (☎97 80 17), off the *vieux port* up rue Clemenceau. Open July-Aug. daily 7am-9pm; Mar.-June and Sept.-Oct. M-Sa 9am-8pm, Su 10am-1pm and 3-8pm.

Laundromat: Laverie du Pin, 13 quai de l'Epi. Wash €5.50, dry €2. Open M-Sa July-Aug. 7am-9pm; Sept.-June 9am-1pm and 3-7pm.

Police: Pl. de la Garonne, on rue François Sibilli and rue Général Leclerc, by the new port (☎54 86 65, at night 97 09 22).

Hospital: Centre Hospitalier de Saint-Tropez, av. du Maréchal Foch (☎79 47 11).

Pharmacy: Pharmacie du Port, 9 quai Suffren (☎97 00 06).

Internet Access: Kreatik Café, 19 av. Général Leclerc (☎97 40 61; www.kreatik.com), down the street from Monoprix. €2 per 10min., €4 per 30min., €7 per hr. Open daily 10am-1am. AmEx/MC/V.

Post Office: Pl. A. Celli (☎55 96 50), between the new and old ports. Open M-F 8:30am-noon and 2-5pm, Sa 8:30am-noon; opens at 9:30am on 2nd and 4th Th of every month. **Postal Code:** 83990.

ACCOMMODATIONS AND CAMPING

Hotels are plentiful in St-Tropez but incredibly expensive, and the cheapest ones require reservations months in advance, particularly during July and August. A

▲■ ACCOMMODATIONS

La Belle Isnarde, **15**
Camping Kon Tiki, **14**
Camping Les Prairies de la Mer, **5**
Lou Cagnard, **13**

🍴 FOOD

Auberge des Maures, **8**
L'Aventure, **6**
Délice des Lices, **10**
La Grange, **1**
Restaurant UGO, **7**
La Tarte Tropézienne, **11**

▮ NIGHTLIFE

Bar de la Maison Blanche, **12**
Chez Maggi, **4**
Les Caves du Roy, **9**
Kelly's Irish Pub, **3**
Nano Salon, **2**

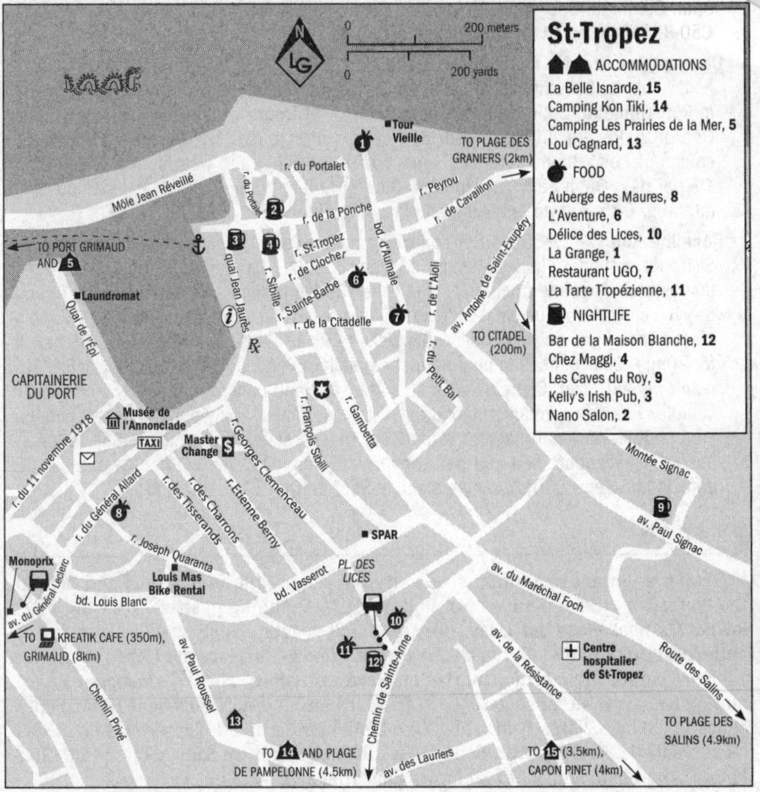

stay in St-Raphaël is easier on the wallet but forces visitors to limit their time and miss out on nightlife. The closest hostel is in Fréjus. Camping is the cheapest option close to St-Tropez, though prices remain shockingly high and no sites are within walking distance of town. A ferry connects the campsite at Port Grimaud (p. 754) with the peninsula, and shuttles run on limited schedules from the center of town to the smaller grounds flanking St-Tropez's beaches. These sites are popular and often full; book months in advance. Camping on the beach is prohibited.

La Belle Isnarde, rte. de Tahiti (☎/fax 97 13 64 or 97 57 74), but closest entrance on chemin de la Belle Isnarde, 15min. from the bus station. From pl. des Lices, turn right on av. du Maréchal Foch, right again onto rue de la Résistance, and left onto av. de la Résistance, which becomes chemin de la Belle Isnarde. The hotel is on the left. This is the cheapest hotel in St-Tropez. Converted farmhouse provides a quiet getaway from the activity of the *centre-ville*. Light pink doors open onto spacious, spotless rooms with feather pillows and large windows equipped with thick shutters. Breakfast €8. Reception 7am-10pm. Open Easter to mid-Oct. Singles and doubles with shower €62-72, with shower and toilet €72-82. Cash only. ⑤

Lou Cagnard, 18 av. Paul Roussel (☎97 04 24; www.hotel-lou-cagnard.com), 3min. from pl. des Lices. 19 impeccably maintained rooms overlook the peaceful garden or the avenue. All with shower and phone. Breakfast €8. Free parking. Reception 8am-

Open late Dec. to early Nov. Apr.-Sept. singles and doubles €62-117; Oct.-Mar. -80. June-Sept. 1-week min. stay. MC/V. ❺

Camping Les Prairies de la Mer, Port Grimaud (☎79 09 09; www.riviera-villages.com). Accessible by **Bateaux Verts** (☎49 29 39) ferries, which leave from the *capitainerie* in Port Grimaud, 3min. from the campsite, for St-Tropez (round-trip every hr., €11). One of 3 "Riviera Villages" near St-Tropez. Huge, social site by a beach and the canals of Port Grimaud. Tennis, supermarket, bowling, and watersports. Bike rental €7 per day. Open early Apr. to early Oct. Early July to mid-Aug. €42; late June and late Aug. €25; Apr. to late June and late Aug. to mid-Oct. €18. MC/V. ❸

Camping Kon Tiki (☎55 96 96; kontiki@campazur.com). Sodetrav buses run from the St-Tropez station daily in July-Aug. (11:45am, 2:20, 4:10, 5:40pm; €1.60). At other times in July-Aug. and from Sept.-June (when Sodetrav serves Pampelonne only Tu and Sa) you can take a municipal shuttle (M-Sa 4 per day, €1) from pl. des Lices to "Capon-Pinet." Then head downhill, follow the signs to Plage Tahiti, and walk along the beach for 20min. Choice location near northern stretch of Pampelonne Beach, but difficult to reach without a car. Campers soak up sun by day and party at the bar by night. Lively complex has a supermarket, laundromat, tennis, archery, ping-pong, and restaurants. Free shuttles to local markets Tu and Sa. On-site scuba diving instruction. Internet access in reception area (€3 per 15min.). July-Aug. €60 for 1-2 people and a tent; early to mid-Sept. €30; Apr.-June and mid-Sept. to Oct. €20. MC/V. ❹

FOOD

St-Tropez's vibrant restaurant scene stretches along the *vieux port* and behind the waterfront. Save pennies for club cover by grabbing pastries from the *boulangeries* near **place des Lices.** For fruits and vegetables, as well as an array of antiques, books, and clothing, try the *grand marché* on **place des Lices** (Tu and Sa 7:30am-1pm) or the morning market on **place aux Herbes.** There's a **Monoprix** supermarket at 9 av. Général Leclerc. (☎97 07 94. Open July-Aug. daily 8am-10pm; Sept.-June M-Sa 8am-8:20pm. AmEx/MC/V.) A **SPAR** market, 16 bd. Vasserot, is on pl. des Lices. (☎97 02 20. Open Apr.-Sept. M-Sa 7:30am-7:30pm, Su 8am-7:30pm; Oct.-Mar. M-Sa 7:30am-1pm and 3:30-7:30pm, Su 8am-1pm and 4-7:30pm.)

La Grange, 9 rue du Petit St-Jean (☎97 09 62). Not the cheapest place in St-Tropez, but the best value. Delicious handmade pastas (€14-25) in a farm-inspired setting. Open daily 8pm-12:30am. AmEx/MC/V. ❸

L'Aventure, 21 rue du Portail Neuf (☎97 44 01.) Worth the splurge. Serves creative, exquisitely presented *plats* of regional cuisine (€19-32). The specialty, *filet de boeuf "aventure"* (€26), is well worth the money. Open mid-June to mid-Sept. daily 7:30-11pm; mid-Sept. to mid-June M-Tu and Th-Su 7:30-11pm. AmEx/MC/V. ❹

Auberge des Maures, 4 rue du Docteur Boutin (☎97 01 51), at the end of pedestrian rue Allard. Join cost-conscious diners in the garden of the Salinesi family and watch them grill fresh fish or meat (€12-25) as you start with a plate of artichoke hearts (€7). Open Apr.-Nov. daily 7:30pm-1am. AmEx/MC/V. ❹

La Tarte Tropézienne, pl. des Lices (☎97 04 69). "Always imitated but never matched," the St-Tropez pie is one of three famous local sweets, along with the *câlin de St-Tropez* and the nougat at Sénequier's. Its cream, orange-flavored sponge cake, and sugar topping delight even the most discerning sweet tooth. Pastries from €1.20. Sandwiches and pizzas €2.60. Open daily July-Aug. 6am-10pm; Sept.-June 6am-8pm. MC/V. ❶

Restaurant UGO, 9 rue Aire du Chemin (☎97 09 21). Budget travelers sample tasty pasta dishes (€6-8) and meats (€15-17) on small yellow and green tables. Open May-Sept. daily noon-4pm and 7pm-midnight or later; closed in winter. MC/V. ❸

Délice des Lices, pl. des Lices (☎54 89 84). The place to hit after a night out. Panini and sandwiches €4.60. June-Aug. open 24hr.; Sept.-May until 2am. Cash only. ❶

SIGHTS AND BEACHES

St-Tropez's pride and joy is its endless white sandy coastline, and most of the "sights" here can be found in—or out of—bathing suits, as the young and beautiful come to the shore to show off their bronzed bodies. Marathon tanning is practically a sport in itself, but those who prefer a more active approach will find a series of watersport companies along the beach.

A *navette* (shuttle bus) leaves from pl. des Lices (schedules vary; ask the tourist office). The bus goes to **Les Salins** (M-Sa 5 per day, last shuttle returns 6:10pm; €1), a rather secluded spot, and to **Capon Pinet** (M-Sa 4 per day, last return shuttle leaves 5:20pm; €1), the first stretch of the famous **Pampelonne** shoreline. Walking is another option. From the old port, head to the citadel and follow the path that passes Tour Portalet, Tour Vieille, and the cemetery. You'll reach **plage des Graniers,** already a decent swimming spot, and wind up in **Baie des Canebiers,** home to **Les Salins** (2.8km, 50min.). Farther South, the trail leads to **Capon Pinet,** and the footpath starting there takes you to **plage Tahiti,** halfway up a cliff (3.5km, 1hr.). Popular beach clubs among the young crowd are **Stefano for Ever, Le Club 55,** and **Key West Beach.** Lounge chairs in these clubs cost at least €14 per day; you're better off walking along the coast to find a swimming spot, getting a glimpse of celebrity villas along the way. Sunbathers who miss the shuttle back to town can take a taxi from Pampelonne to the port (€25-30) or walk along rte. de Tahiti (3km). Many spots allow nude sunbathing—in St-Tropez, only tourists have tan lines.

Travelers don't come to St-Tropez for the museums. Nevertheless, **Le Musée de l'Annonciade,** pl. Grammont, is a good break from sun, sand, and shopping—and it has A/C, which is a welcome relief. This converted chapel houses Fauvist and neo-Impressionist paintings by Bonnard, Matisse, and Signac, among others, as well as a number of Riviera images. (☎97 04 01. Open June-Sept. M and W-Su 10am-noon and 2-6pm; Oct.-May 10am-1pm and 4-7pm. €5.50, students €3.50.) The **Citadel,** a 17th-century fortress above the port, contains rotating artistic and historical exhibits. (☎97 59 43. Open daily Apr.-Sept. 10am-12:30pm and 1:30-6:30pm; Oct. and Dec.-Mar. 10am-12:30pm and 1:30-5:30pm. €4, students €2.50.)

NIGHTLIFE

The height of St-Tropez's excess and exclusivity is its wild nightlife. Bars and clubs can be found in the same areas as restaurants—around the port and surrounding **place des Lices.** For clubbing, dress to impress the strict bouncers.

Les Caves du Roy, av. Paul Signac (☎56 68 00; www.lescavesduroy.com), in the elegant Hotel Byblos. Perfect that bored rich-girl pout or high-society swagger, slip on your Chanel sunglasses, and shell out a cool €25,000 for a bottle of Cristal to share with the celebrity next to you at the bar. If things look shaky on the trust-fund front, you may have to settle for a slightly more mundane €25 vodka and tonic. Open July-Aug. daily 11pm-5am; June and Sept. F-Sa 11:30pm-4am. AmEx/MC/V.

Bar de la Maison Blanche, pl. des Lices (☎97 52 66), on the patio of the Maison Blanche hotel, at the corner of rue Sibilli and bd. Vasserot. Low-hanging trees and a profusion of flowers create a secluded, tranquil atmosphere for champagne (€16-17) and cocktails (€18). Open Mar.-Jan. daily 8pm-1am. Closed Feb. AmEx/MC/V.

Chez Maggi, 7 rue Sibille (☎97 16 12). A diverse crowd gathers at this flamboyant gay restaurant, which turns into a hopping bar and club come midnight. Open mid-Mar. to Sept. daily 7pm-3am. MC/V.

Nano Salon, 2 rue Sibille (☎97 72 59). An older, more sophisticated crowd kicks back under red lights on cozy couches. Mixed drinks €12. Open daily 7pm-3am. MC/V.

Kelly's Irish Pub, (☎54 89 11), quai F. Mistral, at the *vieux port.* A low-key anglophone crowd frequents this rowdy joint. Grab a Guinness (€4) in the intimate bar or enjoy it on the large outdoor patio that overlooks the water. Open daily 8:30am-3am. MC/V.

FESTIVALS

St-Tropez celebrates its historic ties to the idle rich with yearly golf tournaments and sailing regattas, including the famed three-day **Giraglia Rolex Cup** in mid-June, which concludes with an open-sea race from St-Tropez all the way to Genoa, Italy. Every May 16-18, during **Les Bravades,** locals pay homage to their military past and patron saint with costumed parades and celebrations. June 29 brings **St-Peter's Day** and a torch-lit procession honoring the saint of fishermen. Pick up a copy of *Manifestations* from the tourist office for detailed monthly festival information.

DAYTRIP FROM ST-TROPEZ

GRIMAUD

Less ritzy but more endearing than the city, the villages of the St-Tropez Peninsula make excellent daytrips. With their stunning hilltop settings and unforgettable views, these gems are becoming prized real estate and major tourist destinations.

The best of the peninsula is delightfully peaceful Grimaud (GREE-moh), located 100m above the sea and surrounded by the vineyards of 354 wine producers. The castle of Grimaud once controlled the Gulf of St-Tropez, fittingly known as the "Gulf of Grimaud" until the late 19th century. From its high towers, you can look down on the medieval village itself and also get a choice view of the gulf. Few can resist the charm of Grimaud's cobblestone lanes and fountain-filled *places.* Above the fairy-tale **place Neuve,** signs point to the 12th-century Romanesque **Eglise St-Michel.** (Open daily 9am-6pm.)

Sodetrav (☎97 88 51) sends **buses** from St-Tropez to Grimaud (30min., M-Sa 13 per day, €2.50). Or, take the ferry to Port Grimaud (20min., every hr.), and catch the hourly *petit train* at the top of Prairies de la Mer campsite. (☎54 09 09; €3, round-trip €5.60.) For non-campers Grimaud must be a daytrip; it has no budget hotels. The **tourist office,** 1 bd. des Aliziers, is just past the bus stop. (☎43 26 98; www.grimaud-provence.com. Open July-Aug. M-Sa 9am-12:30pm and 3-7pm, Su 10am-1pm; Apr.-June and Sept. M-Sa 9am-12:30pm and 2:30-6:15pm; Oct.-Mar. M-Sa 9am-12:30pm and 2:15-5:30pm.)

ILES D'HYÈRES

Three exotic, underpopulated islands—Porquerolles, Ile du Levant, and Port-Cros—lie off the French coast between the chic resort of St-Tropez and the looming metropolis of Toulon. The coastal town of Hyères and the adjacent Giens peninsula serve as good, if expensive, bases for visiting the islands, which Henri II nicknamed the *Iles d'Or* (Golden Islands) for the way the shale rocks glow in the sun. Today, things look mostly bronze, thanks to the miles of rough, unspoiled beaches and coves that allow for some of the best nude sunbathing in the region.

HYÈRES ☎04 94

While the tiny islands are the highlight of this area, you have to sleep somewhere. That's where Hyères (ee-EHR; pop. 51,500) comes in.

> **IF YOU CAN'T TAKE THE HEAT...** In summer, the Iles d'Hyères don't see much rain and become susceptible to wildfires. Because of this constant fire risk, the islands close to visitors frequently in July and August. Call ☎04 98 10 55 41 to inquire about which trails are open.

TRANSPORTATION AND PRACTICAL INFORMATION. The train station is located at the top of Av. Edith Cavell, off av. Gambetta towards the port. **Trains** run from Hyères to Marseille (1-2hr., 6 per day, €13) and Toulon (25min., 7 per day, €3.60). Sodetrav **buses** (☎12 55 00) run to St-Tropez (1½-2hr., 8 per day, €15) and Toulon (1hr., every 20min., €1.40), while Phocéens-Cars (☎04 93 85 66 61) go to Cannes (1½hr., 2 per day, €25) and Nice (2hr., 2 per day, €25). Buses run from rue du Soldat Ferrari, past the Casino des Palmiers from the tourist office.

The **tourist office** in Hyères, 3 rue Ambroise Thomas, offers free maps and ferry schedules. (☎01 84 50; www.ot-hyeres.fr. Open July-Aug. M-Sa 8:30am-7:30pm, Su 3:30-7:30pm; Sept.-June M-F 9am-6pm, Sa 10am-4pm.) Other services in Hyères include: **police,** pl. Henri Dunant (☎65 02 39); a **pharmacy,** 7B av. Gambetta (☎65 01 15); a **hospital,** 597 bd. du Maréchal Juin (☎00 24 00); **Internet** access at **La M@ison de L'Internet,** rue Soldat Bellon, on the third floor of the Centre Olbia (follow white signs from av. Gambetta; ☎65 92 82; €3 per 30min.; open M-F 9am-12:30pm and 2-5:30pm); and a **post office,** 3 rue Edouard Branley (☎12 43 60; open M-Tu and Th 8:30am-6:30pm, W 9am-6:30pm, Sa 8:30am-noon). **Postal Code:** 83400.

CÔTE D'AZUR

ACCOMMODATIONS AND FOOD. Budget accommodations in Hyères are scarce. A good option near the port is **Hôtel Le Calypso ❹,** 36 av. de la Méditerranée, a small, colorful hotel with bright rooms and a pleasant outdoor patio. A few rooms have balconies overlooking the sea. (☎58 02 09. Breakfast included. June-Sept. singles and doubles €42-52; triples €65; quads €79. Oct.-May €37-47/60/74. MC/V.) The Giens peninsula, extending 8km south of Hyères toward the islands, has several campsites; one of the cheapest is **La Presqu'île de Giens ❷,** 153 rte. de la Madrague, which has clean facilities and organizes windsailing, diving, and kayaking expeditions. (☎58 22 86; www.camping-giens.com. July-Aug. €14 for 1-2 people with a tent; Sept.-June €11.)

Avenue Gambetta is lined with enough cafés, *brasseries*, and *boulangeries* to fulfill all possible cravings. For picnic fare, head to the **Casino** supermarket, 20 av. Gambetta, near the intersection with av. E. Millet. (Open Tu-Sa 7:30am-12:30pm and 4-7:30pm, Su 8am-noon. MC/V.) Try **La Brasserie ❸,** 2 rue Léon Gautier, within La Coupole, for a reasonably priced sit-down meal. This restaurant offers a variety of seafood, pasta, and meat dishes in a plush, ornamental dining room or on an outdoor terrace with umbrellas and a stone fountain. (☎12 88 00. Lunch *menus* €11-13. Dinner *menus* €15-25. Open daily noon-2:30pm and 7-11pm. MC/V.). **Le Jardin ❸,** 19 av. Joseph Clotis, does indeed have a garden, encircled by orange trees. The chef serves creative dishes like octopus stew (€18) and grilled scallop salad (€16) to a young crowd. (☎35 24 12. Open Feb.-Dec. daily noon-midnight.)

ISLANDS

FERRIES. Ferries to the three islands depart from the port d'Hyères or from the *gare maritime* at La Tour Fondue on the Giens peninsula. From the bus or train station, catch bus #67 (dir.: Ports, €1.40), which stops on the side of the road closest to the station. TLV and TVM ferries are the cheapest way to get to any of the three islands (☎57 44 07 or 58 95 14 for service to Porquerolles, 57 44 07 for service to Port-Cros or Ile du Levant; www.tlv-tvm.com). Ferries to **Port-Cros** (1hr.) and **Ile du**

Levant (1½hr.) leave from Port D'Hyères. (Boats depart 8:15 or 9:30am depending on the season; €26 to visit both islands, ages 4-10 €22; €23 to visit 1 island, ages 4-10 €20.) Ferries to **Porquerolles** (20min.) leave from La Tour Fondue. (July-Aug. every 30min.-1hr. 7:30am-7pm; Sept.-June every 1-1½hr. €16, ages 4-10 €14.) Ferry and bus service can be infrequent; pay attention to schedules. **Vedettes Iles d'or et Le Corsaire** offers **shuttles** between the two islands, as well as connections to nearby ports, including St-Tropez. (☎71 01 02. Boats depart from Port-Cros for Ile du Levant 10:15am, 12:15, 5:15pm. €7.)

PORQUEROLLES. The largest of the three islands and the one most easily accessible from the coast, Porquerolles (POHR-kehr-ohll; pop. 342) has a colorful history. It was home to a religious order until François I granted pardons to convicts who promised to live on the island and defend the mainland against pirates. The criminals promptly transformed the island into the ultimate pirate hideout. Today, mainlanders and tourists find respite from the hectic Riviera on shady trails and in sun-drenched coves, while droves of windsurfers ride the waves just off the coast. An **info office** at the end of the main dock offers free maps and ferry schedules.

ILE DU LEVANT. Like its neighbor, Ile du Levant (EEL doo lev-ahn; pop. 100) was originally settled by monks. If they saw the island today, they would be uttering *mea culpas* for the next 50 years. This is the home of Héliopolis, Europe's oldest nudist colony; islanders go *au naturel* on the beaches and wear the legal minimum (not much) in the port and the main square. Bathing *au naturel* is actually mandatory on **plage des Grottes.** The landscape of Ile du Levant also offers eye candy on the winding trails in the Domaine des Arbousiers, a substantial natural reserve. The Héliopolis map includes seven trails, three of which skirt the dramatic coastline for miles. A small **Superette** provides basic snacks and cold drinks. (☎05 90 05. Open M-Sa 9:30am-1pm and 5:30-7:30pm. MC/V over €15.)

PORT-CROS. The smallest and most rugged of the three islands, Port-Cros (POHR-kroh; pop. 30) is a stunning **national park,** offering three main trails that wind through its verdant landscape. The mountainous terrain is home to 114 species of birds and 602 indigenous plants. The well-trodden **sentier des plantes** (plant trail) passes by forts and the crowded **plage de la Palud.** To find a solitary spot, continue on the **sentier de Port Man,** accessible by a 4hr. hike that penetrates the island's unpopulated interior. The national park info booth at the port provides maps (€2 and €3.80) and suggests activities. (☎01 40 70; www.portcrosparcnational.fr. Open July-Aug. daily 9:15am-12:30pm and 3:30-5:30pm; Sept.-June whenever boats arrive and depart.) **Snorkel** in the clear turquoise water off Port-Cros to view a dazzling array of sea life. You can also **scuba dive,** explore the area's many wrecks, and search for the 40 lb. brown *mérou*, a massive grouper once thought to be extinct. **Sun Plongée** runs open-water dives. (☎05 90 16; www.sun-plongee.com. With equipment and diving "buddy" €47, beginners €50; equipment €36. MC/V.)

CORSICA (LA CORSE)

Bathed in turquoise waters, Corsica was dubbed *Kallysté* (most beautiful) by the Greeks. Despite centuries of invasion, it has managed to guard a unique culture that has its own language, cuisine, and customs. In the tiny mountain towns of this island paradise, life proceeds much as it has for hundreds of years. Goats and sheep wander lonely roads, and crumbling hilltop chapels ring with prayers sung in *Corse*, Corsica's traditional dialect. Behind the island's sun-drenched beaches, patches of scrubby underbrush give way to an endless, unspoiled landscape. Nearly one-third of the island is protected nature reserve, and over 100 summits pierce a sky that refuses to rain 310 days of the year. The island's rugged landscape makes it ideal for hikers looking to conquer towering peaks and discover unforgettable views. Though development along the coast has brought a stream of bikini-clad tourists to the spectacular beaches, most of Corsica remains untouched. Even well-trodden resort towns are marked by Genoese towers and unique markets full of fresh Corsican produce. However, all this beauty comes at a price: it is challenging to find budget hotels and restaurants on the island, and camping is often the best—if not the only—budget option.

Fiercely defensive of its independent identity, Corsica has long resisted foreign rule. The Corsicans controlled their island until the Genoese took over in 1284. Almost 500 years later, following the 40-year Corsican War of Independence, General Pasquale Paoli reclaimed the island and created a university, government, currency, and army. Paoli also drafted the island's—and the world's—first modern constitution. Nevertheless, the 1768 Treaty of Versailles allowed France's Louis XV to gain control of the island, and Corsica found itself divided between the nationalist *Paolistes* and the *Populaires*, who swore allegiance to France.

Today, the *Front de Libération National de la Corse* (FLNC) sporadically tries to bomb its way to independence, but most Corsicans deplore this sort of extremism. When President Nicholas Sarkozy, then Interior Minister, proposed increasing Corsican autonomy in July 2003, the referendum was defeated by a 2% margin: only 49% of Corsicans wanted increased autonomy from France. It seems that this island's love-hate relationship with the mainland is destined to continue.

HIGHLIGHTS OF CORSICA

HIKE among the rock formations of **Les Calanches** (p. 771) near Porto or along stunning **Cap Corse** (p. 789) to marvel at the Corsican coast's rugged beauty.

DANCE THE NIGHT AWAY in **Calvi's** (p. 772) nightclubs and sober up on its beaches the next day—both rank among the best on the island.

GET YOUR FEET WET in **Bonifacio** (p. 793), which offers spectacular scuba diving, snorkeling, and windsurfing.

TRANSPORTATION

BY PLANE. Air France and its partner **Compagnie Corse Méditerranée (CCM)** fly to Ajaccio, Bastia, and Calvi from Marseille (€88, students €71), Nice (€85, students €68), and Paris (from €112, students €109). In Ajaccio, the Air France/CCM office

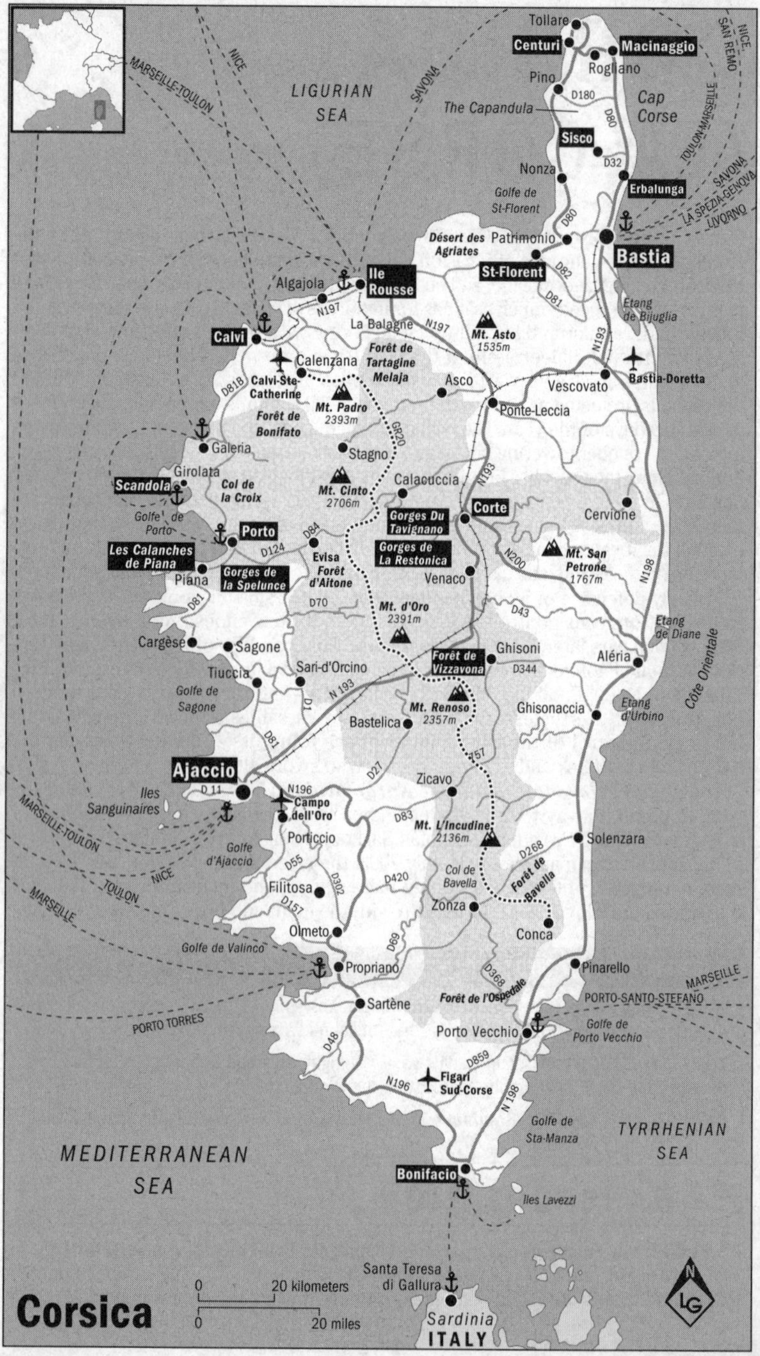
Corsica
LIGURIAN SEA
MEDITERRANEAN SEA
TYRRHENIAN SEA
MARSEILLE-TOULON
NICE
SAVONA
NICE SAN REMO
TOULON-MARSEILLE
SAVONA
LA SPEZIA-GENOVA
LIVORNO
MARSEILLE
PORTO-SANTO-STEFANO
PORTO TORRES
TOULON
Toilare
Centuri
Macinaggio
Rogliano
Pino
D180
Cap Corse
The Capandula
D80
Sisco
D32
Nonza
Erbalunga
Golfe de St-Florent
Désert des Agriates
Patrimonio
Bastia
St-Florent
D82
D81
Etang de Biguglia
Ile Rousse
Algajola
N197
Calvi
La Balagne
Mt. Asto 1535m
N193
Forêt de Tartagine Melaja
Calenzana
Calvi-Ste-Catherine
D81B
Asco
Vescovato
Bastia-Doretta
Mt. Padro 2393m
Ponte-Leccia
Forêt de Bonifato
GR20
Galeria
Stagno
Girolata
Scandola
Col de la Croix
Mt. Cinto 2706m
Calacuccia
Golfe de Porto
Porto
D84
Gorges Du Tavignano
Corte
Cervione
Les Calanches de Piana
D124
Evisa
Gorges de La Restonica
Mt. San Petrone 1767m
Piana
Gorges de la Spelunce
Forêt d'Aitone
Venaco
N200
N198
D81
D70
Mt. d'Oro 2391m
D43
Etang de Diane
Cargèse
Sagone
Forêt de Vizzavona
Ghisoni
Aléria
Côte Orientale
Tiuccia
Sari-d'Orcino
D344
Golfe de Sagone
N 193
D1
Mt. Renoso 2357m
Ghisonaccia
Etang d'Urbino
Bastelica
D81
Ajaccio
D 11
N196
Campo dell'Oro
D27
Zicavo
Iles Sanguinaires
D83
Mt. L'Incudine 2136m
Solenzara
Porticcio
Golfe d'Ajaccio
D55
D302
D420
D268
Col de Bavella
Forêt de Bavella
Filitosa
D157
Zonza
Conca
Olmeto
D69
Golfe de Valinco
Propriano
D368
Pinarello
Forêt de l'Ospedale
Sartène
Golfe de Porto Vecchio
Porto Vecchio
D48
D859
Figari Sud-Corse
N196
N 198
Golfe de Sta-Manza
Bonifacio
Iles Lavezzi
Santa Teresa di Gallura
Sardinia
ITALY
0
20 kilometers
0
20 miles
N
LG

is at 3 bd. du Roi Jérôme (☎08 20 82 08 20). Hunting around can yield significant savings; inquire at a budget travel agency in France.

BY BOAT. **Ferry** travel between the mainland and Corsica can be rough, and it's not always cheaper than a plane. High-speed ferries (3½hr.) run between Nice and Corsica. Overnight ferries from Toulon and Marseille take over 10hr. The **Société National Maritime Corse Méditerranée (SNCM;** ☎08 91 70 18 01; www.sncm.fr) sends ferries from Marseille (€40-58, under 25 €25-45), Nice (€35-47, under 25 €20-35), and Toulon (€40-58, under 25 €25-45) to Ajaccio, Bastia, Calvi, and Ile Rousse. It costs €40-305 to take a car, depending on the day and the type of car. In July and August, nine boats travel between Corsica and the mainland, though only three make the trip the rest of the year. The fastest boats *(Navires à Grande Vitesse)* leave from Nice and head to Ajaccio, Calvi, and Ile Rousse, making the crossing in nearly a third of the time. **Corsica Ferries** (☎08 25 09 50 95; www.corsicaferries.com) has similar destinations and prices with high-speed ferries. **SAREMAR** (☎04 95 73 00 96; fax 04 95 73 13 37) and **Moby Lines** (☎04 95 73 00 29; fax 04 95 73 05 50) run from Santa Teresa, Sardinia to Bonifacio (2-5 per day depending on the season; €14-15 per person, €26-52 per car). Moby Lines (€15-28) and Corsica Ferries (€16-32) cross from Genoa and Livorno in Italy to Bastia.

ON WHEELS AND RAILS. Rumor has it that the Marquis de Sade and Machiavelli collaborated on the design of Corsica's transportation system. **Train** service is slow, limited to the half of the island north of Ajaccio, and doesn't accept mainland rail passes, though a €47 Zoom pass allows for seven consecutive days of travel. **Buses** serve the whole island, but be prepared for twisting roads. If prone to motion sickness, bring medicine. Call **Eurocorse Voyages** (☎04 95 21 06 30) for info.

> **ROCKY ROAD.** Corsica allegedly has the most dangerous roads in France. Those foolhardy enough to **rent a car** should expect to pay €60-90 per day or €250-365 per week. The unlimited mileage deals are best. Gas stations are scarce; the police can help drivers who run out. **Bicycle, moped,** and **scooter** rental can also be pricey. Winding mountain roads and high winds make cycling difficult and risky; drivers should honk before rounding mountain curves. Many roads are too narrow for two cars to pass at one time. Tourists should always give way to buses, which *Let's Go* strongly recommends for island transport.

ON FOOT. Hiking is an excellent way to explore Corsica. *Randonnées* (hikes) exist all over the island, with panoramas of everything from the mountainous interior to the rocky coastline. Campsites, *refuges*, and an active backpacking culture ensure that hikers feel at home in Corsica. The longest marked route, the **GR20,** is a difficult 180km, 12- to 15-day trail that takes hard-core hikers across the island from Calenzana (southeast of Calvi) to Conca (northeast of Porto-Vecchio). The GR20 requires excellent physical fitness but rewards hikers with an unparalleled sampling of Corsica's scenery. Do not tackle this trail alone, and be prepared for cold, snowy weather even in early summer. For a shorter, less challenging route, try the popular **Mare e Monti,** a seven- to 10-day trail from Calenzana to Cargèse that passes through the pristine Aitone Forest and the breathtaking Gorges de Spelunca. The easier **Da Mare a Mare Sud** crosses the southern part of the island between Porto-Vecchio and Propriano (4-6 days), leading hikers through green countryside and past prehistoric remains at Filitosa. Its northern equivalent, the **Mare a Mare Nord,** is a 12-day trek from Moriani to Cargèse that passes through the university town of Corte before traversing the Tavignanu and Restonica river valleys. The **Mare a Mare Centre** transects the middle of the island from Ghisonaccia to Porticcio and can be completed in seven days. Though easier than the GR20, this trail requires advance preparation and is best enjoyed in autumn and spring. All major trails are administered by the **Parc Naturel Régional de la**

Corse, 2 Sargent Casalonga (☎04 95 51 79 00; www.parc-naturel-corse.com), in Ajaccio, whose jurisdiction encompasses most of the Corsican heartland. For any route, a topo-guide is essential (€14-15; available for purchase by fax, email, over the phone, or at a Parc Naturel office). The guide includes trail maps, *gîte* and *refuge* listings, and other important practical info. Prospective GR20 trekkers will want to consider buying *Le Grand Chemin* (€15), a more complete guide that includes elevations and sources of potable water. For more info, contact the Parc Naturel office.

ACCOMMODATIONS

Agence du Tourisme de la Corse, 17 bd. du Roi Jérôme, Ajaccio (☎04 95 51 00 00; www.visit-corsica.com), publishes free guides to Corsica's accommodations, available at tourist offices. Corsica's few budget hotels fill weeks ahead in summer, and it can be nearly impossible to find a room in August. Camping is a great choice all over the island: nearly every city, small town, or half-forgotten village offers at least one spot to pitch a tent. Resist the urge to set up camp on that stunning mountain ledge: **unofficial camping is strictly banned** and will be met with severe fines. *Refuges,* or mountain huts, provide trail-side shelter and camping.

TIP **ÇA VA?** Perhaps more than their mainland compatriots, Corsicans appreciate a little chit-chat before getting down to business. Ask how people are doing and be prepared to spend a few minutes rather than a few seconds talking, and you'll get more helpful answers to your questions.

AJACCIO (AIACCIU) ☎04 95

Napoleon must have insisted on the best from the beginning: the dictator couldn't have picked a better place to call home. With palm-lined boulevards, white sand beaches, and endless sunshine, Corsica's capital city, Ajaccio (ah-JAHKS-ee-o; pop. 60,000), is reminiscent of a Riviera resort. Though Ajaccio's countless boutiques, yacht-filled harbors, and pleasant beaches attract wealthy tourists, the city does not feel overrun and maintains its Corsican culture with pride. It is one of the few Corsican towns with multiple museums and considerable urban energy.

TRANSPORTATION

Flights: Aéroport Campo dell'Oro (**AJA;** ☎23 56 56; www.ajaccio.aeroport.fr), 5km away. TCA bus #8 (€4.50) shuttles to and from the bus station daily 6am-7:25pm and from the airport M-Sa 9am-11:15pm, Su 8am-11:15pm. Flights to **Lyon, Marseille, Nice,** and **Paris.** For info call **Air France,** 3 bd. du Roi Jérôme, or **Compagnie Corse Mediterranée** (☎08 20 82 08 20 for both; www.airfrance.com, www.aircorsica.com.) Airport office open daily 6am-8pm.

Trains: pl. de la Gare (☎23 11 03), off bd. Sampiero, 400m from the *gare maritime,* toward the airport. Open daily mid-June to mid-Sept. 6:30am-9:30pm; mid-Sept. to mid-June 6am-8:30pm. Trains go to: **Bastia** (3-4hr., 4 per day, €21), **Calvi** via **Ponte Leccia** (5hr., 2 per day, €25), and **Corte** (2½hr., 4 per day, €13).

Buses: quai l'Herminier (☎51 55 45), at the *gare maritime.* Open June-Aug. daily 6:30am 7:45pm; Sept.-May M-Sa 6:30am-7:45pm. **Eurocorse Voyages** (☎21 06 30) goes to: **Bastia** (3hr., M-Sa 7:45am and 3pm, €18) via **Corte** (1¾hr., €11); **Bonifacio** (3-4hr., M-Sa 8:30am and 1pm, €20); **Calvi** via Ponte Leccia (3½hr., July-Aug. M-Sa 3pm, €15); **Porto Vecchio** (3-4hr., M-Sa 2 per day, €20). **Autocars SAIB** (☎22 41 99) runs to **Porto** (2hr.; July to mid-Sept. daily 7:30am and 2:15pm, May-June and mid- to late Sept. M-Sa 7:30am and 2:15pm, Oct.-Apr. M-F 7:30am and 2:15pm, Sa 7:30am and 10:30pm; €11).

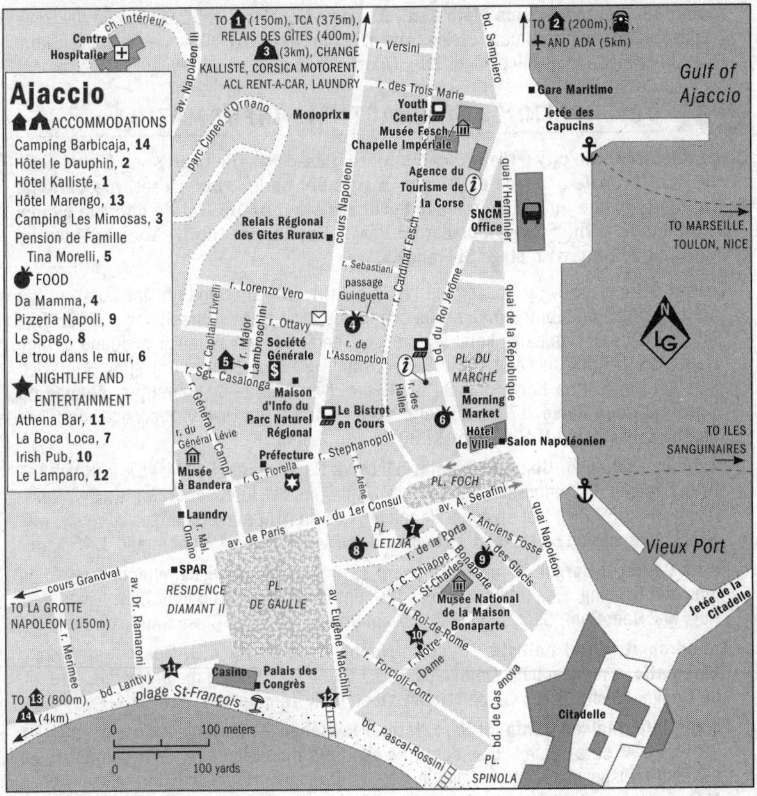

Ferries: Depart from the *gare maritime* (☎51 55 45). Open June-Aug. daily 6:30am-7:45pm; Sept.-May M-Sa 6:30am-7:45pm and for departures and arrivals. **SNCM,** quai l'Herminier (☎29 66 99; www.sncm.fr), across from the bus station, goes to **Marseille** (12hr., 1 per day) and **Nice** (4hr., 2-3 per week). €45-57, ages 12-25 and students €30-52. Office open M-F 8am-8pm, Sa for departures and arrivals (usually 8am-noon). MC/V. **Corsica Ferries** (☎50 78 82), in the *gare maritime,* runs to **Toulon** (5¾hr., 4-6 per week) and **Nice** (4½hr., 1-5 per week). €20-45, ages 12-25 €5-35. MC/V.

Local Transportation: TCA, 75 cours Napoleon (☎23 29 41). Buses run every 20min.-1¼hr., depending on the line. Tickets €1.20, *carnet* of 10 €9; available at the TCA office, in *tabacs,* and on the bus; validate on board. Buses #1, 2, and 3 go from pl. de Gaulle to the train station or down cours Napoleon toward public beaches. Bus #5 from av. Dr. Ramaroni and bd. Lantivy stops at Marinella and the beaches on the way to **Iles Sanguinaires** (7am-7:30pm). Line #8 heads to the airport from the *gare routière* (6am-7:25pm; €4.50). Office open M-Sa 9am-12:30pm and 3:30-6:30pm.

Taxis: Taxi Station, pl. de Gaulle (☎21 00 87) or on av. Pascal Paoli (☎23 25 70). **Ajaccio Voyages** (☎06 07 25 46 or 06 61 16 40 40). 24hr. €20 to the airport.

Car Rental: Ada (☎23 56 57; www.ada-en-corse.com), at the airport. 21+. Open daily 8am-midnight. AmEx/MC/V. **ACL Rent-a-Car,** 51 cours Napoleon (☎51 61 81; www.rentacar.fr), in Hôtel Kallisté and at the airport (☎23 56 36). 23+. Open daily 8am-8pm. MC/V.

Motorcycle Rental: Corsica Moto Rent, 51 cours Napoleon (☎51 61 81), in the Hôtel Kallisté. Scooters and motorcycles from €36 per day, €189 per week; deposit from €600. Helmet and lock included. 23+. Open daily 8am-8pm. MC/V.

ORIENTATION AND PRACTICAL INFORMATION

Cours Napoleon, the city's main thoroughfare, passes by the train station and ends in the *vieille ville* at **Place de Gaulle.** A parallel pedestrian street, **rue Cardinal Fesch,** leads to the more lively **Place Foch.** Between pl. de Gaulle and the **citadel** (still an active military base), **boulevard Pascal Rossini** runs above the city's public beaches, beginning with **plage St-François.**

Tourist Office: 3 bd. du Roi Jérôme (☎51 53 03; www.ajaccio-tourisme.com), pl. du Marché. Staff distributes maps, bus schedules, and festival brochures. 15min. free Internet access. Same-day hotel assistance. Themed tours in French mid-June to mid-Sept.; €5-9. Open July-Aug. M-Sa 8am-8:30pm, Su 9am-1pm and 4-7pm; Sept.-Oct. and Apr.-June M-Sa 8am-7pm, Su 9am-1pm; Nov.-Mar. M-Sa 8am-6pm. **Agence du Tourisme de la Corse,** 17 bd. du Roi Jérôme (☎51 00 00; www.visit-corsica.com), is a nearby annex. Open M-F 8:30am-12:30pm and 2-6pm.

Currency Exchange: Change Kallisté, 51 cours Napoleon (☎51 34 45), in Hôtel Kallisté, charges no commission. Open daily 8am-8pm. **Société Génerale,** rue Sgt. Casalonga (☎51 57 06), just off cours Napoleon, has an **ATM** and exchanges currency, with a high commission on **traveler's checks.** Open M-F 8:15am-12:15pm and 1:45-5pm

Youth Center U Borgu: 52 rue Fesch (☎50 13 44; centre.u.borgu@wanadoo.fr). Info on jobs and housing. Free Internet access (40min. limit, under 25 only). Open July to mid-Aug. M-F 9am-6pm; Sept.-June M-F 8:30am-9pm, Sa 2-7pm. Closed Aug. 15-Sept. 6.

Laundromat: Hotel Kallisté, 51 cours Napoleon (☎51 34 45). Open daily 1-8pm. **Lavomatic,** 1 rue Maréchal Ornano (☎06 13 13 64 21), behind the *préfecture,* near pl. de Gaulle. Wash €6, dry €1 per 10min. Open daily 7am-9pm.

Hiking Info: Maison d'Info du Parc Naturel Régional, 2 rue Sergent Casalonga (☎51 79 00; www.parc-naturel-corse.com), across from the *préfecture.* Free pamphlets on regional trails, wildlife, and lodging in *gîtes* and *refuges.* Hours vary, but officially open M-Sa June-Aug. 8am-7pm; Sept.-May 9am-noon and 2-6pm.

Police: rue Général Fiorella (☎11 17 17), near the *préfecture.*

Hospital: 27 av. Impératrice Eugénie (☎29 90 90).

Internet Access: Free at the **Youth Center** and at the **tourist office. Le Bistrot en Cours,** 10 cours Napoleon (☎21 44 75). 20min. Internet access per 1 drink; €1 per additional 20min. 30min. Wi-Fi per 1 drink or per €1. Open daily 8am-2am.

Post Office: 13 cours Napoleon (☎51 84 75). Open M-F 8am-6:45pm, Sa 8am-noon. **Postal Code:** 20000.

ACCOMMODATIONS AND CAMPING

Ajaccio has many hotels, but prices rival those in Paris. Call six weeks ahead to reserve rooms for June through August, when rates soar and vacancies plummet. Ask hotels for their cheapest room, then ask if there's anything cheaper; some hotels keep a couple of old, unrenovated rooms that they don't initially list. The tourist office will help with same-day reservations, but don't expect them to find something in the budget-range. If you're really stuck, the **Relais Régional des Gîtes Ruraux,** 77 cours Napoleon, posts last-minute availability in *gîtes* across the island, although they tend to be far from major cities. (☎10 54 30. Open M-F 8am-12:30pm and 2-5:30pm.) Ajaccio's campsites are well equipped but far from the city center.

Pension de Famille Tina Morelli, 1 rue Major Lambroschini (☎/fax 21 16 97). This welcoming option is tended by Tina herself and attracts older travelers. French-speakers will get the most out of the familial atmosphere, but all can enjoy the great value. Breakfast included. Reservations recommended far in advance. Singles €50, *demi-pension* €60, with *pension complète* €72; doubles €70/80/124; €45 per additional guest. Cash only. ❺

Hôtel Kallisté, 51 cours Napoleon (☎51 34 45; www.hotel-kalliste-ajaccio.com). Follow signs from quai l'Herminier up rue des Trois Marie, then take a right onto cours Napoleon. Rooms are well-designed, comfortable, and equipped with shower or bath, cable TV, and fan or A/C. Other services include currency exchange and vehicle rental. Breakfast €7.50. Laundry €5, dry €2. Free Internet access in the lobby during reception hours. Free Wi-Fi. Reception 8am-8pm. Aug. singles €64-76; doubles €86; triples €98. Mar.-July and Sept.-Oct. €56/64-72/76. Nov.-Feb. €52-58/64/84. MC/V. ❺

Hôtel Marengo, 2 rue Marengo (☎21 43 66; www.hotel-marengo.com). From city center, walk along the boardwalk with the sea on the left for about 25min.; turn right on bd. Madame Mère, then left onto rue Marengo. Or, take bus #1, 2, or 5 to Trottel. By the beach, airy rooms with shower and A/C are managed by cheerful owners. Breakfast €8. Reception 8am-11pm. Reservations recommended. Open Apr. to mid-Nov. 4 rooms sharing hallway toilet €55-60. July-Sept. singles €60; doubles €79; triples €105. Oct.-Nov. and Apr.-June €40-50/59-69/85-95. AmEx/MC/V. ❹

Hôtel le Dauphin, 11 bd. Sampiero (☎21 12 94; www.ledauphinhotel.com), between the train station and ferry port. Plain but well-kept rooms, all with bath and TV. Traffic makes the port a bit noisy. Breakfast included. A/C €8. Reception 5:30am-midnight. Check-in 2pm. July-Oct. singles €59; doubles €75; triples €89. Apr.-June €54/66/79. Nov.-Mar. €52/60/75. Extra bed €10. AmEx/MC/V. ❹

Camping Les Mimosas, rte. d'Alata (☎20 99 85; www.camping-lesmimosas.com). Follow cours Napoleon away from the city center. Turn left on montée St-Jean, which becomes rue Biancamaria and then rte. d'Alata. Walk straight past the roundabout and take a left onto chemin de la Carrossacia; follow signs 900m inland and uphill to the site (30min.). Or, take bus #4 from cours Napoleon to Brasilia (last bus leaves city center 7pm); walk straight to the roundabout and follow the above directions. Large site in a neighborhood above the centre- ville. Laundry €4, dry €1.80 per 15min. Reception 8:30am-noon and 2:30-8:30pm. June-Sept. €5.30 per person, €2.50 per tent or car. Electricity €2.80. Oct. and Apr.-May prices 10% lower. Cash only. ❶

CLEARING YOUR OWN PATH

The short hikes around Corsican towns make it obvious to anyone that many of the island's sites and monuments are in serious need of repair. To remedy the situation and provide "active leisure" opportunities to local youth, an association called **Chantiers Jeunes Bénévoles** organizes trips to clean paths, beaches, and river banks, as well as restore anything from chapels and mills to old chestnut dryers. Instead of deploring the state of the Roman Chapelle St-Michelle in Sisco (p. 791) or the disappearance of old paths on what is now the GR20 hiking trail (p. 782), why not volunteer to help rehabilitate them?

Trips take place between March and November and can last 5 days, 2 weeks, or 1½ months; several take place during the long weekend of the Toussaint (Nov. 1). Usually, local youth ages 14-25 take part in the trips, but CJB redirects volunteers to local partners (mountain clubs, municipal governments, etc.), who may welcome older travelers. Basic room and board are covered by government subsidies.

Chantiers Jeunes Bénévoles has its headquarters in Ajaccio. (Direction du Sport et de la Jeunesse, Hôtel de Région, 22 cours Grandval BP 231 20187 Ajaccio. ☎50 38 94.) There is also a branch in Bastia (☎30 99 40). Call as early as possible to inquire about future projects.

Camping Barbicaja (☎/fax 52 01 17), 4km away. Take bus #5 from av. Ramaroni, past pl. de Gaulle, to Barbicaja and go straight (last bus July-Aug. 11:25pm, Sept.-June 7:30pm). Friendly, English-speaking staff manages this site, just steps from a popular beach. Campers enjoy snack bar, pizzeria, and shaded sites with views of the sparkling bay. Laundry €7. Reception 7am-10pm. Open mid-Apr. to mid-Oct. €5.70 per person, €2.50 per tent or car. Electricity €2.40. Cash only. ❶

FOOD

Though Ajaccio has no shortage of restaurants, the best option is the affordable, extensive **morning market** on **place du Marché.** The endless rows of stalls offer everything for the perfect Corsican picnic; a baguette, a wedge of goat cheese, and a portion of *charcuterie* (sausage). For dessert, pick up Corsican-grown white peaches or chestnut *canistrelli* (cookies) baked that morning. A smaller market opens at **place Abbatucci,** on cours Napoleon. (Both Tu-Su 8am-noon.) The **Monoprix** supermarket is at 31 cours Napoleon. (☎51 76 50. Open M-Sa July-Sept. 8:30am-8pm; Oct.-June 8:30am-7:20pm. AmEx/MC/V.) A **SPAR** supermarket is at 1 cours Grandval, on the first floor of the Diamant complex. (☎21 51 77. Open M-Sa 8:30am-8pm, Su 8:30am-12:30pm. MC/V.) In and around **place Foch** are inexpensive pizzerias, *panini* shops, and *crêperies*, as well as many spots serving local dishes. For the freshest seafood, try tiny **rue des Halles,** behind the tourist office.

Le Trou dans le mur, 1 bd roi Jérôme (☎21 49 22). Splendid salads and variations on Corsican classics. Le Trou brings in fresh ingredients from the morning market across the street. The "Trou dans le Mur" (with walnuts, cheese, bacon, and cantaloupe; €13) is sure to please. Vegetarians can enjoy the Corsican lasagna (€11) or the spinach canellonni (€11). Open daily 11am-2pm and 7-11pm; Sept.-May closed Su. MC/V. ❷

Da Mamma, passage Guinguetta (☎21 39 44), off cours Napoleon. A eucalyptus tree shades packed tables at this local favorite. Serves Corsican specialties at the end of a narrow side street. Try the *soupe de poisson* (fish soup). A €12 *menu* is offered until 9:30pm. Salads €8-14. Meat dishes €12-22. *Menus* €12-26. Open June-Aug. M and Su 7:30-10:30pm, Tu-Sa noon-2pm and 7:30-10:30pm; Sept.-May M and Su 7:30-10pm, Tu-Sa noon-2pm and 7:30-10pm. Reservations recommended. MC/V. ❸

Le Spago, rue Emmanuel Arène (☎21 15 71), off av. du 1er Consul. Modern metal tables and funky chairs adorn this bustling restaurant. Traditional *plats* like the *entrecôte bergère* (meat with Corsican cheese; €17) and other meat dishes (€13-24) will satisfy large appetites. Vegetarians can enjoy local eggplant dishes and salads (€10-13). Open M-F noon-2pm and 7:30-11pm, Sa 7:30-11pm. MC/V. ❸

Pizzeria Napoli, rue Bonaparte (☎21 32 79). This pleasant street-side terrace eatery caters to a late-night crowd with tasty pizzas. Grab a seat before 9pm for well-priced *menus* like the *Italien,* a trio of pizza, pasta, and dessert (€13). Pizza €7.30-9.30. Pasta €7-9.80. *Menus* €12-15. Open July-Aug. daily 6:45pm-6am; Sept.-June M-Th and Su 6:45pm-4am, F-Sa 6:45pm-6am. Cash only. ❷

SIGHTS

Though most of Ajaccio's museums are full of Napoleonic memorabilia, the city's best gallery generally ignores the dictator and turns to another military man. The **Musée Fesch,** 50-52 rue Cardinal Fesch, houses a collection of stunning 14th- to 19th-century Italian paintings, most of which were gathered by M. Fesch following military campaigns in Lombardy. At the time, it was the largest collection of paintings in the world. If you get tired of the numerous "Virgin and the Child" portraits—including Boticelli's groundbreaking representation of the two *standing*—focus on such treasures as Titian's sensual *Man with a Glove* and Veronese's erotic *Leda and the Swan.* The museum will be closed for renovations at the end of 2007. Next door, the **Chapelle Impériale** pays tribute to Napoleon's roots; the chapel's marble interior holds the tombs of many Bonapartes—though Napoleon himself is buried at Les Invalides in Paris. The altar displays a crucifix offered by Napoleon to his mother upon his 1799 return from military campaigns in Egypt. (☎21 48 17; www.musee-fesch.com. Open July-Aug. M 2-6pm, Tu-Th 10:30am-6pm, F 2-9:30pm, Sa-Su 10:30am-6pm; Sept. and Apr.-June Tu-Su 9:30am-noon and 2-6pm; Oct.-Mar. Tu-Sa 9:30am-noon and 2-5:30pm. Museum €5.35, students €3.80. Chapel €1.50/0.75, under 15 free. MC/V.)

The **Musée National de la Maison Bonaparte,** rue St-Charles, was the boyhood home of France's most famous megalomaniac before he left Corsica to pursue his studies. The sumptuous *casa Bonaparte* now showcases such memorabilia as a family tree made entirely from locks of hair. Don't miss the trapdoor through which Napoleon fled after his brief return in 1799. (☎21 43 89. Open Apr.-Sept. Tu-Su 9am-noon and 2-6pm; Oct.-Mar. M 2-4:45pm, Tu-Su 10am-noon and 2-4:45pm. Last tickets sold 45min. before closing. €5, ages 18-25 €3.50, under 18 free. MC/V.) The glittering **Salon Napoléonien,** pl. Foch, in the Hôtel de Ville, is restored in ornate 19th-century style and houses a lavish display of Napoleon's coronation portrait, funerary mask, and personal items. The room now hosts weddings and official city events. The empty glass display case in the smaller room once held a gold replica of Napoleon's olive-leaf coronation crown, created in 1869 entirely from donations given by the city's inhabitants. To their horror, it was stolen nine years ago during renovations and remains at large. The *Maison Bonaparte,* which originally entrusted the crown to the city's care, now displays a spray-painted model. (☎51 52 62. Open mid-June to mid-Sept. M-F 9-11:45am and 2-5:45pm; mid-Sept. to mid-June M-F 9-11:45am and 2-4:45pm. €2.30, students €1.50. Cash only.)

The **Musée à Bandera,** 1 rue Général Levie, chronicles Corsica's past from prehistory to WWII with a collection of maps, models, and elaborate dioramas. The galleries are supplemented by rotating exhibits on related subjects like "Corsican Women." Though the labels require a good understanding of French, the desk can provide an English booklet with translations of the museum's placards. Free guided tours are available with a week's notice. (☎51 07 34; histoirecorse@wanadoo.fr. Open July to mid-Sept. M-Sa 9am-7pm, Su 9am-noon; mid-Sept. to June M-Sa 9am-noon and 2-6pm. €4, students €2.60. Cash only.) The €10 **Passmusée,** valid for seven days, covers entry fees for all five of the sights listed above and is available at the tourist office or any participating museum.

NIGHTLIFE

Like most Corsican cities, Ajaccio saves wild nights for July and August, when the summer heat brings well-dressed tourists eager to show off their tans. You might want to trade in your hiking boots and trail-weary t-shirt for some classier duds before going out. In the *centre-ville,* the bar and lounge scene is popular year-round, but most young people drive to Bonifacio if they really want to party. In the summer, a few distant clubs and beaches that require car access provide Ajaccio's hottest nightlife, with weekly ragers every Sunday at **l'Ariadne** and **Capo di Fero** (pick up the free *Rendez-Vous* guide for details). Those with cash to spare can head to the **Casino,** bd. Pascal Rossini. (☎50 40 60. 18+. Open July to mid-Sept. daily 1pm-4am; Oct.-June M-Th 1pm-3am, F-Su 1pm-4am. AmEx/MC/V.)

Athena Bar, bd. Pascal Rossini (☎21 22 61). Blasts hip-hop and house to a palm-shaded terrace overlooking the sea in the center of Ajaccio's liveliest strip. Locals sip mixed drinks (€8.30) and enjoy ice cream treats (€5.90-8.90). Beer €3.40-5.30. Open daily June-Aug. 7am-2am; Sept.-May 9am-2am. Cash only.

Le Lamparo, résidence Diamant II, bd. Lantivy (☎51 47 05). Off bd. Pascal Rossini, this elegant *avant boîte* (pre-club scene) caters to a chic, older crowd with dark, rich wood and deep velvet chairs. House and lounge Sept.-Apr. F-Sa. Beer €2.50-5. Wine from €3.50. Mixed drinks €6-8. Open daily 7am-2am. AmEx/MC/V.

La Boca Loca, 2 rue de la Porta (☎06 24 57 43 87). Live flamenco, salsa, and jazz fill the red interior, which is plastered with Spanish bullfight posters. Try the tasty tapas (€3, €13.50 for 5) and strawberry mojitos (€6). Mixed drinks €5.50. Sangria €2.50 per glass, €13 per pitcher. Open Tu-Sa 7pm-2am. Cash only.

Irish Pub, 4 rue Notre Dame (☎21 63 22). Adorned with various national flags and run by Paulo, a friendly Corsican, there is nothing Irish about this bar–save the Guinness on tap. Live music, a laid-back ambience, and over 60 beers are a draw, but the bar is more touristy than most. Beer €3-6. Mixed drinks €7-12. Open daily 6pm-2am. MC/V.

FESTIVALS

In early July, Ajaccio kicks off a series of small summer festivals with the **Festival de Musique d'Ajaccio,** an annual orchestral celebration. August 15 brings the three-day **Fêtes Napoleon,** which commemorates the emperor's birth with war reenactments, a parade, ceremonies, and a huge *pyrosymphonie* (fireworks display). Friday night fever hits Ajaccio during the July and August **Shopping de Nuit,** when stores stay open until midnight on Fridays. July and August also has the popular concert series **Polyphonies de l'Eté,** when traditional Corsican music fills churches throughout Ajaccio (€8, €13 for 2, under 18 €5). For tickets or more information on any of these events, visit the tourist office.

CORSICA

IT'S ALL RELATIVE. Corsica: an island, a region, or what? It's often difficult to discern Corsica's official relation to France. An island it is for sure, but beyond that, things get a bit more complicated. While Corsica is commonly considered one of France's 26 regions, it is by law a territorial collective, which means it has an elected local government–or a certain "freedom of administration." The citizens of Corsica have attempted to gain more independence a number of times but have failed. Additionally, though separated from mainland France by the Ligurian Sea, Corsica is considered part of Metropolitan France, as opposed to an overseas department.

PORTO ☎04 95

Corsica's jagged volcanic mountains, lush pine groves, emerald valleys, and crystalline waters converge at the Gulf of Porto, a hiker's paradise. To the north, a marine reserve conceals grottoes and rare birds and fish. At the center of all the natural wonder lies the tiny town of Porto (POHR-toh; pop. 432), which consists almost entirely of hotels, souvenir shops, and tourist restaurants. Despite the camera-toting sightseers and the inconvenience of getting in and out without a car, Porto is a relatively inexpensive base for the region's hiking trails.

TRANSPORTATION

Buses: Autocars Ceccaldi (☎22 41 99) leave from the top of the main road by the pharmacy for **Ajaccio** (2½hr.; July to mid-Sept. daily 8:15am and 2:15pm, mid-Sept. to June M-Sa 8:15am and 10:45am; €11) and **Calvi** (2½hr.; July-Aug. daily at 10am, mid-May to June and Sept. M-Sa; €17). Purchase tickets on board. **Autocars Mordiconi** (☎48 00 04) leave from the parking lot at the base of the marina, in front of the mini golf course.

From July to mid-Sept. buses run to **Corte** (M-Sa daily at 2pm, €20) via **Evisa** (€17). Buy tickets on board. Buses don't run in bad weather.

Taxis: Taxis Ceccaldi-Ange Félix (☎26 12 92 or 06 85 41 95 89).

Car, Bike, and Scooter Rental: Porto Location (☎26 10 13), opposite Haut Porto's supermarkets. If the desk is unattended, ask at La Cigale. Cars from €58 per day, €298 per week; €298 deposit. 18+; at least 2yr. with license. Scooters €46/198; €610 deposit. Bikes €18/68. Open daily Apr.-Oct. 8:30am-7:30pm. MC/V.

ORIENTATION AND PRACTICAL INFORMATION

Porto consists of two clusters of buildings along a main road, which runs down the town's valley. The upper town, **Haut Porto** or **Quartier Vaita** (**Guaïta** in Corsican), is 800m up and inland from the coastal area, **Porto Marina,** where some 15 hotels and restaurants vie for waterfront space. A stream runs through town, separating shops and boutiques in the north from boat slips and beaches to the south. A pedestrian bridge at the river's mouth provides access to the opposite shorelines.

Tourist Office: (☎26 10 55; www.porto-tourisme.com), a short way up the main road from the *Tour Genoise* and the sea. Distributes topo-guide of 29 regional hikes for all skill levels (€2.50); bus schedules; and info on watersports, boat trips, and lodging. English spoken. Open July-Aug. M-Sa 9am-7pm, Su 9am-5pm; June and Sept. M-Sa 9am-7pm, Su 9am-1pm; Oct.-May M-Sa 9am-5pm.

Laundromat: Lavo 2000 (☎26 10 33), next to Hôtel Bon Accueil. Wash €7, dry €0.10 per min.; detergent €0.50. Open daily 9am-9pm. Cash only.

Police: Gendarmerie Maritime (☎51 75 21), on the port.

Pharmacy: (☎26 11 79), at the entrance to quartier Vaita.

Medical Services: (☎26 13 13). Open 3-6pm or in an emergency.

Post Office: (☎26 10 26), between the marina and *Haut Porto.* Open July-Aug. M-F 9am-12:30pm and 2-5pm, Sa 9-11:30am; Sept.-June M-F 9am-noon and 2-4pm, Sa 9-11am. **Postal Code:** 20150.

ACCOMMODATIONS AND CAMPING

Porto's abundance of indistinguishable hotels makes the town affordable most of the year, but in July and August prices skyrocket for even modest lodgings. Make summer reservations well ahead of time. Some of the cheapest accommodations in Corsica are *gîtes* in the pleasant village of Ota, a departure point for many hikes. From Porto Marina, head up the main road and take a hairpin left just before the supermarkets; follow signs to D124 and Ota (1¼hr.). The bus from Ajaccio to Porto also stops at Ota (30min., 2 per day, €3).

Bon Accueil (☎26 12 10; BA20150@aol.com), on the main road a bit farther from the port. A cheerful staff manages clean, colorful, and conveniently located rooms. All with bath, some with balconies. Social bar downstairs. Breakfast €6. Reception 7am-midnight. 1 room can sleep up to 6 guests (€79). Mid-June to Aug. singles and doubles €35-46; triples €50. Sept.-May prices drop by €5-10. AmEx/MC/V. ❸

Chez Felix (☎26 12 92), in Ota. Homey 4- to 8-bed dorms make this hostel feel more like someone's house. Kitchen access. Breakfast €6. Sheets €3. Dorms €13, *demi-pension* €32; doubles with bath and *demi-pension* €45-50. MC/V. ❶

Hôtel du Golfe (☎26 13 33), in the marina. 20m from the sea. A great budget option. Clean rooms have TVs and phones. Breakfast €7. Reception 7:30am-midnight. July-Aug. singles and doubles €42-48; June and Sept. €40-45; Oct.-May €34-38. MC/V. ❹

Le Lonca (☎26 16 44; hotel.lelonca@wanadoo.fr), route de la Marine, next to the post office. Well-kept, modern rooms with large bathrooms but little charm. Several have balconies overlooking the hills. All equipped with shower or bath, toilet, TV, and A/C. Breakfast €7. Reception 7am-10pm. Open Apr.-Oct. Aug. singles and doubles €70-75, with balcony €85; triples €80/105; quads €125. July and Sept. €45-55/65/55/65/85. Apr.-June €43-50/60/50/60/80. MC/V. ❺

Hôtel Brise de Mer (☎26 10 28; www.brise-de-mer.com), in a central location across from the tourist office. Shockingly bright bedspreads fill 20 clean, functional rooms. All with shower or bath, toilet, and balcony. Request a sea view. Includes a bar, TV room, and terrace restaurant. Breakfast €8. Reception daily 8am-10pm. Open Apr.-Oct. Aug. singles and doubles €60-65, *demi-pension* €105-110; triples €70-75; quads €80. July €50-55/95-100/60-65/70. June €47-52/92-97/57-62/67. Apr.-May and Sept.-Oct. €45-50/90-95/55-60/65. MC/V. ❺

Camping Les Oliviers (☎26 14 49; www.camping-oliviers-porto.com). Walk away from the marina to the end of *Haut Porto;* the campsite is just before the bridge leaving Porto towards Ajaccio on D81. Campers are hardly roughing it at this luxurious site, with a large swimming pool, pizzeria, restaurant, sauna, spa, fitness room, and tennis courts. The staff organizes 6- to 9-person canyoning trips (€50), waterside hiking trips (€31), and climbing excursions (€35), then rejuvenates trekkers with a 20min. seated massage (€15) or a 1hr. *shiatsu* massage (€51). Reception 8:30am-8:30pm. Open Apr.-Oct. €6.50-8.50 per person, €2.50-3.50 per tent, €2.50-3.50 per car. 4- to 8-person bungalows €370-885 per week. Electricity €3.50. Refrigerator space €4 per day, €20 per week. Showers free. AmEx/MC/V. ❶

Camping Le Sole e Vista (☎26 15 71), on the right before the supermarkets when entering Porto. 1km from the beach. Mostly attracts families. Secluded plots offer plenty of shade; nab one at the hilltop to watch the sun set over town. On-site bar and open daily 8am-11pm. Breakfast €5. Laundry €4.50. Reception 8am-10pm. Open Apr.-Sept. €5.50-6 per person, €2.40 per tent or car. Electricity €3.20. Cash only. ❶

CORSICA

FOOD

There are two adjacent supermarkets in *Haut Porto* on D81. One is **SPAR.** (☎26 11 25. Open July-Aug. M-Sa 8am-8pm, Su 8am-noon and 5-8pm; Sept.-June M-Sa 8:30am-noon and 3-7pm. MC/V.) The other is **Supermarché Banco.** (☎26 10 92. Open July-Aug. M-Sa 8am-8pm, Su 8:30am-12:30pm and 4-8pm; Sept.-Oct. and Apr.-June M-Sa 8am-noon and 3-7pm. MC/V.)

La Marine (☎26 10 19), on the main road across from the tourist office. One of the better deals in town makes it easy for hikers to bulk up on carbs. Youthful staff serves up tasty pizzas (€6-9), pastas (€6-8), and a series of extensive *menus* (€10-15) on a streetside terrace. The *menu Pizzaoli,* with choice of salad, pizza, and dessert, is a delicious €10 bargain. Open Apr.-Oct. daily 11:30am-2pm and 6:30-11pm. MC/V. ❷

La Tour Génoise (☎26 17 11), behind the aquarium. Mouthwatering cuisine served by an attentive staff. Spacious terrace at the base of the *Tour Génoise* is great for people-watching and enjoying fresh seafood (traditional Corsican *menus* €17-22). Wheelchair-accessible. Open Apr.-Oct. daily noon-2pm and 7-10:30pm. AmEx/MC/V. ❸

Le César (☎26 14 71), farther up the main road from the port. Restaurant and discotheque with basic fare. A young crowd fuels up on pizzas (€6.50-8) and sandwiches (€3-5) before hitting one of the town's only dance floors, below the restaurant. Open Apr.-Sept. daily noon-2pm and 7-10pm; disco open 11pm-5am. MC/V. ❷

SIGHTS AND HIKING

Hiking enthusiasts could spend weeks exploring the trails that radiate from the Gulf of Porto into the countryside. Though routes range in difficulty, every one provides an unforgettable vista of rugged peaks, verdant valleys, or seaside cliffs.

GORGES DE LA SPELUNCA. The old mule track from Ota to Evisa is a good option for hikers of all skill levels. This 5½-6hr. trail (round-trip) winds through the deep **Gorges de la Spelunca,** past 15th-century bridges and spots for picnics and swimming. To get to the Gorges from Calvi, take a left at the fork and walk 5km to Ota (see **Accommodations and Camping,** p. 769, for buses). Marked in orange, the trail begins at the top of the stairway to the left of the Mairie, but to reduce the walk you can pick it up farther down the main road at the first Genoese bridge (45min.). Another 15min. walk in the *maquis* to **Pont de Zaglia** offers incredible vistas of rose-colored cliffs plunging into the sea. The trail continues uphill until it reaches Evisa (3hr.). The 1hr. hike back to Porto is relatively easy, leaving you time to stop and smell the ever-present cistus (white and pale pink flowers) and lavender. There are no afternoon return buses from Evisa and only one from Ota.

Those with energy to spare can hike on to find chestnut trees and 50m pines in the **Forêt d'Aitone** between Evisa and Col. de Vergio. This trail leads directly out of the village of Evisa, part of the **Tra Mare e Monti,** and is famous for its *piscines naturelles*, swimming holes formed by pooling waterfalls. Follow the orange markers; the pools are slightly more than an hour from town. Beyond the pools, a more difficult and secluded trail to **Col de Vergio** (6-7hr.) takes hikers higher into the **Forêt Domanial,** where a *gîte d'étape* marks its intersection with the **GR20;** in order to do this hike, you'll have to spend the night in Evisa.

LES CALANCHES DE PIANA. The astounding rock formations of the Calanches resemble, in the words of Guy de Maupassant, a "menagerie of nightmares petrified by the whim of some extravagant god." Hikes in this alien landscape range from easy to extremely steep. **Piana,** picturesque with its white houses and beautiful church, is a good base for exploring the Calanches, as it is on the Ota-Ajaccio bus line. The **Château Fort,** a mild hike, begins 6km south of Porto on D81 and rewards minimum effort with expansive views of the gulf and the Calanches (25min.). Ask the Ota-Ajaccio bus driver to stop at **Tête de Chien** and take the path that runs along the mountain crest. A fortified castle overlooks the sea from a large promontory. A more demanding hike awaits 2km farther south, off D81. The marked trail, which begins near the stadium, climbs 900m to the 1294m **Capo d'Orto** (3hr.). From the summit, another trail leads back to Porto but is much more difficult. Hikers should consult the tourist office before attempting the descent.

The gratifying **Sentier des Muletiers** leaves directly from Piana and takes hikers on a quick forest ramble before heading into the heart of the looming rocks. Used until the mid-19th century, when Napoleon III opened the Porto-Piana road, this mule track is an excellent introductory hike. To catch the trail, head uphill immediately to the right of the *syndicat d'initiative;* 1km down the road, 100m after the Mezzanu bridge, take the trail on the right and then the downhill path on the left. Cross the stadium diagonally and walk over a footbridge to reach the right bank of the brook. Turn left onto chemin de Palani and walk for 10min. until you reach a stone wall, which is where the mule track begins (30min.). Another 30min. up the cliffside path lead to dizzying views of the Calanches between Piana and Porto; the trail continues down the other face and ends at a statue of the Virgin by D81 (15min.), which you can take to return to Porto (30min.). Those wishing for a longer hike (3hr. round-trip from Piana) should instead abandon the mule track after 50m and take a right into a small pine forest. The path reaches a small pass, crosses the Palani chestnut field, and arrives at the gorgeous **Fontaine d'Oliva Bona** (15min.). Continue downhill until the ruins of Dispensa, and return to Piana via the **Route des Calanches** (2.5km). As with Capo d'Orto, the return trail is steep and difficult, so retracing your steps might be a wise choice.

Southwest of Piana lies the spectacular **Capo Rosso,** a peninsula that marks the southern boundary of the Gulf of Porto. Perched at the top is the tiny **Tour de Turghiu,** accessible by a demanding 1½-2hr. scramble up the sun-drenched outcropping. The path begins easily enough, leading downhill past crumbling sheep pens and shepherds' huts. As you wind around to the base of the summit, the landscape, covered with underbrush, gives way to burnt-red rock. A nearly vertical 1hr. section leads straight to the tower at the apex of the peninsula. The stone structure is still in excellent condition, and if your calves can carry you up the narrow staircase, you'll find astounding views of the distant Calanches in the Gulf of Porto. To reach the trailhead from Piana, take D824 towards Arone; it is situated on a large bend just next to a tiny snack stand and parking lot (15min. by car, 1¼hr. by foot). There is little shade on this hike; wear plenty of sunscreen and bring extra water.

SCANDOLA. Off-limits to hikers and divers, the caves and wild terrain of the **Réserve Naturelle de Scandola** protect many species of Corsican wildlife and can be explored only by boat tour from Porto. Captain Jean Baptiste Rostini at **Porto Linea Excursions Maritimes** leads a 12-person boat into the reserve from Porto Linea, next to Hôtel Monte Rosso and behind the aquarium. The boat is small enough to access the caves and grottoes that dot the cliffside. *(☎26 11 50. Open Apr.-Oct. Reserve 2 days ahead in person. 3½hr. tour of Scandola €45; 1½hr. sunset tour of Les Calanches €25. Cash only.)* Less intimate but equally spectacular, **Nave Va,** near Hôtel Le Cyrnée, tours Scandola with 70- to 150-person boats. *(☎26 15 16. Open Apr.-Oct. Reserve 1 day ahead. 1½hr. tour of Les Calanches €23, 3hr. tour of Scandola €37, 5hr. trip to Les Calanques and Girolata €45. Cash only.)* Before reaching the reserve, both boats make a swimming stop at **Girolata,** a fishing village accessible only by boat. **Le Goëland,** on the marina next to the mini golf center, rents zodiacs and other small motor craft capable of holding up to 10 passengers. *(☎26 15 88 or 06 81 06 88 08. No permit necessary. €75 per ½-day, €115 per day; ID deposit. Gas €1.50 per L. Cash only.)*

CORSICA

BEACHES AND SIGHTS IN PORTO. The *raison d'être* for Porto's hotels and postcard shops is one of Corsica's oldest Genoese towers, the 1549 **Tour Génoise.** The sturdy lookout was built as part of an effort to improve the coastal defense system. From 1510 to 1620, around 100 towers were built to safeguard Corsica from unrelenting Turkish pirates—any *torregiano* (tower guard) who deserted his post was immediately put to death. *(Open daily July-Aug. 9am-9pm; Sept. and Apr.-May 11am-7pm. €2.50, under 12 free. Cash only.)* At the foot of the tower, the vaulted ceilings of the powder magazine provide a lofty home for the **Aquarium de la Poudrière.** Worth a brief stop, the aquarium identifies aquatic creatures from the Gulf of Porto and (in true French fashion) indicates which species are necessary for a good *bouillabaisse* (fish stew). Each tank is designed to recreate the aquatic regions found in the Scandola nature reserve; if you don't have the chance to see the local sea creatures on a dive or boat tour, the aquarium is definitely worth your euro. *(☎26 19 24. Open daily 8am-10pm; Sept. and Apr. 10am-7pm. €5.50. Ticket for aquarium and* Tour Génoise *€6.50. Cash only.)* The **Ecole de Plongée Generation Bleue,** on the north side of the marina, offers **scuba** and **snorkeling** excursions. The company makes use of 15 sites in the gulf and takes divers to the edge of the Scandola reserve. *(☎26 24 88 or 06 85 58 24 14; www.generation-bleue.com. Open May-Oct. Reserve 1 day ahead. 2hr. dives €40 with equipment. Snorkeling €15. Cash only.)* Directly across the channel from the *Tour Genoise* lies Porto's pebbly public **beach.** Surrounded by plunging cliffs and pounding surf, the broad crescent is the perfect place to catch some rays—just don't forget a beach mat, available at many souvenir shops.

CALVI ☎04 95

Often called Corsica's Côte d'Azur, Calvi (CAL-vee; pop. 5700) shares some of the best and worst traits of that better-known coastline. Beyond the souvenir shops and gleaming white yachts, Calvi has elements of the rugged beauty and solitude that make Corsica unique. A star-shaped citadel above town, endless cliffside beaches, and rocky peaks are a pull for visitors both high- and low-rolling. Rollicking nightlife draws party-seekers from all over the island, and a series of beachfront campsites make Calvi a choice destination on every backpacker's itinerary.

TRANSPORTATION

Flights: Aéroport de Calvi Ste-Catherine (CLY; ☎65 88 88), 7km southeast of town. **Air France** (www.airfrance.com) and subsidiary **Air Corse Mediterranée** (☎65 88 60 or 08 20 82 08 20; www.aircorsica.com) fly to **Lille, Lyon, Marseille, Nice,** and **Paris.**

Trains: pl. de la Gare (☎65 00 61), near Port de Plaisance. Open daily June to mid-Sept. 6:30am-9:30pm; mid-Sept. to June 7am-9pm. Purchase tickets at station. To **Bastia** (3½hr., 2 per day, €19), **Corte** (2½hr., 4 per day, €16), and **Ile Rousse** (1hr., 2 per day, €4.50). In summer, **Tramways de la Balagne** also sends trains to **Ile Rousse** (1hr., June-Sept. 10 per day, €4.50).

Buses: Autocars Ceccaldi (☎22 41 99) depart from the Super U and head to **Porto** (2½hr.; July-Aug. daily 3pm, mid-May to Sept. M-Sa 3pm; €17). **Les Beaux Voyages,** av. Wilson (☎65 11 35), leaves from the agency at pl. Porteuse d'Eau, by the tourist office, which sells tickets. Open May-Oct. M-Sa 9am-noon and 2-7pm; Nov.-Apr. M-F 9am-noon and 3-7pm. Buses to **Bastia** (2½hr., M-Sa 1 per day at 6:45am, €17) via **Ile Rousse** (25min., €3.50). **Corse Voyages** (☎21 06 30) runs buses to **Ajaccio** (4hr., M-Sa 1 per day, €24) via **Ponte-Leccia** (€9). Buses depart from pl. Porteuse d'Eau. Buy tickets on board.

Ferries: For info and tickets, call **Agence TRAMAR** (☎65 01 38), quai Landry, in Port de Plaisance. Open July-Sept. M-F 9am-noon and 2-6pm, Sa 9am-noon; Oct.-June M-F 8:30am-noon and 2-5:30pm, Sa 8:30am-noon. MC/V. Both **SNCM** (☎65 17 77; 3hr.; 7 per week; €30-42, ages 12-25 €15-27) and **Corsica Ferries** (☎65 43 21; 3hr., 5 per week, €20-38) send boats to **Nice** and **Marseille** and have offices near Capitainerie du Port de Commerce. Open 2hr. before boat arrivals. Book early for best prices.

Taxi: At the train station. ☎65 03 10 or 65 30 36. Airport to town center €15-25. 24hr.

Car Rental: Europcar, av. de la République, across from the train station. (☎65 10 35, airport 65 10 19). €69 per day, €285 per week. 21+. Open May-Sept. M-Sa 8am-7pm. AmEx/MC/V. **Hertz,** 2 rue Maréchal Joffre (☎65 06 64, airport 65 02 96). €89 per day, €295 per week. 21+. Under-25 surcharge €29 per day. Open July-Aug. daily 8am-8pm; Sept.-June M-Sa 8am-8pm. AmEx/MC/V.

Bike and Scooter Rental: Loc Motos, av. Christophe Colomb (☎47 31 30; www.calvimoto.com). July-Aug. bikes €20 per day, scooters from €40 per day; Sept.-June €10/30; cheaper deals for 3, 5, or 7 days. Open daily 9am-9pm. MC/V.

ORIENTATION AND PRACTICAL INFORMATION

The city is easy to walk, connected by one main road that follows the curve of the coast and changes names several times, from **boulevard Wilson** between the citadel and the post office, to **avenue de la République,** and to **avenue Christophe Colomb** when leaving the city. The pedestrian, souvenir-shop lined **rue Clemenceau** begins from **place Porteuse d'eau,** below the post office, and runs up to the citadel, below bd. Wilson, parallel to the port. **Quai Landry** is a café-lined walk along the water that connects the ferry port at one end with the Port de Plaisance at the other.

Tourist Office: Port de Plaisance (☎65 16 67; www.balagne-corsica.com). From the back of the train station, turn left past the end of the tracks. On 2nd fl. of the 1st building on the right. Staff offers maps and city guides and suggests private guides for tours of the citadel or the city. Open June to mid-Sept. daily 9am-12:30pm and 2:30-7pm; May M-Sa 9am-noon and 2-6pm; mid-Sept. to Apr. M-F 9am-noon and 2-6pm.

Laundromat: Laverie, av. Christophe Colomb, in Super U Plaza. Wash €6, dry €4. Open daily 7:30am-10:30pm. **Calvi Clean,** bd. Wilson, between the citadel and the post office. Wash €6, dry €5. Open daily 7am-10pm.

Police: Port de Plaisance (☎65 44 77 or 06 11 60 17 96), next to the tourist office.

Internet Access: Cyber-Calvi, av. de la République (☎33 71 35; www.cyber-calvi.com). Across the street from the train station and a few steps to the left. €1.50 per 15min., €5 per hr. Open daily 10am-noon and 3-7pm. Cash only. **Calvi 2B Informatique,** av. Santa Maria (☎65 19 25), 2 streets above pl. Porteuse d'Eau, near Hôtel Regina. €1 per 20min. Open June-Sept. M-F 9:15am-12:30pm and 2-9pm, Sa 9:15am-9pm, Su 3:30-9pm; Oct.-May M-Sa 9:15am-noon and 2-7pm. **Café de L'Orient** (☎65 00 16), on quai Landry. €4 per 30min., €6 per hr., €10 per 2hr. Open daily Apr.-Sept. 9:30am-10pm; café open until 2am. MC/V.

Post Office: bd. Wilson (☎65 90 90). Open July-Aug. M-F 8:30am-6pm, Sa 8:30am-noon; Sept.-June M-F 8:30am-5:30pm, Sa 8:30am-noon. **Postal Code:** 20260.

ACCOMMODATIONS AND CAMPING

Though compact, Calvi packs in many pricey three- and four-star hotels. A few budget options exist, albeit farther from the center of town. In the summer, inexpensive options fill up quickly; reserve far in advance to get the best prices. Calvi has one of the only hostels in all of Corsica, a *"Relais International,"* but it is tucked far in the hills above the city. The best bet may be camping; a series of sites lines the coast toward Bastia. In the summer, most are connected to the center by the slow, fifty-year-old *Tramways de la Balagne*, which drivers humorously call the TGV—for *"trains à grande vibration."*

Il Tramonto, rte. de Porto R.N. 199 (☎65 04 17; www.hotel-iltramonto.com). From the citadel, walk 800m with the sea on your right. Though far from town, Il Tramonto enjoys a prime hilltop location. 18 simple rooms, half with balconies and views of the lighthouse and the Girolata peninsula. Walls are thin, so be prepared for noise. All with bath. Breakfast €5. Reception daily 7:30am-midnight. Open Apr. to mid-Oct. Singles and doubles Aug. €53; July €50; Sept. and June €40; Oct. and May €35; Apr. €30. Rooms with balcony €5 extra, €7 in Aug. Studios and apartments available July-Aug. €458-763 per week; Sept.-June €244-350 per week. Extra bed €13-16. MC/V. ❹

Hôtel Les Arbousiers, rte. de Pietramaggiore (☎65 04 47). Take the 2nd road on the right along av. de la République, after the Super U. 40 rooms and a beautiful courtyard await at Calvi's largest budget hotel. Spiraling wooden staircase, lounge, 2nd fl. breakfast terrace, and elegant 1st fl. restaurant. All rooms have TV, private bath, phone, and balcony. Breakfast €7.50. Free parking. Open May-Sept. July-Aug. singles €46; doubles €54. Sept. and June €38/42. May €36/38. MC/V. ❹

Hôtel du Centre, 14 rue Alsace-Lorraine (☎65 02 01), behind rue Clemenceau. Its location in the heart of Calvi compensates for functional white rooms with basic furniture and hard beds. Friendly manager keeps a sizable stack of dog-eared English-, French-, and German-language paperbacks. Breakfast €6; order the night before. Free luggage storage. Reception daily 8am-9pm. Open Apr. to early Nov. Singles and doubles June-July and Sept. €40-49; Aug. €55-57; Apr.-May and Oct.-Nov. €35-49. Cash only. ❹

Camping International, RN 197 (☎65 01 75), 1km from town. From the train station, walk down av. de la République past Super U and Hôtel L'Onda; after the mini golf sign, turn right (15min.). Lively atmosphere, plenty of shade, and international crowd. Flowering trees surround bar and pizzeria (pizzas €6-13). Showers free. Open Apr.-Oct. July-Aug. €6 per adult, €3 per child under 7, €3.50 per tent, €1.70 per car. Sept.-Oct. and Apr.-June €4.80/3/2.30/1.50. MC/V. ❶

Camping Les Castors, rte. de Pietramaggiore (☎65 13 30; www.castors.fr). The closest campsite to town (700m) is well equipped, with a snack bar and a large pool and water

▲▲⌂ ACCOMMODATIONS		🍴 FOOD		★ NIGHTLIFE AND ENTERTAINMENT	
Camping International, **11**		A Boca Loca, **4**		Acapulco, **16**	
Camping Les Castors, **15**		A Scola, **1**		La Camargue, **13**	
Hôtel Les Arbousiers, **10**		Mar a Beach, **14**		Chez Tao, **2**	
Hôtel du Centre, **5**		U Fornu, **7**		Club 24, **9**	
Il Tramonto, **3**		U Minellu, **6**		L'Escale, **12**	
				Havanita, **8**	

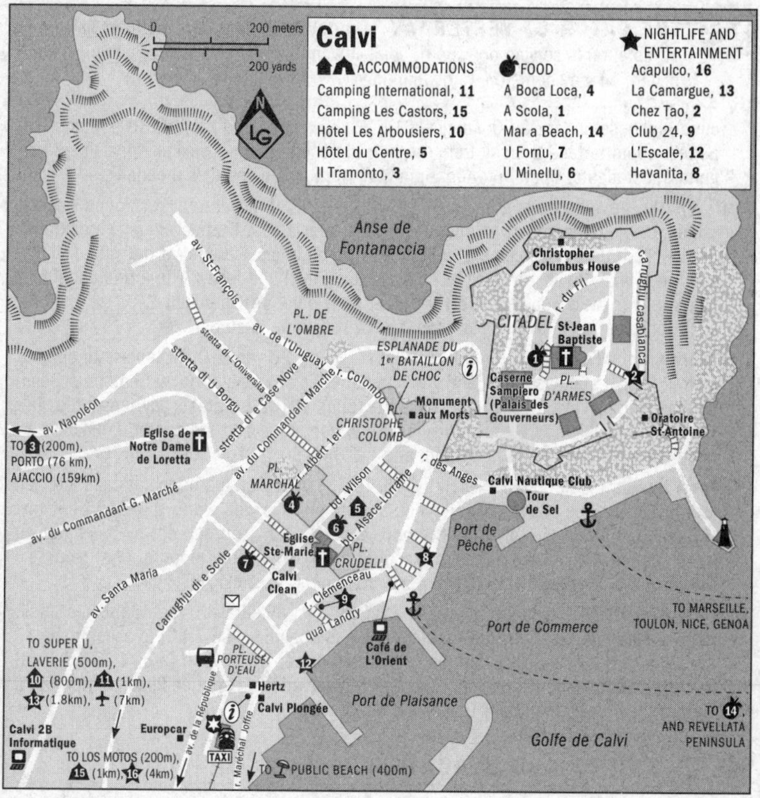

slide, and attracts many families. June and Sept. €7.60 per person; July-Aug. €9.20; Nov.-May and Oct. €6.30. Tents 2.90/3.95/2.70. MC/V. ●

🍴 FOOD

Aside from street-side *panini* vendors and a smattering of pizzerias, cheap pickings are slim in Calvi. For the best deal on sandwiches try the **Super U** supermarket, av. Christophe Colomb. (☎ 65 04 32. Open July-Aug. M-Sa 8:30am-8:30pm, Su 8:30am-1pm; early Sept. and June M-Sa 8:30am-8pm; mid-Sept. to May M-F 8:45am-7:30pm. AmEx/MC/V.) A handful of restaurants set up tables in the lovely **citadel**, with appropriately towering prices. Below, narrow **rue Clemenceau** is filled with specialty food shops and a small covered market beside the **Eglise Ste-Marie.** (Open daily 8am-noon.) **Quai Landry** is packed with pricey cafés, *brasseries*, seafood spots, and *glaciers*. Most restaurants directly on the beach are overpriced but are a good deal for cheap beach chairs (€7) and drinks. **Le Bout du Monde,** quai Landry, is the best of these, sometimes serving dinner in the sand by the water (book one day ahead). For moderately expensive but high quality meals, the pedestrian alleys between the port and bd. Wilson have the best food and ambience.

🍴 **A Boca Loca,** pl. Marchal (☎ 06 26 77 67 42). At the back of pl. Marchal, this intimate restaurant and tapas bar ranges from cheap (*menu* €15; mixed drinks €5) to very

> **TIP** **THE CATCH OF YESTERDAY.** On days following bad weather, beware of restaurants serving *poisson du jour*–it won't be as fresh as they claim, since fishermen stay home on windy mornings.

cheap (cheeseburger €8.50; sangria €1.50). The terrace and Mexican-style interior are perfect spots to take a break from the port atmosphere and Corsican specialties. Live guitar most nights. Open Apr.-Aug. 5pm-2am; for lunch if you call ahead. ❷

U Minellu, traverse de l'Eglise (☎65 05 52). The staff moves quickly around packed tables, serving generous portions of Corsican specialties. Terrace offers a break from tourist-filled rue Clemenceau. Excellent €17 *menu* offers the best of the island. Begin your meal with the savory *tarte aux blettes* (beet tart) and follow with a traditional *plat* like *sanglier* (wild boar) served with fresh corn polenta. Open July-Sept. daily 6:30-11:30pm; Mar.-June M-Sa 11am-2pm and 7-10:30pm. Cash only. ❸

U Fornu, bd. Wilson (☎65 27 60). A local staple for 26 years. Quiet tables surrounded by trees hug a staircase. Pink and gray interior adds an elegant touch. Seafood specialties like shrimp ravioli (€16) and baked octopus (€16) are artistically presented. The €16 *menu* highlights Corsican cuisine with *soupe corse* and *storzapreti* (spinach and fresh cheese). Open M-Sa noon-2pm and 7-11pm, Su 7-11pm. Cash only. ❸

Mar A Beach, plage de la Revellata (☎65 48 30). A day on the beach at this laid-back restaurant, on the spectacular Revellata peninsula, is well worth the €10 boat taxi (Colombo line leaves daily from the port; ☎65 32 10). You can eat by the water on beach chairs (€8 per day). Dishes prepared according to "the mood of Chef Mousse." *Crêpes* €2-5. Meats €11-19. Open Apr.-Oct; hours vary. AmEx/MC/V. ❸

A Scola (☎65 07 09), in the citadel across from the Cathédrale St-Jean Baptiste. Small, elegant *salon de thé* offers delectable homemade pastries (€6-7.80) to accompany 17 varieties of tea (€3-3.20). Salads, omelettes, other light lunch fare (€10-16), and mouthwatering melted chocolate cake (€6.50) served in an antique-filled interior with a view of the coast. Open daily 9am-9pm. MC/V. ❸

SIGHTS AND BEACHES

CITADEL. Calvi's remarkable citadel, looming over Port de Plaisance, is both a symbol of the city's tumultuous history and the centerpiece of modern life. The 18th-century inscription, *"civitas Calvi semper fidelis"* ("the city of Calvi is always faithful"), crowning the entrance, was bestowed on Calvi by the Genoese in thanks for five centuries of loyalty. Just inside the entry, the tourist office annex distributes audio tours and free maps of the citadel. Round the first corner and climb the stairs to reach the citadel's center, dominated by the austere Palais des Gouverneurs. The original *palais* was the oldest building in the citadel, until lightning struck its powder store and the Genoese had to rebuild it.

Like several other Mediterranean towns, Calvi claims to be the birthplace of Christopher Columbus. The theory is that Calvi expatriate Antonio Calvo returned to his hometown in the 15th century to enlist recruits for the Genoese navy. His nephew Christopher caught his eye, so Calvo brought him to Genoa. A few other tenuous leads support the speculation. Calvi is quick to note that Columbus used Corsican dogs in warfare and preferred to keep company with *calvais* officers instead of the Genoese. A plaque in the northern end of the citadel marks the ruins of the house where Columbus was supposedly born. The citadel's other famous residence, the Giubegga house, sheltered Napoleon and his family in 1793, when they fled political opponents in Ajaccio. *(☎36 74 14. Open June-Sept. M-Sa 10am-5pm. Last entry 1hr. before closing. 1½hr. tours in English, French, German, and Italian; €7. MC/V.)*

REVELLATA PENINSULA. The first place to head to with a rented bike or scooter in Calvi is the *presqu'île* of the Girolata, an impressive promontory boasting a lighthouse and sensational isolated beaches. From the citadel, head uphill and away from the town with the sea on your right; the peninsula is only a few kilometers away. Its roads are unbelievably bumpy and only get worse as you go, so it is best to park early and hike around the peninsula. On your way back, a right at the stop sign leads to a chapel with a must-see view of the entire bay of Calvi.

OTHER SIGHTS. Calvi and the surrounding area abound with long stretches of sandy beaches and rocky cliffs, making for some of the best **scuba diving** on the coast. Calvi boasts two particularly well-known sites: **la Bibliothèque,** where rock formations resemble stocked bookshelves, and **le B-17,** a sunken WWII bomber with wings and propellers still intact. **Calvi Plongée,** below the tourist office, runs dives to both sites. High winds sometimes limit dives. *(☎65 33 67 or 06 79 63 57 93; www.calviplongee.com. Open Apr.-Oct. daily 8am-8pm. Reservations highly recommended July-Aug. Dives 20-30min.; 2-4 per day. July-Aug. €35-39, first-timers €43; equipment included. Night dives on request €47. Snorkeling trips €17 with equipment. Apr.-June and Sept.-Oct. €30-34/38/42/12. Cash only.)* Closer to shore, shallow water allows beachgoers to walk many meters from the coast, and strong winds make for great **windsurfing.** The staff at the **Calvi Nautique Club,** near the port, will have you skimming the waves in no time. *(☎65 10 65; www.calvinc.org. Open daily July-Aug. 9am-noon and 1-7pm; Sept.-June 9am-noon and 2-5pm. Windsurfing equipment €15 per hr.; sailboats €32, €230 deposit; kayaks €10-15 per hr. A ticket system allows you to exchange boats and try different types. MC/V.)* If the 6km expanse of **public beach** gets too windy, the rocks surrounding the citadel offer secluded and sun-drenched shelter, as well as a fair number of topless (and bottom-less) sunbathers. The **Tramways de la Balagne** (see **Transportation,** p. 773) run to more remote coves farther out of town.

CORSICA

NIGHTLIFE

Lively bars along **Port de Plaisance** are perfect people-watching venues on sultry summer nights. Two open-air nightclubs on the road to Ile Rousse give St-Tropez a run for its money in the summer: locals come from all over the island for big-name DJs and wild theme parties. Signs posted around town advertise party nights at different spots along the northern coast. In the summer, performers from around the world augment Calvi's nightlife scene with large outdoor festivals.

Acapulco, rte. de Calenzana (☎65 08 03), halfway between Calvi and Ile Rousse. The hottest club in Calvi, with five floors of dancing and drinking, a restaurant, and enough neon lights to keep the young and beautiful crowd happy. DJs Pew-wee and Cuba keep this *boîte* pumping. Free *navette* (shuttle) runs in summer (call ahead). Open May and July-Aug. daily 11pm-dawn; *soirées exceptionelles* Oct. 31 and some nights in winter.

La Camargue (☎65 08 70), 25min. up N197 by foot. Spinning beams of light projected into the night sky lead the way to one of Calvi's hippest clubs. The scantily clad come early and linger late amid 2 large dance floors, waterfalls, outdoor pools, large projection screens, and a jungle-themed bar. An over-30 crowd relives its glory days (albeit fully dressed) in the adjacent piano bar. Free shuttles depart for La Camargue from the port parking lot near the tourist office. Cover €10; includes 1 drink. Big-name events have higher covers. Open May-Sept. daily 10pm-5am. MC/V.

L'Escale, Port de Plaisance (☎65 10 75). Locals yield the dance floor of this popular café to more casually dressed tourists in summer. Top 40 and French classics can be enjoyed with a *piscine* (champagne with ice) or other drinks (€6-9) on the terrace.

Chez Tao (☎65 00 73; www.cheztao.com), in the citadel. Corsica's oldest night spot caters to a swanky crowd with creative mixed drinks (€10-12), wine (€6), and *aperitifs* (€7) served on a candlelit terrace overlooking the sea. Don't be fooled by the subdued appearance: this piano bar turns wild after 1am, when the tables are cleared away and DJs spin disco, funk, house, and 80s until dawn. Happy hour nightly 7-10pm. Open June-Sept. daily 7pm-5am. MC/V.

Club 24, Port de Plaisance (☎06 15 03 65 82). A modest dance floor and excellent DJs keep the party going with an eclectic range of music at this well-known club on the port. Mixed drinks €6-8. Open mid-Mar. to Dec. daily 10pm-2am. AmEx/MC/V.

Havanita, Port de Plaisance (☎04 95 65 00 37). Swaying palms and sexy salsa will remind you of another island. A young crowd knocks back Cuban mixed drinks (€7). Wine €4. Beer €4-6. Happy hour nightly 6-8:30pm. Open Apr.-Oct. daily 6pm-2am.

FESTIVALS

In June, Calvi draws up-and-coming musicians to the **Festival du Jazz** with free lodging and meals. In exchange, they perform in 15 concerts over a two-week period. Bars along the port de Plaisance host nightly performances and jam sessions. (☎65 00 50; €10.) In mid-July, big-name artists come to the open-air music festival **Calvi on the Rocks,** at the base of the citadel. MTV often collaborates, attracting some of the best musicians and DJs in Europe. (www.calviontherocks.com. Contact the tourist office for more information. Nightly pass €15, 4-night Festival Pass €45.) In mid-September, international artists come together for **Rencontres Polyphoniques,** a festival celebrating the worldwide tradition of chanting music. Groups from far-flung locations give individual performances in the citadel, then end the festival with a spectacular joint concert led by *A Fileta*, one of Corsica's best-known traditional groups. (☎65 23 57. Tickets €13-20, under 13 free.) In late October or early November, Calvi pulls out all the stops for the colorful **Festival du Vent,** a three-day celebration of Corsican tradition, art, music, and sport, with a special emphasis on the environment. The festivities, which bring 40,000 visitors, are Calvi's most exciting event. (For more info, contact the Association du Festiventu at ☎04 53 20 93 00 or 01 53 20 93 05; www.lefestivalduvent.com. Tickets €15-20.)

CORSICA

ILE ROUSSE ☎04 95

In 1765, the clever Pascal Paoli decided to build a French port that would give him access to mainland France and divert trade from Genoese-dominated Calvi. Thus, Ile Rousse (EEL ROOSS; pop. 2500) was founded largely out of spite. Though both towns eventually came under French control, their historic rivalry was furthered when Calvi constructed an impressive marina, airport, and other tourism-attracting projects. Today, however, Ile Rousse is a perfect hub for sunbathers and watersports enthusiasts tired of flashy Calvi; it also offers hikers leisurely trails in the countryside of the Balagne. Like much of Corsica's western coast, the town is lined with white-sand beaches that are overrun in July and August. For less crowded spots, take the train toward Calvi and get off when you see an appealing stretch. To take advantage of the town's beaches, stop by the **Club Nautique,** across from the train station, and rent a kayak or catamaran. You can visit Ile Rousse's namesake isles, just off the coast, and access some of the region's best snorkeling. (☎60 22 55; www.cnir.org. Kayaks €12 per hr. Catamarans €31-39 per hr. 2hr. kayak tour of coastal islands €30 per person. Open Jan.-Nov. daily 10am-6pm. Cash only.)

Since Ile Rousse tends to attract the well-moneyed, there's only one budget hotel in town. To find **Hôtel le Grillon ❸,** 10 av. Paul Doumer, go straight on av. Piccioni and take a left. The 16 pastel rooms, some with a balcony and views of the sea (request in advance), were recently refurnished. All are moderately sized and well-equipped with bath, TV, phone, and A/C. (☎60 00 49; fax 60 43 69. Breakfast €5.40. Reception daily 6am-10pm. Reserve far ahead. Open Mar.-Oct. Singles €40, *demi-pension* €53; doubles €45/83; triples €53/111. Aug. *demi-pension* obligatory. MC/V.) An abundance of campsites stretches along the Balagne coast. Sites appear frequently; hop off the train when you see an enticing one. Those set on staying closer to the center of things should head to **Les Oliviers ❶**, in Ile Rousse, which is 800m from downtown on av. Paul Doumer, the main road to Bastia. A bar and pizzeria provide food for happy campers. Two- and four-person bungalows are available for rent. (☎60 19 92; lesolivierskalliste@wanadoo.fr. Laundry €6. July-Aug. closed to cars after 11pm. Open Apr.-Oct. €6.50 per person, €3.50 per tent, €2.50 per car. Electricity €3.50. *Chalet* doubles €85. Bungalows July-Aug. €530 per week; Sept.-June €350. MC/V.) From St-Florent, save yourself the trek from the train station and ask the bus driver to stop at the campsite.

The city's small, signature covered market off **place Paoli** has brought the freshest produce to town since 1850. Now a historical monument, its stalls still burst with ripe local fruits, olives, and the catch of the day. (Open daily 7am-1pm.) The **Casino** supermarket on the Palais des Allées picks up where the market leaves off. (☎60 24 23. Open July-Aug. M-Sa 8:30am-8pm, Su 8:30am-1pm; Sept.-June M-F 8:30am-12:30pm and 3-7:30pm, Sa 8:30am-7:30pm. MC/V.) *Brasseries* and *crêperies* around pl. Paoli fill with diners hungry for inexpensive pizzas, sandwiches, and *crêpes*. For a quieter, sit-down meal, try **U Fucone ❷**, on rue Paoli, down the street from pl. Paoli. This welcoming spot has a *menu* with options like seafood salad, shark steak, and flan (€15), as well as all-you-can-eat *moules-frites* (mussels and fries, €12). The English-speaking staff also serves 10 kinds of pizza (€8.50-9). In winter, the chef serves Alsatian and Savoyard specialties. (☎60 16 67. Open daily May-Sept. 11:30am-2pm and 6:30-11pm; Oct.-June hours vary. MC/V.)

SNCM sends **ferries** to Marseille (5-9hr.; 2 per week; €40-58, students €25-45) and Nice (3-10hr.; 2-7 per week; €35-47, students €20-32). Call Agence CCR on av. J. Calizi for info. (☎60 09 56. Open June-Aug. M-Tu and Th-F 9am-noon and 2-6pm, W 9am-noon and 2:30-6pm, Sa 9am-noon; Sept.-May M-F 8:30am-noon and 2-5:30pm.) The train station provides service to Ajaccio, Bastia, and Calvi. (☎60 00 50. Open daily July-Sept. 6am-8:30pm; Oct.-June 8am-9:30pm.) Tramways de la Balagne **trains** hug the coast on the way to Calvi (50min., June-Sept. 9 per day, €5.10; MC/V). Purchase tickets on board or for less at the station. The train stops at every beach and campsite along the route. The **Aregno Plage** and its lively campsite are three stops from Ile Rousse.

Two kilometers across, Ile Rousse is easy to navigate. To get to the tiny **tourist office** from the train station or ferry depot, walk right for 5min. to the far side of pl. Paoli. (☎60 04 35; www.balagne-corsica.com. Open June-Sept. M-Sa 9am-7pm, Su 10am-1pm and 5-7pm; Oct.-May M-F 9am-noon and 2-6pm. Cash only.) Find **Internet** access at **Movie Store,** rte. de Calvi, across from the Casino supermarket. (☎65 47 97. €2 per 15min., €3 per 30min., €5 per hr. €2 per hr. when bought in bulk. Open M-Sa 10am-2am, Su 2pm-2am. Cash only.) The **post office** is on rte. de Monticello, to the left of the supermarket. (☎63 05 50. Open July-Aug. M-F 8am-6pm, Sa 8am-noon; Sept.-June M-F 8:30am-5pm, Sa 8:30am-noon.) **Postal Code:** 20220.

CORTE (CORTI) ☎04 95

Dynamic Corte (KOHR-tay; pop. 6000, when school is in 10,000) sits near the center of the island between snow-capped peaks. The location is fitting, as Corte is considered the intellectual and political heart of Corsica. The home of the island's university, *Universita di Corsica*, the town gave birth to Pascal Paoli's constitution and remains the center of Corsica's nationalist cause. Locals have made a serious effort to keep Corsican traditions alive; most speak Corse, a language similar to Italian dialects, in addition to French. It's easy to understand the pride of this inland city—perched above the convergence of three rivers, Corte is an eyeful of plunging cliffs and jagged summits, which provide Corsica's best hiking.

TRANSPORTATION. Trains depart from the roundabout at av. Jean Nicoli and N193 (☎00 80 17; station open M-Sa 6:30am-9pm, Su 7:45am-9pm), for Ajaccio

(2½hr., 3 per day, €13), Bastia (2hr., 4 per day, €12), and Calvi (2½hr., 2 per day, €14) via Ponte-Leccia. Eurocorse Voyages **buses** (☎31 73 76) leave from Brasserie Le Majestic, 19 Cours Paoli, for Ajaccio (1¾hr., M-Sa 2 per day, €11) and Bastia (1¼hr., M-Sa 1-2 per day, €10). In July and September Autocars Mordiconi (☎48 00 04) leave from the train station for Porto (2¾hr., M-Sa 1 per day, €19). **Taxis Salviani** can be reached at ☎46 04 88 or 06 03 49 15 24. Rent **cars** at Europcar, next to the train station. (☎46 06 02. From €91 per day, €365 per week; credit card deposit. Insurance included. 22+. Open M-F 8am-noon and 2:30-6pm, Sa 8am-noon. MC/V.)

ORIENTATION AND PRACTICAL INFORMATION. The train station is disagreeably located amidst major roads, 20min. away from hotels or campsites, but don't despair: the *centre-ville* is pleasant and easy to navigate. To reach it from the station, turn right onto N193, cross the bridge, and take a left, crossing a second bridge onto av. Jean Nicoli. Follow the road until it ends at **cours Paoli,** Corte's main drag (it is advisable to look closely at the train station's map before setting off). A left turn leads to **place Paoli,** the town center. At the top right corner, climb the cobblestones of the ascending **rue Scolisca** to reach the citadel, the museum, and the **tourist office,** which provides bus and train schedules and a French-English brochure. (☎46 26 70; www.corte-tourisme.com. Open July-Aug. M, W, Sa 10am-5pm; Tu, Th, F 9am-7pm; Su 10am-6pm. Sept. and June M-Sa 9am-6pm. Apr.-May M-F 9am-noon and 2-6pm. Oct.-Mar. M-F 9am-noon and 2-6pm. Call ahead; hours are subject to change.) Other services include: **Bureau Information Jeunesse de Corte,** rampe Ste-Croix (☎46 80 35; www.a-rinascita.com; open M-Th 8:30am-noon and 1-6pm, F 8:30am-noon and 1:30-5pm); a **laundromat** at **Speed Laverie,** allée du 9 Septembre, in the shopping plaza behind Mr. Bricolage (☎06 82 56 08 31; wash €5, dry €2; open daily 8am-9pm); **police** (☎46 04 81), southeast of town on N200; a **hospital,** allée du 9 Septembre (☎45 05 00); **Internet** access at **Grand Café du Cours,** 22 cours Paoli (☎46 00 33; €0.15 per min., €7 per hr.; free Wi-Fi with a purchase; open daily 7am-2am), and **Le Bar Video-Games,** av. de Président Pierucci (☎47 32 86; €3 per 30min., €5 per hr.; open M-Sa 8am-2am), as well as free **Wi-Fi** with a purchase in several coffee shops, including **Café de France,** pl. Padoue (☎46 20 49; open daily 6am-2am); and a **post office,** av. du Baron Mariani (☎46 81 20; open M-F 8am-12:30pm and 1:30-5pm, Sa 8am-noon). **Postal Code:** 20250.

ACCOMMODATIONS AND CAMPING. Near the train station, **Hôtel-Residence Porette (H-R) ❷,** 6 allée du 9 Septembre, is a no-frills hotel in converted low-income housing. Head left and uphill from the station; at the roundabout, take a right. The hotel is across from the stadium (100m). Rooms overlooking the garden are generally larger, but you'll pay €10 extra in high season. A sauna (€4), weight room, and restaurant are welcome amenities. (☎45 11 11; www.hotel-hr.com. Breakfast buffet €6. Laundry. Reception 24hr. Reservations recommended. Singles €25-30, with bath €42; doubles €30-32/42; triples and quads €65. AmEx.) A more expensive option is **Hôtel de la Paix ❹,** av. du Général de Gaulle, past Hôtel de la Poste and away from the tourists. Pleasant rooms here range from narrow to enormous, and all have toilet, shower or bath, and phone; some have TV. (☎46 06 72. Breakfast €6. May-July and Sept. singles and doubles €48-55; triples €66. Aug. €53-63/75. Oct.-Apr. €36-42/55-63. Cash only.) Gracious owners keep campers happy at **Camping U Sognu ❶,** on D623, a 15min. walk from pl. Paoli. Follow rue Prof. Santiaggi until it ends, then turn left and cross the bridge on your right. At the fork, take a right and follow signs. From the train station, turn left and take a right at the roundabout onto av. du 9 Septembre; walk for 10min. and, after the first bridge, turn left onto D623. This farm-turned-campsite offers homemade wood-fired pizzas (€7), a lively snack bar, and stunning views of the *haute-ville.* Sites on the main section tend to have little shade; nab a spot on one of the tree-lined terraces above or you may as well be sleeping in a sauna. (☎46 09 07. Breakfast €7. Reception 8am-noon and 4-8pm. Closed to cars after 11pm. Open late Mar. to mid-Oct. €6.50 per person, €2.50 per tent or car. Electricity €3. Cash only.) Tents cluster at a small, tree-lined stream perfect for wading at crowded **Camping Restonica ❶,** 20min. from the *centre-ville.* From the train station follow directions to U Sognu, above, but turn left before the bridge. (☎46 11 59; vero.camp@worldonline.fr. Breakfast €6. Laundry €7.50. Reception daily 8am-10pm. Open mid-Apr. to mid-Oct. €6.50 per person, €3.50 per tent, €3 per car. Electricity €3.50. Cash only.)

FOOD. Inexpensive cafés and *brasseries* center around **place Paoli** and along the adjoining **cours Paoli.** For a selection of cheap local cuisine, try **rue Scolisca** and the surrounding streets. Most restaurants in Calvi offer *menus* for €14-18. **SPAR** supermarket, 5 av. Xavier Luciani, is in the town center. (☎45 08 59. Open July-Aug. M-Sa 7:30am-8:30pm, Su 8:30am-noon; Sept.-June M-Sa 8:30am-noon and 3-8pm, Su 8:30am-noon. MC/V.) The mammoth **Casino** supermarket is uphill from the train station on RN 193. (☎45 22 45. Open July-Aug. M-Sa 8:30am-8pm; Sept.-June M-F 8:30am-12:30pm and 3-7:30pm, Sa 8:30am-7:30pm. AmEx/MC/V.)

A friendly staff serves both tourists and locals outstanding regional cuisine at **U Museu ❸,** ramp Ribanelle, off pl. d'Armes at the foot of the citadel. *Civet de sanglier* (wild-boar stew) and trout in a tomato, pepper, and wine sauce will please carnivores, while vegetarians will appreciate salads (€8-12) loaded with fresh *légumes.* (☎61 08 36. Pizza €7.50-9. Pasta €8-13. Fish *plats* €10-16. Meat *plats* €12-18. *Menus* €14-18. Open early Apr. to late Dec. daily noon-2:30pm and 7-10:30pm; Sept.-May M-Sa noon-2:30pm and 7-10:30pm. MC/V.) Though outdoor tables are pleasant at **A Scudella ❷,** 2 pl. Paoli, the best view is inside, where impeccably clad chefs prepare delectable *plats* (€9.20) in view of the dining room tables. (☎46 25 31. *Menus* €10-18. Open M-Sa noon-2pm and 7-10pm. MC/V.) At **U Passa Tempu ❷,** rampe Ste-Croix, off cours Paoli, the staff quickly presents *menus* that feature *brocciu* (local Corsican cheese) for €11 or €13 in a rustic setting. (☎46 18 73. Omelettes and savory *crêpes* €5-7. Pasta €6-15. Meat *plats* €6.50-18. *Menus* €11-15. Open daily 11:30am-3pm and 7-11pm. AmEx/MC/V.)

SIGHTS. Corte's *vieille ville,* with its steep streets and stone citadel that peers over the valleys below, has long been a bastion of Corsican patriotism. The route to the town center honors two men who led the Corsican national movement: Jean Pierre Gaffory wrested control of the city from French hands in 1745 and governed until his 1753 assassination, and the city's best loved son—Pascal Paoli—took control and proclaimed Corte Corsica's capital in 1755. He instituted a constitution and built the university, which now enrolls over 4000 students. In a plain dwelling across from pl. Gaffory, a plaque honors the apartment where Charles Bonaparte, Napoleon's father, lived in the 1760s while a student.

The **Musée de la Corse,** inside the citadel's walls at the top of rue Scolisca, transforms a 19th-century military hospital into a delightful exhibition space with a collection of Corsica's ethnographic history. Traditional *brocciu* cheese strainers and hand looms; rule-books and hooded cloaks from religious brotherhoods; and vintage advertisements for Cap Corse Mattei, the island's best-known *aperitif,* reveal facets of Corsican life and culture from the island's many regions and time periods. 2008 brings a special exhibit on the life of Pascal Paoli. Exhibits are in Corse and French; consider the 1½hr. audio tour, available in several languages (€1.50). Admission includes a visit to Corsica's only inland **citadel,** constructed in 1419. Visitors can explore the pitch-black dungeon, thoughtfully outfitted with a stone mattress and pillow, where Corsican patriots were imprisoned during the Italian occupation of WWII. (☎45 25 45. Museum open late June to late Sept. daily 10am-8pm; late Sept. to Oct. and Apr. to late June Tu-Su 10am-6pm; Nov.-Mar. Tu-Sa 10am-6pm. Citadel closes 1hr. earlier than museum. €5.30, students €3, seniors

€3.80, under 10 free. MC/V.) From pl. Paoli, walk uphill and turn left at the Eglise de l'Annonciation to find the oldest portion of the city walls and a spectacular panorama from the **Belvedere,** a windswept lookout that affords remarkable views of the citadel and of the twisting rivers and tree-covered valleys below. For those who miss the superior views from the citadel, this is a great substitute.

Corte's surroundings offer **hiking** (see **Daytrips** below or call tourist office for maps and info; call ☎08 92 68 32 50 for weather) and **horseback riding.** Try the **Ferme Equestre Albadu,** 1.5km from town on N193 toward Ajaccio. (☎46 24 55. €20 per 1½hr., €24 per 2hr., €35 per 3hr., €40 per ½-day, €65 per full-day including picnic. Reservations required at least 1 day ahead. Cash only.)

DAYTRIPS FROM CORTE

GORGES DE LA RESTONICA

Though the road following the Restonica River from Corte into the gorges is pleasant in itself, hikers will not regret renting a car or scooter to avoid the 15km walk to the base, at parking Grotelle. Some choose to hitchhike, but not every car will stop and for safety reasons, Let's Go does not recommend this option. In July and August, a navette *(shuttle) whisks hikers up from the Parc Naturel Régional's info office, down rue Prof. Santiaggi at the back of pl. Paoli and then right on D623 for 2km; hikers should follow the same route. Call ☎46 02 12 for detailed schedules. July-Aug. daily 8am-1:30pm, return 2:30-5pm. €2, under 18 €1.*

Southwest of Corte, tiny D623 stretches 15km through the Gorges de la Restonica (GOHRJ duh lah rest-ohn-ee-kah), a high-altitude canyon fed by glacial lakes. Both the canyon and its surrounding lakes provide fantastic hikes into some of Corsica's most rugged wilderness. The brave hearted can even take a dip in the gorge's icy water. Air temperatures at these high elevations can drop well below freezing even when it's 25°C (77°F) in town; between October and May hikers should bring warm layers. The area attracts a lot of traffic; it's best to start before 8am to avoid the crowds and, in summer, the extreme heat.

Those with time for only one hike should tour the **glacial lakes** at the top of the gorge, where hikers of all levels enjoy magnificent scenery. From the Grotelle parking lot, a trail marked in yellow crosses the river and ascends to the "most visited lake in Corsica," **Lac de Melo** (1hr.). This snow-fed beauty lies at 1711m and is surrounded by mountains, including Corsica's highest, **Mont Cinto** (2710m). The trail is designated *facile* (easy), but the climb is steep, rocky, and slippery when wet; some parts of the trail require scrambling up ladders or chains. From Melo, the trail continues on the right, still marked in yellow, to an even more impressive lake, **Lac de Capitellu** (1930m; 45min.). Another 30min. up, the trail meets the heavily trafficked red-and-white marked **GR20,** Corsica's most famous and demanding hike. Hikers will find that the steep climb to this point was worth it for the stunning view over the valley. For a full-day adventure, well-equipped trekkers can follow the GR20 to the left until it intersects with a trail leading to the **Refuge de Petra Piana,** where hikers can spend the night or continue on to the **Lac de Rotondo** (4½hr.). Less-trodden but equally spectacular is the hike to **Lac de l'Oriente.** In the summer, take the *navette* (shuttle bus) to **Pont de Tragone** and follow the marked trail, which, after passing shepherds' houses, arrives at the lake (3hr.).

A less-crowded dayhike goes to **Lac de Scapuccioli**, the highest lake in Corsica (2338m), which remains partly frozen until mid-June. From the Grotelle parking lot, begin as if doing the Lac de Capitellu hike, but after crossing the river follow cairns (large stacks of rocks) and climb steeply in the direction of the waterfall. Continue with the brook on your right to find the best way up to the **Lac de Cavacciole** (2015m). Vegetation disappears as you continue to Lac de Scapuccioli (3hr.), which has a perfect lookout onto the glacial lakes below. For more info on Restonica, consult the French-language hiking guide *Tavignano-Restonica* (€12).

GORGES DU TAVIGNANO

Take a right onto rue Colonel Feracci off rue Scoliscia just after pl. Gaffory. From rue Feracci, take the 1st left onto rue St-Joseph. When the road forks, go straight onto chemin de Baliri and follow the signs toward the gorges; the trail is marked in orange (1hr.).

Less rugged and more easily accessible by foot than Restonica, though equally demanding, the Tavignano (tahv-een-YAHNN-oh) gorges are filled with waterfalls, natural pools, and picturesque hiking trails. With no road access, they are likely to be less crowded than their better-known counterpart. The first 2½hr. of hiking along the Tavignano River lead to the **Passerelle du Russulinu** (902m), a suspension bridge surrounded by natural swimming pools and flat, picnic-friendly rocks. Bring sunscreen and wear a hat; there is little shade. Another 3hr. along the same trail lead to the **Refuge de la Sega** (1166m), where hikers can spend the night. (☎46 07 90 or 06 10 71 77 26. Reservations strongly recommended.) On the left, where the road diverges, are ancient *bergeries* (sheep pens) and huts where transient shepherds used to stay on their way to Plateau d'Alzo; those based in Corte will need to turn back at this point, as further hiking will necessitate an overnight stay.

FORÊT DE VIZZAVONA

Vizzavona is easily reached via a magnificent train ride (1hr., 4 per day, €5.80). The track from Corte winds leisurely along picturesque stone tunnels and narrow bridges.

Rugged mountains and miles of pine forest surround tiny Vizzavona (veez-ah-vohn-ah), leaving its 50 inhabitants with plenty of room to stretch their legs. Several hiking trails of varying difficulty converge at the town, making it an excellent base for both serious excursions and ambling daytrips. After reaching Vizzavona, go behind the train station, where a billboard lists hiking routes. The easiest, **Cascade des Anglais,** is a 45min. ramble through the forest that ends at a series of plunging waterfalls. The trail is broad and well marked. Unfortunately, its accessibility draws hordes of hikers in summer. The large, flat rocks and shaded coves make ideal picnic spots, and the lagoons offer opportunities for a dip in the water. Those looking for a more solitary site should continue past the base of the falls.

Hard-core hikers might want to take on the **Monte d'Oro,** an unrelenting 2389m summit whose waters feed the streams and rivers of the entire region. From the top, which is covered in snow even in June, hikers can see all the way to Italy. The base of the trail, marked by cairns and orange circles, begins right in town, at the path leading to Cascade des Anglais. After the footbridge, follow the red and white marks of the GR20 until you reach a second footbridge (1hr.). Just before reaching the crest, leave the GR20 and head right toward the **Col du Porc** (Pork pass); from here, the crest leading to the summit is clear (4hr.). The descent, marked by cairns and yellow paint, leads back to the tall pines of the superb Vizzavona forest and ends at the Vizzavona train station. Monte d'Oro is not for casual hikers; those who attempt a summit bid should be experienced and well equipped, as there is no water along most of the route. Start early (the entire loop takes about 9hr.), and check with the regional park office for weather conditions and detailed maps.

BASTIA ☎04 95

Bastia (BAH-styuh; pop. 40,000), Corsica's second largest city, is a well-trodden gateway to both the mainland and the island's more picturesque vacation spots. A crumbling *vieille ville* and giant ferry port mean that most visitors pass by this city, but Baroque churches, a magnificent citadel, and war monuments give a better taste of Corsica's rich heritage than more touristy spots on the island. Bastia is also the perfect base for the must-see Cap Corse.

TRANSPORTATION

Flights: Bastia-Poretta (**BIA;** ☎54 54 54), 23km from the center of town. An airport bus (☎31 06 65), scheduled to coincide with departing flights, leaves from the *préfecture*, across from train station (30min., €8). Purchase tickets on board. **Air France** (☎08 20 82 08 20) flies to **Marseille** (3-5 per day), **Nice** (3-4 per day), and **Paris** (6 per day).

Trains: Pl. de la Gare (☎32 80 61), to the left of the roundabout at the top of av. Maréchal Sebastiani. Station open July-Aug. daily 6am-9:45pm; Sept.-June M-Sa 6:10am-8:45pm, Su 6:30am-8:45pm. To: **Ajaccio** (3½hr., 3-5 per day, €24) via **Corte; Calvi** (3hr., 2 per day, €19) via **Ponte Leccia** and a bus to **Ile Rousse** (2½hr., 4 per day, €15); **Corte** (45min., 5 per day, €12). Train service is less frequent Oct.-Mar.; check with the tourist office for up-to-date schedules.

Buses: Ask the tourist office for a bus schedule. **Eurocorse,** rte. du Nouveau Port (☎21 06 31), runs to **Ajaccio** (3hr., M-Sa 2 per day, €20). **Autocars Cortenais** (☎46 02 12) leaves for **Corte** (1¼hr.; M, W, F 1 per day; €10). Buy tickets on board.

Ferries: quai de Fango, next to pl. St-Nicolas; turn left from av. Maréchal Sébastiani, past pl. St-Nicolas. **SNCM** (☎54 66 90; fax 54 66 44), by quai de Fango, sails to **Marseille** and **Nice. Corsica Ferries,** 5bis rue du Chanoine Leschi (☎32 95 95), chugs to **Nice** and **Toulon,** as well as **Livorno** and **Savona** in Italy. **Moby Lines,** 4 rue Commandant Luce de Casablanca (☎34 84 94; www.moby-colonna-corse.com), serves **Genoa** and **Livorno** in Italy. For details on ferry connections to mainland France, see **Intercity Transportation,** p. 759.

Taxis: ☎32 24 24, 34 07 00, or 32 70 70. €32-37 to airport. 24hr.

Car Rental: ADA, 35 rue César Campinchi (☎31 48 95; www.ada-encorse.com), with 2nd branch at the airport (☎54 55 44). 21+. Open M-F 8am-noon and 2-6:30pm, Sa 8am-noon. AmEx/MC/V. **Avis, Budget, Europcar,** and **Hertz** share the same locations.

Bike Rental: Objectif Nature, rue Notre-Dame-de-Lourdes (☎32 54 34; www.objectif-nature-corse.com), 1 block beyond the tourist office. Offers excursions and rents bikes. Mountain and city bikes €10 per ½-day, €18 per day, €40 per 3 days. Canyoning €40-50. Paragliding €60. Open M-Sa 9am-noon and 2-7pm. MC/V.

Scooter Rental: Toga Location Nautique, port de Plaisance de Toga (☎34 14 14; www.plaisance-location.com), on the right as you enter the port complex. Scooters €65 per day, €300 per week; €1220 deposit. Open M-Sa 8am-noon and 2-6:30pm. MC/V.

ORIENTATION AND PRACTICAL INFORMATION

Place St-Nicolas sits in the center of the action, dividing the *vieux port* to the south from the new town to the north. Bastia's main thoroughfare, **boulevard du Général de Gaulle,** runs along the inland length of the *place.* Just parallel are two other main arteries, **boulevard Paoli** and **rue César Campinchi.** Facing the mountains, the *vieux port* and citadel are to the left, and the ferry docks are to the right. The tourist office is at the edge of pl. St-Nicolas, near the ferries. The train station is toward the mountains from the tourist office, up av. Maréchal Sébastiani and left on rue Paul. The main bus stop is just behind the tourist office, toward the new port.

Tourist Office: Pl. St-Nicolas (☎54 20 40; www.bastia-tourisme.com), has bus schedules and maps of the city and Cap Corse. Free accommodations service. Open daily July-Aug. 8am-8pm; Sept.-June 8:30am-noon and 2-6pm.

Currency exchange: Société Générale, Pl. St-Nicolas (☎55 19 00), has **ATMs.**

Youth Center: Centre Regional Information Jeunesse (CRIJ), 9 rue César Campinchi (☎32 12 13; www.crij-corse.com). Info on health, housing, and employment. Free Internet access for research only; 40min. max. Open M-F June-July 8am-noon and 1-5pm; Sept.-May 8am-noon and 2-6pm.

Laundromat: Lavoir du Port, 25 rue Luce de Casabianca (☎32 25 51), toward the new port from the tourist office, past the Esso station. Wash €6-9, dry €1 per 10min.; detergent €0.40. Open daily 7am-9pm.

Police: Rue Commandant Luce de Casabianca (☎55 22 22).

Hospital: Rte. Impériale (☎59 11 11).

Internet Access: Free for research at the **CRIJ** (see **Youth Center**). **Le Cyber,** 6 rue des Jardins (☎34 30 34), behind the *vieux port*. 12 computers. Open daily 9:30am-midnight. **Cyber,** 5 av. Maréchal Sébastiani, down the street from Hôtel Univers. Open daily

9am-2am. **Café Albert 1er,** 11 bd. de Gaulle (☎31 76 10), on pl. St-Nicolas. Open noon-2am. All are €1.50 per 30min., €3 per hr.

Post Office: 2 av. Maréchal Sébastiani (☎32 80 78), on the corner of the intersection with bd. Général Graziani. Open M-F 8am-7pm, Sa 8am-noon. **Postal Code:** 20200.

ACCOMMODATIONS AND CAMPING

Most hotel rates in Bastia fall outside the range of budget travelers. Low season brings lower prices and plenty of vacancies, but hotels fill up quickly come June and remain full as late as mid-October. Camping is a viable option, although all sites are too far from town to walk; beachgoers can hop off the train a few stops before Bastia or join hikers on local buses (until 7pm) heading into Cap Corse.

Hôtel Posta Vecchia, 8 rue Posta Vecchia (☎32 32 38; www.hotel-postavecchia.com), just off the quai des Martyrs. Colorful modern hotel with a few *petites chambres* that remain reasonably priced during the high season—reserve ahead. All rooms equipped with private bath, phone, and—except for the *petites chambres*—A/C and TV. Ferry announcements can be heard from some rooms. Breakfast in bed €6.50. July-Sept. singles €45; doubles €55-90; triples €90-100. Oct.-Feb. €40/53-75/80-86. Mar.-June €40/45-70/70-80. AmEx/MC/V. ❹

Hôtel Univers, 3 av. Maréchal Sébastiani (☎31 03 38; www.hotelunivers.org). Plain hallways lead to spotless yellow-and-blue rooms. All have soundproof windows, large bathrooms, A/C, and TV. Ideally located close to the train station. Breakfast €6. Reception 24hr. Aug.-Sept. singles €60; doubles €70; triples €90; quads €110. Jan.-July €50/60/75/90. Extra bed €10. AmEx/MC/V. ❺

Camping Les Orangers (☎33 24 09), in Licciola-Miomo. Take bus #4 (15min., €1.15) from the tourist office. Peaceful site with clean showers and bathrooms. 25 tents and 6 mobile homes for 4-6 people. Restaurant and snack bar. Open May to mid-Oct. €5 per person, €3 per tent, €2.60 per car. Electricity €3.50. ❶

Camping San Damiano (☎33 68 02), Lido de la Marana. Take a bus to "La Marana" from the gare routière (€1.15, 15min.; buses are infrequent; check with tourist office for schedule) to camp under pine trees, literally one step away from the beach. 250 sites. Snack bar and small grocery store. Impeccable showers and bathrooms. €3.50 per person, €2.50 per tent. Open Mar.-Oct. Cash only. ❶

FOOD

Bastia's nonstop sunshine, pleasant squares, and panoramic viewpoints mean plenty of dining *al fresco.* Nearly every inexpensive café on crowded pl. St-Nicholas sets up tables around the perimeter. For better food and a view to match, try the handful of restaurants near the **citadel** or browse the conveniently clustered choices along the **vieux port.** The broad terraces of the **quai des Martyrs de la Libération** offer a more subdued but also more touristy atmosphere; come before sunset to enjoy an uninterrupted view of the sweeping horizon. Early birds hit the **market** on **place de l'Hôtel de Ville.** (Sa-Su 8:15am-12:30pm.) A **SPAR** supermarket is at 14 rue César Campinchi. (☎32 32 40. Open M-Sa 8am-12:30pm and 4-8:30pm, Su 8am-noon. MC/V.) To purchase traditional Corsican delicacies, stop by **U Paese,** 4 rue Napoléon. This pungent shop is the oldest of its kind in Bastia and offers the best of the island's traditional fare, including *brocciu* (sheep's cheese), *canistrelli* (crumbly cookies), and *gâteaux de châtaignes* (chestnut cake). Ask the owner to vacuum-pack your *lonzu* (sausage, €32 per kg) so the aroma doesn't follow you home. (☎32 33 18; www.u-paese.com. Open M-Sa 9am-noon and 3-7pm. MC/V.)

U Tianu, 4 rue Monseigneur Rigo (☎31 36 67). Serving a local clientele for 25 years. Presented in a room plastered with separatist posters, mouthwatering Corsican specialties are well worth the €23 *menu* (with *apéritif*, appetizer, *plat*, cheese, dessert, coffee, and after-dinner drink). The chef will prepare a plate of local *charcuterie* and cheese on request (prices vary). Open Jan.-July and Sept.-Dec. M-Sa 7pm-2am. Cash only. ❸

Chez Vincent, 12 rue St-Michel (☎31 62 50). Enormous pizzas (€7.70-10) only taste better as you enjoy one of the best views of the *vieux port* from the restaurant's terrace within the citadel's walls. Share the popular specialty plate (€18), and reserve ahead to eat it outside. The staff also dishes up meats (€12-19) and reasonably priced traditional *plats* (€8-15). Open M-F noon-1:30pm and 8-10:30pm, Sa 6-10:30pm. MC/V. ❸

A Mandria, 4 pl. du Marché (☎35 17 11). Offers cheap Corsican specialties. Old black-and-white pictures decorate the stone-and-wood interior, while the towers of the Eglise St-Jean-Baptiste frame the view. Homemade lasagna €13. Cannelloni with *brocciu* (Corsican cheese) €12. Open M-Sa 11am-2:30pm and 6pm-midnight. AmEx/MC/V. ❷

Le Pub Assunta, 4 rue Fontaine-Neuve (☎34 11 40). Claims to be a former secret meeting place of Napoleon III and Benedetti Vincent. The well-hidden, leafy courtyard must have been a prime spot for discussing military strategies; luckily, your only tough move is deciding which tasty burger to choose—options include the double-decker royal cheese (€5.50-10). Occasional live music during the summer; regular DJs during the winter. Pizzas €6-8. Open M-Sa 11:30am-2pm and 7pm-2am, Su 7pm-2am. MC/V. ❷

Café Albert 1er, 11 bd. Général de Gaulle (☎31 76 10). On pl. St-Nicolas. Stands out with low prices and wonderful salads. If you don't like what's on the menu, make your own creation out of 31 ingredients (€7-13). The exhaustive ice cream selection competes with profiteroles (€4.90) for dessert. Open mid-May to Sept. daily 8am-11pm. ❷

SIGHTS AND BEACHES

A walk through Bastia's *vieille ville* hints at the town's former glory as the crown jewel of Genoese-ruled Corsica. Many of the buildings in this part of the city are in need of repair, but the 1380 **citadel,** also called *Terra Nova*, has remained imposingly intact. Its ramparts reach down the hill and toward the *vieux port*, dwarfing adjacent shops. Within the walls is a public square, **place du Donjon,** where merchants accused of swindling were once tied to a stone *cul nul* (butt-naked) to be laughed at all day. In **place St-Nicolas,** the central monument showcases Corsica's independent streak; a bronze widow who has lost two of her children in the war of independence offers up her third to the cause, saying "he belongs to the country."

Toward the citadel from pl. St-Nicolas on rue Napoleon sits the 18th-century **Oratoire de L'Imaculée Conception,** the entrance to which is paved with stones in the shape of a large sun. The lavish interior, with glass chandeliers and dark-wood walls and pews, is truly striking. During Corsica's brief 1794-1796 stint as an Anglo-Corsican kingdom, the little Italian organ would lead "God Save the King," sung by Members of Parliament before debates in the church. (Open daily 8am-7pm.) Next door, the 17th-century **Eglise St-Jean Baptiste,** pl. de l'Hôtel de Ville, just behind the *vieux port*, is the largest church in Corsica. The lofty Baroque interior has gilded domes, a large organ, *trompe-l'œil* ceilings, and a relief of a rarely-represented scene: the circumcision of the infant Jesus. Only the windows are unimpressive; all except for three stained-glass pieces at the back of the church were destroyed during WWII when resistors blew up an Italian munitions cache 5km away.

If the church's soaring ceiling makes you feel tiny, the eccentric **Eco-Musée,** in the citadel's old powder magazine (in the corner opposite the *vieux port*), will leave you feeling positively gargantuan. An extraordinarily detailed miniature replica of a traditional mountaintop scene, it features houses, stables, a bakery, a mill, a flowing river, and tiny people who actually move and do work. Each structure is painstakingly precise, right down to the microscopic dishes, working church bells, and authentic vegetation, which the creator René Mattei changes every two weeks to reflect the seasons. The entire setup took 20 years to complete and now weighs over 10 tons. (☎06 10 26 82 08; www.eco-musee.com. Open Apr.-Oct. M-Sa 9am-noon and 2-6pm. €3.50, students €3, ages 8-12 €2.50, under 8 free.)

Bastia does not have **beaches;** they begin 3km to the north and 1km to the south. Though pebbly, the closest ones can get crowded, so head north to **Miomo,** and, farther on, to the beautiful sands of the **Cap Corse** to find seclusion. Bus #4 leaves every 30min. from pl. St-Nicolas (6:30am-7pm), traveling up to the Cap's small towns and beaches. The closest sandy beach lies between **Erbalunga** (€2) and **Sisco** (€2.30); bus #4 heads there nine times per day and continues to **Pietracorba** (30min., €2.60), which also has a sandy stretch. To go snorkeling, rent gear at **Thalassa Location,** 2 rue St-Jean, just behind the *vieux port.* (☎31 08 77; http://perso.wanadoo.fr/thalassashop. Fins, mask, and snorkel €12 per day. Open Mar.-Oct. M-Sa 9am-noon and 2-7pm; Nov.-Feb. M-Sa 2-7pm. AmEx/MC/V.) Thalassa's **Base Nautique,** just past Port Toga on the route du Cap Corse, offers **scuba excursions,** including night dives, for all levels. (☎31 78 90; thalassa.immersion@free.fr. €36 per hr.; equipment included. Certification courses €130-400. AmEx/MC/V.)

TIP **MIND THE MEDUSAS.** Bays on Cap Corse can be filled with jellyfish for an entire week but be *méduse*-free the next. Crowded beaches and empty water are signs you should rethink skinny-dipping. Ask park employees at the Sentier des Douaniers whether the waters are clear; they can also help if you get bitten.

NIGHTLIFE

Though a few clubs spice up the city's nightlife between September and June, Bastians spend their nights either in *avant-boîtes* (bars and lounges) or in Calvi. In town, the local youth head to the **Port de Toga,** a 15min. walk from pl. St-Nicolas along the water, away from the *vieux-port,* and alongside speeding cars. At the roundabout, go right toward the water and under the arches. Here, the party may be happening at **Le White** or at nearby **Maracana,** both lounges with live DJs or bands. (Le White ☎32 11 62, Maracana ☎31 31 77. Beer €3-6. Mixed drinks €7.50. Both open daily 11am-2am.) Next door at **Pub La Pinta** is a young crowd drinking pints and cocktails to music from a live DJ or a karaoke box. (☎34 23 00. Beer €5. Mixed drinks €7.50-9. Open daily 11am-2am.) If you insist on staying in the *vieille ville,* **O'Connor's,** a not-so-Irish pub at 1 rue St-Erasme, offers plenty of beer to a sizable young crowd. A pint is €6.50, or try 2.5L—fittingly named the giraffe—for €29. (☎32 04 97. Live music or DJs on weekends. W karaoke, Th 80s. Open W-Sa 7pm-2am.) Other nightlife options are in the faraway **La Marana** area, home to beachside bars and open-air dance clubs. Unfortunately, public transportation doesn't go there at night, and a taxi ride will cost at least €25.

CAP CORSE ☎04 95

Stretching north from Bastia, the Cap Corse (CAP cohrss) peninsula is Corsica's most stunning frontier. A perilously curving road connects the Cap's numerous former fishing villages and marinas and offers breathtaking views of the jagged coastline. Endangered species flourish in the windswept valleys and atop dizzying cliffs, while peregrine falcons and cormorants soar above the landscape. With its vast natural reserve, the Cap is a hiker's dream. Every other turn reveals a Genoese tower, a hilltop chapel, or an Italian tourist sunbathing in his birthday suit. Unfortunately, there are few budget hotels; camping is a better option, and a handful of sites dot the Cap. Bastia is a good base for those with cars, but visitors planning to hike the Cap (past Pietracorbara) will have to stay on the peninsula itself. When coming back from the rugged northern shores, plop down in a café and try the region's namesake *aperitif,* the Cap Corse, which is like Campari.

CORSICA

> **TIP** **HOLD ONTO YOUR CAP.** Cap Corse and the Balagne region are the windiest areas of Corsica. Check the weather forecast when planning to venture out on the water. Wind also makes forest fires more likely; be cautious when camping and call ☎18 or ☎112 if you see a fire.

Though expensive, the best way to visit the Cap is to drive around the peninsula. While you can complete the trip in three hours without stopping, plan on taking a full day. One look at the stunning coastline and you'll be ready to hop out and start exploring. There are countless places to pull over, including many secluded swimming spots. Consider renting a **car** in Bastia (p. 783) or Calvi (p. 772), but be cautious: the madcap coastal highway is made even more treacherous by local bus drivers, who seem to imagine themselves behind the wheel of a speedster.

> **THE CORSE LESS TRAVELED.** In high season, you can see the Cap by **bus** tour. Up-to-date schedules are available at the tourist office. The eastern side of Cap Corse, including **St-Florent, Erbalunga,** and **Sisco,** is also served by public bus #4 from pl. St-Nicolas in Bastia (see **Bastia: Sights and Beaches,** p. 787). Less frequently, a bus goes all the way to **Macinaggio** (☎31 06 65; 50min.; M-F 2 per day, Sa 1 per day; €6.40). Ask nicely and the driver will stop wherever you feel the urge to explore. When catching a bus back to Bastia, find a bus stop or wave your arms wildly to signal that you want to ride—bus drivers are notorious for ignoring hopeful would-be passengers. Also, keep in mind that most buses serve only coastal towns; to explore the inland villages you'll have to hike. If you are driving, it's best to go during the week, when traffic on D80 thins out. To start on the west side in St-Florent, take bd. Paoli in Bastia, then bd. Auguste Gaudin past the citadel onto N199. For the east-to-west route, follow signs for the Cap on the coastal boulevard north from pl. St-Nicolas.

ST-FLORENT

Across from Bastia at the base of the Cap Corse peninsula, the resort town of St-Florent (sehn FLOHR-ahn; pop. 1500) draws an annual crowd of sun-seekers to its wide beaches and sizable pleasure-boat port. Below the expansive Golfe de St-Florent, the town lies at the intersection of three dramatically different regions: the rugged Cap Corse, the fertile Nebbio, and the unforgiving Desert des Agriates. It is an excellent weekend trip from Bastia; while physically close to the city, bus schedules prevent daytripping (unless you only want to explore from noon-2pm).

St-Florent offers several options for sunbathers. The town's two principal **beaches** meet at the port and host crowds of umbrellas in August. North of the citadel lies **plage de l'Ospedale,** a long, pebbly stretch hidden from traffic by a concrete wall. From town, walk uphill on RN 199 (toward Cap Corse); the beach is 10min. past the post office. Boisterous **plage de la Roya,** south of Port de Plaisance, tempts a tan crowd with a sandy crescent framed by distant mountains. Walk by the parking lot and over a footbridge to reach it. Plenty of wind makes the area perfect for **windsurfing** and **sailing. Base Nautique,** at the southern end of the beach, offers one-stop shopping for **watersport** enthusiasts. (☎06 12 10 23 27; www.corskayak.com. Windsurfing equipment €14 per hr. Kayaks €12-15 per hr. Surf bikes €10 per hr. Catamarans €30-37. Lessons for novices €50. Kayak expeditions €45. Open June-Sept. daily 8am-8:30pm; Oct. by appointment only. Cash only.)

True beach bliss lies farther south at **plage du Lodo** (*Lotu* in Corse), a slice of paradise accessible only by **boat. Le Popeye** makes the 30min. trip from June through September from Port de Plaisance. (☎37 19 07. Round-trip €11, under 18 €6. Purchase tickets 1hr. before departure. Departures at 8:45, 10, 11:30am, 1, 3pm. Return trips depart noon, 1:45, 4, 5:30, 6:30pm. Info desk located on the port;

open daily 8am-7:30pm. Cash only.) From plage du Lodo, a 1hr. hike south takes sunbathers to the pristine **plage de Saleccia,** an isolated, otherworldly spot.

Budget travelers will have to search hard for reasonable accommodations, especially in August. Reserve far in advance. A good bet is the **Hôtel du Centre ❹,** rue du Centre, which has clean, spacious rooms with bold flower-print bedspreads. All rooms have shower and phone, most have TV, and a few allow a glimpse of the sea and port. (☎37 00 68; fax 37 41 01. Breakfast €5. Reception daily 6am-11pm. June-July singles and doubles €45-47; triples €50-55; quads €70. Aug. €65-70/80/80. Sept.-May €42-45/45-50/65-70. Extra bed €8. MC/V.) By far the cheapest option is camping, and a few sites are located south of town along plage de la Roya. To reach **U Pezzo ❶,** head south on CD 81 from the bus station and cross the river via the pedestrian bridge. Walk down the beach until you see the sign for the Base Nautique; the campsite is across the road on your left (15min.). Eucalyptus trees provide plenty of shade for 145 sites just steps from a popular beach. Amenities include a snack bar, pizzeria, and mini-market. Kids will enjoy the tiny on-site animal farm. (☎/fax 37 01 65. Reception 8-11:30am and 3-6:30pm. Open Apr. to mid-Oct. €13 per 2 people, tent, and car. Electricity €3. Showers free. Cash only.)

Create your own three-course meal at **SPAR** supermarket, near the bus stop. (☎37 00 56. Open June-Aug. M-Sa 8am-8pm, Su 8am-1pm and 5-8pm; Sept.-May M-Sa 8am-noon and 3:30-8pm, Su 8am-noon. MC/V.) The quai along Port de Plaisance is home to several unremarkable restaurants. An exception is **U Trogliu ❷,** rue Centrale, which serves the best food in St-Florent for reasonable prices. Specialty homemade pastas are prepared in traditional Corsican dishes (€6.80-10). The *cannelloni au brocciu* and *ravioli à l'ancienne* are definitely worth a try. (☎37 20 73. *Menus* €13 and €16. Open daily mid-May to Sept. 7pm-midnight. Cash only.) If you can't resist the view, head to **César ❸,** along the right-hand side of the port. It has a terrace and a *menu* that won't break the bank. (☎37 15 33. Pizzas €8-13. Pastas €9-15. Meats €15-17. Open daily Apr.-Oct. noon-2:30pm and 7-11:30pm. MC/V.)

Autocars Santini (☎37 02 98) sends **buses** to Bastia (50min., M-Sa 7am and 2pm, €5) and Ile Rousse (1hr., M-Sa 9am and 4:30pm, €10) from the station below Port de Plaisance. Buy tickets on the bus. To get to the **tourist office** from the bus station, walk past pl. des Portes, veer right, and continue uphill; the office is on the left. The staff distributes the St-Florent practical guide, which includes a map. Ask for information about regional festivals. (☎37 06 04; fax 35 30 74. Open July-Aug. M-F 8:30am-12:30pm and 2-7pm, Sa 9am-noon and 3-6pm, Su 9am-noon; Sept.-June M-F 8:30am-12:30pm and 2-6pm, Sa 2-6pm. Hours change weekly.)

ERBALUNGA

The most accessible of Cap Corse's villages, Erbalunga (AYR-bah-loon-gah; pop. 2466) offers a peaceful afternoon alternative to Bastia's crowded streets. Though its busy southern neighbor has steadily grown in size, quiet Erbalunga has gained a mere 180 inhabitants over the past 200 years. "Downtown" in this sleepy hamlet consists of a bakery, a post office, and, of course, the requisite *boules* court. Aging buildings and outdoor cafés cluster around the tiny port, where fishermen tend to their brightly painted wooden dories and occasionally drop lines from their coastal houses. Narrow streets lead to the southern side of the port, where a crumbling Genoese tower overlooks gray-pebble beaches, perfect for an afternoon of sunbathing.

Supermarket **SPAR** is across from the bus station. (☎33 24 24. Open M-Sa 8am-12:30pm and 4-7:30pm, Su 9am-noon. MC/V.) In the hills above the port, the **Monastère des Benedictines du St-Sacrement** is quieter than ever since its last few monks left last year. Pass the monastery to find **L'embrun de folie ❷** down the road, where an Italian cook makes dishes for every budget, including pizzas (€7-8.50) and penne with eggplant and crab (€9.50). Enjoy the sweeping view of the sea or take a quick dip with your order of *huîtres de Diana* (Diana's oysters, €9.50)—to ensure freshness, oysters are kept in a box tied to a rock in the water. (☎33 94 70. Open daily June-Aug. noon-10pm; kitchen open noon-2pm and 6-10pm. Cash only.)

Two-and-a-half kilometers south, **Lavasina** holds the famous 17th-century **Eglise de Notre-Dame des Graces.** Legend has it that a disabled nun from Bonifacio was miraculously granted the use of her legs after praying to an image of the Virgin that hangs in this church. Thousands make an annual torch lit pilgrimage on the evening of September 7 to celebrate this miracle. The holiday itself, the **Fête de la Nativité de la Vierge,** is celebrated the following day. You can hike along the coast or hop on the bus toward Bastia to reach Lavasina. Free weekly guided tours, in French, give the history of Erbalunga's castle and chapel. (Tours mid-June to mid-Sept. Tu at 9am leave from city hall; details at the tourist office in Bastia.)

SISCO VALLEY

Tourist offices hand out a map that lists 21 itineraries on the Cap; hike #9, from **Sisco** (2hr.), is the best. Take bus #4 from pl. St-Nicolas in Bastia to Sisco (30min., every hr., €2.30) and walk with the water on your right until you see signs for **Camping A Casaïola ❷.** The site is a 15min. walk up the road on the left. The English-speaking staff lets sites and offers advice about Sisco's hiking, equestrian, and watersport activities. (☎/fax 35 20 10. Laundry €3. Reception 8am-8pm. €5.50 per person, €2.50 per tent. Cash only.) From the campsite, trail #9 continues to the left of the campsite entrance. Follow the painted orange rectangles along a sun-dappled route that chases a winding streambed before plunging into an expansive valley of wildflowers. Along the way, you'll pass through dense forest and tiny, almost-forgotten villages, where the mountainous backdrop might be enough to convince you to head for the hills—permanently. You'll see only a few other hikers, but geckos and butterflies provide company. The path includes lovely footbridges and ultimately leads to **Petrapiana,** the intersection of several other routes; make sure to take a break at **Barriggioni,** 300m before Petrapiana, and admire the grandiose elegance of **Eglise St-Martin.** From here, it is possible to take a detour to the 11th-century **Chapelle St-Michel,** sitting precariously on a hilltop promontory; follow the signs uphill to the right of the first church. Though it is impossible to enter the chapel, the panoramic view of the bowl-shaped valley below, sprinkled with Renaissance bell towers, is definitely worth the 1hr. climb. Note that this demanding hike requires a good pair of hiking boots as well as long pants to protect against thorny undergrowth; sunscreen and bug repellent are also helpful.

MACINAGGIO TO CENTURI: THE CAPANDULA

Crystal-clear waters, sandy beaches, and deep-green escarpments characterize the arid, windy tip of Cap Corse. Inaccessible to cars, the Capandula is a protected national reserve and the last stop for African migratory birds heading north. Camping is therefore forbidden, but hikers and bikers are blessed by the **sentier de Douaniers,** an extraordinary coastal trail named after the customs officials who first walked it. Crumbling remains of 16th-century towers, an 11th-century lighthouse, and ancient lime quarries can still be seen today.

From the east coast, the trail takes off from **Macinaggio,** a pretty 600-boat port where Corsican leader Pascal Paoli returned in 1790 after 20 years in exile from his beloved island. The **tourist office** has maps of the trail. (☎35 40 34; www.ot-rogliano-macinaggio.com. Internet access €0.20 per min. Open July-Aug. M-Sa 9am-noon and 3-7pm, Su 9am-noon; early to mid-Sept. and June M-Sa 9am-noon and 3-7pm; mid-Sept. to May M-F 9am-noon and 2-5pm.) A warm-up walfk from the beach in Macinaggio leads to **Tamarone beach** (45min.), where reserve employees hand out maps, relieve swimmers bitten by jellyfish, and lead guided hikes (inquire at the tourist office). Here, the *sentier* proper begins. Whenever it splits, hiking uphill offers the best panoramas, but staying closer to the sea will lead to the protected **Finocchiarola**

BACKPACKER'S FOOTPRINT

Ecotourism usually focuses on the exploration of coasts, islands, or mountains–and Corsica has all three. So your stay on the "mountain in the sea," as locals call it, is the perfect occasion to offset your tourist impact and help promote rather than disrupt the local environment and culture.

In the mountains: Is the inviting patch of grass you've been eyeing by that waterfall actually a type of fragile high-altitude plant? Some species of grass and flowers are rare enough to be under scientific study, as in the Gorges de la Restonica near Corte (p. 782), so tread carefully.

Under the sea: Does your diving center follow environmental regulations and teach you to be careful with the marine flora and fauna? Sites outside natural reserves (forbidden to divers) are still fragile; be careful with the sea anemones when you visit Mérouville, off the coast of Bonifacio (p. 793).

On the road: Is the beach close enough that you can trade your scooter for a bike and get a workout before diving into the sea?

For your next visit: Why not come during the winter, to get a more authentic experience and help revive local economies? Try out Corsica's eco-friendly activities, such as Calvi's **Festival du Vent** in early November (p. 778).

—Mathieu Desruisseaux

Islands (30min.). Small boats go to the islands, but landing is forbidden from March to October to protect nesting birds and Europe's smallest daisies. The various paths merge at beaches, which hikers must cross to continue. Beaches give way to cliffs soon after the **tower of Santa Maria** (15min.); the path then leads to Corsica's northernmost village, **Barcaggio** (2hr.), halfway to the end of the trail in **Centuri** (4½hr.). Those turning back toward Macinaggio from the tower of Santa Maria can hike to the crest overlooking **Giraglia island** (1½hr.) for a view of the boisterous tip of the Cap and of the peaceful path behind.

Back in Macinaggio, shady but rocky campsites await at **U Stazzu ❶;** when you get off the bus, continue toward the beach, take the last road on the left, and follow signs along the path (30min.)—or, to save time, walk on the beach and take the first (and only) path inland. (☎35 43 76. Breakfast €4. Open mid-May to Sept. €7.50 per person. Fridge/freezer available. No electricity. Cash only.) If you have your heart set on staying on the Cap and don't want to camp, head to **Campu Stelle ❹,** rte. de Tamarone, across from U Stazzu, where a friendly couple lets two- to six-person apartments with kitchens. A large yard, picnic tables, and a recreation room with TV are also available. (☎35 49 21; www.gitencorse-campustelle.com. Reservations required. July-Aug. 2- to 3-person apartment €390 per week; 4- to 6-person apartment €670. Prices drop 15-50% in low season. Cash only.) The miniature port of **Centuri,** at the other end of the trail from Macinaggio, is one of the Cap's most picturesque spots; sit here at sunset and watch the boats bring in their daily haul of lobsters, mussels, and fish. **Camping Caravaning L'isulotto ❶,** just south of the town, has many amenities, including a mini-market, bar, and a restaurant with a €10 *menu*, 200m from the sea. (☎35 62 81; fax 35 63 63. €6 per person, €2.80 per tent, €2 per car. Electricity €3.50. MC/V.)

There is a **SPAR** supermarket up the road from the Chapelle St-Marc on the right. (☎35 45 65. Open M-Sa 8:30am-12:30pm and 4-8pm, Su 8am-noon. MC/V.) Regional culinary pride and family recipes passed down from the owner's mother drive the menu at **Ostéria di u Portu ❸,** across from the port, where nearly every dish contains local Cap Corse delicacies. The €15 *menu* features three courses, while the hearty €21 *menu* includes an appetizer, salad, ravioli, veal dish, and dessert. Traditional Corsican music from the terrace speakers provides an authentic ambience. (☎35 40 49. *Plats* €9-22. Fish *menu* €22. Open daily 11am-2:30pm and 6-10:30pm. Cash only.) Another local favorite in the port is **U Lampione ❷,** where fresh arrivals like grilled dorado are turned into tasty *plats du jour* (€11), accompanied by a welcome side of A/C. (☎35 34 44. Salads €7.50. Pizzas €7-9. Meats €14-16. *Menus* €18-27. Open daily noon-2:30pm and 6-10:30pm. Cash only.)

Macinaggio offers several options for those who want to see the Capandula but aren't up to tackling it on foot. **Boat tours** aboard the **U San Paulu** depart twice daily from the dock just below the Capitainerie. The 2hr. trips head all the way to **Barcaggio,** the tip of the Cap, and include an optional beach landing for swimming. In July and August, the boat also serves as a **shuttle** between the two towns. (☎35 07 09 or 06 14 78 14 16; www.lebateau.fr.st. Departures 11am and 3:30pm. €20, ages 4-12 €10, under 4 free. Shuttle €12. Cash only.) The shuttles are also a convenient way to shorten the hike to Barcaggio, as you can hike to the village (3½hr.) and then take the shuttle back. Charter your own voyage with a **zodiac** from **Cap Evasion,** in the blue trailer at the end of the port. The tiny boats are perfect for discovering the Cap's hidden inlets and rocky coves. (☎35 12 29 or 06 20 34 48 22. €70-85 per ½-day, €85-110 per day; €800 deposit. Open daily mid-June to Aug. 9am-noon and 2-6pm; Sept. and May to mid-June by appointment. Cash only.) **Loc' Ago,** next to the post office, rents **mountain bikes** for €17 per day. (☎06 76 31 76 69. Open daily July to mid-Sept. 9am-12:30pm and 4-8pm; Oct.-June by appointment. MC/V.) At the edge of the beach, the **Macinaggio Club de Voile** offers **kayak** rental for use in Macinaggio's bay. (☎35 46 82 or 06 86 72 58 40. Kayaks €15 per hr., €35-40 per ½-day. Small sailboats €20/50. Open July-Aug. daily 9am-8pm. Cash only.)

BONIFACIO (BONIFAZIU) ☎04 95

At the extreme southern tip of the island, the imposing fortress that is the city of Bonifacio (bohn-ih-FASS-ee-o; pop. 3000) looms before miles of turquoise sea and distant Sardinia. Enormous stone ramparts enclose the rambling *haute ville,* which sits on top of steep cliffs. Below the city, waves dash across strange limestone formations, making misty grottoes echo with their roar. Its unique landscape, stunning white-sand beaches, and elegant restaurants make Bonifacio a must-see, but be prepared for high price tags and hordes of tourists.

CORSICA

TRANSPORTATION

Buses: Eurocorse Voyages (Ajaccio ☎21 06 30). Buses depart from the port parking lot for **Ajaccio** (3½hr.; M-Sa 3 per day, Su 1 per day; €21) via **Sartène** (1¾hr., €12).

Ferries: SAREMAR (☎73 00 96) and **Moby lines** (☎73 00 29; www.mobylines.de) run to **Santa Teresa, Sardinia** (1hr., 6-7 per day) from the *gare maritime.* 7 rotations per day beginning at 8:30am; last return boat at 7pm. €30 roundtrip per person and per scooter. Offices open daily 7:30-9am, 10:30am-noon, 3-7pm, and 9-10pm. Call the day before to reserve your spot. MC/V.

Taxis: (☎73 19 08). There is a stand at the port.

Car rental: Europcar, av. Sylvère Bohn (☎73 10 99). From €93 per day, €294 per week; credit card deposit. 21+. Open July-Aug. daily 8am-8pm. AmEx/MC/V.

Scooter & Bike rental: Funscoots (☎06 11 16 35 12, www.funscoots.com) delivers around Bonifacio and Porto Vecchio for rentals over 1 day. Bikes €15 per day; scooters €30-40 per day, €900 deposit. Call ahead July-Aug. MC/V. **Corse Moto Services,** quai Nord (☎70 12 88). €40 per day, €245 per week; €1525 deposit. 18+. Open daily July-Aug. 9am-noon and 2-6pm. MC/V.

ORIENTATION AND PRACTICAL INFORMATION

Bonifacio is divided by a steep climb from the **port** to the **haute-ville,** which begins past the pharmacy on the southern side of the port. The main road goes to Ajaccio in one direction and to nearby campgrounds and beaches in the other. Bonifacio is a pedestrian-friendly city and is easy to navigate on foot.

Tourist office: (☎73 11 88; www.bonifacio.fr) at the corner of av. de Gaulle and rue F. Scamaroni in the *haute-ville.* Staff helps with accommodations booking and distributes free maps. Open July-Aug. daily 9am-8pm; Sept. and May-June daily 10am-7pm; Oct. to Apr. M-F 9am-noon and 2-6pm. Annex, at the port, holds the same hours.

Currency exchange: Societé Générale, rue St-Erasme (☎73 02 49), next to the stairs leading to the *haute-ville.* **ATM.** Open M-F 9am-noon and 2-4:30pm.

Laundry: 1 quai Comparetti (☎73 01 03), at the end of the port near the bus stop. Wash €6, dry €1 per 10min. Open daily 7am-10pm. Coins only.

Police: rte. de Santa Manza (☎73 00 17), just off the port.

Hospital: D58 (☎73 95 73), just before the **SPAR** supermarket.

Internet Access: Cybercafé Boni Boom, on the port (☎06 22 25 78 95). Only 7 computers, so be prepared to wait during high season. €0.12 per min., €3 per 30min., €5 per hr. Open daily 8am-2am.

Post office: pl. Carrega (☎73 73 73), uphill from pl. Montepagano in the *haute-ville.* Open M-F 8am-5:30pm, Sa 8am-noon. **Postal Code:** 20169.

ACCOMMODATIONS AND CAMPING

Finding a room in the summer is virtually impossible, and the few available lodgings charge twice their normal prices in July and August. Camping is by far the cheapest option; many sites also offer affordable bungalows or *chalets.*

Hôtel des Etrangers, av. Sylvère Bohn (☎73 01 09), a 10min. walk from the port. Spotless white rooms with tile floors and (relatively) low prices make this the best deal in town. A/C and TV in all but the cheapest rooms. Breakfast €5. Reception 24hr. Reservations recommended July-Aug. Open early Apr. to late Oct. Mid-July to mid-Sept. singles and doubles €48-76; triples €72-76; quads €82-84. Sept. and mid-May to mid-July €42-65/62-66/72-76. Oct. and Apr. to mid-May €35-47/52-57/62-65. MC/V. ❺

Hôtel Le Royal, pl. Bonaparte (☎73 00 51; fax 73 04 68), in the *haute-ville.* Cheerful rooms above a *brasserie* on a lively square. Rooms come with A/C, TV, toilet, and shower or bath. Some have sweeping sea views well worth a few extra euro (ask for *côté mer* rather than *côté ville*). Breakfast €6. Reception 24hr. Reserve at least a month in advance in summer. Aug. singles €95; doubles €100-107. July and Sept. €70/75-82. June and Oct. to early Nov. €50/55-62. Apr.-May €45/50-57. Early Nov.-Mar. €40/45-52. Extra bed €16. AmEx/MC/V. ❺

Camping L'Araguina, av. Sylvère Bohn (☎73 02 96; www.campingaraguina.fr), at the entrance to town. Crowded but shady plots ideally located near the port. Helpful staff offsets the sight of cockroaches in the sinks. Breakfast €7. Laundry €5. Limited parking. Reception 8am-8pm. Non-student ID required. Open April to mid-Oct. High season €6.10 per person, low season €5.80. €2.40 per tent or car. Cash only. ❶

Camping Campo di Liccia, (☎73 03 09). The cheapest of a cluster of campsites accessible by car or on foot (1hr. from the port), on rte. de Porto-Vecchio. Pool, restaurant, mini-market, and ping pong. Laundry €5.50. Reception 8am-10pm. Open Apr.-Oct. €4.40-6 per person, €1.80-2.60 per tent or car. Electricity €1.40-2.60. Cash only. ❶

FOOD

A few supermarkets dot the port, including **SPAR,** at the beginning of rte. de Santa Manza. (☎73 00 26. Open July-Aug. daily 8am-8:30pm; Sept. and June M-Sa 8am-8pm; Oct.-May M-Sa 8am-12:30pm and 3:30-7:30pm. MC/V.) The port is lined with mundane tourist traps; a handful of tiny establishments tucked on streets in the *haute-ville* serve more authentic Corsican cuisine. These charming (but pricey) restaurants are supplemented by a fair number of *crêperies* and pizzerias, allowing diners to enjoy good grub without breaking the bank.

U Molinu, rue Prosper Mérimée (☎10 34 78), in the *haute-ville.* Simple restaurant with a view of the city's smaller port. The perfect place to try local specialties like seafood *à la crème Corse* (€11) or *aubergines à la Bonifacienne* (Bonifacio eggplant, €13). Salads €5.50-11, *plats* €7-16, *menus* €15-17. Call ahead to book a table with a view. Open June-Sept. noon-2pm and 7pm-12am; closes earlier Oct.-May. Cash only. ❸

Kissing Pigs, 15 quai Banda del Ferro (☎73 56 09), on the port. Annually butchers its own Corsican *charcuterie.* Try the savory selections of club sandwiches (€7-8.50) and *petits poelons chauds* (hot casseroles; €7-10). The homey interior of this waterside gem is marked by an open kitchen, where diners can watch the French and English owners at work. Wine €2-6. Salad €7.50-10. *Tartines* €8-11. *Menus* €12-20. Extensive dessert menu €5-7. Open M-Sa 6:30-11pm; closed mid-Nov. to mid-Dec. and Feb. for butchering season. Reservations recommended. MC/V. ❸

L'Archivolto, rue de l'Archivolto (☎73 17 58), in the *haute-ville.* Tables spill out of the rustic, antique-filled interior onto a tiny terrace. The chef's daily whim and the market's offerings dictate the ever-changing *menu,* although dishes are limited to standard Corsican specialties. Tapas for 2 €13. *Plats du jour* €13-15. Desserts €5.80-6.70. Open July to mid-Oct. daily 7:30-11pm; mid-Oct. to June M-Sa noon-2pm and 7:30-11pm. Reservations recommended; call 9-11:30am or after 5:30pm. Cash only. ❹

Cantina Doria, 27 rue Doria (☎73 50 49), in the *haute-ville.* Diners share wooden tables in the Corsican-themed interior, where pots, *brocciu* strainers, and other local artifacts hang from the ceiling. Hungry tourists devour heaping plates of *spaghetti aux aubergines* (spaghetti with eggplant) and other delicious options from the *menu* (€16). *Plats* €11-13. Desserts €4-6. Open June-Sept. daily noon-2pm and 7-11:30pm; Oct. and Apr.-May open M and W-Su noon-2pm and 7:11:30pm. MC/V. ❸

Les Voyageurs, 15 quai Comparetti (☎73 00 46), serves the cheapest meals in the port. A *plat,* fries, and a drink are only €10-15. Try the *bouillabaisse* (fish soup, €9.50) or treat yourself to fresh *langoustes* (crawfish, €14). Open daily May-Sept. 11:30am-12:30am; Oct.-Apr. 11:30am-10:30pm. MC/V. ❷

SIGHTS

A marvel of both constructed and natural architecture, Bonifacio's *haute-ville* boasts 3km-long fortifications atop limestone cliffs. Far below the ochre houses, centuries of pounding surf have carved deep, misshapen grottoes into the impressionable white rock. Be sure to take a **boat tour** of the *bouches de Bonifacio:* a small army of shuttle companies has taken over the base of the port and brings tourists to multicolored coves, cliffs, and stalactite-filled grottoes (*Grottes-Falaises-Calanques tour*). From the water, look up at Bonifacio's *haute-ville,* sticking out 70m above the waves. A different tour takes you on a similar route more quickly and continues onward to the **Iles Lavezzi.** Relax and explore the incredible beaches on this nature reserve before catching a return boat. Seven companies offer tours, including **Les Vedettes Thalassa.** (☎06 86 34 00 49. *Grottes-Falaises-Calanques* tour every 30min. 9am-6:30pm; €17. *Iles Lavezzi-Cavallo* tour 5 departures per day, 3 return boats, last return boat 5:30pm. €25. Cash only.) **Marina Croisières** (☎22 91 57) offers the same tours. (*Grottes-Falaises-Calanques* tour every 30min. 9:30am-6pm. €15. Cash only.)

To explore the *haute-ville,* head up the steep steps of the **montée Rastello,** halfway down the port. The summit offers sweeping views of hazy cliffs stretching to the east. From this point, visitors can see an enormous segment of the chalky rock upon which the *haute-ville* stands. Continue up montée St-Roch to the lookout at

Porte de Gênes, constructed with a drawbridge in 1588 as the town's sole entrance. As you pass through the arch, a series of soaring *arc-boutants* (flying buttresses) are visible on the buildings ahead. If they look a little delicate to be bracing such massive stone structures, it's because they serve no supporting purpose at all: instead, the narrow arches are used to carry rainwater from one rooftop to the next. Immediately to the right of the Porte de Gênes sits the **Bastion de L'Entendard.** Eager to overthrow colonizing Italians, Corsican nationals joined forces with King Henri II to besiege the town, successfully razing the Genoese fortress. The triumphant rebels rebuilt their own stronghold on top of the original. Once a prison, the Bastion now traps tourists; the hokey historical displays aren't worth the €2.50 admission, although the 360° views may be. The Bastion, as well as three other tourist office recommended sites (Aragon's Stairway, Ste-Dominique, and the Palazzu Publicu), each costing €2.50, or €6 for all 4, should generally be avoided.

The Bastion visit includes spectacular panoramas, but you can enjoy the view for free by heading left to **place du Marché,** at the end of rue Doria. The square looks out onto Bonifacio's cliffs, surrounded by sea foam. Immediately ahead is the **Grain de Sable,** a limestone formation that serves as a perch for daring cliff-divers. The mound just out of reach is Sardinia, 12km away. Turn right on rue Cardinal, then left on rue du Sacrement to reach the **Eglise Ste-Mairie-Majeure,** Bonifacio's oldest building. Home to the **true cross,** or at least a fragment of it from a shipwreck, and the **Loggia,** where the city's important affairs were decided, this small church holds a lot of history. (Open daily 8am-6pm.) For an even better vista, continue along the peninsula, past the cemetery, to Bonifacio's southern tip. Far enough away from the *haute-ville*, this viewpoint lets you enjoy cliffs, sea, and Sardinia peacefully. Once there, look for a small sign in the middle of a parking lot for the **Poste du Gouvernail:** an underground tunnel will lead you—for free—to grottoes carved out by Italians and Germans during WWII and to a lookout point only 30 ft. above the sea. (Open daily 9am-6pm.)

BEACHES

Bonifacio's beaches are hard to reach and even harder to leave. The ones within walking distance of town are uninspiring by Corsican standards. The peninsula is otherwise filled with spectacular beaches, accessible only by car or scooter; a taxi will cost €40-60 round-trip. From the port, take av. Sylvère Bohn back to the entrance of town and then N196 toward Ajaccio or N198 toward Porto Vecchio. Virtually every exit leads to a beach, including **Cala Longa,** 6km away from Bonifacio, and **plage Maora,** in a natural harbor. On N198, the poorly indicated right turn-off for camping Rondinara, 20km from town, leads to **plage de Rondinara,** one of Corsica's most famous beaches—and possibly one of the best in Europe.

Even more impressive than the mainland beaches are the pristine sands of the **Iles Lavezzi,** where crumbling rock formations meet turquoise waters. Every ferry company on the port runs boats (every 30min.) to this nature reserve, including **Vedettes Thalassa** and **Marina Croisières** (see **Sights**, p. 795, for schedules and prices). Bring water and food; there are no supplies available. Just off the islands, coral reefs teeming with brightly colored fish make for great **scuba diving.** At **Club Barakouda,** a 15min. walk toward the entrance of town, Capitaine Gérard takes experienced divers on *explos* at 8:30am (€32-45) and first-timers for *baptêmes* (baptisms) at 1:30pm (€50). Call the night before to reserve. (☎73 13 02, www.barakouda.com. Reception July-Aug. 8:30am-6:30pm and less regularly June-Sept. Cash only.) If you prefer to stay above water, **Bonif Kayak** runs kayaking tours of the *bouches de Bonifacio* (the Corsica-Sardinia strait) and other sites. (☎06 27 11 30 73. €30. Tours 9am-noon and 3:30-6:30pm; depart from Piantarella.)

APPENDIX

CLIMATE

The French climate varies by region. Though the center of the country generally experiences fairly moderate weather, the Côte d'Azur and Corsica, like their Mediterranean neighbors, are warmer and drier. Mountainous areas tend to be colder than the rest of France year-round, while the Atlantic and northern coast receive the most precipitation. French summers can be hot and sticky, causing most city-dwellers to flee to the sea, while the winters are snowy in mountainous regions, rainy in Paris and the western and northern coasts, and chilly in the south of France during the weeks when the *mistral*, a fierce wind, blows through.

Avg. Temp. Precipitation	January			April			July			October		
	°C	°F	mm	°C	°F	mm	°C	°F	mm	°C	°F	mm
Cherbourg	4/8	39/46	109	9/15	48/59	49	14/19	57/66	55	10/15	50/59	99
Paris	1/6	32/43	56	6/16	43/61	42	15/25	59/77	12	8/16	46/61	13
Strasbourg	-1/4	30/39	33	4/14	39/57	48	14/24	57/76	57	7/14	45/58	43
Lyon	-1/5	30/41	52	6/16	43/61	56	15/27	59/78	56	7/16	45/61	77
Toulouse	2/10	36/50	51	9/18	48/64	76	13/24	56/78	41	7/17	45/63	43
Bordeaux	2/9	36/48	90	6/17	43/63	48	14/25	57/77	11	8/18	46/64	83
Marseille	2/10	36/50	43	8/18	46/64	42	17/29	63/84	11	10/20	50/68	76
Ajaccio	3/13	38/55	76	7/18	45/64	48	16/28	61/81	10	11/12	52/54	10

MEASUREMENTS

France invented, and still uses, the metric system. The basic unit of length is the **meter (m),** which is divided into 100 **centimeters (cm),** or 1000 **millimeters (mm).** One thousand meters make up one **kilometer (km).** Fluids are measured in **liters (L),** each divided into 1000 **milliliters (ml).** A liter of pure water weighs one **kilogram (kg),** divided into 1000 **grams (g),** while 1000kg make up one metric **ton.**

1 in. = 25.4mm	1mm = 0.039 in.
1 ft.= 0.30m	1m = 3.28 ft.
1 yd. = 0.914m	1m = 1.09 yd.
1 mi. = 1.609km	1km = 0.62 mi.
1 oz. = 28.35g	1g = 0.035 oz.
1 lb. = 0.454kg	1kg = 2.205 lb.
1 fl. oz. = 29.57ml	1ml = 0.034 fl. oz.
1 gal. = 3.785L	1L = 0.264 gal.

FRENCH PHRASEBOOK

ENGLISH	FRENCH	PRONUNCIATION
	THE BASICS	
Hello/Good day	Bonjour	bohn-JHOOR
Good evening	Bonsoir	bohn-SWAH

APPENDIX

Hi!	Salut!	sah-LU!
Goodbye	Au revoir	oh ruh-VWAH
Good night	Bonne nuit	buhn NWEE
Have a good day/evening	Bonne journée/soirée	BUHN jhoor nay/swah ray
Yes/No/Maybe	Oui/Non/Peut-être	wee/nohn/p'TET-ruh
Please	S'il vous plaît	see voo PLAY
Thank you	Merci	mehr-SEE
You're welcome	De rien/je vous en prie	duh rhee-EHN/jh'VOOS on PREE
Pardon me!	Excusez-moi/Pardon!	ex-KU-zay-MWAH/pahr-DOHN!
Go away!	Allez-vous en!	ah-LAY vooz ON!
What time do you open/ close?	Vous ouvrez/fermez à quelle heure?	vooz oo-VRAY/ ferh-MAY ah kel-UHR?
Help!	Au secours!	oh-sek-OOR!
I'm lost.	Je suis perdu(e).	jh'SWEE pehr-DU
I'm sorry.	Je suis désolé(e).	jh'SWEE day-zoh-LAY
Do you speak English?	Parlez-vous anglais?	par-lay-voo ahn-GLAY
JUST BEYOND THE BASICS		
Who?	Qui?	kee?
What?	Quoi?	kwah?
When?	Quand?	kahn?
Where?	Où?	oo?
How?	Comment?	ko-MAHN?
Why?	Pourquoi?	pour-KWAH?
I don't understand.	Je ne comprends pas.	jh'ne KOHM-prahn pah
Please speak slowly.	S'il vous plaît, parlez moins vite.	see voo PLAY, par-lay mwehn veet
I would like...	Je voudrais...	jh'voo-DRAY...
How much does this cost?	Ça coûte combien?	sa coot comb-YEN?
Leave me alone.	Laissez-moi tranquille.	LESS-say mwah trahn-KEEL.
I need help.	J'ai besoin d'assistance.	jhay bezz-WEHN dah-SEE-stahnss
I am (20) years old.	J'ai (vingt) ans.	jhay VEHN-tahn.
I don't speak French.	Je ne parle pas le français.	jh'ne parl pah le frahn-SAY.
My name is ( ). What's your name?	Je m'appelle ( ). Comment vous appelez-vous?	JH'ma-PELL ( ). kuh-MAHN-voo-za-pell-ay-VOO?
No, thank you.	Non, merci.	nohn, MEHR-see.
What is it?	Qu'est-ce que c'est?	kess-kuh-SAY?
this one/that one	ceci/cela	suh-SEE/suh-LAH
Stop/Stop that!	Arrêtez!	ahr-eh-TAY!
Please repeat.	Répétez, s'il vous plaît.	reh-peh-TAY, see voo PLAY.
How do you say ( ) in French?	Comment dit-on ( ) en Français?	kuh-MAHN-deet-OHN ( ) ohn frahn-SAY?
Do you understand?	Comprenez-vous?	kohm-PREHN-ay-voo?
I am a student.	Je suis étudiant(e).	jh'sweez EH-too-dee-ahnt
It's just one step from the sublime to the ridiculous.	"Du sublime au ridicule il n'y a qu'un pas." (Napoléon)	doo soo-BLEEM oh ree-dee-CULE eel nee ah KHUN pah
EMERGENCY		
Where is the nearest hospital?	Où est l'hôpital le plus proche?	OO eh loh-peet-TAL luh ploo proh-sh?
Where is the nearest emergency pharmacy?	Où est la pharmacie de garde la plus proche?	OO eh lah farm-ah-SEE duh gard lah ploo proh-sh

APPENDIX

Where is the police station?	Où est la station de police?	OO eh lah stah-si-OHN duh po-leess?
I am ill/I am hurt.	Je suis malade/Je suis blessé(e).	jh'swee mah-LAHD/jh'swee bleh-SAY
I was attacked.	J'ai été attaqué(e).	jhay ay-TAY ah-tah-KAY
I was raped.	J'ai été violé(e).	jhay ay-TAY VEE-oh-lay
I think I broke my leg.	Je pense que j'ai cassé une jambe.	jh'puhnss kuh jhay CAH-say oon jhahmb
My friend has gone crazy.	Mon ami est devenu fou.	mohn ah-MEE eh DUH-vehn-oo foo
I need a doctor.	J'ai besoin d'un médecin.	jhay bez-WHEN duhn med-SEHN
Help me!	Aidez-moi!	eh-day MWAH!
Someone pick-pocketed me!	J'ai été victime d'un pickpocket!	jhay ay-TAY vick-TEEM duhn peek-poh-ket
Someone stole...	Quelqu'un m'a volé...	kell-KUHN mah VOH-lay
...my camera.	...mon appareil photo.	...mohn a-par-RAY foh-TOH
...my purse.	...mon sac.	...mohn sahk
...my wallet.	...ma portefeuille.	...mah port-FOY
...my passport.	...mon passeport.	...mohn pass-PORE
DIRECTIONS		
Please, where is ...?	S'il vous plaît, où se trouve...?	see voo PLAY, oo suh troov...?
...an ATM?	...un distributeur d'argent?	..uhn dis-TRIB-oo-TEHR dar-JAHNT?
...the bathroom?	...les toilettes/les W.C.?	...lay twahlets/lay DOO-bluh vay say?
...the train station?	...la gare?	...lah GARE?
...the post office?	...la poste?	...lah POH-ST?
(to the) right	(à) droite	ah d-whaht
(to the) left	(à) gauche	ah go-sh
straight	tout droit	too d-whah
near to/far from	près de/loin de	PRAY duh/l-WHEN duh
here/there	ici/là	ee-see/lah
south	sud	sood
east	est	ehst
west	ouest	oo-ehst
north	nord	nord
NUMBERS		
one	un	uhn
two	deux	duh
three	trois	twah
four	quatre	KAH-truh
five	cinq	sank
six	six	seess
seven	sept	set
eight	huit	wheet
nine	neuf	nuhf
ten	dix	deess
fifteen	quinze	kanz
twenty	vingt	vehn
twenty-five	vingt-cinq	vehn-sank

thirty	trente	trahnt
forty	quarante	ka-RAHNT
fifty	cinquante	sang-KAHNT
hundred	cent	sahn
thousand	mille	meel
TIME		
What time is it?	Quelle heure est-il?	kell uhr eh-TEEL?
It's (11) o'clock.	Il est (onze) heures.	eel eh-t-ohnze uhr
open/closed	ouvert/fermé	oo-vair/fair-may
until	jusqu'à	jhooss-KAH
January	janvier	JHAN-vee-eh
February	fevrier	FEH-vree-eh
March	mars	marss
April	avril	ah-vreel
May	mai	may
June	juin	jh-WEHN
July	juillet	jh-WEE-eh
August	août	AH-oot
September	septembre	sehp-TAHM-bruh
October	octobre	ohk-TOH-bruh
November	novembre	no-VAHM-bruh
December	décembre	day-SAHM-bruh
today	aujourd'hui	oh-jhore-DWEE
tomorrow	demain	duh-MEHN
yesterday	hier	ee-air
noon/midnight	midi/minuit	mee-DEE/min-NWEE
public holidays	jours fériés (j.f.)	jhor FAIR-ee-ay
morning	le matin	luh meh-TEHN
afternoon	l'après-midi	lah-PRAY mee-DEE
evening	le soir	luh SWAHR
day/night	le jour/la nuit	luh jhor/lah NWEE
Sunday	dimanche	dee-MAHNSH
Monday	lundi	luhn-dee
Tuesday	mardi	marh-dee
Wednesday	mercredi	mair-kruh-dee
Thursday	jeudi	jheu-dee
Friday	vendredi	vawn-druh-dee
Saturday	samedi	sahm-dee

COMMON SIGNS			
Sortie de secours	Emergency exit	**Complet**	No vacancy
Voie sans issue	Dead end	**En panne/Hors service**	Out of order
Pélouse interdite	Stay off the grass	**Entrée interdite**	Stay out/No entrance
À emporter	To go/Takeout	**Stationnement interdit**	No parking
SIGHTSEEING			
vieille ville	old town	**Quel dommage que tu n'aies qu'un guide Lonely Planet.**	What a shame you only have a Lonely Planet guide.

visite guidée	guided tour	**Est-ce que je pourrais prendre un photo?**	Can I take a picture?
Y a-t-il une visite guidée en anglais?	Is there a guided tour in English?	**Pourriez-vous nous prendre une photo?**	Could you take our picture?
PLANES, TRAINS, AND AUTOMOBILES			
gare SNCF	train station	**faire la correspondance**	transfer (between subway lines, trains, or flights)
gare routière	bus station	**billet aller simple**	one-way ticket
arrêt de taxi	taxi stand	**billet aller-retour**	round-trip ticket
PLANES			
vol	flight	**enregistrer les bagages**	check baggage
place côté fenêtre/côté couloir	window/aisle seat	**Dois-je enregistrer ceci?**	Do I have to check this?
douane	customs	**arrivée/départ**	arrival/departure
TRAINS			
TGV	high-speed train	**guichet/billetterie**	ticket window/office
composter le billet	validate a ticket	**quai**	platform
consigne	luggage locker	**voie**	track
wagon	train car	**À quelle heure part le train?**	What time does the train leave?
AUTOMOBILES			
autoroute	highway	**essence (sans plomb/diesel)**	gasoline (unleaded/diesel)
bus	city bus	**limite de vitesse**	speed limit
boîte de vitesse automatique/manuelle	automatic/manual transmission	**station de service**	gas station
(auto)car	coach bus	**voiture**	car
citation	speeding ticket	**roue de secours**	spare tire
OUTDOORS			
bois	woods	**île**	island
faire du camping	to go camping	**piste**	slope
faire du ski	to go skiing	**randonnée**	hike
faire du vélo	to go biking	**source**	spring
ferme	farm	**téléphérique**	cable car
forêt	forest	**thermes**	hot springs
télésiège	chair lift	**falaise**	cliff
ARCHITECTURAL TERMS			
abbaye	abbey	**haute-ville**	upper town
basse-ville	lower town	**hôtel particulier**	town house, mansion
cave	cellar, often for wine	**hôtel de ville**	city hall
centre-ville	center of town	**monastère**	monastery
chapelle	chapel	**mur**	wall
château	castle, mansion, or vineyard headquarters	**muraille**	fortified city wall
cimitière	cemetery	**palais**	palace
cité	walled city	**parc**	park
clocher	church tower	**place**	town square
cloître	cloister	**pont**	bridge
couvent	convent	**quartier**	neighborhood, section of town

église	church	**tour**	tower
fontaine	fountain	**vitraux**	stained-glass windows

AT A HOTEL			
une chambre avec...	a bedroom with...	**une chambre simple/ double**	single/double room
...un grand lit	...a double bed	**une chambre sur la rue/ sur la cour**	room on the street/on the courtyard
...deux lits	...two single beds	**Le petit déjeuner est compris.**	Breakfast is included.
...une douche	...a shower	**Où est l'auberge de jeu-nesse?**	Where is the youth hos-tel?
...bains	...a bath tub	**Puis-je voir la chambre?**	May I see the room?
chambre d'hôte	bed and breakfast	**gîte**	rural hostel-like home
pension/demi-pension	all meals included/din-ner only included	**accueil**	reception
AT A CAFE OR RESTAURANT			
Je voudrais...	I would like...	**L'addition, s'il vous plaît.**	The check, please.
Qu'est que c'est?	What is this?	**Je suis végétarien(ne).**	I'm a vegetarian (m/f).
Avez-vous des plats kashers?	Do you have kosher food?	**Je suis végétalien(ne).**	I'm a vegan (m/f).
Est-ce que le service est compris?	Is tip included?	**Il me faut un whiskey tout de suite.**	I really need a whiskey right now.
WHERE AND WHAT TO EAT			
boucherie	butcher shop	**épicerie**	grocery store
boulangerie	bakery	**(super)marché**	(super)market
brasserie	bar and restaurant	**pâtisserie**	pastry shop
marché en plein air	open-air market	**bistro**	informal restaurant
charcuterie	shop selling cooked meats (such as salami) and prepared food	**tabac**	cigarette shop and news-stand
BOISSONS (DRINKS)			
café (crème/au lait)	coffee (with cream/milk)	**vin rouge/blanc**	red/white wine
chocolat chaud	hot chocolate	**bière**	beer
thé	tea	**carafe d'eau (du robi-net)**	pitcher of water (from the tap)
eau platte/gazeuse	flat/sparkling water	**une bouteille de cham-pagne exquisite**	a bottle of exquisite champagne
VIANDE (MEAT)			
agneau	lamb	**saucisson**	cooked sausage (like sal-ami)
andouillette	tripe sausage	**faux-filet**	sirloin steak
bavette	flank (cut of meat)	**foie gras d'oie/de canard**	liver pâté of goose/duck
boeuf	beef	**jambon**	ham
une brochette	kebab	**lapin**	rabbit
canard	duck	**poulet**	chicken
cervelles	brains	**rillettes**	meat hash (usually pork or rabbit)
côte	rib or chop (cut of meat)	**ris de veau**	sweetbreads (brains)
cuisses de grenouilles	frog legs	**steak...**	a steak...
coq au vin	rooster stewed in wine	**...saignant**	...rare

dinde	turkey	**...à point**	...medium
entrecôte	chop (cut of meat)	**...bien cuit**	...well done
escalope	thin slice of meat	**steak tartare**	raw steak mixed with raw eggs
saucisse	uncooked sausage	**veau**	veal
FRUITS DE MER (SEAFOOD)			
poisson	fish	**homard**	lobster
coquilles st-jacques	scallops	**huîtres**	oysters
crevettes	shrimp	**moules**	mussels
escargots	snail	**thon**	tuna
FRUITS ET LÉGUMES (FRUITS AND VEGETABLES)			
ananas	pineapple	**fraise**	strawberry
asperges	asparagus	**framboise**	raspberry
aubergine	eggplant	**haricots verts**	green beans
champignons	mushrooms	**petits poids**	peas
choufleur	cauliflower	**poire**	pear
compote	stewed fruit	**poireaux**	leeks
cornichon	pickle	**pomme**	apple
épinards	spinach	**pomme de terre**	potato
figue	fig	**raisins**	grapes
PAIN (BREAD)			
baguette	baguette	**feuilleté**	puff pastry
brioche	light, buttery roll	**galette**	savory dinner crêpe
gaufre	waffle	**pain au chocolat**	chocolate-filled croissant
OTHER			
l'ail	garlic	**crème fraîche**	thick cream
beurre	butter	**froid**	cold
chaud	hot	**moutarde**	mustard
citron	lemon	**oeuf**	egg
citron vert	lime	**poivre**	pepper
crème Chantilly	whipped cream	**sel**	salt
AT THE BAR			
Puis-je t'acheter un demi?	Can I buy you a beer?	**Dis donc, quel est ton numéro?**	So tell me, what's your number?
Mon copain/ma copine m'attend dehors.	My boyfriend/girlfriend is waiting for me outside.	**Il a un verre dans le nez.**	He is drunk.

INDEX

INDEX

INDEX

N

O

P

INDEX

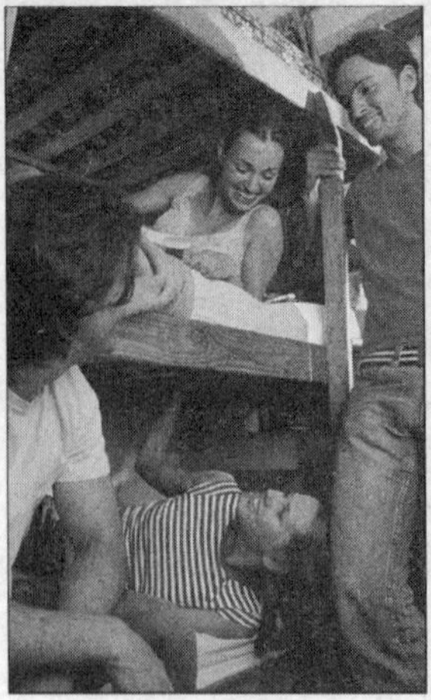

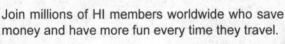

ABOUT LET'S GO

NOT YOUR PARENTS' TRAVEL GUIDE

At Let's Go, we see every trip as the chance of a lifetime. If your dream is to grab a machete and forge through the jungles of Costa Rica, we can take you there. If you'd rather bask in the Riviera sun at a beachside cafe, we'll set you a table. We write for readers who know that there's more to travel than sharing double deckers with tourists and who believe that travel can change both themselves and the world—whether they plan to spend six days in Mexico City or six months in Europe. We'll show you just how far your money can go, and prove that the greatest limitation on your adventures is not your wallet, but your imagination.

BEYOND THE TOURIST EXPERIENCE

To help you gain a deeper connection with the places you travel, our fearless researchers scour the globe to give you the heads-up on both world-renowned and off-the-beaten-track attractions, sights, and destinations. They engage with the local culture only to emerge with the freshest insights on everything from local festivals to regional cuisine. We've also opened our pages to respected writers and scholars to hear their takes on the countries and regions we cover, and asked travelers who have worked, studied, or volunteered abroad to contribute first-person accounts of their experiences. In addition, we increased our coverage of responsible travel and expanded each guide's Beyond Tourism chapter to share more ideas about how to give back while on the road.

FORTY-EIGHT YEARS OF WISDOM

Let's Go got its start in 1960, when a group of creative and well-traveled students compiled their experience and advice into a 20-page mimeographed pamphlet, which they gave to travelers on charter flights to Europe. Four and a half decades later, we've expanded to cover six continents and all kinds of travel—while retaining our founders' adventurous attitude toward the world. Laced with witty prose and total candor, our guides are still researched and written entirely by students on shoestring budgets, experienced travelers who know that train strikes, stolen luggage, food poisoning, and marriage proposals are all part of a day's work.

THE LET'S GO COMMUNITY

More than just a travel guide company, Let's Go is a community. Our small staff comes together because of our shared passion for travel and our desire to help other travelers see the world the way it was meant to be seen. We love it when our readers become part of the Let's Go community as well—when you travel, drop us a postcard (67 Mt. Auburn St., Cambridge, MA 02138, USA), send us an e-mail (feedback@letsgo.com), or post on our forum (http://www.letsgo.com/connect/forum) to tell us about your adventures and discoveries.

For more information, visit us online: www.letsgo.com.

MAP INDEX

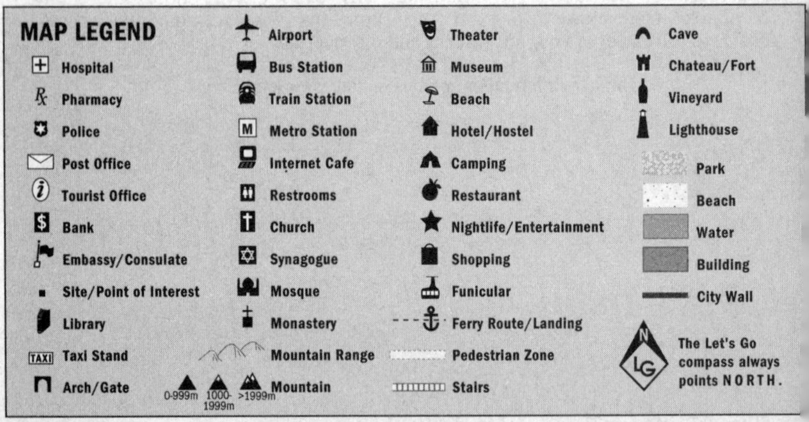

MAP LEGEND
Hospital
Pharmacy
Police
Post Office
Tourist Office
Bank
Embassy/Consulate
Site/Point of Interest
Library
TAXI Taxi Stand
Arch/Gate
Airport
Bus Station
Train Station
M Metro Station
Internet Cafe
Restrooms
Church
Synagogue
Mosque
Monastery
Mountain Range
0-999m 1000-1999m >1999m Mountain
Theater
Museum
Beach
Hotel/Hostel
Camping
Restaurant
Nightlife/Entertainment
Shopping
Funicular
Ferry Route/Landing
Pedestrian Zone
Stairs
Cave
Chateau/Fort
Vineyard
Lighthouse
Park
Beach
Water
Building
City Wall
The Let's Go compass always points NORTH.